IRB
WORLD RUGBY
YEARBOOK
2010

EDITED BY PAUL MORGAN AND JOHN GRIFFITHS

VSP

Vision Sports Publishing
19-23 High Street
Kingston upon Thames
Surrey
KT1 1LL

www.visionsp.co.uk

Published by
Vision Sports Publishing in 2009

ISBN 13: 978-1-905326-67-9

All pictures by Getty Images unless otherwise stated
Illustrations by Ann Cakebread

Typeset by Palimpsest Book Production Ltd, Grangemouth, Stirlingshire

Printed and bound in the UK by Ashford Colour Press Ltd

The IRB World Rugby Yearbook is an independent publication supported by
the International Rugby Board but the views throughout, expressed by
the different authors, do not necessarily reflect the policies and
opinions of the IRB.

International Rugby Board
Huguenot House
35-38 St Stephen's Green
Dublin 2
Ireland

t +353-1-240-9200
f +353-1-240-9201
e irb@irb.com

www.irb.com

INTRODUCTION

FROM THE JOINT EDITOR – PAUL MORGAN

WELCOME **to the** new edition of the IRB World Rugby Yearbook, the fourth since the International Rugby Board and Vision Sports Publishing relaunched it.

It is a book that I was shocked to see disappear from our shelves after the Rugby World Cup 2003 and I am delighted to have played a small part in getting it back there, where it belongs. It is now a unique publication – unrivalled anywhere else in the sporting world.

The 2009 rugby year was epic. It was unquestionably the Year of the Springbok as the Republic strode like a colossus over the rugby world. The signs were there in May when South Africa claimed their first Sevens World Series crown, a title that was quickly followed by The Bulls taking the Super 14 by storm, winning their second title in three years.

This wasn't enough for the country of the world champions though as they went on to beat the British & Irish Lions and then lifted the Tri-Nations trophy for the first time in five years. That is some record and the IRB World Rugby Yearbook takes its hat off to the Springbok Class of 2009!

An Ireland Grand Slam, Leinster's Heineken Cup and that Lions tour ensured the whole of Europe was glued to the field in 2009.

All these momentous events are included in this year's Yearbook plus much, much more in our 616 pages.

This Yearbook is about far more than the top eight and in our pages you can see reports from some of the new tournaments that are lighting up the rugby world and reviews from each of the 20 countries who qualified for the 2007 World Cup.

I am of course just one member of a world-class team so I have many thank yous to offer this time around. My joint editor, John Griffiths heads the list, of course, as without his statistics how could you publish the Yearbook? Jim Drewett and Toby Trotman at Vision Sports, provided good counsel and the crucial support for the project.

Paul Wallace, Gerald Davies, Scott Quinnell and Will Greenwood, supplied their expertise alongside our prodigious principal writer, Iain Spragg.

The International Rugby Board, under new Head of Communications, Dominic Rumbles, stepped up their efforts considerably this time, and I thank them for that.

Alongside Dominic, Andrea Wiggins and the unflappable Karen Bond were stars of the show and I appreciate the many hours they spent on the Yearbook, and the diligence they showed.

And making sense of the many tens of thousands of words we produced was the faithful team at Palimpsest Book Production, where Julie Garvock was again a pillar of strength.

Any comments or recommendations for future editions will be gratefully received at Rugby World Magazine, where I am editor. Email me at paul_morgan@ipcmedia.com

CONTENTS

THE FRONT ROW

INTERNATIONAL TOURNAMENTS

INTERNATIONAL RECORDS AND STATISTICS

THE COUNTRIES

THE COMBINED TEAMS

CROSS-BORDER TOURNAMENTS

THE BACK ROW

INTRODUCTION

RUGBY REACHES OUT TO OLYMPIC GAMES

FROM BERNARD LAPASSET, CHAIRMAN OF THE INTERNATIONAL RUGBY BOARD

In October 2009, members of the International Olympic Committee elected to admit Rugby Sevens to the 2016 Olympic Games in Rio de Janeiro, marking another historic chapter for the game.

We are proud and honoured to be joining the Olympic family. The Olympic Games will be the pinnacle of the sport for all our athletes and the rugby family, who were unified in their support of the campaign. The best men's and women's players are excited to be able to showcase their talent on the world's greatest sporting stage and will be proud to call themselves Olympians.

We are committed to ensuring that Rugby Sevens' debut in the Games will be memorable and ultimately successful. Yet inclusion is more than just the running of a superb Rugby Sevens tournament for men and women.

We will ensure appropriate development programmes are implemented, qualification structures finalised and competition pathways fixed to ensure that Sevens can continue its incredible success story on the global stage.

Much work lies ahead, but we are committed to working with every National Olympic Committee to develop their Sevens teams and working with members of the Olympic family to share knowledge, benefit from one another's experience and promote the growth of sport and its core values worldwide.

Rugby Sevens will be a wonderful addition to the Games. It is fast and exciting and played by our fittest and quickest athletes in stadiums packed with enthusiastic young fans. It is also highly competitive and attractive to broadcasters and sponsors and can be played in one stadium over two or three days.

Indeed Olympic Games inclusion, voted in by a majority of 81–8, is without doubt the biggest event to have happened to our sport since the game going open or the inception of Rugby World Cup. It will have a profound and hugely positive effect for the game, leading to increased playing numbers and even greater levels of interest.

It will also provide the perfect showcase for Sevens. More people in more countries will be inspired by the action and I am sure that we will see great growth within emerging rugby markets such as China, Russia, India and the USA.

We are excited to be joining the Olympic Games and I would like to thank the IOC for believing in our Olympic vision and our values and recognising that Rugby Sevens is a perfect fit for the Games. The rugby family is looking forward to Rugby Sevens in Rio and showcasing our wonderful sport on the world's greatest stage.

A huge factor in the campaign was the staging of a record-breaking Rugby

World Cup Sevens in Dubai. The event, featuring a first-ever women's tournament, was a resounding success showcasing the truly global and competitive nature of Rugby Sevens, reaching out to more fans, television viewers and sponsors than ever before. Wales were worthy winners of the Melrose Cup while Australia made history by claiming the inaugural women's title.

Aside from our Olympic campaign, the IRB's focus on its core business continued in force in 2009, including the roll out of development initiatives across Africa, Asia, Europe, the Americas and Oceania despite the challenging economic climate.

Following the resounding success of the initial phase of the £30 million Strategic Investment Programme (2006–2009), the continued commercial success of Rugby World Cup will allow the IRB to invest a further £48 million in the game in the form of High Performance investment. The total investment in global rugby between 2009–2012 will be an unprecedented £153 million.

Work continues on the review of many of the game's regulations as the IRB aims to ensure that, in a quickly developing global sport, the regulations remain relevant. Regulations 7, 11, 17, 23 are all under review by the IRB's Regulations Committee.

With two years to go until Rugby World Cup 2011 kicks off, the IRB is confident that the tournament, played across 13 venues will be a spectacular, memorable and ultimately successful event. New Zealand will offer an irresistible mix of world class rugby and the unique, colourful experience that only a country with such a rich rugby tradition can offer.

Planning is well advanced with management, operational planning, venue logistics, and the commercial, ticketing, staffing and media programmes all on track. The schedule has been announced and the first phase of ticket sales will begin in early 2010. The challenge now is to ensure that we maintain the excellent momentum and deliver a wonderful RWC.

The RWC 2011 qualifying process is reaching its climax. The play-offs in 2010 will bring to a close the qualifying process that kicked off in April 2008 and has incorporated 185 matches involving 82 teams.

For Rugby World Cup, 2009 was an historic year with the IRB Council awarding RWC 2015 to England and RWC 2019 to Japan. The allocation of the two tournaments enables RWC Limited and the Host Union greater certainty over operational and commercial delivery, further enhancing the ability to deliver world class events.

In another first, the decision concluded a tender process that featured a RWCL Board recommendation. A record number of unions tendered for one or both tournaments with Italy and South Africa also bidding. The tenders were all of a very high standard, which is a tribute to the health of the game and the enormous prestige of RWC.

The succession of England and Japan as host nations will create new opportunities and help maximise commercial revenues for re-investment in the Game. It is an exciting combination for RWC and one we think will enable rugby to reach developing markets and therefore contribute to the continued growth of the game and its values.

Emirates

INTRODUCTION

FROM GARY CHAPMAN – PRESIDENT
GROUP SERVICES & DNATA, EMIRATES GROUP

There are rugby competitions which define history. Rugby World Cup Sevens 2009, hosted by Emirates in Dubai at its new sports facility 7he Sevens in March, was, without question, such a competition.

In terms of global telecast, Rugby World Cup Sevens 2009 was the most viewed Sevens event in the sport's history, demonstrating the sport's phenomenal worldwide appeal. Crucially Rugby Sevens is now set to appear at the Olympic Games 2016 in Rio de Janeiro.

Emirates is honoured to have supported the International Rugby Board's bid to have Sevens accepted into the Olympics and will always look back with pride at what was achieved during those exhilarating three days of world-class sporting action at 7he Sevens. Rugby World Cup Sevens 2009 witnessed some electrifying results, with Wales claiming their first title by beating Argentina in the men's final and Australia putting up a tremendous fight against New Zealand to claim the inaugural women's title.

Emirates continues its support of the annual Dubai Rugby Sevens. Talking of history, this year the tournament celebrates its 40th anniversary since the Staffordshire Regiment claimed victory in that first tournament before a handful of fans dotted along a sandy touchline in the Dubai desert.

Last year's IRB Sevens World Series event saw world record crowds, with over 50,000 fans making the pilgrimage to the new venue at 7he Sevens each day. These figures speak for themselves and clearly demonstrate that the unique Dubai Sevens atmosphere has been both preserved and enhanced at this new facility. 7he Sevens has more than delivered on its promises. The spacious rugby village, the ability to move freely between pitches and, most importantly, it has provided the local community with a first-class facility for rugby to develop and be played and enjoyed at all levels throughout the year.

In addition to its commitment to the Dubai Sevens, Emirates is also actively involved in Sevens tournaments in the United Kingdom and South Africa, as well as its shirt sponsorships of the England and Samoan squads.

Emirates has a wide-ranging and long-term commitment to rugby. Emirates is a Worldwide Partner of Rugby World Cup 2011; it sponsors Emirates Western Force Super 14 team in Australia and is the Official Sponsor of the IRB Referees, the IRB Awards and the IRB World Rugby Yearbook.

I hope that you enjoy the latest edition of the IRB Yearbook and, together with Emirates, look forward to another memorable year of rugby.

THE FRONT ROW

Rugby is Reaching Out

Rugby and the Olympic Movement

INTERNATIONAL RUGBY BOARD

www.irb.com/rugbyandtheolympics

THE KICK OFF

RUGBY ROARS WITH SPIRIT OF THE LIONS

By Gerald Davies

Introducing a new section in the *IRB World Rugby Yearbook* in which a guest writer tackles a pressing issue in the game or a rugby issue close to his or her heart. This year former Wales wing wizard and more recently British & Irish Lions Tour Manager Gerald Davies asks if the spirit of rugby has been irrevocably damaged in 2009?

I know that rugby union has taken something of a battering this year, and all supporters of the game would have preferred not to have seen some of the headlines that have been connected with the game in recent months. But despite some negative incidents I am confident that rugby union hasn't lost its spirit and become a game where it is "win at all costs".

My view may sound idealistic but this summer I was fortunate enough, as the Lions Tour Manager, to get close to the best 40 players in Britain and Ireland and a set of world-class coaches and management, and I can say the game of rugby union is still based on integrity. Our game is still a sport for all, building teamwork and has, I believe, retained its ethos and traditions.

Sport, like many other walks of life is full of clichés. And these clichés get repeated so many times they sound like an eternal truth.

THE FRONT ROW

More than a game: Gerald Davies and Gareth Edwards scrum down with local schoolchildren during the Lions tour of South Africa.

One of the clichés I refer to is, "Winning is everything". Then along comes someone else to outbid it and say, "It is not everything it is the only thing".

If you adopt either of these stances are you taking your first steps down a path which leads to things being done which are not of a sporting nature? Are you on a road which takes you to where Formula One has been recently? Does it lead to what has happened in soccer, in South African athletics and indeed to what happened in rugby this year? That someone will take a massive chance because it is in people's minds that winning is not just everything; winning is the only thing. In Formula One, for example, a man's life was put at risk.

Where do I stand? I don't believe winning is everything, but clearly it is the first thing. When the whistle blows it is the first thing. But when you lose there are second and third things you can take away from the game. The Lions lost the series in South Africa but didn't a lot of people get a lot out of it? Didn't the players get a lot out of touring and battling together? Were we not part of a dramatic series of matches?

Then there is the fact that the supporters who followed us were made to feel good about what we did with the Lions. Those things are important. Sport must reach beyond the basic fundamentals.

Tens of thousands of supporters followed the Lions to South Africa and they must not be forgotten as they embody so many of the great things about rugby. They were great ambassadors for the Lions and the game of rugby football in general. There is a community about the supporters, and never even a hint of problems. Wherever I go around the world I meet loyal supporters who follow their team with exactly the right attitude.

Of course, our first thing was to win the series, but when we didn't the players can look back on having had a real adventure together. People were made to feel good about rugby football. The 2009 tour gave the Lions back its strength, identity and its importance in world rugby.

Don't get me wrong, I didn't enjoy losing to South Africa. I was left bitterly disappointed, but losing will not take away the long-term friendships that were forged in South Africa. We played with smiles on our faces, but with slivers of ice behind our backs.

I played on two Lions tours, one where we lost (1968) and one where we were fortunate enough to win (1971). The team from 1968 may have lost in South Africa but I can confirm the side has had four reunions to date, which shows the bond that was formed. Would we keep meeting as a side if that wasn't the case?

The camaraderie of 1968 and 1971 was there again in 2009. The beauty of the Lions is that it brings together four nations as one.

I remember on the tour talking to Brian O'Driscoll. He said that he would be looking forward to seeing his fellow Lions in the new season and that hadn't always happened on previous Lions tours. Brian told me that when he came down to dinner in the team room he didn't look for who was sitting on a particular table he just looked for the gap, meaning he didn't mind who he sat with.

On another occasion I was in the lift with Tommy Bowe, near the end of the tour. I asked him if he was going on holiday. He told me he was going to Las Vegas with some of the other Lions players, most of whom he would only have met on the trip itself. This squad formed a bond that may never be broken.

With the Lions, the four countries coming together creates an incredible mood and atmosphere, a little like it does for the Barbarians. You talk to Argentineans or people from Japan and they would love to have the Lions. Recently I was at an IRB Conference and I had Australia chief executive John O'Neill and New Zealand's Graham Mourie coming up to me and saying, "Hey, that was terrific!"

We took our legacy very seriously and left facilities and expertise behind that everyone can be proud of.

I was also delighted to see the way that South Africa treated the Lions on and off the pitch. It was great to hear South Africa captain John Smit talk about the Lions at the end of the tour. He described

THE KICK OFF

THE FRONT ROW

Spirit of the Lions: Ugo Monye and Phil Vickery celebrate victory after the Third Test in Johannesburg.

what a privilege it was to play against the Lions, so once again the team helped forge a bond between Britain and Ireland and South Africa.

Some people have suggested that some of rugby's recent problems should be put down to professionalism. Well I disagree with that. Being professional in the main is being disciplined, efficient, doing the best you possibly can and I like Arsène Wenger's comment that the objective is to "win with integrity". I think that is a great line and every sport needs that.

If you put the small transgressions down to professionalism, when does that small transgression become the big one? Once you start down that road where does it end?

The IRB Charter defines the unique character of rugby and the concepts which bind us together: courage, loyalty, sportsmanship, discipline and teamwork. Written to complement the Laws of the Game, all players are encouraged to adhere to principles of spirit and mutual respect balancing the sheer physicality and battle of the sport. Where all these aspects collide, there is glory and sometimes there is winning.

I think this summer's Lions found glory. We lost the series but we found glory from the way the team played, the attitude of the players and management. I believe the spirit of rugby is still strong and the Lions make a big contribution to that spirit.

Gerald Davies was talking to Paul Morgan.

It's time for the IRB World Rugby Yearbook to bring out the crystal ball again and this time gaze into 2010. Let's hope we hit the nail on the head
Paul Morgan – Joint Editor

RBS Six Nations
Providing Jonny Wilkinson stays fit, Martin Johnson's England will see key challengers Ireland and Wales arrive at Twickenham. They have fared well in France in recent years as well.
Winners: **England**

Super 14
How can you look past the South African sides? And with a better squad than last year it's back-to-back for the Bulls.
Winners: **Bulls**

Heineken Cup
The overseas signings have boosted Stade and after years of trying are ready to lift the big one.
Winners: **Stade Français**

Guinness Premiership
London Irish came so close in 2009. I think it will be their year in 2010.
Winners: **London Irish**

Magners League
Leinster have a fabulous group of young players who can supplement the experienced men. Watch Edinburgh push them close!
Winners: **Leinster**

Top 14
I think there will be new kids on the block this year with Stade Français finally getting their hands on the Bouclier de Brennus.
Winners: **Stade Français**

European Challenge Cup
One side, which will be bursting for a trophy is Saracens, and under Steve Borthwick can end their 11-year wait for a title.
Winners: **Saracens**

OLYMPIC GAMES DECISION
SEVENS HEAVEN FOR RUGBY
By Dominic Rumbles

Mike Miller and Bernard Lapasset on hearing that Rugby Sevens will be an Olympic Sport.

October 9, 2009 will be remembered as a monumental date in the history of Rugby Union. It was the day on which the International Olympic Committee Session in Copenhagen elected to include Rugby Sevens in the Olympic Games.

Rugby Sevens will make its debut at the 32nd Olympiad in 2016 when the Games are staged in Rio de Janeiro, an apt new dawn in a country where the sport is experiencing significant increase in popularity off the back of the Brazilian women's exploits at Rugby World Cup Sevens 2009.

The format will have a familiar feel. Twelve men's and 12 women's teams, 144 Olympic athletes competing over two or three days. It is a proven formula at multi-sport events such as the Commonwealth and World Games and a truly exciting prospect.

The top players have pledged their commitment and each and every one will be proud to call themselves Olympians, while a global audience of billions will see a truly high-octane mix of fast and furious action, highly competitive matches, drama, excitement and a festival of a modern sport.

"This is a historic moment for our sport and for the Rugby family around the world," said International Rugby Board Chairman Bernard Lapasset. "Rugby Sevens will be a great addition to the Olympic Games and Olympic Games inclusion will be fabulous for the growth of the Game.

"I want to thank the IOC membership for their decision to include our sport and I would also like to say a special thank you to the global rugby community for their strong support of the campaign and their hard work in promoting Rugby Sevens around the world."

When the dust settles the countdown to the inaugural Olympic Rugby Sevens tournament will begin. The consequences for the sport are far reaching. Inclusion will unlock new funding worldwide and access to facilities and infrastructure as many Governments only fund Olympic sports. It will also further establish Rugby Sevens in new and emerging markets and attract new fans, sponsors and broadcasters to the sport.

The campaign by the International Rugby Board gained universal acclaim across the rugby world with leading players like Lawrence Dallaglio, Agustín Pichot, Jonah Lomu and Cheryl Soon leading the way.

The Olympic Games will be the pinnacle for Rugby Sevens; a festival of the world's fittest and finest players. In order to ensure high standards of competition and a Sevens pathway across all continents, the IRB is already working on the qualifying structure, the role of the annual IRB Sevens World Series and the development of women's tournaments.

"Like the IOC we are committed to inspiring a new generation to play and watch sport. Currently there are over three million playing the game in 116 countries. We are determined to see that grow and that's why we are investing £153 million in development programmes over the next four years," said IRB Chief Executive Mike Miller.

"We will work with National Olympic Committees and our own Unions throughout the whole of the Olympiad, investing in training programmes, facilities and competitions to help them prepare for Rugby Sevens at the Olympic Games.

"We are already doing that in Mexico and India to ensure that the Pan American and Commonwealth Games are a huge success – and that a lasting legacy is in place for the growth of Rugby in those countries."

For smaller nations the opportunity to win an Olympic medal resonates, but so too does the opportunity to inspire more people to take up the sport in new communities bound by the Game's ideals of fair play, team work and respect.

Kenya is a modern day rugby success story. In a short space of time the Sevens team, led by the charismatic Humphrey Kayange, has set the world alight over the past two years, causing upsets, entertaining fans and challenging for honours.

They are not alone, Kenya's exploits has prompted growth across Africa with Uganda, Ethiopia, Nigeria, Ghana, Tunisia, Ivory Coast and Morocco, to name but a few, all making progress on the Sevens circuit. Olympic inclusion will provide another, more significant lift.

The impact that this decision will have on the future of the sport across Africa and in emerging nations around the world should not be underestimated. Rugby Sevens is now firmly on the map, it will be played on the world's greatest sporting stage and there will be significant growth.

"It is every sportsman and woman's dream to participate in an Olympic Games. Now that dream is a reality," said Kayange, a member of the IRB's presentation team in Copenhagen.

"Many sports in Africa are not funded centrally unless they are Olympic sports. Rugby was one of those sports, but now it is an Olympic sport, I would expect to see government support and assistance, NOC support and that means more teams playing at a more competitive level. It is very exciting."

Inclusion will also boost the women's game, which is experiencing significant global appeal. There are now more than 200,000 registered players worldwide and for gold medal winning Australia captain Soon, the heralding of a new era will have a big effect on the development of women's rugby worldwide.

"Women's rugby is experiencing unprecedented growth, but Olympic inclusion will provide further stimulus. We can look forward to the emergence of new nations with Sevens programmes, more competitive tournaments and what I am sure will be a remarkable Olympic Sevens tournament," said Soon.

The campaign, which had its origins a decade ago, was a key goal of the International Rugby Board's Strategic Plan and is testament to the hard work of the IRB, led by Lapasset, the IRB staff and of course the global rugby family.

There may still be six years to go until Sevens makes its debut, but the excitement is palpable. Rugby Sevens has finally been welcomed into the Olympic Games and sports fans from around the world will be in for a treat when the inaugural tournament kicks off in Brazil.

THE 2009 IRB AWARDS

A YEAR TO REMEMBER

By Iain Spragg

Aaron Cruden was named IRB Junior Player of the Year.

Italian First Division side L'Aquila were presented with the IRB Spirit of Rugby Award in 2009 after a tragic yet extraordinary year in which the club distinguished itself in the horrific aftermath of the earthquake that suddenly struck the area in April.

The quake killed 300 people and left many thousands more homeless. L'Aquila Rugby Club was quick to respond and offered local survivors food and accommodation as the prolonged clean up operation began. The club's players were also in the frontline, helping to put up tents on the pitch to ensure no-one was left without shelter.

Sadly, among the many fatalities was promising young L'Aquila prop

Lorenzo Sebastiani, who had had represented Italy at the IRB Junior World Championship in Wales the previous year.

"This is a very special award for a very special club," said IRB Chairman Bernard Lapasset. "The global rugby family were shocked and saddened by the events that unfolded in L'Aquila in April and share the grief at the loss of Lorenzo Sebastiani.

"However, the rugby family can take great pride and inspiration from the members of the club for their selfless action and unwavering spirit in helping their community come to terms with their loss."

L'Aquila was at the epicentre of the earthquake but despite the devastation, the club were playing rugby in their home stadium again just five months after the natural disaster.

"I would like to thank the IRB, to thank Bernard Lapasset and the Italian Federation for this great honour," said club president Giacomo Pasqua after accepting the award. "The city of L'Aquila was very proud to accept this and it has been a night of great emotion."

Elsewhere, England captain Ollie Phillips was named IRB Sevens Player of the Year. Succeeding New Zealand captain DJ Forbes, the Newcastle Falcon led his side to a first ever Series success in the NZI Sevens in Wellington and then the London Sevens at Twickenham for the first time in five years.

Nominated and voted for by the management of the 12 leading teams in the Series, Phillips beat off competition from Fiji's Emosi Vucago, South African World Series winning pair Mpho Mbiyozo and Renfred Dazel and Kenyan brothers Humphrey Kayange and Collins Injera, the season's top try scorer, to land the award.

He is the second Englishman to be named the IRB Sevens Player of the Year, following Simon Amor in 2004.

"It's been a fantastic year personally and collectively for our team and to captain any England side is a huge honour," Phillips said. "I was surprised to be on the shortlist of nominees for the award, so to win it is really very special.

"To do the things that we've done this season, where we've fallen short at some points and then we've had massive highs in Wellington and Twickenham was huge for us. This award is a special thing for me obviously. To be named as the best Sevens player in the world is amazing. There's a lot of players who've graced that turf who are pretty special too, some get recognised, some don't and fortunately for me people have picked me out. I'll be able to tell my grandkids when I'm looking slightly older than I do already that that was me and I was involved in that."

Australian No.8 Debby Hodgkinson was named the IRB Women's Personality of the Year after helping her team to qualify for Women's

Rugby World Cup 2010 with victory over Samoa in August. The powerful and dynamic 28-year-old scored in the Wallaroos' 87–0 win and is the first Australian to claim the award.

"We are delighted for Debby," said John O'Neill, the ARU's Managing Director and CEO. "Her achievements in the women's game and her contribution over a considerable period of time make her a thoroughly deserving recipient of this prestigious IRB Award.

"I had the pleasure of being in Dubai when the Australia Women's team won the World Cup Sevens this year and Debby, as a significant force throughout, was named the Player of the Tournament. Her powerful running has been a feature of the Sevens team and of the Wallaroos side since she made her debut for Australia in 2002."

Hodgkinson was in scintillating form at Rugby World Cup Sevens 2009 in Dubai, starting all six matches and scoring seven tries, including a superb score in a dramatic sudden-death extra-time final victory over New Zealand.

"Her outstanding and consistent performances were a strong feature of Australia's push to become world champions and Debby is a deserving recipient of this prestigious award," said Lapasset. "I would like to extend my congratulations to her on behalf of the International Rugby Board.

"The women's game was firmly positioned on the world sporting map this year with the introduction of the spectacular Women's Rugby World Cup Sevens in Dubai. A strong feature of the groundbreaking tournament was the competitiveness of the matches, the quality of the rugby and the emergence of true stars of the women's game. Debby is certainly one of them."

New Zealand captain Aaron Cruden was unveiled as the IRB Junior Player of the Year 2009, following in the footsteps of countryman Luke Braid who scooped the Award in 2008, to continue the Kiwi domination of the category in recent years and become the seventh Baby Black to receive the recognition.

"It is a huge honour to be named the best player for this age group at the Under 20 level and I am just extremely honoured," Cruden said. "I suppose the hard work that I have put in has paid off now."

The 20-year-old guided New Zealand to their second successive IRB Junior World Championship final against England, leading by example with two tries and creating another three as they triumphed 44–28 in Tokyo.

He had produced a similar performance in the semi-final against Australia four days earlier, creating two tries in as many minutes to turn the match in New Zealand's favour and kicking 11 points in the 31–17 victory. Cruden's composure, vision and inspirational leadership of a new-look New Zealand squad in Japan were the outstanding qualities which saw him claim the coveted award ahead of his New Zealand team-mate Winston Stanley, England No.8 Carl Fearns and Australian scrum-half Richard Kingi.

"He is worth his weight in gold to us," said New Zealand coach Dave Rennie. "I have been lucky enough to have a lot to do with Aaron. He is a very special player. He was very good against Australia and sensational against England.

"He is inspirational. He can put people in space around him or spot space in behind or an opportunity to run and it gives the team a lot of confidence having a guy like him at No. 10."

IRB HALL OF FAME

To coincide with the British & Irish Lions tour of South Africa, this year's IRB Hall of Fame induction is geared towards the encounters between the Lions and South Africa. The 2009 tour was the 13th to South Africa with the first visit by a British team taking place more than a century ago in 1891. A three month public vote on 19th, 20th and 21st century nominees was followed by deliberations by the Induction Panel to select the nine inductees for the IRB Hall of Fame ceremony at Rugby School on October 27. The previous 11 inductees can be viewed at www.irb.com.

Those inducted in 2009 were:

12. **Bill Maclagan** (Scotland and British)
13. **Barry Heatlie** (South Africa)
14. **Bennie Osler** (South Africa)
15. **Cliff Morgan** (Wales and Lions)
16. **Sir Anthony O'Reilly** (Ireland and Lions)
17. **Frik du Preez (**South Africa)
18. **Dr Syd Millar** (Ireland and Lions)
19. **William J McBride** (Ireland and Lions)
20. **Ian McGeechan** (Scotland and Lions)

IRB WORLD RANKINGS
THE MOVERS AND SHAKERS
By Karen Bond

For the 12 automatic qualifiers from Rugby World Cup 2007, the IRB World Rankings took on extra significance during the autumn internationals with the three bands they would be divided into for the Pool Allocation Draw for the 2011 tournament in New Zealand based on their rankings at 1 December 2008.

With the Pacific Islanders alliance touring Europe there were no matches for Fiji or Tonga so they would sit in band three, while going into the final weekend of the November Tests New Zealand, South Africa and Australia were certain to be in the top band.

This left just one place up for grabs with three sides dreaming of ending the year fourth and so ensuring they could not meet any of those World Cup winners until the knockout stages. Argentina held that position after briefly losing it earlier in the month, but England and Wales could unseat them if they got the right results against New Zealand and Australia respectively.

Only one of this trio managed a victory after Argentina lost 17–3 to Ireland and England fell 32–6 to the All Blacks. However, while Wales were the only one of the Home Unions to record a win over southern hemisphere opposition in the autumn, their 21–18 defeat of Australia was not by a big enough margin to displace the Pumas.

Argentina, therefore, would be the top seeds in one of the RWC 2011 pools, while Wales and England joined their Six Nations rivals France and Ireland in band two with Scotland, Fiji, Italy and Tonga making up the final band for the draw inside Tourism New Zealand's giant rugby ball in the heart of London.

The Pumas would not occupy that fourth position by the end of September 2009, having fallen to sixth with both Six Nations Grand Slam winners Ireland and France climbing above them. The Irish were the biggest movers in the Top 10 during this time, rising four places to become the leading northern hemisphere nation.

The most significant change in the Top 10 came at the summit with South Africa's first of three victories over New Zealand in the 2009 Tri-Nations seeing the rivals swap places, ending the All Blacks' 11-month reign at number one. South Africa won 11 of their 12 Tests – three against the British & Irish Lions – in the last year, while New Zealand lost four and could have fallen to third for the first time in nearly six years had they lost to Australia in Wellington.

Georgia were the biggest fallers in the Top 20, the Lelos slipping three places to 17th over the year with defeats by the lower ranked Canada and USA in the Churchill Cup cancelling out any gains by winning the European Nations Cup with an unbeaten record to lead the way in the region's qualifying process for RWC 2011.

While Georgia suffered a fall, there was better news for other European nations with Serbia, Israel and Netherlands all enjoying climbs into double figures. The Dutch climbed 12 places to 36th, Serbia jumped 13 to 60th, while Israel's climb by the same margin to 80th came in a memorable season which saw them beat three sides above them, including Slovenia – then ranked 28 places higher – in the region's first play-off round of RWC qualifying. By contrast Europe also had the three biggest fallers of the year with Monaco sliding 10 places, Latvia 12 and Andorra 13.

There were other notable climbers around the world with Malaysia rising 11 places, the majority of them on the back of beating China in the HSBC Asian Five Nations. Two other Asian sides on the rise were Kazakhstan, who enjoyed their highest ever ranking following victories over Korea and Hong Kong, and Division I winners Arabian Gulf with a six-place climb to 45th.

In Oceania, Papua New Guinea were the biggest climbers, up three to 50th after beating Vanuatu and Cook Islands to earn a RWC qualifying play-off with Samoa. By contrast Niue fell eight places after losing to Cook Islands in that qualifying process. Only Chile and Venezuela enjoyed small climbs among the South American nations, while Zimbabwe were Africa's biggest movers with an eight-place elevation to 46th, although Senegal also rose five to 63rd.

Canada and USA both climbed two places over the year, but the biggest movers in the North America and Caribbean region were Bermuda, up five places to 58th – their highest position for four years – while Cayman Islands also rose a couple of places. Guyana and Jamaica, meanwhile, are two of only 11 countries to remain stationary in the IRB World Rankings over the last 12 months.

The IRB World Rankings were introduced in October 2003 and are published every Monday on www.irb.com. They are calculated using a points exchange system in which teams take points off each other based on the match result. Whatever one team gains, the other team loses. The exchanges are determined by the match result, the relative strength of the team and the margin of victory. There is also an allowance for home advantage.

Ninety-five of the IRB's Member Unions have a rating, typically between 0 and 100 with the top side in the world usually having a rating above 90 – South Africa's was 91.69 at the time of writing. Any match that is not a full international between two countries or a Test against the Lions or Pacific Islanders does not count towards the rankings. Likewise neither does a match against a country that is not a Full Member Union of the IRB. For more details, visit www.irb.com.

POSITION	MEMBER UNION	RATING POINTS	MOVERS
1	South Africa	91.69	Up 1
2	New Zealand	89.61	Down 1
3	Australia	85.15	
4	Ireland	83.27	Up 4
5	France	81.48	Up 2
6	Argentina	81.29	Down 2
7	England	81.23	Down 2
8	Wales	80.74	Down 2
9	Fiji	76.52	Up 2
10	Scotland	75.23	Down 1
11	Samoa	73.48	Up 1
12	Italy	71.23	Down 2
13	Canada	70.07	Up 2
14	Japan	68.37	Up 2
15	Tonga	67.53	Down 2
16	Russia	67.17	Up 2
17	Georgia	66.85	Down 3
18	USA	65.97	Up 2
19	Romania	64.85	Down 2
20	Portugal	62.16	Up 3
21	Uruguay	61.97	Down 2
22	Spain	59.01	Down 1
23	Chile	57.95	Up 1
24	Korea	57.90	Down 2
25	Namibia	56.60	Up 1
26	Germany	55.35	Down 1
27	Tunisia	55.28	Up 2
28	Kazakhstan	55.12	Up 5
29	Brazil	54.97	Down 1
30	Ukraine	54.90	Up 6
31	Poland	53.70	
32	Belgium	53.67	Down 5
33	Morocco	53.06	Up 1
34	Hong Kong	52.07	Down 4
35	Czech Republic	51.48	
36	Netherlands	51.02	Up 12
37	Paraguay	50.93	Down 5
38	Lithuania	50.79	Up 5
39	Ivory Coast	50.31	Up 2
40	Moldova	49.84	Down 3
41	Uganda	49.71	Down 3
42	Kenya	49.68	Down 2
43	Croatia	48.94	Up 1
44	Sweden	48.03	Down 5
45	Arabian Gulf	47.96	Up 6
46	Trinidad & Tobago	47.19	Down 1

47	Zimbabwe	46.91	Up 8
48	Madagascar	46.90	Down 2
49	China	46.25	Down 7
50	Papua New Guinea	46.19	Up 3
51	Chinese Taipei	46.16	Down 2
52	Singapore	45.98	Up 2
53	Sri Lanka	45.90	Down 3
54	Malta	45.11	Up 2
55	Cook Islands	44.61	Up 2
56	Venezuela	43.92	Up 2
57	Switzerland	43.83	Down 5
58	Bermuda	43.59	Up 5
59	Latvia	43.52	Down 12
60	Serbia	43.09	Up 13
61	Slovenia	42.27	Up 5
62	Cayman	42.12	Up 2
63	Senegal	42.12	Up 5
64	Hungary	42.12	Up 6
65	Colombia	42.03	
66	Denmark	41.62	Down 6
67	Guyana	41.52	
68	Malaysia	41.23	Up 11
69	Niue Islands	41.11	Down 8
70	Thailand	40.84	Down 8
71	Peru	40.64	
72	Andorra	40.37	Down 13
73	Zambia	39.31	Down 1
74	St Vincent & The Grenadines	39.30	Up 1
75	Botswana	39.21	Down 1
76	Barbados	39.21	Down 7
77	Solomon Islands	39.06	Down 1
78	Cameroon	38.21	Down 1
79	St Lucia	37.57	Up 1
80	Israel	37.56	Up 13
81	Guam	36.80	Up 1
82	Swaziland	36.68	Up 1
83	India	36.61	Down 2
84	Jamaica	36.61	
85	Norway	36.44	Up 3
86	Bahamas	36.33	
87	Tahiti	36.25	
88	Monaco	35.92	Down 10
89	Bulgaria	35.49	Up 2
90	Bosnia & Herzegovina	35.43	Up 4
91	Nigeria	35.29	Down 2
92	Vanuatu	34.77	
93	Austria	34.01	Down 8
94	Luxembourg	33.52	Down 4
95	Finland	30.32	

INTERNATIONAL TOURNAMENTS

CANADA AND SAMOA BOUND FOR RWC 2011

By Karen Bond

The two-year countdown to Rugby World Cup 2011 may have begun on 9 September, but the qualification road began more than 18 months before and has now produced the first two nations – Canada and Samoa – to emerge from this global qualification process and confirm their place at the seventh edition of the showpiece in New Zealand.

Canada had the honour of becoming the first to join the 12 automatic qualifiers from Rugby World Cup 2007 – beating Samoa by a week – after defeating USA 41-18 to easily overhaul a six-point deficit from their first leg to qualify as Americas 1 and join hosts New Zealand, France, Tonga and the as yet unknown Asian representative in Pool A.

The Eagles had marked Independence Day with a 12-6 victory in Charleston, fly-half Mike Hercus kicking their points. However, a week later, Canada were on a mission to "put things right" in the words of coach Kieran Crowley and ran in six tries to mark prop Kevin Tkachuk's 50th Test in style before a crowd of around 5,000.

USA's cause was not helped by centre Paul Emerick's red card in the 27th minute and they must now regroup to face Uruguay in a home and away play-off with the winner qualifying as Americas 2 – slotting into Pool C with Australia, Ireland, Italy and Europe 2 – and the loser advancing to the final place play-off.

Uruguay lay in wait after recording convincing victories over Brazil and Chile in the South American Championship in late April-early May.

While the Americas qualifying process had been the first to begin – only six months after Springbok captain John Smit lifted the Webb Ellis Cup – by contrast Oceania was the last to get underway on 27 June when Papua New Guinea overwhelmed Vanuatu 86-12 in the West division of the Oceania Cup, to set up a final against Cook Islands, the 29-7 conquerors of Niue in the East division.

The 'prize' awaiting the Oceania Cup winner was a home and away play-off with Samoa, one that PNG Pukpuks claimed with a 29-21 victory in Port Moresby. Samoa were overwhelming favourites and showed just why, running in 17 tries – four of them by Esera Lauina – to win the first leg 115-7 in Apia. A week later it was slightly closer, Samoa triumphing 73-12 with Mikaele Pesamino grabbing a hat-trick.

All of which leaves six places remaining at RWC 2011, two to be claimed when the Americas and African processes conclude. USA or Uruguay will take one, while Namibia and Tunisia meet home and away in the Africa Cup final to secure the last spot in Pool D.

Veterans of three World Cups, Namibia enjoyed contrasting fortunes in their semi-final with Ivory Coast, drawing the first leg 13-13 and then winning 54-14 on home soil. Tunisia's passage was somewhat easier, having beaten Uganda 41-17 away and then 38-13 in Tunis to keep alive their dreams of qualifying for a first ever World Cup and becoming the continent's fifth nation to grace the stage. The loser will enter the final place play-off.

After that, the next two qualifiers will come from Europe in late March 2010, potentially two months before the HSBC Asian Five Nations determines that region's representative. The top two sides in the European Nations Cup, which concludes with a new condensed programme during the Six Nations window, will qualify directly as Europe 1 and Europe 2. Defending champions Georgia and Russia occupy those positions at the halfway stage, albeit only just from Portugal, with Romania not yet out of the picture.

The third placed team in Europe can also still qualify but must negotiate a two-legged European play-off and then the cross-continental play-off to join Argentina, England, Scotland and Europe 1 in Pool B. Three of the four rounds which will culminate in that European play-off have already taken place involving sides who topped their respective divisions at the halfway stage.

Israel, who play in Division 3C, upset Slovenia (3B) 26-19 in their country's first live televised rugby match, but then suffered a 19-3 defeat by Lithuania (3A) in Netanya. Lithuania themselves then caused a surprise, beating Division 2B's unbeaten side Netherlands 6-3 in Vilnius and now await the Division 2A winner in May.

The other continent with a qualifying process still underway is Asia, where the dream of playing at RWC 2011 is still alive for five nations – Japan, Kazakhstan, Korea, Hong Kong and Arabian Gulf. The latter guaranteed their place in the Asian Five Nations Top 5 in 2010 – which will decide the Asia 1 qualifier – by winning Division I in April.

POOLS FOR THE 2011 RUGBY WORLD CUP

POOL A: New Zealand, France. Tonga. Canada and **Asia** 1
POOL B: Argentina, England, Scotland, Europe 1 Play-off Winner
POOL C: Australia, Ireland, Italy, Europe 2, **Americas** 2
POOL D: South Africa, Wales, Fiji, Samoa, Africa 1
Pools as at 30 October 2009

RUGBY WORLD CUP 2011

RUGBY WORLD CUP TOURNAMENTS 1987–2007

SIXTH TOURNAMENT: 2007

IN FRANCE, WALES & SCOTLAND

POOL A

England	28	United States	10
South Africa	59	Samoa	7
United States	15	Tonga	25
England	0	South Africa	36
Samoa	15	Tonga	19
South Africa	30	Tonga	25
England	44	Samoa	22
Samoa	25	United States	21
England	36	Tonga	20
South Africa	64	United States	15

	P	W	D	L	F	A	Pts
South Africa	4	4	0	0	189	47	19
England	4	3	0	1	108	88	14
Tonga	4	2	0	2	89	96	9
Samoa	4	1	0	3	69	143	5
United States	4	0	0	4	61	142	1

POOL B

Australia	91	Japan	3
Wales	42	Canada	17
Japan	31	Fiji	35
Wales	20	Australia	32
Fiji	29	Canada	16
Wales	72	Japan	18
Australia	55	Fiji	12
Canada	12	Japan	12
Australia	37	Canada	6
Wales	34	Fiji	38

	P	W	D	L	F	A	Pts
Australia	4	4	0	0	215	41	20
Fiji	4	3	0	1	114	136	15
Wales	4	2	0	2	168	105	12
Japan	4	0	1	3	64	210	3
Canada	4	0	1	3	51	120	2

POOL C

New Zealand	76	Italy	14
Scotland	56	Portugal	10
Italy	24	Romania	18
New Zealand	108	Portugal	13
Scotland	42	Romania	0
Italy	31	Portugal	5
Scotland	0	New Zealand	40
Romania	14	Portugal	10
New Zealand	85	Romania	8
Scotland	18	Italy	16

	P	W	D	L	F	A	Pts
New Zealand	4	4	0	0	309	35	20
Scotland	4	3	0	1	116	66	14
Italy	4	2	0	2	85	117	9
Romania	4	1	0	3	40	161	5
Portugal	4	0	0	4	38	209	1

POOL D

France	12	Argentina	17
Ireland	32	Namibia	17
Argentina	33	Georgia	3
Ireland	14	Georgia	10
France	87	Namibia	10
France	25	Ireland	3
Argentina	63	Namibia	3
Georgia	30	Namibia	0
France	64	Georgia	7
Ireland	15	Argentina	30

	P	W	D	L	F	A	Pts
Argentina	4	4	0	0	143	33	18
France	4	3	0	1	188	37	15
Ireland	4	2	0	2	64	82	9
Georgia	4	1	0	3	50	111	5
Namibia	4	0	0	4	30	212	0

QUARTER-FINALS

Australia	10	England	12
New Zealand	18	France	20
South Africa	37	Fiji	20
Argentina	19	Scotland	13

SEMI-FINALS

France	9	England	14
South Africa	37	Argentina	13

BRONZE MEDAL MATCH

France	10	Argentina	34

SOUTH AFRICA 15 (5PG)
ENGLAND 6 (2PG)

SOUTH AFRICA: P C Montgomery; J–P R Pietersen, J Fourie, F P L Steyn, B G Habana; A D James, P F du Preez; J P du Randt, J W Smit (*captain*), C J van der Linde, J P Botha, V Matfield, J H Smith, D J Rossouw, S W P Burger *Substitutions:* J L van Heerden for Rossouw (72 mins); B W du Plessis for Smit (temp 71 to 76 mins)

SCORERS *Penalty Goals*: Montgomery (4), Steyn

ENGLAND: J T Robinson; P H Sackey, M Tait, M J Catt, M J Cueto; J P Wilkinson, A C T Gomarsall; A J Sheridan, M P Regan, P J Vickery (*captain*), S D Shaw, B J Kay, M E Corry, N Easter, L W Moody *Substitutions:* M J H Stevens for Vickery (40 mins); D Hipkiss for Robinson (46 mins); T Flood for Catt (50 mins); G S Chuter for Regan (62 mins); J P R Worsley for Moody (62 mins); L B N Dallaglio for Easter (64 mins); P C Richards for Worsley (70 mins)

SCORER *Penalty Goals*: Wilkinson (2)

REFEREE A C Rolland (Ireland)

Dave Rogers/Getty Images

Victorious captain John Smit of South Africa receives the trophy from French President, Nicolas Sarkozy after the 2007 final.

RUGBY WORLD CUP TOURNAMENTS

FIFTH TOURNAMENT: 2003
IN AUSTRALIA

POOL A

Australia	24	Argentina	8
Ireland	45	Romania	17
Argentina	67	Namibia	14
Australia	90	Romania	8
Ireland	64	Namibia	7
Argentina	50	Romania	3
Australia	142	Namibia	0
Ireland	16	Argentina	15
Romania	37	Namibia	7
Australia	17	Ireland	16

	P	W	D	L	F	A	Pts
Australia	4	4	0	0	273	32	18
Ireland	4	3	0	1	141	56	14
Argentina	4	2	0	2	140	57	11
Romania	4	1	0	3	65	192	5
Namibia	4	0	0	4	28	310	0

POOL B

France	61	Fiji	18
Scotland	32	Japan	11
Fiji	19	United States	18
France	51	Japan	29
Scotland	39	United States	15
Fiji	41	Japan	13
France	51	Scotland	9
United States	39	Japan	26
France	41	United States	14
Scotland	22	Fiji	20

	P	W	D	L	F	A	Pts
France	4	4	0	0	204	70	20
Scotland	4	3	0	1	102	97	14
Fiji	4	2	0	2	98	114	9
United States	4	1	0	3	86	125	6
Japan	4	0	0	4	79	163	0

POOL C

South Africa	72	Uruguay	6
England	84	Georgia	6
Samoa	60	Uruguay	13
England	25	South Africa	6
Samoa	46	Georgia	9
South Africa	46	Georgia	19
England	35	Samoa	22
Uruguay	24	Georgia	12
South Africa	60	Samoa	10
England	111	Uruguay	13

	P	W	D	L	F	A	Pts
England	4	4	0	0	255	47	19
South Africa	4	3	0	1	184	60	15
Samoa	4	2	0	2	138	117	10
Uruguay	4	1	0	3	56	255	4
Georgia	4	0	0	4	46	200	0

POOL D

New Zealand	70	Italy	7
Wales	41	Canada	10
Italy	36	Tonga	12
New Zealand	68	Canada	6
Wales	27	Tonga	20
Italy	19	Canada	14
New Zealand	91	Tonga	7
Wales	27	Italy	15
Canada	24	Tonga	7
New Zealand	53	Wales	37

	P	W	D	L	F	A	Pts
New Zealand	4	4	0	0	282	57	20
Wales	4	3	0	1	132	98	14
Italy	4	2	0	2	77	123	8
Canada	4	1	0	3	54	135	5
Tonga	4	0	0	4	46	178	1

QUARTER-FINALS

New Zealand	29	South Africa	9
Australia	33	Scotland	16
France	43	Ireland	21
England	28	Wales	17

SEMI-FINALS

Australia	22	New Zealand	10
England	24	France	7

THIRD PLACE MATCH

New Zealand	40	France	13

Fifth World Cup Final, Telstra Stadium, Sydney, 22 November 2003

ENGLAND 20 (4PG 1DG 1T)
AUSTRALIA 17 (4PG 1T) *

ENGLAND: J Robinson; O J Lewsey, W J H Greenwood, M J Tindall, B C Cohen; J P Wilkinson, M J S Dawson; T J Woodman, S Thompson, P J Vickery, M O Johnson (captain), B J Kay, R A Hill, L B N Dallaglio, N A Back Substitutions: M J Catt for Tindall (78 mins); J Leonard for Vickery (80 mins); I R Balshaw for Lewsey (85 mins); L W Moody for Hill (93 mins)

SCORERS *Try*: Robinson *Penalty Goals*: Wilkinson (4) *Dropped Goal*: Wilkinson

AUSTRALIA: M S Rogers; W J Sailor, S A Mortlock, E J Flatley, L Tuqiri; S J Larkham, G M Gregan (captain); W K Young, B J Cannon, A K E Baxter, J B Harrison, N C Sharpe, G B Smith, D J Lyons, P R Waugh Substitutions: D T Giffin for Sharpe (48 mins); J A Paul for Cannon (56 mins); M J Cockbain for Lyons (56 mins); J W Roff for Sailor (70 mins); M J Dunning for Young (92 mins); M J Giteau for Larkham (temp 18 to 30 mins; 55 to 63 mins; 85 to 93 mins)

SCORERS *Try*: Tuqiri *Penalty Goals*: Flatley (4)

REFEREE A J Watson (South Africa)

* after extra time: 14–14 after normal time

Jonny Wilkinson and Martin Johnson get to grips with 'Bill'.

RUGBY WORLD CUP TOURNAMENTS

FOURTH TOURNAMENT: 1999
IN BRITAIN, IRELAND & FRANCE

INTERNATIONAL TOURNAMENTS

POOL A

Spain	15	Uruguay	27
South Africa	46	Scotland	29
Scotland	43	Uruguay	12
South Africa	47	Spain	3
South Africa	39	Uruguay	3
Scotland	48	Spain	0

	P	W	D	L	F	A	Pts
South Africa	3	3	0	0	132	35	9
Scotland	3	2	0	1	120	58	7
Uruguay	3	1	0	2	42	97	5
Spain	3	0	0	3	18	122	3

POOL B

England	67	Italy	7
New Zealand	45	Tonga	9
England	16	New Zealand	30
Italy	25	Tonga	28
New Zealand	101	Italy	3
England	101	Tonga	10

	P	W	D	L	F	A	Pts
New Zealand	3	3	0	0	176	28	9
England	3	2	0	1	184	47	7
Tonga	3	1	0	2	47	171	5
Italy	3	0	0	3	35	196	3

POOL C

Fiji	67	Namibia	18
France	33	Canada	20
France	47	Namibia	13
Fiji	38	Canada	22
Canada	72	Namibia	11
France	28	Fiji	19

	P	W	D	L	F	A	Pts
France	3	3	0	0	108	52	9
Fiji	3	2	0	1	124	68	7
Canada	3	1	0	2	114	82	5
Namibia	3	0	0	3	42	186	3

POOL D

Wales	23	Argentina	18
Samoa	43	Japan	9
Wales	64	Japan	15
Argentina	32	Samoa	16
Wales	31	Samoa	38
Argentina	33	Japan	12

	P	W	D	L	F	A	Pts
Wales	3	2	0	1	118	71	7
Samoa	3	2	0	1	97	72	7
Argentina	3	2	0	1	83	51	7
Japan	3	0	0	3	36	140	3

POOL E

Ireland	53	United States	8
Australia	57	Romania	9
United States	25	Romania	27
Ireland	3	Australia	23
Australia	55	United States	19
Ireland	44	Romania	14

	P	W	D	L	F	A	Pts
Australia	3	3	0	0	135	31	9
Ireland	3	2	0	1	100	45	7
Romania	3	1	0	2	50	126	5
United States	3	0	0	3	52	135	3

PLAY-OFFS FOR QUARTER-FINAL PLACES

England	45	Fiji	24
Scotland	35	Samoa	20
Ireland	24	Argentina	28

QUARTER-FINALS

Wales	9	Australia	24
South Africa	44	England	21
France	47	Argentina	26
Scotland	18	New Zealand	30

SEMI-FINALS

South Africa	21	Australia	27
New Zealand	31	France	43

THIRD PLACE MATCH

South Africa	22	New Zealand	18

Fourth World Cup Final, Millennium Stadium, Cardiff, 6 November 1999

AUSTRALIA 35 (2G 7PG) FRANCE 12 (4PG)

AUSTRALIA: M Burke; B N Tune, D J Herbert, T J Horan, J W Roff; S J Larkham, G M Gregan; R L L Harry, M A Foley, A T Blades, D T Giffin, J A Eales (captain), M J Cockbain, R S T Kefu, D J Wilson Substitutions J S Little for Herbert (46 mins); O D A Finegan for Cockbain (52 mins); M R Connors for Wilson (73 mins); D J Crowley for Harry (75 mins); J A Paul for Foley (85 mins); C J Whitaker for Gregan (86 mins); N P Grey for Horan (86 mins)

SCORERS *Tries:* Tune, Finegan *Conversions:* Burke (2) *Penalty Goals:* Burke (7)

FRANCE: X Garbajosa; P Bernat Salles, R Dourthe, E Ntamack, C Dominici; C Lamaison, F Galthié; C Soulette, R Ibañez (captain), F Tournaire, A Benazzi, F Pelous, M Lièvremont, C Juillet, O Magne Substitutions O Brouzet for Juillet (HT); P de Villiers for Soulette (47 mins); A Costes for Magne (temp 19 to 22 mins) and for Lièvremont (67 mins); U Mola for Garbajosa (67 mins); S Glas for Dourthe (temp 49 to 55 mins and from 74 mins); S Castaignède for Galthié (76 mins); M Dal Maso for Ibañez (79 mins)

SCORER *Penalty Goals:* Lamaison (4)

REFEREE A J Watson (South Africa)

Dave Rogers/Getty Images

Australia are world champions for the second time.

THIRD TOURNAMENT: 1995
IN SOUTH AFRICA

POOL A

South Africa	27	Australia	18
Canada	34	Romania	3
South Africa	21	Romania	8
Australia	27	Canada	11
Australia	42	Romania	3
South Africa	20	Canada	0

	P	W	D	L	F	A	Pts
South Africa	3	3	0	0	68	26	9
Australia	3	2	0	1	87	41	7
Canada	3	1	0	2	45	50	5
Romania	3	0	0	3	14	97	3

POOL B

Western Samoa	42	Italy	18
England	24	Argentina	18
Western Samoa	32	Argentina	26
England	27	Italy	20
Italy	31	Argentina	25
England	44	Western Samoa	22

	P	W	D	L	F	A	Pts
England	3	3	0	0	95	60	9
Western Samoa	3	2	0	1	96	88	7
Italy	3	1	0	2	69	94	5
Argentina	3	0	0	3	69	87	3

POOL C

Wales	57	Japan	10
New Zealand	43	Ireland	19
Ireland	50	Japan	28
New Zealand	34	Wales	9
New Zealand	145	Japan	17
Ireland	24	Wales	23

	P	W	D	L	F	A	Pts
New Zealand	3	3	0	0	222	45	9
Ireland	3	2	0	1	93	94	7
Wales	3	1	0	2	89	68	5
Japan	3	0	0	3	55	252	3

POOL D

Scotland	89	Ivory Coast	0
France	38	Tonga	10
France	54	Ivory Coast	18
Scotland	41	Tonga	5
Tonga	29	Ivory Coast	11
France	22	Scotland	19

	P	W	D	L	F	A	Pts
France	3	3	0	0	114	47	9
Scotland	3	2	0	1	149	27	7
Tonga	3	1	0	2	44	90	5
Ivory Coast	3	0	0	3	29	172	3

QUARTER-FINALS

France	36	Ireland	12
South Africa	42	Western Samoa	14
England	25	Australia	22
New Zealand	48	Scotland	30

SEMI-FINALS

South Africa	19	France	15
New Zealand	45	England	29

THIRD PLACE MATCH

France	19	England	9

SOUTH AFRICA 15 (3PG 2DG)
NEW ZEALAND 12 (3PG 1DG) *

SOUTH AFRICA: A J Joubert; J T Small, J C Mulder, H P Le Roux, C M Williams; J T Stransky, J H van der Westhuizen; J P du Randt, C L C Rossouw, I S Swart, J J Wiese, J J Strydom, J F Pienaar (captain), M G Andrews, R J Kruger Substitutions: G L Pagel for Swart (68 mins); R A W Straeuli for Andrews (90 mins); B Venter for Small (97 mins)

SCORER *Penalty Goals*: Stransky (3) *Drop Goals*: Stransky (2)

NEW ZEALAND: G M Osborne; J W Wilson, F E Bunce, W K Little, J T Lomu; A P Mehrtens, G T M Bachop; C W Dowd, S B T Fitzpatrick (captain), O M Brown, I D Jones, R M Brooke, M R Brewer, Z V Brooke, J A Kronfeld Substitutions: J W Joseph for Brewer (40 mins); M C G Ellis for Wilson (55 mins); R W Loe for Dowd (83 mins); A D Strachan for Bachop (temp 66 to 71 mins)

SCORER *Penalty Goals*: Mehrtens (3) *Drop Goal*: Mehrtens

REFEREE E F Morrison (England)

* after extra time: 9–9 after normal time

Simon Bruty/Getty Images

Joel Stransky wins the World Cup for South Africa.

RUGBY WORLD CUP TOURNAMENTS

SECOND TOURNAMENT: 1991
IN BRITAIN, IRELAND & FRANCE

INTERNATIONAL TOURNAMENTS

POOL 1

New Zealand	18	England	12
Italy	30	USA	9
New Zealand	46	USA	6
England	36	Italy	6
England	37	USA	9
New Zealand	31	Italy	21

	P	W	D	L	F	A	Pts
New Zealand	3	3	0	0	95	39	9
England	3	2	0	1	85	33	7
Italy	3	1	0	2	57	76	5
USA	3	0	0	3	24	113	3

POOL 2

Scotland	47	Japan	9
Ireland	55	Zimbabwe	11
Ireland	32	Japan	16
Scotland	51	Zimbabwe	12
Scotland	24	Ireland	15
Japan	52	Zimbabwe	8

	P	W	D	L	F	A	Pts
Scotland	3	3	0	0	122	36	9
Ireland	3	2	0	1	102	51	7
Japan	3	1	0	2	77	87	5
Zimbabwe	3	0	0	3	31	158	3

POOL 3

Australia	32	Argentina	19
Western Samoa	16	Wales	13
Australia	9	Western Samoa	3
Wales	16	Argentina	7
Australia	38	Wales	3
Western Samoa	35	Argentina	12

	P	W	D	L	F	A	Pts
Australia	3	3	0	0	79	25	9
Western Samoa	3	2	0	1	54	34	7
Wales	3	1	0	2	32	61	5
Argentina	3	0	0	3	38	83	3

POOL 4

France	30	Romania	3
Canada	13	Fiji	3
France	33	Fiji	9
Canada	19	Romania	11
Romania	17	Fiji	15
France	19	Canada	13

	P	W	D	L	F	A	Pts
France	3	3	0	0	82	25	9
Canada	3	2	0	1	45	33	7
Romania	3	1	0	2	31	64	5
Fiji	3	0	0	3	27	63	3

QUARTER-FINALS

England	19	France	10
Scotland	28	Western Samoa	6
Australia	19	Ireland	18
New Zealand	29	Canada	13

SEMI-FINALS

| England | 9 | Scotland | 6 |
| Australia | 16 | New Zealand | 6 |

THIRD PLACE MATCH

| New Zealand | 13 | Scotland | 6 |

AUSTRALIA 12 (1G 2PG)
ENGLAND 6 (2PG)

AUSTRALIA: M C Roebuck; D I Campese, J S Little, T J Horan, R H Egerton; M P Lynagh, N C Farr-Jones (captain); A J Daly, P N Kearns, E J A McKenzie, R J McCall, J A Eales, S P Poidevin, T Coker, V Ofahengaue

SCORERS *Try*: Daly *Conversion*: Lynagh *Penalty Goals*: Lynagh (2)

ENGLAND: J M Webb; S J Halliday, W D C Carling (captain), J C Guscott, R Underwood; C R Andrew, R J Hill; J Leonard, B C Moore, J A Probyn, P J Ackford, W A Dooley, M G Skinner, M C Teague, P J Winterbottom

SCORER *Penalty Goals*: Webb (2)

REFEREE W D Bevan (Wales)

Getty Images

Nick Farr-Jones and Michael Lynagh bring the Webb Ellis Cup back to Australia.

RUGBY WORLD CUP TOURNAMENTS

FIRST TOURNAMENT: 1987
IN AUSTRALIA & NEW ZEALAND

POOL 1

Australia	19	England	6
USA	21	Japan	18
England	60	Japan	7
Australia	47	USA	12
England	34	USA	6
Australia	42	Japan	23

	P	W	D	L	F	A	Pts
Australia	3	3	0	0	108	41	6
England	3	2	0	1	100	32	4
USA	3	1	0	2	39	99	2
Japan	3	0	0	3	48	123	0

POOL 2

Canada	37	Tonga	4
Wales	13	Ireland	6
Wales	29	Tonga	16
Ireland	46	Canada	19
Wales	40	Canada	9
Ireland	32	Tonga	9

	P	W	D	L	F	A	Pts
Wales	3	3	0	0	82	31	6
Ireland	3	2	0	1	84	41	4
Canada	3	1	0	2	65	90	2
Tonga	3	0	0	3	29	98	0

POOL 3

New Zealand	70	Italy	6
Fiji	28	Argentina	9
New Zealand	74	Fiji	13
Argentina	25	Italy	16
Italy	18	Fiji	15
New Zealand	46	Argentina	15

	P	W	D	L	F	A	Pts
New Zealand	3	3	0	0	190	34	6
Fiji	3	1	0	2	56	101	2
Argentina	3	1	0	2	49	90	2
Italy	3	1	0	2	40	110	2

POOL 4

Romania	21	Zimbabwe	20
France	20	Scotland	20
France	55	Romania	12
Scotland	60	Zimbabwe	21
France	70	Zimbabwe	12
Scotland	55	Romania	28

	P	W	D	L	F	A	Pts
France	3	2	1	0	145	44	5
Scotland	3	2	1	0	135	69	5
Romania	3	1	0	2	61	130	2
Zimbabwe	3	0	0	3	53	151	0

QUARTER-FINALS

New Zealand	30	Scotland	3
France	31	Fiji	16
Australia	33	Ireland	15
Wales	16	England	3

SEMI-FINALS

France	30	Australia	24
New Zealand	49	Wales	6

THIRD PLACE MATCH

Wales	22	Australia	21

NEW ZEALAND 29 (1G 4PG 1DG 2T)
FRANCE 9 (1G 1PG)

NEW ZEALAND: J A Gallagher; J J Kirwan, J T Stanley, W T Taylor, C I Green; G J Fox, D E Kirk (captain); S C McDowell, S B T Fitzpatrick, J A Drake, M J Pierce, G W Whetton, A J Whetton, W T Shelford, M N Jones

SCORERS *Tries***:** Jones, Kirk, Kirwan *Conversion*: Fox *Penalty Goals*: Fox (4) *Drop Goal*: Fox

FRANCE: S Blanco; D Camberabero, P Sella, D Charvet, P Lagisquet; F Mesnel, P Berbizier; P Ondarts, D Dubroca (captain), J–P Garuet, A Lorieux, J Condom, E Champ, L Rodriguez, D Erbani

SCORERS *Try*: Berbizier *Conversion*: Camberabero *Penalty Goal*: Camberabero

REFEREE K V J Fitzgerald (Australia)

Getty Images

Skipper David Kirk crashes over the line in the final, against France.

RUGBY WORLD CUP TOURNAMENTS

RUGBY WORLD CUP RECORDS 1987–2007

(FINAL STAGES ONLY)

OVERALL RECORDS

MOST MATCHES WON IN FINAL STAGES

30	New Zealand
28	Australia
26	France
25	England

MOST OVERALL POINTS IN FINAL STAGES

249	J P Wilkinson	England	1999–2007
227	A G Hastings	Scotland	1987–1995
195	M P Lynagh	Australia	1987–1995
170	G J Fox	New Zealand	1987–1991
163	A P Mehrtens	New Zealand	1995–1999

MOST OVERALL TRIES IN FINAL STAGES

15	J T Lomu	New Zealand	1995–1999
13	D C Howlett	New Zealand	2003–2007
11	R Underwood	England	1987–1995
11	J T Rokocoko	New Zealand	2003–2007
11	C E Latham	Australia	1999–2007

MOST OVERALL CONVERSIONS IN FINAL STAGES

39	A G Hastings	Scotland	1987–1995
37	G J Fox	New Zealand	1987–1991
36	M P Lynagh	Australia	1987–1995
29	D W Carter	New Zealand	2003–2007
27	P J Grayson	England	1999–2003

MOST OVERALL PENALTY GOALS IN FINAL STAGES

53	J P Wilkinson	England	1999–2007
36	A G Hastings	Scotland	1987–1995
35	G Quesada	Argentina	1999–2003
33	M P Lynagh	Australia	1987–1995
33	A P Mehrtens	New Zealand	1995–1999

MOST OVERALL DROPPED GOALS IN FINAL STAGES

13	J P Wilkinson	England	1999–2007
6	J H de Beer	South Africa	1999
5	C R Andrew	England	1987–1995
5	G L Rees	Canada	1987–1999
4	J M Hernández	Argentina	2003–2007

MOST MATCH APPEARANCES IN FINAL STAGES

22	J Leonard	England	1991–2003
20	G M Gregan	Australia	1995–2007
19	M J Catt	England	1995–2007
18	M O Johnson	England	1995–2003
18	B P Lima	Samoa	1991–2007
18	R Ibañez	France	1999–2007

MOST POINTS IN ONE COMPETITION

126	G J Fox	New Zealand	1987
113	J P Wilkinson	England	2003
112	T Lacroix	France	1995
105	P C Montgomery	South Africa	2007
104	A G Hastings	Scotland	1995
103	F Michalak	France	2003
102	G Quesada	Argentina	1999
101	M Burke	Australia	1999

MOST PENALTY GOALS IN ONE COMPETITION

31	G Quesada	Argentina	1999
26	T Lacroix	France	1995
23	J P Wilkinson	England	2003
21	G J Fox	New Zealand	1987
21	E J Flatley	Australia	2003
20	C R Andrew	England	1995

MOST TRIES IN ONE COMPETITION

8	J T Lomu	New Zealand	1999
8	B G Habana	South Africa	2007
7	M C G Ellis	New Zealand	1995
7	J T Lomu	New Zealand	1995
7	D C Howlett	New Zealand	2003
7	J M Muliaina	New Zealand	2003
7	D A Mitchell	Australia	2007

MOST DROPPED GOALS IN ONE COMPETITION

8	J P Wilkinson	England	2003
6	J H de Beer	South Africa	1999
5	J P Wilkinson	England	2007
4	J M Hernández	Argentina	2007

MOST CONVERSIONS IN ONE COMPETITION

30	G J Fox	New Zealand	1987
22	P C Montgomery	South Africa	2007
20	S D Culhane	New Zealand	1995
20	M P Lynagh	Australia	1987
20	L R MacDonald	New Zealand	2003
20	N J Evans	New Zealand	2007

RUGBY WORLD CUP RECORDS

INTERNATIONAL TOURNAMENTS

MOST POINTS IN A MATCH
BY THE TEAM

145	New Zealand v Japan	1995
142	Australia v Namibia	2003
111	England v Uruguay	2003
108	New Zealand v Portugal	2007
101	New Zealand v Italy	1999
101	England v Tonga	1999

BY A PLAYER

45	S D Culhane	New Zealand v Japan	1995
44	A G Hastings	Scotland v Ivory Coast	1995
42	M S Rogers	Australia v Namibia	2003
36	T E Brown	New Zealand v Italy	1999
36	P J Grayson	England v Tonga	1999
34	J H de Beer	South Africa v England	1999
33	N J Evans	New Zealand v Portugal	2007
32	J P Wilkinson	England v Italy	1999

MOST TRIES IN A MATCH
BY THE TEAM

22	Australia v Namibia	2003
21	New Zealand v Japan	1995
17	England v Uruguay	2003
16	New Zealand v Portugal	2007
14	New Zealand v Italy	1999

BY A PLAYER

6	M C G Ellis	New Zealand v Japan	1995
5	C E Latham	Australia v Namibia	2003
5	O J Lewsey	England v Uruguay	2003
4	I C Evans	Wales v Canada	1987
4	C I Green	New Zealand v Fiji	1987
4	J A Gallagher	New Zealand v Fiji	1987
4	B F Robinson	Ireland v Zimbabwe	1991
4	A G Hastings	Scotland v Ivory Coast	1995
4	C M Williams	South Africa v Western Samoa	1995
4	J T Lomu	New Zealand v England	1995
4	K G M Wood	Ireland v United States	1999
4	J M Muliaina	New Zealand v Canada	2003
4	B G Habana	South Africa v Samoa	2007

MOST CONVERSIONS IN A MATCH
BY THE TEAM

20	New Zealand v Japan	1995
16	Australia v Namibia	2003
14	New Zealand v Portugal	2007
13	New Zealand v Tonga	2003
13	England v Uruguay	2003

BY A PLAYER

20	S D Culhane	New Zealand v Japan	1995
16	M S Rogers	Australia v Namibia	2003
14	N J Evans	New Zealand v Portugal	2007
12	P J Grayson	England v Tonga	1999
12	L R MacDonald	New Zealand v Tonga	2003

MOST PENALTY GOALS IN A MATCH
BY THE TEAM

8	Australia v South Africa	1999
8	Argentina v Samoa	1999
8	Scotland v Tonga	1995
8	France v Ireland	1995

BY A PLAYER

8	M Burke	Australia v South Africa	1999
8	G Quesada	Argentina v Samoa	1999
8	A G Hastings	Scotland v Tonga	1995
8	T Lacroix	France v Ireland	1995

MOST DROPPED GOALS IN A MATCH
BY THE TEAM

5	South Africa v England	1999
3	Fiji v Romania	1991
3	England v France	2003
3	Argentina v Ireland	2007

BY A PLAYER

5	J H de Beer	South Africa v England	1999
3	J P Wilkinson	England v France	2003
3	J M Hernández	Argentina v Ireland	2007

EXPECT THE UNEXPECTED!

By Karen Bond

Wales celebrate their stunning victory, confirming them as new world champions.

Rugby World Cup Sevens 2009 was always guaranteed its place in the history books given it was the first ever to include a women's competition alongside the men's, but what transpired on a breathtaking final day at 'The Sevens' in Dubai will live long in the memory as proof that anything can, and often does, happen in the pulsating and non-stop version of the game.

That said, few would have been brave enough to predict that Wales, regarded as 80–1 outsiders for the 24-team men's tournament, would lift the Melrose Cup for the first time, nor that all four of the fancied teams –

New Zealand, Fiji, England and South Africa – would fall by the wayside in the Cup quarter-finals during a remarkable hour and a half of scintillating play.

Wales had kicked off the derailment of the traditional Sevens powers, Tom Isaac's late try dumping New Zealand out of the tournament 15–14 and leaving the 2001 champions to rue the ball dropped by Viliami Waqaseduadua with the try-line at his mercy. This quarter-final, though, was only the appetiser for 30,000 fans enjoying the glorious weather.

Next up was an incredible seesaw battle between England and Samoa, the islanders racing into a 21–7 lead only for Josh Drauniniu to level it at 26–26 with a try after the full-time hooter. Samoa's chance seemed to have gone, but they had one more trick up their sleeve. Ben Gollings hesitated in defence in the knowledge he was offside, Samoa pounced and Simaika Mikaele's try had coach Rudi Moors cart-wheeling on the sidelines.

South Africa, the World Series leaders at the halfway stage, were next to fall with tries from Martin Bustos Moyano giving Argentina a 14–12 win. It was left to Kenya, therefore, to provide the African presence in the last four, the fans' favourites running in three second half tries to end Fiji's reign as champions and keep alive coach Benjamin Ayimba's prediction of six months earlier that his side would lift the Melrose Cup.

Four teams from different continents duly lined up for the semi-finals with the crowd unsure what to expect next. Unfortunately for Ayimba, the exploits against Fiji seemed to take their toll on his side and despite giving it their all they were on the end of a 12–0 loss to Argentina, Bustos Moyano again among the try-scorers. Argentina would therefore face Wales – a side they had beaten 14–0 in the pool stages the day before – in the final, Isaacs again having scored what turned out to be the winning try as Samoa ran out of time to overturn a 12-point deficit, going down 19–12.

The Melrose Cup final was another match which had everyone in 'The Sevens' on the edge of their seats, twisting one way and then the other, with Richie Pugh and Tal Selley scoring tries to give Wales a slender 12–7 half-time advantage. Gonzalo Camacho chased down a cross-field kick to level the scores, but just as another final seemed to be heading for extra-time up popped Aled Thomas to touch down and ensure it was Tom Jones' hit 'Delilah' that rang out at the final whistle.

"It's amazing. It hasn't quite sunk in yet," captain Lee Beach said after lifting the trophy. "We have always said about going for a Cup final and it came at the right time – it's a World Cup final. I guess it will take a while to sink in. I just don't know what to say, we are over the moon."

Wales, though, were not the only European nation celebrating on that balmy March evening with Scotland having beaten Australia 21–17 in the Plate final, Andrew Turnbull having scored two of their three tries.

However, there would be no clean sweep with Zimbabwe beating Ireland 17–14 in the Bowl final, Jacques Leitao's late try ensuring his side left Dubai as Africa's only silverware winners.

The quarter-final exits of the big guns and crowning of surprise champions may have grabbed their fair share of the headlines, but the inaugural women's competition was just as enthralling from start to finish as the 16 participating teams seized their opportunity to showcase all that their game has to offer and more besides with plenty of upsets and nail-biting affairs along the way.

Australia and China had the honour of contesting the first ever women's match in RWC Sevens history on 6 March and so it was perhaps fitting that both nations ended the tournament with some extra luggage to take home after final successes. For the record, Australia ran out 50–12 winners to get their campaign off to the perfect start with Bo de la Cruz and Tricia Brown claiming hat-tricks against a Chinese side who looked dangerous in attack.

The Australians had a number of players from a background of touch football and their winning mentality had rubbed off on the other, more experienced members of the squad. They had arrived in Dubai as Oceania champions, buoyed by their first ever wins over the New Zealand Black Ferns, and determined to write their names into the history books.

They would ultimately realise that goal, but they certainly went about it the hard way after suffering the first loss since the Australia Women's Sevens team was formed in 2008, in their second pool match against France. The French had lost to the Netherlands 17–14 but hit back to beat Australia 14–10, albeit only after a try-saving tackle from Anais Lagougine denied Debby Hodgkinson the winning try.

Hodgkinson did score four tries as Australia saw off the Dutch 36–0, but the defeat by France meant they finished second in Pool A and as a result would face top seeds and tournament favourites England in the Cup quarter-finals. England, under the guidance of former men's captain Simon Amor, hadn't conceded a point in beating USA, Russia and Japan, but Australia would be a different prospect in the standout match.

The loss of key player Jo Yapp to injury before kick-off was a blow to England, but they had held a slender lead at half-time only to see Nicole Beck and Rebecca Tavo tries give Australia a 17–10 victory and leave the English women in tears. Australia would face South Africa in the semi-finals following their come from behind 15–7 defeat of Spain. Carla Hohepa scored a first half hat-trick as New Zealand, the only unbeaten side left in the tournament, overcame Canada 33–12 to earn a meeting with USA, who had stormed to a 19–0 victory over France in the first quarter-final.

New Zealand's pace out wide proved decisive in their semi-final, captain Hannah Porter scoring what proved to be the winning try with Christy Ringgenberg's effort coming too late as USA slipped to a 14–12 defeat.

The other semi was equally tight, South Africa seemingly having stolen it with Phumeza Gadu's try only for Australia to score twice for a 19–10 victory and a rematch with their trans-Tasman rivals.

The final did not disappoint with both sides determined to be crowned world champions, New Zealand hoping to unite the 15-a-side and Sevens World Cups for the first time. Australia raced into a two-try cushion through Beck and Hodgkinson, but the sin-binning of Tavo saw New Zealand score either side of half-time. Both sides went close to breaking the deadlock, but at 10–10 sudden-death extra-time would be needed to crown the champions, Shelly Matcham ultimately sparking Australian celebrations.

"We have worked so hard to get here and to come here and achieve this is just mammoth," enthused captain Cheryl Soon. "We believed in each other and we just knew we had to stick it out for the whole 20 minutes or however long. We just knew we could do it in the end."

England recovered to win the Plate, shutting Canada out in the second half to win 12–0 after tries from Danielle Waterman and Kat Merchant before the break. China, though, were the first women's team to taste RWC Sevens success after overcoming Brazil – unbeaten in five years on home soil and the first nation to qualify for the inaugural tournament – 10–7 in a tight Bowl final with Yang Hong scoring her eighth try in Dubai.

China's success is a sign of their potential, which will increase with Rugby Sevens gaining admittance to the Olympic Games in 2016 and the additional funding that will bring. The same is true for other emerging nations who graced 'The Sevens', with Thailand having beaten Japan and China in regional qualifying to reach Dubai and Uganda having created their own piece of history as their country's first ever side in any sport to qualify for a World Cup finals. The Lady Cranes participation has, in the words of captain Helen Buteme, "changed the face of Women's Rugby forever in Uganda" with player numbers continuing to rise.

The success story of Rugby World Cup Sevens 2009 was not only restricted to the action on the pitch, the three-day tournament broke all previous broadcast records. It was broadcast in 760 million homes – more than double Hong Kong in 2005 – in 141 countries through 29 international broadcasters in 19 languages. A total of 827 hours was screened over the three days, up a massive 141 percent on the 2005 tournament.

"RWC Sevens 2009 was a resounding success. It's winning formula of exciting, explosive action, competitive matches, world class men's and women's players and plenty of spectacular tries was a hit with broadcasters the world over and has proven highly successful in reaching out to new audiences," said IRB Chairman Bernard Lapasset.

The 40 teams had done all they could to showcase Sevens' qualities, now all they could do was wait with the rest of the Rugby family to see if the sport would join the Olympics.

RUGBY WORLD CUP SEVENS 2009 RESULTS

MEN

CUP

QUARTER-FINALS			
New Zealand	14	Wales	15
England	26	Samoa (AET)	31
South Africa	12	Argentina	14
Kenya	26	Fiji	7

SEMI-FINALS			
Argentina	12	Kenya	0
Wales	19	Samoa	12

FINAL			
Wales	19	Argentina	12

PLATE

QUARTER-FINALS			
Tonga	24	Tunisia	7
USA	14	Australia	24
France	19	Scotland	21
Portugal	12	Canada	5

SEMI-FINALS			
Scotland	29	Portugal	7
Tonga	19	Australia	22

FINAL			
Australia	17	Scotland	21

BOWL

QUARTER-FINALS			
Zimbabwe	28	Georgia	10
Japan	12	Uruguay	19
Ireland	24	Arabian Gulf	5
Hong Kong	14	Italy	7

SEMI-FINALS			
Zimbabwe	24	Uruguay	7
Ireland	22	Hong Kong	15

FINAL			
Zimbabwe	17	Ireland	14

WORLD CUP SEVENS

WOMEN

CUP

QUARTER-FINALS			
France	0	USA	19
New Zealand	33	Canada	12
Spain	7	South Africa	15
England	10	Australia	17

SEMI-FINALS			
USA	12	New Zealand	14
South Africa	10	Australia	19

FINAL			
New Zealand	10	Australia (AET)	15

PLATE

SEMI-FINALS			
France	12	Canada	19
Spain	7	England	12

FINAL			
Canada	0	England	12

BOWL

QUARTER-FINALS			
China	21	Japan	5
Italy	17	Thailand	0
Brazil	12	Uganda	7
Russia	12	Netherlands	5

SEMI-FINALS			
China	28	Italy	0
Brazil	17	Russia (AET)	12

FINAL			
China	10	Brazil	7

Warren Little/Getty Images

Australia, led by Cheryl Soon (centre), became the first women's Sevens world champions.

CLAIMING A UNIQUE DOUBLE

By Iain Spragg

South Africa finally get their hands on the IRB Sevens World Series trophy.

South Africa claimed their first ever IRB Sevens World Series crown in the 2008–09 season, clinching the title in Edinburgh on the final weekend and in the process ending New Zealand's virtual monopoly of the competition since its inception in 1999.

In winning the Sevens World Series, South Africa also united the Sevens trophy with the Webb Ellis Cup for the first time.

New Zealand had won all but one of the Series' in its 10-year history, but failed to retain any of the six Cup titles they had won the previous season as South Africa romped to victory by an imposing 30 points ahead of Fiji, the only other nation to have won the overall title in 2006, with England in third place.

The South Africans confirmed themselves as champions on the penultimate day of the season when they made it through to the Cup quarter-finals at Murrayfield, in doing so guaranteeing superiority over England, who had still retained a mathematical chance of victory.

Although Paul Treu's side was eventually beaten 20–19 in the final by Fiji, there was still a celebratory mood in the Springbok camp as they reflected on their achievement.

"It's an unbelievable feeling for me," said the South Africa coach, who has been involved with the Springbok Sevens set-up for a decade. "I can only imagine how the players are feeling.

"I don't think the guys even realise what they've achieved as a team. Maybe when they're 30-years-old or sitting at home when they're old and looking back on their careers, this is definitely going to be one of the highlights.

"Credit to everyone who has contributed to our success. This is something that didn't start this season but four years ago with a vision that we wanted to become one of the best Sevens teams in the world and leave a legacy behind and that's exactly what the guys have done."

The result in London left the South Africans 20 points clear of England with only the Edinburgh Sevens in Murrayfield to play, meaning that they needed to reach the Cup quarter-finals to be confirmed as champions.

On day one in Edinburgh Treu's full-time Sevens players edged closer with pool wins over France and the USA, meaning that a New Zealand victory against France would ironically guarantee South Africa a place in the last eight, and with it the World Series crown. New Zealand duly dispatched France 22–5 and South African celebrations could begin.

"It was nerve-racking, especially when New Zealand were up 17–5 up but the French started to attack," admitted Treu. "I said 'we can't start celebrating yet, we have to wait' but now we're finally there and it takes the pressure off a little bit but we still have some work to do."

In the end, his side maintained their focus to reach the final in Scotland but were turned over by Fiji, propelling Tanivula's side into second place above England, who had failed to make it through to the Cup knockout phase. New Zealand ended the Series in fourth with Argentina fifth, while Kenya's impressive campaign earned them a creditable sixth place finish.

IRB SEVENS WORLD SERIES 2008–09 RESULTS

DUBAI: 28–29 NOVEMBER

South Africa (20), England (16), Fiji (12), New Zealand (12), Samoa (8), Kenya (6), Argentina (4), Australia (4), Portugal (2)

SOUTH AFRICA: 5–6 DECEMBER

South Africa (20), New Zealand (16), Argentina (12), Fiji (12) , England (8), Portugal (6), Samoa (4), USA (4), France (2)

NEW ZEALAND: 6–7 FEBRUARY

England (20), New Zealand (16), Argentina (12), Kenya (12), South Africa (8), Wales (6), USA (4), Fiji (4), Cook Islands (2)

USA: 14–15 FEBRUARY

Argentina (20), England (16), South Africa (12), USA (12), New Zealand (8), Kenya (6), Samoa (4), Fiji (4), Australia (2)

HONG KONG: 27–29 MARCH

Fiji (30), South Africa (24), Kenya (18), Samoa (18), England (8), New Zealand (8), Argentina (8), Australia (8), Tonga (4), Canada (3), Wales (2), France (2), Portugal (1)

AUSTRALIA: 3–5 APRIL

South Africa (20), Kenya (16), Fiji (12), Argentina (12), England (8), Australia (6), New Zealand (4), Wales (4), Samoa (2)

LONDON: 23–24 MAY

England (20), New Zealand (16), South Africa (12), Scotland (12), Fiji (8), Portugal (6), Australia (4), France (4), Kenya (2)

SCOTLAND: 30–31 MAY

Fiji (20), South Africa (16), Scotland (12), Wales (12), New Zealand (8), Australia (6), Kenya (4), Samoa (4), England (2)

FINAL STANDINGS

South Africa – 132 points	Scotland – 24
Fiji – 102	Wales – 24
England – 98	USA – 20
New Zealand – 88	Portugal – 15
Argentina – 68	France – 8
Kenya – 64	Tonga – 4
Samoa – 40	Canada – 3
Australia – 30	Cook Islands – 2

PREVIOUS WINNERS

1999–2000: New Zealand	2004–05: New Zealand
2000–01: New Zealand	2005–06: Fiji
2001–02: New Zealand	2006–07: New Zealand
2002–03: New Zealand	2007–08: New Zealand
2003–04: New Zealand	2008–09: South Africa

Bryn Lennon/Getty Images

Fiji won in Edinburgh to finish second overall

INTERNATIONAL TOURNAMENTS

IRISH EYES ARE BEAMING
AFTER LANDING THE SLAM

By Scott Quinnell

Skipper Brian O'Driscoll leads the celebrations in Cardiff.

In truth, I couldn't say it was a classic Six Nations year but there's no argument that Ireland's Grand Slam was thoroughly deserved and Declan Kidney did an excellent job in his first season as head coach. It had been a long, long time coming for the Irish but I'm sure they made it a party to remember after their historic victory on the final day in Cardiff.

With the exception of their 38–9 win over Italy in Rome, Ireland didn't really cut loose during the tournament but to come to the Millennium Stadium for their last game and beat Wales, the defending champions, was a reflection of the character of the side and they were without doubt the most consistent and complete team in the competition.

We say this every four years but I couldn't shake the feeling a lot of the players had one eye on the Lions tour and it had a strange effect on the atmosphere in some of the matches. You can't always see with the naked eye when a player is holding back a little but it certainly seemed to me a few had South Africa and the summer tour at the back of their minds.

Ireland, of course, had come close to completing the Grand Slam in previous years. They'd come up short before and for me what seemed to be the difference this season was the sense of urgency, an understanding that time really was running out for what is definitely a generation of great Irish players. Some have tried to pension the older players off before but they looked like they believed it themselves this year and didn't want to let the opportunity to slip through their fingers again.

Kidney may have been new to the role but it didn't seem like he was a newcomer and he probably benefitted from not having to work too hard to earn his players' respect. His track record with Munster spoke for itself and his two Heineken Cups demanded people took him seriously from the start.

Tactically, he adopted the same simple but fluid style he used at Munster. Ireland were hard-nosed up front, Ronan O'Gara dictated the play beautifully at 10 but they had a cutting edge out wide with Luke Fitzgerald and Tommy Bowe. It was pragmatic but it wasn't boring.

I think Ireland also benefitted from the success of Leinster and Munster in European competition. Leinster went on to lift the Heineken Cup, Munster were Magners League champions and Kidney was able to select from a pool of confident, in-form players. The Ireland players had a strut, an air of quiet self-belief about them and they translated that into results.

The captaincy of Brian Driscoll was superb but my Ireland player of the tournament was Jamie Heaslip. Maybe it's a bit of the old No.8 union but I thought he carried powerfully, he was dynamic in all areas of the pitch and he put in a great stint at the coal face.

For England, it was a mixed bag. Knowing Martin Johnson, he will have been delighted to end the tournament with two straight wins against France and Scotland and finish second in the table but he's not easily pleased and he'll know there's still huge room for improvement.

The big question was could Johnson translate the talismanic qualities he possessed in spades as England captain into his new role as team manager and the answer is, it's a work in progress. After a truly rotten autumn against the southern hemisphere big three, England's strong finish in the Six Nations was encouraging but the ill-discipline and yellow cards that plagued their earlier performances will have driven Johnson completely mad.

The positives were the emergence of a few new faces and the fact England looked as powerful and as gritty up front as ever. In the pack, Tom Croft was outstanding when he came into the side and he was a massive presence in both the lineout and in the loose. Delon Armitage was another good find and I thought he was unlucky not to get the nod from the Lions while Ugo Monye, who did get the call from Ian McGeechan, was a real threat on the wing.

What can you say about France? Magnificently unpredictable again, they were destroyed by England at Twickenham but cut Italy to ribbons in Rome and it was anyone's guess which team would turn up once the whistle went. It's hard to imagine France ever being any different because unpredictability seems ingrained in their DNA.

I can understand the frustrations of the French supporters but I think Marc Lièvremont was working with a longer term plan in mind than any of his Six Nations counterparts. France have their sights firmly set on the World Cup in 2011 and Lièvremont was very obviously determined to experiment with his combinations and give a lot of players game time.

He was criticised for his mix-and-match approach and his seemingly constant team changes but I'm sure he's convinced the team will reap the rewards in the future. I'd also say the French players perhaps looked a little more jaded than the rest of the sides. In my opinion, the Top 14 is the toughest and longest domestic competition in Europe and that could have had an effect on their performances.

Expectations on Wales were understandably high after the Grand Slam in 2008 and by those high standards it was a disappointing campaign. I'm not saying Wales went backwards but it's hard to argue they took a major step forwards either.

RBS SIX NATIONS

TRIVIA

Ireland's Grand Slam put them in pole position when it came to the composition of Rugby World's Team of the Tournament. The side was: Rob Kearney; Mark Cueto, Brian O'Driscoll, Riki Flutey, Tommy Bowe; Ronan O'Gara, Morgan Parra; Gethin Jenkins, Lee Mears, Euan Murray, Paul O'Connell, Alun Wyn Jones, Thierry Dusautoir, Joe Worsley, Sergio Parisse. Brian O'Driscoll was confirmed as the RBS Man of the Tournament.

Their fourth place was slightly misleading because they finished level on six points with England and France and if they had scored more points in the match against Italy in Rome when Warren Gatland selected an under strength shadow XV, they could have ended up as runners-up.

The coach took a lot of flak for his selection to face the Azzurri and I have to admit I did find it curious he decided to play what was effectively a second XV. A big victory would have seen Wales going into the last game against Ireland with a chance of the Championship but their 20–15 victory left them a mountain to climb.

Wales only scored eight tries in the tournament, which reflects the fact the other teams had begun to work them out. It reminded me of the way New Zealand seem unbeatable in the years between World Cups, throwing the ball about, but seem to come unstuck when it matters. Wales had been unstoppable at times in 2008 but in 2009 the opposition had found some answers to the way they tried to attack and proved Test teams need to constantly evolve in the modern era.

Scotland's poor tournament ultimately cost Frank Hadden his job and I felt a lot of sympathy for him when he decided to step down. He had four years as head coach, so there's no denying he had a fair crack of the whip, but he was always working with limited resources and that left him with very little room for manoeuvre when key players were unavailable.

Paul Gilham/Getty Images

England were left celebrating second place, in the first season under Martin Johnson.

I genuinely think Scotland showed some solid improvement but when they lost Euan Murray and Nathan Hines they really suffered and that highlighted the ongoing lack of strength in depth in Scottish rugby.

Saying that, it certainly isn't all doom and gloom. The pack is looking stronger each season and they looked to play a quick, expansive game. Perhaps a bit more raw pace out wide is needed but Andy Robinson, Hadden's successor, definitely has some positives to build on.

Another Wooden Spoon for Italy was no huge surprise and they really struggled with the ELVs and the reduced threat of the maul. They've always largely played a limited, 10-man game and with the opposition allowed to pull down their rolling mauls, they were bereft of ideas at times.

They were as abrasive as ever but until they develop their game out wide, they will always be easy pickings for the better teams. The coach, Nick Mallett, pointed out Italy rarely play teams below them in the IRB rankings and I thought it was an interesting point. More games against "lesser" opposition would give Italy the chance to play with more ambition and freedom and that, on the evidence of another courageous but disappointing Six Nations, is exactly what they need.

Honourable mention must of course go to No.8 and skipper Sergio Parisse, who was simply outstanding – the only Italian to make it into Rugby World's Team of the Tournament. He was phenomenal throughout the tournament and his work rate, commitment and passion were amazing. He does the work of three players but his energy and skill levels never seemed to drop.

Most impressively though was the fact he kept making a huge impact in a losing team. To be all over the field, as he constantly was, is hard enough from eight at the best of times but to do it in a beaten side, leading the troops, was breathtaking.

FIXTURES 2010

IRELAND'S attempt to win back-to-back Grand Slams for the first time in their history will begin at Croke Park in February with the visit of Italy.

Brian O'Driscoll's men will have to win at the Stade de France and Twickenham if they are to pick up a clean sweep in 2010.

Since 2003, the Championship has been entirely broadcast on terrestrial TV and the audience figures have increased dramatically in all of the participating six nations from 94m in 2003 up to 125m in 2009.

The 2010 tournament will celebrate the centenary of the first Championship between the five original members.

Saturday 6 February
Ireland v Italy (2.30pm)
England v Wales (5pm)

Sunday 7 February
Scotland v France (3pm)

Saturday 13 February
Wales v Scotland (2pm)
France v Ireland (4.30pm)

Sunday 14 February
Italy v England (2.30pm)

Friday 26 February
Wales v France (8pm)

Saturday 27 February
Italy v Scotland (1.30pm)
England v Ireland (4pm)

Saturday 13 March
Ireland v Wales (2.30pm)
Scotland v England (5pm)

Sunday 14 March
France v Italy (2.30pm)

Saturday 20 March
Wales v Italy (2.30pm)
Ireland v Scotland (5pm)
France v England (7.45pm)

All times GMT

SIX NATIONS 2009
FINAL TABLE

	P	W	D	L	For	Against	Pts
Ireland	5	5	0	0	121	73	**10**
England	5	3	0	2	124	70	**6**
France	5	3	0	2	124	101	**6**
Wales	5	3	0	2	100	81	**6**
Scotland	5	1	0	4	79	102	**2**
Italy	5	0	0	5	49	170	**0**

Points: Win 2; Draw 1; Defeat 0.

There were 597 points scored at an average of 39.8 a match. The Championship record (803 points at an average of 53.5 a match) was set in 2000. Ronan O'Gara was the leading individual points scorer with 56, 33 points shy of the Championship record Jonny Wilkinson set in 2001. Riki Flutey and Brian O'Driscoll were the Championship's leading try-scorers with four each, four short of the all-time record shared between England's Cyril Lowe (1914) and Scotland's Ian Smith (1925).

Stu Foster/Getty Images

Brian O'Driscoll (with trophy) led Ireland to their first Grand Slam since 1948.

RBS SIX NATIONS

2009 MATCH STATS

7 February, Twickenham, London

ENGLAND 36 (4G 1PG 1T) ITALY 11 (2PG 1T)

ENGLAND: D A Armitage; P H Sackey, J D Noon, R J Flutey, M J Cueto; A J Goode, H A Ellis; A J Sheridan, L A Mears, P J Vickery, S W Borthwick (*captain*), N J Kennedy, J Haskell, N J Easter, S Armitage *Substitutions:* D M Hartley for Mears (55 mins); J P R Worsley for S Armitage (55 mins); S J J Geraghty for Flutey (59 mins); B J Foden for Ellis (59 mins); J M White for Sheridan (59 mins); M J M Tait for Noon (73 mins); T Croft for Kennedy (73 mins)

SCORERS *Tries:* Ellis (2), Goode, Flutey, Cueto *Conversions:* Goode (4) *Penalty Goal:* Goode

ITALY: A Masi; K Robertson, G-J Canale, G Garcia, Mirco Bergamasco; A Marcato, Mauro Bergamasco; S Perugini, F Ongaro, M-L Castrogiovanni, S Dellape, M Bortolami, J Sole, S Parisse (*captain*), A Zanni *Substitutions:* L McLean for Marcato (28 mins); G Toniolatti for Mauro Bergamasco (40 mins); M Pratichetti for Garcia (55 mins); T Reato for Bortolami (temp 19 to 24 mins and 55 mins); C Festuccia for Ongaro (55 mins); C Nieto for Perugini (60 mins); Perugini back for Castrogiovanni (65 mins); J-F Montauriol for Dellape (75 mins)

SCORERS *Try:* Mirco Bergamasco *Penalty Goals:* McLean (2)

REFEREE S M Lawrence (South Africa)

YELLOW CARDS J Haskell (36 mins); S J J Geraghty (59 mins)

7 February, Croke Park, Dublin

IRELAND 30 (3G 3PG)
FRANCE 21 (1G 1PG 2DG 1T)

IRELAND: R D J Kearney; T J Bowe, B G O'Driscoll (*captain*), P W Wallace, L M Fitzgerald; R J R O'Gara, T G O'Leary; M J Horan, J P Flannery, J J Hayes, D P O'Callaghan, P J O'Connell, S P H Ferris, J P R Heaslip, D P Wallace *Substitutions:* R Best for Flannery (48 mins); G M D'Arcy for P W Wallace (temp 28 to 35 mins and 61 mins); D P Leamy for Ferris (72 mins); G E A Murphy for Kearney (75 mins)

SCORERS *Tries:* Heaslip, O'Driscoll, D'Arcy *Conversions:* O'Gara (3) *Penalty Goals:* O'Gara (3)

FRANCE: C Poitrenaud; M Médard, F Fritz, Y Jauzion, J Malzieu; L Beauxis, S Tillous-Borde; L Faure, D Szarzewski, B Lecouls, L Nallet (*captain*), S Chabal, T Dusautoir, I Harinordoquy, F Ouedraogo *Substitutions:* N Mas for Lecouls (40 mins); B Kayser for Szarzewski (58 mins); R Millo-Chluski for Chabal (61 mins); M Parra for Tillous-Borde (67 mins); L Picamoles for Harinordoquy (70 mins); C Heymans for Poitrenaud (72 mins); B Baby for Fritz (78 mins)

SCORERS *Tries:* Harinordoquy, Médard *Conversion:* Beauxis *Penalty Goal:* Beauxis *Dropped Goals:* Beauxis (2)

REFEREE N Owens (Wales)

8 February, Murrayfield, Edinburgh

SCOTLAND 13 (1G 2PG) WALES 26 (2PG 4T)

SCOTLAND: H F G Southwell; S L Webster, B J Cairns, G A Morrison, S F Lamont; P J Godman, M R L Blair (*captain*); A F Jacobsen, R W Ford, G Cross, J P R White, J L Hamilton, A Hogg, S M Taylor, J A Barclay *Substitutions:* C D Paterson for Webster (20 mins); A G Dickinson for White (temp 26 to 31 mins) and for Cross (31 mins); M B Evans for Cairns (51 mins); S D Gray for Barclay (55 mins); C P Cusiter for Blair (62 mins); D W H Hall for Ford (62 mins); K D R Brown for Hogg (73 mins)

SCORERS *Try:* Evans *Conversion:* Paterson *Penalty Goals:* Paterson (2)

WALES: L M Byrne; S L Halfpenny, T G L Shanklin, J Roberts, S M Williams; S M Jones, W M Phillips; G D Jenkins, M Rees, A R Jones, I M Gough, A-W Jones, D A R Jones, A Powell, M E Williams (*captain*) *Substitutions:* D J Peel for Phillips (59 mins); J Yapp for Jenkins (62 mins); A Bishop for Roberts (62 mins); H Bennett for Rees (62 mins); L C Charteris for Gough (62 mins); J W Hook for S M Jones (62 mins); B Davies for S M Williams (70 mins)

SCORERS *Tries:* Shanklin, A-W Jones, Halfpenny, S M Williams *Penalty Goals:* S M Jones (2)

REFEREE A C Rolland (Ireland)

YELLOW CARDS G Cross (20 mins); M E Williams (66 mins)

14 February, Stade de France, Paris

FRANCE 22 (1G 5PG) SCOTLAND 13 (1G 2PG)

FRANCE: C Poitrenaud; M Médard, Y Jauzion, B Baby, C Heymans; L Beauxis, S Tillous-Borde; F Barcella, D Szarzewski, N Mas, L Nallet (*captain*), R Millo-Chluski, T Dusautoir, I Harinordoquy, F Ouedraogo *Substitutions:* R Boyoud for Mas (40 mins); B Kayser for Szarzewski (54 mins); S Chabal for Millo-Chluski (59 mins); M Mermoz for Baby (59 mins); M Parra for Tillous-Borde (66 mins); L Picamoles for Harinordoquy (70 mins); J Malzieu for Médard (79 mins)

SCORERS *Try:* Ouedraogo *Conversion:* Beauxis *Penalty Goals:* Beauxis (5)

SCOTLAND: H F G Southwell; S C J Danielli, M B Evans, G A Morrison, T H Evans; P J Godman, M R L Blair (*captain*); A F Jacobsen, R W Ford, A G Dickinson, J P R White, J L Hamilton, A K Strokosch, S M Taylor, J A Barclay *Substitutions:* K D R Brown for Hamilton (17 mins); M J Low for Dickinson (46 mins); C D Paterson for Danielli (65 mins); D W H Hall for Ford (65 mins); Dickinson back for Jacobsen (70 mins); N J de Luca for Morrison (72 mins); C P Cusiter for Blair (72 mins)

SCORERS *Try:* T H Evans *Conversion:* Paterson *Penalty Goals:* Godman (2)

REFEREE G Clancy (Ireland)

14 February, Millennium Stadium, Cardiff

WALES 23 (6PG 1T) ENGLAND 15 (1G 1DG 1T)

WALES: L M Byrne; S L Halfpenny, T G L Shanklin, J Roberts, M A Jones; S M Jones, W M Phillips; G D Jenkins, M Rees, A R Jones, I M Gough, A-W Jones, R P Jones (*captain*), A Powell, M E Williams *Substitutions:* D A R Jones for Powell (60 mins); H Bennett for Rees (66 mins); D J Peel for Phillips (72 mins)

SCORERS *Try:* Halfpenny *Penalty Goals:* S M Jones (5), Halfpenny

ENGLAND: D A Armitage; P H Sackey, M J Tindall, R J Flutey, M J Cueto; A J Goode, H A Ellis; A J Sheridan, L A Mears, P J Vickery, S W Borthwick (*captain*), N J Kennedy, J Haskell, N J Easter, J P R Worsley *Substitutions:* T G A L Flood for Goode (52 mins); T Croft for Kennedy (54 mins); D M Hartley for Mears (64 mins); J M White for Vickery (64 mins); M J M Tait for Sackey (64 mins); L J W Narraway for Haskell (64 mins)

SCORERS *Tries:* Sackey, Armitage *Conversion:* Flood *Dropped Goal:* Goode

REFEREE J I Kaplan (South Africa)

YELLOW CARDS M J Tindall (15 mins); A J Goode (41 mins)

15 February, Stadio Flaminio, Rome

ITALY 9 (3PG) IRELAND 38 (5G 1PG)

ITALY: A Masi; K Robertson, G-J Canale, Mirco Bergamasco, M Pratichetti; L McLean, P Griffen; S Perugini, F Ongaro, M-L Castrogiovanni, S Dellape, T Reato, A Zanni, S Parisse (*captain*), Mauro Bergamasco *Substitutions:* A Bacchetti for Robertson (19 mins); C Nieto for Castrogiovanni (32 mins); C Festuccia for Ongaro (41 mins); G Garcia for Canale (47 mins); C-A Del Fava for Dellape (47 mins); J Sole for Reato (47 mins); Castrogiovanni back for Perugini (58 mins); G Toniolatti for McLean (71 mins)

SCORER *Penalty Goals:* McLean (3)

IRELAND: R D J Kearney; T J Bowe, B G O'Driscoll (*captain*), P W Wallace, L M Fitzgerald; R J R O'Gara, T G O'Leary; M J Horan, J P Flannery, J J Hayes, D P O'Callaghan, P J O'Connell, S P H Ferris, J P R Heaslip, D P Wallace *Substitutions:* G M D'Arcy for P W Wallace (40 mins); T Court for Horan (54 mins); R Best for Flannery (59 mins); P A Stringer for P W Wallace (temp 34 to 40 mins) and for O'Leary (71 mins); D P Leamy for Ferris (temp 62 to 74 mins) and for Heaslip (74 mins); G E A Murphy for Kearney (74 mins); M E O'Kelly for O'Connell (76 mins)

SCORERS *Tries:* Fitzgerald (2), Bowe, D P Wallace, O'Driscoll *Conversions:* O'Gara (4), Kearney *Penalty Goal:* O'Gara

REFEREE C White (England)

YELLOW CARDS A Masi (1 mins); R J R O'Gara (30 mins); S Perugini (35 mins)

FRANCE 21 (1G 3PG 1T) WALES 16 (1G 3PG)

FRANCE: M Médard; J Malzieu, M Bastareaud, Y Jauzion, C Heymans; B Baby, M Parra; F Barcella, D Szarzewski, S Marconnet, L Nallet (*captain*), S Chabal, T Dusautoir, I Harinordoquy, F Ouedraogo *Substitutions:* F Trinh-Duc for Baby (36 mins); R Millo-Chluski for Chabal (56 mins); T Domingo for Marconnet (56 mins); B Kayser for Szarzewski (64 mins); S Tillous-Borde for Parra (70 mins); Marconnet back for Domingo (75 mins)

SCORERS *Tries:* Dusautoir, Heymans *Conversion:* Parra *Penalty Goals:* Parra (3)

WALE: L M Byrne; S L Halfpenny, T G L Shanklin, J Roberts, S M Williams; S M Jones, W M Phillips; G D Jenkins, M Rees, A R Jones, I M Gough, A-W Jones, R P Jones (*captain*), A Powell, M E Williams *Substitutions:* H Bennett for Rees (54 mins); D J Peel for Phillips (54 mins); G L Henson for Roberts (54 mins); J W Hook for S M Jones (67 mins); D A R Jones for Powell (67 mins); L C Charteris for Gough (70 mins)

SCORERS *Try:* Byrne *Conversion:* S M Jones *Penalty Goals:* S M Jones (2), Hook

REFEREE S M Lawrence (South Africa)

SCOTLAND 26 (2G 4PG)
ITALY 6 (1PG 1DG)

SCOTLAND: H F G Southwell; S C J Danielli, M B Evans, G A Morrison, T H Evans; P J Godman, M R L Blair (*captain*); A F Jacobsen, R W Ford, E A Murray, J P R White, A D Kellock, A K Strokosch, S M Taylor, J A Barclay *Substitutions:* C D Paterson for Godman (temp 3 to 12 mins) and for Southwell (47 mins); D W H Hall for Ford (52 mins); C P Cusiter for Blair (56 mins); S D Gray for Barclay (56 mins); A G Dickinson for Jacobsen (63 mins); Jacobsen back for Murray (64 mins); N J de Luca for Morrison (67 mins); K D R Brown for Jacobsen (67 mins)

SCORERS *Tries:* Danielli, Gray *Conversions:* Paterson, Godman *Penalty Goals:* Paterson (3), Godman

ITALY: A Marcato; Mirco Bergamasco, G-J Canale, G Garcia, M Pratichetti; L McLean, P Griffen; S Perugini, L Ghiraldini, M-L Castrogiovanni, S Dellape, M Bortolami, A Zanni, S Parisse (*captain*), Mauro Bergamasco *Substitutions:* A Bacchetti for Garcia (3 mins); G Rubini for Marcato (47 mins); P Canavosio for Griffen (56 mins); C-A Del Fava for Dellape (57 mins); F Sbaraglini for Ghiraldini (58 mins); C Nieto for Castrogiovanni (58 mins); J Sole for Bortolami (76 mins)

SCORERS *Penalty Goal:* McLean *Dropped Goal:* Parisse

REFEREE N Owens (Wales)

28 February, Croke Park, Dublin

IRELAND 14 (2PG 1DG 1T)
ENGLAND 13 (1G 2PG)

IRELAND: R D J Kearney; T J Bowe, B G O'Driscoll (*captain*), P W Wallace, L M Fitzgerald; R J R O'Gara, T G O'Leary; M J Horan, J P Flannery, J J Hayes, D P O'Callaghan, P J O'Connell, S P H Ferris, J P R Heaslip, D P Wallace *Substitutions:* P A Stringer for O'Leary (65 mins); R Best for Flannery (68 mins); D P Leamy for Heaslip (68 mins)

SCORERS *Try:* O'Driscoll *Penalty Goals:* O'Gara (2) *Dropped Goal:* O'Driscoll

ENGLAND: D A Armitage; P H Sackey, M J Tindall, R J Flutey, M J Cueto; T G A L Flood, H A Ellis; A J Sheridan, L A Mears, P J Vickery, S W Borthwick (*captain*), N J Kennedy, J Haskell, N J Easter, J P R Worsley *Substitutions:* D S Care for Ellis (57 mins); M J M Tait for Sackey (57 mins); D M Hartley for Mears (65 mins); A J Goode for Flood (65 mins); T Croft for Kennedy (68 mins); L J W Narraway for Easter (75 mins); J M White for Haskell (temp 55 to 65 mins) and for Sheridan (75 mins)

SCORERS *Try:* Armitage *Conversion:* Goode *Penalty Goals:* Flood, Armitage

REFEREE C Joubert (South Africa)

YELLOW CARDS P J Vickery (54 mins); D S Care (69 mins)

14 March, Stadio Flaminio, Rome

ITALY 15 (5PG) WALES 20 (2G 2PG)

ITALY: A Marcato; M Pratichetti, G-J Canale, Mirco Bergamasco, G Rubini; L McLean, P Griffen; S Perugini, L Ghiraldini, C Nieto, S Dellape, M Bortolami, A Zanni, S Parisse (*captain*), Mauro Bergamasco *Substitutions:* M-L Castrogiovanni for Nieto (49 mins); C-A Del Fava for Dellape (49 mins); J Sole for Bortolami (64 mins); P Canavosio for Griffen (65 mins); R Quartaroli for Mirco Bergamasco (73 mins); L Orquera for Marcato (75 mins)

SCORER *Penalty Goals:* Marcato (5)

WALES: L M Byrne; M A Jones, J Roberts, G L Henson, S M Williams; J W Hook, W M Phillips; J Yapp, H Bennett, R Thomas, L C Charteris, A-W Jones (*captain*), J Thomas, A Powell, D A R Jones *Substitutions:* M Rees for Bennett (57 mins); G D Jenkins for R Thomas (57 mins); R P Jones for J Thomas (57 mins); B Davies for Charteris (65 mins); T G L Shanklin for Byrne (68 mins); S M Jones for Hook (75 mins)

SCORERS *Tries:* S M Williams, Shanklin *Conversions:* Hook (2) *Penalty Goals:* Hook (2)

REFEREE D A Lewis (Ireland)

SCOTLAND 15 (5PG) IRELAND 22 (1G 4PG 1DG)

SCOTLAND: C D Paterson; S C J Danielli, M B Evans, G A Morrison, T H Evans; P J Godman, M R L Blair (*captain*); A G Dickinson, R W Ford, E A Murray, J P R White, J L Hamilton, A K Strokosch, S M Taylor, J A Barclay *Substitutions:* N J Hines for White (50 mins); C P Cusiter for Blair (51 mins); D W H Hall for Ford (56 mins); S D Gray for Barclay (67 mins); N J de Luca for Morrison (69 mins)

SCORER *Penalty Goals:* Paterson (5)

IRELAND: R D J Kearney; T J Bowe, B G O'Driscoll (*captain*), G M D'Arcy, L M Fitzgerald; R J R O'Gara, P A Stringer; M J Horan, R Best, J J Hayes, D P O'Callaghan, P J O'Connell, S P H Ferris, D P Leamy, D P Wallace *Substitutions:* J P R Heaslip for Leamy (29 mins); J P Flannery for Best (61 mins); T G O'Leary for Stringer (65 mins); G E A Murphy for Kearney (75 mins)

SCORERS *Try:* Heaslip *Conversion:* O'Gara *Penalty Goals:* O'Gara (4) *Dropped Goal:* O'Gara

REFEREE J I Kaplan (South Africa)

ENGLAND 34 (3G 1PG 2T) FRANCE 10 (2T)

ENGLAND: D A Armitage; M J Cueto, M J Tindall, R J Flutey, Y C C Monye; T G A L Flood, H A Ellis; A J Sheridan, L A Mears, P J Vickery, S W Borthwick (*captain*), S D Shaw, T Croft, N J Easter, J P R Worsley *Substitutions:* A J Goode for Flood (40 mins); D S Care for Ellis (54 mins); D M Hartley for Mears (56 mins); J Haskell for Shaw (56 mins); J M White for Vickery (temp 42 to 56 mins) and for Sheridan (65 mins); N J Kennedy for Worsley (67 mins); M J M Tait for Monye (72 mins)

SCORERS *Tries:* Flutey (2), Cueto, Armitage, Worsley *Conversions:* Flood (3) *Penalty Goal:* Flood

FRANCE: M Médard; J Malzieu, M Bastareaud, Y Jauzion, C Heymans; F Trinh-Duc, M Parra; L Faure, D Szarzewski, S Marconnet, L Nallet (*captain*), J Thion, T Dusautoir, I Harinordoquy, S Chabal *Substitutions:* J Bonnaire for Thion (47 mins); D Traille for Trinh-Duc (47 mins); F Fritz for Bastareaud (47 mins); T Domingo for Faure (50 mins); B Kayser for Szarzewski (58 mins); S Tillous-Borde for Parra (58 mins); L Picamoles for Harinordoquy (67 mins); Faure back for Marconnet (71 mins)

SCORERS *Tries:* Szarzewski, Malzieu

REFEREE S J Dickinson (Australia)

21 March, Stadio Flaminio, Rome

ITALY 8 (1PG 1T)
FRANCE 50 (3G 3PG 4T)

ITALY: A Marcato; M Pratichetti, G-J Canale, Mirco Bergamasco, G Rubini; L McLean, P Griffen; S Perugini, L Ghiraldini, C Nieto, S Dellape, M Bortolami, A Zanni, S Parisse (*captain*), Mauro Bergamasco *Substitutions:* R Quartaroli for Pratichetti (47 mins); C-A Del Fava for Dellape (51 mins); M-L Castrogiovanni for Nieto (57 mins); P Canavosio for Griffen (66 mins); J Sole for Bortolami (68 mins); L Orquera for McLean (71 mins); F Sbaraglini for Orquera (78 mins)

SCORERS *Try:* Parisse *Penalty Goal:* Marcato

FRANCE: D Traille; M Médard, F Fritz, Y Jauzion, C Heymans; F Trinh-Duc, M Parra; F Barcella, D Szarzewski, S Marconnet, L Nallet (*captain*), S Chabal, T Dusautoir, I Harinordoquy, J Bonnaire *Substitutions:* T Domingo for Marconnet (47 mins); W Servat for Szarzewski (51 mins); F Michalak for Parra (51 mins); L Picamoles for Harinordoquy (53 mins); M Bastareaud for Fritz (60 mins); J Thion for Nallet (71 mins); J Malzieu for Heymans (71 mins); Marconnet back for Barcella (73 mins)

SCORERS *Tries:* Médard (2), Chabal, Trinh-Duc, Heymans, Domingo, Malzieu *Conversions:* Parra (3) *Penalty Goals:* Parra (3)

REFEREE A C Rolland (Ireland)

21 March, Twickenham, London

ENGLAND 26 (1G 2PG 1DG 2T)
SCOTLAND 12 (4PG)

ENGLAND: D A Armitage; M J Cueto, M J Tindall, R J Flutey, Y C C Monye; T G A L Flood, H A Ellis; A J Sheridan, L A Mears, P J Vickery, S W Borthwick (*captain*), S D Shaw, T Croft, N J Easter, J P R Worsley *Substitutions:* J M White for Vickery (13 mins); D S Care for Ellis (16 mins); M J M Tait for Monye (47 mins); N J Kennedy for Shaw (57 mins); D M Hartley for Mears (72 mins); A J Goode for Flood (72 mins); J Haskell for Croft (72 mins)

SCORERS *Tries:* Monye, Flutey, Tait *Conversion:* Flood *Penalty Goals:* Flood (2) *Dropped Goal:* Care

SCOTLAND: C D Paterson; S C J Danielli, M B Evans, G A Morrison, T H Evans; P J Godman, M R L Blair (*captain*); A G Dickinson, R W Ford, E A Murray, J P R White, J L Hamilton, A K Strokosch, S M Taylor, S D Gray *Substitutions:* K D R Brown for Taylor (40 mins); N J de Luca for T H Evans (43 mins); N J Hines for White (56 mins); D W H Hall for Ford (56 mins); C P Cusiter for Blair (66 mins); M J Low for Dickinson (75 mins); H F G Southwell for Danielli (75 mins)

SCORERS *Penalty Goals:* Paterson (3), Godman

REFEREE M Jonker (South Africa)

WALES 15 (4PG 1DG)
IRELAND 17 (2G 1DG)

WALES: L M Byrne; M A Jones, T G L Shanklin, G L Henson, S M Williams; S M Jones, W M Phillips; G D Jenkins, M Rees, A R Jones, I M Gough, A-W Jones, D A R Jones, R P Jones (*captain*), M E Williams *Substitutions:* J Roberts for Byrne (30 mins); H Bennett for Rees (55 mins); L C Charteris for Gough (55 mins)

SCORER *Penalty Goals:* S M Jones (4) *Dropped Goal:* S M Jones

IRELAND: R D J Kearney; T J Bowe, B G O'Driscoll (*captain*), G M D'Arcy, L M Fitzgerald; R J R O'Gara, T G O'Leary; M J Horan, J P Flannery, J J Hayes, D P O'Callaghan, P J O'Connell, S P H Ferris, J P R Heaslip, D P Wallace *Substitutions:* D P Leamy for Ferris (6 mins); G E A Murphy for Kearney (66 mins); R Best for Flannery (66 mins); P A Stringer for O'Leary (69 mins); P W Wallace for Fitzgerald (76 mins); T Court for Hayes (temp 23 to 26 mins)

SCORERS *Tries:* O'Driscoll, Bowe *Conversions:* O'Gara (2) *Dropped Goal:* O'Gara

REFEREE W Barnes (England)

Stu Foster/Getty Images

Ronan O'Gara was Ireland's hero in Cardiff with a last-minute drop goal.

INTERNATIONAL CHAMPIONSHIP RECORDS 1883–2009

PREVIOUS WINNERS

1883 England	1884 England	1885 Not completed
1886 England & Scotland	1887 Scotland	1888 Not completed
1889 Not completed	1890 England & Scotland	1891 Scotland
1892 England	1893 Wales	1894 Ireland
1895 Scotland	1896 Ireland	1897 Not completed
1898 Not completed	1899 Ireland	1900 Wales
1901 Scotland	1902 Wales	1903 Scotland
1904 Scotland	1905 Wales	1906 Ireland & Wales
1907 Scotland	1908 Wales	1909 Wales
1910 England	1911 Wales	1912 England & Ireland
1913 England	1914 England	1920 England & Scotland & Wales
1921 England	1922 Wales	1923 England
1924 England	1925 Scotland	1926 Scotland & Ireland
1927 Scotland & Ireland	1928 England	1929 Scotland
1930 England	1931 Wales	1932 England & Ireland & Wales
1933 Scotland	1934 England	1935 Ireland
1936 Wales	1937 England	1938 Scotland
1939 England & Ireland & Wales	1947 England & Wales	1948 Ireland
1949 Ireland	1950 Wales	1951 Ireland
1952 Wales	1953 England	1954 England & Wales & France
1955 Wales & France	1956 Wales	1957 England
1958 England	1959 France	1960 England & France
1961 France	1962 France	1963 England
1964 Scotland & Wales	1965 Wales	1966 Wales
1967 France	1968 France	1969 Wales
1970 Wales & France	1971 Wales	1972 Not completed
1973 Five Nations tie	1974 Ireland	1975 Wales
1976 Wales	1977 France	1978 Wales
1979 Wales	1980 England	1981 France
1982 Ireland	1983 Ireland & France	1984 Scotland
1985 Ireland	1986 Scotland & France	1987 France
1988 Wales & France	1989 France	1990 Scotland
1991 England	1992 England	1993 France
1994 Wales	1995 England	1996 England
1997 France	1998 France	1999 Scotland
2000 England	2001 England	2002 France
2003 England	2004 France	2005 Wales
2006 France	2007 France	2008 Wales
2009 Ireland		

England have won the title outright 25 times; Wales 24; France 16; Scotland 14; Ireland 11; Italy 0.

TRIPLE CROWN WINNERS

England (23 times) 1883, 1884, 1892, 1913, 1914, 1921, 1923, 1924, 1928, 1934, 1937, 1954, 1957, 1960, 1980, 1991, 1992, 1995, 1996, 1997, 1998, 2002, 2003.

Wales (19 times) 1893, 1900, 1902, 1905, 1908, 1909, 1911, 1950, 1952, 1965, 1969, 1971, 1976, 1977, 1978, 1979, 1988, 2005, 2008.

Scotland (10 times) 1891, 1895, 1901, 1903, 1907, 1925, 1933, 1938, 1984, 1990.

Ireland (10 times) 1894, 1899, 1948, 1949, 1982, 1985, 2004, 2006, 2007, 2009.

GRAND SLAM WINNERS

England (12 times) 1913, 1914, 1921, 1923, 1924, 1928, 1957, 1980, 1991, 1992, 1995, 2003.

Wales (10 times) 1908, 1909, 1911, 1950, 1952, 1971, 1976, 1978, 2005, 2008.

France (Eight times) 1968, 1977, 1981, 1987, 1997, 1998, 2002, 2004.

Scotland (Three times) 1925, 1984, 1990.

Ireland (Twice) 1948, 2009.

THE SIX NATIONS CHAMPIONSHIP 2000–2009
COMPOSITE SEVEN-SEASON TABLE

	P	W	D	L	Pts
France	50	36	0	14	72
Ireland	50	36	0	14	72
England	50	33	0	17	66
Wales	50	23	2	25	48
Scotland	50	14	1	35	29
Italy	50	6	1	43	13

CHIEF RECORDS

INTERNATIONAL TOURNAMENTS

RECORD	DETAIL		SET
Most team points in season	229 by England	in five matches	2001
Most team tries in season	29 by England	in five matches	2001
Highest team score	80 by England	80–23 v Italy	2001
Biggest team win	57 by England	80–23 v Italy	2001
Most team tries in match	12 by Scotland	v Wales	1887
Most appearances	56 for Ireland	C M H Gibson	1964 – 1979
Most points in matches	499 for Ireland	R J R O'Gara	2000 – 2009
Most points in season	89 for England	J P Wilkinson	2001
Most points in match	35 for England	J P Wilkinson	v Italy, 2001
Most tries in matches	24 for Scotland	I S Smith	1924 – 1933
Most tries in season	8 for England	C N Lowe	1914
	8 for Scotland	I S Smith	1925
Most tries in match	5 for Scotland	G C Lindsay	v Wales, 1887
Most cons in matches	81 for England	J P Wilkinson	1998 – 2008
Most cons in season	24 for England	J P Wilkinson	2001
Most cons in match	9 for England	J P Wilkinson	v Italy, 2001
Most pens in matches	99 for Ireland	R J R O'Gara	2000 – 2009
Most pens in season	18 for England	S D Hodgkinson	1991
	18 for England	J P Wilkinson	2000
	18 for France	G Merceron	2002
Most pens in match	7 for England	S D Hodgkinson	v Wales, 1991
	7 for England	C R Andrew	v Scotland, 1995
	7 for England	J P Wilkinson	v France, 1999
	7 for Wales	N R Jenkins	v Italy, 2000
	7 for France	G Merceron	v Italy, 2002
	7 for Scotland	C D Paterson	v Wales, 2007
Most drops in matches	9 for France	J-P Lescarboura	1982 – 1988
	9 for England	C R Andrew	1985 – 1997
	9 for England	J P Wilkinson	1998 – 2008
Most drops in season	5 for France	G Camberabero	1967
	5 for Italy	D Dominguez	2000
	5 for Wales	N R Jenkins	2001
	5 for England	J P Wilkinson	2003
Most drops in match	3 for France	P Albaladejo	v Ireland, 1960
	3 for France	J-P Lescarboura	v England, 1985
	3 for Italy	D Dominguez	v Scotland 2000
	3 for Wales	N R Jenkins	v Scotland 2001

BOKS HIT THE HEIGHTS

By Iain Spragg

The annual battle for bragging rights in the southern hemisphere is frequently an epic, titanic struggle between the finest Australia, New Zealand and South Africa can offer, but the 2009 instalment of the tournament proved to be uncharacteristically one-sided as the Springboks marched relentlessly to their first Tri-Nations title since 2004 and in the process asserted their status as the Game's pre-eminent side.

Peter de Villiers' side may have been forced to postpone their celebrations until after their final game against New Zealand in Hamilton in mid September but they were the standout team throughout the competition. In fact had it not been for their surprise 21–6 defeat to the Wallabies in Brisbane in their penultimate fixture, their inevitable coronation would have been confirmed a week earlier.

The world champions went into the Tri-Nations buoyed by their cathartic Series victory over the British & Irish Lions and with old scores finally settled, they proved virtually irresistible home and away against New Zealand and Australia.

Their reverse against the Australians at Suncorp Stadium was the only blemish on what was an otherwise flawless record and when John Smit lifted the trophy after beating the All Blacks in the Waikato Stadium, the Springboks were in possession of both the World Cup and the Tri-Nations crown.

The 14th instalment of the tournament began in July with the visit of Australia to Auckland to tackle the All Blacks. The game was flanker George Smith's 100th in the famous gold shirt of the Wallabies but he and his team-mates were unable to mark the occasion with victory as New Zealand kicked off the defence of their title with a 22–16 win.

The Australians began brightly at Eden Park with a Berrick Barnes try in the third minute. However, New Zealand slowly but surely began to assert their authority and a Richie McCaw score and four penalties from the boot of Stephen Donald, deputising for Dan Carter, were enough to see off the Wallaby challenge.

"At the end of the day there's very little between these two teams and sometimes it's about who really wants to dig deep at the end of 80 minutes," McCaw said after the match. "I'm pretty proud of the guys and the way they did that.

"It did take a while to get into the game and it was a wee bit frustrating but the guys made sure we stuck together and into the wind I thought we got a bit of momentum. In the second half we were swinging backwards and forwards but the wind helped us."

A week later South Africa entered the fray with a game against the All Blacks in Bloemfontein, the first of three successive home fixtures for De Villiers' team.

The Boks had never beaten New Zealand in Bloemfontein but laid that ghost to rest with a gritty, determined performance at Vodacom Park. Fly-half Ruan Pienaar set the tone with his first half try and although Conrad Smith replied for Graham Henry's team after the break, Jaque Fourie settled the contest eight minutes from time and South Africa were 28–19 winners.

The rematch between the two great rivals came in Durban seven days later and served up a host of milestones. The game saw Smit surpass George Gregan and Will Carling's record for the most Tests as captain (59), while Bryan Habana and Jean de Villiers both reached the 50-cap landmark.

The most telling record, though, came from Springbok fly-half Morné Steyn, who scored all of his side's 31 points as the All Blacks were defeated for a second time. The outstanding Bulls fly-half scored a try, converted it and also landed eight penalties to condemn the All Blacks to a 31–19 loss and eclipse the previous tournament record of 29 points set by Andrew Mehrtens a decade earlier.

"He's a wonderful asset to have," said Smit of his match-winning fly-half. "When you've got a guy who's that young, still very inexperienced at international level but seems so composed, it's a huge bonus.

"I think I've been asked about Morné at every single press conference we've had this year so far. It's probably because he keeps on doing so well. It's one thing for a team to create pressure, it's another to convert that into points."

Two wins from two had already installed South Africa as the tournament favourites and they further underlined their title credentials with a 29–17 defeat of the Australians in Cape Town in their next fixture.

The Wallabies sliced through the South African defence at Newlands in the first minute with an Adam Ashley-Cooper try, but Steyn was once again on hand to rescue his side, landing seven penalties and a drop goal for an individual haul of 24 points. He missed the conversion of Victor Matfield's first half try but his contribution proved decisive for the second time in the space of a week.

Defeat was becoming a depressingly familiar experience for Australia and Robbie Deans' team were on the wrong end of a 19–18 scoreline when they crossed swords again with New Zealand in Sydney in late August.

New Zealand welcomed back Carter at fly-half for the game and the talismanic playmaker marked his return to the international fold with a clinical 78th minute penalty, his fourth of the match, to dash Australian hopes of their first victory in the competition.

The visit of the South Africans to the Subiaco Oval in Perth at the end of August was hardly the fixture the beleaguered Wallabies needed and when Fourie du Preez's quick tap penalty resulted in a fifth minute try for the visitors, Australia already had their backs against the wall.

Fly-half Matt Giteau almost single-handedly tried to salvage the Wallaby cause with two converted tries either side of half-time and two penalties, but a try from Fourie and two second half scores from Habana proved too much to contend with and the Springboks claimed a 32–25 win that sent them nine points clear at the top of the table.

The world champions could now claim the title with a game to spare with victory over Australia in Brisbane, but the home side finally found some form and second half scores from Ashley-Cooper and James O'Connor, coupled with 11 points from the boot of Giteau, condemned South Africa to a 21–6 defeat.

It will be a fillip for this group and that was evident in the last 10 minutes," said Deans after watching his team break their competition duck. "We had a few things go against us but they kept their heads up and they played for the full 80 minutes. It was evident at the end that the confidence was starting to kick in, and the spirit was great. We took South Africa outside their comfort zone, which we haven't been able to do previously."

The Boks now knew they needed a victory against New Zealand in Hamilton to guarantee themselves the title but the All Blacks were back in the hunt and a bonus-point win over South Africa, followed by a similar result against Australia in their final game, would be enough to secure a fifth successive Tri-Nations crown.

The clash in the Waikato Stadium was, without question, a classic. Carter landed a first minute penalty for the All Blacks to become the tournament's record points scorer but it was to prove the only period of the match that the defending champions found themselves in the lead.

South Africa were back on level terms five minutes later when full-back Francois Steyn drilled a breathtaking penalty from all of 60 metres out and the Boks then edged in front when he slotted another superb long-range effort.

The first try of the match came in the 19th minute when Joe Rokocoko failed to collect an up-and-under. Flanker Pierre Spies pounced on the loose ball and sent Du Preez scampering over and South Africa were now firmly in the ascendency.

A third huge penalty from Steyn kept the scoreboard ticking over and when De Villiers scored an interception try from an ill-judged Carter pass 10 minutes after the restart, the Springboks appeared to be out of sight.

The All Blacks, however, had other ideas and their second half fight-back had the crowd on the edge of their seats. Wing Sitiveni Sivivatu began the revival with a 55th minute score and when McCaw touched down Carter's cross-field kick with just two minutes remaining, the game hung in the balance.

Carter converted his captain's effort to pull New Zealand to within three points. The fly-half then tried the same tactic again, but this time his kick to the opposite corner was too high and the South Africans clung on for a famous 32–29 triumph.

"At the end my heart was in my throat as we always knew the All Blacks would never give up," said coach De Villiers after the match. "It was as tough as it gets. The All Blacks aren't a walkover. To play them in their backyard, it's a great honour to come out victorious."

The South Africa celebrations could now begin in earnest, but New Zealand had one final assignment in the shape of Australia in Wellington. It may have been rendered something of a dead rubber by the Springboks' success in Hamilton but second place was still up for grabs and it was the All Blacks who ensured they did not suffer the embarrassment of propping up the final table.

The Wallabies were the first to trouble the scorers with an early Giteau penalty but they had no answer to tries from Cory Jane, Ma'a Nonu and Rokocoko as New Zealand cantered to a 33–6 victory.

However, it had undoubtedly been South Africa's tournament. They outscored both their southern hemisphere rivals and conceded fewer points and with a settled, cohesive side, the Springboks will be favourites to defend their title next season.

TRI-NATIONS 2009:
FINAL TABLE

	P	W	D	L	F	A	Bonus Pts	Pts
South Africa	6	5	0	1	158	130	1	21
New Zealand	6	3	0	3	141	131	1	13
Australia	6	1	0	5	103	141	3	7

Points: win 4; draw 2; four or more tries, or defeat by seven or fewer points 1

18 July, Eden Park, Auckland

NEW ZEALAND 22 (1G 5PG)
AUSTRALIA 16 (1G 3PG)

NEW ZEALAND: J M Muliaina; C S Jane, C G Smith, M A Nonu, S W Sivivatu; S R Donald, Q J Cowan; T D Woodcock, A K Hore, N S Tialata, B C Thorn, I B Ross, J Kaino, R So'oialo, R H McCaw (*captain*) *Substitutions:* O T Franks for Tialata (44 mins); K F Mealamu for Hore (44 mins); P A T Weepu for Cowan (52 mins); K J Read for So'oialo (61 mins); J J Eaton for Ross (71 mins)

SCORERS *Try*: McCaw *Conversion*: Donald *Penalty Goals:* Donald (5)

AUSTRALIA: A P Ashley–Cooper; L D Turner, S A Mortlock (*captain*), B S Barnes, D A Mitchell; M J Giteau, L Burgess; B A Robinson, S T Moore, A K E Baxter, J E Horwill, N C Sharpe, R N Brown, W L Palu, G B Smith *Substitutions:* D W Pocock for Brown (50 mins); J D O'Connor for Barnes (61 mins); B E Alexander for Baxter (71 mins); S W Genia for Burgess (73 mins); D W Mumm for Horwill (temp 38 to 44 mins and temp 63 to 70 mins)

SCORERS *Try*: Barnes *Conversion:* Giteau *Penalty Goals*: Giteau (3)

REFEREE C Joubert (South Africa)

25 July, Vodacom Park, Bloemfontein

SOUTH AFRICA 28 (6PG 2T)
NEW ZEALAND 19 (1G 4PG)

SOUTH AFRICA: F P L Steyn; J–P R Pietersen, J Fourie, J de Villiers, B G Habana; R Pienaar, P F du Preez; T Mtawarira, B W du Plessis, J W Smit (*captain*), J P Botha, V Matfield, J H Smith, P J Spies, H W Brüssow *Substitutions*: M Steyn for Pienaar (40 mins); W Olivier for De Villiers (68 mins); D J Rossouw for Botha (68 mins); E R Januarie for Du Preez (73 mins); M C Ralepelle for B du Plessis (79 mins); J N du Plessis for Smit (temp 65 to 73 mins)

SCORERS *Tries*: Pienaar, Fourie *Penalty Goals*: M Steyn (3), F Steyn (2), Pienaar

NEW ZEALAND: J M Muliaina; J T Rokocoko, C G Smith, M A Nonu, S W Sivivatu; S R Donald, B G Leonard; T D Woodcock, A K Hore, N S Tialata, B C Thorn, I B Ross, J Kaino, R So'oialo, R H McCaw (*captain*) *Substitutions*: O T Franks for Tialata (40 mins); P A T Weepu for Leonard (48 mins); K J Read for So'oialo (52 mins); K F Mealamu for Hore (57 mins); J J Eaton for Ross (64 mins); C L McAlister for Smith (75 mins)

SCORERS *Try*: Smith *Conversion*: Donald *Penalty Goals:* Donald (4)

REFEREE A C Rolland (Ireland)

1 August, ABSA Stadium, King's Park, Durban

SOUTH AFRICA 31 (1G 8PG)
NEW ZEALAND 19 (1G 4PG)

SOUTH AFRICA: F P L Steyn; J–P R Pietersen, J Fourie, J de Villiers, B G Habana; M Steyn, P F du Preez; T Mtawarira, B W du Plessis, J W Smit (*captain*), J P Botha, V Matfield, J H Smith, P J Spies, H W Brüssow *Substitutions*: D J Rossouw for Smith (65 mins); A A Jacobs for De Villiers (70 mins); J N du Plessis for Smit (77 mins); E R Januarie for Du Preez (77 mins); A Bekker for Botha (77 mins); W Olivier for Fourie (77 mins); M C Ralepelle for B du Plessis (78 mins)

SCORER *Try*: M Steyn *Conversion*: M Steyn *Penalty Goals*: M Steyn (8)

NEW ZEALAND: J M Muliaina; J T Rokocoko, C G Smith, M A Nonu, S W Sivivatu; S R Donald, Q J Cowan; T D Woodcock, A K Hore, O T Franks, B C Thorn, I B Ross, J Kaino, R So'oialo, R H McCaw (*captain*) *Substitutions*: K F Mealamu for Hore (43 mins); P A T Weepu for Cowan (43 mins); K J Read for Kaino (59 mins); C L McAlister for Donald (60 mins); I F Afoa for Franks (65 mins); Hore back for Mealamu (76 mins)

SCORERS *Try*: Ross *Conversion*: Donald *Penalty Goals:* Donald (3), McAlister

REFEREE N Owens (Wales)

YELLOW CARDS Pietersen (27 mins); Ross (30 mins); Botha (49 mins)

8 August, Newlands, Cape Town

SOUTH AFRICA 29 (7PG 1DG 1T)
AUSTRALIA 17 (2G 1DG)

SOUTH AFRICA: F P L Steyn; J–P R Pietersen, J Fourie, J de Villiers, B G Habana; M Steyn, P F du Preez; T Mtawarira, B W du Plessis, J W Smit (*captain*), J P Botha, V Matfield, J H Smith, P J Spies, H W Brüssow *Substitutions:* D J Rossouw for Smith (52 mins); R Pienaar for F Steyn (60 mins); J N du Plessis for Mtawarira (68 mins); A A Jacobs for De Villiers (71 mins); E R Januarie for Du Preez (75 mins); A Bekker for Botha (75 mins)

SCORERS *Try:* Matfield *Penalty Goals:* M Steyn (7) *Dropped Goal:* M Steyn

AUSTRALIA: A P Ashley–Cooper; L D Turner, S A Mortlock (*captain*), B S Barnes, D A Mitchell; M J Giteau, L Burgess; B A Robinson, S T Moore, A K E Baxter, J E Horwill, N C Sharpe, R N Brown, W L Palu, G B Smith *Substitutions:* J D O'Connor for Mortlock (29 mins); D W Mumm for Horwill (40 mins); T Polota–Nau for Moore (49 mins); B E Alexander for Baxter (49 mins); D W Pocock for Palu (55 mins); S W Genia for Burgess (55 mins)

SCORERS *Tries:* Ashley–Cooper, Giteau *Conversions:* Giteau (2) *Dropped Goal:* Barnes

REFEREE A C Rolland (Ireland)

YELLOW CARDS Giteau (34 mins); Brown (35 mins); G Smith (78 mins)

22 August, ANZ Stadium, Sydney

AUSTRALIA 18 (6PG)
NEW ZEALAND 19 (1G 4PG)

AUSTRALIA: J D O'Connor; L D Turner, A P Ashley–Cooper, B S Barnes, D A Mitchell; M J Giteau, L Burgess; B A Robinson, S T Moore, A K E Baxter, J E Horwill, N C Sharpe, R D Elsom, R N Brown, G B Smith (*captain*) *Substitutions:* B E Alexander for Robinson (temp 21 to 23 mins) and for Baxter (31 mins); R P Cross for Barnes (40 mins); P J Hynes for O'Connor (45 mins); D W Pocock for Brown (66 mins); D W Mumm for Sharpe (68 mins); T Polota–Nau for Moore (temp 21 to 31 mins, temp 49 to 66 mins and 70 mins); S W Genia for Burgess (75 mins)

SCORER *Penalty Goals:* Giteau (6)

NEW ZEALAND: J M Muliaina; J T Rokocoko, C G Smith, C L McAlister, S W Sivivatu; D W Carter, Q J Cowan; T D Woodcock, A K Hore, O T Franks, B C Thorn, I B Ross, J Kaino, K J Read, R H McCaw (*captain*) *Substitutions:* M A Nonu for McAlister (temp 2 to 10 mins) and for Smith (40 mins); S R Donald for McAlister (49 mins); R So'oialo for Kaino (66 mins); I F Afoa for Franks (66 mins)

SCORERS *Try:* Nonu *Conversion:* Carter *Penalty Goals:* Carter (4)

REFEREE J I Kaplan (South Africa)

YELLOW CARD Brown (41 mins)

29 August, Subiaco Oval, Perth

AUSTRALIA 25 (2G 2PG 1T)
SOUTH AFRICA 32 (3G 2PG 1T)

AUSTRALIA: J D O'Connor; L D Turner, R P Cross, A P Ashley–Cooper, P J Hynes; M J Giteau, L Burgess; B A Robinson, S T Moore, B E Alexander, J E Horwill, M D Chisholm, R D Elsom, R N Brown, G B Smith (*captain*) *Substitutions:* D W Pocock for Brown (47 mins); T Polota–Nau for Moore (54 mins); S W Genia for Burgess (56 mins); Q S Cooper for Cross (63 mins); D A Mitchell for O'Connor (76 mins)

SCORERS *Tries:* Giteau (2), Turner *Conversions:* Giteau (2) *Penalty Goals:* Giteau (2)

SOUTH AFRICA: R Pienaar; J–P R Pietersen, J Fourie, J de Villiers, B G Habana; M Steyn, P F du Preez; T Mtawarira, B W du Plessis, J W Smit (*captain*), J P Botha, V Matfield, J H Smith, P J Spies, H W Brüssow *Substitutions:* A Bekker for Botha (54 mins); S W P Burger for Smith (64 mins); A A Jacobs for Pietersen (64 mins); F P L Steyn for Pienaar (72 mins); J N du Plessis for Smit (76 mins); E R Januarie for Du Preez (76 mins); M C Ralapelle for B du Plessis (76 mins)

SCORERS *Tries:* Habana (2), Du Preez, Fourie *Conversions:* M Steyn (3) *Penalty Goals:* M Steyn (2)

REFEREE B J Lawrence (New Zealand)

5 September, Suncorp Stadium, Brisbane

AUSTRALIA 21 (1G 2PG 1DG 1T)
SOUTH AFRICA 6 (1PG 1DG)

AUSTRALIA: J D O'Connor; L D Turner, A P Ashley–Cooper, B S Barnes, D A Mitchell; M J Giteau, S W Genia; B A Robinson, T Polota–Nau, B E Alexander, J E Horwill, M D Chisholm, R D Elsom, G B Smith (*captain*), D W Pocock *Substitutions:* P J Hynes for Turner (30 mins); S T Moore for Polota–Nau (32mins); Q S Cooper for Barnes (74 mins); P J M Cowan for Alexander (76 mins)

SCORERS *Tries:* Ashley–Cooper, O'Connor *Conversion:* Giteau *Penalty Goals:* Giteau (2) *Dropped Goal:* Giteau

SOUTH AFRICA: R Pienaar; O M Ndungane, J Fourie, J de Villiers, B G Habana; M Steyn, P F du Preez; T Mtawarira, B W du Plessis, J W Smit (*captain*), J P Botha, V Matfield, J H Smith, P J Spies, H W Brüssow *Substitutions*: A A Jacobs for Habana (38 mins); D J Rossouw for Botha (59 mins); S W P Burger for Brüssow (59 mins); F P L Steyn for Pienaar (67 mins)

SCORER *Penalty Goal:* M Steyn *Dropped Goal*: M Steyn

REFEREE W Barnes (England)

12 September, Waikato Stadium, Hamilton

NEW ZEALAND 29 (2G 5PG)
SOUTH AFRICA 32 (2G 5PG 1DG)

NEW ZEALAND: J M Muliaina; J T Rokocoko, M A Nonu, S R Donald, S W Sivivatu; D W Carter, Q J Cowan; T D Woodcock, A K Hore, O T Franks, B C Thorn, I B Ross, J Kaino, K J Read, R H McCaw (*captain*) *Substitutions:* I Toeava for Donald (50 mins); I F Afoa for Franks (50 mins); A J Thomson for Kaino (71 mins); C S Jane for Sivivatu (71 mins)

SCORERS *Tries:* Sivivatu, McCaw *Conversions:* Carter (2) *Penalty Goals:* Carter (5)

SOUTH AFRICA: F P L Steyn; O M Ndungane, J Fourie, J de Villiers, B G Habana; M Steyn, P F du Preez; T Mtawarira, B W du Plessis, J W Smit (*captain*), J P Botha, V Matfield, S W P Burger, P J Spies, H W Brüssow *Substitutions:* R Kankowski for Burger (67 mins); D J Rossouw for Botha (71 mins); A A Jacobs for Habana (76 mins); E R Januarie for Du Preez (76 mins); J N du Plessis for Mtawarira (79 mins); M C Ralepelle for B du Plessis (79 mins)

SCORERS *Tries:* Du Preez, De Villiers *Conversions:* M Steyn (2) *Penalty Goals:* F Steyn (3), M Steyn (2) *Dropped Goal:* M Steyn

REFEREE N Owens (Wales)

19 September, Westpac Stadium, Wellington

NEW ZEALAND 33 (3G 4PG)
AUSTRALIA 6 (1PG 1DG)

NEW ZEALAND: J M Muliaina; C S Jane, I Toeava, M A Nonu, J T Rokocoko; D W Carter, Q J Cowan; T D Woodcock, A K Hore, N S Tialata, B C Thorn, T J S Donnelly, A J Thomson, K J Read, R H McCaw (*captain*) *Substitutions:* I F Afoa for Tialata (46 mins); H E Gear for Jane (58 mins); J J Eaton for Donnelly (65 mins); B G Leonard for Cowan (68 mins); R So'oialo for Thomson (72 mins); A P de Malmanche for Hore (78 mins)

SCORERS *Tries:* Jane, Nonu, Rokocoko *Conversions:* Carter (3) *Penalty Goals:* Carter (4)

AUSTRALIA: J D O'Connor; L D Turner, A P Ashley–Cooper, B S Barnes, D A Mitchell; M J Giteau, S W Genia; B A Robinson, S T Moore, B E Alexander, J E Horwill, M D Chisholm, R D Elsom, G B Smith (*captain*), D W Pocock *Substitutions:* S T Moore for Polota–Nau (48 mins); P J M Cowan for Robinson (67 mins); W L Palu for Elsom (temp 61 to 68 mins) and for Smith (68 mins); L Burgess for Genia (76 mins)

SCORERS *Penalty Goal:* Giteau *Dropped Goal:* Barnes

REFEREE C Joubert (South Africa)

YELLOW CARD Toeava (28 mins)

TRI-NATIONS RECORDS
1996–2009

PREVIOUS WINNERS

1996 New Zealand	1997 New Zealand	1998 South Africa	1999 New Zealand
2000 Australia	2001 Australia	2002 New Zealand	2003 New Zealand
2004 South Africa	2005 New Zealand	2006 New Zealand	2007 New Zealand
2008 New Zealand	2009 South Africa		

GRAND SLAM WINNERS

New Zealand (Three times) 1996, 1997, 2003.

South Africa (Once) 1998.

TEAM RECORD	DETAIL		SET
Most team points in season	179 by N Zealand	in six matches	2006
Most team tries in season	18 by S Africa	in four matches	1997
Highest team score	61 by S Africa	61–22 v Australia (h)	1997
Biggest team win	49 by Australia	49–0 v S Africa (h)	2006
Most team tries in match	8 by S Africa	v Australia	1997
	8 by S Africa	v Australia	2008

INDIVIDUAL RECORD	DETAIL		SET
Most appearances	48 for Australia	G M Gregan	1996 to 2007
Most points in matches	363 for N Zealand	D W Carter	2003 to 2009
Most points in season	99 for N Zealand	D W Carter	2006
Most points in match	31 for S Africa	M Steyn	v N Zealand (h) 2009
Most tries in matches	16 for N Zealand	C M Cullen	1996 to 2002
Most tries in season	7 for N Zealand	C M Cullen	2000
Most tries in match	4 for S Africa	J L Nokwe	v Australia (h) 2008
Most cons in matches	43 for N Zealand	D W Carter	2003 to 2009
Most cons in season	14 for N Zealand	D W Carter	2006
Most cons in match	6 for S Africa	J H de Beer	v Australia (h),1997
Most pens in matches	82 for N Zealand	A P Mehrtens	1996 to 2004
	82 for N Zealand	D W Carter	2003 to 2009
Most pens in season	23 for S Africa	M Steyn	2009
Most pens in match	9 for N Zealand	A P Mehrtens	v Australia (h) 1999
Most drops in matches	4 for S Africa	A S Pretorius	2002 to 2006
Most drops in season	3 for S Africa	M Steyn	2009
Most drops in match	2 for S Africa	J H de Beer	v N Zealand (h) 1997
	2 for S Africa	F P L Steyn	v Australia (h) 2007

From 1996 to 2009 inclusive, each nation played four matches in a season, except in 2006, 2008 and 2009 when the nations each played six matches.

TWO IN A ROW FOR BABY BLACKS

By Iain Spragg

Hannah Johnston/Getty Images

Aaron Cruden (centre) with the 2009 trophy

New Zealand's Under 20 side retained their title with a superb display of 15-man rugby in the IRB TOSHIBA Junior World Championship final against England in Tokyo, destroying their opponents 44–28 in a scintillating seven-try romp.

The Baby Blacks claimed the inaugural IRB Junior World Championship crown in 2008 with a 38–3 victory over England and repeated the trick 12 months later to send a clear message to the rugby world that the New Zealand production line of talent remains in rude health.

It was closer this time around as England fought gallantly to contain the fledgling New Zealanders in the Prince Chichibu Memorial Stadium, but there was little doubt New Zealand were the best team in the tournament, scoring an average of 43 points in their five games, crossing for 33 tries and conceding a mere five – all of them in the knockout stages.

The second IRB Junior World Championship, featuring 16 sides from across the globe, began in early June in five venues across Japan with the young hopefuls divided in four pools before the competition reached its play-off phase.

New Zealand were drawn in Pool A alongside Ireland, Argentina and tournament newcomers Uruguay, the inaugural IRB Junior World Rugby Trophy winners in 2008. The Baby Blacks dispatched Uruguay 75–0 in their opening match, but found Ireland a much tougher prospect and it was only when Winston Stanley crashed over in the 54th minute for the first try of the night that they pulled away.

Argentina actually led the pool decider at the Mizuho Rugby Ground in Nagoya at half-time, but the introduction of Zac Guildford and scrum-half Frae Wilson had an instant impact, the pair crossing within minutes to spark New Zealand's seven-try romp into the semi-finals.

In Pool B, England were almost as dominant and left Samoa, Scotland and hosts Japan in their muscular wake. The junior version of the Calcutta Cup in Tokyo was England's closest clash but they still beat the Scots 30–7 as they finished top with three wins from three and having scored 17 tries in the process.

The Pool C decider at the Kintetsu Hanazono Stadium in Osaka produced one of the matches of the Championship with a sublime display of rugby taking France out into a 20–0 lead in the first half hour. South Africa simply had no answer to France's play, but the sin-binning of fly half Pierre Bernard late in the first half proved the turning point, the Baby Boks scoring 18 points in his absence amid an unanswered run of 43 points before the French were awarded a late consolation penalty try.

Australia, boasting a squad packed with Super 14 players, were the standout side of the pool stages as they put Wales, Tonga and Canada to the sword. Canada were the first to feel the full force of attack-minded Australians, suffering an 86–0 loss in Saga with full-back Kurtley Beale and scrum-half Richard Kingi both scoring a JWC record-equalling four tries apiece. The Tongans (40–6) and Wales (38–5) both fared marginally better, but there was no stopping the Australians, who amassed a staggering 164 points as they easily topped Pool D.

At the conclusion of the pool stages the four nations who had finished bottom of their respective groups – Uruguay, Japan, Italy and Canada – already knew they would not be playing in the reduced 12-team Junior World Championship next year and would instead have to come through regional qualifying to contest the second tier Junior World Rugby Trophy.

The Championship – which saw more than 100,000 spectators attend the five match days – came to an end on 21 June with the play-offs to determine the final standings with hosts Japan securing their first win with an eight-try, 54–7 defeat of Uruguay in the 15th place play-off in Nagoya to the delight of the home supporters.

Scotland edged an agonisingly close encounter with Tonga in the ninth place play-off. Both sides scored three tries, converting two of them, and the game was ultimately settled 28–25 in the Scots' favour by a late Robbie McGowan penalty.

The seventh place play-off proved another hard fought encounter in Fukuoka where Samoa battled with Ireland. The Irish took an early lead at the Level 5 Stadium, but successful penalties from Ioane Sefo, Ivy Leleisiuao and Rayhan Laulala were enough to secure a 9–3 win for the Samoans to match their placing in 2008.

It was an all-European affair to determine fifth place as France, the Under 20 Six Nations champions, played Wales and the match followed the form book as Les Bleus crushed the Welsh with an eight-try, 68–13 mauling in which impressive fly half Bernard helped himself to a Junior World Championship record 33 points to surpass Kingi's record of 26 in Australia's defeat of Canada.

Two of the southern hemisphere's "big three" were left to contest the third place play-off as South Africa and Australia crossed swords in Tokyo. Heavy rain at the Prince Chichibu Memorial Stadium meant both teams struggled to hold onto the slippery ball but it was the Baby Boks, who missed out on the final after losing to England – just as they had done in 2008 – in the semi finals, who adapted best to the conditions.

The South Africans were the first to cross the whitewash when fly half Lionel Cronje scored his fourth try of the tournament. Wing Gerhard van den Heever added a second minutes later and although Australia replied through prop Albert Anae, the Baby Boks were in irrepressible form and Cronje's second try after the break sealed a 32–5 win and third place for his side – a repeat of their performance in 2008.

The final itself produced an even more compelling showcase. England's powerful pack and two early penalties from full-back Tom Homer gave the side in white hope in the initial exchanges, but the New Zealanders began to take ominous control on 14 minutes when full-back Robbie Robinson crossed for the first try. England replied with a try from lock James Gaskell, but the Baby Blacks were looking dangerous from open and broken play and their second try came midway through the first half from experienced wing Guildford, the only survivor of New Zealand's triumph 12 months earlier in Wales.

England were never really in genuine contention again and a brace of tries from New Zealand's outstanding captain Aaron Cruden, another from Guildford and further scores from hooker Brayden Mitchell and inside centre Shaun Treeby were more than enough to settle the contest and secure a 44–28 victory.

Cruden had been the standout performer for New Zealand in the knockout stages and was duly named IRB Junior Player of the Year after the final whistle, the fly half – who had been diagnosed with testicular cancer in August 2008 – beating teammate Stanley, England No.8 Carl Fearns and Kingi to the prestigious honour.

JUNIOR WORLD CHAMPIONSHIP

IRB JUNIOR WORLD
CHAMPIONSHIP 2009 RESULTS

POOL A

Round One: **Argentina** 9 **Ireland** 16, **New Zealand** 75 **Uruguay** 0. Round Two: **Argentina** 33 **Uruguay** 15, **Ireland** 0 **New Zealand** 17. Round Three: **Ireland** 45 **Uruguay** 0, **Argentina** 9 **New Zealand** 48.

POOL B

Round One: **Samoa** 17 **Scotland** 14, **England** 43 **Japan** 0. Round Two: **England** 30 **Scotland** 7, **Japan** 20 **Samoa** 29. Round Three: **England** 52 **Samoa** 7, **Japan** 7 **Scotland** 12

POOL C

Round One: **France** 43 **Italy** 13, **Fiji** 10 **South Africa** 36. Round Two: **Fiji** 25 **France** 48, **Italy** 3 **South Africa** 65. Round Three: **Fiji** 20 **Italy** 14, **France** 27 **South Africa** 43.

POOL D

Round One: **Australia** 86 **Canada** 0, **Tonga** 5 **Wales** 51. Round Two: **Australia** 40 **Tonga** 6, **Canada** 15 **Wales** 51. Round Three: **Canada** 20 **Tonga** 36, **Australia** 38 **Wales** 5

PLAY-OFFS – FIRST PHASE

13th Place Semi-Finals	**Uruguay** 11 **Canada** 29
	Japan 15 **Italy** 21
Ninth Place Semi-Finals	**Argentina** 17 **Tonga** 26
	Scotland 39 **Fiji** 26
Fifth Place Semi-Finals	**Ireland** 17 **Wales** 19
	Samoa 6 **France** 16
Semi-Finals	**New Zealand** 31 **Australia** 17
	South Africa 21 **England** 40

PLAY-OFFS – SECOND PHASE

15th Place Play-Off	**Uruguay** 17 **Japan** 54
13th Place Play-Off	**Canada** 22 **Italy** 32
11th Place Play-Off	**Argentina** 27 **Fiji** 10
Ninth Place Play-Off	**Tonga** 25 **Scotland** 28
Seventh Place Play-Off	**Ireland** 3 **Samoa** 9
Fifth Place Play-Off	**Wales** 13 **France** 68

AUSTRALIA 5 (1T) SOUTH AFRICA 32 (3G, 2PG, 1T)

FINAL

21 June, Prince Chichibu Memorial Stadium, Tokyo

NEW ZEALAND 44 (3G, 1PG, 4T) ENGLAND 28 (2G, 3PG, 1T)

NEW ZEALAND: R Robinson; N Tuitavake, W Stanley, S Treeby, Z Guildford; A Cruden (captain), F Wilson; W Afuvai, B Mitchell, M Fia, A Ryan, D Faleafa, B O'Connor, B Hall, T Boswell-Wakefield.

SUBSTITUTIONS: E Dixon for Hall (55 mins); K Siaosi for Tuitavake (55 mins); L Talakai for Afuvai (55 mins); Afuvai for Boswell-Wakefield (69 mins); C Rei for Robinson (72 mins); T Taylor for Wilson (72 mins); L Price for Faleafa for (72 mins); S Tamati for Mitchell (75 mins); Boswell-Wakefield for Afuvai (78 mins).

SCORERS *Tries*: Robinson, Guildford (2), Cruden (2), Mitchell, Treeby *Conversions*: Cruden (3) *Penalty Goal*: Cruden

YELLOW CARD: Talakai (68 mins)

ENGLAND: T Homer; G Lowe, H Trinder, L Eves, C Sharples; R Clegg, B Youngs; B Moon, J George, B Baker, G Kitchener, J Gaskell, C Lawes, C Clark (captain), C Fearns.

SUBSTITUTIONS: D Lewis for Youngs (28 mins); S Knight for Baker (44 mins); R Miller for Clegg (44 mins); J Clark for George (58 mins); J Ovens for Fearns (60 mins); D Williams for Kitchener (66 mins); J Cobden for Homer (69 mins).

SCORERS *Tries*: Gaskell, Fearns, Lewis *Conversions*: Homer (2) *Penalty Goals*: Homer (3)

REFEREE: J Jones (Wales)

FINAL STANDINGS

1. New Zealand	2. England
3. South Africa	4. Australia
5. France	6. Wales
7. Samoa	8. Ireland
9. Scotland	10. Tonga
11. Argentina	12. Fiji
13. Italy	14. Canada
15. Japan	16. Uruguay

JUNIOR WORLD CHAMPIONSHIP

ROMANIA EDGE TIGHT FINALE

By Karen Bond

Romania's Under 20s may have been the ones celebrating in Kenya, but the IRB Junior World Rugby Trophy 2009 was one which all participants will look back on fondly, be it for the ultra competitiveness of the eight-team tournament streamed live and on-demand on the IRB website, the festival atmosphere surrounding it or the hugely successful legacy programme which brought the players and management closer than ever to the local communities.

The raising of the bar in terms of playing standards from the inaugural tournament in Chile was evident with no fewer than five teams – Chile, Kenya, Namibia, Romania and USA – going into the final round of pool matches with a chance of reaching the title decider. It was only after a number of twists and turns that USA booked their place as Pool A winners against Romania, the top side in Pool B.

Neither finalist was known until the last five minutes of their respective pool matches, ensuring maximum drama. Filip Lazar capitalised on a Chile mistake to win the race to touch down and seal a 26–20 victory for Romania, and David Tameilau scored the crucial fourth try for the Junior Eagles to secure the bonus point victory they needed to deny the Kenyans what would have been a much celebrated place in the final.

The hosts had only finished fifth in the 2008 CAR Under 19 Championship and the battle for top spot was expected to be between African champions Namibia and USA, the side relegated from last year's IRB Junior World Championship in Wales. Kenya, however, clearly hadn't read that script and were inspired throughout by their vociferous supporters who created a fantastic match day atmosphere.

Every tackle made by the Kenya Chipu, every ball lost by their opponents and every attack they mounted was greeted with a cacophony of noise and they came within a whisker of the first upset in the all-African affair with Namibia. The hosts' chip and chase philosophy had the crowd on the edge of their seats and produced memorable tries for wing Collins Omae and flanker Joel Omer.

It was not to be their day though, relentless Namibia pressure in the second half finally paid dividends in the dying minutes against a tiring Kenyan side when wing Nathan Ockhuizen chased and gathered his own chip to run under the posts and seal a 22–17 comeback win.

Kenya went away to lick their wounds, returning four days later to face the Junior Eagles with even more determination to give their fans a victory to celebrate. This had seemed unlikely with the Chipu trailing 32–14 after hooker Tim Barford won the race to touch down Zach Test's kick in the 62nd minute. However, there was to be another twist as things finally clicked for the hosts and they duly whipped the crowd into a frenzy by scoring three tries in eight frenetic minutes, two of them by their flying wing Omae, to edge ahead 33–32.

The hosts could have been forgiven for experiencing a sense of déjà vu when Tai Enosa, who together with Test was named in the USA senior squad while in Nairobi, attempted a last gasp drop goal, but the impressive fly-half's effort flew wide and a packed RFUEA Grounds heaved a sigh of relief and the celebrations could begin.

Kenya had the easier task as the pool stages drew to a conclusion, facing the Cayman Islands who had conceded 17 tries in a 104–17 defeat by Namibia last time out. They did produce a much-improved performance and took the game to the hosts early on, but ultimately the relentless pressure from Kenya's forward pack proved the difference and they scored seven of their 10 tries in a 67–0 victory.

The hosts had done all they could, now they and their supporters – including Sevens coach Benjamin Ayimba – had to endure a nervous wait for the USA-Namibia outcome. A win for Namibia and they would finish top; a victory with no bonus point for USA and Kenya would on the head-to-head rule after their 33–32 win.

The crowd started cheering for USA after Namibia went ahead, but they were ultimately silenced when Tameilau scored the Junior Eagles' second try in a nervy final eight minutes to finish top with 12 points.

The decisive Pool B match was always going to be Chile v Romania. Not that either side had it all their own way against Papua New Guinea in particular, the Oceania representatives lighting up the Trophy with several contenders for try of the tournament as a result of their 'run everything' game plan, many of them coming from moves that had started deep in their own 22 when seemingly nothing was on.

Both were eager to reach the final, but Chile had an extra motivation as they were desperate to lift the trophy in memory of Santiago Fuenzalida, one of the stars of their 2008 side who had been killed in a car accident soon after the South American Championship later that year. Throughout the tournament the squad wore t-shirts bearing the name and number (15) of the player who would have captained them in Kenya.

The match was full of twists and turns, Cristian Rizea's two tries in as many minutes giving Romania a 21–8 lead only for a quick-fire Mauricio Rey brace to cut the deficit to one point. It was a mistake, though, that ultimately proved costly, a pass going astray and allowing Lazar to race clear. Chile could still have snatched the win, but lost the ball and the match, 26–20.

Papua New Guinea rounded off the pool stages with a first win, three tries in six first half minutes setting up a 43–19 victory over Korea. They would finish sixth overall, albeit only after losing an enthralling play-off to Namibia 48–43 on the final day, with coach Robin Tarere admitting the tournament "was an eye opener for all of us and every one of the players goes home much more experienced".

A try scorer for Namibia in that victory was Andre de Klerk, who just over a month later became the first schoolboy to play for his country's senior side in Rugby World Cup qualifiers against Ivory Coast. PNG's impressive full-back and captain Christopher Kakah would also make that step up against the might of Samoa in July.

The third place play-off was equally tight with Chile holding off Kenya to win 19–17, while Korea finished on a high with a 62–12 defeat of Cayman Islands, thanks in no small part to No.8 Cha Sung Kun's record haul of five tries.

The final itself lived up to all expectations with end to end play, scything breaks through midfield, near misses and a tense final as Romania scored 19 unanswered points in the second half to triumph 25–13. It was unfortunate, therefore, that an enthralling final that had been all square with 10 minutes remaining swung Romania's way as a result of two USA errors.

A restructuring of the IRB Junior World Championship in 2010 – reducing the participating teams from 16 to 12 – means Romania will not play in the top tier as Trophy champions, but that did not damper their celebrations at the final whistle.

"I am happy and overjoyed," enthused Romania captain Eduard Marinca after receiving the trophy from IRB Chairman Bernard Lapasset.

WOMEN'S RUGBY
A YEAR TO REMEMBER
By Paul Morgan

Women's rugby moved firmly into the spotlight in 2009 with the first ever Women's Rugby World Cup Sevens competition, an enthralling RBS Six Nations and the ascension of the first woman to the IRB Rugby Committee.

Australia captain Cheryl Soon had the honour of being the first woman to lift a World Cup Sevens trophy, while England's domination of the 15-a-side game in Europe took them to their fourth successive Six Nations title.

Dubai was the scene for RWC Sevens in March as the women's competition welcomed Brazil, Thailand, the Lady Cranes from Uganda and China – who would go on to win the Bowl – on to the world stage.

England's powerful squad, led by Sue Day, started as favourites and cruised through their three pool matches without conceding a point. In contrast, Australia lost 14–10 to France, putting them on a collision course with Simon Amor's England side in the Cup quarter-finals.

Australia beat England 17–10 in the last eight, before edging past South Africa to meet New Zealand in the final. The final couldn't have been closer or a better advertisement for the women's game, Shelly Matcham scoring the decisive try in sudden-death extra-time to seal Australia's 15–10 triumph.

"We have worked so hard to get here and to come here and achieve this is just mammoth," said Soon. "We believed in each other and we just knew we had to stick it out for the whole 20 minutes or however long. We just knew we could do it in the end."

In an incredible year for women's rugby in Australia, Debby Hodgkinson followed up the Sevens triumph by being named IRB Women's Personality of the Year 2009 in association with Emirates Airline on the day the Wallaroos qualified for WRWC 2010 with an 87–0 defeat of Samoa in Apia.

In the 15-a-side game the main focus was on the Six Nations and the campaign for some of the sides to qualify for WRWC 2010 in England.

England, in 2009, became the first women's team to record four back-to-back Six Nations titles, although they missed out on a fourth straight Grand Slam. Gary Street's side inflicted a punishing 72–3 defeat on Scotland, running in 12 tries to clinch the crown on points difference after losing 16–15 to Wales at Taff's Well.

"This championship has really been built on team effort and morale. We have a really close knit management and coaching team, and that rubs off on our playing squad," said Street.

"Our defeat against Wales was real motivation for us to pick ourselves up and prove what we can do. Even though we haven't won the Grand Slam, this has been our best Six Nations championship in my opinion."

Wales continued their superb form to finish second, the Grand Slam slipping from their grasp when they lost 27–5 in France, but they will always remember 2009 as the year they finally beat England after 22 years of trying, thanks to Non Evans' penalty with the last kick of the match.

Scotland may have finished fifth, but their Women's Performance Manager Jo Hull believes the future is bright, having seen the Scots qualify for the World Cup after beating Netherlands 38–10 to top their pool at the European Trophy in May.

"We've now got a structure in place for up and coming players, which we didn't have prior to the last World Cup," Hull said. "We're evolving as an organisation and although there is a lot of work to do, things are definitely going in the right direction. We're a long way behind England at the moment as they have so much more staff, players and financial backing, but the future of women's rugby in Scotland is looking pretty good."

Wales and Ireland had qualified for the World Cup through the Six Nations and were joined by Sweden, who upset both Italy and Spain to top the other European Trophy pool. This leaves only one place remaining for Asia's representative.

Following their Six Nations success, England travelled to Canada to defend their Nations Cup title and once again proved what powerful adversaries they will be for world champions New Zealand. Already confirmed as champions after beating USA, France and South Africa, England finished with a 22–0 victory over Canada.

USA finished second with their highlight a first defeat of Canada since 2006. "Overall, I'm happy with our performance over the course of the tournament and impressed by the progress we've made as a team," said head coach Kathy Flores.

But whatever happened in 2009 will be eclipsed when the Women's Rugby World Cup comes to England in August and September. Since

England captain Catherine Spencer got her hands on the Six Nations trophy again.

WOMEN'S RUGBY

the tournament became an official IRB event in 1998, only New Zealand have tasted success, beating England in the last two finals.

"Any World Cup is obviously very special. I was lucky enough to be involved in the last one, but to have it on home soil really does add that extra something. And the support I think we are going to get will be brilliant," said England captain Catherine Spencer.

"New Zealand are still ranked number one but as a team we have been doing tremendously well since the last World Cup. We think we have developed as a squad, as players individually and as a team, so we are very much looking forward to challenging for the World Cup."

New Zealand will themselves have a new coach to spearhead their charge for a fourth successive title following leading Auckland women's and schoolboy coach Brian Evans' appointment in June.

The pools for Women's Rugby World Cup 2010 are:

Pool A: New Zealand, Wales, Australia, South Africa

Pool B: England, USA, Ireland, Asia qualifier

Pool C: France, Canada, Scotland, Sweden

The Women's Rugby World Cup may be the highlight of 2010, but thoughts have turned to the next event with tenders already being invited for the 2014 event. Rugby World Cup Limited will analyse the tenders, prior to the IRB Council selecting the Host Union at its meeting in May.

"The phenomenal growth of Women's Rugby World Cup since its

inaugural tournament is a major success story for the women's game," said RWCL Chairman Bernard Lapasset. "Burgeoning participation, the introduction of Women's Rugby World Cup Sevens and ever increasing standards of competition mean that the women's game has never enjoyed such a strong global profile and the launching of this tender process is another significant milestone for the Women's Game."

• Off the field, the IRB Women's Personality of the Year Award winner in 2008, Carol Isherwood received another accolade in 2009 after being invited to join the IRB Rugby Committee, which deals with all issues related to the playing of the game. The first female to be appointed to the Committee by the IRB Council, Isherwood has been a leading figure in the women's game for over 25 years.

RBS WOMEN'S SIX NATIONS 2009

Team	Wins	Points Diff	Points
England	4	+185	8
Wales	4	+25	8
Ireland	3	+24	6
France	3	-8	6
Scotland	1	-123	2
Italy	0	-103	0

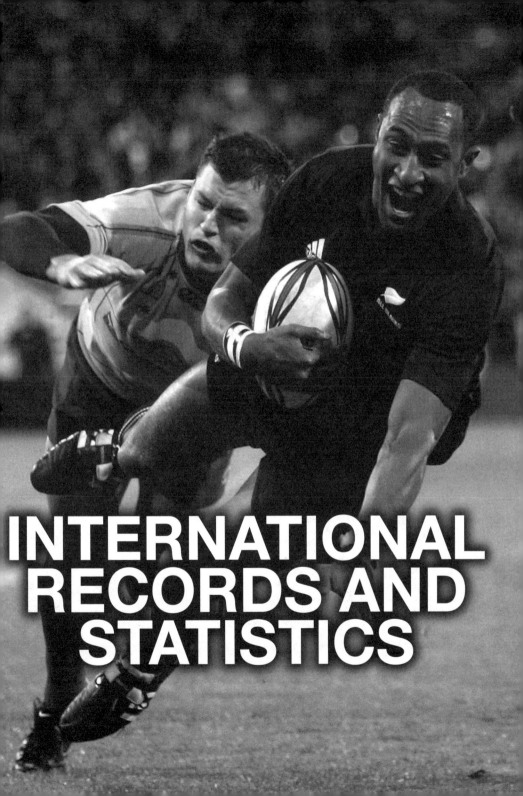

INTERNATIONAL RECORDS AND STATISTICS

World Rankings
Tournaments
Fixtures and Results
Mediazone

Education and Training
Online Resources
Union's Details
Rugby and the Olympic Games

Laws and Regulations
Total Rugby Radio
Total Rugby TV
News & Regional News

and
much
more...

irb.com

The official website of the International Rugby Board

INTERNATIONAL RECORDS

RESULTS OF INTERNATIONAL MATCHES
(UP TO 30TH SEPTEMBER 2009)

Cap matches involving senior executive council member unions only. Years for International Championship matches are for the second half of the season: eg 1972 means season 1971–72. Years for matches against touring teams from the Southern Hemisphere refer to the actual year of the match.

Points-scoring was first introduced in 1886, when an International Board was formed by Scotland, Ireland and Wales. Points values varied among the countries until 1890, when England agreed to join the Board, and uniform values were adopted.

Northern Hemisphere seasons	Try	Conversions	Penalty Goal	Dropped goal	Goal from mark
1890–91	1	2	2	3	3
1891–92 to 1892–93	2	3	3	4	4
1893–94 to 1904–05	3	2	3	4	4
1905–06 to 1947–48	3	2	3	4	3
1948–49 to 1970–71	3	2	3	3	3
1971–72 to 1991–92	4	2	3	3	3*
1992–93 onwards	5	2	3	3	–

*The goal from mark ceased to exist when the free-kick clause was introduced, 1977–78.

WC indicates a fixture played during the Rugby World Cup finals. LC indicates a fixture played in the Latin Cup. TN indicates a fixture played in the Tri Nations.

ENGLAND v SCOTLAND

Played 126 England won 67, Scotland won 42, Drawn 17
Highest scores England 43–3 in 2001 and 43–22 in 2005, Scotland 33–6 in 1986
Biggest wins England 43–3 in 2001, Scotland 33–6 in 1986

1871 Raeburn Place (Edinburgh) **Scotland** 1G 1T to 1T	1910 Inverleith **England** 14–5
1872 The Oval (London) **England** 1G 1DG 2T to 1DG	1911 Twickenham **England** 13–8
1873 Glasgow **Drawn** no score	1912 Inverleith **Scotland** 8–3
1874 The Oval **England** 1DG to 1T	1913 Twickenham **England** 3–0
1875 Raeburn Place **Drawn** no score	1914 Inverleith **England** 16–15
1876 The Oval **England** 1G 1T to 0	1920 Twickenham **England** 13–4
1877 Raeburn Place **Scotland** 1 DG to 0	1921 Inverleith **England** 18–0
1878 The Oval **Drawn** no score	1922 Twickenham **England** 11–5
1879 Raeburn Place **Drawn** Scotland 1DG England 1G	1923 Inverleith **England** 8–6
1880 Manchester **England** 2G 3T to 1G	1924 Twickenham **England** 19–0
1881 Raeburn Place **Drawn** Scotland 1G 1T England 1DG 1T	1925 Murrayfield **Scotland** 14–11
1882 Manchester **Scotland** 2T to 0	1926 Twickenham **Scotland** 17–9
1883 Raeburn Place **England** 2T to 1T	1927 Murrayfield **Scotland** 21–13
1884 Blackheath (London) **England** 1G to 1T	1928 Twickenham **England** 6–0
1885 No Match	1929 Murrayfield **Scotland** 12–6
1886 Raeburn Place **Drawn** no score	1930 Twickenham **Drawn** 0–0
1887 Manchester **Drawn** 1T each	1931 Murrayfield **Scotland** 28–19
1888 No Match	1932 Twickenham **England** 16–3
1889 No Match	1933 Murrayfield **Scotland** 3–0
1890 Raeburn Place **England** 1G 1T to 0	1934 Twickenham **England** 6–3
1891 Richmond (London) **Scotland** 9–3	1935 Murrayfield **Scotland** 10–7
1892 Raeburn Place **England** 5–0	1936 Twickenham **England** 9–8
1893 Leeds **Scotland** 8–0	1937 Murrayfield **England** 6–3
1894 Raeburn Place **Scotland** 6–0	1938 Twickenham **Scotland** 21–16
1895 Richmond **Scotland** 6–3	1939 Murrayfield **England** 9–6
1896 Glasgow **Scotland** 11–0	1947 Twickenham **England** 24–5
1897 Manchester **England** 12–3	1948 Murrayfield **Scotland** 6–3
1898 Powderhall (Edinburgh) **Drawn** 3–3	1949 Twickenham **England** 19–3
1899 Blackheath **Scotland** 5–0	1950 Murrayfield **Scotland** 13–11
1900 Inverleith (Edinburgh) **Drawn** 0–0	1951 Twickenham **England** 5–3
1901 Blackheath **Scotland** 18–3	1952 Murrayfield **England** 19–3
1902 Inverleith **England** 6–3	1953 Twickenham **England** 26–8
1903 Richmond **Scotland** 10–6	1954 Murrayfield **England** 13–3
1904 Inverleith **Scotland** 6–3	1955 Twickenham **England** 9–6
1905 Richmond **Scotland** 8–0	1956 Murrayfield **England** 11–6
1906 Inverleith **England** 9–3	1957 Twickenham **England** 16–3
1907 Blackheath **Scotland** 8–3	1958 Murrayfield **Drawn** 3–3
1908 Inverleith **Scotland** 16–10	1959 Twickenham **Drawn** 3–3
1909 Richmond **Scotland** 18–8	1960 Murrayfield **England** 21–12
	1961 Twickenham **England** 6–0
	1962 Murrayfield **Drawn** 3–3
	1963 Twickenham **England** 10–8
	1964 Murrayfield **Scotland** 15–6

1965	Twickenham **Drawn** 3–3		1987	Twickenham **England** 21–12
1966	Murrayfield **Scotland** 6–3		1988	Murrayfield **England** 9–6
1967	Twickenham **England** 27–14		1989	Twickenham **Drawn** 12–12
1968	Murrayfield **England** 8–6		1990	Murrayfield **Scotland** 13–7
1969	Twickenham **England** 8–3		1991	Twickenham **England** 21–12
1970	Murrayfield **Scotland** 14–5		1991	Murrayfield WC **England** 9–6
1971	Twickenham **Scotland** 16–15		1992	Murrayfield **England** 25–7
1971	Murrayfield **Scotland** 26–6		1993	Twickenham **England** 26–12
	Special centenary match –		1994	Murrayfield **England** 15–14
	non-championship		1995	Twickenham **England** 24–12
1972	Murrayfield **Scotland** 23–9		1996	Murrayfield **England** 18–9
1973	Twickenham **England** 20–13		1997	Twickenham **England** 41–13
1974	Murrayfield **Scotland** 16–14		1998	Murrayfield **England** 34–20
1975	Twickenham **England** 7–6		1999	Twickenham **England** 24–21
1976	Murrayfield **Scotland** 22–12		2000	Murrayfield **Scotland** 19–13
1977	Twickenham **England** 26–6		2001	Twickenham **England** 43–3
1978	Murrayfield **England** 15–0		2002	Murrayfield **England** 29–3
1979	Twickenham **Drawn** 7–7		2003	Twickenham **England** 40–9
1980	Murrayfield **England** 30–18		2004	Murrayfield **England** 35–13
1981	Twickenham **England** 23–17		2005	Twickenham **England** 43–22
1982	Murrayfield **Drawn** 9–9		2006	Murrayfield **Scotland** 18–12
1983	Twickenham **Scotland** 22–12		2007	Twickenham **England** 42–20
1984	Murrayfield **Scotland** 18–6		2008	Murrayfield **Scotland** 15–9
1985	Twickenham **England** 10–7		2009	Twickenham **England** 26–12
1986	Murrayfield **Scotland** 33–6			

ENGLAND v IRELAND

Played 122 England won 70, Ireland won 44, Drawn 8
Highest scores England 50–18 in 2000, Ireland 43–13 in 2007
Biggest wins England 46–6 in 1997, Ireland 43–13 in 2007

1875	The Oval (London) **England** 1G 1DG 1T to 0	1889	No Match
1876	Dublin **England** 1G 1T to 0	1890	Blackheath (London) **England** 3T to 0
1877	The Oval **England** 2G 2T to 0	1891	Dublin **England** 9–0
1878	Dublin **England** 2G 1T to 0	1892	Manchester **England** 7–0
1879	The Oval **England** 2G 1DG 2T to 0	1893	Dublin **England** 4–0
1880	Dublin **England** 1G 1T to 1T	1894	Blackheath **Ireland** 7–5
1881	Manchester **England** 2G 2T to 0	1895	Dublin **England** 6–3
1882	Dublin **Drawn** 2T each	1896	Leeds **Ireland** 10–4
1883	Manchester **England** 1G 3T to 1T	1897	Dublin **Ireland** 13–9
1884	Dublin **England** 1G to 0	1898	Richmond (London) **Ireland** 9–6
1885	Manchester **England** 2T to 1T	1899	Dublin **Ireland** 6–0
1886	Dublin **England** 1T to 0	1900	Richmond **England** 15–4
1887	Dublin **Ireland** 2G to 0	1901	Dublin **Ireland** 10–6
1888	No Match	1902	Leicester **England** 6–3
		1903	Dublin **Ireland** 6–0

1904	Blackheath **England** 19–0	
1905	Cork **Ireland** 17–3	
1906	Leicester **Ireland** 16–6	
1907	Dublin **Ireland** 17–9	
1908	Richmond **England** 13–3	
1909	Dublin **England** 11–5	
1910	Twickenham **Drawn** 0–0	
1911	Dublin **Ireland** 3–0	
1912	Twickenham **England** 15–0	
1913	Dublin **England** 15–4	
1914	Twickenham **England** 17–12	
1920	Dublin **England** 14–11	
1921	Twickenham **England** 15–0	
1922	Dublin **England** 12–3	
1923	Leicester **England** 23–5	
1924	Belfast **England** 14–3	
1925	Twickenham **Drawn** 6–6	
1926	Dublin **Ireland** 19–15	
1927	Twickenham **England** 8–6	
1928	Dublin **England** 7–6	
1929	Twickenham **Ireland** 6–5	
1930	Dublin **Ireland** 4–3	
1931	Twickenham **Ireland** 6–5	
1932	Dublin **England** 11–8	
1933	Twickenham **England** 17–6	
1934	Dublin **England** 13–3	
1935	Twickenham **England** 14–3	
1936	Dublin **Ireland** 6–3	
1937	Twickenham **England** 9–8	
1938	Dublin **England** 36–14	
1939	Twickenham **Ireland** 5–0	
1947	Dublin **Ireland** 22–0	
1948	Twickenham **Ireland** 11–10	
1949	Dublin **Ireland** 14–5	
1950	Twickenham **England** 3–0	
1951	Dublin **Ireland** 3–0	
1952	Twickenham **England** 3–0	
1953	Dublin **Drawn** 9–9	
1954	Twickenham **England** 14–3	
1955	Dublin **Drawn** 6–6	
1956	Twickenham **England** 20–0	
1957	Dublin **England** 6–0	
1958	Twickenham **England** 6–0	
1959	Dublin **England** 3–0	
1960	Twickenham **England** 8–5	
1961	Dublin **Ireland** 11–8	
1962	Twickenham **England** 16–0	
1963	Dublin **Drawn** 0–0	

1964	Twickenham **Ireland** 18–5
1965	Dublin **Ireland** 5–0
1966	Twickenham **Drawn** 6–6
1967	Dublin **England** 8–3
1968	Twickenham **Drawn** 9–9
1969	Dublin **Ireland** 17–15
1970	Twickenham **England** 9–3
1971	Dublin **England** 9–6
1972	Twickenham **Ireland** 16–12
1973	Dublin **Ireland** 18–9
1974	Twickenham **Ireland** 26–21
1975	Dublin **Ireland** 12–9
1976	Twickenham **Ireland** 13–12
1977	Dublin **England** 4–0
1978	Twickenham **England** 15–9
1979	Dublin **Ireland** 12–7
1980	Twickenham **England** 24–9
1981	Dublin **England** 10–6
1982	Twickenham **Ireland** 16–15
1983	Dublin **Ireland** 25–15
1984	Twickenham **England** 12–9
1985	Dublin **Ireland** 13–10
1986	Twickenham **England** 25–20
1987	Dublin **Ireland** 17–0
1988	Twickenham **England** 35–3
1988	Dublin **England** 21–10
	Non-championship match
1989	Dublin **England** 16–3
1990	Twickenham **England** 23–0
1991	Dublin **England** 16–7
1992	Twickenham **England** 38–9
1993	Dublin **Ireland** 17–3
1994	Twickenham **Ireland** 13–12
1995	Dublin **England** 20–8
1996	Twickenham **England** 28–15
1997	Dublin **England** 46–6
1998	Twickenham **England** 35–17
1999	Dublin **England** 27–15
2000	Twickenham **England** 50–18
2001	Dublin **Ireland** 20–14
2002	Twickenham **England** 45–11
2003	Dublin **England** 42–6
2004	Twickenham **Ireland** 19–13
2005	Dublin **Ireland** 19–13
2006	Twickenham **Ireland** 28–24
2007	Dublin **Ireland** 43–13
2008	Twickenham **England** 33–10
2009	Dublin **Ireland** 14–13

ENGLAND v WALES

Played 118 England won 53, Wales won 53, Drawn 12
Highest scores England 62–5 in 2007, Wales 34–21 in 1967
Biggest wins England 62–5 in 2007, Wales 25–0 in 1905

1881	Blackheath (London) **England** 7G 1DG 6T to 0		1928	Swansea **England** 10–8	
			1929	Twickenham **England** 8–3	
1882	No Match		1930	Cardiff **England** 11–3	
1883	Swansea **England** 2G 4T to 0		1931	Twickenham **Drawn** 11–11	
1884	Leeds **England** 1G 2T to 1G		1932	Swansea **Wales** 12–5	
1885	Swansea **England** 1G 4T to 1G 1T		1933	Twickenham **Wales** 7–3	
1886	Blackheath **England** 1GM 2T to 1G		1934	Cardiff **England** 9–0	
1887	Llanelli **Drawn** no score		1935	Twickenham **Drawn** 3–3	
1888	No Match		1936	Swansea **Drawn** 0–0	
1889	No Match		1937	Twickenham **England** 4–3	
1890	Dewsbury **Wales** 1T to 0		1938	Cardiff **Wales** 14–8	
1891	Newport **England** 7–3		1939	Twickenham **England** 3–0	
1892	Blackheath **England** 17–0		1947	Cardiff **England** 9–6	
1893	Cardiff **Wales** 12–11		1948	Twickenham **Drawn** 3–3	
1894	Birkenhead **England** 24–3		1949	Cardiff **Wales** 9–3	
1895	Swansea **England** 14–6		1950	Twickenham **Wales** 11–5	
1896	Blackheath **England** 25–0		1951	Swansea **Wales** 23–5	
1897	Newport **Wales** 11–0		1952	Twickenham **Wales** 8–6	
1898	Blackheath **England** 14–7		1953	Cardiff **England** 8–3	
1899	Swansea **Wales** 26–3		1954	Twickenham **England** 9–6	
1900	Gloucester **Wales** 13–3		1955	Cardiff **Wales** 3–0	
1901	Cardiff **Wales** 13–0		1956	Twickenham **Wales** 8–3	
1902	Blackheath **Wales** 9–8		1957	Cardiff **England** 3–0	
1903	Swansea **Wales** 21–5		1958	Twickenham **Drawn** 3–3	
1904	Leicester **Drawn** 14–14		1959	Cardiff **Wales** 5–0	
1905	Cardiff **Wales** 25–0		1960	Twickenham **England** 14–6	
1906	Richmond (London) **Wales** 16–3		1961	Cardiff **Wales** 6–3	
1907	Swansea **Wales** 22–0		1962	Twickenham **Drawn** 0–0	
1908	Bristol **Wales** 28–18		1963	Cardiff **England** 13–6	
1909	Cardiff **Wales** 8–0		1964	Twickenham **Drawn** 6–6	
1910	Twickenham **England** 11–6		1965	Cardiff **Wales** 14–3	
1911	Swansea **Wales** 15–11		1966	Twickenham **Wales** 11–6	
1912	Twickenham **England** 8–0		1967	Cardiff **Wales** 34–21	
1913	Cardiff **England** 12–0		1968	Twickenham **Drawn** 11–11	
1914	Twickenham **England** 10–9		1969	Cardiff **Wales** 30–9	
1920	Swansea **Wales** 19–5		1970	Twickenham **Wales** 17–13	
1921	Twickenham **England** 18–3		1971	Cardiff **Wales** 22–6	
1922	Cardiff **Wales** 28–6		1972	Twickenham **Wales** 12–3	
1923	Twickenham **England** 7–3		1973	Cardiff **Wales** 25–9	
1924	Swansea **England** 17–9		1974	Twickenham **England** 16–12	
1925	Twickenham **England** 12–6		1975	Cardiff **Wales** 20–4	
1926	Cardiff **Drawn** 3–3		1976	Twickenham **Wales** 21–9	
1927	Twickenham **England** 11–9		1977	Cardiff **Wales** 14–9	

94

1978	Twickenham **Wales** 9–6	1996	Twickenham **England** 21–15
1979	Cardiff **Wales** 27–3	1997	Cardiff **England** 34–13
1980	Twickenham **England** 9–8	1998	Twickenham **England** 60–26
1981	Cardiff **Wales** 21–19	1999	Wembley **Wales** 32–31
1982	Twickenham **England** 17–7	2000	Twickenham **England** 46–12
1983	Cardiff **Drawn** 13–13	2001	Cardiff **England** 44–15
1984	Twickenham **Wales** 24–15	2002	Twickenham **England** 50–10
1985	Cardiff **Wales** 24–15	2003	Cardiff **England** 26–9
1986	Twickenham **England** 21–18	2003	Cardiff **England** 43–9
1987	Cardiff **Wales** 19–12		Non-championship match
1987	Brisbane WC **Wales** 16–3	2003	Brisbane WC **England** 28–17
1988	Twickenham **Wales** 11–3	2004	Twickenham **England** 31–21
1989	Cardiff **Wales** 12–9	2005	Cardiff **Wales** 11–9
1990	Twickenham **England** 34–6	2006	Twickenham **England** 47–13
1991	Cardiff **England** 25–6	2007	Cardiff **Wales** 27–18
1992	Twickenham **England** 24–0	2007	Twickenham **England** 62–5
1993	Cardiff **Wales** 10–9		Non-championship match
1994	Twickenham **England** 15–8	2008	Twickenham **Wales** 26–19
1995	Cardiff **England** 23–9	2009	Cardiff **Wales** 23–15

ENGLAND v FRANCE

Played 92 England won 50, France won 35, Drawn 7
Highest scores England 48–19 in 2001, France 37–12 in 1972
Biggest wins England 37–0 in 1911, France 37–12 in 1972 and 31–6 in 2006

1906	Paris **England** 35–8	1948	Paris **France** 15–0
1907	Richmond (London) **England** 41–13	1949	Twickenham **England** 8–3
1908	Paris **England** 19–0	1950	Paris **France** 6–3
1909	Leicester **England** 22–0	1951	Twickenham **France** 11–3
1910	Paris **England** 11–3	1952	Paris **England** 6–3
1911	Twickenham **England** 37–0	1953	Twickenham **England** 11–0
1912	Paris **England** 18–8	1954	Paris **France** 11–3
1913	Twickenham **England** 20–0	1955	Twickenham **France** 16–9
1914	Paris **England** 39–13	1956	Paris **France** 14–9
1920	Twickenham **England** 8–3	1957	Twickenham **England** 9–5
1921	Paris **England** 10–6	1958	Paris **England** 14–0
1922	Twickenham **Drawn** 11–11	1959	Twickenham **Drawn** 3–3
1923	Paris **England** 12–3	1960	Paris **Drawn** 3–3
1924	Twickenham **England** 19–7	1961	Twickenham **Drawn** 5–5
1925	Paris **England** 13–11	1962	Paris **France** 13–0
1926	Twickenham **England** 11–0	1963	Twickenham **England** 6–5
1927	Paris **France** 3–0	1964	Paris **England** 6–3
1928	Twickenham **England** 18–8	1965	Twickenham **England** 9–6
1929	Paris **England** 16–6	1966	Paris **France** 13–0
1930	Twickenham **England** 11–5	1967	Twickenham **France** 16–12
1931	Paris **France** 14–13	1968	Paris **France** 14–9
1947	Twickenham **England** 6–3	1969	Twickenham **England** 22–8

1970 Paris **France** 35–13	1995 Twickenham **England** 31–10
1971 Twickenham **Drawn** 14–14	1995 Pretoria WC **France 19–9**
1972 Paris **France** 37–12	1996 Paris **France** 15–12
1973 Twickenham **England** 14–6	1997 Twickenham **France** 23–20
1974 Paris **Drawn** 12–12	1998 Paris **France** 24–17
1975 Twickenham **France** 27–20	1999 Twickenham **England** 21–10
1976 Paris **France** 30–9	2000 Paris **England** 15–9
1977 Twickenham **France** 4–3	2001 Twickenham **England** 48–19
1978 Paris **France** 15–6	2002 Paris **France** 20–15
1979 Twickenham **England** 7–6	2003 Twickenham **England** 25–17
1980 Paris **England** 17–13	2003 Marseilles **France** 17–16
1981 Twickenham **France** 16–12	Non-championship match
1982 Paris **England** 27–15	2003 Twickenham **England** 45–14
1983 Twickenham **France** 19–15	Non-championship match
1984 Paris **France** 32–18	2003 Sydney WC **England** 24–7
1985 Twickenham **Drawn** 9–9	2004 Paris **France** 24–21
1986 Paris **France** 29–10	2005 Twickenham **France** 18–17
1987 Twickenham **France** 19–15	2006 Paris **France** 31–6
1988 Paris **France** 10–9	2007 Twickenham **England** 26–18
1989 Twickenham **England** 11–0	2007 Twickenham **France** 21–15
1990 Paris **England** 26–7	Non-championship match
1991 Twickenham **England** 21–19	2007 Marseilles **France** 22–9
1991 Paris WC **England** 19–10	Non-championship match
1992 Paris **England** 31–13	2007 Paris WC **England** 14–9
1993 Twickenham **England** 16–15	2008 Paris **England** 24–13
1994 Paris **England** 18–14	2009 Twickenham **England** 34–10

ENGLAND v SOUTH AFRICA

Played 31 England won 12, South Africa won 18, Drawn 1
Highest scores England 53–3 in 2002, South Africa 58–10 in 2007
Biggest wins England 53–3 in 2002, South Africa 58–10 in 2007

1906 Crystal Palace (London) **Drawn** 3–3	1999 Paris WC **South Africa** 44–21
1913 Twickenham **South Africa** 9–3	2000 *1* Pretoria **South Africa** 18–13
1932 Twickenham **South Africa** 7–0	*2* Bloemfontein **England** 27–22
1952 Twickenham **South Africa** 8–3	Series drawn 1–1
1961 Twickenham **South Africa** 5–0	2000 Twickenham **England** 25–17
1969 Twickenham **England** 11–8	2001 Twickenham **England** 29–9
1972 Johannesburg **England** 18–9	2002 Twickenham **England** 53–3
1984 *1* Port Elizabeth **South Africa** 33–15	2003 Perth WC **England** 25–6
2 Johannesburg **South Africa** 35–9	2004 Twickenham **England** 32–16
South Africa won series 2–0	2006 1 Twickenham **England** 23–21
1992 Twickenham **England** 33–16	2 Twickenham **South Africa** 25–14
1994 *1* Pretoria **England** 32–15	Series drawn 1–1
2 Cape Town **South Africa** 27–9	2007 1 Bloemfontein **South Africa** 58–10
Series drawn 1–1	2 Pretoria **South Africa** 55–22
1995 Twickenham **South Africa** 24–14	South Africa won series 2–0
1997 Twickenham **South Africa** 29–11	2007 Paris WC **South Africa** 36–0
1998 Cape Town **South Africa** 18–0	2007 Paris WC **South Africa** 15–6
1998 Twickenham **England** 13–7	2008 Twickenham **South Africa** 42–6

ENGLAND v NEW ZEALAND

Played 32 England won 6, New Zealand won 25, Drawn 1
Highest scores England 31–28 in 2002, New Zealand 64–22 in 1998
Biggest wins England 13–0 in 1936, New Zealand 64–22 in 1998

1905 Crystal Palace (London) **New Zealand** 15–0	1995 Cape Town WC **New Zealand 45–29**
1925 Twickenham **New Zealand** 17–11	1997 *1* Manchester **New Zealand** 25–8
1936 Twickenham **England** 13–0	*2* Twickenham **Drawn** 26–26
1954 Twickenham **New Zealand** 5–0	New Zealand won series 1–0, with 1 draw
1963 *1* Auckland **New Zealand** 21–11	1998 *1* Dunedin **New Zealand** 64–22
2 Christchurch **New Zealand** 9–6	*2* Auckland **New Zealand** 40–10
New Zealand won series 2–0	New Zealand won series 2–0
1964 Twickenham **New Zealand** 14–0	1999 Twickenham WC **New Zealand** 30–16
1967 Twickenham **New Zealand** 23–11	2002 Twickenham **England** 31–28
1973 Twickenham **New Zealand** 9–0	2003 Wellington **England** 15–13
1973 Auckland **England** 16–10	2004 *1* Dunedin **New Zealand** 36–3
1978 Twickenham **New Zealand** 16–6	*2* Auckland **New Zealand** 36–12
1979 Twickenham **New Zealand** 10–9	New Zealand won series 2–0
1983 Twickenham **England** 15–9	2005 Twickenham **New Zealand** 23–19
1985 *1* Christchurch **New Zealand** 18–13	2006 Twickenham **New Zealand** 41–20
2 Wellington **New Zealand** 42–15	2008 *1* Auckland **New Zealand** 37–20
New Zealand won series 2–0	*2* Christchurch **New Zealand** 44–12
1991 Twickenham WC **New Zealand** 18–12	New Zealand won series 2–0
1993 Twickenham **England** 15–9	2008 Twickenham **New Zealand** 32–6

ENGLAND v AUSTRALIA

Played 36 England won 14, Australia won 21, Drawn 1
Highest scores England 32–31 in 2002, Australia 76–0 in 1998
Biggest wins England 20–3 in 1973 & 23–6 in 1976, Australia 76–0 in 1998

1909 Blackheath (London) **Australia** 9–3	*2* Sydney **Australia** 28–8
1928 Twickenham **England** 18–11	Australia won series 2–0
1948 Twickenham **Australia** 11–0	1988 Twickenham **England** 28–19
1958 Twickenham **England** 9–6	1991 Sydney **Australia** 40–15
1963 Sydney **Australia** 18–9	1991 Twickenham WC **Australia** 12–6
1967 Twickenham **Australia** 23–11	1995 Cape Town WC **England** 25–22
1973 Twickenham **England** 20–3	1997 Sydney **Australia** 25–6
1975 *1* Sydney **Australia** 16–9	1997 Twickenham **Drawn** 15–15
2 Brisbane **Australia** 30–21	1998 Brisbane **Australia** 76–0
Australia won series 2–0	1998 Twickenham **Australia** 12–11
1976 Twickenham **England** 23–6	1999 Sydney **Australia** 22–15
1982 Twickenham **England** 15–11	2000 Twickenham **England** 22–19
1984 Twickenham **Australia** 19–3	2001 Twickenham **England** 21–15
1987 Sydney WC **Australia** 19–6	2002 Twickenham **England** 32–31
1988 *1* Brisbane **Australia** 22–16	2003 Melbourne **England** 25–14

2003	Sydney WC **England** 20–17 (aet)		2 Melbourne **Australia** 43–18
2004	Brisbane **Australia** 51–15		Australia won series 2–0
2004	Twickenham **Australia** 21–19	2007	Marseilles WC **England** 12–10
2005	Twickenham **England** 26–16	2008	Twickenham **Australia** 28–14
2006	1 Sydney **Australia** 34–3		

ENGLAND v NEW ZEALAND NATIVES

Played 1 England won 1
Highest score England 7–0 in 1889, NZ Natives 0–7 in 1889
Biggest win England 7–0 in 1889, NZ Natives no win

1889	Blackheath **England** 1G 4T to 0	

ENGLAND v RFU PRESIDENT'S XV

Played 1 President's XV won 1
Highest score England 11–28 in 1971, RFU President's XV 28–11 in 1971
Biggest win RFU President's XV 28–11 in 1971

1971	Twickenham **President's XV** 28–11	

ENGLAND v ARGENTINA

Played 14 England won 9, Argentina won 4, Drawn 1
Highest scores England 51–0 in 1990, Argentina 33–13 in 1997
Biggest wins England 51–0 in 1990, Argentina 33–13 in 1997

1981	*1* Buenos Aires **Drawn** 19–19	1997	*1* Buenos Aires **England** 46–20
	2 Buenos Aires **England** 12–6		*2* Buenos Aires **Argentina** 33–13
	England won series 1–0 with 1 draw		Series drawn 1–1
1990	*1* Buenos Aires **England** 25–12	2000	Twickenham **England** 19–0
	2 Buenos Aires **Argentina** 15–13	2002	Buenos Aires **England** 26–18
	Series drawn 1–1	2006	Twickenham **Argentina** 25–18
1990	Twickenham **England** 51–0	2009	1 Manchester **England** 37–15
1995	Durban WC **England** 24–18		2 Salta **Argentina** 24–22
1996	Twickenham **England** 20–18		Series drawn 1–1

ENGLAND v ROMANIA

Played 4 England won 4
Highest scores England 134–0 in 2001, Romania 15–22 in 1985
Biggest win England 134–0 in 2001, Romania no win

1985	Twickenham **England** 22–15	1994	Twickenham **England** 54–3
1989	Bucharest **England** 58–3	2001	Twickenham **England** 134–0

ENGLAND v JAPAN

Played 1 England won 1
Highest score England 60–7 in 1987, Japan 7–60 in 1987
Biggest win England 60–7 in 1987, Japan no win

1987	Sydney WC **England** 60–7

ENGLAND v UNITED STATES

Played 5 England won 5
Highest scores England 106–8 in 1999, United States 19–48 in 2001
Biggest win England 106–8 in 1999, United States no win

1987	Sydney WC **England** 34–6	2001	San Francisco **England** 48–19
1991	Twickenham WC **England** 37–9	2007	Lens WC **England** 28–10
1999	Twickenham **England** 106–8		

ENGLAND v FIJI

Played 4 England won 4
Highest scores England 58–23 in 1989, Fiji 24–45 in 1999
Biggest win England 58–23 in 1989, Fiji no win

1988	Suva **England** 25–12	1991	Suva **England** 28–12
1989	Twickenham **England** 58–23	1999	Twickenham WC **England** 45–24

ENGLAND v ITALY

Played 15 England won 15
Highest scores England 80–23 in 2001, Italy 23–80 in 2001
Biggest win England 67–7 in 1999, Italy no win

1991	Twickenham WC **England** 36–6	2003	Twickenham **England** 40–5
1995	Durban WC **England 27–20**	2004	Rome **England** 50–9
1996	Twickenham **England** 54–21	2005	Twickenham **England** 39–7
1998	Huddersfield **England** 23–15	2006	Rome **England** 31–16
1999	Twickenham WC **England** 67–7	2007	Twickenham **England** 20–7
2000	Rome **England** 59–12	2008	Rome **England** 23–19
2001	Twickenham **England** 80–23	2009	Twickenham **England** 36–11
2002	Rome **England** 45–9		

ENGLAND v CANADA

Played 6 England won 6
Highest scores England 70–0 in 2004, Canada 20–59 in 2001
Biggest win England 70–0 in 2004, Canada no win

1992	Wembley **England** 26–13		2 Burnaby **England** 59–20
1994	Twickenham **England** 60–19		England won series 2–0
1999	Twickenham **England** 36–11	2004	Twickenham **England** 70–0
2001	1 Markham **England** 22–10		

ENGLAND v SAMOA

Played 5 England won 5
Highest scores England 44–22 in 1995 and 44–22 in 2007, Samoa 22–44 in 1995, 22–35 in 2003 and 22–44 in 2007
Biggest win England 40–3 in 2005, Samoa no win

1995	Durban WC **England** 44–22	2005	Twickenham **England** 40–3
1995	Twickenham **England** 27–9	2007	Nantes WC **England** 44–22
2003	Melbourne WC **England** 35–22		

ENGLAND v THE NETHERLANDS

Played 1 England won 1
Highest scores England 110–0 in 1998, The Netherlands 0–110 in 1998
Biggest win England 110–0 in 1998, The Netherlands no win

1998	Huddersfield **England** 110–0	

ENGLAND v TONGA

Played 2 England won 2
Highest scores England 101–10 in 1999, Tonga 20–36 in 2007
Biggest win England 101–10 in 1999, Tonga no win

1999 Twickenham WC **England** 101–10	2007 Paris WC **England** 36–20

ENGLAND v GEORGIA

Played 1 England won 1
Highest scores England 84–6 in 2003, Georgia 6–84 in 2003
Biggest win England 84–6 in 2003, Georgia no win

2003 Perth WC **England** 84–6

ENGLAND v URUGUAY

Played 1 England won 1
Highest scores England 111–13 in 2003, Uruguay 13–111 in 2003
Biggest win England 111–13 in 2003, Uruguay no win

2003 Brisbane WC **England** 111–13

ENGLAND v PACIFIC ISLANDS

Played 1 England won 1
Highest scores England 39–13 in 2008, Pacific Islands 13–39 in 2008
Biggest win England 39–13 in 2008, Pacific Islands no win

2008 Twickenham **England** 39–13

SCOTLAND v IRELAND

Played 123 Scotland won 62, Ireland won 55, Drawn 5, Abandoned 1
Highest scores Scotland 38–10 in 1997, Ireland 44–22 in 2000
Biggest wins Scotland 38–10 in 1997, Ireland 36–6 in 2003

1877 Belfast **Scotland** 4G 2DG 2T to 0	1885 Belfast **Abandoned** Ireland 0 Scotland
1878 No Match	1T
1879 Belfast **Scotland** 1G 1DG 1T to 0	1885 Raeburn Place **Scotland** 1G 2T to 0
1880 Glasgow **Scotland** 1G 2DG 2T to 0	1886 Raeburn Place **Scotland** 3G 1DG 2T to
1881 Belfast **Ireland** 1DG to 1T	0
1882 Glasgow **Scotland** 2T to 0	1887 Belfast **Scotland** 1G 1GM 2T to 0
1883 Belfast **Scotland** 1G 1T to 0	1888 Raeburn Place **Scotland** 1G to 0
1884 Raeburn Place (Edinburgh) **Scotland** 2G	1889 Belfast **Scotland** 1DG to 0
2T to 1T	1890 Raeburn Place **Scotland** 1DG 1T to 0

1891	Belfast **Scotland** 14–0	
1892	Raeburn Place **Scotland** 2–0	
1893	Belfast **Drawn** 0–0	
1894	Dublin **Ireland** 5–0	
1895	Raeburn Place **Scotland** 6–0	
1896	Dublin **Drawn** 0–0	
1897	Powderhall (Edinburgh) **Scotland** 8–3	
1898	Belfast **Scotland** 8–0	
1899	Inverleith (Edinburgh) **Ireland** 9–3	
1900	Dublin **Drawn** 0–0	
1901	Inverleith **Scotland** 9–5	
1902	Belfast **Ireland** 5–0	
1903	Inverleith **Scotland** 3–0	
1904	Dublin **Scotland** 19–3	
1905	Inverleith **Ireland** 11–5	
1906	Dublin **Scotland** 13–6	
1907	Inverleith **Scotland** 15–3	
1908	Dublin **Ireland** 16–11	
1909	Inverleith **Scotland** 9–3	
1910	Belfast **Scotland** 14–0	
1911	Inverleith **Ireland** 16–10	
1912	Dublin **Ireland** 10–8	
1913	Inverleith **Scotland** 29–14	
1914	Dublin **Ireland** 6–0	
1920	Inverleith **Scotland** 19–0	
1921	Dublin **Ireland** 9–8	
1922	Inverleith **Scotland** 6–3	
1923	Dublin **Scotland** 13–3	
1924	Inverleith **Scotland** 13–8	
1925	Dublin **Scotland** 14–8	
1926	Murrayfield **Ireland** 3–0	
1927	Dublin **Ireland** 6–0	
1928	Murrayfield **Ireland** 13–5	
1929	Dublin **Scotland** 16–7	
1930	Murrayfield **Ireland** 14–11	
1931	Dublin **Ireland** 8–5	
1932	Murrayfield **Ireland** 20–8	
1933	Dublin **Scotland** 8–6	
1934	Murrayfield **Scotland** 16–9	
1935	Dublin **Ireland** 12–5	
1936	Murrayfield **Ireland** 10–4	
1937	Dublin **Ireland** 11–4	
1938	Murrayfield **Scotland** 23–14	
1939	Dublin **Ireland** 12–3	
1947	Murrayfield **Ireland** 3–0	
1948	Dublin **Ireland** 6–0	
1949	Murrayfield **Ireland** 13–3	
1950	Dublin **Ireland** 21–0	
1951	Murrayfield **Ireland** 6–5	
1952	Dublin **Ireland** 12–8	
1953	Murrayfield **Ireland** 26–8	
1954	Belfast **Ireland** 6–0	
1955	Murrayfield **Scotland** 12–3	
1956	Dublin **Ireland** 14–10	
1957	Murrayfield **Ireland** 5–3	
1958	Dublin **Ireland** 12–6	

1959	Murrayfield **Ireland** 8–3	
1960	Dublin **Scotland** 6–5	
1961	Murrayfield **Scotland** 16–8	
1962	Dublin **Scotland** 20–6	
1963	Murrayfield **Scotland** 3–0	
1964	Dublin **Scotland** 6–3	
1965	Murrayfield **Ireland** 16–6	
1966	Dublin **Scotland** 11–3	
1967	Murrayfield **Ireland** 5–3	
1968	Dublin **Ireland** 14–6	
1969	Murrayfield **Ireland** 16–0	
1970	Dublin **Ireland** 16–11	
1971	Murrayfield **Ireland** 17–5	
1972	No Match	
1973	Murrayfield **Scotland** 19–14	
1974	Dublin **Ireland** 9–6	
1975	Murrayfield **Scotland** 20–13	
1976	Dublin **Scotland** 15–6	
1977	Murrayfield **Scotland** 21–18	
1978	Dublin **Ireland** 12–9	
1979	Murrayfield **Drawn** 11–11	
1980	Dublin **Ireland** 22–15	
1981	Murrayfield **Scotland** 10–9	
1982	Dublin **Ireland** 21–12	
1983	Murrayfield **Ireland** 15–13	
1984	Dublin **Scotland** 32–9	
1985	Murrayfield **Ireland** 18–15	
1986	Dublin **Scotland** 10–9	
1987	Murrayfield **Scotland** 16–12	
1988	Dublin **Ireland** 22–18	
1989	Murrayfield **Scotland** 37–21	
1990	Dublin **Scotland** 13–10	
1991	Murrayfield **Scotland** 28–25	
1991	Murrayfield WC **Scotland** 24–15	
1992	Dublin **Scotland** 18–10	
1993	Murrayfield **Scotland** 15–3	
1994	Dublin **Drawn** 6–6	
1995	Murrayfield **Scotland** 26–13	
1996	Dublin **Scotland** 16–10	
1997	Murrayfield **Scotland** 38–10	
1998	Dublin **Scotland** 17–16	
1999	Murrayfield **Scotland** 30–13	
2000	Dublin **Ireland** 44–22	
2001	Murrayfield **Scotland** 32–10	
2002	Dublin **Ireland** 43–22	
2003	Murrayfield **Ireland** 36–6	
2003	Murrayfield **Ireland** 29–10	
	Non-championship match	
2004	Dublin **Ireland** 37–16	
2005	Murrayfield **Ireland** 40–13	
2006	Dublin **Ireland** 15–9	
2007	Murrayfield **Ireland** 19–18	
2007	Murrayfield **Scotland** 31–21	
	Non-championship match	
2008	Dublin **Ireland** 34–13	
2009	Murrayfield **Ireland** 22–15	

SCOTLAND v WALES

Played 114 Scotland won 48, Wales won 63, Drawn 3
Highest scores Scotland 35–10 in 1924, Wales 46–22 in 2005
Biggest wins Scotland 35–10 in 1924, Wales 46–22 in 2005

1883	Raeburn Place (Edinburgh) **Scotland** 3G to 1G	1930	Murrayfield **Scotland** 12–9
1884	Newport **Scotland** 1DG 1T to 0	1931	Cardiff **Wales** 13–8
1885	Glasgow **Drawn** no score	1932	Murrayfield **Wales** 6–0
1886	Cardiff **Scotland** 2G 1T to 0	1933	Swansea **Scotland** 11–3
1887	Raeburn Place **Scotland** 4G 8T to 0	1934	Murrayfield **Wales** 13–6
1888	Newport **Wales** 1T to 0	1935	Cardiff **Wales** 10–6
1889	Raeburn Place **Scotland** 2T to 0	1936	Murrayfield **Wales** 13–3
1890	Cardiff **Scotland** 1G 2T to 1T	1937	Swansea **Scotland** 13–6
1891	Raeburn Place **Scotland** 15–0	1938	Murrayfield **Scotland** 8–6
1892	Swansea **Scotland** 7–2	1939	Cardiff **Wales** 11–3
1893	Raeburn Place **Wales** 9–0	1947	Murrayfield **Wales** 22–8
1894	Newport **Wales** 7–0	1948	Cardiff **Wales** 14–0
1895	Raeburn Place **Scotland** 5–4	1949	Murrayfield **Scotland** 6–5
1896	Cardiff **Wales** 6–0	1950	Swansea **Wales** 12–0
1897	No Match	1951	Murrayfield **Scotland** 19–0
1898	No Match	1952	Cardiff **Wales** 11–0
1899	Inverleith (Edinburgh) **Scotland** 21–10	1953	Murrayfield **Wales** 12–0
1900	Swansea **Wales** 12–3	1954	Swansea **Wales** 15–3
1901	Inverleith **Scotland** 18–8	1955	Murrayfield **Scotland** 14–8
1902	Cardiff **Wales** 14–5	1956	Cardiff **Wales** 9–3
1903	Inverleith **Scotland** 6–0	1957	Murrayfield **Scotland** 9–6
1904	Swansea **Wales** 21–3	1958	Cardiff **Wales** 8–3
1905	Inverleith **Wales** 6–3	1959	Murrayfield **Scotland** 6–5
1906	Cardiff **Wales** 9–3	1960	Cardiff **Wales** 8–0
1907	Inverleith **Scotland** 6–3	1961	Murrayfield **Scotland** 3–0
1908	Swansea **Wales** 6–5	1962	Cardiff **Scotland** 8–3
1909	Inverleith **Wales** 5–3	1963	Murrayfield **Wales** 6–0
1910	Cardiff **Wales** 14–0	1964	Cardiff **Wales** 11–3
1911	Inverleith **Wales** 32–10	1965	Murrayfield **Wales** 14–12
1912	Swansea **Wales** 21–6	1966	Cardiff **Wales** 8–3
1913	Inverleith **Wales** 8–0	1967	Murrayfield **Scotland** 11–5
1914	Cardiff **Wales** 24–5	1968	Cardiff **Wales** 5–0
1920	Inverleith **Scotland** 9–5	1969	Murrayfield **Wales** 17–3
1921	Swansea **Scotland** 14–8	1970	Cardiff **Wales** 18–9
1922	Inverleith **Drawn** 9–9	1971	Murrayfield **Wales** 19–18
1923	Cardiff **Scotland** 11–8	1972	Cardiff **Wales** 35–12
1924	Inverleith **Scotland** 35–10	1973	Murrayfield **Scotland** 10–9
1925	Swansea **Scotland** 24–14	1974	Cardiff **Wales** 6–0
1926	Murrayfield **Scotland** 8–5	1975	Murrayfield **Scotland** 12–10
1927	Cardiff **Scotland** 5–0	1976	Cardiff **Wales** 28–6
1928	Murrayfield **Wales** 13–0	1977	Murrayfield **Wales** 18–9
1929	Swansea **Wales** 14–7	1978	Cardiff **Wales** 22–14
		1979	Murrayfield **Wales** 19–13

1980	Cardiff **Wales** 17–6
1981	Murrayfield **Scotland** 15–6
1982	Cardiff **Scotland** 34–18
1983	Murrayfield **Wales** 19–15
1984	Cardiff **Scotland** 15–9
1985	Murrayfield **Wales** 25–21
1986	Cardiff **Wales** 22–15
1987	Murrayfield **Scotland** 21–15
1988	Cardiff **Wales** 25–20
1989	Murrayfield **Scotland** 23–7
1990	Cardiff **Scotland** 13–9
1991	Murrayfield **Scotland** 32–12
1992	Cardiff **Wales** 15–12
1993	Murrayfield **Scotland** 20–0
1994	Cardiff **Wales** 29–6
1995	Murrayfield **Scotland** 26–13

1996	Cardiff **Scotland** 16–14
1997	Murrayfield **Wales** 34–19
1998	Wembley **Wales** 19–13
1999	Murrayfield **Scotland** 33–20
2000	Cardiff **Wales** 26–18
2001	Murrayfield **Drawn** 28–28
2002	Cardiff **Scotland** 27–22
2003	Murrayfield **Scotland** 30–22
2003	Cardiff **Wales** 23–9
	Non-championship match
2004	Cardiff **Wales** 23–10
2005	Murrayfield **Wales** 46–22
2006	Cardiff **Wales** 28–18
2007	Murrayfield **Scotland** 21–9
2008	Cardiff **Wales** 30–15
2009	Murrayfield **Wales** 26–13

SCOTLAND v FRANCE

Played 82 Scotland won 34, France won 45, Drawn 3
Highest scores Scotland 36–22 in 1999, France 51–16 in 1998 and 51–9 in 2003
Biggest wins Scotland 31–3 in 1912, France 51–9 in 2003

1910	Inverleith (Edinburgh) **Scotland** 27–0
1911	Paris **France** 16–15
1912	Inverleith **Scotland** 31–3
1913	Paris **Scotland** 21–3
1914	No Match
1920	Paris **Scotland** 5–0
1921	Inverleith **France** 3–0
1922	Paris **Drawn** 3–3
1923	Inverleith **Scotland** 16–3
1924	Paris **France** 12–10
1925	Inverleith **Scotland** 25–4
1926	Paris **Scotland** 20–6
1927	Murrayfield **Scotland** 23–6
1928	Paris **Scotland** 15–6
1929	Murrayfield **Scotland** 6–3
1930	Paris **France** 7–3
1931	Murrayfield **Scotland** 6–4
1947	Paris **France** 8–3
1948	Murrayfield **Scotland** 9–8
1949	Paris **Scotland** 8–0
1950	Murrayfield **Scotland** 8–5
1951	Paris **France** 14–12
1952	Murrayfield **France** 13–11
1953	Paris **France** 11–5
1954	Murrayfield **France** 3–0

1955	Paris **France** 15–0
1956	Murrayfield **Scotland** 12–0
1957	Paris **Scotland** 6–0
1958	Murrayfield **Scotland** 11–9
1959	Paris **France** 9–0
1960	Murrayfield **France** 13–11
1961	Paris **France** 11–0
1962	Murrayfield **France** 11–3
1963	Paris **Scotland** 11–6
1964	Murrayfield **Scotland** 10–0
1965	Paris **France** 16–8
1966	Murrayfield **Drawn** 3–3
1967	Paris **Scotland** 9–8
1968	Murrayfield **France** 8–6
1969	Paris **Scotland** 6–3
1970	Murrayfield **France** 11–9
1971	Paris **France** 13–8
1972	Murrayfield **Scotland** 20–9
1973	Paris **France** 16–13
1974	Murrayfield **Scotland** 19–6
1975	Paris **France** 10–9
1976	Murrayfield **France** 13–6
1977	Paris **France** 23–3
1978	Murrayfield **France** 19–16
1979	Paris **France** 21–17

1980	Murrayfield **Scotland** 22–14	1995	Pretoria WC **France** 22–19
1981	Paris **France** 16–9	1996	Murrayfield **Scotland** 19–14
1982	Murrayfield **Scotland** 16–7	1997	Paris **France** 47–20
1983	Paris **France** 19–15	1998	Murrayfield **France** 51–16
1984	Murrayfield **Scotland** 21–12	1999	Paris **Scotland** 36–22
1985	Paris **France** 11–3	2000	Murrayfield **France** 28–16
1986	Murrayfield **Scotland** 18–17	2001	Paris **France** 16–6
1987	Paris **France** 28–22	2002	Murrayfield **France** 22–10
1987	Christchurch WC **Drawn** 20–20	2003	Paris **France** 38–3
1988	Murrayfield **Scotland** 23–12	2003	Sydney WC **France** 51–9
1989	Paris **France** 19–3	2004	Murrayfield **France** 31–0
1990	Murrayfield **Scotland** 21–0	2005	Paris **France** 16–9
1991	Paris **France** 15–9	2006	Murrayfield **Scotland** 20–16
1992	Murrayfield **Scotland** 10–6	2007	Paris **France** 46–19
1993	Paris **France** 11–3	2008	Murrayfield **France** 27–6
1994	Murrayfield **France** 20–12	2009	Paris **France** 22–13
1995	Paris **Scotland** 23–21		

SCOTLAND v SOUTH AFRICA

Played 20 Scotland won 4, South Africa won 16, Drawn 0
Highest scores Scotland 29–46 in 1999, South Africa 68–10 in 1997
Biggest wins Scotland 21–6 in 2002, South Africa 68–10 in 1997

1906	Glasgow **Scotland** 6–0	1999	Murrayfield WC **South Africa** 46–29
1912	Inverleith **South Africa** 16–0	2002	Murrayfield **Scotland** 21–6
1932	Murrayfield **South Africa** 6–3	2003	1 Durban **South Africa** 29–25
1951	Murrayfield **South Africa** 44–0		2 Johannesburg **South Africa** 28–19
1960	Port Elizabeth **South Africa** 18–10		South Africa won series 2–0
1961	Murrayfield **South Africa** 12–5	2004	Murrayfield **South Africa** 45–10
1965	Murrayfield **Scotland** 8–5	2006	1 Durban **South Africa** 36–16
1969	Murrayfield **Scotland** 6–3		2 Port Elizabeth **South Africa** 29–15
1994	Murrayfield **South Africa** 34–10		South Africa won series 2–0
1997	Murrayfield **South Africa** 68–10	2007	Murrayfield **South Africa** 27–3
1998	Murrayfield **South Africa** 35–10	2008	Murrayfield **South Africa** 14–10

SCOTLAND v NEW ZEALAND

Played 27 Scotland won 0, New Zealand won 25, Drawn 2
Highest scores Scotland 31–62 in 1996, New Zealand 69–20 in 2000
Biggest wins Scotland no win, New Zealand 69–20 in 2000

1905	Inverleith (Edinburgh) **New Zealand** 12–7	1964	Murrayfield **Drawn** 0–0
1935	Murrayfield **New Zealand** 18–8	1967	Murrayfield **New Zealand** 14–3
1954	Murrayfield **New Zealand** 3–0	1972	Murrayfield **New Zealand** 14–9

1975	Auckland **New Zealand** 24–0
1978	Murrayfield **New Zealand** 18–9
1979	Murrayfield **New Zealand** 20–6
1981	1 Dunedin **New Zealand** 11–4
	2 Auckland **New Zealand** 40–15
	New Zealand won series 2–0
1983	Murrayfield **Drawn** 25–25
1987	Christchurch WC **New Zealand** 30–3
1990	1 Dunedin **New Zealand** 31–16
	2 Auckland **New Zealand** 21–18
	New Zealand won series 2–0
1991	Cardiff WC **New Zealand** 13–6
1993	Murrayfield **New Zealand** 51–15

1995	Pretoria WC **New Zealand** 48–30
1996	1 Dunedin **New Zealand** 62–31
	2 Auckland **New Zealand** 36–12
	New Zealand won series 2–0
1999	Murrayfield WC **New Zealand** 30–18
2000	1 Dunedin **New Zealand** 69–20
	2 Auckland **New Zealand** 48–14
	New Zealand won series 2–0
2001	Murrayfield **New Zealand** 37–6
2005	Murrayfield **New Zealand** 29–10
2007	Murrayfield WC **New Zealand** 40–0
2008	Murrayfield **New Zealand** 32–6

SCOTLAND v AUSTRALIA

Played 25 Scotland won 7, Australia won 18, Drawn 0
Highest scores Scotland 24–15 in 1981, Australia 45–3 in 1998
Biggest wins Scotland 24–15 in 1981, Australia 45–3 in 1998

1927	Murrayfield **Scotland** 10–8
1947	Murrayfield **Australia** 16–7
1958	Murrayfield **Scotland** 12–8
1966	Murrayfield **Scotland** 11–5
1968	Murrayfield **Scotland** 9–3
1970	Sydney **Australia** 23–3
1975	Murrayfield **Scotland** 10–3
1981	Murrayfield **Scotland** 24–15
1982	1 Brisbane **Scotland** 12–7
	2 Sydney **Australia** 33–9
	Series drawn 1–1
1984	Murrayfield **Australia** 37–12
1988	Murrayfield **Australia** 32–13
1992	1 Sydney **Australia** 27–12
	2 Brisbane **Australia** 37–13

	Australia won series 2–0
1996	Murrayfield **Australia** 29–19
1997	Murrayfield **Australia** 37–8
1998	1 Sydney **Australia** 45–3
	2 Brisbane **Australia** 33–11
	Australia won series 2–0
2000	Murrayfield **Australia** 30–9
2003	Brisbane WC **Australia** 33–16
2004	1 Melbourne **Australia** 35–15
	2 Sydney **Australia** 34–13
	Australia won series 2–0
2004	1 Murrayfield **Australia** 31–14
	2 Glasgow **Australia** 31–17
	Australia won series 2–0
2006	Murrayfield **Australia** 44–15

SCOTLAND v SRU PRESIDENT'S XV

Played 1 Scotland won 1
Highest scores Scotland 27–16 in 1972, SRU President's XV 16–27 in 1973
Biggest win Scotland 27–16 in 1973, SRU President's XV no win

| 1973 | Murrayfield **Scotland** 27–16 |

SCOTLAND v ROMANIA

Played 12 Scotland won 10 Romania won 2, Drawn 0
Highest scores Scotland 60–19 in 1999, Romania 28–55 in 1987 & 28–22 in 1984
Biggest wins Scotland 48–6 in 2006 and 42–0 in 2007, Romania 28–22 in 1984 & 18–12 in 1991

1981	Murrayfield **Scotland** 12–6		1995	Murrayfield **Scotland** 49–16
1984	Bucharest **Romania** 28–22		1999	Glasgow **Scotland** 60–19
1986	Bucharest **Scotland** 33–18		2002	Murrayfield **Scotland** 37–10
1987	Dunedin WC **Scotland** 55–28		2005	Bucharest **Scotland** 39–19
1989	Murrayfield **Scotland** 32–0		2006	Murrayfield **Scotland** 48–6
1991	Bucharest **Romania** 18–12		2007	Murrayfield WC **Scotland** 42–0

SCOTLAND v ZIMBABWE

Played 2 Scotland won 2
Highest scores Scotland 60–21 in 1987, Zimbabwe 21–60 in 1987
Biggest win Scotland 60–21 in 1987 & 51–12 in 1991, Zimbabwe no win

1987	Wellington WC **Scotland** 60–21		1991	Murrayfield WC **Scotland** 51–12

SCOTLAND v FIJI

Played 4 Scotland won 3, Fiji won 1
Highest scores Scotland 38–17 in 1989, Fiji 51–26 in 1998
Biggest win Scotland 38–17 in 1989, Fiji 51–26 in 1998

1989	Murrayfield **Scotland** 38–17		2002	Murrayfield **Scotland** 36–22
1998	Suva **Fiji** 51–26		2003	Sydney WC **Scotland** 22–20

SCOTLAND v ARGENTINA

Played 9 Scotland won 2, Argentina won 7, Drawn 0
Highest scores Scotland 49–3 in 1990, Argentina 31–22 in 1999
Biggest wins Scotland 49–3 in 1990, Argentina 31–22 in 1999 and 25–16 in 2001

1990	Murrayfield **Scotland** 49–3		*2* Buenos Aires **Argentina** 19–17
1994	*1* Buenos Aires **Argentina** 16–15		Argentina won series 2–0

1999 Murrayfield **Argentina** 31–22	2008 *1* Rosario **Argentina** 21–15
2001 Murrayfield **Argentina** 25–16	*2* Buenos Aires **Scotland** 26–14
2005 Murrayfield **Argentina** 23–19	Series drawn 1–1
2007 Paris WC **Argentina** 19–13	

SCOTLAND v JAPAN

Played 3 Scotland won 3
Highest scores Scotland 100–8 in 2004, Japan 11–32 in 2003
Biggest win Scotland 100–8 in 2004, Japan no win

1991 Murrayfield WC **Scotland** 47–9	2004 Perth **Scotland** 100–8
2003 Townsville WC **Scotland** 32–11	

SCOTLAND v SAMOA

Played 6 Scotland won 5, Drawn 1
Highest scores Scotland 38–3 in 2004, Samoa 20–35 in 1999
Biggest win Scotland 38–3 in 2004, Samoa no win

1991 Murrayfield WC **Scotland** 28–6	2000 Murrayfield **Scotland** 31–8
1995 Murrayfield **Drawn** 15–15	2004 Wellington (NZ) **Scotland** 38–3
1999 Murrayfield WC **Scotland** 35–20	2005 Murrayfield **Scotland** 18–1

SCOTLAND v CANADA

Played 3 Scotland won 2, Canada won 1
Highest scores Scotland 41–0 in 2008, Canada 26–23 in 2002
Biggest win Scotland 41–0 in 2008, Canada 26–23 in 2002

1995 Murrayfield **Scotland** 22–6	2008 Aberdeen **Scotland** 41–0
2002 Vancouver **Canada** 26–23	

SCOTLAND v IVORY COAST

Played 1 Scotland won 1
Highest scores Scotland 89–0 in 1995, Ivory Coast 0–89 in 1995
Biggest win Scotland 89–0 in 1995, Ivory Coast no win

1995 Rustenburg WC **Scotland** 89–0

INTERNATIONAL RECORDS

SCOTLAND v TONGA

Played 2 Scotland won 2
Highest scores Scotland 43–20 in 2001, Tonga 20–43 in 2001
Biggest win Scotland 41–5 in 1995, Tonga no win

1995	Pretoria WC **Scotland** 41–5		2001	Murrayfield **Scotland** 43–20

SCOTLAND v ITALY

Played 15 Scotland won 10, Italy won 5
Highest scores Scotland 47–15 in 2003, Italy 37–17 in 2007
Biggest wins Scotland 47–15 in 2003, Italy 37–17 in 2007

1996	Murrayfield **Scotland** 29–22			Non-championship match
1998	Treviso **Italy** 25–21		2004	Rome **Italy** 20–14
1999	Murrayfield **Scotland** 30–12		2005	Murrayfield **Scotland** 18–10
2000	Rome **Italy** 34–20		2006	Rome **Scotland** 13–10
2001	Murrayfield **Scotland** 23–19		2007	Murrayfield **Italy** 37–17
2002	Rome **Scotland** 29–12		2007	Saint Etienne WC **Scotland** 18–16
2003	Murrayfield **Scotland** 33–25		2008	Rome **Italy** 23–20
2003	Murrayfield **Scotland** 47–15		2009	Murrayfield **Scotland** 26–6

SCOTLAND v URUGUAY

Played 1 Scotland won 1
Highest scores Scotland 43–12 in 1999, Uruguay 12–43 in 1999
Biggest win Scotland 43–12 in 1999, Uruguay no win

1999	Murrayfield WC **Scotland** 43–12

SCOTLAND v SPAIN

Played 1 Scotland won 1
Highest scores Scotland 48–0 in 1999, Spain 0–48 in 1999
Biggest win Scotland 48–0 in 1999, Spain no win

1999	Murrayfield WC **Scotland** 48–0

Played 3 Scotland won 3
Highest scores Scotland 65–23 in 2002, United States 23–65 in 2002
Biggest win Scotland 53–6 in 2000, United States no win

2000	Murrayfield **Scotland** 53–6	2003	Brisbane WC **Scotland** 39–15
2002	San Francisco **Scotland** 65–23		

SCOTLAND v PACIFIC ISLANDS

Played 1 Scotland won 1
Highest scores Scotland 34–22 in 2006, Pacific Islands 22–34 in 2006
Biggest win Scotland 34–22 in 2006, Pacific Islands no win

2006	Murrayfield **Scotland** 34–22

SCOTLAND v PORTUGAL

Played 1 Scotland won 1
Highest scores Scotland 56–10 in 2007, Portugal 10–56 in 2007
Biggest win Scotland 56–10 in 2007, Portugal no win

2007	Saint Etienne WC **Scotland** 56–10

IRELAND v WALES

Played 114 Ireland won 46, Wales won 62, Drawn 6
Highest scores Ireland 54–10 in 2002, Wales 34–9 in 1976
Biggest wins Ireland 54–10 in 2002, Wales 29–0 in 1907

1882	Dublin **Wales** 2G 2T to 0	1891	Llanelli **Wales** 6–4
1883	No Match	1892	Dublin **Ireland** 9–0
1884	Cardiff **Wales** 1DG 2T to 0	1893	Llanelli **Wales** 2–0
1885	No Match	1894	Belfast **Ireland** 3–0
1886	No Match	1895	Cardiff **Wales** 5–3
1887	Birkenhead **Wales** 1DG 1T to 3T	1896	Dublin **Ireland** 8–4
1888	Dublin **Ireland** 1G 1DG 1T to 0	1897	No Match
1889	Swansea **Ireland** 2T to 0	1898	Limerick **Wales** 11–3
1890	Dublin **Drawn** 1G each	1899	Cardiff **Ireland** 3–0

1900	Belfast	**Wales** 3–0
1901	Swansea	**Wales** 10–9
1902	Dublin	**Wales** 15–0
1903	Cardiff	**Wales** 18–0
1904	Belfast	**Ireland** 14–12
1905	Swansea	**Wales** 10–3
1906	Belfast	**Ireland** 11–6
1907	Cardiff	**Wales** 29–0
1908	Belfast	**Wales** 11–5
1909	Swansea	**Wales** 18–5
1910	Dublin	**Wales** 19–3
1911	Cardiff	**Wales** 16–0
1912	Belfast	**Ireland** 12–5
1913	Swansea	**Wales** 16–13
1914	Belfast	**Wales** 11–3
1920	Cardiff	**Wales** 28–4
1921	Belfast	**Wales** 6–0
1922	Swansea	**Wales** 11–5
1923	Dublin	**Ireland** 5–4
1924	Cardiff	**Ireland** 13–10
1925	Belfast	**Ireland** 19–3
1926	Swansea	**Wales** 11–8
1927	Dublin	**Ireland** 19–9
1928	Cardiff	**Ireland** 13–10
1929	Belfast	**Drawn** 5–5
1930	Swansea	**Wales** 12–7
1931	Belfast	**Wales** 15–3
1932	Cardiff	**Ireland** 12–10
1933	Belfast	**Ireland** 10–5
1934	Swansea	**Wales** 13–0
1935	Belfast	**Ireland** 9–3
1936	Cardiff	**Wales** 3–0
1937	Belfast	**Ireland** 5–3
1938	Swansea	**Wales** 11–5
1939	Belfast	**Wales** 7–0
1947	Swansea	**Wales** 6–0
1948	Belfast	**Ireland** 6–3
1949	Swansea	**Ireland** 5–0
1950	Belfast	**Wales** 6–3
1951	Cardiff	**Drawn** 3–3
1952	Dublin	**Wales** 14–3
1953	Swansea	**Wales** 5–3
1954	Dublin	**Wales** 12–9
1955	Cardiff	**Wales** 21–3
1956	Dublin	**Ireland** 11–3
1957	Cardiff	**Wales** 6–5
1958	Dublin	**Wales** 9–6
1959	Cardiff	**Wales** 8–6
1960	Dublin	**Wales** 10–9
1961	Cardiff	**Wales** 9–0
1962	Dublin	**Drawn** 3–3
1963	Cardiff	**Ireland** 14–6
1964	Dublin	**Wales** 15–6
1965	Cardiff	**Wales** 14–8
1966	Dublin	**Ireland** 9–6
1967	Cardiff	**Ireland** 3–0
1968	Dublin	**Ireland** 9–6
1969	Cardiff	**Wales** 24–11
1970	Dublin	**Ireland** 14–0
1971	Cardiff	**Wales** 23–9
1972	No Match	
1973	Cardiff	**Wales** 16–12
1974	Dublin	**Drawn** 9–9
1975	Cardiff	**Wales** 32–4
1976	Dublin	**Wales** 34–9
1977	Cardiff	**Wales** 25–9
1978	Dublin	**Wales** 20–16
1979	Cardiff	**Wales** 24–21
1980	Dublin	**Ireland** 21–7
1981	Cardiff	**Wales** 9–8
1982	Dublin	**Ireland** 20–12
1983	Cardiff	**Wales** 23–9
1984	Dublin	**Wales** 18–9
1985	Cardiff	**Ireland** 21–9
1986	Dublin	**Wales** 19–12
1987	Cardiff	**Ireland** 15–11
1987	Wellington WC	**Wales** 13–6
1988	Dublin	**Wales** 12–9
1989	Cardiff	**Ireland** 19–13
1990	Dublin	**Ireland** 14–8
1991	Cardiff	**Drawn** 21–21
1992	Dublin	**Wales** 16–15
1993	Cardiff	**Ireland** 19–14
1994	Dublin	**Wales** 17–15
1995	Cardiff	**Ireland** 16–12
1995	Johannesburg WC	**Ireland** 24–23
1996	Dublin	**Ireland** 30–17
1997	Cardiff	**Ireland** 26–25
1998	Dublin	**Wales** 30–21
1999	Wembley	**Ireland** 29–23
2000	Dublin	**Wales** 23–19
2001	Cardiff	**Ireland** 36–6
2002	Dublin	**Ireland** 54–10
2003	Cardiff	**Ireland** 25–24
2003	Dublin	**Ireland** 35–12
2004	Dublin	**Ireland** 36–15
2005	Cardiff	**Wales** 32–20
2006	Dublin	**Ireland** 31–5
2007	Cardiff	**Ireland** 19–9
2008	Dublin	**Wales** 16–12
2009	Cardiff	**Ireland** 17–15

IRELAND v FRANCE

Played 85 Ireland won 29, France won 51, Drawn 5
Highest scores Ireland 31–43 in 2006, France 45–10 in 1996
Biggest wins Ireland 24–0 in 1913, France 44–5 in 2002

1909	Dublin **Ireland** 19–8		1972	Paris **Ireland** 14–9
1910	Paris **Ireland** 8–3		1972	Dublin **Ireland** 24–14
1911	Cork **Ireland** 25–5			Non-championship match
1912	Paris **Ireland** 11–6		1973	Dublin **Ireland** 6–4
1913	Cork **Ireland** 24–0		1974	Paris **France** 9–6
1914	Paris **Ireland** 8–6		1975	Dublin **Ireland** 25–6
1920	Dublin **France** 15–7		1976	Paris **France** 26–3
1921	Paris **France** 20–10		1977	Dublin **France** 15–6
1922	Dublin **Ireland** 8–3		1978	Paris **France** 10–9
1923	Paris **France** 14–8		1979	Dublin **Drawn** 9–9
1924	Dublin **Ireland** 6–0		1980	Paris **France** 19–18
1925	Paris **Ireland** 9–3		1981	Dublin **France** 19–13
1926	Belfast **Ireland** 11–0		1982	Paris **France** 22–9
1927	Paris **Ireland** 8–3		1983	Dublin **Ireland** 22–16
1928	Belfast **Ireland** 12–8		1984	Paris **France** 25–12
1929	Paris **Ireland** 6–0		1985	Dublin **Drawn** 15–15
1930	Belfast **France** 5–0		1986	Paris **France** 29–9
1931	Paris **France** 3–0		1987	Dublin **France** 19–13
1947	Dublin **France** 12–8		1988	Paris **France** 25–6
1948	Paris **Ireland** 13–6		1989	Dublin **France** 26–21
1949	Dublin **France** 16–9		1990	Paris **France** 31–12
1950	Paris **Drawn** 3–3		1991	Dublin **France** 21–13
1951	Dublin **Ireland** 9–8		1992	Paris **France** 44–12
1952	Paris **Ireland** 11–8		1993	Dublin **France** 21–6
1953	Belfast **Ireland** 16–3		1994	Paris **France** 35–15
1954	Paris **France** 8–0		1995	Dublin **France** 25–7
1955	Dublin **France** 5–3		1995	Durban WC **France** 36–12
1956	Paris **France** 14–8		1996	Paris **France** 45–10
1957	Dublin **Ireland** 11–6		1997	Dublin **France** 32–15
1958	Paris **France** 11–6		1998	Paris **France** 18–16
1959	Dublin **Ireland** 9–5		1999	Dublin **France** 10–9
1960	Paris **France** 23–6		2000	Paris **Ireland** 27–25
1961	Dublin **France** 15–3		2001	Dublin **Ireland** 22–15
1962	Paris **France** 11–0		2002	Paris **France** 44–5
1963	Dublin **France** 24–5		2003	Dublin **Ireland** 15–12
1964	Paris **France** 27–6		2003	Melbourne WC **France** 43–21
1965	Dublin **Drawn** 3–3		2004	Paris **France** 35–17
1966	Paris **France** 11–6		2005	Dublin **France** 26–19
1967	Dublin **France** 11–6		2006	Paris **France** 43–31
1968	Paris **France** 16–6		2007	Dublin **France** 20–17
1969	Dublin **Ireland** 17–9		2007	Paris WC **France** 25–3
1970	Paris **France** 8–0		2008	Paris **France** 26–21
1971	Dublin **Drawn** 9–9		2009	Dublin **Ireland** 30–21

IRELAND v SOUTH AFRICA

Played 18 Ireland won 3, South Africa won 14, Drawn 1
Highest scores Ireland 32–15 in 2006, South Africa 38–0 in 1912
Biggest wins Ireland 32–15 in 2006, South Africa 38–0 in 1912

1906	Belfast **South Africa** 15–12	1998	*1* Bloemfontein **South Africa** 37–13
1912	Dublin **South Africa** 38–0		*2* Pretoria **South Africa** 33–0
1931	Dublin **South Africa** 8–3		South Africa won series 2–0
1951	Dublin **South Africa** 17–5	1998	Dublin **South Africa** 27–13
1960	Dublin **South Africa** 8–3	2000	Dublin **South Africa** 28–18
1961	Cape Town **South Africa** 24–8	2004	1 Bloemfontein **South Africa** 31–17
1965	Dublin **Ireland** 9–6		*2* Cape Town **South Africa** 26–17
1970	Dublin **Drawn** 8–8		South Africa won series 2–0
1981	*1* Cape Town **South Africa** 23–15	2004	Dublin **Ireland** 17–12
	2 Durban **South Africa** 12–10	2006	Dublin **Ireland** 32–15
	South Africa won series 2–0		

IRELAND v NEW ZEALAND

Played 22 Ireland won 0, New Zealand won 21, Drawn 1
Highest scores Ireland 29–40 in 2001, New Zealand 63–15 in 1997
Biggest win Ireland no win, New Zealand 59–6 in 1992

1905	Dublin **New Zealand** 15–0	1995	Johannesburg WC **New Zealand 43–19**
1924	Dublin **New Zealand** 6–0	1997	Dublin **New Zealand** 63–15
1935	Dublin **New Zealand** 17–9	2001	Dublin **New Zealand** 40–29
1954	Dublin **New Zealand** 14–3	2002	*1* Dunedin **New Zealand** 15–6
1963	Dublin **New Zealand** 6–5		*2* Auckland **New Zealand** 40–8
1973	Dublin **Drawn** 10–10		New Zealand won series 2–0
1974	Dublin **New Zealand** 15–6	2005	Dublin **New Zealand** 45–7
1976	Wellington **New Zealand** 11–3	2006	1 Hamilton **New Zealand** 34–23
1978	Dublin **New Zealand** 10–6		*2* Auckland **New Zealand** 27–17
1989	Dublin **New Zealand** 23–6		New Zealand won series 2–0
1992	*1* Dunedin **New Zealand** 24–21	2008	Wellington **New Zealand** 21–1
	2 Wellington **New Zealand** 59–6	2008	Dublin **New Zealand** 22–3
	New Zealand won series 2–0		

IRELAND v AUSTRALIA

Played 27 Ireland won 8, Australia won 19, Drawn 0
Highest scores Ireland 27–12 in 1979, Australia 46–10 in 1999
Biggest wins Ireland 27–12 in 1979 & 21–6 in 2006, Australia 46–10 in 1999

1927 Dublin **Australia** 5–3	1994 *1* Brisbane **Australia** 33–13
1947 Dublin **Australia** 16–3	*2* Sydney **Australia** 32–18
1958 Dublin **Ireland** 9–6	Australia won series 2–0
1967 Dublin **Ireland** 15–8	1996 Dublin **Australia** 22–12
1967 Sydney **Ireland** 11–5	1999 *1* Brisbane **Australia** 46–10
1968 Dublin **Ireland** 10–3	*2* Perth **Australia** 32–26
1976 Dublin **Australia** 20–10	Australia won series 2–0
1979 *1* Brisbane **Ireland** 27–12	1999 Dublin WC **Australia** 23–3
2 Sydney **Ireland** 9–3	2002 Dublin **Ireland** 18–9
Ireland won series 2–0	2003 Perth **Australia** 45–16
1981 Dublin **Australia** 16–12	2003 Melbourne WC **Australia** 17–16
1984 Dublin **Australia** 16–9	2005 Dublin **Australia** 30–14
1987 Sydney WC **Australia** 33–15	2006 Perth **Australia** 37–15
1991 Dublin WC **Australia** 19–18	2006 Dublin **Ireland** 21–6
1992 Dublin **Australia** 42–17	2008 Melbourne **Australia** 18–12

IRELAND v NEW ZEALAND NATIVES

Played 1 New Zealand Natives won 1
Highest scores Ireland 4–13 in 1888, Zew Zealand Natives 13–4 in 1888
Biggest win Ireland no win, New Zealand Natives 13–4 in 1888

1888 Dublin **New Zealand Natives**
4G 1T to 1G 1T

IRELAND v IRU PRESIDENT'S XV

Played 1 Drawn 1
Highest scores Ireland 18–18 in 1974, IRFU President's XV 18–18 in 1974

1974 Dublin **Drawn** 18–18

IRELAND v ROMANIA

Played 8 Ireland won 8
Highest scores Ireland 60–0 in 1986, Romania 35–53 in 1998
Biggest win Ireland 60–0 in 1986, Romania no win

1986	Dublin **Ireland** 60–0		2001	Bucharest **Ireland** 37–3
1993	Dublin **Ireland** 25–3		2002	Limerick **Ireland** 39–8
1998	Dublin **Ireland** 53–35		2003	Gosford WC **Ireland** 45–17
1999	Dublin WC **Ireland** 44–14		2005	Dublin **Ireland** 43–12

IRELAND v CANADA

Played 5 Ireland won 4 Drawn 1
Highest scores Ireland 55–0 in 2008, Canada 27–27 in 2000
Biggest win Ireland 55–0 in 2008, Canada no win

1987	Dunedin WC **Ireland** 46–19		2008	Limerick **Ireland** 55–0
1997	Dublin **Ireland** 33–11		2009	Vancouver **Ireland** 25–6
2000	Markham **Drawn** 27–27			

IRELAND v TONGA

Played 2 Ireland won 2
Highest scores Ireland 40–19 in 2003, Tonga 19–40 in 2003
Biggest win Ireland 32–9 in 1987, Tonga no win

1987	Brisbane WC **Ireland** 32–9		2003	Nuku'alofa **Ireland** 40–19

IRELAND v SAMOA

Played 4 Ireland won 3, Samoa won 1, Drawn 0
Highest scores Ireland 49–22 in 1988, Samoa 40–25 in 1996
Biggest wins Ireland 49–22 in 1988 and 35–8 in 2001, Samoa 40–25 in 1996

1988	Dublin **Ireland** 49–22		2001	Dublin **Ireland** 35–8
1996	Dublin **Samoa** 40–25		2003	Apia **Ireland** 40–14

IRELAND v ITALY

Played 17 Ireland won 14, Italy won 3, Drawn 0
Highest scores Ireland 61–6 in 2003, Italy 37–29 in 1997 & 37–22 in 1997
Biggest wins Ireland 61–6 in 2003, Italy 37–22 in 1997

1988	Dublin **Ireland** 31–15		Non-championship match
1995	Treviso **Italy** 22–12	2004	Dublin **Ireland** 19–3
1997	Dublin **Italy** 37–29	2005	Rome **Ireland** 28–17
1997	Bologna **Italy** 37–22	2006	Dublin **Ireland** 26–16
1999	Dublin **Ireland** 39–30	2007	Rome **Ireland** 51–24
2000	Dublin **Ireland** 60–13	2007	Belfast **Ireland** 23–20
2001	Rome **Ireland** 41–22		Non-championship match
2002	Dublin **Ireland** 32–17	2008	Dublin **Ireland** 16–11
2003	Rome **Ireland** 37–13	2009	Rome **Ireland** 38–9
2003	Limerick **Ireland** 61–6		

IRELAND v ARGENTINA

Played 11 Ireland won 6 Argentina won 5
Highest scores Ireland 32–24 in 1999, Argentina 34–23 in 2000
Biggest win Ireland 17–3 in 2008, Argentina 16–0 in 2007

1990	Dublin **Ireland** 20–18	2004	Dublin **Ireland** 21–19
1999	Dublin **Ireland** 32–24	2007	1 Santa Fé **Argentina** 22–20
1999	Lens WC **Argentina** 28–24		2 Buenos Aires **Argentina** 16–0
2000	Buenos Aires **Argentina** 34–23		Argentina won series 2–0
2002	Dublin **Ireland** 16–7	2007	Paris WC **Argentina** 30–15
2003	Adelaide WC **Ireland** 16–15	2008	Dublin **Ireland** 17–3

IRELAND v NAMIBIA

Played 4 Ireland won 2, Namibia won 2
Highest scores Ireland 64–7 in 2003, Namibia 26–15 in 1991
Biggest win Ireland 64–7 in 2003, Namibia 26–15 in 1991

1991	1 Windhoek **Namibia** 15–6	2003	Sydney WC **Ireland** 64–7
	2 Windhoek **Namibia** 26–15	2007	Bordeaux WC **Ireland** 32–17
	Namibia won series 2–0		

INTERNATIONAL RECORDS

IRELAND v ZIMBABWE

Played 1 Ireland won 1
Highest scores Ireland 55–11 in 1991, Zimbabwe 11–55 in 1991
Biggest win Ireland 55–11 in 1991, Zimbabwe no win

1991	Dublin WC **Ireland** 55–11

IRELAND v JAPAN

Played 5 Ireland won 5
Highest scores Ireland 78–9 in 2000, Japan 28–50 in 1995
Biggest win Ireland 78–9 in 2000, Japan no win

1991	Dublin WC **Ireland** 32–16	2005	1 Osaka **Ireland** 44–12
1995	Bloemfontein WC **Ireland 50–28**		2 Tokyo **Ireland** 47–18
2000	Dublin **Ireland** 78–9		Ireland won series 2–0

IRELAND v UNITED STATES

Played 6 Ireland won 6
Highest scores Ireland 83–3 in 2000, United States 18–25 in 1996
Biggest win Ireland 83–3 in 2000, United States no win

1994	Dublin **Ireland** 26–15	2000	Manchester (NH) **Ireland** 83–3
1996	Atlanta **Ireland** 25–18	2004	Dublin **Ireland** 55–6
1999	Dublin WC **Ireland** 53–8	2009	Santa Clara **Ireland** 27–10

IRELAND v FIJI

Played 2 Ireland won 2
Highest scores Ireland 64–17 in 2002, Fiji 17–64 in 2002
Biggest win Ireland 64–17 in 2002, Fiji no win

1995	Dublin **Ireland** 44–8	2002	Dublin **Ireland** 64–17

IRELAND v GEORGIA

Played 3 Ireland won 3
Highest scores Ireland 70–0 in 1998, Georgia 14–63 in 2002
Biggest win Ireland 70–0 in 1998, Georgia no win

1998 Dublin **Ireland** 70–0	2007 Bordeaux WC **Ireland** 14–10
2002 Dublin **Ireland** 63–14	

IRELAND v RUSSIA

Played 1 Ireland won 1
Highest scores Ireland 35–3 in 2002, Russia 3–35 in 2002
Biggest win Ireland 35–3 in 2002, Russia no win

2002 Krasnoyarsk **Ireland** 35–3

IRELAND v PACIFIC ISLANDS

Played 1 Ireland won 1
Highest scores Ireland 61–17 in 2006, Pacific Islands 17–61 in 2006
Biggest win Ireland 61–17 in 2006, Pacific Islands no win

2006 Dublin **Ireland** 61–17

WALES v FRANCE

Played 86 Wales won 43, France won 40, Drawn 3
Highest scores Wales 49–14 in 1910, France 51–0 in 1998
Biggest wins Wales 47–5 in 1909, France 51–0 in 1998

1908 Cardiff **Wales** 36–4	1921 Cardiff **Wales** 12–4
1909 Paris **Wales** 47–5	1922 Paris **Wales** 11–3
1910 Swansea **Wales** 49–14	1923 Swansea **Wales** 16–8
1911 Paris **Wales** 15–0	1924 Paris **Wales** 10–6
1912 Newport **Wales** 14–8	1925 Cardiff **Wales** 11–5
1913 Paris **Wales** 11–8	1926 Paris **Wales** 7–5
1914 Swansea **Wales** 31–0	1927 Swansea **Wales** 25–7
1920 Paris **Wales** 6–5	1928 Paris **France** 8–3

1929	Cardiff **Wales** 8–3	1981	Paris **France** 19–15
1930	Paris **Wales** 11–0	1982	Cardiff **Wales** 22–12
1931	Swansea **Wales** 35–3	1983	Paris **France** 16–9
1947	Paris **Wales** 3–0	1984	Cardiff **France** 21–16
1948	Swansea **France** 11–3	1985	Paris **France** 14–3
1949	Paris **France** 5–3	1986	Cardiff **France** 23–15
1950	Cardiff **Wales** 21–0	1987	Paris **France** 16–9
1951	Paris **France** 8–3	1988	Cardiff **France** 10–9
1952	Swansea **Wales** 9–5	1989	Paris **France** 31–12
1953	Paris **Wales** 6–3	1990	Cardiff **France** 29–19
1954	Cardiff **Wales** 19–13	1991	Paris **France** 36–3
1955	Paris **Wales** 16–11	1991	Cardiff **France** 22–9
1956	Cardiff **Wales** 5–3		Non-championship match
1957	Paris **Wales** 19–13	1992	Cardiff **France** 12–9
1958	Cardiff **France** 16–6	1993	Paris **France** 26–10
1959	Paris **France** 11–3	1994	Cardiff **Wales** 24–15
1960	Cardiff **France** 16–8	1995	Paris **France** 21–9
1961	Paris **France** 8–6	1996	Cardiff **Wales** 16–15
1962	Cardiff **Wales** 3–0	1996	Cardiff **France** 40–33
1963	Paris **France** 5–3		Non-championship match
1964	Cardiff **Drawn** 11–11	1997	Paris **France** 27–22
1965	Paris **France** 22–13	1998	Wembley **France** 51–0
1966	Cardiff **Wales** 9–8	1999	Paris **Wales** 34–33
1967	Paris **France** 20–14	1999	Cardiff **Wales** 34–23
1968	Cardiff **France** 14–9		Non-championship match
1969	Paris **Drawn** 8–8	2000	Cardiff **France** 36–3
1970	Cardiff **Wales** 11–6	2001	Paris **Wales** 43–35
1971	Paris **Wales** 9–5	2002	Cardiff **France** 37–33
1972	Cardiff **Wales** 20–6	2003	Paris **France** 33–5
1973	Paris **France** 12–3	2004	Cardiff **France** 29–22
1974	Cardiff **Drawn** 16–16	2005	Paris **Wales** 24–18
1975	Paris **Wales** 25–10	2006	Cardiff **France** 21–16
1976	Cardiff **Wales** 19–13	2007	Paris **France** 32–21
1977	Paris **France** 16–9	2007	Cardiff **France** 34–7
1978	Cardiff **Wales** 16–7		Non-championship match
1979	Paris **France** 14–13	2008	Cardiff **Wales** 29–12
1980	Cardiff **Wales** 18–9	2009	Paris **France** 21–16

WALES v SOUTH AFRICA

Played 23 Wales won 1, South Africa won 21, Drawn 1
Highest scores Wales 36–38 in 2004, South Africa 96–13 in 1998
Biggest win Wales 29–19 in 1999, South Africa 96–13 in 1998

1906	Swansea **South Africa** 11–0	1951	Cardiff **South Africa** 6–3
1912	Cardiff **South Africa** 3–0	1960	Cardiff **South Africa** 3–0
1931	Swansea **South Africa** 8–3	1964	Durban **South Africa** 24–3

1970	Cardiff **Drawn** 6–6		SA won series 2–0
1994	Cardiff **South Africa** 20–12	2004	Pretoria **South Africa** 53–18
1995	Johannesburg **South Africa** 40–11	2004	Cardiff **South Africa** 38–36
1996	Cardiff **South Africa** 37–20	2005	Cardiff **South Africa** 33–16
1998	Pretoria **South Africa** 96–13	2007	Cardiff **South Africa** 34–12
1998	Wembley **South Africa** 28–20	2008	*1* Bloemfontein **South Africa** 43–17
1999	Cardiff **Wales** 29–19		*2* Pretoria **South Africa** 37–21
2000	Cardiff **South Africa** 23–13		SA won series 2–0
2002	*1* Bloemfontein **South Africa** 34–19	2008	Cardiff **South Africa** 20–15
	2 Cape Town **South Africa** 19–8		

WALES v NEW ZEALAND

Played 24 Wales won 3, New Zealand won 21, Drawn 0
Highest scores Wales 37–53 in 2003, New Zealand 55–3 in 2003
Biggest wins Wales 13–8 in 1953, New Zealand 55–3 in 2003

1905	Cardiff **Wales** 3–0	1988	*1* Christchurch **New Zealand** 52–3
1924	Swansea **New Zealand** 19–0		*2* Auckland **New Zealand** 54–9
1935	Cardiff **Wales** 13–12		New Zealand won series 2–0
1953	Cardiff **Wales** 13–8	1989	Cardiff **New Zealand** 34–9
1963	Cardiff **New Zealand** 6–0	1995	Johannesburg WC **New Zealand 34–9**
1967	Cardiff **New Zealand** 13–6	1997	Wembley **New Zealand** 42–7
1969	*1* Christchurch **New Zealand** 19–0	2002	Cardiff **New Zealand** 43–17
	2 Auckland **New Zealand** 33–12	2003	Hamilton **New Zealand** 55–3
	New Zealand won series 2–0	2003	Sydney WC **New Zealand** 53–37
1972	Cardiff **New Zealand** 19–16	2004	Cardiff **New Zealand** 26–25
1978	Cardiff **New Zealand** 13–12	2005	Cardiff **New Zealand** 41–3
1980	Cardiff **New Zealand** 23–3	2006	Cardiff **New Zealand** 45–10
1987	Brisbane WC **New Zealand** 49–6	2008	Cardiff **New Zealand** 29–9

WALES v AUSTRALIA

Played 28 Wales won 10, Australia won 17, Drawn 1
Highest scores Wales 29–29 in 2006, Australia 63–6 in 1991
Biggest wins Wales 28–3 in 1975, Australia 63–6 in 1991

1908	Cardiff **Wales** 9–6		*2* Sydney **Australia** 19–17
1927	Cardiff **Australia** 18–8		Australia won series 2–0
1947	Cardiff **Wales** 6–0	1981	Cardiff **Wales** 18–13
1958	Cardiff **Wales** 9–3	1984	Cardiff **Australia** 28–9
1966	Cardiff **Australia** 14–11	1987	Rotorua WC **Wales** 22–21
1969	Sydney **Wales** 19–16	1991	Brisbane **Australia** 63–6
1973	Cardiff **Wales** 24–0	1991	Cardiff WC **Australia** 38–3
1975	Cardiff **Wales** 28–3	1992	Cardiff **Australia** 23–6
1978	*1* Brisbane **Australia** 18–8	1996	*1* Brisbane **Australia** 56–25

	2 Sydney **Australia** 42–3	2006	Cardiff **Drawn** 29–29
	Australia won series 2–0	2007	1 Sydney **Australia** 29–23
1996	Cardiff **Australia 28–19**		2 Brisbane **Australia** 31–0
1999	Cardiff WC **Australia** 24–9		Australia won series 2–0
2001	Cardiff **Australia** 21–13	2007	Cardiff WC **Australia** 32–20
2003	Sydney **Australia** 30–10	2008	Cardiff **Wales** 21–18
2005	Cardiff **Wales** 24–22		

WALES v NEW ZEALAND NATIVES

Played 1 Wales won 1
Highest scores Wales 5–0 in 1888, New Zealand Natives 0–5 in 1888
Biggest win Wales 5–0 in 1888, New Zealand Natives no win

1888	Swansea **Wales** 1G 2T to 0

WALES v NEW ZEALAND ARMY

Played 1 New Zealand Army won 1
Highest scores Wales 3–6 in 1919, New Zealand Army 6–3 in 1919
Biggest win Wales no win, New Zealand Army 6–3 in 1919

1919	Swansea **New Zealand Army** 6–3

WALES v ROMANIA

Played 8 Wales won 6, Romania won 2
Highest scores Wales 81–9 in 2001, Romania 24–6 in 1983
Biggest wins Wales 81–9 in 2001, Romania 24–6 in 1983

1983	Bucharest **Romania** 24–6	2001	Cardiff **Wales** 81–9
1988	Cardiff **Romania** 15–9	2002	Wrexham **Wales** 40–3
1994	Bucharest **Wales** 16–9	2003	Wrexham **Wales** 54–8
1997	Wrexham **Wales** 70–21	2004	Cardiff **Wales** 66–7

Played 7 Wales won 6, Fiji won 1
Highest scores Wales 58–14 in 2002, Fiji 38–34 in 2007
Biggest win Wales 58–14 in 2002, Fiji 38–34 in 2007

1985	Cardiff **Wales** 40–3	2002	Cardiff **Wales** 58–14
1986	Suva **Wales** 22–15	2005	Cardiff **Wales** 11–10
1994	Suva **Wales** 23–8	2007	Nantes WC **Fiji** 38–34
1995	Cardiff **Wales** 19–15		

WALES v TONGA

Played 6 Wales won 6
Highest scores Wales 51–7 in 2001, Tonga 20–27 in 2003
Biggest win Wales 51–7 in 2001, Tonga no win

1986	Nuku'Alofa **Wales** 15–7	1997	Swansea **Wales** 46–12
1987	Palmerston North WC **Wales** 29–16	2001	Cardiff **Wales** 51–7
1994	Nuku'Alofa **Wales** 18–9	2003	Canberra WC **Wales** 27–20

WALES v SAMOA

Played 6 Wales won 3, Samoa won 3, Drawn 0
Highest scores Wales 50–6 in 2000, Samoa 38–31 in 1999
Biggest wins Wales 50–6 in 2000, Samoa 34–9 in 1994

1986	Apia **Wales** 32–14	1994	Moamoa **Samoa** 34–9
1988	Cardiff **Wales** 28–6	1999	Cardiff WC **Samoa** 38–31
1991	Cardiff WC **Samoa** 16–13	2000	Cardiff **Wales** 50–6

WALES v CANADA

Played 12 Wales won 11, Canada won 1, Drawn 0
Highest scores Wales 61–26 in 2006, Canada 26–24 in 1993 & 26–61 in 2006
Biggest wins Wales 60–3 in 2005, Canada 26–24 in 1993

1987	Invercargill WC **Wales** 40–9	1994	Toronto **Wales** 33–15
1993	Cardiff **Canada** 26–24	1997	Toronto **Wales** 28–25

1999	Cardiff **Wales** 33–19	2006	Cardiff **Wales** 61–26
2002	Cardiff **Wales** 32–21	2007	Nantes WC **Wales** 42–17
2003	Melbourne WC **Wales** 41–10	2008	Cardiff **Wales** 34–13
2005	Toronto **Wales** 60–3	2009	Toronto **Wales** 32–23

WALES v UNITED STATES

Played 7 Wales won 7
Highest scores Wales 77–3 in 2005, United States 23–28 in 1997
Biggest win Wales 77–3 in 2005, United States no win

1987	Cardiff **Wales** 46–0		Wales won series 2–0
1997	Cardiff **Wales** 34–14	2000	Cardiff **Wales** 42–11
1997	*1* Wilmington **Wales** 30–20	2005	Hartford **Wales** 77–3
	2 San Francisco **Wales** 28–23	2009	Chicago **Wales** 48–15

WALES v NAMIBIA

Played 3 Wales won 3
Highest scores Wales 38–23 in 1993, Namibia 30–34 in 1990
Biggest win Wales 38–23 in 1993, Namibia no win

1990	*1* Windhoek **Wales** 18–9		Wales won series 2–0
	2 Windhoek **Wales** 34–30	1993	Windhoek **Wales** 38–23

WALES v BARBARIANS

Played 2 Wales won 1, Barbarians won 1
Highest scores Wales 31–10 in 1996, Barbarians 31–24 in 1990
Biggest wins Wales 31–10 in 1996, Barbarians 31–24 in 1990

1990	Cardiff **Barbarians** 31–24	1996	Cardiff **Wales** 31–10

WALES v ARGENTINA

Played 11 Wales won 7, Argentina won 4
Highest scores Wales 44–50 in 2004, Argentina 50–44 in 2004
Biggest win Wales 35–20 in 2004, Argentina 45–27 in 2006

1991	Cardiff WC **Wales** 16–7		2004	1 Tucumán **Argentina** 50–44
1998	Llanelli **Wales** 43–30			2 Buenos Aires **Wales** 35–20
1999	*1* Buenos Aires **Wales** 36–26			Series drawn 1–1
	2 Buenos Aires **Wales** 23–16		2006	1 Puerto Madryn **Argentina** 27–25
	Wales won series 2–0			2 Buenos Aires **Argentina** 45–27
1999	Cardiff WC **Wales** 23–18			Argentina won series 2–0
2001	Cardiff **Argentina** 30–16		2007	Cardiff **Wales** 27–20

WALES v ZIMBABWE

Played 3 Wales won 3
Highest scores Wales 49–11 in 1998, Zimbabwe 14–35 in 1993
Biggest win Wales 49–11 in 1998, Zimbabwe no win

1993	*1* Bulawayo **Wales** 35–14			Wales won series 2–0
	2 Harare **Wales** 42–13		1998	Harare **Wales** 49–11

WALES v JAPAN

Played 7 Wales won 7
Highest scores Wales 98–0 in 2004, Japan 30–53 in 2001
Biggest win Wales 98–0 in 2004, Japan no win

1993	Cardiff **Wales** 55–5			2 Tokyo **Wales** 53–30
1995	Bloemfontein WC **Wales 57–10**			Wales won series 2–0
1999	Cardiff WC **Wales** 64–15		2004	Cardiff **Wales** 98–0
2001	*1* Osaka **Wales** 64–10		2007	Cardiff WC **Wales** 72–18

WALES v PORTUGAL

Played 1 Wales won 1
Highest scores Wales 102–11 in 1994, Portugal 11–102 in 1994
Biggest win Wales 102–11 in 1994, Portugal no win

1994	Lisbon **Wales** 102–11

WALES v SPAIN

Played 1 Wales won 1
Highest scores Wales 54–0 in 1994, Spain 0–54 in 1994
Bigegst win Wales 54–0 in 1994, Spain no win

1994	Madrid **Wales** 54–0	

WALES v ITALY

Played 16 Wales won 13, Italy won 2, Drawn 1
Highest scores Wales 60–21 in 1999, Italy 30–22 in 2003
Biggest win Wales 60–21 in 1999 and 47–8 in 2008, Italy 30–22 in 2003

1994	Cardiff **Wales** 29–19		2003	Rome **Italy** 30–22
1996	Cardiff **Wales** 31–26		2003	Canberra WC **Wales** 27–15
1996	Rome **Wales** 31–22		2004	Cardiff **Wales** 44–10
1998	Llanelli **Wales** 23–20		2005	Rome **Wales** 38–8
1999	Treviso **Wales** 60–21		2006	Cardiff **Drawn** 18–18
2000	Cardiff **Wales** 47–16		2007	Rome **Italy** 23–20
2001	Rome **Wales** 33–23		2008	Cardiff **Wales** 47–8
2002	Cardiff **Wales** 44–20		2009	Rome **Wales** 20–15

WALES v PACIFIC ISLANDS

Played 1 Wales won 1
Highest scores Wales 38–20 in 2006, Pacific Islands 20–38 in 2006
Biggest win Wales 38–20 in 2006, Pacific Islands no win

2006	Cardiff **Wales** 38–20	

BRITISH/IRISH ISLES v SOUTH AFRICA

Played 46 British/Irish won 17, South Africa won 23, Drawn 6
Highest scores: British/Irish 28–9 in 1974 & 2009, South Africa 35–16 in 1997
Biggest wins: British/Irish 28–9 in 1974 & 2009, South Africa 34–14 in 1962

1891	*1* Port Elizabeth **British/Irish** 4–0			*3* Kimberley **British/Irish** 9–3
	2 Kimberley **British/Irish** 3–0			*4* Cape Town **South Africa** 5–0
	3 Cape Town **British/Irish** 4–0			British/Irish won series 3–1
	British/Irish won series 3–0		1903	*1* Johannesburg **Drawn** 10–10
1896	*1* Port Elizabeth **British/Irish** 8–0			*2* Kimberley **Drawn** 0–0
	2 Johannesburg **British/Irish** 17–8			*3* Cape Town **South Africa** 8–0

South Africa won series 1–0 with two drawn

1910 *1* Johannesburg **South Africa** 14–10
    2 Port Elizabeth **British/Irish** 8–3
    3 Cape Town **South Africa** 21–5
    South Africa won series 2–1

1924 *1* Durban **South Africa** 7–3
    2 Johannesburg **South Africa** 17–0
    3 Port Elizabeth **Drawn** 3–3
    4 Cape Town **South Africa** 16–9
    South Africa won series 3–0, with 1 draw

1938 *1* Johannesburg **South Africa** 26–12
    2 Port Elizabeth **South Africa** 19–3
    3 Cape Town **British/Irish** 21–16
    South Africa won series 2–1

1955 *1* Johannesburg **British/Irish** 23–22
    2 Cape Town **South Africa** 25–9
    3 Pretoria **British/Irish** 9–6
    4 Port Elizabeth **South Africa** 22–8
    Series drawn 2–2

1962 *1* Johannesburg **Drawn** 3–3
    2 Durban **South Africa** 3–0
    3 Cape Town **South Africa** 8–3
    4 Bloemfontein **South Africa** 34–14

South Africa won series 3–0, with 1 draw

1968 *1* Pretoria **South Africa** 25–20
    2 Port Elizabeth **Drawn** 6–6
    3 Cape Town **South Africa** 11–6
    4 Johannesburg **South Africa** 19–6
    South Africa won series 3–0, with 1 draw

1974 *1* Cape Town **British/Irish** 12–3
    2 Pretoria **British/Irish** 28–9
    3 Port Elizabeth **British/Irish** 26–9
    4 Johannesburg **Drawn** 13–13
    British/Irish won series 3–0, with 1 draw

1980 *1* Cape Town **South Africa** 26–22
    2 Bloemfontein **South Africa** 26–19
    3 Port Elizabeth **South Africa** 12–10
    4 Pretoria **British/Irish** 17–13
    South Africa won series 3–1

1997 *1* Cape Town **British/Irish** 25–16
    2 Durban **British/Irish** 18–15
    3 Johannesburg **South Africa** 35–16
    British/Irish won series 2–1

2009 1 Durban **South Africa** 26–21
    2 Pretoria **South Africa** 28–25
    3 Johannesburg **British/Irish** 28–9
    South Africa won series 2–1

BRITISH/IRISH ISLES v NEW ZEALAND

Played 35 British/Irish won 6, New Zealand won 27, Drawn 2
Highest scores: British/Irish 20–7 in 1993, New Zealand 48–18 in 2005
Biggest wins: British/Irish 20–7 in 1993, New Zealand 38–6 in 1983

1904 Wellington **New Zealand** 9–3

1930 *1* Dunedin **British/Irish** 6–3
    2 Christchurch **New Zealand** 13–10
    3 Auckland **New Zealand** 15–10
    4 Wellington **New Zealand** 22–8
    New Zealand won series 3–1

1950 *1* Dunedin **Drawn** 9–9
    2 Christchurch **New Zealand** 8–0
    3 Wellington **New Zealand** 6–3
    4 Auckland **New Zealand** 11–8
    New Zealand won series 3–0, with 1 draw

1959 *1* Dunedin **New Zealand** 18–17
    2 Wellington **New Zealand** 11–8
    3 Christchurch **New Zealand** 22–8
    4 Auckland **British/Irish** 9–6
    New Zealand won series 3–1

1966 *1* Dunedin **New Zealand** 20–3
    2 Wellington **New Zealand** 16–12

    3 Christchurch **New Zealand** 19–6
    4 Auckland **New Zealand** 24–11
    New Zealand won series 4–0

1971 *1* Dunedin **British/Irish** 9–3
    2 Christchurch **New Zealand** 22–12
    3 Wellington **British/Irish** 13–3
    4 Auckland **Drawn** 14–14
    British/Irish won series 2–1, with 1 draw

1977 *1* Wellington **New Zealand** 16–12
    2 Christchurch **British/Irish** 13–9
    3 Dunedin **New Zealand** 19–7
    4 Auckland **New Zealand** 10–9
    New Zealand won series 3–1

1983 *1* Christchurch **New Zealand** 16–12
    2 Wellington **New Zealand** 9–0
    3 Dunedin **New Zealand** 15–8
    4 Auckland **New Zealand** 38–6
    New Zealand won series 4–0

1993	*1* Christchurch **New Zealand** 20–18	2005	1 Christchurch **New Zealand** 21–3
	2 Wellington **British/Irish** 20–7		2 Wellington **New Zealand** 48–18
	3 Auckland **New Zealand** 30–13		3 Auckland **New Zealand** 38–19
	New Zealand won series 2–1		New Zealand won series 3–0

ANGLO-WELSH v NEW ZEALAND

Played 3 New Zealand won 2, Drawn 1
Highest scores Anglo Welsh 5–32 in 1908, New Zealand 32–5 in 1908
Biggest win Anglo Welsh no win, New Zealand 29–0 in 1908

1908	*1* Dunedin **New Zealand** 32–5	New Zealand won series 2–0 with one
	2 Wellington **Drawn** 3–3	drawn
	3 Auckland **New Zealand** 29–0	

BRITISH/IRISH ISLES v AUSTRALIA

Played 20 British/Irish won 15, Australia won 5, Drawn 0
Highest scores: British/Irish 31–0 in 1966, Australia 35–14 in 2001
Biggest wins: British/Irish 31–0 in 1966, Australia 35–14 in 2001

1899	*1* Sydney **Australia** 13–3		*2* Sydney **British/Irish** 24–3
	2 Brisbane **British/Irish** 11–0		British/Irish won series 2–0
	3 Sydney **British/Irish** 11–10	1966	*1* Sydney **British/Irish** 11–8
	4 Sydney **British/Irish** 13–0		*2* Brisbane **British/Irish** 31–0
	British/Irish won series 3–1		British/Irish won series 2–0
1904	*1* Sydney **British/Irish** 17–0	1989	*1* Sydney **Australia** 30–12
	2 Brisbane **British/Irish** 17–3		*2* Brisbane **British/Irish** 19–12
	3 Sydney **British/Irish** 16–0		*3* Sydney **British/Irish** 19–18
	British/Irish won series 3–0		British/Irish won series 2–1
1930	Sydney **Australia** 6–5	2001	*1* Brisbane **British/Irish** 29–13
1950	*1* Brisbane **British/Irish** 19–6		*2* Melbourne **Australia** 35–14
	2 Sydney **British/Irish** 24–3		*3* Sydney **Australia** 29–23
	British/Irish won series 2–0		Australia won series 2–1
1959	*1* Brisbane **British/Irish** 17–6		

BRITISH/IRISH ISLES v ARGENTINA

Played 1 British/Irish won 0, Argentina won 0, Drawn 1
Highest scores: British/Irish 25–25 in 2005, Argentina 25–25 in 2005
Biggest wins: British/Irish no win to date, Argentina no win to date

2005	Cardiff **Drawn** 25–25

FRANCE v SOUTH AFRICA

Played 36 France won 10, South Africa won 20, Drawn 6
Highest scores France 36–26 in 2006, South Africa 52–10 in 1997
Biggest wins France 30–10 in 2002, South Africa 52–10 in 1997

1913 Bordeaux **South Africa** 38–5	1980 Pretoria **South Africa** 37–15
1952 Paris **South Africa** 25–3	1992 *1* Lyons **South Africa** 20–15
1958 *1* Cape Town **Drawn** 3–3	*2* Paris **France** 29–16
2 Johannesburg **France** 9–5	Series drawn 1–1
France won series 1–0, with 1 draw	1993 *1* Durban **Drawn** 20–20
1961 Paris **Drawn** 0–0	*2* Johannesburg **France** 18–17
1964 Springs (SA) **France** 8–6	France won series 1–0, with 1 draw
1967 *1* Durban **South Africa** 26–3	1995 Durban WC **South Africa 19–15**
2 Bloemfontein **South Africa** 16–3	1996 *1* Bordeaux **South Africa** 22–12
3 Johannesburg **France** 19–14	*2* Paris **South Africa** 13–12
4 Cape Town **Drawn** 6–6	*South Africa won series 2–0*
South Africa won series 2–1, with 1 draw	1997 *1* Lyons **South Africa** 36–32
1968 *1* Bordeaux **South Africa** 12–9	*2* Paris **South Africa** 52–10
2 Paris **South Africa** 16–11	South Africa won series 2–0
South Africa won series 2–0	2001 *1* Johannesburg **France** 32–23
1971 *1* Bloemfontein **South Africa** 22–9	*2* Durban **South Africa** 20–15
2 Durban **Drawn** 8–8	Series drawn 1–1
South Africa won series 1–0, with 1 draw	2001 Paris **France** 20–10
1974 *1* Toulouse **South Africa** 13–4	2002 Marseilles **France** 30–10
2 Paris **South Africa** 10–8	2005 1 Durban **Drawn** 30–30
South Africa won series 2–0	*2* Port Elizabeth **South Africa** 27–13
1975 *1* Bloemfontei*n **South Africa** 38–25	South Africa won series 1–0, with 1 draw
2 Pretoria **South Africa** 33–18	2005 Paris **France** 26–20
South Africa won series 2–0	2006 Cape Town **France** 36–26

FRANCE v NEW ZEALAND

Played 48 France won 12, New Zealand won 35, Drawn 1
Highest scores France 43–31 in 1999, New Zealand 61–10 in 2007
Biggest wins France 22–8 in 1994, New Zealand 61–10 in 2007

1906 Paris **New Zealand** 38–8	1967 Paris **New Zealand** 21–15
1925 Toulouse **New Zealand** 30–6	1968 1 Christchurch **New Zealand** 12–9
1954 Paris **France** 3–0	*2* Wellington **New Zealand** 9–3
1961 *1* Auckland **New Zealand** 13–6	*3* Auckland **New Zealand** 19–12
2 Wellington **New Zealand** 5–3	New Zealand won series 3–0
3 Christchurch **New Zealand** 32–3	1973 Paris **France** 13–6
New Zealand won series 3–0	1977 *1* Toulouse **France** 18–13
1964 Paris **New Zealand** 12–3	*2* Paris **New Zealand** 15–3

128

Series drawn 1–1	
1979	1 Christchurch **New Zealand** 23–9
	2 Auckland **France** 24–19
	Series drawn 1–1
1981	1 Toulouse **New Zealand** 13–9
	2 Paris **New Zealand** 18–6
	New Zealand won series 2–0
1984	1 Christchurch **New Zealand** 10–9
	2 Auckland **New Zealand** 31–18
	New Zealand won series 2–0
1986	Christchurch **New Zealand** 18–9
1986	1 Toulouse **New Zealand** 19–7
	2 Nantes **France** 16–3
	Series drawn 1–1
1987	Auckland WC **New Zealand** 29–9
1989	1 Christchurch **New Zealand** 25–17
	2 Auckland **New Zealand** 34–20
	New Zealand won series 2–0
1990	1 Nantes **New Zealand** 24–3
	2 Paris **New Zealand** 30–12
	New Zealand won series 2–0
1994	1 Christchurch **France** 22–8
	2 Auckland **France** 23–20
	France won series 2–0

1995	1 Toulouse **France** 22–15
	2 Paris **New Zealand** 37–12
	Series drawn 1–1
1999	Wellington **New Zealand** 54–7
1999	Twickenham WC **France** 43–31
2000	1 Paris **New Zealand** 39–26
	2 Marseilles **France** 42–33
	Series drawn 1–1
2001	Wellington **New Zealand** 37–12
2002	Paris **Drawn** 20–20
2003	Christchurch **New Zealand** 31–23
2003	Sydney WC **New Zealand** 40–13
2004	Paris **New Zealand** 45–6
2006	1 Lyons **New Zealand** 47–3
	2 Paris **New Zealand** 23–11
	New Zealand won series 2–0
2007	1 Auckland **New Zealand** 42–11
	2 Wellington **New Zealand** 61–10
	New Zealand won series 2–0
2007	Cardiff WC **France** 20–18
2009	1 Dunedin **France** 27–22
	2 Wellington **New Zealand** 14–10
	Series drawn 1–1

FRANCE v AUSTRALIA

Played 40 France won 16, Australia won 22, Drawn 2
Highest scores France 34–6 in 1976, Australia 48–31 in 1990
Biggest wins France 34–6 in 1976, Australia 40–10 in 2008

1928	Paris **Australia** 11–8
1948	Paris **France** 13–6
1958	Paris **France** 19–0
1961	Sydney **France** 15–8
1967	Paris **France** 20–14
1968	Sydney **Australia** 11–10
1971	1 Toulouse **Australia** 13–11
	2 Paris **France** 18–9
	Series drawn 1–1
1972	1 Sydney **Drawn** 14–14
	2 Brisbane **France** 16–15
	France won series 1–0, with 1 draw
1976	1 Bordeaux **France** 18–15
	2 Paris **France** 34–6
	France won series 2–0
1981	1 Brisbane **Australia** 17–15
	2 Sydney **Australia** 24–14

	Australia won series 2–0
1983	1 Clermont-Ferrand **Drawn** 15–15
	2 Paris **France** 15–6
	France won series 1–0, with 1 draw
1986	Sydney **Australia** 27–14
1987	Sydney WC **France** 30–24
1989	1 Strasbourg **Australia** 32–15
	2 Lille **France** 25–19
	Series drawn 1–1
1990	1 Sydney **Australia** 21–9
	2 Brisbane **Australia** 48–31
	3 Sydney **France** 28–19
	Australia won series 2–1
1993	1 Bordeaux **France** 16–13
	2 Paris **Australia** 24–3
	Series drawn 1–1
1997	1 Sydney **Australia** 29–15

	2 Brisbane **Australia** 26–19	2004	Paris **France** 27–14
	Australia won series 2–0	2005	Brisbane **Australia** 37–31
1998	Paris **Australia** 32–21	2005	Marseilles **France** 26–16
1999	Cardiff WC **Australia** 35–12	2008	*1* Sydney **Australia** 34–13
2000	Paris **Australia** 18–13		*2* Brisbane **Australia** 40–10
2001	Marseilles **France** 14–13		Australia won series 2–0
2002	*1* Melbourne **Australia** 29–17	2008	Paris **Australia** 18–13
	2 Sydney **Australia** 31–25	2009	Sydney **Australia** 22–6
	Australia won series 2–0		

FRANCE v UNITED STATES

Played 7 France won 6, United States won 1, Drawn 0
Highest scores France 41–9 in 1991 and 41–14 in 2003, United States 31–39 in 2004
Biggest wins France 41–9 in 1991, United States 17–3 in 1924

1920	Paris **France** 14–5		*Abandoned after 43 mins
1924	Paris **United States** 17–3		France won series 2–0
1976	Chicago **France** 33–14	2003	Wollongong WC **France** 41–14
1991	*1* Denver **France** 41–9	2004	Hartford **France** 39–311
	2 Colorado Springs **France** 10–3*		

FRANCE v ROMANIA

Played 49 France won 39, Romania won 8, Drawn 2
Highest scores France 67–20 in 2000, Romania 21–33 in 1991
Biggest wins France 59–3 in 1924, Romania 15–0 in 1980

1924	Paris **France** 59–3	1974	Bucharest **Romania** 15–10
1938	Bucharest **France** 11–8	1975	Bordeaux **France** 36–12
1957	Bucharest **France** 18–15	1976	Bucharest **Romania** 15–12
1957	Bordeaux **France** 39–0	1977	Clermont-Ferrand **France** 9–6
1960	Bucharest **Romania** 11–5	1978	Bucharest **France** 9–6
1961	Bayonne **Drawn** 5–5	1979	Montauban **France** 30–12
1962	Bucharest **Romania** 3–0	1980	Bucharest **Romania** 15–0
1963	Toulouse **Drawn** 6–6	1981	Narbonne **France** 17–9
1964	Bucharest **France** 9–6	1982	Bucharest **Romania** 13–9
1965	Lyons **France** 8–3	1983	Toulouse **France** 26–15
1966	Bucharest **France** 9–3	1984	Bucharest **France** 18–3
1967	Nantes **France** 11–3	1986	Lille **France** 25–13
1968	Bucharest **Romania** 15–14	1986	Bucharest **France** 20–3
1969	Tarbes **France** 14–9	1987	Wellington WC **France** 55–12
1970	Bucharest **France** 14–3	1987	Agen **France** 49–3
1971	Béziers **France** 31–12	1988	Bucharest **France** 16–12
1972	Constanza **France** 15–6	1990	Auch **Romania** 12–6
1973	Valence **France** 7–6	1991	Bucharest **France** 33–21

INTERNATIONAL RECORDS

1991	Béziers WC **France** 30–3		1997	Bucharest **France** 51–20
1992	Le Havre **France** 25–6		1997	Lourdes LC **France 39–3**
1993	Bucharest **France** 37–20		1999	Castres **France** 62–8
1993	Brive **France** 51–0		2000	Bucharest **France** 67–20
1995	Bucharest **France** 24–15		2003	Lens **France** 56–8
1995	Tucumán LC **France 52–8**		2006	Bucharest **France** 62–14
1996	Aurillac **France** 64–12			

FRANCE v NEW ZEALAND MAORI

Played 1 New Zealand Maori won 1
Highest scores France 3–12 in 1926, New Zealand Maori 12–3 in 1926
Biggest win France no win, New Zealand Maori 12–3 in 1926

1926	Paris **New Zealand Maori** 12–3	

FRANCE v GERMANY

Played 15 France won 13, Germany won 2, Drawn 0
Highest scores France 38–17 in 1933, Germany 17–16 in 1927 & 17–38 in 1933
Biggest wins France 34–0 in 1931, Germany 3–0 in 1938

1927	Paris **France** 30–5		1934	Hanover **France** 13–9
1927	Frankfurt **Germany** 17–16		1935	Paris **France** 18–3
1928	Hanover **France** 14–3		1936	*1* Berlin **France** 19–14
1929	Paris **France** 24–0			*2* Hanover **France** 6–3
1930	Berlin **France** 31–0			France won series 2–0
1931	Paris **France** 34–0		1937	Paris **France** 27–6
1932	Frankfurt **France** 20–4		1938	Frankfurt **Germany** 3–0
1933	Paris **France** 38–17		1938	Bucharest **France** 8–5

FRANCE v ITALY

Played 30 France won 29, Italy won 1, Drawn 0
Highest scores France 60–13 in 1967, Italy 40–32 in 1997
Biggest wins France 60–13 in 1967, Italy 40–32 in 1997

1937	Paris **France** 43–5		1953	Lyons **France** 22–8
1952	Milan **France** 17–8		1954	Rome **France** 39–12

1955	Grenoble **France** 24–0	1995	Buenos Aires LC **France 34–22**
1956	Padua **France** 16–3	1997	Grenoble **Italy** 40–32
1957	Agen **France** 38–6	1997	Auch LC **France 30–19**
1958	Naples **France** 11–3	2000	Paris **France** 42–31
1959	Nantes **France** 22–0	2001	Rome **France** 30–19
1960	Treviso **France** 26–0	2002	Paris **France** 33–12
1961	Chambéry **France** 17–0	2003	Rome **France** 53–27
1962	Brescia **France** 6–3	2004	Paris **France** 25–0
1963	Grenoble **France** 14–12	2005	Rome **France** 56–13
1964	Parma **France** 12–3	2006	Paris **France** 37–12
1965	Pau **France** 21–0	2007	Rome **France** 39–3
1966	Naples **France** 21–0	2008	Paris **France** 25–13
1967	Toulon **France** 60–13	2009	Rome **France** 50–8

FRANCE v BRITISH XVs

Played 5 France won 2, British XVs won 3, Drawn 0
Highest scores France 27–29 in 1989, British XV 36–3 in 1940
Biggest wins France 21–9 in 1945, British XV 36–3 in 1940

1940	Paris **British XV** 36–3	1946	Paris **France** 10–0
1945	Paris **France** 21–9	1989	Paris **British XV** 29–27
1945	Richmond **British XV** 27–6		

FRANCE v WALES XVs

Played 2 France won 1, Wales XV won 1
Highest scores France 12–0 in 1946, Wales XV 8–0 in 1945
Biggest win France 12–0 in 1946, Wales XV 8–0 in 1945

1945	Swansea **Wales XV** 8–0	1946	Paris **France** 12–0

FRANCE v IRELAND XVs

Played 1 France won 1
Highest scores France 4–3 in 1946, Ireland XV 3–4 in 1946
Biggest win France 4–3 in 1946, Ireland XV no win

1946	Dublin **France** 4–3

FRANCE v NEW ZEALAND ARMY

Played 1 New Zealand Army won 1
Highest scores France 9–14 in 1946, New Zealand Army 14–9 in 1946
Biggest win France no win, New Zealand Army 14–9 in 1946

1946   Paris **New Zealand Army** 14–9

FRANCE v ARGENTINA

Played 42 France won 31, Argentina won 10, Drawn 1
Highest scores France 47–12 in 1995 & 47–26 in 1999, Argentina 34–10 in 2007
Biggest wins France 47–12 in 1995, Argentina 34–10 in 2007

1949	*1* Buenos Aires **France** 5–0			*2* Buenos Aires **Argentina** 18–6
	2 Buenos Aires **France** 12–3			Series drawn 1–1
	France won series 2–0		1988	*1* Nantes **France** 29–9
1954	*1* Buenos Aires **France** 22–8			*2* Lille **France** 28–18
	2 Buenos Aires **France** 30–3			France won series 2–0
	France won series 2–0		1992	*1* Buenos Aires **France** 27–12
1960	*1* Buenos Aires **France** 37–3			*2* Buenos Aires **France** 33–9
	2 Buenos Aires **France** 12–3			France won series 2–0
	3 Buenos Aires **France** 29–6		1992	Nantes **Argentina** 24–20
	France won series 3–0		1995	Buenos Aires LC **France** 47–12
1974	*1* Buenos Aires **France** 20–15		1996	*1* Buenos Aires **France** 34–27
	2 Buenos Aires **France** 31–27			*2* Buenos Aires **France** 34–15
	France won series 2–0			*France won series 2–0*
1975	*1* Lyons **France** 29–6		1997	Tarbes LC **France** 32–27
	2 Paris **France** 36–21		1998	*1* Buenos Aires **France** 35–18
	France won series 2–0			*2* Buenos Aires **France** 37–12
1977	*1* Buenos Aires **France** 26–3			*France won series 2–0*
	2 Buenos Aires **Drawn** 18–18		1998	Nantes **France** 34–14
	France won series 1–0, with 1 draw		1999	Dublin WC **France** 47–26
1982	*1* Toulouse **France** 25–12		2002	Buenos Aires **Argentina** 28–27
	2 Paris **France** 13–6		2003	*1* Buenos Aires **Argentina** 10–6
	France won series 2–0			*2* Buenos Aires **Argentina** 33–32
1985	*1* Buenos Aires **Argentina** 24–16			Argentina won series 2–0
	2 Buenos Aires **France** 23–15		2004	Marseilles **Argentina** 24–14
	Series drawn 1–1		2006	Paris **France** 27–26
1986	*1* Buenos Aires **Argentina** 15–13		2007	Paris WC **Argentina** 17–12
	2 Buenos Aires **France** 22–9		2007	Paris WC **Argentina** 34–10
	Series drawn 1–1		2008	Marseilles **France** 12–6
1988	*1* Buenos Aires **France** 18–15			

FRANCE v CZECHOSLOVAKIA

Played 2 France won 2
Highest scores France 28–3 in 1956, Czechoslovakia 6–19 in 1968
Biggest win France 28–3 in 1956, Czechoslovakia no win

1956	Toulouse **France** 28–3	1968	Prague **France** 19–6	

FRANCE v FIJI

Played 7 France won 7
Highest scores France 77–10 in 2001, Fiji 19–28 in 1999
Biggest win France 77–10 in 2001, Fiji no win

1964	Paris **France** 21–3	1999	Toulouse WC **France** 28–19
1987	Auckland WC **France** 31–16	2001	Saint Etienne **France** 77–10
1991	Grenoble WC **France** 33–9	2003	Brisbane WC **France** 61–18
1998	Suva **France** 34–9		

FRANCE v JAPAN

Played 2 France won 2
Highest scores France 51–29 in 2003, Japan 29–51 in 2003
Biggest win France 51–29 in 2003, Japan no win

1973	Bordeaux **France** 30–18	2003	Townsville WC **France** 51–29

FRANCE v ZIMBABWE

Played 1 France won 1
Highest scores France 70–12 in 1987, Zimbabwe 12–70 in 1987
Biggest win France 70–12 in 1987, Zimbabwe no win

1987	Auckland WC **France** 70–12

FRANCE v CANADA

Played 7 France won 6, Canada won 1, Drawn 0
Highest scores France 50–6 in 2005, Canada 20–33 in 1999
Biggest wins France 50–6 in 2005, Canada 18–16 in 1994

1991	Agen WC **France** 19–13	2002	Paris **France** 35–3
1994	Nepean **Canada** 18–16	2004	Toronto **France** 47–13
1994	Besançon **France** 28–9	2005	Nantes **France** 50–6
1999	Béziers WC **France** 33–20		

FRANCE v TONGA

Played 3 France won 2, Tonga won 1
Highest scores France 43–8 in 2005, Tonga 20–16 in 1999
Biggest win France 43–8 in 2005, Tonga 20–16 in 1999

1995	Pretoria WC **France** 38–10	2005	Toulouse **France** 43–8
1999	Nuku'alofa **Tonga** 20–16		

FRANCE v IVORY COAST

Played 1 France won 1
Highest scores France 54–18 in 1995, Ivory Coast 18–54 in 1995
Biggest win France 54–18 in 1995, Ivory Coast no win

1995	Rustenburg WC **France** 54–18

FRANCE v SAMOA

Played 1 France won 1
Highest scores France 39–22 in 1999, Samoa 22–39 in 1999
Biggest win France 39–22 in 1999, Samoa no win

1999	Apia **France** 39–22

Played 2 France won 2
Highest scores France 87–10 in 2007, Namibia 13–47 in 1999
Biggest win France 87–10 in 2007, Namibia no win

1999 Bordeaux WC **France** 47–13	2007 Toulouse WC **France** 87–10

FRANCE v GEORGIA

Played 1 France won 1
Highest scores France 64–7 in 2007, Georgia 7–64 in 2007
Biggest win France 64–7 in 2007, Georgia no win

2007 Marseilles WC **France** 64–7

FRANCE v PACIFIC ISLANDS

Played 1 Wales won 1
Highest scores France 42–17 in 2008, Pacific Islands 17–42 in 2008
Biggest win France 42–17 in 2008, Pacific Islands no win

2008 Sochaux **France** 42–17

SOUTH AFRICA v NEW ZEALAND

Played 78 New Zealand won 42, South Africa won 33, Drawn 3
Highest scores New Zealand 55–35 in 1997, South Africa 46–40 in 2000
Biggest wins New Zealand 52–16 in 2003, South Africa 17–0 in 1928

1921 *1* Dunedin **New Zealand** 13–5
2 Auckland **South Africa** 9–5
3 Wellington **Drawn** 0–0
Series drawn 1–1, with 1 draw
1928 *1* Durban **South Africa** 17–0
2 Johannesburg **New Zealand** 7–6
3 Port Elizabeth **South Africa** 11–6
4 Cape Town **New Zealand** 13–5
Series drawn 2–2
1937 *1* Wellington **New Zealand** 13–7
2 Christchurch **South Africa** 13–6
3 Auckland **South Africa** 17–6
South Africa won series 2–1
1949 *1* Cape Town **South Africa** 15–11
2 Johannesburg **South Africa** 12–6
3 Durban **South Africa** 9–3
4 Port Elizabeth **South Africa** 11–8
South Africa won series 4–0
1956 *1* Dunedin **New Zealand** 10–6

2 Wellington **South Africa** 8–3
3 Christchurch **New Zealand** 17–10
4 Auckland **New Zealand** 11–5
New Zealand won series 3–1
1960 *1* Johannesburg **South Africa** 13–0
2 Cape Town **New Zealand** 11–3
3 Bloemfontein **Drawn** 11–11
4 Port Elizabeth **South Africa** 8–3
South Africa won series 2–1, with 1 draw
1965 *1* Wellington **New Zealand** 6–3
2 Dunedin **New Zealand** 13–0
3 Christchurch **South Africa** 19–16
4 Auckland **New Zealand** 20–3
New Zealand won series 3–1
1970 *1* Pretoria **South Africa** 17–6
2 Cape Town **New Zealand** 9–8
3 Port Elizabeth **South Africa** 14–3
4 Johannesburg **South Africa** 20–17
South Africa won series 3–1

1976	*1* Durban **South Africa** 16–7
	2 Bloemfontein **New Zealand** 15–9
	3 Cape Town **South Africa** 15–10
	4 Johannesburg **South Africa** 15–14
	South Africa won series 3–1
1981	*1* Christchurch **New Zealand** 14–9
	2 Wellington **South Africa** 24–12
	3 Auckland **New Zealand** 25–22
	New Zealand won series 2–1
1992	Johannesburg **New Zealand** 27–24
1994	*1* Dunedin **New Zealand** 22–14
	2 Wellington **New Zealand** 13–9
	3 Auckland **Drawn** 18–18
	New Zealand won series 2–0, with 1 draw
1995	Johannesburg WC **South Africa** 15–12
	(aet)
1996	Christchurch TN **New Zealand** 15–11
1996	Cape Town TN **New Zealand** 29–18
1996	*1* Durban **New Zealand** 23–19
	2 Pretoria **New Zealand** 33–26
	3 Johannesburg **South Africa** 32–22
	New Zealand won series 2–1
1997	Johannesburg TN **New Zealand** 35–32
1997	Auckland TN **New Zealand** 55–35
1998	Wellington TN **South Africa** 13–3
1998	Durban TN **South Africa** 24–23
1999	Dunedin TN **New Zealand** 28–0

1999	Pretoria TN **New Zealand** 34–18
1999	Cardiff WC **South Africa** 22–18
2000	Christchurch TN **New Zealand** 25–12
2000	Johannesburg TN **South Africa** 46–40
2001	Cape Town TN **New Zealand** 12–3
2001	Auckland TN **New Zealand** 26–15
2002	Wellington TN **New Zealand** 41–20
2002	Durban TN **New Zealand** 30–23
2003	Pretoria TN **New Zealand** 52–16
2003	Dunedin TN **New Zealand** 19–11
2003	Melbourne WC **New Zealand** 29–9
2004	Christchurch TN **New Zealand** 23–21
2004	Johannesburg TN **South Africa** 40–26
2005	Cape Town TN **South Africa** 22–16
2005	Dunedin TN **New Zealand** 31–27
2006	Wellington TN **New Zealand** 35–17
2006	Pretoria TN **New Zealand** 45–26
2006	Rustenburg TN **South Africa** 21–20
2007	Durban TN **New Zealand** 26–21
2007	Christchurch TN **New Zealand** 33–6
2008	Wellington TN **New Zealand** 19–8
2008	Dunedin TN **South Africa** 30–28
2008	Cape Town TN **New Zealand** 19–0
2009	Bloemfontein TN **South Africa** 28–19
2009	Durban TN **South Africa** 31–19
2009	Hamilton TN **South Africa** 32–29

SOUTH AFRICA v AUSTRALIA

Played 68 South Africa won 40, Australia won 27, Drawn 1
Highest scores South Africa 61–22 in 1997, Australia 49–0 in 2006
Biggest wins South Africa 53–8 in 2008, Australia 49–0 in 2006

1933	*1* Cape Town **South Africa** 17–3
	2 Durban **Australia** 21–6
	3 Johannesburg **South Africa** 12–3
	4 Port Elizabeth **South Africa** 11–0
	5 Bloemfontein **Australia** 15–4
	South Africa won series 3–2
1937	*1* Sydney **South Africa** 9–5
	2 Sydney **South Africa** 26–17
	South Africa won series 2–0
1953	*1* Johannesburg **South Africa** 25–3
	2 Cape Town **Australia** 18–14
	3 Durban **South Africa** 18–8
	4 Port Elizabeth **South Africa** 22–9
	South Africa won series 3–1
1956	*1* Sydney **South Africa** 9–0
	2 Brisbane **South Africa** 9–0
	South Africa won series 2–0

1961	*1* Johannesburg **South Africa** 28–3
	2 Port Elizabeth **South Africa** 23–11
	South Africa won series 2–0
1963	*1* Pretoria **South Africa** 14–3
	2 Cape Town **Australia** 9–5
	3 Johannesburg **Australia** 11–9
	4 Port Elizabeth **South Africa** 22–6
	Series drawn 2–2
1965	*1* Sydney **Australia** 18–11
	2 Brisbane **Australia** 12–8
	Australia won series 2–0
1969	*1* Johannesburg **South Africa** 30–11
	2 Durban **South Africa** 16–9
	3 Cape Town **South Africa** 11–3
	4 Bloemfontein **South Africa** 19–8
	South Africa won series 4–0
1971	*1* Sydney **South Africa** 19–11

	2 Brisbane **South Africa** 14–6		2001	Perth TN **Drawn** 14–14	
	3 Sydney **South Africa** 18–6		2002	Brisbane TN **Australia** 38–27	
	South Africa won series 3–0		2002	Johannesburg TN **South Africa** 33–31	
1992	Cape Town **Australia** 26–3		2003	Cape Town TN **South Africa** 26–22	
1993	*1* Sydney **South Africa** 19–12		2003	Brisbane TN **Australia** 29–9	
	2 Brisbane **Australia** 28–20		2004	Perth TN **Australia** 30–26	
	3 Sydney **Australia** 19–12		2004	Durban TN **South Africa** 23–19	
	Australia won series 2–1		2005	Sydney **Australia** 30–12	
1995	Cape Town WC **South Africa** 27–18		2005	Johannesburg **South Africa** 33–20	
1996	Sydney TN **Australia** 21–16		2005	Pretoria TN **South Africa** 22–16	
1996	Bloemfontein TN **South Africa** 25–19		2005	Perth TN **South Africa** 22–19	
1997	Brisbane TN **Australia** 32–20		2006	Brisbane TN **Australia** 49–0	
1997	Pretoria TN **South Africa** 61–22		2006	Sydney TN **Australia** 20–18	
1998	Perth TN **South Africa** 14–13		2006	Johannesburg TN **South Africa** 24–16	
1998	Johannesburg TN **South Africa** 29–15		2007	Cape Town TN **South Africa** 22–19	
1999	Brisbane TN **Australia** 32–6		2007	Sydney TN **Australia** 25–17	
1999	Cape Town TN **South Africa** 10–9		2008	Perth TN **Australia** 16–9	
1999	Twickenham WC **Australia** 27–21		2008	Durban TN **Australia** 27–15	
2000	Melbourne **Australia** 44–23		2008	Johannesburg TN **South Africa** 53–8	
2000	Sydney TN **Australia** 26–6		2009	Cape Town TN **South Africa** 29–17	
2000	Durban TN **Australia** 19–18		2009	Perth TN **South Africa** 32–25	
2001	Pretoria TN **South Africa** 20–15		2009	Brisbane TN **Australia** 21–6	

SOUTH AFRICA v WORLD XVs

Played 3 South Africa won 3
Highest scores South Africa 45–24 in 1977, World XV 24–45 in 1977
Biggest win South Africa 45–24 in 1977, World XV no win

1977	Pretoria **South Africa** 45–24		*2* Johannesburg **South Africa** 22–16
1989	*1* Cape Town **South Africa** 20–19		South Africa won series 2–0

SOUTH AFRICA v SOUTH AMERICA

Played 8 South Africa won 7, South America won 1, Drawn 0
Highest scores South Africa 50–18 in 1982, South America 21–12 in 1982
Biggest wins South Africa 50–18 in 1982, South America 21–12 in 1982

1980	*1* Johannesburg **South Africa** 24–9		1982	*1* Pretoria **South Africa** 50–18
	2 Durban **South Africa** 18–9			*2* Bloemfontein **South America** 21–12
	South Africa won series 2–0			Series drawn 1–1
1980	*1* Montevideo **South Africa** 22–13		1984	*1* Pretoria **South Africa** 32–15
	2 Santiago **South Africa** 30–16			*2* Cape Town **South Africa** 22–13
	South Africa won series 2–0			South Africa won series 2–0

INTERNATIONAL RECORDS

SOUTH AFRICA v UNITED STATES

Played 3 South Africa won 3
Highest scores South Africa 64–10 in 2007, United States 20–43 in 2001
Biggest win South Africa 64–10 in 2007, United States no win

1981	Glenville **South Africa** 38–7	2007	Montpellier WC **South Africa** 64–10
2001	Houston **South Africa** 43–20		

SOUTH AFRICA v NEW ZEALAND CAVALIERS

Played 4 South Africa won 3, New Zealand Cavaliers won 1, Drawn 0
Highest scores South Africa 33–18 in 1986, New Zealand Cavaliers 19–18 in 1986
Biggest wins South Africa 33–18 in 1986, New Zealand Cavaliers 19–18 in 1986

1986	*1* Cape Town **South Africa** 21–15		*4* Johannesburg **South Africa** 24–10
	2 Durban **New Zealand Cavaliers** 19–18		South Africa won series 3–1
	3 Pretoria **South Africa** 33–18		

SOUTH AFRICA v ARGENTINA

Played 13 South Africa won 13
Highest scores South Africa 63–9 in 2008, Argentina 33–37 in 2000
Biggest wins South Africa 63–9 in 2008, Argentina no win

1993	*1* Buenos Aires **South Africa** 29–26		South Africa win series 2–0
	2 Buenos Aires **South Africa** 52–23	*2000*	Buenos Aires **South Africa** 37–33
	South Africa won series 2–0	2002	Springs **South Africa** 49–29
1994	*1* Port Elizabeth **South Africa** 42–22	2003	Port Elizabeth **South Africa** 26–25
	2 Johannesburg **South Africa** 46–26	2004	Buenos Aires **South Africa** 39–7
	South Africa won series 2–0	2005	Buenos Aires **South Africa** 34–23
1996	*1* Buenos Aires **South Africa** 46–15	2007	Paris WC **South Africa** 37–13
	2 Buenos Aires **South Africa** 44–21	2008	Johannesburg **South Africa** 63–9

SOUTH AFRICA v SAMOA

Played 6 South Africa won 6
Highest scores South Africa 60–8 in 1995, 60–18 in 2002 and 60–10 in 2003, Samoa 18–60 in 2002
Biggest win South Africa 60–8 in 1995 and 59–7 in 2007, Samoa no win

1995	Johannesburg **South Africa** 60–8	2003	Brisbane WC **South Africa** 60–10
1995	Johannesburg WC **South Africa** 42–14	2007	Johannesburg **South Africa** 35–8
2002	Pretoria **South Africa** 60–18	2007	Paris WC **South Africa** 59–7

SOUTH AFRICA v ROMANIA

Played 1 South Africa won 1
Highest score South Africa 21–8 in 1995, Romania 8–21 in 1995
Biggest win South Africa 21–8 in 1995, Romania no win

1995	Cape Town WC **South Africa** 21–8

SOUTH AFRICA v CANADA

Played 2 South Africa won 2
Highest scores South Africa 51–18 in 2000, Canada 18–51 in 2000
Biggest win South Africa 51–18 in 2000, Canada no win

1995	Port Elizabeth WC **South Africa** 20–0	2000	East London **South Africa** 51–18

SOUTH AFRICA v ITALY

Played 7 South Africa won 7
Highest scores South Africa 101–0 in 1999, Italy 31–62 in 1997
Biggest win South Africa 101–0 in 1999, Italy no win

1995	Rome **South Africa** 40–21		South Africa won series 2–0
1997	Bologna **South Africa** 62–31	2001	Port Elizabeth **South Africa** 60–14
1999	*1* Port Elizabeth **South Africa** 74–3	2001	Genoa **South Africa** 54–26
	2 Durban **South Africa** 101–0	2008	Cape Town **South Africa** 26–0

SOUTH AFRICA v FIJI

Played 2 South Africa won 2
Highest scores South Africa 43–18 in 1996, Fiji 20–37 in 2007
Biggest win South Africa 43–18 in 1996, Fiji no win

1996 Pretoria **South Africa** 43–18	2007 Marseilles WC **South Africa** 37–20

SOUTH AFRICA v TONGA

Played 2 South Africa won 2
Higest scores South Africa 74–10 in 1997, Tonga 25–30 in 2007
Biggest win South Africa 74–10 in 1997, Tonga no win

1997 Cape Town **South Africa** 74–10	2007 Lens WC **South Africa** 30–25

SOUTH AFRICA v SPAIN

Played 1 South Africa won 1
Highest scores South Africa 47–3 in 1999, Spain 3–47 in 1999
Biggest win South Africa 47–3 in 1999, Spain no win

1999 Murrayfield WC **South Africa** 47–3

SOUTH AFRICA v URUGUAY

Played 3 South Africa won 3
Highest scores South Africa 134–3 in 2005, Uruguay 6–72 in 2003
Biggest win South Africa 134–3 in 2005, Uruguay no win

1999 Glasgow WC **South Africa** 39–3	2005 East London **South Africa** 134–3
2003 Perth WC **South Africa** 72–6	

Played 1 South Africa won 1
Highest scores South Africa 46–19 in 2003, Georgia 19–46 in 2003
Biggest win South Africa 46–19 in 2003, Georgia no win

2003	Sydney WC **South Africa** 46–19	

SOUTH AFRICA v PACIFIC ISLANDS

Played 1 South Africa won 1
Highest scores South Africa 38–24 in 2004, Pacific Islands 24–38 in 2004
Biggest win South Africa 38–24 in 2004, Pacific Islands no win

2004	Gosford (Aus) **South Africa** 38–24	

SOUTH AFRICA v NAMIBIA

Played 1 South Africa won 1
Highest scores South Africa 105–13 in 2007, Namibia 13–105 in 2007
Biggest win South Africa 105–13 in 2007, Namibia no win

2007	Cape Town **South Africa** 105–13	

NEW ZEALAND v AUSTRALIA

Played 135 New Zealand won 91, Australia won 39, Drawn 5
Highest scores New Zealand 50–21 in 2003, Australia 35–39 in 2000
Biggest wins New Zealand 43–6 in 1996, Australia 28–7 in 1999

1903	Sydney **New Zealand** 22–3			New Zealand won series 2–1
1905	Dunedin **New Zealand** 14–3	1913	*1* Wellington **New Zealand** 30–5
1907	*1* Sydney **New Zealand** 26–6		*2* Dunedin **New Zealand** 25–13
	2 Brisbane **New Zealand** 14–5		*3* Christchurch **Australia** 16–5
	3 Sydney **Drawn** 5–5		New Zealand won series 2–1
	New Zealand won series 2–0, with 1 draw	1914	*1* Sydney **New Zealand** 5–0
1910	*1* Sydney **New Zealand** 6–0		*2* Brisbane **New Zealand** 17–0
	2 Sydney **Australia** 11–0		*3* Sydney **New Zealand** 22–7
	3 Sydney **New Zealand** 28–13		New Zealand won series 3–0

1929	*1* Sydney **Australia** 9–8	
	2 Brisbane **Australia** 17–9	
	3 Sydney **Australia** 15–13	
	Australia won series 3–0	
1931	Auckland **New Zealand** 20–13	
1932	*1* Sydney **Australia** 22–17	
	2 Brisbane **New Zealand** 21–3	
	3 Sydney **New Zealand** 21–13	
	New Zealand won series 2–1	
1934	*1* Sydney **Australia** 25–11	
	2 Sydney **Drawn** 3–3	
	Australia won series 1–0, with 1 draw	
1936	*1* Wellington **New Zealand** 11–6	
	2 Dunedin **New Zealand** 38–13	
	New Zealand won series 2–0	
1938	*1* Sydney **New Zealand** 24–9	
	2 Brisbane **New Zealand** 20–14	
	3 Sydney **New Zealand** 14–6	
	New Zealand won series 3–0	
1946	*1* Dunedin **New Zealand** 31–8	
	2 Auckland **New Zealand** 14–10	
	New Zealand won series 2–0	
1947	*1* Brisbane **New Zealand** 13–5	
	2 Sydney **New Zealand** 27–14	
	New Zealand won series 2–0	
1949	*1* Wellington **Australia** 11–6	
	2 Auckland **Australia** 16–9	
	Australia won series 2–0	
1951	*1* Sydney **New Zealand** 8–0	
	2 Sydney **New Zealand** 17–11	
	3 Brisbane **New Zealand** 16–6	
	New Zealand won series 3–0	
1952	*1* Christchurch **Australia** 14–9	
	2 Wellington **New Zealand** 15–8	
	Series drawn 1–1	
1955	*1* Wellington **New Zealand** 16–8	
	2 Dunedin **New Zealand** 8–0	
	3 Auckland **Australia** 8–3	
	New Zealand won series 2–1	
1957	*1* Sydney **New Zealand** 25–11	
	2 Brisbane **New Zealand** 22–9	
	New Zealand won series 2–0	
1958	*1* Wellington **New Zealand** 25–3	
	2 Christchurch **Australia** 6–3	
	3 Auckland **New Zealand** 17–8	
	New Zealand won series 2–1	
1962	*1* Brisbane **New Zealand** 20–6	
	2 Sydney **New Zealand** 14–5	
	New Zealand won series 2–0	

1962	*1* Wellington **Drawn** 9–9	
	2 Dunedin **New Zealand** 3–0	
	3 Auckland **New Zealand** 16–8	
	New Zealand won series 2–0, with 1 draw	
1964	*1* Dunedin **New Zealand** 14–9	
	2 Christchurch **New Zealand** 18–3	
	3 Wellington **Australia** 20–5	
	New Zealand won series 2–1	
1967	Wellington **New Zealand** 29–9	
1968	*1* Sydney **New Zealand** 27–11	
	2 Brisbane **New Zealand** 19–18	
	New Zealand won series 2–0	
1972	*1* Wellington **New Zealand** 29–6	
	2 Christchurch **New Zealand** 30–17	
	3 Auckland **New Zealand** 38–3	
	New Zealand won series 3–0	
1974	*1* Sydney **New Zealand** 11–6	
	2 Brisbane **Drawn** 16–16	
	3 Sydney **New Zealand** 16–6	
	New Zealand won series 2–0, with 1 draw	
1978	*1* Wellington **New Zealand** 13–12	
	2 Christchurch **New Zealand** 22–6	
	3 Auckland **Australia** 30–16	
	New Zealand won series 2–1	
1979	Sydney **Australia** 12–6	
1980	*1* Sydney **Australia** 13–9	
	2 Brisbane **New Zealand** 12–9	
	3 Sydney **Australia** 26–10	
	Australia won series 2–1	
1982	*1* Christchurch **New Zealand** 23–16	
	2 Wellington **Australia** 19–16	
	3 Auckland **New Zealand** 33–18	
	New Zealand won series 2–1	
1983	Sydney **New Zealand** 18–8	
1984	*1* Sydney **Australia** 16–9	
	2 Brisbane **New Zealand** 19–15	
	3 Sydney **New Zealand** 25–24	
	New Zealand won series 2–1	
1985	Auckland **New Zealand** 10–9	
1986	*1* Wellington **Australia** 13–12	
	2 Dunedin **New Zealand** 13–12	
	3 Auckland **Australia** 22–9	
	Australia won series 2–1	
1987	Sydney **New Zealand** 30–16	
1988	*1* Sydney **New Zealand** 32–7	
	2 Brisbane **Drawn** 19–19	
	3 Sydney **New Zealand** 30–9	
	New Zealand won series 2–0, with 1 draw	
1989	Auckland **New Zealand** 24–12	

1990 *1* Christchurch **New Zealand** 21–6
     2 Auckland **New Zealand** 27–17
     3 Wellington **Australia** 21–9
     New Zealand won series 2–1
1991 *1* Sydney **Australia** 21–12
     2 Auckland **New Zealand** 6–3
1991 Dublin WC **Australia** 16–6
1992 *1* Sydney **Australia** 16–15
     2 Brisbane **Australia** 19–17
     3 Sydney **New Zealand** 26–23
     Australia won series 2–1
1993 Dunedin **New Zealand** 25–10
1994 Sydney **Australia** 20–16
1995 Auckland **New Zealand** 28–16
1995 Sydney **New Zealand** 34–23
1996 Wellington TN **New Zealand** 43–6
1996 Brisbane TN **New Zealand** 32–25
     New Zealand won series 2–0
1997 Christchurch **New Zealand** 30–13
1997 Melbourne TN **New Zealand** 33–18
1997 Dunedin TN **New Zealand** 36–24
     New Zealand won series 3–0
1998 Melbourne TN **Australia** 24–16
1998 Christchurch TN **Australia** 27–23
1998 Sydney Australia 19–14
     Australia won series 3–0
1999 Auckland TN **New Zealand** 34–15
1999 Sydney TN **Australia** 28–7
     Series drawn 1–1
2000 Sydney TN **New Zealand** 39–35
2000 Wellington TN **Australia** 24–23
     Series drawn 1–1
2001 Dunedin TN **Australia** 23–15

2001 Sydney TN **Australia** 29–26
     Australia won series 2–0
2002 Christchurch TN **New Zealand** 12–6
2002 Sydney TN **Australia** 16–14
     Series drawn 1–1
2003 Sydney TN **New Zealand** 50–21
2003 Auckland TN **New Zealand** 21–17
     New Zealand won series 2–0
2003 Sydney WC **Australia** 22–10
2004 Wellington TN **New Zealand** 16–7
2004 Sydney TN **Australia** 23–18
     Series drawn 1–1
2005 Sydney TN **New Zealand** 30–13
2005 Auckland TN **New Zealand** 34–24
     New Zealand won series 2–0
2006 Christchurch TN **New Zealand** 32–12
2006 Brisbane TN **New Zealand** 13–9
2006 Auckland TN **New Zealand** 34–27
     New Zealand won series 3–0
2007 Melbourne TN **Australia** 20–15
2007 Auckland TN **New Zealand** 26–12
     Series drawn 1–1
2008 Sydney TN **Australia** 34–19
2008 Auckland TN **New Zealand** 39–10
2008 Brisbane TN **New Zealand** 28–24
2008 Hong Kong **New Zealand** 19–14
     New Zealand won series 3–1
2009 Auckland TN **New Zealand** 22–16
2009 Sydney TN **New Zealand** 19–18
2009 Wellington TN **New Zealand** 33–6
     Final match of 2009 series to be played
     on October 31 in Tokyo

NEW ZEALAND v UNITED STATES

Played 2 New Zealand won 2
Highest scores New Zealand 51–3 in 1913, United States 6–46 in 1991
Biggest win New Zealand 51–3 in 1913, United States no win

1913 Berkeley **New Zealand** 51–3

1991 Gloucester WC **New Zealand** 46–6

NEW ZEALAND v ROMANIA

Played 2 New Zealand won 2
Highest score New Zealand 85–8 in 2007, Romania 8–85 in 2007
Biggest win New Zealand 85–8 in 2007, Romania no win

1981 Bucharest **New Zealand** 14–6	2007 Toulouse WC **New Zealand** 85–8

NEW ZEALAND v ARGENTINA

Played 13 New Zealand won 12, Drawn 1
Highest scores New Zealand 93–8 in 1997, Argentina 21–21 in 1985
Biggest win New Zealand 93–8 in 1997, Argentina no win

1985 *1* Buenos Aires **New Zealand** 33–20	New Zealand won series 2–0
2 Buenos Aires **Drawn** 21–21	1997 *1* Wellington **New Zealand** 93–8
New Zealand won series 1–0, with 1 draw	*2* Hamilton **New Zealand** 62–10
1987 Wellington *WC* **New Zealand** 46–15	New Zealand won series 2–0
1989 *1* Dunedin **New Zealand** 60–9	2001 Christchurch **New Zealand** 67–19
2 Wellington **New Zealand** 49–12	2001 Buenos Aires **New Zealand** 24–20
New Zealand won series 2–0	2004 Hamilton **New Zealand** 41–7
1991 *1* Buenos Aires **New Zealand** 28–14	2006 Buenos Aires **New Zealand** 25–19
2 Buenos Aires **New Zealand** 36–6	

NEW ZEALAND v ITALY

Played 10 New Zealand won 10
Highest scores New Zealand 101–3 in 1999, Italy 21–31 in 1991
Biggest win New Zealand 101–3 in 1999, Italy no win

1987 Auckland WC **New Zealand** 70–6	2002 Hamilton **New Zealand** 64–10
1991 Leicester WC **New Zealand** 31–21	2003 Melbourne WC **New Zealand** 70–7
1995 Bologna **New Zealand** 70–6	2004 Rome **New Zealand** 59–10
1999 Huddersfield WC **New Zealand** 101–3	2007 Marseilles WC **New Zealand** 76–14
2000 Genoa **New Zealand** 56–19	2009 Christchurch **New Zealand** 27–6

NEW ZEALAND v FIJI

145

Played 4 New Zealand won 4
Highest scores New Zealand 91–0 in 2005, Fiji 18–68 in 2002
Biggest win New Zealand 91–0 in 2005, Fiji no win

1987	Christchurch WC **New Zealand** 74–13	2002	Wellington **New Zealand** 68–18
1997	Albany **New Zealand** 71–5	2005	Albany **New Zealand** 91–0

NEW ZEALAND v CANADA

Played 4 New Zealand won 4
Highest scores New Zealand 73–7 in 1995, Canada 13–29 in 1991 & 13–64 in 2007
Biggest win New Zealand 73–7 in 1995, Canada no win

1991	Lille WC **New Zealand** 29–13	2003	Melbourne WC **New Zealand** 68–6
1995	Auckland **New Zealand** 73–7	2007	Hamilton **New Zealand** 64–13

NEW ZEALAND v WORLD XVs

Played 3 New Zealand won 2, World XV won 1, Drawn 0
Highest scores New Zealand 54–26 in 1992, World XV 28–14 in 1992
Biggest wins New Zealand 54–26 in 1992, World XV 28–14 in 1992

1992	*1* Christchurch **World XV** 28–14		*3* Auckland **New Zealand** 26–15
	2 Wellington **New Zealand** 54–26		New Zealand won series 2–1

NEW ZEALAND v SAMOA

Played 5 New Zealand won 5
Highest scores New Zealand 101–14 in 2008, Samoa 14–101 in 2008
Biggest win New Zealand 101–14 in 2008, Samoa no win

1993	Auckland **New Zealand** 35–13	2001	Albany **New Zealand** 50–6
1996	Napier **New Zealand** 51–10	2008	New Plymouth **New Zealand** 101–14
1999	Albany **New Zealand** 71–13		

NEW ZEALAND v JAPAN

Played 1 New Zealand won 1
Highest scores New Zealand 145–17 in 1995, Japan 17–145 in 1995
Biggest win New Zealand 145–17 in 1995, Japan no win

1995	Bloemfontein WC **New Zealand** 145–17

NEW ZEALAND v TONGA

Played 3 New Zealand won 3
Highest scores New Zealand 102–0 in 2000, Tonga 9–45 in 1999
Biggest win New Zealand 102–0 in 2000, Tonga no win

1999	Bristol WC **New Zealand** 45–9	2003	Brisbane WC **New Zealand** 91–7
2000	Albany **New Zealand** 102–0		

NEW ZEALAND v PACIFIC ISLANDS

Played 1 New Zealand won 1
Highest scores New Zealand 41–26 in 2004, Pacific Islands 26–41 in 2004
Biggest win New Zealand 41–26 in 2004, Pacific Islands no win

2004	Albany **New Zealand 41–26**

NEW ZEALAND v PORTUGAL

Played 1 New Zealand won 1
Highest scores New Zealand 108–13 in 2007, Portugal 13–108 in 2007
Biggest win New Zealand 108–13 in 2007, Portugal no win

2007	Lyons WC **New Zealand** 108–13

Played 6 Australia won 6
Highest scores Australia 67–9 in 1990, United States 19–55 in 1999
Biggest win Australia 67–9 in 1990, United States no win

1912	Berkeley **Australia** 12–8	1987	Brisbane WC **Australia** 47–12
1976	Los Angeles **Australia** 24–12	1990	Brisbane **Australia** 67–9
1983	Sydney **Australia** 49–3	1999	Limerick WC **Australia** 55–19

AUSTRALIA v NEW ZEALAND XVs

Played 24 Australia won 6, New Zealand XVs won 18, Drawn 0
Highest scores Australia 26–20 in 1926, New Zealand XV 38–11 in 1923 and 38–8 in 1924
Biggest win Australia 17–0 in 1921, New Zealand XV 38–8 in 1924

1920	*1* Sydney **New Zealand XV** 26–15		New Zealand XV won series 2–1
	2 Sydney **New Zealand XV** 14–6	1925	*1* Sydney **New Zealand XV** 26–3
	3 Sydney **New Zealand XV** 24–13		*2* Sydney **New Zealand XV** 4–0
	New Zealand XV won series 3–0		*3* Sydney **New Zealand XV** 11–3
1921	Christchurch **Australia** 17–0		New Zealand XV won series 3–0
1922	*1* Sydney **New Zealand XV** 26–19	1925	Auckland **New Zealand XV** 36–10
	2 Sydney **Australia** 14–8	1926	*1* Sydney **Australia** 26–20
	3 Sydney **Australia** 8–6		*2* Sydney **New Zealand XV** 11–6
	Australia won series 2–1		*3* Sydney **New Zealand XV** 14–0
1923	*1* Dunedin **New Zealand XV** 19–9		*4* Sydney **New Zealand XV** 28–21
	2 Christchurch **New Zealand XV** 34–6		New Zealand XV won series 3–1
	3 Wellington **New Zealand XV** 38–11	1928	*1* Wellington **New Zealand XV** 15–12
	New Zealand XV won series 3–0		*2* Dunedin **New Zealand XV** 16–14
1924	*1* Sydney **Australia** 20–16		*3* Christchurch **Australia** 11–8
	2 Sydney **New Zealand XV** 21–5		New Zealand XV won series 2–1
	3 Sydney **New Zealand XV** 38–8		

AUSTRALIA v SOUTH AFRICA XVs

Played 3 South Africa XVs won 3
Highest scores Australia 11–16 in 1921, South Africa XV 28–9 in 1921
Biggest win Australia no win, South Africa XV 28–9 in 1921

1921	*1* Sydney **South Africa XV** 25–10		*3* Sydney **South Africa XV** 28–9
	2 Sydney **South Africa XV** 16–11		South Africa XV won series 3–0

INTERNATIONAL RECORDS

AUSTRALIA v NEW ZEALAND MAORIS

Played 16 Australia won 8, New Zealand Maoris won 6, Drawn 2
Highest scores Australia 31–6 in 1936, New Zealand Maoris 25–22 in 1922
Biggest wins Australia 31–6 in 1936, New Zealand Maoris 20–0 in 1946

INTERNATIONAL RECORDS

1922	*1* Sydney **New Zealand Maoris** 25–22	1936	Palmerston North **Australia** 31–6
	2 Sydney **Australia** 28–13	1946	Hamilton **New Zealand Maoris** 20–0
	3 Sydney **New Zealand Maoris** 23–22	1949	*1* Sydney **New Zealand Maoris** 12–3
	New Zealand Maoris won series 2–1		*2* Brisbane **Drawn** 8–8
1923	*1* Sydney **Australia** 27–23		*3* Sydney **Australia** 18–3
	2 Sydney **Australia** 21–16		Series drawn 1–1, with 1 draw
	3 Sydney **Australia** 14–12	1958	*1* Brisbane **Australia** 15–14
	Australia won series 3–0		*2* Sydney **Drawn** 3–3
1928	Wellington **New Zealand Maoris** 9–8		*3* Melbourne **New Zealand Maoris** 13–6
1931	Palmerston North **Australia** 14–3		Series drawn 1–1, with 1 draw

AUSTRALIA v FIJI

Played 18 Australia won 15, Fiji won 2, Drawn 1
Highest scores Australia 66–20 in 1998, Fiji 28–52 in 1985
Biggest wins Australia 49–0 in 2007, Fiji 17–15 in 1952 & 18–16 in 1954

1952	*1* Sydney **Australia** 15–9		*2* Brisbane **Australia** 21–9
	2 Sydney **Fiji** 17–15		*3* Sydney **Australia** 27–17
	Series drawn 1–1		Australia won series 3–0
1954	*1* Brisbane **Australia** 22–19	1980	Suva **Australia** 22–9
	2 Sydney **Fiji** 18–16	1984	Suva **Australia** 16–3
	Series drawn 1–1	1985	*1* Brisbane **Australia** 52–28
1961	*1* Brisbane **Australia** 24–6		*2* Sydney **Australia** 31–9
	2 Sydney **Australia** 20–14		Australia won series 2–0
	3 Melbourne **Drawn** 3–3	1998	Sydney **Australia** 66–20
	Australia won series 2–0, with 1 draw	2007	Perth **Australia** 49–0
1972	Suva **Australia** 21–19	2007	Montpellier WC **Australia** 55–12
1976	*1* Sydney **Australia** 22–6		

AUSTRALIA v TONGA

Played 4 Australia won 3, Tonga won 1, Drawn 0
Highest scores Australia 74–0 in 1998, Tonga 16–11 in 1973
Biggest wins Australia 74–0 in 1998, Tonga 16–11 in 1973

1973	*1* Sydney **Australia** 30–12	1993	Brisbane **Australia** 52–14
	2 Brisbane **Tonga** 16–11	1998	Canberra **Australia** 74–0
	Series drawn 1–1		

AUSTRALIA v JAPAN

Played 4 Australia won 4
Highest scores Australia 91–3 in 2007, Japan 25–50 in 1973
Biggest win Australia 91–3 in 2007, Japan no win

1975	*1* Sydney **Australia** 37–7	1987	Sydney WC **Australia** 42–23
	2 Brisbane **Australia** 50–25	2007	Lyons WC **Australia** 91–3
	Australia won series 2–0		

AUSTRALIA v ARGENTINA

Played 17 Australia won 12, Argentina won 4, Drawn 1
Highest scores Australia 53–7 in 1995 & 53–6 in 2000, Argentina 27–19 in 1987
Biggest wins Australia 53–6 in 2000, Argentina 18–3 in 1983

1979	*1* Buenos Aires **Argentina** 24–13	1991	Llanelli WC **Australia** 32–19
	2 Buenos Aires **Australia** 17–12	1995	*1* Brisbane **Australia** 53–7
	Series drawn 1–1		*2* Sydney **Australia** 30–13
1983	*1* Brisbane **Argentina** 18–3		Australia won series 2–0
	2 Sydney **Australia** 29–13	1997	*1* Buenos Aires **Australia** 23–15
	Series drawn 1–1		*2* Buenos Aires **Argentina** 18–16
1986	*1* Brisbane **Australia** 39–19		Series drawn 1–1
	2 Sydney **Australia** 26–0	2000	*1* Brisbane **Australia** 53–6
	Australia won series 2–0		*2* Canberra **Australia** 32–25
1987	*1* Buenos Aires **Drawn** 19–19		Australia won series 2–0
	2 Buenos Aires **Argentina** 27–19	2002	Buenos Aires **Australia** 17–6
	Argentina won series 1–0, with 1 draw	2003	Sydney WC **Australia** 24–8

AUSTRALIA v SAMOA

Played 4 Australia won 4
Highest scores Australia 74–7 in 2005, Samoa 13–25 in 1998
Biggest win Australia 73–3 in 1994, Samoa no win

1991	Pontypool WC **Australia** 9–3	1998	Brisbane **Australia** 25–13
1994	Sydney **Australia** 73–3	2005	Sydney **Australia** 74–7

AUSTRALIA v ITALY

Played 12 Australia won 12
Highest scores Australia 69–21 in 2005, Italy 21–69 in 2005
Biggest win Australia 55–6 in 1988, Italy no win

1983	Rovigo **Australia** 29–7	2002	Genoa **Australia** 34–3
1986	Brisbane **Australia** 39–18	2005	Melbourne **Australia** 69–21
1988	Rome **Australia** 55–6	2006	Rome **Australia** 25–18
1994	1 Brisbane **Australia** 23–20	2008	Padua **Australia** 30–20
	2 Melbourne **Australia** 20–7	2009	1 Canberra **Australia** 31–8
	Australia won series 2–0		2 Melbourne **Australia** 34–12
1996	Padua **Australia** 40–18		Australia won series 2–0

AUSTRALIA v CANADA

Played 6 Australia won 6
Highest scores Australia 74–9 in 1996, Canada 16–43 in 1993
Biggest win Australia 74–9 in 1996, Canada no win

1985	1 Sydney **Australia** 59–3	1995	Port Elizabeth WC **Australia** 27–11
	2 Brisbane **Australia** 43–15	1996	Brisbane **Australia** 74–9
	Australia won series 2–0	2007	Bordeaux WC **Australia** 37–6
1993	Calgary **Australia** 43–16		

AUSTRALIA v KOREA

Played 1 Australia won 1
Highest scores Australia 65–18 in 1987, Korea 18–65 in 1987
Biggest win Australia 65–18 in 1987, Korea no win

1987	Brisbane **Australia** 65–18

AUSTRALIA v ROMANIA

Played 3 Australia won 3
Highest scores Australia 90–8 in 2003, Romania 9–57 in 1999
Biggest win Australia 90–8 in 2003, Romania no win

1995	Stellenbosch WC **Australia** 42–3	2003	Brisbane WC **Australia** 90–8
1999	Belfast WC **Australia** 57–9		

AUSTRALIA v SPAIN

Played 1 Australia won 1
Highest scores Australia 92–10 in 2001, Spain 10–92 in 2001
Biggest win Australia 92–10 in 2001, Spain no win

2001	Madrid **Australia** 92–10

AUSTRALIA v NAMIBIA

Played 1 Australia won 1
Highest scores Australia 142–0 in 2003, Namibia 0–142 in 2003
Biggest win Australia 142–0 in 2003, Namibia no win

2003	Adelaide WC **Australia** 142–0

AUSTRALIA v PACIFIC ISLANDS

Played 1 Australia won 1
Highest scores Australia 29–14 in 2004, Pacific Islands 14–29 in 2004
Biggest win Australia 29–14 in 2004, Pacific Islands no win

2004	Adelaide **Australia** 29–14

August 20 - September 5, 2010
Women's Rugby World Cup 2010, England

England 2010

for further information **www.rwcwomens.com**

INTERNATIONAL WORLD RECORDS

The match and career records cover **official Test matches** *played by the dozen Executive Council Member Unions of the International Board (England, Scotland, Ireland, Wales, France, Italy, South Africa, New Zealand, Australia, Argentina, Canada and Japan) from 1871 up to 30 September 2009. Figures include Test performances for the (British/Irish Isles) Lions and (South American) Jaguars (shown in brackets). Where a world record has been set in a Test match played by another nation in membership of the IRB, this is shown as a footnote to the relevant table.*

MATCH RECORDS

MOST CONSECUTIVE TEST WINS

17 by N Zealand	1965 *SA* 4, 1966 *BI* 1,2,3,4, 1967 *A, E, W, F, S,* 1968 *A* 1,2, *F* 1,2,3, 1969 *W* 1,2
17 by S Africa	1997 *A* 2, *It, F* 1,2, *E, S,* 1998 *I* 1,2, *W* 1, *E* 1, *A* 1, *NZ* 1,2, *A* 2, *W* 2, *S, I* 3

MOST CONSECUTIVE TESTS WITHOUT DEFEAT

Matches	Wins	Draws	Period
23 by N Zealand	22	1	1987 to 1990
17 by N Zealand	15	2	1961 to 1964
17 by N Zealand	17	0	1965 to 1969
17 by S Africa	17	0	1997 to 1998

MOST POINTS IN A MATCH

BY THE TEAM

Pts.	Opponents	Venue	Year
155 by Japan	Chinese Taipei	Tokyo	2002
152 by Argentina	Paraguay	Mendoza	2002
147 by Argentina	Venezuela	Santiago	2004
145 by N Zealand	Japan	Bloemfontein	1995
144 by Argentina	Paraguay	Montevideo	2003
142 by Australia	Namibia	Adelaide	2003
134 by Japan	Chinese Taipei	Singapore	1998
134 by England	Romania	Twickenham	2001
134 by S Africa	Uruguay	East London	2005
120 by Japan	Chinese Taipei	Tainan	2002

Hong Kong scored 164 points against Singapore at Kuala Lumpur in 1994

BY A PLAYER

Pts.	Player	Opponents	Venue	Year
60 for Japan	T Kurihara	Chinese Taipei	Tainan	2002
50 for Argentina	E Morgan	Paraguay	San Pablo	1973
45 for N Zealand	S D Culhane	Japan	Bloemfontein	1995
45 for Argentina	J–M Nuñez-Piossek	Paraguay	Montevideo	2003
44 for Scotland	A G Hastings	Ivory Coast	Rustenburg	1995
44 for England	C Hodgson	Romania	Twickenham	2001
42 for Australia	M S Rogers	Namibia	Adelaide	2003
40 for Argentina	G M Jorge	Brazil	Sao Paulo	1993
40 for Japan	D Ohata	Chinese Taipei	Tokyo	2002
40 for Scotland	C D Paterson	Japan	Perth	2004
39 for Australia	M C Burke	Canada	Brisbane	1996

MOST TRIES IN A MATCH
BY THE TEAM

Tries	Opponents	Venue	Year
24 by Argentina	Paraguay	Mendoza	2002
24 by Argentina	Paraguay	Montevideo	2003
23 by Japan	Chinese Taipei	Tokyo	2002
23 by Argentina	Venezuela	Santiago	2004
22 by Australia	Namibia	Adelaide	2003
21 by N Zealand	Japan	Bloemfontein	1995
21 by S Africa	Uruguay	East London	2005
20 by Argentina	Brazil	Montevideo	1989
20 by Japan	Chinese Taipei	Singapore	1998
20 by England	Romania	Twickenham	2001
19 by Argentina	Brazil	Santiago	1979
19 by Argentina	Paraguay	Asuncion	1985

Hong Kong scored 26 tries against Singapore at Kuala Lumpur in 1994

BY A PLAYER

Tries	Player	Opponents	Venue	Year
11 for Argentina	U O'Farrell	Brazil	Buenos Aires	1951
9 for Argentina	J–M Nuñez–Piossek	Paraguay	Montevideo	2003
8 for Argentina	G M Jorge	Brazil	Sao Paulo	1993
8 for Japan	D Ohata	Chinese Taipei	Tokyo	2002
6 for Argentina	E Morgan	Paraguay	San Pablo	1973
6 for Argentina	G M Jorge	Brazil	Montevideo	1989
6 for N Zealand	M C G Ellis	Japan	Bloemfontein	1995
6 for Japan	T Kurihara	Chinese Taipei	Tainan	2002
6 for S Africa	T Chavhanga	Uruguay	East London	2005
6 for Japan	D Ohata	Hong Kong	Tokyo	2005
5 for Scotland	G C Lindsay	Wales	Raeburn Place	1887
5 for England	D Lambert	France	Richmond	1907
5 for Argentina	H Goti	Brazil	Montevideo	1961
5 for Argentina	M R Jurado	Brazil	Montevideo	1971
5 for England	R Underwood	Fiji	Twickenham	1989
5 for N Zealand	J W Wilson	Fiji	Albany	1997
5 for Japan	T Masuho	Chinese Taipei	Singapore	1998
5 for Argentina	P Grande	Paraguay	Asuncion	1998
5 for S Africa	C S Terblanche	Italy	Durban	1999
5 for England	O J Lewsey	Uruguay	Brisbane	2003
5 for Australia	C E Latham	Namibia	Adelaide	2003
5 for Argentina	F Higgs	Venezuela	Santiago	2004

MOST CONVERSIONS IN A MATCH
BY THE TEAM

Cons	Opponents	Venue	Year
20 by N Zealand	Japan	Bloemfontein	1995
20 by Japan	Chinese Taipei	Tokyo	2002
17 by Japan	Chinese Taipei	Singapore	1998
16 by Argentina	Paraguay	Mendoza	2002
16 by Australia	Namibia	Adelaide	2003
16 by Argentina	Venezuela	Santiago	2004
15 by Argentina	Brazil	Santiago	1979
15 by England	Netherlands	Huddersfield	1998
15 by Japan	Chinese Taipei	Tainan	2002

BY A PLAYER

Cons	Player	Opponents	Venue	Year
20 for N Zealand	S D Culhane	Japan	Bloemfontein	1995
16 for Argentina	J–L Cilley	Paraguay	Mendoza	2002
16 for Australia	M S Rogers	Namibia	Adelaide	2003
15 for England	P J Grayson	Netherlands	Huddersfield	1998
15 for Japan	T Kurihara	Chinese Taipei	Tainan	2002

MOST PENALTIES IN A MATCH
BY THE TEAM

Penalties	Opponents	Venue	Year
9 by Japan	Tonga	Tokyo	1999
9 by N Zealand	Australia	Auckland	1999
9 by Wales	France	Cardiff	1999
9 by N Zealand	France	Paris	2000

Portugal scored nine penalties against Georgia at Lisbon in 2000

BY A PLAYER

Penalties	Player	Opponents	Venue	Year
9 for Japan	K Hirose	Tonga	Tokyo	1999
9 for N Zealand	A P Mehrtens	Australia	Auckland	1999
9 for Wales	N R Jenkins	France	Cardiff	1999
9 for N Zealand	A P Mehrtens	France	Paris	2000

Nine penalties were scored for Portugal by T Teixeira against Georgia at Lisbon in 2000

MOST DROPPED GOALS IN A MATCH
BY THE TEAM

Drops	Opponents	Venue	Year
5 by South Africa	England	Paris	1999
4 by South Africa	England	Twickenham	2006
3 by several nations			

BY A PLAYER

Drops	Player	Opponents	Venue	Year
5 for S Africa	J H de Beer	England	Paris	1999
4 for S Africa	A S Pretorius	England	Twickenham	2006
3 for several nations				

Five drops were scored for Portugal by G Malheiro against both Georgia and Russia in 2003

CAREER RECORDS

MOST TEST APPEARANCES

Caps	Player	Career Span
139	G M Gregan (Australia)	1994 to 2007
119 (5)	J Leonard (England/Lions)	1990 to 2004
118	F Pelous (France)	1995 to 2007
111	P Sella (France)	1982 to 1995
105	G B Smith (Australia)	2000 to 2009
103 (3)	Gareth Thomas (Wales/Lions)	1995 to 2007
102	S J Larkham (Australia)	1996 to 2007
102	P C Montgomery (S Africa)	1997 to 2008
101	D I Campese (Australia)	1982 to 1996
101	A Troncon (Italy)	1994 to 2007
99 (6)	B G O'Driscoll (Ireland/Lions)	1999 to 2009
98	R Ibañez (France)	1996 to 2007
96 (2)	C L Charvis (Wales/Lions)	1996 to 2007
96 (2)	J J Hayes (Ireland/Lions)	2000 to 2009
95	C D Paterson (Scotland)	1999 to 2009
94 (2)	R J R O'Gara (Ireland/Lions)	2000 to 2009
93	S Blanco (France)	1980 to 1991
92	S B T Fitzpatrick (N Zealand)	1986 to 1997
92 (8)	M O Johnson (England/Lions)	1993 to 2003
92	G O Llewellyn (Wales)	1989 to 2004
92	M E O'Kelly (Ireland/Lions)	1997 to 2009
92 (4)	M E Williams (Wales/Lions)	1996 to 2009

MOST POINTS IN TESTS

Points	Player	Tests	Career Span
1099 (67)	J P Wilkinson (England/Lions)	76 (6)	1998 to 2008
1090 (41)	N R Jenkins (Wales/Lions)	91 (4)	1991 to 2002
1010 (27)	D Dominguez (Italy/Argentina)	76 (2)	1989 to 2003
967	A P Mehrtens (N Zealand)	70	1995 to 2004
930	D W Carter (N Zealand)	62	2003 to 2009
919 (0)	R J R O'Gara (Ireland/Lions)	94 (2)	2000 to 2009
911	M P Lynagh (Australia)	72	1984 to 1995
893	P C Montgomery (S Africa)	102	1997 to 2008
878	M C Burke (Australia)	81	1993 to 2004
746 (53)	S M Jones (Wales/Lions)	86 (6)	1998 to 2009
738	C D Paterson (Scotland)	95	1999 to 2009
733 (66)	A G Hastings (Scotland/Lions)	67 (6)	1986 to 1995

MOST CONSECUTIVE TESTS

Tests	Player	Career span
63	S B T Fitzpatrick (N Zealand)	1986 to 1995
62	J W C Roff (Australia)	1996 to 2001
53	G O Edwards (Wales)	1967 to 1978
52	W J McBride (Ireland)	1964 to 1975
51	C M Cullen (N Zealand)	1996 to 2000

MOST TESTS AS CAPTAIN

Tests	Captain	Career span
64	J W Smit (S Africa)	2003 to 2009
59	W D C Carling (England)	1988 to 1996
59	G M Gregan (Australia)	2001 to 2007
57 (1)	B G O'Driscoll (Ireland/Lions)	2002 to 2009
55	J A Eales (Australia)	1996 to 2001
51	S B T Fitzpatrick (N Zealand)	1992 to 1997
46 (8)	H Porta (Argentina/Jaguars)	1971 to 1990
45 (6)	M O Johnson (England/Lions)	1997 to 2003
42	F Pelous (France)	1997 to 2006
41	L Arbizu (Argentina)	1992 to 2002
41	R Ibañez (France)	1996 to 2007
39	R H McCaw (N Zealand)	2004 to 2009
37	M Giovanelli (Italy)	1992 to 1999
36	N C Farr–Jones (Australia)	1988 to 1992
36	G H Teichmann (S Africa)	1996 to 1999
36	K G M Wood (Ireland)	1996 to 2003

MOST TRIES IN TESTS

Tries	Player	Tests	Career Span
69	D Ohata (Japan)	58	1996 to 2007
64	D I Campese (Australia)	101	1982 to 1996
50 (1)	R Underwood (England/Lions)	91 (6)	1984 to 1996
49	D C Howlett (N Zealand)	62	2000 to 2007
48 (2)	S M Williams (Wales/Lions)	69 (4)	2000 to 2009
46	C M Cullen (N Zealand)	58	1996 to 2002
45	J T Rokocoko (N Zealand)	60	2003 to 2009
44	J W Wilson (N Zealand)	60	1993 to 2001
41 (1)	Gareth Thomas (Wales/Lions)	103 (3)	1995 to 2007
40	C E Latham (Australia)	78	1998 to 2007
38	S Blanco (France)	93	1980 to 1991
38	J H van der Westhuizen (S Africa)	89	1993 to 2003
38	H Onozawa (Japan)	52	2001 to 2009
37	J T Lomu (N Zealand)	63	1994 to 2002
37*	J F Umaga (N Zealand)	74	1999 to 2005
37 (1)	B G O'Driscoll (Ireland/Lions)	99 (6)	1999 to 2009

* includes a penalty try

MOST CONVERSIONS IN TESTS

Cons	Player	Tests	Career Span
169	A P Mehrtens (N Zealand)	70	1995 to 2004
161	D W Carter (N Zealand)	62	2003 to 2009
153	P C Montgomery (S Africa)	102	1997 to 2008
151 (7)	J P Wilkinson (England/Lions)	76 (6)	1998 to 2008
144 (0)	R J R O'Gara (Ireland/Lions)	94 (2)	2000 to 2009
140	M P Lynagh (Australia)	72	1984 to 1995
133 (6)	D Dominguez (Italy/Argentina)	76 (2)	1989 to 2003
131 (1)	N R Jenkins (Wales/Lions)	91 (4)	1991 to 2002
124 (7)	S M Jones (Wales/Lions)	86 (6)	1998 to 2009
118	G J Fox (N Zealand)	46	1985 to 1993

MOST DROPPED GOALS IN TESTS

Drops	Player	Tests	Career Span
29 (0)	J P Wilkinson (England/Lions)	76 (6)	1998 to 2008
28 (2)	H Porta (Argentina/Jaguars)	65 (8)	1971 to 1990
23 (2)	C R Andrew (England/Lions)	76 (5)	1985 to 1997
19 (0)	D Dominguez (Italy/Argentina)	76 (2)	1989 to 2003
18	H E Botha (S Africa)	28	1980 to 1992
17	S Bettarello (Italy)	55	1979 to 1988
15	J-P Lescarboura (France)	28	1982 to 1990

MOST PENALTY GOALS IN TESTS

Pens	Player	Tests	Career Span
248 (13)	N R Jenkins (Wales/Lions)	91 (4)	1991 to 2002
225 (16)	J P Wilkinson (England/Lions)	76 (6)	1998 to 2008
214 (5)	D Dominguez (Italy/Argentina)	76 (2)	1989 to 2003
188	A P Mehrtens (N Zealand)	70	1995 to 2004
177	M P Lynagh (Australia)	72	1984 to 1995
174	M C Burke (Australia)	81	1993 to 2004
173 (0)	R J R O'Gara (Ireland/Lions)	94 (2)	2000 to 2009
160 (20)	A G Hastings (Scotland/Lions)	67 (6)	1986 to 1995
159	D W Carter (N Zealand)	62	2003 to 2009

WORLD RECORDS

IRB WORLD RUGBY YEARBOOK 2011

ON SALE: OCTOBER 2010

To order your advanced copy of the IRB World Rugby Yearbook 2011, and get it before it goes in the shops, pre-order from the online shop at **www.visionsp.co.uk**, or to obtain an order form send a stamped addressed envelope to: IRB World Rugby Yearbook 2011, Vision Sports Publishing, 19-23 High Street, Kingston upon Thames, Surrey, KT1 1LL.

ALL THE 2010 WORLD RUGBY STATS

INCLUDING
SIX NATIONS • TRI-NATIONS • AUTUMN INTERNATIONALS
HEINEKEN CUP • SUPER-14 • AND MUCH MUCH MORE

PLUS
FEATURES AND COMMENT BY TOP RUGBY WRITERS
COUNTRY BY COUNTRY STATS • WORLD RUGBY RECORDS
2011 FIXTURES • RUGBY PHOTO OF THE YEAR
DIRECTORY OF UNIONS

Published by Vision Sports Publishing • **VSP** • www.visionsp.co.uk

SPRINGBOK

THE COUNTRIES

INTERNATIONAL
RUGBY BOARD

James Hook
Wales fly half

Tackle Doping
Join us in the fight against doping -
Keep Rugby Clean!

KEEP RUGBY CLEAN

www.irb.com

ARGENTINA

ARGENTINA'S 2008–09 TEST RECORD

OPPONENTS	DATE	VENUE	RESULT
France	8 November	A	**Lost** 6–12
Italy	15 November	A	**Won** 22–14
Ireland	22 November	A	**Lost** 3–17
England	6 June	A	**Lost** 15–37
England	13 June	H	**Won** 24–22

THE BIG BREAKTHROUGH

By Frankie Deges

Having lobbied hard on and off the field, Argentine rugby was finally offered an international home when SANZAR invited them to join a revamped Four Nations from 2012.

Argentina's geographical isolation could now be a thing of the past as the invitation will open a new world to a team that has been, for many years, making sufficient waves asking for inclusion in an international competition. The involvement is conditional to Los Pumas fielding their best players and the Unión Argentina de Rugby coming up with a satisfactory financial package.

This alone will now have to become a renewed focus for those who run the game in the country. Even the international community will have to assist. The International Rugby Board has been assisting Argentina in grand fashion, with funds and leading the process that kicked off at the historic Woking Accord in November 2007, where the game's major stakeholders agreed on a transition programme for Argentina's full integration into a senior international playing calendar.

As the future looks rosy after the September announcement, current affairs for the Argentine Pumas remained the same for a team occupying sixth place in the IRB World Rankings.

When this same book was published a year ago, they were ranked a couple of places higher, at fourth, and facing a similarly empty fixture list. While other Tier One nations had a minimum of ten Test matches in the period covered in this Yearbook, Argentina played only five times and of these, two matches were won and three lost.

Despite the small Test schedule, the game in the country has continued to thrive and the production line of players been working overtime.

Analysing the performance of every major nation in the last two Rugby World Cup tournaments in either form of the game, only Argentina has managed to return home with medals from both of them. After the never to be forgotten bronze medal for third place in RWC 2007, Los Pumas Sevens backed that up with a silver medal at RWC Sevens in Dubai in March. It still hurts them how close they came to claiming gold, but Wales were a deserving champion.

Argentina A, renamed the Jaguars, is the team selected from players still in Argentina. Their performances showed the needs of international rugby are big but with work and preparation these players can compete at the highest level. The Jaguars have become the second best team in the Americas, having beaten USA and Canada in the 2009 Churchill Cup.

A slap in the face was the eleventh place of the Under 20s at the IRB TOSHIBA Junior World Championship in Japan. After solid preparation and selection processes stretching back many months, they came close to dropping out of the now reduced Championship. From 2010, when the tournament comes to Argentina, it will be reduced from 16 to 12 nations.

With substantial International Rugby Board funding, the High Performance Units finally opened their doors on 2 February 2009. "The first day of professional rugby in Argentina," was how UAR President Porfirio Carreras explained the Plan de Alto Rendimiento (PLADAR) launch at the union headquarters. "An historic day," he said.

Thirty-nine senior players were put under a central contract with the UAR allowing them to play for their clubs and provinces. True to Argentine fashion, soon the powerful Unión de Rugby de Buenos Aires decreed that their championship was amateur and could not accept professional players. The pro tag was dropped and players went back to receiving so-called "allowances". If things don't change, these players will not be able to play club rugby in Buenos Aires in the 2010 season.

There are High Performance centres in Buenos Aires, Tucumán, Rosario, Córdoba and Mendoza. They in turn cater for the regions close to those cities. Not only senior players selected take active part in the HP plans, but also Under 20s, Under 19s and Under 18s, bringing the total to some 300.

This High Performance plan aims to provide home-based players with the extra preparation needed for international competition. As an added value, their newly acquired preparation is filtering through to the clubs and soon to the regional nations – Uruguay being the first beneficiary in lieu of their RWC qualifying series against the USA Eagles in November 2009. A growing number of staff members are also learning a new undeveloped trade in the country in which rugby has been taught at clubs with love and passion. This is an extra step in the development of the game.

Since its inception, three new players represented Argentina and did very well. Gonzalo Camacho (who has since joined Harlequins), Lucas González Amorosino (now with Leicester Tigers) and Mauro Comuzzi had their first caps amongst all the established and experienced internationals. In the 2009 June window, six players from the PLADAR were used.

The International Rugby Board is investing in excess of US$2 million per calendar year on Argentine rugby and while the fruits of this huge expenditure are already seen locally, it might take longer to translate into Test performances.

ARGENTINA

The return of players to Argentine rugby is slowly happening. With rugby markets shrinking in the midst of the economic crisis, the leading names continue to stay in Europe but a number of players have returned and if the internal competition is sorted out and the High Performance plan allows for more players to come under the "allowance" system, they will have a new home to come to. The lure of a Four Nations future is something that enters the equation.

The international game saw Los Pumas travel to Europe in November 2008 where France was the first host. Needing to exorcise the demons of two RWC 2007 defeats, the French were desperate for a win at Stade Velodrome in Marseille. Argentina's 12–6 loss was far from enterprising, both sides using a ping-pong-like kicking strategy trying to put the opposition under pressure. Argentina cracked more than France and was punished with its fourth consecutive defeat.

On to Torino and having lost to Italy at home earlier that year, the 22–14 win was much celebrated. The only Puma try came from a rare moment of magic from the mercurial Juan Martín Hernández. Not much else was evident in a game that had a late Italian try to reduce the scoreline.

To continue with this sporting revenge theme, Ireland awaited Argentina in Dublin. Reeling from the defeat of a year earlier in Paris, they found a Puma team in disarray. Captain Felipe Contepomi spent most of the week in hospital with a septic hand, eventually missing the Test, and Hernández had to be replaced during the warm-up at Croke Park. Despite this, Los Pumas performed with a degree of assurance that defied logic. Three all after 40 minutes, Ronan O'Gara's kicking and a late try stretched the score to the 17–3 loss.

Six and a half months later, Argentina hosted England at Old Trafford. Having agreed to take one of their two confirmed home games there pursuing commercial benefits, it was an interesting venture. In front of 42,000 spectators, Los Pumas showed an understandable lack of cohesion and went down without a hint of the rugby they can play. Three English tries broke a feeble defence and Argentina only managed points through the boot of Hernández, back to his best.

A week later, both teams reconvened in the northern Argentina city of Salta where the trademark Puma passion was evident from kick-off. Despite allowing England to come back into the game in the second half, those opening 40 minutes by coach Santiago Phelan's team showed sufficient to dream of a positive future. Then again, with few matches on the agenda, it will always come down to how well they can regroup in a short space of time when they prepare for any given international.

The June window finished with a 32–18 win against the French Barbarians in Buenos Aires.

The Jaguars – a more apt name than Pumas (coined in South Africa 45 years ago) given that this animal does indeed inhabit Argentina – had a successful debut, winning six of seven matches in May and June 2009. This Argentina second XV is selected mostly from players based in the country, showing the benefits of the PLADAR. In those seven games 59 players were used.

Namibia arrived in Argentina and the Jaguars beat them 62–7 and 19–7 – the Namibians lifting their standard from game to game. Then, with new players, Chile and Uruguay were beaten in Montevideo, 89–6 and 33–9 respectively. The only loss (28–20) came against England Saxons during the Churchill Cup in Colorado.

The Jaguars' superiority over their regional rivals from the north was heart-warming. The USA Eagles were downed 35–15 and then Canada 44–29 with a number of relatively unknown players putting their hands up in a tournament which saw only five overseas-based players used.

Argentina, meanwhile, finished fifth in the IRB Sevens World Series after recording their second tournament win at the USA Sevens, in San Diego in February. On the back of that win they were in great form at RWC Sevens in Dubai a month later, beating South Africa and Kenya to reach the final. Firm favourites in the Melrose Cup decider, Argentina could not control a hungry Welsh side that ultimately beat them 19–12 in the final. Two players went on to win full caps (Camacho and González Amorosino) and a lot is expected from Martín Rodríguez Gurruchaga.

Having been confirmed as host venue for the IRB Junior World Championship 2010, Argentina arrived in Japan hoping to regain some of the ground lost in this age group. They didn't and it will be hard for next year's side to slowly claw this back. When the IRB Under 21 World Championship was played in Argentina in 2005 the team finished fifth. A lot is expected of the team in a tournament that, hopefully, will showcase all that is good about Argentine rugby.

On the domestic scene, Buenos Aires missed out on a fourth consecutive NPC title, with Córdoba the strongest side, beating Tucumán 15–12 in a hard final.

Slowly but steadily, the game in Argentina is getting its act together. There is no professional league or a structured international season. Yet players continue to come through, ready for the high demands of top rugby. Around the corner is RWC 2011 and Los Pumas will have to show they are still good enough to mix it with the best again.

The invitation to a Four Nations opens a new era for Argentine rugby. The challenges will be on and off the field to ensure that Los Pumas are ready when they enter this competition.

ARGENTINA

ARGENTINA INTERNATIONAL STATISTICS

MATCH RECORDS UP TO 30TH SEPTEMBER 2009

WINNING MARGIN

Date	Opponent	Result	Winning Margin
01/05/2002	Paraguay	152–0	152
27/04/2003	Paraguay	144–0	144
01/05/2004	Venezuela	147–7	140
02/10/1993	Brazil	114–3	111
09/10/1979	Brazil	109–3	106

MOST PENALTIES IN A MATCH
BY THE TEAM

Date	Opponent	Result	Pens
10/10/1999	Samoa	32–16	8
10/03/1995	Canada	29–26	8
17/06/2006	Wales	45–27	8

MOST POINTS IN A MATCH
BY THE TEAM

Date	Opponent	Result	Points
01/05/2002	Paraguay	152–0	152
01/05/2004	Venezuela	147–7	147
27/04/2003	Paraguay	144–0	144
02/10/1993	Brazil	114–3	114
09/10/1979	Brazil	109–3	109

MOST DROP GOALS IN A MATCH
BY THE TEAM

Date	Opponent	Result	DGs
27/10/1979	Australia	24–13	3
02/11/1985	New Zealand	21–21	3
26/05/2001	Canada	20–6	3
21/09/1975	Uruguay	30–15	3
07/08/1971	SA Gazelles	12–0	3
30/09/2007	Ireland	30–15	3

MOST TRIES IN A MATCH
BY THE TEAM

Date	Opponent	Result	Tries
01/05/2002	Paraguay	152–0	24
27/04/2003	Paraguay	144–0	24
01/05/2004	Venezuela	147–7	23
08/10/1989	Brazil	103–0	20

MOST POINTS IN A MATCH
BY A PLAYER

Date	Player	Opponent	Points
14/10/1973	Eduardo Morgan	Paraguay	50
27/04/2003	José María Nuñez Piossek	Paraguay	45
02/10/1993	Gustavo Jorge	Brazil	40
24/10/1977	Martin Sansot	Brazil	36
13/09/1951	Uriel O'Farrell	Brazil	33

MOST CONVERSIONS IN A MATCH
BY THE TEAM

Date	Opponent	Result	Cons
01/05/2002	Paraguay	152–0	16
01/05/2004	Venezuela	147–7	16
09/10/1979	Brazil	109–3	15
21/09/1985	Paraguay	102–3	13
14/10/1973	Paraguay	98–3	13

MOST TRIES IN A MATCH
BY A PLAYER

Date	Player	Opponent	Tries
13/09/1951	Uriel O'Farrell	Brazil	11
27/04/2003	José María Nuñez Piossek	Paraguay	9
02/10/1993	Gustavo Jorge	Brazil	8
08/10/1989	Gustavo Jorge	Brazil	6
14/10/1973	Eduardo Morgan	Paraguay	6

MOST CONVERSIONS IN A MATCH
BY A PLAYER

Date	Player	Opponent	Cons
01/05/2002	Jose Cilley	Paraguay	16
21/09/1985	Hugo Porta	Paraguay	13
14/10/1973	Eduardo Morgan	Paraguay	13
25/09/1975	Eduardo de Forteza	Paraguay	11

MOST PENALTIES IN A MATCH
BY A PLAYER

Date	Player	Opponent	Pens
10/10/1999	Gonzalo Quesada	Samoa	8
10/03/1995	Santiago Meson	Canada	8
17/06/2006	Federico Todeschini	Wales	8

MOST DROP GOALS IN A MATCH
BY A PLAYER

Date	Player	Opponent	DGs
27/10/1979	Hugo Porta	Australia	3
02/11/1985	Hugo Porta	New Zealand	3
07/08/1971	Tomas Harris-Smith	SA Gazelles	3
26/05/2001	Juan Fernández Miranda	Canada	3
30/09/2007	Juan Martín Hernández	Ireland	3

MOST CAPPED PLAYERS

Name	Caps
Lisandro Arbizu	86
Rolando Martin	86
Pedro Sporleder	78
Federico Méndez	73
Agustín Pichot	71

LEADING TRY SCORERS

Name	Tries
José María Nuñez Piossek	29
Diego Cuesta Silva	28
Gustavo Jorge	24
Facundo Soler	18
Rolando Martin	18

LEADING CONVERSIONS SCORERS

Name	Cons
Hugo Porta	84
Gonzalo Quesada	68
Santiago Meson	68
Felipe Contepomi	56
Juan Fernández Miranda	41

LEADING PENALTY SCORERS

Name	Pens
Gonzalo Quesada	103
Hugo Porta	102
Felipe Contepomi	101
Santiago Meson	63
Federico Todeschini	54

LEADING DROP GOAL SCORERS

Name	DGs
Hugo Porta	26
Lisandro Arbizu	11
Tomas Harris-Smith	6
Gonzalo Quesada	6
Juan Martín Hernández	6

LEADING POINTS SCORERS

Name	Pts.
Hugo Porta	593
Gonzalo Quesada	483
Felipe Contepomi	479
Santiago Meson	370
Federico Todeschini	256

ARGENTINA

ARGENTINA INTERNATIONAL PLAYERS
UP TO 30TH SEPTEMBER 2009

Note: Years given for International Championship matches are for second half of season; eg 1972 means season 1971–72. Years for all other matches refer to the actual year of the match.

A Abadie 2007 *Ch*
A Abella 1969 *Ur, Ch*
C Abud 1975 *Par, Bra, Ch*
H Achaval 1948 *OCC*
J Aguilar 1983 *Ch, Ur*
A Aguirre 1997 *Par, Ch*
ME Aguirre 1990 *E, S,* 1991 *Sa*
H Agulla 2005 *Sa,* 2006 *Ur, E, It,* 2007 *It, F, Nm, I, S, SA, F,* 2008 *S, It, SA, F, It, I,* 2009 *E, E*
P Albacete 2003 *Par, Ur, F, SA, Ur, C, A, R,* 2004 *W, W, NZ, F, I,* 2005 *It, It,* 2006 *E, It, F,* 2007 *W, F, Geo, Nm, I, S, SA, F,* 2008 *SA, F, It, I,* 2009 *E, E*
DL Albanese 1995 *Ur, C, E, F,* 1996 *Ur, F, SA, E,* 1997 *NZ, Ur, R, It, F, A, A,* 1998 *Ur, F, F, R, US, C, It, F, W,* 1999 *WXV, W, W, S, I, W, Sa, J, I, F,* 2000 *I, A, A, SA,* 2001 *NZ, It, W, S, NZ,* 2002 *F, E, SA, A, It, I,* 2003 *F, F, SA, US, C, A, Nm, I*
F Albarracin 2007 *Ch*
M Albina 2001 *Ur, US,* 2003 *Par, Ur, Fj,* 2004 *Ch, Ven, W, W,* 2005 *J*
C Aldao 1961 *Ch, Bra, Ur*
P Alexenicer 1997 *Par, Ch*
C Alfonso 1936 *BI*
H Alfonso 1936 *BI, BI, Ch*
G Allen 1977 *Par*
JG Allen 1981 *C,* 1985 *F, F, Ur, NZ, NZ,* 1986 *F, F, A, A,* 1987 *Ur, Fj, It, NZ, Sp, A, A,* 1988 *F, F, F, F,* 1989 *Bra, Ch, Par, Ur, US*
L Allen 1951 *Ur, Bra, Ch*
M Allen 1990 *C, E, S,* 1991 *NZ, Ch*
A Allub 1997 *Par, Ur, It, F, A, A,* 1998 *Ur, F, F, US, C, J, It, F, W,* 1999 *WXV, W, W, S, I, W, Sa, J, I, F,* 2000 *I, A, A, SA, E,* 2001 *NZ*
M Alonso 1973 *R, R, S,* 1977 *F, F*
A Altberg 1972 *SAG, SAG,* 1973 *R, R, Par*
J Altube 1998 *Par, Ch, Ur*
C Alvarez 1958 *Ur, Per, Ch,* 1959 *JSB, JSB,* 1960 *F*
GM Alvarez 1975 *Ur, Par, Bra, Ch,* 1976 *Ur, NZ,* 1977 *Bra, Ur, Par, Ch*
R Álvarez Kairelis 1998 *Par, Ch, Ur,* 2001 *Ur, US, C, W, S, NZ,* 2002 *F, E, SA, A, It, I,* 2003 *F, SA, Fj, Ur, C, Nm, I,* 2004 *F, I,* 2006 *W, W, NZ, Ch, Ur,* 2007 *I, It, W, F, Geo, Nm, I, S, SA, F,* 2008 *SA, F, It, I,* 2009 *E*
F Amelong 2007 *Ch*
LG Amorosino 2007 *Ch,* 2009 *E, E*
A Amuchastegui 2001 *Ur,* 2002 *Ur, Par, Ch*
GP Angaut 1987 *NZ, Ur, Ch,* 1990 *S,* 1991 *NZ, Sa*
J-J Angelillo 1987 *Ur, Ch, A,* 1988 *F, F, F,* 1989 *It, Bra, Ch, Par, Ur, US,* 1990 *C, US, E, E,* 1994 *US, S, S, US,* 1995 *Par, Ch, R, F*
W Aniz 1960 *F*
R Annichini 1983 *Ch, Ur,* 1985 *F, Ch, Par*
A Anthony 1965 *OCC, Ch,* 1967 *Ur, Ch,* 1968 *W, W,* 1969 *S, S, Ur, Ch,* 1970 *I, I,* 1971 *SAG, SAG, OCC,* 1972 *SAG, SAG,* 1974 *F, F*
F Aranguren 2007 *Ch*
L Arbizu 1990 *I, S,* 1991 *NZ, NZ, Ch, A, W, Sa,* 1992 *F, F, Sp, Sp, R, F,* 1993 *J, J, Bra, Ch, Par, Ur, SA, SA,* 1995 *Ur, A, A, E, Sa, It, Par, Ch, Ur, R, It, F,* 1996 *F, US, Ur,*

C, SA, SA, E, 1997 *E, E, NZ, NZ, R, It, F, A, A,* 1998 *Ur, F, F, R, US, C, It, F, W,* 1999 *W, W, S, I, W, Sa, J, I, F,* 2000 *A, A, SA, E,* 2001 *NZ, It, W, S, NZ,* 2002 *F, A, It, I,* 2003 *F, F, US, C,* 2005 *BI, It, It*
F Argerich 1979 *Ur*
G Aristide 1997 *E*
J Arocena Messones 2005 *C, Sa*
E Arriaga 1936 *Ch, Ch*
S Artese 2004 *SA,* 2005 *C*
M Avellaneda 1948 *OCC, OCC,* 1951 *Bra, Ch*
M Avramovic 2005 *J, C, Sa,* 2006 *Ch, Ur, E, It,* 2007 *I,* 2008 *It, SA, I,* 2009 *E*
M Ayerra 1927 *GBR*
MI Ayerza 2004 *SA,* 2005 *J, It, Sa,* 2006 *W, W, Ch, Ur, E, It, F,* 2007 *I, I, Geo, F,* 2008 *S, S, SA, F, It, I,* 2009 *E, E*
G Azcarate 2007 *Ch*
M Azpiroz 1956 *OCC,* 1958 *Ur, Per, Ch,* 1959 *JSB, JSB*
J Bach 1975 *Par, Bra, Ch*
A Badano 1977 *Bra, Ur, Par, Ch*
J Baeck 1983 *Par*
M Baeck 1985 *Ur, Ch, Par,* 1990 *US, E, E*
DR Baetti Sabah 1980 *WXV, Fj, Fj,* 1981 *E, E, C,* 1983 *WXV,* 1987 *Ur, Par, Ch,* 1988 *F, F,* 1989 *It, NZ, NZ*
L Balfour 1977 *Bra, Ur, Par, Ch*
C Barrea 1996 *Ur, C, SA*
O Bartolucci 1996 *US, C, SA,* 1998 *Ur, Ch, Ur,* 1999 *WXV, W, W, S, I, W, Sa,* 2000 *I, A, A, SA, E,* 2001 *US, C,* 2003 *Par, Ur*
E Basile 1983 *Ch, Ur*
L Bavio 1954 *F*
R Bazan 1951 *Ur, Bra, Ch,* 1956 *OCC*
D Beccar Varela 1975 *Ch, F, F,* 1976 *Ur, W, NZ,* 1977 *F, F*
G Beccar Varela 1976 *W, NZ, NZ,* 1977 *F, F*
M Beccar Varela 1965 *Rho, OCC, OCC*
G Begino 2007 *Ch*
JW Beith 1936 *BI*
J Benzi 1965 *Rho,* 1969 *S, Ur, Ch*
E Bergamaschi 2001 *US*
O Bernacchi 1954 *F,* 1956 *OCC, OCC,* 1958 *Ur, Per, Ch*
G Bernardi 1997 *Ch*
O Bernat 1932 *JSB*
MM Berro 1964 *Ur, Bra, Ch*
MJS Bertranou 1989 *It, NZ, NZ, Ch, Par,* 1990 *C, US, C, E, E, I, E, S,* 1993 *SA*
E Bianchetti 1959 *JSB, JSB*
G Blacksley 1971 *SAG*
T Blades 1938 *Ch*
G Bocca 1998 *J, Par*
C Bofelli 1997 *Ur,* 1998 *Par,* 2004 *Ch, Ur, Ven*
S Boffelli 2005 *C*
L Borges 2001 *Ur,* 2003 *Par, Ch, Ur,* 2004 *Ch, Ur, Ven, W, W, NZ, F, I, SA,* 2005 *SA, S,* 2006 *W, W, Ch, Ur,* 2007 *W, F, Geo, I, S, SA,* 2008 *S, It*
C Bori 1975 *Ch, F*
F Bosch 2004 *Ch, SA,* 2005 *J, Sa*
MA Bosch 1991 *Sa,* 1992 *F, F*
MT Bosch 2007 *It,* 2008 *It*
N Bossicovich 1995 *Ur, C*

CA Bottarini 1973 *Par, Ur, Bra, I*, 1974 *F*, 1975 *F, F*, 1979 *Ur, Ch, Bra*, 1983 *Ch, Par, Ur*
R Botting 1927 *GBR, GBR, GBR*
L Bouza 1992 *Sp*
M Bouza 1966 *SAG, SAG*, 1967 *Ur, Ch*
P Bouza 1996 *Ur, F, F, E*, 1997 *E, NZ, NZ, Ur, R*, 1998 *Ur*, 2002 *Ur, Par, Ch*, 2003 *Par, Ch, Ur, US, Ur, Nm, R*, 2004 *Ch, Ur, Ven, W, NZ, SA*, 2005 *J, BI, It, It, C, SA, S, It*, 2006 *Ch, Ur*, 2007 *I, I*
N Bozzo 1975 *Bra*
JG Braceras 1971 *Bra, Par*, 1976 *W, NZ*, 1977 *F*
W Braddon 1927 *GBR*
EN Branca 1976 *Ur, W, NZ, NZ*, 1977 *F, F*, 1980 *Fj*, 1981 *E, E, C*, 1983 *WXV, A, A*, 1985 *F, F, Ur, Ch, Par, NZ, NZ*, 1986 *F, F, A, A*, 1987 *Ur, Fj, It, NZ, Sp, A, A*, 1988 *F, F, F, F*, 1989 *Bra, Par, Ur*, 1990 *E, E*
M Brandi 1997 *Par, Ch*, 1998 *Par, Ch, Ur*
J Bridger 1932 *JSB*
J Brolese 1998 *Ch, Ur*
E Brouchou 1975 *Ch, Ur, Par, Bra, Ch*
F Buabse 1991 *Ur, Par, Bra*, 1992 *Sp*
PM Buabse 1989 *NZ, US*, 1991 *Sa*, 1993 *Bra*, 1995 *Ur, C, A*
E Buckley 1938 *Ch*
R Bullrich 1991 *Ur, Bra*, 1992 *R*, 1993 *Bra, Ch, SA*, 1994 *SA, SA*
S Bunader 1989 *US*, 1990 *C*
K Bush 1938 *Ch*
E Bustamante 1927 *GBR, GBR, GBR, GBR*
F Bustillo 1977 *F, F, Bra, Ur, Par, Ch*
G Bustos 2001 *Ur*, 2003 *Par, Ur*, 2004 *Ch, Ven*
E Caffarone 1949 *F, F*, 1951 *Bra, Ch*, 1952 *I, I*, 1954 *F, F*
M Caldwell 1956 *OCC*
G Camacho 2009 *E, E*
GF Camardon 1990 *E*, 1991 *NZ, Ch, A, W, Sa*, 1992 *F, F, Sp, R, F*, 1993 *J, Par, Ur, SA, SA*, 1995 *A*, 1996 *Ur, US, Ur, C, SA, E*, 1999 *W, W, Sa, J, I, F*, 2001 *US, C, NZ, It, W, S, NZ*, 2002 *F, E, SA, It, I*
PJ Camerlinckx 1989 *Bra, Par, Ur*, 1990 *C, US*, 1994 *S*, 1995 *Ch*, 1996 *Ur, F, F, US, Ur, C, SA, SA, E*, 1997 *E, E, NZ, NZ, Ur, R, It, F, A, A*, 1998 *R, US, C, F, W*, 1999 *WXV, W*
A Cameron 1936 *BI, BI, Ch, Ch*, 1938 *Ch*
R Cameron 1927 *GBR, GBR*
J Caminotti 1987 *Ur, Par, Ch*
M Campo 1975 *Ch*, 1978 *E, It*, 1979 *NZ, NZ, A, A*, 1980 *WXV, Fj*, 1981 *E, E, C*, 1982 *F, F, Sp*, 1983 *WXV, A, A*, 1987 *Ur, Fj, NZ*
A Campos 2007 *Ch*, 2008 *S, It, F, It*
A Canalda 1999 *S, I, F*, 2000 *A*, 2001 *Ur, US, C, Ur*
R Cano 1997 *Par*
J Capalbo 1975 *Bra*, 1977 *Bra, Ur, Ch*
AE Capelletti 1977 *F, F*, 1978 *E, It*, 1979 *NZ, NZ, A, A*, 1980 *WXV, Fj, Fj*, 1981 *E, E*
R Carballo 2005 *C*, 2006 *W, Ch, Ur*, 2008 *SA, It, I*
N Carbone 1969 *Ur, Ch*, 1971 *SAG*, 1973 *I, S*
PF Cardinali 2001 *US, Ur*, 2002 *Ur, Par*, 2004 *W*, 2007 *I*
M Carizza 2004 *SA*, 2005 *J, BI, SA, S, It*, 2006 *W, Ch, Ur*, 2007 *It*, 2008 *It*, 2009 *E, E*
J Carlos Galvalisi 1983 *Par, Ur*
MA Carluccio 1973 *R, R, Ur, Bra, I*, 1975 *F, F*, 1976 *NZ*, 1977 *F, F*
M Carmona 1997 *Par, Ch*
S Carossio 1985 *NZ*, 1987 *It, NZ*
J Carracedo 1971 *Ch, Bra, Par*, 1972 *SAG, SAG*, 1973 *R, R, Par, Ur, Bra, Ch, I, S*, 1975 *F*, 1976 *W, NZ, NZ*, 1977 *F*
J Carrasco 2001 *Ur*
M Carreras 1991 *NZ, NZ, Ch, A, W, Sa*, 1992 *F*
M Carreras 1987 *Par*
M Carrique 1983 *Par, Ur*
J Casanegra 1959 *JSB, JSB*, 1960 *F, F*
GF Casas 1971 *OCC*, 1973 *Par, Ch, I*, 1975 *F, F*
DM Cash 1985 *F, F, Ur, Ch, NZ, NZ*, 1986 *F, F, A, A*, 1987 *Ur, Fj, It, NZ, Sp, A, A*, 1988 *F, F, F, F*, 1989 *It, NZ, NZ, US*, 1990 *C, US, C, E, I, E, S*, 1991 *NZ, NZ, Ch, A, Sa*, 1992 *F, F*
R Castagna 1977 *F*
A Castellina 2004 *Ch, Ur, Ven*
R Castro 1971 *Ch, Bra, Par*

J Cato 1975 *Ur, Par*
R Cazenave 1965 *Rho, JSB, OCC, Ch*, 1966 *SAG, SAG*
A Cerioni 1975 *F*, 1978 *E, It*, 1979 *Ch, Bra*
G Cernegoy 1938 *Ch*
H Cespedes 1997 *Ur, Ch*
M Chesta 1966 *SAG, SAG*, 1967 *Ur, Ch*, 1968 *W, W*
W Chiswell 1949 *F*
V Christianson 1954 *F, F*, 1956 *OCC*
E Cilley 1932 *JSB, JSB*
J Cilley 1936 *BI, Ch, Ch*, 1938 *Ch*
JL Cilley 1994 *SA*, 1995 *Sa, It, Par, Ch*, 1996 *Ur, F, F, SA, SA*, 1999 *WXV, W*, 2000 *A*, 2001 *Ur*, 2002 *Par*
J Clement 1987 *Par*, 1989 *Bra*
R Cobelo 1987 *Ur, Par, Ch*
I Comas 1951 *Bra, Ch*, 1958 *Per, Ch*, 1960 *F*
A Conen 1951 *Ch*, 1952 *I, I*
J Conrard 1927 *GBR, GBR*
CA Contepomi 1964 *Bra, Ch*
F Contepomi 1998 *Ch, Ur, F, W*, 1999 *W, S, I, J, I, F*, 2000 *I, A, A, SA, E*, 2001 *Ur, US, C, NZ, It, W, S, NZ*, 2002 *E, SA, A, It, I*, 2003 *F, F, SA, US, C, A, Nm, I*, 2004 *W, W, F, I*, 2005 *BI, It, It, SA, S, It*, 2006 *W, NZ, E, F*, 2007 *I, W, F, Geo, Nm, I, S, SA, F*, 2008 *S, S, SA, F, It*
M Contepomi 1998 *US, C, It, F, W*, 1999 *S, I, W, Sa, F*, 2003 *Ur, F, Fj, Ur, A, R*, 2004 *Ch, Ur, Ven, W, W, NZ, F, I, SA*, 2005 *SA, S*, 2006 *It, F*, 2007 *I, It, W, F, Nm, I, S, SA, F*
F Conti 1988 *F*
GEF Cooke 1927 *GBR*
KAM Cookson 1932 *JSB*
N Cooper 1936 *BI, Ch, Ch*
R Cooper 1927 *GBR, GBR, GBR, GBR*
J Copello 1975 *Ch, Ur, Bra*
C Cordeiro 1983 *Par*
J Coria 1987 *Ur, Par, Ch*, 1989 *Bra*
I Corleto 1998 *J, F, W*, 1999 *WXV, I, J, I, F*, 2000 *I, A, SA, E*, 2001 *W, S, NZ*, 2002 *E, SA, A, It, I*, 2003 *F, Fj, US, Ur, C, A, I*, 2006 *It, F*, 2007 *W, F, Geo, Nm, I, S, SA, F*
L Cornella 2001 *Ur*
ME Corral 1993 *J, Bra, Par, Ur, SA, SA*, 1994 *US, S, SA, SA*, 1995 *Ur, C, A, A, E, Sa, It*
M Cortese 2005 *Sa*
F Cortopasso 2003 *Ch, Ur*
A Costa Repetto 2005 *C, Sa*
JD Costante 1971 *OCC, OCC, Ch, Bra, Par, Ur*, 1976 *Ur, W, NZ*, 1977 *F*
AF Courreges 1979 *Ur, Par, Bra*, 1982 *F, F, Sp*, 1983 *WXV, A, A*, 1987 *Sp, A, A*, 1988 *F*
PH Cox 1938 *Ch*
A Creevy 2005 *J, Sa*, 2006 *Ur*
P Cremaschi 1993 *J, J*, 1995 *Par, Ch, Ur, It*
RH Crexell 1990 *I, S*, 1991 *Par*, 1992 *Sp*, 1993 *J*, 1995 *Ur, C, A, E, Sa, It, Par, R*
L Criscuolo 1992 *F*, 1993 *Bra, SA*, 1996 *Ur, F, F*
J Cruz Legora 2001 *Ur*, 2002 *Par, Ch*
J Cruz Meabe 1997 *Par*
AG Cubelli 1977 *Bra, Ur, Ch*, 1978 *E, It*, 1979 *A, A*, 1980 *WXV, Fj*, 1983 *Par*, 1985 *F, F, Ur, Par, NZ, NZ*, 1990 *S*
D Cuesta Silva 1983 *Ch, Ur*, 1985 *F, F, Ur, Ch, NZ, NZ*, 1986 *F, F, A, A*, 1987 *Ur, Fj, It, Sp, A, A*, 1988 *F, F, F, F*, 1989 *It, NZ, NZ*, 1990 *C, E, E, I, E, S*, 1991 *NZ, NZ, Ch, A, W, Sa*, 1992 *F, F, Sp, R, F*, 1993 *J, J, Bra, Par, Ur, SA, SA*, 1994 *US, S, S, US*, 1995 *Ur, C, E, Sa, It, Par, R, It, F*
J Cuesta Silva 1927 *GBR, GBR, GBR, GBR*
B Cuezzo 2007 *Ch*
M Cutler 1969 *Ur*, 1971 *Ch, Bra, Par, Ur*
A Da Milano 1964 *Bra, Ch*
F D'Agnillo 1975 *Ur, Bra*, 1977 *Bra, Ur, Par, Ch*
JL Damioli 1991 *Par, Ch*
H Dande 2001 *Ur, C*, 2004 *Ch, Ven*
J Dartiguelongue 1964 *Bra, Ch*, 1968 *W, W*
S Dassen 1973 *Ch, Par, Ur*
H Davel 1936 *BI*
R de Abelleyra 1932 *JSB, JSB*
L de Chazal 2001 *Ur, C*, 2004 *SA*, 2005 *C*
E de Forteza 1975 *Ur, Par, Bra, Ch*
R de la Arena 1992 *F, Sp*

JC De Pablo 1948 *OCC*
G de Robertis 2005 *Sa*, 2006 *Ch, Ur*
R de Vedia 1982 *F, Sp*
T de Vedia 2007 *I, I*, 2008 *S*
R del Busto 2007 *Ch*
F del Castillo 1994 *US, SA*, 1995 *Ur, C, A*, 1996 *Ur, F*, 1997 *Par, Ur*, 1998 *Ur*
GJ del Castillo 1991 *NZ, NZ, Ch, A, W*, 1993 *J*, 1994 *S, S, US, SA*, 1995 *C, A*
L del Chazal 1983 *Ch, Par, Ur*
R Dell'Acqua 1956 *OCC*
S Dengra 1982 *F, Sp*, 1983 *WXV, A, A*, 1986 *A*, 1987 *It, NZ, Sp, A, A*, 1988 *F, F, F, F*, 1989 *It, NZ, NZ*
C Derkheim 1927 *GBR*
M Devoto 1975 *Par, Bra*, 1977 *Par*
PM Devoto 1982 *F, F, Sp*, 1983 *WXV*
R Devoto 1960 *F*
M Diaz 1997 *Par, Ch*, 1998 *J, Par, Ch*
F Diaz Alberdi 1997 *Ur*, 1999 *WXV, S, I*, 2000 *A, A*
J Diez 1956 *OCC*
R Dillon 1956 *OCC*
P Dinisio 1989 *NZ*, 1990 *C, US*
M Dip 1979 *Par, Bra*
D Dominguez 1989 *Ch, Par*
E Dominguez 1949 *F, F*, 1952 *I, I*, 1954 *F, F*
L Dorado 1949 *F*
J Dumas 1973 *R, R, Ur, Bra, S*
M Dumas 1966 *SAG, SAG*
MA Durand 1997 *Ch*, 1998 *Par, Ch, Ur, It, F, W*, 2000 *SA, 2001 Ur, US, C, It, NZ*, 2002 *F, SA, A, It, I*, 2003 *Ch, Ur, Fj, US, Ur, C, A, Nm, R*, 2004 *Ch, Ur, Ven, W, NZ, F, I, SA*, 2005 *SA, S, It*, 2006 *W, NZ, Ch, Ur, It, F*, 2007 *I, I, It, W, F, Geo, I, F*, 2008 *S, S, It, SA, F, It, I*
C Echeverria 1932 *JSB*
G Ehrman 1948 *OCC*, 1949 *F, F*, 1951 *Ur, Bra, Ch*, 1952 *I, I*, 1954 *F, F*
O Elia 1954 *F*
R Elliot 1936 *BI, BI*, 1938 *Ch*
J Escalante 1975 *Ur, Par, Ch*, 1978 *It*, 1979 *Ur, Ch, Par, Bra*
N Escary 1927 *GBR, GBR*, 1932 *JSB, JSB*
R Espagnol 1971 *SAG*
AM Etchegaray 1964 *Ur, Bra, Ch*, 1965 *Rho, JSB, Ch*, 1967 *Ur, Ch*, 1968 *W, W*, 1969 *S, S*, 1971 *SAG, OCC, OCC*, 1972 *SAG, SAG*, 1973 *Par, Bra, I*, 1974 *F, F*, 1976 *Ur, W, NZ, NZ*
R Etchegoyen 1991 *Ur, Par, Bra*
C Ezcurra 1958 *Ur, Per, Ch*
E Ezcurra 1990 *I, E, S*
R Fariello 1973 *Par, Ur, Ch, S*
M Farina 1968 *W, W*, 1969 *S, S*
D Farrell 1951 *Ur*
P Felisari 1956 *OCC*
JJ Fernandez 1971 *SAG, Ch, Bra, Par, Ur*, 1972 *SAG, SAG, 1973 R, R, Par, Ur, Ch, I, S*, 1974 *F, F*, 1975 *F*, 1976 *Ur, W, NZ, NZ*, 1977 *F, F*
S Fernandez 2008 *It, I*, 2009 *E, E*
Pablo Fernandez Bravo 1993 *SA, SA*
E Fernandez del Casal 1951 *Ur, Bra, Ch*, 1952 *I, I*, 1956 *OCC, OCC*
CI Fernandez Lobbe 1996 *US*, 1997 *E, E*, 1998 *Ur, F, F, R, US, Ur, C, J, It, F*, 1999 *WXV, W, W, S, I, W, Sa, J, I, F*, 2000 *I, A, A, SA, E*, 2001 *NZ, It, W, S, NZ*, 2002 *F, E, SA, A, It, I*, 2003 *F, F, SA, US, C, A, Nm, I*, 2004 *W, W, NZ*, 2005 *SA, S, It*, 2006 *W, W, NZ, E, F*, 2007 *It, W, F, Nm, I, S, SA*, 2008 *S, S*
JM Fernandez Lobbe 2004 *Ur, Ven*, 2005 *S, It, Sa*, 2006 *W, W, NZ, E, It, F*, 2007 *I, I, It, W, F, Geo, Nm, I, S, SA, F*, 2008 *S, S, SA, F, It, I*, 2009 *E, E*
JC Fernández Miranda 1997 *Ur, R, It*, 1998 *Ur, Ur, It*, 1999 *WXV*, 2000 *I*, 2001 *US, C*, 2002 *Ur, Par, Ch, It, I*, 2003 *Par, Ch, Ur, Fj, US, Nm, R*, 2004 *W, NZ, SA*, 2005 *J, C, Sa*, 2006 *Ch, Ur*, 2007 *It*
N Fernandez Miranda 1994 *US, S, S, US*, 1995 *Ch, Ur*, 1996 *F, SA, SA, E*, 1997 *E, E, NZ, NZ, Ur, R*, 1998 *Ur, R, US, C, It*, 1999 *WXV, I, F*, 2002 *Ur, Ch, It*, 2003 *Ch, Ur, F, F, SA, US, Ur, Nm, R*, 2004 *W, NZ*, 2005 *J, BI, It, It*, 2006 *W, It*, 2007 *It, Geo, Nm*

N Ferrari 1992 *Sp, Sp*
G Fessia 2005 *C*, 2007 *I*, 2009 *E*
A Figuerola 2008 *It, I*
R Follett 1948 *OCC, OCC*, 1952 *I, I*, 1954 *F*
G Foster 1971 *Ch, Bra, Par, Ur*
R Foster 1965 *Rho, JSB, OCC, OCC, Ch*, 1966 *SAG, SAG, 1970 I, I*, 1971 *SAG, SAG, OCC*, 1972 *SAG, SAG*
P Franchi 1987 *Ur, Par, Ch*
JL Francombe 1932 *JSB, JSB*, 1936 *BI, BI*
J Freixas 2003 *Ch, Ur*
R Frigerio 1948 *OCC, OCC*, 1954 *F*
J Frigoli 1936 *BI, BI, Ch, Ch*
P Fuselli 1998 *J, Par*
E Gahan 1954 *F, F*
M Gaitán 1998 *Ur*, 2002 *Par, Ch*, 2003 *Fj, US, Nm, R*, 2004 *W*, 2007 *It, W*
AM Galindo 2004 *Ur, Ven*, 2008 *S, It, SA, F, It*, 2009 *E*
R Gallo 1964 *Bra*
P Gambarini 2006 *W, Ch, Ur*, 2007 *I, It, Ch*, 2008 *S*
E Garbarino 1992 *Sp, Sp*
FL Garcia 1994 *SA*, 1995 *A, A, Par, Ch*, 1996 *Ur, F, F*, 1997 *NZ*, 1998 *Ur, R, Ur, J*
J Garcia 1998 *Par, Ur*, 2000 *A*
PT Garcia 1948 *OCC*
E Garcia Hamilton 1993 *Bra*
P Garcia Hamilton 1998 *Ch*
HM Garcia Simon 1990 *I*, 1992 *F*
G Garcia-Orsetti 1992 *R, F*
PA Garreton 1987 *Sp, Ur, Ch, A, A*, 1988 *F, F, F, F*, 1989 *It, NZ, Bra, Ch, Ur, US*, 1990 *C, E, E, I, E, S*, 1991 *NZ, NZ, Ch, A, W, Sa*, 1992 *F, F*, 1993 *J, J*
P Garzon 1990 *C*, 1991 *Par, Bra*
G Gasso 1983 *Ch, Par*
JM Gauweloose 1975 *F, F*, 1976 *W, NZ, NZ*, 1977 *F, F*, 1981 *C*
E Gavina 1956 *OCC, OCC*, 1958 *Ur, Per, Ch*, 1959 *JSB, JSB*, 1960 *F, F*, 1961 *Ch, Bra, Ur*
FA Genoud 2004 *Ch, Ur, Ven*, 2005 *J, BI, It*
J Genoud 1952 *I, I*, 1956 *OCC, OCC*
M Gerosa 1987 *Ur*
D Giambroni 2001 *Ur*
D Giannantonio 1996 *Ur*, 1997 *Par, Ur, It, A, A*, 1998 *Ur, F, F*, 2000 *A*, 2002 *E*
MC Giargia 1973 *Par, Ur, Bra*, 1975 *Par, Ch*
R Giles 1948 *OCC*, 1949 *F, F*, 1951 *Ur*, 1952 *I, I*
C Giuliano 1959 *JSB, JSB*, 1960 *F*
L Glastra 1948 *OCC, OCC*, 1952 *I, I*
M Glastra 1979 *Ur, Ch*, 1981 *C*
FE Gomez 1985 *Ur*, 1987 *Ur, Fj, It, NZ*, 1989 *NZ*, 1990 *C, E, E*
JF Gomez 2006 *It*, 2008 *S, S, It*
N Gomez 1997 *Par, Ch*
PM Gomez Cora 2001 *Ur*, 2004 *NZ, SA*, 2005 *Sa*, 2006 *E*
D Gonzalez 1988 *F, F*
D Gonzalez 1987 *Par*
T Gonzalez 1975 *Ur, Ch*
S Gonzalez Bonorino 2001 *Ur, US, C*, 2002 *Par, Ch*, 2003 *F, SA*, 2007 *I, I, It, W, F, Geo*, 2008 *S, S*
E Gonzalez del Solar 1960 *F*, 1961 *Ch, Bra, Ur*
N Gonzalez del Solar 1964 *Ur, Bra, Ch*, 1965 *Rho, JSB, OCC, OCC, Ch*
H Goti 1961 *Ch, Bra, Ur*, 1964 *Ur, Bra, Ch*, 1965 *Rho*, 1966 *SAG*
LM Gradin 1965 *OCC, OCC, Ch*, 1966 *SAG, SAG*, 1969 *Ch*, 1970 *I, I*, 1973 *R, R, Par, Ur, Ch, S*
P Grande 1998 *Par, Ch, Ur*
RD Grau 1993 *J, Bra, Ch*, 1995 *Par, Ch*, 1996 *F, F, US, Ur, C, SA, SA, E*, 1997 *E, E, NZ, NZ, A, A*, 1998 *Ur, F, It, F*, 1999 *W, W, S, I, W, F*, 2000 *A, SA, E*, 2001 *NZ, W, S, NZ*, 2002 *F, E, It, I*, 2003 *F, SA, US, Ur, C, A, I*
L Gravano 1997 *Ch*, 1998 *Ch, Ur*
B Grigolon 1948 *OCC*, 1954 *F, F*
V Grimoldi 1927 *GBR, GBR*
J Grondona 1990 *C*
R Grosse 1952 *I, I*, 1954 *F, F*
P Guarrochena 1977 *Par*
A Guastella 1956 *OCC*, 1959 *JSB, JSB*, 1960 *F*

J **Guidi** 1958 *Ur, Per, Ch*, 1959 *JSB*, 1960 *F*, 1961 *Ch, Bra, Ur*
E **Guiñazu** 2003 *Par, Ch, Ur*, 2004 *Ch, Ur, Ven, W, W, SA*, 2005 *J, It*, 2007 *I, It, F*, 2009 *E*
JA **Guzman** 2007 *Ch*
D **Halle** 1989 *Bra, Ch, Ur, US*, 1990 *US*
A **Hamilton** 1936 *BI*
R **Handley** 1966 *SAG, SAG*, 1968 *W, W*, 1969 *S, S, Ur, Ch*, 1970 *I, I*, 1971 *SAG, SAG*, 1972 *SAG, SAG*
G **Hardie** 1948 *OCC*
TA **Harris-Smith** 1969 *S, S*, 1971 *SAG, OCC, OCC*, 1973 *Par, Ur*
V **Harris-smith** 1936 *BI*
O **Hasan Jalil** 1995 *Ur*, 1996 *Ur, C, SA, SA*, 1997 *E, E, NZ, R, It, F, A*, 1998 *Ur, F, F, R, US, C, It, F, W*, 1999 *W, W, S, W, Sa, J, I*, 2000 *SA, E*, 2001 *NZ, It, W, S, NZ*, 2002 *F, E, SA, A, It, I*, 2003 *US, C, A, R*, 2004 *W, W, NZ, F, I*, 2005 *It, It, SA, S, It*, 2006 *NZ, E, F*, 2007 *It, Geo, Nm, I, S, SA, F*
P **Henn** 2004 *Ch, Ur, Ven*, 2005 *J, It, C*, 2007 *It*
JM **Hernández** 2003 *Par, Ur, F, F, SA, C, A, Nm, R*, 2004 *F, I, SA*, 2005 *SA, S, It*, 2006 *W, W, NZ, E, It, F*, 2007 *F, Geo, I, S, SA, F*, 2008 *It, F, It*, 2009 *E, E*
M **Hernandez** 1927 *GBR, GBR, GBR*
L **Herrera** 1991 *Ur, Par*
FA **Higgs** 2004 *Ur, Ven*, 2005 *J*
D **Hine** 1938 *Ch*
C **Hirsch** 1960 *F*
C **Hirsch** 1960 *F*
E **Hirsch** 1954 *F*, 1956 *OCC*
R **Hogg** 1958 *Ur, Per, Ch*, 1959 *JSB, JSB*, 1961 *Ch, Bra, Ur*
S **Hogg** 1956 *OCC, OCC*, 1958 *Ur, Per, Ch*, 1959 *JSB, JSB*
E **Holmberg** 1948 *OCC*
B **Holmes** 1949 *F, F*
E **Holmgren** 1958 *Ur, Per, Ch*, 1959 *JSB, JSB*, 1960 *F, F*
G **Holmgren** 1985 *NZ, NZ*
E **Horan** 1956 *OCC*
L **Hughes** 1936 *Ch*
M **Hughes** 1954 *F, F*
M **Hughes** 1949 *F, F*
CA **Huntley Robertson** 1932 *JSB, JSB*
A **Iachetti** 1975 *Ur, Par*, 1977 *Ur, Par, Ch*, 1978 *E, It*, 1979 *NZ, NZ, A, A*, 1980 *WXV, Fj, Fj*, 1981 *E, E*, 1982 *F, F, Sp*, 1987 *Ur, Par, A, A*, 1988 *F, F, F, F*, 1989 *It, NZ*, 1990 *C, E, E*
A **Iachetti** 1977 *Bra*, 1987 *Ch*
ME **Iachetti** 1979 *NZ, NZ, A, A*
M **Iglesias** 1973 *R*, 1974 *F, F*
G **Illia** 1965 *Rho*
JL **Imhoff** 1967 *Ur, Ch*
V **Inchausti** 1936 *BI, Ch, Ch*
F **Insua** 1971 *Ch, Bra, Par, Ur*, 1972 *SAG, SAG*, 1973 *R, R, Bra, Ch, I, S*, 1974 *F, F*, 1976 *Ur, W, NZ, NZ*, 1977 *F, F*
R **Iraneta** 1974 *F*, 1976 *Ur, W, NZ*
FJ **Irarrazabal** 1991 *Sa*, 1992 *Sp, Sp*
S **Irazoqui** 1993 *J, Ch, Par, Ur*, 1995 *E, Sa, Par*
A **Irigoyen** 1997 *Par*
C **Jacobi** 1979 *Ch, Par*
AG **Jacobs** 1927 *GBR, GBR*
Jaugust 1975 *Ch*
AGW **Jones** 1948 *OCC*
GM **Jorge** 1989 *Bra, Ch, Par, Ur*, 1990 *I, E*, 1992 *F, F, Sp, Sp, R, F*, 1993 *J, J, Bra, Ch, Ur, SA, SA*, 1994 *US, S, S, US*
J **Jose Villar** 2001 *Ur, US, C*, 2002 *Par, Ch*
E **Jurado** 1995 *A, A, E, Sa, It, Par, Ch, Ur, R, It, F*, 1996 *SA, E*, 1997 *E, E, NZ, NZ, Ur, R, It, F, A, A*, 1998 *Ur, F, Ur, C, It*, 1999 *W*
E **Karplus** 1959 *JSB, JSB*, 1960 *F, F, F*
A **Ker** 1936 *Ch*, 1938 *Ch*
E **Kossler** 1960 *F, F, F*
EH **Laborde** 1991 *A, W, Sa*
G **Laborde** 1979 *Ch, Bra*
J **Lacarra** 1989 *Par, Ur*
R **Lagarde** 1956 *OCC*
A **Lalanne** 2008 *SA*, 2009 *E*
M **Lamas** 1998 *Par, Ch*
TR **Landajo** 1977 *F, Bra, Ur, Ch*, 1978 *E*, 1979 *A, A*, 1980 *WXV, Fj, Fj*, 1981 *E, E*

M **Lanfranco** 1991 *Ur, Par, Bra*
AR **Lanusse** 1932 *JSB*
M **Lanusse** 1951 *Ur, Bra, Ch*
J **Lanza** 1985 *F, Ur, Par, NZ, NZ*, 1986 *F, F, A, A*, 1987 *Ur, Fj, It, NZ*
P **Lanza** 1983 *Ch, Par, Ur*, 1985 *F, F, Ur, Ch, Par, NZ, NZ*, 1986 *F, F, A, A*, 1987 *It, NZ*
J **Lasalle** 1964 *Ur*
J **Lavayen** 1961 *Ch, Bra, Ur*
CG **Lazcano Miranda** 1998 *Ch*, 2004 *Ch, Ur, Ven*, 2005 *J*
RA **le Fort** 1990 *I, E*, 1991 *NZ, NZ, Ch, A, W*, 1992 *R, F*, 1993 *J, SA, SA*, 1995 *Ur, It*
F **Lecot** 2003 *Par, Ur*, 2005 *J*, 2007 *Ch*
P **Ledesma** 2008 *It, SA*
ME **Ledesma Arocena** 1996 *Ur, C*, 1997 *NZ, NZ, Ur, R, It, F, A, A*, 1998 *Ur, F, F, Ur, C, J, Ur, F, W*, 1999 *WXV, W, W, Sa, J, I, F*, 2000 *SA, E*, 2001 *It, W, NZ*, 2002 *F, E, SA, A, It, I*, 2003 *F, SA, Fj, US, C, A, Nm, R*, 2004 *W, NZ, F, I*, 2005 *BI, It, It, SA, S, It*, 2006 *W, W, NZ, Ch, Ur, E, It, F*, 2007 *W, F, Geo, I, S, SA*, 2008 *SA, F, It, I*, 2009 *E*
J **Legora** 1996 *F, F, US, Ur*, 1997 *Ch*, 1998 *Par*
JM **Leguizamón** 2005 *J, BI, It, It, SA, S, It*, 2006 *W, NZ, Ur, E, It, F*, 2007 *I, I, It, W, F, Geo, Nm, S, SA, F*, 2008 *S, S, It, SA, I*, 2009 *E, E*
GP **Leiros** 1973 *Bra, I*
C **Lennon** 1958 *Ur, Per*
FJ **Leonelli Morey** 2001 *Ur*, 2004 *Ur, Ven*, 2005 *J, BI, It, C, SA, S, It*, 2006 *W, W*, 2007 *I, I, It*, 2008 *F, I*, 2009 *E*
M **Lerga** 1995 *Par, Ch, Ur*
Lesianado 1948 *OCC*
I **Lewis** 1932 *JSB*
GA **Llanes** 1990 *I, E, S*, 1991 *NZ, NZ, Ch, A, W*, 1992 *F, F, Sp, R, F*, 1993 *Bra, Ch, SA, SA*, 1994 *US, S, S, SA, SA*, 1995 *A, A, E, Sa, It, R, It, F*, 1996 *SA, SA, E*, 1997 *E, E, NZ, NZ, R, It, F*, 1998 *Ur, F*, 2000 *A*
G **Llanos** 2005 *C*
L **Lobrauco** 1996 *US*, 1997 *Ch*, 1998 *J, Ch, Ur*
MH **Loffreda** 1978 *E*, 1979 *NZ, NZ, A, A*, 1980 *WXV, Fj, Fj*, 1981 *E, E, C*, 1982 *F, F, Sp*, 1983 *WXV, A, A*, 1985 *Ur, Ch, Par*, 1987 *Ur, Par, Ch, A, A*, 1988 *F, F, F, F*, 1989 *It, NZ, Bra, Ch, Par, Ur, US*, 1990 *C, US, E, E*, 1994 *US, S, S, US, SA, SA*
G **Logan** 1936 *BI, BI*
GM **Longo Elía** 1999 *W, W, S, I, W, Sa, I, F*, 2000 *I, A, A, SA, E*, 2001 *US, NZ, It, W, S, NZ*, 2002 *F, E, SA, A, It, I*, 2003 *F, F, SA, Fj, C, A, I*, 2004 *W, W, NZ, F, I*, 2005 *It, It, SA*, 2006 *W, W, NZ, E, It, F*, 2007 *W, Nm, I, S, SA, F*
L **Lopez Fleming** 2004 *Ur, Ven, W*, 2005 *BI, C, Sa*
A **Lopresti** 1997 *Par, Ch*
J **Loures** 1954 *F*
R **Loyola** 1964 *Ur, Ch*, 1965 *Rho, JSB, OCC, OCC, Ch*, 1966 *SAG, SAG*, 1968 *W, W*, 1969 *S, S*, 1970 *I, I*, 1971 *Ch, Bra, Par, Ur*
E **Lozada** 2006 *E, It*, 2007 *I, I, Geo, F*, 2008 *S, S, It, SA, F, It, I*, 2009 *E*
F **Lucioni** 1927 *GBR*
R **Lucke** 1975 *Ur, Par, Bra, Ch*, 1976 *Ur*, 1981 *C*
M **Lugano** 2001 *Ur*
J **Luna** 1995 *Par, Ch, Ur, R, It, F*, 1997 *Par, Ch*
P **Macadam** 1949 *F, F*
AM **Macome** 1990 *I, E*, 1995 *Ur, C*
RM **Madero** 1978 *E, It*, 1979 *NZ, NZ, A, A*, 1980 *WXV, Fj, Fj*, 1981 *E, E, C*, 1982 *F, F, Sp*, 1983 *WXV, A, A*, 1985 *F, NZ*, 1986 *A, A*, 1987 *Ur, It, NZ, Sp, Ur, Par, Ch, A, A*, 1988 *F, F, F*, 1989 *It, NZ, NZ*, 1990 *E, E*
L **Makin** 1927 *GBR*
A **Mamanna** 1991 *Par*, 1997 *Par*
Manguiamell 1975 *Ch*
J **Manuel Belgrano** 1956 *OCC*
A **Marguery** 1991 *Ur, Bra*, 1993 *Ch, Par*
R **Martin** 1938 *Ch*
RA **Martin** 1994 *US, S, S, US, SA, SA*, 1995 *Ur, C, A, A, E, Sa, It, Ch, Ur, R, It, F*, 1996 *Ur, F, F, Ur, C, SA, SA, E*, 1997 *E, E, NZ, NZ, Ur, R, It, F, R, US, Ur, J, Par, Ch, Ur, It, W*, 1999 *WXV, W, W, S, I, W, Sa, J, I, F*, 2000 *I, A, A, SA, E*, 2001 *Ur, US, C, NZ, It, W, S, NZ*, 2002 *Ur, Par, Ch, F, E, SA, A, It, I*, 2003 *Par, Ch, Ur, F, SA, Ur, C, A, R, I*

F **Martin Aramburu** 2004 *Ch, Ven, W, NZ, F, I*, 2005 *It, SA, S, It*, 2006 *NZ*, 2007 *Geo, F*, 2008 *S, SA, F, It, I*, 2009 *E*
J **Martin Copella** 1989 *Ch, Par*
C **Martinez** 1969 *Ur, Ch*, 1970 *I, I*
E **Martinez** 1971 *Ch, Bra, Ur*
O **Martinez Basante** 1954 *F*
M **Martinez Mosquera** 1971 *Ch*
RC **Mastai** 1975 *Ch, F*, 1976 *Ur, W, NZ, NZ*, 1977 *F, F, Bra, Ur, Par, Ch*, 1980 *WXV*
R **Matarazzo** 1971 *SAG, SAG, Par, Ur*, 1972 *SAG, SAG*, 1973 *R, R, Par, Ur, Ch, I, S*, 1974 *F, F*
H **Maurer** 1932 *JSB, JSB*
L **Maurette** 1948 *OCC, OCC*
C **Mazzini** 1977 *F, F*
G **McCormick** 1964 *Bra, Ch*, 1965 *Rho, OCC, OCC, Ch*, 1966 *SAG, SAG*
M **McCormick** 1927 *GBR*
A **Memoli** 1979 *Ur, Par, Bra*
FE **Méndez** 1990 *I, E*, 1991 *NZ, NZ, Ch, A, W*, 1992 *F, F, Sp, Sp, R, F*, 1994 *S, US, SA, SA*, 1995 *Ur, C, A, A, E, Sa, It, Par, Ch, Ur, R, It, F*, 1996 *SA, SA*, 1997 *E*, 1998 *Ur, F, F, R, US, Ur, C, It, F, W*, 1999 *W, W*, 2000 *I, A, A, SA, E*, 2001 *NZ, It, W, S, NZ*, 2002 *Ur, Ch, F, E, SA, A*, 2003 *F, F, SA, Fj, Ur, Nm, I*, 2004 *Ch, Ur, W, W, NZ, SA*, 2005 *BI*
FJ **Mendez** 1991 *Ur, Par, Bra*, 1992 *Sp, Sp*
H **Mendez** 1967 *Ur, Ch*
L **Mendez** 1958 *Ur, Per, Ch*, 1959 *JSB*
CI **Mendy** 1987 *Ur, Par, Ch, A, A*, 1988 *F, F, F, F*, 1989 *It, NZ, NZ, US*, 1990 *C*, 1991 *Ur, Bra*
D **Mercol** 2001 *Ur*
FJ **Merello** 2007 *Ch*
I **Merlo** 1993 *Bra, Ch*
P **Merlo** 1985 *Ch, Par*
SE **Meson** 1987 *Par*, 1989 *Bra, Par, Ur, US*, 1990 *US, C, S*, 1991 *NZ, NZ, Ch, Sa*, 1992 *F, F, Sp, R, F*, 1993 *J, Bra, Par, Ur, SA, SA*, 1994 *US, S, S, US*, 1995 *Ur, C, A, A*, 1996 *US, C*, 1997 *Ch*
I **Mieres** 2007 *Ch*
BH **Miguens** 1983 *WXV, A, A*, 1985 *F, F, NZ, NZ*, 1986 *F, F, A, A*, 1987 *Sp*
E **Miguens** 1975 *Ch, Ur, Par, Ch*
H **Miguens** 1969 *S, S, Ur, Ch*, 1970 *I, I*, 1971 *OCC*, 1972 *SAG, SAG*, 1973 *R, R, Par, Ur, Bra, Ch, I, S*, 1975 *F*
J **Miguens** 1982 *F*, 1985 *F, F*, 1986 *F, F, A, A*
GE **Milano** 1982 *F, F, Sp*, 1983 *WXV, A, A*, 1985 *F, F, Ur, Ch, Par, NZ, NZ*, 1986 *F, F, A, A*, 1987 *Ur, Fj, Sp, Ur, Ch, A, A*, 1988 *F, F, F*, 1989 *It, NZ, NZ*
A **Mimesi** 1998 *J, Par, Ch*
B **Minguez** 1975 *Par, Bra, Ch*, 1979 *Ur, Ch, Par*, 1983 *WXV, A, A*, 1985 *Ur, Ch*
B **Mitchelstein** 1936 *BI*
E **Mitchelstein** 1956 *OCC*, 1960 *F, F*
LE **Molina** 1985 *Ch*, 1987 *Ur, Fj, It, NZ*, 1989 *NZ, NZ, Bra, Ch, Par*, 1990 *C, E*, 1991 *W*
M **Molina** 1998 *Par, Ch, Ur*
G **Montes de Oca** 1961 *Ch, Bra, Ur*
E **Montpelat** 1948 *OCC, OCC*
G **Morales Oliver** 2001 *Ur, US, C*
C **Morea** 1951 *Ur, Bra, Ch*
FR **Morel** 1979 *A, A*, 1980 *WXV, Fj, Fj*, 1981 *E, E, C*, 1982 *F*, 1985 *F, F, Ur, Par, NZ, NZ*, 1986 *F, F, A*, 1987 *Ur, Fj*
A **Moreno** 1998 *Par, Ch, Ur*
D **Moreno** 1967 *Ch*, 1970 *I, I*, 1971 *SAG, SAG, OCC, OCC*, 1972 *SAG, SAG*
E **Morgan** 1969 *S, S*, 1972 *SAG, SAG*, 1973 *R, R, Par, Ur, Bra, Ch, I, S*, 1975 *Ch, F, F*
G **Morgan** 1977 *Bra, Ur, Par, Ch*, 1979 *Ur, Par, Bra*
M **Morgan** 1971 *SAG, OCC, OCC*
JS **Morganti** 1951 *Ur, Bra, Ch*
J **Mostany** 1987 *Ur, Fj, NZ*
E **Muliero** 1997 *Ch*
S **Muller** 1927 *GBR*
R **Muniz** 1975 *Par, Bra, Ch*
M **Nannini** 2001 *Ur*, 2002 *Ur, Par, Ch*, 2003 *Par, Ch*
A **Navajas** 1932 *JSB, JSB*
E **Naveyra** 1998 *Ch*

G **Nazassi** 1997 *Ch*
ML **Negri** 1979 *Ch, Bra*
E **Neri** 1960 *F, F*, 1961 *Ch, Bra, Ur*, 1964 *Ur, Bra, Ch*, 1965 *Rho, JSB, OCC*, 1966 *SAG, SAG*
CM **Neyra** 1975 *Ch, F, F*, 1976 *W, NZ, NZ*, 1983 *WXV*
A **Nicholson** 1979 *Ur, Par, Bra*
HM **Nicola** 1971 *SAG, OCC, OCC, Ch, Bra, Par, Ur*, 1975 *Ch, F, F*, 1978 *E, It*, 1979 *NZ, NZ*
EP **Noriega** 1991 *Par*, 1992 *Sp, Sp, R, F*, 1993 *J, J, Ch, Par, Ur, SA, SA*, 1994 *US, S, S, US, SA, SA*, 1995 *Ur, C, A, A, E, Sa, It*
JM **Nuñez Piossek** 2001 *Ur, NZ*, 2002 *Ur, Par, Ch, A*, 2003 *Par, Ur, F, SA, Ur, C, A, R, I*, 2004 *Ch, Ur, W, W*, 2005 *BI, It, It*, 2006 *W, W, NZ, E, F*, 2008 *S, SA*
R **Ochoa** 1956 *OCC*
M **Odriozola** 1961 *Ch, Ur*
J **O'Farrell** 1948 *OCC*, 1951 *Ur, Bra*, 1956 *OCC*
U **O'Farrell** 1951 *Ur, Bra, Ch*
C **Ohanian** 1998 *Ur, Par, Ur*
C **Olivera** 1958 *Ur, Per, Ch*, 1959 *JSB, JSB*
R **Olivieri** 1960 *F, F, F*, 1961 *Ch, Bra, Ur*
J **Orengo** 1996 *Ur*, 1997 *Ur, R, It*, 1998 *Ur, F, F, R, US, C, F, W*, 1999 *WXV, W*, 2000 *A, SA, E*, 2001 *Ur, US, C, NZ, W, S, NZ*, 2002 *F, E, SA, A, It, I*, 2003 *F, SA, Ur, C, A, I*, 2004 *W, W*
JP **Orlandi** 2008 *F, It, I*, 2009 *E, E*
C **Orti** 1949 *F, F*
L **Ortiz** 2003 *Par, Ch, Ur*
A **Orzabal** 1974 *F, F*
L **Ostiglia** 1999 *W, W, S, I, W, J, F*, 2001 *NZ, It, W, S*, 2002 *E, SA*, 2003 *Par, Ch, Ur, F, F, SA, Nm, I*, 2004 *W, W, NZ, F, I, SA*, 2007 *F, Nm, I, S, SA*
B **Otaño** 1960 *F, F, F*, 1961 *Ch, Bra, Ur*, 1964 *Ur, Bra, Ch*, 1965 *Rho, JSB, OCC, OCC, Ch*, 1966 *SAG, SAG*, 1968 *W, W*, 1969 *S, S, Ur, Ch*, 1970 *I, I*, 1971 *SAG, OCC, OCC*
J **Otaola** 1970 *I*, 1971 *Ch, Bra, Par, Ur*, 1974 *F, F*
M **Pacheco** 1938 *Ch*
A **Palma** 1949 *F, F*, 1952 *I, I*, 1954 *F, F*
JMC **Palma** 1982 *F, Sp*, 1983 *WXV, A, A*
R **Palma** 1985 *Ch, Par*
M **Palou** 1996 *US, Ur*
M **Parra** 1975 *Ur, Bra, Ch*
A **Pasalagua** 1927 *GBR, GBR*
M **Pascual** 1965 *Rho, JSB, OCC, OCC, Ch*, 1966 *SAG, SAG*, 1967 *Ur, Ch*, 1968 *W, W*, 1969 *S, S, Ur, Ch*, 1970 *I, I*, 1971 *SAG, SAG, OCC, OCC*
HR **Pascuali** 1936 *BI*
H **Pasman** 1936 *Ch*
R **Passaglia** 1977 *Bra, Ur, Ch*, 1978 *E, It*
G **Paz** 1979 *Ur, Ch, Par, Bra*, 1983 *Ch, Par, Ur*
JJ **Paz** 1991 *Ur, Bra*
F **Peralta** 2001 *Ur*
S **Peretti** 1993 *Bra, Par, SA*
N **Perez** 1968 *W*
RN **Perez** 1992 *F, F, Sp, R, F*, 1993 *Bra, Par, Ur, SA*, 1995 *Ur, R, It, F*, 1996 *US, Ur, C, SA, SA*, 1998 *Ur*, 1999 *WXV, I*
J **Perez Cobo** 1979 *NZ, NZ*, 1980 *Fj*, 1981 *E, E, C*
M **Peri Brusa** 1998 *Ch*
R **Pesce** 1958 *Ur, Per, Ch*
TA **Petersen** 1978 *E, It*, 1979 *NZ, NZ, A, A*, 1980 *Fj, Fj*, 1981 *E, E, C*, 1982 *F*, 1983 *WXV, A, A*, 1985 *F, F, Ur, Ch, Par, NZ, NZ*, 1986 *F, F, A*
AD **Petrilli** 2004 *SA*, 2005 *J, C*
J **Petrone** 1949 *F, F*
R **Petti** 1995 *Par, Ch*
M **Pfister** 1994 *SA, SA*, 1996 *F*, 1998 *R, Ur, J*
S **Phelan** 1997 *Ur, Ch, R, It*, 1998 *Ur, F, F, R, US, C, It*, 1999 *S, I, W, Sa, J, I, F*, 2000 *I, A, A, SA, E*, 2001 *NZ, It, W, S, NZ*, 2002 *Ur, Ch, F, E, SA, A, It, I*, 2003 *Ch, Ur, F, SA, Fj, C, A, R*
A **Phillips** 1948 *OCC*, 1949 *F, F*
JP **Piccardo** 1981 *E*, 1983 *Ch, Par, Ur*
A **Pichot** 1995 *A, R, It, F*, 1996 *Ur, F, F*, 1997 *It, F, A, A*, 1998 *F, F, R, It, F, W*, 1999 *WXV, W, W, S, I, W, Sa, J, I, F*, 2000 *I, A, A, SA, E*, 2001 *Ur, US, C, NZ, It, W, S, NZ*, 2002 *F, E, SA, A, It, I*, 2003 *Ur, C, A, R, I*, 2004 *F, I,*

AUSTRALIA

AUSTRALIA'S 2008–09 TEST RECORD

OPPONENTS	DATE	VENUE	RESULT
New Zealand	1 November	N	**Lost** 14–19
Italy	8 November	A	**Won** 30–20
England	15 November	A	**Won** 28–14
France	22 November	A	**Won** 18–13
Wales	29 November	A	**Lost** 18–21
Italy	13 June	H	**Won** 31–8
Italy	20 June	H	**Won** 34–12
France	27 June	H	**Won** 22–6
New Zealand	18 July	A	**Lost** 16–22
South Africa	8 August	A	**Lost** 17–29
New Zealand	22 August	H	**Lost** 18–19
South Africa	29 August	H	**Lost** 25–32
South Africa	5 September	H	**Won** 21–6
New Zealand	19 September	A	**Lost** 6–33

WALLABIES STRUGGLE FOR CONSISTENCY

By Iain Spragg

When **Robbie Deans sat** down to reflect on his first full season as Australia head coach after the climax of the 2009 Tri-Nations, the New Zealander could be forgiven for invoking that oldest of sporting clichés and concluding it was a 12-month campaign of two distinct and contrasting halves.

The first was largely successful. The autumn tour of Europe yielded three wins from four games for Deans' youthful side and although their record was blemished by a narrow defeat to Wales in Cardiff, victories against England and France suggested the Wallabies were in fine fettle.

Three successive wins the following June at home to Italy and the French further fostered the impression that Australia were growing in both confidence and stature, but their subsequent Tri-Nations performances proved a chastening experience as the side finished rock bottom behind South Africa and New Zealand with just one victory from their six outings.

The climax of their season came in September in the Westpac Stadium, a fortnight after a 21–6 triumph over South Africa had gone some way to relieving the mounting pressure on Deans. However, his team's inexperience and naivety were all too obvious in Wellington as the All Blacks cantered to a comprehensive 33–6 victory.

For Deans, a sixth successive loss to his native country must have been particularly sobering and with a modest record of seven wins from 14 games for the season, the sense that his young charges needed to mature sooner rather than later on the international stage was palpable.

The first stop on Australia's year-long itinerary was Hong Kong in early November and a ground-breaking Bledisloe Cup clash with New Zealand, the first time in the 77-year history of the match that the two teams had crossed swords on neutral territory.

The Wallabies had lost two of their three preceding Tri-Nations clashes with the All Blacks but two first half tries from Drew Mitchell in the So Kon Po Stadium, both converted by Matt Giteau, gave Australia hope of a famous win. However, they were ultimately unable to contain the inevitable Kiwi rally in the second half and went down 19–14.

Jonathan Wood/Getty Images

Australia's best win came against South Africa in September.

AUSTRALIA

"From our perspective, our discipline let us down a number of times," said captain Stirling Mortlock after the game. "We gave them possession and territory through penalties. The majority of the guys were on their feet (at the breakdown) but we still let it slip a few times and when we did, the All Blacks pounced on it."

A week later, the Wallabies were in Italy for the first leg of their European foray. They had never lost to the Azzurri in nine previous meetings but were made to work hard for their 10th triumph by the home side in Padova and were heavily indebted to a brilliant solo try from substitute fly-half Quade Cooper in a 30–20 triumph.

England at Twickenham were the next opponents and Deans made eight changes to his starting line-up, recalling Giteau and the fly-half's contribution proved crucial as he landed six penalties to punish English indiscipline. He also converted Australia's only try from Adam Ashley-Cooper and although the home side enjoyed the lions' share of possession, the Wallabies emerged 28–14 victors.

"I'm delighted for the boys," Deans said. "They put in and they got the reward. A lot was asked of them. It was pretty brutal, direct and aggressive but they just kept turning up. They were asked a lot of questions but passed the test.

"It doesn't concern us whether the points were penalties or tries. We'd prefer tries but those decisions are made by the opposition."

The Stade de France was the venue for the third instalment of the tour and once again the Wallabies managed to manufacture a victory despite spending much of the contest against France on the back foot.

Hooker Stephen Moore and wing Peter Hynes scored tries either side of half-time to set up an 18–13 victory, but had David Skrela not missed five penalties for the home side it could have been a different story.

Australia's final match was against Wales in Cardiff, but they were not to record the win they craved in the Millennium Stadium as the home side notched up a rare victory for the northern hemisphere.

Wales went ahead in the third minute when Shane Williams rounded off a fine attacking move but the Wallabies hit back through Mark Chisholm. A Lee Byrne score re-established Wales' lead and although Digby Ioane crossed late on for the visitors, it was not enough to overhaul the home side and Australia were beaten 21–18.

A subsequent seven-month break from Test rugby for Deans' team finally came to an end in June with the arrival of Italy in Canberra. The Azzurri had taken Australia to the brink in November but the Wallabies were a different proposition on home territory and a superb hat-trick from 18-year-old full-back James O'Connor in his first Test start was the highlight of an encouraging 31–8 win.

The second Test against the Italians a week later in Melbourne was equally one-sided. Luke McLean landed four penalties for the visitors but tries from hooker Tatafu Polota-Nau, centre Ryan Cross, wing Lachie Turner and a brace from replacement Ashley-Cooper were testament to Australia's greater cutting edge and they cantered to a 34–12 victory.

The final match before the start of the Tri-Nations saw the Wallabies face France in Sydney for the Trophée des Bicentenaires. Les Bleus were brimming with confidence after beating the All Blacks a fortnight earlier but they were unable to claim another southern hemisphere scalp as Giteau grabbed the match by the scruff of the neck. The fly-half scored the only try of the match, which he converted, and also landed five penalties for all of Australia's points in their 22–6 triumph.

It was now time for the annual arm wrestle between the southern hemisphere giants and Deans and his team began against New Zealand at Eden Park. Australia had not recorded a win in Auckland since 1986 and although an early Barnes try suggested that unwanted record could finally come to an end, a Richie McCaw try sparked an All Black revival which resulted in a 22–16 win for the home side.

A daunting trip to South Africa in early August was the next challenge and once again they started brightly with a try from Ashley-Cooper, but indiscipline was to prove their undoing and seven penalties from Morné Steyn and a Victor Matfield try gave the Springboks a 29–17 success.

Australia now had three successive home games but were unable to take advantage in their first two outings. New Zealand triumphed 19–18 in Sydney courtesy of a Dan Carter penalty in the final minute and the Springboks were victorious 32–25 in Perth a week later to intensify the pressure on Deans.

The Wallabies were now in desperate need of a morale-boosting win and it finally came in Brisbane against South Africa. The first half was a tense affair but Australia exploded into life after the break and tries from Ashley-Cooper and O'Connor proved decisive as the Wallabies recorded a much-needed 21–6 win and left the Springboks waiting to be crowned Tri-Nations champions.

"It will be a fillip for this group and that was evident in the last 10 minutes," Deans said. "We had a few things go against us but they kept their heads up and they played for the full 80 minutes. It was evident at the end that the confidence was starting to kick in, and the spirit was great. We took South Africa outside their comfort zone, which we haven't been able to do previously."

The climax of the competition saw Australia play New Zealand in Wellington. The game was the 500th Test in the history of the Australian Rugby Union but any hopes the Wallabies had of marking the landmark occasion with a victory were ruthlessly dashed by the All Blacks in the Westpac Stadium.

Defeat for the home side would have meant an unprecedented third loss at home in a calendar year but there was never any danger of that happening as Australia failed to break through the Kiwi defence. Giteau landed a solitary penalty and Barnes slotted a drop goal but Deans' side were outclassed from start to finish as the All Blacks wrapped up a 33–6 victory.

The result condemned Australia to a distant third in the final Tri-Nations table and confirmed the men in gold as the southern hemisphere's poor relations.

"We prepared well for this game," said captain George Smith. "The boys were ready to play tonight, it's just in a number of areas we lacked it. We're going to have to fix that up come the spring tour. We didn't have too much possession and full credit to the All Blacks. When you have the other team dominating a number of areas, it's very hard to get any momentum going forward."

AUSTRALIA

AUSTRALIA INTERNATIONAL STATISTICS

MATCH RECORDS UP TO 30TH SEPTEMBER 2009

MOST CONSECUTIVE TEST WINS

10 1991 Arg, WS, W, I, NZ, E, 1992 S 1,2, NZ 1,2
10 1998 NZ 3, Fj, Tg, Sm, F, E 2, 1999 I 1,2, E, SA 1
10 1999 NZ 2, R, I 3, US,W, SA 3, F, 2000 Arg 1,2, SA 1

MOST CONSECUTIVE TESTS WITHOUT DEFEAT

Matches	Wins	Draws	Period
10	10	0	1991 to 1992
10	10	0	1998 to 1999
10	10	0	1999 to 2000

MOST POINTS IN A MATCH

BY THE TEAM

Pts.	Opponents	Venue	Year
142	Namibia	Adelaide	2003
92	Spain	Madrid	2001
91	Japan	Lyons	2007
90	Romania	Brisbane	2003
76	England	Brisbane	1998
74	Canada	Brisbane	1996
74	Tonga	Canberra	1998
74	W Samoa	Sydney	2005
73	W Samoa	Sydney	1994
69	Italy	Melbourne	2005
67	United States	Brisbane	1990

BY A PLAYER

Pts.	Player	Opponents	Venue	Year
42	M S Rogers	Namibia	Adelaide	2003
39	M C Burke	Canada	Brisbane	1996
30	E J Flatley	Romania	Brisbane	2003
29	S A Mortlock	South Africa	Melbourne	2000
28	M P Lynagh	Argentina	Brisbane	1995
27	M J Giteau	Fiji	Montpellier	2007
25	M C Burke	Scotland	Sydney	1998
25	M C Burke	France	Cardiff	1999
25	M C Burke	British/Irish Lions	Melbourne	2001
25	E J Flatley*	Ireland	Perth	2003
25	C E Latham	Namibia	Adelaide	2003
24	M P Lynagh	United States	Brisbane	1990
24	M P Lynagh	France	Brisbane	1990
24	M C Burke	New Zealand	Melbourne	1998
24	M C Burke	South Africa	Twickenham	1999

* includes a penalty try

MOST TRIES IN A MATCH
BY THE TEAM

Tries	Opponents	Venue	Year
22	Namibia	Adelaide	2003
13	South Korea	Brisbane	1987
13	Spain	Madrid	2001
13	Romania	Brisbane	2003
13	Japan	Lyons	2007
12	United States	Brisbane	1990
12	Wales	Brisbane	1991
12	Tonga	Canberra	1998
12	Samoa	Sydney	2005
11	Western Samoa	Sydney	1994
11	England	Brisbane	1998
11	Italy	Melbourne	2005

BY A PLAYER

Tries	Player	Opponents	Venue	Year
5	C E Latham	Namibia	Adelaide	2003
4	G Cornelsen	New Zealand	Auckland	1978
4	D I Campese	United States	Sydney	1983
4	J S Little	Tonga	Canberra	1998
4	C E Latham	Argentina	Brisbane	2000
4	L D Tuqiri	Italy	Melbourne	2005

MOST CONVERSIONS IN A MATCH
BY THE TEAM

Cons	Opponents	Venue	Year
16	Namibia	Adelaide	2003
12	Spain	Madrid	2001
11	Romania	Brisbane	2003
10	Japan	Lyons	2007
9	Canada	Brisbane	1996
9	Fiji	Parramatta	1998
8	Italy	Rome	1988
8	United States	Brisbane	1990
7	Canada	Sydney	1985
7	Tonga	Canberra	1998
7	Samoa	Sydney	2005
7	Italy	Melbourne	2005

BY A PLAYER

Cons	Player	Opponents	Venue	Year
16	M S Rogers	Namibia	Adelaide	2003
11	E J Flatley	Romania	Brisbane	2003
10	M C Burke	Spain	Madrid	2001
9	M C Burke	Canada	Brisbane	1996
9	J A Eales	Fiji	Parramatta	1998
8	M P Lynagh	Italy	Rome	1988
8	M P Lynagh	United States	Brisbane	1990
7	M P Lynagh	Canada	Sydney	1985
7	S A Mortlock	Japan	Lyons	2007

MOST PENALTIES IN A MATCH
BY THE TEAM

Pens	Opponents	Venue	Year
8	South Africa	Twickenham	1999
7	New Zealand	Sydney	1999
7	France	Cardiff	1999
7	Wales	Cardiff	2001
7	England	Twickenham	2008
6	New Zealand	Sydney	1984
6	France	Sydney	1986
6	England	Brisbane	1988
6	Argentina	Buenos Aires	1997
6	Ireland	Perth	1999
6	France	Paris	2000
6	British/Irish Lions	Melbourne	2001
6	New Zealand	Sydney	2004
6	Italy	Padua	2008
6	New Zealand	Sydney	2009

BY A PLAYER

Pens	Player	Opponents	Venue	Year
8	M C Burke	South Africa	Twickenham	1999
7	M C Burke	New Zealand	Sydney	1999
7	M C Burke	France	Cardiff	1999
7	M C Burke	Wales	Cardiff	2001
6	M P Lynagh	France	Sydney	1986
6	M P Lynagh	England	Brisbane	1988
6	D J Knox	Argentina	Buenos Aires	1997
6	M C Burke	France	Paris	2000
6	M C Burke	British/Irish Lions	Melbourne	2001
6	M J Giteau	England	Twickenham	2008
6	M J Giteau	New Zealand	Sydney	2009

MOST DROPPED GOALS IN A MATCH
BY THE TEAM

Drops	Opponents	Venue	Year
3	England	Twickenham	1967
3	Ireland	Dublin	1984
3	Fiji	Brisbane	1985

BY A PLAYER

Drops	Player	Opponent	Venue	Year
3	P F Hawthorne	England	Twickenham	1967
2	M G Ella	Ireland	Dublin	1984
2	D J Knox	Fiji	Brisbane	1985

AUSTRALIA

MOST CAPPED PLAYERS

Caps	Player	Career Span
139	G M Gregan	1994 to 2007
105	G B Smith	2000 to 2009
102	S J Larkham	1996 to 2007
101	D I Campese	1982 to 1996
86	J A Eales	1991 to 2001
86	J W C Roff	1995 to 2004
81	M C Burke	1993 to 2004
80	T J Horan	1989 to 2000
80	S A Mortlock	2000 to 2009
79	D J Wilson	1992 to 2000
79	N C Sharpe	2002 to 2009
79	P R Waugh	2000 to 2009
78	C E Latham	1998 to 2007
75	J S Little	1989 to 2000
73	M J Giteau	2002 to 2009
72	M P Lynagh	1984 to 1995
72	J A Paul	1998 to 2006
69	A K E Baxter	2003 to 2009
67	P N Kearns	1989 to 1999
67	D J Herbert	1994 to 2002
67	L D Tuqiri	2003 to 2008
63	N C Farr Jones	1984 to 1993
63	M J Cockbain	1997 to 2003
60	R S T Kefu	1997 to 2003
59	S P Poidevin	1980 to 1991

MOST CONSECUTIVE TESTS

Tests	Player	Career Span
62	J W C Roff	1996 to 2001
46	P N Kearns	1989 to 1995
44	G B Smith	2003 to 2006
42	D I Campese	1990 to 1995
37	P G Johnson	1959 to 1968

MOST TESTS AS CAPTAIN

Tests	Captain	Career Span
59	G M Gregan	2001 to 2007
55	J A Eales	1996 to 2001
36	N C Farr Jones	1988 to 1992
29	S A Mortlock	2006 to 2009
19	A G Slack	1984 to 1987
16	J E Thornett	1962 to 1967
16	G V Davis	1969 to 1972

MOST POINTS IN TESTS

Pts	Player	Tests	Career Span
911	M P Lynagh	72	1984 to 1995
878	M C Burke	81	1993 to 2004
514	M J Giteau	73	2002 to 2009
489	S A Mortlock	80	2000 to 2009
315	D I Campese	101	1982 to 1996
260	P E McLean	30	1974 to 1982
249*	J W Roff	86	1995 to 2004
200	C E Latham	78	1998 to 2007
187*	E J Flatley	38	1997 to 2005
173	J A Eales	86	1991 to 2001

* Roff and Flatley's totals include a penalty try

MOST TRIES IN TESTS

Tries	Player	Tests	Career Span
64	D I Campese	101	1982 to 1996
40	C E Latham	78	1998 to 2007
31*	J W Roff	86	1995 to 2004
30	T J Horan	80	1989 to 2000
30	L D Tuqiri	67	2003 to 2008
29	M C Burke	81	1993 to 2004
29	S A Mortlock	80	2000 to 2009
26	M J Giteau	73	2002 to 2009
25	S J Larkham	102	1996 to 2007
24	B N Tune	47	1996 to 2006
21	J S Little	75	1989 to 2000

* Roff's total includes a penalty try

MOST CONVERSIONS IN TESTS

Cons	Player	Tests	Career Span
140	M P Lynagh	72	1984 to 1995
104	M C Burke	81	1993 to 2004
75	M J Giteau	73	2002 to 2009
61	S A Mortlock	80	2000 to 2009
31	J A Eales	86	1991 to 2001
30	E J Flatley	38	1997 to 2005
27	P E McLean	30	1974 to 1982
27	M S Rogers	45	2002 to 2006
20	J W Roff	86	1995 to 2004
19	D J Knox	13	1985 to 1997

MOST PENALTY GOALS IN TESTS

Pens	Player	Tests	Career Span
177	M P Lynagh	72	1984 to 1995
174	M C Burke	81	1993 to 2004
74	S A Mortlock	80	2000 to 2009
74	M J Giteau	73	2002 to 2009
62	P E McLean	30	1974 to 1982
34	J A Eales	86	1991 to 2001
34	E J Flatley	38	1997 to 2005
23	M C Roebuck	23	1991 to 1993

MOST DROPPED GOALS IN TESTS

Drops	Player	Tests	Career Span
9	P F Hawthorne	21	1962 to 1967
9	M P Lynagh	72	1984 to 1995
8	M G Ella	25	1980 to 1984
5	B S Barnes	21	2007 to 2009
4	P E McLean	30	1974 to 1982
4	M J Giteau	73	2002 to 2009

TRI-NATIONS RECORDS

RECORD	DETAIL	HOLDER	SET
Most points in season	133	in six matches	2006
Most tries in season	14	in six matches	2006
	14	in six matches	2008
Highest Score	49	49–0 v S Africa (h)	2006
Biggest win	49	49–0 v S Africa (h)	2006
Highest score conceded	61	22–61 v S Africa (a)	1997
Biggest defeat	45	8–53 v S Africa (a)	2008
Most appearances	48	G M Gregan	1996 to 2007
Most points in matches	271	M C Burke	1996 to 2004
Most points in season	72	M J Giteau	2009
Most points in match	24	M C Burke	v N Zealand (h) 1998
Most tries in matches	9	J W C Roff	1996 to 2003
	9	S A Mortlock	2000 to 2009
	9	L D Tuqiri	2003 to 2008
Most tries in season	4	S A Mortlock	2000
Most tries in match	2	B N Tune	v S Africa (h) 1997
	2	S J Larkham	v N Zealand (a) 1997
	2	M C Burke	v N Zealand (h) 1998
	2	J W C Roff	v S Africa (h) 1999
	2	S A Mortlock	v N Zealand (h) 2000
	2	C E Latham	v S Africa (h) 2002
	2	M J Giteau	v S Africa (h) 2006
	2	L D Tuqiri	v N Zealand (a) 2006
	2	M J Giteau	v S Africa (h) 2009
Most cons in matches	25	M J Giteau	2003 to 2009
Most cons in season	12	S A Mortlock	2006
Most cons in match	5	S A Mortlock	v S Africa (h) 2006
Most pens in matches	65	M C Burke	1996 to 2004
Most pens in season	14	M C Burke	2001
	14	M J Giteau	2009
Most pens in match	7	M C Burke	v N Zealand (h) 1999

MISCELLANEOUS RECORDS

RECORD	HOLDER	DETAIL
Longest Test Career	G M Cooke	1932–1948
Youngest Test Cap	B W Ford	18 yrs 90 days in 1957
Oldest Test Cap	A R Miller	38 yrs 113 days in 1967

CAREER RECORDS OF AUSTRALIA INTERNATIONAL PLAYERS
(UP TO 30 SEPTEMBER 2009)

PLAYER BACKS	DEBUT	CAPS	T	C	P	D	PTS
A P Ashley-Cooper	2005 v SA	32	11	0	0	0	55
B S Barnes	2007 v J	21	4	1	0	5	37
L Burgess	2008 v I	19	0	0	0	0	0
Q S Cooper	2008 v It	7	1	0	0	0	5
S J Cordingley	2000 v Arg	22	0	0	0	0	0
R P Cross	2008 v F	15	5	0	0	0	25
S W Genia	2009 v NZ	6	0	0	0	0	0
M J Giteau	2002 v E	73	26	75	74	4	514
P J Hynes	2008 v I	17	3	0	0	0	15
D N Ioane	2007 v W	4	2	0	0	0	10
D A Mitchell	2005 v SA	37	17	0	0	0	85
S A Mortlock	2000 v Arg	80	29	61	74	0	489
S H Norton-Knight	2007 v W	2	1	0	0	0	5
J D O'Connor	2008 v It	10	4	2	1	0	27
P J A Tahu	2008 v NZ	4	0	0	0	0	0
L D Tuqiri	2003 v I	67	30	0	0	0	150
L D Turner	2008 v F	11	3	0	0	0	15
J J Valentine	2006 v E	6	0	0	0	0	0
FORWARDS:							
B E Alexander	2008 v F	13	0	0	0	0	0
A K E Baxter	2003 v NZ	69	1	0	0	0	5
R N Brown	2008 v NZ	11	0	0	0	0	0
M D Chisholm	2004 v S	43	6	0	0	0	30
P J M Cowan	2009 v It	3	0	0	0	0	0
M J Dunning	2003 v Nm	43	0	0	0	0	0
R D Elsom	2005 v Sm	44	7	0	0	0	35
A L Freier	2002 v Arg	25	2	0	0	0	10
S A Hoiles	2004 v S	16	3	0	0	0	15
J E Horwill	2007 v Fj	19	4	0	0	0	20
S M Kepu	2008 v It	2	0	0	0	0	0
P J Kimlin	2009 v It	2	0	0	0	0	0
H J McMeniman	2005 v Sm	21	0	0	0	0	0
S T Moore	2005 v Sm	41	2	0	0	0	10
D W Mumm	2008 v I	16	0	0	0	0	0

W L Palu	2006 v E	31	1	0	0	0	5
D W Pocock	2008 v NZ	11	0	0	0	0	0
T Polota-Nau	2005 v E	18	1	0	0	0	5
B A Robinson	2006 v SA	26	1	0	0	0	5
N C Sharpe	2002 v F	79	7	0	0	0	35
G T Shepherdson	2006 v I	18	1	0	0	0	5
G B Smith	2000 v F	105	9	0	0	0	45
D J Vickerman	2002 v F	55	0	0	0	0	0
P R Waugh	2000 v E	79	4	0	0	0	20

Matt King/Getty Images

AUSTRALIA

Matt Giteau is 26, but has racked up an incredible 73 caps.

AUSTRALIA INTERNATIONAL PLAYERS
UP TO 30TH SEPTEMBER 2009

Note: Years given for International Championship matches are for second half of season; eg 1972 means season 1971–72. Years for all other matches refer to the actual year of the match. Entries in square brackets denote matches played in RWC Finals.

Abrahams, A M F (NSW) 1967 NZ, 1968 NZ 1, 1969 W
Adams, N J (NSW) 1955 NZ 1
Adamson, R W (NSW) 1912 US
Alexander, B E (ACT) 2008 F1(R), 2(R), It, F3, 2009 It1(R), 2, F(R), NZ1(R), SA1(R), NZ2(t&R), SA2, 3, NZ3
Allan, T (NSW) 1946 NZ 1, M, NZ 2, 1947 NZ 2, S, I, W, 1948 E, F, 1949 M 1, 2, 3, NZ 1, 2
Anderson, R P (NSW) 1925 NZ 1
Anlezark, E A (NSW) 1905 NZ
Armstrong, A R (NSW) 1923 NZ 1, 2
Ashley-Cooper, A P (ACT) 2005 SA4(R), 2007 W1, 2, Fj, SA1(R), NZ1, SA2, NZ2, [J, Fj, C, E], 2008 F1(R), 2, SA1, NZ1, 2, SA3, NZ3, 4, It, E, F3, 2009 It1(R), 2(t&R), F, NZ1, SA1, NZ2, SA2, 3, NZ3
Austin, L R (NSW) 1963 E
Baker, R L (NSW) 1904 BI 1, 2
Baker, W H (NSW) 1914 NZ 1, 2, 3
Ballesty, J P (NSW) 1968 NZ 1, 2, F, I, S, 1969 W, SA 2, 3, 4, Bannon, D P** (NSW) 1946 M
Bardsley, E A (NSW) 1928 NZ 1, 3, M (R)
Barker, H S (NSW) 1952 Fj 1, 2, NZ 1, 2, 1953 SA 4, 1954 Fj 1, 2
Barnes, B S (Q) 2007 [J(R), W, Fj, E], 2008 I, F1, 2, SA1, NZ1, 2, SA2, NZ4(R), It, 2009 It1, 2, F, NZ1, SA1, NZ2, SA3, NZ3
Barnett, J T (NSW) 1907 NZ 1, 2, 3, 1908 W, 1909 E
Barry, M J (Q) 1971 SA 3
Bartholomeusz, M A (ACT) 2002 It (R)
Barton, R F D (NSW) 1899 BI 3
Batch, P G (Q) 1975 S, W, 1976 E, Fj 1, 2, 3, F 1, 2, 1978 W 1, 2, NZ 1, 2, 3, 1979 Arg 2
Batterham, R P (NSW) 1967 NZ, 1970 S
Battishall, B R (NSW) 1973 E
Baxter, A J (NSW) 1949 M 1, 2, 3, NZ 1, 2, 1951 NZ 1, 2, 1952 NZ 1, 2
Baxter, A K E (NSW) 2003 NZ 2(R), [Arg, R, I(R), S(R), NZ(R), E], 2004 S1, 2, E1, PI, NZ1, SA1, NZ2, SA2, S3, F, S4, E2, 2005 It, F1, SA1, 2, 3(R), NZ1, SA4, NZ2, F2, E, I(R), W(R), 2006 E1(R), 2(R), I1(R), NZ1(R), SA1(R), NZ3(R), SA3(R), W, It, I2, S(R), 2007 Fj, SA1(R), NZ1(R), SA2(R), NZ2(R), [J, W(R), C, E(R)], 2008 I(R), F1, 2, SA1, NZ1, 2, SA2(R), 3(R), NZ3, 4, E, F3, W, 2009 It1, F, NZ1, SA1, NZ2
Baxter, T J (Q) 1958 NZ 3
Beith, B McN (NSW) 1914 NZ 3, 1920 NZ 1, 2, 3
Bell, K R (Q) 1968 S
Bell, M D NSW) 1996 C
Bennett, W G (Q) 1931 M, 1933 SA 1, 2, 3,
Bermingham, J V (Q) 1934 NZ 1, 2, 1937 SA 1
Berne, J E (NSW) 1975 S
Besomo, K S (NSW) 1979 I 2
Betts, T N (Q) 1951 NZ 2, 3, 1954 Fj 2
Biilmann, R R (NSW) 1933 SA 1, 2, 3, 4
Birt, R S W (Q) 1914 NZ 2
Black, J W (NSW) 1985 C 1, 2, NZ, Fj 1
Blackwood, J G (NSW) 1922 M 1, NZ 1, 2, 3, 1923 M 1, NZ 1, 2, 3, 1924 NZ 1, 2, 3, 1925 NZ 1, 4, 1926 NZ 1, 2, 3, 1927 I, W, S, 1928 E, F
Blades, A T (NSW) 1996 S, I, W 3, 1997 NZ 1(R), E 1(R), SA 1(R), NZ 3, SA 2, Arg 1, 2, E 2, S, 1998 E 1, S 1, 2, NZ 1, SA 1, NZ 2, SA 2, NZ 3, Fj, WS, F, E 2, 1999 I 1(R), SA 2, NZ 2, [R, I 3, W, SA 3, F]
Blades, C D (NSW) 1997 E 1
Blake, R C (Q) 2006 E1, 2, NZ2, SA2, NZ3, SA3, W
Blair, M R (NSW) 1928 F, 1931 M, NZ
Bland, G V (NSW) 1928 NZ 3, M, 1932 NZ 1, 2, 3, 1933 SA 1, 2, 4, 5
Blomley, J (NSW) 1949 M 1, 2, 3, NZ 1, 2, 1950 BI 1, 2
Boland, S B (Q) 1899 BI 3, 4, 1903 NZ
Bond, G S G (ACT) 2001 SA 2(R), Sp (R), E (R), F, W

Bond, J H (NSW) 1920 NZ 1, 2, 3, 1921 NZ
Bondfield, C (NSW) 1925 NZ 2
Bonis, E T (Q) 1929 NZ 1, 2, 3, 1930 BI, 1931 M, NZ, 1932 NZ 1, 2, 3, 1933 SA 1, 2, 3, 4, 5, 1934 NZ 1, 2, 1936 NZ 1, 2, M, 1937 SA 1, 1938 NZ 1
Bonner, J E (NSW) 1922 NZ 1, 2, 3, 1923 M 1, 2, 3, 1924 NZ 1, 2
Bosler, J M (NSW) 1953 SA 1
Bouffler, R G (NSW) 1899 BI 3
Bourke, T K (Q) 1947 NZ 2
Bowden, R (NSW) 1926 NZ 4
Bowen, S (NSW) 1993 SA 1, 2, 3, 1995 [R], NZ 1, 2, 1996 C, NZ 1, SA 2
Bowers, A J A (NSW) 1923 M 2(R), 3, NZ, 3, 1925 NZ 1, 4, 1926 NZ 1, 1927 I
Bowman, T M (NSW) 1998 E 1, S 1, 2, NZ 1, SA 1, NZ 2, SA 2, NZ 3, Fj, WS, F, E 2, 1999 I 1, 2, SA 2, [US]
Boyce, E S (NSW) 1962 NZ 1, 2, 1964 NZ 1, 2, 3, 1965 SA 1, 2, 1966 W, S, 1967 E, I 1, F, I 2
Boyce, J S (NSW) 1962 NZ 3, 4, 5, 1963 E, SA 1, 2, 3, 4, 1964 NZ 1, 3, 1965 SA 1, 2
Boyd, A (NSW) 1899 BI 3
Boyd, A F McC (Q) 1958 M 1
Brass, J E (NSW) 1966 BI 2, W, S, 1967 E, I 1, F, I 2, NZ, 1968 NZ 1, F, I, S
Breckenridge, J W (NSW) 1925 NZ 2(R), 3, 1927 I, W, S, 1928 E, F, 1929 NZ 1, 2, 3, 1930 BI
Brial, M C (NSW) 1993 F 1(R), 2, 1996 W 1(R), 2, C, NZ 1, SA 1, NZ 2, SA 2, It, I, W 3, 1997 NZ 2
Bridle, O L (V) 1931 M, 1932 NZ 1, 2, 3, 1933 SA 3, 4, 5, 1934 NZ 1, 2, 1936 NZ 1, 2, M
Broad, E G (Q) 1949 M 1
Brockhoff, J D (NSW) 1949 M 2, 3, NZ 1, 2, 1950 BI 1, 2, 1951 NZ 2, 3
Brown, B R (Q) 1972 NZ 1, 3
Brown, J V (NSW) 1956 SA 1, 2, 1957 NZ 1, 2, 1958 W, I, E, S, F
Brown, R C (NSW) 1975 E 1, 2
Brown, R N (WF) 2008 NZ3(R), 4, It, E, W, 2009 It1, F, NZ1, SA1, NZ2, SA2
Brown, S W (NSW) 1953 SA 2, 3, 4
Bryant, H (NSW) 1925 NZ 1, 3, 4
Buchan, A J (NSW) 1946 NZ 1, 2, 1947 NZ 1, 2, S, I, W, 1948 E, F, 1949 M 3
Buchanan, P N (NSW) 1923 M 2(R), 3
Bull, D (NSW) 1928 M
Buntine, H (NSW) 1923 NZ 1(R), 1924 NZ 2
Burdon, A (NSW) 1903 NZ, 1904 BI 1, 2, 1905 NZ
Burge, A B (NSW) 1907 NZ 3, 1908 W
Burge, P H (NSW) 1907 NZ 1, 2, 3
Burge, R (NSW) 1928 NZ 1, 2, 3(R), M (R)
Burgess, L (NSW) 2008 I, F1, 2, SA1, NZ1, 2, 4, It, E, F3, W, 2009 It1, 2, F, NZ1, SA1, NZ2, SA2, NZ3(R)
Burke, B T (NSW) 1988 S (R)
Burke, C T (NSW) 1946 NZ 2, 1947 NZ 1, 2, S, I, W, 1948 E, F, 1949 M 2, 3, NZ 1, 2, 1950 BI 1, 2, 1951 NZ 1, 2, 1953 SA 2, 3, 4, 1954 Fj 1, 1955 NZ 1, 2, 3, 1956 SA 1, 2,
Burke, M C (NSW) 1993 SA 3(R), F 1, 1994 I 1, 2, It 1, 2, 1995 [C, R, E], NZ 1, 2, 1996 W 1, 2, C, NZ 1, SA 1, NZ 2, SA 2, It, S, I, W 3, 1997 E 1, NZ 2 , 1998 E 1, S 1, 2, NZ 1, SA 1, NZ 2, SA 2, [R, I 3, US, W, SA 3, F], 2000 F, S, E, 2001 BI 1(R), 2, 3, SA 1, NZ 1, SA 2, NZ 2, Sp, E, F, W, 2002 F 1, 2, NZ 1, SA 1, NZ 2, SA 2, Arg, I, E, It, 2003 SA 1, NZ 1, SA 2(R), [Arg, R, Nm(R), I], 2004 S1(R), PI(R), SA1(R), NZ2(t&R), SA2(R)
Burke, M P (NSW) 1984 E (R), I, 1985 C 1, 2, NZ, Fj 1, 2, 1986 It (R), F, Arg 1, 2, NZ 1, 2, 3, 1987 SK, [US, J, I, F, W], NZ, Arg 1, 2
Burnet, D R (NSW) 1972 F 1, 2, NZ 1, 2, 3, Fj

Butler, O F (NSW) 1969 SA 1, 2, 1970 S, 1971 SA 2, 3, F 1, 2
Calcraft, W J (NSW) 1985 C 1, 1986 It, Arg 2
Caldwell, B C (NSW) 1928 NZ 3
Cameron, A S (NSW) 1951 NZ 1, 2, 3, 1952 Fj 1, 2, NZ 1, 2, 1953 SA 1, 2, 3, 4, 1954 Fj 1, 2, 1955 NZ 1, 2, 3, 1956 SA 1, 2, 1957 NZ 1, 1958 I
Campbell, A M (ACT) 2005 F1(R), 2006 It(R), I2(R), S
Campbell, J D (NSW) 1910 NZ 1, 2, 3
Campbell, W A (Q) 1984 Fj, 1986 It, F, Arg 1, 2, NZ 1, 2, 3, 1987 SK, [E, US, J (R), I, F], NZ, 1988 E, 1989 BI 1, 2, 3, NZ, 1990 NZ 2, 3
Campese, D I (ACT, NSW) 1982 NZ 1, 2, 3, 1983 US, Arg 1, 2, NZ, It, F 1, 2, 1984 Fj, NZ 1, 2, 3, E, I, W, S, 1985 Fj 1, 2, 1986 It, F, Arg 1, 2, NZ 1, 2, 3, 1987 [E, US, J, I, F, W], NZ, 1988 E 1, 2, NZ 1, 2, 3, E, S, It, 1989 BI 1, 2, 3, NZ, F 1, 2, 1990 F 2, 3, US, NZ 1, 2, 3, 1991 W, E, NZ 1, 2, [Arg, WS, W, I, NZ, E], 1992 S 1, 2, NZ 1, 2, 3, SA, I, W, 1993 Tg, NZ, SA 1, 2, 3, C, F 1, 2, 1994 I 1, 2, It 1, 2, WS, NZ, 1995 Arg 1, 2, [SA, C, E], NZ 2(R), 1996 W 1, 2, C, NZ 1, SA 1, NZ 2, SA 2, It, W3
Canniffe, W D (Q) 1907 NZ 2
Cannon, B J (NSW, WF) 2001 BI 2(R), NZ 1(R), Sp (R), F (R), W (R), 2002 F 1(R), 2, SA 1(t), 2(R), I (t), It (R), 2003 I (R), W (R), E (R), SA 1, NZ 1, SA 2, NZ 2, [Arg, R, I, S, NZ, E], 2004 S1, 2, E1, PI, NZ1, 2, SA2, S3(R), 4(R), 2005 NZ1(R), SA4, NZ2, F2, E, I, W, 2006 W(R), It
Caputo, M E (ACT) 1996 W 1, 2, 1997 F 1, 2, NZ 1
Carberry, C M (NSW, Q) 1973 Tg 2, E, 1976 I, US, Fj 1, 2, 3, 1981 F 1, 2, I, W, S, 1982 E
Cardy, A M (NSW) 1966 BI 1, 2, W, S, 1967 E, I 1, F, 1968 NZ 1, 2
Carew, P J (Q) 1899 BI 1, 2, 3, 4
Carmichael, P (Q) 1904 BI 2, 1907 NZ 1, 1908 W, 1909 E
Carozza, P V (Q) 1990 F 1, 2, 3, NZ 2, 3, 1992 S 1, 2, NZ 1, 2, 3, SA, I, W, 1993 Tg
Carpenter, M G (V) 1938 NZ 1, 2,
Carr, E T A (NSW) 1913 NZ 1, 2, 3, 1914 NZ 1, 2, 3
Carr, E W (NSW) 1921 SA 1, 2, 3, NZ (R)
Carroll, D B (NSW) 1908 W, 1912 US
Carroll, J C (NSW) 1953 SA 1
Carroll, J H (NSW) 1958 M 2, 3, NZ 1, 2, 3, 1959 BI 1, 2
Carson, J (NSW) 1899 BI 1
Carson, P J (NSW) 1979 NZ, 1980 NZ 3
Carter, D G (NSW) 1988 E 1, 2, NZ 1, 1989 F 1, 2
Casey, T V (NSW) 1963 SA 2, 3, 4, 1964 NZ 1, 2, 3
Catchpole, K W (NSW) 1961 Fj 1, 2, 3, SA 1, 2, F, 1962 NZ 1, 2, 4, 1963 SA 2, 3, 4, 1964 NZ 1, 2, 3, 1965 SA 1, 2, 1966 BI 1, 2, W, S, 1967 E, I 1, F, I 2, NZ, 1968 NZ 1
Cawsey, R M (NSW) 1949 M 1, NZ 1, 2
Cerutti, W H (NSW) 1928 NZ 1, 2, 3, M, 1929 NZ 1, 2, 3, 1930 BI, 1931 M, NZ, 1932 NZ 1, 2, 3, 1933 SA 1, 2, 3, 4, 5, 1936 M, 1937 SA 1, 2
Challoner, R L (NSW) 1899 BI 2
Chambers, R (NSW) 1920 NZ 1, 3
Chapman, G A (NSW) 1962 NZ 3, 4, 5
Chisholm, M D (ACT) 2004 S3(R), 2005 Sm, It, F1, SA1, 2, 3(R), NZ1(R), 2, F2, E(t&R), I(R), W(R), 2006 E1(R), 2, I1, NZ1, SA1(R), NZ2(R), SA2(R), NZ3(t&R), SA3(R), W(R), It, I2, S(t&R), 2007 W1, 2(R), Fj, SA1(R), NZ1(R), 2(R), [W(R), Fj, C], 2008 NZ4, It, E, F3(R), W, 2009 SA2, NZ3
Clark, J G (Q) 1931 M, 1932 NZ 1, 2, 1933 SA 1
Clarken, J C (NSW) 1905 NZ, 1910 NZ 1, 2, 3
Cleary, M A (NSW) 1961 Fj 1, 2, 3, SA 1, 2, F
Clements, P (NSW) 1982 NZ 3
Clifford, M (NSW) 1938 NZ 3
Cobb, W (NSW) 1899 BI 3, 4
Cockbain, M J (Q) 1997 F 2(R), NZ 1, SA 1, 2, 1998 E 1, S 1, 2, NZ 1, SA 1, NZ 2, SA 2, NZ 3, Fj, Tg (R), WS, F, E 2, 1999 I 1, 2, E, SA 1, NZ 1, SA 2, NZ 2, [US (t&R), W, SA 3, F], 2000 Arg 1, 2, SA 2(t&R), 3(t&R), F, S, E (R), 2001 BI 1(R), 2(R), 3(R), SA 1(R), NZ 1(R), SA 2(R), NZ 1(R), Sp (R), E (R), F (t+R), W, 2002 F 1(R), 2(R), NZ 1(R), SA 1(R), NZ 2(R), SA 2(R), Arg, I, E, It, 2003 [Arg(R), R(R), Nm(R), I(R), S(R), NZ(R), E(R)]
Cocks, M R (NSW, Q) 1972 F 1, 2, NZ 2, 3, Fj, 1973 Tg 1, 2, W, E, 1975 J 1
Codey, D (NSW Country, Q) 1983 Arg 1, 1984 E, W, S, 1985 C 2, NZ, 1986 F, Arg 1, 1987 [US, J, F (R), W], NZ
Cody, E W (NSW) 1913 NZ 1, 2, 3
Coker, T (Q, ACT) 1987 [E, US, F, W], 1991 NZ 2, [Arg, WS, NZ, E], 1992 NZ 1, 2, 3, SA, I, W (R), 1993 Tg, NZ, 1995 Arg 2, NZ (R), 1997 F 1(R), 2, NZ 1, E 1, NZ 2(R), SA 1(R), NZ 3, SA 2, Arg 1, 2
Colbert, R (NSW) 1952 Fj 2, NZ 1, 2, 1953 SA 2, 3, 4
Cole, J W (NSW) 1968 NZ 1, 2, F, I, S, 1969 W, SA 1, 2, 3, 4, 1970 S, 1971 SA 1, 2, 3, F 1, 2, 1972 NZ 1, 2, 3, 1973 Tg 1, 2, 1974 NZ 1, 2, 3

Collins, P K (NSW) 1937 SA 2, 1938 NZ 2, 3
Colton, A J (Q) 1899 BI 1, 3
Colton, T (Q) 1904 BI 1, 2
Comrie-Thomson, I R (NSW) 1926 NZ 4, 1928 NZ 1, 2, 3 M
Connor, D M (Q) 1958 W, I, E, S, F, M 2, 3, NZ 1, 2, 3, 1959 BI 1, 2
Connors, M R (Q) 1999 SA 1(R), NZ 1(R), SA 2(R), NZ 2, [R (R), I 3, US, W (R), SA 3(R), F(R)], 2000 Arg 1(R), 2(R), SA 1, NZ 1, SA 2, NZ 2(t&R), SA 3, F (R), S (R), E (R)
Constable, R (Q) 1994 I 2(t & R)
Cook, M T (Q) 1986 F, 1987 SK, [J], 1988 E 1, 2, NZ 1, 2, 3, E, S, It
Cooke, B P (Q) 1979 I 1
Cooke, G M (Q) 1932 NZ 1, 2, 3, 1933 SA 1, 2, 3, 1946 NZ 2, 1947 NZ 2, S, I, W, 1948 E, F
Coolican, J E (NSW) 1982 NZ 1, 1983 It, F 1, 2
Cooney, R C (NSW) 1922 M 2
Cooper, Q S (Q) 2008 It(R), F3(R), W(R), 2009 It1(R), 2, SA2(R), 3(R)
Cordingley, S J (Q, Grenoble) 2000 Arg 1(R), SA 1(R), F, S, E, 2006 E2, I1(R), NZ1(R), SA1(R), NZ2(R), SA2(R), 2007 Fj(R), [Fj(R), C], 2008 I(R), F1(R), 2(t&R), SA1(R), 2, 3, NZ3, F3(R)
Corfe, A C (Q) 1899 BI 2
Cornelsen, G (NSW) 1974 NZ 2, 3, 1975 J 2, S, W, 1976 E, F 1, 2, 1978 W 1, 2, NZ 1, 2, 3, 1979 I 1, 2, NZ, Arg 1, 2, 1980 NZ 1, 2, 3, 1981 I, W, S, 1982 E
Cornes, J R (Q) 1972 Fj
Cornforth, R G W (NSW) 1947 NZ 1, 1950 BI 2
Cornish, P (ACT) 1990 F 2, 3, NZ 1
Costello, P P S (Q) 1950 BI 2
Cottrell, N V (Q) 1949 M 1, 2, 3, NZ 1, 2, 1950 BI 1, 2, 1951 NZ 1, 2, 3, 1952 Fj 1, 2, NZ 1, 2
Cowan, P J M (WF) 2009 It2, SA3(R), NZ3(R)
Cowper, D L (V) 1931 NZ, 1932 NZ 1, 2, 3, 1933 SA 1, 2, 3, 4, 5
Cox, B P (NSW) 1952 Fj 1, 2, NZ 1, 2, 1954 Fj 2, 1955 NZ 1, 1956 SA 2, 1957 NZ 1, 2
Cox, M H (NSW) 1981 W, S
Cox, P A (NSW) 1979 Arg 1, 2, 1980 Fj, NZ 1, 2, 1981 W (R), S, 1982 S 1, 2, NZ 1, 2, 3, 1984 Fj, NZ 1, 2, 3
Craig, R R (NSW) 1908 W
Crakanthorp, J S (NSW) 1923 NZ 3
Cremin, J F (NSW) 1946 NZ 1, 2, 1947 NZ 1
Crittle, C P (NSW) 1962 NZ 4, 5, 1963 SA 2, 3, 4, 1964 NZ 1, 2, 3, 1965 SA 1, 2, 1966 BI 1, 2, S, 1967 E, I
Croft, B H D (NSW) 1928 M
Croft, D N (Q) 2002 Arg (t&R), I (R), E (t&R), It (R), 2003 [Nm]
Cross, J R (NSW) 1955 NZ 1, 2, 3
Cross, K A (NSW) 1949 M 1, NZ 1, 2, 1950 BI 1, 2, 1951 NZ 2, 3, 1952 NZ 1, 1953 SA 1, 2, 3, 4, 1954 Fj 1, 2, 1955 NZ 3, 1956 SA 1, 2, 1957 NZ 1, 2
Cross, R P (WF) 2008 F1(R), 2(R), SA1(R), NZ1, 2(R), SA2(R), 3(R), NZ3, 4, E, W, 2009 It2, F(R), NZ2(R), SA2
Crossman, O C (NSW) 1923 M 1(R), 2, 3, 1924 NZ 1, 2, 3, 1925 NZ 1, 3, 4, 1926 NZ 1, 2, 3, 4, 1929 NZ 2, 1930 BI
Crowe, P J (NSW) 1976 F 2, 1978 W 1, 2, 1979 I 2, NZ, Arg 1
Crowley, D J (NSW) 1989 BI 1, 2, 3, 1991 [WS], 1992 I, W, 1993 C (R), 1995 Arg 1, 2, [SA, E], NZ 1, 1996 W 2(R), C, NZ 1, SA 1, 2, I, W 3, 1998 E 1(R), S 1(R), 2(R), NZ 1(R), SA 1, NZ 2, SA 2, NZ 3, Tg, WS, 1999 I 1, 2(R), E (R), SA 1, NZ 1(R), [R (R), I 3(t&R), US, F(R)]
Curley, T G P (NSW) 1957 NZ 1, 2, 1958 W, I, E, S, F, M 1, NZ 1, 2, 3
Curran, D J (NSW) 1980 NZ 3, 1981 F 1, 2, W, 1983 Arg 1
Currie, E W (Q) 1899 BI 2
Cutler, S A G (NSW) 1982 NZ 2(R), 1984 NZ 1, 2, 3, E, I, W, S, 1985 C 1, 2, NZ, Fj 1, 2, 1986 It, F, NZ 1, 2, 3, 1987 SK, [E, J, I, F, W], NZ, Arg 1, 2, 1988 E 1, 2, NZ 1, 2, 3, E, S, It, 1989 BI 1, 2, 3, NZ, 1991 [WS]
Daly, A J (NSW) 1989 NZ, F 1, 2, 1990 F 1, 2, 3, US, NZ 1, 2, 3, 1991 W, E, NZ 1, 2, [Arg, W, I, NZ, E], 1992 S 1, 2, NZ 1, 2, 3, SA, 1993 Tg, NZ, SA 1, 2, 3, C, F 1, 2, 1994 I 1, 2, It 1, 2, WS, NZ, 1995 [C, R]
D'Arcy, A M (Q) 1980 Fj, NZ 3, 1981 F 1, 2, I, W, S, 1982 E, S 1, 2
Darveniza, P (NSW) 1969 W, SA 2, 3, 4
Darwin, B J (ACT) 2001 BI 1(R), SA 1(R), NZ 1(R), SA 2(R), NZ 2(t&R), Sp, E, F, W, 2002 NZ 1(R), SA 1(R), NZ 2(R), SA 2, Arg (R), I (R), E (R), It (R), 2003 I (R), W (t&R), E (R), SA 1(R), NZ 1(R), [Arg(R), R(R), Nm, I, S, NZ]
Davidson, R A L (NSW) 1952 Fj 1, 2, NZ 1, 2, 1953 SA 1, 1957 NZ 1, 2, 1958 W, I, E, S, F, M 1
Davis, C C (NSW) 1949 NZ 1, 1951 NZ 1, 2, 3
Davis, E H (V) 1947 S, W, 1949 M 1, 2
Davis, G V (NSW) 1963 E, SA 1, 2, 3, 4, 1964 NZ 1, 2, 3, 1965 SA 1, 1966 BI 1, 2, W, S, 1967 E, I 1, F, I 2, NZ, 1968 NZ 1, 2, F, I, S, 1969 W, SA 1, 2, 3, 4, 1970 S, 1971 SA 1, 2, 3, F 1, 2, 1972 F 1, 2, NZ 1, 2, 3
Davis, G W G (NSW) 1955 NZ 2, 3

Davis, R A (NSW) 1974 NZ 1, 2, 3
Davis, T S R (NSW) 1920 NZ 1, 2, 3, 1921 SA 1, 2, 3, NZ, 1922 M 1, 2, 3, NZ 1, 2, 3, 1923 M 3, NZ 1, 2, 3, 1924 NZ 1, 2, 1925 NZ 1
Davis, W (NSW) 1899 BI 1, 3, 4
Dawson, W L (NSW) 1946 NZ 1, 2
Diett, L J (NSW) 1959 BI 1, 2
Dix, W (NSW) 1907 NZ 1, 2, 3, 1909 E
Dixon, E J (Q) 1904 BI 3
Donald, K J (Q) 1957 NZ 1, 1958 W, I, E, S, M, 2, 3, 1959 BI 1, 2
Dore, E (Q) 1904 BI 1
Dore, M J (Q) 1905 NZ
Dorr, R W (V) 1936 M, 1937 SA 1
Douglas, J A (V) 1962 NZ 3, 4, 5
Douglas, W A (NSW) 1922 NZ 3(R)
Dowse, J H (NSW) 1961 Fj 1, 2, SA 1, 2
Dunbar, A R (NSW) 1910 NZ 1, 2, 3, 1912 US
Duncan, J L (NSW) 1926 NZ 4
Dunlop, E E (V) 1932 NZ 3, 1934 NZ 1
Dunn, P K (NSW) 1958 NZ 1, 2, 3, 1959 BI 1, 2
Dunn, V A (NSW) 1920 NZ 1, 2, 3, 1921 SA 1, 2, 3, NZ
Dunning, M J (NSW) 2003 [Nm, E(R)], 2004 S1(R), 2(R), E1(R), NZ1(R), SA1(R), NZ2(t&R), SA2(R), S3(R), F(R), S4(R), E2(R), 2005 Sm, It(R), F1(t&R), SA1(R), 2(R), 3, NZ1(t&R), SA4(t&R), NZ2(R), F2, E, W, 2007 W1, 2(R), Fj, SA1, NZ1, SA2, NZ2, [J, W, Fj, E], 2008 I, SA1(R), NZ1(R), SA2, 3, NZ4(R), It
Dunworth, D A (Q) 1971 F 1, 2, 1972 F 1, 2, 1976 Fj 2
Dwyer, L J (NSW) 1910 NZ 1, 2, 3, 1912 US, 1913 NZ 3, 1914 NZ 1, 2, 3
Dyson, F J (Q) 2000 Arg 1, 2, SA 1, NZ 1, SA 2, NZ 2, SA 3, F, S, E
Eales, J A (Q) 1991 W, E, NZ 1, 2, [Arg, WS, W, I, NZ, E], 1992 S 1, 2, NZ 1, 2, 3, SA, I, 1994 I 1, 2, It 1, 2, WS, NZ, 1995 Arg 1, 2, [SA, C, R, E], NZ 1, 2, 1996 W 1, 2, C, NZ 1, SA 1, NZ 2, SA 2, It, S, I, 1997 F 1, 2, NZ 1, E 1, NZ 2, SA 1, Arg 1, 2, E 2, S, 1998 E 1, S 1, 2, NZ 1, SA 1, NZ 2, SA 2, NZ 3, Fj, Tg, WS, F, E 2, 1999 [R, I 3, W, SA 3, F], 2000 Arg 1, 2, SA 1, NZ 1, SA 2, NZ 2, SA 3, F, S, E, 2001 BI 1, 2, 3, SA 1, NZ 1, SA 2, NZ 2
Eastes, C C (NSW) 1946 NZ 1, 2, 1947 NZ 1, 2, 1949 M 1, 2
Edmonds, M H M (NSW) 1998 Tg, 2001 SA 1(R)
Egerton, R H (NSW) 1991 W, E, NZ 1, 2, [Arg, W, I, NZ, E]
Ella, G A (NSW) 1982 NZ 1, 2, 1983 F 1, 2, 1988 E 2, NZ 1
Ella, G J (NSW) 1982 S 1, 1983 It, 1985 C 2(R), Fj 2
Ella, M G (NSW) 1980 NZ 1, 2, 3, 1981 F 2, S, 1982 S 1, NZ 1, 2, 3, 1983 US, Arg 1, 2, NZ, It, F 1, 2, 1984 Fj, NZ 1, 2, 3, E, I, W, S
Ellem, M A (NSW) 1976 Fj 3(R)
Elliott, F M (NSW) 1957 NZ 1
Elliott, R E (NSW) 1920 NZ 1, 1921 NZ, 1922 M 1, 2, NZ 1(R), 2, 3, 1923 M 1, 2, 3, NZ 1, 2, 3
Ellis, C S (NSW) 1899 BI 1, 2, 3, 4
Ellis, K J (NSW) 1958 NZ 1, 2, 3, 1959 BI 1, 2
Ellwood, B J (NSW) 1958 NZ 1, 2, 3, 1961 Fj 2, 3, SA 1, F, 1962 NZ 1, 2, 3, 4, 5, 1963 SA 1, 2, 3, 4, 1964 NZ 3, 1965 SA 1, 2, 1966 BI 1
Elsom, R D (NSW, ACT) 2005 Sm, It, F1, SA1, 2, 3(R), 4, NZ2, F2, 2006 E1, 2, I1, NZ1, SA1, NZ2, SA2, NZ3, SA3, W, It, I2, S, 2007 W1, 2, SA1, NZ1, SA2, NZ2, [J, W, Fj, E], 2008 I, F1, 2, SA1, NZ1, SA2, 3, NZ3, 2009 NZ2, SA2, 3, NZ3
Emanuel, D M (NSW) 1957 NZ 2, 1958 W, I, E, S, F, M 1, 2, 3
Emery, N A (NSW) 1947 NZ 2, S, I, W, 1948 E, F, 1949 M 2, 3, NZ 1, 2
Erasmus, D J (NSW) 1923 NZ 1, 2
Erby, A B (NSW) 1923 M 1, 2, NZ 2, 3, 1925 NZ 2
Evans, L J (Q) 1903 NZ, 1904 BI 1, 3
Evans, W T (Q) 1899 BI 1, 2
Fahey, E J (NSW) 1912 US, 1913 NZ 1, 2, 1914 NZ 3
Fairfax, R L (NSW) 1971 F 1, 2, 1972 F 1, 2, NZ 1, Fj, 1973 W, E
Farmer, E H (Q) 1910 NZ 1
Farquhar, C R (NSW) 1920 NZ 2
Farr-Jones, N C (NSW) 1984 E, I, W, S, 1985 C 1, 2, NZ, Fj 1, 2, 1986 It, F, Arg 1, 2, NZ 1, 2, 3, 1987 SK, [E, I, F, W (R)], NZ, Arg 2, 1988 E 1, 2, NZ 1, 2, 3, E, S, It, 1989 BI 1, 2, 3, NZ, F 1, 2, 1990 F 1, 2, 3, US, NZ 1, 2, 3, 1991 W, E, NZ 1, 2, [Arg, WS, I, NZ, E], 1992 S 1, 2, NZ 1, 2, 3, SA, 1993 NZ, SA 1, 2, 3
Fava, S G (ACT, WF) 2005 E(R), I(R), 2006 NZ1(R), SA1, NZ2
Fay, G (NSW) 1971 SA 2, 1972 NZ 1, 2, 3, 1973 Tg 1, 2, W, E, 1974 NZ 1, 2, 3, 1975 E 1, 2, J 1, S, W, 1976 I, US, 1978 W 1, 2, NZ 1, 2, 3, 1979 I 1
Fenwicke, P T (NSW) 1957 NZ 1, 1958 W, I, E, 1959 BI 1, 2

Ferguson, R T (NSW) 1922 M 3, NZ 1, 1923 M 3, NZ 3
Fihelly, J A (Q) 1907 NZ 2
Finau, S F (NSW) 1997 NZ 3
Finegan, O D A (ACT) 1996 W 1, 2, C, NZ 1, SA 1(t), S, W 3, 1997 SA 1, NZ 3, SA 2, Arg 1, 2, E 2, S, 1998 E 1(R), S 1(t + R), 2(t + R), NZ 1(R), SA 1(t), 2(R), NZ 3(R), Fj (R), Tg, WS (t + R), F (R), E 2(R), 1999 NZ 2(R), [R, I 3(R), US, W (R), SA 3(R), F (R)], 2001 BI 1, 2, 3, SA 1, NZ 1, SA 2, NZ 2, Sp, E, F, W, 2002 F 1, SA 1, NZ 1, SA 2, SA 2, I, 2003 SA 1(t&R), NZ2 1(R), SA 2(R), NZ 2(R)
Finlay, A N (NSW) 1926 NZ 1, 2, 3, 1927 I, W, S, 1928 E, F, 1929 NZ 1, 2, 3, 1930 BI
Finley, F G (NSW) 1904 BI 3
Finnane, S C (NSW) 1975 E 1, J 1, 2, 1976 E, 1978 W 1, 2
Fitter, D E S (ACT) 2005 I, W
FitzSimons, P (NSW) 1989 F 1, 2, 1990 F 1, 2, 3, US, NZ 1
Flanagan, P (Q) 1907 NZ 1, 2
Flatley, E J (Q) 1997 E 2, S, 2000 S (R), 2001 BI 1(R), 2(R), 3, SA 1, NZ 1(R), 2(R), Sp (R), F (R), W, 2002 F 1(R), 2(R), NZ 1(t+R), SA 1(R), NZ 2(t), Arg (R), I (R), E, It, 2003 I, W, SA 1, NZ 1, SA 2, NZ 2, [Arg, R, I, S, NZ, E], 2004 S3(R), F(R), S4(R), E2, 2005 NZ1(R)
Flett, J A (NSW) 1990 US, NZ 2, 3, 1991 [WS]
Flynn, J P (Q) 1914 NZ 1, 2
Fogarty, J R (Q) 1949 M 2, 3
Foley, M A (Q) 1995 [C (R), R], 1996 W 2(R), NZ 1, SA 1, NZ 2, SA 2, It, S, I, W 3, 1997 NZ 1(R), E 1, NZ 2, SA 1, NZ 3, SA 2, Arg 1, 2, E 2, S, 1998 Tg (R), F (R), E 2(R), 1999 NZ 2(R), [US, W, SA 3, F], 2000 Arg 1, 2, SA 1, NZ 1, SA 2, NZ 2, SA 3, F, S, E, 2001 BI 1(R), 2, 3, SA 1, NZ 1, SA 2, Sp, E, F, W
Foote, R H (NSW) 1924 NZ 2, 3, 1926 NZ 2
Forbes, C F (Q) 1953 SA 2, 3, 4, 1954 Fj 1, 1956 SA 1, 2
Ford, B (Q) 1957 NZ 2
Ford, E E (NSW) 1927 I, W, S, 1928 E, F, 1929 NZ 1, 3
Ford, J A (NSW) 1925 NZ 4, 1926 NZ 1, 2, 1927 I, W, S, 1928 E, 1929 NZ 1, 2, 3, 1930 BI
Forman, T R (NSW) 1968 I, S, 1969 W, SA 1, 2, 3, 4
Fowles, D G (NSW) 1921 SA 1, 2, 3, 1922 M 2, 3, 1923 M 2, 3
Fox, C L (NSW) 1920 NZ 1, 2, 3, 1921 SA 1, NZ, 1922 M 1, 2, NZ 1, 1924 NZ 1, 2, 3, 1925 NZ 1, 2, 3, 1926 NZ 1, 3, 1928 F
Fox, O G (NSW) 1958 F
Francis, E (Q) 1914 NZ 1, 2
Frawley, D (Q, NSW) 1986 Arg 2(R), 1987 Arg 1, 2, 1988 E 1, 2, NZ 1, 2, 3, S, It
Freedman, J E (NSW) 1962 NZ 3, 4, 5, 1963 SA 1
Freeman, E (NSW) 1946 NZ 1(R), M
Freier, A L (NSW) 2002 Arg 2(R), I, E (R), It, 2003 SA 1(R), NZ 1(t), 2005 NZ2(R), 2006 E2, 2007 W1(R), 2(R), Fj, SA1(R), NZ1(R), SA2, NZ2(R), [JfR), W(R), Fj(R), C, E(R)], 2008 I(R), F1(R), 2(R), NZ3(R), W(t&R)
Freney, M E (Q) 1972 NZ 1, 2, 3, 1973 Tg 1, W, E (R)
Friend, W S (NSW) 1920 NZ 3, 1921 SA 1, 2, 3, 1922 NZ 1, 2, 3, 1923 M 1, 2, 3
Furness, D C (NSW) 1946 M
Futter, F C (NSW) 1904 BI 3
Gardner, J M (Q) 1987 Arg 2, 1988 E 1, NZ 1, E
Gardner, W C (NSW) 1950 BI 1
Garner, R L (NSW) 1949 NZ 1, 2
Gavin, K A (NSW) 1909 E
Gavin, T B (NSW) 1988 NZ 2, 3, S, It (R), 1989 NZ (R), F 1, 2, 1990 F 1, 2, 3, US, NZ 1, 2, 3, 1991 W, E, NZ 1, 1992 S 1, 2, SA, I, W, 1993 Tg, NZ, SA 1, 2, 3, C, F 1, 2, 1994 I 1, 2, It 1, 2, WS, NZ, 1995 Arg 1, 2, [SA, C, R, E], NZ 1, 2, 1996 NZ 2(R), SA 2, W 3
Gelling, A M (NSW) 1972 NZ 1, Fj
Genia, S W (Q) 2009 NZ1(R), SA1(R), NZ2(R), SA2(R), 3, NZ3
George, H W (NSW) 1910 NZ 1, 2, 3, 1912 US, 1913 NZ 1, 3, 1914 NZ 1, 3
George, W G (NSW) 1923 M 1, 3, NZ 1, 2, 1924 NZ 3, 1925 NZ 2, 3, 1926 NZ 4, 1928 NZ 1, 2, 3, M
Gerrard, M A (ACT) 2005 It(R), SA1(R), NZ1, 2, E, I, W, 2006 E1, 2, I1, NZ1, SA1, NZ2, SA2, NZ3(t), SA3(R), I2, S, 2007 W1, 2(R), SA2, NZ2, [J(R)]
Gibbons, E de C (NSW) 1936 NZ 1, 2, M
Gibbs, P R (V) 1966 S
Giffin, D T (ACT) 1996 W 3, 1997 F 1, 2, 1999 I 1, 2, E, SA 1, NZ 1, SA 2, NZ 2, [R, I 3, US (R), W, SA 3, F], 2000 Arg 1, 2, SA 1, NZ 1, SA 2, NZ 2, SA 3, F, S, E, 2001 BI 1, 2, SA 1, NZ 1, SA 2, Sp, E, F, W, 2002 Arg (R), I, E (R), It (R), 2003 I, W, E, SA 1, NZ 1, SA 2, NZ 2, 2, [Arg, Nm(R), I, NZ(t&R), E(R)]
Gilbert, H (NSW) 1910 NZ 1, 2, 3
Girvan, B (ACT) 1988 E
Giteau, M J (ACT, WF) 2002 E (R), It (R), 2003 SA 2(R), NZ 2(R),

Hynes, P J (Q) 2008 I, F1, 2, SA1, NZ1, 2, SA2, 3, NZ3, 4, E, F3, W, 2009 It2, NZ2(R), SA2, 3(R)
Ide, W P J (Q) 1938 NZ 2, 3
Ioane, D N (WF, Q) 2007 W2, 2008 It, F3, W
Ives, W N (NSW) 1926 NZ 1, 2, 3, 4, 1929 NZ 3
James, P M (Q) 1958 M 2, 3
James, S L (NSW) 1987 SK (R), [E (R)], NZ, Arg 1, 2, 1988 NZ 2(R)
Jamieson, A E (NSW) 1925 NZ 3(R)
Jaques, T (ACT) 2000 SA 1(R), NZ 1(R)
Jessep, E M (V) 1934 NZ 1, 2
Johansson, L D T (Q) 2005 NZ2(R), F2(R), E(R)
Johnson, A P (NSW) 1946 NZ 1, M
Johnson, B B (NSW) 1952 Fj 1, 2, NZ 1, 2, 1953 SA 2, 3, 4, 1955 NZ 1, 2
Johnson, P G (NSW) 1959 BI 1, 2, 1961 Fj 1, 2, 3, SA 1, 2, F, 1962 NZ 1, 2, 3, 4, 5, 1963 E, SA 1, 2, 3, 4, 1964 NZ 1, 2, 3, 1965 SA 1, 2, 1966 BI 1, 2, W, S, 1967 E, I 1, F, I 2, NZ, 1968 NZ 1, 2, F, I, S, 1970 S, 1971 SA 1, 2, F 1, 2
Johnstone, B (Q) 1993 Tg (R)
Jones, G G (Q) 1952 Fj 1, 2, 1953 SA 1, 2, 3, 4, 1954 Fj 1, 2, 1955 NZ 1, 2, 3, 1956 SA 1
Jones, H (NSW) 1913 NZ 1, 2, 3
Jones, P A (NSW) 1963 E, SA 1
Jorgensen, P (NSW) 1992 S 1(R), 2(R)
Joyce, J E (NSW) 1903 NZ
Judd, H A (NSW) 1903 NZ, 1904 BI 1, 2, 3, 1905 NZ
Judd, P B (NSW) 1925 NZ 4, 1926 NZ 1, 2, 3, 4, 1927 I, W, S, 1928 E, 1931 M, NZ
Junee, D K (NSW) 1989 F 1(R), 2(R), 1994 WS (R), NZ (R)
Kafer, R B (ACT) 1999 NZ 2, [R, US (R)], 2000 Arg 1(R), 2, SA 1, NZ 1(t&R), SA 2(R), 3(R), F, S, E
Kahl, P R (Q) 1992 W
Kanaar, A (NSW) 2005 NZ2(R)
Kassulke, N (Q) 1985 C 1, 2
Kay, A R (V) 1958 NZ 2, 1959 BI 2
Kay, P (NSW) 1988 E 2
Kearney, K H (NSW) 1947 NZ 1, 2, S, I, W, 1948 E, F
Kearns, P N (NSW) 1989 NZ, F 1, 2, 1990 F 1, 2, 3, US, NZ 1, 2, 3, 1991 W, E, NZ 1, 2, [Arg, WS, W, I, NZ, E], 1992 S 1, 2, NZ 1, 2, 3, SA, I, W, 1993 Tg, NZ, SA 1, 2, 3, C, F 1, 2, 1994 I 1, 2, It 1, 2, WS, NZ, 1995 Arg 1, 2, [SA, C, E], NZ 1, 2, 1998 E 1, S 1, 2, NZ 1, SA 1, NZ 2, SA 2, NZ 3, Fj, WS, F, E 2, 1999 I 2(R), SA 1(R), 2, NZ 2, [R, I 3]
Kefu, R S T (Q) 1997 SA 2(R), 1998 E 1, S 1, 2, NZ 1, SA 1, NZ 2, SA 2, NZ 3, Fj (R), Tg, WS (R), F, E 2, 1999 I 1, 2, E, SA 1, NZ 1(R), SA 2, NZ 2, [R, I 3, SA 3, F], 2000 SA 1(t&R), NZ 1(R), SA 2(R), NZ 2, SA 3(R), F, S, E, 2001 BI 1, 2, 3, SA 1, NZ 1, SA 2, NZ 2, Sp, E, F, W, 2002 F 1, NZ 1, SA 1, NZ 2, SA 2, Arg, I, E, It, 2003 I, W, E, SA 1, NZ 1, SA 2, NZ 2
Kefu, S (Q) 2001 W (R), 2003 I, W, E, SA 1, NZ 1(R)
Kelaher, J D (NSW) 1933 SA 1, 2, 3, 4, 5, 1934 NZ 1, 2, 1936 NZ 1, 2, M, 1937 SA 1, 2, 1938 NZ 3
Kelaher, T P (NSW) 1992 NZ 1, I (R), 1993 NZ
Kelleher, R J (Q) 1969 SA 2, 3
Keller, D H (NSW) 1947 NZ 1, S, I, W, 1948 E, F
Kelly, A J (NSW) 1899 BI 1
Kelly, R L F (NSW) 1936 NZ 1, 2, M, 1937 SA 1, 2, 1938 NZ 1, 2
Kent, A (Q) 1912 US
Kepu, S M (NSW) 2008 It(R), F3(R)
Kerr, F R (V) 1938 NZ 1
Kimlin, P J (ACT) 2009 It1(R), 2
King, S C (NSW) 1926 NZ 1, 2, 3, 4(R), 1927 W, S, 1928 E, F, 1929 NZ 1, 2, 3, 1930 BI, 1932 NZ 1, 2
Knight, M (NSW) 1978 W 1, 2, NZ 1
Knight, S O (NSW) 1969 SA 2, 4, 1970 S, 1971 SA 1, 2, 3
Knox, D J (NSW, ACT) 1985 Fj 1, 2, 1990 US (R), 1994 WS, NZ, 1996 It, S, I, 1997 SA 1, NZ 3, SA 2, Arg 1, 2
Kraefft, D F (NSW) 1947 NZ 2, S, I, W, 1948 E, F
Kreutzer, S D (Q) 1914 NZ 2
Lamb, J S (NSW) 1928 NZ 1, 2, M
Lambie, J K (NSW) 1974 NZ 1, 2, 3, 1975 W
Lane, R E (NSW) 1921 SA 1
Lane, T A (Q) 1985 C 1, 2, NZ
Lang, C W P (V) 1938 NZ 2, 3
Langford, J F (ACT) 1997 NZ 3, SA 2, E 2, S
Larkham, S J (ACT) 1996 W 2(R), 1997 F 1, 2, NZ 1, 2(R), SA 1, NZ 3, SA 2, Arg 1, 2, E 2, S, 1998 E 1, S 1, 2, NZ 1, SA 1, NZ 2, SA 2, NZ 3, Fj, Tg (t), WS, F, E 2, 1999 [I 3, US, W, SA 3, F], 2000 Arg 1, 2, SA 1, NZ 1, SA 2, NZ 2, SA 3, 2001 BI 1, 2, NZ 1, SA 2, NZ 2, Sp, E, F, W, 2002 F 1, 2, NZ 1, SA 1, NZ 2, SA 2, Arg, I, E, 2003 SA 1(R), NZ 1, SA 2, NZ 2, [Arg, R, I, S, NZ, E], 2004S1, 2, E1, PI, NZ1, SA1, NZ2, SA2, S3, F, S4, 2005 Sm(R), It, F1, SA1, 2, 3, 2006 E1, 2, I1, NZ1, SA1, NZ2, SA2, NZ3, SA3, W, It, I2, S, 2007 W2, Fj, SA1, NZ1, SA2, NZ2, [J]
Larkin, E R (NSW) 1903 NZ
Larkin, K K (Q) 1958 M 2, 3
Latham, C E (Q) 1998 F, E 2, 1999 I 1, 2, E, [US], 2000 Arg 1, 2, SA 1, NZ 1, SA 2, NZ 2, SA 3, F, S, E, 2001 BI 1, 2(R), SA 1(R), NZ 1(R), SA 2, NZ 2, Sp, E, F, W (R), 2002 F 1, 2, NZ 1, SA 1, NZ 2, SA 2, 2003 I, W, E, NZ 1(R), SA 2, NZ 2, [Nm], 2004 S1(R), 2(R), E1(R), PI(t&R), NZ1, SA1, NZ2, SA2, S3, F, S4, E2, 2005 Sm, F1, SA2, 3, F2, E, I, W, 2006 E1, 2, I1, NZ1, SA1, NZ2, SA2, NZ3, SA3, W, It, I2, S, 2007 NZ2(R), [J, W, Fj, C, E]
Latimer, N B (NSW) 1957 NZ 2
Lawton, R (Q) 1988 E 1, NZ 2(R), 3, S
Lawton, T (NSW, Q) 1920 NZ 1, 2, 1925 NZ 4, 1927 I, W, S, 1928 E, F, 1929 NZ 1, 2, 3, 1930 BI, 1932 NZ 1, 2
Lawton, T A (Q) 1983 F 1(R), 2, 1984 Fj, NZ 1, 2, 3, E, I, W, S, 1985 C 1, 2, NZ, Fj 1, 1986 It, F, Arg 1, 2, NZ 1, 2, 3, 1987 SK, [E, US, I, F, W], NZ, Arg 1, 2, 1988 E 1, 2, NZ 1, 2, 3, E, S, It, 1989 BI 1, 2, 3
Laycock, W M B (NSW) 1925 NZ 2, 3, 4, 1926 NZ 2
Leeds, A J (NSW) 1986 NZ 3, 1987 [US, W], NZ, Arg 1, 2, 1988 E 1, 2, NZ 1, 2, 3, E, S, It
Lenehan, J K (NSW) 1958 W, E, S, F, M 1, 2, 3, 1959 BI 1, 2, 1961 SA 1, 2, F, 1962 NZ 2, 3, 4, 5, 1965 SA 1, 2, 1966 W, S, 1967 E, I 1, F, I 2
L'Estrange, R D (Q) 1971 F 1, 2, 1972 NZ 1, 2, 3, 1973 Tg 1, 2, W, E, 1974 NZ 1, 2, 3, 1975 S, W, 1976 I, US
Lewis, L S (Q) 1934 NZ 1, 2, 1936 NZ 2, 1938 NZ 1
Lidbury, S (NSW) 1987 Arg 1, 1988 E 2
Lillicrap, C P (Q) 1985 Fj 2, 1987 [US, I, F, W], 1989 BI 1, 1991 [WS]
Lindsay, R T G (Q) 1932 NZ 3
Lisle, R J (NSW) 1961 Fj 1, 2, 3, SA 1
Little, J S (Q, NSW) 1989 F 1, 2, 1990 F 1, 2, 3, US, 1991 W, E, NZ 1, 2, [Arg, W, I, NZ, E], 1992 NZ 1, 2, 3, SA, I, W, 1993 Tg, NZ, SA 1, 2, 3, C, F 1, 2, 1994 WS, NZ, 1995 Arg 1, 2, [SA, C, E], NZ 1, 2, 1996 It (R), I, W 3, 1997 F 1, 2, E 1, NZ 2, SA 1, NZ 3, SA 2, 1998 E 1(R), S 2(R), NZ 2, SA 2(R), NZ 3, Fj, Tg, WS, F, E 2, 1999 I 1(R), 2, SA 2(R), NZ 2, [R, I 3(t&R), US, W (R), SA 3(t&R), F (R)], 2000 Arg 1(R), 2(R), SA 1(R), NZ 1, SA 2, NZ 2, SA 3
Livermore, A E (Q) 1946 NZ 1, M
Loane, M E (Q) 1973 Tg 1, 2, 1974 NZ 1, 1975 E 1, 2, J 1, 1976 E, I, Fj 1, 2, 3, F 1, 2, 1978 W 1, 2, 1979 I 1, 2, NZ, Arg 1, 2, 1981 F 1, 2, I, W, S, 1982 E, S 1, 2
Logan, D L (NSW) 1958 M 1
Loudon, D B (NSW) 1921 NZ, 1922 M 1, 2, 3
Loudon, R B (NSW) 1923 NZ 1(R), 2, 3, 1928 NZ 1, 2, 3, M, 1929 NZ 2, 1933 SA 2, 3, 4, 5, 1934 NZ 2
Love, E W (NSW) 1932 NZ 1, 2, 3
Lowth, D R (NSW) 1958 NZ 1
Lucas, B C (Q) 1905 NZ
Lucas, P W (NSW) 1982 NZ 1, 2, 3
Lutge, D (NSW) 1903 NZ, 1904 BI 1, 2, 3
Lynagh, M P (Q) 1984 Fj, E, I, W, S, 1985 C 1, 2, NZ, 1986 It, F, Arg 1, 2, NZ 1, 2, 3, 1987 [E, US, J, I, F, W], Arg 1, 2, 1988 E 1, 2, NZ 1, 3(R), E, S, It, 1989 BI 1, 2, 3, NZ, F 1, 2, 1990 F 1, 2, 3, US, NZ 1, 2, 3, 1991 W, E, NZ 1, 2, [Arg, WS, W, I, NZ, E], 1992 S 1, 2, NZ 1, 2, 3, SA, I, 1993 Tg, C, F 1, 2, 1994 I 1, 2, It 1, 1995 Arg 1, 2, [SA, C, E]
Lyons, D J (NSW) 2000 Arg 1(t&R), 2(R), 2001 BI 1(R), SA 1(R), 2002 F 1(R), 2, NZ 1(R), SA 1(R), NZ 2(R), SA 2(t+R), 2003 I, W, E, SA 1, [Arg, R, Nm, I, S, NZ, E], 2004 S1, 2, E1, PI, NZ1, SA1, NZ2, SA2, S3(R), F(R), S4, E2, 2005 Sm, It, F1, SA1, 2, NZ1, SA4, 2006 S, 2007 Fj, SA2(R), [C]
McArthur, M (NSW) 1909 E
McBain, M I (Q) 1983 It, F 1, 1985 Fj 2, 1986 It (R), 1987 [J], 1988 E 2(R), 1989 BI 1(R)
MacBride, J W T (NSW) 1946 NZ 1, M, NZ 2, 1947 NZ 1, 2, S, I, W, 1948 E, F
McCabe, A J M (NSW) 1909 E
McCall, R J (Q) 1989 F 1, 2, 1990 F 1, 2, 3, US, NZ 1, 2, 3, 1991 W, E, NZ 1, 2, [Arg, W, I, NZ, E], 1992 S 1, 2, NZ 1, 2, 3, SA, I, W, 1993 Tg, NZ, SA 1, 2, 3, C, F 1, 2, 1994 It 2, 1995 Arg 1, 2, [SA, R, E]
McCarthy, F J C (Q) 1950 BI 1
McCowan, R H (Q) 1899 BI 1, 2, 4
McCue, P A (NSW) 1907 NZ 1, 3, 1908 W, 1909 E
McDermott, L C (Q) 1962 NZ 1, 2
McDonald, B S (NSW) 1969 SA 4, 1970 S
McDonald, J C (Q) 1938 NZ 2, 3
Macdougall, D G (NSW) 1961 Fj 1, SA 1
Macdougall, S G (NSW, ACT) 1971 SA 3, 1973 E, 1974 NZ 1, 2, 3, 1975 E 1, 2, 1976 E
McGhie, G H (Q) 1929 NZ 2, 3, 1930 BI
McGill, A N (NSW) 1968 NZ 1, 2, F, 1969 W, SA 1, 2, 3, 4, 1970 S, 1971 SA 1, 2, 3, F 1, 2, 1972 F 1, 2, NZ 1, 2, 3, 1973 Tg 1, 2

Palu, W L (NSW) 2006 E2(t&R), I1(R), SA2, NZ3, SA3, W, It, I2, S(R), 2007 W1, 2, SA1, NZ1, [J, W, Fj, E], 2008 I, F1, SA1, NZ1, 2, SA2, 3, NZ3, It(R), E(R), F3, 2009 NZ1, SA1, NZ3(t&R)

Panoho, G M (Q) 1998 SA 2(R), NZ 3(R), Fj (R), Tg, WS (R), 1999 I 2, E, SA 1(R), NZ 1, 2000 Arg 1(R), 2(R), SA 1(R), NZ 1(R), SA 2(R), 3(R), F (R), S (R), E (R), 2001 BI 1, 2003 SA 2(R), NZ 2

Papworth, B (NSW) 1985 Fj 1, 2, 1986 It, Arg 1, 2, NZ 1, 2, 3, 1987 [E, US, J (R), I, F], NZ, Arg 1, 2

Parker, A J (Q) 1983 Arg 1(R), 2, NZ

Parkinson, C E (Q) 1907 NZ 2

Pashley, J J (NSW) 1954 Fj 1, 2, 1958 M 1, 2, 3

Paul, J A (ACT) 1998 S 1(R), NZ 1(R), SA 1(t), Fj (R), Tg, 1999 I 1, 2, E, SA 1, NZ 1, [R (R), I 3(R), W (t), F (R)], 2000 Arg 1(R), 2(R), SA 1(R), NZ 1(R), SA 2(R), NZ 2(R), SA 3(R), F (R), S (R), E (R), 2001 BI 1, 2002 F 1, NZ 1, SA 1, NZ 2, SA 2, Arg, E, 2003 I W, E, SA 2(t&R), NZ2(R), [Arg(R), R(R), Nm, I(R), S(R), NZ(R), E(R)], 2004 S1(R), 2(R), E1(R), PI(R), NZ1(t&R), SA1, NZ2(R), SA2(R), S3, F, S4, E2, 2005 Sm, It, F1, SA1, 2, 3, NZ1, 2006 E1(R), 2(R), I1(R), NZ1(R), SA1, NZ2, SA2(R), NZ3, SA3

Pauling, T P (NSW) 1936 NZ 1, 1937 SA 1

Payne, S J (NSW) 1996 W 2, C, NZ 1, S, 1997 F 1(t), NZ 2(R), Arg 2(t)

Pearse, G K (NSW) 1975 W (R), 1976 I, US, Fj 1, 2, 3, 1978 NZ 1, 2, 3

Penman, A P (NSW) 1905 NZ

Perrin, P D (Q) 1962 NZ 1

Perrin, T D (NSW) 1931 M, NZ

Phelps, R (NSW) 1955 NZ 2, 3, 1956 SA 1, 2, 1957 NZ 1, 2, 1958 W, I, E, S, F, M 1, NZ 1, 2, 3, 1961 Fj 1, 2, 3, SA 1, 2, F, 1962 NZ 1, 2

Phipps, J A (NSW) 1953 SA 1, 2, 3, 4, 1954 Fj 1, 2, 1955 NZ 1, 2, 3, 1956 SA 1, 2

Phipps, W J (NSW) 1928 NZ 2

Piggott, H R (NSW) 1922 M 3(R)

Pilecki, S J (Q) 1978 W 1, 2, NZ 1, 2, 1979 I 1, 2, NZ, Arg 1, 2, 1980 NZ 1, 2, 1982 S 1, 2, 1983 US, Arg 1, 2, NZ

Pini, M (Q) 1994 I 1, It 2, WS, NZ, 1995 Arg 1, 2, [SA, R (t)]

Piper, B J C (NSW) 1946 NZ 1, M, NZ 2, 1947 NZ 1, S, I, W, 1948 E, F, 1949 M, 1, 2, 3

Pocock, D W (WF) 2008 NZ4(R), It(R), 2, F(R), NZ1(R), SA1(R), NZ2(R), SA2(R), 3, NZ3

Poidevin, S P (NSW) 1980 Fj, NZ 1, 2, 3, 1981 F 1, 2, I, W, S, 1982 E, NZ 1, 2, 3, 1983 US, Arg 1, 2, NZ, It, F 1, 2, 1984 Fj, NZ 1, 2, 3, E, I, W, S, 1985 C 1, 2, NZ, Fj 1, 2, 1986 It, F, Arg 1, 2, NZ 1, 2, 3, 1987 SK, [E, J, I, F, W], Arg 1, 1988 NZ 1, 2, 3, 1989 NZ, 1991 E, NZ 1, 2, [Arg, W, I, NZ, E]

Polota-Nau, T (NSW) 2005 E(R), I(R), 2006 S(R), 2008 SA1(R), NZ1(R), 2(R), SA2(R), 3, It(R), E(R), 2009 It1(R), 2, F(R), SA1(R), NZ2(t&R), SA2(R), 3, NZ3

Pope, A M (Q) 1968 NZ 2(R)

Potter, R T (Q) 1961 Fj 2

Potts, J M (NSW) 1957 NZ 1, 2, 1958 W, I, 1959 BI 1

Prentice, C W (NSW) 1914 NZ 3

Prentice, W S (NSW) 1908 W, 1909 E, 1910 NZ 1, 2, 3, 1912 US

Price, R A (NSW) 1974 NZ 1, 2, 3, 1975 E 1, 2, J 1, 2, 1976 US

Primmer, C J (Q) 1951 NZ 1, 3

Proctor, I J (NSW) 1967 NZ

Prosser, R B (NSW) 1967 E, I 1, 2, NZ, 1968 NZ 1, 2, F, I, S, 1969 W, SA 1, 2, 3, 4, 1971 SA 1, 2, 3, F 1, 2, 1972 F 1, 2, NZ 1, 2, 3, Fj

Pugh, G H (NSW) 1912 US

Purcell, M P (Q) 1966 W, S, 1967 I 2

Purkis, E M (NSW) 1958 S, M 1

Pym, J E (NSW) 1923 M 1

Rainbow, A E (NSW) 1925 NZ 1

Ramalli, C (NSW) 1938 NZ 2, 3

Ramsay, K M (NSW) 1936 M, 1937 SA 1, 1938 NZ 1, 3

Rankin, R (NSW) 1936 NZ 1, 2, M, 1937 SA 1, 2, 1938 NZ 1, 2

Rathbone, C (ACT) 2004 S1, 2(R), E1, PI, NZ1, SA1, NZ2, SA2, S3, F, S4, 2005 Sm, NZ1(R), SA4, NZ2, 2006E1(R), 2(R), I1(R), SA1(R), NZ2(R), SA2(R), NZ3, SA3, W, It, I2

Rathie, D S (Q) 1972 F 1, 2

Raymond, R L (NSW) 1920 NZ 1, 2, 1921 SA 2, 3, NZ, 1922 M 1, 2, 3, NZ 1, 2, 3, 1923 M 1, 2

Redwood, C (Q) 1903 NZ, 1904 BI 1, 2, 3

Reid, E J (NSW) 1925 NZ 2, 3, 4

Reid, T W (NSW) 1961 Fj 1, 2, 3, SA 1, 1962 NZ 1

Reilly, N P (Q) 1968 NZ 1, 2, F, I, S, 1969 W, SA 1, 2, 3, 4

Reynolds, L J (NSW) 1910 NZ 2(R), 3

Reynolds, R J (NSW) 1984 Fj, NZ 1, 2, 3, 1985 Fj 1, 2, 1986 Arg 1, 2, NZ 1, 1987 [J]

Richards, E W (Q) 1904 BI 1, 3, 1905 NZ, 1907 NZ 1(R), 2

Richards, G (NSW) 1978 NZ 2(R), 3, 1981 F 1

Richards, T J (Q) 1908 W, 1909 E, 1912 US

Richards, V S (NSW) 1936 NZ 1, 2(R), M, 1937 SA 1, 1938 NZ 1

Richardson, G C (Q) 1971 SA 1, 2, 3, 1972 NZ 2, 3, Fj, 1973 Tg 1, 2, W

Rigney, W A (NSW) 1925 NZ 2, 4, 1926 NZ 4

Riley, S A (NSW) 1903 NZ

Ritchie, E V (NSW) 1924 NZ 1, 3, 1925 NZ 2, 3

Roberts, B T (NSW) 1956 SA 2

Roberts, H F (Q) 1961 Fj 1, 3, SA 2, F

Robertson, I J (NSW) 1975 J 1, 2

Robinson, B A (NSW) 2006 SA3, I2(R), S, 2007 W1(R), 2, Fj(R), 2008 I, F1, 2, SA1, NZ1, 2, SA2, 3, NZ3, 4, E, W, 2009 It1, F, NZ1, SA1, NZ2, SA2, 3, NZ3

Robinson, B J (ACT) 1996 It (R), S (R), I (R), 1997 F 1, 2, NZ 1, E 1, NZ 2, SA 1(R), NZ 3(R), SA 2(R), Arg 1, 2, E 2, S, 1998 Tg

Roche, C (Q) 1982 S 1, 2, NZ 1, 2, 3, 1983 US, Arg 1, 2, NZ, It, F 1, 2, 1984 Fj, NZ 1, 2, 3, I

Rodriguez, E E (NSW) 1984 Fj, NZ 1, 2, 3, E, I, W, S, 1985 C 1, 2, NZ, Fj 1, 1986 It, F, Arg 1, 2, NZ 1, 2, 3, 1987 SK, [E, J, W (R)], NZ, Arg 1, 2 Roe, J A (Q) 2003 [Nm(R)], 2004 E1(R), SA1(R), NZ2(R), SA2(t&R), S3, F, 2005 Sm(R), It(R), F1(R), SA1(R), 3, NZ1, SA4(t&R), NZ2(R), F2(R), E, I, W

Roebuck, M C (NSW) 1991 W, E, NZ 1, 2, [Arg, WS, W, I, NZ, E], 1992 S 1, 2, NZ 2, 3, SA, I, W, 1993 Tg, SA 1, 2, 3, C, F 2

Roff, J W (ACT) 1995 [C, R], NZ 1, 2, 1996 W 1, 2, NZ 1, SA 1, NZ 2, SA 2(R), S, I, W 3, 1997 F 1, 2, NZ 1, E 1, NZ 2, SA 1, NZ 3, SA 2, Arg 1, 2, E 2, S, 1998 E 1, S 1, 2, NZ 1, SA 1, NZ 2, SA 2, NZ 3, Fj, Tg, WS, F, E 2, 1999 I 1, 2, E, SA 1, NZ 1, SA 2, NZ 2(R), [R (R), I 3, US (R), W, SA 3, F], 2000 Arg 1, 2, SA 1, NZ 1, SA 2, NZ 2, SA 3, F, S, E, 2001 BI 1, 2, 3, SA 1, NZ 1, SA 2, NZ 2, Sp, E, F, W, 2003 I W, E, SA 1, [Arg, R, I, S(R), NZ(t&R), E(R)], 2004 S1, 2, E1, PI

Rogers, M S (NSW) 2002 F 1(R), 2(R), NZ 1(R), SA 1(R), NZ 2(R), SA 2(t&R), Arg, 2003 E (R), SA 1, NZ 1, SA 2, NZ 2, [Arg, R, Nm, I, S, NZ, E], 2004S3(R), F(R), S4(R), E2(R), 2005 Sm(R), It, F1(R), SA1, 4, NZ2, F2, E, I, W, 2006 E1, 2, I1, NZ1, SA1(R), NZ2(R), SA2(R), NZ3(R), W, It, I2(R), S(R)

Rose, H A (NSW), 1967 I 2, NZ, 1968 NZ 1, 2, F, I, S, 1969 W, SA 1, 2, 3, 4, 1970 S

Rosenblum, M E (NSW) 1928 NZ 1, 2, 3, M

Rosenblum, R G (NSW) 1969 SA 1, 3, 1970 S

Rosewell, J S H (NSW) 1907 NZ 1, 3

Ross, A W (NSW) 1925 NZ 1, 2, 3, 1927 I, W, S, 1928 E, F, 1929 NZ 1, 1930 BI, 1931 M, NZ, 1932 NZ 2, 3, 1933 SA 5, 1934 NZ 1, 2

Ross, W S (Q) 1979 I 1, 2, Arg 2, 1980 Fj, NZ 1, 2, 3, 1982 S 1, 2, 1983 US, Arg 1, 2, NZ

Rothwell, P R (NSW) 1951 NZ 1, 2, 3, 1952 Fj 1

Row, F L (NSW) 1899 BI 1, 3, 4

Row, N E (NSW) 1907 NZ 1, 3, 1909 E, 1910 NZ 1, 2, 3

Rowles, P G (NSW) 1972 Fj, 1973 E

Roxburgh, J R (NSW) 1968 NZ 1, 2, F, 1969 W, SA 1, 2, 3, 4, 1970 S

Ruebner, G (NSW) 1966 BI 1, 2

Russell, C J (NSW) 1907 NZ 1, 2, 3, 1908 W, 1909 E

Ryan, J R (NSW) 1975 J 2, 1976 I, US, Fj 1, 2, 3

Ryan, K J (Q) 1958 E, M 1, NZ 1, 2, 3

Ryan, P F (NSW) 1963 E, SA 1, 1966 BI 1, 2

Rylance, M H (NSW) 1926 NZ 4(R)

Sailor, W J (Q) 2002 F 1, 2, Arg (R), I, E, It, 2003 I, W, E, SA 1, NZ 1, SA 2, NZ 2, [Arg, R, I, S, NZ, E], 2004 S1, 2, NZ1(R), 2(R), SA2(R), S3(R), F(R), S4(R), E2, 2005 Sm, It, F1, SA1, 2, 3, F2, I(R), W(R)

Samo, R U (ACT) 2004 S1, 2, E1, PI, NZ1, S4(R)

Sampson, J H (NSW) 1899 BI 4

Sayle, J L (NSW) 1967 NZ

Schulte, B G (Q) 1946 NZ 1, M

Scott, P R I (NSW) 1962 NZ 1, 2

Scott-Young, S J (Q) 1990 F 2, 3(R), US, NZ 3, 1992 NZ 1, 2, 3

Shambrook, G G (NSW) 1976 Fj 2, 3

Sharpe, N C (Q, WF) 2002 F 1, 2, NZ 1, SA 1, NZ 2, SA 2, 2003 I, W, E, SA 1(R), NZ 1(R), SA 2(R), NZ 2(R), [Arg, R, Nm, I, S, NZ, E], 2004 S1, 2, E1, PI, NZ1, SA1, NZ2, SA2, 2005 Sm, It, F1, SA1, 2, 3, NZ1, SA4, NZ2, F2, E, I, W, 2006 E1, 2, I1, NZ1, SA1, NZ2, SA2, NZ3, SA3, W, It, I2, S, 2007 W1, 2, SA1, NZ1, SA2, [J, W, C, E], 2008 I, F1, SA1, NZ1, 2, 3, 4, E, F3, W, 2009 It1, F, NZ1, SA1, NZ2

Shaw, A A (Q) 1973 W, E, 1975 E 1, 2, J 2, S, W, 1976 E, I, US, Fj 1, 3, F 1, 2, 1978 W 1, 2, NZ 1, 2, 3, 1979 I 1, 2, NZ, Arg 1, 2, 1980 Fj, NZ 1, 2, 3, 1981 F 1, 2, I, W, S, 1982 S 1, 2

Shaw, C (NSW) 1925 NZ 2, 3, 4(R)

Shaw, G A (NSW) 1969 W, SA 1(R), 1970 S, 1971 SA 1, 2, 3, F 1, 2, 1973 W, E, 1974 NZ 1, 2, 3, 1975 E 1, 2, J 1, 2, W, 1976 E, I, US, Fj 1, 2, 3, F 1, 2, 1979 NZ

Sheehan, B R (ACT) 2006 SA3(R), 2008 SA2(R), 3(R)
Sheehan, W B J (NSW) 1921 SA 1, 2, 3, 1922 NZ 1, 2, 3, 1923 M 1, 2, NZ 1, 2, 3, 1924 NZ 1, 2, 1926 NZ 1, 2, 3, 1927 W, S
Shehadie, N M (NSW) 1947 NZ 2, 1948 E, F, 1949 M 1, 2, 3, NZ 1, 2, 1950 Bl 1, 2, 1951 NZ 1, 2, 3, 1952 Fj 1, 2, NZ 2, 1953 SA 1, 2, 3, 4, 1954 Fj 1, 2, 1955 NZ 1, 2, 3, 1956 SA 1, 2, 1957 NZ 2, 1958 W, I
Sheil, A G R (Q) 1956 SA 1
Shepherd, C B (WF) 2006 E1(R), 2(R), I1(R), SA3, W, 2007 [C], 2008 I, F1, 2(R)
Shepherd, D J (V) 1964 NZ 3, 1965 SA 1, 2, 1966 Bl 1, 2
Shepherdson, G T (ACT) 2006 I1, NZ1, SA1, NZ2(R), SA2(R), It, I2, S, 2007 W1, 2, SA1, NZ1, SA2, NZ2, [J(R), W, Fj, E]
Shute, J L (NSW) 1920 NZ 3, 1922 M 2, 3
Simpson, R J (NSW) 1913 NZ 2
Skinner, A J (NSW) 1969 W, SA 4, 1970 S
Slack, A G (Q) 1978 W 1, 2, NZ 1, 2, 1979 NZ, Arg 1, 2, 1980 Fj, 1981 I, W, S, 1982 E, S 1, NZ 3, 1983 US, Arg 1, 2 NZ, It, 1984 Fj, NZ 1, 2, 3, E, I, W, S, 1986 It, F, NZ 1, 2, 3, 1987 SK, [E, US, J, I, F, W]
Slater, S H (NSW) 1910 NZ 3
Slattery, P J (Q) 1990 US (R), 1991 W (R), E (R), [WS (R), W, I (R)], 1992 I, W, 1993 Tg, C, F 1, 2, 1994 I 1, 2, It 1(R), 1995 [C, R (R)]
Smairl, A M (NSW) 1928 NZ 1, 2, 3
Smith, B A (J) 1987 SK, [US, J, I (R), W], Arg 1
Smith, D P (Q) 1993 NZ 1, 2, 3, C F 2, 1994 I 1 2, It 1 2, WS, NZ, 1995 Arg 1, 2, [SA, R, E], NZ 1, 2, 1998 SA 1(R), NZ 3(R), Fj
Smith, F B (NSW) 1905 NZ, 1907 NZ 1, 2, 3
Smith, G B (ACT) 2000 F, S, E, 2001 Bl 1, 2, 3, SA 1, NZ 1, SA 2, NZ 2, Sp, E, F (R), W (R), 2002 F 1, 2, NZ 1, SA 1, NZ 2, SA 2, Arg, I, E, It, 2003 I, NZ 1, SA 2, NZ 2, [Arg, R, Nm, I, S, NZ, E], 2004 S1, 2(R), E1(t&R), PI(R), NZ1(R), SA1, NZ2, SA2, S3, F, S4, E2, 2005 Sm, It, F1, SA1, 2, 3, NZ1, SA4(R), NZ2, F2, E, I, W, 2006 E1, 2, I1, NZ1, SA1, NZ2, SA2, NZ3(t), SA3(R), It, I2(R), S, 2007 W1(R), 2, Fj(R), SA1, NZ1, SA2, NZ2, [J, W, C, E], 2008 I, F1, 2(R), SA1, NZ1, 2, SA2, 3(R), NZ3, 4, E, F3, W(R), 2009 It1, 2, F, NZ1, SA1, NZ2, SA2, 3, NZ3
Smith, L M (NSW) 1905 NZ
Smith, N C (NSW) 1922 NZ 2, 3, 1923 NZ 1, 1924 NZ 1, 3(R), 1925 NZ 2, 3
Smith, P V (NSW) 1967 NZ, 1968 NZ 1, 2, F, I, S, 1969 W, SA 1
Smith, R A (NSW) 1971 SA 1, 2, 1972 F 1, 2, NZ 1, 2(R), 3, Fj, 1975 E 1, 2, J 1, 2, S, W, 1976 E, I, US, Fj 1, 2, 3, F 1, 2
Smith, T S (NSW) 1921 SA 1, 2, 3, NZ, 1922 M 2, 3, NZ 1, 2, 3, 1925 NZ 1, 3, 4
Snell, H W (NSW) 1925 NZ 2, 3, 1928 NZ 3
Solomon, H J (NSW) 1949 M 3, NZ 2, 1950 Bl 1, 2, 1951 NZ 1, 2, 1952 Fj 1, 2, NZ 1, 2, 1953 SA 1, 2, 3, 1955 NZ 1
Spooner, N R (Q) 1999 I 1, 2
Spragg, S A (NSW) 1899 Bl 1, 2, 3, 4
Staniforth, S N G (NSW, WF) 1999 [US], 2002 I, It, 2006 SA3(R), I2(R), S, 2007 Fj, NZ1(R), SA2(R), NZ2(R), [W(R), Fj(R)]
Stanley, R G (NSW) 1921 NZ, 1922 M 1, 2, 3, NZ 1, 2, 3, 1923 M 2, 3, NZ 1, 2, 3, 1924 NZ 1, 3
Stapleton, E T (NSW) 1951 NZ 1, 2, 3, 1952 Fj 1, 2, NZ 1, 2, 1953 SA 1, 2, 3, 4, 1954 Fj 1, 1955 NZ 1, 2, 3, 1958 NZ 1
Steggall, J C (Q) 1931 M, NZ, 1932 NZ 1, 2, 3, 1933 SA 1, 2, 3, 4, 5
Stegman, T R (NSW) 1973 Tg 1, 2
Stephens, O G (NSW) 1973 Tg 1, 2, W, 1974 NZ 2, 3
Stewart, A A (NSW) 1979 NZ, Arg 1, 2
Stiles, N B (Q) 2001 Bl 1, 2, 3, SA 1, NZ 1, SA 2, NZ 2, Sp, E, F, W, 2002 I
Stone, A H (NSW) 1937 SA 2, 1938 NZ 2, 3
Stone, C G (NSW) 1938 NZ 1
Stone, J M (NSW) 1946 M, NZ 2
Storey, G P (NSW) 1926 NZ 4, 1927 I, W, S, 1928 E, F, 1929 NZ 3(R), 1930 Bl
Storey, K P (NSW) 1936 NZ 2
Storey, N J D (NSW) 1962 NZ 1
Strachan, D J (NSW) 1955 NZ 2, 3
Strauss, C P (NSW) 1999 I 1(R), 2(R), E (R), SA 1(R), NZ 1, SA 2(R), NZ 2(R), [R (R), I 3(R), US, W]
Street, N O (NSW) 1899 Bl 1, 2
Streeter, S F (NSW) 1978 NZ 1
Stuart, R (NSW) 1910 NZ 2, 3
Stumbles, B D (NSW) 1972 NZ 1(R), 2, 3, Fj
Sturtridge, G S (V) 1929 NZ 2, 1932 NZ 1, 2, 3, 1933 SA 1, 2, 3, 4, 5
Sullivan, P D (NSW) 1971 SA 1, 2, 3, F 1, 2, 1972 F 1, 2, NZ 1, 2, Fj, 1973 Tg 1, 2, W

Summons, A J (NSW) 1958 W, I, E, S, M 2, NZ 1, 2, 3, 1959 Bl 1, 2
Suttor, D C (NSW) 1913 NZ 1, 2, 3
Swannell, B I (NSW) 1905 NZ
Sweeney, T L (Q) 1953 SA 1
Taafe, B S (NSW) 1969 SA 1, 1972 F 1, 2
Tabua, I (Q) 1993 SA 2, 3, C, F 1, 1994 I 1, 2, It 1, 2, 1995 [C, R]
Tahu, P J A (NSW) 2008 NZ1(R), SA2(R), 3, It
Tancred, A J (NSW) 1927 I, W, S
Tancred, H E (NSW) 1923 M 1, 2
Tancred, J L (NSW) 1926 NZ 3, 4, 1928 F
Tanner, W H (Q) 1899 Bl 1, 2
Tarleton, K (NSW) 1925 NZ 2, 3
Tasker, W G (NSW) 1913 NZ 1, 2, 3, 1914 NZ 1, 2, 3
Tate, M J (NSW) 1951 NZ 3, 1952 Fj 1, 2, NZ 1, 2, 1953 SA 1, 1954 Fj 1, 2
Taylor, D A (Q) 1968 NZ 1, 2, F, I, S
Taylor, H C (NSW) 1923 NZ 1, 2, 3, 1924 NZ 4
Taylor, J I (NSW) 1971 SA 1, 1972 F 1, 2, Fj
Taylor, J M (NSW) 1922 M 1, 2
Teitzel, R G (Q) 1966 W, S, 1967 E, I 1, F, I 2, NZ
Telford, D G (NSW) 1926 NZ 3(R)
Thompson, C E (NSW) 1922 M 1, 1923 M 1, 2, NZ 1, 1924 NZ 2, 3
Thompson, E G (Q) 1929 NZ 1, 2, 3, 1930 Bl
Thompson, F (NSW) 1913 NZ 1, 2, 3, 1914 NZ 1, 3
Thompson, J (Q) 1914 NZ 1, 2
Thompson, P D (Q) 1950 Bl 1
Thompson, R J (WA) 1971 SA 3, F 2(R), 1972 Fj
Thorn, A M (NSW) 1921 SA 1, 2, 3, NZ, 1922 M 1, 3
Thorn, E J (NSW) 1922 NZ 1, 2, 3, 1923 NZ 1, 2, 3, 1924 NZ 1, 2, 3, 1925 NZ 1, 2, 1926 NZ 1, 2, 3, 4
Thornett, J E (NSW) 1955 NZ 1, 2, 3, 1956 SA 1, 2, 1958 W, I, S, F, M 2, 3, NZ 2, 3, 1959 Bl 1, 2, 1961 Fj 2, 3, SA 1, 2, F, 1962 NZ 2, 3, 4, 5, 1963 E, SA 1, 2, 3, 4, 1964 NZ 1, 2, 3, 1965 SA 1, 2, 1966 Bl 1, 2, 1967 F
Thornett, R N (NSW) 1961 Fj 1, 2, 3, SA 1, 2, F, 1962 NZ 1, 2, 3, 4, 5
Thorpe, A C (NSW) 1929 NZ 1(R)
Timbury, F R V (Q) 1910 NZ 1, 2,
Tindall, E N (NSW) 1973 Tg 2
Toby, A E (NSW) 1925 NZ 1, 4
Tolhurst, H A (NSW) 1931 M, NZ
Tombs, R C (NSW) 1992 S 1, 2, 1994 I 2, It 1, 1996 NZ 2
Tonkin, A E J (NSW) 1947 S, I, W, 1948 E, F, 1950 Bl 2
Tooth, R M (NSW) 1951 NZ 1, 2, 3, 1954 Fj 1, 2, 1955 NZ 1, 2, 3, 1957 NZ 1, 2
Towers, C H T (NSW) 1926 NZ 1, 3(R), 4, 1927 I, 1928 E, F, NZ 1, 2, 3, M, 1929 NZ 1, 3, 1930 Bl, 1931 M, NZ, 1934 NZ 1, 2, 1937 SA 1, 2
Trivett, R K (Q) 1966 Bl 1, 2
Tune, B N (Q) 1996 W 2, C, NZ 1, SA 1, NZ 2, SA 2, 1997 F 1, 2, NZ 1, E 1, NZ 2, SA 1, NZ 3, SA 2, Arg, 1, 2, E 2, S, 1998 E 1, S 1, 2, NZ 1, SA 1, 2, 3, 1999 I 1, E, SA 1, NZ 2, SA 2, NZ 2, [R, I 3, W, SA 3, F], 2000 SA 2(R), NZ 2(t&R), SA 3(R), 2001 F (R), W, 2002 NZ 1, SA 1, NZ 2, SA 2, Arg, 2006 NZ1(R)
Tuqiri, L D (NSW) 2003 I (R), W (R), E (R), SA 1(R), NZ 1, SA 2, [Arg(R), R(R), Nm, I(R), S, NZ, E], 2004 S1, 2, E1, PI, NZ1, SA1, SA2, S3, F, S4, E2, 2005 It, F1, SA1, 2, 3, NZ1, SA4, NZ2, F2, E, I, W, 2006 E1, 2, I1, NZ1, SA1, NZ2, SA2, NZ3, W, It, I2, S, 2007 Fj, SA1, NZ1, [J, W, Fj, C, E], 2008 I, F1, SA1, NZ1, 2, SA2, 3, NZ3, W(R)
Turinui, M P (NSW) 2003 I, W, E, 2003 [Nm(R)], 2004 S1(R), 2, E2, 2005 Sm, It(R), F1(R), SA1, 2(t&R), 3, NZ1, SA4, NZ2, F2, E, I, W
Turnbull, A (V) 1961 Fj 3
Turnbull, R V (NSW) 1968 I
Turner, D J (NSW) 2008 F2, It, 2009 It1, 2, F, NZ1, SA1, NZ2, SA2, 3, NZ3
Tuynman, S N (NSW) 1983 F 1, 2, 1984 E, I, W, S, 1985 C 1, 2, NZ, Fj 1, 2, 1986 It, F, Arg 1, 2, NZ 1, 2, 3, 1987 SK, [E, US, J, I, W], NZ, Arg 1(R), 2, 1988 E, It, 1989 Bl 1, 2, 3, NZ, 1990 NZ 1
Tweedale, E (NSW) 1946 NZ 1, 2, 1947 NZ 2, S, I, 1948 E, F, 1949 M 1, 2, 3
Valentine, J J (Q, WF) 2006 E1(R), W(R), I2(R), S(R), 2009 It2(R), F(R)
Vaughan, D (NSW) 1983 US, Arg 1, It, F 1, 2
Vaughan, G N (V) 1958 E, S, F, M 1, 2, 3
Verge, A (NSW) 1904 Bl 1, 2
Vickerman, D J (ACT, NSW) 2002 F 2(R), Arg, E, It, 2003 I (R), W (R), E (R), SA 1, NZ 1, SA 2, NZ 2, [Arg(R), R, I(R), S(R)], 2004 S1(t&R), 2(R), E1(R), PI(R), NZ1(R), SA1(R), NZ2(R), SA2(R), S3,

CANADA

CANADA'S 2008–09 TEST RECORD

OPPONENTS	DATE	VENUE	RESULT
Portugal	1 November	A	**Won** 21–13
Ireland	8 November	A	**Lost** 0–55
Wales	14 November	A	**Lost** 13–34
Scotland	22 November	A	**Lost** 0–41
Ireland	23 May	H	**Lost** 6–25
Wales	30 May	H	**Lost** 23–32
Georgia	6 June	A	**Won** 42–10
Ireland A	10 June	A	**Lost** 19–30
Argentina Jaguars	21 June	A	**Lost** 29–44
USA	4 July	A	**Lost** 6–12
USA	11 July	H	**Won** 41–18

MISSION ACCOMPLISHED

By Tom Chick

The last 12 months may have yielded only three victories from 11 internationals, but one of these came in the most important match of Kieran Crowley's tenure and saw Canada become the first nation to emerge through the global qualifying process and secure their place at Rugby World Cup 2011.

Crowley, himself a World Cup winner with New Zealand in 1987, was appointed in 2008 with a view to taking Canada to Rugby's premier tournament and maintaining their record of having appeared in every edition to date.

Canada had to overcome a first leg defeat by the USA Eagles to qualify as Americas 1 and join hosts New Zealand, France, Tonga and the Asia 1 qualifier in Pool A. The Eagles had beaten their neighbours for the first time in nearly five years on American Independence Day, albeit only by a slender 12–6 margin.

There was a sense among the Canadian ranks of having "let themselves down" with their performance in Charleston, but the following weekend the Canucks recorded a comfortable 41–18 victory in Edmonton to fittingly mark prop Kevin Tkachuk's 50th Test by qualifying for RWC 2011.

The last time the two sides had met in a RWC qualifier on Canadian soil in August 2006 the home side had triumphed 56–7 and this time around Canada knew that victory at Ellerslie Rugby Park would ensure their rivals did not move above them in the IRB World Rankings.

Canada had cancelled out the deficit by the 25th minute when James Pritchard converted his own try, having earlier kicked a penalty. Things got worse for the Eagles when minutes later centre Paul Emerick was sent off and the Canucks never looked back with tries from Adam Kleeberger, Justin Mensah-Coker, Ed Fairhurst, the impressive DTH van der Merwe and Matt Evans cementing a 47–30 aggregate win.

The result meant that Canada retained the 13th position in the Rankings they had achieved with victory over Georgia in the Churchill Cup the previous month and they fittingly became the 13th team bound for RWC 2011, joining the 12 automatic qualifiers from the 2007 tournament in France.

"It was the main objective and to achieve it was great," admitted

Crowley. "The first game in Charleston we let ourselves down a fair bit. It was on American Independence Day and I think we thought that we focused too much on what they would bring rather than what we could bring. I felt let down hugely and it was a matter of putting it right."

While there will be tougher tests to come for Canada, the result means they won't need to face another potentially dangerous play-off in November. Instead USA will face Uruguay to determine the Americas 2 qualifier, while Canada can concentrate on the countdown to 2011.

"It was a huge win at home against the USA and everything we do now is building to the next World Cup," admitted captain Pat Riordan. "We are back on the big stage and it is really exciting, it means we can plan autumn tours knowing we don't have to go to Uruguay. The last World Cup we got close a couple of times and we have got two years to get ready."

The build up to the crucial play-off began last November when Canada travelled to Europe for four matches, kicking off with a 21–13 victory over Portugal. Losses to Ireland, Wales and Scotland ensued, but the improvements made under Crowley were clear in the coming months. Canada met Ireland and Wales again on home soil six months later and despite two more losses they cut the deficit considerably and then continued to progress in the Churchill Cup.

In the first pool match Evans helped himself to a brace and Pritchard kicked 17 points to ensure an emphatic bonus point 42–10 win over Georgia – the first ever match between the two nations. Four days later Ireland A were the opponents for the buoyant Canadians and for much of the game it seemed as though they might pull off a major shock. Leading 16–13 thanks to a Phil Mack try, Canada were eventually over-hauled by a late penalty try. They then faced the Argentina Jaguars in the Plate final, but it was the South Americans left celebrating despite a remarkable fightback with Evans once again the catalyst with two tries.

Canada were always guaranteed a second bite at the cherry had they lost in the play-off against the Eagles with Los Teros awaiting them, but the Churchill Cup campaign proved vital in ensuring Crowley's charges were the best prepared they had ever been.

"We had great preparation going into the match against USA. We had the games against Wales and Ireland and then we had the Churchill Cup games which were outstanding preparation for the two games," admitted Crowley. "Between USA and Canada it was the best prepared side we have had because of that competition."

Looking forward, Crowley will prepare his troops for an end of year

CANADA

tour of Japan, a side they are likely to meet again at RWC 2011, and he is keen to add more matches to their run in to New Zealand.

"We need to learn how to win games," admitted Crowley. "There is an art to winning games and not to let close games slip. We have stayed in against teams a lot better than us but not quite finished off, so we have to learn how to win. We have to be playing games and at a level of competition and it's pleasing to have Japan, they are round about us. But you also want to play a couple above you."

With the Women's Rugby World Cup 2010 around the corner in England, Canada hosted a five-team Women's Nations Cup in Ontario in August. They started brightly with a 30–17 victory over South Africa, but ultimately finished fourth after losing to France 12–7, USA 15–10 – their first defeat by their rivals since 2006 – and champions England 22–0.

It was also another busy year for Canada's Sevens teams with the RWC Sevens taking place in Dubai. Despite no longer being a core side on the IRB Sevens World Series, they still played in five of the eight events – Wellington, San Diego, Hong Kong, London and Edinburgh. Shane Thompson's men won two Shield finals, but their only points in the standings came from a 14–12 Plate final loss to Tonga in Hong Kong.

Canada's women enjoyed more success than their male counterparts at RWC Sevens, captain Maria Gallo leading them to the Plate final in the inaugural women's competition where they were beaten 33–12 by England. The men's team had narrowly missed out on the Cup quarter-finals after finishing second in Pool C and were then beaten 12–5 by Portugal in the Plate quarter-finals.

The Under 20 side travelled to Japan for the IRB TOSHIBA Junior World Championship, but could only manage 14th spot with one win – 29–11 over Uruguay – and as such will not play in the revised 12-team format of the 2010 tournament. Instead Canada must look to qualify for the second tier IRB Junior World Rugby Trophy. Their female counterparts, meanwhile, took part in the Under 20 Women's Nations Cup in England and finished third.

Domestically, the Rugby Canada Super League didn't take place with the new Americas Rugby Championship involving four Canadian provincial teams, USA Selects and the Argentina Jaguars starting in October. Replaced by a National Junior Championship, the Vancouver Wave side – with Canada U20 captain Harry Jones in their ranks – won the title, beating Toronto Rebellion 41–21 in the final. Meanwhile, in the third year of the National Women's League, Ontario claimed the honours after beating defending champions British Columbia 20–14.

CANADA INTERNATIONAL STATISTICS

MATCH RECORDS UP TO 30TH SEPTEMBER 2009

WINNING MARGIN

Date	Opponent	Result	Winning Margin
24/06/2006	Barbados	69–3	66
14/10/1999	Namibia	72–11	61
12/08/2006	USA	56–7	49
06/07/1996	Hong Kong	57–9	48

MOST POINTS IN A MATCH
BY THE TEAM

Date	Opponent	Result	Pts.
14/10/1999	Namibia	72–11	72
24/06/2006	Barbados	69–3	69
15/07/2000	Japan	62–18	62
06/07/1996	Hong Kong	57–9	57
12/08/2006	USA	56–7	56

MOST TRIES IN A MATCH
BY THE TEAM

Date	Opponent	Result	Tries
24/06/2006	Barbados	69–3	11
14/10/1999	Namibia	72–11	9
11/05/1991	Japan	49–26	8
15/07/2000	Japan	62–18	8

MOST CONVERSIONS IN A MATCH
BY THE TEAM

Date	Opponent	Result	Cons
14/10/1999	Namibia	72–11	9
15/07/2000	Japan	62–18	8
24/06/2006	Barbados	69–3	7
02/06/2007	USA	52–10	7
11/05/1991	Japan	49–26	7

MOST PENALTIES IN A MATCH
BY THE TEAM

Date	Opponent	Result	Pens
25/05/1991	Scotland	24–19	8
22/08/1998	Argentina	28–54	7

MOST DROP GOALS IN A MATCH
BY THE TEAM

Date	Opponent	Result	DGs
08/11/1986	USA	27–16	2
04/07/2001	Fiji	23–52	2
08/06/1980	USA	16–0	2
24/05/1997	Hong Kong	35–27	2

MOST POINTS IN A MATCH
BY A PLAYER

Date	Player	Opponent	Pts.
12/08/2006	James Pritchard	USA	36
24/06/2006	James Pritchard	Barbados	29
14/10/1999	Gareth Rees	Namibia	27
13/07/1996	Bobby Ross	Japan	26
25/05/1991	Mark Wyatt	Scotland	24

MOST TRIES IN A MATCH
BY A PLAYER

Date	Player	Opponent	Tries
15/07/2000	Kyle Nichols	Japan	4
24/06/2006	James Pritchard	Barbados	3
12/08/2006	James Pritchard	USA	3
10/05/1987	Steve Gray	USA	3

CANADA

MOST CONVERSIONS IN A MATCH
BY A PLAYER

Date	Player	Opponent	Cons
14/10/1999	Gareth Rees	Namibia	9
15/07/2000	Jared Barker	Japan	8
24/06/2006	James Pritchard	Barbados	7
02/06/2007	James Pritchard	USA	7
11/05/1991	Mark Wyatt	Japan	7

MOST PENALTIES IN A MATCH
BY A PLAYER

Date	Player	Opponent	Pens
25/05/1991	Mark Wyatt	Scotland	8
22/08/1998	Gareth Rees	Argentina	7

MOST DROP GOALS IN A MATCH
BY A PLAYER

Date	Player	Opponent	DGs
04/07/2001	Bobby Ross	Fiji	2
24/05/1997	Bobby Ross	Hong Kong	2

MOST CAPPED PLAYERS

Name	Caps
Al Charron	76
Winston Stanley	66
Scott Stewart	64
Rod Snow	62
Bobby Ross	58

LEADING TRY SCORERS

Name	Tries
Winston Stanley	24
Morgan Williams	13
Pat Palmer	10
Kyle Nichols	10
James Pritchard	10

LEADING CONVERSIONS SCORERS

Name	Cons
Bobby Ross	52
Gareth Rees	51
James Pritchard	51
Jared Barker	24
Mark Wyatt	24

LEADING PENALTY SCORERS

Name	Pens
Gareth Rees	110
Bobby Ross	84
Mark Wyatt	64
Jared Barker	55
James Pritchard	41

LEADING DROP GOAL SCORERS

Name	DGs
Bobby Ross	10
Gareth Rees	9
Mark Wyatt	5

LEADING POINTS SCORERS

Name	Pts.
Gareth Rees	491
Bobby Ross	421
James Pritchard	275
Mark Wyatt	263
Jared Barker	226

CANADIAN INTERNATIONAL PLAYERS
UP TO 30TH SEPTEMBER 2009

Note: Years given for International Championship matches are for second half of season; eg 1972 means season 1971–72. Years for all other matches refer to the actual year of the match.

AD Abrams 2003 *US, NZ, Tg,* 2004 *US, J, EngA, US, F, It, E,* 2005 *US, J, W, EngA, US, Ar, F, R,* 2006 *S, E, US, It*
MJ Alder 1976 *Bb*
P Aldous 1971 *W*
AS Arthurs 1988 *US*
M Ashton 1971 *W*
F Asselin 1999 *Fj,* 2000 *Tg, US, SA,* 2001 *Ur, Ar, Fj,* 2002 *S, US, US, Ur, Ur, Ch, W, F*
O Atkinson 2005 *J, Ar,* 2006 *E, US, It*
S Ault 2006 *W, It,* 2008 *US, Pt,* 2009 *Geo, US, US*
JC Bain 1932 *J*
RG Banks 1999 *I, Fj, Sa, US, Tg, W, E, F, Nm,* 2000 *US, SA, I, J, It,* 2001 *US, Ur, Ar, E, Fj, J,* 2002 *S, US, US, Ur, Ch, Ur, Ch, W, F,* 2003 *E, US, M, M, Ur, NZ, It*
S Barber 1973 *W,* 1976 *Bb*
M Barbieri 2006 *E, US*
B Barker 1966 *BI,* 1971 *W*
J Barker 2000 *Tg, J, It,* 2002 *S, US, US, Ur, Ch, Ur, Ch, W,* 2003 *US, NZ, It,* 2004 *US, J, F, It*
T Bauer 1977 *US, E,* 1978 *US, F,* 1979 *US*
D Baugh 1998 *J, HK, US, HK, J, Ur, Ar,* 1999 *J, Fj, Sa, US, Tg, W, E, F, Fj, Nm,* 2000 *US, SA, I, It,* 2001 *E, E,* 2002 *S, US, Ur, Ch*
A Bianco 1966 *BI*
AJ Bibby 1979 *US, F,* 1980 *W, US, NZ,* 1981 *US, Ar*
R Bice 1996 *US, A,* 1997 *US, J, W, I,* 1998 *US, US, HK, J, Ur, US, Ar,* 1999 *J, Fj, Sa, US, Tg, W, F*
P Bickerton 2004 *US, J*
D Biddle 2006 *S, E, Bar,* 2007 *M, W, Fj, A*
JM Billingsley 1974 *Tg,* 1977 *US,* 1978 *F,* 1979 *US,* 1980 *W,* 1983 *US, It, It,* 1984 *US*
WG Bjarneson 1962 *Bb*
TJH Blackwell 1973 *W*
B Bonenberg 1983 *US, It, It*
J Boone 1932 *J, J*
T Bourne 1967 *E*
R Breen 1986 *US,* 1987 *W,* 1990 *US,* 1991 *J, S, US, R,* 1993 *E, US*
R Breen 1983 *E,* 1987 *US*
R Brewer 1967 *E*
STT Brown 1989 *I, US*
N Browne 1973 *W,* 1974 *Tg*
T Browne 1964 *Fj*
S Bryan 1996 *Ur, US, Ar,* 1997 *HK, J, US, W,* 1998 *HK, US, Ar,* 1999 *Fj, Sa, US, Tg, W, E, F, Fj, Nm*
T Bunyan 1964 *Fj*
M Burak 2004 *US, J, EngA, US, F, It, E,* 2005 *EngA, US, Ar, F, R,* 2006 *US, Bar, W,* 2007 *IrA, M, NZ, Pt, W, Fj, J, A,* 2008 *I, W, S,* 2009 *I, W, Geo, IrA, US, US*
C Burford 1970 *Fj*
D Burgess 1962 *Bb, W23,* 1964 *Fj*
D Burleigh 2001 *Ur, Ar, E, E*
JB Burnham 1966 *BI,* 1967 *E,* 1970 *Fj,* 1971 *W*
H Buydens 2006 *E,* 2008 *US*
H Calder 1964 *Fj*
GE Cameron 1932 *J*
JWD Cannon 2001 *US, Ar, E, E, Fj, J,* 2002 *S, US, Ur, Ch, Ur, Ch, W, F,* 2003 *E, M, M, Ur, US, Ar, NZ, It,* 2004 *US, F, It, E,* 2005 *W, EngA, US, F*
R Card 1996 *US, A, Ur, US, Ar,* 1997 *US, J, HK*

ME Cardinal 1986 *US,* 1987 *US, Tg, I, US,* 1991 *S,* 1993 *A,* 1994 *US, F, E, F,* 1995 *S, Fj, NZ, R, SA,* 1996 *US, US, HK, J, A, HK, J,* 1997 *US, US, W, I,* 1998 *US, HK,* 1999 *Fj, US, W, E, Fj, Nm*
LAG Carlson 2002 *Ur, W,* 2003 *E*
A Carpenter 2005 *US, J, EngA, US, Ar, F, R,* 2006 *S, E, US, W, It,* 2007 *IrA, M, US, NZ, Pt, W, Fj, J, A,* 2008 *US, Pt, I, W, S,* 2009 *I, W, Geo, IrA, ArJ, US*
NS Carr 1985 *A, A*
DJ Carson 1980 *W, US, NZ,* 1981 *US, Ar,* 1982 *J, E, US,* 1983 *It, It*
SFB Carson 1977 *E*
MP Chambers 1962 *Bb, W23,* 1964 *Fj,* 1966 *BI*
AJ Charron 1990 *Ar, US, Ar,* 1991 *J, S, Fj, F, NZ,* 1992 *US,* 1993 *E, E, US, A, W,* 1994 *US, F, W,* 1995 *Fj, NZ, R, A, SA, US,* 1996 *US, US, A, HK, J, Ur, US, Ar,* 1997 *US, J, HK, HK, J, US, W, I,* 1998 *US, HK, J, Ur, US, Ar,* 1999 *Fj, Sa, US, Tg, W, E, F, Fj, Nm,* 2000 *Tg, US, SA, Sa, Fj, J, It,* 2001 *Ur, Ar, E, E,* 2002 *S, US, Ur, Ch, Ur, Ch, F,* 2003 *W, It, Tg*
L Chung 1978 *F*
N Clapinson 1995, 1996 *US*
RM Clark 1962 *Bb*
D Clarke 1996 *A*
ME Clarkin 1985 *A, A*
B Collins 2004 *US, J*
W Collins 1977 *US, E*
GG Cooke 2000 *Tg, US,* 2001 *Fj, J,* 2003 *E, US, M, M, Ur, US, Ar, W, NZ, Tg,* 2004 *EngA, US, It, E,* 2005 *US, J, W, Ar, F, R,* 2006 *US*
I Cooper 1993 *W*
JA Cordle 1998 *HK, J,* 1999 *J, Fj, Sa,* 2001 *J*
GER Cox 1932 *J*
S Creagh 1988 *US*
J Cudmore 2002 *US, Ch, W, F,* 2003 *E, US, W, NZ, It, Tg,* 2004 *US, F, It, E,* 2005 *W, F,* 2006 *US,* 2007 *Pt, W, Fj*
L Cudmore 2008 *US*
C Culpan 2006 *E,* 2007 *IrA, M, US, NZ, Pt, W, Fj, J*
TJ Cummings 1964 *Fj,* 1966 *BI,* 1973 *W*
Z Cvitak 1983 *E*
N Dala 2007 *IrA, US,* 2008 *US,* 2009 *I, W, Geo, IrA, ArJ, US, US*
MJW Dandy 1977 *E, E*
M Danskin 2001 *J,* 2004 *EngA, F*
D Daypuck 2004 *EngA, F, It, E,* 2005 *US, J, W, EngA, Ar, F, R,* 2006 *S, US, US, W, It,* 2007 *IrA, M, A*
H de Goede 1976 *Bb,* 1977 *US, E, E,* 1978 *US,* 1979 *US, F,* 1980 *W, US, NZ,* 1981 *US,* 1982 *J, J, E, US,* 1984 *US,* 1985 *US,* 1986 *US,* 1987 *US, Tg, I, W*
HW de Goede 1974 *Tg*
F Deacy 1973 *W*
J Delaney 1983 *E*
P Densmore 2005 *EngA*
JD Devlin 1985 *US,* 1986 *US*
M di Girolamo 2001 *Ur, Ar,* 2002 *US, Ur, Ch, Ur, W, F,* 2003 *US, M, M, Ur, W, NZ, It, Tg,* 2004 *EngA, US, F, It, E*
GA Dixon 2000 *US, SA, I, Sa, Fj, J, It,* 2001 *US, Ar, E, E*
D Docherty 1973 *W*
WJ Donaldson 1978 *F,* 1979 *US, F,* 1980 *W, US, NZ,* 1981 *US,* 1982 *E, US,* 1983 *US, It, It,* 1984 *US*
A Douglas 1974 *Tg*

2002 S, US, US, Ur, Ch, Ur, Ch, W, F, 2003 Ur, US, Ar, W, NZ, It, Tg, 2006 US, Bar, US, 2007 Pt, W, Fj, J, A
DA Speirs 1988 US, 1989 I, US, 1991 Fj, NZ
D Spicer 2004 E, 2005 R, 2006 S, E, US, Bar, US, W, 2007 IrA, US, NZ, Pt, W, Fj, J, 2008 US, 2009 I, W
WE Spofford 1981 Ar
W Stanley 1994 US, F, 1995 S, Ur, Ar, R, A, SA, US, 1996 US, US, A, HK, J, 1997 US, J, HK, HK, US, W, I, 1998 US, US, HK, Ur, US, Ar, 1999 I, Fj, Sa, US, Tg, W, E, F, Fj, Nm, 2000 Tg, US, SA, I, Sa, Fj, It, 2001 E, E, 2002 S, US, US, Ur, Ch, Ur, Ch, W, F, 2003 E, US, M, M, Ur, US, Ar, W, It, Tg
AI Stanton 1971 W, 1973 W, 1974 Tg
E Stapleton 1978 US, F
D Steen 1966 BI
SM Stephen 2005 EngA, US, 2006 S, E, US, Bar, US, W, 2007 US, NZ, Pt, W, Fj, A, 2008 I, W, S, 2009 I, W
C Stewart 1991 S, US, Fj, R, F, NZ, 1994 E, F, 1995 S, Fj, NZ, R, A, SA
DS Stewart 1989 US, 1990 Ar, 1991 US, Fj, R, F, NZ, 1992 E, 1993 E, E, US, A, W, 1994 US, F, W, E, F, 1995 S, Fj, NZ, R, A, SA, US, 1996 US, US, A, HK, J, Ur, US, Ar, 1997 US, J, HK, HK, J, US, W, I, 1998 US, J, Ur, Ar, 1999 Sa, US, Tg, W, E, F, Fj, Nm, 2000 US, SA, I, Sa, Fj, It, 2001 US, Ur, Ar, E, E
R Stewart 2005 R
B Stoikos 2001 Ur
G Stover 1962 Bb
R Strang 1983 E
C Strubin 2004 EngA
IC Stuart 1984 US, 1985 A, A, 1986 J, 1987 US, Tg, I, W, US, 1988 US, 1989 US, 1990 Ar, US, Ar, 1992 E, 1993 A, W, 1994 US, F, W, E
JD Stubbs 1962 Bb, W23
FJ Sturrock 1971 W
CW Suter 1932 J
KF Svoboda 1985 A, A, US, 1986 J, US, 1987 W, 1990 Ar, US, Ar, 1991 J, US, R, F, 1992 US, E, 1993 E, E, US, 1994 F, W, F, 1995 Fj, A, US
P Szabo 1989 I, US, 1990 Ar, US, Ar, 1991 NZ, 1993 US, A, W
JN Tait 1997 US, J, HK, HK, J, US, W, I, 1998 US, Ur, Ar, 1999 J, Fj, Sa, US, Tg, W, E, F, Fj, Nm, 2000 Tg, US, SA, I, Sa, Fj, J, It, 2001 US, Ar, E, E, 2002 US, W, F
L Tait 2005 US, J, W, EngA, 2006 S, E, US, Bar, US, W, It, 2007 M, US, NZ, Pt, W, Fj, A, 2009 I, W
WG Taylor 1978 F, 1979 US, F, 1980 W, US, NZ, 1981 US, Ar, 1983 US, It
J Thiel 1998 HK, J, Ur, 1999 I, Fj, Sa, US, Tg, W, E, F, Fj, Nm, 2000 SA, I, Sa, Fj, J, 2001 US, Ar, E, E, 2002 S, US, US, Ur, Ch, Ur, W, F, 2003 Ur, US, Ar, W, It, 2004 F, 2007 Pt, W, Fj, J, A, 2008 I, W
S Thompson 2001 Fj, J
W Thomson 1970 Fj
A Tiedemann 2009 W, Geo, IrA, US
K Tkachuk 2000 Tg, US, SA, Sa, Fj, It, 2001 Fj, J, 2002 Ch, Ur, Ch, W, F, 2003 E, US, M, M, Ur, US, Ar, W, NZ, It, Tg, 2004 EngA, US, F, It, E, 2005 US, J, W, Ar, F, R, 2006 US, W, It, 2007 IrA, M, US, NZ, 2008 US, Pt, I, W, S, 2009 I, W, Geo, US, US
H Toews 1997 HK, 1998 J, HK, HK, Ur, 1999 Tg, 2000 US, Sa, J, It, 2001 Fj, J
R Toews 1993 W, 1994 US, F, W, E, 1995 S, Ur, Ar, Fj, 1996 US, HK, J, A, 1997 US, I
J Tomlinson 1996 A, 2001 Ur
N Trenkel 2007 A
DM Tucker 1985 A, A, US, 1986 US, 1987 US, W
A Tyler 2005 Ar
A Tynan 1995 Ur, Ar, US, 1997 J
CJ Tynan 1987 US, 1988 US, 1990 Ar, US, Ar, 1991 J, US, Fj,

F, NZ, 1992 US, 1993 E, E, US, W, 1995 NZ, 1996 US, J, 1997 HK, J, 1998 US
DN Ure 1962 Bb, W23
PC Vaesen 1985 US, 1986 J, 1987 US, Tg, US
D van Camp 2005 J, R, 2006 It, 2007 IrA, M, US, NZ, 2008 Pt, W, 2009 I, Geo, ArJ
R van den Brink 1986 US, 1987 Tg, 1988 US, 1991 J, US, R, F, NZ
D van der Merwe 2006 Bar, It, 2007 Pt, W, Fj, J, A, 2009 I, W, Geo, IrA, ArJ, US, US
D Van Eeuwen 1978 F, 1979 US
A van Staveren 2000 Tg, Sa, Fj, 2002 US, US, Ur, Ch, Ur, Ch, W, F, 2003 E, US, M, M, Ur, US, W, NZ, Tg
J Verstraten 2000 US, SA, Fj, J
J Vivian 1983 E, 1984 US
F Walsh 2008 I, W, S, 2009 IrA, ArJ, US
KC Walt 1976 Bb, 1977 US, E, E, 1978 US, F
JM Ward 1962 W23
M Webb 2004 US, J, US, F, It, 2005 US, J, W, EngA, US, Ar, F, 2006 US, W, It, 2007 M, J, A, 2008 US
M Weingart 2004 J, 2005 J, EngA, US, F, R, 2007 Pt
GJM Wessels 1962 W23
WR Wharton 1932 J, J
K Whitley 1995 S
C Whittaker 1993 US, A, 1995 Ur, 1996 A, 1997 J, 1998 J, HK, US, US, HK, J, US, Ar, 1999 J, Fj, US
LW Whitty 1967 E
DW Whyte 1974 Tg, 1977 US, E, E
RR Wickland 1966 BI, 1967 E
JP Wiley 1977 US, E, E, 1978 US, F, 1979 US, 1980 W, US, NZ, 1981 US
K Wilke 1971 W, 1973 W, 1976 Bb, 1978 US
K Wilkinson 1976 Bb, 1978 F, 1979 F
BN Williams 1962 W23
J Williams 2001 US, Ur, Ar, Fj, J
M Williams 1999 W, E, F, Fj, Nm, 2000 Tg, SA, I, Sa, Fj, J, It, 2001 E, E, Fj, J, 2002 S, US, US, Ur, Ch, W, F, 2003 E, US, M, M, Ur, US, Ar, W, It, Tg, 2004 EngA, US, F, 2005 W, Ar, F, R, 2006 E, US, Bar, US, W, It, 2007 IrA, M, US, NZ, W, Fj, J, A, 2008 Pt, W, S
M Williams 1992 E, 1993 A, W
MH Williams 1978 US, F, 1980 US
MH Williams 1982 J
A Wilson 2008 US
PG Wilson 1932 J, J
RS Wilson 1962 Bb
K Wirachowski 1992 E, 1993 US, 1996 US, HK, Ur, US, Ar, 1997 US, HK, 2000 It, 2001 Ur, E, Fj, J, 2002 S, Ch, 2003 E, US, M
T Wish 2004 US, J
K Witkowski 2005 EngA, Ar, 2006 E
N Witkowski 1998 US, J, 2000 Tg, US, SA, I, Sa, Fj, J, It, 2001 US, E, E, 2002 S, US, US, Ur, Ch, W, F, 2003 E, US, M, M, Ur, Ar, W, NZ, Tg, 2005 EngA, US, 2006 E
AH Woller 1967 E
S Wood 1977 E
TA Woods 1984 US, 1986 J, US, 1987 US, Tg, I, W, 1988 US, 1989 I, US, 1990 Ar, US, 1991 S, F, NZ, 1996 US, US, 1997 US, J
D Wooldridge 2009 I, Geo, IrA, ArJ
MA Wyatt 1982 J, J, E, US, 1983 US, It, It, E, 1985 A, A, US, 1986 J, US, 1987 Tg, I, W, US, 1988 US, 1989 I, US, 1990 Ar, US, Ar, 1991 J, S, US, R, F, NZ
H Wyndham 1973 W
JJ Yeganegi 2009 US, 1998 J
C Yukes 2001 Ur, Fj, J, 2002 S, US, Ur, Ur, 2003 E, US, M, M, US, Ar, W, NZ, It, Tg, 2004 US, J, EngA, US, F, It, E, 2005 W, EngA, US, 2006 Bar, US, 2007 IrA, US, NZ, Pt, W, Fj, J, A

ENGLAND

ENGLAND'S 2008–09 TEST RESULTS

OPPONENTS	DATE	VENUE	RESULT
Pacific Islanders	8 November	H	**Won** 39–13
Australia	15 November	H	**Lost** 14–28
South Africa	22 November	H	**Lost** 6–42
New Zealand	29 November	H	**Lost** 6–32
Italy	7 February	H	**Won** 36–11
Wales	14 February	A	**Lost** 15–23
Ireland	28 February	A	**Lost** 13–14
France	15 March	H	**Won** 34–10
Scotland	21 March	H	**Won** 26–12
Barbarians	30 May	H	**Lost** 26–33
Argentina	6 June	H	**Won** 37–15
Argentina	13 June	A	**Lost** 22–24

JOHNSON BEGINS REBUILDING PROCESS

By Paul Morgan

Shaun Botterill/Getty Images

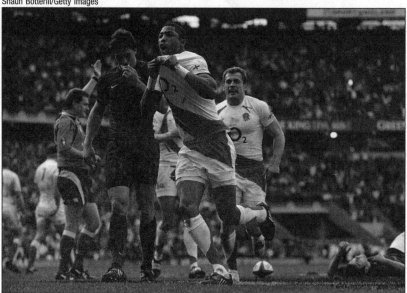

A great win over France took England into runners-up spot in the Six Nations.

When Martin Johnson was installed as the new England team manager in July 2008, there was widespread if tentative hope that the former World Cup-winning captain could recapture the elusive magic of 2003 and transform a struggling side back into a genuine Test match force once again.

A year on from his appointment and it was apparent that there would be no overnight solution to England's problems. Johnson was infamously difficult to please during his record-breaking reign as captain and the 39-year-old found the experience of his side losing seven of their 12 outings in his first season at the helm as frustrating as it was unfamiliar.

It is debatable whether a more experienced coach could have squeezed better results from a team lacking both confidence and continuity but despite the signs of improvement England showed in the Six Nations,

there was scant gloss that could be put on their heavy defeats to the
Wallabies, Springboks and All Blacks at Twickenham in the autumn.

England finished their season with a two-Test series against Argentina and their victory at Old Trafford in the first game, followed by defeat in the return match a week later in Salta, summed up the campaign. Johnson had presided over some solid performances and a dynamic victory over France in the Championship but there was clearly no silver bullet that would cure his side's fundamental failings.

"The season got better through the Six Nations and that was clear in our performances and results, the French game in particular," Johnson said after the second Test against the Pumas. "Generally we're improving, as is the confidence of the players and the belief they have in themselves.

"We understand what we're trying to do on the field and it's certainly far better than in the autumn. You always hope to be further than you are but we've made significant strides as a team. I really do believe that.

"There's no point writing off a Test match to blood some players. You want to blood Test players and win. Every game is a development game because we have the chance to get better from it, but we want to win. We wanted to beat Argentina. I don't want to look guys in the face and say it doesn't matter if we don't win because we're a development team."

England began their new era in early November against the Pacific Islanders and Johnson picked four new caps for the Twickenham clash, drafting in full-back Delon Armitage, wing Ugo Monye, inside centre Riki Flutey and lock Nick Kennedy. The visitors provided a predictably physical challenge but two tries from Paul Sackey and further scores from Danny Cipriani, Kennedy and Lee Mears laid the foundation for a comfortable 39–13 victory.

Australia were in London a week later looking for revenge for their World Cup quarter-final defeat to England a year earlier and they took full advantage of a performance littered with basic errors and ill-discipline to record a 28–14 win. Both sides scored a try apiece but Matt Giteau landed six penalties to Cipriani's two and Johnson tasted defeat for the first time.

The new manager resisted the temptation to make wholesale changes to his starting XV for the South Africa game. James Haskell replaced Tom Croft in the back row but otherwise the same personnel were given another opportunity to impress against the Springboks.

In the World Cup final England had pushed South Africa close but at Twickenham they were simply blown away by the same side, conceding five unanswered tries in a record 42–6 defeat by the Springboks on home soil. England were woeful in every department and the gulf in

THE COUNTRIES

England ended the Championship on a high, beating Scotland at Twickenham.

class was painfully obvious to every supporter at Twickenham who witnessed the brutal and humiliating dismantling of their side.

"The changing room is a very quiet place," admitted disappointed captain Steve Borthwick. "International rugby is all about fine margins and we made too many errors. Credit to South Africa, their work around the breakdown, their defensive work and the way they took their chances was a lesson to us.

"We want to be better and we want to improve. All we can do is work hard, study the tape of what happened today and put it right next week. We had plenty of ball, we've just got to use it better."

Cipriani was the high-profile casualty for the final game of the autumn against New Zealand but the introduction of Toby Flood at fly half did little to revive England fortunes as the All Blacks completed the Home Union 'Grand Slam' with a routine 32–6 triumph.

For a second successive match at Twickenham, England failed to cross the whitewash but their ill-discipline – resulting in four yellow cards during the match and 15 penalties conceded – was their real downfall as they slumped to another defeat.

The Six Nations offered England the chance of redemption after an appalling autumn and to an extent, they took it.

First up was Italy at Twickenham and although the men in white ultimately ran out 36–11 winners, the performance raised as many questions about the direction of the side as it answered. England did score five tries, including two for scrum-half Harry Ellis, but they benefited hugely from Nick Mallett's bizarre decision to play flanker Mauro Bergamasco at nine which backfired badly and in truth the home side failed to create many clear-cut chances against the Azzurri.

A week later it was the reigning champions Wales in Cardiff and although England went down 23–15 at the Millennium Stadium, it was arguably the side's best performance since Johnson took charge and they had the small satisfaction of outscoring their hosts two tries to one.

Ill-discipline again blighted England's chances with Mike Tindall and Andy Goode both spending time in the bin, while 18 of the points Wales scored came from penalties, and Johnson was left to rue what might have been.

"We let the Test match slip by," he said. "Despite the penalties and sin-bins we kept ourselves in the game. We could have been good enough to overcome that if we'd backed ourselves."

England were similarly stoic but ultimately unsuccessful in their next match against Ireland at Croke Park. Phil Vickery and Danny Care joined the team's growing and inglorious list of players shown yellow cards but a late try from Armitage and Goode's conversion gave the visitors a glimmer of hope only for Ireland to hold out for a 14–13 victory.

England finished the Championship with back-to-back home games against France and Scotland. Hopes were not high ahead of the clash with Les Bleus but Johnson's troops amazed a packed Twickenham with a devastating first half blitz that decimated the French and yielded a 34–10 final scoreline.

Mark Cueto, Flutey, Armitage and Joe Worsley all crossed in an astonishing first period, with Flutey grabbing a second try after the break and although France did score twice themselves late on, England were resounding winners.

Scotland were dispatched 26–12 a week later at Twickenham despite a mediocre second-half display and England finished the Six Nations in second, edging out France and Wales on points difference. It had not been a vintage campaign but three wins in five Championship outings represented a decent return.

But if Johnson privately felt his side had taken a tentative step forward, they were to take a stride backwards in their final three games of the season.

Their game with the Barbarians at the end of May was supposed to be a warm-up for the more serious games with the Pumas coming up, but England were outclassed by the BaaBaas, outscored five tries to four and condemned to a 33–26 defeat.

ENGLAND

England ended their 2008–09 season with defeat in Argentina.

The first Test against Argentina at Old Trafford a week later saw England rally and two tries from Armitage, who had been surprisingly overlooked by the British & Irish Lions, and a third from Matt Banahan provided the platform for an encouraging and timely 37–15 win.

England made the long trip to South America for the return game seven days later but Johnson's hopes of ending his debut season in charge with victory were dashed by a resolute Pumas display on home soil.

The Pumas crossed after just minutes through Juan Manuel Leguizamón and scored a second try after the break through Gonzalo Camacho. Four Goode penalties and a late score from Banahan reduced the arrears but the visitors had left their fightback too late and the Pumas were narrow 24–22 winners.

"This game was always going to be different from the first Test we won at Old Trafford because Argentina are a proud team, especially when they're at home," Johnson admitted. "You have to make them work a lot harder to score than that but the guys battled hard and played very well to come back in the second half."

Defeat was the seventh of Johnson's brief tenure. Positives over the previous 12 months were not impossible to pinpoint, particularly the side's vastly-improved defence, but the negatives were equally apparent, not least England's disastrous discipline problems. Johnson knows he still has his work cut out.

ENGLAND TO HOST RWC 2015

By Paul Morgan

England's 2009–10 pre-season was given a massive boost when Rugby World Cup Limited confirmed they would host Rugby World Cup 2015.

"The RFU, and every rugby fan in England, will be thrilled that we have been chosen to host RWC 2015," said Francis Baron, CEO of the Rugby Football Union. "This is a fantastic addition to the UK's Decade of World Sport which started this year with the Cricket Twenty20 World Cup and which continues in 2010 with the Women's Rugby World Cup, followed by the Olympics in 2012 and now the Rugby World Cup in 2015."

England's bid rested on their use of some of the country's biggest stadiums like Arsenal's Emirates Stadium and Old Trafford in Manchester, which the RFU believe will allow them to sell three million tickets for the event, the first time this barrier has been breached.

"The world's best players will now have a chance to play in some of the world's best stadia and supporters can look forward to a feast of rugby. It's almost enough to bring me out of retirement!" said World Cup winner Lawrence Dallaglio.

Will Greenwood, another member of England's RWC 2003 winning squad, added: "What excites me about a tournament in England is the opportunity to use rugby as a force for good in the world and the opportunity to leave a lasting legacy. I have seen at first hand how rugby can change lives on an individual basis – now we have a chance to change many lives in England and around the world. It is a huge opportunity and a wonderful challenge."

The RFU proposed that Rugby World Cup 2015 be staged in 10 cities across England and Wales: Wembley (London, 90,000 capacity), Twickenham (London, 82,000), Old Trafford (Manchester, 76,100), Millennium Stadium (Cardiff, 73,350), Emirates Stadium (London, 60,000), St James' Park (Newcastle, 52,387), Anfield (Liverpool, 45,000), Elland Road (Leeds, 40,204), St Mary's Stadium (Southampton, 32,689), Ricoh Arena (Coventry, 32,500), Kingsholm (Gloucester, 18,000).

ENGLAND

ENGLAND INTERNATIONAL STATISTICS

MATCH RECORDS UP TO 30TH SEPTEMBER 2009

MOST CONSECUTIVE TEST WINS

14	2002 W,It,Arg,NZ,A,SA, 2003 F1,W1,It,S,I,NZ,A,W2
11	2000 SA 2,A,Arg,SA3, 2001 W,It,S,F,C1,2,US
10	1882 W, 1883 I,S, 1884 W,I,S, 1885 W,I, 1886 W,I
10	1994 R,C, 1995 I,F,W,S, Arg, It, WS, A
10	2003 F,Gg,SA,Sm,U,W,F,A, 2004 It,S

MOST CONSECUTIVE TESTS WITHOUT DEFEAT

Matches	Wins	Draws	Periods
14	14	0	2002 to 2003
12	10	2	1882 to 1887
11	10	1	1922 to 1924
11	11	0	2000 to 2001

MOST POINTS IN A MATCH

BY THE TEAM

Pts	Opponents	Venue	Year
134	Romania	Twickenham	2001
111	Uruguay	Brisbane	2003
110	Netherlands	Huddersfield	1998
106	U S A	Twickenham	1999
101	Tonga	Twickenham	1999
84	Georgia	Perth	2003
80	Italy	Twickenham	2001

BY A PLAYER

Pts	Player	Opponents	Venue	Year
44	C Hodgson	Romania	Twickenham	2001
36	P J Grayson	Tonga	Twickenham	1999
35	J P Wilkinson	Italy	Twickenham	2001
32	J P Wilkinson	Italy	Twickenham	1999
30	C R Andrew	Canada	Twickenham	1994
30	P J Grayson	Netherlands	Huddersfield	1998
30	J P Wilkinson	Wales	Twickenham	2002
29	D J H Walder	Canada	Burnaby	2001
27	C R Andrew	South Africa	Pretoria	1994
27	J P Wilkinson	South Africa	Bloemfontein	2000
27	C C Hodgson	South Africa	Twickenham	2004
27	J P Wilkinson	Scotland	Twickenham	2007
26	J P Wilkinson	United States	Twickenham	1999

MOST TRIES IN A MATCH

BY THE TEAM

Tries	Opponents	Venue	Year
20	Romania	Twickenham	2001
17	Uruguay	Brisbane	2003
16	Netherlands	Huddersfield	1998
16	United States	Twickenham	1999
13	Wales	Blackheath	1881
13	Tonga	Twickenham	1999
12	Georgia	Perth	2003
12	Canada	Twickenham	2004
10	Japan	Sydney	1987
10	Fiji	Twickenham	1989
10	Italy	Twickenham	2001

BY A PLAYER

Tries	Player	Opponents	Venue	Year
5	D Lambert	France	Richmond	1907
5	R Underwood	Fiji	Twickenham	1989
5	O J Lewsey	Uruguay	Brisbane	2003
4	G W Burton	Wales	Blackheath	1881
4	A Hudson	France	Paris	1906
4	R W Poulton	France	Paris	1914
4	C Oti	Romania	Bucharest	1989
4	J C Guscott	Netherlands	Huddersfield	1998
4	N A Back	Netherlands	Huddersfield	1998
4	J C Guscott	United States	Twickenham	1999
4	J Robinson	Romania	Twickenham	2001
4	N Easter	Wales	Twickenham	2007

MOST CONVERSIONS IN A MATCH
BY THE TEAM

Cons	Opponents	Venue	Year
15	Netherlands	Huddersfield	1998
14	Romania	Twickenham	2001
13	United States	Twickenham	1999
13	Uruguay	Brisbane	2003
12	Tonga	Twickenham	1999
9	Italy	Twickenham	2001
9	Georgia	Perth	2003
8	Romania	Bucharest	1989
7	Wales	Blackheath	1881
7	Japan	Sydney	1987
7	Argentina	Twickenham	1990
7	Wales	Twickenham	1998
7	Wales	Twickenham	2007

BY A PLAYER

Cons	Player	Opponents	Venue	Year
15	P J Grayson	Netherlands	Huddersfield	1998
14	C Hodgson	Romania	Twickenham	2001
13	J P Wilkinson	United States	Twickenham	1999
12	P J Grayson	Tonga	Twickenham	1999
11	P J Grayson	Uruguay	Brisbane	2003
9	J P Wilkinson	Italy	Twickenham	2001
8	S D Hodgkinson	Romania	Bucharest	1989
7	J M Webb	Japan	Sydney	1987
7	S D Hodgkinson	Argentina	Twickenham	1990
7	P J Grayson	Wales	Twickenham	1998
7	J P Wilkinson	Wales	Twickenham	2007

MOST PENALTIES IN A MATCH
BY THE TEAM

Pens	Opponents	Venue	Year
8	South Africa	Bloemfontein	2000
7	Wales	Cardiff	1991
7	Scotland	Twickenham	1995
7	France	Twickenham	1999
7	Fiji	Twickenham	1999
7	South Africa	Paris	1999
7	South Africa	Twickenham	2001
6	Wales	Twickenham	1986
6	Canada	Twickenham	1994
6	Argentina	Durban	1995
6	Scotland	Murrayfield	1996
6	Ireland	Twickenham	1996
6	South Africa	Twickenham	2000
6	Australia	Twickenham	2002
6	Wales	Brisbane	2003

BY A PLAYER

Pens	Player	Opponents	Venue	Year
8	J P Wilkinson	South Africa	Bloemfontein	2000
7	S D Hodgkinson	Wales	Cardiff	1991
7	C R Andrew	Scotland	Twickenham	1995
7	J P Wilkinson	France	Twickenham	1999
7	J P Wilkinson	Fiji	Twickenham	1999
7	J P Wilkinson	South Africa	Twickenham	2001
6	C R Andrew	Wales	Twickenham	1986
6	C R Andrew	Canada	Twickenham	1994
6	C R Andrew	Argentina	Durban	1995
6	P J Grayson	Scotland	Murrayfield	1996
6	P J Grayson	Ireland	Twickenham	1996
6	P J Grayson	South Africa	Paris	1999
6	J P Wilkinson	South Africa	Twickenham	2000
6	J P Wilkinson	Australia	Twickenham	2002
6	J P Wilkinson	Wales	Brisbane	2003

MOST DROPPED GOALS IN A MATCH
BY THE TEAM

Drops	Opponents	Venue	Year
3	France	Sydney	2003
2	Ireland	Twickenham	1970
2	France	Paris	1978
2	France	Paris	1980
2	Romania	Twickenham	1985
2	Fiji	Suva	1991
2	Argentina	Durban	1995
2	France	Paris	1996
2	Australia	Twickenham	2001
2	Wales	Cardiff	2003
2	Ireland	Dublin	2003
2	South Africa	Perth	2003
2	Samoa	Nantes	2007
2	Tonga	Paris	2007
2	Argentina	Manchester	2009

BY A PLAYER

Drops	Player	Opponents	Venue	Year
3	J P Wilkinson	France	Sydney	2003
2	R Hiller	Ireland	Twickenham	1970
2	A G B Old	France	Paris	1978
2	J P Horton	France	Paris	1980
2	C R Andrew	Romania	Twickenham	1985
2	C R Andrew	Fiji	Suva	1991
2	C R Andrew	Argentina	Durban	1995
2	P J Grayson	France	Paris	1996
2	J P Wilkinson	Australia	Twickenham	2001
2	J P Wilkinson	Wales	Cardiff	2003
2	J P Wilkinson	Ireland	Dublin	2003
2	J P Wilkinson	South Africa	Perth	2003
2	J P Wilkinson	Samoa	Nantes	2007
2	J P Wilkinson	Tonga	Paris	2007
2	A J Goode	Argentina	Manchester	2009

ENGLAND

CAREER RECORDS

MOST CAPPED PLAYERS

Caps	Player	Career Span
114	J Leonard	1990 to 2004
85	R Underwood	1984 to 1996
85	L B N Dallaglio	1995 to 2007
84	M O Johnson	1993 to 2003
77	M J S Dawson	1995 to 2006
75	M J Catt	1994 to 2007
73	P J Vickery	1998 to 2009
72	W D C Carling	1988 to 1997
72	J P R Worsley	1999 to 2009
71	C R Andrew	1985 to 1997
71	R A Hill	1997 to 2004
70	J P Wilkinson	1998 to 2008
69	D J Grewcock	1997 to 2007
66	N A Back	1994 to 2003
65	J C Guscott	1989 to 1999
64	B C Moore	1987 to 1995
64	M E Corry	1997 to 2007
62	B J Kay	2001 to 2009
60	M J Tindall	2000 to 2009
58	P J Winterbottom	1982 to 1993
57	B C Cohen	2000 to 2006
55	W A Dooley	1985 to 1993
55	W J H Greenwood	1997 to 2004
55	O J Lewsey	1998 to 2007
54	G C Rowntree	1995 to 2006
53	L W Moody	2001 to 2008
52	S D Shaw	1996 to 2009
51	A S Healey	1997 to 2003
51	K P P Bracken	1993 to 2003
51	J T Robinson	2001 to 2007
51	J M White	2000 to 2009

MOST CONSECUTIVE TESTS

Tests	Player	Span
44	W D C Carling	1989 to 1995
40	J Leonard	1990 to 1995
36	J V Pullin	1968 to 1975
33	W B Beaumont	1975 to 1982
30	R Underwood	1992 to 1996

MOST TESTS AS CAPTAIN

Tests	Captain	Span
59	W D C Carling	1988 to 1996
39	M O Johnson	1998 to 2003
22	L B N Dallaglio	1997 to 2004
21	W B Beaumont	1978 to 1982
17	M E Corry	2005 to 2007
15	P J Vickery	2002 to 2008
14	S W Borthwick	2008 to 2009
13	W W Wakefield	1924 to 1926
13	N M Hall	1949 to 1955
13	E Evans	1956 to 1958
13	R E G Jeeps	1960 to 1962
13	J V Pullin	1972 to 1975

MOST POINTS IN TESTS

Points	Player	Tests	Career
1032	J P Wilkinson	70	1998 to 2008
400	P J Grayson	32	1995 to 2004
396	C R Andrew	71	1985 to 1997
296	J M Webb	33	1987 to 1993
259	C C Hodgson	31	2001 to 2008
240	W H Hare	25	1974 to 1984
210	R Underwood	85	1984 to 1996

MOST TRIES IN TESTS

Tries	Player	Tests	Career
49	R Underwood	85	1984 to 1996
31	W J H Greenwood	55	1997 to 2004
31	B C Cohen	57	2000 to 2006
30	J C Guscott	65	1989 to 1999
28	J T Robinson	51	2001 to 2007
24	D D Luger	38	1998 to 2003
22	O J Lewsey	55	1998 to 2007
18	C N Lowe	25	1913 to 1923
17	L B N Dallaglio	85	1995 to 2007
16	N A Back	66	1994 to 2003
16	M J S Dawson	77	1995 to 2006
15	A S Healey	51	1997 to 2003
15	M J Cueto	31	2004 to 2009
13	T Underwood	27	1992 to 1998
13	M J Tindall	60	2000 to 2009
13	I R Balshaw	35	2000 to 2008

MOST CONVERSIONS IN TESTS

Cons	Player	Tests	Career
144	J P Wilkinson	70	1998 to 2008
78	P J Grayson	32	1995 to 2004
44	C C Hodgson	31	2001 to 2008
41	J M Webb	33	1987 to 1993
35	S D Hodgkinson	14	1989 to 1991
33	C R Andrew	71	1985 to 1997
17	L Stokes	12	1875 to 1881

MOST PENALTY GOALS IN TESTS			
Pens	Player	Tests	Career
209	J P Wilkinson	70	1998 to 2008
86	C R Andrew	71	1985 to 1997
72	P J Grayson	32	1995 to 2004
67	W H Hare	25	1974 to 1984
66	J M Webb	33	1987 to 1993
44	C C Hodgson	31	2001 to 2008
43	S D Hodgkinson	14	1989 to 1991

MOST DROPPED GOALS IN TESTS			
Drops	Player	Tests	Career
29	J P Wilkinson	70	1998 to 2008
21	C R Andrew	71	1985 to 1997
6	P J Grayson	32	1995 to 2004
4	J P Horton	13	1978 to 1984
4	L Cusworth	12	1979 to 1988
4	A J Goode	16	2005 to 2009

INTERNATIONAL CHAMPIONSHIP RECORDS

ENGLAND

RECORD	DETAIL		SET
Most points in season	229	in five matches	2001
Most tries in season	29	in five matches	2001
Highest Score	80	80–23 v Italy	2001
Biggest win	57	80–23 v Italy	2001
Highest score conceded	43	13–43 v Ireland	2007
Biggest defeat	30	13–43 v Ireland	2007
Most appearances	54	J Leonard	1991–2004
Most points in matches	479	J P Wilkinson	1998–2008
Most points in season	89	J P Wilkinson	2001
Most points in match	35	J P Wilkinson	v Italy, 2001
Most tries in matches	18	C N Lowe	1913–1923
	18	R Underwood	1984–1996
Most tries in season	8	C N Lowe	1914
Most tries in match	4	R W Poulton	v France, 1914
Most cons in matches	81	J P Wilkinson	1998–2008
Most cons in season	24	J P Wilkinson	2001
Most cons in match	9	J P Wilkinson	v Italy, 2001
Most pens in matches	90	J P Wilkinson	1998–2008
Most pens in season	18	S D Hodgkinson	1991
	18	J P Wilkinson	2000
Most pens in match	7	S D Hodgkinson	v Wales, 1991
	7	C R Andrew	v Scotland, 1995
	7	J P Wilkinson	v France, 1999
Most drops in matches	9	C R Andrew	1985–1997
	9	J P Wilkinson	1998–2008
Most drops in season	5	J P Wilkinson	2003
Most drops in match	2	R Hiller	v Ireland, 1970
	2	A G B Old	v France, 1978
	2	J P Horton	v France, 1980
	2	P J Grayson	v France, 1996
	2	J P Wilkinson	v Wales, 2003
	2	J P Wilkinson	v Ireland, 2003

MISCELLANEOUS RECORDS

RECORD	HOLDER	DETAIL
Longest Test Career	J Leonard	1990 to 2004
Youngest Test Cap	H C C Laird	18 yrs 134 days in 1927
Oldest Test Cap	F Gilbert	38 yrs 362 days in 1923

CAREER RECORDS OF ENGLAND INTERNATIONAL PLAYERS
(UP TO 30 SEPTEMBER 2009)

PLAYER BACKS	DEBUT	CAPS	T	C	P	D	PTS
N J Abendanon	2007 v SA	2	0	0	0	0	0
A O Allen	2006 v NZ	2	0	0	0	0	0
D A Armitage	2008 v PI	11	5	0	2	1	34
I R Balshaw	2000 v I	35	13	0	0	0	65
M A Banahan	2009 v Arg	2	2	0	0	0	10
O J Barkley	2001 v US	23	2	9	18	0	82
M N Brown	2007 v SA	3	0	0	0	0	0
D S Care	2008 v NZ	11	1	0	0	1	8
D J Cipriani	2008 v W	7	1	7	10	0	49
B C Cohen	2000 v I	57	31	0	0	0	155
M J Cueto	2004 v C	31	15	0	0	0	75
H A Ellis	2004 v SA	27	5	0	0	0	25
T G A L Flood	2006 v Arg	26	3	7	10	1	62
R J Flutey	2008 v PI	9	4	0	0	0	20
B J Foden	2009 v It	1	0	0	0	0	0
S J J Geraghty	2007 v F	3	0	1	1	0	5
A J Goode	2005 v It	16	1	15	20	4	107
D J Hipkiss	2007 v W	9	0	0	0	0	0
C C Hodgson	2001 v R	31	6	44	44	3	259
P K Hodgson	2008 v I	3	0	0	0	0	0
T A May	2009 v Arg	2	0	0	0	0	0
Y C C Monye	2008 v PI	6	1	0	0	0	5
O Morgan	2007 v S	2	0	0	0	0	0
J D Noon	2001 v C	38	7	0	0	0	35
T O Ojo	2008 v NZ	2	2	0	0	0	10
S A Perry	2006 v NZ	14	2	0	0	0	10
P C Richards	2006 v A	13	0	0	0	0	0
P H Sackey	2006 v NZ	22	11	0	0	0	55
D G R Scarbrough	2003 v W	2	1	0	0	0	5
J D Simpson-Daniel	2002 v NZ	10	3	0	0	0	15
D Strettle	2007 v I	6	1	0	0	0	5
M J M Tait	2005 v W	31	4	0	0	0	20
M J Tindall	2000 v I	60	13	2	0	0	69
L P I Vainikolo	2008 v W	5	0	0	0	0	0

T W Varndell	2005 v Sm	4	3	0	0	0	15
S B Vesty	2009 v Arg	2	0	0	0	0	0
R E P Wigglesworth	2008 v It	5	1	0	0	0	5
J P Wilkinson	1998 v I	70	6	144	209	29	1032

ENGLAND

FORWARDS

S E Armitage	2009 v It	3	0	0	0	0	0
S W Borthwick	2001 v F	50	2	0	0	0	10
A T Brown	2006 v A	3	0	0	0	0	0
M I Cairns	2007 v SA	1	0	0	0	0	0
G S Chuter	2006 v A	22	1	0	0	0	5
J S Crane	2008 v SA	2	0	0	0	0	0
T Croft	2008 v F	13	0	0	0	0	0
L P Deacon	2005 v Sm	10	0	0	0	0	0
N J Easter	2007 v It	27	5	0	0	0	25
P T Freshwater	2005 v Sm	10	0	0	0	0	0
D M Hartley	2008 v PI	11	0	0	0	0	0
J A W Haskell	2007 v W	19	0	0	0	0	0
J D Hobson	2008 v NZ	1	0	0	0	0	0
B J Kay	2001 v C	62	2	0	0	0	10
N J Kennedy	2008 v PI	7	1	0	0	0	5
M R Lipman	2004 v NZ	10	0	0	0	0	0
L A Mears	2005 v Sm	34	1	0	0	0	5
L W Moody	2001 v C	53	9	0	0	0	45
L J W Narraway	2008 v W	7	0	0	0	0	0
D J Paice	2008 v NZ	2	0	0	0	0	0
T P Palmer	2001 v US	13	0	0	0	0	0
T A N Payne	2004 v A	12	0	0	0	0	0
T Rees	2007 v S	15	1	0	0	0	5
C D C Robshaw	2009 v Arg	1	0	0	0	0	0
S D Shaw	1996 v It	52	2	0	0	0	10
A J Sheridan	2004 v C	32	0	0	0	0	0
B D Skirving	2007 v SA	1	0	0	0	0	0
M J H Stevens	2004 v NZ	32	0	0	0	0	0
S G Thompson	2002 v S	48	3	0	0	0	15
S C Turner	2007 v W	3	0	0	0	0	0
P J Vickery	1998 v W	73	2	0	0	0	10
J M White	2000 v SA	51	0	0	0	0	0
D G Wilson	2009 v Arg	2	0	0	0	0	0
J P R Worsley	1999 v Tg	72	10	0	0	0	50

ENGLAND

ENGLAND INTERNATIONAL PLAYERS
UP TO 30TH SEPTEMBER 2009

Note: Years given for International Championship matches are for second half of season; eg 1972 means season 1971–72. Years for all other matches refer to the actual year of the match. Entries in square brackets denote matches played in RWC Finals.

THE COUNTRIES

Aarvold, C D (Cambridge U, W Hartlepool, Headingley, Blackheath) 1928 A, W, I, F, S, 1929 W, I, F, 1931 W, S, F, 1932 SA, W, I, S, 1933 W

Abbott, S R (Wasps, Harlequins) 2003 W2, F3, [Sm, U, W(R)], 2004 NZ1(t&R), 2, 2006 I, A2(R)

Abendanon, N A (Bath) 2007 SA2(R),F2

Ackford, P J (Harlequins) 1988 A, 1989 S, I, F, W, R, Fj, 1990 I, F, W, S, Arg 3, 1991 W, S, I, F, A, [NZ, It, F, S, A]

Adams, A A (London Hospital) 1910 F

Adams, F R (Richmond) 1875 I, S, 1876 S, 1877 I, 1878 S, 1879 S, I

Adebayo, A A (Bath) 1996, It, 1997 Arg 1,2, A 2, NZ 1, 1998 S

Adey, G J (Leicester) 1976 I, F

Adkins, S J (Coventry) 1950 I, F, S, 1953 W, I, F, S

Agar, A E (Harlequins) 1952 SA, W, S, I, F, 1953 W, I

Alcock, A (Guy's Hospital) 1906 SA

Alderson, F H R (Hartlepool R) 1891 W, I, S, 1892 W, S, 1893 W

Alexander, H (Richmond) 1900 I, S, 1901 W, I, S, 1902 W, I

Alexander, W (Northern) 1927 F

Allen, A O (Gloucester) 2006 NZ,Arg

Allison, D F (Coventry) 1956 W, I, S, F, 1957 W, 1958 W, S

Allport, A (Blackheath) 1892 W, 1893 I, 1894 W, I, S

Anderson, S (Rockcliff) 1889 I

Anderson, W F (Orrell) 1973 NZ 1

Anderton, C (Manchester FW) 1889 M

Andrew, C R (Cambridge U, Nottingham, Wasps, Toulouse, Newcastle) 1985 R, F, S, I, W, 1986 W, S, I, F, 1987 I, F, W, [J (R), US], 1988 S, I 1,2, A 1,2, Fj, A, 1989 S, I, F, W, R, Fj, 1990 I, F, W, S, Arg 3, 1991 W, S, I, F, Fj, A, [NZ, It, US, F, S, A], 1992 S, I, F, W, C, SA, 1993 F, W, NZ, 1994 S, I, F, W, SA 1,2, R, C, 1995 I, F, W, S, [Arg, It, A, NZ, F], 1997 W (R)

Appleford, G N (London Irish) 2002 Arg

Archer, G S (Bristol, Army, Newcastle) 1996 S, I, 1997 A 2, NZ 1, SA, NZ 2, 1998 F, W, S, I, A 1, NZ 1, H, It, 1999 Tg, Fj, 2000 I, F, W, It, S

Archer, H (Bridgwater A) 1909 W, F, I

Armitage, D A (London Irish) 2008 PI, A, SA, NZ3, 2009 It, W, I, F, S, Arg 1,2

Armitage, S E (London Irish) 2009 It,Arg 1,2

Armstrong, R (Northern) 1925 W

Arthur, T G (Wasps) 1966 W, I

Ashby, R C (Wasps) 1966 I, F, 1967 A

Ashcroft, A (Waterloo) 1956 W, I, S, F, 1957 W, I, F, S, 1958 W, A, I, F, S, 1959 I, F, S

Ashcroft, A H (Birkenhead Park) 1909 A

Ashford, W (Richmond) 1897 W, I, 1898 S, W

Ashworth, A (Oldham) 1892 I

Askew, J G (Cambridge U) 1930 W, I, F

Aslett, A R (Richmond) 1926 W, I, F, S, 1929 S, F

Assinder, E W (O Edwardians) 1909 A, W

Aston, R L (Blackheath) 1890 S, I

Auty, J R (Headingley) 1935 S

Back, N A (Leicester) 1994 S, I, 1995 [Arg (t), It, WS], 1997 NZ 1(R), SA, NZ 2, 1998 F, W, S, I, H, It, A 2, SA 2, 1999 S, I, F, W, A, US, C, [It, NZ, Fj, SA], 2000 I, F, W, S, A, Arg, SA 3, 2001 W, It, S, F, I, A, R, SA, 2002 S, I, F, W, It, NZ (t + R), A, SA, 2003 F 1, W 1, S, I, NZ, A,

F 3, [Gg, SA, Sm, W, F, A]

Bailey, M D (Cambridge U, Wasps) 1984 SA 1,2, 1987 [US], 1989 Fj, 1990 I, F, S (R)

Bainbridge, S (Gosforth, Fylde) 1982 F, W, 1983 F, W, S, I, NZ, 1984 S, I, F, W, 1985 NZ 1,2, 1987 F, W, S, [J, US]

Baker, D G S (OMTs) 1955 W, I, F, S

Baker, E M (Moseley) 1895 W, I, S, 1896 W, I, S, 1897 W

Baker, H C (Clifton) 1887 W

Balshaw, I R (Bath, Leeds, Gloucester) 2000 I (R), F (R), It (R), S (R), A (R), Arg, SA 3(R), 2001 W, It, S, F, I, 2002 S (R), I (R), 2003 F2,3, [Sm, U, A(R)], 2004 It, S, I, 2005 It, S, 2006 A1, 2, NZ,Arg, 2007 It,SA1, 2008 W, It, F, S, I

Banahan, M A (Bath) 2009 Arg 1,2

Bance, J F (Bedford) 1954 S

Barkley, O J (Bath) 2001 US (R), 2004 It(R), I(t), W, F, NZ2(R), A1(R), 2005 W(R), F, I, It, S, A(R), Sm(R), 2006 A1, 2(R), 2007 F2,3(R), [US,Sm,Tg], 2008 NZ1,2(R)

Barley, B (Wakefield) 1984 I, F, W, A, 1988 A 1,2, Fj

Barnes, S (Bristol, Bath) 1984 A, 1985 R (R), NZ 1,2, 1986 S (R), F (R), 1987 I (R), 1988 Fj, 1993 S, I

Barr, R J (Leicester) 1932 SA, W, I

Barrett, E I M (Lennox) 1903 S

Barrington, T J M (Bristol) 1931 W, I

Barrington-Ward, L E (Edinburgh U) 1910 W, I, F, S

Barron, J H (Bingley) 1896 S, 1897 W, I

Bartlett, J T (Waterloo) 1951 W

Bartlett, R M (Harlequins) 1957 W, I, F, S, 1958 I, F, S

Barton, J (Coventry) 1967 I, E, W, 1972 F

Batchelor, T B (Oxford U) 1907 F

Bates, S M (Wasps) 1989 R

Bateson, A H (Otley) 1930 W, I, F, S

Bateson, H D (Liverpool) 1879 I

Batson, T (Blackheath) 1872 S, 1874 S, 1875 I

Batten, J M (Cambridge U) 1874 S

Baume, J L (Northern) 1950 S

Baxendell, J J N (Sale) 1998 NZ 2, SA 1

Baxter, J (Birkenhead Park) 1900 W, I, S

Bayfield, M C (Northampton) 1991 Fj, A 1992 S, I, F, W, C, SA, 1993 F, W, S, I, 1994 S, I, SA 1,2, R, C, 1995 I, F, W, S, [Arg, It, A, NZ, F], SA, WS, 1996 F, W

Bazley, R C (Waterloo) 1952 I, F, 1953 W, I, F, S, 1955 W, I, F, S

Beal, N D (Northampton) 1996 Arg, 1997 A 1, 1998 NZ 1,2, SA 1, H (R), SA 2, 1999 S, F (R), A (t), C (R), [It (R), Tg (R), Fj, SA]

Beaumont, W B (Fylde) 1975 I, A 1(R),2, 1976 A, W, S, I, F, 1977 S, I, F, W, 1978 F, W, S, I, NZ, 1979 S, I, F, W, NZ, 1980 I, F, W, S, 1981 I, W, S, I, F, Arg 1,2, 1982 A, S

Bedford, H (Morley) 1889 M, 1890 S, I

Bedford, L L (Headingley) 1931 W, I

Beer, I D S (Harlequins) 1955 F, S

Beese, M C (Liverpool) 1972 W, I, F

Beim, T D (Sale) 1998 NZ 1(R),2

Bell, D S C (Bath) 2005 It(R), S

Bell, F J (Northern) 1900 W

Bell, H (New Brighton) 1884 I

Bell, J L (Darlington) 1878 I

Bell, P J (Blackheath) 1968 W, I, F, S

Bell, R W (Northern) 1900 W, I, S
Bendon, G J (Wasps) 1959 W, I, F, S
Bennett, N O (St Mary's Hospital, Waterloo) 1947 W, S, F, 1948 A, W, I, S
Bennett, W N (Bedford, London Welsh) 1975 S, A1, 1976 S (R), 1979 S, I, F, W
Bennetts, B B (Penzance) 1909 A, W
Bentley, J (Sale, Newcastle) 1988 I 2, A 1, 1997 A 1, SA
Bentley, J E (Gipsies) 1871 S, 1872 S
Benton, S (Gloucester) 1998 A 1
Berridge, M J (Northampton) 1949 W, I
Berry, H (Gloucester) 1910 W, I, F, S
Berry, J (Tyldesley) 1891 W, I, S
Berry, J T W (Leicester) 1939 W, I, S
Beswick, E (Swinton) 1882 I, S
Biggs, J M (UCH) 1878 S, 1879 I
Birkett, J G G (Harlequins) 1906 S, F, SA, 1907 F, W, S, 1908 F, W,I , S, 1910 W, I, S, 1911 W, F, I , S, 1912 W, I , S, F
Birkett L (Clapham R) 1875 S, 1877 I, S
Birkett, R H (Clapham R) 1871 S, 1875 S, 1876 S, 1877 I
Bishop, C C (Blackheath) 1927 F
Black, B H (Blackheath) 1930 W, I, F, S, 1931 W, I, S, F, 1932 S, 1933 W
Blacklock, J H (Aspatria) 1898 I, 1899 I
Blakeway, P J (Gloucester) 1980 I, F, W, S, 1981 W, S, I, F, 1982 I, F, W, 1984 I, F, W, SA 1, 1985 R, F, S, I
Blakiston, A F (Northampton) 1920 S, 1921 W, I, S, F, 1922 W, 1923 S, F, 1924 W, I, F, S, 1925 NZ, W, I, S, F
Blatherwick, T (Manchester) 1878 I
Body, J A (Gipsies) 1872 S, 1873 S
Bolton, C A (United Services) 1909 F
Bolton, R (Harlequins) 1933 W, 1936 S, 1937 S, 1938 W, I
Bolton, W N (Blackheath) 1882 I, S, 1883 W, I, S, 1884 W, I, S, 1885 I, 1887 I, S
Bonaventura, M S (Blackheath) 1931 W
Bond, A M (Sale) 1978 NZ, 1979 S, I, NZ, 1980 I, 1982 I
Bonham-Carter, E (Oxford U) 1891 S
Bonsor, F (Bradford) 1886 W, I, S, 1887 W, S, 1889 M
Boobbyer, B (Rosslyn Park) 1950 W, I, F, S, 1951 W, F, 1952 S, I, F
Booth, L A (Headingley) 1933 W, I, S, 1934 S, 1935 W, I, S
Borthwick, S W (Bath, Saracens) 2001 F, C 1, 2(R), US, R, 2003 A(t), W 2(t), F 2, 2004 I, F(R), NZ1(R), 2, A1, C, SA, A2, 2005 W(R), It(R), S(R), A, NZ, Sm, 2006 W, It, S, F, I, 2007 W2, F3, [SA1(t&R), Sm(R), Tg], 2008 W, It, F, S, I, NZ1, 2, PI, A, SA, NZ3, 2009 It, W, I, F, S, Arg 1,2
Botting, I J (Oxford U) 1950 W, I
Boughton, H J (Gloucester) 1935 W, I, S
Boyle, C W (Oxford U) 1873 S
Boyle, S B (Gloucester) 1983 W, S, I
Boylen, F (Hartlepool R) 1908 F, W, I, S
Bracken, K P P (Bristol, Saracens) 1993 NZ, 1994 S, I, C, 1995 I, F, W, S, [It, WS (t)], SA, 1996 It (R), 1997 Arg 1,2, A 2, NZ 1,2, 1998 F, W, 1999 S(R), I, F, A, 2000 SA 1,2, A, 2001 It (R), S (R), F (R), C 1,2, US, I (R), A, R (R), SA, 2002 S, I, F, W, It, 2003 W 1, It(R), I(t), NZ, A, F3, [SA, U(R), W(R), F(t&R)]
Bradby, M S (United Services) 1922 I, F
Bradley, R (W Hartlepool) 1903 W
Bradshaw, H (Bramley) 1892 S, 1893 W, I, S, 1894 W, I, S
Brain, S E (Coventry) 1984 SA 2, A (R), 1985 R, F, S, I, W, NZ 1,2, 1986 W, S, I, F
Braithwaite, J (Leicester) 1905 NZ
Braithwaite-Exley, B (Headingley) 1949 W
Brettargh, A T (Liverpool OB) 1900 W, 1903 I, S, 1904 W, I, S, 1905 I, S
Brewer, J (Gipsies) 1876 I
Briggs, A (Bradford) 1892 W, I, S
Brinn, A (Gloucester) 1972 W, I, S
Broadley, T (Bingley) 1893 W, S, 1894 W, I, S, 1896 S
Bromet, W E (Richmond) 1891 W, I, 1892 W, I, S, 1893 W, I, S, 1895 W, I, S, 1896 I
Brook, P W P (Harlequins) 1930 S, 1931 F, 1936 S
Brooke, T J (Richmond) 1968 F, S
Brooks, F G (Bedford) 1906 SA
Brooks, M J (Oxford U) 1874 S
Brophy, T J (Liverpool) 1964 I, F, 1965 W, I, 1966 W, I, F

Brough, J W (Silloth) 1925 NZ, W
Brougham, H (Harlequins) 1912 W, I, S, F
Brown, A A (Exeter) 1938 S
Brown, A T (Gloucester) 2006 A1, 2007 SA1,2
Brown, L G (Oxford U, Blackheath) 1911 W, F, I, S, 1913 SA, W, F, I, S, 1914 W, I, S, F, 1921 W, I, S, F, 1922 W
Brown, M N (Harlequins) 2007 SA1,2, 2008 NZ1
Brown S P (Richmond) 1998 A 1, SA 1
Brown, T W (Bristol) 1928 S, 1929 W, I, S, F, 1932 S, 1933 W, I, S
Brunton, J (N Durham) 1914 W, I, S
Brutton, E B (Cambridge U) 1886 S
Bryden, C C (Clapham R) 1876 I, 1877 S
Bryden, H A (Clapham R) 1874 S
Buckingham, R A (Leicester) 1927 F
Bucknall, A L (Richmond) 1969 SA, 1970 I, W, S, F, 1971 W, I, F, S (2[1C])
Buckton, J R D (Saracens) 1988 A (R), 1990 Arg 1,2
Budd, A J (Blackheath) 1878 I, 1879 S, I, 1881 W, S
Budworth, R T D (Blackheath) 1890 W, 1891 W, S
Bull, A G (Northampton) 1914 W
Bullough, E (Wigan) 1892 W, I, S
Bulpitt, M P (Blackheath) 1970 S
Bulteel, A J (Manchester) 1876 I
Bunting, W L (Moseley) 1897 I, S, 1898 I, S, W, 1899 S, 1900 S, 1901 I, S
Burland, D W (Bristol) 1931 W, I, F, 1932 I, S, 1933 W, I, S
Burns, B H (Blackheath) 1871 S
Burton, G W (Blackheath) 1879 S, I, 1880 S, 1881 I, W, S
Burton, H C (Richmond) 1926 W
Burton, M A (Gloucester) 1972 W, I, F, S, SA, 1974 F, W, 1975 S, A 1,2, 1976 A, W, S, I, F, 1978 F, W
Bush, J A (Clifton) 1872 S, 1873 S, 1875 S, 1876 I, S
Butcher, C J S (Harlequins) 1984 SA 1,2, A
Butcher, W V (Streatham) 1903 S, 1904 W, I, S, 1905 W, I, S
Butler, A G (Harlequins) 1937 W, I
Butler, P E (Gloucester) 1975 A 1, 1976 F
Butterfield, J (Northampton) 1953 F, S, 1954 W, NZ, I, S, F, 1955 W, I, F, S, 1956 W, I, S, F, 1957 W, I, F, S, 1958 W, A, I, F, S, 1959 W, I, F, S
Byrne, F A (Moseley) 1897 W
Byrne, J F (Moseley) 1894 W, I, S, 1895 I, S, 1896 I, 1897 W, I, S, 1898 I, S, W, 1899 I
Cain, J J (Waterloo) 1950 W
Cairns, M I (Saracens) 2007 SA1(R)
Callard, J E B (Bath) 1993 NZ, 1994 S, I, 1995 [WS], SA
Campbell, D A (Cambridge U) 1937 W, I
Candler, P L (St Bart's Hospital) 1935 W, 1936 NZ, W, I, S, 1937 W, I, S, 1938 W, S
Cannell, L B (Oxford U, St Mary's Hospital) 1948 F, 1949 W, I, F, S, 1950 W, I, F, S, 1952 SA, W, 1953 W, I, F, 1956 I, S, F, 1957 W, I
Caplan, D W N (Headingley) 1978 S, I
Cardus, R M (Roundhay) 1979 F, W
Care, D S (Harlequins) 2008 NZ1(R),2,PI,A,SA,NZ3, 2009 I(R), F(R), S(R), Arg 1, 2
Carey, G M (Blackheath) 1895 W, I, S, 1896 W, I
Carleton, J (Orrell) 1979 NZ, 1980 I, F, W, S, 1981 W, S, I, F, Arg 1,2, 1982 A, S, I, F, W, 1983 F, W, S, I, NZ, 1984 S, I, F, W, A
Carling, W D C (Durham U, Harlequins) 1988 F, W, S, I 1,2, A2, Fj, A, 1989 S, I, F, W, Fj, 1990 I, F, W, S, Arg 1,2,3, 1991 W, S, I, F, Fj, A, [NZ, It, US, F, S, A], 1992 S, I, F, W, C, SA, 1993 F, W, S, I, NZ, 1994 S, I, F, W, SA 1,2, R, C, 1995 I, F, W, S, [Arg, WS, A, NZ, F], SA, WS, 1996 F, W, S, I, It, Arg, 1997 S, I, F, W
Carpenter, A D (Gloucester) 1932 SA
Carr, R S L (Manchester) 1939 W, I, S
Cartwright, V H (Nottingham) 1903 W, I, S, 1904 W, S, 1905 W, I, S, NZ, 1906 W, I, S, F, SA
Catcheside, H C (Percy Park) 1924 W, I, F, S, 1926 W, I, 1927 I, S
Catt, M J (Bath, London Irish) 1994 W (R), C (R), 1995 I, F, W, S, [Arg, It, WS, A, NZ, F], SA, WS, 1996 F, W, S, I, It, Arg, 1997 W, Arg 1, A 1,2, NZ 1, SA, 1998 F, W (R), I, A 2(R), SA 2, 1999 S, F, W, A, C (R), [Tg (R), Fj, SA (R)], 2000

I, F, W, It, S, SA 1,2, A, Arg, 2001 W, It, S, F, I, A, R (R), SA, 2003 [Sm(R), U, W(R), F, A(R)], 2004 W(R), F(R), NZ1, A1, 2006 A1, 2, 2007 F1,W1,F2, [US,SA1,A,F,SA2]

Cattell, R H B (Blackheath) 1895 W, I, S, 1896 W, I, S, 1900 W

Cave, J W (Richmond) 1889 M

Cave, W T C (Blackheath) 1905 W

Challis, R (Bristol) 1957 I, F, S

Chambers, E L (Bedford) 1908 F, 1910 W, I

Chantrill, B S (Bristol) 1924 W, I, F, S

Chapman, C E (Cambridge U) 1884 W

Chapman D E (Richmond) 1998 A 1(R)

Chapman, F E (Hartlepool) 1910 W, I, F, S, 1912 W, 1914 W, I

Cheesman, W I (OMTs) 1913 SA, W, F, I

Cheston, E C (Richmond) 1873 S, 1874 S, 1875 I, S, 1876 S

Chilcott, G J (Bath) 1984 A, 1986 I, F, 1987 F (R), W, [J, US, W (R)], 1988 I 2(R), Fj, 1989 I (R), F, W, R

Christophers, P D (Bristol) 2002 Arg, SA, 2003 W 1 (R)

Christopherson, P (Blackheath) 1891 W, S

Chuter, G S (Leicester) 2006 A1(R), 2, NZ, Arg, SA1, 2(R), 2007 S, It, I, F1, W1, 2(R), [US(R), SA1(R), Sm, Tg, A(R), F(R), SA2(R)], 2008 S(R), I(R), 2009 Arg 2(R)

Cipriani, D J (Wasps) 2008 W(R), It(R), I, PI, A, SA, NZ3(R)

Clark, C W H (Liverpool) 1876 I

Clarke, A J (Coventry) 1935 W, I, S, 1936 NZ, W, I

Clarke, B B (Bath, Richmond) 1992 SA, 1993 F, W, S, I, NZ, 1994 S, F, W, SA 1,2, R, C, 1995 I, F, W, S, [Arg, It, A, NZ, F], SA, WS, 1996 F, W, S, I, Arg (R), 1997 W, Arg 1,2, A 1(R), 1998 A 1(t),NZ 1,2, SA 1, H, It, 1999 A (R)

Clarke, S J S (Cambridge U, Blackheath) 1963 W, I, F, S, NZ 1,2, A, 1964 NZ, W, I, 1965 I, F, S

Clayton, J H (Liverpool) 1871 S

Clements, J W (O Cranleighans) 1959 I, F, S

Cleveland, C R (Blackheath) 1887 W, S

Clibborn, W G (Richmond) 1886 W, I, S, 1887 W, I, S

Clough, F J (Cambridge U, Orrell) 1986 I, F, 1987 [J (R), US]

Coates, C H (Yorkshire) W 1880 S, 1881 S, 1882 S

Coates, V H M (Bath) 1913 SA, W, F, I, S

Cobby, W (Hull) 1900 W

Cockerham, A (Bradford Olicana) 1900 W

Cockerill, R (Leicester) 1997 Arg 1(R),2, A 2(t+R), NZ 1, SA, NZ 2, 1998 W, S, I, A 1, NZ 1,2, SA 1, H, It, A 2, SA 2, 1999 S, I, F, W, A, C (R), [It, NZ, Tg (R), Fj (R)]

Codling, A J (Harlequins) 2002 Arg

Cohen, B C (Northampton) 2000 I, F, W, It, S, SA 2, Arg, SA 3, 2001 W, It, S, F, R, 2002 S, I, F, W, It, NZ, A, SA, 2003 F 1, W 1, S, I, NZ, A, F2, 3, [Gg, SA, Sm, W, F, A], 2004 It, S, I, W, F, NZ1, 2, A1,C(R), A2(R), 2005 F(R), A, NZ, 2006 W, It, S, F, I, Arg, SA1, 2

Colclough, M J (Angoulême, Wasps, Swansea) 1978 S, I, 1979 NZ, 1980 F, W, S, 1981 W, S, I, F, 1982 A, S, I, F, W, 1983 F, NZ, 1984 S, I, F, W, 1986 W, S, I, F

Coley, E (Northampton) 1929 F, 1932 W

Collins, P J (Camborne) 1952 S, I, F

Collins, W E (O Cheltonians) 1874 S, 1875 I, S, 1876 I, S

Considine, S G U (Bath) 1925 F

Conway, G S (Cambridge U, Rugby, Manchester) 1920 F, I, S, 1921 F, 1922 W, I, F, S, 1923 W, I, S, F, 1924 W, I, F, S, 1925 NZ, 1927 W

Cook, J G (Bedford) 1937 S

Cook, P W (Richmond) 1965 I, F

Cooke, D A (Harlequins) 1976 W, S, I, F

Cooke, D H (Harlequins) 1981 W, S, I, F, 1984 I, 1985 R, F, S, I, W, NZ 1,2

Cooke, P (Richmond) 1939 W, I

Coop, T (Leigh) 1892 S

Cooper, J G (Moseley) 1909 A, W

Cooper, M J (Moseley) 1973 F, S, NZ 2(R), 1975 F, W, 1976 A, W, 1977 S, I, F, W

Coopper, S F (Blackheath) 1900 W, 1902 W, I, 1905 W, I, S, 1907 W

Corbett, L J (Bristol) 1921 F, 1923 W, I, 1924 W, I, F, S, 1925 NZ, W, I, S, F, 1927 W, I, S, F

Corless, B J (Coventry, Moseley) 1976 A, I (R), 1977 S, I, F, W, 1978 F, W, S, I

Corry, M E (Bristol, Leicester) 1997 Arg 1,2, 1998 H, It, SA 2(t), 1999 F(R), A, C (t), [It (R), NZ (t+R), SA (R)], 2000

I (R), F (R), W (R), It (R), S (R), Arg (R), SA 3(t), 2001 W (R), It (R), F (t), C 1, I, 2002 F (t+R), W (t), 2003 W 2, F 2,3, [U], 2004 A1(R), C, SA, A2, 2005 F, I, It, S, A, NZ, Sm, 2006 W, It, S, F, I, NZ,Arg, SA1,2, 2007 S, It, I, F1, W1, 2, F2(R), 3, [US(R), SA1, Sm, Tg, A, F, SA2]

Cotton, F E (Loughborough Colls, Coventry, Sale) 1971 S (2[1C]), P, 1973 W, I, F, S, NZ 2, A, 1974 S, I, 1975 I, F, W, 1976 A, W, S, I, F, 1977 S, I, F, W, 1978 S, I, 1979 NZ, 1980 I, F, W, S, 1981 W

Coulman, M J (Moseley) 1967 A, I, F, S, W, 1968 W, I, F, S

Coulson, T J (Coventry) 1927 W, 1928 A, W

Court, E D (Blackheath) 1885 W

Coverdale, H (Blackheath) 1910 F, 1912 I, F, 1920 W

Cove-Smith, R (OMTs) 1921 S, F, 1922 I, F, S, 1923 W, I, S, F, 1924 W, I, S, F, 1925 NZ, W, I, S, F, 1927 W, I, S, F, 1928 A, W, I, F, S, 1929 W, I

Cowling, R J (Leicester) 1977 S, I, F, W, 1978 F, NZ, 1979 S, I

Cowman, A R (Loughborough Colls, Coventry) 1971 S (2[1C]), P, 1973 W, I

Cox, N S (Sunderland) 1901 S

Crane, J S (Leicester) 2008 SA(R), 2009 Arg 1(R)

Cranmer, P (Richmond, Moseley) 1934 W, I, S, 1935 W, I, S, 1936 NZ, W, I, S, 1937 W, I, S, 1938 W, I, S

Creed, R N (Coventry) 1971 P

Cridlan, A G (Blackheath) 1935 W, I, S

Croft, T (Leicester) 2008 F(R), S, I, NZ2(R), PI, A, SA(R), NZ3(R), 2009 It(R), W(R), I(R), F, S

Crompton, C A (Blackheath) 1871 S

Crompton, D E (Bristol) 2007 SA1(R)

Crosse, C W (Oxford U) 1874 S, 1875 I

Cueto, M J (Sale) 2004 C, SA, A2, 2005 W, F, I, It, S, A, NZ, Sm, 2006 W, It, S, F, I, SA1, 2, 2007 W1, F3, [US, Sm, Tg, SA2], 2009 It, W, I, F, S, Arg 1, 2

Cumberlege, B S (Blackheath) 1920 W, I, S, 1921 W, I, S, F, 1922 W

Cumming, D C (Blackheath) 1925 S, F

Cunliffe, F L (RMA) 1874 S

Currey, F I (Marlborough N) 1872 S

Currie, J D (Oxford U, Harlequins, Bristol) 1956 W, I, S, F, 1957 W, I, F, S, 1958 W, A, I, F, S, 1959 W, I, F, S, 1960 W, I, F, S, 1961 SA, 1962 W, I, F

Cusani, D A (Orrell) 1987 I

Cusworth, L (Leicester) 1979 NZ, 1982 F, W, 1983 F, W, NZ, 1984 S, I, F, W, 1988 F, W

D'Aguilar, F B G (Royal Engineers) 1872 S

Dallaglio, L B N (Wasps) 1995 SA (R), WS, 1996 F, W, S, I, It, Arg, 1997 S, I, F, A 1,2, NZ 1, SA, NZ 2, 1998 F, W, S, I, A 2, SA 2, 1999 S, I, F, W, US, C, [It, NZ, Tg, Fj, SA], 2000 I, F, W, It, S, SA 1,2, A, Arg, SA 3, 2001 W, It, S, F, 2002 It (R), NZ, A (t), SA(R), 2003 F 1 (R), W 1, It, S, I, NZ, A, [Gg, SA, Sm, U, W, F, A], 2004 It, S, I, W, F, NZ1, 2, A1,2006 W(t&R), It(R), S(R), F(R), 2007 W2(R), F2, 3(R), [US, Tg(R), A(R), F(R), SA2(R)]

Dalton, T J (Coventry) 1969 S(R)

Danby, T (Harlequins) 1949 W

Daniell, J (Richmond) 1899 W, 1900 I, S, 1902 I, S, 1904 I, S

Darby, A J L (Birkenhead Park) 1899 I

Davenport, A (Ravenscourt Park) 1871 S

Davey, J (Redruth) 1908 S, 1909 W

Davey, R F (Teignmouth) 1931 W

Davidson, Jas (Aspatria) 1897 S, 1898 S, W, 1899 I, S

Davidson, Jos (Aspatria) 1899 W, S

Davies, G H (Cambridge U, Coventry, Wasps) 1981 S, I, F, Arg 1,2, 1982 A, S, I, 1983 F, W, S, 1984 S, SA 1,2, 1985 R (R), NZ 1,2, 1986 W, S, I, F

Davies, P H (Sale) 1927 I

Davies, V G (Harlequins) 1922 W, 1925 NZ

Davies, W J A (United Services, RN) 1913 SA, W, F, I, S, 1914 I, S, F, 1920 F, I, S, 1921 W, I, S, F, 1922 I, F, S, 1923 W, I, S, F

Davies, W P C (Harlequins) 1953 S, 1954 NZ, I, 1955 W, I, F, S, 1956 W, 1957 F, S, 1958 W

Davis, A M (Torquay Ath, Harlequins) 1963 W, I, S, NZ 1,2, 1964 NZ, W, I, F, S, 1966 W, 1967 A, 1969 SA, 1970 I, W, S

Dawe, R G R (Bath) 1987 I, F, W, [US], 1995 [WS]
Dawson, E F (RIEC) 1878 I
Dawson, M J S (Northampton, Wasps) 1995 WS, 1996 F, W, S, I, 1997 A 1, SA, NZ 2(R), 1998 W (R), S, I, NZ 1,2, SA 1, H, It, A 2, SA 2, 1999 S, F(R), W, A(R), US, C, [It, NZ, Tg, Fj (R), SA], 2000 I, F, W, It, S, A (R), Arg, SA 3, 2001 W, It, S, F, I, 2002 W (R), It (R), NZ, A, SA, 2003 It, S, I, A(R), F3(R), [Gg, Sm, W, F, A], 2004It(R), S(R), I, W, F, NZ1, 2(R), A1(R), 2005 W, F(R), I(R), It(R), S(R), A, NZ, 2006 W(R), It(R), S(t&R), F, I(R)
Day, H L V (Leicester) 1920 W, 1922 W, F, 1926 S
Deacon, L P (Leicester) 2005 Sm, 2006 A1, 2(R), 2007 S, It, I, F1(R), W1(R), 2009 Arg 1, 2
Dean, G J (Harlequins) 1931 I
Dee, J M (Hartlepool R) 1962 S, 1963 NZ 1
Devitt, Sir T G (Blackheath) 1926 I, F, 1928 A, W
Dewhurst, J H (Richmond) 1887 W, I, S, 1890 W
De Glanville, P R (Bath) 1992 SA (R), 1993 W (R), NZ, 1994 S, I, F, W, SA 1,2, C (R), 1995 [Arg (R), It, WS], SA (R), 1996 W (R), I (R), It, 1997 S, I, F, W, Arg 1,2, A 1,2, NZ 1,2, 1998 W (R), S (R), I (R), A 2, SA 2, 1999 A (R), US, [It, NZ, Fj (R), SA]
De Winton, R F C (Marlborough N) 1893 W
Dibble, R (Bridgwater A) 1906 S, F, SA, 1908 F, W, I, S, 1909 A, W, F, I, S, 1910 S, 1911 W, F, S, 1912 W, I, S
Dicks, J (Northampton) 1934 W, I, S, 1935 W, I, S, 1936 S, 1937 I
Dillon, E W (Blackheath) 1904 W, I, S, 1905 W
Dingle, A J (Hartlepool R) 1913 I, 1914 S, F
Diprose, A J (Saracens) 1997 Arg 1,2, A 2, NZ 1, 1998 W (R), S (R), I, A 1, NZ 2, SA 1
Dixon, P J (Harlequins, Gosforth) 1971 P, 1972 W, I, F, S, 1973 I, F, S, 1974 S, I, F, W, 1975 I, 1976 F, 1977 S, I, F, W, 1978 F, S, I, NZ
Dobbs, G E B (Devonport A) 1906 W, I
Doble, S A (Moseley) 1972 SA, 1973 NZ 1, W
Dobson, D D (Newton Abbot) 1902 W, I, S, 1903 W, I, S
Dobson, T H (Bradford) 1895 S
Dodge, P W (Leicester) 1978 W, S, I, NZ, 1979 S, I, F, W, 1980 W, S, 1981 W, S, I, F, Arg 1,2, 1982 A, S, F, W, 1983 F, W, S, I, NZ, 1985 R, F, S, I, W, NZ 1,2
Donnelly, M P (Oxford U) 1947 I
Dooley, W A (Preston Grasshoppers, Fylde) 1985 R, F, S, I, W, NZ 2(R), 1986 W, S, I, F, 1987 F, W, [A, US, W], 1988 F, W, S, I 1,2, A 1,2, Fj, A, 1989 S, I, F, W, R, Fj, 1990 I, F, W, S, Arg 1,2,3, 1991 W, S, I, F, [NZ, US, F, S, A], 1992 S, I, F, W, C, SA, 1993 W, S, I
Dovey, B A (Rosslyn Park) 1963 W, I
Down, P J (Bristol) 1909 A
Dowson, A O (Moseley) 1899 S
Drake-Lee, N J (Cambridge U, Leicester) 1963 W, I, F, S, 1964 NZ, W, I, 1965 W
Duckett, H (Bradford) 1893 I, S
Duckham, D J (Coventry) 1969 I, F, S, W, SA, 1970 I, W, S, F, 1971 I, F, S (2[1C]), P, 1972 W, I, F, S, 1973 NZ 1, W, I, F, S, NZ 2, A, 1974 S, I, F, W, 1975 I, F, W, 1976 A, W, S
Dudgeon, H W (Richmond) 1897 S, 1898 I, S, W, 1899 W, I, S
Dugdale, J M (Ravenscourt Park) 1871 S
Dun, A F (Wasps) 1984 W
Duncan, R F H (Guy's Hospital) 1922 I, F, S
Duncombe, N S (Harlequins) 2002 S (R), I (R)
Dunkley, P E (Harlequins) 1931 I, S, 1936 NZ, W, I, S
Duthie, J (W Hartlepool) 1903 W
Dyson, J W (Huddersfield) 1890 W, 1892 S, 1893 I, S
Easter, N J (Harlequins) 2007 It, F1, SA1, 2, W2, F3, [SA1, Sm, Tg, A, F, SA2], 2008 It, F, S, I, PI, A, SA, NZ3, 2009 It, W, I, F, S, Arg 1, 2
Ebdon, P J (Wellington) 1897 W, I
Eddison, J H (Headingley) 1912 W, I, S, F
Edgar, C S (Birkenhead Park) 1901 S
Edwards, R (Newport) 1921 W, I, S, F, 1922 W, F, 1923 W, 1924 W, F, S, 1925 NZ
Egerton, D W (Bath) 1988 I 2, A 1, Fj (R), A, 1989 Fj, 1990 I, Arg 2(R)
Elliot, C H (Sunderland) 1886 W
Elliot, E W (Sunderland) 1901 W, I, S, 1904 W

Elliot, W (United Services, RN) 1932 I, S, 1933 W, I, S, 1934 W, I
Elliott, A E (St Thomas's Hospital) 1894 S
Ellis, H A (Leicester) 2004 SA(R), A2(R), 2005 W(R), F, I, It, S, Sm, 2006 W, It, S, F(R), I, 2007 S, It, I, F1, W1, 2008 PI(R), A(R), SA(R), NZ3(R), 2009 It, W, I, F, S
Ellis, J (Wakefield) 1939 S
Ellis, S S (Queen's House) 1880 I
Emmott, C (Bradford) 1892 W
Enthoven, H J (Richmond) 1878 I
Estcourt, N S D (Blackheath) 1955 S
Evans, B J (Leicester) 1988 A 2, Fj
Evans, E (Sale) 1948 A, 1950 W, 1951 I, F, S, 1952 SA, W, S, I, F, 1953 I, F, S, 1954 W, NZ, I, F, 1956 W, I, S, F, 1957 W, I, F, S, 1958 W, A, I, F, S
Evans, G W (Coventry) 1972 S, 1973 W (R), F, S, NZ 2, 1974 S, I, F, W
Evans, N L (RNEC) 1932 W, I, S, 1933 W, I
Evanson, A M (Richmond) 1883 W, I, S, 1884 S
Evanson, W A D (Richmond) 1875 S, 1877 S, 1878 S, 1879 S, I
Evershed, F (Blackheath) 1889 M, 1890 W, S, I, 1892 W, I, S, 1893 W, I, S
Eyres, W C T (Richmond) 1927 I
Fagan, A R St L (Richmond) 1887 I
Fairbrother, K E (Coventry) 1969 I, F, S, W, SA, 1970 I, W, S, F, 1971 W, I, F
Faithfull, C K T (Harlequins) 1924 I, 1926 F, S
Fallas, H (Wakefield T) 1884 I
Farrell, A D (Saracens) 2007 S,It,I,W2,F3, [US(R),SA1,Tg (R)]
Fegan, J H C (Blackheath) 1895 W, I, S
Fernandes, C W L (Leeds) 1881 I, W, S
Fidler, J H (Gloucester) 1981 Arg 1,2, 1984 SA 1,2
Fidler, R J (Gloucester) 1998 NZ 2, SA 1
Field, E (Middlesex W) 1893 W, I
Fielding, K J (Moseley, Loughborough Colls) 1969 I, F, S, SA, 1970 I, F, 1972 W, I, F, S
Finch, R T (Cambridge U) 1880 S
Finlan, J F (Moseley) 1967 I, F, S, W, NZ, 1968 W, I, 1969 I, F, S, W, 1970 F, 1973 NZ 1
Finlinson, H W (Blackheath) 1895 W, I, S
Finney, S (RIE Coll) 1872 S, 1873 S
Firth, F (Halifax) 1894 W, I, S
Flatman, D L (Saracens) 2000 SA 1(t),2(t+R), A (t), Arg (t+R), 2001 F (t), C 2(t+R), US (t+R), 2002 Arg
Fletcher, N C (OMTs) 1901 W, I, S, 1903 S
Fletcher, T (Seaton) 1897 W
Fletcher, W R B (Marlborough N) 1873 S, 1875 S
Flood, T G A L (Newcastle, Leicester) 2006 Arg(R), 2007 S(R), It(R), F1, W1, SA1, 2, W2(t), [A(R), F(R), SA2(R)], 2008 W, It, F, S, I, NZ2, PI(R), A(R), SA(R), NZ3, 2009 W(R), I, F, S
Flutey, R J (Wasps) 2008 PI,A,SA,NZ3, 2009 It,W,I,F,S
Foden, B J (Northampton) 2009 It(R)
Fookes, E F (Sowerby Bridge) 1896 W, I, S, 1897 W, I, S, 1898 I, W, 1899 I, S
Ford, P J (Gloucester) 1964 W, I, F, S
Forrest, J W (United Services, RN) 1930 W, I, F, S, 1931 W, I, S, F, 1934 I, S
Forrest, R (Wellington) 1899 W, 1900 S, 1902 I, S, 1903 I, S
Forrester, J (Gloucester) 2005 W(t), Sm(t&R)
Foulds, R T (Waterloo) 1929 W, I
Fowler, F D (Manchester) 1878 S, 1879 S
Fowler, H (Oxford U) 1878 S, 1881 W, S
Fowler, R H (Leeds) 1877 I
Fox, F H (Wellington) 1890 W, S
Francis, T E S (Cambridge U) 1926 W, I, F, S
Frankcom, G P (Cambridge U, Bedford) 1965 W, I, F, S
Fraser, E C (Blackheath) 1875 I
Fraser, G (Richmond) 1902 W, I, S, 1903 W, I
Freakes, H D (Oxford U) 1938 W, 1939 W, I
Freeman, H (Marlborough N) 1872 S, 1873 S, 1874 S
French, R J (St Helens) 1961 W, I, F, S
Freshwater, P T (Perpignan) 2005 v Sm(R), 2006 S(t&R), I(R), Arg, 2007 S, It, I, F3, [SA1(R), Sm(R)]
Fry, H A (Liverpool) 1934 W, I, S

Haskell, J A W (Wasps) 2007 W1,F2, 2008 W, It, F, I(R), NZ1, 2, PI(t&R), A(R), SA, NZ3, 2009 It, W, I, F(R), S(R), Arg 1, 2(R)
Haslett, L W (Birkenhead Park) 1926 I, F
Hastings, G W D (Gloucester) 1955 W, I, F, S, 1957 W, I, F, S, 1958 W, A, I, F, S
Havelock, H (Hartlepool R) 1908 F, W, I
Hawcridge, J J (Bradford) 1885 W, I
Hayward, L W (Cheltenham) 1910 I
Hazell, A R (Gloucester) 2004 C, SA(t&R), 2005 W, F(t), It(R), S(R), 2007 SA1
Hazell, D St G (Leicester) 1955 W, I, F, S
Healey, A S (Leicester) 1997 I (R), W, A 1(R),2(R), NZ 1(R), SA (R), NZ 2, 1998 F, W, S, I, A 1, NZ 1,2, H, It, A 2, SA 2(R), 1999 US, C, [It, NZ, Tg, Fj, SA (R)], 2000 I, F, W, It, S, SA 1,2, A, SA 3(R), 2001 W (R), It, S, F, I (R), A, R, SA, 2002 S, I, F, W, It (R), NZ (R), A (R), SA(R), 2003 F2
Hearn, R D (Bedford) 1966 F, S, 1967 I, F, S, W
Heath, A H (Oxford U) 1876 S
Heaton, J (Waterloo) 1935 W, I, S, 1939 W, I, S, 1947 I, S, F
Henderson, A P (Edinburgh Wands) 1947 W, I, S, F, 1948 I, S, F, 1949 W, I
Henderson, R S F (Blackheath) 1883 W, S, 1884 W, S, 1885 W
Heppell, W G (Devonport A) 1903 I
Herbert, A J (Wasps) 1958 F, S, 1959 W, I, F, S
Hesford, R (Bristol) 1981 S (R), 1982 A, S, F (R), 1983 F (R), 1985 R, F, S, I, W
Heslop, N J (Orrell) 1990 Arg 1,2,3, 1991 W, S, I, F, [US, F], 1992 W (R)
Hetherington, J G G (Northampton) 1958 A, I, 1959 W, I, F, S
Hewitt, E N (Coventry) 1951 W, I, F
Hewitt, W W (Queen's House) 1881 I, W, S, 1882 I
Hickson, J L (Bradford) 1887 W, I, S, 1890 W, S, I
Higgins, R (Liverpool) 1954 W, NZ, I, S, 1955 W, I, F, S, 1957 W, I, F, S, 1959 W
Hignell, A J (Cambridge U, Bristol) 1975 A 2, 1976 A, W, S, I, 1977 S, I, F, W, 1978 W, 1979 S, I, F, W
Hill, B A (Blackheath) 1903 I, S, 1904 W, I, 1905 W, NZ, 1906 SA, 1907 F, W
Hill, R A (Saracens) 1997 S, I, F, W, A 1,2, NZ 1, SA, NZ 2, 1998 F, W, H (R), It (R), A 2, 1999 S, I, F, W, A, US, C, [It, NZ, Tg, Fj (R), SA], 2000 I, F, W, It, S, SA 1,2, A, Arg, SA 3, 2001 W, It, S, F, I, A, SA 2, S, I, F, W, It, NZ, A, SA, 2003 F 1, W 1, It, S, I, NZ, A, F 3, [Gg, F, A], 2004 It, S, I, W, F, NZ1, 2, A1
Hill, R J (Bath) 1984 SA 1,2, 1985 I (R), NZ 2(R), 1986 F (R), 1987 I, F, W, [US], 1989 Fj, 1990 I, F, W, S, Arg 1,2,3, 1991 W, S, I, F, Fj, A, [NZ, It, US, F, S, A]
Hillard, R J (Oxford U) 1925 NZ
Hiller, R (Harlequins) 1968 W, I, F, S, 1969 I, F, S, W, SA, 1970 I, W, S, 1971 I, F, S (2[1C]), P, 1972 W, I
Hind, A E (Leicester) 1905 NZ, 1906 W
Hind, G R (Blackheath) 1910 S, 1911 I
Hipkiss, D J (Leicester) 2007 W2, F3, [Sm(R), Tg(R), F(R), SA2(R)], 2008 NZ3(R), 2009 Arg 1, 2
Hobbs, R F A (Blackheath) 1899 S, 1903 W
Hobbs, R G S (Richmond) 1932 SA, W, I, S
Hobson, J D (Bristol) 2008 NZ2(R)
Hodges, H A (Nottingham) 1906 W, I
Hodgkinson, S D (Nottingham) 1989 R, Fj, 1990 I, F, W, S, Arg 1,2,3, 1991 W, S, I, F, [US]
Hodgson, C C (Sale) 2001 R, 2002 S (R), I (R), It (R), Arg, 2003 F 1, W 1, It (R), 2004 NZ1, 2, A1, C, SA, A2, 2005 W, F, I, It, S, A, NZ, Sm, 2006 W, It, S, F,NZ, Arg, SA1, 2008 S(R),NZ1
Hodgson, J McD (Northern) 1932 SA, W, I, S, 1934 W, I, 1936 I
Hodgson, P K (London Irish) 2008 I(R), 2009 Arg 1(R),2 (R)
Hodgson, S A M (Durham City) 1960 W, I, F, S, 1961 SA, W, 1962 W, I, F, S, 1964 W
Hofmeyr, M B (Oxford U) 1950 W, F, S
Hogarth, T B (Hartlepool R) 1906 F
Holford, G (Gloucester) 1920 W, F
Holland, D (Devonport A) 1912 W, I, S
Holliday, T E (Aspatria) 1923 S, F, 1925 I, S, F, 1926 F, S
Holmes, C B (Manchester) 1947 S, 1948 I, F

Holmes, E (Manningham) 1890 S, I
Holmes, W A (Nuneaton) 1950 W, I, F, S, 1951 W, I, F, S, 1952 SA, S, I, F, 1953 W, I, F, S
Holmes, W B (Cambridge U) 1949 W, I, F, S
Hook, W G (Gloucester) 1951 S, 1952 SA, W
Hooper, C A (Middlesex W) 1894 W, I, S
Hopley, D P (Wasps) 1995 [WS (R)], SA, WS
Hopley, F J V (Blackheath) 1907 F, W, 1908 I
Horak, M J (London Irish) 2002 Arg
Hordern, P C (Gloucester) 1931 I, S, F, 1934 W
Horley, C H (Swinton) 1885 I
Hornby, A N (Manchester) 1877 I, S, 1878 S, I, 1880 I, 1881 I, S, 1882 I, S
Horrocks-Taylor, J P (Cambridge U, Leicester, Middlesbrough) 1958 W, A, 1961 S, 1962 S, 1963 NZ 1,2, A, 1964 NZ, W
Horsfall, E L (Harlequins) 1949 W
Horton, A L (Blackheath) 1965 W, I, F, S, 1966 F, S, 1967 NZ
Horton, J P (Bath) 1978 W, S, I, NZ, 1980 I, F, W, S, 1981 W, 1983 S, I, 1984 SA 1,2
Horton, N E (Moseley, Toulouse) 1969 I, F, S, W, 1971 I, F, S, 1974 S, 1975 W, 1977 S, I, F, W, 1978 F, W, 1979 S, I, F, W, 1980 I
Hosen, R W (Bristol, Northampton) 1963 NZ 1,2, A, 1964 F, S, 1967 A, I, F, S, W
Hosking, G R d'A (Devonport Services) 1949 W, I, F, S, 1950 W
Houghton, S (Runcorn) 1892 I, 1896 W
Howard, P D (O Millhillians) 1930 W, I, F, S, 1931 W, I, S, F
Hubbard, G C (Blackheath) 1892 W, I
Hubbard, J C (Harlequins) 1930 S
Hudson, A (Gloucester) 1906 W, I, F, 1908 F, W, I, S, 1910 F
Hughes, G E (Barrow) 1896 S
Hull, P A (Bristol, RAF) 1994 SA 1,2, R, C
Hulme, F C (Birkenhead Park) 1903 W, I, 1905 W, I
Hunt, J T (Manchester) 1882 I, S, 1884 W
Hunt, R (Manchester) 1880 I, 1881 W, S, 1882 I
Hunt, W H (Manchester) 1876 S, 1877 I, S, 1878 I
Hunter, I (Northampton) 1992 C, 1993 F, W, 1994 F, W, 1995 [WS, F]
Huntsman, R P (Headingley) 1985 NZ 1,2
Hurst, A C B (Wasps) 1962 S
Huskisson, T F (OMTs) 1937 W, I, S, 1938 W, I, 1939 W, I, S
Hutchinson, F (Headingley) 1909 F, I, S
Hutchinson, J E (Durham City) 1906 I
Hutchinson, W C (RIE Coll) 1876 S, 1877 I
Hutchinson, W H H (Hull) 1875 I, 1876 I
Huth, H (Huddersfield) 1879 S
Hyde, J P (Northampton) 1950 F, S
Hynes, W B (United Services, RN) 1912 F
Ibbitson, E D (Headingley) 1909 W, F, I, S
Imrie, H M (Durham City) 1906 NZ, 1907 I
Inglis, R E (Blackheath) 1886 W, I, S
Irvin, S H (Devonport A) 1905 W
Isherwood, F W (Ravenscourt Park) 1872 S
Jackett, E J (Leicester, Falmouth) 1905 NZ, 1906 W, I, S, F, SA, 1907 W, I, S, 1909 W, F, I, S
Jackson, A H (Blackheath) 1878 I, 1880 I
Jackson, B S (Broughton Park) 1970 S (R), F
Jackson, P B (Coventry) 1956 W, I, F, 1957 W, I, F, S, 1958 W, A, F, S, 1959 W, I, F, S, 1961 S, 1963 W, I, F, S
Jackson, W J (Halifax) 1894 S
Jacob, F (Cambridge U) 1897 W, I, S, 1898 I, S, W, 1899 W, I
Jacob, H P (Blackheath) 1924 W, I, F, S, 1930 F
Jacob, P G (Blackheath) 1898 I
Jacobs, C R (Northampton) 1956 W, I, S, F, 1957 W, I, F, S, 1958 W, A, I, F, S, 1960 W, I, F, S, 1961 SA, W, I, F, S, 1963 NZ 1,2, A, 1964 W, I, F, S
Jago, R A (Devonport A) 1906 W, I, SA, 1907 W, I
Janion, J P A G (Bedford) 1971 W, I, F, S (2[1C]), P, 1972 W, S, SA, 1973 A, 1975 A 1, 2
Jarman, J W (Bristol) 1900 W
Jeavons, N C (Moseley) 1981 S, I, F, Arg 1,2, 1982 A, S, I, F, W, 1983 F, W, S, I
Jeeps, R E G (Northampton) 1956 W, 1957 W, I, F, S, 1958 W, A, I, F, S, 1959 W, I, F, S, 1960 W, I, F, S, 1961 SA, W, I, F, S, 1962 W, I, F, S

Oakley, **L F L** (Bedford) 1951 W
Obolensky, **A** (Oxford U) 1936 NZ, W, I, S
Ojo, **T O** (London Irish) 2008 NZ1,2
Ojomoh, **S O** (Bath, Gloucester) 1994 I, F, SA 1(R),2, R, 1995 S (R), [Arg, WS, A (t), F], 1996 F, 1998 NZ 1
Old, **A G B** (Middlesbrough, Leicester, Sheffield) 1972 W, I, F, S, SA, 1973 NZ 2, A, 1974 S, I, F, W, 1975 I, A 2, 1976 S, I, 1978 F
Oldham, **W L** (Coventry) 1908 S, 1909 A
Olver, **C J** (Northampton) 1990 Arg 3, 1991 [US], 1992 C
O'Neill, **A** (Teignmouth, Torquay A) 1901 W, I, S
Openshaw, **W E** (Manchester) 1879 I
Orwin, **J** (Gloucester, RAF, Bedford) 1985 R, F, S, I, W, NZ 1,2, 1988 F, W, S, I 1,2, A 1,2
Osborne, **R R** (Manchester) 1871 S
Osborne, **S H** (Oxford U) 1905 S
Oti, **C** (Cambridge U, Nottingham, Wasps) 1988 S, I 1, 1989 S, I, F, W, R, 1990 Arg 1,2, 1991 Fj, A, [NZ, It]
Oughtred, **B** (Hartlepool R) 1901 S, 1902 W, I, S, 1903 W, I
Owen, **J E** (Coventry) 1963 W, I, F, S, A, 1964 NZ, 1965 W, I, F, S, 1966 I, F, S, 1967 NZ
Owen-Smith, **H G O** (St Mary's Hospital) 1934 W, I, S, 1936 NZ, W, I, S, 1937 W, I, S
Page, **J J** (Bedford, Northampton) 1971 W, I, F, S, 1975 S
Paice, **D J** (London Irish) 2008 NZ1(R), 2(R)
Pallant, **J N** (Notts) 1967 I, F, S
Palmer, **A C** (London Hospital) 1909 I, S
Palmer, **F H** (Richmond) 1905 W
Palmer, **G V** (Richmond) 1928 I, F, S
Palmer, **J A** (Bath) 1984 SA 1,2, 1986 I (R)
Palmer, **T P** (Leeds, Wasps) 2001 US (R), 2006 Arg(R), SA1, 2, 2007 It(R), I(R), F1, W1, 2008 NZ1, 2, PI(R), A, SA
Pargetter, **T A** (Coventry) 1962 S, 1963 F, NZ 1
Parker, **G W** (Gloucester) 1938 I, S
Parker, **Hon S** (Liverpool) 1874 S, 1875 S
Parsons, **E I** (RAF) 1939 S
Parsons, **M J** (Northampton) 1968 W, I, F, S
Patterson, **W M** (Sale) 1961 SA, S
Pattisson, **R M** (Blackheath) 1883 I, S
Paul, **H R** (Gloucester) 2002 F(R), 2004 It(t&R), S(R), C, SA, A2
Paul, **J E** (RIE Coll) 1875 S
Payne, **A T** (Bristol) 1935 I, S
Payne, **C M** (Harlequins) 1964 I, F, S, 1965 I, F, S, 1966 W, I, F, S
Payne, **J H** (Broughton) 1882 S, 1883 W, I, S, 1884 I, 1885 W, I
Payne, **T A N** (Wasps) 2004 A1, 2006 A1(R), 2(R), 2007 F1, W1, 2008 It,NZ1(R),2, SA,NZ3, 2009 Arg 1,2
Pearce, **G S** (Northampton) 1979 S, I, F, W, 1981 Arg 1,2, 1982 A, S, 1983 F, W, S, I, NZ, 1984 S, SA 2, A, 1985 R, F, S, I, W, NZ 1,2, 1986 W, S, I, F, 1987 I, F, W, S, [A, US, W], 1988 Fj, 1991 [US]
Pears, **D** (Harlequins) 1990 Arg 1,2, 1992 F (R), 1994 F
Pearson, **A W** (Blackheath) 1875 I, S, 1876 I, S, 1877 S, 1878 S, I
Peart, **T G A H** (Hartlepool R) 1964 F, S
Pease, **F E** (Hartlepool R) 1887 I
Penny, **S H** (Leicester) 1909 A
Penny, **W J** (United Hospitals) 1878 I, 1879 S, I
Percival, **L J** (Rugby) 1891 I, 1892 I, 1893 S
Periton, **H G** (Waterloo) 1925 W, 1926 W, I, F, S, 1927 W, I, S, F, 1928 A, I, F, S, 1929 W, I, S, F, 1930 W, I, F, S
Perrott, **E S** (O Cheltonians) 1875 I
Perry, **D G** (Bedford) 1963 F, S, NZ 1,2, A 1964 NZ, W, 1965 W, I, F, S, 1966 W, I, F
Perry, **M B** (Bath) 1997 A 2, NZ 1, SA, NZ 2, 1998 W, S, I, A 1, NZ 1,2, SA 1, H, It, A 2, 1999 I, F, W, A US, C, [It, NZ, Tg, Fj, SA], 2000 I, F, W, It, S, SA 1,2, A, SA 3, 2001 W (R), F (R)
Perry, **S A** (Bristol) 2006 NZ,Arg,SA1(R),2(R), 2007 I(R),F1(R),W1(R),SA1(R),2(R),W2,F2,3, [US,SA1]
Perry, **S V** (Cambridge U, Waterloo) 1947 W, I, 1948 A, W, I, S, F
Peters, **J** (Plymouth) 1906 S, F, 1907 I, S, 1908 W
Phillips, **C** (Birkenhead Park) 1880 S, 1881 I, S
Phillips, **M S** (Fylde) 1958 A, I, F, S, 1959 W, I, F, S, 1960 W, I, F, S, 1961 W, 1963 W, I, F, S, NZ 1,2, A, 1964 NZ, W, I, F, S

Pickering, **A S** (Harrogate) 1907 I
Pickering, **R D A** (Bradford) 1967 I, F, S, W, 1968 F, S
Pickles, **R C W** (Bristol) 1922 I, F
Pierce, **R** (Liverpool) 1898 I, 1903 S
Pilkington, **W N** (Cambridge U) 1898 S
Pillman, **C H** (Blackheath) 1910 W, I, F, S, 1911 W, F, I, S, 1912 W, F, 1913 SA, W, F, I, S, 1914 W, I, S
Pillman, **R L** (Blackheath) 1914 F
Pinch, **J** (Lancaster) 1896 W, I, 1897 S
Pinching, **W W** (Guy's Hospital) 1872 S
Pitman, **I J** (Oxford U) 1922 S
Plummer, **K C** (Bristol) 1969 W, 1976 S, I, F
Pool-Jones, **R J** (Stade Francais) 1998 A 1
Poole, **F O** (Oxford U) 1895 W, I, S
Poole, **R W** (Hartlepool R) 1896 S
Pope, **E B** (Blackheath) 1931 W, S, F
Portus, **G V** (Blackheath) 1908 F, I
Potter, **S** (Leicester) 1998 A 1(t)
Poulton, **R W** (later Poulton Palmer) (Oxford U, Harlequins, Liverpool) 1909 F, I, S, 1910 W, 1911 S, 1912 W, I, S, 1913 SA, W, F, I, S, 1914 W, I, S, F
Powell, **D L** (Northampton) 1966 W, I, 1969 I, F, S, W, 1971 W, I, F, S (2[1C])
Pratten, **W E** (Blackheath) 1927 S, F
Preece, **I** (Coventry) 1948 I, S, F, 1949 F, S, 1950 W, I, F, S, 1951 W, I, F
Preece, **P S** (Coventry) 1972 SA, 1973 NZ 1, W, I, F, S, NZ 2, 1975 I, F, W, A 2, 1976 W (R)
Preedy, **M** (Gloucester) 1984 SA 1
Prentice, **F D** (Leicester) 1928 I, F, S
Prescott, **R E** (Harlequins) 1937 W, I, 1938 I, 1939 W, I, S
Preston, **N J** (Richmond) 1979 NZ, 1980 I, F
Price, **H L** (Harlequins) 1922 I, S, 1923 W, I
Price, **J** (Coventry) 1961 I
Price, **P L A** (RIE Coll) 1877 I, S, 1878 S
Price, **T W** (Cheltenham) 1948 S, F, 1949 W, I, F, S
Probyn, **J A** (Wasps, Askeans) 1988 F, W, S, I 1,2, A 1, 2, A, 1989 S, I, R (R), 1990 I, F, W, S, Arg 1,2,3, 1991 W, S, I, F, Fj, A, [NZ, It, F, S, A], 1992 S, I, F, W, 1993 F, W, S, I
Prout, **D H** (Northampton) 1968 W, I
Pullin, **J V** (Bristol) 1966 W, 1968 W, I, F, S, 1969 I, F, S, W, SA, 1970 I, W, S, F, 1971 W, I, F, S (2[1C]), P, 1972 W, I, F, S, SA, 1973 NZ 1, W, I, F, S, NZ 2, A, 1974 S, I, F, W, 1975 I, W (R), S, A 1,2, 1976 F
Purdy, **S J** (Rugby) 1962 S
Pyke, **J** (St Helens Recreation) 1892 W
Pym, **J A** (Blackheath) 1912 W, I, S, F
Quinn, **J P** (New Brighton) 1954 W, NZ, I, S, F
Rafter, **M** (Bristol) 1977 S, F, W, 1978 F, W, S, I, NZ, 1979 S, I, F, W, NZ, 1980 W(R), 1981 W, Arg 1,2
Ralston, **C W** (Richmond) 1971 S (C), P, 1972 W, I, F, S, SA, 1973 NZ 1, W, I, F, S, NZ 2, A, 1974 S, I, F, W, 1975 I, F, W, S
Ramsden, **H E** (Bingley) 1898 S, W
Ranson, **J M** (Rosslyn Park) 1963 NZ 1,2, A, 1964 W, I, F, S
Raphael, **J E** (OMTs) 1902 W, I, S, 1905 W, S, NZ, 1906 W, S, F
Ravenscroft, **J** (Birkenhead Park) 1881 I
Ravenscroft, **S C W** (Saracens) 1998 A 1, NZ 2(R)
Rawlinson, **W C W** (Blackheath) 1876 S
Redfern, **S P** (Leicester) 1984 I (R)
Redman, **N C** (Bath) 1984 A, 1986 S (R), 1987 I, S, [A, J, W], 1988 Fj, 1990 Arg 1,2, 1991 Fj, [It, US], 1993 NZ, 1994 F, W, SA 1,2, 1997 Arg 1, A 1
Redmond, **G F** (Cambridge U) 1970 F
Redwood, **B W** (Bristol) 1968 W, I
Rees, **D L** (Sale) 1997 A 2, NZ 1, SA, NZ 2, 1998 F, W, SA 2(R), 1999 S, I, F, A
Rees, **G W** (Nottingham) 1984 SA 2(R), A, 1986 I, F, 1987 F, W, S, [A, J, US, W], 1988 S, I 1,2, A 1,2, Fj, 1989 W (R), R (R), Fj (R), 1990 Arg 3(R), 1991 Fj, [US]
Rees, **T** (Wasps) 2007 S(R), It(R), I(R), F1, W1, F3, [US, SA1], 2008 W(R),NZ1,2,PI,A, SA,NZ3(R)
Reeve, **J S R** (Harlequins) 1929 F, 1930 W, I, F, S, 1931 W, I, S
Regan, **M** (Liverpool) 1953 W, I, F, S, 1954 W, NZ, I, S, F, 1956 I, F, S
Regan, **M P** (Bristol, Bath, Leeds) 1995 SA, WS, 1996 F,

W, S, I, It, Arg, 1997 S, I, F, W, A 1, NZ 2(R), 1998 F,
2000 SA 1(t), A(R), Arg, SA 3(t), 2001 It(R), S(R), C 2(R),
R, 2003 F 1(t), It(R), W 2, [Gg(R), Sm], 2004 It(R), I(R),
NZ1(R), 2, A1, 2007 SA1,2,W2, F2,3, [US,SA1,A,F,SA2],
2008 W,It,F

Rendall, P A G (Wasps, Askeans) 1984 W, SA 2, 1986 W, S,
1987 I, F, S, [A, J, W], 1988 F, W, S, I 1,2, A 1,2, A, 1989
S, I, F, W, R, 1990 I, F, W, S, 1991 [It (R)]

Rew, H (Blackheath) 1929 S, F, 1930 F, S, 1931 W, S, F, 1934
W, I, S

Reynolds, F J (O Cranleighans) 1937 S, 1938 I, S

Reynolds, S (Richmond) 1900 W, I, S, 1901 I

Rhodes, J (Castleford) 1896 W, I, S

Richards, D (Leicester) 1986 I, F, 1987 S, [A, J, US, W], 1988
F, W, S, I 1, A 1,2, Fj, A, 1989 S, I, F, W, R, 1990 Arg 3,
1991 W, S, I, F, Fj, A, [NZ, It, US], 1992 S (R), F, W, C,
1993 NZ, 1994 W, SA 1, C, 1995 I, F, W, S, [WS, A, NZ],
1996 F (t), S, I

Richards, E E (Plymouth A) 1929 S, F

Richards, J (Bradford) 1891 W, I, S

Richards, P C (Gloucester, London Irish) 2006 A1, 2, NZ(R),
Arg(R), SA1, 2, 2007 [US(R), SA1(R), Tg(R), A(t), F(R),
SA2(R)], 2008 NZ2(R)

Richards, S B (Richmond) 1965 W, I, F, S, 1967 A, I, F, S, W

Richardson, J V (Birkenhead Park) 1928 A, W, I, F, S

Richardson, W R (Manchester) 1881 I

Rickards, C H (Gipsies) 1873 S

Rimmer, G (Waterloo) 1949 W, I, 1950 W, 1951 W, I, F, 1952
SA, W, 1954 W, NZ, I, S

Rimmer, L I (Bath) 1961 SA, W, I, F, S

Ripley, A G (Rosslyn Park) 1972 W, I, F, S, SA, 1973 NZ 1,
W, I, F, S, NZ 2, A, 1974 S, I, F, W, 1975 I, F, S, A 1,2,
1976 A, W, S

Risman, A B W (Loughborough Coll) 1959 W, I, F, S, 1961
SA, W, I, F

Ritson, J A S (Northern) 1910 F, S, 1912 F, 1913 SA, W, F, I, S

Rittson-Thomas, G C (Oxford U) 1951 W, I, F

Robbins, G L (Coventry) 1986 W, S

Robbins, P G D (Oxford U, Moseley, Coventry) 1956 W, I, S,
F, 1957 W, I, F, S, 1958 W, A, I, S, 1960 W, I, F, S, 1961
SA, W, 1962 S

Roberts, A D (Northern) 1911 W, F, I, S, 1912 I, S, F, 1914 I

Roberts, E W (RNE Coll) 1901 W, I, 1905 NZ, 1906 W, I,
1907 S

Roberts, G D (Harlequins) 1907 S, 1908 F, W

Roberts, J (Sale) 1960 W, I, F, S, 1961 SA, W, I, F, S, 1962
W, I, F, S, 1963 W, I, F, S, 1964 NZ

Roberts, R S (Coventry) 1932 I

Roberts, S (Swinton) 1887 W, I

Roberts, V G (Penryn, Harlequins) 1947 F, 1949 W, I, F, S,
1950 I, F, S, 1951 W, I, F, S, 1956 W, I, S, F

Robertshaw, A R (Bradford) 1886 W, I, S, 1887 W, S

Robinson, A (Blackheath) 1889 M, 1890 W, S, I

Robinson, E T (Coventry) 1954 S, 1961 I, F, S

Robinson, G C (Percy Park) 1897 I, S, 1898 I, 1899 W, 1900
I, S, 1901 I, S

Robinson, J T (Sale) 2001 It (R), S (R), F (R), I, A, R, SA, 2002
S, I, F, It, NZ, A, SA, 2003 F 1, W 1, S, I, NZ, A, F 3, [Gg,
SA, Sm, U(R), W, F, A], 2004 It, S, I, W, F, C, SA, A2, 2005
W, F, I, 2007 S,It,F1,W1,SA1,W2,F3, [US,SA1,A,F,SA2]

Robinson, J J (Headingley) 1893 S, 1902 W, I, S

Robinson, R A (Bath) 1988 A 2, Fj, A, 1989 S, I, F, W, 1995 SA

Robshaw, C D C (Harlequins) 2009 Arg 2

Robson, A (Northern) 1924 W, I, F, S, 1926 W

Robson, M (Oxford U) 1930 W, I, F, S

Rodber, T A K (Army, Northampton) 1992 S, I, 1993 NZ, 1994
I, F, W, SA 1,2, R, C, 1995 I, F, W, S, [Arg, It, WS (R), A,
NZ, F], SA, WS, 1996 W, S (R), I (t), It, Arg, 1997 S, I, F,
W, A 1, 1998 H (R), It (R), A 2, SA 2, 1999 S, I, F, W, A,
US (R), [NZ (R), Fj (R)]

Rogers, D P (Bedford) 1961 I, F, S, 1962 W, I, F, 1963 W, I,
F, S, NZ 1,2, A, 1964 NZ, W, I, F, S, 1965 W, I, F, S, 1966
W, I, F, S, 1967 A, S, W, NZ, 1969 I, F, S, W

Rogers, J H (Moseley) 1890 W, S, I, 1891 S

Rogers, W L Y (Blackheath) 1905 W, I

Rollitt, D M (Bristol) 1967 I, F, S, W, 1969 I, F, S, W, 1975 S,
A 1,2

Roncoroni, A D S (West Herts, Richmond) 1933 W, I, S

Rose, W M H (Cambridge U, Coventry, Harlequins) 1981 I,
F, 1982 A, S, I, 1987 I, F, W, S, [A]

Rossborough, P A (Coventry) 1971 W, 1973 NZ 2, A, 1974
S, I, 1975 I, F

Rosser, D W A (Wasps) 1965 W, I, F, S, 1966 W

Rotherham, Alan (Richmond) 1883 W, S, 1884 W, S, 1885
W, I, 1886 W, I, S, 1887 W, I, S

Rotherham, Arthur (Richmond) 1898 S, W, 1899 W, I, S

Roughley, D (Liverpool) 1973 A, 1974 S, I

Rowell, R E (Leicester) 1964 W, 1965 W

Rowley, A J (Coventry) 1932 SA

Rowley, H C (Manchester) 1879 S, I, 1880 I, S, 1881 I, W,
S, 1882 I, S

Rowntree, G C (Leicester) 1995 S (t), [It, WS], WS, 1996 F,
W, S, I, It, Arg, 1997 S, I, F, W, A 1, 1998 A 1, NZ 1, 2, SA
1, H (R), It (R), 1999 US, C, [It (R), Tg, Fj (R)], 2001 C 1,2,
US, I(R), A, R, SA, 2002 S, I, F, W, It, 2003 F 1(R), W 1, It,
S, I, NZ, F 2, 2004 C, SA, A2, 2005 W, F, I, It, 2006 A1, 2

Royds, P M R (Blackheath) 1898 S, W, 1899 W

Royle, A V (Broughton R) 1889 M

Rudd, E L (Liverpool) 1965 W, I, S, 1966 W, I, S

Russell, R F (Leicester) 1905 NZ

Rutherford, D (Percy Park, Gloucester) 1960 W, I, F, S, 1961
SA, 1965 W, I, F, S, 1966 W, I, F, S, 1967 NZ

Ryalls, H J (New Brighton) 1885 W, I

Ryan, D (Wasps, Newcastle) 1990 Arg 1,2, 1992 C, 1998 S

Ryan, P H (Richmond) 1955 W, I

Sackey, P H (Wasps) 2006 NZ,Arg, 2007 F2,3(R), [SA1, Sm,
Tg, A, F, SA2], 2008 W, It, F, S, I, PI, A, SA, NZ3, 2009 It,
W, I

Sadler, E H (Army) 1933 I, S

Sagar, J W (Cambridge U) 1901 W, I

Salmon, J L B (Harlequins) 1985 NZ 1,2, 1986 W, S, 1987
I, F, W, S, [A, J, US, W]

Sample, C H (Cambridge U) 1884 I, 1885 I, 1886 S

Sampson, P C (Wasps) 1998 SA 1, 2001 C 1,2

Sanders, D L (Harlequins) 1954 W, NZ, I, S, F, 1956 W, I, S, F

Sanders, F W (Plymouth A) 1923 I, S, F

Sanderson, A (Sale) 2001 R (R), 2002 Arg, 2003 It(t + R), W
2(R), F 2

Sanderson, P H (Sale, Harlequins, Worcester) 1998 NZ 1,2,
SA 1, 2001 C 1(R), 2(R), US(t+R), 2005 A, NZ, Sm, 2006
A1, 2, NZ, Arg, SA1,2, 2007 SA1(R)

Sandford, J R P (Marlborough N) 1906 I

Sangwin, R D (Hull and E Riding) 1964 NZ, W

Sargent, G A F (Gloucester) 1981 I (R)

Savage, K F (Northampton) 1966 W, I, F, S, 1967 A, I, F, S,
W, NZ, 1968 W, I, F, S

Sawyer, C M (Broughton) 1880 S, 1881 I

Saxby, L E (Gloucester) 1932 SA, W

Scarbrough, D G R (Leeds, Saracens) 2003 W 2, 2007 SA2

Schofield, D F (Sale) 2007 SA1,2(R)

Schofield, J W (Manchester) 1880 I

Scholfield, J A (Preston Grasshoppers) 1911 W

Schwarz, R O (Richmond) 1899 S, 1901 W, I

Scorfield, E S (Percy Park) 1910 F

Scott, C T (Blackheath) 1900 W, I, 1901 W, I

Scott, E K (St Mary's Hospital, Redruth) 1947 W, 1948 A, W,
I, S

Scott, F S (Bristol) 1907 W

Scott, H (Manchester) 1955 F

Scott, J P (Rosslyn Park, Cardiff) 1978 F, W, S, I, NZ, 1979
S (R), I, F, NZ, 1980 I, F, W, S, 1981 W, S, I, F, Arg 1,2,
1982 I, F, W, 1983 F, W, S, I, NZ, 1984 S, I, F, W, SA 1,2

Scott, J S M (Oxford U) 1958 F

Scott, M T (Cambridge U) 1887 I, 1890 S, I

Scott, W M (Cambridge U) 1889 M

Seddon, R L (Broughton R) 1887 W, I, S

Sellar, K A (United Services, RN) 1927 W, I, S, 1928 A, W, I, F

Sever, H S (Sale) 1936 NZ, W, I, S, 1937 W, I, S, 1938 W, I, S

Shackleton, I R (Cambridge U) 1969 SA, 1970 I, W, S

Sharp, R A W (Oxford U, Wasps, Redruth) 1960 W, I, F, S,
1961 I, F, 1962 W, I, F, 1963 W, I, F, S, 1967 A

Shaw, C H (Moseley) 1906 S, SA, 1907 F, W, I, S

Shaw, F (Cleckheaton) 1898 I

Shaw, J F (RNE Coll) 1898 S, W

Shaw, S D (Bristol, Wasps) 1996 It, Arg, 1997 S, I, F, W, A 1, SA (R), 2000 I, F, W, It, S, SA 1(R),2(R), 2001 C 1(R), 2, US, I, 2003 It (R), W 2, F 2(R), 3(R), 2004 It(t&R), S(R), NZ1, 2, A1, 2005 Sm(R), 2006 W(R), It(R), S(R), F(R), I, 2007 W2, F2, 3, [US, SA1, Sm, A, F, SA2], 2008 W, It, F, S, I, A(R), SA(R), 2009 F,S

Sheasby, C M A (Wasps) 1996 It, Arg, 1997 W (R), Arg 1(R),2(R), SA (R), NZ 2(t)

Sheppard, A (Bristol) 1981 W (R), 1985 W

Sheridan, A J (Sale) 2004 C(R), 2005 A, NZ, Sm, 2006 W, It, S, F(R), I, NZ, SA1, 2007 W2, F2, [US, SA1, Sm, Tg, A, F, SA2], 2008 W,F,S,I,NZ1,PI,A, 2009 It,W,I,F,S

Sherrard, C W (Blackheath) 1871 S, 1872 S

Sherriff, G A (Saracens) 1966 S, 1967 A, NZ

Shewring, H E (Bristol) 1905 I, NZ, 1906 W, S, F, SA, 1907 F, W, I, S

Shooter, J H (Morley) 1899 I, S, 1900 I, S

Shuttleworth, D W (Headingley) 1951 S, 1953 S

Sibree, H J H (Harlequins) 1908 F, 1909 I, S

Silk, N (Harlequins) 1965 W, I, F, S

Simms, K G (Cambridge U, Liverpool, Wasps) 1985 R, F, S, I, W, 1986 I, F, 1987 I, F, W, [A, J, W], 1988 F, W

Simpson, C P (Harlequins) 1965 W

Simpson, P D (Bath) 1983 NZ, 1984 S, 1987 I

Simpson, T (Rockcliff) 1902 S, 1903 W, I, S, 1904 I, S, 1905 I, S, 1906 S, SA, 1909 F

Simpson-Daniel, J D (Gloucester) 2002 NZ, A, 2003 W 1(t + R), It, W 2, 2004 I(R), NZ1, 2005 Sm, 2006 It(R), 2007 SA1(R)

Sims, D (Gloucester) 1998 NZ 1(R),2, SA 1

Skinner, M G (Harlequins) 1988 F, W, S, I 1,2, 1989 Fj, 1990 I, F, W, S, Arg 1,2, 1991 Fj (R), [US, F, S, A], 1992 S, I, F, W

Skirving, B D (Saracens) 2007 SA2

Sladen, G M (United Services, RN) 1929 W, I, S

Sleightholme, J M (Bath) 1996 F, W, S, I, It, Arg, 1997 S, I, F, W, Arg 1,2

Slemen, M A C (Liverpool) 1976 I, F, 1977 S, I, F, W, 1978 F, W, S, I, NZ, 1979 S, I, F, W, NZ, 1980 I, F, W, S, 1981 W, S, I, F, 1982 A, S, I, F, W, 1983 NZ, 1984 S

Slocock, L A N (Liverpool) 1907 F, W, I, S, 1908 F, W, I, S

Slow, C F (Leicester) 1934 S

Small, H D (Oxford U) 1950 W, I, F, S

Smallwood, A M (Leicester) 1920 F, I, 1921 W, I, S, F, 1922 I, S, 1923 W, I, S, F, 1925 I, S

Smart, C E (Newport) 1979 F, W, NZ, 1981 S, I, F, Arg 1,2, 1982 A, S, I, F, W, 1983 F, W, S, I

Smart, S E J (Gloucester) 1913 SA, W, F, I, S, 1914 W, I, S, F, 1920 W, I, S

Smeddle, R W (Cambridge U) 1929 W, I, S, 1931 F

Smith, C C (Gloucester) 1901 W

Smith, D F (Richmond) 1910 W, I

Smith, J V (Cambridge U, Rosslyn Park) 1950 W, I, F, S

Smith, K (Roundhay) 1974 F, W, 1975 W, S

Smith, M J K (Oxford U) 1956 W

Smith, O J (Leicester) 2003 It (R), W 2(R), F 2, 2005 It(R), S(R)

Smith, S J (Sale) 1973 I, F, S, A, 1974 I, F, 1975 W (R), 1976 F, 1977 F (R), 1979 NZ, 1980 I, F, W, S, 1981 W, S, I, F, Arg 1,2, 1982 A, S, I, F, W, 1983 F, W, S

Smith, S R (Richmond) 1959 W, F, S, 1964 F, S

Smith, S T (Wasps) 1985 R, F, S, I, W, NZ 1,2, 1986 W, S

Smith, T H (Northampton) 1951 W

Soane, F (Bath) 1893 S, 1894 W, I, S

Sobey, W H (O Millhillians) 1930 W, F, S, 1932 SA, W

Solomon, B (Redruth) 1910 W

Sparks, R H W (Plymouth A) 1928 I, F, S, 1929 W, I, S, 1931 I, S, F

Speed, H (Castleford) 1894 W, I, S, 1896 S

Spence, F W (Birkenhead Park) 1890 I

Spencer, J (Harlequins) 1966 W

Spencer, J S (Cambridge U, Headingley) 1969 I, F, S, W, SA, 1970 I, W, S, F, 1971 W, I, S (2[1C]), P

Spong, R S (O Millhillians) 1929 F, 1930 W, I, F, S, 1931 F, 1932 SA, W

Spooner, R H (Liverpool) 1903 W

Springman, H H (Liverpool) 1879 S, 1887 S

Spurling, A (Blackheath) 1882 I

Spurling, N (Blackheath) 1886 I, S, 1887 W

Squires, P J (Harrogate) 1973 F, S, NZ 2, A, 1974 S, I, F, W, 1975 I, F, W, S, A 1,2, 1976 A, W, 1977 S, I, F, W, 1978 F, W, S, I, NZ, 1979 S, I, F, W

Stafford R C (Bedford) 1912 W, I, S, F

Stafford, W F H (RE) 1874 S

Stanbury, E (Plymouth A) 1926 W, I, S, 1927 W, I, S, F, 1928 A, W, I, F, S, 1929 W, I, S, F

Standing, G (Blackheath) 1883 W, I

Stanger-Leathes, C F (Northern) 1905 I

Stark, K J (O Alleynians) 1927 W, I, S, F, 1928 A, W, I, F, S

Starks, A (Castleford) 1896 W, I

Starmer-Smith, N C (Harlequins) 1969 SA, 1970 I, W, S, F, 1971 S (C), P

Start, S P (United Services, RN) 1907 S

Steeds, J H (Saracens) 1949 F, S, 1950 I, F, S

Steele-Bodger, M R (Cambridge U) 1947 W, I, S, F, 1948 A, W, I, S, F

Steinthal, F E (Ilkley) 1913 W, F

Stephenson, M (Newcastle) 2001 C 1,2, US

Stevens, C B (Penzance-Newlyn, Harlequins) 1969 SA, 1970 I, W, S, 1971 P, 1972 W, I, F, S, SA, 1973 NZ 1, W, I, F, S, NZ 2, A, 1974 S, I, F, W, 1975 I, F, W, S

Stevens, M J H (Bath) 2004 NZ1(R), 2(t), 2005 I, It, S, NZ(R), Sm, 2006 W, It, F, 2007 SA2, W2(R), F2, 3(R), [US(R), SA1, Sm, Tg, A(R), F(R), SA2(R)], 2008 W(R), It, F(R), S(R), I(R), NZ1, 2, PI, A(t&R), SA(R), NZ3(R)

Still, E R (Oxford U, Ravenscourt P) 1873 S

Stimpson, T R G (Newcastle, Leicester) 1996 It, 1997 S, I, F, W, A 1, NZ 2(t+R), 1998 A 1, NZ 1,2(R), SA 1(R), 1999 US (R), C (R), 2000 SA 1, 2001 C 1(t),2(R), 2002 W (R), Arg, SA (R)

Stirling, R V (Leicester, RAF, Wasps) 1951 W, I, F, S, 1952 SA, W, S, I, F, 1953 W, I, F, S, 1954 W, NZ, I, S, F

Stoddard, A E (Blackheath) 1885 W, I, 1886 W, I, S, 1889 M, 1890 W, I, 1893 W, S

Stoddart, W B (Liverpool) 1897 W, I, S

Stokes, F (Blackheath) 1871 S, 1872 S, 1873 S

Stokes, L (Blackheath) 1875 I, 1876 S, 1877 I, S, 1878 S, 1879 S, I, 1880 I, S, 1881 I, W, S

Stone, F le S (Blackheath) 1914 F

Stoop, A D (Harlequins) 1905 S, 1906 S, F, SA, 1907 F, W, 1910 W, I, S, 1911 W, F, I, S, 1912 W, S

Stoop, F M (Harlequins) 1910 S, 1911 F, I, 1913 SA

Stout, F M (Richmond) 1897 W, I, 1898 I, S, W, 1899 I, S, 1903 S, 1904 W, I, S, 1905 W, I, S

Stout, P W (Richmond) 1898 S, W, 1899 W, I, S

Strettle, D (Harlequins) 2007 I,F1,W1,2, 2008 W,NZ1

Stringer, N C (Wasps) 1982 A (R), 1983 NZ (R), 1984 SA 1(R), A, 1985 R

Strong, E L (Oxford U) 1884 W, I, S

Sturnham B (Saracens) 1998 A 1, NZ 1(t),2(t)

Summerscales, G E (Durham City) 1905 NZ

Sutcliffe, J W (Heckmondwike) 1889 M

Swarbrick, D W (Oxford U) 1947 W, I, F, 1948 A, W, 1949 I

Swayne, D H (Oxford U) 1931 W

Swayne, J W R (Bridgwater) 1929 W

Swift, A H (Swansea) 1981 Arg 1,2, 1983 F, W, S, 1984 SA 2

Syddall, J P (Waterloo) 1982 I, 1984 A

Sykes, A R V (Blackheath) 1914 F

Sykes, F D (Northampton) 1955 F, S, 1963 NZ 2, A

Sykes, P W (Wasps) 1948 F, 1952 S, I, F, 1953 W, I, F

Syrett, R E (Wasps) 1958 W, A, I, F, 1960 W, I, F, S, 1962 W, I, F

Tait, M J M (Newcastle, Sale) 2005 W, 2006 A1, 2, SA1, 2, 2007 It(R), I(R), F1(R), W1, SA1, 2, W2, [US(R), SA1(R), Sm, Tg, A, F, SA2], 2008 It(t), F(R), S(R), I(t&R), NZ2, 2009 It(R), W(R), I(R), F(R), S(R), Arg 1(R), 2(R)

Tallent, J A (Cambridge U, Blackheath) 1931 S, F, 1932 SA, W, 1935 I

Tanner, C C (Cambridge U, Gloucester) 1930 S, 1932 SA, W, I, S

Tarr, F N (Leicester) 1909 A, W, F, 1913 S

Tatham, W M (Oxford U) 1882 S, 1883 W, I, S, 1884 W, I, S

Taylor, A S (Blackheath) 1883 W, I, 1886 W, I

Taylor, E W (Rockcliff) 1892 I, 1893 I, 1894 W, I, S, 1895 W, I, S, 1896 W, I, 1897 W, I, S, 1899 I

Taylor, F (Leicester) 1920 F, I

Taylor, F M (Leicester) 1914 W
Taylor, H H (Blackheath) 1879 S, 1880 S, 1881 I, W, 1882 S
Taylor, J T (W Hartlepool) 1897 I, 1899 I, 1900 I, 1901 W, I, 1902 W, I, S, 1903 W, I, 1905 S
Taylor, P J (Northampton) 1955 W, I, 1962 W, I, F, S
Taylor, R B (Northampton) 1966 W, 1967 I, F, S, W, NZ, 1969 F, S, W, SA, 1970 I, W, S, F, 1971 S (2[1C])
Taylor, W J (Blackheath) 1928 A, W, I, F, S
Teague, M C (Gloucester, Moseley) 1985 F (R), NZ 1, 2, 1989 S, I, F, W, R, 1990 F, W, S, 1991 W, S, I, F, Fj, A, [NZ, It, F, S, A], 1992 SA, 1993 F, W, S, I
Teden, D E (Richmond) 1939 W, I, S
Teggin, A (Broughton R) 1884 I, 1885 W, 1886 I, S, 1887 I, S
Tetley, T S (Bradford) 1876 S
Thomas, C (Barnstaple) 1895 W, I, S, 1899 I
Thompson, P H (Headingley, Waterloo) 1956 W, I, S, F, 1957 W, I, F, S, 1958 W, A, I, F, S, 1959 W, I, F, S
Thompson, S G (Northampton, Brive) 2002 S, I, F, W, It, Arg, NZ, A, SA, 2003 F 1, W 1, It, S, I, NZ, A, F 2(R), 3, [Gg, SA, Sm(R), W, F, A], 2004 It, S, I, W, F, NZ1, A1(R), C, SA, A2, 2005 W, F, I, It, S, A, NZ, Sm, 2006 W, It, S, F, I(R), 2009 Arg 1(R)
Thomson, G T (Halifax) 1878 S, 1882 I, S, 1883 W, I, S, 1884 I, S, 1885 I
Thomson, W B (Blackheath) 1892 W, 1895 W, I, S
Thorne, J D (Bristol) 1963 W, I, F
Tindall, M J (Bath, Gloucester) 2000 I, F, W, It, S, SA 1,2, A Arg, SA 3, 2001 W (R), R, SA (R), 2002 S, I, F, W, It, NZ, A, SA, 2003 It, S, I, NZ, A, F 2, [Gg, SA, Sm, W, F(R), A], 2004 W, F, NZ1, 2, A, C, SA, A2, 2005 A, NZ, Sm, 2006 W, It, S, F, I(t&R), 2007 S,It,I,F1, 2008 W,NZ1,2, 2009 W,I,F,S
Tindall, V R (Liverpool U) 1951 W, I, F, S
Titterrell, A J (Sale) 2004 NZ2(R), C(R), 2005 It(R), S(R), 2007 SA2(R)
Tobin, F (Liverpool) 1871 S
Todd, A F (Blackheath) 1900 I, S
Todd, R (Manchester) 1877 S
Toft, H B (Waterloo) 1936 S, 1937 W, I, S, 1938 W, I, S, 1939 W, I, S
Toothill, J T (Bradford) 1890 S, I, 1891 W, I, 1892 W, I, S, 1893 W, I, S, 1894 W, I
Tosswill, L R (Exeter) 1902 W, I, S
Touzel, C J C (Liverpool) 1877 I, S
Towell, A C (Bedford) 1948 F, 1951 S
Travers, B H (Harlequins) 1947 W, I, 1948 A, W, 1949 F, S
Treadwell, W T (Wasps) 1966 I, F, S
Trick, D M (Bath) 1983 I, 1984 SA 1
Tristram, H B (Oxford U) 1883 S, 1884 W, S, 1885 W, 1887 S
Troop, C L (Aldershot S) 1933 I, S
Tucker, J S (Bristol) 1922 W, 1925 NZ, W, I, S, F, 1926 W, I, F, S, 1927 W, I, S, F, 1928 A, W, I, F, S, 1929 W, I, F, 1930 W, I, F, S, 1931 W
Tucker, W E (Blackheath) 1894 W, I, 1895 W, I, S
Tucker, W E (Blackheath) 1926 I, 1930 W, I
Turner, D P (Richmond) 1871 S, 1872 S, 1873 S, 1874 S, 1875 I, S
Turner, E B (St George's Hospital) 1876 I, 1877 I, 1878 I
Turner, G R (St George's Hospital) 1876 S
Turner, H J C (Manchester) 1871 S
Turner, M F (Blackheath) 1948 S, F
Turner, S C (Sale) 2007 W1(R), SA1,2(R)
Turquand-Young, D (Richmond) 1928 A, W, 1929 I, S, F
Twynam, H T (Richmond) 1879 I, 1880 I, 1881 W, 1882<j> I, 1883 I, 1884 W, I, S
Ubogu, V E (Bath) 1992 C, SA, 1993 NZ, 1994 S, I, F, W, SA 1,2, R, C, 1995 I, F, W, S, [Arg, WS, A, NZ, F], SA, 1999 F (R), W (R), A (R)
Underwood, A M (Exeter) 1962 W, I, F, S, 1964 I
Underwood, R (Leicester, RAF) 1984 I, F, W, A, 1985 R, F, S, I, W, 1986 W, I, F, 1987 I, F, W, S, [A, J, W], 1988 F, W, S, I 1,2, A 1,2, Fj, A, 1989 S, I, F, W, R, Fj, 1990 I, F, W, S, Arg 3, 1991 W, S, I, F, Fj, A, [NZ, It, US, F, S, A], 1992 S, I, F, W, SA, 1993 F, W, S, I, NZ, 1994 S, I, F, W, SA 1,2, R, C, 1995 I, F, W, S, [Arg, It, WS, A, NZ, F], SA, WS, 1996 F, W, S, I
Underwood, T (Leicester, Newcastle) 1992 C, SA, 1993 S, I, NZ, 1994 S, I, W, SA 1,2, R, C, 1995 I, F, W, S, [Arg, It, A, NZ], 1996 Arg, 1997 S, I, F, W, 1998 A 2, SA 2

Unwin, E J (Rosslyn Park, Army) 1937 S, 1938 W, I, S
Unwin, G T (Blackheath) 1898 S
Uren, R (Waterloo) 1948 I, S, F, 1950 I
Uttley, R M (Gosforth) 1973 I, F, S, NZ 2, A, 1974 I, F, W, 1975 F, W, S, A 1,2, 1977 S, I, F, W, 1978 NZ 1979 S, 1980 I, F, W, S
Vainikolo, L P I (Gloucester) 2008 W(R),It,F,S,I
Valentine J (Swinton) 1890 W, 1896 W, I, S
Vanderspar, C H R (Richmond) 1873 S
Van Gisbergen, M C (Wasps) 2005 A(t)
Van Ryneveld, C B (Oxford U) 1949 W, I, F, S
Varley, H (Liversedge) 1892 S
Varndell, T W (Leicester) 2005 Sm(R), 2006 A1,2, 2008 NZ2
Vassall, H (Blackheath) 1881 W, S, 1882 I, S, 1883 W
Vassall, H H (Blackheath) 1908 I
Vaughan, D B (Headingley) 1948 A, W, I, S, 1949 I, F, S, 1950 W
Vaughan-Jones, A (Army) 1932 I, S, 1933 W
Verelst, C L (Liverpool) 1876 I, 1878 I
Vernon, G F (Blackheath) 1878 S, I, 1880 I, S, 1881 I
Vesty, S B (Leicester) 2009 Arg 1(R),2(R)
Vickery, G (Aberavon) 1905 I
Vickery, P J (Gloucester, Wasps) 1998 W, A 1, NZ 1,2, SA 1, 1999 US, C, [It, NZ, Tg, SA], 2000 I, F, W, S, A, Arg (R), SA 3(R), 2001 W, It, S, A, SA, 2002 I, F, Arg, NZ, A, SA, 2003 NZ(R), A, [Gg, SA, Sm(R), U, W, F, A], 2004 It, S, I, W, F, 2005 W(R), F, A, NZ, 2006 SA1(R),2, 2007 S, It, I, W, F2(R),3, [US, Tg(R), A, F, SA2], 2008 W,F,S,I,PI(R),A,SA,NZ3, 2009 It,W,I,F,S
Vivyan, E J (Devonport A) 1901 W, 1904 W, I, S
Voyce, A T (Gloucester) 1920 I, S, 1921 W, I, S, F, 1922 W, I, F, S, 1923 W, I, S, F, 1924 W, I, F, S, 1925 NZ, W, I, S, F, 1926 W, I, S
Voyce, T M D (Bath, Wasps) 2001 US (R), 2004 NZ2, A1, 2005 Sm, 2006 W(R), It, F(R), I, A1
Vyvyan, H D (Saracens) 2004 C(R)
Wackett, J A S (Rosslyn Park) 1959 W, I
Wade, C G (Richmond) 1883 W, I, S, 1884 W, S, 1885 W, 1886 W, I
Wade, M R (Cambridge U) 1962 W, I, F
Wakefield, W W (Harlequins) 1920 W, F, I, S, 1921 W, I, S, F, 1922 W, I, F, S, 1923 W, I, S, F, 1924 W, I, F, S, 1925 NZ, W, I, S, F, 1926 W, I, F, S, 1927 S, F
Walder, D J H (Newcastle) 2001 C 1,2, US, 2003 W 2(R)
Walker, G A (Blackheath) 1939 W, I
Walker, H W (Coventry) 1947 W, I, S, F, 1948 A, W, I, S, F
Walker, R (Manchester) 1874 S, 1875 I, 1876 S, 1879 S, 1880 S
Wallens, J N S (Waterloo) 1927 F
Walshe, N P J (Bath) 2006 A1(R), 2(R)
Walton, E J (Castleford) 1901 W, I, 1902 I, S
Walton, W (Castleford) 1894 S
Ward, G (Leicester) 1913 W, F, S, 1914 W, I, S
Ward, H (Bradford) 1895 W
Ward, J I (Richmond) 1881 I, 1882 I
Ward, J W (Castleford) 1896 W, I, S
Wardlow, C S (Northampton) 1969 SA (R), 1971 W, I, F, S (2[1C])
Warfield, P J (Rosslyn Park, Durham U) 1973 NZ 1, W, I, 1975 I, F, S
Warr, A L (Oxford U) 1934 W, I
Waters, F H H (Wasps) 2001 US, 2004 NZ2(R), A1(R)
Watkins, J A (Gloucester) 1972 SA, 1973 NZ 1, W, NZ 2, A, 1975 F, W
Watkins, J K (United Services, RN) 1939 W, I, S
Watson, F B (United Services, RN) 1908 S, 1909 S
Watson, J H D (Blackheath) 1914 W, S, F
Watt, D E J (Bristol) 1967 I, F, S, W
Webb, C S H (Devonport Services, RN) 1932 SA, W, I, S, 1933 W, I, S, 1935 S, 1936 NZ, W, I, S
Webb, J M (Bristol, Bath) 1987 [A (R), J, US, W], 1988 F, W, S, I 1,2, A 1,2, Fj, A, 1989 S, I, F, W, 1991 Fj, A, [NZ, It, F, S, A], 1992 S, I, F, W, C, SA, 1993 F, W, S, I
Webb, J W G (Northampton) 1926 F, S, 1929 S
Webb, R E (Coventry) 1967 S, W, NZ, 1968 I, F, S, 1969 I, F, S, W, 1972 I, F
Webb, St L H (Bedford) 1959 W, I, F, S

Webster, J G (Moseley) 1972 W, I, SA, 1973 NZ 1, W, NZ 2, 1974 S, W, 1975 I, F, W

Wedge, T G (St Ives) 1907 F, 1909 W

Weighill, R H G (RAF, Harlequins) 1947 S, F, 1948 S, F 1896 S, 1897 W, S

Wells, C M (Cambridge U, Harlequins) 1893 S, 1894 W, S, 1896 S, 1897 W, S

West, B R (Loughborough Colls, Northampton) 1968 W, I, F, S, 1969 SA, 1970 I, W, S

West, D E (Leicester) 1998 F (R), S (R), 2000 Arg (R), 2001 W, It, S, F (t), C 1,2, US, I (R), A, SA, 2002 F (R), W (R), It (R), 2003 W 2(R), F 2,3(t+R), [U, F(R)]

West, R (Gloucester) 1995 [WS]

Weston, H T F (Northampton) 1901 S

Weston, L E (W of Scotland) 1972 F, S

Weston, M P (Richmond, Durham City) 1960 W, I, F, S, 1961 SA, W, I, F, S, 1962 W, I, F, 1963 W, I, F, S, NZ 1,2, A, 1964 NZ, W, I, F, S, 1965 F, S, 1966 S, 1968 F, S

Weston, W H (Northampton) 1933 I, S, 1934 I, S, 1935 W, I, S, 1936 NZ, W, S, 1937 W, I, S, 1938 W, I, S

Wheatley, A A (Coventry) 1937 W, I, S, 1938 W, S

Wheatley, H F (Coventry) 1936 I, 1937 S, 1938 W, S, 1939 W, I, S

Wheeler, P J (Leicester) 1975 F, W, 1976 A, W, S, I, 1977 S, I, F, W, 1978 F, W, S, I, NZ, 1979 S, I, F, W, NZ, 1980 I, F, W, S, 1981 W, S, I, F, 1982 A, S, I, F, W, 1983 F, S, I, NZ, 1984 S, I, F, W

White, C (Gosforth) 1983 NZ, 1984 S, I, F

White, D F (Northampton) 1947 W, I, S, 1948 I, F, 1951 S, 1952 SA, W, S, I, F, 1953 W, I, S

White, J M (Saracens, Bristol, Leicester) 2000 SA 1,2, Arg, SA 3, 2001 F, C 1,2, US, I, R (R), 2002 S, W, It, 2003 F 1(R), W 2, F 2,3, [Sm, U(R)], 2004 W(R), F(R), NZ1,2, A1,C, SA, A2, 2005 W, 2006 W(R), It(R), S, F, I, A1, 2, NZ, Arg, SA1, 2, 2007 S(R), It(R), I(R), F1, W1, 2009 It(R), W(R), I(t&R), F(t&R), S(R), Arg 1(R), 2

White-Cooper, S (Harlequins) 2001 C 2, US

Whiteley, E C P (O Alleynians) 1931 S, F

Whiteley, W (Bramley) 1896 W

Whitely, H (Northern) 1929 W

Wightman, B J (Moseley, Coventry) 1959 W, 1963 W, I, NZ 2, A

Wigglesworth, H J (Thornes) 1884 I

Wigglesworth, R E P (Sale) 2008 It(R), F, S, I, NZ1

Wilkins, D T (United Services, RN, Roundhay) 1951 W, I, F, S, 1952 SA, W, S, I, F, 1953 W, I, F, S

Wilkinson, E (Bradford) 1886 W, I, 3, 1887 W, 3

Wilkinson, H (Halifax) 1929 W, I, S, 1930 F

Wilkinson, H J (Halifax) 1889 M

Wilkinson, J P (Newcastle) 1998 I (R), A 1, NZ 1, 1999 S, I, F, W, A, US, C, [It, NZ, Fj, SA (R)], 2000 I, F, W, It, S, SA 2, A, Arg, SA 3, 2001 W, It, S, F, I, A, SA, 2002 S, I, F, W, NZ, A, SA, 2003 F 1, W 1, It, S, I, NZ, A, F 3, [Gg, SA, Sm, W, F, A], 2007 S, It, I, SA1, 2, W2, F2(R), F3, [Sm, Tg, A, F, SA2], 2008 W, It, F, S, I(R)

Wilkinson, P (Law Club) 1872 S

Wilkinson, R M (Bedford) 1975 A 2, 1976 A, W, S, I, F

Willcocks, T J (Plymouth) 1902 W

Willcox, J G (Oxford U, Harlequins) 1961 I, F, S, 1962 W, I, F, S, 1963 W, I, F, S, 1964 NZ, W, I, F, S

William-Powlett, P B R W (United Services, RN) 1922 S

Williams, C G (Gloucester, RAF) 1976 F

Williams, C S (Manchester) 1910 F

Williams, J E (O Millhillians, Sale) 1954 F, 1955 W, I, F, S, 1956 I, S, F, 1965 W

Williams, J M (Penzance-Newlyn) 1951 I, S

Williams, P N (Orrell) 1987 S, [A, J, W]

Williams, S G (Devonport A) 1902 W, I, S, 1903 I, S, 1907 I, S

Williams, S H (Newport) 1911 W, F, I, S

Williamson, R H (Oxford U) 1908 W, I, S, 1909 A, F

Wilson, A J (Camborne S of M) 1909 I

Wilson, C E (Blackheath) 1898 I

Wilson, C P (Cambridge U, Marlborough N) 1881 W

Wilson, D G (Newcastle) 2009 Arg 1,2(R)

Wilson, D S (Met Police, Harlequins) 1953 F, 1954 W, NZ, I, S, F, 1955 F, S

Wilson, G S (Tyldesley) 1929 W, I

Wilson, K J (Gloucester) 1963 F

Wilson, R P (Liverpool OB) 1891 W, I, S

Wilson, W C (Richmond) 1907 I, S

Winn, C E (Rosslyn Park) 1952 SA, W, S, I, F, 1954 W, S, F

Winterbottom, P J (Headingley, Harlequins) 1982 A, S, I, F, W, 1983 F, W, S, I, NZ, 1984 S, F, W, SA 1,2, 1986 W, S, I, F, 1987 I, F, W, [A, J, US, W], 1988 F, W, S, 1989 R, Fj, 1990 I, F, W, S, Arg 1,2,3, 1991 W, S, I, F, A, [NZ, It, F, S, A], 1992 S, I, F, W, C, SA, 1993 F, W, S, I

Winters, R A (Bristol) 2007 SA1(R),2

Wintle, T C (Northampton) 1966 S, 1969 I, F, S, W

Wodehouse, N A (United Services, RN) 1910 F, 1911 W, F, I, S, 1912 W, I, S, F, 1913 SA, W, F, I, S

Wood, A (Halifax) 1884 I

Wood, A E (Gloucester, Cheltenham) 1908 F, W, I

Wood, G W (Leicester) 1914 W

Wood, M B (Wasps) 2001 C 2(R), US (R)

Wood, R (Liversedge) 1894 I

Wood, R D (Liverpool OB) 1901 I, 1903 W, I

Woodgate, E E (Paignton) 1952 W

Woodhead, E (Huddersfield) 1880 I

Woodman, T J (Gloucester) 1999 US (R), 2000 I (R), It (R), 2001 W (R), It (R), 2002 NZ, 2003 S (R), I(t + R), A, F 3, [Gg, SA, W(R), F, A], 2004 It, S, I, W, F, NZ1, 2

Woodruff, C G (Harlequins) 1951 W, I, F, S

Woods, S M J (Cambridge U, Wellington) 1890 W, S, I, 1891 W, I, S, 1892 I, S, 1893 W, I, 1895 W, I, S

Woods, T (Bridgwater) 1908 S

Woods, T (United Services, RN) 1920 S, 1921 W, I, S, F

Woodward, C R (Leicester) 1980 I (R), F, W, S, 1981 W, S, I, F, Arg 1,2, 1982 A, S, I, F, W, 1983 I, NZ, 1984 S, I, F, W

Woodward, J E (Wasps) 1952 SA, W, S, 1953 W, I, F, S, 1954 W, NZ, I, S, F, 1955 W, I, 1956 S

Wooldridge, C S (Oxford U, Blackheath) 1883 W, I, S, 1884 W, I, S, 1885 I

Wordsworth, A J (Cambridge U) 1975 A 1(R)

Worsley, J P R (Wasps) 1999 [Tg, Fj], 2000 It (R), S (R), SA 1(R),2(R), 2001 It (R), S (R), F (R), C 1,2, US, A, R, SA, 2002 S, I, F, W (t+R), Arg, 2003 W 1(R), It, S(R), I(t), NZ(R), A(R), W 2, [SA(t), Sm, U], 2004 It, I, W(R), F, NZ1(R), 2, A1, SA, A2, 2005 W, F, I, It, S, 2006 W, It, S, F, I, A1(R), 2, SA1,2, 2007 S, I, F1,W1,2, F2,3(R), [US, Sm, A(R), F(R), SA2(R)], 2008 NZ1(R),2(R), 2009 It(R),W,I,F,S

Worsley, M A (London Irish, Harlequins) 2003 It(R), 2004 A1(R), 2005 S(R)

Worton, J R B (Harlequins, Army) 1926 W, 1927 W

Wrench, D F B (Harlequins) 1964 F, S

Wright, C C G (Cambridge U, Blackheath) 1909 I, S

Wright, F T (Edinburgh Acady, Manchester) 1881 S

Wright, I D (Northampton) 1971 W, I, F, S (R)

Wright. J C (Met Police) 1934 W

Wright, J F (Bradford) 1890 W

Wright, T P (Blackheath) 1960 W, I, F, S, 1961 SA, W, I, F, S, 1962 W, I, F, S

Wright, W H G (Plymouth) 1920 W, F

Wyatt, D M (Bedford) 1976 S (R)

Yarranton, P G (RAF, Wasps) 1954 W, NZ, I, 1955 F, S

Yates, K P (Bath, Saracens) 1997 Arg 1,2, 2007 SA1,2

Yiend, W (Hartlepool R, Gloucester) 1889 M, 1892 W, I, S, 1893 I, S

Young, A T (Cambridge U, Blackheath, Army) 1924 W, I, F, S, 1925 NZ, F, 1926 I, F, S, 1927 I, S, F, 1928 A, W, I, F, S, 1929 I

Young, J R C (Oxford U, Harlequins) 1958 I, 1960 W, I, F, S, 1961 SA, W, I, F

Young, M (Gosforth) 1977 S, I, F, W, 1978 F, W, S, I, NZ, 1979 S

Young, P D (Dublin Wands) 1954 W, NZ, I, S, F, 1955 W, I, F, S

Youngs, N G (Leicester) 1983 I, NZ, 1984 S, I, F, W

TIGERS RETURN TO SUMMIT OF THE ENGLISH GAME

By Iain Spragg

David Rogers/Getty Images

Geordan Murphy lifts the Guinness Premiership trophy.

ENGLAND

When **Heyneke Meyer resigned** as Leicester head coach at the end of January 2009, forced to return to his native South Africa for personal reasons, his Tigers side were languishing in fifth in the Premiership table and their prospects of being crowned champions of England appeared to be fading fast.

Four months later, however, Leicester were at Twickenham for a fifth successive appearance in the play-off final and their eventual 10–9 victory over London Irish represented a miraculous transformation of the team's fortunes masterminded by former England hooker Richard Cockerill.

Appointed caretaker coach by the Welford Road hierarchy in February, Cockerill was eventually given the job on a permanent basis in April, but from the moment he succeeded Meyer, the Tigers were a side reborn and a sequence of 10 wins in their final 11 league games ensured Leicester finished the regular season in top spot.

Bath were duly dispatched in the play-off semi-finals and although the victory over the Exiles courtesy of Jordan Crane's try and the boot of Julien Dupuy lacked the pyrotechnics befitting a showpiece final, it was a result that gave Leicester a record eighth English league title and confirmed the 38-year-old Cockerill as a bona fide head coach in his own right.

It also went some way to banishing the club's painful memories of recent play-off final defeats at Twickenham. The Tigers had fallen at the final hurdle three times in the previous four years and although Cockerill was far from enamoured with his team's performance after the final whistle, he was relieved to have got over the winning line.

"We've choked a little bit with three wins in eight finals in all competitions in the last few seasons," he said after Leicester became the first side since Sale in 2006 to top the table and then go on to claim the title.

"So I'm happy and we deserve it on the basis of the last four months. Our performance today was poor and we didn't play well but stuck to our task. Over the balance of the year I think we deserve to be champions. I'm pleased with the win because the pressure was on."

For London Irish, appearing in their first final, such a narrow defeat was a particularly bitter pill to swallow for veteran Mike Catt, who became the oldest ever player to appear in English rugby's showpiece game at the grand old age of 37.

"We had opportunities but didn't take them and that's what finals are all about," he conceded. "They took their chances and took us apart. It's a tough one to take, emotions are running high. We'll have a good summer and go again next year. This team are young enough and have enough talent to bounce back."

The 2008–09 campaign was nothing if not eventful. Relegated Bristol sacked coach Richard Hill in February after five years at the Memorial Ground, while director of rugby Eddie Jones abruptly parted company with Saracens in February.

Elsewhere, there was heated debate about the Premiership salary cap in the wake of the economic downturn and the news in February that England flanker James Haskell was joining Stade Français for next season sparked a mini exodus of players to France including Jamie Noon, Riki Flutey, Tom Palmer, Iain Balshaw and Jonny Wilkinson and raised real concerns about further damaging, high-profile defections across the Channel.

London Irish, with Seilala Mapusua to the fore, had a magnificent season, ending in the Guinness Premiership final at Twickenham.

ENGLAND

On the pitch, it was equally enthralling. The campaign kicked off in early September and although it was Leicester who signalled their intent in the initial exchanges with three successive victories it was Bath, London Irish, Gloucester and Harlequins who made the early running.

Coached by Toby Booth in his first season at the helm following Brian Smith's decision to join the England set-up, the Exiles in particular were quick out of the blocks and a six-match winning streak from October through to December proved Irish would be a force to be reckoned with.

Bath also made a strong start, defeating Leicester 25–21 at the Recreation Ground in mid November thanks to Butch James' last-gasp try which extended his side's lead at the top of the table to six points, while Harlequins were proving a tough proposition under the no-nonsense leadership of coach Dean Richards.

In contrast, the Tigers suffered five defeats in 10 league outings but the anointment of Cockerill and their rivals' alarming slump in form in the second half of the campaign opened the door and Leicester gleefully seized their unexpected chance to claim top spot.

Harlequins steeled themselves when it mattered most with four wins in their last five fixtures to claim second, Irish finished third after victory over Worcester on the final day of the season and Bath secured the last semi-final play-off place in fourth.

The first semi-final in early May saw Leicester entertain Bath at the Walkers Stadium. The two sides had each won their home league games against the other and home advantage, albeit at the city's football rather than rugby ground, was to prove decisive once again as the Tigers muscled their way to a 24–10 victory.

Leicester raced into a first half lead with converted tries from Dan Hipkiss and the in-form Sam Vesty, but Bath replied after the break through Michael Claassens and Stuart Hooper and it needed a late try from Lewis Moody to settle the contest.

"We have done well in Europe and the Premiership this season but we need to kick on again and freshen up mentally," admitted Bath coach Steve Meehan after the defeat. "We were just not on our game in the first half and I don't really know why."

Harlequins entertained London Irish at the Stoop in the second semi-final but missed four crucial first half penalties and were made to pay for their profligacy after the break when James Hudson raced over for the first try of the match. A second score from Catt put the Exiles out of sight and Booth's side cantered to an impressive 17–0 win.

"We had opportunities to get points on the board but didn't take them," said Richards after the defeat. "It might have been a totally different game had we taken those points at the start but that's life. I like to think this is just the beginning. We'll learn from today and will be a better side next year."

Despite their less than impressive record in recent play-off finals, Leicester went into the Twickenham game against the Exiles as favourites but were unable to assert any real dominance and the game proved to be a tense and fretful affair.

The Irish drew first blood with a 35-metre drop goal from Peter Hewat after just 22 seconds, but the Tigers hit back with a Dupuy penalty and although Crane was sin-binned on the half-hour mark, neither side could add to their respective tallies and they went in at half time locked at 3–3.

The second period saw Delon Armitage land a penalty for the Exiles to edge them into the lead but the crucial moment came on the hour when Crane atoned for his earlier indiscretion, stretching over from close range for the game's only try.

Dupuy converted and although Armitage's second penalty eight minutes from time ensured Leicester were unable to relax as the final whistle loomed, they held out to hand Cockerill his first piece of silverware since stepping into Meyer's shoes.

"It was nice to get over the line for a little try," said Crane after the match. "I just reached out and luckily I got there. I thought it was not going to be our day but we came through in the end and the way we have backed up over the last three weeks has been awesome."

Elsewhere in England, Leeds Carnegie bounced back from relegation from the Premiership the previous season by claiming the National League One title and earning themselves an immediate return to the top flight.

The Yorkshire side finished 14 points clear of second placed Exeter and having satisfied the Professional Game Board's minimum standards criteria for promotion, their return to the top tier of the English game was confirmed.

"Our goal is to develop Leeds Carnegie from good to great over the coming years," said head coach Neil Back. "And the infrastructure is in place to certainly do that."

In National League Two, Birmingham & Solihull clinched promotion at the end of April with a 31–7 triumph over Redruth, their 12th consecutive league win. Nuneaton were the runaway winners of National League Three North while London Scottish were National League Three South champions with an impressive 25 wins and one draw from their 26 league fixtures.

In the Bill Beaumont Cup final at Twickenham, Lancashire were crowned the English County champions for the first time since 2006 with a 32–18 victory over Gloucestershire.

The North Pool winners crossed the try-line three times through Nicholas Royle, Matthew Riley and Juan Crous which, along with five penalties from Plymouth Albion fly half Alex Davies, were enough to see off the challenge of their West Country opponents.

David Rogers/Getty Images

Andy Key (left) and Neil Back take Leeds back into the Premiership.

ENGLAND

GUINNESS PREMIERSHIP
2008–09 RESULTS

6 September: **London Irish** 26 **Wasps** 14, **Saracens** 21 **Harlequins** 24. 7 September: **Northampton** 21 **Worcester** 13, **Bristol** 20 **Bath** 33, **Newcastle** 9 **Sale** 14, **Gloucester** 8 **Leicester** 20. 12 September: **Sale** 18 **Saracens** 15. 13 September: **Bath** 17 **Gloucester** 21, **Harlequins** 31 **Bristol** 13, **Leicester** 24 **London Irish** 22. 14 September: **Wasps** 10 **Worcester** 11, **Newcastle** 32 **Northampton** 22. 19 September: **Bristol** 6 **Sale** 9. 20 September: **Gloucester** 24 **Harlequins** 20, **London Irish** 16 **Bath** 20, **Northampton** 24 **Wasps** 20, **Worcester** 17 **Leicester** 19. 21 September: **Saracens** 44 **Newcastle** 14. 26 September: **Sale** 23 **Gloucester** 9, **Newcastle** 17 **Bristol** 3, **Leicester** 19 **Wasps** 28. 27 September: **Bath** 37 **Worcester** 19, **Saracens** 26 **Northampton** 12, **Harlequins** 27 **London Irish** 28. 30 September: **Gloucester** 39 **Newcastle** 23. 1 October: **Wasps** 23 **Bath** 27, **Bristol** 16 **Saracens** 23, **Leicester** 29 **Northampton** 19, **London Irish** 28 **Sale** 6. 2 October: **Worcester** 23 **Harlequins** 30. 14 November: **Sale** 9 **Worcester** 17. 15 November: **Bath** 25 **Leicester** 21. 16 November: **Bristol** 14 **Northampton** 13, **Harlequins** 32 **Wasps** 10, **Newcastle** 8 **London Irish** 24, **Saracens** 21 **Gloucester** 25. 21 November: **Gloucester** 39 **Bristol** 10, **Worcester** 26 **Newcastle** 11. 22 November: **Northampton** 28 **Bath** 28, **Leicester** 27 **Harlequins** 14. 23 November: **London Irish** 27 **Saracens** 14, **Wasps** 12 **Sale** 13. 28 November: **Sale** 27 **Leicester** 13, **Newcastle** 17 **Wasps** 23. 29 November: **Gloucester** 33 **Northampton** 10. 30 November: **Bristol** 13 **London Irish** 18, **Harlequins** 21 **Bath** 14, **Saracens** 23 **Worcester** 6. 20 December: **Leicester** 20 **Newcastle** 3, **Wasps** 33 **Saracens** 24, **Bath** 24 **Sale** 20, **London Irish** 42 **Gloucester** 12, **Northampton** 23 **Harlequins** 13, **Worcester** 20 **Bristol** 20. 26 December: **Sale** 31 **Wasps** 3. 27 December: **Saracens** 16 **London Irish** 13, **Bath** 25 **Northampton** 14, **Bristol** 10 **Gloucester** 29, **Newcastle** 16 **Worcester** 16, **Harlequins** 26 **Leicester** 26. 3 January: **Gloucester** 22 **Saracens** 16, **London Irish** 48 **Newcastle** 8, **Northampton** 30 **Bristol** 8. 4 January: **Leicester** 24 **Bath** 22, **Wasps** 24 **Harlequins** 18. 9 January: **Sale** 14 **London Irish** 8. 10 January: **Northampton** 17 **Leicester** 13. 11 January: **Newcastle** 10 **Gloucester** 7, **Saracens** 37 **Bristol** 13. 31 January: **Gloucester** 23 **London Irish** 21, **Harlequins** 27 **Northampton** 6, **Worcester** 20 **Sale** 37. 13 February: **Bristol** 3 **Newcastle** 35. 14 February: **London Irish** 9 **Harlequins** 14, **Gloucester** 24 **Sale** 17, **Northampton** 20 **Saracens** 15, **Worcester** 17 **Bath** 34. 15 February: **Wasps** 36 **Leicester** 29. 20 February: **Sale** 32 **Bristol** 13, **Newcastle** 13 **Saracens** 9. 21 February: **Bath** 20 **London Irish** 20, **Harlequins** 14 **Gloucester** 9, **Leicester** 38 **Worcester** 5. 22 February: **Wasps** 9 **Northampton** 5. 28 February: **Gloucester** 36 **Bath** 27, **Northampton** 13 **Newcastle** 19, **Worcester** 13 **Wasps** 12. 1 March: **London Irish** 28 **Leicester** 31, **Bristol** 14 **Harlequins** 21, **Saracens** 24 **Sale** 23. 7 March: **Bath** 45 **Bristol** 8, **Leicester** 24 **Gloucester** 10, **Harlequins** 21 **Saracens** 15, **Worcester** 12 **Northampton** 22. 8 March: **Sale** 25 **Newcastle** 32, **Wasps** 21 **London Irish** 16. 13 March: **Bristol** 17 **Leicester** 23. 14 March: **Gloucester** 24 **Wasps** 22, **Northampton** 38 **Sale** 3. 15 March: **London Irish** 38 **Worcester** 17, **Newcastle** 24 **Harlequins** 16, **Saracens** 20 **Bath** 16. 21 March: **Bath** 36 **Newcastle** 25, **Leicester** 46 **Saracens** 16. 22 March: **London Irish** 32 **Northampton** 27, **Harlequins** 38 **Sale** 20, **Wasps** 21 **Bristol** 19, **Worcester** 14 **Gloucester** 10. 27 March: **Sale** 23 **Bath** 16, **Newcastle** 14 **Leicester** 10. 29 March: **Bristol** 37 **Worcester** 18, **Saracens** 19 **Wasps** 14. 1 April: **Harlequins** 60 **Worcester** 14, **Bath** 22 **Wasps** 14. 4 April: **Bath** 3 **Harlequins** 19, **London Irish** 38 **Bristol** 21, **Northampton** 40 **Gloucester** 22, **Worcester** 22 **Saracens** 8, **Leicester** 37 **Sale** 31. 5 April: **Wasps** 12 **Newcastle** 6. 17 April: **Sale** 28 **Harlequins** 6. 18 April: **Northampton** 21 **London Irish** 17. 19 April: **Bristol** 18 **Wasps** 36, **Saracens** 13 **Leicester** 16, **Newcastle** 14 **Bath** 15. 21 April: **Gloucester** 6 **Worcester** 13. 25 April: **Bath** 33 **Saracens** 18, **Harlequins** 31 **Newcastle** 12, **Leicester** 73 **Bristol** 3, **Wasps** 34 **Gloucester** 3, **Sale** 24 **Northampton** 18, **Worcester** 15 **London Irish** 32.

FINAL TABLE

	P	W	D	L	F	A	BP	PTS
Leicester	22	15	1	6	582	401	9	**71**
Harlequins	22	14	1	7	519	387	8	**66**
London Irish	22	12	1	9	551	386	16	**66**
Bath	22	13	2	7	539	441	9	**65**
Sale	22	13	0	9	447	410	10	**61**
Gloucester	22	12	0	10	435	448	9	**57**
Wasps	22	11	0	11	431	416	9	**53**
Northampton	22	10	1	11	443	434	7	**49**
Saracens	22	9	0	13	437	447	11	**47**
Newcastle	22	9	1	12	362	456	6	**44**
Worcester	22	7	2	13	348	530	2	**34**
Bristol	22	2	1	19	299	637	7	**17**

ENGLAND

PREVIOUS ENGLISH CHAMPIONS

1987/1988: Leicester	1998/1999: Leicester
1988/1989: Bath	1999/2000: Leicester
1989/1990: Wasps	2000/2001: Leicester
1990/1991: Bath	2001/2002: Leicester
1991/1992: Bath	2002/2003: Wasps
1992/1993: Bath	2003/2004: Wasps
1993/1994: Bath	2004/2005: Wasps
1994/1995: Leicester	2005/2006: Sale
1995/1996: Bath	2006/2007: Leicester
1996/1997: Wasps	2007/2008: London Wasps
1997/1998: Newcastle	2008/2009: Leicester

PLAY-OFF
SEMI-FINALS

9 May, Walkers Stadium, Leicester

LEICESTER 24 (3G, 1PG) BATH 10 (2T)

LEICESTER: G Murphy (captain); S Hamilton, A Erinle, D Hipkiss, J Murphy; S Vesty, J Dupuy; M Ayerza, G Chuter, M Castrogiovanni (J White, 61), T Croft, B Kay, C Newby, J Crane, B Woods.

SUBSTITUTIONS: M Wentzel for Croft (temp 44 to 57 mins); B Kayser for Chuter (58 mins); L Moody for Woods (66 mins); H Ellis for Dupuy (72 mins); M Smith for Erinle (75 mins); T Varndell for G Murphy (77 mins); Wentzel for Newby (78 mins)

SCORERS: *Tries:* Hipkiss, Vesty, Moody, *Conversions:* Dupuy (3), *Penalty Goal:* Dupuy

BATH: N Abendanon; J Maddock, A Crockett (captain), S Hape, M Banahan; R Davis, M Claassens; D Flatman, L Mears, D Bell, J Harrison, P Short, A Beattie, S Hooper, J Scaysbrook

SUBSTITUTIONS : D Barnes for Flatman (64 mins); P Dixon for Mears (64 mins); S Bemand for Claassens (72 mins); S Berne for Abendanon (78 mins); A Higgins for Crockett (78 mins)

SCORERS: *Tries:* Claassens, Hooper

REFEREE: D Pearson (Northumberland)

9 May, Twickenham Stoop, London

HARLEQUINS 0 LONDON IRISH 17 (2G, 1PG)

HARLEQUINS: M Brown; T Williams, G Tiesi, J Turner-Hall, U Monye; N Evans, D Care; C Jones, T Fuga, M Ross, J Percival, G Robson, C Robshaw, N Easter, W Skinner (captain)

SUBSTITUTIONS: G Botha for Fuga (53 mins); J Evans for Percival (54 mins); A Gomarsall for Care (61 mins); T Guest for Robshaw (62 mins); W Luveniyali for Evans (61 mins); DW Barry for Williams (68 mins); M Lambert for Ross (70 mins)

LONDON IRISH: P Hewat; A Thompstone, D Armitage, S Mapusua, S Tagicakibau; M Catt, P Hodgson; C Dermody, D Coetzee, R Skuse, N Kennedy, B Casey (captain), D Danaher, C Hala'ufia, S Armitage

SUBSTITUTIONS: J Hudson for Kennedy (26 mins); A Corbisiero for Skuse (49 mins); R Thorpe for Hala'ufia (49 mins); J Buckland for Coetzee (61 mins); T Homer for Thompstone (61 mins); E Seveali'i for Mapusua (70 mins); P Richards for Catt (76 mins)

SCORERS: *Tries:* Hudson, Catt, *Conversions:* D Armitage (2), *Penalty Goal:* D Armitage

YELLOW CARD: Tagicakibau (40 mins)

REFEREE: C White (Gloucestershire)

PLAY-OFF FINAL

16 May, Twickenham, London

LEICESTER 10 (1G, 1PG)
LONDON IRISH 9 (2PG, 1DG)

LEICESTER: G Murphy (captain); S Hamilton, A Erinle, D Hipkiss, J Murphy; S Vesty, J Dupuy; M Ayerza, G Chuter, J White, T Croft, B Kay, C Newby, B Woods, J Crane

SUBSTITUTIONS : M Short for J Murphy (20 mins); L Moody for Woods (61 mins)

SCORERS: *Try*: Crane *Conversion*: Dupuy, *Penalty Goal*: Dupuy

LONDON IRISH: P Hewat, A Thompstone, D Armitage, S Mapusua, S Tagickibau, M Catt, P Hodgson; C Dermody, D Coetzee, R Skuse, J Hudson, B Casey (captain), D Danaher, S Armitage, C Hala'ufia

SUBSTITUTIONS : T Homer for Thompstone (41 mins)

SCORERS: *Penalty Goals*: D Armitage (2), *Drop Goal*: Hewat

YELLOW CARD: Crane (40 mins)

REFEREE: W Barnes (England)

ENGLAND

Warren Little/Getty Images

Jordan Crane crashes over for Leicester's only try in the final.

OTHER MAJOR DOMESTIC WINNERS

NATIONAL ONE

Leeds Carnegie

NATIONAL TWO

Birmingham & Solihull

NATIONAL THREE NORTH

Nuneaton

NATIONAL THREE SOUTH

London Scottish

NORTH ONE

Westoe

SOUTH WEST ONE

Clifton

MIDLANDS ONE

Broadstreets

LONDON ONE

Shelford

FIJI

FIJI'S 2008–09 TEST RECORD

OPPONENTS	DATE	VENUE	RESULT
Tonga	13 June	A	**Won** 36–22
Junior All Blacks	18 June	H	**Lost** 17–45
Samoa	27 June	H	**Won** 19–14
Japan	3 July	H	**Won** 40–39

CLIMBING BACK UP THE HILL

By Jeremy Duxbury

The euphoria of 2007 when Fiji beat Wales, Canada and Japan and then took eventual world champions South Africa down to the wire is in danger of becoming a distant memory unless Fiji's preparations for Rugby World Cup 2011 get a radical revamp.

Despite the glowing recognition two years ago, the Fiji Rugby Union have so far not been able to add any meaningful fixtures to their calendar. In the whole of 2008, Fiji played just five matches, four of which were classified as Tests, and in the 12 months between July 2008 and August 2009, those figures dropped to just four and three respectively.

Before RWC 2011, Fiji have two Northern Hemisphere tours planned and will compete in two ANZ Pacific Nations Cups. That means only 14 matches over the two years leading to the World Cup, when they join South Africa, Wales, Samoa and the Africa 1 qualifier, in Pool d.

There is also concern over player availability and the perennial club versus country dispute with a dozen of Fiji's top professionals from overseas not joining the squad for the Pacific Nations Cup. That meant there was no Napolioni Nalaga (Clermont Auvergne), no Rupeni Caucau (Agen), Vilimoni Delasau (Montauban), Sireli Bobo (Metro Racing), Maleli Kunavore (Toulouse), Sisa Koyamaibole (Sale Sharks), Akapusi Qera and Apolosi Satala (Gloucester), Sireli Naqelevuki (Stormers), Gabby Lovobalavu (Toulon) or Isoa Neivua (Padova). The majority of these players were injury-free and in Fiji during the PNC, but chose not to play.

Hopefully, that view of things will change now that a new coaching panel has been appointed after the previous national coach Ilivasi Tabua was sacked in August. Heading into town from overseas as technical advisors are Australian rugby icon Glen Ella and former All Blacks captain Mike Brewer.

From Fiji's side, the FRU have named former Test No.8 Inoke Male and former Test lock Samuela Domoni as part of the coaching panel with the latter earmarked to become head coach.

So while the coaching side of things appears to be in good hands, the FRU is still searching for a strong manager to perform the important role that Pio Bosco Tikoisuva did so admirably in 2007.

Tikoisuva, the former Harlequins pivot who skippered Fiji when they beat the British Lions in 1977 and is now the Fiji High Commissioner to London, says he has retired from rugby, but those words have been heard before.

The Pacific Islanders toured Europe in autumn 2008, which meant that Fiji had no fixtures in that Test window. Samoa have since pulled out of the Pacific Islanders alliance, meaning it is highly unlikely this consortium will play any more matches.

With the Test window in June-July being pushed back a little, those professionals returning from Europe had a little more time to get ready. Some, like Worcester No.8 Netani Talei, had played a very long season in Europe but still managed to lace up their boots for the whole of the Pacific Nations Cup.

Other Europe-based representatives making it back in time included centre Seru Rabeni, who later picked up a contract with Leeds Carnegie.

After five years with Leicester, Rabeni had signed with Gloucester but an injury picked up in the PNC led the west country club to pull out of the agreement. And herein lies one of the reasons why some overseas-based professionals may be hesitant to play in Fiji: insurance.

An injury to Akapusi Qera in 2008 put him out for nine months. The FRU does not currently carry insurance for loss of income in such instances, so Rabeni would have been mightily relieved to sign for Leeds.

It's a scenario that may have led to Sisa Koyamaibole sidestepping the PNC in 2009, as he was moving from Toulon to Sale.

So Fiji entered the Pacific Nations Cup on home soil with a relatively inexperienced squad, and thus did well to finish second overall with two or three young players coming through with distinction.

Fiji's Test side began with a 36–22 victory in the Tongan capital of Nuku'alofa, never an easy venue at which to get maximum points. Though Fiji scored five tries – including two from Ulster wing Jim Nagusa – the play was disjointed and many of the tries came from turnovers or slack defence rather than sustained pressure.

An interesting element to this victory was the inclusion of fly-half Alipate Tani and centre Waisale Suka, both of whom featured at the 2008 Rugby League World Cup. Suka played for Fiji U18s and U21s from 2002–04 so he is no stranger to the game. Tani, however, is a new recruit to the code and did particularly well on debut.

To face the Junior All Blacks a week later in the western Fijian city of Lautoka, Tabua astounded fans by making five changes to his team, mysteriously dropping top players like flanker Semisi Naevo.

Much to the disappointment of the crowd that had seen Fiji narrowly lose to New Zealand Maori a year earlier on the same ground, this time their play lacked passion or cohesion. The Junior All Blacks had what turned out to be a cruise, winning 45–17 with Hosea Gear grabbing a brace towards his record total of eight tries in the tournament.

A week later, Tabua made another 11 changes to face Samoa including all seven backline positions. Samoa had the experience on paper to take this match, and they dominated the first half in terms of possession and territory but only led 9–3 at the interval.

Steadied by Clermont's Bai at inside centre, Fiji grew with confidence after the break as Samoa failed to make their advantages tell on the scoreboard. Bai kicked 14 points and Fiji Sevens skipper Vereniki Goneva picked up the winning try with a great dash through the Samoan line to take the match 19–14.

Goneva, the quiet and unassuming Nadi captain, had led the Fiji Sevens side to victories over South Africa in the finals of the Hong Kong and Edinburgh tournaments with outstanding all-round play.

So, onto Suva and Fiji just had to beat Japan to finish runners-up behind the Junior All Blacks and record their best ever position in the tournament's history.

Playing at home in the heat and with a buoyant crowd in support, Fiji ought not to have been troubled by Japan despite finding the Japanese tricky opponents in recent times and so nearly coming unstuck against their smaller opponents on several occasions.

Leading 20–14 at half-time with tries from Goneva and impressive young half-back Nemia Kenatale, Fiji looked set to rack up a good score. But the Japanese had the audacity to push the Fijians around in the scrums and mauls, and scored four of their eventual five tries from the rolling maul.

As questions were silently mouthed about Fiji's perennial pack problems, John Kirwan's Japan had the bit between their teeth. They had earlier beaten Tonga and scored well against Samoa and the Junior All Blacks. Here was a chance to really show what they could achieve.

Converted tries for hooker Yusuke Aoki and No.8 Takashi Kikutani (2) saw Japan eke out a 10-point lead, 36–26, with only four minutes of normal time remaining. Few, though, could have predicted the flurry of action at both ends to round off a superb Pacific Nations Cup.

First Fiji's replacement hooker Sireli Ledua picked up a loose ball and scooted away for a surprise try. Then on full-time Ryan Nicholas replied for Japan with another penalty to take the score to 39–33 in Japan's favour.

However, well after the full-time hooter had sounded, Fiji had the ball alive and were pounding the Japanese defence. With the last play of the match Talei forced his way over by the posts to give Bai an easy conversion and send the Fijians into a frenzy of delight as they took the match 40–39.

Bai's 20-point haul took his Test tally to 151, fourth in Fiji's all-time list behind Nicky Little, Severo Koroduadua and Waisale Serevi. Goneva earned a contract with France Pro2 side Colomiers, but he is surely headed for higher honours, while young openside flanker Samuela Bola also stood out.

This, however, was Tabua's last match in charge. His tinkering with selections, his inability to give Fiji a competitive scrum and his off-field misdemeanours led the FRU to take corrective action as they plan for 2011. But there is still much work to be done.

On the Sevens scene, the big news was the sacking in late January of coach Serevi. His replacement, former Auckland Blues back Iliesa Tanivula, had led Nadi to all the domestic trophies on offer in 2008.

And after a shaky start that saw Fiji lose their hold on the Melrose Cup with a quarter-final defeat to Kenya at Rugby World Cup Sevens in Dubai, Tanivula slowly built up a creditable team and pipped England for second place in the IRB Sevens World Series behind first time champions South Africa.

On the domestic front, Nadi had to relinquish their provincial crown to Nadroga, who took top honours with a 19–13 win in the Digicel Cup final.

The year 2009 was also a sad one for the demise of the Colonial Cup, a semi-professional franchise tournament that had run so well for five years and set up a superb pathway for players all over Fiji. Despite the huge loss to the elite programme, the FRU decided for financial and operational reasons to cancel the competition.

FIJI INTERNATIONAL STATISTICS

MATCH RECORDS UP TO 30TH SEPTEMBER 2009

WINNING MARGIN

Date	Opponent	Result	Winning Margin
10/09/1983	Niue Island	120–4	116
21/08/1969	Solomon Islands	113–13	100
08/09/1983	Solomon Islands	86–0	86
30/08/1979	Papua New Guinea	86–0	86
23/08/1969	Papua New Guinea	88–3	85

MOST TRIES IN A MATCH BY THE TEAM

Date	Opponent	Result	Tries
21/08/1969	Solomon Islands	113–13	25
10/09/1983	Niue Island	120–4	21
18/08/1969	Papua New Guinea	79–0	19
30/08/1979	Papua New Guinea	86–0	18
08/09/1983	Solomon Islands	86–0	16

MOST POINTS IN A MATCH BY THE TEAM

Date	Opponent	Result	Pts.
10/09/1983	Niue Island	120–4	120
21/08/1969	Solomon Islands	113–13	113
23/08/1969	Papua New Guinea	88–3	88
08/09/1983	Solomon Islands	86–0	86
30/08/1979	Papua New Guinea	86–0	86

MOST CONVERSIONS IN A MATCH BY THE TEAM

Date	Opponent	Result	Cons
21/08/1969	Solomon Islands	113–13	19
10/09/1983	Niue Island	120–4	18

MOST PENALTIES IN A MATCH
BY THE TEAM

Date	Opponent	Result	Pens
08/07/2001	Samoa	28–17	7

MOST DROP GOALS IN A MATCH
BY THE TEAM

Date	Opponent	Result	DGs
02/07/1994	Samoa	20–13	3
12/10/1991	Romania	15–17	3

MOST POINTS IN A MATCH
BY A PLAYER

Date	Player	Opponent	Pts.
10/09/1983	Severo Koroduadua	Niue Island	36
07/10/1989	Waisale Serevi	Belgium	26
28/08/1999	Nicky Little	Italy	25

MOST TRIES IN A MATCH
BY A PLAYER

Date	Player	Opponent	Tries
30/08/1979	Tevita Makutu	Papua New Guinea	6
18/08/1969	George Sailosi	Papua New Guinea	5

MOST CONVERSIONS IN A MATCH
BY A PLAYER

Date	Player	Opponent	Cons
10/09/1983	Severo Koroduadua	Niue Island	18
21/08/1969	Semesa Sikivou	Solomon Islands	12
07/10/1989	Waisale Serevi	Belgium	11

MOST PENALTIES IN A MATCH
BY A PLAYER

Date	Player	Opponent	Pens
08/07/2001	Nicky Little	Samoa	7
26/05/2000	Nicky Little	Tonga	6
25/05/2001	Nicky Little	Tonga	6
05/10/1996	Nicky Little	Hong Kong	6
08/07/1967	Inoke Tabualevu	Tonga	6

MOST DROP GOALS IN A MATCH
BY A PLAYER

Date	Player	Opponent	Pens
02/07/1994	Opeti Turuva	Samoa	3
12/10/1991	Tomasi Rabaka	Romania	2

MOST CAPPED PLAYERS

Name	Caps
Nicky Little	63
Jacob Rauluni	50
Joeli Veitayaki	49
Emori Katalau	47

LEADING TRY SCORERS

Name	Tries
Senivalati Laulau	19
Norman Ligairi	16
Viliame Satala	16
Fero Lasagavibau	16

LEADING CONVERSIONS SCORERS

Name	Cons
Nicky Little	113
Waisale Serevi	51
Severo Koroduadua	43
Seremaia Bai	25

LEADING PENALTY SCORERS

Name	Pens
Nicky Little	133
Severo Koroduadua	37
Waisale Serevi	27
Seremaia Bai	26

LEADING DROP GOAL SCORERS

Name	DGs
Opeti Turuva	5
Severo Koroduadua	5
Waisale Serevi	3

LEADING POINTS SCORERS

Name	Pts.
Nicky Little	641
Waisale Serevi	239
Severo Koroduadua	212
Seremaia Baikeinuku	151

FRANCE

FRANCE'S 2008–09 TEST RECORD

OPPONENTS	DATE	VENUE	RESULT
Argentina	8 November	H	**Won** 12–6
Pacific Islanders	15 November	H	**Won** 42–17
Australia	22 November	H	**Lost** 13–18
Ireland	7 February	A	**Lost** 21–30
Scotland	14 February	H	**Won** 22–13
Wales	27 February	H	**Won** 21–16
England	15 March	A	**Lost** 10–34
Italy	21 March	A	**Won** 50–8
New Zealand	13 June	A	**Won** 27–22
New Zealand	20 June	A	**Lost** 14–10
Australia	27 June	A	**Lost** 6–22

FINISHING ON A HIGH

By Iain Spragg

France celebrate their incredible win in Dunedin.

When **Marc Lièvremont surveyed** the wreckage of his side's 34–10 Six Nations mauling by England at Twickenham in March, it is debatable whether even the usually philosophical France coach could find any crumbs of comfort after what was a woeful and demoralising display.

Three months later, however, and Lièvremont and Les Bleus were celebrating in earnest after lowering New Zealand's colours in Dunedin, a first French success on Kiwi soil in 15 years and a repeat of their shock victory over the All Blacks in Cardiff in the World Cup quarter-final of 2007.

But such is the ridiculous and then frequently sublime nature of the French team. Lièvremont is not the first coach to strive to marry consistency with the traditional Gallic traits of flair and adventure and irrespective of how long he remains at the helm, he almost certainly will not be the last. France are nothing if not predictably unpredictable.

In total, Les Bleus lost five of their 11 Tests in 2008–09 but the triumph in New Zealand, only their fourth win in 22 attempts in the All Blacks' backyard, underlined the huge potential of the side and made a mockery of their third place in the Six Nations. Overall it was a season of frustrating glimpses of brilliance coupled with mediocrity and under achievement.

The campaign kicked off in November with Argentina. The Pumas had beaten France twice the previous year in the World Cup but although the home side brought the losing streak to an end with a 12–6 win, the performance was far from convincing. Neither side could muster a try in the Stade de France and Lièvremont's team were indebted to two penalties and a drop goal from David Skrela.

A week later it was the Pacific Islanders in Sochaux and a match that was ended as a meaningful contest after just 18 minutes when Napolioni Nalaga was sent off for a high and late tackle that knocked Jean-Baptiste Elissalde unconscious. Les Bleus duly took advantage of their numerical superiority and tries from Dimitri Szarzewski, Sebastien Tillous-Borde, Cedric Heymans, Louis Picamoles and Maxime Médard set up a 42–17 victory.

A week later Les Bleus were always in contention against the Wallabies but five missed penalty attempts by fly-half Skela cost his side dearly and Australia held out for an 18–13 win.

"We could have taken that match but we didn't and there is an enormous frustration," Lièvremont said. "Against teams like Australia, you don't get 10 chances, you get three or four. We are able to compete against the biggest teams in the world but we can't express ourselves."

The Six Nations offered the French the chance of redemption after a disappointing Autumn and Lièvremont decided to shuffle his cards ahead of his team's opener against Ireland at Croke Park, selecting Tillous-Borde at scrum-half ahead of Morgan Parra and recalling Florian Fritz at centre and Clément Poitrenaud at full-back.

The clash certainly did not disappoint the 80,000-plus fans who descended on Dublin. An early Imanol Harinordoquy try established a 7–3 lead for the visitors but Ireland hit back with scores from Jamie Heaslip and Brian O'Driscoll either side of the break, only for Les Bleus to reply with a Médard try. The match was finely balanced but it was Ireland who got the all-important next score through Gordon D'Arcy and France were beaten 30–21.

Scotland were in Paris a week later and although the home side dispatched Frank Hadden's team 22–13, they were far from fluent and were restricted to a single try when Fulgence Ouedraogo crashed over in the second half from what looked like a forward pass from Médard. France had their first Championship win but there was scant evidence of the side playing in the manner their coach or supporters craved.

Defending champions Wales were next up in Paris and although France once again failed to find their famed cutting edge, they were in resolute mood at the Stade de France and despite trailing 13–3 after just 25 minutes, they battled back with tries from Dusautoir and Heymans to record a hard-fought 21–16 win.

That French spirit was severely tested at Twickenham a fortnight later but while against Wales they were up to the challenge, Lièvremont's side crumbled when the pressure was applied by the English and the match was effectively over by half-time.

England careered into a 29–0 lead at the break with four tries and were the first on the scoreboard after the restart and although France did score through Szarzewski and Julien Malzieu, it could not disguise the extent to which Les Bleus had been outplayed in every department.

France finished the tournament against Italy in Rome and to their credit bounced back from their Twickenham nightmare with their own seven-try blitz of the Azzurri, galloping to a 50–8 victory and a degree of closure for the events of six days earlier in London.

The greater challenge of the All Blacks lay ahead, however, and although New Zealand were missing a number of senior players as the two sides prepared for battle in Carisbrook in mid-June, the French cannot have been at their most confident after their Six Nations trials and tribulations.

A third minute penalty from scrum half Julien Dupuy certainly helped to ease French anxieties in front of a hostile Dunedin crowd and when fly half François Trinh-Duc burst through two tacklers for the first try after 18 minutes, there was a growing sense that Les Bleus were indeed capable of beating New Zealand.

Hooker William Servat added a second score before half-time to put his side firmly in the driving seat and although the All Blacks hauled themselves level at 17–17 in the 57th minute, Médard provided the coup de grace with a long-range interception try with 10 minutes on the clock and France had their first win in New Zealand since they triumphed in Auckland in 1994.

"It was very tough," admitted captain Dusautoir. "We were very nervous before the match but we gave our all and won. We are very proud. Our defence was good but we also scored three tries, which is very important against the All Blacks. We are going to enjoy this victory and prepare again for next week."

The second Test in Wellington was reduced to little more than a lottery by the blustery and rain-soaked conditions and France ultimately paid the price for their profligacy with the boot as Dupuy missed two penalties and Damien Traille a drop goal. New Zealand also suffered in the kicking department but Ma'a Nonu's try provided the platform for a 14–10 win and French hopes of a series victory were dashed.

There was, however, some consolation for the tourists even in defeat. Their five-point margin of victory in Dunedin against the four-point loss in Wellington meant that they claimed the Dave Gallaher Cup for the first time since its inception in 2000.

The French ended their season in Sydney against Australia and it was a tired-looking team that took to the field against the Wallabies. Matt Giteau was the star turn for the Australians, scoring all 22 points for the home side and France could only muster a penalty apiece from Lionel Beauxis and Dimitri Yachvili in defeat.

Domestically, Perpignan ended more than half a century of patient waiting to be crowned French club champions by beating Clermont Auvergne in the Top 14 final at the Stade de France and in the process condemned Les Jaunards to a third consecutive and heartbreaking defeat in the battle for the Bouclier de Brennus.

The Catalans triumphed 22–13 in Paris thanks largely to centre David Marty's second half try and the prolific boot of full-back Jerome Porical to be crowned champions for the first time since 1955 when they beat Lourdes in Bordeaux. It was the seventh league title in the club's history and revenge for their semi-final defeat at the hands of Vern Cotter's side the previous season.

For the 23-year-old Porical, victory was particularly sweet as he maintained a proud family tradition. His father had been part of the Perpignan side beaten in the final in 1977 by Béziers while his grandfather had played in the team that had emerged victorious against Biarritz back in 1938.

In stark contrast, defeat in the 108th Championship final to be staged was a body blow for Clermont. Beaten 23–18 by Stade Français in 2007 and 26–20 Toulouse 12 months later, the result meant Les Jaunards had appeared in 10 finals and lost them all.

The French domestic season began in late August and of the big four sides who once again monopolised the semi-final places for a second successive season, it was Stade Français who made the strongest start to their campaign with seven wins on the bounce.

Coached by Australian Ewan McKenzie, the Parisians dispatched Dax and Mont-de-Marsan in their two opening fixtures before travelling to the Stade Aimé Giral in early September to face Perpignan.

The Catalans were unbeaten at home since April 2007 and had begun their own season impressively with wins over Brive and Bourgoin but were brought abruptly down to earth with tries in each half for Dave Vainqueur and wing Julien Arias for the visitors. Full back Lionel Beauxis added two conversions and three penalties and although Christophe Manas touched down seven minutes from time for Perpignan, it was too little too late and Stade were 26–11 victors.

Toulouse struggled in the early months. Beaten 16–11 at Montpellier on the first day of the season, they lost to Clermont in their fourth match and by the end of October they were in dire need of a morale-boosting victory.

The opportunity presented itself in the shape of a daunting trip to the Stade de France and a clash with McKenzie's unbeaten side, but Toulouse stunned the 80,000 fans in the ground with a superb display that made a mockery of the form book and ended in a shock 26–13 victory, and it turned out to be a season-defining triumph.

The victory over Stade was the spark for a formidable seven-match winning streak and as the competition entered the New Year, it was Toulouse and Perpignan who were the form teams.

The results left the two clubs level on 92 points. Despite recording an inferior points difference, as well as winning one less game, Perpignan were awarded top spot courtesy of an idiosyncratic Top 14 rule that states that in such circumstances, the winner of the last meeting between the two sides finishes higher. That was the Catalans, who beat Toulouse 32–8 in early March.

The first play-off semi-final saw Toulouse and Clermont cross swords in the Stade Jacques Chaban-Delmas in Bordeaux in a repeat of the 2008 final, but this time it was Clermont who emerged victorious after a 19–9 triumph.

A day later, Perpignan tackled Stade in the Stade de Gerland in Lyon and it was to be an epic tussle that could have gone either way, Perpignan relieved to cling on for a 25–21 win.

The final at the Stade de France was an emotional one for all involved, the difference being full-back Porical, who was at the heart of the Perpignan cause.

Clermont had scored the first try of the match after just 10 minutes through Fijian wing Napolioni Nalaga but they could not find a way through the Catalan defence for the remaining 70 minutes and duly completed an unwanted hat-trick of final disappointments.

"It is a dream, a unique moment in a lifetime," Porical said after the match. "Every player dreams of this. I am only 23 and I am a champion. I can hardly believe it. This is fantastic, the best day of my life."

FRANCE INTERNATIONAL STATISTICS

MATCH RECORDS UP TO 30TH SEPTEMBER 2009

MOST CONSECUTIVE TEST WINS

10	1931 E,G, 1932 G, 1933 G, 1934 G, 1935 G, 1936 G1,2, 1937 G,It
8	1998 E, S, I, W, Arg 1,2, Fj, Arg 3
8	2001 SA 3 A, Fj 2002 It, W, E, S,I
8	2004 I, It, W, S, E, US, C, A

MOST CONSECUTIVE TESTS WITHOUT DEFEAT

Matches	Wins	Draws	Period
10	10	0	1931 to 1938
10	8	2	1958 to 1959
10	9	1	1986 to 1987

MOST POINTS IN A MATCH

BY THE TEAM

Pts.	Opponents	Venue	Year
87	Namibia	Toulouse	2007
77	Fiji	Saint Etienne	2001
70	Zimbabwe	Auckland	1987
67	Romania	Bucharest	2000
64	Romania	Aurillac	1996
64	Georgia	Marseilles	2007
62	Romania	Castres	1999
62	Romania	Bucharest	2006
61	Fiji	Brisbane	2003
60	Italy	Toulon	1967
59	Romania	Paris	1924
56	Romania	Lens	2003
56	Italy	Rome	2005

BY A PLAYER

Pts.	Player	Opponents	Venue	Year
30	D Camberabero	Zimbabwe	Auckland	1987
28	C Lamaison	New Zealand	Twickenham	1999
28	F Michalak	Scotland	Sydney	2003
27	G Camberabero	Italy	Toulon	1967
27	C Lamaison	New Zealand	Marseilles	2000
27	G Merceron	South Africa	Johannesburg	2001
27	J-B Elissalde	Namibia	Toulouse	2007
26	T Lacroix	Ireland	Durban	1995
26	F Michalak	Fiji	Brisbane	2003
25	J-P Romeu	United States	Chicago	1976
25	P Berot	Romania	Agen	1987
25	T Lacroix	Tonga	Pretoria	1995

MOST TRIES IN A MATCH

BY THE TEAM

Tries	Opponents	Venue	Year
13	Romania	Paris	1924
13	Zimbabwe	Auckland	1987
13	Namibia	Toulouse	2007
12	Fiji	Saint Etienne	2001
11	Italy	Toulon	1967
10	Romania	Aurillac	1996
10	Romania	Bucharest	2000

BY A PLAYER

Tries	Player	Opponents	Venue	Year
4	A Jauréguy	Romania	Paris	1924
4	M Celhay	Italy	Paris	1937

MOST CONVERSIONS IN A MATCH

BY THE TEAM

Cons	Opponents	Venue	Year
11	Namibia	Toulouse	2007
9	Italy	Toulon	1967
9	Zimbabwe	Auckland	1987
8	Romania	Wellington	1987
8	Romania	Lens	2003

BY A PLAYER

Cons	Player	Opponents	Venue	Year
11	J–B Elissalde	Namibia	Toulouse	2007
9	G Camberabero	Italy	Toulon	1967
9	D Camberabero	Zimbabwe	Auckland	1987
8	G Laporte	Romania	Wellington	1987

MOST PENALTIES IN A MATCH
BY THE TEAM

Pens	Opponents	Venue	Year
8	Ireland	Durban	1995
7	Wales	Paris	2001
7	Italy	Paris	2002
6	Argentina	Buenos Aires	1977
6	Scotland	Paris	1997
6	Italy	Auch	1997
6	Ireland	Paris	2000
6	South Africa	Johannesburg	2001
6	Argentina	Buenos Aires	2003
6	Fiji	Brisbane	2003
6	England	Twickenham	2005
6	Wales	Paris	2007
6	England	Twickenham	2007

BY A PLAYER

Pens	Player	Opponents	Venue	Year
8	T Lacroix	Ireland	Durban	1995
7	G Merceron	Italy	Paris	2002
6	J-M Aguirre	Argentina	Buenos Aires	1977
6	C Lamaison	Scotland	Paris	1997
6	C Lamaison	Italy	Auch	1997
6	G Merceron	Ireland	Paris	2000
6	G Merceron	South Africa	Johannesburg	2001
6	F Michalak	Fiji	Brisbane	2003
6	D Yachvili	England	Twickenham	2005

MOST DROPPED GOALS IN A MATCH
BY THE TEAM

Drops	Opponents	Venue	Year
3	Ireland	Paris	1960
3	England	Twickenham	1985
3	New Zealand	Christchurch	1986
3	Australia	Sydney	1990
3	Scotland	Paris	1991
3	New Zealand	Christchurch	1994

BY A PLAYER

Drops	Player	Opponents	Venue	Year
3	P Albaladejo	Ireland	Paris	1960
3	J-P Lescarboura	England	Twickenham	1985
3	J-P Lescarboura	New Zealand	Christchurch	1986
3	D Camberabero	Australia	Sydney	1990

CAREER RECORDS

MOST CAPPED PLAYERS

Caps	Player	Career Span
118	F Pelous	1995 to 2007
111	P Sella	1982 to 1995
98	R Ibañez	1996 to 2007
93	S Blanco	1980 to 1991
89	O Magne	1997 to 2007
78	A Benazzi	1990 to 2001
76	S Marconnet	1998 to 2009
71	J-L Sadourny	1991 to 2001
71	O Brouzet	1994 to 2003
71	C Califano	1994 to 2007
71	D Traille	2001 to 2009
69	R Bertranne	1971 to 1981
69	P Saint-André	1990 to 1997
69	P de Villiers	1999 to 2007
67	C Dominici	1998 to 2007
64	F Galthié	1991 to 2003
63	M Crauste	1957 to 1966
63	B Dauga	1964 to 1972
63	S Betsen	1997 to 2007

MOST CONSECUTIVE TESTS

Tests	Player	Career Span
46	R Bertranne	1973 to 1979
45	P Sella	1982 to 1987
44	M Crauste	1960 to 1966
35	B Dauga	1964 to 1968

MOST TESTS AS CAPTAIN

Tests	Captain	Span
42	F Pelous	1997 to 2006
41	R Ibanez	1998 to 2007
34	J-P Rives	1978 to 1984
34	P Saint-André	1994 to 1997
25	D Dubroca	1986 to 1988
25	F Galthié	1999 to 2003
24	G Basquet	1948 to 1952
22	M Crauste	1961 to 1966

MOST POINTS IN TESTS

Pts	Player	Tests	Career
380	C Lamaison	37	1996 to 2001
367	T Lacroix	43	1989 to 1997
354	D Camberabero	36	1982 to 1993
267	G Merceron	32	1999 to 2003
265	J-P Romeu	34	1972 to 1977
264	D Yachvili	41	2002 to 2009
247	T Castaignède	54	1995 to 2007
246	F Michalak	51	2001 to 2009
233	S Blanco	93	1980 to 1991
214	J-B Elissalde	35	2000 to 2008
200	J-P Lescarboura	28	1982 to 1990

MOST TRIES IN TESTS

Tries	Player	Tests	Career
38	S Blanco	93	1980 to 1991
33*	P Saint-André	69	1990 to 1997
30	P Sella	111	1982 to 1995
26	E Ntamack	46	1994 to 2000
26	P Bernat Salles	41	1992 to 2001
25	C Dominici	67	1998 to 2007
23	C Darrouy	40	1957 to 1967

*Saint-Andre's total includes a penalty try against Romania in 1992

MOST CONVERSIONS IN TESTS

Cons	Player	Tests	Career
59	C Lamaison	37	1996 to 2001
48	D Camberabero	36	1982 to 1993
45	M Vannier	43	1953 to 1961
42	T Castaignède	54	1995 to 2007
40	J–B Elissalde	35	2000 to 2008
37	D Yachvili	41	2002 to 2009
36	R Dourthe	31	1995 to 2001
36	G Merceron	32	1999 to 2003
36	F Michalak	51	2001 to 2009
32	T Lacroix	43	1989 to 1997
29	P Villepreux	34	1967 to 1972

MOST PENALTY GOALS IN TESTS

Pens	Player	Tests	Career
89	T Lacroix	43	1989 to 1997
78	C Lamaison	37	1996 to 2001
59	D Camberabero	36	1982 to 1993
58	D Yachvili	41	2002 to 2009
57	G Merceron	32	1999 to 2003
56	J–P Romeu	34	1972 to 1977
38	F Michalak	51	2001 to 2009
38	J–B Elissalde	35	2000 to 2008
33	P Villepreux	34	1967 to 1972
33	P Bérot	19	1986 to 1989

MOST DROPPED GOALS IN TESTS

Drops	Player	Tests	Career
15	J–P Lescarboura	28	1982 to 1990
12	P Albaladejo	30	1954 to 1964
11	G Camberabero	14	1961 to 1968
11	D Camberabero	36	1982 to 1993
9	J–P Romeu	34	1972 to 1977

FRANCE

INTERNATIONAL CHAMPIONSHIP RECORDS

RECORD	DETAIL		SET
Most points in season	156	in five matches	2002
Most tries in season	18	in four matches	1998
	18	in five matches	2006
Highest Score	56	56–13 v Italy	2005
Biggest win	51	51–0 v Wales	1998
Highest score conceded	49	14–49 v Wales	1910
Biggest defeat	37	0–37 v England	1911
Most appearances	50	P Sella	1983–1995
Most points in matches	180	D Yachvili	2003–2008
Most points in season	80	G Merceron	2002
Most points in match	24	S Viars	v Ireland, 1992
	24	C Lamaison	v Scotland, 1997
	24	J-B Elissalde	v Wales, 2004
Most tries in matches	14	S Blanco	1981–1991
	14	P Sella	1983–1995
Most tries in season	5	P Estève	1983
	5	E Bonneval	1987
	5	E Ntamack	1999
	5	P Bernat Salles	2001
	5	V Clerc	2008
Most tries in match	3	M Crauste	v England, 1962
	3	C Darrouy	v Ireland, 1963
	3	E Bonneval	v Scotland, 1987
	3	D Venditti	v Ireland, 1997
	3	E Ntamack	v Wales, 1999
	3	V Clerc	v Ireland, 2008
Most cons in matches	25	D Yachvili	2003–2008
Most cons in season	9	C Lamaison	1998
	9	G Merceron	2002
	9	D Yachvili	2003
Most cons in match	6	D Yachvili	v Italy, 2003
Most pens in matches	40	D Yachvili	2003–2008
Most pens in season	18	G Merceron	2002
Most pens in match	7	G Merceron	v Italy, 2002
Most drops in matches	9	J-P Lescarboura	1982–1988
Most drops in season	5	G Camberabero	1967
Most drops in match	3	P Albaladejo	v Ireland, 1960
	3	J-P Lescarboura	v England, 1985

RECORD	HOLDER	DETAIL
Longest Test Career	F Haget	1974 to 1987
	C Califano	1994 to 2007
Youngest Test Cap	C Dourthe	18 yrs 7 days in 1966
Oldest Test Cap	A Roques	37 yrs 329 days in 1963

CAREER RECORDS OF FRANCE INTERNATIONAL PLAYERS
(UP TO 30TH SEPTEMBER 2009)

PLAYER BACKS	DEBUT	CAPS	T	C	P	D	PTS
J Arias	2009 v A	1	0	0	0	0	0
B Baby	2005 v I	9	1	0	1	0	8
M Bastareaud	2009 v W	4	0	0	0	0	0
L Beauxis	2007 v It	15	1	18	21	2	110
V Clerc	2002 v SA	36	20	0	0	0	100
J Dupuy	2009 v NZ	3	0	4	2	0	14
J-B Elissalde	2000 v S	35	4	40	38	0	214
A Floch	2008 v E	3	1	0	0	0	5
M Forest	2007 v NZ	2	0	0	0	0	0
F Fritz	2005 v SA	18	3	0	0	2	21
C Heymans	2000 v It	52	15	0	0	0	75
D Janin	2008 v A	2	0	0	0	0	0
Y Jauzion	2001 v SA	61	17	0	0	1	88
J Malzieu	2008 v S	11	3	0	0	0	15
M Médard	2008 v Arg	11	5	0	0	1	28
M Mermoz	2008 v A	4	0	0	0	0	0
F Michalak	2001 v SA	51	9	36	38	5	246
A Palisson	2008 v A	5	1	0	0	0	5
M Parra	2008 v S	9	0	4	7	0	29
C Poitrenaud	2001 v SA	34	6	0	0	0	30
A Rougerie	2001 v SA	55	21	0	0	0	105
D Skrela	2001 v NZ	18	0	13	27	1	110
B Thiéry	2007 v NZ	4	0	0	0	0	0
S Tillous-Borde	2008 v A	8	1	0	0	0	5
J Tomas	2008 v It	2	0	0	0	0	0
D Traille	2001 v SA	71	12	8	12	1	115
F Trinh-Duc	2008 v S	12	3	1	1	0	20
D Yachvili	2002 v C	41	2	37	58	2	264

FRANCE

FORWARDS	DEBUT	CAPS	T	C	P	D	PTS
F Barcella	2008 v It	9	0	0	0	0	0
J Bonnaire	2004 v S	44	6	0	0	0	30
R Boyoud	2008 v A	3	0	0	0	0	0
S Chabal	2000 v S	49	6	0	0	0	30
D Chouly	2007 v NZ	4	0	0	0	0	0
P Correia	2008 v A	1	0	0	0	0	0
I Diarra	2008 v It	1	0	0	0	0	0
T Domingo	2009 v W	4	1	0	0	0	5
T Dusautoir	2006 v R	25	4	0	0	0	20
L Faure	2008 v S	8	0	0	0	0	0
G Guirado	2008 v It	2	0	0	0	0	0
I Harinordoquy	2002 v W	56	11	0	0	0	55
B Kayser	2008 v A	9	0	0	0	0	0
B Lecouls	2008 v A	6	0	0	0	0	0
S Marconnet	1998 v Arg	76	3	0	0	0	15
R Martin	2002 v E	23	3	0	0	0	15
N Mas	2003 v NZ	27	0	0	0	0	0
A Mela	2008 v S	4	0	0	0	0	0
R Millo-Chluski	2005 v SA	10	0	0	0	0	0
F Montanella	2007 v NZ	1	0	0	0	0	0
L Nallet	2000 v R	47	6	0	0	0	30
F Ouedraogo	2007 v NZ	17	1	0	0	0	5
P Papé	2004 v I	22	2	0	0	0	10
L Picamoles	2008 v I	14	1	0	0	0	5
J Puricelli	2009 v NZ	2	0	0	0	0	0
W Servat	2004 v I	23	1	0	0	0	5
O Sourgens	2007 v NZ	1	0	0	0	0	0
D Szarzewski	2004 v C	38	5	0	0	0	25
J Thion	2003 v Arg	47	1	0	0	0	5

Note: Years given for International Championship matches are for second half of season; eg 1972 means season 1971–72. Years for all other matches refer to the actual year of the match. Entries in square brackets denote matches played in RWC Finals.

Abadie, A (Pau) 1964 I
Abadie, A (Graulhet) 1965 R, 1967 SA 1,3,4, NZ, 1968 S, I
Abadie, L (Tarbes) 1963 R
Accoceberry, G (Bègles) 1994 NZ 1,2, C 2, 1995 W, E, S, I, R 1, [Iv, S], It, 1996 I, W 1, R, Arg 1, W 2(R), SA 2, 1997 S, It 1
Aguerre, R (Biarritz O) 1979 S
Aguilar, D (Pau) 1937 G
Aguirre, J-M (Bagnères) 1971 A 2, 1972 S, 1973 W, I, J, R, 1974 I, W, Arg 2, R, SA 1, 1976 W (R), E, US, A 2, R, 1977 W, E, S, I, Arg 1,2, NZ 1,2, R, 1978 E, S, I, W, R, 1979 I, W, E, S, NZ 1,2, R, 1980 W, I
Ainciart, E (Bayonne) 1933 G, 1934 G, 1935 G, 1937 G, It, 1938 G 1
Albaladéjo, P (Dax) 1954 E, It, 1960 W, I, It, R, 1961 S, SA, E, W, I, NZ 1,2, A, 1962 S, E, W, I, 1963 S, I, E, W, It, 1964 S, NZ, W, It, I, SA, Fj
Albouy, A (Castres) 2002 It (R)
Alvarez, A-J (Tyrosse) 1945 B2, 1946 B, I, K, W, 1947 S, I, W, E, 1948 I, A, S, W, E, 1949 I, E, W, 1951 S, E, W
Amand, H (SF) 1906 NZ
Ambert, A (Toulouse) 1930 S, I, E, G, W
Amestoy, J-B (Mont-de-Marsan) 1964 NZ, E
André, G (RCF) 1913 SA, E, W, I, 1914 I, W, E
Andrieu, M (Nîmes) 1986 Arg 2, NZ 1, R 2, NZ 2, 1987 [R, Z], R, 1988 E, S, I, W, Arg 1,2,3,4, R, 1989 I, W, E, S, NZ 2, B, A 2, 1990 W, E, I (R)
Anduran, J (SCUF) 1910 W
Aqua, J-L (Toulon) 1999 R, Tg, NZ 1(R)
Araou, R (Narbonne) 1924 R
Arcalis, R (Brive) 1950 S, I, 1951 I, E, W
Arias, J (SF) 2009 A(R)
Arino, M (Agen) 1962 R
Aristouy, P (Pau) 1948 S, 1949 Arg 2, 1950 S, I, E, W
Arlettaz, P (Perpignan) 1995 R 2
Armary, L (Lourdes) 1987 [R], R, 1988 S, I, W, Arg 3,4, R, 1989 W, S, A 1,2, 1990 W, E, S, I, A 1,2,3, NZ 1, 1991 W 2, 1992 S, I, R, Arg 1,2, SA 1,2, Arg, 1993 E, S, I, W, SA 1,2, R 2, A 1,2, 1994 I, W, NZ 1(t),2(t), 1995 I, R 1 [Tg, I, SA]
Arnal, J-M (RCF) 1914 I, W
Arnaudet, M (Lourdes) 1964 I, 1967 It, W
Arotca, R (Bayonne) 1938 R
Arrieta, J (SF) 1953 E, W
Arthapignet, P (see Harislur-Arthapignet)
Artiguste, E (Castres) 1999 WS
Astre, R (Béziers) 1971 R, 1972 I 1, 1973 E (R), 1975 E, S, I, SA 1,2, Arg 2, 1976 A 2, R
Attoub, D (Castres) 2006 R
Aucagne, D (Pau) 1997 W (R), S, It 1, R 1(R), A 1, R 2(R), SA 2(R), 1998 S (R), W (R), Arg 2(R), Fj (R), Arg 3, A, 1999 W 1(R), S (R)
Audebert, A (Montferrand) 2000 R, 2002 W (R)
Aué, J-M (Castres) 1998 W (R)
Augé, J (Dax) 1929 S, W
Augras-Fabre, L (Agen) 1931 I, S, W
August, B (Biarritz) 2007 W1(R)
Auradou, D (SF) 1999 E (R), S (R), WS (R), Tg, NZ 1, W 2(R), [Arg (R)], 2000 A (R), NZ 1,2, 2001 S, I, It, W, E (R), SA 1,2, NZ (R), SA 3, A, Fj, 2002 It, E, I (R), C (R), 2003 S (R), It (R), W (R), Arg, 1,2, NZ 2(R), R (R), E 2(R),3, [J(R),US,NZ] , 2004 I(R), It(R),S(R),E(R)

Averous, J-L (La Voulte) 1975 S, I, SA 1,2, 1976 I, W, E, US, A 1,2, R, 1977 W, E, S, I, Arg 1, R, 1978 E, S, I, 1979 NZ 1,2, 1980 E, S, 1981 A 2
Avril, D (Biarritz) 2005 A1
Azam, O (Montferrand, Gloucester) 1995 R 2, Arg (R), 2000 A (R), NZ 2(R), 2001 SA 2(R), NZ, 2002 E (R), I (R), Arg (R), A 1
Azarete, J-L (Dax, St Jean-de-Luz) 1969 W, R, 1970 S, I, W, R, 1971 S, I, E, SA 1,2, A 1, 1972 E, W, I 2, A 1, R, 1973 NZ, W, I, R, 1974 I, R, SA 1,2, 1975 W
Baby, B (Toulouse, Clermont-Auvergne) 2005 I,SA2(R),A1, 2008 Arg,PI,A3, 2009 I(R),S,W
Bacqué, N (Pau) 1997 R 2
Bader, E (Primevères) 1926 M, 1927 I, S
Badin, C (Chalon) 1973 W, I, 1975 Arg 1
Baillette, M (Perpignan) 1925 I, NZ, S, 1926 W, M, 1927 I, W, G 2, 1929 G, 1930 S, I, E, G, 1931 I, S, E, 1932 G
Baladie, G (Agen) 1945 B 1,2, W, 1946 B, I, K
Ballarin, J (Tarbes) 1924 E, 1925 NZ, S
Baquey, J (Toulouse) 1921 I
Barbazanges, A (Roanne) 1932 G, 1933 G
Barcella, F (Auch, Biarritz) 2008 It,W,Arg, 2009 S,W,It,NZ1,2,A
Barrau, M (Beaumont, Toulouse) 1971 S, E, W, 1972 E, W, A 1,2, 1973 S, NZ, E, J, R, 1974 I, S
Barrau, M (Agen) 2004 US,C(R),NZ(R)
Barrère, P (Toulon) 1929 G, 1931 W
Barrière, P (Béziers) 1960 R
Barthe, F (SBUC) 1925 W, E
Barthe, J (Lourdes) 1954 Arg 1,2, 1955 S, 1956 I, W, It, E, Cz, 1957 S, I, E, W, R 1,2, 1958 S, E, A, W, It, I, SA 1,2, 1959 S, E, It, W
Basauri, R (Albi) 1954 Arg 1
Bascou, P (Bayonne) 1914 E
Basquet, G (Agen) 1945 W, 1946 B, I, K, W, 1947 S, I, W, E, 1948 I, A, S, W, E, 1949 S, I, E, W, Arg 1, 1950 S, I, E, W, 1951 S, I, E, W, 1952 S, I, SA, W, E, It
Bastareaud, M (SF) 2009 W,E,It(R),NZ1
Bastiat, J-P (Dax) 1969 R, 1970 S, I, W, 1971 S, I, SA 2, 1972 S, A 1, 1973 E, 1974 Arg 1,2, SA 2, 1975 W, Arg 1,2, R, 1976 S, I, W, E, A 2, R, 1977 W, E, S, I, 1978 S, I, W
Baudry, N (Montferrand) 1949 S, I, W, Arg 1,2
Baulon, R (Vienne, Bayonne) 1954 S, NZ, W, E, It, 1955 I, E, W, It, 1956 S, I, W, It, E, Cz, 1957 S, I, W
Baux, J-P (Lannemezan) 1968 NZ 1,2, SA 1,2
Bavozet, J (Lyon) 1911 S, E, W
Bayard, J (Toulouse) 1923 S, W, E, 1924 W, R, US
Bayardon, J (Chalon) 1964 S, NZ, E
Beaurin-Gressier, C (SF) 1907 E, 1908 E
Beauxis, L (SF) 2007 It(R), I(R), W1(R), E1(R), S, W2, [Nm(R), I(R), Gg, NZ, E, Arg 2(R)], 2009 I, S, A
Bégu, J (Dax) 1982 Arg 2(R), 1984 E, S
Béguerie, C (Agen) 1979 NZ 1
Béguet, L (RCF) 1922 I, 1923 S, W, E, I, 1924 S, I, E, R, US
Béhotéguy, A (Bayonne, Cognac) 1923 E, 1924 S, I, E, W, R, US, 1926 E, 1927 E, G 1,2, 1928 A, I, E, G, W, 1929 S, W, E
Béhotéguy, H (RCF, Cognac) 1923 W, 1928 A, I, E, G, W
Bélascain, C (Bayonne) 1977 R, 1978 E, S, I, W, R, 1979 I, W, E, S, 1982 W, E, S, I, 1983 E, S, I, W
Belletante, G (Nantes) 1951 I, E, W
Belot, F (Toulouse) 2000 I (R)

Arg, NZ 2(R), A (R)], 2000 W, E, S, I, It, A, NZ 1(R),2(R), 2001 SA 1,2, NZ, 2002 W, E, S, I, Arg, A 1(R),2, SA, NZ, C, 2003 E 1, S, I, It, W, E 3, [Fj(R),J,S(R),US,I(R)]

Bru, Y (Toulouse) 2001 A (R), Fj (R), 2002 It, 2003 Arg 2, NZ, R, E 2, 3(R), [J,S(R), US, I(t&R), NZ], 2004 I(R), It(R), W(R), S(R), E(R)

Brugnaut, J (Dax) 2008 S,I(R)

Brun, G (Vienne) 1950 E, W, 1951 S, E, W, 1952 S, I, SA, W, E, It, 1953 E, W, It

Bruneau, M (SBUC) 1910 W, E, 1913 SA, E

Brunet, Y (Perpignan) 1975 SA 1, 1977 Arg 1

Bruno, S (Béziers, Sale) 2002 W (R), 2004 A(R), NZ(t&R), 2005 S(R),E,W,I,It,SA1, 2(R), A1(R), 2(R), C, SA3(R), 2006 S(R), I(R), 2007 I(R), E1(R), NZ1, 2, E3(R), W2(R), [Gg,Arg 2(t&R)], 2008 A1,2

Brusque, N (Pau, Biarritz) 1997 R 2(R), 2002 W, E, S, I, Arg, A 2, SA, NZ, C, 2003 E 2, [Fj,S,I,E,NZ(R)], 2004 I,It,W,S,E,A,Arg, 2005 SA1(R),2,A1, 2006 S

Buchet, E (Nice) 1980 R, 1982 E, R (R), Arg 1,2

Buisson, H (see Empereur-Buisson)

Buonomo, Y (Béziers) 1971 A 2, R, 1972 I 1

Burgun, M (RCF) 1909 I, 1910 W, S, I, 1911 S, E, 1912 I, S, 1913 S, E, 1914 E

Bustaffa, D (Carcassonne) 1977 Arg 1,2, NZ 1,2, 1978 W, R, 1980 W, E, S, SA, R

Buzy, C-E (Lourdes) 1946 K, W, 1947 S, I, W, E, 1948 I, A, S, W, E, 1949 S, I, E, W, Arg 1,2

Caballero, Y (Montauban) 2008 A2(R)

Cabanier, J-M (Montauban) 1963 R, 1964 S, Fj, 1965 S, I, W, It, R, 1966 S, I, E, W, It, R, 1967 S, A, E, W, I, SA 1,3, NZ, R, 1968 S, I

Cabannes, L (RCF, Harlequins) 1990 NZ 2(R), 1991 S, I, W, E, US 2, W 2, [R, Fj, C, E], 1992 W, E, S, I, R, Arg 2, SA 1,2, 1993 E, S, I, W R 1, SA 1,2, 1994 E, S, C 1, NZ 1,2, 1995 W, E, S, R 1, [Tg (R), Iv, S, I, SA, E], 1996 E, S, I, W 1, 1997 It 2, Arg, SA 1,2

Cabrol, H (Béziers) 1972 A 1(R),2, 1973 J, 1974 SA 2

Cadenat, J (SCUF) 1910 S, E, 1911 W, I, 1912 W, E, 1913 I

Cadieu, J-M (Toulouse) 1991 R, US 1, [R, Fj, C, E], 1992 W, I, R, Arg 1,2, SA 1

Cahuc, F (St Girons) 1922 S

Califano, C (Toulouse, Saracens, Gloucester) 1994 NZ 1,2, C 2, 1995 W, E, S, I, [Iv, S, I, SA, E], It, Arg, NZ 1,2, 1996 E, S, I, W 1, R, Arg 1,2, SA 1,2, 1997 I, W, E, A 1,2, It 2, R 2(R), Arg, SA 1,2, 1998 E, S, I, W, 1999 I, W 1, E (R), S, WS, Tg (R), NZ 1, W 2, [C, Nm, Fj], 2000 W, E, S, I, It, R, A, NZ 1,2(R), 2001 S (R), I (R), It, W, SA 1(R),2(R), NZ, 2003 E 1, S (R), I (R), 2007 NZ1,2

Cals, R (RCF) 1938 G 1

Calvo, G (Lourdes) 1961 NZ 1,3

Camberabero, D (La Voulte, Béziers) 1982 R, Arg 1,2, 1983 E, W, 1987 [R (R), Z, Fj (R), A, NZ], 1988 I, 1989 B, A 1, 1990 W, S, I, R, A 1,2,3, NZ 1,2, 1991 S, I, W 1, E, R, US 1,2, W 2, [R, Fj, C], 1993 E, S, I

Camberabero, G (La Voulte) 1961 NZ 3, 1962 R, 1964 R, 1967 A, E, It, W, I, SA 1,3,4, 1968 S, E, W

Camberabero, L (La Voulte) 1964 R, 1965 S, I, 1966 E, W, 1967 A, E, It, W, I, 1968 S, E, W

Cambré, T (Oloron) 1920 E, W, I, US

Camel, A (Toulouse) 1928 S, A, I, E, G, W, 1929 W, E, G, 1930 S, I, E, G, W, 1935 G

Camel, M (Toulouse) 1929 S, W, E

Camicas, F (Tarbes) 1927 G 2, 1928 S, I, E, G, W, 1929 I, S, W, E

Camo, E (Villeneuve) 1931 I, S, W, E, G, 1932 G

Campaès, A (Lourdes) 1965 W, 1967 NZ, 1968 S, I, E, W, Cz, NZ 1,2, A, 1969 S, W, 1972 R, 1973 NZ

Campan, O (Agen) 1993 SA 1(R),2(R), R 2(R), 1996 I, W 1, R

Candelon, J (Narbonne) 2005 SA1,A1(R)

Cantoni, J (Béziers) 1970 W, R, 1971 S, I, E, W, SA 1,2, R 1972 S, I 1, 1973 S, NZ, W, I, 1975 W (R)

Capdouze, J (Pau) 1964 SA, Fj, R, 1965 S, I, E

Capendeguy, J-M (Bègles) 1967 NZ, R

Capitani, P (Toulon) 1954 Arg 1,2

Capmau, J-L (Toulouse) 1914 E

Carabignac, G (Agen) 1951 S, I, 1952 SA, W, E, 1953 S, I

Carbonne, J (Perpignan) 1927 W

Carbonneau, P (Toulouse, Brive, Pau) 1995 R 2, Arg, NZ 1,2,

1996 E, S, R (R), Arg 2, W 2, SA 1, 1997 I (R), W, E, S (R), R 1(R), A 1,2, 1998 E, S, I, W, Arg 1,2, Fj, Arg 3, A, 1999 I, W 1, E, S, 2000 NZ 2(R), 2001 I

Carminati, A (Béziers, Brive) 1986 R 2, NZ 2, 1987 [R, Z], 1988 I, W, Arg 1,2, 1989 I, W, S, NZ 1(R),2, A 2, 1990 S, 1995 It, R 2, Arg, NZ 1,2

Caron, L (Lyon O, Castres) 1947 E, 1948 I, A, W, E, 1949 S, I, E, W, Arg 1

Carpentier, M (Lourdes) 1980 E, SA, R, 1981 S, I, A 1, 1982 E, S

Carrère, C (Toulon) 1966 R, 1967 S, A, E, W, I, SA 1,3,4, NZ, R, 1968 S, I, E, W, Cz, NZ 3, A, R, 1969 S, I, 1970 S, I, W, E, 1971 E, W

Carrère, J (Vichy, Toulon) 1956 S, 1957 W, R 2, 1958 S, SA 1,2, 1959 I

Carrère, R (Mont-de-Marsan) 1953 E, It

Casadei, D (Brive) 1997 S, R 1, SA 2(R)

Casaux, L (Tarbes) 1959 I, It, 1962 S

Cassagne, P (Pau) 1957 It

Cassayet-Armagnac, A (Tarbes, Narbonne) 1920 S, E, W, US, 1921 W, E, I, 1922 S, E, W, 1923 S, W, E, I, 1924 S, E, W, R, 1925 I, NZ, S, W, 1926 S, I, E, W, M, 1927 I, S, W

Cassiède, M (Dax) 1961 NZ 3, A, R

Castaignède, S (Mont-de-Marsan) 1999 W 2, [C (R), Nm (R), Fj, Arg (R), NZ 2(R), A (R)]

Castaignède, T (Toulouse, Castres, Saracens) 1995 R 2, Arg, NZ 1,2, 1996 E, S, I, W, Arg 1,2, 1997 I, A 1,2, It 2, 1998 E, S, I, W, Arg 1,2, Fj, 1999 I, W 1, E, S, R, WS, Tg (R), NZ 1, W 2, [C], 2000 W, E, S, H, Arg, NZ, C 2003 E 1(R), S (R), It, W, Arg 1, 2005 A2(R),C,Tg,SA3, 2006 It,E,W,R,SA(R), 2007 NZ1,2

Castel, R (Toulouse, Béziers) 1996 I, W 1, W 2, SA 1(R),2, 1997 I (R), W, E (R), S (R), A 1(R), 1998 Arg 3(R), A (R), 1999 W 1(R), E, S

Castets, J (Toulon) 1923 W, E, I

Caujolle, J (Tarbes) 1909 E, 1913 SA, E, 1914 W, E

Caunègre, R (SB) 1938 R, G 2

Caussade, A (Lourdes) 1978 R, 1979 I, W, E, NZ 1,2, R, 1980 W, E, S, 1981 S (R), I

Caussarieu, P (Pau) 1929 I

Cayrefourcq, E (Tarbes) 1921 E

Cazalbou, J (Toulouse) 1997 It 2(R), R 2, Arg, SA 2(R)

Cazals, P (Mont-de-Marsan) 1961 NZ 1, A, R

Cazenave, A (Pau) 1927 E, G 1, 1928 S, A, G

Cazenave, F (RCF) 1950 E, 1952 S, 1954 I, NZ, W, E

Cécillon, M (Bourgoin) 1988 I, W, Arg 2,3,4, R, 1989 I, E, NZ 1,2, A 1, 1991 S, I, E (R), R, US 1, W 2, [E], 1992 W, E, S, I, R, Arg 1,2, SA 1,2, 1993 E, S, I, W, R 1, SA 1,2, R 2, A 1,2, 1994 I, W, NZ 1(R), 1995 I, R 1, [Tg, S (R), I, SA]

Celaya, M (Biarritz O, SBUC) 1953 E, W, It, 1954 I, E, It, Arg 1,2, 1955 S, I, E, W, It, 1956 S, I, W, It, E, Cz 1957 S, I, E, W, R 2, 1958 S, E, A, W, It, 1959 S, E, W, I, Arg 1,2,3, 1960 S, A, W, I, NZ 1,2,3, A, R

Celhay, R (Bayonne) 1935 G, 1936 G 1, 1937 G, It, 1938 G 1, 1940 B

Cermeno, F (Perpignan) 2000 R

Cessieux, N (Lyon) 1906 NZ

Cester, E (TOEC, Valence) 1966 S, I, E, 1967 W, 1968 S, I, E, W, Cz, NZ 1,3, A, SA 1,2, R, 1969 S, I, E, W, 1970 S, I, W, E, 1971 A 1, 1972 R, 1973 S, NZ, W, I, J, R, 1974 I, W, E, S

Chabal, S (Bourgoin, Sale) 2000 S, 2001 SA 1,2, NZ (R), Fj (R), 2002 Arg (R), A 2, SA (R), NZ (t), C (R), 2003 E 1(R), S (R), I (R), Arg (R),2, [J(R),US,NZ], 2005 S,E,A2(R),Tg, 2007 It,I,E1,NZ1,2,E2(R),W2, [Arg 1(R),Nm,I,NZ(R),E(R),Arg 2(R)], 2008 A1,2,Arg(R),PI(R),A3, 2009 I,S(R),W,E,It,NZ1(R),2

Chaban-Delmas, J (CASG) 1945 B 2

Chabowski, H (Nice, Bourgoin) 1985 Arg 2, 1986 R 2, NZ 2, 1989 B (R)

Chadebech, P (Brive) 1982 R, Arg 1,2, 1986 S, I

Champ, E (Toulon) 1985 Arg 1,2, 1986 I, W, E, R 1, Arg 1,2, A, NZ 1, R 2, NZ 2,3, 1987 W, E, S, I, [S, R, Fj, A, NZ], 1988 E, S, Arg 1,3,4, R, 1989 W, S, A 1,2, 1990 W, E, 1991 R, US 1, [R, Fj, C, E]

Chaban-Delmas, J (CASG) 1945 B 2

Charpentier, G (SF) 1911 E, 1912 W, E

Charton, P (Montferrand) 1940 B

Charvet, D (Toulouse) 1986 W, E, R 1, Arg 1, A, NZ 1,3, 1987

W, E, S, I, [S, R, Z, Fj, A, NZ], R, 1989 E (R), 1990 W, E, 1991 S, I

Chassagne, J (Montferrand) 1938 G 1

Chatau, A (Bayonne) 1913 SA

Chaud, E (Toulon) 1932 G, 1934 G, 1935 G

Chazalet, A (Bourgoin) 1999 Tg

Chenevay, C (Grenoble) 1968 SA 1

Chevallier, B (Montferrand) 1952 S, I, SA, W, E, It, 1953 E, W, It, 1954 S, I, NZ, W, Arg 1, 1955 S, I, E, W, It, 1956 S, I, W, It, E, Cz, 1957 S

Chiberry, J (Chambéry) 1955 It

Chilo, A (RCF) 1920 S, W, 1925 I, NZ

Cholley, G (Castres) 1975 E, S, I, SA 1,2, Arg 1,2, R, 1976 S, I, W, E, A 1,2, R, 1977 W, E, S, I, Arg 1,2, NZ 1,2, R, 1978 E, S, I, W, R, 1979 I, S

Chouly, D (Brive, Perpignan) 2007 NZ1(R),2, 2009 NZ2(R),A(R)

Choy J (Narbonne) 1930 S, I, E, G, W, 1931 I, 1933 G, 1934 G, 1935 G, 1936 G 2

Cigagna, A (Toulouse) 1995 [E]

Cimarosti, J (Castres) 1976 US (R)

Cistacq, J-C (Agen) 2000 R (R)

Clady, A (Lezignan) 1929 G, 1931 I, S, E, G

Clarac, H (St Girons) 1938 G 1

Claudel, R (Lyon) 1932 G, 1934 G

Clauzel, F (Béziers) 1924 E, W, 1925 W

Clavé, J (Agen) 1936 G 2, 1938 R, G 2

Claverie, H (Lourdes) 1954 NZ, W

Cléda, T (Pau) 1998 E (R), S (R), I (R), W (R), Arg 1(R), Fj (R), Arg 3(R), 1999 I (R), S

Clément, G (RCF) 1931 W

Clément, J (RCF) 1921 S, W, E, 1922 S, E, W, I, 1923 S, W, I

Clemente, M (Oloron) 1978 R, 1980 S, I

Clerc, V (Toulouse) 2002 SA, NZ, C, 2003 E 1, S, I, It (R), W (R), Arg 2, NZ, 2004 I,It, W, 2005 SA2,Tg, 2006 SA, 2007 I, W1, E1, S, E2, W2, [Nm, I, Gg(R), NZ, E, Arg 2(R)], 2008 S, I, E, It(t), W, 2009 NZ1, 2, A(R)

Cluchague, L (Biarritz O) 1924 S, 1925 E

Coderc, J (Chalon) 1932 G, 1933 G, 1934 G, 1935 G, 1936 G 1

Codorniou, D (Narbonne) 1979 NZ 1,2, R, 1980 W, E, S, I, 1981 S, W, E, A 2, 1983 E, S, I, W, A 1,2, R, 1984 I, W, E, S, NZ 1,2, R, 1985 E, S, I, W, Arg 1,2

Coeurveille, C (Agen) 1992 Arg 1(R),2

Cognet, L (Montferrand) 1932 G, 1936 G 1,2, 1937 G, It

Collazo, P (Bègles) 2000 R

Colombier, J (St Junien) 1952 SA, W, E

Colomine, G (Narbonne) 1979 NZ 1

Comba, F (SF) 1998 Arg 1,2, Fj, Arg 3, 1999 I, W 1, E, S, 2000 A, NZ 1,2, 2001 S, I

Combe, J (SF) 1910 S, E, I, 1911 S

Combes, G (Fumel) 1945 B 2

Communeau, M (SF) 1906 NZ, E, 1907 E, 1908 E, W, 1909 E, W, I, 1910 S, E, I, 1911 S, E, I, 1912 I, S, W, E, 1913 SA, E, W

Condom, J (Boucau, Biarritz O) 1982 R, 1983 E, S, I, W, A 1,2, R, 1984 I, W, E, S, NZ 1,2, R, 1985 E, S, I, W, Arg 1,2, 1986 S, I, W, E, R 1, Arg 1,2, NZ 1, R 2, NZ 2,3, 1987 W, [S, R, Z, A, NZ], R, 1988 E, S, W, Arg 1,2,3,4, R, 1989 I, W, E, S, NZ 1,2, A 1, 1990 I, R, A 2,3(R)

Conilh de Beyssac, J-J (SBUC) 1912 I, S, 1914 I, W, E

Constant, G (Perpignan) 1920 W

Correia, P (Albi) 2008 A2

Coscolla, G (Béziers) 1921 S, W

Costantino, J (Montferrand) 1973 R

Costes, A (Montferrand) 1994 C 2, 1995 R 1, [Iv], 1997 It 1, 1999 WS, Tg (R), NZ 1, [Nm (R), Fj (R), Arg (R), NZ 2(R), A (t&R)], 2000 S (R), I

Costes, F (Montferrand) 1979 E, S, NZ 1,2, R, 1980 W, I

Couffignal, H (Colomiers) 1993 R 1

Coulon, E (Grenoble) 1928 S

Courtiols, M (Bègles) 1991 R, US 1, W 2

Coux, J-F (Bourgoin) 2007 NZ1,2

Couzinet, D (Biarritz) 2004 US,C(R), 2008 A1(R)

Crabos, R (RCF) 1920 S, E, W, I, US, 1921 S, W, E, I, 1922 S, E, W, I, 1923 S, I, 1924 S, I

Crampagne, J (Bègles) 1967 SA 4

Crancée, R (Lourdes) 1960 Arg 3, 1961 S

Crauste, M (RCF, Lourdes) 1957 R 1,2, 1958 S, E, A, W, It, I, 1959 E, It, W, I, 1960 S, E, W, I, It, R, Arg 1,3, 1961 S, SA, E, W, It, I, NZ 1,2,3, A, R, 1962 S, E, W, I, It, R, 1963 S, I, E, W, It, R, 1964 S, NZ, E, W, It, I, SA, Fj, R, 1965 S, I, E, W, It, R, 1966 S, I, E, W, It

Cremaschi, M (Lourdes) 1980 R, 1981 R, NZ 1,2, 1982 W, S, 1983 A 1,2, R, 1984 I, W

Crenca, J-J (Agen) 1996 SA 2(R), 1999 R, Tg, WS (R), NZ 1(R), 2001 SA 1,2, NZ 2(R), SA 3, A, Fj, 2002 It, W, E, S, I, Arg, A 2, SA, NZ, C, 2003 E 1, S, I, It, W, R, E 2, [Fj, J(t&R),S,I,E,NZ(R)], 2004 I(R),It(R),W(R),S(R),E(R)

Crichton, W H (Le Havre) 1906 NZ, E

Cristina, J (Montferrand) 1979 R

Cussac, P (Biarritz O) 1934 G

Cutzach, A (Quillan) 1929 G

Daguerre, F (Biarritz O) 1936 G 1

Daguerre, A (CASG) 1933 G

Dal Maso, M (Mont-de-Marsan, Agen, Colomiers) 1988 R (R), 1990 NZ 2, 1996 SA 1(R),2, 1997 I, W, E, S, It 1, R 1(R), A 1,2, It 2, Arg, SA 1,2, 1998 W (R), Arg 1(t), Fj (R), 1999 R (R), WS (R), Tg, NZ 1(R), W 2(R), [Nm (R), Fj (R), Arg (R), A (R)], 2000 W, E, S, I, It

Danion, J (Toulon) 1924 I

Danos, P (Toulon, Béziers) 1954 Arg 1,2, 1957 R 2, 1958 S, E, W, It, I, SA 1,2, 1959 S, E, It, W, I, 1960 S, E

Dantiacq, D (Pau) 1997 R 1

Darbos, P (Dax) 1969 R

Darracq, R (Dax) 1957 It

Darrieussecq, A (Biarritz O) 1973 E

Darrieussecq, J (Mont-de-Marsan) 1953 It

Darrouy, C (Mont-de-Marsan) 1957 I, E, W, It, R 1, 1959 E, 1961 R, 1963 S, I, E, W, It, 1964 NZ, E, W, It, I, SA, Fj, R, 1965 S, I, E, It, R, 1966 S, I, E, W, It, R, 1967 S, A, E, It, W, I, SA 1,2,4

Daudé, J (Bourgoin) 2000 S

Daudignon, G (SF) 1928 S

Dauga, B (Mont-de-Marsan) 1964 S, NZ, E, W, It, I, SA, Fj, R, 1965 S, I, E, W, It, R, 1966 S, I, E, W, It, R, 1967 S, A, E, It, W, I, SA 1,2,3,4, NZ, R, 1968 S, I, NZ 1,2,3, A, SA 1,2, R, 1969 S, I, E, R, 1970 S, I, W, E, R, 1971 S, I, E, W, SA 1,2, A 1,2, R, 1972 S, I 1, W

Dauger, J (Bayonne) 1945 B 1,2, 1953 S

Daulouède, P (Tyrosse) 1937 G, It, 1938 G 1, 1940 B

David, Y (Bourgoin) 2008 It

Debaty, V (Perpignan) 2006 R(R)

De Besombes, S (Perpignan) 1998 Arg 1(R), Fj (R)

Decamps, P (RCF) 1911 S

Dedet, J (SF) 1910 S, E, I, 1911 W, I, 1912 S, 1913 E, I

Dedeyn, P (RCF) 1906 NZ

Dedieu, P (Béziers) 1963 E, It, 1964 W, It, I, SA, Fj, R, 1965 S, I, E, W

De Gregorio, J (Grenoble) 1960 S, E, W, I, It, R, Arg 1,2, 1961 S, SA, E, W, It, I, 1962 S, E, W, 1963 S, W, It, W, 1964 NZ, E

Dehez, J-L (Agen) 1967 SA 2, 1969 R

De Jouvencel, E (SF) 1909 W, I

De Laborderie, M (RCF) 1921 I, 1922 I, 1925 W, E

Delage, C (Agen) 1983 S, I

De Malherbe, H (CASG) 1932 G, 1933 G

De Malmann, R (RCF) 1908 E, W, 1909 E, W, I, 1910 E, I

De Muizon, J J (SF) 1910 I

Delaigue, G (Toulon) 1973 J, R

Delaigue, Y (Toulon, Toulouse, Castres) 1994 S, NZ 2(R), C 2, 1995 I, [Tg, Iv], It, R 2(R), 1997 It 1, 2003 Arg 1,2, 2005 S,E,W,I,It,A2(R),Tg,SA3(R)

Delmotte, G (Toulon) 1999 R, Tg

Delque, A (Toulouse) 1937 It, 1938 G 1, R, G 2

De Rougemont, M (Toulon) 1995 E (t), R 1(t), [Iv], NZ 1,2, 1996 I (R), Arg 1,2, W 2, SA 1, 1997 E (R), S (R), It 1

Desbrosse, C (Toulouse) 1999 [Nm (R)], 2000 I

Descamps, P (SB) 1927 G 2

Desclaux, F (RCF) 1949 Arg 1,2, 1953 It

Desclaux, J (Perpignan) 1934 G, 1935 G, 1936 G 1,2, 1937 G, It, 1938 G 1, R, G 2, 1945 B 1

Deslandes, C (RCF) 1990 A 1, NZ 2, 1991 W 1, 1992 R, Arg 1,2

Desnoyer, L (Brive) 1974 R

Destarac, L (Tarbes) 1926 S, I, E, W, M, 1927 W, E, G 1,2

Desvouges, R (SF) 1914 W

Detrez, P-E (Nîmes) 1983 A 2(R), 1986 Arg 1(R),2, A (R), NZ1

Devergie, T (Nîmes) 1988 R, 1989 NZ 1,2, B, A 2, 1990 W, E, S, I, R, A 1,2,3, 1991 US 2, W 2, 1992 R (R), Arg 2(R)

De Villiers, P (SF) 1999 W 2, [Arg (R), NZ 2(R), A (R)], 2000 W (R), E (R), S (R), I (R), It (R), NZ 1(R),2, 2001 S, I, It, W, E, SA 1,2, NZ (R), SA 3, A, Fj, 2002 It, W, E, I, SA, NZ, C, 2003 Arg 1,2, NZ (R), 2004 I,It,W,S,E,US,C,NZ, 2005 S, I(R), It(R), SA1(R), 2, A1(R), 2, C, Tg(R), SA3, 2006 S, I, It, E, W, SA, NZ1, 2, Arg, 2007 It, I, E1, S, W2, [Arg1, Nm, I, NZ,E]

Deygas, M (Vienne) 1937 It

Deylaud, C (Toulouse) 1992 R, Arg 1,2, SA 1, 1994 C 1, NZ 1,2, 1995 W, E, S, [Iv (R), S, I, SA], It, Arg

Diarra, I (Montauban) 2008 It

Dintrans, P (Tarbes) 1979 NZ 1,2, R, 1980 E, S, I, SA, R, 1981 S, I, W, E, A 1,2, R, NZ 1,2, 1982 W, E, S, I, R, Arg 1,2, 1983 E, W, A 1,2, R, 1984 I, W, E, S, NZ 1,2, R, 1985 E, S, I, W, Arg 1,2, 1987 [R], 1988 Arg 1,2,3, 1989 W, E, S, 1990 R

Dispagne, S (Toulouse) 1996 I (R), W 1

Dizabo, P (Tyrosse) 1948 A, S, E, 1949 S, I, E, W, Arg 2, 1950 S, I, 1960 Arg 1,2,3

Domec, A (Carcassonne) 1929 W

Domec, H (Lourdes) 1953 W, It, 1954 S, I, NZ, W, E, It, 1955 S, I, E, W, 1956 I, W, It, 1958 E, A, W, It, I

Domenech, A (Vichy, Brive) 1954 W, E, It, 1955 S, I, E, W, 1956 S, I, W, It, E, Cz, 1957 S, I, E, W, It, R 1,2, 1958 S, E, It, 1959 It, 1960 S, E, W, I, It, R, Arg 1,2,3, 1961 S, SA, E, W, It, I, NZ 1,2,3, A, R, 1962 S, E, W, I, It, R, 1963 W, It

Domercq, J (Bayonne) 1912 I, S

Domingo, T (Clermont-Auvergne) 2009 W(R),E(R),It(R),NZ2(R)

Dominici, C (SF) 1998 E, S, Arg 1,2, 1999 E, S, WS, NZ 1, W 2, [C, Fj, Arg, NZ 2, A], 2000 W, E, 2001 I (R), It, W, E, SA 1,2, NZ, Fj, 2003 Arg 1, R, E 2, 3, [Fj, J, S, I, E], 2004 I, It, W, S, E, A(R), NZ(R), 2005 S, E, W, I, It, 2006 S, I, It, E, W, NZ1, 2(R), Arg, 2007 It, I, W1, E1, S(R), E3, W2(R), [Arg 1, Gg, NZ(R), E(R),Arg 2]

Dorot, J (RCF) 1935 G

Dospital, P (Bayonne) 1977 R, 1980 I, 1981 S, I, W, E, 1982 I, R, Arg 1,2, 1983 E, S, I, W, 1984 E, S, NZ 1,2, R, 1985 E, S, I, W, Arg 1

Dourthe, C (Dax) 1966 R, 1967 S, A, E, W, I, SA 1,2,3, NZ, 1968 W, NZ 3, SA 1,2, 1969 W, 1971 SA 2(R), R, 1972 I 1,2, A 1,2, R, 1973 S, NZ, E, 1974 I, Arg 1,2, SA 1,2, 1975 W, E, S

Dourthe, M (Dax) 2000 NZ 2(t)

Dourthe, R (Dax, SF, Béziers) 1995 R 2, Arg, NZ 1,2, 1996 E, R, 1996 Arg 1,2, W 2, SA 1,2, 1997 W, A 1, 1999 I, W 1,2, [C, Nm, Fj, Arg, NZ 2, A], 2000 W, E, It, R, A, NZ 1,2, 2001 S, I

Doussau, E (Angoulême) 1938 R

Droitecourt, M (Montferrand) 1972 R, 1973 NZ (R), E, 1974 E, S, Arg 1, SA 2, 1975 SA 1,2, Arg 1,2, R, 1976 S, I, W, A 1, 1977 Arg 2

Dubertrand, A (Montferrand) 1971 A 1,2, 1972 I 2, 1974 I, W, E, SA 2, 1975 Arg 1,2, R, 1976 S, US

Dubois, D (Bègles) 1971 S

Dubroca, D (Agen) 1979 NZ 2, 1981 NZ 2(R), 1982 E, S, 1984 W, E, S, 1985 Arg 2, 1986 S, I, W, E, R 1, Arg 2, A, NZ 1, R 2, NZ 2,3, 1987 W, E, S, I, [S, Z, Fj, A, NZ], R, 1988 E, S, I, W

Duché, A (Limoges) 1929 G

Duclos, A (Lourdes) 1931 S

Ducousso, J (Tarbes) 1925 S, W, E

Dufau, G (RCF) 1948 I, A, 1949 I, W, 1950 S, E, W, 1951 S, I, E, W, 1952 SA, W, 1953 S, I, E, W, 1954 S, I, NZ, W, E, It, 1955 S, I, E, W, It, 1956 S, I, W, It, 1957 S, I, E, W, It, R 1

Dufau, J (Biarritz) 1912 I, S, W, E

Duffaut, Y (Agen) 1954 Arg 1,2

Duffour, R (Tarbes) 1911 W

Dufourcq, J (SBUC) 1906 NZ, E, 1907 E, 1908 W

Duhard, R (Bagnères) 1980 E

Duhau, J (SF) 1928 I,1930 I, G, 1931 I, S, W, 1933 G

Dulaurens, C (Toulouse) 1926 I, 1928 S, 1929 W

Duluc, A (Béziers) 1934 G

Du Manoir, Y le P (RCF) 1925 I, NZ, S, W, E, 1926 S, 1927 I, S

Dupont, C (Lourdes) 1923 S, W, I, 1924 S, I, W, R, US, 1925 S, 1927 E, G 1,2, 1928 A, G, W, 1929 I

Dupont, J-L (Agen) 1983 S

Dupont, L (RCF) 1934 G, 1935 G, 1936 G 1,2, 1938 R, G 2

Dupouy, A (SB) 1924 W, R

Duprat, B (Bayonne) 1966 E, W, It, R, 1967 S, A, E, SA 2,3, 1968 S, I, 1972 E, W, I 2, A 1

Dupré, P (RCF) 1909 W

Dupuy, J (Leicester) 2009 NZ1,2,A(R)

Dupuy, J-V (Tarbes) 1956 S, I, W, It, E, Cz, 1957 S, I, E, W, It, R 2, 1958 S, E, SA 1,2, 1959 S, E, It, W, I, 1960 W, I, It, Arg 1,3, 1961 S, SA, E, NZ 2, R, 1962 S, E, W, I, It, 1963 W, It, R, 1964 S

Durand, N (Perpignan) 2007 NZ1,2

Dusautoir, T (Biarritz, Toulouse) 2006 R, SA, NZ1, 2007 E3, W2(R), [Nm, I, NZ, E, Arg 2], 2008 S, I, E, W, Arg, PI, A3, 2009 I, S, W, E, It, NZ1, 2, A

Du Souich, C J (see Judas du Souich)

Dutin, B (Mont-de-Marsan) 1968 NZ 2, A, SA 2, R

Dutour, F X (Toulouse) 1911 E, I, 1912 S, W, E, 1913 S

Dutrain, H (Toulouse) 1945 W, 1946 B, I, 1947 E, 1949 I, E, W, Arg 1

Dutrey, J (Lourdes) 1940 B

Duval, R (SF) 1908 E, W, 1909 E, 1911 E, W, I

Echavé, L (Agen) 1961 S

Elhorga, P (Agen) 2001 NZ, 2002 A 1,2, 2003 Arg 2, NZ (R), R, [Fj(R),US,I(R),NZ], 2004 I(R),It(R),S,E, 2005 S,E, 2006 NZ2,Arg, 2008 A1

Elissalde, E (Bayonne) 1936 G 2, 1940 B

Elissalde, J-B (La Rochelle, Toulouse) 2000 S (R), R (R), 2003 It (R), W (R), 2004 I, It, W, A, Arg, 2005 SA1, 2(R), A1, 2, SA3, 2006 S, I, It, W(R), NZ1(R), 2, 2007 E2(R), 3, W2(R), [Arg 1(R), Nm, I, Gg(R), NZ, E, Arg 2], 2008 S, I, W, Arg, PI

Elissalde, J-P (La Rochelle) 1980 SA, R, 1981 A 1,2, R

Empereur-Buisson, H (Béziers) 1931 E, G

Erbani, D (Agen) 1981 A 1,2, NZ 1,2, 1982 Arg 1,2, 1983 S (R), I, W, A 1,2, R, 1984 W, E, R, 1985 E W (R), Arg 2, 1986 S, I, W, E, R 1, Arg 2, NZ 1,2(R),3, 1987 W, E, S, I, [S, R, Fj, A, NZ], 1988 E, S, 1989 I (R), W, E, S, NZ 1, A 2, 1990 W, E

Escaffre, P (Narbonne) 1933 G, 1934 G

Escommier, M (Montelimar) 1955 It

Esponda, J-M (RCF) 1967 SA 1,2, R, 1968 NZ 1,2, SA 2, R, 1969 S, I (R), E

Estève, A (Béziers) 1971 SA 1, 1972 I 1, E, W, I 2, A 2, R, 1973 S, NZ, E, I, 1974 I, W, E, S, R, SA 1,2, 1975 W, E

Estève, P (Narbonne, Lavelanet) 1982 R, Arg 1,2, 1983 E, S, I, W, A 1,2, R, 1984 I, W, E, S, NZ 1,2, R, 1985 E, S, I, W, 1986 S, I, 1987 [S, Z]

Etcheberry, J (Rochefort, Cognac) 1923 W, I, 1924 S, I, E, W, R, US, 1926 S, I, E, M, 1927 I, S, W, G 2

Etchenique, J-M (Biarritz O) 1974 R, SA 1, 1975 E, Arg 2

Etchepare, A (Bayonne) 1922 I

Etcheverry, M (Pau) 1971 S, I

Eutrope, A (SCUF) 1913 I

Fabre, E (Toulouse) 1937 It, 1938 G 1,2

Fabre, J (Toulouse) 1963 S, I, E, W, It, 1964 S, NZ, E

Fabre, L (Lezignan) 1930 G

Fabre, M (Béziers) 1981 A 1, R, NZ 1,2, 1982 I, R

Failliot, P (RCF) 1911 S, W, I, 1912 I, S, E, 1913 E, W

Fargues, G (Dax) 1923 I

Fauré, F (Tarbes) 1914 I, W, E

Faure, L (Sale) 2008 S,I,E,A1,PI,A3, 2009 I,E

Fauvel, J-P (Tulle) 1980 R

Favre, M (Lyon) 1913 E, W

Ferrand, L (Chalon) 1940 B

Ferrien, R (Tarbes) 1950 S, I, E, W

Finat, R (CASG) 1932 G, 1933 G

Fite, R (Brive) 1963 W, It

Floch, A (Clermont-Auvergne) 2008 E(R),It,W

Forest, M (Bourgoin) 2007 NZ1(R),2(R)

Forestier, J (SCUF) 1912 W

Forgues, F (Bayonne) 1911 S, E, W, 1912 I, W, E, 1913 S, SA, W, 1914 I, E

Fort, J (Agen) 1967 It, W, I, SA 1,2,3,4

Fourcade, G (BEC) 1909 E, W

Foures, H (Toulouse) 1951 S, I, E, W

Fournet, F (Montferrand) 1950 W

Fouroux, J (La Voulte) 1972 I 2, R, 1974 W, E, Arg 1,2, R, SA 1,2, 1975 W, Arg 1, R, 1976 S, I, W, E, US, A 1, 1977 W, E, S, I, Arg 1,2, NZ 1,2, R

263

FRANCE

Francquenelle, A (Vaugirard) 1911 S, 1913 W, I

Fritz, F (Toulouse) 2005 SA1,A2,SA3, 2006 S, I, It, E, W, SA, NZ1, 2, Arg, 2007 It, 2009 I, E(R), It, NZ2(R), A

Froment, R (Castres) 2004 US(R)

Furcade, R (Perpignan) 1952 S

Gabernet, S (Toulouse) 1980 E, S, 1981 S, I, W, E, A 1,2, R, NZ 1,2, 1982 I, 1983 A 2, R

Gachassin, J (Lourdes) 1961 S, I, 1963 R, 1964 S, NZ, E, W, It, I, SA, Fj, R, 1965 S, I, E, W, It, R, 1966 S, I, E, W, 1967 S, A, It, W, I, NZ, 1968 I, E, 1969 S, I

Galasso, A (Toulon, Montferrand) 2000 R (R), 2001 E (R)

Galau, H (Toulouse) 1924 S, I, E, W, US

Galia, J (Quillan) 1927 E, G 1,2, 1928 S, A, I, E, W, 1929 I, E, G, 1930 S, I, E, G, W, 1931 S, W, E, G

Gallart, P (Béziers) 1990 R, A 1,2(R),3, 1992 S, I, R, Arg 1,2, SA 1,2, Arg, 1994 I, W, E, 1995 I (t), R 1, [Tg]

Gallion, J (Toulon) 1978 E, S, I, W, 1979 I, W, E, S, NZ 2, R, 1980 W, E, S, I, 1983 A 1,2, R, 1984 I, W, E, S, R, 1985 E, S, I, W, 1986 Arg 2

Galthié, F (Colomiers, SF) 1991 R, US 1, [R, Fj, C, E], 1992 W, E, S, R, Arg, 1994 I, W, E, 1995 [SA, E], 1996 W 1(R), 1997 I, It 2, SA 1,2, 1998 W (R), Fj (R), 1999 R, WS (R), Tg, NZ 1(R), [Fj (R), Arg, NZ 2, A], 2000 W, E, A, NZ 1,2, 2001 S, It, W, E, SA 1,2, NZ, SA 3, A, Fj, 2002 E, S, I, SA, NZ, C, 2003 E 1, S, Arg 1,2, NZ, R, E 2, [Fj,J,S,I,E]

Galy, J (Perpignan) 1953 W

Garbajosa, X (Toulouse) 1998 I, W, Arg 2(R), Fj, 1999 W 1(R), E, S, WS, NZ 1, W 2, [C, Nm (R), Fj (R), Arg, NZ 2, A], 2000 A, NZ 1,2, 2001 S, I, E, 2002 It (R), W, SA (R), C (R), 2003 E 1, S, I, It, W, E 3

Gasc, J (Graulhet) 1977 NZ 2

Gasparotto, G (Montferrand) 1976 A 2, R

Gauby, G (Perpignan) 1956 Cz

Gaudermen, P (RCF) 1906 E

Gayraud, W (Toulouse) 1920 I

Gelez, F (Agen) 2001 SA 3, 2002 I (R), A 1, SA, NZ, C (R), 2003 S, I

Geneste, R (BEC) 1945 B 1, 1949 Arg 2

Genet, J-P (RCF) 1992 S, I, R

Gensane, R (Béziers) 1962 S, E, W, I, It, R, 1963 S

Gérald, G (RCF) 1927 E, G 2, 1928 S, 1929 I, S, W, E, G, 1930 S, I, E, G, W, 1931 I, S, E, G

Gérard, D (Bègles) 1999 Tg

Gérintes, G (CASG) 1924 R, 1925 I, 1926 W

Geschwind, P (RCF) 1936 G 1,2

Giacardy, M (SBUC) 1907 E

Gimbert, P (Bègles) 1991 R, US 1, 1992 W, E

Giordani, P (Dax) 1999 E, S

Glas, S (Bourgoin) 1996 S (t), I (R), W 1, R, Arg 2(R), W 2, SA 1,2, 1997 I, W, E, S, It 2(R), R 2, Arg, SA 1,2, 1998 E, S, I, W, Arg 1,2, Fj, Arg 3, A, 1999 W 2, [C,Nm, Arg (R), NZ 2(R), A (t&R)], 2000 I, 2001 E, SA 1,2, NZ

Gomès, A (SF) 1998 Arg 1,2, Fj, Arg 3, A, 1999 I (R)

Gommes, J (RCF) 1909 I

Gonnet, C-A (Albi) 1921 E, I, 1922 E, W, 1924 S, E, 1926 S, I, E, W, M, 1927 I, S, W, E, G 1

Gonzalez, J-M (Bayonne) 1992 Arg 1,2, SA 1,2, Arg, 1993 R 1, SA 1,2, R 2, A 1,2, 1994 I, W, E, S, C 1, NZ 1,2, C 2, 1995 W, E, S, I, R 1, [Tg, S, I, SA, E], It, Arg, 1996 E, S, I, W 1

Got, R (Perpignan) 1920 I, US, 1921 S, W, 1922 S, E, W, I, 1924 I, E, W, R, US

Gourdon, J-F (RCF, Bagnères) 1974 S, Arg 1,2, R, SA 1,2, 1975 W, E, S, I, R, 1976 S, I, W, E, 1978 E, S, 1979 W, E, S, R, 1980 I

Gourragne, J-F (Béziers) 1990 NZ 2, 1991 W 1

Goutta, B (Perpignan) 2004 C

Goyard, A (Lyon U) 1936 G 1,2, 1937 G, It, 1938 G 1, R, G 2

Graciet, R (SBUC) 1926 I, W, 1927 S, G 1, 1929 E, 1930 W

Grandclaude, J-P (Perpignan) 2005 E(R),W(R), 2007 NZ1

Graou, S (Auch, Colomiers) 1992 Arg (R), 1993 SA 1,2, R 2, A 2(R), 1995 R 2, Arg (t), NZ 2(R)

Gratton, J (Agen) 1984 NZ 2, R, 1985 E, S, I, W, Arg 1,2, 1986 S, NZ 1

Graule, V (Arl Perpignan) 1926 I, E, W, 1927 S, W, 1931 G

Greffe, M (Grenoble) 1968 W, Cz, NZ 1,2, SA 1

Griffard, J (Lyon U) 1932 G, 1933 G, 1934 G

Gruarin, A (Toulon) 1964 W, It, I, SA, Fj, R, 1965 S, I, E, W, It, 1966 S, I, E, W, It, R, 1967 S, A, E, It, W, I, NZ, 1968 S, I

Guélorget, P (RCF) 1931 E, G

Guichemerre, A (Dax) 1920 E, 1921 E, I, 1923 S

Guilbert, A (Toulon) 1975 E, S, I, SA 1,2, 1976 A 1, 1977 Arg 1,2, NZ 1,2, R, 1979 I, W, E

Guillemin, P (RCF) 1908 E, W, 1909 E, I, 1910 W, S, E, I, 1911 S, E, W

Guilleux, P (Agen) 1952 SA, It

Guirado, G (Perpignan) 2008 It(R), 2009 A(R)

Guiral, M (Agen) 1931 G, 1932 G, 1933 G

Guiraud, H (Nîmes) 1996 R

Haget, A (PUC) 1953 E, 1954 I, NZ, E, Arg 2, 1955 E, W, It, 1957 I, E, It, R 1, 1958 It, SA 2

Haget, F (Agen, Biarritz O) 1974 Arg 1,2, 1975 SA 2, Arg 1,2, R, 1976 S, 1978 S, I, W, R, 1979 I, W, E, S, NZ 1,2, R, 1980 W, S, I, 1984 S, NZ 1,2, R, 1985 E, S, I, 1986 S, I, W, E, R 1, Arg 1, A, NZ 1, 1987 S, I, [R, Fj]

Haget, H (CASG) 1928 S, 1930 G

Halet, R (Strasbourg) 1925 NZ, S, W

Hall, S (Béziers) 2002 It, W

Harinordoquy, I (Pau, Biarritz)) 2002 W, E, S, I, A 1,2, SA, NZ, C, 2003 E 1, S, I, It, W, Arg 1(R),2, NZ, R, E 2,3(R), [Fj,S,I,E], 2004 I,It,W,E,A,Arg,NZ, 2005 W(R),2006 R(R),SA, 2007 It(R),I,W1(R),E1(R),S,E3,W2, [Arg 1,Nm(R),NZ(R),E(R),Arg 2], 2008 A1,2,Arg,PI,A3, 2009 I,S,W,E,It

Harislur-Arthapignet, P (Tarbes) 1988 Arg 4(R)

Harize, D (Cahors, Toulouse) 1975 SA 1,2, 1976 A 1,2, R, 1977 W, E, S, I

Hauc, J (Toulon) 1928 E, G, 1929 I, S, G

Hauser, M (Lourdes) 1969 E

Hedembaigt, M (Bayonne) 1913 S, SA, 1914 W

Hericé, D (Bègles) 1950 I

Herrero, A (Toulon) 1963 R, 1964 NZ, E, W, It, I, SA, Fj, R, 1965 S, I, E, W, 1966 W, It, R, 1967 S A, E, It, I, R

Herrero, B (Nice) 1983 I, 1986 Arg 1

Heyer, F (Montferrand) 1990 A 2

Heymans, C (Agen, Toulouse) 2000 It (R) R, 2002 A 2(R), SA, NZ, 2004 W(R), US, C(R), A, Arg, NZ, 2005 I, It, SA1, 2, A1, 2, C, SA3, 2006 S, I, W(R), R, SA, NZ2, Arg, 2007 It, I(R), E1(R), S, E3, W2, [Arg 1, Nm, I, NZ, E], 2008 S, I, E, W(R), Arg, PI, A3, 2009 I(R), S, W, E, It, NZ1, 2, A

Hiquet, J-C (Agen) 1964 E

Hoche, M (PUC) 1957 I, E, W, It, R 1

Hondagné-Monge, M (Tarbes) 1988 Arg 2(R)

Hontas, P (Biarritz) 1990 S, I, R, 1991 R, 1992 Arg, 1993 E, S, I, W

Hortoland, J-P (Béziers) 1971 A 2

Houblain, H (SCUF) 1909 E, 1910 W

Houdet, R (SF) 1927 S, W, G 1, 1928 G, W, 1929 I, S, E, 1930 S, E

Hourdebaigt, A (SBUC) 1909 I, 1910 W, S, E, I

Hubert, A (ASF) 1906 E, 1907 E, 1908 E, W, 1909 E, W, I

Hueber, A (Lourdes, Toulon) 1990 A 3, NZ 1, 1991 US 2, 1992 I, Arg 1,2, SA 1,2, 1993 E, S, I, W, R 1, SA 1,2, R 2, A 1,2, 1995 [Tg, S (R), I], 2000 It, R

Hutin, R (CASG) 1927 I, S, W

Hyardet, A (Castres) 1995 It, Arg (R)

Ibañez, R (Dax, Perpignan, Castres, Saracens, Wasps) 1996 W 1(R), 1997 It 1(R), R 1, It 2(R), R 2, SA 2(R), 1998 E, S, I, W, Arg 1,2, Fj, Arg 3, A, 1999 I, W 1, E, S, R, WS, Tg (R), NZ 1, W 2, [C, Nm, Fj, Arg, NZ 2, A], 2000 W (R), E (R), S (R), I (R), It (R), R, 2001 S, I, It, W, E, SA 1,2, NZ (R), SA 3, A, Fj, 2002 It (R), W, E, S, I, Arg, A 1(R),2, SA, NZ, C, 2003 E 1, S, I, It, W, R (R), E 2(R), 3, [Fj, J(R), S, I, E, NZ(R)], 2005 C(R), Tg, 2006 I, It, E, W, R, SA(R), NZ1(R), 2, Arg, 2007 It, I, W1, E1, S, NZ1(R), 2(R), E2, 3, [Arg 1, Nm(R), I, NZ, E, Arg 2]

Icard, J (SF) 1909 E, W

Iguiniz, M (Bayonne) 1914 E

Ihingoué, D (BEC) 1912 I, S

Imbernon, J-F (Perpignan) 1976 I, W, E, US, A 1, 1977 W, E, S, I, Arg 1,2, NZ 1,2, 1978 E, R, 1979 I, 1981 S, I, W, E, 1982 I, 1983 I, W

Iraçabal, J (Bayonne) 1968 NZ 1,2, SA 1, 1969 S, I, W, R, 1970

S, I, W, E, R, 1971 W, SA 1,2, A 1, 1972 E, W, I 2, A 2, R, 1973 S, NZ, E, W, I, J, 1974 I, W, E, S, Arg 1,2, SA 2(R)
Isaac, H (RCF) 1907 E, 1908 E
Ithurra, E (Biarritz O) 1936 G 1,2, 1937 G
Jacquet, L (Clermont-Auvergne) 2006 NZ2(R),Arg, 2008 S,I(t&R)
Janeczek, T (Tarbes) 1982 Arg 1,2, 1990 R
Janik, K (Toulouse) 1987 R
Janin, D (Bourgoin) 2008 A1(R),2
Jarasse, A (Brive) 1945 B 1
Jardel, J (SB) 1928 I, E
Jauréguy, A (RCF, Toulouse, SF) 1920 S, E, W, I, US, 1922 S, W, 1923 S, W, E, I, 1924 S, W, R, US, 1925 I, NZ, 1926 S, E, W, M, 1927 I, E, 1928 S, A, E, G, W, 1929 I, S, E
Jauréguy, P (Toulouse) 1913 S, SA, W, I
Jauzion, Y (Colomiers, Toulouse) 2001 SA 1,2, NZ, 2002 A 1(R), 2(R), 2003 Arg 2, NZ, R, E 2, 3, [Fj, S, I, E], 2004 I, It, W, S, E, A, Arg, NZ(t), 2005 W, I, It, SA1, 2, A1, 2, C, Tg(R), SA3, 2006 R, SA, NZ1, 2, Arg, 2007 It, I, W1, E1, S, E3, W2, [Arg 1, Nm(R), I(R), Gg, NZ, E], 2008 It, W, Arg, PI, A3, 2009 I, S, W, E, It, NZ1(R)
Jeangrand, M-H (Tarbes) 1921 I
Jeanjean, N (Toulouse) 2001 SA 1,2, NZ, SA 3(R), A (R), Fj (R), 2002 It, Arg, A 1
Jeanjean, P (Toulon) 1948 I
Jérôme, G (SF) 1906 NZ, E
Joinel, J-L (Brive) 1977 NZ 1, 1978 R, 1979 I, W, E, S, NZ 1,2, R, 1980 W, E, S, I, SA, 1981 S, I, W, E, R, NZ 1,2, 1982 E, S, I, R, 1983 E, S, I, W, A 1,2, R, 1984 I, W, E, S, NZ 1,2, 1985 S, I, W, Arg 1, 1986 S, I, W, E, R 1, Arg 1,2, A, 1987 [Z]
Jol, M (Biarritz O) 1947 S, I, W, E, 1949 S, I, E, W, Arg 1,2
Jordana, J-L (Pau, Toulouse) 1996 R (R), Arg 1(t),2, W 2, 1997 I (t), W, S (R)
Judas du Souich, C (SCUF) 1911 W, I
Juillet, C (Montferrand, SF) 1995 R 2, Arg, 1999 E, S, WS, NZ 1, [C, Fj, Arg, NZ 2, A], 2000 A, NZ 1,2, 2001 S, I, It, W
Junquas, L (Tyrosse) 1945 B 1,2, W, 1946 B, I, K, W, 1947 S, I, W, E, 1948 S, W
Kaczorowski, G (Le Creusot) 1974 I (R)
Kaempf, A (St Jean-de-Luz) 1946 B
Kayser, B (Leicester) 2008 A1(R),2(R),Arg(R),PI(R),A3(R), 2009 I(R),S(R),W(R),E(R)
Labadie, P (Bayonne) 1952 S, I, SA, W, E, It, 1953 S, I, It, 1954 S, I, NZ, W, E, Arg 2, 1955 S, I, E, W, 1956 I, 1957 I
Labarthète, R (Pau) 1952 S
Labazuy, A (Lourdes) 1952 I, 1954 S, W, 1956 E, 1958 A, W, I, 1959 S, E, It, W
Labit, C (Toulouse) 1999 S, R (R), WS (R), Tg, 2000 R (R), 2002 Arg, A 1(R), 2003 Arg 1,2, NZ (R), R (R), E 3, [Fj(R),J,US,E(R),NZ]
Laborde, C (RCF) 1962 It, R, 1963 R, 1964 SA, 1965 E
Labrousse, T (Brive) 1996 R, SA 1
Lacans, P (Béziers) 1980 SA, 1981 W, E, A 2, R, 1982 W
Lacassagne, H (SBUC) 1906 NZ, 1907 E
Lacaussade, R (Bègles) 1948 A, S
Lacaze, C (Lourdes, Angoulême) 1961 NZ 2,3, A, R, 1962 E, W, I, It, 1963 W, R, 1964 S, NZ, E, 1965 It, R, 1966 S, I, E, W, It, R, 1967 S, E, SA 1,3,4, R, 1968 S, E, W, Cz, NZ 1, 1969 E
Lacaze, H (Périgueux) 1928 I, G, W, 1929 I, W
Lacaze, P (Lourdes) 1958 SA 1,2, 1959 S, E, It, W, I
Lacazedieu, C (Dax) 1923 W, I, 1928 A, I, 1929 S
Lacombe, B (Agen) 1989 B, 1990 A 2
Lacome, M (Pau) 1960 Arg 2
Lacoste, R (Tarbes) 1914 I, W, E
Lacrampe, F (Béziers) 1949 Arg 2
Lacroix, P (Mont-de-Marsan, Agen) 1958 A, 1960 W, I, It, R, Arg 1,2,3, 1961 S, SA, E, W, I, NZ 1,2,3, A, R, 1962 S, E, W, I, R, 1963 S, I, E, W
Lacroix, T (Dax, Harlequins) 1989 A 1(R),2, 1991 W 1(R),2(R), [R, C (R), E], 1992 SA 2, 1993 E, S, I, W, SA 1,2, R 2, A 1,2, 1994 I, W, E, S, C 1, NZ 1,2, C 2, 1995 W, E, S, R 1, [Tg, Iv, S, I, SA, E], 1996 E, S, I, 1997 It 2, R 2, Arg, SA 1,2
Lacroix, T (Albi) 2008 A1,2
Lafarge, T (Montferrand) 1978 R, 1979 NZ 1, 1981 I (R)
Laffitte, A (SCUF) 1910 W, S
Laffont, H (Narbonne) 1926 W
Lafond, A (Bayonne) 1922 E
Lafond, J-B (RCF) 1983 A 1, 1985 Arg 1,2 1986 S, I, W, E, R 1, 1987 I (R), 1988 W, 1989 I, W, E, 1990 W, A 3(R), NZ 2,

1991 S, I, W 1, E, R, US 1, W 2, [R (R), Fj, C, E], 1992 W, E, S, I (R), SA 2, 1993 E, S, I, W
Lagisquet, P (Bayonne) 1983 A 1,2, R, 1984 I, W, NZ 1,2, 1986 R 1(R), Arg 1,2, A, NZ 1, 1987 [S, R, Fj, A, NZ], R, 1988 S, I, W, Arg 1,2,3,4, R, 1989 I, W, E, S, NZ 1,2, B, A 1,2, 1990 W, E, S, I, A 1,2,3, 1991 S, I, US 2, [R]
Lagrange, J-C (RCF) 1966 It
Laharrague, J (Brive, Perpignan, Sale) 2005 W, I, It, SA1, A1, 2, C(R), Tg, 2006 R(R), SA, NZ1, 2007 NZ2
Laharrague, N (Perpignan) 2007 NZ1(R),2(R)
Lalande, M (RCF) 1923 S, W, I
Lalanne, F (Mont-de-Marsan) 2000 R
Lamaison, C (Brive, Agen) 1996 SA 1(R),2, 1997 W, E, S, R 1, A 2, It 2, R 2, Arg, SA 1,2, 1998 E, S, I, W, Arg 3(R), A, 1999 R, WS (R), Tg, NZ 1(R), W 2(R), [C (R), Nm, Fj, Arg, NZ 2, A], 2000 W, A, NZ 1,2, 2001 S, I, It, W (R)
Lamboley, G (Toulouse) 2005 S(R), E(R), W(R), I(R), It(R), SA1(R), 2(R),A1, 2(R), C(R), Tg, SA3(R), 2007 W1(R)
Landreau, F (SF) 2000 A, NZ 1,2, 2001 E (R)
Lane, G (RCF) 1906 NZ, E, 1907 E, 1908 E, W, 1909 E, W, I, 1910 W, E, 1911 S, W, 1912 I, W, E, 1913 S
Langlade, J-C (Hyères) 1990 R, A 1, NZ 1
Laperne, D (Dax) 1997 R 1(R)
Laporte, G (Graulhet) 1981 I, W, E, R, NZ 1,2, 1986 S, I, W, E, R 1, Arg 1, A (R), 1987 [R, Z (R), Fj]
Larreguy, G (Bayonne) 1954 It
Larribau, J (Périgueux) 1912 I, S, W, E, 1913 S, 1914 I, E
Larrieu, J (Tarbes) 1920 I, US, 1921 W, 1923 S, W, E, I
Larrieux, M (SBUC) 1927 G 2
Larrue, H (Carmaux) 1960 W, I, It, R, Arg 1,2,3
Lasaosa, P (Dax) 1950 I, 1952 S, I, E, It, 1955 It
Lascubé, G (Agen) 1991 S, I, W 1, E, US 2, W 2, [R, Fj, C, E], 1992 W, E
Lassegue, J-B (Toulouse) 1946 W, 1947 S, I, W, 1948 W, 1949 I, E, W, Arg 1
Lasserre, F (René) (Bayonne, Cognac, Grenoble) 1914 I, 1920 S, 1921 S, W, I, 1922 S, E, W, I, 1923 W, E, 1924 S, I, R, US
Lasserre, J-C (Dax) 1963 It, 1964 S, NZ, E, W, It, I, Fj, 1965 W, It, R, 1966 R, 1967 S
Lasserre, M (Agen) 1967 SA 2,3, 1968 E, W, Cz, NZ 3, A, SA 1,2, 1969 S, I, E, 1970 E, 1971 E, W
Laterrade, G (Tarbes) 1910 E, I, 1911 S, E, I
Laudouar, J (Soustons, SBUC) 1961 NZ 1,2, R, 1962 I, R
Lauga, P (Vichy) 1950 S, I, E, W
Laurent, A (Biarritz O) 1925 NZ, S, W, E, 1926 W
Laurent, J (Bayonne) 1920 S, E, W
Laurent, M (Auch) 1932 G, 1933 G, 1934 G, 1935 G, 1936 G 1
Laussucq, C (SF) 1999 S (R), 2000 W (R), S, I
Lavail, G (Perpignan) 1937 G, 1940 B
Lavaud, R (Carcassonne) 1914 I, W
Lavergne, P (Limoges) 1950 S
Lavigne, B (Agen) 1984 R, 1985 E
Lavigne, J (Dax) 1920 E, W
Laziès, H (Auch) 1954 Arg 2, 1955 It, 1956 E, 1957 S
Le Bourhis, R (La Rochelle) 1961 R
Lecointre, M (Nantes) 1952 It
Le Corvec, G (Perpignan) 2007 NZ1
Lecouls, B (Biarritz) 2008 A1,2(R),Arg,PI(R),A3(R), 2009 I
Le Droff, J (Auch) 1963 It, R, 1964 S, NZ, E, 1970 E, R, 1971 S, I
Lefèvre, R (Brive) 1961 NZ 2
Leflamand, L (Bourgoin) 1996 SA 2, 1997 W, E, S, It 2, Arg, SA 1, 2(R)
Lefort, J-B (Biarritz O) 1938 G 1
Le Goff, R (Métro) 1938 R, G 2
Legrain, M (SF) 1909 I, 1910 I, 1911 S, E, W, I, 1913 SA, E, I, 1914 I, W
Lemeur, Y (RCF) 1993 R 1
Lenient, J-J (Vichy) 1967 R
Lepatey, J (Mazamet) 1954 It, 1955 S, I, E, W
Lepatey, L (Mazamet) 1924 S, I, E
Lescarboura, J-P (Dax) 1982 W, E, S, I, 1983 A 1,2, R, 1984 I, W, E, S, NZ 1,2, R, 1985 E, S, I, W, Arg 1,2, 1986 Arg 2, A, NZ 1, R 2, NZ 2, 1988 S, W, 1990 R
Lesieur, E (SF) 1906 E, 1908 E, W, 1909 E, W, I, 1910 S, E, I, 1911 E, I, 1912 W

265

FRANCE

Leuvielle, M (SBUC) 1908 W, 1913 S, SA, E, W, 1914 W, E
Levasseur, R (SF) 1925 W, E
Levée, H (RCF) 1906 NZ
Lewis, E W (Le Havre) 1906 E
Lhermet, J-M (Montferrand) 1990 S, I, 1993 R 1
Libaros, G (Tarbes) 1936 G 1, 1940 B
Liebenberg, B (SF) 2003 R (R), E 2(R),3, [US,I(R),NZ(R)], 2004 I(R),US,C,NZ, 2005 S,E
Lièvremont, M (Perpignan, SF) 1995 It, R 2, Arg (R), NZ 2(R), 1996 R, Arg 1(R), SA 2(R), 1997 R 1, A 2(R), 1998 E (R), S, I, W, Arg 1,2, Fj, Arg 3, A, 1999 W 2, [C, Nm, Fj, Arg, NZ 2, A]
Lièvremont, M (Dax) 2008 A1(R),2
Lièvremont, T (Perpignan, SF, Biarritz) 1996 W 2(R), 1998 E, S, I, W, Arg 1,2, Fj, Arg 3, A, 1999 I, W 1, E, W 2, [Nm] 2000 W (R), E (R), S (R), I, It, 2001 E (R), 2004 I(R), It(R), W, S, US, C, 2005 A2, C, Tg(t&R), SA3(R), 2006 S(R), It, E, W
Lira, M (La Voulte) 1962 R, 1963 I, E, W, It, R, 1964 W, It, I, SA, 1965 S, I, R
Llari, R (Carcassonne) 1926 S
Lobies, J (RCF) 1921 S, W, E
Lombard, F (Narbonne) 1934 G, 1937 It
Lombard, T (SF) 1998 Arg 3, A, 1999 I, W 1, S (R), 2000 W, E, S, A, NZ 1, 2001 It, W
Lombarteix, R (Montferrand) 1938 R, G 2
Londios, J (Montauban) 1967 SA 3
Loppy, L (Toulon) 1993 R 2
Lorieux, A (Grenoble, Aix) 1981 A 1, R, NZ 1,2, 1982 W, 1983 A 2, R, 1984 I, W, E, 1985 Arg 1,2(R), 1986 R 2, NZ 2,3, 1987 W, E, [S, Z, Fj, A, NZ], 1988 S, I, W, Arg 1,2,4, 1989 W, A 2
Loury, A (RCF) 1927 E, G 1,2, 1928 S, A, I
Loustau, L (Perpignan) 2004 C
Loustau, M (Dax) 1923 E
Lubin-Lebrère, M-F (Toulouse) 1914 I, W, E, 1920 S, E, W, I, US, 1921 S, 1922 S, E, W, 1924 W, US, 1925 I
Lubrano, A (Béziers) 1972 A 2, 1973 S
Lux, J-P (Tyrosse, Dax) 1967 E, It, W, I, SA 1,2,4, R, 1968 I, E, Cz, NZ 3, A, SA 1,2, 1969 S, I, E, 1970 S, I, W, E, R, 1971 S, I, E, W, A 1,2, 1972 S, I 1, E, W, I 2, A 1,2, R, 1973 S, NZ, E, 1974 I, W, E, S, Arg 1,2, 1975 W
Macabiau, A (Perpignan) 1994 S, C 1
Maclos, P (SF) 1906 E, 1907 E
Magne, O (Dax, Brive, Montferrand, Clermont-Auvergne, London Irish) 1997 W (n), C, S, n 1(n), A 1,2, It 2(n), n 2, Arg (n), 1998 E, S, I, W, Arg 1,2, Fj, Arg 3, A, 1999 I, R, WS, NZ 1, W 2, [C, Nm, Fj, Arg, NZ 2, A], 2000 W, E, S, It, R, A, NZ 1,2, 2001 S, I, It, W, E, SA 1,2, NZ, SA 3, Fj, 2002 It, E, S, I, Arg, A 1,2(R), SA, NZ, C, 2003 E 1, S, I, It, W, R, E 2,3(R), [Fj,J,S,I,E,NZ(R)], 2004 I,It,W(R),S,E,A,Arg,NZ, 2005 SA1,2(R),A1, 2006 I,It,E,W(R), 2007 NZ1,2
Magnanou, C (RCF) 1923 E, 1925 W, E, 1926 S, 1929 S, W, 1930 S, I, E, W
Magnol, L (Toulouse) 1928 S, 1929 S, W, E
Magois, H (La Rochelle) 1968 SA 1,2, R
Majérus, R (SF) 1928 W, 1929 I, S, 1930 S, I, E, G, W
Malbet, J-C (Agen) 1967 SA 2,4
Maleig, A (Oloron) 1979 W, E, NZ 2, 1980 W, E, SA, R
Mallier, L (Brive) 1999 R, W 2(R), [C (R)], 2000 I (R), It
Malquier, Y (Narbonne) 1979 S
Malzieu, J (Clermont-Auvergne) 2008 S,It,W,Arg,PI,A3, 2009 I,S(R),W,E,It(R)
Manterola, T (Lourdes) 1955 It, 1957 R 1
Mantoulan, C (Pau) 1959 I
Marcet, J (Albi) 1925 I, NZ, S, W, E, 1926 I, E
Marchal, J-F (Lourdes) 1979 S, R, 1980 W, S, I
Marconnet, S (SF) 1998 Arg 3, A, 1999 I (R), W 1(R), E, S (R), R, Tg, 2000 A, NZ 1,2, 2001 S, I, It (R), W (R), E, 2002 S (R), Arg (R), A 1,2, SA (R), C (R), 2003 E 1(R), S, I, It, W, Arg 1(t+R), 2, NZ, R, E 2, 3(t+R), [S, US(R), I, E, NZ], 2004 I, It, W, S, E, A, Arg, NZ, 2005 S, E, W, I, It, SA1, 2, A1(R), 2(R), C, Tg, SA3(R), 2006 S, I(R), It(R), E, W, R, SA, NZ1, 2(R), Arg(R), 2007 It(R), I, W1(R), 2009 W, E, It, NZ1, A
Marchand, R (Poitiers) 1920 S, W
Marfaing, M (Toulouse) 1992 R, Arg 1
Marlu, J (Montferrand, Biarritz) 1998 Fj (R), 2002 S (R), I (R), 2005 E
Marocco, P (Montferrand) 1968 S, I, W, E, R 1, Arg 1,2, A, 1988

Arg 4, 1989 I, 1990 E (R), NZ 1(R), 1991 S, I, W 1, E, US 2, [R, Fj, C, E]
Marot, A (Brive) 1969 R, 1970 S, I, W, 1971 SA 1, 1972 I 2, 1976 A 1
Marquesuzaa, A (RCF) 1958 It, SA 1,2, 1959 S, E, It, W, 1960 S, E, Arg 1
Marracq, H (Pau) 1961 R
Marsh, T (Montferrand) 2001 SA 3, A, Fj, 2002 It, W, E, S, I, Arg, A, 1,2, 2003 [Fj,J,S,I, E,NZ], 2004 C,A,Arg,NZ
Martin, C (Lyon) 1909 I, 1910 W, S
Martin, H (SBUC) 1907 E, 1908 W
Martin, J-L (Béziers) 1971 A 2, R, 1972 S, I 1
Martin, L (Pau) 1948 I, A, S, W, E, 1950 S
Martin, R (SF, Bayonne) 2002 E (t+R), S (R), I (R), 2005 SA1(t&R),2,A1,2,C,SA3, 2006 S,I(t&R),R,SA(R),NZ1(R),2, Arg, 2007 E2,W2, [Arg 1,Gg(R),Arg 2(R)], 2009 NZ2(R), A(R)
Martine, R (Lourdes) 1952 S, I, It, 1953 It, 1954 S, I, NZ, W, E, It, Arg 2, 1955 S, I, W, 1958 A, W, It, I, SA 1,2, 1960 S, E, Arg 3, 1961 S, It
Martinez, A (Narbonne) 2002 A 1, 2004 C
Martinez, G (Toulouse) 1982 W, E, S, Arg 1,2, 1983 E, W
Marty, D (Perpignan) 2005 It,C,Tg, 2006 I,It(R),R(R),NZ1(R),Arg(R), 2007 I,W1,E1,S, E2, [Nm,I,Gg,NZ,E,Arg 2], 2008 S,I,E
Mas, F (Béziers) 1962 R, 1963 S, I, E, W
Mas, N (Perpignan) 2003 NZ, 2005 E, W, I, It, 2007 W1, NZ1, 2(R), E2(R), 3(R), W2, [Nm(R), Gg(R), Arg 2], 2008 S(R), I, E, It, W, Arg(R), PI, A3, 2009 I(R), S, NZ1(R), 2, A(R)
Maso, J (Perpignan, Narbonne) 1966 It, R, 1967 S, R, 1968 S, W, Cz, NZ 1,2,3, A, R, 1969 S, I, W, 1971 SA 1,2, R, 1972 E, W, A 2, 1973 W, I, J, R
Massare, J (PUC) 1945 B 1,2, W, 1946 B, I, W
Massé, A (SBUC) 1908 W, 1909 E, W, 1910 W, S, E, I
Masse, H (Grenoble) 1937 G
Matheu-Cambas, J (Agen) 1945 W, 1946 B, I, K, W, 1947 S, I, W, E, 1948 I, A, S, W, E, 1949 S, I, E, W, Arg 1,2, 1950 E, W, 1951 S, I
Matiu, L (Biarritz) 2000 W, E
Mauduy, G (Périgueux) 1957 It, R 1,2, 1958 S, E, 1961 W, It
Mauran, J (Castres) 1952 SA, W, E, It, 1953 I, E
Mauriat, P (Lyon) 1907 E, 1908 E, W, 1909 W, I, 1910 W, S, E, I, 1011 8, E, W, I, 1012 I, 8, 1013 8, 8A, W, I
Maurin, G (ASF) 1906 E
Maury, A (Toulouse) 1925 I, NZ, G, W, E, 1926 S, I, E
Mayssonnié, A (Toulouse) 1908 E, W, 1910 W
Mazars, L (Narbonne) 2007 NZ2
Mazas, L (Colomiers, Biarritz) 1992 Arg, 1996 SA 1
Médard, M (Toulouse) 2008 Arg, PI, A3, 2009 I, S, W, E, It, NZ1, 2, A
Mela, A (Albi) 2008 S(R),I,It(R),W(R)
Melville, G (Toulon) 1990 I (R), A 1,2,3, NZ 1, 1991 US 2
Menrath, R (SCUF) 1910 W
Menthiller, Y (Romans) 1964 W, It, SA, R, 1965 E
Merceron, G (Montferrand) 1999 R (R), Tg, 2000 S, I, R, 2001 S (R), W, E, SA 1,2, NZ (R), Fj, 2002 It, W, E, S, I, Arg, A 2, C, 2003 E 1, It (R), W (R), NZ (t+R), R (R), E 3, [Fj(R), J(R), S(R), US, E(R), NZ]
Meret, F (Tarbes) 1940 B
Mericq, S (Agen) 1959 I, 1960 S, E, W, 1961 I
Merle, O (Grenoble, Montferrand) 1993 SA 1,2, R 2, A 1,2, 1994 I, W, E, S, C 1, NZ 1,2, C 2, 1995 W, I, R 1, [Tg, S, I, SA, E], It, R 2, Arg, NZ 1,2, 1996 E, S, R, Arg 1,2, W 2, SA 2, 1997 I, W, E, S, It 1, R 1, A 1,2, It 2, R 2, SA 1(R),2
Mermoz, M (Toulouse, Perpignan) 2008 A2, 2009 S(R),NZ2,A
Merquey, J (Toulon)1950 S, I, E, W
Mesnel, F (RCF) 1986 NZ 2(R), 3, 1987 W, E, S, I, [S, Z, Fj, A, NZ], R, 1988 E, Arg 1, 2, 3, 4, R, 1989 I, W, E, S, NZ 1, A 1, 2, 1990 E, S, I, A 2, 3, NZ 1, 2, 1991 S, I, W, 1, E, R, US 1,2, W 2, [R, Fj, C, E], 1992 W, E, S, I, SA 1, 2, 1993 E (R), W, 1995 I, R 1, [Iv, E]
Mesny, P (RCF, Grenoble) 1979 NZ 1, 2, 1980 SA R, 1981 I, W (R), A 1, 2, R, NZ 1, 2, 1982 I, Arg 1, 2
Meyer, G-S (Périgueux) 1960 S, E, It, R, Arg 2
Meynard, J (Cognac) 1954 Arg 1, 1956 Cz
Mias, L (Mazamet) 1951 S, I, E, W, 1952 I, SA, W, E, It, 1953 S,

I, W, It, 1954 S, I, NZ, W, 1957 R 2, 1958 S, E, A, W, I, SA 1, 2, 1959 S, It, W, I

Michalak, F (Toulouse) 2001 SA 3(R), A, Fj (R), 2002 It, A 1, 2, 2003 It, W, Arg 2(R), NZ, R, E 2, [Fj, J, S, I, E, NZ(R)], 2004 I, W, S, E, A, Arg, NZ, 2005 S(R), E(R), W(R), I(R), It(R), SA1, 2, A1, 2, C, Tg(R), SA3, 2006 S, I, It, E, W, 2007 E2(R), 3, [Arg1(t&R), Nm, I, NZ(R), E(R), Arg 2], 2009 It(R)

Mignardi, A (Agen) 2007 NZ1, 2

Mignoni, P (Béziers, Clermont-Auvergne)) 1997 R 2(R), Arg (t), 1999 R (R), WS, NZ 1, W 2(R), [C, Nm], 2002 W, E (R), I (R), Arg, A 2(R), 2005 S, It(R), C(R), 2006 R, 2007 It, I, W1, E1(R), S, E2, 3(R), W2, [Arg 1, Gg, Arg 2(R)]

Milhères, C (Biarritz) 2001 E

Milliand, P (Grenoble) 1936 G 2, 1937 G, It

Millo-Chlusky, R (Toulouse) 2005 SA1, 2008 Arg, PI, A3(R), 2009 I(R), S, W(R), NZ1, 2, A

Milloud, O (Bourgoin) 2000 R (R), 2001 NZ, 2002 W (R), E (R), 2003 It, W (R), Arg 1, R (R), E 2(t+R), 3, [J, S(R), US, I(R), E(R)], 2004 US, C(R), A, Arg, NZ(R), 2005 S(R), E(R), W(R), SA1, 2(R), A1, 2, C(R), Tg, SA3, 2006 S(R), I, It, E(R), W(R), NZ1(R), 2, Arg, 2007 It, I(R), W1, E1, S, E2, 3, [Arg 1, I, Gg, NZ, E]

Minjat, R (Lyon) 1945 B 1

Miorin, H (Toulouse) 1996 R, SA 1, 1997 I, W, E, S, It 1, 2000 It (R), R (R)

Mir, J-H (Lourdes) 1967 R, 1968 I

Mir, J-P (Lourdes) 1967 A

Modin, R (Brive) 1987 [Z]

Moga, A-M-A (Bègles) 1945 B 1, 2, W, 1946 B, I, K, W, 1947 S, I, W, E, 1948 I, A, S, W, E, 1949 S, I, E, W, Arg 1, 2

Mola, U (Dax, Castres) 1997 S (R), 1999 R (R), WS, Tg (R), NZ 1, W 2, [C, Nm, Fj, Arg (R), NZ 2(R), A (R)]

Momméjat, B (Cahors, Albi) 1958 It, I, SA 1, 2, 1959 S, E, It, W, I, 1960 S, E, It, R, 1962 S, E, W, I, It, R, 1963 S, I, W, 1960 S, E, W, It, W, I, 1960 S, E, W, I, It, R, Arg 1, 2, 3, 1961 S, SA, E, W, It, I, NZ 1, 2, 3

Moni, C (Nice, SF) 1996 R, 2000 A, NZ 1, 2, 2001 S, I, It, W

Monié, R (Perpignan) 1956 Cz, 1957 E

Monier, R (SBUC) 1911 I, 1912 S

Monniot, M (RCF) 1912 W, E

Montade, A (Perpignan) 1925 I, NZ, S, W, 1926 W

Montanella, F (Auch) 2007 NZ1(R)

Montlaur, P (Agen) 1992 E (R), 1994 S (R)

Moraitis, B (Toulon) 1969 E, W

Morel, A (Grenoble) 1954 Arg 2

Morère, J (Toulouse) 1927 E, G 1, 1928 S, A

Moscato, V (Bègles) 1991 R, US 1, 1992 W, E

Mougeot, C (Bègles) 1992 W, E, Arg

Mouniq, P (Toulouse) 1911 S, E, W, I, 1912 I, E, 1913 S, SA, E

Moure, H (SCUF) 1908 E

Moureu, P (Béziers) 1920 I, US, 1921 W, E, I, 1922 S, W, I, 1923 S, W, E, I, 1924 S, I, E, W, 1925 E

Mournet, A (Bagnères) 1981 A 1(R)

Mouronval, F (SF) 1909 I

Muhr, A H (RCF) 1906 NZ, E, 1907 E

Murillo, G (Dijon) 1954 It, Arg 1

Nallet, L (Bourgoin, Castres) 2000 R, 2001 E, SA 1(R), 2(R), NZ, SA 3(R), A (R), Fj (R), 2003 NZ, 2005 A2(R), C, Tg(R), SA3, 2006 I(R), It(R), E(R), W(R), R, SA(R), NZ1(R), 2, Arg, 2007 It, I, W1, E1, S, E3(R), [Nm, I(R), Gg, Arg 2], 2008 S, I, E, It, W, A1, 2, Arg, PI, A3, 2009 I, S, W, E, It

Namur, R (Toulon) 1931 E, G

Noble, J-C (La Voulte) 1968 E, W, Cz, NZ 3, A, R

Normand, A (Toulouse) 1957 R 1

Novès, G (Toulouse) 1977 NZ 1, 2, R, 1978 W, R, 1979 I, W

Ntamack, E (Toulouse) 1994 W, C 1, NZ 1, 2, 2, C 2, 1995 W, I, R 1, [Tg, S, I, SA, E], It, R 2, Arg, NZ 1, 2, 1996 E, S, I, W 1, R (R), Arg 1, 2, W 2, 1997 I, 1998 Arg 3, 1999 I, W 1, E, S, WS, NZ 1, W 2(R), [C (R, Nm, Fj, Arg, NZ 2, A], 2000 W, E, S, I, It

Ntamack F (Colomiers) 2001 SA 3

Nyanga, Y (Béziers, Toulouse) 2004 US, C, 2005 S(R), E(R), W, I, It, SA1, 2, A1(R), 2, C(t&R), Tg, SA3, 2006 S, I, It, E, W, 2007 E2(R), 3, [Nm, I(R), Gg, Arg 2]

Olibeau, O (Perpignan) 2007 NZ1(R), 2(R)

Olive, D (Montferrand) 1951 I, 1952 I

Ondarts, P (Biarritz O) 1986 NZ 3, 1987 W, E, S, I, [S, Z, Fj, A,

NZ], R, 1988 E, I, W, Arg 1, 2, 3, 4, R, 1989 I, W, E, NZ 1, 2, A 2, 1990 W, E, S, I, R (R), NZ 1, 2, 1991 S, I, W 1, E, US 2, W 2, [R, Fj, C, E]

Orso, J-C (Nice, Toulon) 1982 Arg 1, 2, 1983 E, S, A 1, 1984 E (R), S, NZ 1, 1985 I (R), W, 1988 I

Othats, J (Dax) 1960 Arg 2, 3

Ouedraogo, F (Montpellier) 2007 NZ2(R), 2008 S, I, E(R), It, W, A1, 2, Arg(R), PI, A3, 2009 I, S, W, NZ1, 2, A

Ougier, S (Toulouse) 1992 R, Arg 1, 1993 E (R), 1997 It 1

Paco, A (Béziers) 1974 Arg 1, 2, R, SA 1, 2, 1975 W, E, Arg 1, 2, R, 1976 S, I, W, E, US, A 1, 2, R, 1977 W, E, S, I, NZ 1, 2, R, 1978 E, S, I, W, R, 1979 I, W, E, S, 1980 W

Palat, J (Perpignan) 1938 G 2

Palisson, A (Brive) 2008 A1, 2, Arg(R), PI(R), A3(R)

Palmié, M (Béziers) 1975 SA 1, 2, Arg 1, 2, R, 1976 S, I, W, E, US, 1977 W, E, S, I, Arg 1, 2, NZ 1, 2, R, 1978 E, S, I, W

Paoli, R (see Simonpaoli)

Paparemborde, R (Pau) 1975 SA 1, 2, Arg 1, 2, R, 1976 S, I, W, E, US, A 1, 2, R, 1977 W, E, S, I, Arg 1, NZ 1, 2, 1978 E, S, I, W, R, 1979 I, W, E, S, NZ 1, 2, R, 1980 W, E, S, SA, R, 1981 S, I, W, E, A 1, 2, R, NZ 1, 2, 1982 W, I, R, Arg 1, 2

Papé, P (Bourgoin, Castres, SF) 2004 I, It, W, S, E, C, NZ(R), 2005 I(R), It(R), SA1, 2, A1, 2006 NZ1, 2, 2007 It(R), I, S(R), NZ1, 2, 2008 E, 2009 NZ1, A

Pardo, L (Hendaye) 1924 I, E

Pardo, L (Bayonne) 1980 SA, R, 1981 S, I, W, E, A 1, 1982 W, E, S, 1983 A 1(R), 1985 S, I, Arg 2

Pargade, J-H (Lyon U) 1953 It

Pariès, L (Biarritz O) 1968 SA 2, R, 1970 S, I, W, 1975 E, S, I

Parra, M (Bourgoin) 2008 S(R), I(R), E, Arg(R), 2009 I(R), S(R), W, E, It

Pascalin, P (Mont-de-Marsan) 1950 I, E, W, 1951 S, I, E, W

Pascarel, J-R (TOEC) 1912 W, E, 1913 S, SA, E, I

Pascot, J (Perpignan) 1922 S, E, I, 1923 S, 1926 I, 1927 G 2

Paul, R (Montferrand) 1940 B

Pauthe, G (Graulhet) 1956 E

Pebeyre, E-J (Fumel, Brive) 1945 W, 1946 I, K, W, 1947 S, I, W, E

Pebeyre, M (Vichy, Montferrand) 1970 E, W, 1971 I, SA 1, 2, A 1, 1973 W

Péclier, A (Bourgoin) 2004 US, C

Pécune, J (Tarbes) 1974 W, E, S, 1975 Arg 1, 2, R, 1976 I, W, E, US

Pédeutour, P (Bègles) 1980 I

Pellissier, L (RCF) 1928 A, I, E, G, W

Pelous, F (Dax, Toulouse) 1995 R 2, Arg, NZ 1, 2, 1996 E, S, I, R (R), Arg 1, 2, W 2, SA, I 1, 1997 I, W, E, S, It 1, R 1, A 1, 2, It 2, R 2, Arg, SA 1, 2(R), 1998 E, S, I, W, Arg 1, 2, Fj, Arg 3, A, 1999 I, W 1, E, R (R), WS, Tg (R), NZ 1, W 2, [C, Nm, Fj, NZ 2, A], 2000 W, E, S, I, It, A, NZ 1, 2, 2001 S, I, It, W, E, 2002 It (R), W (R), E(R), S, I, Arg, A 1, 2, SA, NZ, C, 2003 E 1, S, I, It, W, R, E 2, 3(R), [Fj, J, S, I, E, NZ(R)], 2004 I, It, W, S, E, US, C, A, Arg, NZ, 2005 S, E, W, I, It, A2, 2006 S, I, It, E, W, R, SA, NZ1, 2007 E2, 3, W2(R), [Arg1, Nm(R), Gg(R), NZ, E]

Penaud, A (Brive, Toulouse) 1992 W, E, S, I, R, Arg 1, 2, SA 1, 2, Arg, 1993 R 1, SA 1, 2, R 2, A 1, 2, 1994 I, W, E, 1995 NZ 1, 2, 1996 S, R, Arg 1, 2, W 2, 1997 I, E, R 1, A 2, 2000 W (R), It

Périé, M (Toulon) 1996 E, S, I (R)

Péron, P (RCF) 1975 SA 1, 2

Perrier, P (Bayonne) 1982 W, E, S, I (R)

Pesteil, J-P (Béziers) 1975 SA 1, 1976 A 2, R

Petit, C (Lorraine) 1931 W

Peyras, R (Bayonne) 2008 A2(R)

Peyrelade, H (Tarbes) 1940 B

Peyrelongue, J (Biarritz) 2004 It, S(R), C(R), A(R), Arg(R), NZ

Peyroutou, G (Périgueux) 1911 S, E

Phliponeau, J-F (Montferrand) 1973 W, I

Piazza, A (Montauban) 1968 NZ 1, A

Picamoles, L (Montpellier) 2008 I(R), E, It, A1, 2(t&R), Arg, PI(R), A3(R), 2009 I(R), S(R), E(R), It(R), NZ1, 2

Picard, T (Montferrand) 1985 Arg 2, 1986 R 1(R), Arg 2

Pierre, J (Bourgoin) 2007 NZ1, 2

Pierrot, G (Pau) 1914 I, W, E

Pilon, J (Périgueux) 1949 E, 1950 E

Piqué, J (Pau) 1961 NZ 2, 3, A, 1962 S, It, 1964 NZ, E, W, It, I, SA, Fj, R, 1965 S, I, E, W, It

Piquemal, M (Tarbes) 1927 I, S, 1929 I, G, 1930 S, I, E, G, W

Piquiral, E (RCF) 1924 S, I, E, W, R, US, 1925 E, 1926 S, I, E, W, M, 1927 I, S, W, E, G 1, 2, 1928 E

Piteu (Pau) 1921 S, W, E, I, 1922 S, E, W, I, 1923 E, 1924 E, 1925 I, NZ, W, E, 1926 E

Plantefol, A (RCF) 1967 SA 2, 3, 4, NZ, R, 1968 E, W, Cz, NZ 2, 1969 E, W

Plantey, S (RCF) 1961 A, 1962 It

Podevin, G (SF) 1913 W, I

Poeydebasque, F (Bayonne) 1914 I, W

Poirier, A (SCUF) 1907 E

Poitrenaud, C (Toulouse) 2001 SA 3, A, Fj, 2003 E 1, S, I, It, W, Arg 1, NZ, E 3, [J, US, E(R), NZ], 2004 E(R), US, C, Arg(R), NZ, 2006 R, 2007 It, I, W1, E1, S, E2, 3, [Nm, I, Gg, Arg 2], 2009 I, S

Pomathios, M (Agen, Lyon U, Bourg) 1948 I, A, S, W, E, 1949 S, I, E, W, Arg 1, 2, 1950 S, I, W, 1951 S, I, E, W, 1952 W, E, 1953 S, I, W, 1954 S

Pons, P (Toulouse) 1920 S, E, W, 1921 S, W, 1922 S

Porcu, C (Agen) 2002 Arg (R), A 1, 2(R)

Porra, M (Lyon) 1931 I

Porthault, A (RCF) 1951 S, E, W, 1952 I, 1953 S, I, It

Portolan, C (Toulouse) 1986 A, 1989 I, E

Potel, A (Begles) 1932 G

Poux, J-B (Narbonne, Toulouse) 2001 Fj (R), 2002 S, I (R), Arg, A 1(R), 2(R), 2003 E 3, [Fj, J, US, NZ], 2007 E2, 3, W2(R), [Nm, I(R), Gg, NZ(R), E(R), Arg 2], 2008 E(R), It(R), W(R)

Prat, J (Lourdes) 1945 B 1, 2, W, 1946 B, I, K, W, 1947 S, I, W, E, 1948 I, A, S, W, E, 1949 S, I, E, W, Arg 1, 2, 1950 S, I, E, W, 1951 S, E, W, 1952 S, I, SA, W, E, It, 1953 S, I, E, W, It, 1954 S, I, NZ, W, E, It, 1955 S, I, E, W, It

Prat, M (Lourdes) 1951 I, 1952 S, I, SA, W, E, 1953 S, I, E, 1954 I, NZ, W, E, It, 1955 S, I, E, W, It, 1956 I, W, It, Cz, 1957 S, I, W, It, R 1, 1958 A, W, I

Prévost, A (Albi) 1926 M, 1927 I, S, W

Prin-Clary, J (Cavaillon, Brive) 1945 B 1, 2, W, 1946 B, I, K, W, 1947 S, I, W

Privat, T (Béziers, Clermont-Auvergne) 2001 SA 3, A, Fj, 2002 It, W, S (R), SA (R), 2003 [NZ], 2005 SA2, A1(R)

Puech, L (Toulouse) 1920 S, E, 1921 E, I

Puget, M (Toulouse) 1961 It, 1966 S, I, It, 1967 SA 1, 3, 4, NZ, 1968 Cz, NZ 1, 2, SA 1, 2, R, 1969 E, R, 1970 W

Puig, A (Perpignan) 1926 S, E

Pujol, A (SOE Toulouse) 1906 NZ

Pujolle, M (Nice) 1989 B, A 1, 1990 S, I, R, A 1, 2, NZ 2

Puricelli, J (Bayonne) 2009 NZ1(R), A

Quaglio, A (Mazamet) 1957 R 2, 1958 S, E, A, W, I, SA 1, 2, 1959 S, E, It, W, I

Quilis, A (Narbonne) 1967 SA 1, 4, NZ, 1970 R, 1971 I

Rabadan, P (SF) 2004 US(R), C(R)

Ramis, R (Perpignan) 1922 E, I, 1923 W

Rancoule, H (Lourdes, Toulon, Tarbes) 1955 E, W, It, 1958 A, W, It, I, SA 1, 1959 S, It, W, 1960 I, It, R, Arg 1, 2, 1961 SA, E, W, It, NZ 1, 2, 1962 S, E, W, I, It

Rapin, A (SBUC) 1938 R

Raymond, F (Toulouse) 1925 S, 1927 W, 1928 I

Raynal, F (Perpignan) 1935 G, 1936 G 1, 2, 1937 G, It

Raynaud, F (Carcassonne) 1933 G

Raynaud, M (Narbonne) 1999 W 1, E (R)

Razat, J-P (Agen) 1962 R, 1963 S, I, R

Rebujent, R (RCF) 1963 E

Revailler, D (Graulhet) 1981 S, I, W, E, A 1, 2, R, NZ 1, 2, 1982 W, S, I, R, Arg 1

Revillon, J (RCF) 1926 I, E, 1927 S

Ribère, E (Perpignan, Quillan) 1924 I, 1925, I, NZ, S, 1926 S, I, W, M, 1927 I, S, W, E, G 1, 2, 1928 S, A, I, E, G, W, 1929 I, E, G, 1930 S, I, E, W, 1931 I, S, W, E, G, 1932 G, 1933 G

Rives, J-P (Toulouse, RCF) 1975 E, S, I, Arg 1, 2, R, 1976 S, I, W, E, US, A 1, 2, R, 1977 W, E, S, I, Arg 1, 2, R, 1978 E, S, I, W, R, 1979 I, W, E, S, NZ 1, 2, R, 1980 W, E, S, SA, 1981 S, I, W, E, A 2, 1982 W, E, S, I, R, 1983 E, S, I, W, A 1, 2, R, 1984 I, W, E, S

Rochon, A (Montferrand) 1936 G 1

Rodrigo, M (Mauléon) 1931 I, W

Rodriguez, L (Mont-de-Marsan, Montferrand, Dax) 1981 A 1, 2, R, NZ 1, 2, 1982 W, E, S, I, R, 1983 E, S, 1984 I, NZ 1, 2, R, 1985 E, S, I, W, 1986 Arg 1, A, R 2, NZ 2, 3, 1987 W, E, S, I, [S, Z, Fj, A, NZ], R, 1988 E, S, I, W, Arg 1, 2, 3, 4, R, 1989 I, E, S, NZ 1, 2, B, A 1, 1990 W, E, S, I, NZ 1

Rogé, L (Béziers) 1952 It, 1953 E, W, It, 1954 S, Arg 1, 2, 1955 S, I, 1956 W, It, E, 1957 S, 1960 S, E

Rollet, J (Bayonne) 1960 Arg 3, 1961 NZ 3, A, 1962 It, 1963 I

Romero, H (Montauban) 1962 S, E, W, I, It, R, 1963 E

Romeu, J-P (Montferrand) 1972 R, 1973 S, NZ, E, W, I, R, 1974 W, E, S, Arg 1, 2, R, SA 1, 2(R), 1975 W, SA 2, Arg 1, 2, R, 1976 S, I, W, E, US, 1977 W, E, S, I, Arg 1, 2, NZ 1, 2, R

Roques, A (Cahors) 1958 A, W, It, I, SA 1, 2, 1959 S, E, W, I, 1960 S, E, W, I, It, Arg 1, 2, 3, 1961 S, SA, E, W, It, I, 1962 S, E, W, I, It, 1963 S

Roques, J-C (Brive) 1966 S, I, It, R

Rossignol, J-C (Brive) 1972 A 2

Rouan, J (Narbonne) 1953 S, I

Roucariès, G (Perpignan) 1956 S

Rouffia, L (Narbonne) 1945 B 2, W, 1946 W, 1948 I

Rougerie, A (Montferrand, Clermont-Auvergne) 2001 SA 3, A, Fj (R), 2002 It, W, E, S, I, Arg, A 1, 2, 2003 E 1, S, I, It, W, Arg 1, 2, NZ, R, E 2, 3(R), [Fj, J, S, I, E], 2004 US, C, A, Arg, NZ, 2005 S, W, A2, C, Tg, SA3, 2006 I, It, E, W, NZ1, 2, 2007 E2, W2, [Arg1, Nm(R), I(R), Gg, Arg 2], 2008 S(R), I, E, It

Rougerie, J (Montferrand) 1973 J

Rougé-Thomas, P (Toulouse) 1989 NZ 1, 2

Roujas, F (Tarbes) 1910 I

Roumat, O (Dax) 1989 NZ 2(R), B, 1990 W, E, S, I, R, A 1, 2, 3, NZ 1, 2, 1991 S, I, W 1, E, R, US 1, W 2, [R, Fj, C, E], 1992 W (R), E (R), S, I, SA 1, 2, Arg, 1993 E, S, I, W, R 1, SA 1, 2, R 2, A 1, 2, 1994 I, W, E, C 1, NZ 1, 2, C 2, 1995 W, E, S, [Iv, S, I, SA, E], 1996 E, S, I, W 1, Arg 1, 2

Rousie, M (Villeneuve) 1931 S, G, 1932 G, 1933 G

Rousset, G (Béziers) 1975 SA 1, 1976 US

Rué, J-B (Agen) 2002 SA (R), C (R), 2003 E 1(R), S (R), It (R), W (R), Arg 1, 2(R)

Ruiz, A (Tarbes) 1968 SA 2, R

Rupert, J-J (Tyrosse) 1963 R, 1964 S, Fj, 1965 E, W, It, 1966 S, I, E, W, 1967 It, R, 1968 S

Sadourny, J-L (Colomiers) 1991 W 2(R), [C (R)], 1992 E (R), S, I, Arg 1(R), 2, 1993 R 1, SA 1, 2, R 2, A 1, 2, 1994 I, W, E, S, C 1, NZ 1, 2, C 2, 1995 W, E, S, I, R 1, [Tg, S, I, SA, E], It, R 2, Arg, NZ 1, 2, 1996 E, S, I, W 1, Arg 1, 2, W 2, SA 2, 1997 I, W, E, S, It 1, R 1, A 1, 2, It 2 R 2, Arg, SA 1, 2, 1998 E, S, I, W, 1999 R, Tg, NZ 1(R), 2000 NZ 2, 2001 It, W, E

Sagot, P (SF) 1906 NZ, 1908 E, 1909 W

Sahuc, A (Métro) 1945 B 1, 2

Sahuc, F (Toulouse) 1936 G 2

Saint-André, P (Montferrand, Gloucester) 1990 R, A 3, NZ 1, 2, 1991 I (R), W 1, E, US 1, W 2, [R, Fj, C, E], 1992 W, E, S, I, R, SA 1, 2, 1993 E, S, I, W, SA 1, 2, A 1, 2, 1994 I, W, E, S, C 1, NZ 1, 2, C 2, 1995 W, E, S, I, R 1, [Tg, Iv, S, I, SA, E], It, R 2, Arg, NZ 1, 2, 1996 E, S, I, W 1, R, Arg 1, 2, W 2, 1997 It 1, 2, R 2, Arg, SA 1, 2

Saisset, O (Béziers) 1971 R, 1972 S, I I, A 1, 2, 1973 S, NZ, E, W, I, J, R, 1974 I, Arg 2, SA 1, 2, 1975 W

Salas, P (Narbonne) 1979 NZ 1, 2, R, 1980 W, E, 1981 A 1, 1982 Arg 2

Salinié, R (Perpignan) 1923 E

Sallefranque, M (Dax) 1981 A 2, 1982 W, E, S

Salut, J (TOEC) 1966 R, 1967 S, 1968 I, E, Cz, NZ 1, 1969 I

Samatan, R (Agen) 1930 S, I, E, G, W, 1931 I, S, W, E, G

Sanac, A (Perpignan) 1952 It, 1953 S, I, 1954 S, 1956 Cz, 1957 S, I, E, W, It

Sangalli, F (Narbonne) 1975 I, SA 1, 2, 1976 S, A 1, 2, R, 1977 W, E, S, I, Arg 1, 2, NZ 1, 2

Sanz, H (Narbonne) 1988 Arg 3, 4, R, 1989 A 2, 1990 S, I, R, A 1, 2, NZ 2, 1991 W 2

Sappa, M (Nice) 1973 J, R, 1977 R

Sarrade, R (Pau) 1929 I

Sarraméa, O (Castres) 1999 R, WS (R), Tg, NZ 1

Saux, J-P (Pau) 1960 W, It, Arg 1, 2, 1961 SA, E, W, It, I, NZ 1, 2, 3, A, 1962 S, E, W, I, It, 1963 S, I, E, It

Savitsky, M (La Voulte) 1969 R

Savy, M (Montferrand) 1931 I, S, W, E, 1936 G 1

Sayrou, J (Perpignan) 1926 W, M, 1928 E, G, W, 1929 S, W, E, G

Viviès, B (Agen) 1978 E, S, I, W, 1980 SA, R, 1981 S, A 1, 1983 A 1(R)

Volot, M (SF) 1945 W, 1946 B, I, K, W

Weller, S (Grenoble) 1989 A 1, 2, 1990 A 1, NZ 1

Wolf, J-P (Béziers) 1980 SA, R, 1981 A 2, 1982 E

Yachvili, D (Biarritz) 2002 C (R), 2003 S (R), I, It, W, R (R), E 3, [US, NZ], 2004 I(R), It(R), W(R), S, E, 2005 S(R), E, W, I, It, SA1(R), 2, C, Tg, 2006 S(R), I(R), It(R), E, W, SA, NZ1, 2(R), Arg, 2007 E1, 2008 E(R), It, W(R), A1, 2(R), 2009 NZ1(R), 2(R), A

Yachvili, M (Tulle, Brive) 1968 E, W, Cz, NZ 3, A, R, 1969 S, I, R, 1971 E, SA 1, 2 A 1, 1972 R, 1975 SA 2

Zago, F (Montauban) 1963 I, E

Phil Walter/Getty Images

Damien Traille went through the 70-cap barrier in 2009, into the top ten of France's most-capped players.

THE COUNTRIES

GEORGIA

GEORGIA'S 2008–09 TEST RECORD

OPPONENTS	DATE	VENUE	RESULT
Scotland A	14 November	A	**Lost** 3–69
Germany	7 February	A	**Won** 38–5
Portugal	14 February	H	**Drew** 20–20
Spain	28 February	A	**Won** 55–11
Romania	14 March	H	**Won** 28–23
Russia	22 March	N	**Won** 29–21
Canada	6 June	N	**Lost** 10–42
Ireland A	14 June	N	**Lost** 5–40
USA	21 June	A	**Lost** 13–31

FULL OF EASTERN PROMISE

By Frankie Deges

Georgia's rugby development received a big boost in 2009, with a young side taking part in the Churchill Cup.

With the top tier of the European Nations Cup to determine the region's two direct qualifiers for Rugby World Cup 2011, Georgia are halfway to realising their goal of a playing in a third successive tournament having ended the 2008–09 season on top of the standings with the only unbeaten record after four wins and a draw.

The Georgian Lelos began the season as defending ENC champions and also ended it in the same manner, following the decision at the Annual General Meeting of the FIRA-AER – the largest of the IRB's Regional Associations – in December to recognise champions at the end of each season, rather than every other year.

Promotion and relegation will still be determined over the two-year format, but if Georgia can replicate their performances when the top division picks up again in February and March and again finish top they will join England, Argentina, Scotland and the cross-continental play-off winner in Pool B. A runners-up finish will see them qualify as Europe 2 and slot into Pool C with Australia, Ireland, Italy and Americas 2. Even a third place finish will still keep their RWC 2011 hopes alive, but throw them into the play-offs.

Qualifying for another Rugby World Cup would reflect fairly on a Union that is working positively to ensure sustained growth. Five new clubs were formed in the last year – the number now reaches 41 nation-wide – and registered players rose by almost 20 percent, going from 3,200 to 4,100. The national government is supportive of rugby, with a special four-year support programme that has been of great assistance in spreading the game outside of Tbilisi.

Crowds in excess of 12,000 per game attended the two home matches of the Lelos, a great indication of the strength of the game in a country of some 4.2 million inhabitants.

Georgia's 2008–09 international season started with a first ever trip to Scotland. On a cold night at Firhill Stadium in Glasgow, Scotland A proved too strong for the visitors. With many capped players, the Scots crossed for 11 unanswered tries for a 69–3 win. The two-match tour finished in darkness when the floodlights at Boroughmuir's ground failed after 25 minutes with Edinburgh Gunners leading 19–0, courtesy of three early tries.

Tim Lane's side then went their own ways, the majority returning to their clubs in France. This continues to be the situation with the Georgian national side; its best players have to abandon the country in search of a better future in stronger economic climates. The best players continue to shine for Top 14 sides and other French clubs.

When the squad regrouped, it was with the goal of defending the European Nations Cup title they had won over the previous two seasons. Lane, a much travelled coach who worked with the 1999 world champion Wallabies and also with the Springboks and has been instrumental in taking the Georgian national side to a new level, was able to select most of his first choice players and the road began in Heidelberg where Germany were beaten 38–5. Mamuka Gorgodze scored a brace to lead the way as Georgia showed their intent for the campaign ahead with a six-try romp.

Twelve thousand spectators attended a key game against Portugal at the National Stadium in Tbilisi. Portugal, having lost 18–14 to Russia seven days earlier in their first match, could not afford a second loss and so Os Lobos and the Lelos met in an exciting encounter. Portugal edged the first half 10–3 and then with both teams locked at 13–13, the visitors scored a converted try in the 79th minute. Georgia, though, did not give up and minutes later lock Ilia Zedginidze scored his 14th and most important Test try, full-back Merab Kvirikashvili kicking the conversion to earn the celebrated draw.

Two weeks later Lane's side faced Spain at the Ciudad Universitaria in their capital Madrid and after a quiet first half Georgia turned on the afterburners to win 55–11, scoring six of their eight tries in the final 35 minutes.

GEORGIA

Tbilisi hosted a second Lelos match with more than 15,000 spectators witnessing another thrilling battle against the Romanian Oaks. Two very proud rugby nations, with the smell of Rugby World Cup 2011 in their nostrils, were always going to play an exciting game. Georgia would come out on top 28–23, securing the Antim Cup at stake whenever the two countries meet.

After going into half-time with a 15–13 advantage, the Lelos continued to dominate, at one stage leading 28–16 before a last minute Romanian try made the match appear closer. This win almost assured the Lelos of the 2008–09 title, although standing between them and the silverware was Russia in a match which would take place on neutral soil in the Ukraine.

Two quick tries in the space of five minutes in the first quarter, followed by a third almost on half-time generated sufficient comfort for Georgia to go into the break leading 19–6. Despite stretching that lead to 24–6, Russia, with the vocal support of the Mariupol crowd, fought back to within three points going into the final minutes. Wing Irakli Machkaneli came to the rescue with a try in the 42nd minute to seal the title and ensure Georgia goes into the second half of the RWC 2011 qualifying process in prime position.

A depleted squad – the top Georgian players were involved in the French league finals – travelled to Colorado, USA, in June to play in the Churchill Cup. It was a great opportunity for a number of young aspiring players, still playing in Georgia, to sample a higher degree of rugby.

Georgia's first participation in a tournament that dates back to 2003 showed that there is still a gap with some of the more established nations, yet given that this tournament, as well as other IRB supported events, are a major component in the development of professional player pools for national teams, the benefits will be seen longer term. Nine of the 28 players in the squad were based in Georgia with the top five clubs, RC AIA, Lelo, Locomotiv, Kochebi and Universteti.

Having said this, their opening game of the Churchill Cup was a 42–10 defeat at the hands of Canada, David Dadunashvili scoring his team's only try with the Canucks crossing for five of their own. A week later, eventual champions Ireland A proved too strong and again a single try in the first half was all Georgia managed, the Irish scoring six tries for a 40–5 win.

To round off the three-week tour, hosts USA stood between Georgia and a fifth place finish. The Eagles were better drilled and with the assistance of vocal crowd support won the Bowl final 31–13. Georgia scored, again, a solitary converted try against USA's three.

In a season in which Rugby Sevens took centre stage because of Rugby World Cup Sevens and the voting for Olympic inclusion, the short version of the game was not kind to Georgia. Invited to four IRB Sevens World Series tournaments and having qualified for RWC Sevens, the Sevens Lelos went through a winless period that included 24 consecutive losses against 13 different opponents and scoring an average of one try per game. Six of the games were in fact try-less and the most they scored was a brace in seven of those 24 games.

What was most worrying was the fact that there were no close losses in the five tournaments. With the dream of Rugby Sevens going to the Olympic Games and the importance this is given by governments such as the Georgian, this is a facet of the game that needs to be worked upon.

Some belated happiness came at the Hanover Sevens, the European region's showpiece event, where Georgia beat Portugal, Romania and Moldova to take some silverware back home to Tbilisi in the form of the Plate.

At Age Grade level, the Georgia Under 19s lost the final of the European Championship and with it a ticket to the IRB Junior World Rugby Trophy 2009 in Kenya. In an entertaining and hard-fought final Romania beat the young Lelos 31–28 in Poland. The Oaks would go on to win the Junior World Rugby Trophy in Nairobi.

Locomotiv continued to dominate the domestic club scene, winning the 2008 title, the Palm Cup, for the sixth time – to go with successes in 2000, 2001, 2003, 2005 and 2006. They beat Lelo 19–9 in the final, which was played in the city of Vake. Locomotiv duly had five players named in the Domestic XV for the season.

GEORGIA

John Gichigi/Getty Images

Alexander Nizharadze of Georgia scores against England during the Edinburgh Sevens at Murrayfield.

GEORGIA INTERNATIONAL RECORDS
MATCH RECORDS UP TO 30TH SEPTEMBER 2009

WINNING MARGIN

Date	Opponent	Result	Winning Margin
07/04/2007	Czech Republic	98–3	95
03/02/2002	Netherlands	88–0	88
26/02/2005	Ukraine	65–0	65
12/06/2005	Czech Republic	75–10	65

MOST POINTS IN A MATCH
BY THE TEAM

Date	Opponent	Result	Pts.
07/04/2007	Czech Republic	98–3	98
03/02/2002	Netherlands	88–0	88
12/06/2005	Czech Republic	75–10	75
23/03/1995	Bulgaria	70–8	70

MOST TRIES IN A MATCH
BY THE TEAM

Date	Opponent	Result	Tries
07/04/2007	Czech Republic	98–3	16
03/02/2002	Netherlands	88–0	14
23/03/1995	Bulgaria	70–8	11
26/02/2005	Ukraine	75–10	11
12/06/2005	Czech Republic	70–8	11

MOST CONVERSIONS IN A MATCH
BY THE TEAM

Date	Opponent	Result	Cons
03/02/2002	Netherlands	88–0	9
07/04/2007	Czech Republic	98–3	9
12/06/2005	Czech Republic	75–10	7
23/03/1995	Bulgaria	70–8	6

MOST PENALTIES IN A MATCH
BY THE TEAM

Date	Opponent	Result	Pens
08/03/2003	Russia	23–17	6

MOST DROP GOALS IN A MATCH
BY THE TEAM

Date	Opponent	Result	DGs
20/10/1996	Russia	29–20	2
21/11/1991	Ukraine	19–15	2
15/07/1992	Ukraine	15–0	2
04/06/1994	Switzerland	22–21	2

MOST POINTS IN A MATCH
BY A PLAYER

Date	Player	Opponent	Pts.
08/03/2003	Pavle Jimsheladze	Russia	23
07/04/2007	Merab Kvirikashvili	Czech Republic	23
12/06/2005	Malkhaz Urjukashvili	Czech Republic	20
28/10/2006	Malkhaz Urjukashvili	Spain	19
06/04/2002	Malkhaz Urjukashvili	Romania	18
03/02/2002	Pavle Jimsheladze	Netherlands	18

MOST TRIES IN A MATCH
BY A PLAYER

Date	Player	Opponent	Tries
23/03/1995	Pavle Jimsheladze	Bulgaria	3
23/03/1995	Archil Kavtarashvili	Bulgaria	3
12/06/2005	Mamuka Gorgodze	Czech Republic	3
07/04/2007	David Dadunashvili	Czech Republic	3
07/04/2007	Malkhaz Urjukashvili	Czech Republic	3
26/04/2008	Mamuka Gorgodze	Spain	3

MOST CONVERSIONS IN A MATCH
BY A PLAYER

Date	Player	Opponent	Cons
03/02/2002	Pavle Jimsheladze	Netherlands	9
07/04/2007	Merab Kvirikashvili	Czech Republic	9
12/06/2005	Malkhaz Urjukashvili	Czech Republic	7
23/03/1995	Kakha Machitidze	Bulgaria	6

MOST PENALTIES IN A MATCH
BY A PLAYER

Date	Player	Opponent	Pens
08/03/2003	Pavle Jimsheladze	Russia	6

MOST DROP GOALS IN A MATCH
BY A PLAYER

Date	Player	Opponent	DGs
15/07/1992	Davit Chavleishvili	Ukraine	2

MOST CAPPED PLAYERS

Player	Caps
Malkhaz Urjukashvili	58
Pavle Jimsheladze	57
Irakli Abuseridze	57
Besiki Khamashuridze	53
Akvsenti Giorgadze	53
Grigol Labadze	53

LEADING TRY SCORERS

Player	Tries
Malkhaz Urjukashvili	17
Mamuka Gorgodze	15
Ilia Zedginidze	14
Irakli Machkhaneli	13
Besiki Khamashuridze	12

LEADING CONVERSIONS SCORERS

Player	Cons
Pavle Jimsheladze	61
Malkhaz Urjukashvili	40
Merab Kvirikashvili	32
Nugzar Dzagnidze	9

LEADING PENALTY SCORERS

Player	Pens
Pavle Jimsheladze	48
Malkhaz Urjukashvili	37
Nugzar Dzagnidze	22
Merab Kvirikashvili	20

LEADING DROP GOAL SCORERS

Player	DGs
Kakha Machitidze	4
Nugzar Dzagnidze	3
Pavle Jimsheladze	3

LEADING POINTS SCORERS

Player	Pts.
Pavle Jimsheladze	320
Malkhaz Urjukashvili	279
Merab Kvirikashvili	137
Nugzar Dzagnidze	105

GEORGIA

GEORGIA INTERNATIONAL PLAYERS
UP TO 30TH SEPTEMBER 2009

Note: Years given for International Championship matches are for second half of season; eg 1972 means season 1971–72. Years for all other matches refer to the actual year of the match.

V Abashidze 1998 *It, Ukr, I,* 1999 *Tg, Tg,* 2000 *It, Mor, Sp,* 2001 *H, Pt, Rus, Sp, R,* 2006 *J*

N Abdaladze 1997 *Cro, De*

I Abuseridze 2000 *It, Pt, Mor, Sp, H, R,* 2001 *H, Pt, Rus, Sp, R,* 2002 *Pt, Rus, Sp, R, I, Rus,* 2003 *Pt, Rus, CZR, R, It, E, Sa, SA,* 2004 *Rus,* 2005 *Pt, Ukr, R,* 2006 *Rus, R, Pt, Ukr, J, R, Sp, Pt, Pt,* 2007 *R, Rus, CZR, Nm, ESp, ItA, Ar, I, Nm, F,* 2008 *Pt, R, Pt, Rus, Sp,* 2009 *Ger, Pt, R, Rus*

V Akhvlediani 2007 *CZR*

K Alania 1993 *Lux,* 1994 *Swi,* 1996 *CZR, CZR, Rus,* 1997 *Pt, Pol, Cro, De,* 1998 *It,* 2001 *H, Pt, Sp, F, SA,* 2002 *H, Pt, Rus, Sp, R, I, Rus,* 2003 *Rus,* 2004 *Pt, Sp*

N Andghuladze 1997 *Pol,* 2000 *It, Pt, Mor, Sp, H, R,* 2004 *Sp, Rus, CZR, R*

D Ashvetia 1998 *Ukr,* 2005 *Pt,* 2006 *R,* 2007 *Sp*

K Asieshvili 2008 *ItA*

G Babunashvili 1992 *Ukr, Ukr, Lat,* 1993 *Rus, Pol, Lux,* 1996 *CZR*

Z Bakuradze 1989 *Z,* 1990 *Z,* 1991 *Ukr, Ukr,* 1993 *Rus, Pol*

D Baramidze 2000 *H*

O Barkalaia 2002 *I,* 2004 *Sp, Rus, CZR, R, Ur, Ch, Rus,* 2005 *Pt, Ukr, R, CZR, Ch,* 2006 *Rus, R, Pt, Ukr, J, Bb, R, Sp,* 2007 *Nm, ItA, I, F,* 2008 *Pt, R, Pt, Rus, Sp, ESp, Ur, ItA,* 2009 *Ger, R*

D Basilaia 2008 *Pt, R, Pt, CZR, Rus, Sp,* 2009 *Ger, R, C, US*

R Belkania 2004 *Sp,* 2005 *Ch,* 2007 *Sp, Rus*

G Beriashvili 1993 *Rus, Pol,* 1995 *Ger*

M Besselia 1991 *Ukr,* 1993 *Rus, Pol,* 1996 *Rus,* 1997 *Pt*

D Bolgashvili 2000 *It, Pt, H, R,* 2001 *H, Pt, Rus, Sp, R, F, SA,* 2002 *H, Pt, Rus, I,* 2003 *Pt, Sp, Rus, CZR, R, E, Sa, SA,* 2004 *Rus, Ur, Ch, Rus,* 2005 *CZR,* 2007 *Sp*

J Bregvadze 2008 *ESp, ItA,* 2009 *C, IrA*

G Buguianishvili 1996 *CZR, Rus,* 1997 *Pol,* 1998 *It, Rus, I, R,* 2000 *Sp, H, R,* 2001 *H, F, SA,* 2002 *Rus*

D Chavleishvili 1990 *Z, Z,* 1992 *Ukr, Ukr, Lat,* 1993 *Pol, Lux*

M Cheishvili 1989 *Z,* 1990 *Z, Z,* 1995 *H*

D Chichua 2008 *CZR*

I Chikava 1993 *Pol, Lux,* 1994 *Swi,* 1995 *Bul, Mol, H,* 1996 *CZR, CZR,* 1997 *Pol,* 1998 *I*

R Chikvaidze 2004 *Ur, Ch*

L Chikvinidze 1994 *Swi,* 1995 *Bul, Mol, Ger, H,* 1996 *CZR, Rus*

G Chkhaidze 2002 *H, R, I, Rus,* 2003 *Pt, CZR, It, E, SA, Ur,* 2004 *CZR, R,* 2006 *Pt, Ukr,* 2007 *R, Rus, CZR, Nm, ESp, ItA, Ar, I, Nm, F,* 2008 *R, Pt, CZR, Rus, Sp,* 2009 *Ger, Pt, R, Rus*

S Chkhenkeli 1997 *Pol*

I Chkhikvadze 2005 *Ch,* 2007 *Sp,* 2008 *Pt, R, Pt, CZR, Rus, ESp, Ur, ItA,* 2009 *Ger*

I Chkonia 2007 *ESp, ItA*

D Dadunashvili 2003 *It, E, SA, Ur,* 2004 *Sp, Rus, CZR, R,* 2005 *Ch,* 2007 *Sp, Rus, CZR, Nm, ItA,* 2008 *Pt, R, Pt, CZR, Rus, Sp,* 2009 *C, IrA, US*

L Datunashvili 2004 *Sp,* 2005 *Pt, Ukr, R, CZR,* 2006 *Rus, R, Pt, Ukr, J, Bb, CZR, Pt,* 2007 *R, Rus, Nm, ESp, ItA, I, Nm, F,* 2008 *Pt, Pt,* 2009 *R, Rus, C, US*

V Didebulidze 1991 *Ukr,* 1994 *Kaz,* 1995 *Bul, Mol,* 1996 *CZR,* 1997 *De,* 1999 *Tg,* 2000 *H,* 2001 *H, Pt, Rus, Sp, R, F, SA,* 2002 *H, Pt, Rus, Sp, R, I, Rus,* 2003 *Pt, Sp, Rus, CZR, R, It, E, Sa, SA,* 2004 *Rus,* 2005 *Pt,* 2006 *R, R,* 2007 *R, Sp, Rus, CZR, Nm, ESp, ItA, Ar, Nm, F*

E Dzagnidze 1992 *Ukr, Ukr, Lat,* 1993 *Rus, Pol,* 1995 *Bul, Mol, Ger, H,* 1998 *I*

N Dzagnidze 1989 *Z,* 1990 *Z, Z,* 1991 *Ukr,* 1992 *Ukr, Ukr, Lat,* 1993 *Rus, Pol,* 1994 *Swi,* 1995 *Ger, H*

T Dzagnidze 2008 *ESp*

D Dzneladze 1992 *Ukr, Lat,* 1993 *Lux,* 1994 *Kaz*

P Dzotsenidze 1995 *Ger, H,* 1997 *Pt, Pol*

G Elizbarashvili 2002 *Rus,* 2003 *Sp,* 2004 *Ch,* 2005 *CZR,* 2006 *Pt, Ukr, J, Bb, CZR, Sp, Pt,* 2007 *R, Sp, Rus, I, F,* 2009 *C, IrA*

O Eloshvili 2002 *H,* 2003 *SA,* 2006 *Bb, CZR,* 2007 *Sp, CZR, Nm, ESp, ItA, I, F*

S Essakia 1999 *Tg, Tg,* 2000 *It, Mor, Sp, H,* 2004 *CZR, R*

M Gagnidze 1991 *Ukr, Ukr*

D Gasviani 2004 *Sp, Rus,* 2005 *CZR, Ch,* 2006 *Ukr, J,* 2007 *Rus, CZR,* 2008 *ESp, Ur, ItA*

A Ghibradze 1992 *Ukr, Ukr, Lat,* 1994 *Swi,* 1995 *Bul, Mol, Ger,* 1996 *CZR*

D Ghudushauri 1989 *Z,* 1991 *Ukr, Ukr*

L Ghvaberidze 2004 *Pt*

R Gigauri 2006 *Ukr, J, Bb, CZR, Sp, Pt, Pt,* 2007 *R, Nm, ESp, ItA, Ar, Nm, F,* 2008 *Pt, R, Pt, Rus, Sp, ESp, Ur,* 2009 *C, IrA, US*

A Giorgadze 1996 *CZR,* 1998 *It, Ukr, Rus, R,* 1999 *Tg, Tg,* 2000 *It, Pt, Mor, H, R,* 2001 *H, Pt, Rus, Sp, R, F, SA,* 2002 *H, Pt, Rus, Sp, R, I, Rus,* 2003 *Pt, Sp, Rus, R, It, E, Sa, SA, Ur,* 2005 *Pt, Ukr, R, CZR,* 2006 *Rus, R, Pt, Bb, CZR, Sp, Pt,* 2007 *R, Ar, I, Nm, F,* 2009 *Ger, Pt*

I Giorgadze 2001 *F, SA,* 2003 *Pt, Sp, Rus, R, It, E, Sa, Ur,* 2004 *Rus,* 2005 *Pt, R, CZR,* 2006 *Rus, R, Pt, Bb, CZR, Pt,* 2007 *Pt,* 2007 *R, Sp, Rus, CZR, Ar, Nm, F,* 2008 *R,* 2009 *Ger, Pt, Rus*

M Gorgodze 2003 *Sp, Rus,* 2004 *Pt, Sp, Rus, CZR, R, Ur, Ch, Rus,* 2005 *Pt, Ukr, R, CZR, Ch,* 2006 *Rus, Pt, Bb, CZR, R, Sp, Pt, Pt,* 2007 *Ar, I, Nm,* 2008 *R, Rus, Sp,* 2009 *Ger, Pt, R, Rus*

E Gueguchadze 1990 *Z, Z*

L Gugava 2004 *Sp, Rus, CZR, Ur, Ch, Rus,* 2005 *Pt, Ukr,* 2006 *Bb, CZR,* 2009 *C, IrA*

I Guiorkhelidze 1998 *R,* 1999 *Tg, Tg*

G Guiunashvili 1989 *Z,* 1990 *Z,* 1991 *Ukr, Ukr,* 1992 *Ukr, Ukr, Lat,* 1993 *Rus, Pol, Lux,* 1994 *Swi,* 1996 *Rus,* 1997 *Pt*

K Guiunashvili 1990 *Z, Z,* 1991 *Ukr, Ukr,* 1992 *Ukr, Ukr, Lat*

B Gujaraidze 2008 *ESp*

S Gujaraidze 2003 *SA, Ur*

I Gundishvili 2002 *I,* 2003 *Pt, Sp, Rus, CZR,* 2008 *ESp, Ur, ItA,* 2009 *C, US*

D Gurgenidze 2007 *Sp, ItA*

A Gusharashvili 1998 *Ukr*

D Iobidze 1993 *Rus, Pol*

E Iovadze 1993 *Lux,* 1994 *Kaz,* 1995 *Bul, Mol, Ger, H,* 2001 *Sp, F, SA,* 2002 *H, Rus, Sp, R, I*

A Issakadze 1989 *Z*

N Iurini 1991 *Ukr,* 1994 *Swi,* 1995 *Ger, H,* 1996 *CZR, Rus,* 1997 *Pt, Pol, Cro, De,* 1998 *Ukr, Rus,* 2000 *It, Sp, H, R*

S Janelidze 1991 *Ukr, Ukr,* 1993 *Rus,* 1994 *Kaz,* 1995 *Ger,* 1997 *Pt,* 1998 *Ukr, I, R,* 1999 *Tg,* 2000 *R*

R Japarashvili 1992 *Ukr, Ukr, Lat,* 1993 *Pol, Lux,* 1996 *CZR,* 1997 *Pt*

L Javelidze 1997 *Cro,* 1998 *I,* 2001 *H, R, F, SA,* 2002 *H, R,* 2004 *R,* 2005 *Ukr,* 2007 *Sp*

G Jgenti 2004 *Ur*, 2005 *Ch*, 2007 *Sp, CZR, Nm, ESp, ItA*, 2009 *C, IrA, US*
D Jghenti 2004 *CZR, R*
D Jhamutashvili 2005 *Ch*
P Jimsheladze 1995 *Bul, Mol, H*, 1996 *CZR, CZR, Rus*, 1997 *De*, 1998 *It, Ukr, Rus, I, R*, 1999 *Tg, Tg*, 2000 *Pt, Mor, Sp, H, R*, 2001 *H, Pt, Rus, Sp, R, F, SA*, 2002 *H, Pt, Rus, Sp, I, Rus*, 2003 *Pt, Sp, Rus, CZR, R, It, E, Sa, SA, Ur*, 2004 *Rus*, 2005 *R*, 2006 *Rus, R, Pt, Ukr, J, Bb, CZR, Pt, Pt*, 2007 *R, Rus, CZR, Ar*
K Jintcharadze 1993 *Rus, Pol*, 2000 *It, Mor*
D Kacharava 2006 *Ukr, J, R, Sp, Pt*, 2007 *R, Sp, Rus, CZR, Nm, ESp, ItA, I, Nm*, 2008 *Pt, R, Pt, CZR, Rus, Sp*, 2009 *Ger, Pt, R, Rus, C, IrA, US*
G Kacharava 2005 *Ukr*, 2006 *J, Bb, CZR, R*, 2007 *Sp*, 2008 *CZR*
G Kakhiani 1995 *Bul, Mol*
V Kakovin 2009 *C, IrA, US*
V Katsadze 1997 *Pol*, 1998 *It, Ukr, Rus, I, R*, 1999 *Tg, Tg*, 2000 *Pt, Mor, Sp, H, R*, 2001 *H, Pt, Rus, Sp, R*, 2002 *Pt, Rus, Sp, R, I, Rus*, 2003 *Pt, Sp, CZR, R, E, Sa, SA, Ur*, 2004 *Sp*, 2005 *Ukr*
A Kavtarashvili 1994 *Swi*, 1995 *Bul, Mol, Ger*, 1996 *CZR, Rus*, 1997 *Pt, Cro, De*, 1998 *It, Rus, I, R*, 1999 *Tg, Tg*, 2000 *It, H, R*, 2001 *H*, 2003 *SA, Ur*
I Kerauli 1991 *Ukr, Ukr*, 1992 *Ukr, Ukr*
L Khachirashvili 2005 *Ukr*
T Khakhaleishili 1994 *Kaz*
B Khamashuridze 1998 *It, Ukr, Rus, I, R*, 1999 *Tg, Tg*, 2000 *It, Pt, Sp, H, R*, 2001 *Pt, Rus, Sp, R, F, SA*, 2002 *H, Pt, Rus, Sp, R, I, Rus*, 2003 *Pt, CZR, R, It, E, Sa, SA, Ur*, 2004 *Pt, Rus, Rus*, 2005 *Pt, Ukr, Ch*, 2006 *Rus, R, Pt, R, Sp, Pt, Pt*, 2007 *Rus, CZR, ESp, Ar, Nm, F*, 2008 *Pt*
B Khamashuridze 1989 *Z*
M Kharshiladze 1991 *Ukr*
B Khekhelashvili 1999 *Tg, Tg*, 2000 *It, Pt, Mor, Sp, H, R*, 2001 *H, Pt, R, F, SA*, 2002 *H, Pt, Rus, Sp, R, I*, 2003 *Sp, Rus, CZR, R, E, Sa*, 2004 *Sp*
D Khinchagashvili 2003 *Sp, CZR*, 2004 *Pt, Sp, Rus*, 2006 *Bb, CZR, Sp, Pt*, 2007 *R, Rus, Nm, ESp, ItA, Ar, I, Nm*, 2009 *Ger, Pt, R, Rus*
L Khmaladze 2008 *ESp, ItA*
G Khonelidze 2003 *SA*
G Khositashvili 2008 *ESp, Ur, ItA*
N Khuade 1989 *Z*, 1990 *Z, Z*, 1991 *Ukr, Ukr*, 1993 *Rus, Pol, Lux*, 1994 *Swi*, 1995 *Ger*
Z Khutsishvili 1993 *Lux*, 1994 *Kaz, Swi*, 1995 *Bul*, 1996 *CZR*
A Khvedelidze 1989 *Z*, 1990 *Z, Z*, 1991 *Ukr, Ukr*, 1992 *Ukr, Ukr, Lat*, 1993 *Rus, Pol*
I Kiasashvili 2008 *Pt, CZR, Ur*
D Kiknadze 2004 *Rus*, 2005 *Pt, Ukr*
A Kobakhidze 1997 *Cro*, 1998 *I*
K Kobakhidze 1995 *Ger, H*, 1996 *Rus*, 1997 *Pt*, 1998 *It, Ukr, Rus, I, R*, 1999 *Tg*, 2000 *It*
Z Koberidze 2004 *Ur*
V Kolelishvili 2008 *ItA*
A Kopaleishvili 2004 *Ur*
A Kopaliani 2003 *It, SA, Ur*, 2004 *Pt*, 2005 *Ukr, R*, 2006 *Rus, R, Ukr, J, Bb, CZR, R, Sp, Pt*, 2007 *R, Sp, Rus, CZR, Ar, I, Nm, F*
D Kubriashvili 2008 *Pt, R, Pt, Rus, Sp*, 2009 *Pt, R, Rus*
E Kuparadze 2007 *ESp*
G Kutarashvili 2004 *Pt, Sp, CZR, R*, 2005 *Ch*, 2006 *Rus, R, Pt, Ukr, J, R*
B Kvinikhidze 2002 *R*, 2004 *Pt, Sp, CZR, R*, 2005 *Ch*
M Kvirikashvili 2003 *Pt, Sp, CZR, E, Sa, SA, Ur*, 2004 *Rus, CZR, R, Ch*, 2005 *CZR, Ch*, 2007 *R, Sp, Rus, CZR, Nm, ESp, ItA, Ar, I, Nm, F*, 2008 *Pt, CZR, Rus, Sp*, 2009 *Ger, Pt, R, Rus, C, IrA, US*
G Labadze 1996 *CZR, Rus*, 1997 *Pt, Pol, Cro, De*, 1998 *It, Ukr, Rus, I, R*, 1999 *Tg, Tg*, 2000 *It, Pt, Sp, H, R*, 2001 *H, Pt, Rus, Sp, F, SA*, 2002 *Pt, Rus, Sp, R, I, Rus*, 2003 *Pt, Sp, CZR, R, It, E, Sa*, 2004 *Rus*, 2005 *R*, 2006 *Rus, R, Pt, J, R, Pt, Pt*, 2007 *Rus, Ar, Nm*, 2008 *Pt, R, Pt, Rus, R, C, IrA, US*
I Lezhava 1991 *Ukr, Ukr*, 1992 *Ukr, Ukr*, 1995 *Bul*
Z Lezhava 1991 *Ukr*, 1995 *Ger*, 1996 *CZR, CZR, Rus*, 1997 *Pt, Cro, De*, 1998 *It, Rus, R*, 1999 *Tg*

B Liluashvili 1989 *Z*, 1990 *Z, Z*
L Liluashvili 1997 *Pt*
O Liparteliani 1989 *Z*, 1990 *Z, Z*
S Liparteliani 1991 *Ukr*, 1994 *Kaz, Swi*, 1996 *CZR*
Z Liparteliani 1994 *Kaz, Swi*, 1995 *Bul, Mol, Ger, H*
G Lomgadze 2009 *US*
D Losaberidze 2009 *IrA*
M Lossaberidze 1989 *Z*
K Machitidze 1989 *Z*, 1993 *Rus*, 1995 *Bul, Mol, Ger, H*, 1996 *CZR, CZR, Rus*, 1997 *Pt, Pol, Cro, De*, 1998 *It, Ukr, Rus, R*, 1999 *Tg*
I Machkhaneli 2002 *H, R*, 2003 *It, E, Sa, SA, Ur*, 2004 *Pt, Ur, Ch, Rus*, 2005 *Pt, Ukr, R, CZR, Ch*, 2006 *Rus, R, Pt, Bb, CZR, R, Pt*, 2007 *R, Ar, I, Nm*, 2009 *Ger, Pt, R, Rus, US*
M Magrakvelidze 1998 *Ukr*, 2000 *Mor*, 2001 *F*, 2002 *Pt, Sp, R*, 2004 *Rus*, 2005 *Pt, R*, 2006 *Bb, CZR, Pt, Pt*, 2007 *R, CZR, Nm, ESp, ItA, I, F*
I Maisuradze 1997 *Cro*, 1998 *It, Ukr*, 1999 *Tg, Tg*, 2004 *Rus, R*, 2005 *CZR*, 2006 *Bb, CZR, R, Pt, Pt*, 2007 *R, Sp, Rus, CZR, ESp, ItA, I, F*
S Maisuradze 2008 *Pt, CZR, Rus, Sp, ESp, Ur, ItA*, 2009 *IrA, US*
Z Maisuradze 2004 *Pt, Sp, CZR, Ur, Ch, Rus*, 2005 *Ukr, R*, 2006 *Rus, R, Pt, Ukr, J, Bb, CZR, Sp*, 2007 *Nm, ESp, ItA, Ar, I, F*, 2008 *Pt*, 2009 *C, IrA, US*
L Malaguradze 2008 *Pt, R, Pt, CZR, Rus, Sp, ESp, Ur, ItA*, 2009 *Ger, Pt, R, Rus, C, IrA, US*
K Margvelashvili 2003 *It, E, Sa, SA*
M Marjanishvili 1990 *Z, Z*, 1992 *Ukr, Ukr, Lat*, 1993 *Rus, Pol, Lux*
A Matchutadze 1993 *Lux*, 1994 *Kaz*, 1995 *Bul, Mol*, 1997 *Pt, Pol, Cro, De*
Z Matiashvili 2003 *Sp*, 2005 *Ch*
G Mchedlishvili 2008 *CZR*
S Melikidze 2008 *CZR, Sp, ESp, ItA*
L Mgueladze 1992 *Ukr, Ukr*
N Mgueladze 1995 *Bul, Mol, H*, 1997 *Pol*
I Modebadze 2003 *SA, Ur*, 2004 *Sp*
S Modebadze 1994 *Kaz*, 1995 *Mol*, 1996 *CZR, CZR, Rus*, 1997 *Pt, Pol, Cro, De*, 1998 *It, Ukr, Rus*, 1999 *Tg*, 2000 *It, Pt*, 2001 *Sp, F, SA*, 2002 *H, Pt, Rus, Sp, R*
A Mtchedlishvili 2004 *Ur, Ch*, 2008 *CZR*
S Mtchedlishvili 2000 *It*, 2007 *Sp*
Z Mtchedlishvili 1995 *Mol*, 1996 *CZR*, 1997 *Cro, De*, 1998 *It, Ukr, Rus, I, R*, 1999 *Tg, Tg*, 2000 *Pt, Mor, Sp, H, R*, 2001 *Rus, Sp, R, F, SA*, 2002 *H, Pt, Rus, I, Rus*, 2003 *Pt, Sp, Rus, CZR, R, It, E, Sa, Ur*, 2004 *Pt, Rus*, 2005 *Pt*, 2006 *J*, 2007 *Rus, CZR, Nm, ESp, ItA, F*
M Mtiulishvili 1991 *Ukr*, 1994 *Kaz*, 1996 *CZR, CZR, Rus*, 1997 *Pt, Pol, Cro, De*, 1998 *It, Ukr, Rus, R*, 2001 *H, Pt, Rus, Sp, R*, 2002 *H, Pt, Rus, Sp, R, I*, 2003 *Rus, CZR, R*, 2004 *Rus, CZR, R*
V Nadiradze 1994 *Kaz, Swi*, 1995 *H*, 1996 *Rus*, 1997 *Pt, De*, 1998 *I, R*, 1999 *Tg*, 2000 *Pt, Mor, Sp, H, R*, 2001 *H, Pt, Rus, Sp, R, F, SA*, 2002 *H, Pt, Rus, Sp, R, I, Rus*, 2003 *Rus, CZR, R, It, E, Sa*
A Natchqebia 1990 *Z, Z*
I Natriashvili 2006 *Ukr, J*, 2007 *ItA*, 2008 *Pt, R, Pt, Rus, Sp*, 2009 *Ger, Pt, R, Rus*
I Natriashvili 2008 *ESp, Ur, ItA*, 2009 *C, IrA, US*
N Natroshvili 1992 *Ukr, Ukr, Lat*
G Nemsadze 2005 *Ch*, 2006 *Ukr*, 2007 *Sp*, 2008 *CZR, Sp, ESp, Ur, ItA*, 2009 *IrA, US*
A Nijaradze 2008 *CZR*
I Nikolaenko 1999 *Tg, Tg*, 2000 *It, Mor, Sp, H, R*, 2001 *R, F*, 2003 *Pt, Sp, E, Sa, SA, Ur*
I Ninidze 2004 *Ur, Ch*
D Oboladze 1993 *Rus, Pol, Lux*, 1994 *Swi*, 1995 *Bul, Mol, Ger, H*, 1996 *CZR, CZR, Rus*, 1997 *Pt, Pol*, 1998 *It, Ukr*
T Odisharia 1989 *Z*, 1994 *Kaz*
S Papashvili 2001 *SA*, 2004 *CZR, R*, 2006 *Bb, CZR*, 2007 *Sp*
S Partsikanashvili 1994 *Kaz*, 1996 *CZR, Rus*, 1997 *Pol*, 1999 *Tg, Tg*, 2000 *It, Pt, Mor*
A Peikrishvili 2008 *Pt, Pt*, 2009 *R*
G Peradze 1991 *Ukr*

Z Peradze 1997 *Pol*, 1998 *Rus*
Z Petriashvili 2009 *C, IrA*
D Pinchukovi 2004 *CZR*
L Pirpilashvili 2004 *Rus, CZR, R, Ur, Ch*, 2005 *Ukr, R, CZR*
G Pirtskhalava 1989 *Z*, 1995 *Ger*, 1996 *CZR, Rus*, 1997 *Pt, Pol*
T Pkhakadze 1989 *Z*, 1990 *Z, Z*, 1993 *Rus, Pol, Lux*, 1994 *Kaz*, 1996 *CZR*
G Rapava-Ruskini 1990 *Z*, 1992 *Ukr, Lat*, 1994 *Kaz*, 1996 *Rus*, 1997 *Pt, Cro, De*, 1998 *It, Ukr, Rus, R*, 1999 *Tg*
T Ratianidze 2000 *It*, 2001 *H, Pt, Sp, R, SA*, 2002 *Pt, Rus, Sp, R, I, Rus*, 2003 *Pt, Sp, Rus, CZR, R*
Z Rekhviashvili 1995 *H*, 1997 *Pt, Pol*
G Rokhvadze 2008 *ItA*, 2009 *C, IrA, US*
S Sakandelidze 1996 *CZR*, 1998 *Ukr*
B Samkharadze 2004 *Pt, Sp, Rus, CZR, R, Ur, Ch*, 2005 *CZR, Ch*, 2006 *Rus, R, Pt, Ukr, Bb, CZR, R, Sp, Pt, Pt*, 2007 *R, Sp, Rus, CZR, Nm, ESp, Ar, I, Nm, F*, 2008 *Pt, R, Pt, Sp, ESp, Ur, ItA*, 2009 *Ger, R*
A Sanadze 2004 *Ch*
P Saneblidze 1994 *Kaz*
G Sanikidze 2004 *Ur, Ch*
B Sardanashvili 2004 *Ch*
V Satseradze 1989 *Z*, 1990 *Z*, 1991 *Ukr*, 1992 *Ukr, Ukr, Lat*
E Shanidze 1994 *Swi*
G Shkinin 2004 *CZR, R, Ch*, 2005 *Ch*, 2006 *Rus, R, Ukr, J, R, Sp, Pt, Pt*, 2007 *R, Sp, Rus, CZR, Nm, ESp, ItA, Ar, I, Nm*, 2008 *R, Pt, CZR, Rus, Sp, ESp, Ur, ItA*, 2009 *Pt*
B Shvanguiradze 1990 *Z, Z*, 1992 *Ukr, Ukr, Lat*, 1993 *Rus, Pol, Lux*
G Shvelidze 1998 *I, R*, 1999 *Tg, Tg*, 2000 *It, Pt, Sp, H, R*, 2001 *H, Pt, Sp, F, SA*, 2002 *H, Rus, I, Rus*, 2003 *Pt, Sp, Rus, CZR, R, It, E, Sa, Ur*, 2004 *Rus*, 2005 *Pt, CZR*, 2006 *Rus, R, Pt, R, Sp, Pt, Pt*, 2007 *Ar, I, Nm, F*, 2008 *Pt, R, Pt, CZR, Rus*, 2009 *Ger, Pt, R, Rus*
I Sikharulidze 1994 *Kaz*
T Sokhadze 2005 *CZR*, 2006 *Rus, R, Pt, Ukr, J, Pt, Pt*, 2009 *C, IrA*
M Sujashvili 2004 *Pt, Rus*, 2005 *Pt, Ukr, R, CZR*, 2006 *Pt, Ukr, J, Bb, CZR*
S Sultanishvili 1998 *Ukr*
S Sutiashvili 2005 *Ch*, 2006 *Ukr*, 2007 *CZR, Nm, ESp*, 2008 *Pt, R, CZR, Rus*
P Svanidze 1992 *Ukr*
T Tavadze 1991 *Ukr, Ukr*
N Tchavtchavadze 1998 *It, Ukr*, 2004 *CZR, R, Ur, Ch*
B Tepnadze 1995 *H*, 1996 *CZR*, 1997 *Cro*, 1998 *I, R*, 1999 *Tg*

A Todua 2008 *CZR, Rus, Sp, ESp, Ur, ItA*, 2009 *R, C, IrA, US*
P Tqabladze 1993 *Lux*, 1995 *Bul*
L Tsabadze 1994 *Kaz, Swi*, 1995 *Bul, Ger, H*, 1996 *CZR, Rus*, 1997 *Cro, De*, 1998 *It, Rus, I, R*, 1999 *Tg, Tg*, 2000 *Pt, Mor, Sp, R*, 2001 *H, Pt, Rus, Sp, R, F, SA*, 2002 *H, Pt, Rus, Sp, R, I, Rus*
B Tsiklauri 2008 *ItA*
G Tsiklauri 2003 *SA, Ur*
D Tskhvediani 1998 *Ukr*
V Tskitishvili 1994 *Swi*, 1995 *Bul, Mol*
T Turdzeladze 1989 *Z*, 1990 *Z, Z*, 1991 *Ukr*, 1995 *Ger, H*
K Uchava 2002 *Sp*, 2004 *Sp*, 2008 *Pt, R, Pt, Rus, Sp, ESp, Ur, ItA*, 2009 *Ger, Pt, R, C, IrA*
B Udesiani 2001 *Sp, F*, 2002 *H*, 2004 *Pt, Sp, CZR, R, Rus*, 2005 *Pt, Ukr, R, CZR, Ch*, 2006 *Rus, R, Ukr, J, Bb, CZR, R, Sp, Pt, Pt*, 2007 *R, Rus, CZR, Ar, Nm*, 2008 *CZR, Sp, ESp, Ur, ItA*
M Urjukashvili 1997 *Cro, De*, 1998 *Ukr, Rus, R*, 1999 *Tg, Tg*, 2000 *It, Pt, Mor, Sp*, 2001 *Pt, Rus, Sp, R, F, SA*, 2002 *H, Pt, Sp, R, I, Rus*, 2003 *Pt, Sp, Rus, R, It, E, Sa, Ur*, 2004 *Pt, Rus, Ur, Ch, Rus*, 2005 *Pt, R, CZR*, 2006 *Rus, R, Pt, Ukr, J, R, Sp*, 2007 *Rus, CZR, Nm, ESp, ItA, Ar, I, Nm, F*, 2008 *Sp*, 2009 *R, Rus*
R Urushadze 1997 *Pol*, 2002 *R*, 2004 *Pt, Rus, Rus*, 2005 *Pt, Ukr, R, CZR, Ch*, 2006 *Rus, R, Pt, Bb, CZR, R, Sp, Pt, Pt*, 2007 *Nm, ESp, ItA, I, Nm, F*, 2008 *Pt, R, Pt, Rus, Sp*, 2009 *Ger, Pt, R, Rus, C, IrA, US*
Z Valishvili 2004 *Ch*
D Vartaniani 1991 *Ukr, Ukr*, 1992 *Ukr, Ukr, Lat*, 1997 *Pol*, 2000 *Sp, H, R*
L Vashadze 1991 *Ukr*, 1992 *Ukr, Ukr, Lat*
G Yachvili 2001 *H, Pt, R*, 2003 *Sp, Rus, CZR, R, It, E, Sa, Ur*
I Zedginidze 1998 *I*, 2000 *It, Pt, Mor, Sp, H, R*, 2001 *H, Pt, Rus, Sp, R*, 2002 *H, Rus, Sp, I, Rus*, 2003 *Pt, Sp, Rus, CZR, R, It, Sa, SA, Ur*, 2004 *Pt, Sp, Rus, CZR, R, Rus*, 2005 *Pt, Ukr, R, CZR*, 2006 *Rus, R, Pt, Ukr, CZR, R, Sp, Pt, Pt*, 2007 *R, Ar, I*, 2009 *Ger, Pt, Rus*
T Zibzibadze 2000 *It, Pt, Mor, Sp*, 2001 *H, Pt, Rus, Sp, R, F, SA*, 2002 *H, Pt, Rus, Sp, R, I, Rus*, 2003 *Pt, Sp, Rus, CZR, R, It, E, Sa, Ur*, 2004 *Pt, Sp, Rus, CZR, R, Rus*, 2005 *Pt, Ukr, R, CZR*, 2009 *Ger, Pt, R*
D Zirakashvili 2004 *Ur, Ch, Rus*, 2005 *Ukr, R, CZR*, 2006 *Rus, R, Pt, R, Sp, Pt*, 2007 *R, Ar, Nm, F*, 2008 *R*, 2009 *Ger*

IRELAND

IRELAND'S 2008–09 TEST RECORD

OPPONENTS	DATE	VENUE	RESULT
Canada	8 November	H	**Won** 55–0
New Zealand	15 November	H	**Lost** 3–22
Argentina	22 November	H	**Won** 17–3
France	7 February	H	**Won** 30–21
Italy	15 February	A	**Won** 38–9
England	28 February	H	**Won** 14–13
Scotland	14 March	A	**Won** 22–15
Wales	21 March	A	**Won** 17–15
Canada	23 May	A	**Won** 25–6
USA	31 May	A	**Won** 27–10

THE GRAND SLAMMERS
By Iain Spragg

Ireland finally win their first Grand Slam since 1948.

In the year Ireland last won the Grand Slam, Laurence Olivier won an Oscar for his screen version of Hamlet, Warner Brothers showed the first ever colour newsreel and the Cold War was getting distinctly chillier. For the Irish, the 61-year wait for a second Championship clean sweep had been a long, arduous and frequently painful one.

Many Ireland coaches had tried and failed to emulate the feat of the legendary class of 1948 before Declan Kidney took control of the national side in July 2008. The former Munster coach certainly had an impeccable pedigree having led the Red Army to four Heineken Cup finals in just eight years and two triumphs but even the most ardent Ireland fan must have had some doubts whether he could achieve the Holy Grail of the Grand Slam in his first season, let alone a first title success since 1985.

It all came down to Ireland's visit to Cardiff to face Wales in March. France, Italy, England and Scotland had all been dispatched with varying degrees of blood, sweat and tears and all that stood between Kidney's side and their date with destiny were the defending Six Nations champions, a noisy and partisan Millennium Stadium crowd and, most importantly, the weight of a patient but long-suffering nation's expectations.

In the end, Ireland held their nerve. Six points to nil down at half-time in the Welsh capital, Kidney worked wonders in the dressing room and his side came storming back into the game after the break with tries from skipper Brian O'Driscoll and Tommy Bowe in a six-minute salvo and with five, tantalising minutes left on the clock, the men in green led 14–12.

The drama, of course, was not over. Fly half Stephen Jones landed a drop goal to edge Wales back in front only for opposite number Ronan O'Gara to return the favour two minutes from time to give Ireland a precarious 17–15 advantage. Kidney's troops were almost there but still had to endure the agony of watching Jones strike but miss a last minute penalty attempt and the party, just over six decades in the planning, could finally begin.

"To go down at the end, it would have broken my heart, " O'Driscoll said after the final whistle in Cardiff. "I'm so proud of the boys. We took a lot of flak over the last 18 months but to be champions, I'm delighted.

"At half-time Declan said we were still completely in it, we just hadn't converted our pressure into points. We came out firing and got two quick tries and we couldn't have asked for a more dramatic end. Two drop goals and then for Stephen Jones to miss a penalty – you couldn't ask for more."

The opening game of the 2008–09 campaign and Kidney's first in charge was the visit of Canada to Thomond Park in November, but the Canucks were simply overpowered by the home side. Debutant full back Keith Earls set the tone with a third minute try and Ireland cantered to a 55–0 win.

The All Blacks were in Dublin a week later but Irish hopes of a first ever victory over the New Zealanders were shattered by a clinical Kiwi performance. Dan Carter and O'Gara traded early penalties but the visitors pulled effortlessly clear with a first half penalty try and further scores after the break from Ma'a Nonu and Brad Thorn to ease to a 22–3 success.

Ireland finished their autumn series with a potentially tricky clash with Argentina and the match at Croke Park was predictably fractious. The Pumas took the lead with a 35th minute Santiago Fernandez penalty but O'Gara levelled and the sides went in at the break all square.

The home side, however, pulled clear in the second half with two more O'Gara penalties, a drop goal and a late Tommy Bowe try for a 17–3 win that secured their place among the second tier of seeds for the draw for Rugby World Cup 2011.

"We were not going to take a backwards step," said O'Driscoll as he reflected on the hard-fought win against the physical Argentineans. "When teams come to Croke Park we are not here to be bullied or shoved around. We did not initiate too much but if anything was going on then we certainly were not backing down. It showed great camaraderie that everyone was there for one another."

Ireland's Six Nations challenge began with France at Croke Park and was in stark contrast to the Pumas clash as the two sides produced a five-try thriller in front of 80,000 fans. Les Bleus surged into the lead courtesy of an Imanol Harinordoquy try but Kidney's side hit back through Jamie Heaslip and O'Driscoll. Maxime Médard reduced the arrears for France but the pivotal moment of the match came on 66 minutes when Gordon D'Arcy barged his way over and Ireland ran out 30–21 winners.

One of the biggest obstacles to the Grand Slam had been safely negotiated and Italy offered little resistance a week later in Rome as Luke Fitzgerald crossed the whitewash twice in a 38–9 triumph.

The third instalment was the visit of England to Dublin. Kidney kept faith with the XV who had demolished the Azzurri but the men in white presented an altogether sterner challenge and at the final whistle, Ireland breathed a collective sigh of relief after clinging on for a 14–13 win.

With O'Gara's kicking uncharacteristically inaccurate, the home side badly needed O'Driscoll's 57th-minute try from close range but were nearly overhauled when Delon Armitage scored for England late on. Desperate defence kept England at bay and Ireland had preserved their unbeaten record by the skin of their teeth.

A visit to Murrayfield to face Scotland followed and it was another scrappy but ultimately effective performance from Kidney's team. The Scots led 12–9 at the break after Chris Paterson and O'Gara traded penalties, the Munster fly half becoming the Six Nations all-time leading point scorer in the process, but Ireland pulled clear in the second half courtesy of Heaslip's pivotal try to emerge 22–15 victors.

Only Wales, who still had the chance to land the title if they won by 13 clear points, now stood between Ireland and the Grand Slam.

Kidney made three changes to his side for the all-important clash, recalling Tomas O'Leary, Heaslip and Jerry Flannery at the expense of Peter Stringer, Denis Leamy and Rory Best respectively.

Wales drew first blood with two Stephen Jones penalties to put the home side 6–0 up at the break but O'Driscoll's fourth try of the tournament from close range, followed by Bowe's score just two minutes

later sent Ireland surging ahead and set the stage for the nerve-jangling **285**
drama of the dying minutes.

Kidney and his players had finally ended Ireland's long wait for the Grand Slam but in the euphoric aftermath of victory in the Millennium Stadium, the coach was quick to pay tribute to his predecessor Eddie O'Sullivan who had won three Triple Crowns but twice missed out on the Championship clean sweep.

"This is all due to the groundwork done by Eddie, all the coaching team, all that's done in the provinces and more so in the schools, as they're the ones who enrich the kids," Kidney said. "Brian [O'Driscoll] would say this is far from a one man team – we have 30 odd people who make this team. After 80 minutes, you take what's there. Some days it swings for you, some it doesn't."

Ireland's season, however, was not quite over. There were still two summer Tests away to Canada and the USA to play and shorn of 13 senior players either on Lions duty or involved with Leinster in the Heineken Cup final, Kidney named an experimental squad captained by Ulster hooker Rory Best for the North America tour.

The side to face the Canadians in Vancouver in May featured six new caps – Darren Cave, Ian Whitten, Ian Dowling, Ian Keatley, John Muldoon and Niall Ronan – and it was little surprise that the unfamiliar looking side struggled for fluency.

Ireland did score three tries through Barry Murphy, Whitten and Tony Buckley but it was a far from convincing performance despite the final 25–6 scoreline in the visitors' favour.

It was a similar story eight days later against the USA in Santa Clara as the Eagles battled hard to claim a major scalp. Best scored the last of Ireland's four tries in a 27–10 victory as the second string side ensured the Irish finished with a record of nine wins from 10 Test outings for the season, the All Black defeat back in November the only blemish on the record.

"It was a very poor game with a lot of mistakes," Kidney admitted. "We said this was the start of our World Cup build-up and the players will know about the errors they made, but you have to start somewhere.

"The lads trained very well during the week but you have to front up week in, week out if you are to compete in international rugby. We were not too euphoric after the Six Nations and we will not get too despondent now."

IRELAND INTERNATIONAL STATISTICS

MATCH RECORDS UP TO 30TH SEPTEMBER 2009

MOST CONSECUTIVE TEST WINS

10	2002 R,Ru,Gg,A,Fj,Arg,	2003 S1,It1,F,W1
8	2003 Tg, Sm,W2 ,It2, S2, R ,Nm, Arg	
8	2008 Arg, 2009 F, It ,E, S, W ,C, US	
6	1968 S,W,A,	1969 F,E,S
6	2004 SA,US,Arg,	2005 It,S,E

MOST CONSECUTIVE TEST WITHOUT DEFEAT

Matches	Wins	Draws	Period
10	10	0	2002 to 2003
8	8	0	2003
8	8	0	2008 to 2009
7	6	1	1968 to 1969
6	6	0	2004 to 2005

MOST POINTS IN A MATCH

BY THE TEAM

Pts.	Opponents	Venue	Year
83	United States	Manchester (NH)	2000
78	Japan	Dublin	2000
70	Georgia	Dublin	1998
64	Fiji	Dublin	2002
64	Namibia	Sydney	2003
63	Georgia	Dublin	2002
61	Italy	Limerick	2003
61	Pacific Islands	Dublin	2006
60	Romania	Dublin	1986
60	Italy	Dublin	2000
55	Zimbabwe	Dublin	1991
55	United States	Dublin	2004
55	Canada	Limerick	2008
54	Wales	Dublin	2002
53	Romania	Dublin	1998
53	United States	Dublin	1999
51	Italy	Rome	2007
50	Japan	Bloemfontein	1995

BY A PLAYER

Pts.	Player	Opponents	Venue	Year
32	R J R O'Gara	Samoa	Apia	2003
30	R J R O'Gara	Italy	Dublin	2000
26	D G Humphreys	Scotland	Murrayfield	2003
26	D G Humphreys	Italy	Limerick	2003
26	P Wallace	Pacific Islands	Dublin	2006
24	P A Burke	Italy	Dublin	1997
24	D G Humphreys	Argentina	Lens	1999
23	R P Keyes	Zimbabwe	Dublin	1991
23	R J R O'Gara	Japan	Dublin	2000
22	D G Humphreys	Wales	Dublin	2002
21	S O Campbell	Scotland	Dublin	1982
21	S O Campbell	England	Dublin	1983
21	R J R O'Gara	Italy	Rome	2001
21	R J R O'Gara	Argentina	Dublin	2004
21	R J R O'Gara	England	Dublin	2007
20	M J Kiernan	Romania	Dublin	1986
20	E P Elwood	Romania	Dublin	1993
20	S J P Mason	Samoa	Dublin	1996
20	E P Elwood	Georgia	Dublin	1998
20	K G M Wood	United States	Dublin	1999
20	D A Hickie	Italy	Limerick	2003
20	D G Humphreys	United States	Dublin	2004

MOST TRIES IN A MATCH
BY THE TEAM

Tries	Opponents	Venue	Year
13	United States	Manchester (NH)	2000
11	Japan	Dublin	2000
10	Romania	Dublin	1986
10	Georgia	Dublin	1998
10	Namibia	Sydney	2003
9	Fiji	Dublin	2003
8	Western Samoa	Dublin	1988
8	Zimbabwe	Dublin	1991
8	Georgia	Dublin	2002
8	Italy	Limerick	2003
8	Pacific Islands	Dublin	2006
8	Italy	Rome	2007
8	Canada	Limerick	2008
7	Japan	Bloemfontein	1995
7	Romania	Dublin	1998
7	United States	Dublin	1999
7	United States	Dublin	2004
7	Japan	Tokyo	2005

BY A PLAYER

Tries	Player	Opponents	Venue	Year
4	B F Robinson	Zimbabwe	Dublin	1991
4	K G M Wood	United States	Dublin	1999
4	D A Hickie	Italy	Limerick	2003
3	R Montgomery	Wales	Birkenhead	1887
3	J P Quinn	France	Cork	1913
3	E O'D Davy	Scotland	Murrayfield	1930
3	S J Byrne	Scotland	Murrayfield	1953
3	K D Crossan	Romania	Dublin	1986
3	B J Mullin	Tonga	Brisbane	1987
3	M R Mostyn	Argentina	Dublin	1999
3	B G O'Driscoll	France	Paris	2000
3	M J Mullins	United States	Manchester (NH)	2000
3	D A Hickie	Japan	Dublin	2000
3	R A J Henderson	Italy	Rome	2001
3	B G O'Driscoll	Scotland	Dublin	2002
3	K M Maggs	Fiji	Dublin	2002

MOST CONVERSIONS IN A MATCH
BY THE TEAM

Cons	Opponents	Venue	Year
10	Georgia	Dublin	1998
10	Japan	Dublin	2000
9	United States	Manchester (NH)	2000
7	Romania	Dublin	1986
7	Georgia	Dublin	2002
7	Namibia	Sydney	2003
7	United States	Dublin	2004
6	Japan	Bloemfontein	1995
6	Romania	Dublin	1998
6	United States	Dublin	1999
6	Italy	Dublin	2000
6	Italy	Limerick	2003
6	Japan	Tokyo	2005
6	Pacific Islands	Dublin	2006
6	Canada	Limerick	2008

BY A PLAYER

Cons	Player	Opponents	Venue	Year
10	E P Elwood	Georgia	Dublin	1998
10	R J R O'Gara	Japan	Dublin	2000
8	R J R O'Gara	United States	Manchester (NH)	2000
7	M J Kiernan	Romania	Dublin	1986
7	R J R O'Gara	Namibia	Sydney	2003
7	D G Humphreys	United States	Dublin	2004
6	P A Burke	Japan	Bloemfontein	1995
6	R J R O'Gara	Italy	Dublin	2000
6	D G Humphreys	Italy	Limerick	2003
6	D G Humphreys	Japan	Tokyo	2005
6	P Wallace	Pacific Islands	Dublin	2006
5	M J Kiernan	Canada	Dunedin	1987
5	E P Elwood	Romania	Dublin	1999
5	R J R O'Gara	Georgia	Dublin	2002
5	D G Humphreys	Fiji	Dublin	2002
5	D G Humphreys	Romania	Dublin	2005
5	R J R O'Gara	Canada	Limerick	2008

THE COUNTRIES

MOST PENALTIES IN A MATCH
BY THE TEAM

Pens	Opponents	Venue	Year
8	Italy	Dublin	1997
7	Argentina	Lens	1999
6	Scotland	Dublin	1982
6	Romania	Dublin	1993
6	United States	Atlanta	1996
6	Western Samoa	Dublin	1996
6	Italy	Dublin	2000
6	Wales	Dublin	2002
6	Australia	Dublin	2002
6	Samoa	Apia	2003
6	Japan	Osaka	2005

BY A PLAYER

Pens	Player	Opponents	Venue	Year
8	P A Burke	Italy	Dublin	1997
7	D G Humphreys	Argentina	Lens	1999
6	S O Campbell	Scotland	Dublin	1982
6	E P Elwood	Romania	Dublin	1993
6	S J P Mason	Western Samoa	Dublin	1996
6	R J R O'Gara	Italy	Dublin	2000
6	D G Humphreys	Wales	Dublin	2002
6	R J R O'Gara	Australia	Dublin	2002

MOST DROPPED GOALS IN A MATCH
BY THE TEAM

Drops	Opponents	Venue	Year
2	Australia	Dublin	1967
2	France	Dublin	1975
2	Australia	Sydney	1979
2	England	Dublin	1981
2	Canada	Dunedin	1987
2	England	Dublin	1993
2	Wales	Wembley	1999
2	New Zealand	Dublin	2001
2	Argentina	Dublin	2004
2	England	Dublin	2005

BY A PLAYER

Drops	Player	Opponents	Venue	Year
2	C M H Gibson	Australia	Dublin	1967
2	W M McCombe	France	Dublin	1975
2	S O Campbell	Australia	Sydney	1979
2	E P Elwood	England	Dublin	1993
2	D G Humphreys	Wales	Wembley	1999
2	D G Humphreys	New Zealand	Dublin	2001
2	R J R O'Gara	Argentina	Dublin	2004
2	R J R O'Gara	England	Dublin	2005

MOST CAPPED PLAYERS

Caps	Player	Career Span
94	J J Hayes	2000 to 2009
93	B G O'Driscoll	1999 to 2009
92	M E O'Kelly	1997 to 2009
92	R J R O'Gara	2000 to 2009
91	P A Stringer	2000 to 2009
82	G T Dempsey	1998 to 2008
72	D G Humphreys	1996 to 2005
70	K M Maggs	1997 to 2005
69	C M H Gibson	1964 to 1979
66	M J Horan	2000 to 2009
65	S H Easterby	2000 to 2008
64	S P Horgan	2000 to 2008
63	W J McBride	1962 to 1975
63	G E A Murphy	2000 to 2009
62	A G Foley	1995 to 2005
62	D A Hickie	1997 to 2007
62	P J O'Connell	2002 to 2009
61	J F Slattery	1970 to 1984
59	P S Johns	1990 to 2000
58	P A Orr	1976 to 1987
58	K G M Wood	1994 to 2003
55	B J Mullin	1984 to 1995
55	D P O'Callaghan	2003 to 2009
55	D P Wallace	2000 to 2009
54	T J Kiernan	1960 to 1973
54	P M Clohessy	1993 to 2002
52	D G Lenihan	1981 to 1992
51	M I Keane	1974 to 1984

MOST CONSECUTIVE TESTS

Tests	Player	Span
52	W J McBride	1964 to 1975
49	P A Orr	1976 to 1986
43	D G Lenihan	1981 to 1989
39	M I Keane	1974 to 1981
38	P A Stringer	2003 to 2007
37	G V Stephenson	1920 to 1929

MOST TESTS AS CAPTAIN

Tests	Captain	Span
56	B G O'Driscoll	2002 to 2009
36	K G M Wood	1996 to 2003
24	T J Kiernan	1963 to 1973
19	C F Fitzgerald	1982 to 1986
17	J F Slattery	1979 to 1981
17	D G Lenihan	1986 to 1990

MOST POINTS IN TESTS

Pts	Player	Tests	Career
919	R J R O'Gara	92	2000 to 2009
565*	D G Humphreys	72	1996 to 2005
308	M J Kiernan	43	1982 to 1991
296	E P Elwood	35	1993 to 1999
217	S O Campbell	22	1976 to 1984
195	B G O'Driscoll	93	1999 to 2009
158	T J Kiernan	54	1960 to 1973
145	D A Hickie	62	1997 to 2007
113	A J P Ward	19	1978 to 1987

* Humphreys's total includes a penalty try against Scotland in 1999

MOST TRIES IN TESTS

Tries	Player	Tests	Career
36	B G O'Driscoll	93	1999 to 2009
29	D A Hickie	62	1997 to 2007
20	S P Horgan	64	2000 to 2008
19	G T Dempsey	82	1998 to 2008
18	G E A Murphy	63	2000 to 2009
17	B J Mullin	55	1984 to 1995
15	K G M Wood	58	1994 to 2003
15	K M Maggs	70	1997 to 2005
14	G V Stephenson	42	1920 to 1930
14	R J R O'Gara	92	2000 to 2009
12	K D Crossan	41	1982 to 1992
11	A T A Duggan	25	1963 to 1972
11	S P Geoghegan	37	1991 to 1996
11	D P Wallace	55	2000 to 2009

MOST CONVERSIONS IN TESTS

Cons	Player	Tests	Career
144	R J R O'Gara	92	2000 to 2009
88	D G Humphreys	72	1996 to 2005
43	E P Elwood	35	1993 to 1999
40	M J Kiernan	43	1982 to 1991
26	T J Kiernan	54	1960 to 1973
16	R A Lloyd	19	1910 to 1920
15	S O Campbell	22	1976 to 1984

MOST PENALTY GOALS IN TESTS

Pens	Player	Tests	Career
173	R J R O'Gara	92	2000 to 2009
110	D G Humphreys	72	1996 to 2005
68	E P Elwood	35	1993 to 1999
62	M J Kiernan	43	1982 to 1991
54	S O Campbell	22	1976 to 1984
31	T J Kiernan	54	1960 to 1973
29	A J P Ward	19	1978 to 1987

MOST DROPPED GOALS IN TESTS

Drops	Player	Tests	Career
14	R J R O'Gara	92	2000 to 2009
8	D G Humphreys	72	1996 to 2005
7	R A Lloyd	19	1910 to 1920
7	S O Campbell	22	1976 to 1984
6	C M H Gibson	69	1964 to 1979
6	B J McGann	25	1969 to 1976
6	M J Kiernan	43	1982 to 1991

INTERNATIONAL CHAMPIONSHIP RECORDS

RECORD	DETAIL		SET
Most points in season	168	in five matches	2000
Most tries in season	17	in five matches	2000
	17	in five matches	2004
	17	in five matches	2007
Highest Score	60	60–13 v Italy	2000
Biggest win	47	60–13 v Italy	2000
Highest score conceded	50	18-50 v England	2000
Biggest defeat	40	6–46 v England	1997
Most appearances	56	C M H Gibson	1964–1979
Most points in matches	499	R J R O'Gara	2000–2009
Most points in season	82	R J R O'Gara	2007
Most points in match	30	R J R O'Gara	v Italy, 2000
Most tries in matches	21	B G O'Driscoll	2000–2009
Most tries in season	5	J E Arigho	1928
	5	B G O'Driscoll	2000
Most tries in match	3	R Montgomery	v Wales, 1887
	3	J P Quinn	v France, 1913
	3	E O'D Davy	v Scotland, 1930
	3	S J Byrne	v Scotland, 1953
	3	B G O'Driscoll	v France, 2000
	3	R A J Henderson	v Italy, 2001
	3	B G O'Driscoll	v Scotland, 2002
Most cons in matches	71	R J R O'Gara	2000–2009
Most cons in season	11	R J R O'Gara	2000
	11	R J R O'Gara	2004
Most cons in match	6	R J R O'Gara	v Italy, 2000
Most pens in matches	99	R J R O'Gara	2000–2009
Most pens in season	17	R J R O'Gara	2006
Most pens in match	6	S O Campbell	v Scotland, 1982
	6	R J R O'Gara	v Italy, 2000
	6	D G Humphreys	v Wales, 2002
Most drops in matches	7	R A Lloyd	1910–1920
Most drops in season	2	on several	Occasions
Most drops in match	2	W M McCombe	v France, 1975
	2	E P Elwood	v England, 1993
	2	D G Humphreys	v Wales, 1999
	2	R J R O'Gara	v England, 2005

RECORD	HOLDER	DETAIL
Longest Test Career	A J F O'Reilly	1955 to 1970
	C M H Gibson	1964 to 1979
Youngest Test Cap	F S Hewitt	17 yrs 157 days in 1924
Oldest Test Cap	C M H Gibson	36 yrs 195 days in 1979

CAREER RECORDS OF IRELAND INTERNATIONAL PLAYERS
(UP TO 30 SEPTEMBER 2009)

PLAYER BACKS	DEBUT	CAPS	T	C	P	D	PTS
I J Boss	2006 v NZ	12	2	0	0	0	10
T J Bowe	2004 v US	23	10	0	0	0	50
D M Cave	2009 v C	2	0	0	0	0	0
G W D'Arcy	1999 v R	41	5	0	0	0	25
G T Dempsey	1998 v Gg	82	19	0	0	0	95
I Dowling	2009 v C	2	0	0	0	0	0
G W Duffy	2004 v SA	10	3	0	1	0	18
K Earls	2008 v C	2	1	0	0	0	5
L M Fitzgerald	2006 v PI	12	2	0	0	0	10
S P Horgan	2000 v S	64	20	0	0	0	100
D Hurley	2009 v US	1	0	0	0	0	0
R D J Kearney	2007 v Arg	16	4	1	0	0	22
I J Keatley	2009 v C	2	0	4	3	0	17
B J Murphy	2007 v Arg	4	1	0	0	0	5
G E A Murphy	2000 v US	63	18	1	1	1	98
B G O'Driscoll	1999 v A	93	36	0	0	5	195
R J R O'Gara	2000 v S	92	14	144	173	14	919
T G O'Leary	2007 v Arg	8	0	0	0	0	0
E G Reddan	2006 v F	16	0	0	0	0	0
J W Staunton	2001 v Sm	5	1	2	4	0	21
P A Stringer	2000 v S	91	6	0	0	0	30
A D Trimble	2005 v A	24	8	0	0	0	40
P W Wallace	2006 v SA	16	2	11	6	0	50
I Whitten	2009 v C	2	2	0	0	0	10

IRELAND

FORWARDS

N A Best	2005 v NZ	18	2	0	0	0	10
R Best	2005 v NZ	34	4	0	0	0	20
T D Buckley	2007 v Arg	13	1	0	0	0	5
R Caldwell	2009 v C	2	0	0	0	0	0
R E Casey	1999 v A	7	1	0	0	0	5
T Court	2009 v It	4	0	0	0	0	0
L F M Cullen	2002 v NZ	19	0	0	0	0	0
S Ferris	2006 v PI	13	0	0	0	0	0
J P Flannery	2005 v R	31	3	0	0	0	15
J J Hayes	2000 v S	94	2	0	0	0	10
J P R Heaslip	2006 v PI	18	3	0	0	0	15
M J Horan	2000 v US	66	6	0	0	0	30
B J Jackman	2005 v J	9	0	0	0	0	0
S Jennings	2007 v Arg	5	0	0	0	0	0
D P Leamy	2004 v US	41	2	0	0	0	10
J Muldoon	2009 v C	2	0	0	0	0	0
D P O'Callaghan	2003 v W	55	1	0	0	0	5
P J O'Connell	2002 v W	62	6	0	0	0	30
J H O'Connor	2004 v SA	12	1	0	0	0	5
M R O'Driscoll	2001 v R	17	0	0	0	0	0
M E O'Kelly	1997 v NZ	92	8	0	0	0	40
A N Quinlan	1999 v R	27	6	0	0	0	30
N Ronan	2009 v C	2	0	0	0	0	0
M R Ross	2009 v C	2	0	0	0	0	0
D Ryan	2008 v Arg	3	0	0	0	0	0
D P Wallace	2000 v Arg	55	11	0	0	0	55
B G Young	2006 v NZ	8	0	0	0	0	0

Clive Mason/Getty Images

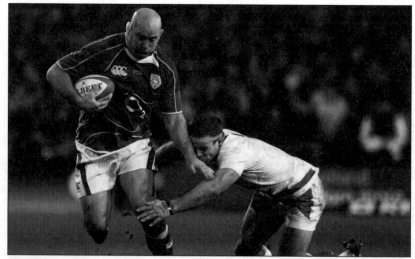

John Hayes is one of four members of the 90-cap club in the Ireland squad.

IRELAND INTERNATIONAL PLAYERS
UP TO 30TH SEPTEMBER 2009

Note: Years given for International Championship matches are for second half of season; eg 1972 means season 1971–72. Years for all other matches refer to the actual year of the match. Entries in square brackets denote matches played in RWC Finals.

Abraham, M (Bective Rangers) 1912 E, S, W, SA, 1914 W

Adams, C (Old Wesley), 1908 E, 1909 E, F, 1910 F, 1911 E, S, W, F, 1912 S, W, SA, 1913 W, F, 1914 F, E, S

Agar, R D (Malone) 1947 F, E, S, W, 1948 F, 1949 S, W, 1950 F, E, W

Agnew, P J (CIYMS) 1974 F (R), 1976 A

Ahearne, T (Queen's Coll, Cork) 1899 E

Aherne, L F P (Dolphin, Lansdowne) 1988 E 2, WS, It, 1989 F, W, E, S, NZ, 1990 E, S, F, W (R), 1992 E, S, F, A

Alexander, R (NIFC, Police Union) 1936 E, S, W, 1937 E, S, W, 1938 E, S, 1939 E, S, W

Allen, C E (Derry, Liverpool) 1900 E, S, W, 1901 E, S, W, 1903 S, W, 1904 E, S, W, 1905 E, S, W, NZ, 1906 E, S, W, SA, 1907 S, W

Allen, G G (Derry, Liverpool) 1896 S, W, 1897 E, S, 1898 E, S, 1899 E, W

Allen, T C (NIFC) 1885 E, S 1

Allen, W S (Wanderers) 1875 E

Allison, J B (Edinburgh U) 1899 E, S, 1900 E, S, W, 1901 E, S, W, 1902 E, S, W, 1903 S

Anderson, F E (Queen's U, Belfast, NIFC) 1953 F, E, S, W, 1954 NZ, F, E, S, W, 1955 F, E, S, W

Anderson, H J (Old Wesley) 1903 E, S, 1906 E, S

Anderson, W A (Dungannon) 1984 A, 1985 S, F, W, E, 1986 F, S, R, 1987 E, S, F, W, [W, C, Tg, A], 1988 S, F, W, E 1, 2, 1989 F, W, E, NZ, 1990 E, S

Andrews, G (NIFC) 1875 E, 1876 E

Andrews, H W (NIFC) 1888 M, 1889 S, W

Archer, A M (Dublin U, NIFC) 1879 S

Arigho, J E (Lansdowne) 1928 F, E, W, 1929 F, E, S, W, 1930 F, E, S, W, 1931 F, E, S, W, SA

Armstrong, W K (NIFC) 1960 NZ, 1961 E

Arnott, D T (Lansdowne) 1876 E

Ash, W H (NIFC) 1875 E, 1876 E, 1877 S

Aston, H R (Dublin U) 1908 E, W

Atkins, A P (Bective Rangers) 1924 F

Atkinson, J M (NIFC) 1927 F, A

Atkinson, J R (Dublin U) 1882 W, S

Bagot, J C (Dublin U, Lansdowne) 1879 S, E, 1880 E, S, 1881 S

Bailey, A H (UC Dublin, Lansdowne) 1934 W, 1935 E, S, W, NZ, 1936 E, S, W, 1937 E, S, W, 1938 E, S

Bailey, N (Northampton) 1952 E

Bardon, M E (Bohemians) 1934 E

Barlow, M (Wanderers) 1875 E

Barnes, R J (Dublin U, Armagh) 1933 W

Barr, A (Methodist Coll, Belfast) 1898 W, 1899 S, 1901 E, S

Barry, N J (Garryowen) 1991 Nm 2(R)

Beamish, C E St J (RAF, Leicester) 1933 W, S, 1934 S, W, 1935 E, S, W, NZ, 1936 E, S, W, 1938 W

Beamish, G R (RAF, Leicester) 1925 E, S, W, 1928 F, E, S, W, 1929 F, E, S, W, 1930 F, S, W, 1931 F, E, S, W, SA, 1932 E, S, W, 1933 E, W, S

Beatty, W J (NIFC, Richmond) 1910 F, 1912 F, W

Becker, V A (Lansdowne) 1974 F, W

Beckett, G G P (Dublin U) 1908 E, S, W

Bell, J C (Ballymena, Northampton, Dungannon) 1994 A 1, 2, US, 1995 S, It, [NZ, W, F], Fj, 1996 US, S, F, W, E, WS, A, 1997 It 1, F, W, E, S, 1998 Gg, R, SA 3, 1999 F, W, S It (R), A 2, [US (R), A 3(R), R], 2001 R (R), 2003 Tg, Sm, It 2(R)

Bell, R J (NIFC) 1875 E, 1876 E

Bell, W E (Belfast Collegians) 1953 F, E, S, W

Bennett, F (Belfast Collegians) 1913 S

Bent, G C (Dublin U) 1882 W, E

Berkery, P J (Lansdowne) 1954 W, 1955 W, 1956 S, W, 1957 F, E, S, W, 1958 A, E, S

Bermingham, J J C (Blackrock Coll) 1921 E, S, W, F

Best, N A (Ulster) 2005 NZ(R), R, 2006 NZ1, 2, A1, SA, A2, 2007 F(R), E(R), S1(R), Arg1, 2(R), S2, It2, [Nm(R), Gg(R), F(R), Arg(t&R]

Best, R (Ulster) 2005 NZ(R), A(t), 2006 W(R), A1(R), SA, A2, PI(R), 2007 W, F, E, S1, It1, S2(R), It2, [Nm, Gg, Arg(R)], 2008 It, F(R), S(R), W, E, NZ1(R), A, C(R), NZ2, Arg(R), 2009 F(R), It(R), E(R), S, W(R), C, US

Best, S J (Belfast Harlequins, Ulster) 2003 Tg (R), W 2, S 2(R), 2003 [Nm(R)], 2004 W(R), US(R), 2005 J1, 2, NZ, R, 2006 F(R), W(R), PI(R), 2007 E(R), S1, It1(R), Arg1, 2, S2, It2(R), [Nm(R), Gg(R), F(R)]

Bishop, J P (London Irish) 1998 SA, 1, 2, Gg, R, SA 3, 1999 F, W, E, S, It, A 1, 2, Arg 1, [US, A 3, Arg 2], 2000 E, Arg, C, 2002 NZ 1, 2, Fj, Arg, 2003 W 1, E

Blackham, J C (Queen's Coll, Cork) 1909 S, W, F, 1910 E, S, W

Blake-Knox, S E F (NIFC) 1976 E, S, 1977 F (R)

Blayney, J J (Wanderers) 1950 S

Bond, A T W (Derry) 1894 S, W

Bornemann, W W (Wanderers) 1960 E, S, W, SA

Boss, I J (Ulster) 2006 NZ2(R), A1(R), SA(R), A2, PI(R), 2007 F, E(R), Arg1, S2, It2(R), [Gg(R), Arg(R)]

Bowe, T J (Ulster, Ospreys) 2004 US, 2005 J1, 2, NZ, A, R, 2006 It, F, 2007 Arg1, S2, 2008 S, W, E, NZ1, A, C, NZ2, Arg, 2009 F, It, E, S, W

Bowen, D St J (Cork Const) 1977 W, E, S

Boyd, C A (Dublin U) 1900 S, 1901 S, W

Boyle, C V (Dublin U) 1935 NZ, 1936 E, S, W, 1937 E, S, W, 1938 W, 1939 W

Brabazon, H M (Dublin U) 1884 E, 1885 S 1, 1886 E

Bradley, M J (Dolphin) 1920 W, F, 1922 E, S, W, F, 1923 E, S, W, F, 1925 F, S, W, 1926 F, E, S, W, 1927 F, W

Bradley, M T (Cork Constitution) 1984 A, 1985 S, F, W, E, 1986 F, W, E, S, R, 1987 E, S, F, W, [W, C, Tg, A], 1988 S, F, W, E 1, 1990 W, 1992 NZ 1, 2, 1993 S, F, W, E, R, 1994 F, W, E, S, A 1, 2, US, 1995 S, F, [NZ]

Bradshaw, G (Belfast Collegians) 1903 W

Bradshaw, R M (Wanderers) 1885 E, S 1, 2

Brady, A M (UC Dublin, Malone) 1966 S, 1968 E, S, W

Brady, J A (Wanderers) 1976 E, S

Brady, J R (CIYMS) 1951 S, W, 1953 F, E, S, W, 1954 W, 1956 W, 1957 F, E, S, W

Bramwell, T (NIFC) 1928 F

Brand, T N (NIFC) 1924 NZ

Brennan, J I (CIYMS) 1957 S, W

Brennan, T (St Mary's Coll, Barnhall) 1998 SA 1(R), 2(R), 1999 F (R), S (R), It, A 2, Arg 1, [US, A 3], 2000 E (R), 2001 W (R), E (R), Sm (R)

Bresnihan, F P K (UC Dublin, Lansdowne, London Irish) 1966 E, W, 1967 A 1, E, S, W, F, 1968 E, S, W, A, 1969 F, E, S, W, 1970 SA, E, S, W, 1971 F, E, S, W

Brett, J T (Monkstown) 1914 W

Bristow, J R (NIFC) 1879 E

Brophy, N H (Blackrock Coll, UC Dublin, London Irish) 1957 F, E, 1959 E, S, W, F, 1960 F, SA, 1961 S, W, 1962 E, S, W, 1963 E, W, 1967 E, S, W, F, A 2

Brown, E L (Instonians) 1958 F

Brown, G S (Monkstown, United Services) 1912 S, W, SA
Brown, H (Windsor) 1877 E
Brown, T (Windsor) 1877 E, S
Brown, W H (Dublin U) 1899 E
Brown, W J (Malone) 1970 SA, F, S, W
Brown, W S (Dublin U) 1893 S, W, 1894 E, S, W
Browne, A W (Dublin U) 1951 SA
Browne, D (Blackrock Coll) 1920 F
Browne, H C (United Services and RN) 1929 E, S, W
Browne, W F (United Services and Army) 1925 E, S, W, 1926
  S, W, 1927 F, E, S, W, A, 1928 E, S
Browning, D R (Wanderers) 1881 E, S
Bruce, S A M (NIFC) 1883 E, S, 1884 E
Brunker, A A (Lansdowne) 1895 E, W
Bryant, C H (Cardiff) 1920 E, S
Buchanan, A McM (Dublin U) 1926 E, S, W, 1927 S, W, A
Buchanan, J W B (Dublin U) 1882 S, 1884 E, S
Buckley, J H (Sunday's Well) 1973 E, S
Buckley, T D (Munster) 2007 Arg1(R), 2(R), 2008 It(R), F(R), S(R),
  W(R), E(R), NZ1(R), A(R), C, NZ2(R), 2009 C, US
Bulger, L Q (Lansdowne) 1896 E, S, W, 1897 E, S, 1898 E, S, W
Bulger, M J (Dublin U) 1888 M
Burges, J H (Rosslyn Park) 1950 F, E
Burgess, R B (Dublin U) 1912 SA
Burke, P A (Cork Constitution, Bristol, Harlequins) 1995 E, S,
  W (R), It, [J], Fj, 1996 US (R), A, 1997 It 1, S (R), 2001 R (R),
  2003 S 1(R), Sm (R)
Burkitt, J C S (Queen's Coll, Cork) 1881 E
Burns, I J (Wanderers) 1980 E (R)
Butler, L G (Blackrock Coll) 1960 W
Butler, N (Bective Rangers) 1920 E
Byers, R M (NIFC) 1928 S, W, 1929 E, S, W
Byrne, E (St Mary's Coll) 2001 It (R), F (R), S (R), W (R), E (R),
  Sm, NZ (R), 2003 A (R), Sm (R)
Byrne, E M J (Blackrock Coll) 1977 S, F, 1978 F, W, E, NZ
Byrne, J S (Blackrock Coll, Leinster, Saracens) 2001 R (R), 2002
  W (R), E (R), S (R), It, NZ 2(R), R, Ru (R), Gg, A, Arg, 2003 S
  1, It 1, F, W, It 1, A, E, A, Tg, Sm, W 2(R), It 2, S2(R), [R(R), Nm(R)],
  2004 F, W, E, It, S, SA1, 2, 3, Arg, 2005 It, S, E, F, W, NZ,
  A, R
Byrne, N F (UC Dublin) 1962 F
Byrne, S J (UC Dublin, Lansdowne) 1953 S, W, 1955 F
Byron, W G (NIFC) 1896 E, S, W, 1897 E, S, 1898 E, S, W, 1899
  E, S, W
Caddell, E D (Dublin U, Wanderers) 1904 S, 1905 E, S, W, NZ,
  1906 E, S, W, SA, 1907 E, S, 1908 S, W
Cagney, S J (London Irish) 1925 W, 1926 F, E, S, W, 1927 F,
  1928 E, S, W, 1929 F, E, S, W
Caldwell, R (Ulster) 2009 C(R), US(R)
Callan, C P (Lansdowne) 1947 F, E, S, W, 1948 F, E, S, W,
  1949 F, E
Cameron, E D (Bective Rangers) 1891 S, W
Campbell, C E (Old Wesley) 1970 SA
Campbell, E F (Monkstown) 1899 S, W, 1900 E, W
Campbell, K P (Ulster) 2005 J1(R), 2(R), R
Campbell, S B B (Derry) 1911 E, S, W, F, 1912 F, E, S, W, SA,
  1913 E, S, F
Campbell, S O (Old Belvedere) 1976 A, 1979 A 1, 2, 1980 E,
  S, F, W, 1981 F, W, E, S, SA 1, 1982 W, E, S, F, 1983 S, F,
  W, E, 1984 F, W
Canniffe, D M (Lansdowne) 1976 W, E
Cantrell, J L (UC Dublin, Blackrock Coll) 1976 A, F, W, E, S,
  1981 S, SA 1, 2, A
Carey, R W (Dungannon) 1992 NZ 1, 2
Carney, B B (Munster) 2007 Arg1, 2, S2, It2(R)
Carpendale, M J (Monkstown) 1886 S, 1887 W, 1888 W, S
Carr, N J (Ards) 1985 S, F, W, E, 1986 W, E, S, R, 1987 E, S, W
Carroll, C (Bective Rangers) 1930 F
Carroll, R (Lansdowne) 1947 F, 1950 S, W
Casement, B N (Dublin U) 1875 E, 1876 E, 1879 E
Casement, F (Dublin U) 1906 E, S, W
Casey, J C (Young Munster) 1930 S, 1932 E
Casey, P J (UC Dublin, Lansdowne) 1963 F, E, S, W, NZ, 1964
  E, S, W, 1965 F, E, S
Casey, R E (Blackrock Coll, London Irish) 1999 [A 3(t), Arg 2(R)],
  2000 E, US (R), C (R), 2009 C, US
Cave, D M (Ulster) 2009 C, US
Chambers, J (Dublin U) 1886 E, S, 1887 E, S, W
Chambers, R R (Instonians) 1951 F, E, S, W, 1952 F, W
Clancy, T P J (Lansdowne) 1988 W, E 1, 2, WS, It, 1989 F, W, E, S

Clarke, A T H (Northampton, Dungannon) 1995 Fj (R), 1996 W,
  E, WS, 1997 F (R), It 2(R), 1998 Gg (R), R
Clarke, C P (Terenure Coll) 1993 F, W, E, 1998 W, E
Clarke, D J (Dolphin) 1991 W, Nm 1, 2, [J, A], 1992 NZ 2(R)
Clarke, J A B (Bective Rangers) 1922 S, W, F, 1923 F, 1924 E,
  S, W
Clegg, R J (Bangor) 1973 F, 1975 E, S, F, W
Clifford, J T (Young Munster) 1949 F, E, S, W, 1950 F, E, S, W,
  1951 F, E, SA, 1952 F, S, W
Clinch, A D (Dublin U, Wanderers) 1892 S, 1893 W, 1895 E, S,
  W, 1896 E, S, W, 1897 E, S
Clinch, J D (Wanderers, Dublin U) 1923 W, 1924 F, E, S, W, NZ,
  1925 F, E, S, 1926 E, S, W, 1927 F, 1928 F, E, S, W, 1929 F,
  E, S, W, 1930 F, E, S, W, 1931 F, E, S, W, SA
Clohessy, P M (Young Munster) 1993 F, W, E, 1994 F, W, E, S,
  A 1, 2, US, 1995 E, S, F, W, 1996 S, F, 1997 It 2, 1998 F (R),
  W (R), SA 2(R), Gg, R, SA 3, 1999 F, W, E, S, It, A 1, 2 Arg
  1, [US, A 3(R)], 2000 E, S, It, F, W, Arg, J, SA, 2001 It, F, R,
  S, W, E, Sm (R), NZ, 2002 W, E, S, It, F
Clune, J J (Blackrock Coll) 1912 SA, 1913 W, F, 1914 F, E, W
Coffey, J J (Lansdowne) 1900 E, 1901 W, 1902 E, S, W, 1903
  E, S, W, 1905 E, S, W, NZ, 1906 E, S, W, SA, 1907 E, 1908
  W, 1910 F
Cogan, W St J (Queen's Coll, Cork) 1907 E, S
Collier, S R (Queen's Coll, Belfast) 1883 S
Collins, P C (Lansdowne, London Irish) 1987 [C], 1990 S (R)
Collis, W R F (KCH, Harlequins) 1924 F, W, NZ, 1925 F, E, S,
  1926 F
Collis, W S (Wanderers) 1884 W
Collopy, G (Bective Rangers) 1891 S, 1892 S
Collopy, R (Bective Rangers) 1923 E, S, W, F, 1924 F, E, S, W,
  NZ, 1925 F, E, S, W
Collopy, W P (Bective Rangers) 1914 F, E, S, W, 1921 E, S, W,
  F, 1922 E, S, W, F, 1923 S, W, F, 1924 F, E, S, W
Combe, A (NIFC) 1875 E
Condon, H C (London Irish) 1984 S (R)
Cook, H G (Lansdowne) 1884 W
Coote, P B (RAF, Leicester) 1933 S
Corcoran, J C (London Irish) 1947 A, 1948 F, W
Corken, T S (Belfast Collegians) 1937 E, S, W
Corkery, D S (Cork Constitution, Bristol) 1994 A 1, 2, US, 1995
  E, [NZ, J, W, F], Fj, 1996 US, E, F, W, WS, A, 1997 It 1, F,
  W, E, S, 1998 S, F, W, E, 1999 A 1(R), 2(R)
Corley, H H (Dublin U, Wanderers) 1902 E, S, W, 1903 E, S, W,
  1904 E, S
Cormac, H S T (Clontarf) 1921 E, S, W
Corrigan, R (Greystones, Lansdowne, Leinster) 1997 C (R), It
  2, 1998 S, F, W, E, SA 3(R), 1999 A 1(R), 2(R), [Arg 2], 2002
  NZ 1, 2, R, Ru, Gg, A, Fj (R), Arg, 2003 S 1, It 1, A, Tg, Sm,
  W 2, It 2, S 2, [R, Arg, A, F], 2004 F, W, E, It, S, SA1, 2, 3,
  Arg, 2005 It, S, E, F, W, J1(R), 2(R), 2006 F
Costello, P (Bective Rangers) 1960 F
Costello, R A (Garryowen) 1993 S
Costello, V C P (St Mary's Coll, London Irish) 1996 US, F, W, E,
  WS (R), 1997 C, It 2(R), 1998 S (R), F, W, E, SA 1, 2, Gg, R, SA
  3, 1999 F, W (R), E, S (R), It, A 1, 2002 R (R), A, Arg, 2003 S 1,
  It 1, F, E, A, It 2, S 2, [R, Arg, F], 2004 F(R), W(R), It(R), S(R)
Cotton, J (Wanderers) 1889 W
Coulter, H H (Queen's U, Belfast) 1920 E, S, W
Court, T (Ulster) 2009 It(R), W(t), C, US(R)
Courtney, A W (UC Dublin) 1920 S, W, F, 1921 E, S, W, F
Cox, H L (Dublin U) 1875 E, 1876 E, 1877 E, S
Craig, R G (Queen's U, Belfast) 1938 S, W
Crawford, E C (Dublin U) 1885 E, S 1
Crawford, W E (Lansdowne) 1920 E, S, W, F, 1921 E, S, W, F,
  1922 E, S, 1923 E, S, W, F, 1924 F, E, W, NZ, 1925 F, E, S,
  W, 1926 F, E, S, W, 1927 F, E, S, W
Crean, T J (Wanderers) 1894 E, S, W, 1895 E, S, W, 1896 E,
  S, W
Crichton, R Y (Dublin U) 1920 E, S, W, F, 1921 F, 1922 E, 1923
  W, F, 1924 F, E, S, W, NZ, 1925 E, S
Croker, E W D (Limerick) 1878 E
Cromey, G E (Queen's U, Belfast) 1937 E, S, W, 1938 E, S, W,
  1939 E, S, W
Cronin, B (Garryowen) 1995 S, 1997 S
Cronyn, A P (Dublin U, Lansdowne) 1875 E, 1876 E, 1880 S
Crossan, K D (Instonians) 1982 S, 1984 F, W, E, S, 1985 S, F,
  W, E, 1986 E, S, R, 1987 E, S, F, W, [W, C, Tg, A], 1988 S,
  F, W, E 1, WS, It, 1989 W, S, NZ, 1990 E, S, F, W, Arg, 1991
  E, S, Nm 2 [Z, J, S], 1992 W

Crotty, D J (Garryowen) 1996 A, 1997 It 1, F, W, 2000 C
Crowe, J F (UC Dublin) 1974 NZ
Crowe, L (Old Belvedere) 1950 E, S, W
Crowe, M P (Lansdowne) 1929 W, 1930 E, S, W, 1931 F, S, W, SA, 1932 S, W, 1933 W, S, 1934 E
Crowe, P M (Blackrock Coll) 1935 E, 1938 E
Cullen, L F M (Blackrock Coll, Leinster, Leicester) 2002 NZ 2(R), R (R), Ru (R), Gg (R), A (R), Fj, Arg 2(R), 2003 S 1(R), It 1(R), F (R), W 1, Tg, Sm, It 2, 2004 US(R), 2005 J1, 2, R, 2007 Arg2
Cullen, T J (UC Dublin) 1949 F
Cullen, W J (Monkstown and Manchester) 1920 E
Culliton, M G (Wanderers) 1959 E, S, W, F, 1960 E, S, W, F, SA, 1961 E, S, W, F, 1962 S, F, 1964 E, S, W, F
Cummins, W E A (Queen's Coll, Cork) 1879 S, 1881 E, 1882 E
Cunningham, D McC (NIFC) 1923 E, S, W, 1925 F, E, W
Cunningham, M J (UC Cork) 1955 F, E, S, W, 1956 F, S, W
Cunningham, V J G (St Mary's Coll) 1988 E 2, It, 1990 Arg (R), 1991 Nm 1, 2, [Z, J(R)], 1992 NZ 1, 2, A, 1993 S, F, W, E, R, 1994 F
Cunningham, W A (Lansdowne) 1920 W, 1921 E, S, W, F, 1922 E, 1923 S, W
Cuppaidge, J L (Dublin U) 1879 E, 1880 E, S
Currell, J (NIFC) 1877 S
Curtis, A B (Oxford U) 1950 F, E, S
Curtis, D M (London Irish) 1991 W, E, S, Nm 1, 2, [Z, J, S, A], 1992 W, E, S (R), F
Cuscaden, W A (Dublin U, Bray) 1876 E
Cussen, D J (Dublin U) 1921 E, S, W, F, 1922 E, 1923 E, S, W, F, 1926 F, E, S, W, 1927 F, E
Daly, J C (London Irish) 1947 F, E, S, W, 1948 E, S, W
Daly, M J (Harlequins) 1938 E
Danaher, P P A (Lansdowne, Garryowen) 1988 S, F, W, WS, It, 1989 F, NZ (R), 1990 F, 1992 S, F, NZ 1, A, 1993 S, F, W, E, R, 1994 F, W, E, S, A 1, 2, US, 1995 E, S, F, W
D'Arcy, G W (Lansdowne, Leinster) 1999 [R (R)], 2002 Fj (R), 2003 Tg (R), Sm (R), W 2(R), 2004 F, W, E, It, S, SA1, 2005 It, NZ, A, R, 2006 It, F, W, S, E, NZ1, 2, A1, SA, A2, PI(R), 2007 W, F, E, S1, It1, 2, [Nm, Gg, F, Arg], 2008 It, 2009 F(t&R), It(R), S, W
Dargan, M J (Old Belvedere) 1952 S, W
Davidson, C T (NIFC) 1921 F
Davidson, I G (NIFC) 1899 E, 1900 S, W, 1901 E, S, W, 1902 E, S, W
Davidson, J C (Dungannon) 1969 F, E, S, W, 1973 NZ, 1976 NZ
Davidson, J W (Dungannon, London Irish, Castres) 1995 Fj, 1996 S, F, W, E, WS, A, 1997 It 1, F, W, E, S, 1998 Gg (R), R (R), SA 3(R), 1999 F, W, E, S, It, A 1, [US, R (R), Arg 2], 2000 S (R), W (R), US, C, 2001 It (R), S
Davies, F E (Lansdowne) 1892 S, W, 1893 E, S, W
Davis, J L (Monkstown) 1898 E, S
Davis, W J N (Edinburgh U, Bessbrook) 1890 S, W, E, 1891 E, S, W, 1892 E, S, 1895 S
Davison, W (Belfast Academy) 1887 W
Davy, E O'D (UC Dublin, Lansdowne) 1925 W, 1926 F, E, S, W, 1927 F, E, S, W, A, 1928 F, E, S, W, 1929 F, E, S, W, 1930 F, E, S, W, 1931 F, E, S, W, SA, 1932 E, S, W, 1933 E, W, S, 1934 F
Dawson, A R (Wanderers) 1958 A, E, S, W, F, 1959 E, S, W, F, 1960 F, SA, 1961 E, S, W, F, SA, 1962 S, F, W, 1963 F, E, S, W, NZ, 1964 E, S, F
Dawson, K (London Irish) 1997 NZ, C, 1998 S, 1999 [R, Arg 2], 2000 E, S, It, F, W, J, SA, 2001 R, S, W (R), E (R), Sm, 2002 Fj, 2003 Tg, It 2(R), S 2(R)
Dean, P M (St Mary's Coll) 1981 SA 1, 2, A, 1982 W, E, S, F, 1984 A, 1985 S, F, W, E, 1986 F, W, 1987 E, S, F, W, [W, A], 1988 S, F, W, E 1, 2, WS, It, 1989 F, W, E, S
Deane, E C (Monkstown) 1909 E
Deering, M J (Bective Rangers) 1929 W
Deering, S J (Bective Rangers) 1935 E, S, W, NZ, 1936 E, S, W, 1937 E, S
Deering, S M (Garryowen, St Mary's Coll) 1974 W, 1976 F, W, E, S, 1977 W, E, 1978 NZ
De Lacy, H (Harlequins) 1948 E, S
Delany, M G (Bective Rangers) 1895 W
Dempsey, G T (Terenure Coll, Leinster) 1998 Gg (R). SA 3, 1999 F, E, S, It, A 2, 2000 E (R), S, It, F, W, SA, 2001 It, F, S, W, E, NZ, 2002 W, E, S, It, F, NZ 1, 2, R, Ru, Gg, A, Arg, 2003 S 1, E (R), A, Sm, W 2(R), It 2, S 2(R), [R, Nm, Arg, A, F], 2004 F, W, E, It, S, SA1, 2, 3, US(R), Arg, 2005 It(R), S, E, F, W, J1, 2, NZ(R), R(R), 2006 E(R), NZ1(R), 2(t&R), A1, A2(R), PI, 2007 W, F, E, S1, It1, 2, [Nm, Gg, F], 2008 It, F, A(R), NZ2

Dennison, S P (Garryowen) 1973 F, 1975 E, S
Dick, C J (Ballymena) 1961 W, F, SA, 1962 W, 1963 F, E, S, W
Dick, J S (Queen's U, Belfast) 1962 E
Dick, J S (Queen's U, Cork) 1887 E, S, W
Dickson, J A N (Dublin U) 1920 E, W, F
Doherty, A E (Old Wesley) 1974 P (R)
Doherty, W D (Guy's Hospital) 1920 E, S, W, 1921 E, S, W, F
Donaldson, J A (Belfast Collegians) 1958 A, E, S, W
Donovan, T M (Queen's Coll, Cork) 1889 S
Dooley, J F (Galwegians) 1959 E, S, W
Doran, B R W (Lansdowne) 1900 S, W, 1901 E, S, W, 1902 E, S, W
Doran, E F (Lansdowne) 1890 S, W
Doran, G P (Lansdowne) 1899 W, 1900 E, S, 1902 S, W, 1903 W, 1904 E
Douglas, A C (Instonians) 1923 F, 1924 E, S, 1927 A, 1928 S
Dowling, I (Munster) 2009 C, US
Downing, A J (Dublin U) 1882 W
Dowse, J C A (Monkstown) 1914 F, S, W
Doyle, J A P (Greystones) 1984 E, S
Doyle, J T (Bective Rangers) 1935 W
Doyle, M G (Blackrock Coll, UC Dublin, Cambridge U, Edinburgh Wands) 1965 F, E, S, W, SA, 1966 F, E, S, W, 1967 A 1, E, S, W, F, A 2, 1968 F, E, S, W, A
Doyle, T J (Wanderers) 1968 E, S, W
Duffy, G W (Harlequins, Connacht) 2004 SA 2(R), 2005 S(R), J1, 2, 2007 Arg1, 2, S2, [Arg(R)], 2009 C, US
Duggan, A T A (Lansdowne) 1963 NZ, 1964 F, 1966 W, 1967 A 1, S, W, A 2, 1968 F, E, S, W, 1969 F, E, S, W, 1970 SA, F, E, S, W, 1971 F, E, S, W, 1972 F 2
Duggan, W (UC Cork) 1920 S, W
Duggan, W P (Blackrock Coll) 1975 E, S, F, W, 1976 A, F, W, S, NZ, 1977 W, E, S, F, 1978 S, F, W, E, NZ, 1979 E, S, A 1, 2, 1980 E, 1981 F, W, E, S, SA 1, 2, A, 1982 F, W, E, S, 1983 S, F, W, E, 1984 F, W, E, S
Duignan, P (Galwegians) 1998 Gg, R
Duncan, W R (Malone) 1984 W, E
Dunlea, F J (Lansdowne) 1989 W, E, S
Dunlop, R (Dublin U) 1889 W, 1890 S, W, E, 1891 E, S, W, 1892 E, S, 1893 W, 1894 W
Dunn, P E F (Bective Rangers) 1923 S
Dunn, T B (NIFC) 1935 NZ
Dunne, M J (Lansdowne) 1929 F, E, S, 1930 F, E, S, W, 1932 E, S, W, 1933 E, W, S, 1934 E, S, W
Dwyer, P J (UC Dublin) 1962 W, 1963 F, NZ, 1964 S, W
Earls, K (Munster) 2008 C, NZ2(R)
Easterby, S H (Llanelli Scarlets) 2000 S, It, F, W, Arg, US, C, 2001 S, Sm (R), 2002 W, E (R), S (R), It, F, NZ 1, 2, R, Ru, Gg, 2003 Tg, Sm, It 2, S 2(t+R), [Nm, Arg, A, F], 2004 F, W, E, It, S, SA1, 2, 3, US, Arg, 2005 It, S, E, F, W, NZ, A, 2006 It, F, W, S, E, SA(R), A2(R), PI, 2007 W, F, E, S1, It1, 2, [Nm, Gg, F, Arg], 2008 It, S(R), E(R)
Easterby, W G (Ebbw Vale, Ballynahinch, Llanelli, Leinster) 2000 US, C, 2001 R (R), S, W (R), Sm (R), 2002 W (R), S (R), R (R), Ru (R), Gg (R), Fj, 2003 S 1(R), It 1(R), Tg, Sm, W 2(R), It 2, S 2(R), [R(R), Nm(R), F(R)], 2004 W(R), It(R), S(R), SA2(R), US, 2005 S(R)
Edwards, H G (Dublin U) 1877 E, 1878 E
Edwards, R W (Malone) 1904 W
Edwards, T (Lansdowne) 1888 M, 1890 S, W, E, 1892 W, 1893 E
Edwards, W V (Malone) 1912 F, E
Egan, J D (Bective Rangers) 1922 S
Egan, J T (Cork Constitution) 1931 F, E, SA
Egan, M S (Garryowen) 1893 E, 1895 S
Ekin, W (Queen's Coll, Belfast) 1888 W, S
Elliott, W R J (Bangor) 1979 S
Elwood, E P (Lansdowne, Galwegians) 1993 W, E, R, 1994 F, W, E, S, A 1, 2, 1995 F, W, [NZ, W, F], 1996 US, S, 1997 F, W, E, NZ, C, It 2(R), 1998 F, W, E, SA 1, 2, Gg, R, SA 3, 1999 It, Arg 1(R), [US (R), A 3(R), R]
English, M A F (Lansdowne, Limerick Bohemians) 1958 W, F, 1959 E, S, F, 1960 E, S, 1961 S, W, F, 1962 F, W, 1963 E, S, W, NZ
Ennis, F N G (Wanderers) 1979 A 1(R)
Ensor, A H (Wanderers) 1973 W, F, 1974 F, W, E, S, P, NZ, 1975 E, S, F, W, 1976 A, F, W, E, NZ, 1977 E, 1978 S, F, W, E
Entrican, J C (Queen's U, Belfast) 1931 S
Erskine, D J (Sale) 1997 NZ (R), C, It 2
Fagan, G L (Kingstown School) 1878 E
Fagan, W B C (Wanderers) 1956 F, E, S

Hamilton, G F (NIFC) 1991 F, W, E, S, Nm 2, [Z, J, S, A], 1992 A
Hamilton, R L (NIFC) 1926 F
Hamilton, R W (Wanderers) 1893 W
Hamilton, W J (Dublin U) 1877 E
Hamlet, G T (Old Wesley) 1902 E, S, W, 1903 E, S, W, 1904 S, W, 1905 E, S, W, NZ, 1906 SA, 1907 E, S, W, 1908 E, S, W, 1909 E, S, W, F, 1910 E, S, F, 1911 E, S, W, F
Hanrahan, C J (Dolphin) 1926 S, W, 1927 E, S, W, A, 1928 F, E, S, 1929 F, E, S, W, 1930 F, E, S, W, 1931 F, 1932 S, W
Harbison, H T (Bective Rangers) 1984 W (R), E, S, 1986 R, 1987 E, S, F, W
Hardy, G G (Bective Rangers) 1962 S
Harman, G R A (Dublin U) 1899 E, W
Harper, J (Instonians) 1947 F, E, S
Harpur, T G (Dublin U) 1908 E, S, W
Harrison, T (Cork) 1879 S, 1880 S, 1881 E
Harvey, F M W (Wanderers) 1907 W, 1911 F
Harvey, G A D (Wanderers) 1903 E, S, 1904 W, 1905 E, S
Harvey, T A (Dublin U) 1900 W, 1901 S, W, 1902 E, S, W, 1903 E, W
Haycock, P P (Terenure Coll) 1989 E
Hayes, J J (Shannon, Munster) 2000 S, It, F, W, Arg, C, J, SA, 2001 It, F, R, S, W, E, Sm, NZ, 2002 W, E, S, It, F, NZ 1, 2, R, Ru, Gg, A, Fj, Arg, 2003 S 1, It 1, F, W 1, E, [R(R), Nm, Arg, A, F], 2004 F, W, E, It, S, SA1, 2, 3, US, Arg, 2005 It, S, E, F, W, NZ, A, R(R), 2006 It, F, W, S, E, NZ1, 2, A1, SA, A2, PI, 2007 W, F, E, S1, It1, S2(R), It2, [Nm, Gg, F, Arg], 2008 It, F, S, W, E, NZ1, A, C, NZ2, Arg, 2009 F, It, E, S, W
Headon, T A (UC Dublin) 1939 S, W
Healey, P (Limerick) 1901 E, S, W, 1902 E, S, W, 1903 E, S, W, 1904 S
Heaslip, J P R (Leinster) 2006 PI, 2007 Arg1, S2, 2008 It(R), F, S, W, E, NZ1, A, C, NZ2, Arg, 2009 F, It, E, S(R), W
Heffernan, M R (Cork Constitution) 1911 E, S, W
Hemphill, D (Dublin U) 1912 F, E, S, W
Henderson, N J (Queen's U, Belfast, NIFC) 1949 S, W, 1950 F, 1951 F, E, S, W, SA, 1952 F, S, W, E, 1953 F, E, S, W, 1954 NZ, F, E, S, W, 1955 F, E, S, W, 1956 S, W, 1957 F, E, S, W, 1958 A, E, S, W, F, 1959 E, S, W, F
Henderson, R A J (London Irish, Wasps, Young Munster) 1996 WS, 1997 NZ, C, 1998 F, W, SA 1(R), 2(R), 1999 F (R), E, S (R), It, 2000 S (R), It (R), F, W, Arg, US, J, SA, 2001 It, F, 2002 W (R), E (R), F, R (R), Ru (t), Gg (R), 2003 It 1(R), 2
Henebrey, G J (Garryowen) 1906 E, S, W, SA, 1909 W, F
Heron, A G (Queen's Coll, Belfast) 1901 E
Heron, J (NIFC) 1877 S, 1879 E
Heron, W T (NIFC) 1880 E, S
Herrick, R W (Dublin U) 1886 S
Heuston, F S (Kingstown) 1882 W, 1883 E, S
Hewitt, D (Queen's U, Belfast, Instonians) 1958 A, E, S, F, 1959 S, W, 1960 E, S, W, F, 1961 E, S, W, F, 1962 S, F, 1965 W
Hewitt, F S (Instonians) 1924 W, NZ, 1925 F, E, S, 1926 E, 1927 E, S, W
Hewitt, J A (NIFC) 1981 SA 1(R), 2(R)
Hewitt, T R (Queen's U, Belfast) 1924 W, NZ, 1925 F, E, S, 1926 F, E, S, W
Hewitt, V A (Instonians) 1935 S, W, NZ, 1936 E, S, W
Hewitt, W J (Instonians) 1954 E, 1956 S, 1959 W, 1961 SA
Hewson, F T (Wanderers) 1875 E
Hickie, D A (St Mary's Coll, Leinster) 1997 W, E, S, NZ, C, It 2, 1998 S, F, W, E, SA 1, 2, 2000 S, It, F, W, J, SA, 2001 F, R, S, W, E, NZ, 2002 W, E, S, It, F, R, Ru, Gg, A, 2003 S 1, It 1, F, W 1, E, It 2, S 2, [R, Nm, Arg, A], 2004 SA3, Arg, 2005 It, S, E, F, W, 2006 A2, PI, 2007 W, F, E, S1, It1, 2, [Nm, Gg, Arg]
Hickie, D J (St Mary's Coll) 1971 F, E, S, W, 1972 F 1, E
Higgins, J A D (Civil Service) 1947 S, W, A, 1948 F, S, W
Higgins, W W (NIFC) 1884 E, S
Hillary, M F (UC Dublin) 1952 E
Hingerty, D J (UC Dublin) 1947 F, E, S, W
Hinton, W P (Old Wesley) 1907 W, 1908 E, S, W, 1909 E, S, 1910 E, S, W, F, 1911 E, S, W, 1912 F, E, W
Hipwell, M L (Terenure Coll) 1962 E, S, 1968 F, A, 1969 F (R), S (R), W, 1971 F, E, S, W, 1972 F 2
Hobbs, T H M (Dublin U) 1884 S, 1885 E
Hobson, E W (Dublin U) 1876 E
Hogan, N A (Terenure Coll, London Irish) 1995 E, W, [J, W, F], 1996 F, W, E, WS, 1997 F, W, E, It 2
Hogan, P (Garryowen) 1992 F
Hogan, T (Munster, Leinster) 2005 J1(R), 2(R), 2007 It1(R), Arg1
Hogg, W (Dublin U) 1885 S 2

Holland, J J (Wanderers) 1981 SA 1, 2, 1986 W
Holmes, G W (Dublin U) 1912 SA, 1913 E, S
Holmes, L J (Lisburn) 1889 S, W
Hooks, K J (Queen's U, Belfast, Ards, Bangor) 1981 S, 1989 NZ, 1990 F, W, Arg, 1991 F
Horan, A K (Blackheath) 1920 E, W
Horan, M J (Shannon, Munster) 2000 US (R), 2002 Fj, Arg (R), 2003 S 1(R), It 1(R), F, W 1, E, A, Sm, It 2, S 2, [R, Nm, Arg(t&R), A(R), F(R)], 2004 It(R), S(R), SA1(R), 2(t&R), 3(R), US, 2005 It(R), S(R), E(R), F(R), W(R), J1, 2, NZ, A, R, 2006 It, W, S, E, NZ1, 2, A1, SA, A2(R), 2007 W, F, E, It1, 2, [Nm, Gg, F, Arg], 2008 It, F, S, W, E, NZ1, A, C, NZ2, Arg, 2009 F, It, E, S, W
Horgan, A P (Cork Const, Munster) 2003 Sm, W 2, S 2, 2004 F(R), 2005 J1, 2, NZ
Horgan, S P (Lansdowne, Leinster) 2000 S, It, W, Arg, C, J, SA (R), 2001 It, S, W, E, NZ, 2002 S, It, F, A, Fj, Arg, 2003 S 1, [R, Nm, Arg, A, F], 2004 F, W, E, It, S, SA1, 2, 3, US, Arg, 2005 It, S, E, NZ, A, R, 2006 It, F, W, S, E, NZ1, 2, A1, SA, A2, PI, 2007 F, E, S1, It1, [Gg, F, Arg], 2008 S(R), W, E, NZ1, A, C(R)
Houston, K J (Oxford U, London Irish) 1961 SA, 1964 S, W, 1965 F, E, SA
Howe, T G (Dungannon, Ballymena, Ulster) 2000 US, J, SA, 2001 It, F, R, Sm, 2002 It (R), 2003 Tg, W 2, 2004 F, W, E, SA2
Hughes, R W (NIFC) 1878 E, 1880 E, S, 1881 S, 1882 E, S, 1883 E, S, 1884 E, S, 1885 E, 1886 E
Humphreys, D G (London Irish, Dungannon, Ulster) 1996 F, W, E, WS, 1997 E (R), S, It 2, 1998 S, E (R), SA 2(t + R), R (R), 1999 F, W, E, S, A 1, 2, Arg 1, [US, A 3, Arg 2], 2000 E, S (R), F (t&R), W (R), Arg, US (R), C, J (R), SA (R), 2001 It (R), R, S (R), W, E, NZ, 2002 W, E, S, It, F, NZ 1, 2(R), R (t+R), Ru (R), Gg (R), Fj, 2003 S 1, It 1, F, W 1, E, A, W 2, It 2 S 2(R), [R, Arg, A(R), F(R)], 2004W(R), It(R), S(R), SA2(R), US, 2005 S(R), W(R), J1, 2, NZ(R), A(R), R
Hunt, E W F de Vere (Army, Rosslyn Park) 1930 F, 1932 E, S, W, 1933 E
Hunter, D V (Dublin U) 1885 S 2
Hunter, L M (Civil Service) 1968 W, A
Hunter, W R (CIYMS) 1962 E, S, W, F, 1963 F, E, S, 1966 F, E, S
Hurley, D (Munster) 2009 US(t&R)
Hurley, H D (Old Wesley, Moseley) 1995 Fj (t), 1996 WS
Hutton, S A (Malone) 1967 S, W, F, A 2
Ireland, J (Windsor) 1876 E, 1877 E
Irvine, H A S (Collegians) 1901 S
Irwin, D G (Queen's U, Belfast, Instonians) 1980 F, W, 1981 F, W, E, S, SA 1, 2, A, 1982 W, 1983 S, F, W, E, 1984 F, W, 1987 [Tg, A (R)], 1989 F, W, E, S, NZ, 1990 E, S
Irwin, J W S (NIFC) 1938 E, S, 1939 E, S, W
Irwin, S T (Queen's Coll, Belfast) 1900 E, S, W, 1901 E, W, 1902 E, S, W, 1903 S
Jack, H W (UC Cork) 1914 S, W, 1921 W
Jackman, B J (Leinster) 2005 J1(R), 2(R), 2007 Arg1(R), 2(R), 2008 It(R), F, S, W(R), E(R)
Jackson, A R V (Wanderers) 1911 E, S, W, F, 1913 W, F, 1914 F, E, S, W
Jackson, F (NIFC) 1923 E
Jackson, H W (Dublin U) 1877 E
Jameson, J S (Lansdowne) 1888 M, 1889 S, W, 1891 W, 1892 E, W, 1893 S
Jeffares, E W (Wanderers) 1913 E, S
Jennings, S (Leicester, Leinster) 2007 Arg 2, 2008 NZ1(R), A, C, NZ2(R)
Johns, P S (Dublin U, Dungannon, Saracens) 1990 Arg, 1992 NZ 1, 2, A, 1993 S, F, W, E, R, 1994 F, W, E, S, A 1, 2, US, 1995 E, S, W, It, [NZ, J, W, F], Fj, 1996 US, S, F, WS, 1997 It 1(R), F, W, E, S, NZ, C, It 2, 1998 S, F, W, E, SA 1, 2, Gg, R, SA 3, 1999 F, W, E, S, It, A 1, 2, Arg 1, [US, A 3, R], 2000 F (R), J
Johnston, J (Belfast Acad) 1881 S, 1882 S, 1884 S, 1885 S 1, 2, 1886 E, 1887 E, S, W
Johnston, M (Dublin U) 1880 E, S, 1881 E, S, 1882 E, 1884 E, S, 1886 E
Johnston, R (Wanderers) 1893 E, W
Johnston, R W (Dublin U) 1890 S, W, E
Johnston, T J (Queen's Coll, Belfast) 1892 E, S, W, 1893 E, S, 1895 E
Johnstone, W E (Dublin U) 1884 W
Johnstone-Smyth, T R (Lansdowne) 1882 E
Kavanagh, J R (UC Dublin, Wanderers) 1953 F, E, S, W, 1954

NZ, S, W, 1955 F, E, 1956 E, S, W, 1957 F, E, S, W, 1958 A, E, S, W, 1959 E, S, W, F, 1960 E, S, W, F, SA, 1961 E, S, W, F, SA, 1962 F

Kavanagh, P J (UC Dublin, Wanderers) 1952 E, 1955 W

Keane, K P (Garryowen) 1998 E (R)

Keane, M I (Lansdowne) 1974 F, W, E, S, P, NZ, 1975 E, S, F, W, 1976 A, F, W, E, S, NZ, 1977 W, E, S, F, 1978 S, F, W, E, NZ, 1979 F, W, E, S, A 1, 2, 1980 E, S, F, W, 1981 F, W, E, S, 1982 W, E, S, F, 1983 S, F, W, E, 1984 F, W, E, S

Kearney, R D J (Leinster) 2007 Arg 2, 2008 It(R), F, S, W, E, NZ1, A, C, NZ2, Arg, 2009 F, It, E, S, W

Kearney, R K (Wanderers) 1982 F, 1984 A, 1986 F, W

Keatley, I J (Connacht) 2009 C, US

Keeffe, E (Sunday's Well) 1947 F, E, S, W, A, 1948 F

Kelly, H C (NIFC) 1877 E, S, 1878 E, 1879 S, 1880 E, S

Kelly, J C (UC Dublin) 1962 F, W, 1963 F, E, S, W, NZ, 1964 E, S, W, F

Kelly, J P (Cork Constitution) 2002 It, NZ 1, 2, R, Ru, Gg, A (R), 2003 It 1, F, A, Tg, Sm, It 2, [R(R), Nm(R), A(R), F]

Kelly, S (Lansdowne) 1954 S, W, 1955 S, 1960 W, F

Kelly, W (Wanderers) 1884 S

Kennedy, A G (Belfast Collegians) 1956 F

Kennedy, A P (London Irish) 1986 W, E

Kennedy, F (Wanderers) 1880 E, 1881 E, 1882 W

Kennedy, F A (Wanderers) 1904 E, W

Kennedy, H (Bradford) 1938 S, W

Kennedy, J M (Wanderers) 1882 W, 1884 W

Kennedy, K W (Queen's U, Belfast, London Irish) 1965 F, E, S, W, SA, 1966 F, E, W, 1967 A 1, E, S, W, F, A 2, 1968 F, A, 1969 F, E, S, W, 1970 SA, F, E, S, W, 1971 F, E, S, W, 1972 F 1, E, F 2, 1973 E, S, W, F, 1974 F, W, E, S, P, NZ, 1975 F, W

Kennedy, T J (St Mary's Coll) 1978 NZ, 1979 F, W, E (R), A 1, 2, 1980 E, S, F, W, 1981 SA 1, 2, A

Kenny, P (Wanderers) 1992 NZ 2(R)

Keogh, F S (Bective Rangers) 1964 W, F

Keon, J J (Limerick) 1879 E

Keyes, R P (Cork Constitution) 1986 E, 1991 [Z, J, S, A], 1992 W, E, S

Kidd, F W (Dublin U, Lansdowne) 1877 E, S, 1878 E

Kiely, M D (Lansdowne) 1962 W, 1963 F, E, S, W

Kiernan, M J (Dolphin, Lansdowne) 1982 W (R), E, S, F, 1983 S, F, W, E, 1984 F, S, A, 1985 S, F, W, E, 1986 F, W, E, S, R, 1987 E, S, F, W, [W, C, A], 1988 S, F, W, E 1, 2, WS, 1989 F, W, E, S, 1990 S, F, W, Arg, 1991 F

Kiernan, T J (UC Cork, Cork Const) 1960 E, S, W, F, SA, 1961 E, S, W, F, SA, 1962 E, W, 1963 F, S, W, NZ, 1964 E, S, 1965 F, E, S, W, SA, 1966 F, E, S, W, 1967 A 1, E, S, W, F, A 2, 1968 F, E, S, W, A, 1969 F, E, S, W, 1970 SA, F, E, S, W, 1971 F, 1972 F 1, E, F 2, 1973 NZ, E, S

Killeen, G V (Garryowen) 1912 E, S, W, 1913 E, S, W, F, 1914 E, S, W

King, H (Dublin U) 1883 E, S

Kingston, T J (Dolphin) 1987 [W, Tg, A], 1988 S, F, W, E 1, 1990 F, W, 1991 [J], 1993 F, W, E, R, 1994 F, W, E, S, 1995 F, W, It, [NZ, J (R), W, F], Fj, 1996 US, S, F

Knox, J H (Dublin U, Lansdowne) 1904 W, 1905 E, S, W, NZ, 1906 S, W, 1907 W, 1908 S

Kyle, J W (Queen's U, Belfast, NIFC) 1947 F, E, S, W, A, 1948 F, E, S, W, 1949 F, E, S, W, 1950 F, E, S, W, 1951 F, E, S, W, SA, 1952 F, S, W, E, 1953 F, E, S, W, 1954 NZ, F, 1955 F, E, W, 1956 F, E, S, W, 1957 F, E, S, W, 1958 A, E, S

Lambert, N H (Lansdowne) 1934 S, W

Lamont, R A (Instonians) 1965 F, E, SA, 1966 F, E, S, W, 1970 SA, F, E, S, W

Landers, M F (Cork Const) 1904 W, 1905 E, S, W, NZ

Lane, D J (UC Cork) 1934 S, W, 1935 E, S

Lane, M F (UC Cork) 1947 W, 1949 F, E, S, W, 1950 F, E, S, W, 1951 F, S, W, SA, 1952 F, S, 1953 F, E

Lane, P (Old Crescent) 1964 W

Langan, D J (Clontarf) 1934 W

Langbroek, J A (Blackrock Coll) 1987 [Tg]

Lavery, P (London Irish) 1974 W, 1976 W

Lawlor, P J (Clontarf) 1951 S, SA, 1952 F, S, W, E, 1953 F, 1954 NZ, E, S, 1956 F, E

Lawlor, P J (Bective Rangers) 1935 E, S, W, 1937 E, S, W

Lawlor, P J (Bective Rangers) 1990 Arg, 1992 A, 1993 S

Leahy, K T (Wanderers) 1992 NZ 1

Leahy, M W (UC Cork) 1964 W

Leamy, D P (Munster) 2004 US, 2005 It, J2, NZ, A, R, 2006 It,

F, W, S, E, NZ1, 2, A1, SA, A2, PI(R), 2007 W, F, E, S1, It1, 2, [Nm, Gg, F, Arg], 2008 It, F, S, W, E, NZ1, A, 2009 F(R), It(t&R), E(R), S, W(R), C, US

Lee, S (NIFC) 1891 E, S, W, 1892 E, S, W, 1893 E, S, W, 1894 E, S, W, 1895 E, W, 1896 E, S, W, 1897 E, 1898 E

Le Fanu, V C (Cambridge U, Lansdowne) 1886 E, S, 1887 E, W, 1888 S, 1889 W, 1890 E, 1891 E, 1892 E, S, W

Lenihan, D G (UC Cork, Cork Const) 1981 A, 1982 W, E, S, F, 1983 S, F, W, E, 1984 F, W, E, S, A, 1985 S, F, W, E, 1986 F, W, E, S, R, 1987 E, S, F, W, [W, C, Tg, A], 1988 S, F, W, E 1, 2, WS, It, 1989 F, W, E, S, NZ, 1990 S, F, W, Arg, 1991 Nm 2, [Z, S, A], 1992 W

L'Estrange, L P F (Dublin U) 1962 E

Levis, F H (Wanderers) 1884 E

Lewis, K P (Leinster) 2005 J2(R), 2007 Arg1, 2(R)

Lightfoot, E J (Lansdowne) 1931 F, E, S, W, SA, 1932 E, S, W, 1933 E, W, S

Lindsay, H (Dublin U, Armagh) 1893 E, S, W, 1894 E, S, W, 1895 E, 1896 E, S, W, 1898 E, S, W

Little, T J (Bective Rangers) 1898 W, 1899 S, W, 1900 S, W, 1901 E, S

Lloyd, R A (Dublin U, Liverpool) 1910 E, S, 1911 E, S, W, F, 1912 F, E, S, W, SA, 1913 E, S, W, F, 1914 F, E, 1920 E, F

Longwell, G W (Ballymena) 2000 J (R), SA, 2001 F (R), R, S (R), Sm, NZ (R), 2002 W (R), E (R), S (R), It, F, NZ 1, 2, R, Ru, Gg, A, Arg, 2003 S 1, It 1, F, E, A, It 2, 2004 It(R)

Lydon, C T J (Galwegians) 1956 S

Lyle, R K (Dublin U) 1910 W, F

Lyle, T R (Dublin U) 1885 E, S 1, 2, 1886 E, 1887 E, S

Lynch, J F (St Mary's Coll) 1971 F, E, S, W, 1972 F 1, E, F 2, 1973 NZ, E, S, W, 1974 F, W, E, S, P, NZ

Lynch, L M (Lansdowne) 1956 S

Lytle, J H (NIFC) 1894 E, S, W, 1895 W, 1896 E, S, W, 1897 E, S, 1898 E, S, 1899 S

Lytle, J N (NIFC) 1888 M, 1889 W, 1890 E, 1891 E, S, 1894 E, S, W

Lyttle, V J (Collegians, Bedford) 1938 E, 1939 E, S

McAleese, D R (Ballymena) 1992 F

McAllan, G H (Dungannon) 1896 S, W

Macauley, J (Limerick) 1887 E, S

McBride, W D (Malone) 1988 W, E 1, WS, It, 1989 S, 1990 F, W, Arg, 1993 S, F, W, E, R, 1994 W, E, S, A 1(R), 1995 S, F, [NZ, W, F], Fj (R), 1996 W, E, WS, A, 1997 It 1(R), F, W, E, S

McBride, W J (Ballymena) 1962 E, S, F, W, 1963 F, E, S, W, NZ, 1964 E, S, F, 1965 F, E, S, W, SA, 1966 F, E, S, W, 1967 A 1, E, S, W, F, A 2, 1968 F, E, S, W, A, 1969 F, E, S, W, 1970 SA, F, E, S, W, 1971 F, E, S, W, 1972 F 1, E, F 2, 1973 NZ, E, S, W, F, 1974 F, W, E, S, P, NZ, 1975 E, S, F, W

McCahill, S A (Sunday's Well) 1995 Fj (t)

McCall, B W (London Irish) 1985 F (R), 1986 E, S

McCall, M C (Bangor, Dungannon, London Irish) 1992 NZ 1(R), 2, 1994 W, 1996 E (R), A, 1997 It 1, NZ, C, It 2, 1998 S, E, SA 1, 2

McCallan, B (Ballymena) 1960 E, S

McCarten, R J (London Irish) 1961 E, W, F

McCarthy, E A (Kingstown) 1882 W

McCarthy, J S (Dolphin) 1948 F, E, S, W, 1949 F, E, S, W, 1950 W, 1951 F, E, S, SA, 1952 F, S, W, E, 1953 F, E, S, 1954 NZ, F, E, S, W, 1955 F, E

McCarthy, P D (Cork Const) 1992 NZ 1, 2, A, 1993 S, R (R)

MacCarthy, St G (Dublin U) 1882 W

McCarthy, T (Cork) 1898 W

McClelland, T A (Queen's U, Belfast) 1921 E, S, W, F, 1922 E, W, F, 1923 E, S, W, F, 1924 F, E, S, W, NZ

McClenahan, R O (Instonians) 1923 E, S, W

McClinton, A N (NIFC) 1910 W, F

McCombe, W McM (Dublin U, Bangor) 1968 F, 1975 E, S, F, W

McConnell, A A (Collegians) 1947 A, 1948 F, E, S, W, 1949 F, E

McConnell, G (Derry, Edinburgh U) 1912 F, E, 1913 W, F

McConnell, J W (Lansdowne) 1913 S

McCormac, F M (Wanderers) 1909 W, 1910 W, F

McCormick, W J (Wanderers) 1930 E

McCoull, H C (Belfast Albion) 1895 E, S, W, 1899 E

McCourt, D (Queen's U, Belfast) 1947 A

McCoy, J J (Dungannon, Bangor, Ballymena) 1984 W, A, 1985 S, F, W, E, 1986 F, 1987 [Tg], 1988 E 2, WS, It, 1989 F, W, E, S, NZ

McCracken, H (NIFC) 1954 W

McCullen, A (Lansdowne) 2003 Sm

McCullough, M T (Ulster) 2005 J1, 2, NZ(R), A(R)
McDermott, S J (London Irish) 1955 S, W
Macdonald, J A (Methodist Coll, Belfast) 1875 E, 1876 E, 1877 S, 1878 E, 1879 S, 1880 E, 1881 S, 1882 E, S, 1883 E, S, 1884 E, S
McDonald, J P (Malone) 1987 [C], 1990 E (R), S, Arg
McDonnell, A C (Dublin U) 1889 W, 1890 S, W, 1891 E
McDowell, J C (Instonians) 1924 F, NZ
McFarland, B A T (Derry) 1920 S, W, F, 1922 W
McGann, B J (Lansdowne) 1969 F, E, S, W, 1970 SA, F, E, S, W, 1971 F, E, S, W, 1972 F 1, E, F 2, 1973 NZ, E, S, W, 1976 F, W, E, S, NZ
McGowan, A N (Blackrock Coll) 1994 US
McGown, T M W (NIFC) 1899 E, S, 1901 S
McGrath, D G (UC Dublin, Cork Const) 1984 S, 1987 [W, C, Tg, A]
McGrath, N F (Oxford U, London Irish) 1934 W
McGrath, P J (UC Cork) 1965 E, S, W, SA, 1966 F, E, S, W, 1967 A 1, A 2
McGrath, R J M (Wanderers) 1977 W, E, F (R), 1981 SA 1, 2, A, 1982 W, E, S, F, 1983 S, F, W, E, 1984 F, W
McGrath, T (Garryowen) 1956 W, 1958 F, 1960 E, S, W, F, 1961 SA
McGuinness, C D (St Mary's Coll) 1997 NZ, C, 1998 F, W, E, SA 1, 2, Gg, R (R), SA 3, 1999 F, W, E, S
McGuire, E P (UC Galway) 1963 E, S, W, NZ, 1964 E, S, W, F
MacHale, S (Lansdowne) 1965 F, E, S, W, SA, 1966 F, E, S, W, 1967 S, W, F
McHugh, M (St Mary's Coll) 2003 Tg
McIldowie, G (Malone) 1906 SA, 1910 E, S, W
McIlrath, J A (Ballymena) 1976 A, F, NZ, 1977 W, E
McIlwaine, E H (NIFC) 1895 S, W
McIlwaine, E N (NIFC) 1875 E, 1876 E
McIlwaine, J E (NIFC) 1897 S, 1898 E, S, W, 1899 E, W
McIntosh, L M (Dublin U) 1884 S
MacIvor, C V (Dublin U) 1912 F, E, S, W, 1913 E, S, F
McIvor, S C (Garryowen) 1996 A, 1997 It 1, S (R)
McKay, J W (Queen's U, Belfast) 1947 F, E, S, W, A, 1948 F, E, S, W, 1949 F, E, S, W, 1950 F, E, S, W, 1951 F, E, S, W, SA, 1952 F
McKee, W D (NIFC) 1947 A, 1948 F, E, S, W, 1949 F, E, S, W, 1950 F, E, 1951 SA
McKeen, A J W (Lansdowne) 1999 [R (R)]
McKelvey, J M (Queen's U, Belfast) 1956 F, E
McKenna, P (St Mary's Coll) 2000 Arg
McKibbin, A R (Instonians, London Irish) 1977 W, E, S, 1978 S, F, W, E, NZ, 1979 F, W, E, S, 1980 E, S
McKibbin, C H (Instonians) 1976 S (R)
McKibbin, D (Instonians) 1950 F, E, S, W, 1951 F, E, S, W
McKibbin, H R (Queen's U, Belfast) 1938 W, 1939 E, S, W
McKinney, S A (Dungannon) 1972 F 1, E, F 2, 1973 W, F, 1974 F, E, S, P, NZ, 1975 E, S, 1976 A, F, E, S, NZ, 1977 W, E, S, 1978 S (R), F, W, E
McLaughlin, J H (Derry) 1887 E, S, 1888 W, S
McLean, R E (Dublin U) 1881 S, 1882 W, E, S, 1883 E, S, 1884 E, S, 1885 E, S 1
Maclear, B (Cork County, Monkstown) 1905 E, S, W, NZ, 1906 E, S, W, SA, 1907 E, S, W
McLennan, A C (Wanderers) 1977 F, 1978 S, F, W, E, NZ, 1979 F, W, E, S, 1980 E, F, 1981 F, W, E, S, SA 1, 2
McLoughlin, F M (Northern) 1976 A
McLoughlin, G A J (Shannon) 1979 F, W, E, S, A 1, 2, 1980 E, 1981 SA 1, 2, 1982 W, E, S, F, 1983 S, F, W, E, 1984 F
McLoughlin, R J (UC Dublin, Blackrock Coll, Gosforth) 1962 E, S, F, 1963 E, S, W, NZ, 1964 E, S, 1965 F, E, S, W, SA, 1966 F, E, S, W, 1971 F, E, S, W, 1972 F 1, E, F 2, 1973 NZ, E, S, W, F, 1974 F, W, E, S, P, NZ, 1975 E, S, F, W
McMahon, L B (Blackrock Coll, UC Dublin) 1931 E, SA, 1933 E, 1934 E, 1936 E, S, W, 1937 E, S, W, 1938 E, S
McMaster, A W (Ballymena) 1972 F 1, E, F 2, 1973 NZ, E, S, W, F, 1974 E, S, P, 1975 F, W, 1976 A, F, W, NZ
McMordie, J (Queen's Coll, Belfast) 1886 S
McMorrow, A (Garryowen) 1951 W
McMullen, A R (Cork) 1881 E, S
McNamara, V (UC Cork) 1914 E, S, W
McNaughton, P P (Greystones) 1978 S, F, W, E, 1979 F, W, E, S, A 1, 2, 1980 E, S, F, W, 1981 F
MacNeill, H P (Dublin U, Oxford U, Blackrock Coll, London Irish) 1981 F, W, E, S, A, 1982 W, E, S, F, 1983 S, F, W, E, 1984 F, W, E, A, 1985 S, F, W, E, 1986 F, W, E, S, R, 1987 E, S, F, W, [W, C, Tg, A], 1988 S (R), E 1, 2

McQuilkin, K P (Bective Rangers, Lansdowne) 1996 US, S, F, 1997 F (t & R), S
MacSweeney, D A (Blackrock Coll) 1955 S
McVicker, H (Army, Richmond) 1927 E, S, W, A, 1928 F
McVicker, J (Collegians) 1924 F, E, S, W, NZ, 1925 F, E, S, W, 1926 F, E, S, W, 1927 F, E, S, W, A, 1928 W, 1930 F
McVicker, S (Queen's U, Belfast) 1922 E, S, W, F
McWeeney, J P J (St Mary's Coll) 1997 NZ
Madden, M N (Sunday's Well) 1955 E, S, W
Magee, A M (Louis) (Bective Rangers, London Irish) 1895 E, S, W, 1896 E, S, W, 1897 E, S, 1898 E, S, W, 1899 E, S, W, 1900 E, S, W, 1901 E, S, W, 1902 E, S, W, 1903 E, S, W, 1904 W
Magee, J T (Bective Rangers) 1895 E, S
Maggs, K M (Bristol, Bath, Ulster) 1997 NZ (R), C, It 2, 1998 S, F, W, E, SA 1, 2, Gg, R (R), SA 3, 1999 F, W, E, S, It, A 1, 2, Arg 1, [US, A 3, Arg 2], 2000 E, F, Arg, US (R), C, 2001 It (R), F (R), R, S (R), W, E, Sm, NZ, 2002 W, E, S, R, Ru, Gg, A, Fj, Arg, 2003 S 1, It 1, F, W 1, E, A, W 2, S 2, [R, Nm, Arg, A, F], 2004 F, W(R), E(R), It(R), S(R), SA1(R), 2, US, 2005 S, F, W, J1
Maginiss, R M (Dublin U) 1875 E, 1876 E
Magrath, R M (Cork Constitution) 1909 S
Maguire, J F (Cork) 1884 S
Mahoney, J (Dolphin) 1923 E
Malcolmson, G L (RAF, NIFC) 1935 NZ, 1936 E, S, W, 1937 E, S, W
Malone, N G (Oxford U, Leicester) 1993 S, F, 1994 US (R)
Mannion, N P (Corinthians, Lansdowne, Wanderers) 1988 WS, It, 1989 F, W, E, S, NZ, 1990 E, S, F, W, Arg, 1991 Nm 1(R), 2, [J], 1993 S
Marshall, B D E (Queen's U, Belfast) 1963 E
Mason, S J P (Orrell, Richmond) 1996 W, E, WS
Massey-Westropp, R H (Limerick, Monkstown) 1886 E
Matier, R N (NIFC) 1878 E, 1879 S
Matthews, P M (Ards, Wanderers) 1984 A, 1985 S, F, W, E, 1986 R, 1987 E, S, F, W, [W, Tg, A], 1988 S, F, W, E 1, 2, WS, It, 1989 F, W, E, S, NZ, 1990 E, S, 1991 F, W, E, S, Nm 1 [Z, S, A], 1992 W, E, S
Mattsson, J (Wanderers) 1948 E
Mayne, R B (Queen's U, Belfast) 1937 W, 1938 E, W, 1939 E, S, W
Mayne, R H (Belfast Academy) 1888 W, S
Mayne, T (NIFC) 1921 E, S, F
Mays, K M A (UC Dublin) 1973 NZ, E, S, W
Meares, A W D (Dublin U) 1899 S, W, 1900 E, W
Megaw, J (Richmond, Instonians) 1934 W, 1938 E
Millar, A (Kingstown) 1880 E, S, 1883 E
Millar, H J (Monkstown) 1904 W, 1905 E, S, W
Millar, S (Ballymena) 1958 F, 1959 E, S, W, F, 1960 E, S, W, F, SA, 1961 E, S, W, F, SA, 1962 E, S, F, 1963 F, E, S, W, 1964 F, 1968 F, E, S, W, A, 1969 F, E, S, W, 1970 SA, F, E, S, W
Millar, W H J (Queen's U, Belfast) 1951 E, S, W, 1952 S, W
Miller, E R P (Leicester, Tererure Coll, Leinster) 1997 It 1, F, W, E, NZ, It 2, 1998 S, W (R), Gg, R, 1999 F, W, E, S, Arg 1(R), [US (R), A 3(t&R), Arg 2(R)], 2000 US, C (R), SA, 2001 R, W, E, Sm, NZ, 2002 E, S, It (R), Fj (R), 2003 W 1(t+R), Tg, Sm, It 2, S 2, [Nm, Arg(R), A(t&R), F(R)], 2004 SA3(R), US, Arg(R), 2005 It(R), S(R), F(R), W(R), J1(R), 2
Miller, F H (Wanderers) 1886 S
Milliken, R A (Bangor) 1973 E, S, W, F, 1974 F, W, E, S, P, NZ, 1975 E, S, F, W
Millin, T J (Dublin U) 1925 W
Minch, J B (Bective Rangers) 1912 SA, 1913 E, S, 1914 E, S
Moffat, J (Belfast Academy) 1888 W, S, M, 1889 S, 1890 S, W, 1891 S
Moffatt, J E (Old Wesley) 1904 S, 1905 E, S, W
Moffett, J W (Ballymena) 1961 E, S
Molloy, M G (UC Galway, London Irish) 1966 F, E, 1967 A 1, E, S, W, F, A 2, 1968 F, E, S, W, A, 1969 F, E, S, W, 1970 F, E, S, W, 1971 F, E, S, W, 1973 F, 1976 A
Moloney, J J (St Mary's Coll) 1972 F 1, E, F 2, 1973 NZ, E, S, W, F, 1974 F, W, E, S, P, NZ, 1975 E, S, F, W, 1976 S, 1978 S, F, W, E, 1979 A 1, 2, 1980 S, W
Moloney, L A (Garryowen) 1976 W (R), S, 1978 S (R), NZ
Molony, J U (UC Dublin) 1950 S
Monteith, J D E (Queen's U, Belfast) 1947 E, S, W
Montgomery, A (NIFC) 1895 S
Montgomery, F P (Queen's U, Belfast) 1914 E, S, W
Montgomery, R (Cambridge U) 1887 E, S, W, 1891 E, 1892 W
Moore, C M (Dublin U) 1887 S, 1888 W, S

Moore, D F (Wanderers) 1883 E, S, 1884 E, W
Moore, F W (Wanderers) 1884 W, 1885 E, S 2, 1886 S
Moore, H (Windsor) 1876 E, 1877 S
Moore, H (Queen's U, Belfast) 1910 S, 1911 W, F, 1912 F, E, S, W, SA
Moore, T A P (Highfield) 1967 A 2, 1973 NZ, E, S, W, F, 1974 F, W, E, S, P, NZ
Moore, W D (Queen's Coll, Belfast) 1878 E
Moran, F G (Clontarf) 1936 E, 1937 E, S, W, 1938 S, W, 1939 E, S, W
Morell, H B (Dublin U) 1881 E, S, 1882 W, E
Morgan, G J (Clontarf) 1934 E, S, W, 1935 E, S, W, NZ, 1936 E, S, W, 1937 E, S, W, 1938 E, S, W, 1939 E, S, W
Moriarty, C C H (Monkstown) 1899 W
Moroney, J C M (Garryowen) 1968 W, A, 1969 F, E, S, W
Moroney, R J M (Lansdowne) 1984 F, W, 1985 F
Moroney, T A (UC Dublin) 1964 W, 1967 A 1, E
Morphy, E McG (Dublin U) 1908 E
Morris, D P (Bective Rangers) 1931 W, 1932 E, 1935 E, S, W, NZ
Morrow, J W R (Queen's Coll, Belfast) 1882 S, 1883 E, S, 1884 E, W, 1885 S 1, 2, 1886 E, S, 1888 S
Morrow, R D (Bangor) 1986 F, E, S
Mortell, M (Bective Rangers, Dolphin) 1953 F, E, S, W, 1954 NZ, F, E, S, W
Morton, W A (Dublin U) 1888 S
Mostyn, M R (Galwegians) 1999 A 1, Arg 1, [US, A 3, R, Arg 2]
Moyers, L W (Dublin U) 1884 W
Moylett, M M F (Shannon) 1988 E 1
Mulcahy, W A (UC Dublin, Bective Rangers, Bohemians) 1958 A, E, S, W, F, 1959 E, S, W, F, 1960 E, S, W, SA, 1961 E, S, W, SA, 1962 E, S, F, W, 1963 F, E, S, W, NZ, 1964 E, S, W, F, 1965 F, E, S, W, SA
Muldoon, J (Connacht) 2009 C, US
Mullan, B (Clontarf) 1947 F, E, S, W, 1948 F, E, S, W
Mullane, J P (Limerick Bohemians) 1928 W, 1929 F
Mullen, K D (Old Belvedere) 1947 F, E, S, W, A, 1948 F, E, S, W, 1949 F, E, S, W, 1950 F, E, S, W, 1951 F, E, S, W, SA, 1952 F, S, W
Mulligan, A A (Wanderers) 1956 F, E, 1957 F, E, S, W, 1958 A, E, S, F, 1959 E, S, W, F, 1960 E, S, W, F, SA, 1961 W, F, SA
Mullin, B J (Dublin U, Oxford U, Blackrock Coll, London Irish) 1984 A, 1985 S, W, E, 1986 F, W, E, S, R, 1987 E, S, F, W, [W, C, Tg, A], 1988 S, F, W, E 1, 2, WS, It, 1989 F, W, E, S, NZ, 1990 E, S, W, Arg, 1991 F, W, E, S, Nm 1, 2, [J, S, A], 1992 W, E, S, 1994 US, 1995 E, S, F, W, It, [NZ, J, W, F]
Mullins, M J (Young Munster, Old Crescent) 1999 Arg 1(R), [R], 2000 E, S, It, Arg (t&R), US, C, 2001 It, R, W (R), E (R), Sm (R), NZ (R), 2003 Tg, Sm
Murphy, B J (Munster) 2007 Arg 1(R), 2, 2009 C, US
Murphy, C J (Lansdowne) 1939 E, S, W, 1947 F, E
Murphy, G E A (Leicester) 2000 US, C (R), J, 2001 R, S, Sm, 2002 W, E, NZ 1, 2, Fj, 2003 S 1(R), It 1, F, W 1, E, A, W 2, It 2(R), S 2, 2004 It, S, SA1, 3, US, Arg, 2005 It, S, E, F, W, NZ, A, R, 2006 It, F, W, S, E, NZ1, 2, A1(R), SA(R), A2, 2007 W(t&R), F, Arg1(t&R), 2, S2, It2, [Nm(R), Arg], 2008 It, F, S, E, NZ1(R), A(R), Arg, 2009 F(R), It(R), S(R), W(R)
Murphy, J G M W (London Irish) 1951 SA, 1952 S, W, E, 1954 NZ, 1958 W
Murphy, J J (Greystones) 1981 SA 1, 1982 W (R), 1984 S
Murphy, J N (Greystones) 1992 A
Murphy, K J (Cork Constitution) 1990 E, S, F, W, Arg, 1991 F, W (R), S (R), 1992 S, F, NZ 2(R)
Murphy, N A A (Cork Constitution) 1958 A, E, S, W, F, 1959 E, S, W, F, 1960 E, W, F, SA, 1961 E, S, W, 1962 E, 1963 NZ, 1964 E, S, W, F, 1965 F, E, S, W, SA, 1966 F, E, S, W, 1967 A 1, E, S, W, F, 1969 F, E, S, W
Murphy, N F (Cork Constitution) 1930 E, W, 1931 F, E, S, W, SA, 1932 E, S, W, 1933 E
Murphy-O'Connor, J (Bective Rangers) 1954 E
Murray, H W (Dublin U) 1877 S, 1878 E, 1879 E
Murray, J B (UC Dublin) 1963 F
Murray, P F (Wanderers) 1927 F, 1929 F, E, S, 1930 F, E, S, W, 1931 F, E, S, W, SA, 1932 E, S, W, 1933 E, W, S
Murtagh, C W (Portadown) 1977 S
Myles, J (Dublin U) 1875 E
Nash, L C (Queen's Coll, Cork) 1889 S, 1890 W, E, 1891 F, E, S, W
Neely, M R (Collegians) 1947 F, E, S, W
Neill, H J (NIFC) 1885 E, S 1, 2, 1886 S, 1887 E, S, W, 1888 W, S

Neill, J McF (Instonians) 1926 F
Nelson, J E (Malone) 1947 A, 1948 E, S, W, 1949 F, E, S, W, 1950 F, E, S, W, 1951 F, E, W, 1954 F
Nelson, R (Queen's Coll, Belfast) 1882 E, S, 1883 S, 1886 S
Nesdale, R P (Newcastle) 1997 W, E, S, NZ (R), C, 1998 F (R), W (R), Gg, SA 3(R), 1999 It, A 2(R), [US (R), R]
Nesdale, T J (Garryowen) 1961 F
Neville, W C (Dublin U) 1879 S, E
Nicholson, P C (Dublin U) 1900 E, S, W
Norton, G W (Bective Rangers) 1949 F, E, S, W, 1950 F, E, S, W, 1951 F, E, S
Notley, J R (Wanderers) 1952 F, S
Nowlan, K W (St Mary's Coll) 1997 NZ, C, It 2
O'Brien, B (Derry) 1893 S, W
O'Brien, B A P (Shannon) 1968 F, E, S
O'Brien, D J (London Irish, Cardiff, Old Belvedere) 1948 E, S, W, 1949 F, E, S, W, 1950 F, E, S, W, 1951 F, E, S, W, SA, 1952 F, S, W, E
O'Brien, K A (Broughton Park) 1980 E, 1981 SA 1(R), 2
O'Brien-Butler, P E (Monkstown) 1897 S, 1898 E, S, 1899 S, W, 1900 E
O'Callaghan, C T (Carlow) 1910 W, F, 1911 E, S, W, F, 1912 F
O'Callaghan, D P (Cork Const, Munster) 2003 W 1(R), Tg (R), Sm (R), W 2(R), It2(R), [(R), A(t&R)], 2004 F(t&R), W, It, S(t&R), SA2(R), US, 2005 It(R), S(R), W(R), NZ, A, R, 2006 It(R), F(R), W, S(R), E(R), NZ1, 2, A1, SA, A2, PI(R), 2007 W, F, E, S1, It1, 2, [Nm, Gg, F, Arg], 2008 It, F, S, W, E, NZ1, A, C, NZ2, Arg, 2009 F, It, E, S, W
O'Callaghan, M P (Sunday's Well) 1962 W, 1964 E, F
O'Callaghan, P (Dolphin) 1967 A 1, E, A 2, 1968 F, E, S, W, 1969 F, E, S, W, 1970 SA, F, E, S, W, 1976 F, W, E, S, NZ
O'Connell, K D (Sunday's Well) 1994 F, S, E (t)
O'Connell, P (Bective Rangers) 1913 W, F, 1914 F, E, S, W
O'Connell, P J (Young Munster, Munster) 2002 W, It (R), F (R), NZ 1, 2003 E (R), A (R), Tg, Sm, W 2, S 2, [R, Nm, Arg, A, F], 2004 F, W, E, S, SA1, 2, 3, US, Arg, 2005 It, S, E, F, W, 2006 It, F, S, E, NZ1, 2, A1, SA, A2, PI, 2007 W, F, E, S1, It1, 2, It2, [Nm, Gg, F, Arg], 2008 S(R), W, E, NZ1, A, C, NZ2, Arg, 2009 F, It, E, S, W
O'Connell, W J (Lansdowne) 1955 F
O'Connor, H S (Dublin U) 1957 F, E, S, W
O'Connor, J (Garryowen) 1895 S
O'Connor, J H (Bective Rangers) 1888 M, 1890 S, W, E, 1891 E, S, 1892 E, W, 1893 E, S, 1894 E, S, W, 1895 E, 1896 E, S, W
O'Connor, J H (Wasps) 2004 SA3, Arg, 2005 S, E, F, W, J1, NZ, A, R, 2006 W(R), E(t&R)
O'Connor, J J (Garryowen) 1909 F
O'Connor, J J (UC Cork) 1933 S, 1934 E, S, W, 1935 E, S, W, NZ, 1936 S, W, 1938 S
O'Connor, P J (Lansdowne) 1887 W
O'Cuinneagain, D (Sale, Ballymena) 1998 SA 1, 2, Gg (R), R (R), SA 3, 1999 F, W, E, S, It, A 1, 2, Arg 1, [US, A 3, R, Arg 2], 2000 E, It (R)
Odbert, R V M (RAF) 1928 F
O'Donnell, R C (St Mary's Coll) 1979 A 1, 2, 1980 S, F, W
O'Donoghue, P J (Bective Rangers) 1955 F, E, S, W, 1956 W, 1957 F, E, 1958 A, E, S, W
O'Driscoll, B G (Blackrock Coll, Leinster) 1999 A 1, 2, Arg 1, [US, A 3, R (R), Arg 2], 2000 E, S, It, F, W, J, SA, 2001 F, S, W, E, Sm, NZ, 2002 W, E, S, It, F, NZ 1, 2, R, Ru, Gg, A, Fj, Arg, 2003 S 1, It 1, F, W 1, E, W 2, It 2, S 2, [R, Nm, Arg, A, F], 2004 W, E, It, S, SA1, 2, 3, US, Arg, 2005 It, E, F, W, 2006 It, F, W, S, E, NZ1, 2, A1, SA, A2, PI, 2007 W, E, S1, It1, S2, [Nm, Gg, F, Arg], 2008 It, F, S, W, NZ1, A, C, NZ2, Arg, 2009 F, It, E, S, W
O'Driscoll, B J (Manchester) 1971 F (R), E, S, W
O'Driscoll, J B (London Irish, Manchester) 1978 S, 1979 A 1, 2, 1980 E, S, F, W, 1981 F, W, E, S, SA 1, 2, A, 1982 W, E, S, F, 1983 S, F, W, E, 1984 F, W, E, S
O'Driscoll, M R (Cork Const, Munster) 2001 R (R), 2002 Fj (R), 2005 R(R), 2006 W(R), NZ1(R), 2(R), A1(R), 2007 E(R), It1, Arg1(t&R), 2, 2008 It(R), F(R), S, E(R), 2009 C, US
O'Flanagan, K P (London Irish) 1947 A
O'Flanagan, M (Lansdowne) 1948 S
O'Gara, R J R (Cork Const, Munster) 2000 S, It, F, W, Arg (R), US, C (R), J, SA, 2001 It, F, S, W (R), E (R), Sm, 2002 W (R), E (R), S (R), It (R), F (R), NZ 1, 2, R, Ru, Gg, A, Arg, 2003 W 1(R), E (R), A (t+R), Tg, Sm, S 2, [R(R), Nm, Arg(R), A, F], 2004 F, W, E, It, S, SA1, 2, 3, Arg, 2005 It, S, E, F, W, NZ, A, R(R), 2006 It, F, W, S, E, NZ1, 2, A1, SA, A2, PI(R), 2007 W, F, E, S1, It1, S2(R), It2,

[Nm, Gg, F, Arg], 2008 It, F, S, W, E, NZ1, A, C, NZ2, Arg, 2009 F, It, E, S, W

O'Grady, D (Sale) 1997 It 2

O'Hanlon, B (Dolphin) 1947 E, S, W, 1948 F, E, S, W, 1949 F, E, S, W, 1950 F

O'Hara, P T J (Sunday's Well, Cork Const) 1988 WS (R), 1989 F, W, E, NZ, 1990 E, S, F, W, 1991 Nm 1, [J], 1993 F, W, E, 1994 US

O'Kelly, M E (London Irish, St Mary's Coll, Leinster) 1997 NZ, C, It 2, 1998 S, F, W, E, SA 1, 2, Gg, R, SA 3, 1999 A 1(R), 2, Arg 1(R), [US (R), A 3, R, Arg 2], 2000 E, S, It, F, W, Arg, US, J, SA, 2001 It, F, S, W, E, NZ, 2002 E, S, It, F, NZ 1(R), 2, R, Ru, Gg, A, Fj, Arg, 2003 S 1, It 1, F, W 1, E, A, W 2, S 2, [R, Nm, Arg, A, F], 2004 F, W(R), E, It, S, SA1, 2, 3, Arg, 2005 It, S, E, F, W, NZ, A, 2006 It, F, W, S, E, SA(R), A2(R), PI, 2007 Arg1, 2(R), S2, It2(R), [F(R), Arg(R)], 2008 It, F, 2009 It(R)

O'Leary, A (Cork Constitution) 1952 S, W, E

O'Leary, T G (Munster) 2007 Arg1(R), 2008 NZ2, Arg, 2009 F, It, E, S(R), W

O'Loughlin, D B (UC Cork) 1938 E, S, W, 1939 E, S, W

O'Mahony, D W (UC Dublin, Moseley, Bedford) 1995 It, [F], 1997 It 2, 1998 R

O'Mahony, David (Cork Constitution) 1995 It

O'Meara, B T (Cork Constitution) 1997 E (R), S, NZ (R), 1998 S, 1999 [US (R), R (R)], 2001 It (R), 2003 Sm (R), It 2(R)

O'Meara, J A (UC Cork, Dolphin) 1951 F, E, S, W, SA, 1952 F, S, W, E, 1953 F, E, S, W, 1954 NZ, F, E, S, 1955 F, E, 1956 S, W, 1958 W

O'Neill, H O'H (Queen's U, Belfast, UC Cork) 1930 E, S, W, 1933 E, S

O'Neill, J B (Queen's U, Belfast) 1920 S

O'Neill, W A (UC Dublin, Wanderers) 1952 E, 1953 F, E, S, W, 1954 NZ

O'Reilly, A J F (Old Belvedere, Leicester) 1955 F, E, S, W, 1956 F, E, S, W, 1957 F, E, S, W, 1958 A, E, S, W, F, 1959 E, S, W, F, 1960 E, 1961 E, F, SA, 1963 F, S, W, 1970 E

Orr, P A (Old Wesley) 1976 F, W, E, S, NZ, 1977 W, E, S, F, 1978 S, F, W, E, NZ, 1979 F, W, E, S, A 1, 2, 1980 E, S, F, W, 1981 F, W, E, SA 1, 2, A, 1982 W, E, S, F, 1983 S, F, W, E, 1984 F, W, E, S, A, 1985 S, F, W, E, 1986 F, S, R, 1987 E, S, F, W, [W, C, A]

O'Shea, C M P (Lansdowne, London Irish) 1993 R, 1994 F, W, E, S, A 1, 2, US, 1995 E, S, [J, W, F], 1997 It 1, F, S (R), 1998 S, F, SA 1, 2, Gg, R, SA 3, 1999 F, W, E, S, It, A 1, Arg 1, [US, A 3, R, Arg 2], 2000 E

O'Sullivan, A C (Dublin U) 1882 S

O'Sullivan, J M (Limerick) 1884 S, 1887 S

O'Sullivan, P J A (Galwegians) 1957 F, E, S, W, 1959 E, S, W, F, 1960 SA, 1961 E, S, 1962 F, W, 1963 F, NZ

O'Sullivan, W (Queen's Coll, Cork) 1895 S

Owens, R H (Dublin U) 1922 E, S

Parfrey, P (UC Cork) 1974 NZ

Parke, J C (Monkstown) 1903 W, 1904 E, S, W, 1905 W, NZ, 1906 E, S, W, SA, 1907 E, S, W, 1908 E, S, W, 1909 E, S, W, F

Parr, J S (Wanderers) 1914 F, E, S, W

Patterson, C S (Instonians) 1978 NZ, 1979 F, W, E, S, A 1, 2, 1980 E, S, F, W

Patterson, R d'A (Wanderers) 1912 F, S, W, SA, 1913 E, S, W, F

Payne, C T (NIFC) 1926 E, 1927 F, E, S, A, 1928 F, E, S, W, 1929 F, E, W, 1930 F, E, S, W

Pedlow, A C (CIYMS) 1953 W, 1954 NZ, F, E, 1955 F, E, S, W, 1956 F, E, S, W, 1957 F, E, S, W, 1958 A, E, S, W, F, 1959 E, 1960 E, S, W, F, SA, 1961 S, 1962 W, 1963 F

Pedlow, J (Bessbrook) 1882 S, 1884 W

Pedlow, R (Bessbrook) 1891 W

Pedlow, T B (Queen's Coll, Belfast) 1889 S, W

Peel, T (Limerick) 1892 E, S, W

Peirce, W (Cork) 1881 E

Phipps, G C (Army) 1950 E, W, 1952 F, W, E

Pike, T O (Lansdowne) 1927 E, S, W, A, 1928 F, E, S, W

Pike, V J (Lansdowne) 1931 E, S, W, SA, 1932 E, S, W, 1933 E, W, S, 1934 E, S, W

Pike, W W (Kingstown) 1879 E, 1881 E, S, 1882 E, 1883 S

Pinion, G (Belfast Collegians) 1909 E, S, W, F

Piper, O J S (Cork Constitution) 1909 E, S, W, F, 1910 E, S, W, F

Polden, S E (Clontarf) 1913 W, F, 1914 F, 1920 F

Popham, I (Cork Constitution) 1922 S, W, F, 1923 F

Popplewell, N J (Greystones, Wasps, Newcastle) 1989 NZ, 1990 Arg, 1991 Nm 1, 2, [Z, S, A], 1992 W, E, S, F, NZ 1, 2, A, 1993 S, F, W, E, R, 1994 F, W, E, S, US, 1995 E, S, F, W,

It, [NZ, J, W, F], Fj, 1996 US, S, F, W, E, A, 1997 It 1, F, W, E, NZ, C, 1998 S (t), F (R)

Potterton, H N (Wanderers) 1920 W

Pratt, R H (Dublin U) 1933 E, W, S, 1934 E, S

Price, A H (Dublin U) 1920 S, F

Pringle, J C (NIFC) 1902 S, W

Purcell, N M (Lansdowne) 1921 E, S, W, F

Purdon, H (NIFC) 1879 S, E, 1880 E, 1881 E, S

Purdon, W B (Queen's Coll, Belfast) 1906 E, S, W

Purser, F C (Dublin U) 1898 E, S, W

Quinlan, A N (Shannon, Munster) 1999 [R (R)], 2001 It, F, 2002 NZ 2(R), Ru (R), Gg (R), A (R), Fj, Arg (R), 2003 S 1(R), It 1(R), F (R), W 1, E (R), A, W 2, [R(R), Nm, Arg], 2004 SA1(R), 2(R), 2005 J1, 2(t&R), 2007 Arg2, S2(t&R), 2008 C(R), NZ2

Quinlan, D P (Northampton) 2005 J1(R), 2

Quinlan, S V J (Blackrock Coll) 1956 F, E, W, 1958 W

Quinn, B T (Old Belvedere) 1947 F

Quinn, F P (Old Belvedere) 1981 F, W, E

Quinn, J P (Dublin U) 1910 E, S, 1911 E, S, W, F, 1912 E, S, W, 1913 E, W, F, 1914 F, E, S

Quinn, K (Old Belvedere) 1947 F, A, 1953 F, E, S

Quinn, M A M (Lansdowne) 1973 F, 1974 F, W, E, S, P, NZ, 1977 S, F, 1981 SA 2

Quirke, J M T (Blackrock Coll) 1962 E, S, 1968 S

Rainey, P I (Ballymena) 1989 NZ

Rambaut, D F (Dublin U) 1887 E, S, W, 1888 W

Rea, H H (Edinburgh U) 1967 A 1, 1969 F

Read, H M (Dublin U) 1910 E, S, 1911 E, S, W, F, 1912 F, E, S, W, SA, 1913 E, S

Reardon, J V (Cork Constitution) 1934 E, S

Reddan, E G (Wasps) 2006 F (R), 2007 Arg2, S2(R), [F, Arg], 2008 It, F, S, W, E, NZ1, A(R), C, NZ2(R), 2009 C(R), US(R)

Reid, C (NIFC) 1899 S, W, 1900 E, 1903 W

Reid, J L (Richmond) 1934 S, W

Reid, P J (Garryowen) 1947 A, 1948 F, E, W

Reid, T E (Garryowen) 1953 E, S, W, 1954 NZ, F, 1955 E, S, 1956 F, E, 1957 F, E, S, W

Reidy, C J (London Irish) 1937 W

Reidy, G F (Dolphin, Lansdowne) 1953 W, 1954 F, E, S, W

Richey, H A (Dublin U) 1889 W, 1890 S

Ridgeway, E C (Wanderers) 1932 S, W, 1935 E, S, W

Rigney, B J (Greystones) 1991 F, W, E, S, Nm 1, 1992 F, NZ 1(R), 2

Ringland, T M (Queen's U, Belfast, Ballymena) 1981 A, 1982 W, E, 1983 S, F, W, E, 1984 F, W, E, S, A, 1985 S, F, W, E, 1986 F, W, E, S, R, 1987 F, W, [W, C, Tg, A], 1988 S, F, W, E 1

Riordan, W F (Cork Constitution) 1910 E

Ritchie, J S (London Irish) 1956 F, E

Robb, C G (Queen's Coll, Belfast) 1904 E, S, W, 1905 NZ, 1906 S

Robbie, J C (Dublin U, Greystones) 1976 A F, NZ, 1977 S, F, 1981 F, W, E, S

Robinson, B F (Ballymena, London Irish) 1991 F, W, E, S, Nm 1, 2, [Z, S, A], 1992 W, E, S, F, NZ 1, 2, A, 1993 W, E, R, 1994 F, W, E, S, A 1, 2

Robinson, T T H (Wanderers) 1904 E, S, 1905 E, S, W, NZ, 1906 SA, 1907 E, S

Roche, J (Wanderers) 1890 S, W, E, 1891 E, S, W, 1892 W

Roche, R E (UC Galway) 1955 E, S, 1957 S, W

Roche, W J (UC Cork) 1920 E, S, F

Roddy, P J (Bective Rangers) 1920 S, F

Roe, R (Lansdowne) 1952 E, 1953 F, E, S, W, 1954 F, E, S, W, 1955 F, E, S, W, 1956 F, E, S, W, 1957 F, E, S, W

Rolland, A C (Blackrock Coll) 1990 Arg, 1994 US (R), 1995 It (R)

Ronan, N (Munster) 2009 C, US

Rooke, C V (Dublin U) 1891 E, W, 1892 E, S, W, 1893 E, S, W, 1894 E, S, W, 1895 E, S, W, 1896 E, S, W, 1897 E, S

Ross, D J (Belfast Academy) 1884 E, 1885 S 1, 2, 1886 E, S

Ross, G R P (CIYMS) 1955 W

Ross, J F (NIFC) 1886 S

Ross, J P (Lansdowne) 1885 E, S 1, 2, 1886 E, S

Ross, M R (Harlequins) 2009 C(R), US

Ross, N G (Malone) 1927 F, E

Ross, W McC (Queen's U, Belfast) 1932 E, S, W, 1933 E, W, S, 1934 E, S, 1935 NZ

Russell, J (UC Cork) 1931 F, E, S, W, SA, 1933 E, W, S, 1934 E, S, W, 1935 E, S, W, 1936 E, S, W, 1937 E, S

Russell, P (Instonians) 1990 E, 1992 NZ 1, 2, A

Rutherford, W G (Tipperary) 1884 E, S, 1885 E, S 1, 1886 E, 1888 W

Ryan, D (Munster) 2008 Arg(R), 2009 C(R), US(R)

Ryan, E (Dolphin) 1937 W, 1938 E, S

Ryan, J (Rockwell Coll) 1897 E, 1898 E, S, W, 1899 E, S, W, 1900 S, W, 1901 E, S, W, 1902 E, 1904 E

Ryan, J G (UC Dublin) 1939 E, S, W

Ryan, M (Rockwell Coll) 1897 E, 1898 E, S, W, 1899 E, S, W, 1900 E, S, W, 1901 E, S, W, 1903 E, 1904 E, S

Saunders, R (London Irish) 1991 F, W, E, S, Nm 1, 2, [Z, J, S, A], 1992 W, 1994 F (t)

Saverimutto, C (Sale) 1995 Fj, 1996 US, S

Sayers, H J M (Lansdowne) 1935 E, S, W, 1936 E, S, W, 1938 W, 1939 E, S, W

Scally, C J (U C Dublin) 1998 Gg (R), R, 1999 S (R), It

Schute, F (Wanderers) 1878 E, 1879 E

Schute, F G (Dublin U) 1912 SA, 1913 E, S

Scott, D (Malone) 1961 F, SA, 1962 S

Scott, R D (Queen's U, Belfast) 1967 E, F, 1968 F, E, S

Scovell, R H (Kingstown) 1883 E, 1884 E

Scriven, G (Dublin U) 1879 S, E, 1880 E, S, 1881 E, 1882 S, 1883 E, S

Sealy, J (Dublin U) 1896 E, S, W, 1897 S, 1899 E, S, W, 1900 E, S

Sexton, J F (Dublin U, Lansdowne) 1988 E 2, WS, It, 1989 F

Sexton, W J (Garryowen) 1984 A, 1988 S, E 2

Shanahan, T (Lansdowne) 1885 E, S 1, 2, 1886 E, 1888 S, W

Shaw, G M (Windsor) 1877 S

Sheahan, F J (Cork Const, Munster) 2000 US (R), 2001 It (R), R, W (R), Sm, 2002 W, E, S, Gg (R), A (t+R), Fj, 2003 S 1(R), It 1(R), 2004 F(R), W(R), It(R), S(R), SA1(R), US, 2005 It(R), S(R), W(R), J1, 2, 2006 SA(R), A2(R), PI, 2007 Arg2, [F(t&R)]

Sheehan, M D (London Irish) 1932 E

Sherry, B F (Terenure Coll) 1967 A 1, E, S, A 2, 1968 F, E

Sherry, M J A (Lansdowne) 1975 F, W

Shields, P M (Ballymena) 2003 Sm (R), It 2(R)

Siggins, J A E (Belfast Collegians) 1931 F, E, S, W, SA, 1932 E, S, W, 1933 E, W, S, 1934 E, S, W, 1935 E, S, W, NZ, 1936 E, S, W, 1937 E, S, W

Slattery, J F (UC Dublin, Blackrock Coll) 1970 SA, F, E, S, W, 1971 F, E, S, W, 1972 F 1, E, F 2, 1973 NZ, E, S, W, F, 1974 F, W, E, S, P, NZ, 1975 E, S, F, W, 1976 A, 1977 S, F, 1978 S, F, W, E, NZ, 1979 F, W, E, S, A 1, 2, 1980 E, S, W, 1981 F, W, E, S, SA 1, 2, A, 1982 W, E, S, F, 1983 S, F, W, E, 1984 F

Smartt, F N B (Dublin U) 1908 E, S, 1909 E

Smith, B A (Oxford U, Leicester) 1989 NZ, 1990 S, F, W, Arg, 1991 F, W, E, S

Smith, J H (London Irish) 1951 F, E, S, W, SA, 1952 F, S, W, E, 1954 NZ, W, F

Smith, R E (Lansdowne) 1892 E

Smith, S J (Ballymena) 1988 E 2, WS, It, 1989 F, W, E, S, NZ, 1990 E, 1991 F, W, E, S, Nm 1, 2, [Z, S, A], 1992 W, E, S, F, NZ 1, 2, 1993 S

Smithwick, F F S (Monkstown) 1898 S, W

Smyth, J T (Queen's U, Belfast) 1920 F

Smyth, P J (Belfast Collegians) 1911 E, S, F

Smyth, R S (Dublin U) 1903 E, S, 1904 E

Smyth, T (Malone, Newport) 1908 E, S, W, 1909 E, S, W, 1910 E, S, W, F, 1911 E, S, W, 1912 E

Smyth, W S (Belfast Collegians) 1910 W, F, 1920 E

Solomons, B A H (Dublin U) 1908 E, S, W, 1909 E, S, W, F, 1910 E, S, W

Spain, A W (UC Dublin) 1924 NZ

Sparrow, W (Dublin U) 1893 W, 1894 E

Spillane, B J (Bohemians) 1985 F, W, E, 1986 F, W, E, 1987 F, W, [W, C, A (R)], 1989 E (R)

Spring, D E (Dublin U) 1978 NZ, 1979 S, 1980 S, F, W, 1981 W

Spring, R M (Lansdowne) 1979 F, W, E

Spunner, H F (Wanderers) 1881 E, S, 1884 W

Stack, C R R (Dublin U) 1889 S

Stack, G H (Dublin U) 1875 E

Staples, J E (London Irish, Harlequins) 1991 W, E, S, Nm 1, 2, [Z, J, S, A], 1992 W, E, NZ 1, 2, A, 1995 F, W, It, [NZ], Fj, 1996 US, S, F, A, 1997 W, E, S

Staunton, J W (Garryowen, Wasps) 2001 Sm, 2005 J1(R), 2(R), 2006 A1(R), 2007 Arg2

Steele, H W (Ballymena) 1976 E, 1977 F, 1978 F, W, E, 1979 F, W, E, A 1, 2

Stephenson, G V (Queen's U, Belfast, London Hosp) 1920 F, 1921 E, S, W, F, 1922 E, S, W, F, 1923 E, S, W, F, 1924 F, E, S, W, NZ, 1925 F, E, S, W, 1926 F, E, S, W, 1927 F, E, S, W, A, 1928 F, E, S, W, 1929 F, E, W, 1930 F, E, S, W

Stephenson, H W V (United Services) 1922 S, W, F, 1924 F, E, S, W, NZ, 1925 F, E, S, W, 1927 A, 1928 E

Stevenson, J (Dungannon) 1888 M, 1889 S

Stevenson, J B (Instonians) 1958 A, E, S, W, F

Stevenson, R (Dungannon) 1887 E, S, W, 1888 M, 1889 S, W, 1890 S, W, E, 1891 W, 1892 W, 1893 E, S, W

Stevenson, T H (Belfast Acad) 1895 E, W, 1896 E, S, W, 1897 E, S

Stewart, A L (NIFC) 1913 W, F, 1914 F

Stewart, J W (Queen's U, Belfast, NIFC) 1922 F, 1924 S, 1928 F, E, S, W, 1929 F, E, S, W

Stoker, E W (Wanderers) 1888 W, S

Stoker, F O (Wanderers) 1886 S, 1888 W, M, 1889 S, 1891 W

Stokes, O S (Cork Bankers) 1882 E, 1884 E

Stokes, P (Garryowen) 1913 E, S, 1914 F, 1920 E, S, W, F, 1921 E, S, F, 1922 W, F

Stokes, R D (Queen's Coll, Cork) 1891 S, W

Strathdee, E (Queen's U, Belfast) 1947 E, S, W, A, 1948 W, F, 1949 E, S, W

Stringer, P A (Shannon, Munster) 2000 S, It, F, W, Arg, C, J, SA, 2001 It, F, R, S (R), W, E, Sm, NZ, 2002 W, E, S, It, F, NZ 1 2, R, Ru, Gg, A, Arg, 2003 S 1, It 1, F, W 1, E, A, W 2, S 2, [R, Nm, Arg, A, F], 2004 F, W, E, It, S, SA1, 2, 3, US(R), Arg, 2005 It, S, E, F, W, J1, 2, NZ, A, R(R), 2006 It, F, W, S, E, NZ1, 2, A1, SA, A2(R), PI, 2007 W, E, S1, It1, 2, [Nm, Gg], 2008 It(R), S(R), E(R), NZ1(R), A, C(R), 2009 It(t&R), E(R), S, W(R), C, US

Stuart, C P (Clontarf) 1912 SA

Stuart, I M B (Dublin U) 1924 E, S

Sugars, H S (Dublin U) 1905 NZ, 1906 SA, 1907 S

Sugden, M (Wanderers) 1925 F, E, S, W, 1926 F, E, S, W, 1927 E, S, W, A, 1928 F, E, S, W, 1929 F, E, S, W, 1930 F, E, S, W, 1931 F, E, S, W

Sullivan, D B (UC Dublin) 1922 E, S, W, F

Sweeney, J A (Blackrock Coll) 1907 E, S, W

Symes, G R (Monkstown) 1895 E

Synge, J S (Lansdowne) 1929 S

Taggart, T (Dublin U) 1887 W

Taylor, A S (Queen's Coll, Belfast) 1910 E, S, W, 1912 F

Taylor, D R (Queen's Coll, Belfast) 1903 E

Taylor, J (Belfast Collegians) 1914 E, S, W

Taylor, J W (NIFC) 1879 S, 1880 E, S, 1881 S, 1882 E, S, 1883 E, S

Tector, W R (Wanderers) 1955 F, E, S

Tedford, A (Malone) 1902 E, S, W, 1903 E, S, W, 1904 E, S, W, 1905 E, S, W, NZ, 1906 E, S, W, SA, 1907 E, S, W, 1908 E, S, W

Teehan, C (UC Cork) 1939 E, S, W

Thompson, C (Belfast Collegians) 1907 E, S, 1908 E, S, W, 1909 E, S, W, F, 1910 E, S, W, F

Thompson, J A (Queen's Coll, Belfast) 1885 S 1, 2

Thompson, J K S (Dublin U) 1921 W, 1922 E, S, F, 1923 E, S, W, F

Thompson, R G (Lansdowne) 1882 W

Thompson, R H (Instonians) 1951 SA, 1952 F, 1954 NZ, F, E, S, W, 1955 F, S, W, 1956 W

Thornhill, T (Wanderers) 1892 E, S, W, 1893 E

Thrift, H (Dublin U) 1904 W, 1905 E, S, W, NZ, 1906 E, W, SA, 1907 E, S, W, 1908 E, S, W, 1909 E, S, W, F

Tierney, D (UC Cork) 1938 S, W, 1939 E

Tierney, T A (Garryowen) 1999 A 1, 2, Arg 1, [US, A 3, R, Arg 2], 2000 E

Tillie, C R (Dublin U) 1887 E, S, 1888 W, S

Todd, A W P (Dublin U) 1913 W, F, 1914 F

Topping, J A (Ballymena) 1996 WS, A, 1997 It 1, F, E, 1999 [R], 2000 US, 2003 A

Torrens, J D (Bohemians) 1938 W, 1939 E, S, W

Trimble, A D (Ulster) 2005 A, R, 2006 F(R), W, S, E, NZ1, 2, A1, SA, 2007 W, F(R), E(R), It1(R), Arg1, S2(R), It2, [Nm, F], 2008 It, F, S, W, E

Tucker, C C (Shannon) 1979 F, W, 1980 F (R)

Tuke, B B (Bective Rangers) 1890 E, 1891 E, S, 1892 E, 1894 E, S, W, 1895 E, S

Turley, N (Blackrock Coll) 1962 E

Tweed, D A (Ballymena) 1995 F, W, It, [J]

Tydings, J J (Young Munster) 1968 A

Tyrrell, W (Queen's U, Belfast) 1910 F, 1913 E, S, W, F, 1914 F, E, S, W

Uprichard, R J H (Harlequins, RAF) 1950 S, W

Waide, S L (Oxford U, NIFC) 1932 E, S, W, 1933 E, W

Waites, J (Bective Rangers) 1886 S, 1888 M, 1889 W, 1890 S, W, E, 1891 E

Waldron, O C (Oxford U, London Irish) 1966 S, W, 1968 A

Walker, S (Instonians) 1934 E, S, 1935 E, S, W, NZ, 1936 E, S, W, 1937 E, S, W, 1938 E, S, W

Walkington, D B (NIFC) 1887 E, W, 1888 W, 1890 W, E, 1891 E, S, W

Walkington, R B (NIFC) 1875 E, 1876 E, 1877 E, S, 1878 E, 1879 S, 1880 E, S, 1882 E, S

Wall, H (Dolphin) 1965 S, W

Wallace, D P (Garryowen, Munster) 2000 Arg, US, 2001 It, F, R (R), S (R), W, E, NZ, 2002 W, E, S, It, F, 2003 Tg (R), Sm (R), W 2(t+R), S 2, 2004 S, SA1, 2, 2005 J2, 2006 It, F, W, S, E, NZ1, 2, A1, SA, A2, 2007 W, F, E, S1, It1, [Nm, Gg, F, Arg], 2008 It, F, S, W, E, NZ1, C(R), NZ2, Arg, 2009 F, It, E, S, W

Wallace, Jas (Wanderers) 1904 E, S

Wallace, Jos (Wanderers) 1903 S, W, 1904 E, S, W, 1905 E, S, W, NZ, 1906 W

Wallace, P S (Blackrock Coll, Saracens) 1995 [J], Fj, 1996 US, W, E, WS, A, 1997 It 1, F, W, E, S, NZ, C, 1998 S, F, W, E, SA 1, 2, Gg, R, 1999 F, W, E, S, It (R), 1999 A 1, 2, Arg 1, [US, A 3, R, Arg 2], 2000 F, E, US, C (R), 2002 W (R), E (R), S (R), It (R), F (R), NZ 2(R), Ru (R), Gg (R)

Wallace, P W (Ulster) 2006 SA(R), PI, 2007 E(R), Arg1, S2, [Nm(R)], 2008 S(R), E(R), NZ1, A, C(R), NZ2(R), 2009 F, It, E, W(R)

Wallace, R M (Garryowen, Saracens) 1991 Nm 1(R), 1992 W, E, S, F, A, 1993 S, F, W, E, R, 1994 F, W, E, S, 1995 W, It, [NZ, J, W], Fj, 1996 US, S, F, WS, 1998 S, F, W, E

Wallace, T H (Cardiff) 1920 E, S, W

Wallis, A K (Wanderers) 1892 E, S, W, 1893 E, W

Wallis, C O'N (Old Cranleighans, Wanderers) 1935 NZ

Wallis, T G (Wanderers) 1921 F, 1922 E, S, W, F

Wallis, W A (Wanderers) 1880 S, 1881 E, S, 1882 W, 1883 S

Walmsley, G (Bective Rangers) 1894 E

Walpole, A (Dublin U) 1888 S, M

Walsh, E J (Lansdowne) 1887 E, S, W, 1892 E, S, W, 1893 E

Walsh, H D (Dublin U) 1875 E, 1876 E

Walsh, J C (UC Cork, Sunday's Well) 1960 S, SA, 1961 E, S, F, SA, 1963 E, S, W, NZ, 1964 E, S, W, F, 1965 F, S, W, SA, 1966 F, S, W, 1967 E, S, W, F, A 2

Ward, A J (Ballynahinch) 1998 F, W, E, SA 1, 2, Gg, R, SA 3, 1999 W, E, S, It (R), A 1, 2, Arg 1, [US, A 3, R, Arg 2], 2000 F (R), W (t&R), Arg (R), US (R), C, J, SA (R), 2001 It (R), F (R)

Ward, A J P (Garryowen, St Mary's Coll, Greystones) 1978 S, F, W, E, NZ, 1979 F, W, E, S, 1981 W, E, S, A, 1983 E (R), 1984 E, S, 1986 S, 1987 [C, Tg]

Warren, J P (Kingstown) 1883 E

Warren, R G (Lansdowne) 1884 W, 1885 E, S 1, 2, 1886 E, 1887 E, S, W, 1888 W, S, M, 1889 S, W, 1890 S, W, E

Watson, R (Wanderers) 1912 SA

Wells, H G (Bective Rangers) 1891 S, W, 1894 E, S

Westby, A J (Dublin U) 1876 E

Wheeler, G H (Queen's Coll, Belfast) 1884 S, 1885 E

Wheeler, J R (Queen's U, Belfast) 1922 E, S, W, F, 1924 E

Whelan, P C (Garryowen) 1975 E, S, 1976 NZ, 1977 W, E, S, F, 1978 S, F, W, E, NZ, 1979 F, W, E, S, 1981 F, W, E

White, M (Queen's Coll, Cork) 1906 E, S, W, SA, 1907 E, W

Whitestone, A M (Dublin U) 1877 E, 1879 S, E, 1880 E, 1883 S

Whitten, I (Ulster) 2009 C, US

Whittle, D (Bangor) 1988 F

Wilkinson, C R (Malone) 1993 S

Wilkinson, R W (Wanderers) 1947 A

Willis, W J (Lansdowne) 1879 E

Wilson, F (CIYMS) 1977 W, E, S

Wilson, H G (Glasgow U, Malone) 1905 E, S, W, NZ, 1906 E, S, W, SA, 1907 E, S, W, 1908 E, S, W, 1909 E, S, W, 1910 W

Wilson, R G (Ulster) 2005 J1

Wilson, W H (Bray) 1877 E, S

Withers, H H C (Army, Blackheath) 1931 F, E, S, W, SA

Wolfe, E J (Armagh) 1882 E

Wood, G H (Dublin U) 1913 W, 1914 F

Wood, B G M (Garryowen) 1954 E, S, 1956 F, E, S, W, 1957 F, E, S, W, 1958 A, E, S, W, F, 1959 E, S, W, F, 1960 E, S, W, F, SA, 1961 E, S, W, F, SA

Wood, K G M (Garryowen, Harlequins) 1994 A 1, 2, US, 1995 E, S, [J], 1996 A, 1997 It 1, F, 1997 NZ, It 2, 1998 S, F, W, E, SA 1, 2, R (R), SA 3, 1999 F, W, E, S, It (R), A 1, 2, Arg 1, [US, A 3, R (R), Arg 2], 2000 E, S, It, F, W, Arg, US, C, J, SA, 2001 It, F, S, W, E, NZ, 2002 F, NZ 1, 2, Ru, 2003 W 2, S 2, [R, Nm, Arg, A, F]

Woods, D C (Bessbrook) 1888 M, 1889 S

Woods, N K P J (Blackrock Coll, London Irish) 1994 A 1, 2, 1995 E, F, 1996 F, W, E, 1999 W

Wright, R A (Monkstown) 1912 S

Yeates, R A (Dublin U) 1889 S, W

Young, B G (Ulster) 2006 NZ2(R), A1(R), SA(R), A2, PI, 2007 Arg1, 2, S2

Young, G (UC Cork) 1913 E

Young, R M (Collegians) 1965 F, E, S, W, 1966 F, E, S, W, 1967 W, F, 1968 W, A, 1969 F, E, S, W, 1970 SA, F, E, S, W, 1971 F, E, S, W

Supporting Clubs.
Supporting Communities.

PARISHMEN CLAIM DRAMATIC WIN

Shannon were crowned AIB Division One champions for a record-extending ninth time after the most dramatic and arguably cruel victories over Clontarf in the play-off final at Thomond Park.

Their dramatic victory confirmed the Munster side's reputation as the most successful team in Irish club rugby, and gave the Parishmen their first league title since 2006.

It also ensured Geoff Moylan enjoyed a triumphant first season as head coach after succeeding Mick Galwey, but defeat could not have been more heartbreaking for 'Tarf. Looking for their first win in three appearances in the showpiece game, they were denied by the narrowest of margins.

The two teams produced an epic encounter but after 80 minutes of battle, they were locked at 19–19. Extra time beckoned but there were no further scores and the moment of reckoning had arrived.

The sides could not been split on try count with two apiece and the rule book came into play, dictating the team who had scored the first try would take the spoils.

That was Shannon courtesy of full-back David O'Donovan, who had powered over in the 23rd minute of the first half. The Parishmen, who had finished second to Cork in the regular season, were champions and Clontarf were left to rue yet another near miss.

"It's an awful way to lose a match. I have to say, I feel for Clontarf," admitted Parish captain David Quinlan. "The way the game went, they ended up having to go for it and we ended up having to hold on. It could easily have been the other way around had they scored the first try."

Clontarf captain Daragh O'Shea was stunned by the result but admitted his side had gone into extra-time fully aware of what they had to do.

"I'd prefer to get hammered than lose it like that, it's even worse than losing by a point," he said. "It's hard to swallow because it doesn't feel like we have lost. We do feel hard done by, but we did know going into extra-time that we needed to get a score, so I suppose when you know that going into the game, you can't complain about it."

Shannon had finished the regular season second in the table behind Cork Constitution with Garryowen in third and Clontarf edging out St Mary's on points difference for fourth and the last semi-final place, but all four sides had contrasting campaigns.

Cork began hesitantly and three defeats in their opening six games, including a surprise 16–21 reverse to Young Munster at Temple Hill in October to end an 11-match winning run in the league dating back to January, initially suggested the defending champions might struggle.

But Con proved they were made of sterner stuff and a six-game winning sequence that was finally ended by Blackrock in March at Stradbrook was enough to secure top spot.

Shannon were also unconvincing in their first six outings but put their shop in order quickly and although they were beaten by Clontarf in December, they were to suffer just one further defeat before the play-off semi-finals.

Garryowen failed to register a victory in their first three fixtures, but a storming run of 10 wins between October and April made a mockery of their early inconsistency and they prepared for the play-offs as the in-form side in the competition.

In contrast, Clontarf began their season in imperious fashion with six wins out of six but they hit the wall in December when they were beaten 16–10 by Dolphin at Musgrave Park. The result sparked a minor slump with three further defeats in their next four games and they needed four wins from their last four fixtures to see off St Mary's by the narrowest of margins.

If the play-off final was a tragic story for Clontarf, then the AIB Cup was a fairytale for Division Two side Ballynahinch, who pulled off arguably the biggest ever shock in the history of the competition with a 17–6 victory over Cork at Dubarry Park.

"We gave our all and I could not have asked any more of the boys," said captain Stuart Lamb, who was named Man of the Match. "This has been done the hard way, beating Shannon, Garryowen, Galwegians and now Cork."

Triumphant coach Derek Suffern was quick to pay tribute to the vocal support of the Ballynahinch fans: "We have had a couple of difficult away matches on the way to the final but today it was like playing at home with the amount of support we had. We like to play rugby and keep the ball and the plan was to starve Cork of possession early on. I cannot explain how proud I am. The players were magnificent, they really play for each other."

IRELAND

AIB DIVISION ONE 2008–09 RESULTS

4 October: **Ballymena** 21 **Young Munster** 10, **Blackrock** 41 **Shannon** 27, **Buccaneers** 28 **Dolphin** 19, **Clontarf** 14 **Garryowen** 13, **Cork Constitution** 43 **Terenure** 19, **Dungannon** 10 **St Mary's** 27, **Old Belvedere** 30 **UCD** 14, **Bohemian** 14 **Galwegians** 6. 11 October: **Galwegians** 27 **Dungannon** 21, **Garryowen** 26 **Blackrock** 30, **Shannon** 25 **Buccaneers** 21, **St Mary's** 31 **Ballymena** 20, **Terenure** 16 **Clontarf** 19, **UCD** 7 **Cork Constitution** 9, **Young Munster** 9 **Old Belvedere** 13. 12 October: **Dolphin** 35 **Bohemian** 33. 17 October: **Shannon** 17 **Garryowen** 17. 18 October: **Ballymena** 5 **Galwegians** 19, **Blackrock** 28 **Terenure** 3, **Buccaneers** 8 **Bohemian** 9, **Clontarf** 30 **St Mary's** 19, **Cork Constitution** 16 **Young Munster** 21, **Dungannon** 15 **UCD** 13, **Old Belvedere** 16 **Dolphin** 11. 25 October: **Ballymena** 14 **Bohemian** 9, **Dungannon** 22 **Dolphin** 16, **Galwegians** 14 **Old Belvedere** 12, **St Mary's** 16 **Cork Constitution** 9, **Terenure** 10 **Shannon** 35, **UCD** 10 **Blackrock** 6, **Young Munster** 0 **Clontarf** 7, **Garryowen** 19 **Buccaneers** 8. 29 November: **Ballymena** 34 **Terenure** 3, **Clontarf** 26 **Blackrock** 8, **Cork Constitution** 25 **Galwegians** 7, **Dolphin** 38 **St Mary's** 3, **Dungannon** 23 **Buccaneers** 36, **Old Belvedere** 14 **Garryowen** 26, **Shannon** 36 **UCD** 9, **Bohemian** 24 **Young Munster** 6. 6 December: **Blackrock** 29 **Buccaneers** 12, **Galwegians** 14 **Dolphin** 29, **Garryowen** 20 **Cork Constitution** 19, **Shannon** 6 **Clontarf** 8, **St Mary's** 18 **Bohemian** 6, **Terenure** 19 **Old Belvedere** 15, **UCD** 6 **Ballymena** 16, **Young Munster** 16 **Dungannon** 17. 13 December: **Dungannon** 19 **Garryowen** 26, **Galwegians** 15 **Young Munster** 10, **Old Belvedere** 17 **Blackrock** 22, **Terenure** 18 **UCD** 19, **Buccaneers** 17 **Ballymena** 21. 14 December: **Dolphin** 16 **Clontarf** 10, **Shannon** 26 **St Mary's** 20, **Bohemian** 19 **Cork Constitution** 25. 17 January: **Ballymena** 0 **Old Belvedere** 12, **Clontarf** 8 **UCD** 14, **Dolphin** 19 **Blackrock** 15, **Bohemian** 11 **Dungannon** 0, **Young Munster** 15 **Terenure** 3. 24 January: **Galwegians** 9 **Shannon** 18, **Ballymena** 12 **Dolphin** 25, **Blackrock** 33 **Young Munster** 19, **Dungannon** 3 **Cork Constitution** 49, **Old Belvedere** 9 **St Mary's** 20, **Terenure** 15 **Garryowen** 22, **Bohemian** 17 **Clontarf** 13, **UCD** 30 **Buccaneers** 24. 31 January: **Cork Constitution** 47 **Buccaneers** 7, **Garryowen** 20 **Bohemian** 18, **Shannon** 22 **Dungannon** 10. 7 February: **Buccaneers** 8 **Galwegians** 9. 21 February: **Buccaneers** 43 **Terenure** 11, **Dungannon** 15 **Ballymena** 19, **Galwegians** 13 **Clontarf** 25, **St Mary's** 18 **Blackrock** 8, **Bohemian** 6 **Old Belvedere** 13, **UCD** 7 **Garryowen** 14, **Young Munster** 10 **Shannon** 28. 22 February: **Dolphin** 22 **Cork Constitution** 41. 7 March: **Ballymena** 6 **Shannon** 7, **Blackrock** 48 **Galwegians** 10, **Buccaneers** 6 **St Mary's** 21, **Cork Constitution** 17 **Clontarf** 13, **Garryowen** 20 **Young Munster** 13, **Old Belvedere** 5 **Dungannon** 6, **Bohemian** 34 **Terenure** 0. 8 March: **Dolphin** 29 **UCD** 12. 17 March: **Cork Constitution** 16 **Shannon** 9, **St Mary's** 8 **Garryowen** 20. 21 March: **Blackrock** 27 **Ballymena** 10, **Clontarf** 24 **Old Belvedere** 23, **Galwegians** 28 **UCD** 3, **Terenure** 10 **Dolphin** 39. 28 March: **Blackrock** 23 **Cork Constitution** 7, **Clontarf** 46 **Buccaneers** 26, **Garryowen** 45 **Ballymena** 7, **Shannon** 23 **Old Belvedere** 19, **St Mary's** 38 **Galwegians** 17, **Terenure** 8 **Dungannon** 22, **UCD** 25 **Bohemian** 30, **Young Munster** 7 **Dolphin** 10. 4 April: **Young Munster** 9 **St Mary's** 11. 11 April: **Ballymena** 0 **Clontarf** 22, **Buccaneers** 0 **Young Munster** 18, **Dolphin** 14 **Garryowen** 9, **Dungannon** 22 **Blackrock** 14, **Galwegians** 26 **Terenure** 14, **Old Belvedere** 20 **Cork Constitution** 22, **St Mary's** 24 **UCD** 17, **Bohemian** 6 **Shannon** 12. 18 April: **Blackrock** 30 **Bohemian** 19, **Buccaneers** 22 **Old Belvedere** 16, **Clontarf** 50 **Dungannon** 0, **Cork Constitution** 54 **Ballymena** 23, **Garryowen** 54 **Galwegians** 5, **Shannon** 27 **Dolphin** 17, **Terenure** 11 **St Mary's** 58, **UCD** 14 **Young Munster** 17.

FINAL TABLE

	P	W	D	L	F	A	Pts
Cork Constitution	15	11	0	4	399	229	52
Shannon	15	11	1	3	318	219	52
Garryowen	15	11	1	3	340	208	51
Clontarf	15	11	0	4	315	188	51
St Mary's	15	11	0	4	332	225	51
Blackrock	15	10	0	5	362	245	49
Dolphin	15	10	0	5	339	259	47
Bohemian	15	7	0	8	255	225	37
Galwegians	15	7	0	8	219	324	30
Old Belvedere	15	5	0	10	234	238	29
Dungannon	15	6	0	9	205	339	27
Buccaneers	15	4	0	11	266	343	26
Ballymena	15	6	0	9	208	302	26
Young Munster	15	4	0	11	180	232	23
UCD	15	4	0	11	200	304	23
Terenure	15	1	0	14	160	452	7

PLAY-OFF SEMI-FINALS

25 April, 2009

Cork Constitution 6 Clontarf 25   Shannon 16 Garryowen 12

IRELAND

PLAY-OFF FINAL

9 May, Thomond Park, Limerick

CLONTARF 19 (3PG, 2T)
SHANNON 19 (2PG, 2T, 1DG) AET

CLONTARF: P Howard; N O'Brien, D O'Shea (captain), B O'Donnell, M Keating; M Dufficy, P O'Donohoe; K Dorian, A Dundon, N Treston, B Reilly, S Crawford, H Stride, N Carson, M Garvey.   **SUBSTITUTIONS:** J Wickham for Dorian (61 mins); M Rantz-McDonald for O'Brien (72 mins); C Keegan for O'Donnell (80 mins); B Focas for Carson (90 mins).
SCORERS *Tries*: Stride, Crawford *Penalty Goals*: O'Shea (3)

SHANNON: D O'Donovan; R Mullane, F McLoughlin, J Clogan, S Kelly; T Bennett, F McNamara; K O'Neill, M Essex, K Griffin, P O'Brien, F Walsh, D Ryan, E Grace, D Quinlan (captain).   **SUBSTITUTIONS:** L Hogan for O'Neill (60 mins); E McLoughlin for O'Brien (90 mins); M O'Driscoll for Kelly (90 mins).
SCORER *Tries*: O'Donovan (2) *Penalty Goals*: Bennett (2) *Drop Goal*: Bennett
REFEREE A Rolland (Ireland)

AIB Division Two: Winners: Ballynahinch
AIB Division Three: Winners: Old Wesley

AIB CUP 2008–09 RESULTS

Play-off Quarter-Finals: 14 February: **Dolphin** 16 **Cork Constitution** 18, **Galwegians** 22 **Ballynahinch** 26, **Garryowen** 28 **Buccaneers** 17, **Young Munster** 12 **UCC** 10

Play-off Semi-Finals: 21 March: **Ballynahinch** 24 **Garryowen** 17, **Young Munster** 13 **Cork Constitution** 27

PLAY-OFF FINAL

5 April, Dubarry Park, Athlone

BALLYNAHINCH 17 (2G, 1PG)
CORK CONSTITUTION 6 (2PG)

BALLYNAHINCH: J Cullen; A Ferris, S Morrow, D Harris, K Corrigan; R Bambry, H McAleese; C Stevenson, N Hanna, G Cronin, G Rourke, C Napier, M Graham, W Faloon, S Lamb (captain).   **SUBSTITUTIONS:** P McAllister for Stevenson (70 mins); J Gunson for Rourke (70 mins); R Greer for Graham (71 mins); D McGregor for Hanna (75 mins); L Johnston for Cronin (77 mins).
SCORERS *Tries*: Graham, Gunson *Conversions*: Bambry (2) *Penalty Goal*: Bambry

CORK CONSTITUTION: D Lyons; C Healy, T Gleeson, E Ryan, S Zebo; J Manning, C Nolan; G Murray, L Gabriel, T Ryan, M O'Connell, D Kelly, B Holland (captain), P O'Mahony, F Cogan.   **SUBSTITUTIONS:** J Moloney for Kelly (48 mins); R Lane for Nolan (52 mins); T Kenneally for Manning (55 mins); E Leamy for O'Mahony (60 mins).
SCORERS *Penalty Goals*: Manning (2)
REFEREE: A Rolland (Ireland)

ITALY

ITALY'S 2008–09 TEST RECORD

OPPONENTS	DATE	VENUE	RESULT
Australia	8 November	H	Lost 20–30
Argentina	15 November	H	Lost 14–22
Pacific Islanders	22 November	H	Lost 17–25
England	7 February	A	Lost 11–36
Ireland	15 February	H	Lost 9–38
Scotland	28 February	A	Lost 6–26
Wales	14 March	H	Lost 15–20
France	21 March	H	Lost 8–50
Australia	13 June	A	Lost 8–31
Australia	20 June	A	Lost 12–34
New Zealand	27 June	A	Lost 6–27

WAITING FOR A NEW DAWN

By Gianluca Barca

THE COUNTRIES

Dave Rogers/Getty Images

Nick Mallett is starting to turn the corner with the Italians.

The last 12 months have proven a testing time for Italian rugby with the national squad losing all 11 of their matches and the Under 20 and women's sides fairing little better, while the two clubs involved in the Heineken Cup – Benetton Treviso and Calvisano – finished bottom of their pools without a win between them.

These disappointments led to calls for a rethink of the domestic set-up in Italy, a situation worsened by the global economic crisis, which saw sponsors pull out and clubs subsequently collapse. A quick solution was required with the only option seemingly being to replicate the system in Wales, Ireland and Scotland with a small number of professional teams, supported by the Federation and taking part in a cross-border competition.

Everything is now in place from the 2010–11 season for two Italian franchises to play in the Magners League and the Heineken Cup. The aim of this new approach being to create the right environment to nurture quality players for the international stage and also downsize the domestic league to a semi-professional status to reduce costs for clubs who are struggling to make ends meet in a difficult climate.

These changes will not be without their teething problems and the disappointment of the Federazione Italiana Rugby's bid to host Rugby World Cup 2015 or 2019 not being successful – with England and Japan respectively earning that honour – will have been felt across the whole of Italy and the loss of a great opportunity to boost the game in the country.

Italy's 2008–09 season had begun in Padova on a sunny November afternoon when more than 30,000 gathered to see the Azzurri play against Australia on the first match of their European tour.

Andrea Masi, who had uncomfortably donned the No.10 jersey in the Six Nations had turned down the option of another spell at fly-half and Nick Mallett decided to give Treviso's Andrea Marcato the green light for the role.

With Marcato settled at fly-half and Masi at full-back the real question hung over the scrum-half position, which had been vacant since Alessandro Troncon's retirement. This position was to be a headache for the coaching staff, later turning into a nightmare when the 2009 Six Nations got underway.

Against the Wallabies, the number nine jersey was handed to Argentinean-born Pablo Canavosio. The match saw Italy stretch Australia until the last quarter when, with 20 minutes remaining and the sides locked at 20–20, Luciano Orquera – who had replaced Marcato – missed a penalty, which would have put Italy ahead. From that moment on the Azzurri faded and Quade Cooper's try, together with a Matt Giteau conversion and penalty, sealed the victory for Australia.

It was Italy's umpteenth honourable defeat, but this time Mallett had plenty to smile about having seen his charges give one of the world's leading nations a run for their money.

Enthusiasm was running high for Italy's next fixture against Argentina at the Stadio Olimpico in Turin, the home of Juventus FC who had agreed to change their league schedule in order to accommodate international rugby. It was a first for soccer mad Italy and this newly found passion for rugby in the country was one of the few ups in a season littered with disappointments.

The pre-match programme included an exhibition of tango dancing on the pitch, although the game itself turned out to be another type of tango with the Pumas leading the show.

It was a ragged and niggly family affair, with Italy fielding no less than five Argentineans – two forwards, two backs and one more on the bench – and it took almost 30 minutes before any points were scored with some poor kicking by half backs Canavosio and Marcato failing to take advantage of the dominant Azzurri pack.

The decisive moment came in the 50th minute when a cheeky chip and chase by fly-half Juan Martín Hernández and a masterful offload to wing Rafael Carballo split open the Italian defence for the Pumas' first and only try. As the match progressed, Italy's chances of recovering looked increasingly dim. Their 80th minute try by Masi arrived just too late, the Azzurri were beaten fair and square 22–14.

All of a sudden, after the excitement of a "near win" against Australia, Italy had to beat the Pacific Islanders to save face and salvage at least one win from the autumn series. But, in Reggio Emilia, on a chilly winter Saturday afternoon, Italian rugby went back to square one, collapsing in front of a team with plenty of individual talent, but which had never won a Test before.

The Islanders triumphed 25–17 and in the post-match press conference Mallett lamented the lack of game breakers as Italy had enjoyed more possession but failed to turn it into tries. The gloom and doom of the defeat added to the whitewash the Italian clubs were suffering in the Heineken Cup.

It was on the back of this that the idea that Italy should join the Magners League started gaining momentum. By Christmas the Italian Federation Board had voted in favour of asking the Magners League Board to admit Italian squads to the tournament. Italy pushed for four, but got two. A result that was to throw Italian rugby into a state of turmoil, as it was impossible to squeeze teams the length and breadth of Italy into only two selections.

But now it was already time for the Six Nations. Italy's first game was against England at Twickenham and Mallett's number nine problems came back to haunt him. Canavosio, who had not made a great impact in November, was not fit, neither was Treviso's Simon Picone, while La Capitolina Roma's Giulio Toniolatti had made only a couple of brief appearances in the autumn and was considered too inexperienced to fit the bill.

On the eve of the match Mallett made a very bold move by naming Mauro Bergamasco, a buccaneer spirit at flanker, as Italy's scrum-half, backing up his selection by declaring that the older Bergamasco brother could be the Azzurri's number nine for the 2011 World Cup.

The experiment backfired horribly as Bergamasco played what Welsh pundit Jonathan Davies labelled "the worst ever performance by an international". Wayward passes were costly not only in terms of points but made fly-half Marcato a sitting duck for the England back rowers and before half-time he left the pitch injured. After the break Bergamasco made way for Toniolatti, but the damage was already done with England winning 36–11.

The next day Mallett had no choice but to recall veteran Kiwi Paul Griffen at scrum-half. For the Ireland game in Rome, with Marcato out, Italy once more reshuffled their half backs with Luke McLean, a full-back

THE IRB/EMIRATES AIRLINE RUGBY PHOTOGRAPH OF THE YEAR 2009

In its fourth year, the IRB/Emirates Airline Rugby Photograph of the Year competition continues to go from strength to strength.

This year a record number of over 500 hundred entries were received from across the world depicting a range of rugby scenes, from the cauldron of the British & Irish Lions tour of South Africa to friends playing on a Fijian Island in bare feet. All the pictures depict the 'Spirit of Rugby' at their core and the judging panel had a challenge to select the six images you see here which make up the shortlist, and of course, the one winner.

This year's judging panel was: Paul Morgan, editor of the IRB Yearbook and Rugby World magazine; Barry Newcombe, Chair of the Sports Journalists Association; Dave Rogers from Getty Images, sports photographer Patrick Eagar, Joelle Watkins, corporate communications manager, Emirates Airline; Andrea Wiggins, IRB communications manager, Lynda Glennon, graphic designer from the IRB and Jim Drewett, editorial director of Vision Sports Publishing.

The prize for the winner is a trip for two to the Emirates Dubai Sevens, courtesy of Emirates Airlines.

For details of how to enter the 2010 competition, see the back page of this picture section.

THE RUNNERS-UP: IN NO PARTICULAR ORDER

◀ **Aussie, Aussie, Aussie!**

Warren Little

Taken at the Rugby World Cup Sevens 2009 in Dubai on 7 March 2009.

Warren Little says: "The men's Australian team cheers their women's team as they leave the pitch after they had beaten New Zealand to win the Women's Rugby World Cup Sevens. This image sums up the changing of the times where the men look to the women to bring home the silverware. Anything you can do I can do better!"

▲ **Winners Circle**

Clive Rose

The Welsh team celebrate on the pitch with a team huddle after winning the final against Argentina at the Rugby World Cup Sevens 2009 in Dubai, 7 March 2009.

Clive Rose says: "As you might expect when an 'underdog' beats one of the favourites to win the World Cup all hell breaks loose on the pitch at the final whistle. I was pleased to capture this intimate moment of the celebration team huddle from underneath and even more pleased not to get trampled on in the process!"

▲ **Rich Kid**

Jeremy Duxbury

Taken at the re-opening of the rugby field at Navuso Methodist High School, Fiji.

Jeremy Duxbury says: *"One boy shows how a pair of boots can help in muddy conditions as his would-be tacklers fall away. After the political upheaval in May 2000, the Navuso grounds in Naitasiri were closed for several years and had become a cow field. The students themselves worked for some time to get the ground into a reasonable condition. It's a pretty typical Fijian rugby scene with mud, a hodge-podge of uniforms, and even a barefoot touch judge."*

▲ Friendship Over Rivalry

Warren Little

Taken at the Emirates Airline Dubai
Rugby Sevens on 28 November 2008.

Warren Little says: "This picture depicting Tomasi Cama of New Zealand helping up Richard Kingi of Australia during the first day of the Emirates Airline Dubai Sevens for me really sums the nature of this great game. Here are two of the greatest teams in the world playing against each other in a huge event with fierce rivalry, but there is an underlying humanity towards each other."

▲ The Flying Hair Bear

Christiaan Kotze

Taken during the Second Test
between the Lions and the Springboks
at Loftus Versfeld in Pretoria.

*Christiaan Kotze says: "The outstanding factor in this image
is that Adam Jones is a prop. The Lions were on the attack
at this point and Adam picked up a loose ball from a ruck
where the scrum-half was buried in and without hesitation
produced a stunning scrumhalf flying leap pass to get
the ball quickly to the backline to keep the pressure on in
their attack."*

AND THE WINNER IS...

Henry Browne
Taken at the Guinness Premiership
match between London Irish and
Leicester on 1 March 2009 at
Reading.

*Henry Browne says: "Mapusua
dived through the posts after
breaking clean through the
Leicester defence. He's usually
good for a celebration picture
when he scores, and this was
a nice one to get. I like this shot
as he's looking straight ahead
and his flowing hair is giving the
picture a sense of movement."*

The Flying Samoan

THE IRB/EMIRATES AIRLINE RUGBY PHOTOGRAPH OF THE YEAR 2010

The IRB/Emirates Airline Rugby Photograph of the Year competition is open to all photographers, professional or amateur, and the subject matter can be from any level of the game, from tag rugby to the Rugby World Cup Final.

To enter the 2010 competition, please visit **www.irb.com/photooftheyear** and you can download an application form and view terms and conditions. The 2010 competition will open on 1 December 2009 and close on 7 September 2010.

for his club, paired with 34-year-old Griffen. Italy, however, could do nothing to prevent a 38–9 loss by an Ireland side on track for a first Grand Slam in 61 years and for the first time ever the Azzurri were booed off the field.

They then lost 26–6 to Scotland, the traditional barometer of the Azzurri's fortunes in the Six Nations. The tournament also ended badly for Italy when they were defeated 50–8 by France in Rome, having given defending champions Wales a scare – losing 20–15 – the week before. Italy had only scored two tries in the whole Championship and conceded 21, looking ineffective in attack and uncomfortable in defence.

Captain Sergio Parisse was one of the few positive notes, leading from the front, and was often voted man of the match despite playing on a losing side. The rest of the team looked anything but settled with Marcato sent back to full-back and McLean fielded at 10 in a perennial switching of roles that put the coaching staff under fire.

In April, Mallett was given a clean slate by the Federation Board to pick the staff he wanted alongside him as up till then he had been working with the men chosen by former coach Pierre Berbizier. Eyebrows were raised when Mallett said he was happy with the current backroom team, which included former scrum-half Troncon in his first coaching role.

Ahead loomed the summer tour to Australia and New Zealand, a task Mallett said that not even two heavyweights like France or England could take lightly. The Azzurri coach, however, had a card up his sleeve and named former National Rugby League star Craig Gower, the Australian now playing Union for Bayonne in France, in the touring party.

Gower, who is eligible to play for Italy through a grandparent, is a centre by trade but was quickly shifted to fly-half in the hope of filling one of Italy's long-standing vacancies. Playing alongside scrum-half Canavosio in the first Test against the Wallabies in Canberra, and new cap Tito Tebaldi in the following two (Australia in Melbourne and New Zealand in Christchurch), Gower showed he might have what it takes to spark Italy's backline in the build up to Rugby World Cup 2011.

Italy did not win any of the three summer Tests but definitely managed to save face with the tour proving that there might, after all, be some light at the end of the tunnel.

Meanwhile on the domestic front, Benetton Treviso won their 14th – and sixth in nine years – title by beating Viadana in the final. However, the season ended on an uncertain note with 2008 national champions Calvisano and La Capitolina Roma both withdrawing from the 2009–10 competitions for financial reasons. They were just two of the casualties of the new era set to start in a year's time with two franchises joining the Magners League.

Will this prove to be the long awaited "new dawn" of Italian rugby?

ITALY INTERNATIONAL STATISTICS
MATCH RECORDS UP TO 30TH SEPTEMBER 2009

WINNING MARGIN

Date	Opponent	Result	Winning Margin
18/05/1994	Czech Republic	104–8	96
07/10/2006	Portugal	83–0	83
17/06/1993	Croatia	76–11	65
19/06/1993	Morocco	70–9	61
02/03/1996	Portugal	64–3	61

MOST POINTS IN A MATCH
BY THE TEAM

Date	Opponent	Result	Pts.
18/05/1994	Czech Republic	104–8	104
07/10/2006	Portugal	83–0	83
17/06/1993	Croatia	76–11	76
19/06/1993	Morocco	70–9	70

MOST TRIES IN A MATCH
BY THE TEAM

Date	Opponent	Result	Tries
18/05/1994	Czech Republic	104–8	16
07/10/2006	Portugal	83–0	13
18/11/1998	Netherlands	67–7	11
17/06/1993	Croatia	76–11	11

MOST CONVERSIONS IN A MATCH
BY THE TEAM

Date	Opponent	Result	Cons
18/05/1994	Czech Republic	104–8	12
19/06/1993	Morocco	70–9	10
17/06/1993	Croatia	76–11	9
07/10/2006	Portugal	83–0	9

MOST PENALTIES IN A MATCH
BY THE TEAM

Date	Opponent	Result	Pens
01/10/1994	Romania	24–6	8
10/11/2001	Fiji	66–10	7

MOST DROP GOALS IN A MATCH
BY THE TEAM

Date	Opponent	Result	DGs
07/10/1990	Romania	29–21	3
05/02/2000	Scotland	34–20	3
11/07/1973	Transvaal	24–28	3

MOST POINTS IN A MATCH
BY A PLAYER

Date	Player	Opponent	Pts.
10/11/2001	Diego Dominguez	Fiji	29
05/02/2000	Diego Dominguez	Scotland	29
01/07/1983	Stefano Bettarello	Canada	29
21/05/1994	Diego Dominguez	Netherlands	28
20/12/1997	Diego Dominguez	Ireland	27

MOST TRIES IN A MATCH
BY A PLAYER

Date	Player	Opponent	Tries
19/06/1993	Ivan Francescato	Morocco	4
10/10/1937	Renzo Cova	Belgium	4

MOST CONVERSIONS IN A MATCH
BY A PLAYER

Date	Player	Opponent	Cons
18/05/1994	Luigi Troiani	Czech Republic	12
19/06/1993	Gabriel Filizzola	Morocco	10
17/06/1993	Luigi Troiani	Croatia	9

MOST PENALTIES IN A MATCH BY A PLAYER

Date	Player	Opponent	Pens
01/10/1994	Diego Dominguez	Romania	8
10/11/2001	Diego Dominguez	Fiji	7

MOST DROP GOALS IN A MATCH BY A PLAYER

Date	Player	Opponent	DGs
05/02/2000	Diego Dominguez	Scotland	3
11/07/1973	Rocco Caligiuri	Transvaal	3

MOST CAPPED PLAYERS

Player	Caps
Alessandro Troncon	101
Carlo Checchinato	83
Andrea Lo Cicero	77
Marco Bortolami	76
Mauro Bergamasco	74
Diego Dominguez	74

LEADING TRY SCORERS

Player	Tries
Marcello Cuttitta	25
Paolo Vaccari	22
Manrico Marchetto	21
Carlo Checchinato	21
Alessandro Troncon	19

LEADING CONVERSIONS SCORERS

Player	Cons
Diego Dominguez	127
Luigi Troiani	57
Stefano Bettarello	46
David Bortolussi	35
Ramiro Pez	33

LEADING PENALTY SCORERS

Player	Pens
Diego Dominguez	209
Stefano Bettarello	106
Luigi Troiani	57
Ramiro Pez	52
Ennio Ponzi	31

LEADING DROP GOAL SCORERS

Player	DGs
Diego Dominguez	19
Stefano Bettarello	15
Ramiro Pez	6
Massimo Bonomi	5
Oscar Collodo	5

LEADING POINT SCORERS

Player	Pts.
Diego Dominguez	983
Stefano Bettarello	483
Luigi Troiani	294
Ramiro Pez	260
David Bortolussi	153

ITALY

ITALY INTERNATIONAL PLAYERS
UP TO 30TH SEPTEMBER 2009

Note: Years given for International Championship matches are for second half of season; eg 1972 means season 1971–72. Years for all other matches refer to the actual year of the match.

E Abbiati 1968 *WGe*, 1970 *R*, 1971 *Mor*, *F*, 1972 *Pt*, *Sp*, *Sp*, *Yug*, 1973 *Pt*, *ETv*, 1974 *Leo*
A Agosti 1933 *Cze*
M Aguero 2005 *Tg*, *Ar*, *Fj*, 2006 *Fj*, 2007 *Ur*, *Ar*, *I*, *Pt*, 2008 *A*, *Ar*, *Pl*, 2009 *A*
A Agujari 1967 *Pt*
E Aio 1974 *WGe*
G Aiolfi 1952 *Sp*, *Ger*, *F*, 1953 *F*, 1955 *Ger*, *F*
A Alacevich 1939 *R*
A Albonico 1934 *R*, 1935 *F*, 1936 *Ger*, *R*, 1937 *Ger*, *R*, *Bel*, *Ger*, *F*, 1938 *Ger*
N Aldorvandi 1994 *Sp*, *CZR*, *H*
M Alfonsetti 1994 *F*
E Allevi 1929 *Sp*, 1933 *Cze*
I Aloisio 1933 *Cze*, *Cze*, 1934 *Cat*, *R*, 1935 *Cat*, 1936 *Ger*, *R*
A Altigeri 1973 *Rho*, *WTv*, *Bor*, *NEC*, *Nat*, *Leo*, *FS*, *Tva*, *Cze*, *Yug*, *A*, 1974 *Pt*, *WGe*, 1975 *F*, *E*, *Pol*, *H*, *Sp*, 1976 *F*, *R*, *J*, 1978 *Ar*, *USS*, *Sp*, 1979 *F*, *Pol*, *R*
T Altissimi 1929 *Sp*
V Ambron 1962 *Ger*, *R*, 1963 *F*, 1964 *Ger*, *F*, 1965 *F*, *Cze*, 1966 *F*, *Ger*, *R*, 1967 *Pt*, *R*, 1968 *Pt*, *WGe*, *Yug*, 1969 *Bul*, *Sp*, *Bel*, 1970 *Mad*, *Mad*, *R*, 1971 *Mor*, 1972 *Sp*, *Sp*
R Ambrosio 1987 *NZ*, *USS*, *Sp*, 1988 *F*, *R*, *A*, *I*, 1989 *R*, *Sp*, *Ar*, *Z*, *USS*
B Ancillotti 1978 *Sp*, 1979 *F*, *Pol*, *R*
E Andina 1952 *F*, 1955 *F*
C Angelozzi 1979 *E*, *Mor*, 1980 *Coo*
A Angioli 1960 *Ger*, *F*, 1961 *Ger*, *F*, 1962 *F*, *Ger*, *R*, 1963 *F*
A Angrisiani 1979 *Mor*, *F*, *Pol*, *USS*, *Mor*, 1980 *Coo*, 1984 *Tun*
S Annibal 1980 *Fj*, *Coo*, *Pol*, *Sp*, 1981 *F*, *WGe*, 1982 *R*, *E*, *WGe*, 1983 *F*, *USS*, *Sp*, *Mor*, *F*, *A*, 1984 *F*, 1985 *F*, *Z*, *Z*, 1986 *Tun*, *F*, *Pt*, 1990 *F*
JM Antoni 2001 *Nm*, *SA*
C Appiani 1976 *Sp*, 1977 *Mor*, *Pol*, *Sp*, 1978 *USS*
S Appiani 1985 *R*, 1986 *Pt*, 1988 *A*, 1989 *F*
O Arancio 1993 *Rus*, 1994 *CZR*, *H*, *A*, *R*, *W*, *F*, 1995 *S*, *I*, *Sa*, *E*, *Ar*, *F*, *R*, *NZ*, *SA*, 1996 *W*, *Pt*, *W*, *A*, *E*, *S*, 1997 *I*, *I*, 1998 *S*, *Geo*, *Ar*, *E*, 1999 *F*, *W*, *I*, *SA*, *E*, *NZ*
D Armellin 1965 *Cze*, 1966 *Ger*, 1968 *Pt*, *WGe*, *Yug*, 1969 *Bul*, *Sp*, *Bel*, *F*
A Arrigoni 1949 *Cze*
G Artuso 1977 *Pol*, *R*, 1978 *Sp*, 1979 *F*, *E*, *NZ*, *Mor*, 1980 *F*, *R*, *JAB*, 1981 *F*, 1982 *F*, *E*, *Mor*, 1983 *F*, *R*, *USS*, *C*, *C*, 1984 *USS*, 1985 *R*, *EngB*, *USS*, *R*, 1986 *Tun*, *F*, *Tun*, 1987 *Pt*, *F*, *R*, *NZ*
E Augeri 1962 *F*, *Ger*, *R*, 1963 *F*
A Autore 1961 *Ger*, *F*, 1962 *F*, 1964 *Ger*, 1966 *Ger*, 1968 *Pt*, *WGe*, *Yug*, 1969 *Bul*, *Sp*, *Bel*, *F*
L Avigo 1959 *F*, 1962 *F*, *Ger*, *R*, 1963 *F*, 1964 *Ger*, *F*, 1965 *F*, *Cze*, 1966 *Ger*, *R*
R Aymonod 1933 *Cze*, 1934 *Cat*, *R*, 1935 *F*
A Azzali 1981 *WGe*, 1982 *F*, *R*, *WGe*, 1983 *F*, *R*, *USS*, *Sp*, *Mor*, *F*, 1984 *F*, *Mor*, *R*, 1985 *F*, *EngB*, *Sp*
S Babbo 1996 *Pt*
A Bacchetti 2009 *I*, *S*
A Balducci 1929 *Sp*
F Baraldi 1973 *Cze*, *Yug*, 1974 *Mid*, *Sus*, *Oxo*, 1975 *E*, *Pol*, *H*, *Sp*, 1976 *F*, *R*, *A*, 1977 *F*, *Mor*, *Cze*
R Baraldi 1971 *R*
A Barattin 1996 *A*, *E*, 1997 *De*
S Barba 1985 *R*, *EngB*, 1986 *E*, *A*, 1987 *Pt*, *F*, *R*, *Ar*, *Fj*, 1988 *R*, *USS*, *A*, 1990 *F*, *Pol*, *Sp*, *H*, *R*, *USS*, 1991 *F*, *R*, *Nm*, *Nm*, *US*, *E*, *USS*, 1992 *Sp*, *F*, *R*, *R*, *S*, 1993 *Sp*, *F*, *Cro*, *Mor*, *Sp*
RJ Barbieri 2006 *J*, *Fj*, *Pt*, 2007 *Ur*, *Ar*, *I*, 2008 *SA*
G Barbini 1978 *USS*
M Barbini 2002 *NZ*, *Sp*, *Ar*, *A*, 2003 *I*, *NZ*, 2004 *F*, *I*, *R*, *J*, *NZ*, *US*, 2005 *W*, *E*, 2007 *I*
N Barbini 1953 *Ger*, *R*, 1954 *Sp*, *F*, 1955 *Ger*, *F*, *Sp*, *Cze*, 1956 *Ger*, 1957 *Ger*, 1958 *R*, 1960 *Ger*, *F*
F Bargelli 1979 *E*, *Sp*, *Mor*, *F*, *Pol*, *USS*, *NZ*, *Mor*, 1980 *F*, *R*, *Fj*, *Sp*, 1981 *F*, *R*
S Barilari 1948 *Cze*, 1953 *Ger*, *R*
M Baroni 1999 *F*, *W*, *I*, *SA*, *SA*, 2000 *C*
V Barzaghi 1929 *Sp*, 1930 *Sp*, 1933 *Cze*
JL Basei 1979 *E*, *Sp*, *Mor*, *F*, *Pol*, *USS*, *NZ*, *Mor*, 1980 *F*, *R*, *Fj*, *JAB*, *Coo*, *USS*, 1981 *R*
A Battagion 1948 *F*, *Cze*
F Battaglini 1948 *F*
M Battaglini 1940 *R*, *Ger*, 1951 *Sp*, 1953 *F*, *R*
A Becca 1937 *R*, 1938 *Ger*, 1939 *R*, 1940 *Ger*
E Bellinazzo 1958 *R*, 1959 *F*, 1960 *Ger*, *F*, 1961 *Ger*, *F*, 1962 *F*, *Ger*, 1964 *F*, *Ger*, *F*, 1966 *F*, *Ger*, *R*, 1967 *F*
A Benatti 2001 *Fj*, *SA*, *Sa*, 2002 *W*, 2003 *NZ*
C Bentivoglio 1977 *Pol*
D Beretta 1993 *S*
A Bergamasco 1973 *Bor*, *Tva*, 1977 *Pol*, 1978 *USS*
M Bergamasco 1998 *H*, *E*, 1999 *SA*, *E*, 2000 *Geo*, *S*, *W*, *I*, *E*, *F*, *C*, 2001 *I*, *E*, *F*, *S*, *W*, *Fj*, *SA*, *Sa*, 2002 *F*, *S*, *W*, *I*, *E*, *NZ*, *Sp*, *R*, *A*, 2003 *W*, *I*, *S*, *I*, *Geo*, *NZ*, *W*, 2004 *J*, *C*, *NZ*, 2005 *I*, *W*, *Ar*, *A*, *Ar*, *Fj*, 2006 *I*, *F*, *F*, *J*, *Fj*, *Pt*, *Rus*, *A*, *Ar*, *C*, 2007 *F*, *S*, *W*, *J*, *NZ*, *R*, *Pt*, *S*, 2008 *I*, *E*, *W*, *Ar*, *A*, *Ar*, *Pl*, 2009 *E*, *I*, *S*, *W*, *F*, *A*, *NZ*
M Bergamasco 2002 *F*, *S*, *W*, *Ar*, *A*, 2003 *W*, *I*, *E*, *F*, *S*, *S*, *Geo*, *NZ*, *C*, 2004 *E*, *F*, *S*, *I*, *W*, 2005 *I*, *W*, *S*, *Tg*, *Ar*, *Fj*, 2006 *I*, *E*, *F*, *W*, *S*, *J*, *Fj*, *Pt*, *Rus*, *Ar*, *C*, 2007 *F*, *E*, *S*, *W*, *I*, *J*, *I*, *NZ*, *R*, *S*, 2008 *I*, *E*, *W*, *F*, *S*, *Ar*, *A*, *Ar*, *Pl*, 2009 *E*, *I*, *S*, *W*, *F*, *A*, *NZ*
L Bernabo 1970 *Mad*, *Mad*, *R*, 1972 *Sp*, *Sp*
V Bernabò 2004 *US*, 2005 *Tg*, *Fj*, 2007 *E*, *S*, *W*, *I*, *Ur*, *Ar*, *J*, *I*, *NZ*, *R*
F Berni 1985 *R*, *Sp*, *Z*, *Z*, 1986 *E*, *A*, 1987 *R*, *NZ*, 1988 *A*, 1989 *F*
D Bertoli 1967 *R*
V Bertolotto 1936 *Ger*, *R*, 1937 *Ger*, *R*, 1942 *R*, 1948 *F*
O Bettarello 1958 *F*, 1959 *F*, 1961 *Ger*
R Bettarello 1953 *Ger*, *R*
S Bettarello 1979 *Pol*, *E*, *Sp*, *F*, *NZ*, *Mor*, 1980 *F*, *R*, *Fj*, *JAB*, *Coo*, *Pol*, *USS*, *Sp*, 1981 *F*, *R*, *USS*, *WGe*, 1982 *F*, *R*, *E*, *WGe*, *Mor*, 1983 *F*, *R*, *USS*, *C*, *Sp*, *Mor*, *F*, *A*, 1984 *F*, *Mor*, *R*, *Tun*, *USS*, 1985 *F*, *R*, *EngB*, *Sp*, *Z*, *USS*, *R*, 1986 *Tun*, *F*, *Pt*, *E*, *A*, *Tun*, *USS*, 1987 *R*, *USS*, *Sp*, 1988 *USS*, *A*
L Bettella 1969 *Sp*, *Bel*, *F*
R Bevilacqua 1937 *Bel*, *Ger*, *F*, 1938 *Ger*, 1939 *Ger*, *R*, 1940 *R*, *Ger*, 1942 *R*
C Bezzi 2003 *W*, *I*, *E*, *F*, *S*, *I*, *NZ*, *W*, 2004 *US*, 2005 *Ar*, *A*
G Biadene 1958 *F*, 1959 *F*
G Bigi 1930 *Sp*, 1933 *Cze*
M Bimbati 1989 *Z*
M Birtig 1998 *H*, 1999 *F*
F Blessano 1975 *F*, *R*, *Pol*, *H*, *Sp*, 1976 *F*, *R*, *J*, 1977 *F*, *Mor*, *Pol*, *R*, *Cze*, *Sp*, 1978 *F*, *Ar*, *Sp*, 1979 *F*, *Pol*, *R*
L Boccaletto 1969 *Bul*, *Bel*, *F*, 1970 *Cze*, *Mad*, *Mad*, *R*, 1971 *F*, *R*, 1972 *Pt*, *Sp*, *Sp*, 1975 *E*

S Boccazzi 1985 *Z*, 1988 *USS*
M Bocconelli 1967 *R*
M Bollesan 1963 *F*, 1964 *F*, 1965 *F*, 1966 *F*, Ger, 1967 *F*, Pt, 1968 *Pt*, WGe, Yug, 1969 *Bul*, Sp, Bel, *F*, 1970 *Cze*, Mad, Mad, *R*, 1971 *Mor*, F, R, 1972 *Pt*, Pt, Sp, Sp, Yug, 1973 *Pt*, Rho, WTv, Bor, NEC, Nat, ETv, Leo, FS, Tva, Yug, A, 1974 *Pt*, Mid, Sus, Oxo, WGe, Leo, 1975 *F*, Sp, Cze
A Bona 1972 *Sp*, Yug, 1973 *Rho*, WTv, Bor, NEC, Nat, ETv, Leo, FS, Tva, Cze, Yug, A, 1974 *Pt*, WGe, Leo, 1975 *F*, Sp, R, Cze, E, Pol, H, Sp, 1976 *F*, R, J, A, Sp, 1977 *F*, Mor, 1978 *Ar*, USS, Sp, 1979 *F*, Sp, Mor, F, Pol, USS, NZ, Mor, 1980 *F*, R, Fj, JAB, Pol, Sp, 1981 *F*
L Bonaiti 1979 *R*, 1980 *Pol*
G Bonati 1939 *Ger*, *R*
S Bonetti 1972 *Yug*, 1973 *Rho*, WTv, Bor, NEC, Nat, ETv, Leo, FS, Tva, 1974 *Pt*, Mid, Sus, Oxo, Leo, 1975 *F*, Sp, R, Cze, E, Pol, H, Sp, 1976 *R*, J, A, Sp, 1977 *F*, Mor, R, Sp, 1978 *F*, 1979 *F*, 1980 *USS*
S Bonfante 1936 *Ger*, *R*
G Bonino 1949 *F*
M Bonomi 1988 *F*, R, 1990 *Sp*, H, R, USS, 1991 *F*, R, Nm, Nm, E, NZ, USS, 1992 *R*, R, 1993 *Cro*, Mor, Sp, F, S, 1994 *Sp*, R, H, A, A, W, 1995 *S*, I, Sa, F, Ar, R, NZ, 1996 *W*
S Bordon 1990 *R*, USS, 1991 *Nm*, USS, 1992 *F*, R, 1993 *Sp*, F, Pt, Rus, F, 1994 *R*, A, A, R, W, F, 1995 *I*, E, Ar, F, Ar, NZ, SA, 1996 *W*, A, E, 1997 *I*, F
L Borsetto 1977 *Pol*
V Borsetto 1948 *F*, Cze
M Bortolami 2001 *Nm*, SA, Fj, SA, Sa, 2002 *F*, S, W, I, E, NZ, Sp, R, Ar, A, 2003 *W*, I, E, S, Geo, Tg, C, 2004 *E*, F, S, I, W, R, J, C, NZ, 2005 *I*, W, S, E, F, Ar, A, A, Tg, Ar, Fj, 2006 *I*, E, F, W, S, J, Fj, Pt, Rus, A, Ar, C, 2007 *F*, E, S, W, I, J, I, NZ, R, Pt, 2008 *W*, F, S, A, Ar, Pl, 2009 *E*, S, W, F, A, A, NZ
G Bortolini 1933 *Cze*, 1934 *Cat*
D Bortolussi 2006 *J*, Fj, Pt, Rus, Ar, C, 2007 *Ur*, Ar, J, I, NZ, R, Pt, S, 2008 *I*, E
L Boscaino 1967 *Pt*
L Bossi 1940 *R*, Ger
A Bottacchiara 1991 *NZ*, USS, 1992 *Sp*, F, R, R
G Bottacin 1956 *Cze*
O Bottonelli 1929 *Sp*, 1934 *R*, 1935 *Cat*, F, 1937 *Ger*, 1939 *Ger*
L Bove 1948 *Cze*, 1949 *F*, Cze
O Bracaglia 1939 *R*
M Braga 1958 *R*
L Bricchi 1929 *Sp*, 1930 *Sp*, 1933 *Cze*
L Brighetti 1934 *Cat*
A Brunelli 1969 *Bel*, 1970 *Mad*, 1971 *F*
M Brunello 1988 *I*, 1989 *F*, 1990 *F*, Sp, H, R, USS, 1993 *Pt*
S Brusin 1957 *Ger*
KS Burton 2007 *Ur*, Ar, 2009 *A*, NZ
P Buso 2008 *W*
G Busson 1957 *Ger*, 1958 *R*, 1959 *F*, 1960 *Ger*, F, 1961 *Ger*, F, 1962 *F*, Ger, 1963 *F*
F Caccia-Dominioni 1935 *F*, 1937 *Ger*
C Caione 1995 *R*, 1996 *Pt*, 1997 *F*, R, De, 1998 *Geo*, Rus, Cro, Ar, H, E, 1999 *F*, S, SA, Ur, Sp, Fj, Tg, NZ, 2000 *Sa*, Fj, C, R, NZ, 2001 *I*, E, S, Fj
R Caligiuri 1969 *F*, 1973 *Pt*, Rho, WTv, NEC, Nat, ETv, Leo, FS, Tva, 1975 *E*, Pol, H, Sp, 1976 *F*, R, J, A, Sp, 1978 *F*, Ar, USS, Sp, 1979 *F*, Pol, R
A Caluzzi 1970 *R*, 1971 *Mor*, F, 1972 *Pt*, Pt, Sp, Sp, 1973 *Pt*, 1974 *Oxo*, WGe, Leo
P Camiscioni 1975 *E*, 1976 *R*, J, A, Sp, 1977 *F*, 1978 *F*
M Campagna 1933 *Cze*, 1934 *Cat*, 1936 *Ger*, R, 1937 *Ger*, R, Bel, 1938 *Ger*
G-J Canale 2003 *S*, Geo, NZ, Tg, C, W, 2004 *S*, I, W, R, J, C, 2005 *I*, Ar, Ar, A, Tg, Ar, Fj, 2006 *I*, E, F, W, S, A, Ar, C, 2007 *F*, E, S, W, J, I, R, Pt, S, 2008 *I*, E, W, F, S, A, 2009 *E*, I, S, W, F, A, NZ
PL Canavosio 2005 *A*, Tg, Fj, 2006 *I*, E, F, W, S, Fj, Pt, Rus, A, Ar, 2007 *Ar*, J, I, Pt, 2008 *I*, SA, Ar, A, Ar, 2009 *S*, W, F, A
C Cantoni 1956 *Ger*, F, Cze, 1957 *Ger*
L Capitani 1989 *F*, R, Sp, Ar, Z, USS
M Capuzzoni 1993 *Cro*, 1995 *I*
A Caranci 1989 *R*
M Carli 1955 *Sp*, Cze
C Carloni 1935 *F*

D Carpente 2004 *R*, *J*
T Carraro 1937 *R*
T Casagrande 1977 *R*
U Cassellato 1990 *Sp*, 1992 *R*, S, 1993 *Sp*, F, Pt, Cro, Mor, F, S
R Cassina 1992 *R*, S
A Castellani 1994 *CZR*, 1995 *Ar*, R, 1996 *W*, S, 1997 *Ar*, R, De, I, 1998 *S*, W, Geo, Rus, Cro, H, E, 1999 *F*, W, Ur, Sp, Fj, Tg, NZ
LM Castrogiovanni 2002 *NZ*, Sp, R, Ar, A, 2003 *I*, E, F, S, I, Geo, NZ, Tg, C, W, 2004 *E*, F, S, I, W, J, 2005 *I*, W, S, E, F, Ar, A, Ar, Fj, 2006 *I*, E, F, W, S, Pt, Rus, A, Ar, C, 2007 *F*, E, S, J, I, NZ, R, Pt, S, 2008 *I*, E, W, F, S, 2009 *E*, I, S, W, F
L Catotti 1979 *Pol*, E
Cavelleri 1997 *De*
A Cazzini 1933 *Cze*, Cze, 1934 *Cat*, R, 1935 *Cat*, F, 1936 *Ger*, R, 1937 *Ger*, R, Bel, Ger, F, 1939 *R*, 1942 *R*
G Cecchetto 1955 *F*
A Cecchetto-Milani 1952 *Sp*, Ger, F
G Cecchin 1970 *Cze*, R, 1971 *F*, R, 1972 *Pt*
G Ceccotti 1972 *Pt*, Sp
A Centinari 1930 *Sp*
R Centinari 1935 *F*, 1936 *Ger*, R, 1937 *Bel*, F, 1939 *Ger*
A Cepolino 1999 *Ur*, Sp, Fj, Tg, NZ
L Cesani 1929 *Sp*, 1930 *Sp*, 1935 *Cat*, F
C Ceselin 1989 *F*, R
C Checchinato 1990 *Sp*, 1991 *Nm*, Nm, US, NZ, USS, 1992 *Sp*, F, R, S, 1993 *Pt*, Cro, Sp, F, Rus, F, S, 1994 *Sp*, R, CZR, A, A, R, W, F, 1995 *Sa*, F, Ar, R, NZ, 1996 *W*, E, 1997 *I*, F, Ar, R, SA, I, 1998 *Geo*, Rus, Ar, H, F, 1999 *F*, S, SA, SA, Ur, Fj, E, Tg, NZ, 2000 *Geo*, S, W, I, E, F, Sa, Fj, 2001 *I*, E, F, S, W, Nm, SA, Ur, Ar, Fj, SA, Sa, 2002 *F*, S, W, Sp, R, 2003 *Geo*, NZ, Tg, C, W, 2004 *E*, F, I
G Chechinato 1973 *Cze*, Yug, A, 1974 *WGe*, Leo
G Cherubini 1949 *Cze*, 1951 *Sp*
T Ciccio 1992 *R*, 1993 *Sp*, F, Mor, F
E Cicognani 1940 *Ger*
R Cinelli 1968 *Pt*, 1969 *Sp*
G Cinti 1973 *Rho*, WTv, ETv
F Cioni 1967 *Pt*, R, 1968 *Pt*, 1969 *Bul*, Sp, Bel, 1970 *Cze*, Mad, Mad, R
L Cittadini 2008 *I*
L Clerici 1939 *Ger*
A Colella 1983 *R*, USS, C, C, Sp, Mor, F, A, USS, 1984 *R*, Tun, USS, 1985 *F*, R, EngB, Sp, Z, Z, USS, R, 1986 *Tun*, F, Pt, E, A, Tun, USS, 1987 *Pt*, F, Ar, Fj, USS, Sp, 1988 *F*, R, USS, 1989 *R*, Sp, Ar, 1990 *Pol*, R
O Collodo 1977 *Pol*, Cze, R, Sp, 1978 *F*, 1986 *Pt*, E, A, USS, 1987 *Pt*, F, R, NZ, Ar, Fj
S Colombini 1971 *R*
F Colombo 1933 *Cze*
G Colussi 1957 *F*, 1958 *F*, 1964 *F*, 1965 *F*, Cze, 1968 *Pt*
C Colusso 1982 *F*
A Comin 1955 *Ger*, F, Sp, F, Cze, 1956 *F*, Cze, 1958 *F*
U Conforto 1965 *Cze*, 1966 *Ger*, R, 1967 *F*, R, 1968 *Pt*, WGe, Yug, 1969 *Bul*, Sp, Bel, F, 1970 *Cze*, 1971 *Mor*, F, 1972 *Yug*, 1973 *R*
F Coppio 1973 *F*, Pt, Cro, Mor, Sp
L Cornella 1999 *Sp*
R Corvo 1985 *F*, Sp, Z
U Cossara 1971 *Mor*, F, R, 1972 *Pt*, Sp, 1973 *Pt*, Rho, NEC, Nat, Leo, FS, Tva, Cze, 1975 *F*, Sp, R, Cze, E, Pol, H, 1976 *F*, J, A, 1977 *Pol*
A Costa 1940 *R*, Ger, 1942 *R*
S Costanzo 2004 *R*, C, NZ, US
E Cottafava 1973 *Pt*
R Cova 1937 *Bel*, Ger, F, 1938 *Ger*, R, 1939 *Ger*, R, 1942 *R*
C Covi 1988 *F*, R, USS, A, I, 1989 *F*, R, Sp, Ar, Z, USS, 1990 *F*, Pol, R, 1991 *F*, R, Nm, Nm, 1996 *E*
F Crepaz 1972 *Pt*
M Crescenzo 1984 *R*
U Crespi 1933 *Cze*, Cze, 1934 *Cat*, R, 1935 *Cat*, 1937 *Ger*
W Cristofoletto 1992 *R*, 1993 *Mor*, Sp, F, 1996 *Pt*, A, E, S, 1997 *I*, F, F, Ar, SA, I, 1998 *S*, W, Rus, Ar, E, 1999 *F*, S, W, I, SA, SA, Sp, Fj, E, NZ, 2000 *E*, F
G Croci 1990 *Sp*, H, R, USS, 1991 *F*, R, Nm, US, E, NZ, USS, 1992 *Sp*, R, 1993 *S*, 1996 *S*, 1997 *I*, F, F, Ar, R, SA, I, 1998 *S*, W, Cro

R Crotti 1993 *S*, 1995 *SA*
L Cuccharelli 1966 *R*, 1967 *R*
G Cucchiella 1973 *A*, 1974 *Sus*, 1979 *Sp, F, Pol, USS, NZ, Mor*, 1980 *F, R, Fj, JAB, Coo*, 1985 *USS, R*, 1986 *Tun, F, Pt, E*, 1987 *Pt, F, Fj*
M Cuttitta 1990 *Pol, R, Sp, H, R, USS*, 1991 *F, Nm, Nm, US, E, NZ, USS*, 1992 *Sp, F, R, R, S*, 1993 *Sp, F, Pt, Cro, Mor, Sp, F, Rus, F, S*, 1994 *Sp, F, CZR, H, A, A, W, F*, 1995 *S, I, Sa, E, Ar, F, Ar, R, NZ, SA*, 1996 *W, Pt, W, E, S*, 1997 *I, F, F, Ar, SA, I*, 1998 *W, Rus, Cro, Ar, H, E*, 1999 *F, S, W*, 2000 *Geo, S, W, I, E*
M Cuttitta 1987 *Pt, F, R, NZ, Ar, Fj, USS, Sp*, 1988 *F, R*, 1989 *Z, USS*, 1990 *Pol, R*, 1991 *F, R, Nm, US, E, NZ, USS*, 1992 *Sp, F, R, R, S*, 1993 *Sp, F, Mor, Sp, F, F*, 1994 *Sp, R, H, A, A, F*, 1995 *S, I, Sa*, 1996 *S*, 1997 *I, F, F, Ar, R, SA, I*, 1998 *S, W, Rus, Cro, Ar*, 1999 *F*
G Dagnini 1949 *F*
D Dal Maso 2000 *Sa, Fj*, 2001 *I, E*, 2004 *J, C, NZ, US*, 2005 *I, W, S, E, F, A*
M Dal Sie 1993 *Pt*, 1994 *R, W, F*, 1995 *F, Ar*, 1996 *A*
A D'Alberton 1966 *F, Ger, R*, 1967 *F, R*
D Daldoss 1979 *Pol, R, E, Sp, Mor*
C D'Alessio 1937 *R, Bel, F*, 1938 *Ger*, 1939 *Ger*
F Dalla Nora 1997 *De*
D Dallan 1997 *De*, 1999 *F, S, W*, 2000 *S, W, I, E, F, C, R, NZ*, 2001 *I, E, F, W, Fj, SA, Sa*, 2002 *F, S, I, E, NZ, Sp, R*, 2003 *W, I, E, F, S, Tg, C, W*, 2004 *E, F, S, I, W, C*, 2006 *J*, 2007 *F, E*
M Dallan 1997 *Ar, R, De, I*, 1998 *Geo, Ar, H, E*, 1999 *SA, SA*, 2000 *S, Sa, C*, 2001 *F, S*, 2003 *Tg, C*, 2004 *E, F, S*
A Danieli 1955 *Ger, F, Sp, F, Cze*
V D'Anna 1993 *Rus*
P Dari 1951 *Sp*, 1952 *Sp, Ger, F*, 1953 *Ger, R*, 1954 *Sp, F*
D Davo 1998 *Geo*
G De Angelis 1934 *Cat, R*, 1935 *Cat, F*, 1937 *R*
E De Anna 1972 *Yug*, 1973 *Cze, A*, 1975 *F, Sp, R, Cze, E, Pol, H, Sp*, 1976 *F, R*, 1978 *Ar, USS, Sp*, 1979 *F, R, Sp, Mor, F, USS, NZ*, 1980 *F, R, Fj, JAB*
R De Bernardo 1980 *USS, Sp*, 1981 *F, R, USS, WGe*, 1982 *R, E*, 1983 *R, USS, C, C, Sp, Mor, F, A, USS*, 1984 *F, USS*, 1985 *R, EngB*, 1988 *I*, 1989 *Ar, Z*
CF De Biase 1987 *Sp*, 1988 *F, A*
G De Carli 1996 *W*, 1997 *R, De*, 1998 *S, Geo, Rus, Ar, H, E*, 1999 *F, I, SA, SA, Ur, Fj*, 2000 *S, Sa, Fj*, 2001 *I, E, W, SA, Ur, Fj, SA, Sa*, 2002 *F, S, W, I, E*, 2003 *W, I, E*
B de Jager 2006 *J*
L De Joanni 1983 *C, Mor, F, A, USS*, 1984 *R, Tun, USS*, 1985 *F, R, EngB, Sp, Z*, 1986 *A, Tun*, 1989 *F, R, Sp, Ar, Z*, 1990 *R*
D De Luca 1998 *Cro*
R De Marchis 1935 *F*
H De Marco 1993 *Pt*
JR de Marigny 2004 *E, F, S, I, W, US*, 2005 *I, W, S*, 2007 *F, E, S, W, I, Ur, J, I, NZ, Pt*
A de Rossi 1999 *Ur, Sp, E*, 2000 *I, E, F, Sa, C, R, NZ*, 2001 *SA, Ur, Ar*, 2002 *I, E, NZ, Sp, R*, 2003 *W, I, E, F, S, I, Geo, Tg, C, W*, 2004 *E, F, S, I, W, R*
C De Rossi 1994 *Sp, H, R*
L De Santis 1952 *Sp*
M De Stefani 1989 *Z*
C De Vecchi 1948 *F*
G Degli Antoni 1963 *F*, 1965 *F*, 1966 *F, Ger, R*, 1967 *F*
G Del Bono 1951 *Sp*
M Del Bono 1960 *F, Ger, F*, 1961 *Ger, F*, 1962 *F, Ger, R*, 1963 *F*, 1964 *Ger, F*
CA Del Fava 2004 *W, R, J*, 2005 *I, W, S, E, F, Tg, Ar, Fj*, 2006 *I, E, F, W, S, J, Fj, Pt*, 2007 *Ur, Ar, Pt, S*, 2008 *I, E, W, F, S, SA, Ar, A, Ar*, 2009 *I, S, W, F, A, NZ*
C Della Valle 1968 *WGe, Yug*, 1969 *F*, 1970 *Mad, Mad*, 1971 *F*
S Dellapè 2002 *F, S, I, E, NZ, Sp, Ar*, 2003 *F, S, S, Geo, Tg, C, W*, 2004 *E, F, S, I, W, C, NZ*, 2005 *I, W, S, E, F, Ar*, 2006 *I, E, W, S, J, Fj, Pt, Rus, A, Ar, C*, 2007 *F, E, S, W, I, J, NZ, R, S*, 2008 *I, E, W, SA, Ar*, 2009 *E, I, S, W, F*
G Delli Ficorilli 1969 *F*
PE Derbyshire 2009 *A*
A Di Bello 1930 *Sp*, 1933 *Cze, Cze*, 1934 *Cat*
F Di Carlo 1975 *Sp, R, Cze, Sp*, 1976 *F, Sp*, 1977 *Pol, R, Pol*, 1978 *Ar, USS*
B Di Cola 1973 *A*
G Di Cola 1972 *Sp, Sp*, 1973 *A*

F Di Maura 1971 *Mor*
A Di Zitti 1958 *R*, 1960 *Ger*, 1961 *Ger, F*, 1962 *F, Ger, R*, 1964 *Ger, F*, 1965 *F, Cze*, 1966 *F, Ger, R*, 1967 *F, Pt, R*, 1969 *Bul, Sp, Bel*, 1972 *Pt, Sp*
R Dolfato 1985 *F*, 1986 *A*, 1987 *Pt, Fj, USS, Sp*, 1988 *F, R, USS*
D Dominguez 1991 *F, R, Nm, Nm, US, E, NZ, USS*, 1992 *Sp, F, R, S*, 1993 *Sp, F, Rus, F, S*, 1994 *R, H, R, W*, 1995 *S, I, Sa, E, Ar, SA*, 1996 *W, Pt, W, A, A, E, S*, 1997 *I, F, F, Ar, R, SA, I*, 1998 *S, W, Rus, Ar, H, E*, 1999 *F, S, W, I, Ur, Sp, Fj, E, Tg, NZ*, 2000 *Geo, S, W, I, E, F*, 2001 *F, S, W, Fj, SA, Sa*, 2002 *S, I, E, Ar*, 2003 *W, I*
D Donadona 1929 *Sp*, 1930 *Sp*
G Dora 1929 *Sp*
R D'Orazio 1969 *Bul*
M Dotti IV 1939 *R*, 1940 *R, Ger*
F Dotto 1971 *Mor, F*, 1972 *Pt, Pt, Sp*
P Dotto 1993 *Sp, Cro*, 1994 *Sp, R*
J Erasmus 2008 *F, S, SA*
U Faccioli 1948 *F*
A Falancia 1975 *E, Pol*
G Faliva 1999 *SA*, 2002 *NZ, Ar, A*
G Faltiba 1993 *Pt*
G Fanton 1979 *Pol*
P Farina 1987 *F, NZ, Fj*
P Farinelli 1949 *F*, 1950 *F, Cze*, 1951 *Sp*, 1952 *Sp*
T Fattori 1936 *Ger, R*, 1937 *R, Ger, F*, 1938 *Ger*, 1939 *Ger, R*, 1940 *R, Ger*
E Fava 1948 *F, Cze*
P Favaretto 1951 *Sp*
R Favaro 1988 *F, USS, A, I*, 1989 *F, R, Sp, Ar, Z, USS*, 1990 *F, Pol, R, H, R, USS*, 1991 *F, R, Nm, Nm, US, E, NZ, USS*, 1992 *Sp, F, R*, 1993 *Sp, F, Cro, Sp, F*, 1994 *CZR, A, A, R, W, F*, 1995 *S, I, Sa*, 1996 *F*
S Favaro 2009 *A, NZ*
G Favretto 1948 *Cze*, 1949 *Cze*
A Fedrigo 1972 *Yug*, 1973 *Pt, Rho, WTv, Bor, NEC, Nat, ETv, Leo, FS, Cze, Yug, A*, 1974 *Pt, Mid, Sus, Oxo, WGe, Leo*, 1975 *F, Sp, R, Cze, E, Pol, H, Sp*, 1976 *F, J, A, Sp*, 1977 *F, Pol, R, Cze, R, Sp*, 1978 *F, Ar*, 1979 *Pol, R*
P Fedrigo 1973 *Pt*
I Fernandez Rouyet 2008 *SA, Ar*, 2009 *A, NZ*
P Ferracin 1975 *R, Cze, E, Pol, H, Sp*, 1976 *F*, 1977 *Mor, Pol*, 1978 *USS*
C Festuccia 2003 *W, I, E, F, S, S, I, Geo, NZ, Tg, C, W*, 2004 *E, F, S, I*, 2005 *F, Ar, Ar, A, Tg, Ar*, 2006 *E, F, W, S, Pt, Rus, A, Ar, C*, 2007 *F, E, S, W, I, Ur, Ar, J, NZ, R, S*, 2008 *I, E, W*, 2009 *E, I*
G Figari 1940 *R, Ger*, 1942 *R*
EG Filizzola 1993 *Pt, Mor, Sp, F, Rus, F, S*, 1994 *Sp, CZR, A*, 1995 *R, NZ*
M Finocchi 1968 *Yug*, 1969 *F*, 1970 *Cze, Mad, Mad, R*, 1971 *Mor, R*
G Fornari 1952 *Sp, Ger*, 1953 *F, Ger, R*, 1954 *Sp, F*, 1955 *Ger, F, Sp, F, Cze*, 1956 *Ger, F, Cze*
B Francescato 1977 *Cze, R, Sp*, 1978 *F, Sp*, 1979 *F*, 1981 *R*
I Francescato 1990 *R, USS*, 1991 *F, R, US, E, NZ, USS*, 1992 *R, S*, 1993 *Mor, F*, 1994 *Sp, H, R, W, F*, 1995 *S, I, Sa, E, Ar, F, Ar, R, NZ, SA*, 1996 *W, Pt, W, A, E, S*, 1997 *F, F, Ar, R, SA*
N Francescato 1972 *Yug*, 1973 *Rho, WTv, Bor, NEC, Nat, ETv, Leo*, 1974 *Pt*, 1976 *J, A, Sp*, 1977 *F, Mor, Pol, R, R, Sp*, 1978 *F, Ar, USS, Sp*, 1979 *F, R, E, Sp, Mor, F, Pol, USS, NZ*, 1980 *F, R, Fj, JAB, Coo, Pol, USS, Sp*, 1981 *F, R,·1982 Mor*
R Francescato 1976 *Sp*, 1978 *Ar, USS*, 1979 *Sp, F, Pol, USS, NZ, Mor*, 1980 *F, R, Fj, JAB, Coo, Pol, USS, Sp*, 1981 *F, R*, 1982 *WGe*, 1983 *F, R, USS, C, C, Sp, Mor, F, A*, 1984 *Mor, R, Tun*, 1985 *F, Sp, Z, USS*, 1986 *Tun, F, Cze*
G Franceschini 1975 *H, Sp*, 1976 *F, J*, 1977 *F, Pol, Pol, Cze, R, Sp*
A Francese 1939 *R*, 1940 *R*
J Francesio 2000 *W, I, Sa*, 2001 *Ur*
F Frati 2000 *C, NZ*, 2001 *I, S*
F Frelich 1955 *Cze*, 1957 *F, Ger*, 1958 *F, R*
M Fumei 1984 *F*
A Fusco 1982 *E*, 1985 *R*, 1986 *Tun, F, Tun*
E Fusco 1960 *Ger, F*, 1961 *F*, 1962 *F, Ger, R*, 1963 *F*, 1964 *Ger, F*, 1965 *F*, 1966 *F*
R Gabanella 1951 *Sp*, 1952 *Sp*

P Gabrielli 1948 *Cze,* 1949 *F, Cze,* 1951 *Sp,* 1954 *F*
F Gaetaniello 1975 *H,* 1976 *R, A, Sp,* 1977 *F, Pol, R, Pol, R, Sp,* 1978 *Sp,* 1979 *Pol, R, E, Sp, Mor, F, Pol, USS, NZ, Mor,* 1980 *Fj, JAB, Sp,* 1981 *F, R, USS, WGe,* 1982 *F, R, E, WGe, Mor,* 1983 *F, R, USS, C, C, Sp*
F Gaetaniello 1980 *Sp,* 1982 *E,* 1984 *USS,* 1985 *R, Sp, Z, Z, USS, R,* 1986 *Pt, E, A, Tun, USS,* 1987 *Pt, F, NZ, Ar, Fj, USS, Sp,* 1988 *F,* 1990 *F, R, Sp, H,* 1991 *Nm, US, E, NZ*
A Galante 2007 *Ur, Ar*
A Galeazzo 1985 *Sp,* 1987 *Pt, R, Ar, USS*
M Galletto 1972 *Pt, Sp, Yug*
E Galon 2001 *I,* 2005 *Tg, Ar, Fj,* 2006 *W, S, Rus,* 2007 *I, Ur, Ar, I, NZ, R, S,* 2008 *I, E, W, F, S*
R Ganzerla 1973 *Bor, NEC*
G Garcia 2008 *SA, Ar, A, Ar, Pl,* 2009 *E, I, S, A, NZ*
M Gardin 1981 *USS, WGe,* 1982 *Mor,* 1983 *F, R,* 1984 *Mor, R, USS,* 1985 *EngB, USS, R,* 1986 *Tun, F, Pt, Tun, USS,* 1987 *Pt, F, R, NZ, Ar, Fj, USS, Sp,* 1988 *R*
JM Gardner 1992 *R, S,* 1993 *Rus, F,* 1994 *Sp, R, H, F,* 1995 *S, I, Sa, E, Ar,* 1996 *W,* 1997 *I, F, De, SA, I,* 1998 *S, W*
P Gargiullo 1973 *FS,* 1974 *Mid, Sus, Oxo*
F Garguillo 1972 *Yug*
F Garguilo 1967 *F, Pt,* 1968 *Yug,* 1974 *Sus*
S Garozzo 2001 *Ur, Ar,* 2002 *Ar*
M Gatto 1967 *Pt, R*
G Gattoni 1933 *Cze, Cze*
Q Geldenhuys 2009 *A, A, NZ*
A Gerardo 1968 *Yug,* 1969 *Sp,* 1970 *Cze, Mad,* 1971 *R,* 1972 *Sp*
F Geremia 1980 *JAB, Pol*
G Geremia 1956 *Cze*
E Gerosa 1952 *Sp, Ger, F,* 1953 *F, Ger, R,* 1954 *Sp*
M Gerosa 1994 *CZR, A, A, R, W,* 1995 *E, Ar*
C Ghezzi 1938 *Ger,* 1939 *Ger, R,* 1940 *R, Ger*
A Ghini 1981 *USS, WGe,* 1982 *F, R, E, Mor,* 1983 *F, R, C, Mor, F, A, USS,* 1984 *F, Mor, R, USS,* 1985 *F, R, EngB, Z, Z, USS,* 1987 *Fj,* 1988 *R, USS*
L Ghiraldini 2006 *J, Fj,* 2007 *I, J, Pt,* 2008 *I, E, W, F, S, SA, Ar, A, Ar, Pl,* 2009 *S, W, F, A, A, NZ*
S Ghizzoni 1977 *F, Mor, Pol, R, Pol, Cze, R, Sp,* 1978 *F, Ar, USS,* 1979 *F, Pol, Sp, Mor, F, Pol,* 1980 *R, Fj, JAB, Coo, Pol, USS, Sp,* 1981 *F,* 1982 *F, R, E, WGe, Mor,* 1983 *F, USS, C, C, Sp, Mor, F, A, USS,* 1984 *F, Mor, R, Tun, USS,* 1985 *F, R, EngB, Z, Z, USS, R,* 1986 *F, E, A, Tun, USS,* 1987 *Pt, F, R, NZ*
M Giacheri 1992 *R,* 1993 *Sp, F, Pt, Rus, F, S,* 1994 *Sp, R, CZR, H, A, A, F,* 1995 *S, I, E, Ar, F, Ar, R, NZ, SA,* 1996 *W,* 1998 *Geo, Cro,* 1999 *S, W, I, Ur, Fj, E, Tg, NZ,* 2001 *Nm, SA, Ur, Ar, SA,* 2002 *F, S, W, I, E, NZ, A,* 2003 *E, F, S, I*
G Giani 1966 *Ger, R,* 1967 *F, Pt, R*
G Gini 1968 *Pt, WGe, Yug,* 1969 *Bul, Sp, Bel, F,* 1970 *Cze, Mad, Mad, R,* 1971 *Mor, F,* 1972 *Pt, Pt,* 1974 *Mid, Oxo*
G Giorgio 1968 *Pt, WGe*
M Giovanelli 1989 *Z, USS,* 1990 *Pol, Sp, H, R, USS,* 1991 *F, R, Nm, E, NZ, USS,* 1992 *Sp, F, S,* 1993 *Sp, F, Pt, Cro, Mor, Sp, F,* 1994 *R, CZR, H, A, A,* 1995 *F, Ar, R, NZ, SA,* 1996 *A, E, S,* 1997 *F, F, Ar, R, SA, I,* 1998 *S, W, Rus, Cro, Ar, H, E,* 1999 *S, W, I, SA, SA, Ur, Sp, Fj, E, Tg, NZ,* 2000 *Geo, S*
E Giugovaz 1965 *Cze,* 1966 *F*
R Giuliani 1951 *Sp*
V Golfetti 1997 *De*
M Gorni 1939 *R,* 1940 *R, Ger*
M Goti 1990 *H*
C Gower 2009 *A, A, NZ*
G Grasselli 1952 *Ger*
G Grespan 1989 *F, Sp, USS,* 1990 *F, R,* 1991 *R, NZ, USS,* 1992 *R, S,* 1993 *Sp, F, Cro, Sp, F, Rus,* 1994 *Sp, CZR, R, W*
PR Griffen 2004 *E, F, S, I, W, R, J, C, NZ, US,* 2005 *W, S, F, Ar, Ar, A, Tg, Ar, Fj,* 2006 *I, E, F, W, S, J, Fj, Rus, A, Ar, C,* 2007 *F, I, Ur, Ar, I, NZ, R, Pt,* 2009 *I, S, W, F*
A Gritti 1996 *F,* 1997 *De,* 2000 *Geo, S, W, I, E, F, Sa, Fj, C, R, NZ,* 2001 *E, F, S, W*
G Guidi 1996 *Pt, E,* 1997 *F, Ar, R,* 1998 *Cro*
F Gumiero 1997 *De*
M Innocenti 1981 *WGe,* 1982 *F, R, E, WGe, Mor,* 1983 *F, USS, C, C, Mor, F, A, USS,* 1984 *F, Mor, Tun, USS,* 1985 *F, R, EngB, Sp, USS, R,* 1986 *Tun, F, Pt, E, A, Tun, USS,* 1987 *Pt, F, R, NZ, Ar, Fj, USS, Sp,* 1988 *F, R, A*

G Intoppa 2004 *R, J, C, NZ,* 2005 *I, W, E*
C Jannone 1981 *USS,* 1982 *F, R*
S Lanfranchi 1949 *F, Cze,* 1953 *F, Ger, R,* 1954 *Sp, F,* 1955 *F,* 1956 *Ger, Cze,* 1957 *F,* 1958 *F,* 1959 *F,* 1960 *F,* 1961 *F,* 1962 *F, Ger, R,* 1963 *F,* 1964 *Ger, F*
G Lanzi 1998 *Cro, Ar, H, E,* 1999 *Sp,* 2000 *S, W, I,* 2001 *I*
G Lari 1972 *Yug,* 1973 *Yug, A,* 1974 *Pt, Mid, Sus, Oxo, Leo*
E Lazzarini 1970 *Cze,* 1971 *Mor, F, R,* 1972 *Pt, Pt, Sp, Sp,* 1973 *Pt, Rho, WTv, Bor, NEC, Leo, FS, Tva, Cze, Yug, A,* 1974 *Pt, Mid, Sus, Oxo, WGe*
U Levorato 1956 *Ger, F,* 1957 *F,* 1958 *F, R,* 1959 *F,* 1961 *Ger, F,* 1962 *F, Ger, R,* 1963 *F,* 1964 *Ger, F,* 1965 *F*
A Lijoi 1977 *Pol, R,* 1978 *Sp,* 1979 *R, Mor*
G Limone 1979 *E, Mor, USS, Mor,* 1980 *JAB, Sp,* 1981 *USS, WGe,* 1982 *E,* 1983 *USS*
A Lo Cicero 2000 *E, F, Sa, Fj, C, R, NZ,* 2001 *I, E, F, S, W, Fj, SA, Sa,* 2002 *F, S, W, Sp, R, A,* 2003 *F, S, S, I, Geo, Tg, C, W,* 2004 *E, F, S, I, W, R, J, C, NZ, US,* 2005 *I, W, S, E, F, Ar, Ar, A, Tg, Ar,* 2006 *E, F, W, S, J, Fj, Pt, Rus, A, Ar, C,* 2007 *F, E, S, W, Ur, Ar, J, NZ, R, Pt, S,* 2008 *I, E, W, F, S, Ar, Pl*
C Loranzi 1973 *Nat, ETv, Leo, FS, Tva*
F Lorigiola 1979 *Sp, F, Pol, USS, NZ, Mor,* 1980 *F, R, Fj, JAB, Pol, USS, Sp,* 1981 *F, R, USS,* 1982 *WGe,* 1983 *R, USS, C, Sp,* 1984 *Tun,* 1985 *Sp,* 1986 *Pt, E, A, USS,* 1987 *Pt, F, R,* 1988 *F*
G Luchini 1973 *Rho, Nat*
L Luise 1955 *Ger, F, Sp, F, Cze,* 1956 *Ger, F, Cze,* 1957 *Ger,* 1958 *F*
R Luise III 1959 *F,* 1960 *Ger, F,* 1961 *Ger, F,* 1962 *F, Ger, R,* 1965 *F, Cze,* 1966 *F,* 1971 *R,* 1972 *Pt, Sp, Sp*
T Lupini 1987 *R, NZ, Ar, Fj, USS, Sp,* 1988 *F, R, USS, A,* 1989 *R*
O Maestri 1935 *Cat, F,* 1937 *Ger*
R Maffioli 1933 *Cze, Cze,* 1934 *Cat, R,* 1935 *Cat,* 1936 *Ger, R,* 1937 *Ger, R, Bel, Ger*
R Maini 1948 *F, Cze*
G Malosti 1953 *F,* 1954 *Sp,* 1955 *F,* 1956 *Ger, F,* 1957 *F,* 1958 *F*
G Mancini 1952 *Ger, F,* 1953 *F, Ger, R,* 1954 *Sp, F,* 1955 *Cze,* 1956 *Ger, F, Cze,* 1957 *F*
R Mandelli 2004 *I, W, R, J, US,* 2007 *F, E, Ur, Ar*
A Mannato 2004 *US,* 2005 *Ar, A*
E Manni 1976 *J, A, Sp,* 1977 *Mor*
L Manteri 1996 *W, A, E, S*
A Marcato 2006 *J, Pt,* 2008 *I, E, W, F, S, SA, Ar, A, Ar, Pl,* 2009 *E, S, W, F*
M Marchetto 1972 *Yug,* 1973 *Pt, Cze, Yug,* 1974 *Pt, Mid, Sus, WGe, Leo,* 1975 *F, Sp, R, Cze, E, Pol, H, Sp,* 1976 *F, R, J, A, Sp,* 1977 *F, Mor, Pol, R, Cze, R, Sp,* 1978 *F, USS, Sp,* 1979 *F, Pol, R, E, Pol, USS, NZ, Mor,* 1980 *F, Coo,* 1981 *USS*
A Marescalchi 1933 *Cze,* 1935 *F,* 1937 *R*
P Mariani 1976 *R, A, Sp,* 1977 *F, Pol,* 1978 *F, Ar, USS, Sp,* 1979 *F, Pol, R, Sp, F, Pol, USS, NZ, Mor,* 1980 *F, R, Fj, JAB*
P Marini 1949 *F, Cze,* 1951 *Sp,* 1953 *F, Ger, R,* 1955 *Ger*
L Martin 1997 *F, R, De,* 1998 *S, W, Geo, Rus, H, E,* 1999 *F, S, W, I, SA, SA, Ur, Sp, Fj, E,* 2000 *S, W, I, E, F, Sa, Fj, C, R, NZ,* 2001 *I, E, S, W, SA, Ar, Fj, SA, Sa,* 2002 *F, S*
F Martinenghi 1952 *Sp, Ger*
R Martinez-Frugoni 2002 *NZ, Sp, R,* 2003 *W, I, E, F, S, S, NZ*
G Martini 1965 *F,* 1967 *F,* 1968 *Pt*
R Martini 1959 *F,* 1960 *Ger, F,* 1961 *Ger, F,* 1964 *Ger, F,* 1965 *F,* 1968 *WGe, Yug*
P Masci 1948 *Cze,* 1949 *F, Cze,* 1952 *Sp, Ger, F,* 1953 *F,* 1954 *Sp,* 1955 *F*
M Mascioletti 1977 *Mor, Pol,* 1978 *Ar, USS, Sp,* 1979 *Pol, E, Sp, Mor, F, Pol, USS, NZ, Mor,* 1980 *F, R, Fj,* 1981 *WGe,* 1982 *F, R, WGe,* 1983 *F, R, USS, C, C, Sp, Mor, F, A, USS,* 1984 *F, Mor, Tun,* 1985 *F, R, Z, Z, USS, R,* 1986 *Tun, F, Pt, E, Tun, USS,* 1987 *NZ, Ar, Fj,* 1989 *Sp, Ar, Z, USS,* 1990 *Pol*
A Masi 1999 *Sp,* 2003 *E, F, S, S, I, NZ, Tg, C, W,* 2004 *E, I, W, R, J, C,* 2005 *I, W, S, E, F, Ar, Ar, A,* 2006 *J, Fj, Pt, Rus,* 2007 *F, S, J, NZ, R, Pt, S,* 2008 *I, E, W, F, S, SA, A, Ar, Pl,* 2009 *E, I*
L Mastrodomenico 2000 *Sa, C, NZ,* 2001 *Nm, Ar*
I Matacchini 1948 *F, Cze,* 1949 *F, Cze,* 1954 *Sp,* 1955 *Ger, F, Sp, F*

JAPAN

JAPAN'S 2008–09 TEST RECORD

OPPONENTS	DATE	VENUE	RESULT
USA	16 November	H	**Won** 29–19
USA	22 November	H	**Won** 32–17
Kazakhstan	25 April	H	**Won** 87–10
Hong Kong	2 May	A	**Won** 59–6
Korea	16 May	H	**Won** 80–9
Singapore	23 May	A	**Won** 45–15
Samoa	18 June	N	**Lost** 15–34
Junior All Blacks	23 June	N	**Lost** 21–52
Tonga	27 June	N	**Won** 21–19
Fiji	3 July	A	**Lost** 39–40

THE WORLD CUP BECKONS

By Rich Freeman

If **Jonathan Kaplan had** blown his whistle five seconds earlier during Japan's final Test of the year against Fiji in the ANZ Pacific Nations Cup, it is fair to say the Brave Blossoms would have been celebrating their best ever international season.

But the referee's whistle stayed in his pocket, preventing Japan from upsetting the ninth-ranked team in the world on home soil and followers of Japanese rugby were once again left wondering what might have been.

Not that it was a bad year. The successful hosting of the IRB TOSHIBA Junior World Championship, and the record crowds attending matches in the Under 20 event, showed Japan was capable of hosting a major rugby tournament and was very much a forerunner of things to come with the country announced as Rugby World Cup 2019 hosts in July.

The problem was Japan really needed a great year on the field to offset some of the problems that had arisen during the domestic season, which had seen the headlines dominated by off the field incidents and a near death experience for one of the Top League's most popular players.

The international season began in November in Nagoya with the visit of the USA Eagles, who had last played, and beaten, Japan in Gosford during RWC 2003. Going into the game, the two sides had played 16 times with Japan winning on just three occasions and it looked like their miserable record would continue with injuries preventing coach John Kirwan from picking 17 players.

However, the improvement in the standard of the Top League meant Kirwan no longer had players who cowered at the thought of playing international rugby. And in Takashi Kikutani, the Brave Blossoms had a new young captain who, like his predecessor Takuro Miuchi, led from the front and wasn't afraid to get involved in the physical side of the game.

Tries by Kosuke Endo and Ryo Koliniasi Holani, together with the boot of Ryan Nicholas and Shaun Webb, saw a Japanese side fielding five uncapped players win the first Test 29–19. A week later in Tokyo, they ran out 32–17 winners thanks to tries from Kensuke Hatakeyama, Koji Tomioka, Webb and Kikutani in an entertaining game played under the lights at the Prince Chichibu Memorial Stadium.

Kirwan was delighted and had particular praise for his new captain. "Kiku has really stood up and taken on the leadership role," he said. "This has been a really positive month."

It was another five months before Kirwan got to work with his

players, and once again he was forced to include a number of young **325**
uncapped players following injuries to the likes of Endo and Holani.

Japan opened their defence of the HSBC Asian Five Nations with an
emphatic 87–10 rout of Kazakhstan, but Kirwan gave his team just four
points out of ten for their performance. A week later, he was slightly
happier, raising their mark to six, following a 59–6 win away to Hong
Kong. "We were able to play with some of the new systems we put in
place but we should have played with more discipline," was the verdict.

Japan wrapped up the title two weeks later when Hirotoki Onozawa
marked his 50th appearance for his country with four tries in an 80–9
rout of Korea in Osaka.

It seemed that Japan were timing things right for the more challenging
Pacific Nations Cup, but they were brought down to earth in Singapore,
winning just 45–15 against the weakest side in the Top 5. "There are times
out there when we self destructed," admitted Kikutani. "That's something
we need to accept honestly and learn from and take to the next games."

Following a narrow defeat to a Queensland Reds side, Japan headed
to Fiji for the Pacific Nations Cup and things looked good as they led
Samoa 15–12 a few minutes into the second half. However, defensive
lapses came back to haunt the Brave Blossoms and they eventually lost
34–15, a game Kirwan would later say they lost rather than Samoa won.

Japan had just four days off before they took on the Junior All Blacks
and the lack of preparation showed as they trailed 40–0 at the break.
A rout seemed on the cards but Japan raised their game to score three
converted tries, only to give up two late tries to lose 52–21.

The confidence gained from this second half performance saw Japan
beat Tonga 21–19 – the third successive year they have beaten the Pacific
islanders – before they came so close to beating Fiji in a thrilling encounter
in Suva. Japan had led 39–33 with time up on the clock, but Fiji No.8
Netani Talei powered over with Kaplan poised to blow his whistle and
Seremaia Bai added the all-important conversion to snatch a 40–39 victory.

The domestic season was marred by controversy with Toshiba Brave
Lupus, the Top League champions, pulling out of the All-Japan
Championship. Having earlier in the year seen one of their players
arrested for robbing a taxi driver, Toshiba made the decision after
Christian Loamanu tested positive for marijuana following a league
game against Suntory Sungoliath.

That paved the way for league runners-up Sanyo Wild Knights to
celebrate the miraculous return of Tony Brown with some silverware.
Earlier in the season Brown had been told by doctors he had come close
to dying after a heavy tackle had resulted in the fly-half rupturing his
pancreas and developing pancreatitis.

JAPAN INTERNATIONAL STATISTICS

MATCH RECORDS UP TO 30TH SEPTEMBER 2009

WINNING MARGIN

Date	Opponent	Result	Winning Margin
06/07/2002	Chinese Taipei	155–3	152
27/10/1998	Chinese Taipei	134–6	128
21/07/2002	Chinese Taipei	120–3	117
03/05/2008	Arabian Gulf	114–6	108
08/05/2005	Hong Kong	91–3	88

MOST POINTS IN A MATCH
BY THE TEAM

Date	Opponent	Result	Pts.
06/07/2002	Chinese Taipei	155–3	155
27/10/1998	Chinese Taipei	134–6	134
21/07/2002	Chinese Taipei	120–3	120
03/05/2008	Arabian Gulf	114–6	114
08/05/2005	Hong Kong	91–3	91

MOST TRIES IN A MATCH
BY THE TEAM

Date	Opponent	Result	Tries
06/07/2002	Chinese Taipei	155–3	23
27/10/1998	Chinese Taipei	134–6	20
21/07/2002	Chinese Taipei	120–3	18
03/05/2008	Arabian Gulf	114–6	18

MOST CONVERSIONS IN A MATCH
BY THE TEAM

Date	Opponent	Result	Cons
06/07/2002	Chinese Taipei	155–3	20
27/10/1998	Chinese Taipei	134–6	17
21/07/2002	Chinese Taipei	120–3	15
03/05/2008	Arabian Gulf	114–6	12

MOST PENALTIES IN A MATCH
BY THE TEAM

Date	Opponent	Result	Pens
08/05/1999	Tonga	44–17	9
08/04/1990	Tonga	28–16	6

MOST DROP GOALS IN A MATCH
BY THE TEAM

Date	Opponent	Result	DGs
15/09/1998	Argentina	44–29	2

MOST POINTS IN A MATCH
BY A PLAYER

Date	Player	Opponent	Pts.
21/07/2002	Toru Kurihara	Chinese Taipei	60
06/07/2002	Daisuke Ohata	Chinese Taipei	40
16/06/2002	Toru Kurihara	Korea	35
08/05/1999	Keiji Hirose	Tonga	34
08/05/2005	Keiji Hirose	Hong Kong	31

MOST TRIES IN A MATCH
BY A PLAYER

Date	Player	Opponent	Tries
06/07/2002	Daisuke Ohata	Chinese Taipei	8
21/07/2002	Toru Kurihara	Chinese Taipei	6
08/05/2005	Daisuke Ohata	Hong Kong	6
27/10/1998	Terunori Masuho	Chinese Taipei	5

MOST CONVERSIONS IN A MATCH
BY A PLAYER

Date	Player	Opponent	Cons
21/07/2002	Toru Kurihara	Chinese Taipei	15
06/07/2002	Andy Miller	Chinese Taipei	12
16/06/2002	Toru Kurihara	Korea	11
08/05/2005	Keiji Hirose	Hong Kong	11

MOST PENALTIES IN A MATCH
BY A PLAYER

Date	Player	Opponent	Pens
08/05/1999	Keiji Hirose	Tonga	9
08/04/1990	Takahiro Hosokawa	Tonga	6

MOST DROP GOALS IN A MATCH
BY A PLAYER

Date	Player	Opponent	DGs
15/09/1998	Kensuke Iwabuchi	Argentina	2

MOST CAPPED PLAYERS

Name	Caps
Yukio Motoki	79
Takeomi Ito	62
Daisuke Ohata	58
Hirotoki Onozawa	51

LEADING TRY SCORERS

Name	Tries
Daisuke Ohata	69
Hirotoki Onozawa	38
Terunori Masuho	28
Toru Kurihara	20
Yoshihito Yoshida	17

LEADING CONVERSIONS SCORERS

Name	Cons
Keiji Hirose	77
Toru Kurihara	71
James Arlidge	36
Ryan Nicholas	32

LEADING PENALTY SCORERS

Name	Pens
Keiji Hirose	76
Toru Kurihara	35
Takahiro Hosokawa	24

LEADING DROP GOAL SCORERS

Name	DGs
Kyohei Morita	5
Yuji Matsuo	2
Katsuhiro Matsuo	2
Keiji Hirose	2
Kensuke Iwabuchi	2

LEADING POINTS SCORERS

Name	Pts.
Keiji Hirose	413
Toru Kurihara	347
Daisuke Ohata	345
Hirotoki Onozawa	190
Terunori Masuho	142

JAPAN

JAPAN INTERNATIONAL PLAYERS
UP TO 30TH SEPTEMBER 2009

Note: Years given for International Championship matches are for second half of season; eg 1972 means season 1971–72. Years for all other matches refer to the actual year of the match.

THE COUNTRIES

T Adachi 1932 *C, C*
M Aizawa 1984 *Kor*, 1986 *US, C, S, E, Kor*, 1987 *A, NZ, NZ*, 1988 *Kor*
H Akama 1973 *F*, 1975 *A, W*, 1976 *S, E, It, Kor*, 1977 *S*
T Akatsuka 1994 *Fj, SL, M*, 1995 *Tg, NZ*, 2005 *Sp*, 2006 *HK, Kor*
J Akune 2001 *W, C*
M Amino 2000 *Kor, C*, 2003 *Rus, AuA, Kor, E, E, S, Fj, US*
E Ando 2006 *AG, Kor, Geo, Tg, Sa, JAB, Fj*, 2007 *HK, Fj, Tg, Sa, JAB, It*
D Anglesey 2002 *Tg, Tai, Tai*
T Aoi 1959 *BCo, BCo*, 1963 *BCo*
S Aoki 1989 *S*, 1990 *Fj*, 1991 *US, C*, 1993 *W*
Y Aoki 2007 *Kor, AuA, JAB*, 2008 *Kor, Kaz, HK, AuA, Tg, Fj, Sa, US, US*, 2009 *Kaz, Sin, Sa, JAB, Tg, Fj*
S Arai 1959 *BCo, BCo*
JA Arlidge 2007 *Kor*, 2008 *Kor, AG, Kaz, HK, AuA, Tg, Fj, M, Sa*, 2009 *Sa, JAB, Tg, Fj*
G Aruga 2006 *HK, Kor*, 2007 *Kor, HK, AuA, Sa, JAB, It, Fj, C*, 2008 *Kor, HK*
K Aruga 1974 *NZU*, 1975 *A, A, W, W*, 1976 *S, E, It, Kor*
R Asano 2003 *AuA, AuA, F, Fj*, 2005 *Ar, HK, Kor, R, C, I, I, Sp*, 2006 *Kor, Geo, Tg, It, HK, Kor*, 2007 *Kor, It, W*
M Atokawa 1969 *HK*, 1970 *Tha, BCo*, 1971 *E, E*
H Atou 1976 *BCo*
T Baba 1932 *C*
GTM Bachop 1999 *C, Tg, Sa, Fj, Sp, Sa, W, Ar*
I Basiyalo 1997 *HK, US, US, C, HK*
D Bickle 1996 *HK, HK, C, US, US, C*
KCC Chang 1930 *BCo*, 1932 *C, C*
T Chiba 1930 *BCo*
M Chida 1980 *Kor*, 1982 *HK, C, C, Kor*, 1983 *W*, 1984 *F, F, Kor*, 1985 *US, I, I, F, F*, 1986 *US, C, S, E, Kor*, 1987 *US, E*
H Daimon 2004 *S, W*
K Endo 2004 *It*, 2006 *AG, Kor, Geo, Tg, It, JAB, Fj*, 2007 *HK, Fj, Tg, AuA, Sa, It, Fj, W, C*, 2008 *AuA, Tg, Fj, M, US, US*
J Enomoto 2005 *Sp*
R Enomoto 1959 *BCo, BCo*
B Ferguson 1993 *W*, 1994 *Fj, HK, Tai, M, Kor*, 1995 *Tg, Tg, R, W, I, NZ*, 1996 *HK, HK, C, US, US, C*
K Fijii 2000 *Sa*
S Fuchigami 2000 *I*, 2002 *Rus, Tai*, 2003 *US, Rus*
A Fuji 1959 *BCo, BCo*
M Fuji 1930 *BCo*
M Fujikake 1993 *W*, 1994 *HK, SL, M*, 1995 *Tg*
T Fujimoto-Kamohara 1969 *HK*, 1970 *BCo*, 1971 *E, E*, 1972 *HK*, 1973 *W*
T Fujita 1980 *H, F*, 1983 *W*, 1984 *F, F, Kor*, 1985 *US, I, I, F, F*, 1986 *US, C, S, E*, 1987 *US, E, A, NZ, NZ*, 1989 *S*, 1990 *Fj, Tg, Kor, Sa*, 1991 *US, US, I*
M Fujiwara 1973 *W*, 1974 *NZU*, 1975 *A, A, W, W*, 1976 *S, E, It*, 1977 *S*, 1978 *F, Kor*, 1979 *HK, E*, 1980 *H, F*
K Fukumuro 1990 *Kor*
K Fukuoka 2000 *Fj*
S Fukuoka 1990 *Kor*
R Fukurodate 1976 *BCo, Kor*, 1979 *E, E*, 1980 *H, F, Kor*
T Fumihara 2000 *I*
T Goda 1990 *Fj, Tg, Kor, Sa, US, Kor*, 1991 *US*, 1994 *SL, M*, 1995 *Tg*

WR Gordon 1997 *HK, C, US, US*, 1998 *C, US, HK, HK, US, C*, 1999 *C, Sa, Fj, Sp, Sa, W, Ar*
A Goromaru 2005 *Ur, R, C, I*, 2009 *Kaz, HK, Kor, Sin, JAB*
S Goto 2005 *Ur, Ar, Kor, R, C, I, I*, 2006 *HK*
M Hagimoto 1987 *E*
T Hagiwara-Maekawa 1930 *BCo*
K Hamabe 1996 *C, US, US, C, Kor*, 1997 *HK, C, US, US, C*, 2001 *Sa, C*
T Haneda 1994 *Tai, SL, M*, 1995 *Tg*
S Hara 1970 *BCo*, 1971 *E, E*, 1973 *W, F*, 1974 *NZU, SL*, 1975 *A, W*, 1976 *E*
T Harada 1959 *BCo*
S Hasegawa 1997 *HK*, 1998 *C, US, HK, HK, US, C, Ar, Kor, Tai, HK, Kor*, 1999 *C, Tg, Sa, Fj, US, Sa, W*, 2000 *Fj, US, Tg, Sa, C*, 2001 *W, W, Sa, C*, 2002 *Tg, Kor, Tai, Kor*, 2003 *US, AuA, E, S, F, Fj, US*
K Hatakeyama 2008 *US, US*, 2009 *HK, Sin, Sa, JAB, Tg, Fj*
T Hatakeyama 1976 *It, Kor*, 1977 *S*, 1978 *F, Kor*, 1979 *HK, E, E*
T Hayashi 1980 *F*, 1982 *C, C, Kor*, 1983 *W*, 1984 *F, F*, 1985 *US, I, I, F, F*, 1986 *US, C, S, E, Kor*, 1987 *US, E, A, NZ, NZ*, 1990 *Tg, Sa*, 1991 *US, C, HK, S, I, Z*, 1992 *HK*
T Hayashi 1989 *S*
T Higashida 1983 *W*
T Hirai 1980 *Kor*, 1982 *HK*
S Hirao 1983 *W*, 1984 *F, F*, 1985 *US, I, I*, 1986 *US, C, S, E*, 1987 *US, E, A, NZ, NZ*, 1988 *Kor*, 1989 *S*, 1990 *Fj, Tg, Kor, US, Kor*, 1991 *US, C, HK, S, I, Z*, 1995 *R, W, I*
S Hirao 1932 *C, C*
T Hirao 1998 *Kor*, 1999 *Tg, Sa, W*, 2001 *Tai, Sa, C*, 2004 *Kor, Rus, C, It*
H Hirashima 2008 *US, US*, 2009 *Kaz, Kor, Sa, JAB, Tg, Fj*
T Hirata 2000 *US, C*
J Hiratsuka 1999 *US*
K Hirose 1994 *Tai, Kor*, 1995 *Tg, NZ*, 1996 *HK, HK, C, US, US, Kor*, 1998 *HK, HK, US, C, Kor, Tai, HK, Kor*, 1999 *C, Tg, Sa, Fj, US, Sp, Sa, W, Ar*, 2000 *Fj, US, Kor, C, I*, 2003 *AuA, AuA, Kor, E, E, S*, 2005 *HK, I, Sp*
T Hirose 1988 *Kor*
T Hirose 2007 *HK*
E Hirotsu 1995 *Tg*
Y Hisadomi 2002 *Rus*, 2003 *Rus, AuA, Kor, E*, 2004 *Kor, C, It, S, R*, 2005 *Sp*, 2006 *AG, Kor, Geo, Tg, It, Sa, JAB, Fj, HK, Kor*
M Hohokabe 1978 *F, Kor*
RK Holani 2008 *Kaz, HK, AuA, Fj, M, Sa, US, US*
K Honjo 1982 *C, C*, 1985 *US, I, F*
K Horaguchi 1979 *E, E*, 1980 *F*, 1982 *HK, C, C, Kor*, 1983 *W*, 1984 *F*, 1985 *US, I, I, F, F*, 1987 *US, E*
M Horikoshi 1988 *Kor*, 1989 *S*, 1990 *Fj, Tg, Kor, US, Kor*, 1991 *US, C, HK, I, Z*, 1992 *HK*, 1993 *Ar, Ar*, 1994 *Tai, Kor*, 1995 *Tg, R, W, I*, 1997 *C*, 1998 *C, US, Tai, HK, Kor*
S Hoshino 1975 *W*, 1976 *S*, 1978 *Kor*, 1979 *HK*
T Hosokawa 1990 *Tg, Kor, Sa, US*, 1991 *US, S, I, Z*, 1993 *Ar, Ar*
S Iburi 1972 *HK*
M Iguchi 1973 *F*, 1974 *NZU*, 1975 *A, A, W*
H Ijyuin 1932 *C, C*
W Ikeda 2004 *Kor, Rus, C, It, S, R, W*, 2005 *Sp*, 2006 *AG, Geo, Tg, It, JAB, Fj*
Y Ikeda 1980 *Kor*, 1983 *W*, 1984 *F, F*

Y Ikegaya 2008 *AG, HK, M*
H Ikuta 1987 *US, A, NZ*
K Imaizumi 1988 *Kor*, 1994 *Fj, HK*, 1996 *US*, 1997 *C, US, US, C*
k Imakoma 1988 *Kor*
K Imamura 1959 *BCo, BCo*
R Imamura 1959 *BCo, BCo*
Y Imamura 2006 *AG, Geo, It, Sa, Fj*, 2007 *HK, Fj, Tg, AuA, Sa, JAB, It, Fj, W, C*, 2008 *AG, Kaz, HK, AuA, M*, 2009 *Kaz, Kor, Sin, Sa, JAB, Tg, Fj*
R Imazato 1969 *HK*, 1970 *Tha, BCo*, 1971 *E, E*, 1972 *HK*, 1973 *W, F*, 1975 *A, A, W, W*, 1976 *S, E, It*
T Inokuchi 2007 *It, A, W*, 2008 *AG, HK, AuA, M*
Y Inose 2008 *AG, Kaz, AuA, Tg, M, Sa*
M Inoue 1982 *C, C, Kor*
M Irie 2008 *US*
R Ishi 1999 *Sp*
K Ishii 1986 *S*
J Ishiyama 1980 *H, F, Kor*, 1982 *HK, C, Kor*, 1983 *W*, 1985 *US, I, I, F, F*
K Ishizuka 1963 *BCo*
T Ishizuka 1974 *NZU, SL*, 1975 *A, W, W*, 1978 *F, Kor*, 1979 *HK, E, E*, 1980 *H, F, Kor*, 1982 *HK, C, C, Kor*
H Ito 2004 *Kor, Rus*
M Ito 2000 *Tg, Sa, Kor, C, I*, 2004 *Kor, C*, 2006 *AG, Kor, Geo, Tg, Sa, Fj, HK, Kor*
M Ito 1999 *HK*
T Ito 1996 *HK, HK, C, US, US, C, Kor*, 1997 *HK, C, US, US, 1998 C, US, HK, HK, US, C, Ar, Kor, Tai, HK, Kor*, 1999 *Tg, Sa, Fj, US, Sp, Sa, W, Ar*, 2000 *I*, 2001 *Kor, W, Sa, C*, 2002 *Rus, Tg, Kor, Tai, Kor*, 2003 *US, Rus, AuA, AuA, Kor, E, E, S, F, Fj, US*, 2004 *Kor, Rus, C, It*, 2005 *Ur, Ar, R, C, I, Sp*
T Ito 1963 *BCo*, 1969 *HK*, 1970 *Tha, BCo*, 1971 *E*, 1972 *HK*, 1973 *W, F*, 1974 *NZU*
T Ito 1980 *H, F*, 1982 *HK, C, Kor*
K Iwabuchi 1997 *HK, C, US, US, C, HK*, 1998 *C, US, Ar, Tai, HK*, 1999 *C*, 2001 *Tai, W, W, Sa*, 2002 *Tg, Kor, Tai, Kor*
Y Iwama 2000 *US, Tg, Sa, Kor, C*, 2001 *Tai*
H Iwashita 1930 *BCo*
Y Izawa 1970 *Tha, BCo*, 1971 *E, E*, 1972 *HK*, 1973 *W, F*, 1974 *NZU*, 1975 *A, A, W*, 1976 *S, E, It*
K Izawa-Nakamura 1994 *Tai, SL, M*, 1995 *Tg, Tg, I, NZ*, 1996 *US, Kor*, 1997 *HK, C, US, US, C, HK*, 1998 *Ar, Kor, Tai, HK, Kor*
JW Joseph 1999 *C, Tg, Sa, Fj, US, Sp, Sa, W, Ar*
H Kajiwara 1989 *S*, 1990 *Fj, Tg, Kor, Sa*, 1991 *US, US, HK, S, I, Z*, 1993 *Ar, Ar*, 1994 *Fj, Fj, M, Kor*, 1995 *Tg, R, W, I, NZ*, 1996 *HK, HK, C, US, US, C, Kor*, 1997 *C*
S Kaleta 1992 *HK*, 1993 *Ar, Ar, W*
K Kamata 1970 *BCo*
T Kanai 2009 *Kaz, HK, Sin, JAB, Fj*
F Kanaya 1980 *F*, 1982 *HK, C, C*, 1983 *W*, 1984 *F, F, Kor*, 1985 *US*
Kanbara 1971 *E*
H Kaneshiro 1993 *Ar*
H Kano 1974 *SL*, 1982 *Kor*
T Kasahara 1932 *C, C*
K Kasai 1999 *C*, 2005 *Ar, HK, Kor, R, C, I, I*, 2006 *AG, Tg*
Y Kasai 1985 *F, F*
Y Katakura 1959 *BCo*
A Kato 2001 *Tai*
H Kato 1993 *Ar, Ar*
D Katsuno 2002 *Kor*
T Katsuraguchi 1970 *Tha*
H Kawachi 1980 *H, Kor*, 1982 *C*, 1983 *W*, 1984 *F, F, Kor*
K Kawachi 1984 *Kor*
R Kawai 2000 *I*
N Kawamata 2008 *US*, 2009 *HK, Kor*
K Kawasaki 1963 *BCo*
M Kawasaki 1970 *Tha*
T Kawasaki 2000 *US, Tg*
Y Kawase 1983 *W*, 1985 *US, I, I, F*, 1986 *Kor*, 1987 *A*
T Kikutani 2005 *Sp*, 2006 *AG, Kor, Geo, Tg, It, Sa, JAB, Fj, Kor*, 2008 *Kor, AG, AuA, Tg, Fj, Sa, US, US*, 2009 *Kaz, HK, Kor, Sin, Sa, JAB, Tg, Fj*

CW Kim 2007 *W, C*
K Kimura 1996 *C*
T Kimura 1984 *F, F, Kor*, 1985 *US*, 1986 *E, Kor*, 1987 *E, A, NZ*
T Kinashita 2002 *Tg, Kor*
T Kinoshita 1932 *C, C*
H Kiso 2001 *Kor, Tai*, 2003 *AuA, AuA, Kor, E, E, S, Fj, US*, 2004 *S, R, W*, 2005 *HK, I, Sp*, 2006 *AG, Kor, Geo, It, Sa, JAB, Fj, HK, Kor*, 2007 *Kor, Fj, AuA, A, W, C*, 2008 *US*
T Kitagawa 2005 *Sp*, 2006 *AG, Kor, Tg, Sa, JAB*, 2008 *Kor, AG, Kaz, HK, AuA, Tg, Fj, M, Sa, US, US*, 2009 *Kaz, Kor, Sa, JAB, Tg, Fj*
T Kitagawa 2006 *HK*, 2007 *HK, A*
Y Kitagawa 2007 *Kor*, 2009 *HK, Kor, Sin, JAB*
T Kitahara 1978 *Kor*, 1979 *HK*
H Kitajima 1963 *BCo*
T Kitano 1930 *BCo*, 1932 *C, C*
S Kitaoka 1959 *BCo*
H Kobayashi 1983 *W*, 1984 *F, Kor*, 1985 *I, F*, 1986 *Kor*
I Kobayashi 1975 *A, A, W, W*, 1976 *BCo, S, E, It, Kor*, 1977 *S*, 1978 *F, Kor*, 1979 *HK, E, E*
K Kobayashi 1959 *BCo, BCo*
K Koizumi 1997 *US, C, HK*, 2000 *Fj, US, Tg, Sa, C*, 2001 *W, C*, 2002 *Tg, Tai*
J Komura 1992 *HK*, 1998 *Kor*, 2000 *Kor, C*
GN Konia 2003 *US, AuA, AuA, F, Fj, US*
K Konishi 1986 *US, Kor*
Y Konishi 1980 *F, Kor*, 1982 *HK, Kor*, 1983 *W*, 1984 *F, F, Kor*, 1985 *US, I, I, F, F*, 1986 *US, C, S, E, Kor*, 1987 *NZ*
M Koshiyama 1984 *F, F, Kor*, 1985 *US, I, I*, 1986 *C, Kor*, 1987 *NZ, NZ*
T Kouda 1988 *Kor*
O Koyabu 1974 *SL*
K Kubo 2000 *I*, 2001 *Kor, W, Sa, C*, 2002 *Rus, Kor, Tai, Kor*, 2003 *US, Rus, E, F, Fj*, 2004 *Kor, C, It*
K Kubota 2004 *S, R, W*
T Kudo-Nakayama 1979 *E*
T Kumagae 2004 *Kor, Rus, C, It, S, R, W*, 2005 *Ur, Ar, Kor, R, C, I, I, Sp*, 2006 *AG, Kor, Geo, It, Sa, Fj*, 2007 *HK, Fj, AuA, Sa, A*
N Kumagai 1977 *S*, 1978 *F*, 1979 *HK*
M Kunda 1990 *Sa, US, Kor*, 1991 *C, HK, S, I, Z*, 1992 *HK*, 1993 *Ar, Ar, W*, 1994 *Fj, Fj, HK, Tai, Kor*, 1995 *Tg, R, W, I, NZ*, 1996 *HK, HK, C*, 1997 *HK, C, US, US*, 1998 *C, HK, HK, US, C, Ar, Kor, HK, Kor*, 1999 *Sa, Fj, US, Sp, Sa, W, Ar*
S Kurihara 1986 *S, E*, 1987 *E*
S Kurihara 1974 *SL*
T Kurihara 2000 *Fj, US, Tg, Sa, Kor, C*, 2001 *Kor, W, W, Sa, C*, 2002 *Rus, Tg, Kor, Tai, Kor, Tai*, 2003 *US, Rus, AuA, AuA, E, E, S, F, Fj, US*
M Kurokawa 1998 *Tai, HK, Kor*, 2000 *Fj, Tg, Sa, Kor, C*
T Kurosaka 1970 *BCo*, 1974 *SL*, 1975 *A, A, W, W*
M Kusatsu 1963 *BCo*
T Kusumi 2007 *A, W*, 2008 *Kor*
E Kutsuki 1985 *F*, 1986 *US, C, S, E*, 1987 *US, E, A, NZ, NZ*, 1989 *S*, 1990 *Fj, Tg, Kor, Sa, US, Kor*, 1991 *US, US, C, HK, S, I, Z*, 1992 *HK*, 1993 *W*, 1994 *Fj, HK*
S Latu 1993 *W*, 1994 *Fj, Fj, HK, Tai, SL, Kor*, 1995 *Tg, R, W, I*
S Latu 1987 *US, A, NZ, NZ*, 1989 *S*, 1990 *Fj, Tg, Kor, Sa, US, Kor*, 1991 *US, C, HK, S, I, Z*, 1992 *HK*, 1993 *Ar, Ar*, 1994 *Fj, Fj, HK, Tai, Kor*, 1995 *Tg, R, W, I, NZ*
MG Leitch 2008 *US, US*, 2009 *Kaz, HK, Kor, Sa, JAB*
CED Loamanu 2005 *Ur, HK*, 2007 *Kor, Fj, Tg, Sa, JAB, It, Fj, W, C*, 2008 *AuA, Tg, Fj, M, Sa*
ET Luaiufi 1990 *Fj, Kor, US, Kor*, 1991 *US, US, C, HK, S, I, Z*
T Madea 1991 *US, C, HK*, 1994 *SL, M*, 1995 *Tg*
P Mafileo 2008 *US*
HAW Makiri 2005 *Ur, Ar, HK, Kor, R, I, I*, 2006 *AG, Tg, Sa, JAB*, 2007 *Kor, Tg, AuA, Sa, JAB, It, A, Fj, W, C*, 2008 *AuA, Tg, Fj, M, Sa*
M Mantani 1969 *HK*, 1970 *Tha, BCo*, 1971 *E, E*, 1972 *HK*
G Marsh 2007 *AuA, Sa, JAB*
T Masuho 1991 *US, C, HK, S, I, Z*, 1993 *Ar, Ar*, 1994 *Fj, Fj, Tai, SL, Kor*, 1995 *Tg, W*, 1996 *HK, C, US, US, C*, 1997 *HK, C, US, C, HK*, 1998 *C, US, HK, HK, US, C, Ar, Kor,*

Tai, HK, 1999 C, US, Sp, Sa, 2000 Fj, US, Tg, Sa, Kor, C, 2001 Kor, W, Sa, C
Y Masutome 1986 Kor
K Matsubara 1930 BCo
T Matsubara 1932 C, C
Y Matsubara 2004 Kor, Rus, C, It, 2005 Sp, 2006 AG, Kor, Geo, Tg, It, Sa, JAB, Fj, Kor, 2007 Kor, Fj, Tg, Sa, JAB, It, Fj, W, C
T Matsuda 1992 HK, 1993 W, 1994 Fj, HK, Tai, Kor, 1995 Tg, R, W, I, NZ, 1996 HK, HK, C, US, US, C, Kor, 1998 US, HK, HK, US, C, Ar, Kor, Tai, HK, Kor, 1999 C, Fj, US, Sp, Sa, Ar, 2001 Kor, Tai, W, 2003 US, AuA, Kor, E, S, Fj, US
J Matsumoto 1977 S, 1978 F, 1980 H, 1982 C, C
T Matsunaga 1985 F, F
Y Matsunobu 1963 BCo
H Matsuo 2003 AuA, AuA, Kor, E, E
H Matsuo 1994 SL
K Matsuo 1986 US, C, S, E, Kor, 1987 E, NZ, 1988 Kor, 1990 Tg, Kor, Sa, US, 1991 US, HK, S, I, Z, 1993 Ar, Ar, 1994 Fj, Fj, HK, M, 1995 Tg
Y Matsuo 1974 SL, 1976 BCo, E, It, Kor, 1977 S, 1979 HK, E, E, 1982 HK, C, C, 1983 W, 1984 F, F, Kor
S Matsuoka 1963 BCo, 1970 Tha
K Matsushita 2008 US, US
F Mau 2004 Rus, C, It, S, R, W
AF McCormick 1996 HK, HK, US, 1997 HK, C, US, US, C, HK, 1998 C, US, HK, Ar, Kor, Tai, HK, 1999 C, Tg, Sa, Fj, US, Sp, Sa, W, Ar
R Miki 1999 Sp, 2002 Tg, Tai, Kor, Tai, Kor, 2004 S, R, W
A Miller 2002 Rus, Kor, Tai, Kor, Tai, 2003 Kor, S, F, Fj, US
S Miln 1998 C, US, HK, HK, US
Y Minamikawa 1976 BCo, 1978 F, Kor, 1979 HK, E, E, 1980 H, F, Kor, 1982 HK, C, C, Kor
M Mishima 1930 BCo, 1932 C, C
T Miuchi 2002 Rus, Kor, Kor, Tai, Kor, 2003 US, Rus, AuA, Kor, E, E, S, F, Fj, US, 2004 Rus, C, It, S, R, W, 2005 Ur, Ar, HK, Kor, R, C, I, I, 2006 HK, Kor, 2007 Kor, HK, Fj, Tg, Sa, It, Fj, W, C, 2008 Kor, AG, Kaz, HK, AuA, Tg, Fj, Sa
S Miura 1963 BCo
K Miyai 1959 BCo, BCo, 1963 BCo
K Miyaji 1969 HK
K Miyajima 1959 BCo, BCo
H Miyaji-Yoshizawa 1930 BCo
T Miyake 2005 Sp, 2006 Sa, JAB, Fj
K Miyamoto 1986 S, E, 1987 US, E, A, 1988 Kor, 1991 I
K Miyata 1971 E, E, 1972 HK
M Miyauchi 1975 W, 1976 It, Kor
K Mizobe 1997 C
K Mizoguchi 1997 C
K Mizube 1997 HK
H Mizuno 2004 R, 2005 HK, Kor, R, C, I, 2006 AG, Geo, Tg, It, Sa, JAB
M Mizutani 1970 Tha, 1971 E
N Mizuyama 2008 Tg, M, Sa, US
S Mori 1974 NZU, SL, 1975 A, A, W, W, 1976 BCo, S, E, It, Kor, 1977 S, 1978 F, 1979 HK, E, E, 1980 H, F, Kor
K Morioka 1982 Kor
K Morita 2004 C, It, 2005 Ur, Ar, Kor, R, C, I
A Moriya 2006 Tg, It, Sa, JAB, Fj, 2008 AG, Kaz
Y Motoki 1991 US, US, C, 1992 HK, 1993 Ar, Ar, 1994 Fj, Fj, Tai, SL, Kor, 1995 Tg, Tg, R, W, I, NZ, 1996 HK, HK, C, US, US, C, Kor, 1997 HK, C, US, US, C, HK, 1998 C, US, HK, HK, US, C, Ar, Kor, HK, Kor, 1999 C, Tg, Sa, Fj, US, Sp, Sa, W, Ar, 2001 W, W, Sa, C, 2002 Rus, Tg, Kor, Tai, Kor, Tai, 2003 Kor, E, E, S, Fj, US, 2004 Kor, Rus, C, It, S, R, W, 2005 Ur, Ar, HK, Kor, R, C, I, I
K Motoyoshi 2001 Tai
S Mukai 1985 I, I, F, 1986 US, C, E, Kor, 1987 US, A, NZ, NZ
M Mukoyama 2004 Kor, C, It, S, R, W
K Muraguchi 1976 S, Kor
D Murai 1985 I, I, F, F, 1987 E
K Murata 1963 BCo
W Murata 1991 US, S, 1995 Tg, NZ, 1996 HK, HK, C, US, US, C, Kor, 1997 HK, C, US, US, HK, 1998 HK, HK, US, C, Ar, Kor, Kor, 1999 US, W, 2001 W, W, Sa, 2002 Rus,

Tg, Kor, Tai, Kor, Tai, 2003 US, AuA, E, 2005 Ur, Ar, Kor, I, I
Y Murata 1971 E, E, 1972 HK, 1973 W, 1974 NZU, SL
M Nagai 1988 Kor
Y Nagatomo 1993 W, 1994 Fj, HK, SL, M, 1995 Tg, 1996 US, US, 1997 C
M Nakabayashi 2005 HK, Kor, R, I
T Nakai 2005 Ur, HK, C, I, I, Sp, 2006 AG, Kor, Geo, Tg, It, Fj
T Nakamichi 1996 HK, HK, US, US, C, 1998 Ar, Kor, 1999 C, Sa, Fj, Sp, W, Ar, 2000 Fj, US, Tg
N Nakamura 1998 C, US, HK, HK, US, C, Ar, Kor, Tai, HK, Kor, 1999 C, Tg, Sa, Fj, US, Sp, W, Ar, 2000 I
S Nakamura 2009 Kaz, Sin
S Nakashima 1989 S, 1990 Fj, Tg, Kor, Sa, US, 1991 US, US, C, HK, S
T Nakayama 1976 BCo, 1978 F, 1979 E, 1980 H, 1982 C, C
Y Nakayama 2008 Kor, AG, Kaz, HK, Tg, 2009 HK, Kor, Sin, Tg, Fj
H Namba 2000 Fj, US, Tg, Sa, Kor, C, I, 2001 Tai, W, W, C, 2002 Rus, Tg, Kor, Tai, Kor, 2003 US, Rus, AuA, AuA, Kor, E, E, F
R Nicholas 2008 Kor, Kaz, HK, AuA, Tg, Fj, Sa, US, US, 2009 HK, Kor, Sa, JAB, Tg, Fj
H Nishida 1994 Fj
S Nishigaki 1932 C, C
T Nishiura 2004 W, 2006 HK, Kor, 2007 Kor, Fj, Tg, Sa, It, Fj, W, C, 2008 Kor, HK, AuA, Tg, Fj, Sa
H Nishizumi 1963 BCo
M Niwa 1932 C
I Nogami 1932 C
T Nozawa 2000 Tg, Sa, Kor, C
M Oda 2000 US, Tg, Sa, Kor, I
H Ogasawara 1969 HK, 1970 Tha, BCo, 1971 E, E, 1973 F, 1974 NZU, 1975 A, A, W, W, 1977 S
K Oguchi 1997 US, C, HK, 1998 Tai, 1999 Sa, Ar, 2000 Fj, Tg, Sa, Kor
K Ohara 1998 Kor, Tai, 2000 Kor, C, I
D Ohata 1996 Kor, 1997 HK, C, US, 1998 HK, C, Ar, Kor, HK, 1999 C, Tg, Sa, Fj, US, Sp, Sa, W, Ar, 2000 Fj, US, Kor, C, I, 2002 Rus, Kor, Tai, Kor, Tai, Kor, 2003 US, Rus, AuA, AuA, Kor, E, E, S, F, Fj, US, 2004 Kor, Rus, C, It, 2005 Ur, Ar, HK, Kor, R, C, I, I, 2006 AG, Kor, Geo, Tg, HK, Kor
K Ohigashi 1973 W, F, 1974 NZU, SL
K Ohigashi 2004 Kor, Rus, C, 2007 Kor, HK, AuA, JAB
K Ohotsuka 1959 BCo
S Oikawa 1980 H
E Okabe 1963 BCo
Y Okada 1932 C, C
M Okidoi 1987 A, NZ, NZ
N Okubo 1999 Tg, Sa, Fj, US, Sp, Sa, W, Ar, 2000 Fj, US, Tg, Sa, Kor, C, 2002 Rus, Tg, Kor, Tai, Kor, Tai, 2003 US, Rus, S, F, Fj, US, 2004 S, R, W
T Omata 1970 BCo
S Onishi 2000 Fj, US, Tg, Sa, Kor, C, 2001 Kor, Tai, W, C, 2005 Sp, 2006 AG, Kor, Geo, Tg, It, JAB, HK, Kor, 2007 HK, Tg, AuA, Sa, JAB, It, Fj, W, C, 2008 Kor, AG, HK, M, Sa
H Ono 2004 Kor, Rus, C, S, 2005 Ar, Kor, I, 2006 Kor, Geo, It, Sa, JAB, Fj, HK, Kor, 2007 Kor, Fj, Tg, Sa, JAB, It, Fj, W, C, 2008 Kor, AG, AuA, Tg, Fj, US, 2009 HK, Sin, Sa, JAB, Tg
K Ono 2007 Kor, AuA, JAB, It, A
S Ono 1932 C, C
H Onozawa 2001 W, Sa, C, 2002 Rus, Kor, Tai, Kor, 2003 Rus, AuA, AuA, Kor, E, E, S, F, Fj, US, 2004 Kor, Rus, C, It, 2005 Ur, Ar, HK, Kor, R, C, I, Sp, 2006 HK, Kor, 2007 Kor, Tg, AuA, JAB, A, Fj, W, C, 2008 Kor, AG, Kaz, HK, AuA, Tg, Fj, Sa, 2009 Kaz, HK, Kor, Sa, Tg
S Onuki 1984 F, F, Kor, 1985 US, I, I, F, F, 1986 US, C, S, E, Kor, 1987 US, E
PD O'Reilly 2005 Kor, 2006 JAB, Fj, HK, Kor, 2007 It, Fj, C, 2009 Kaz
G Ota 1930 BCo
O Ota 1986 US, S, 1989 S, 1990 Fj, Tg, Kor, Sa, US, Kor, 1991 US, C, HK, S, I, Z, 1992 HK, 1993 Ar, Ar, W, 1994 Fj, HK, Tai, Kor, 1995 Tg, R, W, I, NZ

NAMIBIA

NAMIBIA'S 2008–09 TEST RECORD

OPPONENTS	DATE	VENUE	RESULT
Argentina Jaguars	8 May	A	**Lost** 7–62
Argentina Jaguars	15 May	A	**Lost** 7–19
Ivory Coast	14 June	A	**Drew** 13–13
Ivory Coast	27 June	H	**Won** 54–14

THE ROAD TO RECOVERY

By Helge Schutz

Getty Images

Jacques Burger (centre) one of Namibia's outstanding loose forwards.

Namibia's primary focus this year was securing qualification for a fourth successive Rugby World Cup, beginning 2009 with the target of four victories to seal the Africa 1 spot and a place in Pool D with defending champions South Africa, Fiji, Wales and Samoa in New Zealand.

Having topped their pool in the Africa Cup the previous year, Namibia faced Ivory Coast in the semi-finals with the first leg taking place in Abidjan on 14 June. The Ivory Coast have only graced the World Cup stage once, back in 1995, but gave themselves every chance of improving that record by drawing their home leg 13–13.

Namibia, though, made no mistakes in the return leg in Windhoek a fortnight later with a dominant performance seeing them to a 54–14 victory and taking them to within sight of their qualification target. All now standing between Namibia and RWC 2011 is a home and away play-off with Tunisia in November.

The Namibians ran in seven tries in a great display of attacking rugby with 20-year-old full-back Chrysander Botha scoring two tries, three penalties and five conversions for a haul of 29 points and adding to his eight-point tally in the first leg.

However, it was Namibia's forwards who laid the foundations with their constant pressure and dominance of the set pieces. Here the loose trio of Tinus du Plessis, Jacques Burger and Jacques Nieuwenhuis were outstanding, with their terrier-like tackling and relentless drives, while substitute PJ van Lill also had a storming game.

Locks Wacca Kazombiaze and Nico Esterhuizen won a glut of possession in the lineouts, while Namibia also dominated the scrums, pushing the visitors back at will and disrupting their possession in the Hage Geingob Stadium.

Another player to impress was 18-year-old schoolboy Andre de Klerk, who had made his senior international debut off the bench in Abidjan less than two months after appearing for Namibia's Under 20s at the IRB Junior World Rugby Trophy in Kenya.

"There's a lot of talent within this team," admitted Namibia coach John Williams. "We have an 18-year-old, who plays as if he is 35 years old and I think it is one of the most exciting teams that Namibia has had in quite a while.

"There has definitely been growth in the development of the game over the past year, in terms of the number and improvement of the players. But we will have to become more professional to take the players to a higher level."

Namibia currently has a well-balanced side with a good mixture of youth and experience. The bulk of the forwards are made up of experienced players who represented Namibia at RWC 2007, including the front row trio of Kees Lensing, Hugo Horn and Marius Visser.

Most of the newcomers are in the backs, where only half-backs Eugene Jantjies, Jurie van Tonder and Emile Wessels, along with centre Piet van Zyl have remained from that World Cup squad.

Botha and De Klerk head the exciting new generation of talent coming through, while others include wings Llewellyn Winckler and McGrath van Wyk, centres David Philander and Tinus Venter, fly-half Jacky Bock and No.8 Van Lill.

To prepare for the qualifiers against Ivory Coast, Namibia travelled to Argentina for two matches against the Jaguars in May on a tour that was made possible through financial support from the International Rugby Board.

They found life hard-going against the Jaguars, Argentina's second string, in the first encounter and were on the wrong end of a 62–7 defeat with their hosts running in ten tries to Namibia's one. Namibia's

NAMIBIA

Captain Kees Lensing is still at the centre of the Namibia effort.

only points came ten minutes after the break when Philander intercepted the ball in his own half and raced through to score under the posts, with fly-half Jaco van Zyl adding the conversion.

The following week Namibia produced a much better performance and this time it took Francisco Merello's try three minutes from time to seal a 19–7 victory for the Jaguars in Buenos Aires.

Namibia returned home and on 29 May staged an historic match between a South Africa XV and a Namibia Invitation XV, which included several Springboks. It was the first time that the Springboks had played on the African continent outside of South Africa and a bumper crowd of around 10,000 fans turned up.

It was a great spectacle, with the Namibian XV producing a superb performance to trail only 8–7 at half-time. Springbok coach Peter de Villiers, however, brought on some of his top players like Jean de Villiers and Juan Smith and the visitors eventually ran out comfortable 36–7 victors.

Namibia's loose forwards Nieuwenhuis and Burger were outstanding in the rucks and defence, while Esterhuizen gave a fine performance in the lineouts and in the loose. Captain Lensing also had a great game, winning his battle in the scrum against his Springbok counterpart John Smit and capping a fine display with a try.

While Namibia's senior national side seems to be improving, the

Under 20s stumbled in their attempt to qualify for the IRB Junior World Rugby Trophy 2010, Zimbabwe denying them a third successive African Under 19 title with a 39–7 victory in Kenya in August.

Namibia had played at the Junior World Rugby Trophy in April but again had to settle for fifth after edging a thrilling encounter with Papua New Guinea 48–43. Namibia had been unlucky not to reach the final, snatching a last gasp win over hosts Kenya but then crucially losing to USA to finish third in their pool.

NAMIBIA INTERNATIONAL RECORDS
UP TO 30TH SEPTEMBER 2009

WINNING MARGIN

Date	Opponent	Result	Winning Margin
15/06/2002	Madagascar	112–0	112
21/04/1990	Portugal	86–9	77
27/05/2006	Kenya	82–12	70
26/05/2007	Zambia	80–10	70

MOST POINTS IN A MATCH
BY THE TEAM

Date	Opponent	Result	Pts.
15/06/2002	Madagascar	112–0	112
21/04/1990	Portugal	86–9	86
31/08/2003	Uganda	82–13	82
27/05/2006	Kenya	82–12	82

MOST TRIES IN A MATCH
BY THE TEAM

Date	Opponent	Result	Tries
15/06/2002	Madagascar	112–0	18
21/04/1990	Portugal	86–9	16
17/10/1999	Germany	79–13	13

MOST CONVERSIONS IN A MATCH
BY THE TEAM

Date	Opponent	Result	Cons
15/06/2002	Madagascar	112–0	11
21/04/1990	Portugal	86–9	11
31/08/2003	Uganda	82–13	11
27/05/2006	Kenya	82–12	11

MOST PENALTIES IN A MATCH
BY THE TEAM

Date	Opponent	Result	Pens
22/06/1991	Italy	33–19	5
23/01/1998	Portugal	36–19	5
30/06/1990	France A	20–25	5

MOST DROP GOALS IN A MATCH
BY THE TEAM

1 on 7 Occasions

MOST POINTS IN A MATCH
BY A PLAYER

Date	Player	Opponent	Pts.
06/07/1993	Jaco Coetzee	Kenya	35
26/05/2007	Justinus van der Westhuizen	Zambia	33
27/06/2009	Chrysander Botha	Cote D'Ivoire	29
21/04/1990	Moolman Olivier	Portugal	26
15/06/2002	Riaan van Wyk	Madagascar	25

MOST TRIES IN A MATCH
BY A PLAYER

Date	Player	Opponent	Tries
21/04/1990	Gerhard Mans	Portugal	6
15/06/2002	Riaan van Wyk	Madagascar	5
16/05/1992	Eden Meyer	Zimbabwe	4
16/08/2003	Melrick Africa	Kenya	4

NAMIBIA

MOST CONVERSIONS IN A MATCH
BY A PLAYER

Date	Player	Opponent	Cons
21/04/1990	Moolman Olivier	Portugal	11
27/05/2006	Morne Schreuder	Kenya	11
26/05/2007	Justinus van der Westhuizen	Zambia	9
31/08/2003	Rudi van Vuuren	Uganda	8
04/07/1993	Jaco Coetzee	Arabian Gulf	8

MOST PENALTIES IN A MATCH
BY A PLAYER

Date	Player	Opponent	Pens
22/06/1991	Jaco Coetzee	Italy	5
23/01/1998	Rudi van Vuuren	Portugal	5
30/06/1990	Shaun McCulley	France A	5

MOST DROP GOALS IN A MATCH
BY A PLAYER

1 on 7 Occasions

MOST CAPPED PLAYERS

Name	Caps
Herman Lindvelt	32
Jaco Coetzee	28
Casper Derks	28
Hugo Horn	28

LEADING TRY SCORERS

Name	Tries
Gerhard Mans	27
Eden Meyer	21
Melrick Africa	12

LEADING CONVERSIONS SCORERS

Name	Cons
Jaco Coetzee	84
Morne Schreuder	36
Rudi van Vuuren	26
Emile Wessels	13

LEADING PENALTY SCORERS

Name	Pens
Jaco Coetzee	46
Morne Schreuder	18
Rudi van Vuuren	14
Lean van Dyk	11

LEADING DROP GOAL SCORERS

Name	DGs
Jaco Coetzee	3

LEADING POINTS SCORERS

Name	Points.
Jaco Coetzee	344
Morne Schreuder	146
Gerhard Mans	118
Rudi van Vuuren	109
Eden Meyer	98

NAMIBIA INTERNATIONAL PLAYERS
UP TO 30TH SEPTEMBER 2009

Note: Years given for International Championship matches are for second half of season; eg 1972 means season 1971–72. Years for all other matches refer to the actual year of the match.

MJ Africa 2003 *Sa, Ken, Uga, Ar, I, A,* 2005 *Mad, Mor,* 2006 *Ken, Tun, Ken, Tun, Mor, Mor,* 2007 *Za, Geo, ArA, R, Uga, SA, I, F, Ar, Geo*

W Alberts 1991 *Sp, Pt, It, It, Z, Z, I, I, Z, Z, Z,* 1995 *Z,* 1996 *Z, Z*

H Amakali 2005 *Mad*

J Augustyn 1991 *Z,* 1998 *Iv, Mor, Z*

RS Bardenhorst 2007 *Geo, ArA, R*

J Barnard 1990 *Z, Pt, W, W, F, F,* 1991 *Sp, Pt, It, It, Z, Z, I, I, Z, Z, Z,* 1992 *Z, Z*

D Beukes 2000 *Z, Ur,* 2001 *Z, Z*

E Beukes 1990 *Z, F, WGe*

J Beukes 1994 *Z, Mor,* 1995 *Z*

AJ Blaauw 1996 *Z, Z,* 1997 *Tg, Z,* 1998 *Pt, Tun, Z, Iv, Mor, Z,* 1999 *Z, Fj, F, C, Ger,* 2000 *SA23, Z, SA23, Z, Ur,* 2001 *SA23, SA23, It,* 2003 *Ar, I, A, R,* 2004 *Mor*

J Bock 2005 *Mad, Mor,* 2009 *Iv, Iv*

JH Bock 2005 *Mad, Mor,* 2006 *Ken, Tun, Ken, Tun, Mor, Mor,* 2007 *Za, ArA, R, SA, I, F, Ar, Geo*

J Booysen 2003 *Sa, Ken, Ar, A,* 2007 *Uga*

M Booysen 1993 *W, AG, Z,* 1994 *Rus, Z, HK,* 1996 *Z, Z*

LW Botes 2006 *Ken, Mor,* 2007 *Za, Geo, ArA, R, Uga, SA, F*

Botha 2008 *Z,* 2009 *Iv, Iv*

HP Botha 2000 *SA23, Z, SA23, Z, Ur*

H Breedt 1997 *Z,* 1998 *Tun, Z*

H Brink 1992 *Z,* 1993 *W, Ken, Z,* 1994 *Rus, Z, Iv, Mor, HK*

J Britz 1996 *Z*

B Buitendag 1990 *W, W, F, F, WGe, EngB,* 1991 *Sp, Pt, It, It, Z, Z, I, I, Z, Z, Z,* 1992 *Z, Z,* 1993 *W, AG, Ken, Z*

J Burger 2004 *Za, Ken, Z, Mor,* 2006 *Tun, Tun, Mor, Mor,* 2007 *Za, Geo, ArA, R, SA, I, F, Ar, Geo,* 2008 *Z,* 2009 *Iv, Iv*

B Calitz 1995 *Z*

C Campbell 2008 *Z*

DJ Coetzee 1990 *Pt, W, F, F, WGe,* 1991 *Sp, Pt, It, It, Z, Z, I, I, Z, Z, Z,* 1992 *Z, Z,* 1993 *W, AG, Ken, Z,* 1994 *Z, Iv, Mor, HK,* 1995 *Z, Z*

JC Coetzee 1990 *W*

M Couw 2006 *Ken*

B Cronjé 1994 *Rus*

J Dames 1997 *Z,* 1998 *Tun, Z*

D de Beer 2000 *Z*

S de Beer 1995 *Z,* 1997 *Tg, Z,* 1998 *Tun, Z, Iv, Mor, Z,* 1999 *Z*

AD de Klerk 2009 *Iv, Iv*

H de Waal 1990 *Z, Pt*

N de Wet 2000 *Ur*

R Dedig 2004 *Mor, Za, Ken, Z, Mor*

CJH Derks 1990 *Z, Pt, W, W, F, F, WGe, EngB,* 1991 *Sp, Pt, It, It, Z, Z, I, I, Z, Z, Z,* 1992 *Z, Z,* 1993 *W, AG, Z,* 1994 *Rus, Z, Iv, Mor, HK*

J Deysel 1990 *Z, Pt, W, W, EngB,* 1991 *Sp, Pt, It, It, Z, Z, I, I, Z, Z, Z,* 1992 *Z*

V Dreyer 2002 *Z,* 2003 *Ar, I*

J Drotsky 2006 *Ken,* 2008 *Sen*

I du Plessis 2005 *Mor*

M du Plessis 2001 *Z,* 2005 *Mor*

N du Plessis 1993 *Ken,* 1994 *Rus,* 1995 *Z*

O du Plessis 2008 *Sen*

T du Plessis 2006 *Ken, Tun, Mor, Mor,* 2007 *Geo, R, Uga, SA, I, F, Ar, Geo,* 2008 *Sen, Z,* 2009 *Iv, Iv*

P du Plooy 1992 *Z, Z,* 1994 *Z, Mor, HK*

S du Rand 2007 *Geo, ArA, R, Uga*

JA du Toit 2007 *Za, Geo, ArA, R, Uga, SA, I, F, Geo,* 2008 *Sen, Z*

N du Toit 2002 *Tun,* 2003 *Sa, Ar, I, A, R*

V du Toit 1990 *Pt, W, W, F*

JH Duvenhage 2000 *SA23, Z, SA23, Z,* 2001 *SA23, SA23, It, Z, Z,* 2002 *Mad,* 2003 *Sa, Uga, Ar, I, R,* 2007 *Za, ArA, R, Uga*

A Engelbrecht 2000 *SA23, Z*

J Engelbrecht 1990 *WGe,* 1994 *Rus, Z, Iv, Mor, HK,* 1995 *Z, Z*

N Engelbrecht 1996 *Z*

H Engels 1990 *F, WGe*

E Erasmus 1997 *Tg, Z*

G Esterhuizen 2008 *Sen, Z*

N Esterhuizen 2006 *Ken, Tun, Mor,* 2007 *Za, Geo, ArA, R, Uga, SA, I, F, Ar, Geo,* 2008 *Z,* 2009 *Iv, Iv*

SF Esterhuizen 2008 *Z,* 2009 *Iv, Iv*

D Farmer 1997 *Tg, Z,* 1998 *Pt, Iv, Mor, Z,* 1999 *Z, Fj, Ger*

F Fisch 1999 *Z, Ger*

S Furter 1999 *Z, Fj, F, C, Ger,* 2001 *SA23, SA23, It,* 2002 *Mad, Z, Tun, Tun,* 2003 *Sa, Ken, Uga, Ar, I, A, R,* 2004 *Mor,* 2006 *Ken, Tun, Ken*

E Gaoab 2005 *Mad, Mor*

I Gaya 2004 *Za, Ken*

J Genis 2000 *SA23, Z, SA23, Z, Ur,* 2001 *Z*

N Genis 2006 *Mor*

R Gentz 2001 *It*

R Glundeung 2006 *Ken*

CJ Goosen 1991 *Sp, Pt, It, It,* 1993 *W*

D Gouws 1997 *Z,* 2000 *SA23, Z, SA23, Z, Ur,* 2001 *SA23, SA23, It, Z, Z*

T Gouws 2003 *Ken, Uga,* 2004 *Za, Ken,* 2006 *Ken, Tun*

A Graham 2001 *SA23, SA23, It, Z, Z,* 2002 *Mad, Tun,* 2003 *Ken, Uga, I,* 2004 *Mor*

A Greeff 1997 *Tg*

D Grobelaar 2008 *Z*

DP Grobler 2001 *Z,* 2002 *Mad, Tun, Tun,* 2003 *Sa, Ken, Uga, Ar, I, A, R,* 2004 *Mor, Za, Ken, Z, Mor,* 2006 *Ken, Tun, Ken,* 2007 *Za, Geo, ArA, R, SA, Ar*

HJ Grobler 1990 *Z, Pt, W, W, F, F, WGe, EngB,* 1991 *Sp, Pt, It, It, Z, Z, I, I, Z, Z, Z,* 1992 *Z, Z*

T Grünewald 1990 *Z*

D Grunschloss 2003 *A, R*

F Hartung 1996 *Z, Z*

L Holtzhausen 1997 *Tg, Z,* 1998 *Pt, Tun, Z, Iv, Mor, Z,* 1999 *Ger*

F Horn 2005 *Mad, Mor,* 2006 *Ken*

H Horn 1997 *Tg,* 1998 *Pt, Iv, Mor, Z,* 1999 *Z, Fj, F, C, Ger,* 2001 *SA23, SA23, It,* 2002 *Mad, Z, Tun,* 2003 *Sa,* 2007 *Za, Geo, R, Uga, SA, I, F, Ar, Geo,* 2008 *Sen, Z,* 2009 *Iv, Iv*

K Horn 1997 *Tg,* 1998 *Pt*

Q Hough 1995 *Z, Z,* 1997 *Z,* 1998 *Pt, Tun, Z, Iv, Mor, Z,* 1999 *Z, Fj, F, C*

D Husselman 1993 *AG,* 1994 *Z, Mor,* 2002 *Mad, Z, Tun,* 2003 *Sa, Ar, I, A*

JJ Husselman 2004 *Za, Ken*

E Isaacs 1993 *Ken,* 1994 *Iv*

P Isaacs 2000 *SA23, Z, SA23, Z, Ur,* 2001 *Z, Z,* 2003 *A,* 2005 *Mad, Mor*

E Izaacs 1998 *Pt,* 1999 *Z, Ger,* 2000 *Z, SA23, Z, Ur,* 2001 *SA23, SA23, It, Z, Z,* 2002 *Mad, Z, Tun, Tun,* 2003 *Sa, Ken, Ar, A, R*

M Jacobs 1999 *Z, Fj, F, Ger*

E Jansen 2006 *Ken*

EA Jantjies 2006 Ken, Tun, Ken, Tun, 2007 Za, Geo, ArA, R, Uga, SA, I, F, Ar, Geo, 2008 Sen, Z, 2009 Iv, Iv
R Jantjies 1994 HK, 1995 Z, Z, 1996 Z, 1997 Z, 1998 Pt, Tun, Iv, Mor, Z, 1999 Z, Fj, F, C, 2000 SA23, Z, SA23, Z
M Jeary 2003 Uga, 2004 Ken, Z, Mor
R Jeary 2000 SA23, SA23, Z, Ur
D Jeffrey 1990 F
J Jenkins 2002 Mad, Tun, 2003 Ken
D Kamonga 2004 Mor, Za, Ken, Z, Mor, 2007 Uga, Geo
M Kapitako 2000 Z, SA23, Z, 2001 It, Z, Z, 2003 Uga, 2004 Za, 2006 Tun
M Katjiuanjo 2005 Mad, Mor
M Kazombiaze 2006 Ken, Tun
U Kazombiaze 2006 Ken, Tun, Mor, Mor, 2007 Za, ArA, Uga, SA, I, F, Ar, Geo, 2008 Sen, Z, 2009 Iv, Iv
DPW Koen 2006 Tun
A Kotze 1991 Sp, Z, Z, I, I, 1993 W, AG, Z
D Kotze 1993 W, AG, Ken, Z, 1994 Rus, HK
J Kotze 1995 Z, Z, 1996 Z, Z, 2000 SA23, Z, SA23, Z, 2001 SA23, SA23, It, Z, Z, 2002 Mad, Z, Tun, Tun, 2004 Za, Ken, Z, Mor
P Kotze 2001 SA23, SA23, It
P Kotze 1996 Z
L Kotzee 2008 Z
JL Kruger 2001 SA23, It, Z, Z
R Kruger 2003 Ken, Uga, 2005 Mad, Mor
R Kruger 2004 Mor, Za, Ken, Mor
SO Lambert 2000 SA23, Z, Ur, 2001 SA23, It, Z, Z, 2003 Ken, Uga, 2004 Mor, 2005 Mad, 2006 Tun, Ken
B Langenhoven 2007 SA, I, F, Ar, Geo, 2008 Sen, Z
G Lensing 2002 Mad, Z, Tun, Tun, 2003 Sa, Ar, I, A, R, 2004 Mor, 2006 Ken, Mor, Mor, 2007 ArA, R, SA, I, F, Ar, Geo, 2009 Iv, Iv
C Lesch 2005 Mad, Mor
HD Lindvelt 1998 Iv, Z, 1999 F, C, Ger, 2001 It, Z, Z, 2002 Mad, Z, Tun, Tun, 2003 Sa, Ken, Uga, Ar, I, A, 2004 Mor, Za, Ken, Z, Mor, 2006 Ken, Tun, Mor, 2007 Za, Geo, ArA, SA, F, Ar
J Lombaard 1996 Z
H Loots 1990 Z
J Losper 2005 Mor
S Losper 1990 Z, Pt, W, W, F, F, WGe, EngB, 1991 Sp, Pt, It, It, Z, Z, I, I, Z, Z, Z
TC Losper 2007 Za, Geo, ArA, R, Uga, SA, I, F, 2008 Sen
W Lötter 1990 Z
RC Loubser 1999 F, 2005 Mad, Mor
O Louw 1993 Ken, Z, 1994 Z, Iv, 1996 Z
W Ludwig 2001 SA23
M MacKenzie 2004 Mor, 2006 Ken, Tun, 2007 Uga, I, F, Ar
B Malgas 1991 Z, Z, Z, 1993 W, AG, Ken, Z, 1994 Rus, Z, Iv, Mor, HK, 1995 Z, Z, 1996 Z
G Mans 1990 Z, Pt, W, W, F, EngB, 1991 Sp, Pt, It, It, Z, Z, I, I, Z, Z, Z, 1992 Z, Z, 1993 W, AG, Ken, Z, 1994 Rus, Z, Iv, Mor, HK
M Marais 1992 Z, 1993 W, AG, Z
W Maritz 1990 Z, EngB, 1991 Z, Z, I, I, Z, Z, Z
S McCulley 1990 W, W, F, WGe
E Meyer 1991 Sp, Pt, It, It, Z, Z, I, I, Z, Z, Z, 1992 Z, Z, 1993 W, 1994 Z, Iv, Mor, HK, 1995 Z, Z, 1996 Z
H Meyer 2004 Za, Ken, Z, Mor
JM Meyer 2003 Ken, Uga, Ar, I, R, 2006 Ken, Tun, Tun, Mor, Mor, 2007 Uga, SA, I, F, Ar, Geo
P Meyer 2005 Mad
DA Mouton 1999 Z, Fj, Ger, 2000 SA23, Z, SA23, Z, Ur, 2001 SA23, 2002 Mad, Z, Tun, 2003 Sa, Ken, Uga, Ar, I, A, R, 2004 Mor, 2005 Mad, Mor, 2006 Tun, Ken, Tun, Mor, 2007 Ar, 2008 Sen
H Mouton 2000 Z
P Mouton 2005 Mad, Mor
H Neethling 1993 Ken
G Nel 2006 Mor, Mor
S Nell 2000 SA23, Z, SA23, Z
J Nienaber 1998 Pt, Tun, Z, Mor, Z
J Nieuwenhuis 2007 Za, Geo, ArA, R, Uga, SA, I, F, Geo, 2008 Sen, Z, 2009 Iv, Iv
J Olivier 1999 Z, Fj, Ger, 2000 SA23, Z, Z, Ur
M Olivier 1990 Pt, F, EngB
LT Oosthuizen 1990 Z, Pt, W, W, F, F, WGe, EngB
J Opperman 1999 Z, Fj, F, C, Ger
T Opperman 2002 Mad, Z

WJ Otto 1993 AG, Z, 1994 Rus
R Pedro 1998 Z, 1999 Ger, 2000 Ur, 2001 SA23, SA23, It, Z, Z, 2003 Sa, Ken, Uga, Ar, I, A, R, 2004 Mor
D Philander 2008 Sen, 2009 Iv, Iv
F Pienaar 2006 Ken
D Pieters 2008 Sen
L Plaath 2001 SA23, SA23, It, Z, Z
CJ Powell 2001 SA23, It, Z, Z, 2002 Mad, Z, Tun, Tun, 2003 Sa, Ken, Uga, Ar, I, R, 2004 Mor, Ken, Z, Mor, 2006 Ken, Tun, Tun, Mor, Mor, 2007 Za, Geo, ArA, R, Ar, Geo
JH Redelinghuys 2006 Ken, Tun, Mor, 2007 Za, Geo, R, Uga, SA, I, F, Ar, Geo, 2008 Sen, Z, 2009 Iv, Iv
C Redlinghaus 2001 SA23, SA23, It
H Reinders 1996 Z
G Rich 1993 W
C Roets 1995 Z
P Rossouw 2004 Za, Ken, Z, Mor, 2005 Mad, Mor, 2006 Mor, Mor, 2007 Za, Geo, ArA, R
A Samuelson 1995 Z, 1996 Z, Z, 1997 Tg, Z, 1998 Pt, Tun, Z, Iv, Mor, Z, 1999 Z, Fj, F, C, Ger
M Schreuder 2002 Mad, Z, Tun, Tun, 2003 Sa, Ken, Uga, I, A, R, 2004 Mor, Za, Ken, Z, Mor, 2006 Ken, Ken, 2007 Ar, Geo
C Schumacher 1995 Z, 1997 Z
JH Senekal 1998 Iv, Mor, Z, 1999 Z, Fj, F, C, Ger, 2002 Mad, Z, 2003 Sa, Ken, Uga, Ar, I, A, R, 2005 Mad, 2006 Ken, Mor, Mor, 2007 Geo, ArA, R, Uga, I, Ar, Geo
A Skinner 1990 Z, Pt, W, W, F, F, WGe, EngB
G Smit 1990 F
E Smith 1998 Tun, Iv, Mor, Z, 1999 Fj, F, C, 2002 Mad
P Smith 1993 Ken, 1994 Iv, 1995 Z, Z
S Smith 1990 Pt, W, W, F, EngB, 1992 Z, Z, 1993 W, AG, Ken, Z, 1994 Rus, Z, Iv, Mor, HK, 1996 Z
W Smith 2002 Mad, Z, Tun
D Snyders 2003 Uga, 2005 Mad
H Snyman 1990 F, F, 1991 Sp, Pt, It, It, Z, Z, I, I, Z, Z, Z, 1992 Z, Z, 1993 W, AG, Ken, Z, 1994 Z, Iv, Mor, HK, 1995 Z, Z, 1996 Z, Z
M Snyman 1994 Rus, Z, Iv, Mor, HK
D Spangenberg 2005 Mad, Mor
A Steenkamp 1994 Iv, Mor
C Steenkamp 2007 Uga
T Steenkamp 1992 Z, Z, 1993 Ken, 1994 Rus, Iv, 1995 Z, 1996 Z, 1998 Pt, Tun, Z
P Steyn 1996 Z, Z, 1997 Tg, Z, 1998 Pt, Tun, Z, Iv, Mor, 1999 Z, Fj, F, C
A Stoop 1990 Z, Pt, W, EngB, 1991 Sp, Pt, It, It, Z, I, I, Z
L Stoop 1994 Iv
G Suze 2005 Mad
N Swanepoel 2003 Ken, Ar, I, A, R, 2004 Mor, Za, Ken, Z, Mor
H Swart 1995 Z, 1996 Z, 1997 Tg, Z, 1998 Pt, Tun, Z
JL Swart 1990 F, WGe
BM Swartz 1990 W, W, F, F, WGe, EngB
R Theart 1990 Pt
J Theron 1998 Iv, Mor, Z, 1999 Fj, F, C, Ger, 2004 Mor
RHR Thompson 2004 Za, Ken, Mor, 2005 Mad, 2006 Ken, Tun, Ken, Tun, Mor, Mor
D Tredoux 2001 Z
H Undveld 2006 Ken
L van Coller 1993 AG, Ken, 1994 Rus, Iv
GE van der Berg 2006 Ken, Tun, Tun, Mor
L van der Linde 2006 Tun
A van der Merwe 1990 Pt, W, W, F, F, WGe, EngB, 1991 Sp, Pt, It, It, Z, Z, I, I, Z, Z, Z, 1992 Z, Z
D van der Merwe 1990 WGe
S van der Merwe 1997 Tg, Z, 1998 Iv, Mor, Z, 1999 Z, Fj, F, C, 2002 Z, Tun, Tun, 2003 Sa, Ken, Ar, I, A, R, 2004 Za, Ken, Z, Mor, 2006 Tun, Mor
J van der Westhuizen 2007 Za, Geo
L van Dyk 1998 Tun, Z, Iv, Mor, Z, 1999 Fj, F, C, Ger, 2002 Mad
JA van Lill 2002 Mad, Tun, Tun, 2003 Sa, Ar, I, A, R, 2004 Mor, 2006 Tun, 2007 Za, ArA
PJ van Lill 2006 Ken, 2008 Sen, Z, 2009 Iv
F van Rensburg 1995 Z, 1996 Z, Z, 1997 Tg, 1998 Tun, Z, 1999 Z, Fj, F, C, Ger, 2000 Z, 2001 It, Z, Z
SJ van Rensburg 1998 Z, Iv, Mor, Z, 1999 Z, Fj, F, Ger, 2000 Z, Ur

S van Rooi 2003 *Uga, A,* 2004 *Mor,* 2005 *Mor*
A van Rooyen 1991 *Sp, Pt, It, It, I,* 1992 *Z, Z*
M van Rooyen 1996 *Z,* 1998 *Pt, Tun, Z, Mor, Z,* 1999 *Z, F, C*
C van Schalkwyk 1993 *AG, Z*
A Van Tonder 1995 *Z*
CJ van Tonder 2002 *Tun,* 2003 *Sa, Ken, Uga, I, A, R,*
    2004 *Mor, Za, Ken, Z, Mor,* 2006 *Ken, Ken,* 2007 *Za*
JH van Tonder 2004 *Mor, Ken, Z, Mor,* 2006 *Ken, Tun,*
    2007 *Uga, SA, I, F, Ar, Geo,* 2008 *Z,* 2009 *Iv, Iv*
N van Vuuren 1993 *AG*
RJ van Vuuren 1997 *Tg, Z,* 1998 *Pt, Tun, Z,* 1999 *Z, Ger,*
    2000 *SA23, Z, SA23, Z, Ur,* 2002 *Mad, Z,* 2003 *Ken, Uga,*
    R
A van Wyk 1993 *W, Ken,* 1994 *Iv, HK*
G van Wyk 1999 *Z, Fj, F, C,* 2000 *Z, SA23, Z, Ur,* 2001 *It*
L van Wyk 2004 *Mor*
M van Wyk 2009 *Iv, Iv*
R van Wyk 2002 *Mad, Z, Tun, Tun,* 2003 *Sa,* 2004 *Mor,*
    Za, Ken, Z, Mor
R van Wyk 2004 *Za, Ken, Z, Mor*
J van Zyl 2008 *Sen*
P van Zyl 2007 *SA, I, F, Ar, Geo,* 2008 *Z,* 2009 *Iv, Iv*

R van Zyl 1997 *Tg, Z,* 1998 *Tun, Z, Iv, Mor, Z*
T Venter 2003 *Uga,* 2004 *Mor,* 2008 *Z,* 2009 *Iv, Iv*
D Vermaak 1998 *Z*
JJ Vermaak 1990 *Pt,* 1994 *Rus,* 1996 *Z*
B Vermeulen 1995 *Z*
D Vermeulen 1996 *Z, Z,* 1997 *Tg, Z,* 1998 *Pt*
G Vermeulen 1990 *EngB,* 1991 *Z*
M Visser 2007 *Za, Geo, ArA, R, Uga, SA, Ar, Geo,* 2009
    Iv, Iv
P von Wielligh 1991 *It, Z,* 1992 *Z,* 1993 *AG, Z,* 1994 *Iv,*
    Mor, 1995 *Z,* 1996 *Z*
G Walters 2008 *Z,* 2009 *Iv*
W Wentzel 1991 *Sp, Z, Z*
E Wessels 2002 *Tun, Tun,* 2003 *Sa, Ar, I, A, R,* 2006 *Tun,*
    Mor, Mor, 2007 *SA, I, F,* 2009 *Iv*
L Winkler 2008 *Z,* 2009 *Iv, Iv*
RC Witbooi 2004 *Za, Z,* 2005 *Mor,* 2006 *Ken, Tun, Ken,*
    2007 *Za, Geo, R, Uga, I, F, Geo,* 2008 *Sen*
J Wohler 2005 *Mad, Mor*
J Zaayman 1997 *Tg, Z,* 1998 *Pt, Tun, Z, Iv, Mor, Z,* 1999
    Z, Fj, F, C, Ger

Gallo Images/Getty Images

Herman Lindvelt, Namibia's most capped player.

NEW ZEALAND

NEW ZEALAND'S 2008–09 TEST RECORD

OPPONENTS	DATE	VENUE	RESULT
Australia	1 November	N	**Won** 19–14
Scotland	8 November	A	**Won** 32–6
Ireland	15 November	A	**Won** 22–3
Wales	22 November	A	**Won** 29–9
England	29 November	A	**Won** 32–6
France	13 June	H	**Lost** 27–22
France	20 June	H	**Won** 14–10
Italy	27 June	H	**Won** 27–6
Australia	18 July	H	**Won** 22–16
South Africa	25 July	A	**Lost** 19–28
South Africa	1 August	A	**Lost** 19–31
New Zealand	22 August	A	**Won** 19–18
South Africa	12 September	H	**Lost** 29–32
Australia	19 September	H	**Won** 33–6

ALL BLACKS BELOW PAR

By Iain Spragg

New Zealand's Ma'a Nonu (L) and Mils Muliana (R) may have finished the Tri-Nations without a trophy, but at least with a win over Australia.

There is an old saying that one player, however great, does not make a team. The inimitable Dan Carter would probably agree but the painful truth for the All Blacks as their 2008–09 campaign unfolded was that without the Crusaders fly-half orchestrating the troops, they struggled to dominate the rugby landscape in the manner to which they have become accustomed.

Carter headed into a self-imposed international exile after New Zealand's all-conquering tour of Britain and Ireland in the autumn of 2008. The NZRU had agreed to his request for a sabbatical with Top 14 side Perpignan and the outstanding No.10 headed to France for a breather from the rigours of Test match rugby.

Whether the All Blacks' subsequent woes could be solely attributed to Carter's absence is a matter of debate but the fact remained the team lost three of the six internationals they played without the talismanic fly-half in the ranks. New Zealand and their adoring public were certainly not used to such modest returns.

Carter returned to international action in August after recovering from a ruptured Achilles tendon sustained playing in France in January and although New Zealand duly won two of their three remaining games with their star turn back in harness, it was not enough to stop the Springboks dethroning Graham Henry's side as Tri-Nations champions after a four-year reign.

Their uncharacteristic slump was all the more disappointing given that the Kiwis had begun the 2008–09 campaign in more characteristically bullish fashion. With a fourth successive Tri-Nations crown safely secured in September, they headed to Hong Kong in November for a ground-breaking clash with Australia and a first encounter on neutral soil in the 77-year history of the Bledisloe Cup.

The All Blacks had beaten the Wallabies in three of their last four meetings and the unfamiliar surroundings of the So Kon Po Stadium did not unduly upset the rhythm of Henry's team, who replied to two first half tries from Australia's Drew Mitchell with scores after the break from Sitiveni Sivivatu and Richie McCaw to record a 19–14 win.

Carter started the game at inside centre to facilitate a first Test start for Chiefs' fly-half Stephen Donald but Henry abandoned the experiment after 50 minutes and it was ultimately to be Carter's three penalties that was the difference between the two teams.

New Zealand then packed their bags for their annual northern hemisphere trip. Scotland were their first opponents a week later and Henry opted for a largely second-string line-up with Carter and McCaw both named among the substitutes. The All Blacks, however, were still too strong for the home side at Murrayfield and tries from Anthony Tuitavake, Piri Weepu, Richard Kahui and Anthony Boric sealed a routine 32–6 success and a winning start to the tour.

In recognition of the greater threat posed by Ireland, Henry recalled his big guns for their first appearance at Croke Park the following week. The Irish had high hopes of claiming a famous scalp to mark Brian O'Driscoll's 50th game as captain but they were never in the hunt and New Zealand cantered to a 22–3 victory on the back of second half tries from Ma'a Nonu and Brad Thorn.

Reigning Six Nations champions Wales lay in wait in Cardiff and Carter's importance to the side was all too apparent as the All Blacks were forced to recover from a 9–6 half-time deficit to emerge 29–9 victors. The Welsh gave the tourists a stern examination and New Zealand were indebted to 19 points from their fly-half as they kept their dreams of an unbeaten tour alive.

"To hang in there under pressure and come through is a mark of the character of this side," a relieved Henry admitted. "We scored 23 points to none in the second half and that is huge.

"I thought we were superb in the second half which was probably the best 40 minutes of rugby we had produced all year. It was a hell of a good Test match that was mightily competitive. We can start talking about the grand slam now it is a reality."

The climax of the tour came at Twickenham at the end of November. There was only one change to the side that had triumphed at the Millennium Stadium with the recall of the fit-again Conrad Smith in the midfield in place of Kahui and the All Blacks were ready for battle.

England were desperate for a morale-boosting performance, if not victory, after heavy defeats to Australia and South Africa but it was not to be as the All Blacks shrugged off their first half lethargy to produce a dominate performance and 32–6 win.

The home side had four players sin-binned during the course of the game but New Zealand were nonetheless dominate from the start and a brace of tries after the break from Mils Muliaina and a third from Nonu merely underlined their superiority.

"We've got great character and we've shown that all tour with the way we've played in the second half," said Carter, who amassed a personal tally of 17 points at Twickenham. "The grand slam hasn't happened very often and to be part of two is something that means a lot to me.

"We lost a lot of experienced players this year and we've had a lot of new faces coming into the team who've really stepped up – that's been huge. To bounce back and have a year like we've had, winning a few trophies and introduce some new guys to Test match footy has been great. It's been a great season and what a way to finish it off."

Carter headed off to France for his Gallic sojourn while the All Blacks went into hibernation until the summer and a two-Test series at home against France followed by a one-off game with Italy in Christchurch.

With McCaw unavailable for the games through injury, Henry named Muliaina as captain when he announced his squad in May while second row Isaac Ross, prop Wyatt Crockett and flanker Tanerau Latimer were among the uncapped players included.

The French went into the first Test in Dunedin looking for their first win on New Zealand soil in 15 years – and only their third ever – and with a youthful-looking All Black side between them and an historic victory.

Les Bleus clearly sensed an opportunity and in a destructive 27-minute first half burst they breached the Kiwi defence twice through fly-half Francois Trinh-Duc and hooker William Servat to establish a commanding 17–3 lead. New Zealand rallied with a try from No.8 **347** Liam Messam and three penalties from Donald but an interception try from full-back Maxime Médard put pay to the revival and France won 27–22.

"We were out-muscled in the first half hour," admitted Muliaina after the final whistle. "You don't want to use it as an excuse but we are a relatively young side and the way they came back from 17–3 down showed a bit of ticker there."

The opportunity for Henry's side to redeem themselves came seven days later in the shape of the second Test in Wellington. The rain lashed down in the Westpac Stadium and the contest became a war of attrition as the New Zealand pack produced a much improved performance. Nonu crossed the whitewash for the home side while Cedric Heymans scored a superb solo try for Les Bleus but at the final whistle it was the All Blacks who had their noses in front to emerge 14–10 winners. The result, however, was not enough to secure the Dave Gallaher Cup, awarded to the series victors, and for the first time in nine years of competing for the trophy, the French claimed the silverware on points difference.

The final warm-up game before the start of the Tri-Nations was against Italy in Christchurch, but the Azzurri never threatened to pull off a shock victory and tries from Joe Rokocoko, Ross and George Whitelock in a 27–6 win ensured the Kiwis maintained their 100 percent record against the Italians.

New Zealand's Tri-Nations opener against Australia at Eden Park in mid July was a titanic tussle. The Wallabies built an early lead with a Berrick Barnes try but Henry's troops rallied and a score from McCaw and 17 points from the boot of Donald secured a 22–16 triumph and continued the Wallabies' dismal record in Auckland, where they have not won since 1986.

The All Blacks now faced three successive games on the road, two in South Africa followed by a trip across the Tasman Sea to face Australia.

The Test in Bloemfontein saw the All Blacks struggle in the set pieces against the Springboks, buoyed by their recent series victory over the British & Irish Lions, and although the impressive Smith scored for the visitors, tries from Jaque Fourie and Ruan Pienaar proved decisive as South Africa claimed a 28–19 win.

"We weren't smart enough to play at the right end of the field in that first half," admitted McCaw. "I thought we defended pretty well but it was what we were doing post-tackle, going off our feet. The Springboks played particularly well and simple mistakes forced us to play at our own end of the field. Points came from there."

Henry resisted the temptation to make sweeping changes for the following game in Durban, naming Owen Franks at tight-head in place of Neemia Tialata and recalling Jimmy Cowan at scrum-half at the expense of Brendon Leonard.

The All Blacks took an early lead at King's Park through lock Ross but indiscipline was to prove costly and they were eventually beaten 31–19 after a record-breaking display from Morné Steyn. The Springbok fly-half scored and converted his side's only try and also landed eight penalties for a personal haul of 31 points to eclipse the previous Tri-Nations record of 29 points set by Andrew Mehrtens against Australia a decade earlier.

New Zealand were now faced with the unfamiliar prospect of losing three successive Test matches but avoided setting an unwanted milestone with a narrow 19–18 victory over the Australians in Sydney. The match marked Carter's return to the All Blacks fold and his contribution of a conversion to Nonu's try and four penalties was crucial.

"I was just very proud of the character shown by the players tonight," a relieved Henry admitted afterwards. "It was just mental toughness, because we didn't get the roll of the dice. The Australians are a very good side and they really stretched us tonight and there was just a feeling of pride after the game for what the guys achieved. Our guys showed

Ross Land/Getty Images

The year started so well for the All Blacks with a Grand Slam in Europe, under skipper Richie McCaw.

a huge amount of intestinal fortitude. It just shows the guys have got the guts to hang in and keep going."

The result revived New Zealand hopes of stopping South Africa's march to the title. Victory over the Springboks in Hamilton would ensure the champions would not be decided until the final game of the competition and the two sides prepared for battle in the Waikato Stadium and one of the biggest matches in the 88-year history of the fixture.

New Zealand drew first blood with an early penalty from Carter but two long-range kicks from inside his own half by Frans Steyn gave South Africa the advantage. A mistake from Rokocoko gifted Fourie du Preez the first try of the match and a third monster penalty from Steyn ensured the Springboks went in at half-time with a 10-point lead.

The pivotal point of the game came soon after the restart when Carter attempted an ambitious pass to Isaia Toeava only to see it intercepted by Jean de Villiers, who raced over for South Africa's second try. New Zealand were now playing catch-up rugby and although Henry's side did respond with scores from McCaw and Sivivatu, they had left themselves too much to do and South Africa held on for a dramatic 32–29 victory that saw them crowned Tri-Nations champions for the third time.

"It's hard to see those ones go over," McCaw said as he reflected on defeat and Frans Steyn's crucial long-range penalties. "You can't afford to have ill discipline. In the first half we were slow to get into the game. One positive is we did stick at it. We wanted to put some pressure on them, which I think we did quite well. It did come right and it's testament to the guys hanging in there. In Test match rugby, you've got to do it right from the start."

New Zealand ended the campaign with a comfortable 33–6 win over the Wallabies in Wellington to confirm the All Blacks as runners-up, but the three defeats to South Africa were a bitter pill to swallow for Henry and his misfiring team. The All Blacks have two years to rebuild before they host Rugby World Cup 2011 and on the evidence of their performances in 2008–09, Henry will be acutely aware that he has plenty to work on.

NEW ZEALAND INTERNATIONAL STATISTICS

MATCH RECORDS UP TO 30TH SEPTEMBER 2009

MOST CONSECUTIVE TEST WINS

17 1965 SA 4, 1966 BI 1,2,3,4, 1967 A,E,W,F,S, 1968 A 1,2, F 1,2,3, 1969 W 1,2

15 2005 A 1, SA 2, A 2, W,I E,S, 2006 I 1,2, Arg, A 1, SA 1, A 2, 3, SA 2

12 1988 A 3, 1989 F 1,2, Arg 1,2, A,W,I, 1990 S 1,2, A 1,2

MOST CONSECUTIVE TESTS WITHOUT DEFEAT

Matches	Wins	Draws	Periods
23	22	1	1987 to 1990
17	17	0	1965 to 1969
17	15	2	1961 to 1964
15	15	0	2005 to 2006

MOST POINTS IN A MATCH
BY THE TEAM

Pts.	Opponents	Venue	Year
145	Japan	Bloemfontein	1995
108	Portugal	Lyons	2007
102	Tonga	Albany	2000
101	Italy	Huddersfield	1999
101	Samoa	N Plymouth	2008
93	Argentina	Wellington	1997
91	Tonga	Brisbane	2003
91	Fiji	Albany	2005
85	Romania	Toulouse	2007
76	Italy	Marseilles	2007
74	Fiji	Christchurch	1987
73	Canada	Auckland	1995
71	Fiji	Albany	1997
71	Samoa	Albany	1999

BY A PLAYER

Pts.	Player	Opponents	Venue	Year
45	S D Culhane	Japan	Bloemfontein	1995
36	T E Brown	Italy	Huddersfield	1999
33	C J Spencer	Argentina	Wellington	1997
33	A P Mehrtens	Ireland	Dublin	1997
33	D W Carter	British/Irish	Wellington	2005
33	N J Evans	Portugal	Lyons	2007
32	T E Brown	Tonga	Albany	2000
30	M C G Ellis	Japan	Bloemfontein	1995
30	T E Brown	Samoa	Albany	2001
29	A P Mehrtens	Australia	Auckland	1999
29	A P Mehrtens	France	Paris	2000
29	L R MacDonald	Tonga	Brisbane	2003
29	D W Carter	Canada	Hamilton	2007

MOST TRIES IN A MATCH
BY THE TEAM

Tries	Opponents	Venue	Year
21	Japan	Bloemfontein	1995
16	Portugal	Lyons	2007
15	Tonga	Albany	2000
15	Fiji	Albany	2005
15	Samoa	N Plymouth	2008
14	Argentina	Wellington	1997
14	Italy	Huddersfield	1999
13	U S A	Berkeley	1913
13	Tonga	Brisbane	2003
13	Romania	Toulouse	2007
12	Italy	Auckland	1987
12	Fiji	Christchurch	1987

BY A PLAYER

Tries	Player	Opponents	Venue	Year
6	M C G Ellis	Japan	Bloemfontein	1995
5	J W Wilson	Fiji	Albany	1997
4	D McGregor	England	Crystal Palace	1905
4	C I Green	Fiji	Christchurch	1987
4	J A Gallagher	Fiji	Christchurch	1987
4	J J Kirwan	Wales	Christchurch	1988
4	J T Lomu	England	Cape Town	1995
4	C M Cullen	Scotland	Dunedin	1996
4	J W Wilson	Samoa	Albany	1999
4	J M Muliaina	Canada	Melbourne	2003
4	S W Sivivatu	Fiji	Albany	2005

THE COUNTRIES

MOST CONVERSIONS IN A MATCH
BY THE TEAM

Cons	Opponents	Venue	Year
20	Japan	Bloemfontein	1995
14	Portugal	Lyons	2007
13	Tonga	Brisbane	2003
13	Samoa	N Plymouth	2008
12	Tonga	Albany	2000
11	Italy	Huddersfield	1999
10	Fiji	Christchurch	1987
10	Argentina	Wellington	1997
10	Romania	Toulouse	2007
9	Canada	Melbourne	2003
9	Italy	Marseilles	2007
8	Italy	Auckland	1987
8	Wales	Auckland	1988
8	Fiji	Albany	1997
8	Italy	Hamilton	2003
8	Fiji	Albany	2005

BY A PLAYER

Cons	Player	Opponents	Venue	Year
20	S D Culhane	Japan	Bloemfontein	1995
14	N J Evans	Portugal	Lyons	2007
12	T E Brown	Tonga	Albany	2000
12	L R MacDonald	Tonga	Brisbane	2003
11	T E Brown	Italy	Huddersfield	1999
10	G J Fox	Fiji	Christchurch	1987
10	C J Spencer	Argentina	Wellington	1997
9	D W Carter	Canada	Melbourne	2003
8	G J Fox	Italy	Auckland	1987
8	G J Fox	Wales	Auckland	1988
8	A P Mehrtens	Italy	Hamilton	2002

MOST DROPPED GOALS IN A MATCH
BY THE TEAM

Drops	Opponent	Venue	Year
3	France	Christchurch	1986

BY A PLAYER

Drops	Player	Opponents	Venue	Year
2	O D Bruce	Ireland	Dublin	1978
2	F M Botica	France	Christchurch	1986
2	A P Mehrtens	Australia	Auckland	1995

MOST PENALTIES IN A MATCH
BY THE TEAM

Pens	Opponents	Venue	Year
9	Australia	Auckland	1999
9	France	Paris	2000
7	Western Samoa	Auckland	1993
7	South Africa	Pretoria	1999
7	South Africa	Wellington	2006
7	Australia	Auckland	2007
6	British/Irish Lions	Dunedin	1959
6	England	Christchurch	1985
6	Argentina	Wellington	1987
6	Scotland	Christchurch	1987
6	France	Paris	1990
6	South Africa	Auckland	1994
6	Australia	Brisbane	1996
6	Ireland	Dublin	1997
6	South Africa	Cardiff	1999
6	Scotland	Murrayfield	2001
6	South Africa	Christchurch	2004
6	Australia	Sydney	2004
6	South Africa	Dunedin	2008

BY A PLAYER

Pens	Player	Opponents	Venue	Year
9	A P Mehrtens	Australia	Auckland	1999
9	A P Mehrtens	France	Paris	2000
7	G J Fox	Western Samoa	Auckland	1993
7	A P Mehrtens	South Africa	Pretoria	1999
7	D W Carter	South Africa	Wellington	2006
7	D W Carter	Australia	Auckland	2007
6	D B Clarke	British/Irish Lions	Dunedin	1959
6	K J Crowley	England	Christchurch	1985
6	G J Fox	Argentina	Wellington	1987
6	G J Fox	Scotland	Christchurch	1987
6	G J Fox	France	Paris	1990
6	S P Howarth	South Africa	Auckland	1994
6	A P Mehrtens	Australia	Brisbane	1996
6	A P Mehrtens	Ireland	Dublin	1997
6	A P Mehrtens	South Africa	Cardiff	1999
6	A P Mehrtens	Scotland	Murrayfield	2001
6	D W Carter	South Africa	Dunedin	2008

CAREER RECORDS

MOST CAPPED PLAYERS

Caps	Player	Career Span
92	S B T Fitzpatrick	1986 to 1997
81	J W Marshall	1995 to 2005
79	I D Jones	1990 to 1999
77	J M Muliaina	2003 to 2009
76	R H McCaw	2001 to 2009
74	J F Umaga	1997 to 2005
71	K F Mealamu	2002 to 2009
70	A P Mehrtens	1995 to 2004
67	C R Jack	2001 to 2007
66	G M Somerville	2000 to 2008
63	J J Kirwan	1984 to 1994
63	J T Lomu	1994 to 2002
62	R M Brooke	1992 to 1999
62	D C Howlett	2000 to 2007
62	D W Carter	2003 to 2009
61	A J Williams	2002 to 2008
60	C W Dowd	1993 to 2001
60	J W Wilson	1993 to 2001
60	J T Rokocoko	2003 to 2009
60	R So'oialo	2002 to 2009
59	A D Oliver	1997 to 2007
58	G W Whetton	1981 to 1991
58	Z V Brooke	1987 to 1997
58	C M Cullen	1996 to 2002
58	T D Woodcock	2002 to 2009
57	B T Kelleher	1999 to 2007
56	O M Brown	1992 to 1998
56	L R MacDonald	2000 to 2008
55	C E Meads	1957 to 1971
55	F E Bunce	1992 to 1997
55	M N Jones	1987 to 1998

MOST CONSECUTIVE TESTS

Tests	Player	Career span
63	S B T Fitzpatrick	1986 to 1995
51	C M Cullen	1996 to 2000
49	R M Brooke	1995 to 1999
41	J W Wilson	1996 to 1999
40	G W Whetton	1986 to 1991

MOST TESTS AS CAPTAIN

Tests	Player	Career span
51	S B T Fitzpatrick	1992 to 1997
39	R H McCaw	2004 to 2009
30	W J Whineray	1958 to 1965
23	R D Thorne	2002 to 2007
22	T C Randell	1998 to 2002
21	J F Umaga	2004 to 2005
19	G N K Mourie	1977 to 1982
18	B J Lochore	1966 to 1970
17	A G Dalton	1981 to 1985

MOST POINTS IN TESTS

Points	Player	Tests	Career
967	A P Mehrtens	70	1995 to 2004
930	D W Carter	62	2003 to 2009
645	G J Fox	46	1985 to 1993
291	C J Spencer	35	1997 to 2004
245	D C Howlett	62	2000 to 2007
236	C M Cullen	58	1996 to 2002
234	J W Wilson	60	1993 to 2001
225	J T Rokocoko	60	2003 to 2009
207	D B Clarke	31	1956 to 1964
201	A R Hewson	19	1981 to 1984
185	J T Lomu	63	1994 to 2002
185	J F Umaga	74	1997 to 2005

MOST TRIES IN TESTS

Tries	Player	Tests	Career
49	D C Howlett	62	2000 to 2007
46	C M Cullen	58	1996 to 2002
45	J T Rokocoko	60	2003 to 2009
44	J W Wilson	60	1993 to 2001
37	J T Lomu	63	1994 to 2002
37*	J F Umaga	74	1999 to 2005
35	J J Kirwan	63	1984 to 1994
25	D W Carter	62	2003 to 2009
25	S W Sivivatu	39	2005 to 2009
24	J W Marshall	81	1995 to 2005
24	J M Muliaina	77	2003 to 2009
20	F E Bunce	55	1992 to 1997
19	S S Wilson	34	1977 to 1983
19*	T J Wright	30	1986 to 1991

* Umaga and Wright's hauls each include a penalty try

MOST CONVERSIONS IN TESTS

Cons	Player	Tests	Career
169	A P Mehrtens	70	1995 to 2004
161	D W Carter	62	2003 to 2009
118	G J Fox	46	1985 to 1993
49	C J Spencer	35	1997 to 2004
43	T E Brown	18	1999 to 2001
33	D B Clarke	31	1956 to 1964
32	S D Culhane	6	1995 to 1996

MOST PENALTY GOALS IN TESTS

Penalties	Player	Tests	Career
188	A P Mehrtens	70	1995 to 2004
159	D W Carter	62	2003 to 2009
128	G J Fox	46	1985 to 1993
43	A R Hewson	19	1981 to 1984
41	C J Spencer	35	1997 to 2004
38	D B Clarke	31	1956 to 1964
24	W F McCormick	16	1965 to 1971

THE COUNTRIES

MOST DROPPED GOALS IN TESTS

Drops	Player	Tests	Career
10	A P Mehrtens	70	1995 to 2004
7	G J Fox	46	1985 to 1993
5	D B Clarke	31	1956 to 1964
5	M A Herewini	10	1962 to 1967
5	O D Bruce	14	1976 to 1978

TRI-NATIONS RECORDS

RECORD	DETAIL	HOLDER	SET
Most points in season	179	in six matches	2006
Most tries in season	17	in four matches	1997
	17	in four matches	2003
	17	in six matches	2006
Highest Score	55	55–35 v S Africa (h)	1997
Biggest win	37	43–6 v Australia (h)	1996
Highest score conceded	46	40–46 v S Africa (a)	2000
Biggest defeat	21	7–28 v Australia (a)	1999
Most appearances	35	J W Marshall	1996 to 2004
Most points in matches	363	D W Carter	2003 to 2009
Most points in season	99	D W Carter	2006
Most points in match	29	A P Mehrtens	v Australia (h) 1999
Most tries in matches	16	C M Cullen	1996 to 2002
Most tries in season	7	C M Cullen	2000
Most tries in match	3	J T Rokocoko	v Australia (a) 2003
	3	D C Howlett	v Australia (h) 2005
Most cons in matches	43	D W Carter	2003 to 2009
Most cons in season	14	D W Carter	2006
Most cons in match	4	C J Spencer	v S Africa (h) 1997
	4	A P Mehrtens	v Australia (a) 2000
	4	A P Mehrtens	v S Africa (a) 2000
	4	C J Spencer	v S Africa (a) 2003
	4	D W Carter	v S Africa (a) 2006
	4	D W Carter	v Australia (a) 2008
Most pens in matches	82	A P Mehrtens	1996 to 2004
	82	D W Carter	2003 to 2009
Most pens in season	21	D W Carter	2006
Most pens in match	9	A P Mehrtens	v Australia (h) 1999

NEW ZEALAND

MISCELLANEOUS RECORDS

RECORD	HOLDER	DETAIL
Longest Test Career	E Hughes/C E Meads	1907–21/1957–71
Youngest Test Cap	J T Lomu	19 yrs 45 days in 1994
Oldest Test Cap	E Hughes	40 yrs 123 days in 1921

CAREER RECORDS OF NEW ZEALAND INTERNATIONAL PLAYERS
(UP TO 30TH SEPTEMBER 2009)

PLAYER	DEBUT	CAPS	T	C	P	D	PTS
BACKS							
D W Carter	2003 v W	62	25	161	159	2	930
Q J Cowan	2004 v It	28	2	0	0	0	10
S R Donald	2008 v E	16	1	13	20	0	91
A M Ellis	2006 v E	11	2	0	0	0	10
N J Evans	2004 v E	16	5	30	6	0	103
H E Gear	2008 v A	2	0	0	0	0	0
R L Gear	2004 v PI	19	11	0	0	0	55
C S Jane	2008 v A	8	1	0	0	0	5
R D Kahui	2008 v E	8	4	0	0	0	20
B G Leonard	2007 v F	12	2	0	0	0	10
C L McAlister	2005 v BI	28	7	26	17	0	138
L R MacDonald	2000 v S	56	15*	25	7	0	146
L T C Masaga	2009 v It	1	0	0	0	0	0
J M Muliaina	2003 v E	77	24	0	0	0	120
M A Nonu	2003 v E	42	14	0	0	0	70
J T Rokocoko	2003 v E	60	45	0	0	0	225
S W Sivivatu	2005 v Fj	39	25	0	0	0	125
C G Smith	2004 v It	29	11	0	0	0	55
I Toeava	2005 v S	26	6	0	0	0	30
A S M Tuitavake	2008 v I	6	1	0	0	0	5
P A T Weepu	2004 v W	35	6	1	1	0	35
R N Wulf	2008 v E	4	0	0	0	0	0

FORWARDS :

I F "John" Afoa	2005 v I	20	0	0	0	0	0
A F Boric	2008 v E	10	1	0	0	0	5
W W V Crockett	2009 v It	1	0	0	0	0	0
A P de Malmanche	2009 v It	2	0	0	0	0	0
T J S Donnelly	2009 v A	1	0	0	0	0	0
J J Eaton	2005 v I	13	1	0	0	0	5
B R Evans	2009 v F	2	0	0	0	0	0
R A Filipo	2007 v C	4	0	0	0	0	0
C R Flynn	2003 v C	5	1	0	0	0	5
O T Franks	2009 v It	6	0	0	0	0	0
A K Hore	2002 v E	43	4	0	0	0	20
C R Jack	2001 v Arg	67	5	0	0	0	25
J Kaino	2006 v I	22	3	0	0	0	15
T D Latimer	2009 v F	3	0	0	0	0	0
S T Lauaki	2005 v Fj	17	3	0	0	0	15
R H McCaw	2001 v I	76	17*	0	0	0	85
J L Mackintosh	2008 v S	1	0	0	0	0	0
M C Masoe	2005 v W	20	3	0	0	0	15
K F Mealamu	2002 v W	71	9	0	0	0	45
L J Messam	2008 v S	2	1	0	0	0	5
K J O'Neill	2008 v SA	1	0	0	0	0	0
G P Rawlinson	2006 v I	4	0	0	0	0	0
K J Read	2008 v S	12	0	0	0	0	0
I B Ross	2009 v F	8	2	0	0	0	10
J A C Ryan	2005 v Fj	9	0	0	0	0	0
G M Somerville	2000 v Tg	66	1	0	0	0	5
R So'oialo	2002 v W	60	6	0	0	0	30
A J Thomson	2008 v I	12	1	0	0	0	5
B C Thorn	2003 v W	33	3	0	0	0	15
N S Tialata	2005 v W	37	1	0	0	0	5
G B Whitelock	2009 v It	1	1	0	0	0	5
A J Williams	2002 v E	61	7	0	0	0	35
T D Woodcock	2002 v W	58	5	0	0	0	25

NB MacDonald's figures include a penalty try awarded against South Africa in 2001 and McCaw figures include a penalty try awarded against ireland in 2008.

NEW ZEALAND

NEW ZEALAND INTERNATIONAL PLAYERS
UP TO 30TH SEPTEMBER 2009

Note: Years given for International Championship matches are for second half of season; eg 1972 means season 1971–72. Years for all other matches refer to the actual year of the match. Entries in square brackets denote matches played in RWC Finals.

Abbott, H L (Taranaki) 1906 F

Afoa, I F (Auckland) 2005 I,S, 2006 E(R), 2008 I1,SA2,A1(R),2(R),SA3(R),A3(R),S, I2(t&R),W(R),E3(R), 2009 F1(R),2(R),It1,SA2(R),A2(R),SA3(R),A3(R)

Aitken, G G (Wellington) 1921 SA 1,2

Alatini, P F (Otago) 1999 F 1(R), [It, SA 3(R)], 2000 Tg, S 1, A 1, SA 1, A 2, SA 2, It, 2001 Sm, Arg 1, F, SA 1, A 1, SA 2, A 2

Allen, F R (Auckland) 1946 A 1,2, 1947 A 1,2, 1949 SA 1,2

Allen, M R (Taranaki, Manawatu) 1993 WS (t), 1996 S 2 (t), 1997 Arg 1(R),2(R), SA 2(R), A 3(R), E 2, W (R)

Allen, N H (Counties) 1980 A 3, W

Alley, G T (Canterbury) 1928 SA 1,2,3

Anderson, A (Canterbury) 1983 S, E, 1984 A 1,2,3, 1987 [Fj]

Anderson, B L (Wairarapa-Bush) 1986 A 1

Anesi, S R (Waikato) 2005 Fj(R)

Archer, W R (Otago, Southland) 1955 A 1,2, 1956 SA 1,3

Argus, W G (Canterbury) 1946 A 1,2, 1947 A 1,2

Arnold, D A (Canterbury) 1963 I, W, 1964 E, F

Arnold, K D (Waikato) 1947 A 1,2

Ashby, D L (Southland) 1958 A 2

Asher, A A (Auckland) 1903 A

Ashworth, B G (Auckland) 1978 A 1,2

Ashworth, J C (Canterbury, Hawke's Bay) 1978 A 1, 2, 3, 1980 A 1, 2, 3, 1981 SA 1, 2, 3, 1982 A 1, 2, 3, 1983 BI 1, 2, 3, 4, A, 1984 F 1, 2, A 1, 2, 3, 1985 E 1, 2, A

Atiga, B A C (Auckland) 2003 [Tg(R)]

Atkinson, H (West Coast) 1913 A 1

Avery, H E (Wellington) 1910 A 1, 2, 3

Bachop, G T M (Canterbury) 1989 W, I, 1990 S 1, 2, A 1, 2, 3, F 1, 2, 1991 Arg 1, 2, A 1, 2, [E, US, C, A, S], 1992 Wld 1, 1994 SA 1, 2, 3, A, 1995 C, [I, W, S, E, SA], A 1, 2

Bachop, S J (Otago) 1994 F 2, SA 1, 2, 3, A

Badeley, C E O (Auckland) 1921 SA 1, 2

Baird, J A S (Otago) 1913 A 2

Ball, N (Wellington) 1931 A, 1932 A 2, 3, 1935 W, 1936 E

Barrett, J (Auckland) 1913 A 2, 3

Barry, E F (Wellington) 1934 A 2

Barry, L J (North Harbour) 1995 F 2

Bates, S P (Waikato) 2004 It(R)

Batty, G B (Wellington, Bay of Plenty) 1972 W, S, 1973 E 1, I, F, E 2, 1974 A 1, 3, 1975 S, 1976 SA 1, 2, 3, 4, 1977 BI 1

Batty, W (Auckland) 1930 BI 1, 3, 4, 1931 A

Beatty, G E (Taranaki) 1950 BI 1

Bell, R H (Otago) 1951 A 3, 1952 A 1, 2

Bellis, E A (Wanganui) 1921 SA 1, 2, 3

Bennet, R (Otago) 1905 A

Berghan, T (Otago) 1938 A 1, 2, 3

Berry, M J (Wairarapa-Bush) 1986 A 3(R)

Berryman, N R (Northland) 1998 SA 2(R)

Bevan, V D (Wellington) 1949 A 1, 2, 1950 BI 1, 2, 3, 4

Birtwistle, W M (Canterbury) 1965 SA 1, 2, 3, 4, 1967 E, W, S

Black, J E (Canterbury) 1977 F 1, 1979 A, 1980 A 3

Black, N W (Auckland) 1949 SA 3

Black, R S (Otago) 1914 A 1

Blackadder, T J (Canterbury) 1998 E 1(R), 2, 2000 Tg, S 1, 2, A 1, SA 1, A 2, SA 2, F 1, 2, It

Blair, B A (Canterbury) 2001 S (R), Arg 2, 2002 E, W

Blake, A W (Wairarapa) 1949 A 1

Blowers, A F (Auckland) 1996 SA 2(R), 4(R), 1997 I, E 1(R), W (R), 1999 F 1(R), SA 1, A 1(R), SA 2, A 2(R), [It]

Boggs, E G (Auckland) 1946 A 2, 1949 SA 1

Bond, J G (Canterbury) 1949 A 2

Booth, E E (Otago) 1906 F, 1907 A 1, 3

Boric, A F (North Harbour) 2008 E1(R), 2(R), SA2, A2(R), SA3(R), Sm, A3(R), 4(R), S, E3(R)

Boroevich, K G (Wellington) 1986 F 1, A 1, F 3(R)

Botica, F M (North Harbour) 1986 F 1, A 1, 2, 3, F 2, 3, 1989 Arg 1(R)

Bowden, N J G (Taranaki) 1952 A 2

Bowers, R G (Wellington) 1954 I, F

Bowman, A W (Hawke's Bay) 1938 A 1, 2, 3

Braid, D J (Auckland) 2002 W, 2003 [C(R), Tg], 2008 A1

Braid, G J (Bay of Plenty) 1983 S, E

Bremner, S G (Auckland, Canterbury) 1952 A 2, 1956 SA 2

Brewer, M R (Otago, Canterbury) 1986 F 1, A 1, 2, 3, F 2, 3, 1988 A 1, 1989 A, W, I, 1990 S 1, 2, A 1, 2, 3, F 1, 2, 1992 I 2, A 1, 1994 F 1, 2, SA 1, 2, 3, A, 1995 C, [I, W, E, SA], A 1, 2

Briscoe, K C (Taranaki) 1959 BI 2, 1960 SA 1, 2, 3, 4, 1963 I, W, 1964 E, S

Brooke, R M (Auckland) 1992 I 2, A 1, 2, 3, SA, 1993 BI 1, 2, 3, A, WS, 1994 SA 2, 3, 1995 C, [J, S, E, SA], A 1, 2, It, F 1, 2, 1996 WS, S 1, 2, A 1, SA 1, 2, A 2, 3, 4, 5, 1997 Fj, Arg 1, 2, A 1, SA 1, A 2, SA 2, A 3, I, E 1, W, E 2, 1998 E 1, 2, A 1, SA 1, A 2, SA 2, A 3, 1999 WS, F 1, SA 1, A 1, SA 2, A 2, [Tg, E, It (R), S, F 2]

Brooke, Z V (Auckland) 1987 [Arg], 1989 Arg 2(R), 1990 A 1, 2, 3, F 1(R), 1991 Arg 2, A 1, 2, [E, It, C, A, S], 1992 A 2, 3, SA, 1993 BI 1, 2, 3(R), WS (R), S, E, 1994 F 2, SA 1, 2, 3, A, 1995 [J, S, E, SA], A 1, 2, It, F 1, 2, 1996 WS, S 1, 2, A 1, SA 1, 2, A 2, 3, 4, 5, 1997 Arg 1, 2, A 1, SA 1, A 2, SA 2, A 3, I, E 1, W, E 2

Brooke-Cowden, M (Auckland) 1986 F 1, A 1, 1987 [W]

Broomhall, S R (Canterbury) 2002 SA 1(R), 2(R), E, F

Brown, C (Taranaki) 1913 A 2, 3

Brown, O M (Auckland) 1992 I 2, A 1, 2, 3, SA, 1993 BI 1, 2, 3, A, S, E, 1994 F 1, 2, SA 1, 2, 3, A, 1995 C, [I, W, S, E, SA], A 1, 2, It, F 1, 2, 1996 WS, S 1, 2, A 1, SA 1, A 2, SA 2, A 3, I, E 1, W, E 2, 1998 E 1, 2, A 1, SA 1, A 2, SA 2

Brown, R H (Taranaki) 1955 A 3, 1956 SA 1, 2, 3, 4, 1957 A 1, 2, 1958 A 1, 2, 3, 1959 BI 1, 3, 1961 F 1, 2, 3, 1962 A 1

Brown, T E (Otago) 1999 WS, F (R), SA 1(R), A 1(R), 2(R), [E (R), It, S (R)], 2000 Tg, S 2(R), A 1(R), SA 1(R), A 2(R), 2001 Sm, Arg 1(R), F, SA 1, A 1

Brownlie, C J (Hawke's Bay) 1924 W, 1925 E, F

Brownlie, M J (Hawke's Bay) 1924 I, W, 1925 E, F, 1928 SA 1, 2, 3, 4

Bruce, J A (Auckland) 1914 A 1, 2

Bruce, O D (Canterbury) 1976 SA 1, 2, 4, 1977 BI 2, 3, 4, F 1, 2, 1978 A 1, 2, I, W, E, S

Bryers, R F (King Country) 1949 A 1

Budd, T A (Southland) 1946 A 2, 1949 A 2

Bullock-Douglas, G A H (Wanganui) 1932 A 1, 2, 3, 1934 A 1, 2

Bunce, F E (North Harbour) 1992 Wld 1, 2, 3, I 1, 2, A 1, 2, 3, SA, 1993 BI 1, 2, 3, A, WS, S, E, 1994 F 1, 2, SA 1, 2, 3, A, 1995 C, [I, W, S, E, SA], A 1, 2, It, F 1, 2, 1996 WS, S 1, 2, A1, SA 1, 2, A 2, 3, 4, 5, 1997 Fj, Arg 1, 2, A 1, SA 1, A 2, SA 2, A 3, I, E 1, W, E 2

Burgess, G A J (Auckland) 1981 SA 2

Burgess, G F (Southland) 1905 A

Burgess, R E (Manawatu) 1971 BI 1, 2, 3, 1972 A 3, W, 1973 I, F

Burke, P S (Taranaki) 1955 A 1, 1957 A 1, 2

Burns, P J (Canterbury) 1908 AW 2, 1910 A 1, 2, 3, 1913 A 3

Bush, R G (Otago) 1931 A

Bush, W K (Canterbury) 1974 A 1, 2, 1975 S, 1976 I, SA 2, 4, 1977 BI 2, 3, 4(R), 1978 I, W, 1979 A

Buxton, J B (Canterbury) 1955 A 3, 1956 SA 1
Cain, M J (Taranaki) 1913 US, 1914 A 1, 2, 3
Callesen, J A (Manawatu) 1974 A 1, 2, 3, 1975 S
Cameron, D (Taranaki) 1908 AW 1, 2, 3
Cameron, L M (Manawatu) 1980 A 3, 1981 SA 1(R), 2, 3, R
Carleton, S R (Canterbury) 1928 SA 1, 2, 3, 1929 A 1, 2, 3
Carrington, K R (Auckland) 1971 BI 1, 3, 4
Carter, D W (Canterbury) 2003 W, F, A 1(R), [It, C, Tg, SA(R), F(R)], 2004 E1, 2, PI, A1, SA1, A2, It, W, F, 2005 Fj, BI1, 2, SA1, A1, W, E, 2006 Arg, A1, SA1, A2, 3, SA2, 3, E, F1, 2, W, 2007 F1, C, SA1, A1, SA2, A2, [It, S, F], 2008 I1, E1, 2, SA1, 2, A1, 2, SA3, Sm, A3, 4, S(R), I2, W, E3, 2009 A2, SA3, A3
Carter, M P (Auckland) 1991 A 2, [It, A], 1997 Fj (R), A 1(R), 1998 E 2(R), A 2
Casey, S T (Otago) 1905 S, I, E, W, 1907 A 1, 2, 3, 1908 AW 1
Cashmore, A R (Auckland) 1996 S 2(R), 1997 A 2(R)
Catley, E H (Waikato) 1946 A 1, 1947 A 1, 2, 1949 SA 1, 2, 3, 4
Caughey, T H C (Auckland) 1932 A 1, 3, 1934 A 1, 2, 1935 S, I, 1936 E, A 1, 1937 SA 3
Caulton, R W (Wellington) 1959 BI 2, 3, 4, 1960 SA 1, 4, 1961 F 2, 1963 E 1, 2, I, W, 1964 E, S, F, A 1, 2, 3
Cherrington, N P (North Auckland) 1950 BI 1
Christian, D L (Auckland) 1949 SA 4
Clamp, M (Wellington) 1984 A 2, 3
Clark, D W (Otago) 1964 A 1, 2
Clark, W H (Wellington) 1953 W, 1954 I, E, S, 1955 A 1, 2, 1956 SA 2, 3, 4
Clarke, A H (Auckland) 1958 A 3, 1959 BI 4, 1960 SA 1
Clarke, D B (Waikato) 1956 SA 3, 4, 1957 A 1, 2, 1958 A 1, 3, 1959 BI 1, 2, 3, 4, 1960 SA 1, 2, 3, 4, 1961 F 1, 2, 3, 1962 A 1, 2, 3, 4, 5, 1963 E 1, 2, I, W, 1964 E, S, F, A 2, 3
Clarke, E (Auckland) 1992 Wld 2, 3, I 1, 2, 1993 BI 1, 2, S (R), E, 1998 SA 2, A 3
Clarke, I J (Waikato) 1953 W, 1955 A 1, 2, 3, 1956 SA 1, 2, 3, 4, 1957 A 1, 2, 1958 A 1, 3, 1959 BI 1, 2, 1960 SA 2, 4, 1961 F 1, 2, 3, 1962 A 1, 2, 3, 1963 E 1, 2
Clarke, R L (Taranaki) 1932 A 2, 3
Cobden, D G (Canterbury) 1937 SA 1
Cockerill, M S (Canterbury) 1951 A 1, 2, 3
Cockroft, E A P (South Canterbury) 1913 A 3, 1914 A 2, 3
Codlin, B W (Counties) 1980 A 1, 2, 3
Collins, A H (Taranaki) 1932 A 2, 3, 1934 A 1
Collins, J (Wellington) 2001 Arg 1, 2003 E (R), W, F, SA 1, A 1, SA 2, A 2, [It, W, SA, A, F], 2004 E2(R), Arg, PI(R), A1(R), SA1, It, F, 2005 Fj, BI1, 2, 3, SA1, A1, SA2, W, E, 2006 Arg, A1, 2, 3, SA2(R), 3, F1, 2, W, 2007 F2, C, SA1, A1, SA2(R), A2, [It, Pt, R, F]
Collins, J L (Poverty Bay) 1964 A 1, 1965 SA 1, 4
Colman, J T H (Taranaki) 1907 A 1, 2, 1908 AW 1, 3
Connor, D M (Auckland) 1961 F 1, 2, 3, 1962 A 1, 2, 3, 4, 5, 1963 E 1, 2, 1964 A 2, 3
Conway, R J (Otago, Bay of Plenty) 1959 BI 2, 3, 4, 1960 SA 1, 3, 4, 1965 SA 1, 2, 3, 4
Cooke, A E (Auckland, Wellington) 1924 I, W, 1925 E, F, 1930 BI 1, 2, 3, 4
Cooke, R J (Canterbury) 1903 A
Cooksley, M S B (Counties, Waikato) 1992 Wld 1, 1993 BI 2, 3(R), A, 1994 F 1, 2, SA 1, 2, A, 2001 A 1(R), SA 2(t&R)
Cooper, G J L (Auckland, Otago) 1986 F 1, A 1, 2, 1992 Wld 1, 2, 3, I 1
Cooper, M J A (Waikato) 1992 I 2, SA (R), 1993 BI 1(R), 3(t), WS (t), 1994 F 1, 2
Corner, M M N (Auckland) 1930 BI 2, 3, 4, 1931 A, 1934 A 1, 1936 E
Cossey, R R (Counties) 1958 A 1
Cottrell, A I (Canterbury) 1929 A 1, 2, 3, 1930 BI 1, 2, 3, 4, 1931 A, 1932 A 1, 2, 3
Cottrell, W D (Canterbury) 1968 A 1, 2, F 2, 3, 1970 SA 1, 1971 BI 1, 2, 3, 4
Couch, M B R (Wairarapa) 1947 A 1, 1949 A 1, 2
Coughlan, T D (South Canterbury) 1958 A 1
Cowan, Q J (Southland) 2004 It(R), 2005 W(R), I(R), S(R), 2006 I1(R), SA1(R), A2(R), SA2(R), 3, 2008 E1(R), 2(R), SA1(R), A1(t&R), 2, SA3, Sm, A3, 4, I2, W, E3, 2009 F1, 2, A1, SA2, A2, SA3, A3
Creighton, J N (Canterbury) 1962 A 4

Cribb, R T (North Harbour) 2000 S 1, 2, A 1, SA 1, A 2, SA 2, F 1, 2, It, 2001 Sm, F, SA 1, A 1, SA 2, A 2
Crichton, S (Wellington) 1983 S, E
Crockett, W W V (Canterbury) 2009 It1
Cross, T (Canterbury) 1904 BI, 1905 A
Crowley, K J (Taranaki) 1985 E 1, 2, A, Arg 1, 2, 1986 A 3, F 2, 3, 1987 [Arg], 1990 S 1, 2, A 1, 2, 3, F 1, 2, 1991 Arg 1, 2, [A]
Crowley, P J B (Auckland) 1949 SA 3, 4, 1950 BI 1, 2, 3, 4
Culhane, S D (Southland) 1995 [J], It, F 1, 2, 1996 SA 3, 4
Cullen C M (Manawatu, Central Vikings, Wellington) 1996 WS, S 1, 2, A 1, SA 1, A 2, SA 2, 3, 4, 5, 1997 Fj, Arg 1, 2, A 1, SA 1, A 2, SA 2, A 3, I, E 1, W, E 2, 1998 E 1, 2, A 1, SA 1, A 2, SA 2, A 3, 1999 WS, F 1, SA 1, A 1, SA 2, A 2, [Tg, E, It (R), S, F 2, SA 3], 2000 Tg, S 1, 2, A 1, SA 1, A 2, SA 2, F 1, 2, It, 2001 A 2(R), 2002 It, Fj, A 1, SA 1, A 2, F
Cummings, W (Canterbury) 1913 A 2, 3
Cundy, R T (Wairarapa) 1929 A 2(R)
Cunningham, G R (Auckland) 1979 A, S, E, 1980 A 1, 2
Cunningham, W (Auckland) 1905 S, I, 1906 F, 1907 A 1, 2, 3, 1908 AW 1, 2, 3
Cupples, L F (Bay of Plenty) 1924 I, W
Currie, C J (Canterbury) 1978 I, W
Cuthill, J E (Otago) 1913 A 1, US
Dalley, W C (Canterbury) 1924 I, 1928 SA 1, 2, 3, 4
Dalton, A G (Counties) 1977 F 2, 1978 A 1, 2, 3, I, W, E, S, 1979 F 1, 2, S, 1981 S 1, 2, SA 1, 2, 3, R, F 1, 2, 1982 A 1, 2, 3, 1983 BI 1, 2, 3, 4, A, 1984 F 1, 2, A 1, 2, 3, 1985 E 1, 2, A
Dalton, D (Hawke's Bay) 1935 I, W, 1936 A 1, 1937 SA 1, 2, 3, 1938 A 1, 2
Dalton, R A (Wellington) 1947 A 1, 2
Dalzell, G N (Canterbury) 1953 W, 1954 I, E, S, F
Davie, M G (Canterbury) 1983 E (R)
Davies, W A (Auckland, Otago) 1960 SA 4, 1962 A 4, 5
Davis, K (Auckland) 1952 A 2, 1953 W, 1954 I, E, S, F, 1955 A 2, 1958 A 1, 2, 3
Davis, L J (Canterbury) 1976 I, 1977 BI 3, 4
Davis, W L (Hawke's Bay) 1967 A, E, W, F, S, 1968 A 1, 2, F 1, 1969 W 1, 2, 1970 SA 2
Deans, I B (Canterbury) 1988 W 1, 2, A 1, 2, 3, 1989 F 1, 2, Arg 1, 2, A
Deans, R G (Canterbury) 1905 S, I, E, W, 1908 AW 3
Deans, R M (Canterbury) 1983 S, E, 1984 A 1(R), 2, 3
Delamore, G W (Wellington) 1949 SA 4
De Malmanche, A P (Waikato) 2009 It1(R), A3(R)
Dermody, C (Southland) 2006 I1, 2, E(R)
Devine, S J (Auckland) 2002 E, W 2003 E (R), W, F, SA 1, A 1(R), [C, SA(R), F]
Dewar, H (Taranaki) 1913 A 1, US
Diack, E S (Otago) 1959 BI 2
Dick, J (Auckland) 1937 SA 1, 2, 1938 A 3
Dick, M J (Auckland) 1963 I, W, 1964 E, S, F, 1965 SA 3, 1966 BI 4, 1967 A, E, W, F, 1969 W 1, 2, 1970 SA 1, 4
Dixon, M J (Canterbury) 1954 I, E, S, F, 1956 SA 1, 2, 3, 4, 1957 A 1, 2
Dobson, R L (Auckland) 1949 A 1
Dodd, E H (Wellington) 1905 A
Donald, A J (Wanganui) 1983 S, E, 1984 F 1, 2, A 1, 2, 3
Donald, J G (Wairarapa) 1921 SA 1, 2
Donald, Q (Wairarapa) 1924 I, W, 1925 E, F
Donald, S R (Waikato) 2008 E1(R), 2(R), A2(R), SA3(R), Sm(R), A3(R), 4, S, I2(R), 2009 F1, 2, A1, SA1, 2, A2(R), SA3
Donaldson, M W (Manawatu) 1977 F 1, 2, 1978 A 1, 2, 3, I, E, S, 1979 F 1, 2, A, S (R), 1981 SA 3(R)
Donnelly, T J S (Otago) 2009 A3
Dougan, J P (Wellington) 1972 A 1, 1973 E 2
Dowd, C W (Auckland) 1993 BI 1, 2, 3, A, WS, S, E, 1994 SA 1(R), 1995 C, [I, W, J, E, SA], A 1, 2, It, F 1, 2, 1996 WS, S 1, 2, A 1, SA 1, A 2, SA 2, 3, 4, 5, 1997 Fj, Arg 1, 2, A 1, SA 1, A 2, SA 2, A 3, I, E 1, W, 1998 E 1, 2, A 1, SA 1, A 2, 3(R), 1999 SA 2(R), A 2(R), [Tg (R), E, It, S, F 2, SA 3], 2000 Tg, S 1(R), 2(R), A 1(R), SA 1(R), A 2(R)
Dowd, G W (North Harbour) 1992 I 1(R)
Downing, A J (Auckland) 1913 A 1, US, 1914 A 1, 2, 3
Drake, J A (Auckland) 1986 F 2, 3, 1987 [Fj, Arg, S, W, F], A

Grant Fox hasn't played Test rugby for 16 years but still sits third on New Zealand's all-time points list.

Duff, R H (Canterbury) 1951 A 1, 2, 3, 1952 A 1, 2, 1955 A 2, 3, 1956 SA 1, 2, 3, 4

Duggan, R J L (Waikato) 1999 [It (R)]

Duncan, J (Otago) 1903 A

Duncan, M G (Hawke's Bay) 1971 BI 3(R), 4

Duncan, W D (Otago) 1921 SA 1, 2, 3

Dunn, E J (North Auckland) 1979 S, 1981 S 1

Dunn, I T W (North Auckland) 1983 BI 1, 4, A

Dunn, J M (Auckland) 1946 A 1

Earl, A T (Canterbury) 1986 F 1, A 1, F 3(R), 1987 [Arg], 1989 W, I, 1991 Arg 1(R), 2, A 1, [E (R), US, S], 1992 A 2, 3(R)

Eastgate, B P (Canterbury) 1952 A 1, 2, 1954 S

Eaton, J J (Taranaki) 2005 I, E(t), S(R), 2006 Arg, A1, 2(R), 3, SA3(R), F1(R), 2(R), 2009 A1(R), SA1(R), A3(R)

Elliott, K G (Wellington) 1946 A 1, 2

Ellis, A M (Canterbury) 2006 E(R), F2(R), 2007 [Pt(R), R], 2008 I1, E1, 2, SA1, 2, A1, S(R)

Ellis, M C G (Otago) 1993 S, E, 1995 C, [I (R), W, J, S, SA (R)]

Elsom, A E G (Canterbury) 1952 A 1, 2, 1953 W, 1955 A 1, 2, 3

Elvidge, R R (Otago) 1946 A 1, 2, 1949 SA 1, 2, 3, 4, 1950 BI 1, 2, 3

Erceg, C P (Auckland) 1951 A 1, 2, 3, 1952 A 1

Evans, B R (Hawke's Bay) 2009 F1(R), 2(R)

Evans, D A (Hawke's Bay) 1910 A 2

Evans, N J (North Harbour, Otago) 2004 E1(R), 2, Arg, PI(R), 2005 I, S, 2006 F2(R), W(R), 2007 F1(R), 2, SA2(R), A2(R), [Pt, S(R), R, F(R)]

Eveleigh, K A (Manawatu) 1976 SA 2, 4, 1977 BI 1, 2

Fanning, A H N (Canterbury) 1913 A 3

Fanning, B J (Canterbury) 1903 A, 1904 BI

Farrell, C P (Auckland) 1977 BI 1, 2

Fawcett, C L (Auckland) 1976 SA 2, 3

Fea, W R (Otago) 1921 SA 3

Feek, C E (Canterbury) 1999 WS (R), A 1(R), SA 2, [E (t), It], 2000 F 1, 2, It, 2001 I, S

Filipo, R A (Wellington) 2007 C, SA1(R), A1(R), 2008 S(R)

Finlay, B E L (Manawatu) 1959 BI 1

Finlay, J (Manawatu) 1946 A 1

Finlayson, I (North Auckland) 1928 SA 1, 2, 3, 4, 1930 BI 1, 2

Fitzgerald, J T (Wellington) 1952 A 1

Fitzpatrick, B B J (Wellington) 1953 W, 1954 I, F

Fitzpatrick, S B T (Auckland) 1986 F 1, A 1, F 2, 3, 1987 [It, Fj, Arg, S, W, F], A, 1988 W 1, 2, A 1, 2, 3, 1989 F 1, 2, Arg 1, 2, A, W, I, 1990 S 1, 2, A 1, 2, 3, F 1, 2, 1991 Arg 1, 2, A 1, 2, [E, US, It, C, A], 1992 Wld 1, 2, 3, I 1, 2, A 1, 2, 3, SA, 1993 BI 1, 2, 3, A, WS, S, 1994 F 1, 2, SA 1, 2, 3, A, 1995 C, [I, W, S, E, SA], A 1, 2, F 1, 2, 1996 WS, S 1, 2, A 1, SA 1, A 2, SA 2, 3, 4, 5, 1997 Fj, Arg 1, 2, A 1, SA 1, A 2, SA 2, A 3, W (R)

Flavell, T V (North Harbour, Auckland) 2000 Tg, S 1(R), A 1(R), SA 1, 2(t), F 1(R), 2(R), It, 2001 Sm, Arg 1, F, SA 1, A 1, SA 2, A 2, 2006 I1(R), 2, 2007 F1(R), 2(R), C, SA1, A1

Fleming, J K (Wellington) 1979 S, E, 1980 A 1, 2, 3

Fletcher, C J C (North Auckland) 1921 SA 3

Flynn, C R (Canterbury) 2003 [C(R), Tg], 2004 It(R), 2008 S(R), I2(R)

Fogarty, R (Taranaki) 1921 SA 1, 3

Ford, B R (Marlborough) 1977 BI 3, 4, 1978 I, 1979 E

Forster, S T (Otago) 1993 S, E, 1994 F 1, 2, 1995 It, F 1

Fox, G J (Auckland) 1985 Arg 1, 1987 [It, Fj, Arg, S, W, F], A, 1988 W 1, 2, A 1, 2, 3, 1989 F 1, 2, Arg 1, 2, A, W, I, 1990 S 1, 2, A 1, 2, 3, F 1, 2, 1991 Arg 1, 2, A 1, 2, [E, It, C, A], 1992 Wld 1, 2(R), A 1, 2, 3, SA, 1993 BI 1, 2, 3, A, WS

Francis, A R H (Auckland) 1905 A, 1907 A 1, 2, 3, 1908 AW 1, 2, 3, 1910 A 1, 2, 3

Francis, W C (Wellington) 1913 A 2, 3, 1914 A 1, 2, 3

Franks, O T (Canterbury) 2009 It1(R), A1(R), SA1(R), 2, A2, SA3

Fraser, B G (Wellington) 1979 S, E, 1980 A 3, W, 1981 S 1, 2, SA 1, 2, 3, F 1, 2, 1982 A 1, 2, 3, 1983 BI 1, 2, 3, 4, A, S, E, 1984 A 1

Frazer, H F (Hawke's Bay) 1946 A 1, 2, 1947 A 1, 2, 1949 SA 2

Fryer, F C (Canterbury) 1907 A 1, 2, 3, 1908 AW 2

Fuller, W B (Canterbury) 1910 A 1, 2

Furlong, B D M (Hawke's Bay) 1970 SA 4

Gallagher, J A (Wellington) 1987 [It, Fj, S, W, F], A, 1988 W 1, 2, A 1, 2, 3, 1989 F 1, 2, Arg 1, 2, A, W, I

Gallaher, D (Auckland) 1903 A, 1904 BI, 1905 S, E, W, 1906 F

Gard, P C (North Otago) 1971 BI 4

Gardiner, A J (Taranaki) 1974 A 3

Gear, H E (Wellington) 2008 A4, 2009 A3(R)

Gear, R L (North Harbour, Nelson Bays, Tasman) 2004 PI, It, 2005 BI1(R), 2, 3, SA1, A1, SA2, W, S, 2006 Arg, A1, 2, SA2, 3(R), E, W, 2007 C(R), A1

Geddes, J H (Southland) 1929 A 1

Geddes, W McK (Auckland) 1913 A 2

Gemmell, B McL (Auckland) 1974 A 1, 2

George, V L (Southland) 1938 A 1, 2, 3

Gibbes, J B (Waikato) 2004 E1, 2, Arg(R), PI, A1, 2, SA2, 2005 BI2(R)

Gibson, D P E (Canterbury) 1999 WS, F 1, SA 1, A 1, SA 2, A 2, [Tg (R), E (R), It, S (R), F 2(R)], 2000 F 1, 2, 2002 It, I 1(R), 2(R), Fj, A 2(R), SA 2(R)

Gilbert, G D M (West Coast) 1935 S, I, W, 1936 E

Gillespie, C T (Wellington) 1913 A 2

Gillespie, W D (Otago) 1958 A 3

Gillett, G A (Canterbury, Auckland) 1905 S, I, E, W, 1907 A 2, 3, 1908 AW 1, 3

Gillies, C C (Otago) 1936 A 2

Gilray, C M (Otago) 1905 A

Glasgow, F T (Taranaki, Southland) 1905 S, I, E, W, 1906 F, 1908 AW 3

Glenn, W S (Taranaki) 1904 BI, 1906 F

Goddard, M P (South Canterbury) 1946 A 2, 1947 A 1, 2, 1949 SA 3, 4

Going, S M (North Auckland) 1967 A, F, 1968 F 3, 1969 W 1, 2, 1970 SA 1(R), 4, 1971 BI 1, 2, 3, 4, 1972 A 1, 2, 3, W, S, 1973 E 1, I, F, E 2, 1974 I, 1975 S, 1976 I (R), SA 1, 2, 3, 4, 1977 BI 1, 2

Gordon, S B (Waikato) 1993 S, E

Graham, D J (Canterbury) 1958 A 1, 2, 1960 SA 2, 3, 1961 F 1, 2, 3, 1962 A 1, 2, 3, 4, 5, 1963 E 1, 2, I, W, 1964 E, S, F, A 1, 2, 3

Graham, J B (Otago) 1913 US, 1914 A 1, 3

Graham, W G (Otago) 1979 F 1(R)

Grant, L A (South Canterbury) 1947 A 1, 2, 1949 SA 1, 2

Gray, G D (Canterbury) 1908 AW 2, 1913 A 1, US

Gray, K F (Wellington) 1963 I, W, 1964 E, S, F, A 1, 2, 3, 1965 SA 1, 2, 3, 4, 1966 BI 1, 2, 3, 4, 1967 W, F, S, 1968 A 1, F 2, 3, 1969 W 1, 2

Gray, W N (Bay of Plenty) 1955 A 2, 3, 1956 SA 1, 2, 3, 4

Green, C I (Canterbury) 1983 S (R), E, 1984 A 1, 2, 3, 1985 E 1, 2, A, Arg 1, 2, 1986 A 2, 3, F 2, 3, 1987 [It, Fj, S, W, F], A

Grenside, B A (Hawke's Bay) 1928 SA 1, 2, 3, 4, 1929 A 2, 3

Griffiths, J L (Wellington) 1934 A 2, 1935 S, I, W, 1936 A 1, 2, 1938 A 3

Guy, R A (North Auckland) 1971 BI 1, 2, 3, 4

Haden, A M (Auckland) 1977 BI 1, 2, 3, 4, F 1, 2, 1978 A 1, 2, 3, I, W, E, S, 1979 F 1, 2, A, S, E, 1980 A 1, 2, 3, W, 1981 S 2, SA 1, 2, 3, R, F 1, 2, 1982 A 1, 2, 3, 1983 BI 1, 2, 3, 4, A, 1984 F 1, 2, 1985 Arg 1, 2

Hadley, S (Auckland) 1928 SA 1, 2, 3, 4

Hadley, W E (Auckland) 1934 A 1, 2, 1935 S, I, W, 1936 E, A 1, 2

Haig, J S (Otago) 1946 A 1, 2

Haig, L S (Otago) 1950 BI 2, 3, 4, 1951 A 1, 2, 3, 1953 W, 1954 E, S

Hales, D A (Canterbury) 1972 A 1, 2, 3, W

Hamilton, D C (Southland) 1908 AW 2

Hamilton, S E (Canterbury) 2006 Arg, SA1

Hammett, M G (Canterbury) 1999 F 1(R), SA 2(R), [It, S (R), SA 3], 2000 Tg, S 1(R), 2(t&R), A 1(R), SA 1(R), A 2(R), SA 2(R), F 2(H), It (R), 2001 Arg 1(t), 2002 It (R), I 1, 2, A 1, SA 1, 2(R), 2003 SA 1(R), A 1(R), SA 2, [It(R), C, W(R), SA(R), F(R)]

Hammond, I A (Marlborough) 1952 A 2

Harper, E T (Canterbury) 1904 BI, 1906 F

Harding, S (Otago) 2002 Fj

Harris, P C (Manawatu) 1976 SA 3

Hart, A H (Taranaki) 1924 I

Hart, G F (Canterbury) 1930 BI 1, 2, 3, 4, 1931 A 1, 1934 A 1, 1935 S, I, W, 1936 A 1, 2

Harvey, B A (Wairarapa-Bush) 1986 F 1

Harvey, I H (Wairarapa) 1928 SA 4

Harvey, L R (Otago) 1949 SA 1, 2, 3, 4, 1950 BI 1, 2, 3, 4

Harvey, P (Canterbury) 1904 BI

Hasell, E W (Canterbury) 1913 A 2, 3

Hayman, C J (Otago) 2001 Sm (R), Arg 1, F (R), A 1(R), SA 2(R), A 2(R), 2002 F (t), W, 2004 E1, 2, PI, A1, 2, SA2, It,

W(R), F, 2005 BI1, SA1, A1, SA2, A2, W, E, 2006 I1, 2, A1, SA1, A2, 3, SA3, E, F1, 2, W, 2007 F1, 2, SA1, A1, SA2, A2, [It, Pt(R), S, F]

Hayward, H O (Auckland) 1908 AW 3

Hazlett, E J (Southland) 1966 BI 1, 2, 3, 4, 1967 A, E

Hazlett, W E (Southland) 1928 SA 1, 2, 3, 4, 1930 BI 1, 2, 3, 4

Heeps, T R (Wellington) 1962 A 1, 2, 3, 4, 5

Heke, W R (North Auckland) 1929 A 1, 2, 3

Hemi, R C (Waikato) 1953 W, 1954 I, E, S, F, 1955 A 1, 2, 3, 1956 SA 1, 3, 4, 1957 A 1, 2, 1959 BI 1, 3, 4

Henderson, P (Wanganui) 1949 SA 1, 2, 3, 4, 1950 BI 2, 3, 4

Henderson, P W (Otago) 1991 Arg 1, [C], 1992 Wld 1, 2, 3, I 1, 1995 [J]

Herewini, M A (Auckland) 1962 A 5, 1963 I, 1964 S, F, 1965 SA 4, 1966 BI 1, 2, 3, 4, 1967 A

Hewett, D N (Canterbury) 2001 I (R), S (R), Arg 2, 2002 It (R), I 1, 2, A 1, SA 1, A 2, SA 2, 2003 E, F, SA 1, A 1, SA 2, A 2, [It, Tg(R), W, SA, A, F]

Hewett, J A (Auckland) 1991 [It]

Hewitt, N J (Southland) 1995 [I (t), J], 1996 A 1(R), 1997 SA 1(R), I, E 1, W, E 2, 1998 E 2(t + R)

Hewson, A R (Wellington) 1981 S 1, 2, SA 1, 2, 3, R, F 1, 2, 1982 A 1, 2, 3, 1983 BI 1, 2, 3, 4, A, 1984 F 1, 2, A 1

Higginson, G (Canterbury, Hawke's Bay) 1980 W, 1981 S 1, SA 1, 1982 A 1, 2, 1983 A

Hill, D W (Waikato) 2006 I2(R)

Hill, S F (Canterbury) 1955 A 3, 1956 SA 1, 3, 4, 1957 A 1, 2, 1958 A 3, 1959 BI 1, 2, 3, 4

Hines, G R (Waikato) 1980 A 3

Hobbs, M J B (Canterbury) 1983 BI 1, 2, 3, 4, A, S, E, 1984 F 1, 2, A 1, 2, 3, 1985 E 1, 2, A, Arg 1, 2, 1986 A 2, 3, F 2, 3

Hoeft, C H (Otago) 1998 E 2(t + R), A 2(R), SA 2, A 3, 1999 WS, F 1, SA 1, A 1, 2, [Tg, E, S, F 2, SA 3(R)], 2000 S 1, 2, A 1, SA 1, A 2, SA 2, 2001 Sm, Arg 1, F, SA 1, A 1, SA 2, A 2, 2003 W, [C, F(R)]

Holah, M R (Waikato) 2001 Sm, Arg 1(t&R), F (R), SA 1(R), A 1(R), SA 2(R), A 2(R), 2002 It, I 2(R), A 2(t), E, F, W (R), 2003 W, F (R), A 1(R), SA 2, [It(R), C, Tg(R), W(R), SA(t&R), A(R), F(t&R)], 2004 E1(R), 2, Arg(R), PI, A1, SA1, A2, SA2, 2005 BI3(R), A1(R), 2006 I1, SA3(t)

Holder, E C (Buller) 1934 A 2

Hook, L S (Auckland) 1929 A 1, 2, 3

Hooper, J A (Canterbury) 1937 SA 1, 2, 3

Hopkinson, A E (Canterbury) 1967 S, 1968 A 2, F 1, 2, 3, 1969 W 2, 1970 SA 1, 2, 3

Hore, A K (Taranaki) 2002 E, F, 2004 E1(t), 2(R), Arg, A1(t), 2005 W(R), I(R), S(R), 2006 I2(R), Arg(R), A1(R), SA1(R), A2(R), SA3, E(R), F2(R), W(R), 2007 F1(R), C, SA2(R), [Pt, S(R), R(R), F(R)], 2008 I1, E1, 2, SA1, 2, A1, 2, SA3, Sm, A3, 4, 2009 F1, A1, SA1, 2, A2, SA3, A3

Hore, J (Otago) 1930 BI 2, 3, 4, 1932 A 1, 2, 3, 1934 A 1, 2, 1935 S, 1936 E

Horsley, R H (Wellington) 1960 SA 2, 3, 4

Hotop, J (Canterbury) 1952 A 1, 2, 1955 A 3

Howarth, S P (Auckland) 1994 SA 1, 2, 3, A

Howlett, D C (Auckland) 2000 Tg (R), F 1, 2, It, 2001 Sm, Arg 1(R), F (R), SA 1, A 1, 2, I, S, Arg 2, 2002 It, I 1, 2(R), Fj, A 1, SA 1, A 2, SA 2, E, F, W, 2003 E, W, F, SA 1, A 1, 2, [It, C(R), Tg, W, SA, A, F], 2004 E1, A1, SA1, A2, SA2, W, F, 2005 Fj, BI1, A2, I, E, 2006 I1, 2, SA1, A3, SA3, 2007 F2(R), C, SA2, A2, [It, S, R(R)]

Hughes, A M (Auckland) 1949 A 1, 2, 1950 BI 1, 2, 3, 4

Hughes, E (Southland, Wellington) 1907 A 1, 2, 3, 1908 AW 1, 1921 SA 1, 2

Hunter, B A (Otago) 1971 BI 1, 2, 3

Hunter, J (Taranaki) 1905 S, I, E, W, 1906 F, 1907 A 1, 2, 3, 1908 AW 1, 2, 3

Hurst, I A (Canterbury) 1973 I, F, E 2, 1974 A 1, 2

Ieremia, A (Wellington) 1994 SA 1, 2, 3, 1995 [J], 1996 SA 2(R), 5(R), 1997 A 1(R), SA 1(R), A 2, SA 2, A 3, I, E 1, 1999 WS, F 1, SA 1, A 1, SA 2, A 2, [Tg, E, S, F 2, SA 3], 2000 Tg, S 1, 2, A 1, 2, SA 2

Ifwersen, K D (Auckland) 1921 SA 3

Innes, C R (Auckland) 1989 W, I, 1990 F 1, 2, 3, F 1, 2, 1991 Arg 1, 2, A 1, 2, [E, US, It, C, A, S]

Innes, G D (Canterbury) 1932 A 2

Irvine, I B (North Auckland) 1952 A 1

Irvine, J G (Otago) 1914 A 1, 2, 3

Irvine, W R (Hawke's Bay, Wairarapa) 1924 I, W, 1925 E, F, 1930 BI 1

Irwin, M W (Otago) 1955 A 1, 2, 1956 SA 1, 1958 A 2, 1959 BI 3, 4, 1960 SA 1

Jack, C R (Canterbury, Tasman) 2001 Arg 1(R), SA 1(R), 2, A 2, I, S, Arg 2, 2002 I 1, 2, A 1, SA 1, A 2, SA 2, 2003 E, W, F, SA 1, A 1, SA 2(R), A 2, [It, C, SA, A, F], 2004 E1, 2, Arg, PI, A1, SA1, A2, SA2, It, W, F, 2005 Fj(R), BI1, 2, 3, SA1, A1, SA2, A2, W, E, S, 2006 I1, 2, A1, SA1, A2, 3, SA2(R), 3, E, F2, 2007 F1, 2, A1, SA2, A2, [It, Pt, S(R), R(R), F(R)]

Jackson, E S (Hawke's Bay) 1936 A 1, 2, 1937 SA 1, 2, 3, 1938 A 3

Jaffray, J L (Otago, South Canterbury) 1972 A 2, 1975 S, 1976 I, SA 1, 1977 BI 2, 1979 F 1, 2

Jane, C S (Wellington) 2008 A4(R), S(R), 2009 F1, 2, It1(R), A1, SA3(R), A3

Jarden, R A (Wellington) 1951 A 1, 2, 1952 A 1, 2, 1953 W, 1954 I, E, S, F, 1955 A 1, 2, 3, 1956 SA 1, 2, 3, 4

Jefferd, A C R (East Coast) 1981 S 1, 2, SA 1

Jessep, E M (Wellington) 1931 A, 1932 A 1

Johnson, L M (Wellington) 1928 SA 1, 2, 3, 4

Johnston, W (Otago) 1907 A 1, 2, 3

Johnstone, B R (Auckland) 1976 SA 2, 1977 BI 1, 2, F 1, 2, 1978 I, W, E, S, 1979 F 1, 2, S, E

Johnstone, C R (Canterbury) 2005 Fj(R), BI2(R), 3(R)

Johnstone, P (Otago) 1949 SA 2, 4, 1950 BI 1, 2, 3, 4, 1951 A 1, 2, 3

Jones, I D (North Auckland, North Harbour) 1990 S 1, 2, A 1, 2, 3, F 1, 2, 1991 Arg 1, 2, A 1, 2, [E, US, It, C, A, S], 1992 Wld 1, 2, 3, I 1, 2, A 1, 2, 3, SA, 1993 BI 1, 2(R), 3, WS, S, E, 1994 F 1, 2, SA 1, 3, A, 1995 C, [I, W, S, E, SA], A 1, 2, It, F 1, 2, 1996 WS, S 1, 2, A 1, SA 1, A 2, SA 2, 3, 4, 5, 1997 Fj, Arg 1, 2, A 1, SA 1, A 2, SA 2, A 3, I, E 1, W, E 2, 1998 E 1, 2, A 1, SA 1, A 2, 3(R), 1999 F 1(R), [It, S (R)]

Jones, M G (North Auckland) 1973 E 2

Jones, M N (Auckland) 1987 [It, Fj, S, F], A, 1988 W 1, 2, A 2, 3, 1989 F 1, 2, Arg 1, 2, 1990 F 1, 2, 1991 Arg 1, 2, A 1, 2, [E, US, S], 1992 Wld 1, 3, I 2, A 1, 3, SA, 1993 BI 1, 2, 3, A, WS, 1994 SA 3(R), A, 1995 A 1(R), 2, It, F 1, 2, 1996 WS, S 1, 2, A 1, SA 1, A 2, SA 2, 3, 4, 5, 1997 Fj, 1998 E 1, A 1, SA 1, A 2

Jones, P F H (North Auckland) 1954 E, S, 1955 A 1, 2, 1956 SA 3, 4, 1958 A 1, 2, 3, 1959 BI 1, 1960 SA 1

Joseph, H T (Canterbury) 1971 BI 2, 3

Joseph, J W (Otago) 1992 Wld 2, 3(R), I 1, A 1(R), 3, SA, 1993 BI 1, 2, 3, A, WS, S, E, 1994 SA 2(t), 1995 C, [I, W, J (R), S, SA (R)]

Kahui, R D (Waikato) 2008 E2, A1, 2, SA3, Sm, A3, S, W

Kaino, J (Auckland) 2006 I1(R), 2, 2008 I1, E1, SA1, 2, A1, 2, SA3, Sm, A3, 4, I2, W, E3, 2009 F2, It1, A1, SA1, 2, A2, SA3

Karam, J F (Wellington, Horowhenua) 1972 W, S, 1973 E 1, I, F, 1974 A 1, 2, 3, I, 1975 S

Katene, T (Wellington) 1955 A 2

Kearney, J C (Otago) 1947 A 2, 1949 SA 1, 2, 3

Kelleher, B T (Otago, Waikato) 1999 WS (R), SA 1(R), A 2(R), [Tg (R), E (R), It, F 2], 2000 S 1, 2, A 2(R), It (R), 2001 Sm, F (R), A 1(R), SA 2, A 2, I, S, 2002 It, I 2(R), Fj, SA 1(R), 2(R), 2003 F (R), [A(R)], 2004 Arg, PI(R), SA1(R), 2(R), It, W(R), F, 2005 Fj, BI1(R), 2, 3, SA1, W, E, 2006 I1, 2, A1, 2, 3, SA3(R), E, F1(R), 2, W, 2007 F2, C, SA1, A1, 2, [It, S, F]

Kelly, J W (Auckland) 1949 A 1, 2

Kember, G F (Wellington) 1970 SA 4

Ketels, R C (Counties) 1980 W, 1981 S 1, 2, R, F 1

Kiernan, H A D (Auckland) 1903 A

Kilby, F D (Wellington) 1932 A 1, 2, 3, 1934 A 2

Killeen, B A (Auckland) 1936 A 1

King, R M (Waikato) 2002 W

King, R R (West Coast) 1934 A 2, 1935 S, I, W, 1936 E, A 1, 2, 1937 SA 1, 2, 3, 1938 A 1, 2, 3

Kingstone, C N (Taranaki) 1921 SA 1, 2, 3

Kirk, D E (Auckland) 1985 E 1, 2, A, Arg 1, 1986 F 1, A 1, 2, 3, F 2, 3, 1987 [It, Fj, Arg, S, W, F], A

Kirkpatrick, I A (Canterbury, Poverty Bay) 1967 F, 1968 A 1(R), 2, F 1, 2, 3, 1969 W 1, 2, 1970 SA 1, 2, 3, 4, 1971 BI 1, 2, 3, 4, 1972 A 1, 2, 3, W, S, 1973 E 1, I, F, E 2, 1974 A 1, 2, 3, I 1975 S, 1976 I, SA 1, 2, 3, 4, 1977 BI 1, 2, 3, 4

Kirton, E W (Otago) 1967 E, W, F, S, 1968 A 1, 2, F 1, 2, 3, 1969 W 1, 2, 1970 SA 2, 3

Kirwan, J J (Auckland) 1984 F 1, 2, 1985 E 1, 2, A, Arg 1, 2, 1986 F 1, A 1, 2, 3, F 2, 3, 1987 [It, Fj, Arg, S, W, F], A,

361

NEW ZEALAND

MacRae, I R (Hawke's Bay) 1966 BI 1, 2, 3, 4, 1967 A, E, W, F, S, 1968 F 1, 2, 1969 W 1, 2, 1970 SA 1, 2, 3, 4
McRae, J A (Southland) 1946 A 1(R), 2
McWilliams, R G (Auckland) 1928 SA 2, 3, 4, 1929 A 1, 2, 3, 1930 BI 1, 2, 3, 4
Mackintosh, J L (Southland) 2008 S
Mackrell, W H C (Auckland) 1906 F
Macky, J V (Auckland) 1913 A 2
Maguire, J R (Auckland) 1910 A 1, 2, 3
Mahoney, A (Bush) 1935 S, I, W, 1936 E
Mains, L W (Otago) 1971 BI 2, 3, 4, 1976 I
Major, J (Taranaki) 1967 A
Maka, I (Otago) 1998 E 2(R), A 1(R), SA 1(R), 2
Maling, T S (Otago) 2002 It, I 2(R), Fj, A 1, SA 1, A 2, SA 2, 2004 Arg, A1, SA1, 2
Manchester, J E (Canterbury) 1932 A 1, 2, 3, 1934 A 1, 2, 1935 S, I, W, 1936 E
Mannix, S J (Wellington) 1994 F 1
Marshall, J W (Southland, Canterbury) 1995 F 2, 1996 WS, S 1, 2, A 1, SA 1, A 2, SA 2, 3, 4, 5, 1997 Fj, Arg 1, 2, A 1, SA 1, A 2, SA 2, A 3, I, E 1, W, E 2, 1998 A 1, SA 1, A 2, SA 2, A 3, 1999 WS, F 1, SA 1, A 1, SA 2, A 2, [Tg, E, S, F 2(R), SA 3], 2000 Tg, S 2, A 1, SA 1, A 2, SA 2, F 1, 2, It, 2001 Arg 1, F, SA 1, A 1, 2(R), 2002 I 1, 2, Fj (R), A 1, SA 1, A 2, SA 2, 2003 E, SA 1(R), A 1, SA 2, A 2, [It, Tg, W, SA, A], 2004 E1, 2, Pl, A1, SA1, A2, SA2, 2005 Fj(R), BI1, 2(R), 3(R)
Masaga, L T C (Counties Manukau) 2009 It1
Masoe, M C (Taranaki, Wellington) 2005 W, E, 2006Arg, A1(R), SA1(R), A2(R), 3(R), SA2, E, F2(R), 2007(R), C, A1(R), SA2(R), [It(R), Pt, S, R, F(R)]
Mason, D F (Wellington) 1947 A 2(R)
Masters, R R (Canterbury) 1924 I, W, 1925 E, F
Mataira, H K (Hawke's Bay) 1934 A 2
Matheson, J D (Otago) 1972 A 1, 2, 3, W, S
Mauger, A J D (Canterbury) 2001 I, S, Arg 2, 2002 It (R), I 1, 2, Fj, A 1, SA 1, A 2, SA 2, 2003 SA 1, A 1, SA 2, A 2, [W, SA, A, F], 2004 SA2(R), It(R), W, F(R), 2005 Fj, BI1, 2, SA1, A1, SA2, A2, I, E, 2006 I1, 2, A1, 2, A1, 2, SA3, E, 2007 F1, C, SA1, A1, [It(R), Pt, R]
Max, D S (Nelson) 1931 A, 1934 A 1, 2
Maxwell, N M C (Canterbury) 1999 WS, F 1, SA 1, A 1, SA 2, A 2, [Tg, E, S, F 2, SA 3], 2000 S 1, 2, A 1, SA 1(R), A 2, SA 2, F 1, 2, It (R), 2001 Sm, Arg 1, F, SA 1, A 1, SA 2, A2, I, S, Arg 2, 2002 It, I 1, 2, Fj, 2004 It, F
Mayerhofler, M A (Canterbury) 1998 E 1, 2, SA 1, A 2, SA 2, A 3
Meads, C E (King Country) 1957 A 1, 2, 1958 A 1, 2, 3, 1959 BI 2, 3, 4, 1960 SA 1, 2, 3, 4, 1961 F 1, 2, 3, 1962 A 1, 2, 3, 5, 1963 E 1, 2, I, W, 1964 E, S, F, A 1, 2, 3, 1965 SA 1, 2, 3, 4, 1966 BI 1, 2, 3, 4, 1967 A, E, W, F, S, 1968 A 1, 2, F 1, 2, 3, 1969 W 1, 2, 1970 SA 3, 4, 1971 BI 1, 2, 3, 4
Meads, S T (King Country) 1961 F 1, 1962 A 4, 5, 1963 I, 1964 A 1, 2, 3, 1965 SA 1, 2, 3, 4, 1966 BI 1, 2, 3, 4
Mealamu, K F (Auckland) 2002 W, 2003 E (R), W, F (R), SA 1, A 1, SA 2(R), A 2, [It, W, SA, A, F], 2004 E1, 2, Pl, A1, SA1, A2, SA2, W, F(R), 2005 Fj(R), BI1, 2, 3, SA1, A1, SA2, A2, I, E, 2006 I1, 2, A1, 2, 3, SA2(R), E, F1(R), 2, 2007 F1, 2(R), SA1(R), A1(R), SA2, A2(R), 2008 I1(R), E1(t&R), 2(t&R), SA1(R), 2(R), A1(R), 2(R), SA3(R), Sm(R), A3(R), 4(R), S, I2, W, E3, 2009 F1(R), 2, It1, A1(R), SA1(R), 2(R)
Meates, K F (Canterbury) 1952 A 1, 2
Meates, W A (Otago) 1949 SA 2, 3, 4, 1950 BI 1, 2, 3, 4
Meeuws, K J (Otago, Auckland) 1998 A 3, 1999 WS, F 1, SA 1, A 1, SA 2, A 2, [Tg, It (R), S (R), F 2(R), SA 3], 2000 Tg (R), S 2, A 1, SA 1, A 2, SA 2, 2001 Arg 2, 2002 It, Fj, E, F, W (R), 2003 W, F (R), SA 1(R), A 1(R), SA 2, [It(R), C, Tg, W(R), SA(R), A(R)], 2004 E1, 2, Pl, A1, SA1, A2, SA2
Mehrtens, A P (Canterbury) 1995 C, [I, W, S, E, SA], A 1, 2, 1996 WS, S 1, 2, A 1, SA 1, A 2, SA 2, 5, 1997 Fj, SA 2(R), I, E 1, W, E 2, 1998 E 1, 2, A 1, SA 1(R), A 2, SA 2, A 3, 1999 F 1, SA 1, A 1, SA 2, A 2, [Tg, E, S, F 2, SA 3], 2000 S 1, 2, A 1, SA 1, A 2, SA 2, F 1, 2, It, 2001 Sm, A 1, SA 1, A 2, SA 2, A 2, I, S, Arg 2, 2002 It, I 1, 2, Fj (R), A 1, SA 1, A 2, SA 2, E (R), F, W, 2004 E2(R), Arg, A2(R), SA2
Messam, L J (Waikato) 2008 S, 2009 F1
Metcalfe, T C (Southland) 1931 A, 1932 A 1
Mexted, G G (Wellington) 1950 BI 4
Mexted, M G (Wellington) 1979 S, E, 1980 A 1, 2, 3, W, 1981 S 1, 2, SA 1, 2, 3, R, F 1, 2, 1982 A 1, 2, 3, 1983 BI 1, 2, 3, 4, A, S, E, 1984 F 1, 2, A 1, 2, 3, 1985 E 1, 2, A, Arg 1, 2
Mika, B M (Auckland) 2002 E (R), F, W (R)

Mika, D G (Auckland) 1999 WS, F 1, SA 1(R), A 1, 2, [It, SA 3(R)]
Mill, J J (Hawke's Bay, Wairarapa) 1924 W, 1925 E, F, 1930 BI 1
Milliken, H M (Canterbury) 1938 A 1, 2, 3
Milner, H P (Wanganui) 1970 SA 3
Mitchell, N A (Southland, Otago) 1935 S, I, W, 1936 E, A 2, 1937 SA 3, 1938 A 1, 2
Mitchell, T W (Canterbury) 1976 SA 4(R)
Mitchell, W J (Canterbury) 1910 A 2, 3
Mitchinson, F E (Wellington) 1907 A 1, 2, 3, 1908 AW 1, 2, 3, 1910 A 1, 2, 3, 1913 A 1(R), US
Moffitt, J E (Wellington) 1921 SA 1, 2, 3
Moore, G J T (Otago) 1949 A 1
Moreton, R C (Canterbury) 1962 A 3, 4, 1964 A 1, 2, 3, 1965 SA 2, 3
Morgan, J E (North Auckland) 1974 A 3, I, 1976 SA 2, 3, 4
Morris, T J (Nelson Bays) 1972 A 1, 2, 3
Morrison, T C (South Canterbury) 1938 A 1, 2, 3
Morrison, T G (Otago) 1973 E 2(R)
Morrissey, P J (Canterbury) 1962 A 3, 4, 5
Mourie, G N K (Taranaki) 1977 BI 3, 4, F 1, 2, 1978 I, W, E, S, 1979 F 1, 2, A, S, E, 1980 W, 1981 S 1, 2, F 1, 2, 1982 A 1, 2, 3
Muliaina, J M (Auckland, Waikato) 2003 E (R), W, F, SA 1, A 1, SA 2, A 2, [It, C, Tg, W, SA, A, F], 2004 E1, 2, Arg, Pl, A1, SA1, A2, SA2, It, W, F, 2005 Fj, BI1(R), 2, 3, SA1, A1, SA2, A2, W, E, 2006 I1, 2, A1, SA1, A2, 3, SA2, E, F1(R), 2, W, 2007 C, SA1, A1, SA2, A2, [It, Pt, F], 2008 I1, E1, 2(t), SA1, 2, A1, 2, SA3, Sm, A3, I2, W, E3, 2009 F1, 2, It1, A1, SA1, 2, A2, SA3, A3
Muller, B L (Taranaki) 1967 A, E, W, F, 1968 A 1, F 1, 1969 W 1, 1970 SA 1, 2, 4, 1971 BI 1, 2, 3, 4
Mumm, W J (Buller) 1949 A 1
Murdoch, K (Otago) 1970 SA 4, 1972 A 3, W
Murdoch, P H (Auckland) 1964 A 2, 3, 1965 SA 1, 2, 3
Murray, H V (Canterbury) 1913 A 1, US, 1914 A 2, 3
Murray, P C (Wanganui) 1908 AW 2
Myers, R G (Waikato) 1978 A 3
Mynott, H J (Taranaki) 1905 I, W, 1906 F, 1907 A 1, 2, 3, 1910 A 1, 3
Nathan, W J (Auckland) 1962 A 1, 2, 3, 4, 5, 1963 E 1, 2, W, 1964 F, 1966 BI 1, 2, 3, 4, 1967 A
Nelson, K A (Otago) 1962 A 4, 5
Nepia, G (Hawke's Bay, East Coast) 1924 I, W, 1925 E, F, 1929 A 1, 1930 BI 1, 2, 3, 4
Nesbit, S R (Auckland) 1960 SA 2, 3
Newby, C A (North Harbour) 2004 E2(t), SA2(R), 2006 I2(R)
Newton, F (Canterbury) 1905 E, W, 1906 F
Nicholls, H E (Wellington) 1921 SA 1
Nicholls, M F (Wellington) 1921 SA 1, 2, 3, 1924 I, W, 1925 E, F, 1928 SA 4, 1930 BI 2, 3
Nicholson, G W (Auckland) 1903 A, 1904 BI, 1907 A 2, 3
Nonu, M A (Wellington) 2003 E, [It(R), C, Tg(R)], 2004 It(R), W(R), F(R), 2005 BI2(R), W(R), I, S(R), 2006 I1, E, F1(R), 2, W(R), 2007 F1(R), 2(R), 2008 I1, E1, 2, SA1, 2, A1, 2, SA3, Sm, A3, 4(R), S, I2, W, E3, 2009 F1, 2, It1, A1, SA1, 2, A2(t&R), SA3, A3
Norton, R W (Canterbury) 1971 BI 1, 2, 3, 4, 1972 A 1, 2, 3, W, S, 1973 E 1, I, F, E 2, 1974 A 1, 2, 3, I, 1975 S, 1976 I, SA 1, 2, 3, 4, 1977 BI 1, 2, 3, 4
O'Brien, J G (Auckland) 1914 A 1
O'Callaghan, M W (Manawatu) 1968 F 1, 2, 3
O'Callaghan, T R (Wellington) 1949 A 2
O'Donnell, D H (Wellington) 1949 A 2
O'Halloran, J D (Wellington) 2000 It (R)
Old, G H (Manawatu) 1981 SA 3, R (R), 1982 A 1(R)
O'Leary, M J (Auckland) 1910 A 1, 3, 1913 A 2, 3
Oliver, A D (Otago) 1997 Fj (t), 1998 E 1, 2, A 1, SA 1, A 2, SA 2, A 3, 1999 WS, F 1, SA 1, A 1, SA 2, A 2, [Tg, E, S, F 2, SA 3(R)], 2000 Tg (R), S 1, 2, A 1, SA 1, A 2, SA 2, F 1, 2, It, 2001 Sm, Arg 1, F, SA 1, A 1, SA 2, A 2, I, S, Arg 2, 2003 E, F, 2004 It, F, 2005 W, S, 2006 Arg, SA1, 2, 3(R), F1, W, 2007 F2, SA1, A1, 2, [It(R), Pt(R), S, F]
Oliver, C J (Canterbury) 1929 A 1, 2, 1934 A 1, 1935 S, I, W, 1936 E
Oliver, D J (Wellington) 1930 BI 1, 2
Oliver, D O (Otago) 1954 I, F
Oliver, F J (Southland, Otago, Manawatu) 1976 SA 4, 1977 BI 1, 2, 3, 4, F 1, 2, 1978 A 1, 2, 3, I, W, E, S, 1979 F 1, 2, 1981 SA 2

O'Neill, K J (Canterbury) 2008 SA2(R)

Orr, R W (Otago) 1949 A 1

Osborne, G M (North Harbour) 1995 C, [I, W, J, E, SA], A 1, 2, F 1(R), 2, 1996 SA 2, 3, 4, 5, 1997 Arg 1(R), A 2, 3, I, 1999 [It]

Osborne, W M (Wanganui) 1975 S, 1976 SA 2(R), 4(R), 1977 BI 1, 2, 3, 4, F 1(R), 2, 1978 I, W, E, S, 1980 W, 1982 A 1, 3

O'Sullivan, J M (Taranaki) 1905 S, I, E, W, 1907 A 3

O'Sullivan, T P A (Taranaki) 1960 SA 1, 1961 F 1, 1962 A 1, 2

Page, J R (Wellington) 1931 A, 1932 A 1, 2, 3, 1934 A 1, 2

Palmer, B P (Auckland) 1929 A 2, 1932 A 2, 3

Parker, J H (Canterbury) 1924 I, W, 1925 E

Parkhill, A A (Otago) 1937 SA 1, 2, 3, 1938 A 1, 2, 3

Parkinson, R M (Poverty Bay) 1972 A 1, 2, 3, W, S, 1973 E 1, 2

Paterson, A M (Otago) 1908 AW 2, 3, 1910 A 1, 2, 3

Paton, H (Otago) 1910 A 1, 3

Pene, A R B (Otago) 1992 Wld 1(R), 2, 3, I 1, 2, A 1, 2(R), 1993 BI 3, A, WS, S, E, 1994 F 1, 2(R), SA 1(R)

Phillips, W J (King Country) 1937 SA 2, 1938 A 1, 2

Philpott, S (Canterbury) 1991 [It R), S (R)]

Pickering, E A R (Waikato) 1958 A 2, 1959 BI 1, 4

Pierce, M J (Wellington) 1985 E 1, 2, A, Arg 1, 1986 A 2, 3, F 2, 3, 1987 [It, Arg, S, W, F], A, 1988 W 1, 2, A 1, 2, 3, 1989 F 1, 2, Arg 1, 2, A, W, I

Pokere, S T (Southland, Auckland) 1981 SA 3, 1982 A 1, 2, 3, 1983 BI 1, 2, 3, 4, A, S, E, 1984 F 1, 2, A 2, 3, 1985 E 1, 2, A

Pollock, H R (Wellington) 1932 A 1, 2, 3, 1936 A 1, 2

Porter, C G (Wellington) 1925 F, 1929 A 2, 3, 1930 BI 1, 2, 3, 4

Preston, J P (Canterbury, Wellington) 1991 [US, S], 1992 SA (R), 1993 BI 2, 3, A, WS, 1996 SA 4(R), 1997 I (R), E 1(R)

Procter, A C (Otago) 1932 A 1

Purdue, C A (Southland) 1905 A

Purdue, E (Southland) 1905 A

Purdue, G B (Southland) 1931 A, 1932 A 1, 2, 3

Purvis, G H (Waikato) 1991 [US], 1993 WS

Purvis, N A (Otago) 1976 I

Quaid, C E (Otago) 1938 A 1, 2

Ralph, C S (Auckland, Canterbury) 1998 E 2, 2002 It 1 1, 2, A 1, SA 1, 2, SA 2, 2003 E, A 1(R), [C, Tg, SA(R), F(t&R)]

Ranby, R M (Waikato) 2001 Sm (R)

Randell, T C (Otago) 1997 Fj, Arg 1, 2, A 1, SA 1, A 2, SA 2, A 3, I, E 1, W, E 2, 1998 E 1, 2, A 1, SA 1, A 2, SA 2, A 3, 1999 WS, F 1, SA 1, A 1, SA 2, A 2, [Tg, E, It, S, F 2, SA 3], 2000 Tg, S 1, 2(R), A 1, SA 1, A 2, SA 2, F 2(R), It (R), 2001 Arg 1, F, SA 1, A 1, SA 2, A 2, 2002 It, Fj, E, F, W

Rangi, R E (Auckland) 1964 A 2, 3, 1965 SA 1, 2, 3, 4, 1966 BI 1, 2, 3, 4

Rankin, J G (Canterbury) 1936 A 1, 2, 1937 SA 2

Rawlinson, G P (North Harbour) 2006 I1, 2(R), SA2, 2007 SA1

Read, K J (Canterbury) 2008 S, I2(R), E3(R), 2009 F1, 2, It1, A1(R), SA1(R), 2(R), A2, SA3, A3

Reedy, W J (Wellington) 1908 AW 2, 3

Reid, A R (Waikato) 1952 A 1, 1956 SA 3, 4, 1957 A I, 2

Reid, H R (Bay of Plenty) 1980 A 1, 2, W, 1983 S, E, 1985 Arg 1, 2, 1986 A 2, 3

Reid, K H (Wairarapa) 1929 A 1, 3

Reid, S T (Hawke's Bay) 1935 S, I, W, 1936 E, A 1, 2, 1937 SA 1, 2, 3

Reihana, B T (Waikato) 2000 F 2, It

Reside, W B (Wairarapa) 1929 A 1

Rhind, P K (Canterbury) 1946 A 1, 2

Richardson, J (Otago, Southland) 1921 SA 1, 2, 3, 1924 I, W, 1925 E, F

Rickit, H (Waikato) 1981 S 1, 2

Riechelmann, C C (Auckland) 1997 Fj (R), Arg 1(R), A 1(R), SA 2(t), I (R), E 2(t)

Ridland, A J (Southland) 1910 A 1, 2, 3

Roberts, E J (Wellington) 1914 A 1, 2, 3, 1921 SA 2, 3

Roberts, F (Wellington) 1905 S, I, E, W, 1907 A 1, 2, 3, 1908 AW 1, 3, 1910 A 1, 2, 3

Roberts, R W (Taranaki) 1913 A 1, US, 1914 A 1, 2, 3

Robertson, B J (Counties) 1972 A 1, 3, S, 1973 E 1, I, F, 1974 A 1, 2, 3, I, 1976 I, SA 1, 2, 3, 4, 1977 BI 1, 3, 4, F 1, 2, 1978 A 1, 2, 3, W, E, S, 1979 F 1, 2, A, 1980 A 2, 3, W, 1981 S 1, 2

Robertson, D J (Otago) 1974 A 1, 2, 3, I, 1975 S, 1976 I, SA 1, 3, 4, 1977 BI 1

Robertson, S M (Canterbury) 1998 A 2(R), SA 2(R), A 3(R),

1999 [It (R)], 2000 Tg (R), S 1, 2(R), A 1, SA 1(R), 2(R), F 1, 2, It, 2001 I, S, Arg 2, 2002 I 1, 2, Fj (R), A 1, SA 1, A 2, SA 2

Robilliard, A C C (Canterbury) 1928 SA 1, 2, 3, 4

Robinson, C E (Southland) 1951 A 1, 2, 3, 1952 A 1, 2

Robinson, K J (Waikato) 2002 E, F (R), W, 2004 E1, 2, PI, 2006 E, 2007 SA2, A2, [R, F]

Robinson, M D (North Harbour) 1998 E 1(R), 2001 S (R), Arg 2

Robinson, M P (Canterbury) 2000 S 2, SA 1, 2002 It, I 2, A 1, SA 1, E (t&R), F, W (R)

Rokocoko, J T (Auckland) 2003 E, W, F, SA 1, A 1, SA 2, A 2, [It, W, SA, A, F], 2004 E1, 2, Arg, PI, A1, SA1, A2, SA2, It, W, F, 2005 SA1(R), A1, SA2, A2, W, E(R), S, 2006 I1, 2, A1, 2, 3, SA3, E, F1, 2, 2007 F1, 2, SA1, A1, SA2, A2, [Pt, R, F], 2008 S, I2, W, E3, 2009 F1, 2, It1, SA1, 2, A2, SA3, A3

Rollerson, D L (Manawatu) 1980 W, 1981 S 2, SA 1, 2, 3, R, F 1(R), 2

Roper, R A (Taranaki) 1949 A 2, 1950 BI 1, 2, 3, 4

Ross, I B (Canterbury) 2009 F1, 2, It1, A1, SA1, 2, A2, SA3

Rowley, H C B (Wanganui) 1949 A 2

Rush, E J (North Harbour) 1995 [W (R), J], It, F 1, 2, 1996 S 1(R), 2, A 1(t), SA 1(R)

Rush, X J (Auckland) 1998 A 3, 2004 E1, 2, PI, A1, SA1, A2, SA2

Rutledge, L M (Southland) 1978 A 1, 2, 3, I, W, E, S, 1979 F 1, 2, A, 1980 A 1, 2, 3

Ryan, J (Wellington) 1910 A 2, 1914 A 1, 2, 3

Ryan, J A C (Otago) 2005 Fj, BI3(R), A1(R), SA2(R), A2(R), W, S, 2006 F1, W(R)

Sadler, B S (Wellington) 1935 S, I, W, 1936 A 1, 2

Salmon, J L B (Wellington) 1981 R, F 1, 2(R)

Savage, L T (Canterbury) 1949 SA 1, 2, 4

Saxton, C K (South Canterbury) 1938 A 1, 2, 3

Schuler, K J (Manawatu, North Harbour) 1990 A 2(R), 1992 A 2, 1995 [I (R), J]

Schuster, N J (Wellington) 1988 A 1, 2, 3, 1989 F 1, 2, Arg 1, 2, A, W, I

Schwalger, J E (Wellington) 2007 C, 2008 I1(R)

Scott, R W H (Auckland) 1946 A 1, 2, 1947 A 1, 2, 1949 SA 1, 2, 3, 4, 1950 BI 1, 2, 3, 4, 1953 W, 1954 I, E, S, F

Scown, A I (Taranaki) 1972 A 1, 2, 3, W (R), S

Scrimshaw, G (Canterbury) 1928 SA 1

Seear, G A (Otago) 1977 F 1, 2, 1978 A 1, 2, 3, I, W, E, S, 1979 F 1, 2, A

Seeling, C E (Auckland) 1904 BI, 1905 S, I, E, W, 1906 F, 1907 A 1, 2, 1908 AW 1, 2, 3

Sellars, G M V (Auckland) 1913 A 1, US

Senio, K (Bay of Plenty) 2005 A2(R)

Shaw, M W (Manawatu, Hawke's Bay) 1980 A 1, 2, 3(R), W, 1981 S 1, 2, SA 1, 2, R, F 1, 2, 1982 A 1, 2, 3, 1983 BI 1, 2, 3, 4, A, S, E, 1984 F 1, 2, A 1, 1985 E 1, 2, A, Arg 1, 2, 1986 A 3

Shelford, F N K (Bay of Plenty) 1981 SA 3, R, 1984 A 2, 3

Shelford, W T (North Harbour) 1986 F 2, 3, 1987 [It, Fj, S, W, F], A, 1988 W 1, 2, A 1, 2, 3, 1989 F 1, 2, Arg 1, 2, A, W, I, 1990 S 1, 2

Siddells, S K (Wellington) 1921 SA 3

Simon, H J (Otago) 1937 SA 1, 2, 3

Simpson, J G (Auckland) 1947 A 1, 2, 1949 SA 1, 2, 3, 4, 1950 BI 1, 2, 3

Simpson, V L J (Canterbury) 1985 Arg 1, 2

Sims, G S (Otago) 1972 A 2

Sivivatu, S W (Waikato) 2005 Fj, BI1, 2, 3, I, E, 2006 SA2, 3, E(H), F1, 2, W, 2007 F1, 2, C, SA1, A1(R), [It, S, R, F], 2008 I1, E1, SA1, 2, A1, 2, SA3, A3, 4, I2, W, E3, 2009 A1, SA1, 2, A2

Skeen, J R (Auckland) 1952 A 2

Skinner, K L (Otago, Counties) 1949 SA 1, 2, 3, 4, 1950 BI 1, 2, 3, 4, 1951 A 1, 2, 3, 1952 A 1, 2, 1953 W, 1954 I, E, S, F, 1956 SA 3, 4

Skudder, G R (Waikato) 1969 W 2

Slater, G L (Taranaki) 2000 F 1(R), 2(R), It (R)

Sloane, P H (North Auckland) 1979 E

Smith, A E (Taranaki) 1969 W 1, 2, 1970 SA 1

Smith, B W (Waikato) 1984 F 1, 2, A 1

Smith, C G (Wellington) 2004 It, F, 2005 Fj(R), BI3, W, S, 2006 F1, W, 2007 SA2(R), [Pt, S, R(R)], 2008 I1, E1, SA1, 2, A1(R), 2, SA3, Sm, A3, 4, I2, E3, 2009 F2, A1, SA1, 2, A2

Smith, G W (Auckland) 1905 S, I

NEW ZEALAND

NEW ZEALAND DOMESTIC RUGBY

By Gregor Paul

Auckland's Ranfurly Shield clash with Wellington captured New Zealand hearts.

It was another year for New Zealanders to worry more about what was happening off the field than what was taking place on it.

In early May, all 26 provinces met in Wellington to discuss the future of the Air New Zealand Cup. Even the two giants, Auckland and Canterbury, were feeling the financial strain while other unions such as Bay of Plenty and Tasman were in need of a New Zealand Rugby Union hand-out to survive.

The decision to increase the Premier Division in 2006 to 14 teams from 10 had finally taken its toll. Adding four teams had sent player costs spiralling out of control and too many unions were paying what they couldn't afford.

Other factors such as the global recession and a reduction in attendances conspired to make the perfect storm and in May it was agreed that the competition had to be slimmed down to 10 teams from 2010.

It was hardly the ideal way to begin the competition in mid-July – with the axe hovering over four teams. Making it even tougher was the knowledge that final positions in the table would not determine the four sides who would be relegated. The process was going to be more complex, with every team assessed on a range of criteria from their financial strength, the number of players registered and the number who made age grade or representative teams.

With such disruption looming, the championship kicked off with little public expectation and virtually no fanfare. It did, however, prove to be the undisputed highlight of the entire season.

Television audiences were up almost 85 percent on 2008 with Auckland's clash with Wellington for the Ranfurly Shield in round four gaining an audience of 260,000 – a figure no Super 14 clash was remotely close to gaining.

It wasn't just the major unions, though, who captured the imagination. In fact the real story of the competition was the way the likes of Bay of Plenty, Southland and Tasman stole the show. These three teams, as well as Hawke's Bay and Taranaki, enjoyed their best campaigns in years – with Tasman defeating Auckland and Bay of Plenty toppling Canterbury and Wellington. The quality of rugby was outstanding and even the real minnows, Counties Manukau, Northland and Manawatu, ran everyone a lot closer than they ever had.

It was genuinely exciting – the competition the NZRU had always wanted it to be and the irony of course was that they had already decided to make dramatic changes.

The unprecedented popularity of the provincial championship may also have had much to do with Super 14's failure to excite. Starting in early February, New Zealanders were slow to get behind the competition. Crowds and TV audiences were poor for the early rounds and so was much of the rugby. There was also a distinct lack of new heroes, with no one emerging from obscurity to push for an All Black place.

It said much for the lack of overall quality that an erratic and flawed Hurricanes team were able to make the semi-finals as were a vastly inexperienced Crusaders unit who only once managed to secure a try-scoring bonus point. The Chiefs also made the play-offs for the first time since 2004, but they deserved their place and went on to the final where they were hammered by the Bulls in Pretoria.

Defeat in South Africa was to become a familiar theme with the All Blacks beaten there twice by the Springboks, before losing again in Hamilton to be relieved of their Tri-Nations title. The struggles of the national team – who lost four of their first nine Tests – saw the long-serving coaching panel of Graham Henry, Steve Hansen and Wayne Smith come under severe pressure but all three had their contracts extended through to Rugby World Cup 2011.

The coaching panel were the last piece in a jigsaw that was begun last year with the retention of both Richie McCaw and Dan Carter. That was when the NZRU began a targeted recruitment campaign to keep their senior players in New Zealand. The signatures of Ali Williams, Tony Woodcock, Mils Muliaina, Rodney So'oialo and Brad Thorn gave them a scarcely believable 100 per cent return.

Preparations off the field for 2011 also took some giant steps with the redevelopment of Auckland's Eden Park running ahead of schedule and budgets found to carry out construction work at Okara Park in Northland and McLean Park in Napier.

The other highlight of the year on the national stage was the performance of the Under 20 team who cruised to the Junior World Championship title in June. They were led by the hugely impressive Aaron Cruden, who took his place in the side after recovering from testicular cancer. The success did carry a sad edge as shortly after the final, the father of Hurricanes wing Zac Guildford died from a heart attack. Cruden was named IRB Junior Player of the Year and the performance of the Under 20s made up for the Sevens team losing their IRB Sevens World Series title to South Africa.

Making it a year of truly mixed success was the confirmation that player numbers grew one percent in 2009. While the overall rise was not as high as the previous year, the key Under 12 age group experienced significant growth.

A week before these numbers were announced, an ugly brawl in the semi-final of the Auckland Schools Championship between Auckland Boys Grammar School and Kelston Grammar did much to damage rugby's reputation. The game was televised and attended by All Black coach Henry, a former teacher at both institutions, and was headline news for several days.

That made news for all the wrong reasons, unlike the final of the women's provincial competition. The encounter between Auckland and Canterbury – which Auckland won – was the first time ever that a top-level domestic match had a female referee and female assistant referees. Waikato's Lee Jeffrey had the whistle, with Cantabrians Nicky Inwood and Chelsea Gurr running the sidelines.

PORTUGAL

PORTUGAL'S 2008–09 TEST RECORD

OPPONENTS	DATE	VENUE	RESULT
Canada	1 November	H	**Lost** 13–21
England Saxons	30 January	A	**Lost** 0–66
Russia	7 February	H	**Lost** 14–18
Georgia	14 February	A	**Drew** 20–20
Germany	21 February	H	**Won** 44–6
Spain	15 March	H	**Won** 24–19
Romania	21 March	A	**Won** 22–21

THE FUTURE IS BRIGHT

By Frankie Deges

The Portuguese are very clear on their Rugby World Cup 2011 intentions. Having played in the 2007 tournament in France, fully aware of how important it has become for the growth of the game in their country, Os Lobos are desperate to qualify for consecutive World Cups.

They also know very well that in their current position (third at the halfway stage) in the European qualifying system they would face, again, the Repechage. They know how hard that is and how close they came to missing out against Uruguay in 2007, winning by a single point on aggregate, so the goal is clear – qualify directly either as Europe 1 or Europe 2.

Their ambitions are supported by good performances and important wins in the European Nations Cup and by what at first look seems a favourable draw for 2010, when all the matches in the top division will take place in February and March, during the Six Nations window.

If Portugal drew 1,000 spectators for a Test match before RWC 2007, they now attract over 5,000 and the playing numbers have also ballooned, ensuring a bright future for the geographically western-most European nation.

Tomaz Morais continues to be in charge of all that occurs on a rugby field when it comes to senior rugby. As he has been doing since he took charge in 2002, he wears the hat of XVs and Sevens coach, although it was clearly understood that the bigger version of the game will need all his attention in the quest for a place at RWC 2011.

The 2008/09 season all began against Canada, who visited Lisbon's Universitario Stadium on the first day of November. The Canucks managed to win a tight game 21–11, one that saw the home side generate a lot of possession they were unable to turn into points because of a strong Canadian defence and the inability to generate try-scoring chances. "We lost some very valuable possession," rued Morais after the game.

A side containing some new players travelled to Ireland for a two-match tour which showed the gulf existing with professional sides. Connacht beat them 27–11 and four days later, the mighty Munster – who a week later tackled New Zealand – overpowered the Portuguese 62–6.

After an international break for the national squad, in preparation for the start of their 2009 European Nations Cup campaign – which would account for half of the two-year qualifying process – Portugal travelled to Edgeley Park to tackle the England Saxons in late January. Despite never giving in, the very strong home side still defeated them 66–0. Reflecting on that night, former Test captain Vasco Uva admitted "it helped us see where exactly we were as a team."

They would not gel instantly as a week later they hosted Russia at home. Two first half mistakes led to Russian tries that paved the way for the visitors to win 18–14. "After that game we met as a team, regrouped, refocused and going to Tbilisi proved a turning point," explained Uva.

Twelve thousand vociferous fans at the National Stadium were kept on the edge of their seats throughout an enthralling game. As the first half was coming to a 3–3 end, David Mateus crossed for the first of two Portuguese tries. Georgia soon reacted and by the 57th minute the hosts were back in the lead 13–10, although once more Portugal levelled the match. The final minutes would be incredible – centre Pedro Silva scored a try which full-back Pedro Leal converted in the 80th minute, but Georgia did not lie down and three minutes later scored their own converted try to tie the game.

Buoyed by an important draw at an always difficult venue, back on home soil Portugal were too efficient for Germany, dispatching them 44–6 with cruel efficiency.

Given the rather thin pool of talented players, eight players from the Rugby World Cup Sevens squad that two weeks later played in Dubai had been involved in the Tbilisi and Lisbon games. Morais was also in charge for both and when the ENC recommenced, a ninth was added. This meant that the win against Spain was disjointed.

"It's not easy for those playing fifteens and sevens," admitted Morais. "Sometimes they have problems with fatigue, but they are very good players so they cope. Next season we hope to have two separate teams competing in the different disciplines because it's impossible to do really well in both." Wise words from a wise coach.

The 24–19 win against neighbours Spain proved harder than expected – probably because the team was still making the switch back from the Sevens format. "We thought it would be easier and we misjudged the passion of the Spaniards," admitted Uva.

The final ENC match of the season was in Bucharest, where Portugal had never won. Crucial in many ways, it was important that João Correia's side won to ensure they were in a good starting position for the resumption in 2010. This was also going to be Portugal's last Test of the season as there were no June tournaments for Os Lobos.

The stadionul National Arcul de Triumf in the Romanian capital was

PORTUGAL

not prepared for what transpired with Portugal winning the tightest of games 22–21.

Romania dominated at will during the first hour, scoring two tries in the opening half for a 15–6 lead, stretched to 21–9 with two penalties before the 50th minute mark. Portugal soon clicked back into action and full-back Pedro Cabral, with penalties in the 61st and 77th minute, left Os Lobos within a converted try of winning the game.

From an attacking lineout, the forwards kept it tight and drove the maul into the in-goal area where Argentina-born Juan Severino scored in the last minute. Leal, kicking from right to left, 15 yards from the upright, added the extra two points for the win.

"The celebrations on the final whistle showed how close we are as a squad and how important the win was for us," said Severino.

As the curtain fell for the fifteens squad, the win gave them sufficient momentum for a long off-season in which a hard fitness regime was to be adhered to.

Portugal has always made a name for itself in Sevens and this year they shared joy and dejection, almost in equal measure. After a long and well-planned preparation, they beat France to win the Bowl in Dubai and then having reached the top eight, lost the final of the Plate to England in George.

The next tournament was the Rugby World Cup Sevens where the record was won two, lost three. The wins coming against Canada and Ireland, the losses to Scotland, Australia and Samoa.

Silverware in the form of the Bowl was picked up in Hong Kong with a 14–12 defeat of Uruguay in the final and in Adelaide the road ended in the Shield semi-finals. London saw them lose the Plate final 24–10 to Fiji, while in the final leg in Edinburgh it was England who beat them 31–7 in the Bowl semi-final.

Os Lobos' Sevens season continued with wins in Sopot and Ostrava, two legs of the European Sevens circuit. However Portugal were unable to successfully defend their European title in Hanover, a series of injuries suffered on day one ultimately seeing them finish seventh.

One of eight nations to attend the World Games in July, Portugal won the silver medal after beating Argentina 19–0 in the semi-final before running out of steam in the final against Fiji, although the 43–10 loss didn't take any gloss off the medal won in Kaohsiung, Chinese Taipei.

When Rugby Sevens is included in the Olympic Games, the boost the game can receive in Portugal is huge. However the growth since RWC 2007 has been sustained and the pool of players is growing. The Under 19 side finished fourth in the FIRA–AER Championship, drawing the semi-final with Romania but having to play off for third place against Russia, beating them 32–29 for the bronze medal.

The domestic championship was as always extremely hard fought. Eight teams make up the national tournament – Campeonato Super Bock – with six of them from Lisbon and one each from Porto and Coimbra.

Grupo Desportivo Direito won the tournament, beating AEIS Agronomia 32–25 in the final. It was the sixth time they had won the national title with Portugal captain Correia, Eduardo Acosta, Pedro Leal and José Pinto among their stars.

Rugby in Portugal has continued its growth curve, understandably losing some momentum from the previous season where, thanks to the performance in RWC 2007, the numbers multiplied. The Federaçao Portuguesa de Rugby, by all accounts, has been doing good work ensuring the growth is well supported.

With the smell of a second Rugby World Cup in their nostrils, some wind on their back thanks to a good fixture schedule and some good wins in the European Nations Cup, the future looks positive for Portugal.

PORTUGAL

PORTUGAL INTERNATIONAL STATISTICS
MATCH RECORDS UP TO 30TH SEPTEMBER 2009

WINNING MARGIN

Date	Opponent	Result	Winning Margin
23/11/1996	Netherlands	55–11	44
30/05/1998	Andorra	53–11	42
28/02/1981	Switzerland	39–0	39
13/05/2006	Ukraine	52–14	38
21/02/2009	Germany	44–6	38

MOST TRIES IN A MATCH
BY THE TEAM

Date	Opponent	Result	Tries
30/05/1998	Andorra	53–11	9
15/05/1981	Denmark	45–16	9
13/05/2006	Ukraine	52–14	8
23/11/1996	Netherlands	55–11	8

MOST POINTS IN A MATCH
BY THE TEAM

Date	Opponent	Result	Pts.
23/11/1996	Netherlands	55–11	55
30/05/1998	Andorra	53–11	53
13/05/2006	Ukraine	52–14	52
15/05/1981	Denmark	45–16	45
21/02/2009	Germany	44–6	44

MOST CONVERSIONS IN A MATCH
BY THE TEAM

Date	Opponent	Result	Cons
13/05/2006	Ukraine	52–14	6
23/11/2006	Netherlands	55–11	6
21/02/2009	Germany	44–6	5

MOST PENALTIES IN A MATCH
BY THE TEAM

Date	Opponent	Result	Pens
06/02/2000	Georgia	30–32	9
23/03/2003	Spain	35–16	7
20/02/2000	Spain	21–19	7
29/03/2003	Russia	25–14	6

MOST DROP GOALS IN A MATCH
BY THE TEAM

Date	Opponent	Result	DGs
17/03/1985	Marocco	12–6	2
05/05/1990	Belgium	24–12	2

MOST POINTS IN A MATCH
BY A PLAYER

Date	Player	Opponent	Pts.
06/02/2000	Thierry Teixeira	Georgia	30
23/03/2003	Gonçalo Malheiro	Spain	25
08/03/2003	Gonçalo Malheiro	Czech Republic	24
16/02/2008	Pedro Cabral	Czech Republic	22
10/06/2004	Gonçalo Malheiro	Barbarians	21

MOST TRIES IN A MATCH
BY A PLAYER

Date	Player	Opponent	Tries
21/03/2004	Nuno Garvão	Spain	3
10/06/2004	Gonçalo Malheiro	Barbarians	3
23/11/1996	Rohan Hoffman	Netherlands	3

MOST CONVERSIONS IN A MATCH
BY A PLAYER

Date	Player	Opponent	Cons
23/11/1996	Nuno Maria Vilar Gomes	Netherlands	6
30/05/1998	Nuno Mourao	Andorra	4
08/04/1984	Joao Queimado	Denmark	4
13/05/2006	João Diogo Mota	Ukraine	4
16/02/2008	Pedro Cabral	Czech Republic	4

MOST PENALTIES IN A MATCH
BY A PLAYER

Date	Player	Opponent	Pens
06/02/2000	Thierry Teixeira	Georgia	9
23/03/2003	Gonçalo Malheiro	Spain	7
29/03/2003	Gonçalo Malheiro	Russia	6

MOST DROP GOALS IN A MATCH
BY A PLAYER

Date	Player	Opponent	DGs
17/03/1985	Joao Queimado	Morocco	2

MOST CAPPED PLAYERS

Name	Caps
Joaquim Ferreira	84
Luis Pissarra	72
Diogo Mateus	64
Marcello D'Orey	57
Miguel Portela	56

LEADING TRY SCORERS

Name	Tries
Diogo Mateus	14
Nuno Durão	14
António Aguilar	14
Rohan Hoffman	13

LEADING CONVERSIONS SCORERS

Name	Cons
Joao Queimado	22
Gonçalo Malheiro	21
Pedro Leal	19
Nuno Mourao	16
Duarte Cardoso Pinto	15

LEADING PENALTY SCORERS

Name	Pens
Joao Queimado	63
Gonçalo Malheiro	53
José Maria Vilar Gomes	28
Pedro Cabral	24

LEADING DROP GOAL SCORERS

Name	DGs
Joao Queimado	12
Gonçalo Malheiro	2

LEADING POINTS SCORERS

Name	Pts.
Joao Queimado	294
Gonçalo Malheiro	242
José Maria Vilar Gomes	134
Nuno Mourao	115
Duarte Cardoso Pinto	106

PORTUGAL INTERNATIONAL
PLAYERS
UP TO 30TH SEPTEMBER 2009

Note: Years given for International Championship matches are for second half of season; eg 1972 means season 1971–72. Years for all other matches refer to the actual year of the match.

ED Acosta 2006 *Rus, ArA, Ur*, 2007 *R*, 2008 *Geo, Rus, R*, 2009 *Rus, R*

A Águas 1984 *H, Bel, De*, 1985 *Mor, Cze, Pol, Z*, 1986 *R, R*, 1987 *Z, Z, Tun, Bel*, 1988 *Ger*

D Aguiar 1970 *H, Mor, Sp*, 1981 *Swi, De, Swe*, 1982 *Mor, Sp*

R Aguiar 2005 *Ur*, 2006 *Ukr, CZR*, 2008 *Geo, CZR, Geo, Rus, R*

A Aguilar 1999 *H, Ur, Ur*, 2000 *Geo, Sp, SA23*, 2001 *R, H, Rus*, 2002 *R, Geo, Sp, H, Rus, Pol, Sp*, 2003 *Geo, Sp*, 2004 *Geo, R, CZR, Sp, Rus, Bb*, 2005 *Rus, R, Ch, Ur, Fj*, 2006 *Rus, Geo, R, Ukr, CZR, Rus, ArA, Ur, It, Rus, Geo, Geo* 2007 *C, NZ, It, R, R*, 2008 *Geo, R, Sp*, 2009 *Ger, R*

E Albergaria 1935 *Sp*

JM Albergaria 1981 *Swi*

M Albuquerque 1987 *USS*, 1988 *Yug*

AV Almeida 1983 *Sp, H, Pol, Swe*, 1984 *Sp, H, Bel, De*, 1985 *Mor, Cze, Pol, Z*, 1986 *R, F, It, Tun, R*, 1987 *It, Bel*, 1988 *H, Ger, Yug*, 1989 *H, Bel, Yug, Ger, Cze, H*, 1990 *Bel, Tun, Sp*, 1991 *Nm*

J Almeida 1954 *Sp*

PM Almeida 1974 *Ger*

G Alpuim 1998 *US, And*, 2006 *CZR, ArA*

FP Álvares 1954 *Sp*

AF Amaral 1965 *Sp*, 1969 *Sp*

SF Amaral 1997 *Geo, Sp*, 1998 *Nm, Ger, US, CZR, Mor, Sp, And, S, Sp*, 1999 *H, Ur, Ur*, 2000 *Geo, Sp, R, Mor, H*

A Andrade 1970 *H, Mor*, 1972 *It*

AR Andrade 1994 *Bel, Ger, Mor, Tun, W, Sp*, 1995 *Mor*

LR Andrade 2002 *Sp*, 2003 *Rus*, 2004 *Geo, R, CZR, Sp, Rus, Bb, Ch, Ur, Ukr*, 2005 *Geo, CZR, Rus*, 2006 *Ukr, CZR*, 2007 *CZR*

T Antunes 1970 *Sp*

FX Araújo 1935 *Sp*, 1936 *Sp*

M Ascenção 1999 *Ur*

JC Augusto 1970 *Sp*, 1972 *It, It*

GB Ávila 1973 *It, Yug, Swi, Pol, Pol*

AM Avilez 1936 *Sp*

S Azevedo 1997 *Sp*, 1998 *Nm, Ger, US, CZR, Mor, Sp, And*

J Baptista 1998 *US, And*, 2002 *R*

M Baptista 1993 *It, Bel*, 1994 *Bel, Ger, Mor, Tun, W, Sp*

R Barata 1998 *Nm, Ger*

M Barbosa 1996 *Sp, H, Tun*, 1998 *S, Sp*, 1999 *H, Ur, Ur*, 2000 *Geo, Sp, R, Mor, H*, 2001 *H, Rus*

J Barceló 1936 *Sp*

J Bardy 2008 *C*, 2009 *R*

R Bastos 1935 *Sp*

R Begonha 1966 *Sp, Bel*

FL Belo 1986 *R*, 1987 *It, F, Z*, 1988 *H, Ger, Yug*

J Belo 1954 *Sp*

JFL Belo 1985 *Mor, Cze, Pol*, 1986 *F, It, Tun, USS, R*, 1987 *It, F, Z, Z, Tun, USS*, 1988 *H, Ger, Yug*, 1989 *H, Bel, Yug, Ger, Cze, H*, 1990 *Sp*

R Benedito 2000 *SA23*, 2001 *Geo, Sp*

J Bento 1997 *Geo, Sp*, 1998 *Nm*

H Bergh 2003 *R, CZR, Sp, Rus*

JP Bessa 1969 *Sp, Mor*, 1972 *It, It*, 1974 *It*

A Borges 1966 *Sp, Bel*

F Borges 1989 *H*, 1991 *Mor, Nm*, 1992 *And, Mor, Tun*, 1993 *It, Tun, Swi*

O Borges 1979 *Swi*, 1981 *Swi, De, Swe*

R Borges 1997 *Geo, Sp*

F Braga 1995 *Mor, Sp*

A Branco 1968 *Sp, Bel, Mor, It*, 1970 *Sp*, 1974 *Ger*

E Branco 2000 *Mor, H*, 2001 *R*, 2002 *Geo, Sp, H, Rus*

E Branco 1935 *Sp*, 1936 *Sp*

MA Branco 1965 *Sp*, 1970 *H, Sp*

MdePC Branco 1965 *Sp*, 1966 *Sp, Bel*, 1967 *Sp, F, R*, 1968 *Sp, Bel, Mor, It*, 1969 *Sp, Mor*, 1970 *H, Mor*

GVB Bravo 1954 *Sp*

JS Brito 1973 *It, Yug, Swi, Pol, Pol*, 1974 *It, Ger*

L Briz 1973 *Yug, Pol, Pol*

C Bruxelas 1935 *Sp*

P Cabral 2006 *Ur*, 2007 *Sp, Rus, CZR, C, S, It, R*, 2008 *Geo, CZR, Geo, Rus, R, Sp, C*, 2009 *Rus, Geo, Ger, Sp, R*

P Cabrita 1966 *Sp, Bel*

L Caldas 1954 *Sp*

F Calheiros 1935 *Sp*

J Canha 1999 *Ur, Ur*

A Carapuço 1987 *It*

F Cardoso 1999 *H, Ur, Ur*

M Cardoso 2000 *Geo, Sp, R, Mor, H*, 2001 *R, Geo, Sp, H, Rus*

AM Carqueijeiro 1965 *Sp*

A Cartucho 1970 *Sp*

J Carvalho 1998 *Sp, Sp*, 1999 *H*, 2000 *Geo, Sp, R*

P Carvalho 2004 *Ch, Ur, Ukr*, 2005 *Geo, CZR, Rus, Fj*, 2006 *Ukr, CZR, Rus, ItA, ArA, Ur, It, Rus, Geo, Geo*, 2007 *Mor, Mor, Sp, Ur, Ur, CZR, C, S, NZ, R*

R Carvoeira 1990 *Mor, Nm*, 1991 *And, Nm*

C Castro 1993 *R, H, SA23*, 2001 *R, Sp, Rus*

PM Castro 1995 *Sp, CZR, Ger*, 1996 *It, Bel, R, Pol, Tun*, 1997 *Geo, Sp*, 1998 *Ger, CZR, Sp, And, S, Sp*, 2002 *Geo*, 2006 *Geo*

F Cather 2001 *Sp, H, Rus*

J Catulo 1993 *R*, 1996 *It, Bel, Pol*

V Cayola 1935 *Sp*

J Chança 1990 *Mor, Nm*, 1992 *Tun*

R Chança 1998 *Nm, Ger, US, CZR*

LM Chaves 1965 *Sp*, 1966 *Sp, Bel*, 1967 *It, F, R*, 1969 *Sp*, 1970 *Sp*

L Claro 1981 *Swi*

A Cláudio 1997 *Geo, Sp*, 1998 *Sp, And*

A Coelho 1935 *Sp*

B Conceicao 2006 *Rus, Geo, H*

P Consciência 1979 *Swi*

R Cordeiro 2002 *R, Geo, Sp, H, Rus, Pol, Sp*, 2003 *Geo, R, CZR, Sp, Rus*, 2004 *Geo, R, CZR, Sp, Rus, Bb, Ch, Ur, Ukr*, 2005 *Rus, R, Ch, Ur, Fj*, 2006 *Rus, Geo, R, CZR, Rus, ItA, ArA, Ur, It, Rus, Geo, Geo*, 2007 *Mor, Mor, Sp, Ur, CZR, S, NZ, It, R*

E Correia 1998 *US, Mor*

H Correia 1935 *Sp*, 1936 *Sp*

J Correia 1999 *Ur*

J Correia 2003 *CZR, Sp*, 2004 *Bb, Ch, Ur, Ukr*, 2005 *Geo, CZR, Rus, R, Ch, Ur, Fj*, 2006 *Rus, R, Ukr, Rus, It, Rus, Geo, Geo*, 2007 *Mor, Mor, Sp, Ur, Ur, C, S, NZ, It, R, R, R*, 2008 *Geo, CZR, Geo, Rus, R, Sp, C*, 2009 *Rus, Geo, Ger, Sp, R*

P Correia 1990 *Mor, Nm, Bel, Tun*, 1993 *R, It, Swi, Sp*

AP Costa 1967 *Sp*, 1968 *Bel, It*, 1969 *Sp, Mor*, 1970 *H, Mor*

JP Costa 1996 *It, Bel, R, Pol*

LC Costa 1979 *Swi*, 1981 *Bel*, 1982 *Mor, Sp, Tun, Pol*

LP Costa 1969 *Sp, Mor*, 1970 *H, Mor*

MF Costa 1973 *Yug*, 1981 *Swi, De, Swe*, 1982 *Mor, Sp, H, Pol*, 1983 *Sp*, 1984 *Sp, H, Bel, De*

MMd Costa 1987 *Bel*

P Costa 2000 *R*

RB Costa 1969 *Sp, Mor*

T Costa 1998 *Nm*

V Couceiro 2004 *Sp*

D Coutinho 2000 *SA23*, 2001 *H, Rus*, 2002 *Sp, Pol, Sp*, 2004

Bb, 2005 Geo, CZR, Ur, Fj, 2006 Rus, Geo, R, Ukr, CZR, Rus, ItA, ArA, Ur, It, Rus, Geo, Geo, 2007 Mor, Sp, Ur, Rus, CZR, C, S, NZ, R, R

P Coutinho 1986 USS

C Cruz 1935 Sp, 1936 Sp

A Cunha 1990 Nm, Tun, Sp, 1991 Nm, 1992 And, Mor, Tun, 1993 R, It, Tun, Bel, Swi, Sp, 1994 Mor, W, Sp, 1995 Mor, Sp, CZR, Ger, 1996 It, R, Pol, Sp, H, Tun, 2000 SA23, 2001 Geo, H, 2002 R, Geo, Sp, H, Rus, Pol, Sp, 2003 Geo, R, CZR, Sp, Rus, 2004 Geo, R, CZR, Sp, Rus, Bb, Ch, Ur, Ukr, 2005 Geo, CZR

J Cunha 1969 Mor

S Cunha 1992 And, Mor, Tun, 1993 R, It, Tun, Bel, Swi, Sp, 1994 Bel

S Cunha 2004 R, Ch, Ukr, 2005 Geo, CZR, Ch, Ur, 2006 Rus, 2008 Geo, CZR, Geo, Rus, Sp

P Curvelo 1989 Bel, Yug, Ger

V Dias 1968 Bel, Mor, It

P Domingos 1994 Bel, Ger, Mor, Tun, W, Sp

A Dores 1979 Swi, 1981 Swi, Bel, De

M d'Orey 1996 Sp, H, Tun, 1997 Geo, Sp, 1998 Nm, Ger, US, CZR, Mor, Sp, And, Sp, 1999 Ur, 2002 R, Geo, Sp, H, Rus, Pol, Sp, 2003 Geo, R, CZR, Sp, Rus, 2004 Geo, R, CZR, Sp, Rus, Bb, Ch, Ur, Ukr, 2005 Geo, CZR, Rus, R, Ch, Ur, Fj, 2006 Rus, Geo, R, Ukr, CZR, ItA, ArA, Ur, It, Rus, Geo, Geo, 2007 Mor, Mor, Ur, Ur, NZ

R D'Orey Branco 2007 Rus, CZR

D dos Reis 2008 C, 2009 Ger

A Duarte 2008 Geo, CZR, Geo, Rus, R

B Duarte 2008 Geo, CZR, Rus, R, Sp, 2009 Ger

G Duarte 2006 Geo, 2007 Mor, Sp, Rus, CZR, 2008 Geo, CZR, Geo, Rus

J Duarte 1999 Ur

J Duarte 1936 Sp

AG Duque 1972 It, 1973 It, Yug, Pol, Pol, 1974 It, 1981 De, Swe, 1982 Mor, Sp, Tun, Pol

N Durão 1983 Sp, 1984 H, Bel, De, 1985 Mor, Cze, Pol, Z, 1986 R, F, It, Tun, USS, R, 1987 It, F, Z, Z, Tun, USS, Bel, 1988 H, Ger, Yug, 1989 H, Bel, Yug, Ger, Cze, H, 1990 Sp, 1991 And, Tun, Mor, 1992 And, Mor, Tun, 1994 Bel, Ger, 1995 Mor, Sp, CZR, Ger

R Durão 1986 R, F, R, 1987 Z, Z, Tun, Bel, 1988 H, Ger, Yug

V Durão 1990 Mor, Nm, Bel, Tun, 1991 And, Mor, Nm, 1992 And, Mor, Tun, 1995 Mor, Sp, CZR, Ger, 1996 It, Bel, R, Pol, Sp, H, Tun

P Eiró 1979 Swi, 1981 Swi, Bel, De, Swe, 1982 Mor, Tun, H, Pol

R Escarduça 1998 And

A Esteves 1995 Mor, Sp

A Esteves 2006 Rus, It, 2007 Mor, 2008 Geo, CZR, Geo, Rus, R, Sp, C, 2009 Sp, R

F Esteves 1995 Ger

O Fachada 1987 It, Z, USS

DL Faria 1979 Swi, 1981 Bel

G Faria 2001 Geo, 2002 Pol, Sp

J Faria 1967 Sp, It, 1968 Sp, Bel, It

LL Faria 1966 Sp, Bel, 1967 Sp, It, F, R, 1968 Sp, Bel, Mor, It

NL Faria 1968 Sp, Bel, Mor, It, 1970 Sp, 1972 It, It, 1973 It, Yug, Swi, Pol, Pol, 1974 It, Ger

PL Faria 1966 Sp, Bel, 1967 Sp, It, F, R, 1970 H, Mor, Sp, 1973 It, Yug, Swi, Pol, Pol

VL Faria 1981 De, Swe, 1982 Mor, Sp, Tun, H

A Fernandes 1973 Swi

AC Fernandes 1970 H, Mor, Sp, 1972 It, It, 1973 Swi, 1974 Ger

JC Fernandes 1972 It, It, 1974 It, 1979 Swi, 1981 Swi, Bel, De, Swe, 1982 Mor, Sp, Tun, H, Pol

PN Fernandes 1993 R, Tun, Bel, 1994 Mor, Tun, W, Sp, 1996 Sp, H

R Fernandes 1991 Mor, Nm

A Ferreira 2005 Rus, R, Ur, Fj

AB Ferreira 1982 Sp, Tun, H, Pol, 1983 Sp, H, Pol, 1984 Sp, H, Bel, De, 1985 Mor, Cze, Pol, Z, 1986 R, F, It, Tun, USS, 1987 Z, Z, Tun, USS, Bel, 1988 H, Ger, Yug, 1989 H, Bel, Yug, Ger, Cze, H

CD Ferreira 1979 Swi, 1981 Swi, Bel

CN Ferreira 1965 Sp, 1966 Sp, Bel, 1967 Sp, It, F, R, 1968 Sp, Mor, It, 1969 Sp, Mor, 1970 H, Mor, Sp, 1972 It, 1973 It, Yug, Swi, Pol, Pol

J Ferreira 1993 R, It, Tun, Swi, 1995 Mor, Sp, CZR, Ger, 1996 It, Bel, R, Pol, Sp, H, Tun, 1997 Geo, Sp, 1998 Nm, Ger, US,

CZR, Mor, Sp, And, S, Sp, 1999 H, Ur, Ur, 2000 Geo, Sp, R, Mor, H, 2001 R, Geo, Sp, H, Rus, 2002 H, Pol, 2003 Geo, R, CZR, Sp, Rus, 2004 Geo, R, CZR, Sp, Rus, Bb, Ch, Ur, Ukr, 2005 Geo, CZR, Rus, R, Ch, Ur, Fj, 2006 Rus, Geo, R, Ukr, CZR, Rus, ItA, ArA, Ur, It, Rus, Geo, Geo, 2007 Mor, Mor, Sp, Ur, Ur, Rus, CZR, C, S, NZ, R

PB Ferreira 1983 H, Pol, Swe, 1984 Sp, Bel, De, 1985 Mor, Cze, Pol, Z, 1986 R, F, It, Tun, USS, R, 1987 Bel

S Ferreira 1991 Mor, Nm, 1994 Bel, Ger, Mor, Tun, W, Sp, 1995 CZR, Ger, 1996 H, Tun, 1997 Geo, Sp, 1998 Nm, Ger, 2000 SA23

D Fialho 2008 Geo, CZR, C

DAA Figueiredo 2007 Ur, Rus, CZR, It, R, 2008 C

P Fonseca 1996 Bel, 1998 Nm, 2000 SA23, 2001 R, Geo, H, Rus, 2002 R, Geo, Sp, H, Rus, Pol, Sp, 2003 Geo, R, CZR, Sp, Rus, 2004 CZR, Sp, Rus, Bb, 2005 Ch, Ur, Fj

F Fontes 2003 Geo, R, CZR

G Foro 2007 Rus, CZR, It, R, 2008 Geo, CZR, Geo, Rus, R, C, 2009 Rus, Geo, Ger, Sp, R

F Fragateima 2007 CZR, 2008 Geo

JS Franco 1974 Ger

SM Franco 1983 Pol, Swe

NCR Frazão 1974 Ger

A Freitas 1992 Tun, 1993 R

RM Gaio 1982 Pol, 1983 Sp, Swe

E Galvão 1996 It, Bel

D Gama 2006 Rus, Geo, R, 2007 Mor, Mor, Ur, Ur, Rus, CZR, It, R, 2008 Sp, C, 2009 Geo, Ger

F Gameiro 1954 Sp

FR Garcia 1983 H, Pol, Swe, 1984 H, Bel, De, 1985 Cze, Pol, Z, 1986 R, F, 1987 It, Z, USS

M Garcia 1935 Sp

N Garvão 2001 R, H, Rus, 2002 R, Geo, Sp, H, Rus, Pol, Sp, 2003 R, CZR, Sp, Rus, 2004 CZR, Sp, Bb, 2005 CZR

JR Gaspar 1967 Sp, F, R

V Gaspar 2008 Geo, CZR, Rus

T Girão 2006 Geo, R, It, 2007 NZ, It, R, R, 2008 Geo, CZR, Geo, Rus, R, Sp, C, 2009 Rus, Geo, Ger, Sp, R

F Goes 2000 SA23

JMV Gomes 1989 Cze, H, 1990 Mor, Nm, Bel, Tun, Sp, 1991 And, Tun, Mor, Nm, 1992 And, Mor, Tun, 1993 R, Tun, Bel, Swi, 1994 Bel, Ger, Mor, Tun, W, Sp, 1995 Mor, Sp, CZR, Ger, 1996 It, Bel, Sp, 1998 S, 2000 SA23

NMV Gomes 1996 It, Bel, R, Pol, H

R Gomes 1998 S, Sp

G Gonçalves 1983 Sp, H, Pol, Swe

G Gonçalves 1935 Sp

P Gonçalves 2000 SA23, 2001 R, Geo, Sp, 2002 R, Geo, Sp, H, Rus, Pol, Sp, 2003 Geo, R, CZR, Sp

V Goncalves 2005 Ch

F Grenho 2001 R, Geo, Rus, 2004 Geo, R, CZR, Ukr, 2005 Ch, Ur, Fj, 2006 Rus, Geo, R

F Grenho 1979 Swi

FN Guedes 1969 Sp, Mor, 1972 It, It

JFN Guedes 1967 It, F, R, 1968 Sp, Bel, Mor, It, 1969 Mor, 1972 It

R Heitor 2001 Geo, Sp, H, Rus, 2005 Ch

J Herédia 1991 And, Tun, Mor, Nm, 1992 And, Mor, Tun, 1993 It, Tun, Bel, Swi, Sp, 1994 Bel

PR Hoffman 1996 It, Pol, Sp, H, Tun, 1997 Geo, Sp, 1998 Nm, Ger, US, CZR, Sp, S, Sp, 1999 H, Ur, Ur, 2000 Geo, R, SA23, 2002 R, Geo, Sp, H, Rus, Pol, Sp

A Jalles 1983 H, Pol, 1986 R, 1987 Z, Tun, 1988 Yug

F Jesus 1968 Mor

H Jónatas 1989 Cze, H

J Jonet 1990 Mor, Nm, Bel, Tun, Sp, 1991 And, Tun, Mor, Nm, 1992 And, Mor, Tun, 1993 R, It, Swi, Sp, 1994 Bel, Ger, 1995 Mor, Sp, CZR, Ger

V Jorge 2008 Sp, C

J Junior 2008 C, 2009 Rus, Sp, R

L Kadosh 2008 Geo, CZR, Geo, Rus

T King 2000 Sp, And, 2001 R, Geo, Sp, H, Rus

L Lamas 1998 S, 2000 R, Mor, H, 2001 Geo, Sp

J Laureano 1989 Bel, Yug, Ger, 1990 Mor, Nm, Bel, Sp

P Leal 2005 CZR, R, Ch, Ur, Fj, 2006 Rus, R, Rus, ItA, ArA, Ur, It, Rus, Geo, 2007 Mor, Mor, Ur, Ur, Rus, CZR, C, S, NZ, R, R, 2008 R, Sp, C, 2009 Rus, Geo, Ger, Sp, R

AL Leitão 1982 Sp, Tun, H, Pol, 1983 Sp, H, Pol, Swe, 1984 Sp, De

O **Leite** 1970 *Sp*, 1972 *It*
J **Lencastre** 1999 *Ur*
P **Lencastre** 1967 *Sp, It, F, R*
A **Lima** 1995 *Mor, Sp, CZR, Ger*, 1996 *It, R, Sp, H, Tun*, 1997 *Sp*
F **Lima** 2000 *SA23*, 2001 *R*
JA **Lima** 2002 *Pol, Sp*, 2003 *R, CZR, Sp*, 2004 *R*
MS **Lima** 1979 *Swi*, 1981 *Bel, Swe*, 1982 *Tun*
FR **Lince** 1954 *Sp*
L **Lino** 1968 *Bel, Mor*, 1969 *Sp, Mor*
AC **Lopes** 1987 *It, Z*
JM **Lopes** 1954 *Sp*
AdS **Lourenço** 2000 *Geo, Sp, R, Mor, H*, 2001 *Geo, Sp, H, Rus*
F **Lucena** 1969 *Sp, Mor*, 1970 *H, Mor*
L **Luís** 1986 *F, It*, 1987 *It, F, Z, Z, USS*, 1988 *H, Ger, Yug*, 1989 *Bel, Yug, Ger, Cze, H*, 1990 *Mor, Nm, Bel, Tun, Sp*, 1991 *And, Tun, Mor, Nm*, 1993 *It, Tun, Bel, Swi, Sp*
S **Luz** 1987 *Z*
E **Macedo** 1989 *H, Bel, Cze, H*, 1990 *Mor, Nm, Bel, Tun, Sp*, 1991 *And, Tun, Nm*, 1992 *And, Mor, Tun*, 1993 *R, It, Tun, Bel, Swi, Sp*, 1994 *Mor, W, Sp*
H **Macieira** 1979 *Swi*, 1981 *Swi, Bel, Swe*, 1982 *Mor, Tun*
F **Magalhaes** 2008 *Geo, Geo, Rus*
JP **Magalhães** 1981 *Bel, De, Swe*
VP **Magalhães** 1936 *Sp*
MG **Maia** 1981 *Bel, De, Swe*
E **Maleitas** 1979 *Swi*, 1983 *Sp*
G **Malheiro** 1998 *Mor*, 1999 *H, Ur*, 2000 *SA23*, 2001 *R, Geo, Sp, H, Rus*, 2003 *Geo, R, CZR, Sp, Rus*, 2004 *Geo, R, CZR, Sp, Rus, Bb, Ch, Ur*, 2005 *Geo, CZR, Rus*, 2006 *Ukr, CZR, ItA, ArA, Rus, Geo, Geo*, 2007 *Mor, Ur, Ur, Rus, NZ, R, R*
P **Malo** 1986 *R, It, Tun, USS*
A **Marques** 1996 *Bel, R*
JD **Marques** 1996 *Pol, Sp, H, Tun*
MS **Marques** 1936 *Sp*
P **Marques** 1998 *Ger, US, CZR, Mor, Sp, And, S*
MB **Martins** 1954 *Sp*
R **Martins** 1967 *Sp, It, F, R*, 1968 *Sp, Bel, Mor, It*, 1970 *Sp*, 1972 *It, It*, 1973 *It, Yug, Swi, Pol, Pol*, 1974 *It, Ger*, 1981 *Swi, De, Swe*
D **Mateus** 2003 *Geo, R, CZR, Sp, Rus*, 2004 *Geo, R, CZR, Rus, Bb, Ch, Ur*, 2006 *Rus, ItA, It*, 2007 *Mor, Ur, Rus, S, It*, 2008 *CZR, Geo, Rus, R, Sp, C*, 2009 *Rus, Geo, Ger, Sp, R*
D **Mateus** 2000 *Geo, Sp, R, Mor*, 2001 *R, Geo, Sp, H, Rus*, 2002 *Pol, Sp*, 2003 *Geo, R, CZR, Sp, Rus*, 2004 *Geo, R, CZR, Sp, Rus, Bb, Ch, Ur, Ukr*, 2005 *Geo, CZR, Rus, R, Ch, Ur, Fj*, 2006 *Rus, Geo, R, Ukr, CZR, Rus, ItA, ArA, Ur, It, Rus, Geo, Geo*, 2007 *Mor, Mor, Sp, Ur, Rus, CZR, C, S, NZ, It*, 2008 *CZR, Geo, Rus, R, Sp, C*, 2009 *Rus, Geo, Ger, Sp, R*
M **Mauricio** 1990 *Sp*
T **Mayer** 1965 *Sp*, 1966 *Sp, Bel*, 1967 *It, F, R*, 1970 *H, Mor*, 1972 *It*
D **Megre** 1974 *Ger*, 1979 *Swi*, 1981 *Swi, Bel, De, Swe*, 1982 *Mor, Tun, H, Pol*, 1983 *Sp, H, Pol, Swe*, 1984 *Sp, H, Bel, De*, 1985 *Mor, Cze, Pol, Z*, 1986 *R, F, It, Tun, USS, R*, 1987 *It, F, Z, Z, Tun, USS, Bcl*, 1989 *H, Bel, Yug, Ger*
J **Megre** 1979 *Swi*
A **Meira** 1936 *Sp*
H **Melo** 2008 *Geo*
JA **Melo** 1974 *It*
M **Melo** 1998 *Nm, US, S*, 1999 *H, Ur*, 2000 *Geo, Sp, R*, 2001 *R, H, Rus*, 2002 *R, H*
J **Metelo** 1968 *Bel, Mor, It*
A **Minhoto** 1972 *It*, 1973 *It, Yug, Swi, Pol*
F **Mira** 2007 *Sp, R*, 2008 *Geo, CZR, Rus, R*
D **Miranda** 2008 *Geo, Rus*
J **Miranda** 1965 *Sp*, 1966 *Sp, Bel*, 1967 *Sp, It, F, H*, 1968 *Sp*
A **Moita** 1986 *R*, 1987 *F, Z*, 1989 *Bel, Cze, H*
C **Moita** 1974 *It*, 1979 *Swi*, 1981 *Swi, Bel, De, Swe*, 1982 *Mor, Sp, Tun, H, Pol*, 1983 *Sp, H, Pol, Swe*, 1984 *Sp*, 1985 *Cze, Z*
A **Monteiro** 1982 *Sp*
B **Monteiro** 1965 *Sp*, 1966 *Sp, Bel*, 1967 *Sp, It, F, R*, 1968 *Sp*
E **Morais** 1982 *Sp, Tun*, 1986 *It, Tun, USS*, 1987 *It, F, Z*
L **Morais** 1984 *Sp, H, Bel, De*, 1986 *F, It, R*, 1987 *F, Z, Tun, Bel*, 1988 *H*, 1989 *H, Bel, Yug, Ger, Cze, H*
N **Morais** 1984 *Mor, Cze, Pol, Z*, 1986 *R, F, Tun, USS*, 1987 *It, Z, USS*, 1988 *Ger, Yug*, 1995 *Mor, Sp, CZR, Ger*
T **Morais** 1991 *Tun, Mor, Nm*, 1992 *And, Mor, Tun*, 1993 *R, It, Tun, Bel, Swi, Sp*, 1994 *Mor, Tun, W, Sp*, 1995 *Mor, Sp, CZR, Ger*
A **Morgado** 1935 *Sp*

B **Mota** 2000 *SA23*, 2004 *Geo, R, Ukr*, 2005 *Rus*, 2006 *Geo*
JD **Mota** 1998 *S, Sp*, 1999 *H, Ur*, 2000 *Sp, R, Mor, H, SA23*, 2001 *Sp*, 2004 *Ch, Ur*, 2006 *Geo, R, Ukr, CZR*
M **Moura** 1999 *H, Ur*, 2002 *Sp*, 2004 *Ch, Ur, Ukr*, 2005 *Geo, CZR*
N **Mourao** 1993 *R, It, Tun, Bel, Swi, Sp*, 1994 *Bel, Ger, Mor, Tun, W, Sp*, 1995 *CZR, Ger*, 1996 *It, Bel, R, Pol, Sp, H, Tun*, 1997 *Geo, Sp*, 1998 *Nm, Ger, US, CZR, Mor, Sp, And, S, Sp*, 1999 *H, Ur, Ur*, 2000 *Sp*
JM **Muré** 2006 *ItA*, 2007 *C, S, It, R, R*, 2008 *Geo, Geo, Rus, R, Sp, C*, 2009 *Rus, Ger, Sp, R*
P **Murinello** 2003 *Rus*, 2004 *Geo, R, CZR, Sp, Rus, Bb, Ch, Ur, Ukr*, 2005 *Geo, CZR*, 2006 *Ukr, CZR, Rus, ItA, ArA, It, Rus, Geo, Geo*, 2007 *Mor, Mor, Ur, Ur, C, S, NZ, It, R*
P **Murinello** 1993 *R, It, Tun, Bel, Swi, Sp*, 1994 *Bel, Ger, Mor, Tun, W, Sp*, 1995 *Mor, Sp, CZR, Ger*, 1996 *It, Bel, R, Sp, H, Tun*, 2000 *Mor, H*
A **Neto** 1968 *Sp*, 1969 *Sp, Mor*, 1970 *Sp, It, It*, 1973 *Yug, Swi, Pol, Pol*, 1974 *It, Ger*
G **Neto** 1997 *Sp*, 1998 *US, Mor*
N **Neto** 1995 *Mor*
M **Neves** 2002 *R, H*
R **Neves** 2002 *R*
VP **Neves** 1986 *R*
J **Norton** 1935 *Sp*
AC **Nunes** 1954 *Sp*
FP **Nunes** 2000 *Geo, Sp, R, Mor, H, SA23*, 2001 *R, Sp, H*, 2002 *R, Geo, Sp, H, Rus, Pol, Sp*, 2003 *Geo, R, CZR, Sp, Rus*, 2004 *Ch, Ur*, 2005 *Ch*
M **Nunes** 1982 *Tun, H, Pol*
R **Nunes** 1998 *Nm, Ger, US, CZR, And, Sp*, 1999 *H*, 2002 *R, H*
LF **Oliveira** 1974 *It*, 1981 *Swe*, 1982 *Mor, Sp, Tun, H, Pol*, 1983 *Sp, H, Pol, Swe*
M **Paisana** 1981 *De*, 1982 *Mor, Sp, Tun, H, Pol*
JM **Paixao** 1974 *It*
S **Palha** 2006 *Geo*, 2007 *Rus, R*, 2008 *Geo, C*, 2009 *Geo, Ger, Sp, R*
CV **Pardal** 1965 *Sp*, 1967 *It*, 1969 *Sp, Mor*
M **Pardal** 1989 *Yug, Ger*
A **Peças** 1994 *Ger, Mor, Tun, W, Sp*
C **Pegado** 1972 *It*
D **Penalva** 2002 *Sp, H*, 2004 *Sp, Ur*, 2005 *Rus, R, Ch, Ur, Fj*, 2006 *Rus, Geo, R, Ukr, CZR, Rus, ItA, ArA, Geo*, 2007 *Ur, Ur, Rus, C, S, NZ, It, R*, 2009 *Rus, Geo, Sp, R*
J **Pereira** 1965 *Sp*, 1966 *Sp, Bel*, 1967 *Sp, R*, 1970 *H, Mor, Sp*, 1974 *Ger*, 1981 *De*, 1982 *Pol*, 1983 *Sp, H, Pol, Swe*, 1984 *Sp*
JC **Pereira** 1984 *H, Bel, De*, 1986 *R, USS*, 1987 *F, Z, Z, Tun*, 1989 *Cze, H*, 1990 *Mor, Nm, Bel, Tun*
JC **Pereira** 1969 *Mor*, 1970 *H*, 1972 *It*
MC **Pereira** 1965 *Sp*, 1966 *Sp*, 1967 *Sp, R*, 1968 *Bel, Mor, It*, 1969 *Sp*
MM **Pereira** 2006 *Ukr, CZR, Rus, ItA, ArA, It*
RC **Pereira** 1987 *Bel*, 1988 *H*, 1989 *H*, 1991 *And, Tun*, 1992 *And, Mor, Tun*, 1993 *R, It, Tun, Bel*, 1994 *Bel, Ger, Mor, Tun, W, Sp*, 1995 *Mor, Sp*
VS **Pereira** 1973 *It, Yug, Swi, Pol, Pol*, 1974 *Ger*
P **Picão** 1994 *Ger, Mor, Tun, W, Sp*
PS **Pimentel** 1973 *It, Yug, Swi, Pol, Pol*
A **Pinto** 1998 *US, Mor, And*, 1999 *H, Ur, Ur*
AC **Pinto** 1970 *Mor*, 1972 *It, It*, 1973 *It, Yug, Swi, Pol, Pol*, 1974 *It, Ger*
AF **Pinto** 1998 *And*, 2000 *SA23*, 2001 *Sp, H*
BM **Pinto** 1979 *Swi*, 1981 *Swi, Bel, De, Swe*, 1982 *Mor, Sp, Tun, H, Pol*, 1983 *Sp, H, Pol, Swe*, 1984 *Sp, H*, 1985 *Mor, Cze, Pol, Z*, 1986 *R, F, It, Tun, USS, R*, 1987 *It, F, Z, Z, Tun, USS, Bel*, 1988 *H, Ger, Yug, 1989 H, Bel, Yug, Ger, Cze, H*
CR **Pinto** 1972 *It, It*, 1973 *It*
DC **Pinto** 2003 *CZR, Rus*, 2004 *Sp, Bb, Ch, Ur*, 2005 *Rus, R, Ch, Ur, Fj*, 2006 *Geo, R, Ukr, CZR, Rus, Geo, Geo*, 2007 *Mor, Mor, Sp, Ur, Ur, Rus, CZR, C, S, NZ, It, R*, 2008 *CZR, Geo, Sp, C*, 2009 *Rus, Geo, Ger, Sp, R*
EA **Pinto** 1969 *Mor*, 1981 *Swi, Bel, Swe*, 1982 *H*
J **Pinto** 2001 *H, Rus*, 2002 *R*, 2004 *Sp, Bb, Ch, Ur, Ukr*, 2005 *Rus, R, Ch, Ur, Fj*, 2006 *Rus, Geo, R, Ukr, CZR, Rus, ItA, ArA, Ur, It, Rus, Geo, Geo*, 2007 *Mor, Sp, Ur, C, S, NZ, It, R, R*, 2008 *CZR, Geo, Sp, C*, 2009 *Rus, Geo, Ger, Sp, R*
JM **Pinto** 1982 *Mor, Sp, H, Pol*, 1983 *H, Pol, Swe*, 1984 *Sp, H, Bel, De*, 1985 *Mor, Cze, Pol, Z*, 1986 *R, F, USS, R*, 1987 *Tun, USS, Bel*, 1988 *H, Ger, Yug*, 1989 *H, Bel, Yug, Ger, Cze, H*

F Pires 1982 *Mor, H, Pol,* 1983 *Sp, H, Pol, Swe,* 1984 *Sp, H, Bel, De,* 1985 *Mor, Cze, Pol, Z,* 1986 *R, F, It, Tun, USS*

JC Pires 1990 *Mor, Nm, Bel, Tun,* 1991 *And, Tun, Mor, Nm,* 1993 *R, Tun, Bel, Swi, Sp,* 1994 *Bel, Ger, Mor, Tun, W, Sp,* 1996 *Pol,* 1997 *Geo, Sp,* 1998 *Nm*

L Pissarra 1996 *It, Bel, R, Pol, H, Tun,* 1997 *Geo, Sp,* 1998 *Nm, Ger, Sp, And, Sp,* 1999 *H, Ur, Ur,* 2000 *Geo, Sp, R, Mor, H, SA23,* 2001 *R, Geo,* 2002 *R, Geo, Sp, H, Rus, Pol, Sp,* 2003 *Geo, R, CZR, Sp, Rus,* 2004 *Geo, R, CZR, Sp, Rus, Bb, Ch, Ur, Ukr,* 2005 *Geo, CZR, Rus, Ur, Fj,* 2006 *Rus, Geo, R, Ukr, CZR, Rus, ItA, Rus, Geo, Geo,* 2007 *Mor, Mor, Sp, Ur, Ur, Rus, CZR, C, S, NZ, It, R, R*

M Portela 1996 *R, H, Tun,* 1997 *Geo, Sp,* 1998 *US, CZR, Mor, Sp, S, Sp,* 1999 *H, Ur,* 2000 *Geo, Sp, Mor, H, SA23,* 2002 *R, Geo, Sp, H, Rus, Pol, Sp,* 2004 *Sp, Rus, Bb, Ukr,* 2005 *Geo, CZR, Rus, R, Ch, Ur, Fj,* 2006 *Rus, Geo, R, Ukr, Rus, ItA, ArA, It, Rus, Geo, Geo,* 2007 *Mor, Mor, Sp, Ur, Ur, Rus, CZR, C, S, NZ, R*

A Quadrio 1966 *Sp, Bel,* 1967 *It, F*

JF Queimado 1984 *Sp, H, Bel, De,* 1985 *Mor, Cze, Pol, Z,* 1986 *F, It, Tun, USS, R,* 1987 *It, F, Z, Z, Tun, USS, Bel,* 1989 *H, Bel, Cze, H,* 1990 *Mor, Nm, Bel, Tun, Sp,* 1991 *And, Tun, Mor, Nm,* 1992 *And, Mor, Tun,* 1993 *R, It, Tun, Bel, Swi, Sp,* 1994 *Bel, Ger, Mor, Tun, W, Sp*

JA Rafachinho 1973 *It,* 1974 *It, Ger*

JG Ramos 1967 *Sp,* 1968 *Sp, Bel, Mor, It,* 1969 *Sp, Mor,* 1970 *H, Mor, Sp,* 1972 *It, It,* 1973 *It, Yug, Swi, Pol, Pol,* 1974 *It*

T Rankine 2000 *Geo, Sp, R, Mor, H*

D Raws 1936 *Sp*

CC Reis 1965 *Sp,* 1966 *Sp, Bel,* 1967 *Sp,* 1968 *Sp*

CJ Reis 1984 *H, Bel,* 1985 *Mor, Cze, Pol, Z,* 1986 *Tun, USS, R,* 1987 *Tun, USS, Bel,* 1988 *Yug,* 1989 *H, Bel, Yug, Ger*

LN Reis 1983 *Sp, H, Pol, Swe,* 1984 *Sp, H, Bel, De,* 1985 *Mor*

P Reis 1981 *Swi*

JC Ribeiro 1973 *Yug, Pol*

MS Ribeiro 1998 *Nm, Ger, US, CZR, Mor, Sp, And, S, Sp,* 1999 *H, Ur, Ur,* 2000 *Geo, Sp, R, H, SA23,* 2001 *R, Geo, Sp,* 2008 *Geo, Rus*

E Rocha 1973 *Swi, Pol*

F Rocha 1998 *Nm, Ger, US, CZR, Mor, S,* 1999 *H, Ur, Ur*

O Rocha 1954 *Sp*

J Rocheta 1990 *Mor, Nm, Bel, Tun, Sp,* 1991 *And, Tun, Nm,* 1992 *And, Mor, Tun,* 1993 *R, Tun, Bel, Swi, Sp*

JL Rodrigues 1982 *Mor,* 1984 *Sp, H, Bel, De,* 1985 *Mor, Cze, Pol, Z,* 1986 *R, F, It, Tun, USS, R,* 1987 *It, F, Z, Z, Tun, USS, Bel,* 1988 *H, Ger, Yug,* 1989 *H, Bel, Yug, Ger, Cze, H,* 1990 *Mor, Nm, Tun, Sp,* 1991 *And, Tun, Mor, Nm,* 1996 *It, Bel*

P Rodrigues 1990 *Nm, Bel, Sp,* 1991 *And, Tun, Mor, Nm,* 1993 *R, Swi*

M Rogério 1990 *Bel, Tun, Sp,* 1991 *And, Tun, Mor, Nm,* 1992 *And, Mor, Tun,* 1993 *It, Tun, Bel, Sp,* 1994 *Bel, Ger, Mor, Tun, W, Sp,* 1995 *Mor, Sp, CZR, Ger,* 1996 *It, Bel, R, Pol, Sp, H, Tun,* 1998 *Ger, US, CZR, Mor, Sp,* 2000 *Mor*

JB Roque 1954 *Sp*

LV Rosa 1954 *Sp*

LF Roxo 1981 *Bel,* 1982 *Mor, Sp*

JM Rozendo 1936 *Sp*

N Sá 1998 *Sp,* 1999 *Ur, Ur*

F Saldanha 1998 *Mor, Sp, S,* 1999 *Ur, Ur,* 2001 *Geo*

M Salgado 1968 *Sp, Bel, Mor, It,* 1970 *Mor*

JM Sampaio 1987 *F,* 1988 *H, Ger*

F Santos 1936 *Sp*

M Santos 1973 *It, Yug, Swi, Pol, Pol,* 1974 *It*

P Santos 2004 *Geo, R, CZR,* 2005 *CZR*

M Saraiva 1979 *Swi*

A Sarmento 2004 *R,* 2007 *R,* 2008 *Rus, R*

J Segurado 2005 *Ch,* 2009 *Rus, Geo, Ger*

F Sequeira 1974 *Ger*

JC Sequeira 2001 *H, Rus,* 2002 *R, Geo, Sp, H, Pol, Sp,* 2004 *R, CZR, Sp, Rus,* 2005 *Geo*

L Sequeira 1997 *Geo, Sp*

R Sequeira 1988 *Ger*

A Silva 1996 *Sp, H, Tun,* 1997 *Geo, Sp,* 1998 *Nm, S*

A Silva 1935 *Sp,* 1936 *Sp*

A Silva 2007 *Ur, Ur, Rus, NZ, It*

D Silva 1993 *Tun*

JG Silva 1972 *It, It*

JN Silva 1967 *It, F, R,* 1968 *Sp, Bel, Mor, It*

M Silva 2000 *R*

P Silva 1992 *And, Mor, Tun,* 1996 *It, Bel, R, Pol, Sp, H, Tun,* 1997 *Geo, Sp,* 1998 *Nm, Ger, US, CZR, Mor, Sp, And, S,* 1999 *H, Ur, Ur,* 2000 *H,* 2002 *R, Geo, H, Pol, Sp,* 2003 *CZR, Sp*

P Silva 2008 *C,* 2009 *Rus, Geo, Ger, Sp, R*

V Silva 2000 *Geo, Sp, R, Mor, H,* 2001 *R, Geo, Sp, H, Rus*

A Silvestre 1969 *Sp, Mor,* 1970 *H, Mor,* 1972 *It,* 1973 *It, Swi, Pol, Pol,* 1974 *It*

AC Simões 1995 *Ger,* 1996 *Bel, R, Tun,* 2000 *SA23,* 2001 *R*

C Soares 1987 *Bel,* 1988 *H, Ger, Yug,* 1989 *H, Bel, Yug, Ger*

M Soares 1954 *Sp*

JS Somoza 2006 *Rus, Geo, Geo,* 2007 *Mor, Mor, Sp, Ur, Ur, Rus, CZR, C, S,* 2008 *Geo, CZR, Geo, R, C,* 2009 *Rus, Geo, Ger, Sp, R*

F Sousa 2000 *Geo, Sp,* 2001 *R, Geo, Sp, H, Rus,* 2002 *R, Geo, Sp, H, Rus,* 2003 *Geo, R, CZR, Sp, Rus,* 2004 *Geo, R, CZR, Sp, Rus, Bb, Ukr,* 2005 *Geo, CZR, Rus, R, Ch, Ur, Fj,* 2006 *Ukr, CZR, Rus, ItA, ArA, Ur, It, Geo, Geo,* 2007 *CZR, C, S, It, R, R*

O Sousa 1986 *R, F, It, Tun, USS,* 1987 *It*

V Sousa 1979 *Swi,* 1987 *F,* 1988 *H*

RC Spachuck 2005 *Geo, CZR, Rus, R,* 2006 *Rus, Geo, R, Ukr, CZR, Rus, ItA, ArA, It, Rus, Geo, Geo,* 2007 *Rus, CZR, C, S, NZ, It, R, R,* 2008 *R, Sp,* 2009 *Rus, Geo, Ger, Sp, R*

N Taful 2006 *Ur, It*

AH Tavares 1970 *It*

J Teixeira 1935 *Sp*

T Teixeira 1998 *Sp,* 1999 *H, Ur,* 2000 *Geo, Sp, R, Mor, H*

A Telles 1988 *Yug*

LF Thomáz 1991 *Mor,* 1996 *Pol*

NF Thomáz 1990 *Mor, Nm, Bel, Tun, Sp,* 1991 *Tun, Mor, Nm,* 1993 *Swi, Sp*

J Tiago 1995 *CZR, Ger*

M Tomé 2002 *R, Geo, Sp, H, Rus, Pol, Sp,* 2003 *Geo, R, CZR, Sp,* 2004 *Ch, Ur, Ukr,* 2005 *Geo, CZR*

AN Trindade 1969 *Sp,* 1973 *It, Swi*

G Uva 2004 *Bb, Ukr,* 2005 *Geo, CZR, Rus, R, Ch, Ur, Fj,* 2006 *Rus, Geo, R, Ukr, CZR, Rus, ItA, ArA, Ur, It, Rus, Geo, Geo,* 2007 *Mor, Mor, Sp, Ur, Ur, Rus, C, S, NZ, It, R, R,* 2008 *CZR, R, Sp,* 2009 *Rus, Geo, Ger, Sp*

JS Uva 2000 *SA23,* 2001 *R, Geo, Sp,* 2003 *Geo, R, CZR, Sp, Rus,* 2004 *Geo, R, CZR, Rus, Ch, Ur, Ukr,* 2005 *Rus, R, Ch, Ur, Fj,* 2006 *It, Rus, Geo,* 2007 *Mor, Mor, Sp, Ur, Ur, CZR, C, S, NZ, It, R,* 2008 *CZR, Geo, Sp,* 2009 *Rus, Ger, Sp, R*

VS Uva 2003 *Geo, R, Sp,* 2004 *Geo, R, CZR, Sp, Rus, Bb, Ch, Ur, Ukr,* 2005 *Geo, CZR, Rus, R, Ch, Ur, Fj,* 2006 *Rus, Geo, R, Ukr, CZR, Rus, ItA, ArA, Ur, It, Rus, Geo, Geo,* 2007 *Mor, Mor, Sp, Ur, Ur, Rus, CZR, C, S, NZ, It, R,* 2008 *CZR, Rus, Sp, C,* 2009 *Rus, Geo, Ger, Sp, R*

AO Valente 1954 *Sp*

G Vareiro 2002 *R, Geo, Sp, Rus*

JP Varela 1997 *Geo, Sp,* 1998 *Ger, US, CZR, Mor, Sp, And, S,* 1999 *Ur, Ur,* 2000 *H*

JM Vargas 2006 *Rus, ItA, ArA, Ur*

JM Vasconcelos 1965 *Sp,* 1966 *Bel,* 1967 *It, F,* 1970 *Mor*

CR Vaz 1981 *Bel,* 1987 *F, Z, Tun, USS*

L Vaz 1935 *Sp,* 1936 *Sp*

D Vicente 1965 *Sp*

ÁM Vieira 1936 *Sp*

P Vieira 1998 *Nm, Sp, And,* 1999 *H, Ur,* 2000 *Sp, R, Mor, H,* 2001 *Geo, Sp, H, Rus,* 2003 *CZR, Sp, Rus,* 2007 *Mor, Mor, Sp*

R Vieira 1997 *Geo, Sp*

JC Vilela 1973 *Swi*

ROMANIA

ROMANIA'S 2008–09 TEST RECORD

OPPONENTS	DATE	VENUE	RESULT
Spain	7 February	A	**Won** 19–10
Germany	14 February	A	**Won** 22–0
Russia	28 February	H	**Lost** 19–28
Georgia	14 March	A	**Lost** 23–28
Portugal	21 March	H	**Lost** 21–22
Uruguay	12 June	H	**Won** 17–11
France A	16 June	H	**Lost** 16–20
Italy A	21 June	H	**Lost** 13–24

OAKS START TO RALLY

By Chris Thau

A **difficult year that yielded** three successive defeats in the European Nations Cup, denting hopes of Rugby World Cup 2011 qualification, finished on a relative high as a rejuvenated Romania displayed signs of a return to form.

Finishing the 2008–09 season lying fourth in the European Nations Cup and trailing leaders Georgia by five points is nothing short of a disaster for the Oaks, who have appeared at every Rugby World Cup to date.

With a mountain to climb to overhaul Portugal and Russia to secure direct qualification for the 2011 tournament in New Zealand, new head coach Serge Lairle will probably be contemplating the challenge of qualifying through the cross-continental play-offs when the top tier of the European Nations Cup resumes in February.

Off the field over the last 12 months, Technical Director Ellis Meachen was struggling to assemble a squad that was capable of challenging the best in Europe. Facing difficulties in persuading seasoned professionals based in France to pull on the Romanian jersey did not help, while it was clear that the New Zealander had a lot on his plate with also overseeing the development of the national age grade teams.

After barely a year at the helm, Meachen – a leading figure in Tonga's improved fortunes at Rugby World Cup 2007 – and the Romanian Federation had parted company in March 2009 following the back-to-back European Nations Cup defeats to Russia (28–19) in Bucharest and Georgia (28–23) in Tbilisi.

With only a week before the visit of Portugal, an interim coaching team was appointed with former internationals Alexandru Achim, Marin Mot, Cristian Hildan and New Zealander Steve McDowall given the brief of restoring pride and performance against the Portuguese. It was a tough assignment.

Unable to build on their 15–6 half-time lead following tries from forwards Alin Coste and Alexandru Manta, the Romanians collapsed to a Portuguese surge of pride and adrenalin in the closing stages of an intense match to lose 22–21 at the stadionul National Arcul de Triumf and further compound Romania's World Cup qualifying woes.

Romania are left trailing Russia by four points and Portugal by three in the standings at the halfway stage of the region's qualifying process for Rugby World Cup 2011 in New Zealand, their only victories having come on the road against Spain (19–10) and Germany (22–0). This fourth position is Romania's lowest standing since the European Nations Cup started at the beginning of the decade.

After Meachen's remarkable contribution to Tonga's sizzling performances at Rugby World Cup 2007, hopes were high that his arrival would herald a new beginning for Romanian rugby. The then President of the Romanian Federation, the charismatic George Straton, pointed out that Meachen had a complex brief, which on the one hand concerned the elite, with Rugby World Cup 2011 qualification the main target, but also required a significant input into the development work with the country's various age groups.

Meachen was very much a victim of circumstances, being unable to field the best available Romanian team in any significant match. Since Rugby World Cup 2007 the Union had been forced to look at home grown talent after struggling to secure a group of leading players based in France, with Bath prop Paulica Ion and Florin Corodeanu of Grenoble the only overseas-based players involved.

Long-serving centre Romeo Gontineac, a veteran of 75 Tests who had made his farewell appearance against Emerging South Africa in the IRB Nations Cup in 2008, resisted Meachen's call to return to the international stage. "He is by far the most accomplished back in Romania," observed Meachen when faced by a worrying shortage of experienced players.

Confronted with the fast approaching European Nations Cup, Meachen decided, in a good New Zealand tradition, that a tour of the South Pacific, stopping off for matches in New Zealand, Fiji and Samoa, could help develop the players and more significantly the team spirit and cohesion for the crucial matches against Russia, Georgia and Portugal.

"The tour of New Zealand and the Pacific will be invaluable for our RWC qualifying programme, which will kick off in February next year. We will be squaring off against the Georgians, Russia, Spain, Germany and Portugal for a spot at the Rugby World Cup, which is not an easy task at all, so this tour will provide an excellent stepping stone for our players leading into the challenges that we face next season," Meachen said at the time.

Somehow the tour covering the whole of September failed to deliver the expected improvements in playing standards and skill levels. It was a difficult tour and left Meachen scratching his head as to the options available to him. An attempt to bring some of the France-based veterans back into the fold ended in failure and the defeats at the hands of Russia

ROMANIA

and Georgia, with what was very much a second-string team, sealed his fate.

After dismissing Meachen, Straton also decided to stand down as Romanian Federation President after nearly seven years at the helm. This had significant consequences, as under the newly-elected President Alin Petrache, a former Romanian captain and a wealthy businessman, Romania revived the French connection, inviting the experienced Robert Antonin to manage the national team with former Toulouse front row stalwart Lairle appointed as coach.

The first true test for the new-look Romanian coaching team of Lairle and backs coach Olivier Nier was the IRB Nations Cup on home soil in June, when a large number of the French-based players turned up in Bucharest after two years of absence to support Petrache, their former captain.

The team blew hot and cold, playing very well in their second match against France A – the sterling performance and a remarkable recovery from 17–0 down inside 25 minutes to ultimately lose 20–16 undoubtedly the highlight. This contrasted with disappointing displays in beating Uruguay 17–11 and losing 24–13 to Italy A to finish fourth of the six teams in the standings, above Russia only on points difference.

Fifty-three-year-old Lairle is a very experienced coach and will not leave a stone unturned in his quest for success, which in the immediate future is reviving Romania's chances of preserving their ever-present record in Rugby World Cups. The Oaks' battle to qualify for New Zealand 2011 could go right down to the final weekend of the European Nations Cup in March, when they travel to Lisbon to play Portugal on the same day Georgia tackle Russia on neutral soil in Turkey.

The Romanians made a modest step in the right direction in August when they travelled to Narbonne to play in the Armand Vaquerin memorial tournament and sprung a surprise or two. Captained by Augustin Petrichei, Romania beat Narbonne 18–3 and then Albi, newly-promoted to the French Top 14, 26–7 to complete a first undefeated tour of France by a Romanian team since the 1970s.

A remarkable achievement and one which, allied to Romania's Under 20s being crowned IRB Junior World Rugby Trophy champions in Kenya earlier in the year, provided signs that the sleeping giant of European rugby is perhaps stirring once again.

ROMANIA INTERNATIONAL STATISTICS
MATCH RECORDS UP TO 30TH SEPTEMBER 2009

BIGGEST WINNING MARGIN

Date	Opponent	Result	Winning Margin
21/09/1976	Bulgaria	100–0	100
19/03/2005	Ukraine	97–0	97
13/04/1996	Portugal	92–0	92
17/11/1976	Morocco	89–0	89
19/04/1996	Belgium	83–5	78

MOST POINTS IN A MATCH
BY THE TEAM

Date	Opponent	Result	Points
21/09/1976	Bulgaria	100–0	100
19/03/2005	Ukraine	97–0	97
13/04/1996	Portugal	92–0	92
17/11/1976	Morocco	89–0	89

BY A PLAYER

Date	Name	Opponent	Points
05/10/2002	Ionut Tofan	Spain	30
13/04/1996	Virgil Popisteanu	Portugal	27
04/02/2001	Petre Mitu	Portugal	27
13/04/1996	Ionel Rotaru	Portugal	25

MOST TRIES IN A MATCH
BY THE TEAM

Date	Opponent	Result	Tries
17/11/1976	Morocco	89–0	17
21/10/1951	East Germany	64–26	16
19/03/2005	Ukraine	97–0	15
16/04/1978	Spain	74–3	14

BY A PLAYER

Date	Name	Opponent	Tries
30/04/1972	Gheorghe Rascanu	Morocco	5
18/10/1986	Cornel Popescu	Portugal	5
13/04/1996	Ionel Rotaru	Portugal	5

MOST CONVERSIONS IN A MATCH
BY THE TEAM

Date	Opponent	Result	Cons
13/04/1996	Portugal	92–0	12
19/03/2005	Ukraine	97–0	11
04/10/1997	Belguim	83–13	10

BY A PLAYER

Date	Name	Opponent	Cons
13/04/1996	Virgil Popisteanu	Portugal	12
04/10/1997	Serban Guranescu	Belgium	10
19/03/2005	Dan Dumbrava	Ukraine	8
22/03/2008	Florin Vlaicu	Czech Republic	8

MOST PENALTIES IN A MATCH
BY THE TEAM

Date	Opponent	Result	Pens
14/05/1994	Italy	26–12	6
04/02/2001	Portugal	47–0	6

BY A PLAYER

Date	Name	Opponent	Pens
14/05/1994	Neculai Nichitean	Italy	6
04/02/2001	Petre Mitu	Portugal	6

MOST DROP GOALS IN A MATCH
BY THE TEAM

Date	Opponent	Result	DGs
29/10/1967	West Germany	27–5	4
14/10/1965	West Germany	9–8	3
17/10/1976	Poland	38–8	3
03/10/1990	Spain	19–6	3

BY A PLAYER

Date	Name	Opponent	DGs
29/10/1967	Valeriu Irimescu	West Germany	3
17/10/1976	Dumitru Alexandru	Poland	3

ROMANIA

MOST CAPPED PLAYERS	
Name	Caps
Adrian Lungu	77
Romeo Gontineac	75
Gabriel Brezoianu	71
Florica Morariu	70

LEADING PENALTY SCORERS	
Name	Pens
Neculai Nichitean	54
Petre Mitu	53
Ionut Tofan	46
Gelu Ignat	39

LEADING TRY SCORERS	
Name	Tries
Petre Motrescu	33
Gabriel Brezoianu	28
Florica Murariu	26
Mihai Vusec	22

LEADING DROP GOAL SCORERS	
Name	DGs
Dumitru Alexandru	13
Neculai Nichitean	10
Valeriu Irimescu	10
Gelu Ignat	7

LEADING CONVERSIONS SCORERS	
Name	Cons
Petre Mitu	53
Ionut Tofan	51
Dan Dumbrava	39
Ion Constantin	34

LEADING POINTS SCORERS	
Name	Points
Petre Mitu	335
Ionut Tofan	315
Neculai Nichitean	246
Dumitru Alexandru	240
Ion Constantin	222

ROMANIA INTERNATIONAL PLAYERS
UP TO 30TH SEPTEMBER 2009

Note: Years given for International Championship matches are for second half of season; eg 1972 means season 1971–72. Years for all other matches refer to the actual year of the match.

A Achim 1974 *Pol*, 1976 *Pol, Mor*

M Adascalitei 2007 *Rus*, 2009 *Pt, Ur, F, ItA*

M Aldea 1979 *USS, W, Pol, F*, 1980 *It, USS, I, F*, 1981 *It, Sp, USS, S, NZ, F*, 1982 *WGe, It, USS, Z, Z, F*, 1983 *Mor, WGe, It, USS, Pol, W, USS, F*, 1984 *It, S, F*, 1985 *E, USS*

C Alexandrescu 1934 *It*

D Alexandru 1974 *Pol*, 1975 *Sp, JAB*, 1976 *Sp, USS, Bul, Pol, F, Mor*, 1977 *Sp, It, F, Pol, F*, 1978 *Cze, Sp*, 1979 *It, Sp, USS, W, F*, 1980 *It, I, Pol, F*, 1981 *Sp, USS, S, NZ, F*, 1982 *Z*, 1983 *It, USS, Pol, W*, 1984 *It, S, F, Sp*, 1985 *E*, 1987 *It, USS, Z, S, USS, F*, 1988 *USS*

N Anastasiade 1927 *Cze*, 1934 *It*

V Anastasiade 1939 *It*

I Andrei 2003 *W, I, Ar, Nm*, 2004 *CZR, Pt, Sp, Rus, Geo, It, W, J, CZR*, 2005 *Rus, US, S, Pt*, 2006 *CZR*, 2007 *Pt*, 2008 *Sp, Pt, Rus*

I Andriesi 1937 *It, H, Ger*, 1938 *F, Ger*, 1939 *It*, 1940 *It*

E Apjoc 1996 *Bel*, 2000 *It*, 2001 *Pt*

D Armasel 1924 *F, US*

A Atanasiu 1970 *It, F*, 1971 *It, Mor, F*, 1972 *Mor, Cze, WGe*, 1973 *Sp, Mor, Ar, Ar, WGe*, 1974 *Pol*

I Bacioiu 1976 *USS, Bul, Pol, F, Mor*

N Baciu 1964 *Cze, EGe*, 1967 *It, F*, 1968 *Cze, Cze, F*, 1969 *Pol, WGe, F*, 1970 *It*, 1971 *It, Mor, F*, 1972 *Mor, Cze, WGe*, 1973 *Ar, Ar*, 1974 *Cze, EGe*

B Balan 2003 *Pt, Sp, Geo*, 2004 *W*, 2005 *Rus, Ukr, J, US, S, Pt*, 2006 *Geo, Pt, Ukr, Rus, F, Geo, Sp, S*, 2007 *Sp, ESp, ItA, Nm, It, S, Pt, NZ*

D Balan 1983 *F*

PV Balan 1998 *H, Pol, Ukr, Ar, Geo, I*, 1999 *F, S, A, US, I*, 2000 *Mor, H, Pt, Sp, Geo, F, It*, 2001 *Pt, Sp, H, Rus, Geo, I, E*, 2002 *Pt, Sp, H, Rus, Geo, Sp, S*, 2003 *CZR, F, W, I, Nm*, 2004 *It, W, J, CZR*, 2005 *Geo, C, I*, 2006 *Geo, Pt, F, Geo, Sp, S*, 2007 *Geo*, 2009 *Ur, F*

L Balcan 1963 *Bul, EGe, Cze*

F Balmus 2000 *Mor, H, Pt*

S Bals 1927 *F, Ger, Cze*

G Baltaretu 1965 *WGe, F*

C Barascu 1957 *F*

M Baraulea 2004 *CZR, Pt, Geo*

A Barbu 1958 *WGe, It*, 1959 *EGe, Pol, Cze, EGe*, 1960 *F*

A Barbuliceanu 2008 *Rus, ESp*, 2009 *Sp, Ger, Rus, Geo, Pt*

S Bargaunas 1971 *It, Mor*, 1972 *F*, 1974 *Cze*, 1975 *It*

S Barsan 1934 *It*, 1936 *F, It*, 1937 *It, H, F, Ger*, 1938 *F, Ger*, 1939 *It*, 1940 *It*, 1942 *It*

RC Basalau 2007 *Pt*, 2008 *Geo, Pt, Rus, CZR, Ur, Rus, ESp*

CD Beca 2009 *Sp, Ger, Rus, Geo, Pt*

E Beches 1979 *It, Sp, USS*, 1982 *WGe, It*, 1983 *Pol*

M Bejan 2001 *I, W*, 2002 *Pt*, 2003 *Geo, CZR*, 2004 *It*

C Beju 1936 *F, It, Ger*

G Bentia 1919 *US, F*, 1924 *F, US*

V Bezarau 1995 *Ar, F, It*

R Bezuscu 1985 *It*, 1987 *F*

G Bigiu 2007 *Pt*, 2008 *Geo, Sp, Pt, Rus, CZR, Ur, Rus*

M Blagescu 1952 *EGe, EGe*, 1953 *It*, 1955 *Cze*, 1957 *F, Cze, Bel, F*

G Blasek 1937 *It, H, F, Ger*, 1940 *It*, 1942 *It*

A Bogheanu 1980 *Mor*

D Boldor 1988 *It, Sp, US, USS, USS, W*, 1989 *It, E, Sp, Z*
A Boroi 1975 *Sp*
P Bors 1975 *JAB*, 1976 *Sp*, 1977 *It*, 1980 *It, USS, I, Pol, F*, 1981 *It, Sp, USS, S, NZ, F*, 1982 *WGe*, 1983 *Mor, WGe, It, USS*, 1984 *It*
I Botezatu 2009 *Ger, Rus, Geo*
D Bozian 1997 *Bel*, 1998 *H, Pol, Ukr*
V Brabateanu 1919 *US, F*
M Braga 1970 *It, F*
C Branescu 1994 *It, E*, 1997 *F*
I Bratulescu 1927 *Ger, Cze*
G Brezoianu 1996 *Bel*, 1997 *F*, 1998 *H, Pol, Ukr, Ar, Geo, I*, 1999 *F, S, A, US, I*, 2000 *H, Pt, Sp, Geo, F, It*, 2001 *Sp, S*, 2003 *Pt, Sp, Rus, Geo, I, It, Sp, W, S*, 2003 *Pt, Sp, Rus, Geo, CZR, F, W, I, A, Ar, Nm*, 2005 *Rus, Ukr, J, US, S, Pt, C, I*, 2006 *CZR, Pt, Ukr, Rus, F, Geo, Sp, S*, 2007 *Geo, Sp, CZR, ESp, ItA, Nm, It, S, NZ*
V Brici 1991 *NZ*, 1992 *USS, F, It*, 1993 *Tun, F, Sp, I*, 1994 *Sp, Ger, Rus, It, W, It, E*, 1995 *F, S, J, J, SA, A*, 1996 *Pt, F*, 1997 *WalA, F*
TE Brinza 1990 *It, USS*, 1991 *C*, 1992 *It, Ar*, 1993 *Pt, Tun, F, F, I*, 1994 *Sp, Ger, It, W, It, E*, 1995 *F, S, J, J, SA, A*, 1996 *Pt, F, Pol*, 1997 *WalA, F, W, Ar, F, It*, 1998 *Ukr*, 1999 *A, US, I*, 2000 *H, Geo*, 2002 *H*
I Bucan 1976 *Bul*, 1977 *Sp*, 1978 *Cze*, 1979 *F*, 1980 *It, USS, I, Pol, F*, 1981 *It, Sp, USS, S, NZ, F*, 1982 *WGe, It, USS, Z, Z, F*, 1983 *Mor, WGe, It, USS, Pol, W, USS, F*, 1984 *It, S, F, Sp*, 1985 *E, Tun, USS, USS, It*, 1986 *Pt, S, F, Pt*, 1987 *It, USS, Z, S, USS, F*
M Bucos 1972 *Mor, Cze, WGe*, 1973 *Sp*, 1975 *JAB, Pol, F*, 1976 *H, It, Sp, USS, Bul, Pol, F, Mor*, 1977 *Sp, It, F, Pol, It, F*, 1978 *Pol, F*, 1979 *W*, 1980 *It, Mor*
P Buda 1953 *It*, 1955 *Cze*, 1957 *F, Cze*
C Budica 1974 *Cze, EGe, Cze*
S Burcea 2006 *F*, 2007 *ESp, ItA, Nm, Rus, Pt*, 2008 *Geo, Pt, CZR, Ur, Rus, ESp*, 2009 *Sp, Ger, Rus, Geo, Pt*
M Burghelea 1974 *Cze, EGe, F*, 1975 *It*
S Burlescu 1936 *F, It, Ger*, 1938 *F, Ger*, 1939 *It*
M Butugan 2003 *Pt*
VN Calafeteanu 2004 *J*, 2005 *Ukr*, 2006 *CZR, Pt, Ukr, F, Sp, S*, 2007 *Geo, Sp, CZR, ESp, ItA, Nm, It, S, Pt, NZ*, 2008 *Geo, Sp, Pt, CZR*, 2009 *Ger, Geo, Pt, Ur, F, ItA*
A Caligari 1951 *EGe*, 1953 *It*
S Caliman 1958 *EGe*, 1960 *Pol, EGe, Cze*
P Calistrat 1940 *It*, 1942 *It*
Ion Camenita 1939 *It*
CF Caplescu 2007 *Sp, CZR, Rus, Pt*, 2008 *Rus, CZR, Ur*
C Capmare 1983 *Pol*, 1984 *It*
N Capusan 1960 *F*, 1961 *Pol, Cze, EGe, F*, 1962 *Cze, EGe, Pol, It*
R Capusan 1963 *Bul, EGe, Cze*
G Caracostea 1919 *US, F*
G Caragea 1980 *I, Pol, F*, 1981 *It, Sp, USS, S, NZ, F*, 1982 *WGe, It, USS, Z, Z, F*, 1983 *Mor, WGe, It, USS, Pol, W, F*, 1984 *F, Sp*, 1985 *E, Tun*, 1986 *S, F, Tun, Tun, Pt, F, I*, 1988 *It, Sp, US, USS*, 1989 *E*
C Carp 1989 *Z, Sa, USS*
D Carpo 2007 *ItA*, 2008 *Sp, Pt, Rus, CZR, Ur, Rus, ESp*, 2009 *Sp, Ger, Rus, Geo, Pt, Ur, F*
G Celea 1963 *EGe*
D Chiriac 1999 *S, A, I*, 2001 *H*
G Chiriac 1996 *Bel*, 2001 *Pt, Rus*, 2002 *Sp, H, Rus, Geo, I, Sp, W, S*, 2003 *Sp, Rus, Geo, F, W, I, A, Ar, Nm*
R Chiriac 1952 *EGe*, 1955 *Cze*, 1957 *F, Bel, F*, 1958 *Sp, WGe*, 1960 *F*, 1961 *Pol, EGe, Cze, EGe, F*, 1962 *Cze, EGe, Pol, It, F*, 1963 *Bul, EGe, Cze, F*, 1964 *Cze, EGe, WGe, F*
M Chiricencu 1980 *It, Pol*
S Chirila 1989 *Sp, S*, 1990 *F, H, Sp, It, USS*, 1991 *It*
V Chirita 1999 *S*
G Cilinca 1993 *Pt*
N Cioarec 1974 *Pol*, 1976 *It*, 1979 *Pol*
P Ciobanel 1961 *Pol, EGe, Cze, F*, 1962 *Cze, EGe, Pol, It, F*, 1963 *F*, 1964 *Cze, EGe, WGe, F*, 1965 *WGe, F*, 1966 *Cze, It, F*, 1967 *F*, 1968 *Cze, Cze, F*, 1969 *Pol, WGe, Cze, F*, 1970 *F*, 1971 *F*
I Ciobanu 1952 *EGe*

M Ciobanu 1949 *Cze*, 1951 *EGe*
R Cioca 1994 *Sp, Ger, Rus, It, It, E*, 1995 *S, J*, 1996 *Bel*
I Ciofu 2000 *It*, 2003 *Pt*
ML Ciolacu 1998 *Ukr, Ar, Geo, I*, 1999 *F*, 2001 *Sp, H, Rus, Geo, W, E*
S Ciorascu 1988 *US, USS, USS, F, W*, 1989 *It, E, Sp, Z, Sa, USS, S*, 1990 *It, F, H, Sp, USS*, 1991 *It, NZ, S, F, C, Fj*, 1992 *Sp, It, It, Ar*, 1994 *Ger, Rus, It, W*, 1995 *F, S, J, C, SA, A*, 1996 *F*, 1997 *F, It*, 1999 *F*
M Ciornei 1972 *WGe, F*, 1973 *Ar, Ar, WGe, F*, 1974 *Mor, Pol, EGe, F, Cze*, 1975 *It, Sp*
SE Ciuntu 2007 *NZ, Rus, Pt*, 2008 *Geo, Sp, Pt, Rus, CZR, Ur, ESp*, 2009 *Sp, Ger, Rus, Geo, Pt, Ur, F, ItA*
C Cocor 1940 *It*, 1949 *Cze*
M Codea 1998 *Ukr*, 2001 *E*
L Codoi 1980 *I, Pol*, 1984 *F*, 1985 *Tun, USS*
C Cojocariu 1990 *It, F, H, Sp, It, USS*, 1991 *It, NZ, F, S, F, C, Fj*, 1992 *Sp, It, USS, F, Ar*, 1993 *Pt, F, F, I*, 1994 *Sp, Ger, Rus, It, W, It, E*, 1995 *F, S, J, J, C, SA, A, Ar, F, It*, 1996 *F*
L Colceriu 1991 *S, Fj*, 1992 *Sp, It, It*, 1993 *I*, 1994 *Sp, Ger, Rus, It, W, It*, 1995 *F, J, J, C, SA, A*, 1997 *WalA, F, W, Bel, Ar, F, It*, 1998 *Pol, Ukr*
D Coliba 1987 *USS, F*
M Coltuneac 2002 *Sp, W, S*
T Coman 1984 *Sp*, 1986 *F, Tun, Tun, I*, 1988 *Sp, US, USS, USS*, 1989 *It*, 1992 *F*
C Constantin 2001 *Pt*, 2002 *Geo, W*
F Constantin 1972 *Mor, Cze, WGe*, 1973 *Ar, Ar, WGe*, 1980 *Mor*, 1982 *It*
I Constantin 1971 *Mor*, 1972 *WGe*, 1973 *Ar, Ar, WGe, F*, 1974 *Mor, Pol, Sp, F, Cze*, 1975 *It, Sp, JAB, Pol, F*, 1976 *H, It, Sp, USS, Bul, Pol*, 1977 *It, F*, 1978 *Pol, F*, 1979 *It, Sp, USS, W, Pol, F*, 1980 *It, USS, I, Pol, F*, 1981 *It, Sp, USS, S, NZ, F*, 1982 *WGe, It, USS, Z, Z*, 1983 *WGe, USS, 1985 It*
L Constantin 1983 *USS, F*, 1984 *It, S, F, Sp*, 1985 *E, It, Tun, USS, USS, It*, 1986 *Pt, S, F, Tun, Tun, Pt, F, I*, 1987 *It, USS, Z, F, S, USS, F*, 1991 *It, NZ, F*
LT Constantin 1985 *USS*
S Constantin 1980 *Mor*, 1982 *Z, Z*, 1983 *Pol, W, USS, F*, 1984 *S, F*, 1985 *USS*, 1986 *Pt, S, F, Tun*, 1987 *It, Z, S*
T Constantin 1992 *USS, F, It*, 1993 *Pt, F, Sp*, 1996 *Pt*, 1997 *It*, 1999 *F, US, I*, 2000 *Pt, Sp, Geo, F*, 2002 *Rus, Geo*
T Constantin 1985 *USS*
N Copil 1985 *USS, It*, 1986 *S*
D Coravu 1968 *F*
N Cordos 1958 *EGe*, 1961 *EGe*, 1963 *Bul, Cze*, 1964 *Cze, EGe*
V Cornel 1977 *F*, 1978 *Cze, Sp*
G Corneliu 1980 *Mor, USS*, 1982 *WGe, It, Z, Z*, 1986 *Tun, Pt, F*, 1993 *I*, 1994 *W*
G Corneliu 1976 *USS, Bul*, 1977 *F*, 1979 *It*, 1981 *S*, 1982 *Z*
M Corneliu 1979 *USS*
F Corodeanu 1997 *WalA, F, W*, 1998 *H, Pol, Ar, Geo*, 1999 *F, S, A, US, I*, 2000 *H, Sp, Geo, F, It*, 2001 *Pt, Sp, H, Rus, Geo, I, E*, 2002 *Pt, Sp, Rus, Geo, It, Sp, W, S*, 2003 *Sp, Rus, Geo, J, US, S, Pt, C, I*, 2006 *Geo, CZR, Pt, Geo, Sp, S*, 2007 *Geo, ESp, ItA, Nm, It, S, Pt, NZ*, 2008 *Ur, Rus, ESp*, 2009 *Sp, Ger, Rus, Pt*
Coste 2007 *Pt*, 2008 *Geo, Sp, Pt, Rus, CZR, Ur*, 2009 *Sp, Rus, Geo, Pt, F*
L Costea 1994 *E*, 1995 *S, J, J, Ar, F*, 1997 *WalA, F*
L Coter 1957 *F, Cze*, 1959 *EGe, Pol, Cze*, 1960 *F*
F Covaci 1936 *Ger*, 1937 *H, F, Ger*, 1940 *It*, 1942 *It*
C Cratunescu 1919 *US, F*
N Crissoveloni 1936 *F, It*, 1937 *H, F, Ger*, 1938 *F, Ger*
S Cristea 1973 *Mor*
C Cristoloveanu 1952 *EGe*
G Crivat 1938 *F, Ger*
V Csoma 1983 *WGe*
D Curea 2005 *Rus, Ukr, J, US, S, Pt*
D Daiciulescu 1966 *Cze, F*, 1967 *It, Pol*, 1968 *F*, 1969 *Pol*
A Damian 1934 *It*, 1936 *F, It, Ger*, 1937 *It*, 1938 *F, Ger*, 1939 *It*, 1949 *Cze*
G Daraban 1969 *Cze*, 1972 *Mor, Cze, WGe, F*, 1973 *Sp,*

Mor, Ar, Ar, 1974 Cze, EGe, F, Cze, 1975 It, Sp, JAB, Pol, F, 1976 H, It, Sp, USS, Bul, Pol, F, Mor, 1977 Sp, It, F, 1978 Cze, Sp, Pol, F, 1982 F, 1983 Mor, WGe, It, USS, W

CR Dascalu 2006 Ukr, F, Geo, Sp, S, 2007 Sp, CZR, ESp, NZ, Rus, Pt, 2008 Geo, Rus, Ur, Rus, ESp, 2009 Sp, Rus, Geo, Ur, ItA

V David 1984 Sp, 1986 Pt, S, F, Tun, 1987 USS, Z, F, 1992 USS

S Demci 1998 Ar, 2001 H, Rus, Geo, I, W

R Demian 1959 EGe, 1960 F, 1961 Pol, EGe, Cze, EGe, F, 1962 Cze, Pol, It, F, 1963 Bul, EGe, Cze, F, 1964 WGe, F, 1965 WGe, F, 1966 Cze, It, F, 1967 It, Pt, Pol, WGe, F, 1968 Cze, F, 1969 Pol, WGe, F, 1971 It, Mor

E Denischi 1949 Cze, 1952 EGe, EGe

I Diaconu 1942 It

C Diamandi-Telu 1938 Ger, 1939 It

ND Dima 1999 A, US, I, 2000 H, Pt, Geo, F, It, 2001 Sp, H, Rus, Geo, W, E, 2002 Pt, Sp, Rus, W, S, 2004 CZR, Pt, Sp, Rus, Geo, 2009 ItA

TI Dimofte 2004 It, W, CZR, 2005 C, I, 2006 Geo, CZR, Pt, Ukr, Rus, F, Geo, Sp, S, 2007 ESp, ItA, Nm, It, S, Pt, NZ, Rus, Pt, 2008 Geo, Sp, Pt, Rus, CZR, Ur, Rus, ESp, 2009 Sp, Ger, Rus, Geo, Pt, Ur, F, ItA

C Dinescu 1934 It, 1936 F, It, Ger, 1937 It, H, F, Ger, 1938 F, Ger, 1940 It, 1942 It

C Dinu 1965 WGe, F, 1966 Cze, It, F, 1967 It, Pt, Pol, WGe, 1968 F, 1969 Pol, WGe, Cze, F, 1970 It, F, 1971 Mor, F, 1972 Mor, Cze, WGe, F, 1973 Sp, Mor, Ar, Ar, WGe, F, 1974 Mor, Pol, Sp, Cze, F, Cze, 1975 It, Sp, 1976 H, It, Sp, Pol, F, Mor, 1977 Sp, It, F, Pol, It, F, 1978 Sp, Pol, F, 1979 Sp, USS, W, Pol, 1980 I, Pol, F, 1981 It, Sp, USS, NZ, F, 1982 F, 1983 Mor, WGe, It, USS

F Dinu 2000 Mor, H

G Dinu 1990 It, F, H, Sp, It, USS, 1991 It, S, F, C, Fj, 1992 Sp, It, USS, F, It, 1993 F

G Dinu 1975 Pol, 1979 It, Sp, 1983 Pol, USS

F Dobre 2001 E, 2004 W, CZR, 2007 Pt, 2008 CZR

I Dobre 1951 EGe, 1952 EGe, 1953 It, 1955 Cze, 1957 Cze, Bel, F, 1958 Sp

I Doja 1986 Tun, Pt, F, I, 1988 F, W, 1989 Sp, Z, Sa, S, 1990 It, 1991 It, NZ, F, C, 1992 Sp

V Doja 1997 Bel, 1998 Pol, Geo, I

A Domocos 1989 Z, Sa, USS

I Dorutiu 1957 Cze, Bel, F, 1958 Sp, WGe

A Draghici 1919 US

C Dragnea 1995 F, 1996 Pol, 1997 WalA, F, Bel, Ar, F, It, 1998 H, Pol, 1999 F, 2000 F

I Dragnea 1985 Tun

S Dragnea 2002 S

M Dragomir 1996 Bel, 1997 Bel, 1998 H, Pol, Ukr, Geo, I, 2001 I, W, E

M Dragomir 2001 H, Geo, 2002 I

V Dragomir 1964 Cze, EGe, 1966 It, 1967 Pol, WGe

G Dragomirescu 1919 F

G Dragomirescu-Rahtopol 1963 Bul, EGe, Cze, F, 1964 Cze, EGe, WGe, F, 1965 WGe, F, 1966 Cze, 1967 It, Pt, Pol, WGe, F, 1968 Cze, Cze, F, 1969 Pol, WGe, Cze, F, 1970 It, F, 1971 It, Mor, 1972 Mor, Cze, WGe, F, 1973 WGe, F

N Dragos 1995 Ar, It, 1997 WalA, F, Ar, F, It, 1998 H, Pol, Ukr, Ar, Geo, I, 1999 F, S, 2000 Sp, Geo, F

CS Draguceanu 1994 Sp, Geo, F, W, It, E, 1995 S, J, Ar, F, It, 1996 Bel, 1997 W, Bel, Ar, F, It, 1998 H, Pol, Ukr, Ar, Geo, I, 1999 S, A, US, I, 2000 Mor, H, Pt, Sp, Geo, F, It

C Dragulescu 1969 Cze, 1970 F, 1971 It, 1972 Cze

G Drobota 1960 Pol, Cze, 1961 EGe, EGe, F, 1962 Cze, EGe, Pol, F, 1964 Cze, EGe, F

D Dumbrava 2002 W, 2003 Sp, Rus, Geo, CZR, F, W, I, A, Nm, 2004 CZR, Pt, Sp, Rus, Geo, It, J, CZR, 2005 Rus, Geo, Ukr, J, US, S, Pt, C, 2006 Geo, Pt, Rus, 2007 Sp, CZR, Pt, Rus, Pt, 2008 Sp, Pt, Rus, CZR, Ur, Rus, ESp

H Dumitras 1984 It, 1985 E, It, USS, 1986 Pt, F, I, 1987 It, USS, Z, S, USS, F, 1988 It, Sp, US, USS, USS, F, W, 1989 It, E, Z, Sa, USS, S, 1990 It, F, H, Sp, USS, 1991 It, NZ, F, S, F, C, Fj, 1992 Sp, USS, F, Ar, 1993 Pt, Tun, F, Sp, F, I

I Dumitras 2002 H, 2006 Geo, CZR, Ukr, Rus, F, 2007 Geo, Sp, CZR, ESp, ItA, Nm, It, S, Pt, NZ, 2009 Ur, F, ItA

E Dumitrescu 1953 It, 1958 Sp, WGe

G Dumitrescu 1988 It, Sp, F, W, 1989 It, E, Sp, Z, Sa, USS, S, 1990 It, F, H, Sp, It, USS, 1991 It, NZ, F, 1997 It

L Dumitrescu 1997 Bel, Ar, 2001 W

G Dumitriu 1937 H, F, Ger

D Dumitru 2009 Ur, F, ItA

G Dumitru 1973 Sp, Mor, Ar, Ar, WGe, F, 1974 Mor, Sp, Cze, EGe, F, 1975 JAB, Pol, F, 1976 H, It, Sp, 1977 Sp, Pol, F, 1978 Cze, Sp, Pol, F, 1979 It, Sp, USS, W, Pol, F, 1980 It, Mor, USS, I, Pol, F, 1981 It, Sp, USS, S, NZ, F, 1982 WGe, It, USS, Z, Z, F, 1983 Mor, WGe, It, USS, Pol, USS, F, 1984 It, S, F, 1985 E, It, Tun, USS, 1986 F, I, 1987 USS, F, S, USS, F

M Dumitru 1990 F, H, Sp, It, USS, 1991 NZ, F, F, C, 1992 F, 1993 F, Sp, F

M Dumitru 1997 WalA, 1998 Ar, 1999 F, 2000 Mor, H, Pt, Sp, Geo, F, 2002 H, 2003 Sp

M Dumitru 2002 Pt, Sp, H, I

S Dumitru 2004 It, 2005 Rus, Ukr, US, S, Pt

R Durbac 1968 Cze, 1969 WGe, Cze, 1970 It, F, 1971 It, Mor, F, 1972 WGe, F, 1973 Ar, Ar, WGe, F, 1974 Mor, Pol, Sp, Cze, EGe, F, Cze, 1975 It, Sp, JAB, Pol, F

A Duta 1973 Ar

R Eckert 1927 F, Ger, Cze

I Enache 1977 It

M Ezaru 2000 Pt, Geo, F

V Falcusanu 1974 Sp, Cze

G Fantaneanu 1934 It, 1936 F, It, Ger, 1937 It, H, F, Ger

C Fercu 2005 C, I, 2006 Geo, CZR, Pt, Ukr, Rus, F, Geo, Sp, 2007 Geo, Sp, CZR, ESp, ItA, Nm, It, S, Pt, 2008 Geo, Sp, Pt, Rus, CZR, Ur, Rus, 2009 Sp, Ger, Rus, Pt, Ur, F

C Florea 1937 It, F, Ger

G Florea 1981 S, NZ, F, 1982 WGe, It, USS, Z, Z, 1984 Sp, 1985 USS, 1986 Pt, F

S Florea 2000 It, 2001 Sp, 2002 It, Sp, W, 2003 Sp, Rus, Geo, CZR, A, Ar, Nm, 2007 Sp, CZR, S, NZ, 2009 Sp, Ger

I Florescu 1957 F, Cze

M Florescu 1995 F

P Florescu 1967 It, Pt, Pol, WGe, F, 1968 Cze, Cze, F, 1969 Pol, WGe, Cze, F, 1971 Mor, 1973 Sp, Mor, Ar, Ar, 1974 Cze, EGe, F

P Florian 1927 F, 1934 It

T Florian 1927 F, Ger

V Flutur 1994 Ger, 1995 J, J, C, SA, A, Ar, F, It, 1996 Bel, Pol, 1997 WalA, F

M Foca 1992 It, USS, It, Ar, 1993 Pt, Tun, F

C Fugigi 1964 Cze, 1969 Cze, 1972 Mor, Cze, WGe, F, 1973 Sp, Ar, Ar, WGe, F, 1974 Mor, Sp, Cze, EGe, 1975 It, Sp, JAB

C Fugigi 1992 Ar

R Fugigi 1995 It, 1996 Pt, F, Pol, 1998 Ukr, Ar, I, 1999 S, I

S Fuicu 1976 H, 1980 USS, I, Pol, F, 1981 It, Sp, USS, S, NZ, F, 1982 Z, Z, F, 1983 Mor, WGe, It, USS, W, 1984 It

N Fulina 1988 F, W, 1989 It, E, Sp, Sa, USS, 1990 It, F, H, Sp, USS, 1991 NZ, C, Fj, 1992 It, It, 1993 Pt, F, Sp, F, I, 1994 Sp, Ger, Rus, It, W, It

C Gal 2005 I, 2006 Geo, CZR, Pt, S, 2007 Geo, CZR, ESp, ItA, Nm, It, S, NZ, Rus, Pt, 2008 Geo, Sp, Pt, Rus, 2009 Ger, Pt, ItA

S Galan 1985 It, It

I Garlesteanu 1924 F, US, 1927 F, Cze

A Gealapu 1994 It, E, 1995 F, S, J, J, C, SA, A, Ar, F, It, 1996 Pt, F, Pol

C Gheara 2004 CZR, Sp, Rus, Geo

C Gheorghe 1992 It, 1993 Tun, F, Sp, 1994 Sp, Ger, Rus, E

D Gherasim 1959 Cze

V Ghiata 1951 EGe

S Ghica 1937 H, F, 1942 It

V Ghioc 2000 It, 2001 Pt, Sp, Rus, Geo, I, W, E, 2002 Pt, Sp, H, W, S, 2003 CZR, Ar, 2004 It, W, CZR, 2005 Ukr, J, S, 2008 Pt

N Ghiondea 1949 Cze, 1951 EGe

P **Petrisor** 1985 *It*, 1987 *USS*
H **Peuciulescu** 1927 *F*
M **Picoiu** 2001 *Pt, H*, 2002 *Pt, Sp, H, Rus, I, It, Sp, W*
C **Pinghert** 1996 *Bel*
I **Pintea** 1974 *Pol*, 1976 *Pol, F, Mor*, 1977 *Sp, It, F, Pol, It, F*, 1979 *It, Sp, USS, W, Pol, F*, 1980 *It, USS*
D **Piti** 1987 *USS, F*, 1988 *It, Sp, US*, 1991 *S*
A **Plotschi** 1985 *It, Tun*, 1987 *S*
Plumea 1927 *Ger*
S **Podarescu** 1979 *Pol, F*, 1980 *USS*, 1982 *WGe, It, USS, F*, 1983 *Mor, WGe, USS, F*, 1984 *It*, 1985 *E, It*
C **Podea** 2001 *Geo, I*, 2002 *I, It, Sp, W*, 2003 *Pt, Sp, Rus, F, A*
R **Polizu** 1919 *US*
A **Pop** 1970 *It*, 1971 *It, Mor*, 1972 *Mor, Cze, F*, 1973 *WGe, F*, 1974 *Mor, Pol, Sp, EGe, F, Cze*, 1975 *It, Sp, JAB, Pol, F*
D **Popa** 1993 *Tun, F, Sp*
D **Popa** 1994 *Ger*
I **Popa** 1934 *It*, 1936 *F, It, Ger*, 1937 *H, F*, 1938 *F, Ger*, 1939 *It*, 1940 *It*, 1942 *It*
M **Popa** 1962 *EGe*
N **Popa** 1952 *EGe*
V **Poparlan** 2007 *Nm, Pt*, 2008 *Geo, Sp, Pt, Ur, Rus, ESp*, 2009 *Sp, Ger, Rus, Geo*
A **Popean** 1999 *S*, 2001 *Pt, H*
C **Popescu** 1986 *Tun, Pt, F*
CD **Popescu** 1997 *Bel*, 2003 *CZR, F, W, I, A, Ar, Nm*, 2004 *CZR, Pt, Sp, Rus, Geo, J, CZR*, 2005 *Rus, S, Pt, C*, 2006 *CZR, Ukr, Rus, F, Geo, Sp, S*, 2007 *Geo, Sp, CZR, ESp, ItA, Nm, It, Pt*, 2009 *Ur, F, ItA*
I **Popescu** 1958 *USS*
I **Popescu** 2001 *Pt, Sp, H, Rus, Geo*
C **Popescu-Colibasi** 1934 *It*
V **Popisteanu** 1996 *Pt, F, Pol*
F **Popovici** 1973 *Sp, Mor*
N **Postolache** 1972 *WGe, F*, 1974 *Mor, Pol, Sp, EGe, F, Cze*, 1975 *It, Sp, Pol, F*, 1976 *H, It Mor, Pol, Sp, EGe, F, Cze*, 1964 *Cze, EGe, WGe, F*
C **Preda** 1961 *Pol, Cze*, 1962 *EGe, F*, 1963 *Bul, EGe, Cze, F*, 1964 *Cze, EGe, WGe, F*
NF **Racean** 1988 *USS, USS, F, W*, 1989 *It, E, Z, Sa, USS*, 1990 *H, Sp, It, USS*, 1991 *NZ, F, F, C, Fj*, 1992 *Sp, It, USS, F, It, Ar*, 1993 *Pt, Tun, F, Sp, USS, It, W*, 1995 *F, S, J, J, C, SA, A*
A **Radoi** 2008 *CZR*
M **Radoi** 1995 *F*, 1996 *Pt, Pol*, 1997 *WalA, F, W, Bel, Ar, F, It*, 1998 *H, Pol, Ukr*
P **Radoi** 1980 *Mor*
T **Radu** 1991 *NZ*
C **Raducanu** 1985 *It*, 1987 *It, USS, Z, F, S*, 1989 *It, E, Sp, Z*
A **Radulescu** 1980 *USS, Pol*, 1981 *It, Sp, USS, S, F*, 1982 *WGe, It, USS, Z, Z*, 1983 *Pol, W, USS, F*, 1984 *It, S, F, Sp*, 1985 *E, USS*, 1988 *It, Sp, US, USS, USS, F, W*, 1989 *It, E, Sa, USS*, 1990 *It, F, H, Sp, It, USS*
T **Radulescu** 1958 *Sp, WGe*, 1959 *EGe, Pol, Cze, EGe*, 1963 *Bul, EGe, Cze*, 1964 *F*, 1965 *WGe, F*, 1966 *Cze*
D **Rascanu** 1972 *WGe, F*
G **Rascanu** 1966 *It, F*, 1967 *It, Pt, Pol, WGe, F*, 1968 *Cze, Cze, F*, 1969 *Pol, WGe, Cze, F*, 1970 *It, F*, 1971 *It, Mor, F*, 1972 *Mor, Cze, WGe, F*, 1974 *Sp*
C **Ratiu** 2003 *CZR*, 2005 *J, US, S, Pt, C, I*, 2006 *CZR, Pt, Ukr, Rus, F, Geo, Sp, S*, 2007 *Sp, CZR, ESp, It, S, Pt, NZ, Rus, Pt*, 2009 *Geo, Pt*
I **Ratiu** 1992 *It*
S **Rentea** 2000 *Mor*
I **Roman** 1976 *Bul*
C **Rosu** 1993 *I*
I **Rotaru** 1995 *J, C, Ar, It*, 1996 *Pt, F, Pol*, 1997 *W, Bel, Ar, F*
L **Rotaru** 1999 *F, A, I*
N **Rus** 2007 *Rus*
VS **Rus** 2007 *Rus, Pt*, 2008 *Geo, Pt, Rus*, 2009 *F, ItA*
M **Rusu** 1959 *EGe*, 1960 *F*, 1961 *Pol, Cze*, 1962 *Cze, EGe, Pol, It, F*, 1963 *Bul, EGe, Cze, F*, 1964 *WGe, F*, 1965 *WGe, F*, 1966 *Cze, It, F*, 1967 *It, Pt, Pol*
V **Rusu** 1960 *Pol, EGe, Cze*, 1961 *EGe, F*, 1962 *Cze, EGe,*

Pol, It, F, 1964 *Cze, EGe, WGe, F*, 1965 *WGe*, 1966 *It, F*, 1967 *WGe*, 1968 *Cze*
I **Sadoveanu** 1939 *It*, 1942 *It*
AA **Salageanu** 1995 *Ar, F, It*, 1996 *Pt, F, Pol*, 1997 *W, Bel, F*
V **Samuil** 2000 *It*, 2001 *Pt, E*, 2002 *Pt, Sp, Geo*
C **Sasu** 1989 *Z*, 1991 *It, NZ, F, S, F, C, Fj*, 1993 *I*
C **Sauan** 1999 *S, A, US, I*, 2000 *It*, 2002 *Geo, I, It, Sp*, 2003 *Pt, Rus, Geo, CZR, F, W, I, A, Ar, Nm*, 2004 *CZR, Pt, Sp, Rus, Geo, It, W, J, CZR*, 2005 *Rus, Geo, Ukr, J, US, S, Pt, 2006 Rus, 2007 Geo*
G **Sava** 1989 *Z, S*, 1990 *H, Sp, It, USS*, 1991 *It, F, S, F, C, 1992 Sp*
I **Sava** 1959 *EGe, Pol, Cze, EGe*, 1960 *F*, 1961 *Pol, EGe, Cze, EGe, F*, 1962 *Cze, Pol, It, F*
C **Scarlat** 1976 *H, Sp*, 1977 *F*, 1978 *Cze, Sp*, 1979 *It, Sp, USS, W, Pol, F*, 1980 *It, USS*, 1982 *USS*
R **Schmettau** 1919 *US, F*
V **Sebe** 1960 *Pol, EGe, Cze*
I **Seceleanu** 1992 *It, USS, F, It, Ar*, 1993 *Pt, Tun, F, Sp, F*
S **Seceleanu** 1986 *Pt, F, I*, 1990 *It*
E **Septar** 1996 *Bel, Pol*, 1997 *WalA, W*, 1998 *Pol, Ukr, I*, 1999 *F, S, A, US, I*, 2000 *It*
B **Serban** 1989 *Sa, USS, S*, 1990 *It*, 1992 *It, USS*
C **Serban** 1964 *Cze, EGe, WGe*, 1967 *Pol*, 1968 *Cze, F*, 1969 *Pol, WGe, Cze, F*, 1970 *It, F*, 1971 *It, Mor, F*, 1972 *F*, 1973 *WGe, F*, 1974 *Mor*
M **Serbu** 1967 *It*
E **Sfetescu** 1924 *F, US*, 1927 *Cze*
E **Sfetescu** 1934 *It*, 1936 *F, Ger*, 1937 *It*
G **Sfetescu** 1927 *F, Ger*
M **Sfetescu** 1924 *F, US*, 1927 *Ger, Cze*
N **Sfetescu** 1927 *F, Ger, Cze*
G **Simion** 1998 *H*
G **Simion** 1919 *US*
I **Simion** 1976 *H, It, Sp*, 1979 *Pol, F*, 1980 *F*
L **Sirbe** 2008 *CZR*
L **Sirbu** 1996 *Pt*, 2000 *Mor, H, Pt, Geo, F*, 2001 *H, Rus, Geo, I, W, E*, 2002 *Pt, Sp, H, Rus, I, It, S*, 2003 *Pt, Sp, CZR, F, W, I, A, Ar, Nm*, 2004 *Pt, Sp, Rus, Geo, It, W, CZR*, 2005 *Rus, Geo, Ukr, J, US, S, Pt, C*, 2006 *Pt, Ukr, Rus, F, Geo, Sp*, 2007 *Geo, ItA, It, S, Pt, NZ*, 2009 *Ur, F, ItA*
M **Slobozeanu** 1936 *F*, 1937 *H, F, Ger*, 1938 *F, Ger*
OS **Slusariuc** 1993 *Tun*, 1995 *J, J, C*, 1996 *F, Pt*, 1997 *Bel, Ar, F*, 1998 *H, Ar, Geo, I*, 1999 *F, S, A*
S **Soare** 2001 *I, W*, 2002 *Geo*
S **Soare** 1924 *F, US*
M **Socaciu** 2000 *It*, 2001 *I, W, E*, 2002 *It, W, S*, 2003 *Pt, Sp, Rus, Geo, CZR, F, W, I, A, Nm*, 2004 *CZR, Pt, Sp, Rus, Geo, It, W, J, CZR*, 2005 *Rus, Geo, Ukr, J, US, Pt, C, I*, 2006 *CZR*
S **Socol** 2001 *Sp, H, Rus, Geo*, 2002 *Pt, It, Sp, W*, 2003 *Sp, Rus, Geo, F, W, I, A, Ar, Nm*, 2004 *CZR, Pt, Sp, Rus, Geo*, 2005 *Rus, Geo, Ukr, C, I*, 2006 *Geo, CZR, Pt, Ukr, Rus, F, Geo, Sp, S*, 2007 *Geo, Sp, CZR, It, S, Pt, NZ*, 2009 *Ur, F, ItA*
N **Soculescu** 1949 *Cze*, 1951 *EGe*, 1952 *EGe, EGe*, 1953 *It*, 1955 *Cze*
N **Soculescu** 1927 *Ger*
V **Soculescu** 1927 *Cze*
GL **Solomie** 1992 *Sp, F, It, Ar*, 1993 *Pt, Tun, F, Sp, F, I*, 1994 *Sp, Ger, W, It, E*, 1995 *F, S, J, J, C, SA, A, Ar, F, It*, 1996 *Pt, F, Pol*, 1997 *WalA, F, W, Bel, Ar, F, It*, 1998 *H, Pol, Ukr, Ar, Geo, I*, 1999 *S, A, US, I*, 2000 *Sp, F, Pt*, 2001 *Sp, H, Rus*
C **Stan** 1990 *H, USS*, 1991 *It, F, S, F, C, Fj*, 1992 *Sp, It, It, Ar*, 1996 *Pt, Bel, F, Pol*, 1997 *WalA, F, W, Bel, Ar, Geo*, 1999 *F, S, A, US, I*
A **Stanca** 1996 *Pt, Pol*
R **Stanca** 1997 *F*, 2003 *Sp, Rus*, 2009 *Geo, Pt*
A **Stanciu** 1958 *EGe, It*
G **Stanciu** 1958 *EGe, It*
C **Stanescu** 1957 *Bel*, 1958 *WGe*, 1959 *EGe*, 1960 *F*, 1961 *Pol, EGe, Cze*, 1962 *Cze, It, F*, 1963 *Bul, EGe, Cze, F*, 1964 *WGe, F*, 1966 *Cze, It*
C **Stefan** 1951 *EGe*, 1952 *EGe*
E **Stoian** 1927 *Cze*

E **Stoica** 1973 *Ar, Ar,* 1974 *Cze,* 1975 *Sp, Pol, F,* 1976 *Sp, USS, Bul, F, Mor,* 1977 *Sp, It, F, Pol, It, F,* 1978 *Cze, Sp, Pol, F,* 1979 *It, Sp, USS, W, Pol, F,* 1980 *It, USS, I, Pol, F,* 1981 *It, Sp, USS, S, NZ, F,* 1982 *WGe, It, USS, Z, Z, F*

G **Stoica** 1963 *Bul, Cze,* 1964 *WGe,* 1966 *It, F,* 1967 *Pt, F,* 1968 *Cze, Cze, F,* 1969 *Pol*

I **Stroe** 1986 *Pt*

E **Suciu** 1976 *Bul, Pol,* 1977 *It, F, It,* 1979 *USS, Pol, F,* 1981 *Sp*

M **Suciu** 1968 *F,* 1969 *Pol, WGe, Cze,* 1970 *It, F,* 1971 *It, Mor, F,* 1972 *Mor, F*

O **Sugar** 1983 *It,* 1989 *Z, Sa, USS, S,* 1991 *NZ, F*

K **Suiogan** 1996 *Bel*

F **Surugiu** 2008 *Ur, Rus, ESp*

D **Talaba** 1996 *Bel,* 1997 *F, It*

C **Tanase** 1938 *F, Ger,* 1939 *It,* 1940 *It*

A **Tanasescu** 1919 *F,* 1924 *F, US*

N **Tanoviceanu** 1937 *It, H, F,* 1939 *It*

I **Tarabega** 1934 *It,* 1936 *It*

F **Tasca** 2008 *Ur, Rus, ESp,* 2009 *Sp, Ger, Rus, Geo, Pt*

V **Tata** 1971 *F,* 1973 *Ar, Ar*

CF **Tatu** 2003 *Ar,* 2004 *CZR, Pt, Sp, Rus, Geo, It, W,* 2005 *Ukr, J*

I **Tatucu** 1973 *Sp, Mor,* 1974 *Cze, F*

D **Teleasa** 1971 *It,* 1973 *Sp, Ar, Ar*

D **Tenescu** 1951 *EGe*

I **Teodorescu** 2001 *I, W, E,* 2002 *Pt, Sp, S,* 2003 *Pt, Sp, Rus, W, I, A, Ar, Nm,* 2004 *CZR, Pt, Sp, Rus, Geo, W, J, CZR,* 2005 *Rus, Geo, Ukr, J, US, S, Pt, C, I,* 2006 *Geo, CZR, Pt, Ukr, F, Geo, S,* 2007 *ESp, ItA*

I **Teodorescu** 1958 *Sp, WGe, EGe, It,* 1960 *Pol, EGe, Cze,* 1963 *Bul, EGe, Cze,* 1965 *WGe, F*

A **Teofilovici** 1957 *F, Cze, Bel, F,* 1958 *Sp, WGe,* 1959 *EGe,* 1960 *F,* 1961 *Pol, EGe, Cze, EGe, F,* 1962 *Cze, Pol, It, F,* 1963 *Bul, EGe, Cze, F,* 1964 *WGe*

O **Tepurica** 1985 *USS*

M **Tibuleac** 1957 *Bel, F,* 1959 *Pol, Cze,* 1966 *Cze,* 1967 *It, Pt, Pol, WGe,* 1968 *Cze, Cze*

G **Ticlean** 1919 *F*

M **Tigora** 2004 *CZR*

A **Tinca** 1987 *USS, F*

VM **Tincu** 2002 *Pt, Sp, H, Rus, Geo, I, It, Sp, S,* 2003 *Pt, Sp, Rus, Geo, F, W,* 2004 *Sp, USS, Geo, Ukr, C, I,* 2006 *Geo, CZR, F, S,* 2007 *Geo, Sp, CZR, ESp, ItA, Nm, It, S, Pt, NZ,* 2008 *Geo,* 2009 *F, ItA*

M **Toader** 1982 *WGe,* 1984 *Sp,* 1985 *E, It, Tun, USS,* 1986 *S, F, Tun, Tun, Pt, F, I,* 1987 *It, USS, Z, F, S, USS, F,* 1988 *F, W,* 1989 *It, E, Sp, Sa, USS, S,* 1990 *It, F, It*

P **Toderasc** 2000 *It,* 2001 *Pt, Sp, Geo, W, E,* 2002 *H, Rus, Geo, I, It, Sp, W, S,* 2003 *Sp, Rus, Geo, CZR, F, W, I, A, Ar, Nm,* 2004 *CZR, Pt, Sp, Rus, Geo, It, J, CZR,* 2005 *J, US, S, Pt, C, I,* 2006 *Geo, Pt, Ukr, Sp,* 2007 *Geo, ESp, ItA, Nm, It, S*

IR **Tofan** 1997 *Bel, Ar, F, It,* 1998 *H, Ar,* 1999 *I,* 2000 *Mor, Sp, Geo,* 2001 *Pt, Sp, H, Geo, I, W, E,* 2002 *Pt, Sp, H, Rus, Geo, I, It, Sp, W, S,* 2003 *Pt, Sp, Rus, Geo, CZR, F, W, I, A, Ar, Nm,* 2004 *Sp, Geo, It, W, J,* 2005 *Rus, Geo, Ukr, J, US, I,* 2006 *Geo, CZR, Pt, Geo, Sp, S,* 2007 *Geo, ESp, ItA, Nm, S*

S **Tofan** 1985 *USS, It,* 1986 *Tun, Pt, F, I,* 1987 *It, USS, Z, F, S, USS, F,* 1988 *It, Sp, US, USS,* 1991 *NZ,* 1992 *Ar,* 1993 *Pt,* 1994 *It, E*

O **Tonita** 2000 *Mor, H, Pt, Sp, F,* 2001 *Pt, Sp, H, Rus, Geo, I,* 2002 *Sp, It, Sp, W,* 2003 *Rus, Geo, F, W, I, A, Ar, Nm,* 2004 *Sp, Rus, Geo, It,* 2005 *Rus, Pt, C, I,* 2006 *Geo, Pt, Geo, Sp, S,* 2007 *Sp, CZR, It, S, Pt, NZ,* 2009 *Ur, F, ItA*

Traian 1942 *It*

N **Tranca** 1992 *Sp*

B **Tudor** 2003 *CZR, A*

F **Tudor** 1924 *F, US*

M **Tudor** 1924 *F, US*

AM **Tudori** 2003 *F, W, I, A, Ar, Nm,* 2004 *Sp, Rus, Geo, W, J, CZR,* 2005 *Rus, Geo, Ukr, J, US, S, Pt,* 2006 *Geo, CZR,*

Ukr, Rus, F,* 2007 *Sp, CZR, ESp, ItA, Nm, It, S, Pt,* 2009 *Geo, Ur, ItA*

D **Tudosa** 1999 *S,* 2002 *Geo, I, It,* 2003 *Pt, W*

T **Tudose** 1977 *It,* 1978 *Cze, Sp, Pol, F,* 1979 *It, Sp, USS,* 1980 *USS*

V **Tufa** 1985 *USS,* 1986 *Pt, S,* 1990 *It,* 1991 *F,* 1995 *F, S, J, J, SA, A,* 1996 *Pt, F, Pol*

D **Tunaru** 1985 *It*

V **Turlea** 1974 *Sp,* 1975 *JAB, Pol, F,* 1977 *Pol*

C **Turut** 1937 *H,* 1938 *F*

I **Tutuianu** 1960 *Pol, EGe,* 1963 *Bul, EGe, Cze,* 1964 *Cze, EGe, WGe,* 1965 *WGe, F,* 1966 *Cze, It, F,* 1967 *Pt, Pol, WGe, F,* 1968 *Cze, Cze, F,* 1969 *Pol, WGe, Cze,* 1970 *It, F,* 1971 *F*

G **Tutunea** 1992 *Sp*

M **Ungur** 1996 *Bel*

V **Ungureanu** 1979 *It*

V **Urdea** 1979 *F*

V **Ursache** 2004 *It, W, CZR,* 2005 *S, C,* 2006 *Geo, Ukr, Rus, F, S,* 2007 *Geo, Sp, CZR, ESp, ItA, Nm, Pt, NZ, Rus,* 2008 *Pt, Rus, CZR, Rus*

R **Vacioiu** 1977 *It, F, It*

E **Valeriu** 1949 *Cze,* 1952 *EGe*

M **Vardala** 1924 *F, US*

N **Vardela** 1927 *F, Ger*

G **Varga** 1976 *It, USS, Bul, Pol, F, Mor,* 1977 *Sp, It, F, Pol,* 1978 *Sp*

N **Varta** 1958 *EGe*

G **Varzaru** 1980 *Mor, I, Pol, F,* 1981 *It, Sp, USS, F,* 1983 *Mor, WGe, It, USS, F,* 1984 *S, F,* 1985 *Tun, USS,* 1986 *F,* 1988 *It, Sp, US, USS, USS*

Z **Vasluianu** 1989 *Sp, Z, Sa*

P **Veluda** 1967 *It, Pt, Pol, WGe, F,* 1968 *Cze, Cze*

R **Veluda** 1949 *Cze,* 1952 *EGe*

N **Veres** 1986 *Tun, Pt,* 1987 *F, USS, F,* 1988 *It, Sp, USS*

M **Vidrascu** 1919 *US, F*

P **Vidrascu** 1919 *US,* 1924 *F, US,* 1927 *Cze*

M **Vioreanu** 1994 *E,* 1998 *H, Pol, Ukr, Ar, Geo, I,* 1999 *F, S, A, US, I,* 2000 *Mor, Pt, Sp, Geo, F,* 2001 *Geo,* 2002 *Rus, Geo, I, It, Sp,* 2003 *Sp, Rus, F, I, A, Ar, Nm*

A **Visan** 1949 *Cze*

D **Vlad** 2005 *US, S, C, I,* 2006 *Rus,* 2007 *Sp, CZR, It, Rus, Pt,* 2008 *Sp, CZR*

G **Vlad** 1991 *C, Fj,* 1992 *Sp, It, USS, F, It, Ar,* 1993 *Pt, F, I,* 1994 *Sp, Ger, Rus, It, W, It, E,* 1995 *F, C, SA, A, Ar, It,* 1996 *Pt, F,* 1997 *W, Ar, F, It,* 1998 *Ar*

V **Vlad** 1980 *Mor*

FA **Vlaicu** 2006 *Ukr, F, Geo, Sp, S,* 2007 *Geo, Sp, CZR, ESp, ItA, Nm, S, NZ, Pt,* 2008 *Geo, Pt, Rus, CZR, Ur,* 2009 *Sp, Ger, Rus, Geo, Pt, Ur, F, ItA*

C **Vlasceanu** 2000 *Mor, Pt, Sp, Geo, F*

B **Voicu** 2003 *CZR,* 2004 *CZR, Pt, Sp, Rus, It, J,* 2005 *J, Pt*

M **Voicu** 1979 *Pol*

M **Voicu** 2002 *Pt*

V **Voicu** 1951 *EGe,* 1952 *EGe, EGe,* 1953 *It,* 1955 *Cze*

R **Voinov** 1985 *It,* 1986 *Pt, S, F, Tun*

P **Volvoreanu** 1924 *US*

G **Vraca** 1919 *US, F*

M **Vusec** 1959 *EGe, Pol, Cze, EGe,* 1960 *F,* 1961 *Pol, EGe, Cze, EGe, F,* 1962 *Cze, EGe, Pol, It, F,* 1963 *Bul, EGe, Cze, F,* 1964 *WGe, F,* 1965 *WGe, F,* 1966 *It, F,* 1967 *It, Pt, Pol, WGe, F,* 1968 *Cze, F,* 1969 *Pol, F*

RL **Vusec** 1998 *Geo, I,* 1999 *F, S, A, US, I,* 2000 *Mor, H, Pt, Sp, F,* 2002 *H, Rus, I*

F **Wirth** 1934 *It*

I **Zafiescu** 1979 *W, Pol, F*

M **Zafiescu** 1980 *Mor,* 1986 *I*

D **Zamfir** 1949 *Cze*

B **Zebega** 2004 *CZR, Pt, Rus, Geo, It, W, CZR,* 2005 *Rus, Ukr, US, S,* 2006 *Ukr, Sp,* 2007 *Rus, Pt,* 2008 *Geo, Pt, Rus, CZR, Ur*

D **Zlatoianu** 1958 *Sp, WGe, EGe, It,* 1959 *EGe,* 1960 *Pol, EGe, Cze,* 1961 *EGe, EGe, F,* 1964 *Cze, EGe,* 1966 *Cze*

SAMOA

SAMOA'S 2008–09 TEST RECORD

OPPONENTS	DATE	VENUE	RESULT
Junior All Blacks	12 June	H	**Lost** 16–17
Japan	18 June	N	**Won** 34–15
Tonga	23 June	N	**Won** 27–13
Fiji	27 June	A	**Lost** 14–19
Papua New Guinea	11 July	H	**Won** 115–7
Papua New Guinea	18 July	A	**Won** 73–12

FINDING THE PROMISED LAND

By Jeremy Duxbury

Manu Samoa may have finished below Fiji in the ANZ Pacific Nations Cup for the first time in the tournament's four-year history, but new coach Fuimaono Titimaea "Dicky" Tafua can still consider his inaugural season in charge a big success with the main goal of Rugby World Cup 2011 qualification achieved following victories over Papua New Guinea in July.

Samoa needed to qualify after finishing fourth in their pool at RWC 2007, but Tafua's men were nonetheless overwhelming favourites to secure the Oceania 1 spot in Pool D alongside defending champions South Africa, Fiji, Wales and the Africa 1 qualifier.

Papua New Guinea had overcome Vanuatu and Cook Islands over consecutive weekends to win the Oceania Cup and earn the home and away play-off with Samoa. The first leg took place at Apia Park on 11 July, but after the visitors took the lead with Jack Maraha's early try it was Samoa who cut loose to score 17 tries – four of them by wing Esera Lauina – to record a 115–7 victory.

Samoa seemingly only had to turn up to confirm their place at RWC 2011, but on the historic occasion of a fully-fledged Samoan national side playing in Papua New Guinea for the first time, the Pukpuks were determined to play with great pride and passion to better showcase their abilities. Samoa, with a side made up of predominantly locally-based players, still ran in a number of tries to win 73–12, but they had been made to work harder for the victory by the courageous hosts.

With qualification confirmed, Samoa can now turn their attention to their tour of Europe and matches against Wales, France and Italy in November as they build towards 2011. After the win in Port Moresby, team manager Matthew Vaea was quick to acknowledge the importance of this tour to Samoa's hopes for the next World Cup.

"The tour is going to be important for us in terms of blooding in our squad for 2011, so we are looking forward to that," said Vaea. "The boys will deserve a break now after qualifying, but we have got a lot of background work to do."

Samoa's qualification came five months after Tafua took over the reins following the sudden dismissal of Niko Palamo in January. The former Manu Samoa skipper had also overseen a Pacific Nations Cup campaign in June, which yielded comfortable victories over Tonga and

Japan, a narrow loss to Fiji and a near upset after pushing the Junior All Blacks all the way to the wire only to lose 17–16.

The future also looked bright with Samoa's Under 20s having finished seventh at the IRB TOSHIBA Junior World Championship in Japan with victories over Six Nations sides Scotland and Ireland the highlights. Samoan sides also finished as runners-up in the IRB Pacific Rugby Cup (Upolu Samoa losing the final 19–7 to Fiji Warriors) and the Oceania Under 19 Championship on home soil.

Possibly the only low point in the year was the performance of the Samoa Sevens team, who failed to win an IRB Sevens World Series event for the first time in three seasons. Their best result was the Cup semi-finals in Hong Kong, a stage they also reached at Rugby World Cup Sevens in March after beating England 31–26 in the quarter-finals thanks to Simaika Mikaele's extra-time try, before narrowly losing 19–12 to eventual champions Wales at 'The Sevens' in Dubai.

Tafua had previously coached the Sevens team to great success in the 2006–07 IRB Sevens World Series, when they reached the final in five tournaments and won in Hong Kong and Wellington. He was also the Elite Development Coach for Samoa's High Performance Unit and was voted Coach of the Year at the 2007 Samoa Sports Awards.

For a nation that only started taking rugby seriously in the 1980s, Samoa have done remarkably well in the past 25 years, and have proven to have one of the most fertile breeding grounds for raw rugby talent with players spread across the globe competing in high level competitions.

Following the disappointment of RWC 2007, Tafua appears to be looking far and wide to ensure he has the best players available for Test duty in the build-up to 2011. In April, the Samoa Rugby Union Board increased its National Selection Panel to include a member in New Zealand (Peter Fatialofa) and Australia (Tavita Sio) in an effort to keep up with the level of rugby played in Tier One countries.

For the national trials in June, Tafua named 56 overseas-based players and 32 from Samoa's rapidly improving domestic scene, which shows the success of the country's High Performance Unit. By comparison, the RWC 1999 squad comprised 29 overseas-based players in a squad of 30.

Though Samoa's top professionals from European clubs will naturally command the majority of the positions in the starting line-ups, the local players had a big part to play with 10 in the match-day 22 against Tonga. The whole of the Samoa Sevens squad are also locally based and players like Uale Mai, Lolo Lui and Ofisa Treviranus have graduated to full Test honours.

While the Pacific Nations Cup was based primarily in one country – Fiji – for the first time, Samoa opened the tournament by hosting the Junior All Blacks in Apia. The former champions, who returned in place of 2008 winners the New Zealand Maori, had to defend desperately to hold off the hosts in the final minutes at Apia Park after taking a 14–0 lead into half-time with outstanding wing Hosea Gear scoring one try and making another for full-back Israel Dagg.

Samoa's inspirational No.8 and captain George Stowers admitted afterwards that his team had started too slowly, ultimately paying the price for missing two scoring opportunities in the first half and failing to convert their two tries after the break.

Gavin Williams, the son of All Black great Bryan 'BG' Williams, brought Samoa back into contention with two penalties and an unconverted try, before Lauina went over in the corner to put the hosts within a point with 13 minutes remaining. Mai tried to snatch victory with two drop goal attempts, but the New Zealanders hung on to leave the Samoans ruing the scalp that got away, especially given the number of clear chances that went begging.

A week later in the western Fiji town of Sigatoka, Samoa saw off the plucky Japanese 35–14 with four late tries snuffing out a spirited challenge. Japan, who later defeated Tonga and should have also beaten Fiji, led 15–12 midway through the second half only to run out of steam with a late flurry of Samoan tries increasing the margin of victory to 19 points.

Japan dominated territory in the early stages but were undone by handling and tactical errors. Samoa's first half tries underlined the dominance of their pack with prop Justin Va'a emerging from the back of the maul to score and give his side a 12–3 advantage at the interval after an earlier penalty try.

Tries from full-back Jack Tarrant and wing Hirotoki Onozawa saw Japan take a brief lead, but London Irish wing Sailosi Tagicakibau picked up his sixth Test try for Samoa when he broke through several tackles and outpaced the cover defence to score. Mahonri Schwalger, Lauina and veteran Semo Sititi also crossed for Samoa as the Japanese challenge wilted.

With the Pacific Nations Cup condensed into a smaller window, Samoa faced rivals Tonga five days later in Lautoka and ran out 27–13 winners. Led by captain Nili Latu and Hale T-Pole, Tonga's forwards dominated the early exchanges at Churchill Park but failed to take advantage and instead Samoa scored the first try through Joe Tekori.

Samoa added another just before half-time after London Irish centre Seilala Mapusua spun out of a tackle to touch down, but to their credit

Tonga stayed in touch with two Pierre Hola penalties to trail only 10–6. Samoa threatened to run away with it after the break with tries from Treviranus and scrum-half Junior Polu, but on the hour mark Teu'imuli Kaufusi charged over for Tonga's only try.

Their final PNC match saw Samoa face old foes Fiji in a rivalry that dates back to 1924. Samoa fielded their strongest side of the year with the starting 15 including seven players from Guinness Premiership clubs and another three from France's Top 14. Fiji coach Ilivasi Tabua, by contrast, rested some of his key representatives.

As expected from the line-ups on paper, Samoa enjoyed the lion's share of possession and territory, yet were unable to convert this into points on the scoreboard. An exchange of penalties saw Samoa eke out a 9–3 lead, which was scant reward for their endeavours.

After the break, a couple of big hits from Fiji sparked the home crowd into life, and suddenly their players responded by throwing the ball around with their trademark carefree abandon. A second Seremaia Bai penalty was followed by Sevens captain Vereniki Goneva sidestepping his way to give Fiji the lead after 52 minutes. Notise Tauafao gave Samoa hope when he pounced to score their only try with 10 minutes remaining, but ultimately Fiji ran out surprise 19–14 winners.

Fiji went on to scrape past Japan 40–39 at the death in the tournament's final fixture to push Samoa into third place, but their overall performance in the four matches would not give Tafua much cause for concern.

Domestically, the SRU have made great strides to improve both development and elite players. In addition to the National Provincial Cup, Samoa has its own competitive 10s and Sevens series. This important work, combined with the broad view of Tafua, should see Samoa go to Rugby World Cup 2011 with renewed confidence.

SAMOA

SAMOA INTERNATIONAL STATISTICS
MATCH RECORDS UP TO 30TH SEPTEMBER 2009

WINNING MARGIN

Date	Opponent	Result	Winning Margin
11/07/2009	PNG	115–7	108
08/04/1990	Korea	74–7	67
18/07/2009	PNG	73–12	61
10/06/2000	Japan	68–9	59
29/06/1997	Tonga	62–13	49

MOST POINTS IN A MATCH
BY THE TEAM

Date	Opponent	Result	Pts.
11/07/2009	PNG	115–7	115
08/04/1990	Korea	74–7	74
18/07/2009	PNG	73–12	73
10/06/2000	Japan	68–9	68
29/06/1997	Tonga	62–13	62

MOST TRIES IN A MATCH
BY THE TEAM

Date	Opponent	Result	Tries
11/07/2009	PNG	115–7	17
18/07/2009	PNG	73–12	13
08/04/1990	Korea	74–7	11

MOST CONVERSIONS IN A MATCH
BY THE TEAM

Date	Opponent	Result	Cons
11/07/2009	PNG	115–7	15
18/07/2009	PNG	73–12	9
08/04/1990	Korea	74–7	8

MOST PENALTIES IN A MATCH
BY THE TEAM

Date	Opponent	Result	Pens
29/05/2004	Tonga	24–14	8

MOST DROP GOALS IN A MATCH
BY THE TEAM

1 on 9 Occasions

MOST POINTS IN A MATCH
BY A PLAYER

Date	Player	Opponent	Pts.
11/07/2009	Gavin Williams	PNG	30
29/05/2004	Roger Warren	Tonga	24
03/10/1999	Silao Leaega	Japan	23
08/04/1990	Andy Aiolupo	Korea	23
08/07/2000	Toa Samania	Italy	23

MOST TRIES IN A MATCH
BY A PLAYER

Date	Player	Opponent	Tries
28/05/1991	Tupo Fa'amasino	Tonga	4
10/06/2000	Elvis Seveali'I	Japan	4
02/07/2005	Alesana Tuilagi	Tonga	4
11/07/2009	Esera Lauina	PNG	4

MOST CONVERSIONS IN A MATCH
BY A PLAYER

Date	Player	Opponent	Cons
11/07/2009	Gavin Williams	PNG	10
18/07/2009	Titi Jnr Esau	PNG	9
08/04/1990	Andy Aiolupo	Korea	8

MOST PENALTIES IN A MATCH
BY A PLAYER

Date	Player	Opponent	Pens
29/05/2004	Roger Warren	Tonga	8

MOST DROP GOALS IN A MATCH
BY A PLAYER

1 on 9 Occasions

MOST CAPPED PLAYERS	
Name	Caps
Brian Lima	65
To'o Vaega	60
Semo Sititi	59
Opeta Palepoi	42
Steve So'oialo	38

LEADING PENALTY SCORERS	
Name	Pens
Darren Kellett	35
Earl Va'a	31
Silao Leaega	31
Roger Warren	29
Andy Aiolupo	24

LEADING TRY SCORERS	
Name	Tries
Brian Lima	31
Semo Sititi	17
Afato So'oialo	15
To'o Vaega	15
Rolagi Koko	12

LEADING DROP GOAL SCORERS	
Name	DGs
Darren Kellett	2
Roger Warren	2
Steve Bachop	2

LEADING CONVERSIONS SCORERS	
Name	Cons
Andy Aiolupo	35
Earl Va'a	33
Silao Leaega	26
Tanner Vili	21
Gavin Williams	18

LEADING POINTS SCORERS	
Name	Pts.
Earl Va'a	184
Andy Aiolupo	172
Silao Leaega	160
Darren Kellett	155
Brian Lima	150

SAMOA

SAMOA INTERNATIONAL PLAYERS
(UP TO 30TH SEPTEMBER 2009)

Note: Years given for International Championship matches are for second half of season; eg 1972 means season 1971–72. Years for all other matches refer to the actual year of the match.

A'ati 1932 *Tg*
Agnew 1924 *Fj, Fj*
S Ah Fook 1947 *Tg*
F Ah Long 1955 *Fj*
Ah Mu 1932 *Tg*
Ah Sue 1928 *Fj*
T Aialupo 1986 *W*
F Aima'asu 1981 *Fj, 1982 Fj, Fj, Fj, Tg, 1988 Tg, Fj*
AA Aiolupo 1983 *Tg, 1984 Fj, Tg, 1985 Fj, Tg, Tg, 1986 Fj, Tg, 1987 Fj, Tg, 1988 Fj, I, W, 1989 Fj, WGe, Bel, R, 1990 Kor, Tg, J, Tg, Fj, 1991 W, A, Ar, S, 1992 Tg, Fj, 1993 Tg, Fj, S, NZ, 1994 Tg, W, A*
A Aiono 2009 *PNG*
Aitofele 1924 *Fj, Fj, 1928 Fj*
P Alalatoa 1986 *W*
V Alalatoa 1988 *I, W, 1989 Fj, 1991 Tg, W, A, Ar, S, 1992 Tg, Fj*
P Alauni 2009 *PNG*
R Ale 1997 *M, Tg, Fj, 1999 J, Ar, W, S*
A Alelupo 1994 *Fj*
T Aleni 1982 *Tg, 1983 Tg, 1985 Tg, 1986 W, Fj, Tg, 1987 Fj*
S Alesana 1979 *Tg, Fj, 1980 Tg, 1981 Fj, Fj, 1982 Fj, Tg, 1983 Tg, Fj, 1984 Fj, Tg, 1985 Fj, Tg*
T Allen 1924 *Fj, Fj*

K Anufe 2009 *JAB, Tg*
L Aoelua 2008 *NZ*
T Aoese 1981 *Fj, Fj, 1982 Fj, Fj, Fj, Tg, 1983 Tg*
J Apelu 1985 *Tg*
F Asi 1963 *Fj, Fj, Tg*
F Asi 1975 *Tg, Tg*
SP Asi 1999 *S, 2000 Fj, J, Tg, C, It, US, W, S, 2001 Tg, Fj, NZ, Fj, Tg, Fj*
Atiga 1924 *Fj*
S Ati'ifale 1979 *Tg, 1980 Tg, 1981 Fj, Fj*
J Atoa 1975 *Tg, Tg, 1981 Fj*
SJ Bachop 1991 *Tg, Fj, W, A, Ar, S, 1998 Tg, Fj, 1999 J, C, F, NZ, US, Fj, J, Ar, W, S*
C Betham 1955 *Fj*
ML Birtwistle 1991 *Fj, W, A, Ar, S, 1993 Fj, NZ, 1994 Tg, W, Fj, A, 1996 I*
W Brame 2009 *JAB, J, Fj*
FE Bunce 1991 *W, A, Ar, S*
CH Capper 1924 *Fj*
J Cavanagh 1955 *Fj, Fj, Fj*
J Clarke 1997 *Tg, 1998 A, 1999 US, Fj, J*
A Collins 2005 *S, Ar*
A Cortz 2007 *Fj*

G **Cowley** 2005 *S, Ar, 2006 JAB, J, Tg*
T **Cowley** 2000 *J, C, It*
L **Crichton** 2006 *Fj, Tg, 2007 Fj, JAB, AuA, SA, J, Tg, SA, Tg, E, US*
O **Crichton** 1988 *Tg*
O **Crichton** 1955 *Fj, Fj, Fj, 1957 Tg, Tg*
T **Curtis** 2000 *Fj, J, Tg, C, It, US*
H **Ekeroma** 1972 *Tg, Tg*
G **Elisara** 2003 *I, Nm*
S **Enari** 1975 *Tg, Tg*
S **Epati** 1972 *Tg*
T **Esau** 2009 *PNG, PNG*
K **Ese** 1947 *Tg*
S **Esera** 1981 *Fj*
L **Eves** 1957 *Tg, Tg*
H **Faafili** 2008 *Fj, AuA, M, Tg, J, 2009 J, Tg, Fj, PNG*
T **Fa'afou** 2007 *Fj*
P **Fa'alogo** 1963 *Fj*
Fa'amaile 1947 *Tg*
T **Fa'amasino** 1988 *W, 1989 Bel, R, 1990 Kor, Tg, J, Tg, Fj, 1991 Tg, Fj, A, 1995 It, Ar, E, SA, Fj, Tg, 1996 NZ, M, Tg, Fj*
JS **Faamatuainu** 2005 *S, Ar, 2006 JAB, 2008 Fj, AuA, J, 2009 JAB, J, Tg, Fj, PNG*
S **Fa'aofo** 1990 *Tg*
Fa'asalele 1957 *Tg, Tg*
F **Fa'asau** 1963 *Fj, Tg*
M **Fa'asavalu** 2002 *SA, 2003 I, Nm, Ur, Geo, E, SA*
V **Faasua** 1987 *Fj, 1988 Tg, Fj, W*
S **Fa'asua** 2000 *W*
F **Fa'asuaga** 1947 *Tg*
L **Fa'atau** 2000 *Fj, Tg, C, US, 2001 I, It, 2002 Fj, Tg, Fj, Tg, SA, 2003 I, Ur, E, SA, 2004 Tg, S, Fj, 2005 A, Tg, Fj, S, E, Ar, 2006 JAB, J, Fj, Tg, 2007 Fj, JAB, AuA, SA, J, Tg, SA, US*
K **Faiva'ai** 1998 *Tg, Fj, A, 1999 J, C, Tg, NZ, US, Fj*
L **Falaniko** 1990 *Fj, Fj, 1991 Tg, 1993 Tg, Fj, S, NZ, 1995 SA, It, Ar, E, SA, Fj, Tg, S, E, 1996 NZ, M, 1999 US, Fj, W, S*
E **Fale** 2008 *Tg*
S **Fale** 1955 *Fj*
A **Faleata** 1960 *M, M*
S **Fanolua** 1990 *Tg, Fj, 1991 Tg, Fj*
TL **Fanolua** 1996 *NZ, Fj, 1997 Tg, 1998 Tg, Fj, A, 1999 W, S, 2000 J, Tg, C, It, US, 2001 Tg, Fj, NZ, Fj, Tg, J, Fj, 2002 Fj, 2003 Nm, Ur, Geo, E, 2005 A, Tg, Fj, Fj*
R **Fanuatanu** 2003 *I, Geo*
M **Faoagali** 1999 *J, C*
A **Faosilivia** 2006 *J, Tg, 2008 M, Tg, NZ*
DS **Farani** 2005 *Tg, Fj, S, E, Ar, 2006 J, Fj, Tg*
J **Fatialofa** 2008 *M*
M **Fatialofa** 1996 *Tg*
PM **Fatialofa** 1988 *I, W, 1989 Bel, R, 1990 Kor, Tg, J, 1991 Tg, W, A, Ar, S, 1992 Tg, Fj, 1993 Tg, Fj, S, NZ, 1994 Tg, W, Fj, A, 1995 SA, It, Ar, E, SA, Fj, Tg, S, E, 1996 NZ, M, Fj*
Fatu 1947 *Tg*
E **Feagai** 1963 *Fj, Tg*
S **Feagai** 1963 *Fj, Fj*
D **Feaunati** 2003 *Nm, Ur, Geo, E, SA, 2006 JAB*
I **Fea'unati** 1996 *I, 1997 M, Tg, 1999 Tg, NZ, Fj, Ar, 2000 Fj, J, Tg, C, It, US, 2006 JAB, Fj, Tg*
M **Fepuleai** 1957 *Tg*
V **Fepuleai** 1988 *W, 1989 Fj, WGe, R*
I **Fesuiai'i** 1985 *Fj, Tg*
T **Fetu** 1960 *M, M*
S **Fiaola** 1960 *M, M*
JA **Filemu** 1995 *S, E, 1996 NZ, M, Tg, Fj, I, 1997 M, Fj, 1999 J, C, Tg, F, NZ, 2000 Fj, J, Tg, C, It, US, 2001 Tg, Fj, Tg, J*
F **Fili** 2003 *I, Nm*
F **Filisoa** 2005 *Tg*
Filivaa 1928 *Fj*
T **Fong** 1983 *Tg, Fj, 1984 Fj, Tg, 1986 W, Fj, Tg, 1987 Fj, Tg*
S **Fretton** 1947 *Tg*
Fruean 1932 *Tg*
J **Fruean** 1972 *Tg, 1975 Tg, Tg*
S **Fruean** 1955 *Fj, Fj*
P **Fuatai** 1988 *Tg, Fj, 1989 Fj, WGe, R*
S **Fuatai** 1972 *Tg*
T **Fuga** 1999 *F, NZ, US, 2000 Fj, J, Tg, C, It, US, 2007 SA, Tg*
E **Fuimaono-Sapolu** 2005 *S, E, Ar, 2006 Fj, Tg, 2007 SA, E, US, 2008 Fj, AuA, M, Tg, J, 2009 JAB, J, Fj, PNG, PNG*
T **Gage** 1960 *M, M*
T **Galuvao** 1972 *Tg*
N **George** 2004 *Tg, Fj*
C **Glendinning** 1999 *J, C, Tg, F, NZ, US, Fj, J, W, S, 2000 Fj, J, Tg, C, It, US, 2001 Tg, Fj, NZ, Fj, Tg, Fj*
A **Grey** 1957 *Tg, Tg*
I **Grey** 1985 *Fj, Tg*
P **Grey** 1975 *Tg, Fj, 1979 Tg, Fj, 1980 Tg*
G **Harder** 1995 *SA, It, Ar, SA*
Hellesoe 1932 *Tg*
M **Hewitt** 1955 *Fj, Fj*
J **Huch** 1982 *Fj, Fj, 1986 Fj, Tg*
J **Hunt** 1957 *Tg, Tg*
A **Ieremia** 1992 *Tg, Fj, 1993 Tg, Fj, S, NZ*
Iese 1928 *Tg*
I **Imo** 1924 *Fj*
T **Imo** 1955 *Fj, Fj, 1957 Tg, Tg*

A **Ioane** 1957 *Tg, Tg, Tg*
E **Ioane** 1990 *Tg, Fj, 1991 Tg, Fj, S*
T **Iona** 1975 *Tg*
T **Iosua** 2006 *JAB, J*
Iupati 1924 *Fj*
M **Iupeli** 1988 *Tg, Fj, I, W, 1989 Fj, WGe, R, 1993 Tg, S, NZ, 1994 Tg, W, Fj, A, 1995 SA, E*
S **Iuta** 1947 *Tg*
T **Jensen** 1987 *Tg, 1989 Bel*
CAI **Johnston** 2005 *A, Tg, Fj, S, E, Ar, 2006 Fj, Tg, 2007 JAB, AuA, SA, J, Tg, SA, Tg, E, US, 2008 Fj, AuA, M, J, 2009 JAB, J, Tg, Fj, PNG*
J **Johnston** 2008 *AuA, M, Tg, J*
MN **Jones** 1986 *W*
S **Kalapu** 1957 *Tg, 1960 M*
D **Kaleopa** 1990 *Kor, Tg, J, 1991 A, 1992 Fj, 1993 Tg, Fj, S*
S **Kaleta** 1994 *Tg, W, 1995 S, E, 1996 NZ, M, 1997 Tg, Fj*
T **Kali** 1975 *Tg, Tg*
L **Kamu** 1955 *Fj, Fj, Fj*
MG **Keenan** 1991 *W, A, Ar, 1992 Tg, Fj, 1993 NZ, 1994 Tg, W, Fj, A*
JR **Keil** 2007 *JAB*
F **Kelemete** 1984 *Fj, Tg, 1985 Tg, 1986 W*
DK **Kellet** 1993 *Fj, S, NZ, 1994 Tg, W, Fj, A, 1995 It, Ar, Fj, Tg, S, E*
DA **Kerslake** 2005 *Tg, Fj, Tg, Fj, 2006 J, Tg, 2007 Fj, JAB, AuA, SA, J, Tg*
A **Koko** 1999 *J*
R **Koko** 1983 *Tg, Fj, Fj, 1984 Fj, Tg, 1985 Fj, Tg, Tg, 1986 W, Fj, Tg, 1987 Fj, Tg, 1988 Tg, Fj, I, W, 1989 WGe, R, 1993 Tg, S, NZ, 1994 Tg*
M **Krause** 1942 *Tg, 1986 W*
H **Kruse** 1963 *Fj, Fj, Tg*
JA **Kuoi** 1987 *Fj, Tg, 1988 I, W, 1990 Kor, Tg*
B **Laban** 1955 *Fj, 1957 Tg, Tg*
SL **Lafaiali'i** 2001 *Tg, Fj, NZ, Tg, 2002 Fj, Tg, Fj, Tg, SA, 2003 I, Nm, Ur, Geo, E, SA, 2004 Tg, S, Fj, 2005 A, S, E, 2007 Fj, JAB, J, Tg, Tg, US*
I **Laga'aia** 1975 *Tg, Tg, 1979 Tg, Fj*
F **Lalomilo** 2001 *I, It*
PR **Lam** 1991 *W, Ar, S, 1994 W, Fj, A, 1995 SA, Ar, E, SA, Fj, Tg, S, E, 1996 NZ, M, Fj, I, 1997 M, Tg, Fj, 1998 Tg, Fj, A, 1999 J, C, Tg, F, NZ, US, Fj, J, Ar, W, S*
F **Lameta** 1990 *Tg, Fj*
S **Lameta** 1982 *Fj*
Latai 1928 *Fj*
G **Latu** 1994 *Tg, W, Fj, A, 1995 SA, Ar, E, SA, Fj, Tg*
E **Lauina** 2008 *Fj, AuA, M, Tg, J, NZ, 2009 JAB, J, Tg, Fj, PNG, PNG*
M **Lautau** 1985 *Fj*
S **Leaega** 1997 *M, Tg, Fj, 1999 J, J, Ar, W, S, 2001 Tg, Fj, NZ, Fj, Tg, Fj, I, It, 2002 Fj, SA*
K **Lealamanua** 2000 *Fj, J, Tg, C, It, 2001 NZ, Fj, Tg, J, Fj, 2002 Fj, Fj, Tg, SA, 2003 I, Nm, Ur, Geo, E, SA, 2004 Tg, S, Fj, 2005 S, E, 2007 SA, Tg, Fj, US*
GE **Leaupepe** 1995 *SA, Ar, E, Fj, Tg, S, E, 1996 NZ, M, Tg, Fj, I, 1997 Tg, Fj, 1998 Tg, A, 1999 J, C, Tg, F, NZ, US, Fj, J, Ar, W, 2005 A*
S **Leaupepe** 1979 *Tg, Fj, 1980 Tg*
P **Leavai** 1990 *J*
A **Leavasa** 1979 *Tg, Fj, 1980 Tg*
P **Leavasa** 1955 *Fj, Fj, 1957 Tg, Tg, Tg*
PL **Leavasa** 1993 *Tg, Fj, S, 1995 It, Ar, E, S, E, 1996 NZ, M, Tg, Fj, I, 1997 M, Fj, 2002 Tg, Fj, Tg, SA*
S **Leavasa** 1955 *Fj, Fj, 1957 Tg*
T **Leiasamaivao** 1993 *Tg, S, NZ, 1994 Tg, W, Fj, 1995 SA, It, Ar, E, SA, S, E, 1996 NZ, M, Tg, Fj, I, 1997 M, Tg, Fj*
N **Leleimalefaga** 2007 *Fj, US*
S **Lemalu** 2003 *Ur, Geo, E, 2004 Tg, S, Fj, 2008 M, Tg, J, NZ*
S **Lemamea** 1988 *I, W, 1989 Fj, WGe, Bel, R, 1990 J, 1992 Tg, Fj, 1995 E, SA, Fj, Tg*
D **Lemi** 2004 *Tg, S, Fj, 2005 Tg, Fj, Tg, Fj, 2007 Fj, JAB, AuA, SA, J, Tg, SA, Tg, E, US, 2008 Fj, AuA, M, Tg, J*
DA **Leo** 2005 *A, Tg, Fj, Tg, Fj, S, E, Ar, 2006 JAB, J, Fj, Tg, 2007 AuA, SA, J, Tg, SA, Tg, E, 2008 AuA, M, Tg, J, 2009 J, Fj, PNG*
M **Leota** 2000 *Fj, Tg, C*
P **Leota** 1990 *Kor, Tg, J*
T **Leota** 1997 *Tg, Fj, 1998 Tg, Fj, A, 1999 J, C, Tg, F, Fj, J, Ar, W, S, 2000 Fj, J, 2001 Tg, Fj, NZ, Fj, J, Fj, 2002 Fj, Tg, Fj, Tg, SA, 2003 I, 2005 A*
A **Le'u** 1987 *Fj, 1989 WGe, R, 1990 Kor, J, Tg, Fj, 1993 Tg, Fj, S, NZ, 1996 I*
T **Leupolu** 2001 *I, It, 2002 Fj, Tg, Fj, Tg, SA, 2003 I, Nm, SA, 2004 Tg, S, Fj, 2005 Ar, 2007 AuA*
R **Levasa** 2008 *NZ, 2009 J, PNG*
FH **Levi** 2007 *Fj, JAB, AuA, SA, J, Tg, 2008 Fj, AuA, M, J, NZ, 2009 JAB, J, Tg, Fj, PNG*
A **Liaina** 1963 *Fj, Fj, Tg*
S **Liaina** 1963 *Fj, Fj, Tg*
P **Lilomaiava** 1993 *NZ*
BP **Lima** 1991 *Fj, W, A, Ar, S, 1992 Tg, Fj, 1993 Fj, S, NZ, 1994 Tg, W, Fj, A, 1995 SA, It, Ar, E, SA, Fj, Tg, S, E, 1996 NZ, M, Tg, Fj, 1997 M, Fj, 1999 Tg, F, NZ, US, J, Ar, W, S, 2000 C, It, US, 2001 Tg, Fj, I, It, 2002 Fj, Tg, 2003 I, Nm, Ur, Geo, E, SA, 2004 Tg, S, Fj, 2005 A, Fj, 2006 JAB, J, Fj, 2007 Fj, JAB, Tg, SA, E*

S Smith 1995 *S, E*, 1996 *Tg, Fj*, 1999 *C, Tg, F, NZ*
P Solia 1955 *Fj, Fj*
I Solipo 1981 *Fj*
F Solomona 1985 *Tg*
A So'oialo 1996 *I*, 1997 *M, Tg, Fj*, 1998 *Tg*, 1999 *Tg, F, NZ, US, Fj, J, Ar*, 2000 *Tg, It*, 2001 *Tg, Fj, NZ, Fj, Tg, J, I*
S So'oialo 1998 *Tg, Fj*, 1999 *NZ, US, Fj, J, Ar, W, S*, 2000 *W, S*, 2001 *Tg, Fj, NZ, Fj, J, Fj, I*, 2002 *Tg, Fj, Tg, SA*, 2003 *I, Nm, Ur, Geo, E, SA*, 2004 *Tg, S, Fj*, 2005 *E*, 2007 *Fj, JAB, AuA, SA, J, Tg, E, US*
F So'olefai 1999 *C, Tg*, 2000 *W, S*, 2001 *Tg, Fj, NZ, Fj, J*
L Sosene 1960 *M*
V Stet 1963 *Fj*
A Stewart 2005 *A, Tg*
G Stowers 2001 *I*, 2008 *Fj, AuA, M, Tg, J, NZ*, 2009 *JAB, J, Tg, Fj, PNG*
R Stowers 2008 *Fj*
T Stowers 1960 *M*
F Sua 1982 *Fj, Fj, Fj, Tg*, 1983 *Tg, Fj*, 1984 *Fj*, 1985 *Fj, Tg, Tg*, 1986 *Fj, Tg*, 1987 *Fj*
P Swepson 1957 *Fj*
S Ta'ala 1996 *Tg, Fj, I*, 1997 *M, Tg, Fj*, 1998 *Tg, Fj, A*, 1999 *J, C, Tg, US, Fj, J, Ar, W, S*, 2001 *J*
T Taega 1997 *Fj*
P Taele 2005 *Tg, Fj, E, Ar*, 2006 *JAB, J, Fj, Tg*
D Tafeamalii 2000 *W, S*
D Tafua 1981 *Fj, Fj*, 1982 *Fj, Fj, Fj, Tg*, 1983 *Tg, Fj*, 1985 *Fj, Tg, Tg, 1986 W, Fj, Tg*, 1987 *Tg*, 1989 *Fj, WGe, R*
L Tafunai 2004 *Tg, Fj*, 2005 *Tg, Fj, Tg, Fj, S, Ar*, 2008 *AuA, M, Tg, J, NZ*
TDL Tagaloa 1990 *Kor, Tg, J, Tg, Fj*, 1991 *W, A, Ar, S*
S Tagicakibau 2003 *Nm, Ur, Geo, E, SA*, 2004 *Tg, S, Fj*, 2005 *S, E, Ar*, 2007 *Tg*, 2009 *JAB, J, Tg, Fj*
Tagimanu 1924 *Tg*
I Taina 2005 *Tg, Fj, Tg, Fj, S*
F Taiomaivao 1989 *Bel*
L Talapo'o 1960 *M, M*
F Talapusi 1979 *Tg, Fj*, 1980 *Tg*
F Talapusi 2005 *A, Fj, Tg, Fj*
Tamalua 1932 *Tg*
F Tanoa'i 1996 *Tg, Fj*
S Tanuko 1987 *Tg*
P Tapelu 2002 *SA*
V Tasi 1981 *Fj*, 1982 *Fj, Fj, Fj, Tg*, 1983 *Tg, Fj*, 1984 *Fj, Tg*
S Tatupu 1990 *Fj, Tg*, 1993 *Tg, Fj, NZ*, 1995 *It, Ar, E, SA, Fj, Tg*
N Tauafao 2005 *A, Tg, Fj, Tg, Fj, S, Ar*, 2007 *Fj*, 2008 *Fj, AuA, J, NZ*, 2009 *J, Tg, Fj, PNG, PNG*
I Tautau 1985 *Fj*, 1986 *W*
T Tavita 1984 *Fj, Tg*
H Tea 2008 *Fj, AuA, Tg, J, NZ*, 2009 *PNG*
I Tekori 2007 *JAB, AuA, SA, J, SA, Tg, E, US*, 2009 *JAB, Tg, Fj*
AT Telea 1995 *S, E*, 1996 *NZ, M, Tg, Fj*
E Telea 2008 *Fj*
S Telea 1989 *Bel*
A Teo 1947 *Tg*
F Teo 1955 *Fj*
V Teo 1957 *Tg, Tg*
KG Thompson 2007 *Fj, JAB, AuA, SA, Tg, SA, Tg, E, US*, 2008 *M, Tg, J*
H Thomson 1947 *Tg*
A Tiatia 2001 *Tg, Fj, NZ, Fj, Tg, J, Fj*
R Tiatia 1972 *Tg*
S Tilialo 1972 *Tg*
M Timoteo 2009 *Tg*
F Tipi 1998 *Fj, A*, 1999 *J, C, F, NZ, Fj*
F Toala 1998 *Fj*, 1999 *J, C, S*, 2000 *W, S*
L Toelupe 1979 *Fj*
P Toelupe 2008 *Fj, AuA, J, NZ*
T Tofaeono 1989 *Fj, Bel*
A Toleafoa 2000 *W, S*, 2002 *SA*
K Toleafoa 1955 *Fj, Fj*
PL Toleafoa 2006 *JAB, Fj*
K Tole'afoa 1998 *Tg, A*, 1999 *Ar*
F Toloa 1979 *Tg*, 1980 *Tg*
S Toloia 1975 *Tg*
R Tolufale 2008 *NZ*, 2009 *PNG*
J Tomuli 2001 *I, It*, 2002 *Fj, Tg, Fj, Tg, SA*, 2003 *I, Nm, Ur, Geo, E, SA*, 2006 *JAB, J*
L Tone 1998 *Tg, Fj, A*, 1999 *J, C, Tg, F, NZ, US, J, Ar, W, S*, 2000 *Fj, J, Tg, C, It, US, S*, 2001 *NZ, Fj, Tg, J, Fj*
S Tone 2000 *W*
Toni 1924 *Fj*, 1928 *Fj*
OFJ Tonu'u 1992 *Tg*, 1993 *Tg, Fj, S, NZ*
F To'omalatai 1989 *Bel*
S To'omalatai 1985 *Fj, Tg*, 1986 *W, Fj, Tg*, 1988 *Tg, Fj, I, W*, 1989

Fj, WGe, Bel, R, 1990 *Kor, Tg, J, Tg, Fj*, 1991 *Tg, Fj, W, A, Ar, S*, 1992 *Tg, Fj*, 1993 *Fj, S*, 1994 *A*, 1995 *Fj*
O Treviranus 2009 *JAB, J, Tg, Fj, PNG, PNG*
Tualai 1924 *Fj, Fj*
I Tualaulelei 1963 *Fj, Fj, Tg*
F Tuatagaloa 1957 *Tg*
K Tuatagaloa 1963 *Fj, Fj, Tg*, 1972 *Tg*
S Tuatagaloa 1975 *Tg*
V Tuatagaloa 1963 *Fj, Tg*
Tufele 1924 *Fj*
D Tuiavi'I 2003 *I, Nm, Ur, E, SA*
VL Tuigamala 1996 *Fj, I*, 1997 *M, Tg, Fj*, 1998 *Tg, Fj, A*, 1999 *F, NZ, US, Fj, J, Ar, W, S*, 2000 *Fj, J, Tg, US*, 2001 *J, Fj, I, It*
AF Tuilagi 2005 *Tg, Fj, Tg, Fj, S, Ar*, 2006 *J, Tg*, 2007 *Fj, JAB, AuA, SA, J*, 2008 *AuA, M, Tg, J*
AT Tuilagi 2002 *Fj, Tg, SA*, 2005 *A, Tg, Fj, Tg, Fj, S, E*, 2007 *AuA, SA, J, Tg, SA, Tg, E, US*, 2009 *JAB*
F Tuilagi 1992 *Tg*, 1994 *W, Fj, A*, 1995 *SA, SA, Fj*, 2000 *W, S*, 2001 *Fj, NZ, Tg*, 2002 *Fj, Tg, Fj, Tg, SA*
H Tuilagi 2002 *Fj, Tg, Fj, Tg*, 2007 *SA, E*, 2008 *J*
T Tuisaula 1947 *Tg*
R Tuivaiti 2004 *Fj*
A Tunupopo 1963 *Fj*
P Tupa'i 2005 *A, Tg, S, E, Ar*
A Tupou 2008 *NZ*, 2009 *PNG*
S Tupuola 1982 *Fj, Fj, Tg*, 1983 *Tg, Fj*, 1985 *Tg*, 1986 *Fj, Tg*, 1987 *Fj, Tg*, 1988 *W*, 1989 *R*
P Tu'uau 1972 *Tg, Tg*, 1975 *Tg, Tg*
Tuvale 1928 *Fj*
D Tyrrell 2000 *Fj, J, C*, 2001 *It*, 2002 *Fj, Tg, SA*, 2003 *I, Nm, Ur, Geo, E, SA*
S Uati 1988 *Tg, Fj*
T Ugapo 1988 *Tg, Fj, I, W*, 1989 *Fj, WGe, Bel*
U Ulia 2004 *Tg, S, Fj*, 2005 *Ar*, 2006 *JAB, J, Fj, Tg*, 2007 *Fj, JAB, AuA, Tg, Tg, US*
J Ulugia 1985 *Fj, Tg*
M Umaga 1995 *SA, It, Ar, E, SA*, 1998 *Tg, Fj, A*, 1999 *Tg, F, NZ, US, Fj*
S Urika 1960 *M, M*
A Utu'utu 1979 *Tg, Fj*
L Utu'utu 1975 *Tg*
E Va'a 1996 *I*, 1997 *M, Fj*, 1998 *A*, 1999 *Tg, NZ, Fj, J, W, S*, 2001 *Tg, Fj, NZ, Fj, J, Fj, I*, 2002 *Fj, Tg, Fj, Tg, SA*, 2003 *I, Nm, Ur, Geo, E, SA*
JH Va'a 2005 *A, Fj, Tg, Fj, S, E, Ar*, 2006 *Fj, Tg*, 2007 *JAB, AuA, SA, J, Tg, SA*, 2009 *JAB, J, Tg, Fj*
MT Vaea 1991 *Tg, Fj, W, A, Ar, S*, 1992 *Fj*, 1995 *S*
K Vaega 1982 *Fj, Tg*, 1983 *Fj*
TM Vaega 1986 *W*, 1989 *WGe, Bel, R*, 1990 *Kor, Tg, J, Tg, Fj*, 1991 *Tg, Fj, W, A, Ar, S*, 1992 *Tg, Fj*, 1993 *Tg, Fj, S, NZ*, 1994 *Tg, W, Fj, A*, 1995 *SA, It, Ar, E, SA, Fj, Tg, S*, 1996 *NZ, M, Tg, Fj, I*, 1997 *M, Tg*, 1998 *Fj, A*, 1999 *J, C, F, NZ, Fj, J, Ar, W, S*, 2000 *Fj, J, Tg, C, It, US*, 2001 *Fj, Tg, J, Fj, I*
A Vaeluaga 2000 *W, S*, 2001 *Tg, Fj, Tg, J, Fj, I*, 2007 *JAB, AuA, SA, J, SA, E, US*
F Vagaia 1972 *Tg*
K Vai 1987 *Fj, Tg*, 1989 *Bel*
S Vaifale 1989 *R*, 1990 *Kor, Tg, J, Tg, Fj*, 1991 *Tg, Fj, W, Ar, S*, 1992 *Tg, Fj*, 1993 *S, NZ*, 1994 *Tg, W, Fj, A*, 1995 *SA, It, SA, Fj, S, E*, 1996 *NZ, M, Tg*, 1997 *Tg, Fj*
S Vaili 2001 *I, It*, 2002 *Fj, Tg, Fj, Tg*, 2003 *Geo*, 2004 *Tg, S, Fj*
L Vailoaloa 2005 *A*
T Vaise 1960 *M, M*
S Vaisola Sefo 2007 *US*
T Veiru 2000 *W, S*
M Vili 1957 *Tg*
M Vili 1975 *Tg, Tg*
M Vili 1960 *M, M*
T Vili 1999 *C, Tg, US, Ar*, 2000 *Fj, J, Tg, C, It, US*, 2001 *Tg, Fj, J, Fj, I, It*, 2003 *Ur, Geo, E, SA*, 2004 *Tg, S, Fj*, 2005 *A, Tg, Fj, S, E*, 2006 *J, Fj, Tg*
K Viliamu 2001 *I, It*, 2002 *Fj, SA*, 2003 *I, Ur, Geo, E, SA*, 2004 *S*
T Viliamu 1947 *Tg*
Visesio 1932 *Tg*
FV Vitale 1994 *W, Fj, A*, 1995 *Fj, Tg*
F Vito 1972 *Tg*, 1975 *Tg, Tg*
M von Dincklage 2004 *S*
R Warren 2004 *Tg, S*, 2005 *Tg, Fj, Tg, Fj, S, Ar*, 2008 *Fj, M, Tg, J, NZ*
S Wendt 1955 *Fj, Fj, Fj*
AF Williams 2009 *JAB, J, Fj, PNG, PNG*
DR Williams 1988 *I, W*, 1995 *SA, It, E*
G Williams 2007 *I, JAB, AuA, SA, SA, Tg*, 2008 *M, Tg, J*, 2009 *JAB, J, Tg, Fj, PNG, PNG*
H Williams 2001 *Tg, Tg, J*
P Young 1988 *I*, 1989 *Bel*

SCOTLAND

SCOTLAND'S 2008–09 TEST RECORD

OPPONENTS	DATE	VENUE	RESULT
New Zealand	8 November	H	**Lost** 6–32
South Africa	15 November	H	**Lost** 10–14
Canada	22 November	H	**Won** 41–0
Wales	8 February	H	**Lost** 13–26
France	14 February	A	**Lost** 13–22
Italy	28 February	H	**Won** 26–6
Ireland	14 March	H	**Lost** 15–22
England	21 March	A	**Lost** 12–26

HADDEN RESIGNS AS SCOTS STRUGGLE AGAIN

By Iain Spragg

Andy Robinson is the new man in charge in Scotland.

When **Frank Hadden was** charged with the task of revitalising the Scotland side in September 2005, he could have been under no illusions of the magnitude of the task ahead of him. Less than four years later, it was painfully obvious the former Edinburgh coach had not been able to revive the fortunes of the national team.

Hadden fell on his own sword in April, less than a fortnight after his team surrendered the Calcutta Cup to England at Twickenham to conclude another disappointing Six Nations campaign, and although there were justifiably kind words from his players and Scottish Rugby as he departed, the harsh reality was Scotland had stagnated in terms of both results and performances.

The Six Nations brought a solitary victory for the third successive campaign and the international season as a whole yielded just two wins against Canada and Italy. Hadden may have been both popular and well-respected but in the end he was not the man to move Scotland to the next level.

The search for his successor took two months and in early June Andy Robinson was unveiled as the new head coach. The 45-year-old had just led Edinburgh to an impressive second place in the Magners League and although his record of just nine wins in 22 games as England coach between 2004 and 2006 was far from spectacular, Scottish Rugby were convinced he was the right man to replace Hadden.

"I have enjoyed my time with Edinburgh immensely and to be appointed Scotland head coach is something that I am greatly honoured and excited about," Robinson said. "This is a wonderful opportunity for me to get back into Test rugby.

"I have enjoyed being part of the national and A team set-up in Scotland in the past two seasons and working with the players has fuelled my optimism. I am confident that I can take them and the national team onto bigger and better things.

"With the World Cup in New Zealand in 2011, I believe we have a crop of players who can really challenge the world's best and preparation for that starts now.

"I am very proud to be taking up the Scotland head coach role and I can assure all our supporters both at home and abroad that I will be doing everything I possibly can to bring success to the national team."

On the evidence of Scotland's performances in 2008–09, Robinson's challenge is just as great as that faced by his predecessor and in terms of the resources at his disposal, the fact just two Scotland players – Euan Murray and Nathan Hines – were named in Ian McGeechan's initial British & Irish Lions tour party told its own, chastening story.

The omens for the campaign were not good from the start. Before the team had even taken to the pitch for the autumn Tests, a row erupted between Scottish Rugby and the English Premiership sides about the release of players. A compromise was eventually reached that gave Hadden 12 days with his squad before the first match but the coach himself conceded it was 'not ideal' as Scotland prepared to tackle the All Blacks at Murrayfield.

The match was predictably one-sided despite New Zealand fielding an experimental side and they ran in four tries to nil as the home side slumped to a 32–6 defeat. The green shoots of recovery were proving as elusive as ever.

A week later South Africa, the reigning world champions, were in Edinburgh but suddenly Scotland sparked into life and almost toppled the Springboks. The home side had not scored a try at Murrayfield for 14 months but when Hines crashed over just before half-time, Scotland sensed a shock was on the cards.

SCOTLAND

The Springboks rallied after the break, however, and three penalties from Ruan Pienaar and a try from Jaque Fourie put the visitors in front and when Scotland agonisingly fluffed a try scoring chance in the dying minutes, the match was lost 14–10.

"We will never have a better chance to beat the world champions than we did today," Hadden admitted. "Everyone is gutted. They knew the game was there for the taking. Our discipline let us down just after half-time and our concentration let us down in the last 10 minutes.

"At the moment we can't see many positives because we thought we did enough to win the game. People will not really sit up and take notice until we actually win matches."

His side returned to winning ways seven days later with a 41–0 demolition of Canada, with Nikki Walker helping himself to a brace, but the real challenges lay ahead in the Six Nations and the coach was acutely aware debate about his future would only be silenced by results.

Hadden dropped record points scorer Chris Paterson for the Championship opener against Wales and handed Geoff Cross a debut at prop, but the changes backfired badly and the Welsh ran out comfortable 26–13 winners.

Cross was sin-binned in the first half after taking out Lee Byrne in the air and while he was contemplating his misdemeanour on the sidelines, Wales crossed twice through Tom Shanklin and Alun Wyn Jones to effectively settle the contest. The visitors scored two more tries and Max Evans' late score for the Scots was no more than a consolation.

A daunting trip to Paris to face Les Bleus followed with Scotland looking for what would be only their second win in 11 years in the French capital and for much of the match they looked capable of improving on their poor run.

Scotland trailed by just three points at the break but slipped further behind in the second half when Fulgence Ouedraogo barged over for the first try. The scoring pass looked forward but Hadden's team rallied and when Thom Evans crossed, they were within six points of the French. The home side eventually closed the game out for a 22–13 victory but Scotland had come close.

"Referees and linesmen have to take split second decisions and yes while I believe the try was created by a forward pass, it is down to them in the end," said captain Mike Blair afterwards. "However, I saw a lot that was a big improvement on last weekend's defeat by Wales. We feel that we played a lot of positive rugby against France. We have a lot to be proud of."

At the end of February Italy were the visitors to Murrayfield and Hadden knew he desperately needed a result. Scotland had lost to the

Azzurri in both 2007 and 2008 and Murray and Alastair Kellock were restored to the Scottish pack in anticipation of another fierce forward slog between the two sides.

It was out wide, however, that the home side gained a critical advantage when Simon Danielli scored a superb try and at the break they were 16–3 up. Scott Gray added a second in the second half and they ultimately cantered to a comfortable 26–6 triumph. Scotland were finally up and running.

Next up were Ireland in Edinburgh and initially at least the confidence Scotland had garnered from victory over the Italians was very much in evidence as Hadden's side refused to take a backwards step against the men in green.

The Scots led 12–9 at half-time as Paterson traded penalties with Ronan O'Gara but the turning point came after the break when replacement Jamie Heaslip crashed over following a break from Peter Stringer for the only try of the match. O'Gara converted and then added a drop goal and a fourth penalty to condemn Scotland to a 22–15 defeat.

England at Twickenham was Scotland's final assignment of the Championship but once again the Scots' inability to cross the whitewash proved the difference between the two sides and the home team emerged 26–12 winners. Scotland did close the gap in the second half to just six points but a late Danny Care drop goal and Mathew Tait try were decisive and in the end England outscored their visitors three tries to none.

Scotland had avoided the Wooden Spoon courtesy of their win over Italy but Hadden knew he was under severe pressure after the final whistle at Twickenham. He tried to remain positive when quizzed about his future in his post-match interview but there was also a sense of resignation as he reflected on his side's indifferent campaign.

"It's not something I'm thinking about at the moment," he said. "It has been a massive honour and privilege to be involved with the Scotland side. Other people will have a say in the matter, so we'll just have to wait and see.

"We've made progress. There's a massive issue over preparation time that we and Italy get in comparison to the other countries. The players are pretty flat at the moment. We put in an enormous amount of work but it comes to down to the little margins."

In the end, the pressure on him had reached critical mass and less than two weeks later Hadden announced he was stepping down as head coach. It was an honourable decision from an honourable man who had ultimately not been able to get the results the beleaguered Scottish supporters so badly craved.

SCOTLAND INTERNATIONAL STATISTICS

MATCH RECORDS UP TO 30TH SEPTEMBER 2009

MOST CONSECUTIVE TEST WINS

6 1925 F,W,I,E, 1926 F,W
6 1989 Fj, R, 1990 I,F,W,E

MOST CONSECUTIVE TESTS WITHOUT DEFEAT

Matches	Wins	Draws	Period
9	6*	3	1885 to 1887
6	6	0	1925 to 1926
6	6	0	1989 to 1990
6	4	2	1877 to 1880
6	5	1	1983 to 1984

includes an abandoned match

MOST POINTS IN A MATCH

BY THE TEAM

Pts	Opponents	Venue	Year
100	Japan	Perth	2004
89	Ivory Coast	Rustenburg	1995
65	United States	San Francisco	2002
60	Zimbabwe	Wellington	1987
60	Romania	Hampden Park	1999
56	Portugal	Saint Etienne	2007
55	Romania	Dunedin	1987
53	United States	Murrayfield	2000
51	Zimbabwe	Murrayfield	1991
49	Argentina	Murrayfield	1990
49	Romania	Murrayfield	1995

BY A PLAYER

Pts	Player	Opponents	Venue	Year
44	A G Hastings	Ivory Coast	Rustenburg	1995
40	C D Paterson	Japan	Perth	2004
33	G P J Townsend	United States	Murrayfield	2000
31	A G Hastings	Tonga	Pretoria	1995
27	A G Hastings	Romania	Dunedin	1987
26	K M Logan	Romania	Hampden Park	1999
24	B J Laney	Italy	Rome	2002
23	G Ross	Tonga	Murrayfield	2001
21	A G Hastings	England	Murrayfield	1986
21	A G Hastings	Romania	Bucharest	1986
21	C D Paterson	Wales	Murrayfield	2007

MOST TRIES IN A MATCH

BY THE TEAM

Tries	Opponents	Venue	Year
15	Japan	Perth	2004
13	Ivory Coast	Rustenburg	1995
12	Wales	Raeburn Place	1887
11	Zimbabwe	Wellington	1987
10	United States	San Francisco	2002
9	Romania	Dunedin	1987
9	Argentina	Murrayfield	1990

BY A PLAYER

Tries	Player	Opponents	Venue	Year
5	G C Lindsay	Wales	Raeburn Place	1887
4	W A Stewart	Ireland	Inverleith	1913
4	I S Smith	France	Inverleith	1925
4	I S Smith	Wales	Swansea	1925
4	A G Hastings	Ivory Coast	Rustenburg	1995

MOST CONVERSIONS IN A MATCH

BY THE TEAM

Cons	Opponents	Venue	Year
11	Japan	Perth	2004
9	Ivory Coast	Rustenburg	1995
8	Zimbabwe	Wellington	1987
8	Romania	Dunedin	1987
8	Portugal	Saint Etienne	2007

BY A PLAYER

Cons	Player	Opponents	Venue	Year
11	C D Paterson	Japan	Perth	2004
9	A G Hastings	Ivory Coast	Rustenburg	1995
8	A G Hastings	Zimbabwe	Wellington	1987
8	A G Hastings	Romania	Dunedin	1987

MOST PENALTIES IN A MATCH
BY THE TEAM

Penalties	Opponents	Venue	Year
8	Tonga	Pretoria	1995
7	Wales	Murrayfield	2007
6	France	Murrayfield	1986
6	Italy	Murrayfield	2005
6	Ireland	Murrayfield	2007
6	Italy	Saint Etienne	2007

BY A PLAYER

Pens	Player	Opponents	Venue	Year
8	A G Hastings	Tonga	Pretoria	1995
7	C D Paterson	Wales	Murrayfield	2007
6	A G Hastings	France	Murrayfield	1986
6	C D Paterson	Italy	Murrayfield	2005
6	C D Paterson	Ireland	Murrayfield	2007
6	C D Paterson	Italy	Saint Etienne	2007

MOST DROPPED GOALS IN A MATCH
BY THE TEAM

Drops	Opponents	Venue	Year
3	Ireland	Murrayfield	1973
2	on several	occasions	

BY A PLAYER

Drops	Player	Opponents	Venue	Year
2	R C MacKenzie	Ireland	Belfast	1877
2	N J Finlay	Ireland	Glasgow	1880
2	B M Simmers	Wales	Murrayfield	1965
2	D W Morgan	Ireland	Murrayfield	1973
2	B M Gossman	France	Parc des Princes	1983
2	J Y Rutherford	New Zealand	Murrayfield	1983
2	J Y Rutherford	Wales	Murrayfield	1985
2	J Y Rutherford	Ireland	Murrayfield	1987
2	C M Chalmers	England	Twickenham	1995

CAREER RECORDS

MOST CAPPED PLAYERS

Caps	Player	Career Span
95	C D Paterson	1999 to 2009
87	S Murray	1997 to 2007
82	G P J Townsend	1993 to 2003
75	G C Bulloch	1997 to 2005
74	J P R White	2000 to 2009
71	S B Grimes	1997 to 2005
70	K M Logan	1992 to 2003
66	S M Taylor	2000 to 2009
65	S Hastings	1986 to 1997
61	A G Hastings	1986 to 1995
61	G W Weir	1990 to 2000
61	T J Smith	1997 to 2005
60	C M Chalmers	1989 to 1999
60	B W Redpath	1993 to 2003
58	M R L Blair	2002 to 2009
58	N J Hines	2000 to 2009
53	A R Henderson	2001 to 2008
52	J M Renwick	1972 to 1984
52	C T Deans	1978 to 1987
52	A G Stanger	1989 to 1998
52	A P Burnell	1989 to 1999
51	A R Irvine	1972 to 1982
51	G Armstrong	1988 to 1999

MOST CONSECUTIVE TESTS

Tests	Player	Span
49	A B Carmichael	1967 to 1978
44	C D Paterson	2004 to 2008
40	H F McLeod	1954 to 1962
37	J M Bannerman	1921 to 1929
35	A G Stanger	1989 to 1994

MOST TESTS AS CAPTAIN

Tests	Captain	Span
25	D M B Sole	1989 to 1992
21	B W Redpath	1998 to 2003
20	A G Hastings	1993 to 1995
19	J McLauchlan	1973 to 1979
19	J P R White	2005 to 2008
16	R I Wainwright	1995 to 1998
15	M C Morrison	1899 to 1904
15	A R Smith	1957 to 1962
15	A R Irvine	1980 to 1982

MOST POINTS IN TESTS

Points	Player	Tests	Career
738	C D Paterson	95	1999 to 2009
667	A G Hastings	61	1986 to 1995
273	A R Irvine	51	1972 to 1982
220	K M Logan	70	1992 to 2003
210	P W Dods	23	1983 to 1991
166	C M Chalmers	60	1989 to 1999
164	G P J Townsend	82	1993 to 2003
141	B J Laney	20	2001 to 2004
123	D W Hodge	26	1997 to 2002
106	A G Stanger	52	1989 to 1998

SCOTLAND

MOST TRIES IN TESTS

Tries	Player	Tests	Career
24	I S Smith	32	1924 to 1933
24	A G Stanger	52	1989 to 1998
22	C D Paterson	95	1999 to 2009
17	A G Hastings	61	1986 to 1995
17	A V Tait	27	1987 to 1999
17	G P J Townsend	82	1993 to 2003
15	I Tukalo	37	1985 to 1992
13	K M Logan	70	1992 to 2003
12	A R Smith	33	1955 to 1962

MOST PENALTY GOALS IN TESTS

Penalties	Player	Tests	Career
150	C D Paterson	95	1999 to 2009
140	A G Hastings	61	1986 to 1995
61	A R Irvine	51	1972 to 1982
50	P W Dods	23	1983 to 1991
32	C M Chalmers	60	1989 to 1999
29	K M Logan	70	1992 to 2003
29	B J Laney	20	2001 to 2004
21	M Dods	8	1994 to 1996
21	R J S Shepherd	20	1995 to 1998

MOST CONVERSIONS IN TESTS

Cons	Player	Tests	Career
86	A G Hastings	61	1986 to 1995
86	C D Paterson	95	1999 to 2009
34	K M Logan	70	1992 to 2003
26	P W Dods	23	1983 to 1991
25	A R Irvine	51	1972 to 1982
19	D Drysdale	26	1923 to 1929
17	B J Laney	20	2001 to 2004
15	D W Hodge	26	1997 to 2002
14	F H Turner	15	1911 to 1914
14	R J S Shepherd	20	1995 to 1998

MOST DROPPED GOALS IN TESTS

Drops	Player	Tests	Career
12	J Y Rutherford	42	1979 to 1987
9	C M Chalmers	60	1989 to 1999
7	I R McGeechan	32	1972 to 1979
7	G P J Townsend	82	1993 to 2003
6	D W Morgan	21	1973 to 1978
5	H Waddell	15	1924 to 1930

Last season Chris Paterson became the first Scot to kick 150 penalties, in Tests.

RECORD	DETAIL	HOLDER	SET
Most points in season	120	in four matches	1999
Most tries in season	17	in four matches	1925
Highest Score	38	38–10 v Ireland	1997
Biggest win	28	31–3 v France	1912
	28	38–10 v Ireland	1997
Highest score conceded	51	16–51 v France	1998
Biggest defeat	40	3–43 v England	2001
Most appearances	48	C D Paterson	2000–2009
Most points in matches	361	C D Paterson	2000–2009
Most points in season	65	C D Paterson	2007
Most points in match	24	B J Laney	v Italy, 2002
Most tries in matches	24	I S Smith	1924–1933
Most tries in season	8	I S Smith	1925
Most tries in match	5	G C Lindsay	v Wales, 1887
Most cons in matches	31	C D Paterson	2000–2009
Most cons in season	11	K M Logan	1999
Most cons in match	5	F H Turner	v France, 1912
	5	J W Allan	v England, 1931
	5	R J S Shepherd	v Ireland, 1997
Most pens in matches	87	C D Paterson	2000–2009
Most pens in season	16	C D Paterson	2007
Most pens in match	7	C D Paterson	v Wales, 2007
Most drops in matches	8	J Y Rutherford	1979–1987
	8	C M Chalmers	1989–1998
Most drops in season	3	J Y Rutherford	1987
Most drops in match	2	on several	Occasions

SCOTLAND

MISCELLANEOUS RECORDS

RECORD	HOLDER	DETAIL
Longest Test Career	W C W Murdoch	1935 to 1948
Youngest Test Cap	N J Finlay	17 yrs 36 days in 1875*
Oldest Test Cap	J McLauchlan	37 yrs 210 days in 1979

* C Reid, also 17 yrs 36 days on debut in 1881, was a day *older* than Finlay, having lived through an extra leap-year day.

CAREER RECORDS OF SCOTLAND INTERNATIONAL PLAYERS
(UP TO 30 SEPTEMBER 2009)

PLAYER BACKS	DEBUT	CAPS	T	C	P	D	PTS
M R L Blair	2002 v C	58	5	0	0	0	25
B J Cairns	2008 v Arg	6	1	0	0	0	5
C P Cusiter	2004 v W	44	3	0	0	0	15
S C J Danielli	2003 v It	20	6	0	0	0	30
R E Dewey	2006 v R	13	4	0	0	0	20
N J de Luca	2008 v F	11	0	0	0	0	0
M P di Rollo	2002 v US	21	2	0	0	1	13
M B Evans	2008 v C	6	1	0	0	0	5
T H Evans	2008 v Arg	7	1	0	0	0	5
P J Godman	2005 v R	17	1	10	7	0	46
A R Henderson	2001 v I	53	8	0	0	0	40
R P Lamont	2005 v W	19	6	0	0	0	30
S F Lamont	2004 v Sm	37	7	0	0	0	35
R G.M.Lawson	2006 v A	15	0	0	0	0	0
G A Morrison	2004 v A	16	2	0	0	0	10
D A Parks	2004 v W	47	4	9	11	4	83
C D Paterson	1999 v Sp	95	22	86	150	2	738
H F G Southwell	2004 v Sm	48	8	0	0	0	40
N Walker	2002 v R	15	4	0	0	0	20
S L Webster	2003 v I	37	8	0	0	0	40
FORWARDS							
J A Barclay	2007 v NZ	11	1	0	0	0	5
J W Beattie	2006 v R	4	1	0	0	0	5
K D R Brown	2005 v R	30	3	0	0	0	15
D A Callam	2006 v R	11	1	0	0	0	5
G Cross	2009 v W	1	0	0	0	0	0
A G Dickinson	2007 v NZ	13	0	0	0	0	0
R W Ford	2004 v A	30	2	0	0	0	10
S D Gray	2004 v A	8	1	0	0	0	5
D W H Hall	2003 v W	28	1	0	0	0	5
J L Hamilton	2006 v R	23	0	0	0	0	0
N J Hines	2000 v NZ	58	2	0	0	0	10
A Hogg	2004 v W	48	10	0	0	0	50

A F Jacobsen	2002 v C	37	0	0	0	0	0
A D Kellock	2004 v A	17	0	0	0	0	0
G Kerr	2003 v I	50	1	0	0	0	5
S Lawson	2005 v R	16	2	0	0	0	10
M J Low	2009 v F	2	0	0	0	0	0
S J MacLeod	2004 v A	21	0	0	0	0	0
E A Murray	2005 v R	28	2	0	0	0	10
M L Mustchin	2008 v Arg	5	0	0	0	0	0
R M Rennie	2008 v I	1	0	0	0	0	0
C J Smith	2002 v C	25	0	0	0	0	0
A K Strokosch	2006 v A	11	1	0	0	0	5
S M Taylor	2000 v US	66	6	0	0	0	30
F M A Thomson	2007 v I	8	0	0	0	0	0
J P R White	2000 v E	74	4	0	0	0	20

SCOTLAND

With 66 caps, Simon Taylor is now eighth on the Scotland's all-time list.

SCOTLAND INTERNATIONAL PLAYERS
UP TO 30TH SEPTEMBER 2009

Note: Years given for International Championship matches are for second half of season; eg 1972 means season 1971–72. Years for all other matches refer to the actual year of the match. Entries in square brackets denote matches played in RWC Finals.

Abercrombie, C H (United Services) 1910 I, E, 1911 F, W, 1913 F, W

Abercrombie, J G (Edinburgh U) 1949 F, W, I, 1950 F, W, I, E

Agnew, W C C (Stewart's Coll FP) 1930 W, I

Ainslie, R (Edinburgh Inst FP) 1879 I, E, 1880 I, E, 1881 E, 1882 I, E

Ainslie, T (Edinburgh Inst FP) 1881 E, 1882 I, E, 1883 W, I, E, 1884 W, I, E, 1885 W, I 1, 2

Aitchison, G R (Edinburgh Wands) 1883 I

Aitchison, T G (Gala) 1929 W, I, E

Aitken, A I (Edinburgh Inst FP) 1889 I

Aitken, G G (Oxford U) 1924 W, I, E, 1925 F, W, I, E, 1929 F

Aitken, J (Gala) 1977 E, I, F, 1981 F, W, E, I, NZ 1, 2, R, A, 1982 E, I, F, W, 1983 F, W, E, NZ, 1984 W, E, I, F, R

Aitken, R (London Scottish) 1947 W

Allan, B (Glasgow Acads) 1881 I

Allan, J (Edinburgh Acads) 1990 NZ 1, 1991, W, I, R, [J, I, WS, E, NZ]

Allan, J L (Melrose) 1952 F, W, I, 1953 W

Allan, J L F (Cambridge U) 1957 I, E

Allan, J W (Melrose) 1927 F, 1928 I, 1929 F, W, I, E, 1930 F, E, 1931 F, W, I, E, 1932 SA, W, I, 1934 I, E

Allan, R C (Hutchesons' GSFP) 1969 I

Allardice, W D (Aberdeen GSFP) 1947 A, 1948 F, W, I, 1949 F, W, I, E

Allen, H W (Glasgow Acads) 1873 E

Anderson, A H (Glasgow Acads) 1894 I

Anderson, D G (London Scottish) 1889 I, 1890 W, I, E, 1891 W, E, 1892 W, E

Anderson, E (Stewart's Coll FP) 1947 I, E

Anderson, J W (W of Scotland) 1872 E

Anderson, T (Merchiston Castle School) 1882 I

Angus, A W (Watsonians) 1909 W, 1910 F, W, E, 1911 W, I, 1912 F, W, I, E, SA, 1913 F, W, 1914 E, 1920 F, W, I, E

Anton, P A (St Andrew's U) 1873 E

Armstrong, G (Jedforest, Newcastle) 1988 A, 1989 W, E, I, F, Fj, R, 1990 I, F, W, E, NZ 1, 2, Arg, 1991 F, W, E, I, R, [J, I, WS, E, NZ], 1993 I, F, W, E, 1994 E, I, 1996 NZ, 1, 2, A, 1997 W, SA (R), 1998 It, I, F, W, E, SA (R), 1999 W, E, I, F, Arg, R, [SA, U, Sm, NZ]

Arneil, R J (Edinburgh Acads, Leicester and Northampton) 1968 I, E, A, 1969 F, W, I, E, SA, 1970 F, W, I, E, A, 1971 F, W, I, E (2[1C]), 1972 F, W, E, NZ

Arthur, A (Glasgow Acads) 1875 E, 1876 E

Arthur, J W (Glasgow Acads) 1871 E, 1872 E

Asher, A G G (Oxford U) 1882 I, 1884 W, I, E, 1885 W, 1886 I, E

Auld, W (W of Scotland) 1889 W, 1890 W

Auldjo, L J (Abertay) 1878 E

Bain, D McL (Oxford U) 1911 E, 1912 F, W, E, SA, 1913 F, W, I, E, 1914 W, I

Baird, G R T (Kelso) 1981 A, 1982 E, I, F, W, A 1, 2, 1983 I, F, W, E, NZ, 1984 W, E, I, F, A, 1985 I, W, E, 1986 F, W, E, I, R, 1987 NZ, 1988 I

Balfour, A (Watsonians) 1896 W, I, E, 1897 E

Balfour, L M (Edinburgh Acads) 1872 E

Bannerman, E M (Edinburgh Acads) 1872 E, 1873 E

Bannerman, J M (Glasgow HSFP) 1921 F, W, I, E, 1922 F, W, I, E, 1923 F, W, I, E, 1924 F, W, I, E, 1925 F, W, I, E, 1926 F, W, I, E, 1927 F, W, I, E, A, 1928 F, W, I, E, 1929 F, W, I, E

Barclay, J A (Glasgow Warriors) 2007 [NZ], 2008 F, W, Arg 2, NZ, SA, C, 2009 W, F, It, I

Barnes, I A (Hawick) 1972 W, 1974 F (R), 1975 E (R), NZ, 1977 I, F, W

Barrie, R W (Hawick) 1936 E

Bearne, K R F (Cambridge U, London Scottish) 1960 F, W

Beattie, J A (Hawick) 1929 F, W, 1930 W, 1931 F, W, I, E, 1932 SA, W, I, E, 1933 W, E, I, 1934 I, E, 1935 W, I, E, NZ, 1936 W, I, E

Beattie, J R (Glasgow Acads) 1980 I, F, W, E, 1981 F, W, E, I, 1983 F, W, E, NZ, 1984 E (R), R, A, 1985 I, 1986 F, W, E, I, R, 1987 I, F, W, E

Beattie, J W (Glasgow Warriors) 2006 R, PI, 2007 F, 2008 Arg 1

Beattie, R S (Newcastle, Bristol) 2000 NZ 1, 2(R), Sm (R), 2003 E(R), It(R), I 2, [J(R), US, Fj]

Bedell-Sivright, D R (Cambridge U, Edinburgh U) 1900 W, 1901 W, I, E, 1902 W, I, E, 1903 W, I, 1904 W, I, E, 1905 NZ, 1906 W, I, E, SA, 1907 W, I, E, 1908 W, I

Bedell-Sivright, J V (Cambridge U) 1902 W

Begbie, T A (Edinburgh Wands) 1881 I, E

Bell, D L (Watsonians) 1975 I, F, W, E

Bell, J A (Clydesdale) 1901 W, I, E, 1902 W, I, E

Bell, L H I (Edinburgh Acads) 1900 E, 1904 W, I

Berkeley, W V (Oxford U) 1926 F, 1929 F, W, I

Berry, C W (Fettesian-Lorettonians) 1884 I, E, 1885 W, I 1, 1887 I, W, E, 1888 W, I

Bertram, D M (Watsonians) 1922 F, W, I, E, 1923 F, W, I, E, 1924 W, I, E

Beveridge, G A (Glasgow) 2000 NZ 2(R), US (R), Sm (R), 2002 Fj(R), 2003 W 2, 2005 R(R)

Biggar, A G (London Scottish) 1969 SA, 1970 F, I, E, A, 1971 F, W, I, E (2[1C]), 1972 F, W

Biggar, M A (London Scottish) 1975 I, F, W, E, 1976 W, E, I, 1977 I, F, W, 1978 I, F, W, E, NZ, 1979 W, E, I, F, NZ, 1980 I, F, W, E

Birkett, G A (Harlequins, London Scottish) 1975 NZ

Bishop, J M (Glasgow Acads) 1893 I

Bisset, A A (RIE Coll) 1904 W

Black, A W (Edinburgh U) 1947 F, W, 1948 E, 1950 W, I, E

Black, W P (Glasgow HSFP) 1948 F, W, I, E, 1951 E

Blackadder, W F (W of Scotland) 1938 E

Blaikie, C F (Heriot's FP) 1963 I, E, 1966 E, 1968 A, 1969 F, W, I, E

Blair, M R L (Edinburgh) 2002 C, US, 2003 F(t+R), W 1(R), SA 2(R), It 2, I 2, [US], 2004 W(R), E(R), It(R), F(R), I(R), Sm(R), A1(R), 3(R), J(R), A4(R), SA(R), 2005 I(t&R), It(R), W(R), E, R, Arg, Sm(R), NZ(R), 2006 F, W, E, I, It(R), SA 1, 2, R, PI(R), A, 2007 I2, SA, [Pt, R, It, Arg], 2008 F, W, E, It, Arg 1, 2, NZ, SA, C, 2009 W, F, It, I, E

Blair, P C B (Cambridge U) 1912 SA, 1913 F, W, I, E

Bolton, W H (W of Scotland) 1876 E

Borthwick, J B (Stewart's Coll FP) 1938 W, I

Bos, F H ten (Oxford U, London Scottish) 1959 E, 1960 F, W, SA, 1961 F, SA, W, I, E, 1962 F, W, I, E, 1963 F, W, I, E

Boswell, J D (W of Scotland) 1889 W, I, 1890 W, I, E, 1891 W, I, E, 1892 W, I, E, 1893 I, 1894 I, E

Bowie, T C (Watsonians) 1913 I, E, 1914 I, E

Boyd, G M (Glasgow HSFP) 1926 E

Boyd, J L (United Services) 1912 E, SA

Boyle, A C W (London Scottish) 1963 F, W, I

Boyle, A H W (St Thomas's Hospital, London Scottish) 1966 A, 1967 F, NZ, 1968 F, W, I

Brash, J C (Cambridge U) 1961 E
Breakey, R W (Gosforth) 1978 E
Brewis, N T (Edinburgh Inst FP) 1876 E, 1878 E, 1879 I, E, 1880 I, E
Brewster, A K (Stewart's-Melville FP) 1977 E, 1980 I, F, 1986 E, I, R
Brotherstone, S J (Melrose, Brive, Newcastle) 1999 I (R), 2000 F, W, E, US, A, Sm, 2002 C (R)
Brown, A H (Heriot's FP) 1928 E, 1929 F, W
Brown, A R (Gala) 1971 E (2[1C]), 1972 F, W, E
Brown, C H C (Dunfermline) 1929 E
Brown, D I (Cambridge U) 1933 W, E, I
Brown, G L (W of Scotland) 1969 SA, 1970 F, W (R), I, E, A, 1971 F, W, I, E (2[1C]), 1972 F, W, E, NZ, 1973 E (R), P, 1974 W, E, I, F, 1975 I, F, W, E, A, 1976 F, W, E, I
Brown, J A (Glasgow Acads) 1908 W, I
Brown, J B (Glasgow Acads) 1879 I, E, 1880 I, E, 1881 I, E, 1882 I, E, 1883 W, I, E, 1884 W, I, E, 1885 I 1, 2, 1886 W, I, E
Brown, K D R (Borders, Glasgow Warriors) 2005 R, Sm(R), NZ(R), 2006 SA 1(R), 2(R), R, PI, A, 2007 E, W, It, I1, 2(R), SA, [Pt(R), R(R), NZ, It(R), Arg(R)], 2008 F(R), W, I, E(R), It(R), Arg 1(R), 2(R), 2009 W(R), F(R), It(R), E(R)
Brown, P C (W of Scotland, Gala) 1964 F, NZ, W, I, E, 1965 I, E, SA, 1966 A, 1969 I, E, 1970 W, E, 1971 F, W, I, E (2[1C]), 1972 F, W, E, NZ, 1973 F, W, I, E, P
Brown, T G (Heriot's FP) 1929 W
Brown, W D (Glasgow Acads) 1871 E, 1872 E, 1873 E, 1874 E, 1875 E
Brown, W S (Edinburgh Inst FP) 1880 I, E, 1882 I, E, 1883 W, E
Browning, A (Glasgow HSFP) 1920 I, 1922 F, W, I, 1923 W, I, E
Bruce, C R (Glasgow Acads) 1947 F, W, I, E, 1949 F, W, I, E
Bruce, N S (Blackheath, Army and London Scottish) 1958 F, A, I, E, 1959 F, W, I, E, 1960 F, W, I, E, SA, 1961 F, SA, W, I, E, 1962 F, W, I, E, 1963 F, W, I, E, 1964 F, NZ, W, I, E
Bruce, R M (Gordonians) 1947 A, 1948 F, W, I
Bruce-Lockhart, J H (London Scottish) 1913 W, 1920 E
Bruce-Lockhart, L (London Scottish) 1948 E, 1950 F, W, 1953 I, E
Bruce-Lockhart, R B (Cambridge U and London Scottish) 1937 I, 1939 I, E
Bryce, C C (Glasgow Acads) 1873 E, 1874 E
Bryce, R D H (W of Scotland) 1973 I (R)
Bryce, W E (Selkirk) 1922 W, I, E, 1923 F, W, I, E, 1924 F, W, I, E
Brydon, W R C (Heriot's FP) 1939 W
Buchanan, A (Royal HSFP) 1871 E
Buchanan, F G (Kelvinside Acads and Oxford U) 1910 F, 1911 F, W
Buchanan, J C R (Stewart's Coll FP) 1921 W, I, E, 1922 W, I, E, 1923 F, W, I, E, 1924 F, W, I, E, 1925 F, I
Buchanan-Smith, G A E (London Scottish, Heriot's FP) 1989 Fj (R), 1990 Arg
Bucher, A M (Edinburgh Acads) 1897 E
Budge, G M (Edinburgh Wands) 1950 F, W, I, E
Bullmore, H H (Edinburgh U) 1902 I
Bulloch, A J (Glasgow) 2000 US, A, Sm, 2001 F (t+R), E
Bulloch, G C (West of Scotland, Glasgow) 1997 SA, 1998 It, I, F, W, E, Fj, A 1, SA, 1999 W, E, It, I, F, Arg, [SA, U, Sm, NZ], 2000 It, I, W (R), NZ 1, 2, A (R), Sm (R), 2001 F, W, E, It, I, Tg, Arg, NZ, 2002 E, It, I, F, W, C, US, R, SA, Fj, 2003 I 1, F, W 1, E, It 1, SA 1, 2, It 2(R), W2, I 2, [US, F, Fj, A], 2004 W, E, It, F, I, Sm, A1, 2, 3, J, A4, SA, 2005 F, I, It, W, E
Burnell, A P (London Scottish, Montferrand) 1989 E, I, F, Fj, R, 1990 I, F, W, E, Arg, 1991 F, W, E, I, R, [J, Z, I, WS, E, NZ], 1992 E, I, F, W, 1993 I, F, W, E, NZ, 1994 W, E, I, F, Arg 1, 2, SA, 1995 [Iv, Tg (R), F (R)], WS, 1998 E, SA, 1999 W, E, It, I, F, Arg, [Sp, Sm (R), NZ]
Burnet, P J (London Scottish and Edinburgh Acads) 1960 SA
Burnet, W (Hawick) 1912 E
Burnet, W A (W of Scotland) 1934 W, 1935 W, I, E, NZ, 1936 W, I, E
Burnett, J N (Heriot's FP) 1980 I, F, W, E
Burns, G G (Watsonians, Edinburgh) 1999 It (R), 2001 Tg (R), NZ (R), 2002 US (R)
Burrell, G (Gala) 1950 F, W, I, 1951 SA
Cairns, A G (Watsonians) 1903 W, I, E, 1904 W, I, E, 1905 W, I, E, 1906 W, I, E
Cairns, B J (Edinburgh) 2008 Arg 1, 2, NZ, SA, C, 2009 W
Calder, F (Stewart's-Melville FP) 1986 F, W, E, I, R, 1987 I, F, W,

E, [F, Z, R, NZ], 1988 I, F, W, E, 1989 W, E, I, F, R, 1990 I, F, W, E, NZ 1, 2, 1991 F, [J, I, WS, E, NZ]
Calder, J H (Stewart's-Melville FP) 1981 F, W, E, I, NZ 1, 2, R, A, 1982 E, I, F, W, A 1, 2, 1983 I, F, W, E, NZ, 1984 W, E, I, F, A, 1985 I, F, W
Callam, D A (Edinburgh) 2006 R(R), PI(R), A, 2007 E, W, It, I1, F(R), SA, [NZ], 2008 F
Callander, G J (Kelso) 1984 R, 1988 I, F, W, E, A
Cameron, A (Glasgow HSFP) 1948 W, 1950 I, E, 1951 F, W, I, E, SA, 1953 I, E, 1955 F, W, I, E, 1956 F, W, I
Cameron, A D (Hillhead HSFP) 1951 F, 1954 F, W
Cameron, A W C (Watsonians) 1887 W, 1893 W, 1894 I
Cameron, D (Glasgow HSFP) 1953 I, E, 1954 F, NZ, I, E
Cameron, N W (Glasgow U) 1952 E, 1953 F, W
Campbell, A J (Hawick) 1984 I, F, R, 1985 I, F, W, E, 1986 F, W, E, I, R, 1988 F, W, A
Campbell, G T (London Scottish) 1892 W, I, E, 1893 I, E, 1894 W, I, E, 1895 W, I, E, 1896 W, I, E, 1897 I, 1899 I, 1900 E
Campbell, H H (Cambridge U, London Scottish) 1947 I, E, 1948 I, E
Campbell, J A (W of Scotland) 1878 E, 1879 I, E, 1881 I, E
Campbell, J A (Cambridge U) 1900 I
Campbell, N M (London Scottish) 1956 F, W
Campbell, S J (Dundee HSFP) 1995 C, I, F, W, E, R, [Iv, NZ (R)], WS (t), 1996 I, F, W, E, 1997 A, SA, 1998 Fj (R), A 2(R)
Campbell-Lamerton, J R E (London Scottish) 1986 F, 1987 [Z, R(R)]
Campbell-Lamerton, M J (Halifax, Army, London Scottish) 1961 F, SA, W, I, 1962 F, W, I, E, 1963 F, W, I, E, 1964 I, E, 1965 F, W, I, E, SA, 1966 F, W, I, E
Carmichael, A B (W of Scotland) 1967 I, NZ, 1968 F, W, I, E, A, 1969 F, W, I, E, SA, 1970 F, W, I, E, A, 1971 F, W, I, E (2[1C]), 1972 F, W, E, NZ, 1973 F, W, I, E, P, 1974 W, E, I, F, 1975 I, F, W, E, NZ, A, 1976 F, W, E, I, 1977 E, I (R), F, W, 1978 I
Carmichael, J H (Watsonians) 1921 F, W, I
Carrick, J S (Glasgow Acads) 1876 E, 1877 E
Cassels, D Y (W of Scotland) 1880 E, 1881 I, 1882 I, E, 1883 W, I, E
Cathcart, C W (Edinburgh U) 1872 E, 1873 E, 1876 E
Cawkwell, G L (Oxford U) 1947 F
Chalmers, C M (Melrose) 1989 W, E, I, F, Fj, 1990 I, F, W, E, NZ 1, 2, Arg, 1991 F, W, E, I, R, [J, Z (R), I, WS, E, NZ], 1992 E, I, F, W, A 1, 2, 1993 I, F, W, E, NZ, 1994 W, SA, 1995 C, I, F, W, E, R, [Iv, Tg, F, NZ], WS, 1996 A, It, 1997 W, I, F, A (R), SA, 1998 It, I, F, W, E, 1999 Arg (R)
Chalmers, T (Glasgow Acads) 1871 E, 1872 E, 1873 E, 1874 E, 1875 E, 1876 E
Chambers, H F T (Edinburgh U) 1888 W, I, 1889 W, I
Charters, R G (Hawick) 1955 W, I, E
Chisholm, D H (Melrose) 1964 I, E, 1965 F, SA, 1966 F, I, E, A, 1967 F, W, NZ, 1968 F, W, I
Chisholm, R W T (Melrose) 1955 I, E, 1956 F, W, I, E, 1958 F, W, A, I, 1960 SA
Church, W C (Glasgow Acads) 1906 W
Clark, R L (Edinburgh Wands, Royal Navy) 1972 F, W, E, NZ, 1973 F, W, I, E, P
Clauss, P R A (Oxford U) 1891 W, I, E, 1892 W, E, 1895 I
Clay, A T (Edinburgh Acads) 1886 W, I, E, 1887 I, W, E, 1888 W
Clunies-Ross, A (St Andrew's U) 1871 E
Coltman, S (Hawick) 1948 I, 1949 F, W, I, E
Colville, A G (Merchistonians, Blackheath) 1871 E, 1872 E
Connell, G C (Trinity Acads and London Scottish) 1968 E, A, 1969 F, E, 1970 F
Cooper, M McG (Oxford U) 1936 W, I
Corcoran, I (Gala) 1992 A 1(R)
Cordial, I F (Edinburgh Wands) 1952 F, W, I, E
Cotter, J L (Hillhead HSFP) 1934 I, E
Cottington, G S (Kelso) 1934 I, E, 1935 W, I, 1936 E
Coughtrie, S (Edinburgh Acads) 1959 F, W, I, E, 1962 W, I, E, 1963 F, W, I, E
Coutts, F H (Melrose, Army) 1947 W, I, E
Coutts, I D F (Old Alleynians) 1951 F, 1952 E
Cowan, R C (Selkirk) 1961 F, 1962 F, W, I, E
Cowie, W L K (Edinburgh Wands) 1953 E
Cownie, W B (Watsonians) 1893 W, I, E, 1894 W, I, E, 1895 W, I, E
Crabbie, G E (Edinburgh Acads) 1904 W

Crabbie, J E (Edinburgh Acads, Oxford U) 1900 W, 1902 I, 1903 W, I, 1904 E, 1905 W

Craig, A (Orrell, Glasgow) 2002 C, US, R, SA, Fj, 2003 I 1, F(R), W 1(R), E, It 1, SA 1, 2, W 2, I 2, [J, US, F], 2004 A3(R), 2005 F, I, It, W, E

Craig, J B (Heriot's FP) 1939 W

Craig, J M (West of Scotland, Glasgow) 1997 A, 2001 W (R), E (R), It

Cramb, R I (Harlequins) 1987 [R(R)], 1988 I, F, A

Cranston, A G (Hawick) 1976 W, E, I, 1977 E, W, 1978 F (R), W, E, NZ, 1981 NZ 1, 2

Crawford, J A (Army, London Scottish) 1934 I

Crawford, W H (United Services, RN) 1938 W, I, E, 1939 W, E

Crichton-Miller, D (Gloucester) 1931 W, I, E

Crole, G B (Oxford U) 1920 F, W, I, E

Cronin, D F (Bath, London Scottish, Bourges, Wasps) 1988 I, F, W, E, A, 1989 W, E, I, F, Fj, R, 1990 I, F, W, E, NZ 1, 2, 1991 F, W, E, I, R, [Z], 1992 A 2, 1993 I, F, W, E, NZ, 1995 C, I, F, [Tg, F, NZ], WS, 1996 NZ 1, 2, A, It, 1997 F (R), 1998 I, F, W, E

Cross, G (Edinburgh) 2009 W

Cross, M (Merchistonians) 1875 E, 1876 E, 1877 I, E, 1878 E, 1879 I, E, 1880 I, E

Cross, W (Merchistonians) 1871 E, 1872 E

Cumming, R S (Aberdeen U) 1921 F, W

Cunningham, G (Oxford U) 1908 W, I, 1909 W, E, 1910 F, I, E, 1911 E

Cunningham, R F (Gala) 1978 NZ, 1979 W, E

Currie, L R (Dunfermline) 1947 A, 1948 F, W, I, 1949 F, W, I, E

Cusiter, C P (Borders, Perpignan) 2004 W, E, It, F, I, Sm, A1, 2, 3, J, A4, SA, 2005 F, I, It, W, SA, NZ, 2006 F(R), W(R), E(R), I(R), It, R(R), Pl, 2007 E, W, It, I1, F(R), I2(R), [R(R), NZ, It(R), Arg(R)], 2008 F(R), W(R), I(R), 2009 W(R), F(R), It(R), I(R), E(R)

Cuthbertson, W (Kilmarnock, Harlequins) 1980 I, 1981 W, E, I, NZ 1, 2, R, A, 1982 E, I, F, W, A 1, 2, 1983 I, F, W, NZ, 1984 W, E, A

Dalgleish, A (Gala) 1890 W, E, 1891 W, I, 1892 W, 1893 W, 1894 W, I

Dalgleish, K J (Edinburgh Wands, Cambridge U) 1951 I, E, 1953 F, W

Dall, A K (Edinburgh) 2003 W 2(R)

Dallas, J D (Watsonians) 1903 E

Danielli, S C J (Bath, Borders, Ulster) 2003 It 2, W 2, [J(R), US, Fj, A], 2004 W, E, It, F, I, 2005 F, I, 2008 W(R), It, Arg 1, 2009 F, It, I, E

Davidson, J A (London Scottish, Edinburgh Wands) 1959 E, 1960 I, E

Davidson, J N G (Edinburgh U) 1952 F, W, I, E, 1953 F, W, 1954 F

Davidson, J P (RIE Coll) 1873 E, 1874 E

Davidson, R S (Royal HSFP) 1893 E

Davies, D S (Hawick) 1922 F, W, I, E, 1923 F, W, I, E, 1924 F, E, 1925 W, I, E, 1926 F, W, I, E, 1927 F, W, I

Dawson, J C (Glasgow Acads) 1947 A, 1948 F, W, 1949 F, W, I, 1950 F, W, I, E, 1951 F, W, I, E, SA, 1952 F, W, I, E, 1953 E

Deans, C T (Hawick) 1978 F, W, E, NZ, 1979 W, E, I, F, NZ, 1980 I, F, 1981 F, W, E, I, NZ 1, 2, R, A, 1982 E, I, F, W, A 1, 2, 1983 I, F, W, E, NZ, 1984 W, E, I, F, A, 1985 I, F, W, E, 1986 F, W, E, I, R, 1987 I, F, W, E, [F, Z, R, NZ]

Deans, D T (Hawick) 1968 E

Deas, D W (Heriot's FP) 1947 F, W

De Luca, N J (Edinburgh) 2008 F, W, I(t&R), Arg 2(R), NZ, SA, C, 2009 F(R), It(R), I(R), E(R)

Dewey, R E (Edinburgh, Ulster) 2006 R, 2007 E(R), W, It, I1, F, I2, SA, [Pt, R, NZ(R), It, Arg]

Dick, L G (Loughborough Colls, Jordanhill, Swansea) 1972 W (R), E, 1974 W, E, I, F, 1975 I, F, W, E, NZ, A, 1976 F, 1977 E

Dick, R C S (Cambridge U, Guy's Hospital) 1934 W, I, E, 1935 W, I, E, NZ, 1936 W, I, E, 1937 W, 1938 W, I, E

Dickinson, A G (Gloucester) 2007 [NZ], 2008 E(R), It(R), Arg 1(R), 2(t&R), NZ(R), SA(R), C(R), 2009 W(t&R), F, It(R), I, E

Dickson, G (Gala) 1978 NZ, 1979 W, E, I, F, NZ, 1980 W, 1981 F, 1982 W (R)

Dickson, M R (Edinburgh U) 1905 I

Dickson, W M (Blackheath, Oxford U) 1912 F, W, E, SA, 1913 F, W, I

Di Rollo, M P (Edinburgh) 2002 US (R), 2005 R, Arg, Sm, NZ, 2006 F, E, I, It, SA 1, 2, R, Pl, 2007 E, W, It, I1, F(R), [Pt, NZ]

Dobson, J (Glasgow Acads) 1911 E, 1912 F, W, I, E, SA

Dobson, J D (Glasgow Acads) 1910 I

Dobson, W G (Heriot's FP) 1922 W, I, E

Docherty, J T (Glasgow HSFP) 1955 F, W, 1956 E, 1958 F, W, A, I, E

Dods, F P (Edinburgh Acads) 1901 I

Dods, J H (Edinburgh Acads) 1895 W, I, E, 1896 W, I, E, 1897 I, E

Dods, M (Gala, Northampton) 1994 I (t), Arg 1, 2, 1995 WS, 1996 I, F, W, E

Dods, P W (Gala) 1983 I, F, W, E, NZ, 1984 W, E, I, F, R, A, 1985 I, F, W, E, 1989 W, E, I, F, 1991 I (R), R, [Z, NZ (R)]

Donald, D G (Oxford U) 1914 W, I

Donald, R L H (Glasgow HSFP) 1921 W, I, E

Donaldson, W P (Oxford U, W of Scotland) 1893 I, 1894 I, 1895 E, 1896 I, E, 1899 I

Don-Wauchope, A R (Fettesian-Lorettonians) 1881 E, 1882 E, 1883 W, 1884 W, I, E, 1885 W, I 1, 2, 1886 W, I, E, 1888 I

Don-Wauchope, P H (Fettesian-Lorettonians) 1885 I 1, 2, 1886 W, 1887 I, W, E

Dorward, A F (Cambridge U, Gala) 1950 F, 1951 SA, 1952 W, I, E, 1953 F, W, E, 1955 F, 1956 I, E, 1957 F, W, I, E

Dorward, T F (Gala) 1938 W, I, E, 1939 I, E

Douglas, B A F (Borders) 2002 R, SA, Fj, 2003 I 1, F, W 1, E, It 1, SA 1, 2, It 2, W 2, [J, US(t&R), F(R), Fj, A], 2004 W, E, It, F, I, Sm, A1, 2, 3, A4(R), SA(R), 2005 F(R), It(R), W(R), E(R), R, Arg, NZ, 2006 F, W, E, I, It, SA 1, 2(R)

Douglas, G (Jedforest) 1921 W

Douglas, J (Stewart's Coll FP) 1961 F, SA, W, I, E, 1962 F, W, I, E, 1963 F, W, I

Douty, P S (London Scottish) 1927 A, 1928 F, W

Drew, D (Glasgow Acads) 1871 E, 1876 E

Druitt, W A H (London Scottish) 1936 W, I, E

Drummond, A H (Kelvinside Acads) 1938 W, I

Drummond, C W (Melrose) 1947 F, W, I, E, 1948 F, I, E, 1950 F, W, I, E

Drybrough, A S (Edinburgh Wands, Merchistonians) 1902 I, 1903 I

Dryden, R H (Watsonians) 1937 E

Drysdale, D (Heriot's FP) 1923 F, W, I, E, 1924 F, W, I, E, 1925 F, W, I, E, 1926 F, W, I, E, 1927 F, W, I, E, A, 1928 F, W, I, E, 1929 F

Duff, P L (Glasgow Acads) 1936 W, I, 1938 W, I, E, 1939 W

Duffy, H (Jedforest) 1955 F

Duke, A (Royal HSFP) 1888 W, I, 1889 W, I, 1890 W, I

Dunbar, J P A (Leeds) 2005 F(R), It(R)

Duncan, A W (Edinburgh U) 1901 W, I, E, 1902 W, I, E

Duncan, D D (Oxford U) 1920 F, W, I, E

Duncan, M D F (W of Scotland) 1986 F, W, E, R, 1987 I, F, W, E, [F, Z, R, NZ], 1988 I, F, W, E, A, 1989 W

Duncan, M M (Fettesian-Lorettonians) 1888 W

Dunlop, J W (W of Scotland) 1875 E

Dunlop, Q (W of Scotland) 1971 E (2[1C])

Dykes, A S (Glasgow Acads) 1932 E

Dykes, J C (Glasgow Acads) 1922 F, E, 1924 I, 1925 F, W, I, 1926 F, W, I, E, 1927 F, W, I, E, A, 1928 F, I, 1929 F, W, I

Dykes, J M (Clydesdale, Glasgow HSFP) 1898 I, E, 1899 W, E, 1900 W, I, 1901 W, I, E, 1902 E

Edwards, D B (Heriot's FP) 1960 I, E, SA

Edwards, N G B (Harlequins, Northampton) 1992 E, I, F, W, A 1, 1994 W

Elgie, M K (London Scottish) 1954 NZ, I, E, W, 1955 F, W, I, E

Elliot, C (Langholm) 1958 E, 1959 F, 1960 F, 1963 E, 1964 F, NZ, W, I, E, 1965 F, W, I

Elliot, M (Hawick) 1895 W, 1896 W, 1897 I, E, 1898 I, E

Elliot, T (Gala) 1905 E

Elliot, T (Gala) 1955 W, I, E, 1956 F, W, I, E, 1957 F, W, I, E, 1958 W, A, I

Elliot, T G (Langholm) 1968 W, A, 1969 F, W, 1970 E

Elliot, W I D (Edinburgh Acads) 1947 F, W, E, A, 1948 F, W, I, E, 1949 F, W, I, E, 1950 F, W, I, E, 1951 F, W, I, E, SA, 1952 F, W, I, E, 1954 NZ, I, E, W

Ellis, D G (Currie) 1997 W, E, I, F

Emslie, W D (Royal HSFP) 1930 F, 1932 I

Eriksson, B R S (London Scottish) 1996 NZ 1, A, 1997 E

Evans, H L (Edinburgh U) 1885 I 1, 2

Evans, M B (Glasgow Warriors) 2008 C(R), 2009 W(R), F, It, I, E

Evans, T H (Glasgow Warriors) 2008 Arg 1, NZ, SA, 2009 F, It, I, E

Ewart, E N (Glasgow Acads) 1879 E, 1880 I, E

Fahmy, E C (Abertillery) 1920 F, W, I, E

Fairley, I T (Kelso, Edinburgh) 1999 It, I (R), [Sp (R)]
Fasson, F H (London Scottish, Edinburgh Wands) 1900 W, 1901 W, I, 1902 W, E
Fell, A N (Edinburgh U) 1901 W, I, E, 1902 W, E, 1903 W, E
Ferguson, J H (Gala) 1928 W
Ferguson, W G (Royal HSFP) 1927 A, 1928 F, W, I, E
Fergusson, E A J (Oxford U) 1954 F, NZ, I, E, W
Finlay, A B (Edinburgh Acads) 1875 E
Finlay, J F (Edinburgh Acads) 1871 E, 1872 E, 1874 E, 1875 E
Finlay, N J (Edinburgh Acads) 1875 E, 1876 E, 1878 E, 1879 I, E, 1880 I, E, 1881 I, E
Finlay, R (Watsonians) 1948 E
Fisher, A T (Waterloo, Watsonians) 1947 I, E
Fisher, C D (Waterloo) 1975 NZ, A, 1976 W, E, I
Fisher, D (W of Scotland) 1893 I
Fisher, J P (Royal HSFP, London Scottish) 1963 E, 1964 F, NZ, W, I, E, 1965 F, W, I, E, SA, 1966 F, W, I, E, A, 1967 F, W, I, E, NZ, 1968 F, W, I, E
Fleming, C J N (Edinburgh Wands) 1896 I, E, 1897 I
Fleming, G R (Glasgow Acads) 1875 E, 1876 E
Fletcher, H N (Edinburgh U) 1904 E, 1905 W
Flett, A B (Edinburgh U) 1901 W, I, E, 1902 W, I
Forbes, J L (Watsonians) 1905 W, 1906 I, E
Ford, D St C (United Services, RN) 1930 I, E, 1931 E, 1932 W, I
Ford, J A (Gala) 1893 I
Ford, R W (Borders, Glasgow, Edinburgh) 2004 A3(R), 2006 W(R), E(R), PI(R), A(R), 2007 E(R), W(R), It(R), I1(R), F, I2, SA, [Pt(R), R, It, Arg], 2008 F, W, I, E, Arg 1, 2, NZ, SA, C, 2009 W, F, It, I, E
Forrest, J E (Glasgow Acads) 1932 SA, 1935 E, NZ
Forrest, J G S (Cambridge U) 1938 W, I, E
Forrest, W T (Hawick) 1903 W, I, E, 1904 W, I, E, 1905 W, I
Forsayth, H H (Oxford U) 1921 F, W, I, E, 1922 W, I, E
Forsyth, I W (Stewart's Coll FP) 1972 NZ, 1973 F, W, I, E, P
Forsyth, J (Edinburgh U) 1871 E
Foster, R A (Hawick) 1930 W, 1932 SA, I, E
Fox, J (Gala) 1952 F, W, I, E
Frame, J N M (Edinburgh U, Gala) 1967 NZ, 1968 F, W, I, E, 1969 W, I, E, SA, 1970 F, W, I, E, A, 1971 F, W, I, E (2[1C]), 1972 F, W, E, 1973 P, E
France, C (Kelvinside Acads) 1903 I
Fraser, C F P (Glasgow U) 1888 W, 1889 W
Fraser, J W (Edinburgh Inst FP) 1881 E
Fraser, R (Cambridge U) 1911 F, W, I, E
French, J (Glasgow Acads) 1886 W, 1887 I, W, E
Frew, A (Edinburgh U) 1901 W, I, E
Frew, G M (Glasgow HSFP) 1906 SA, 1907 W, I, E, 1908 W, I, E, 1909 W, I, E, 1910 F, W, I, 1911 I, E
Friebe, J P (Glasgow HSFP) 1952 E
Fullarton, I A (Edinburgh) 2000 NZ 1(R), 2, 2001 NZ (R), 2003 It 2(R), I 2(t), 2004 Sm(R), A1(R), 2
Fulton, A K (Edinburgh U, Dollar Acads) 1952 F, 1954 F
Fyfe, K C (Cambridge U, Sale, London Scottish) 1933 W, E, 1934 E, 1935 W, I, E, NZ, 1936 W, E, 1939 I
Gallie, G H (Edinburgh Acads) 1939 W
Gallie, R A (Glasgow Acads) 1920 F, W, I, E, 1921 F, W, I, E
Gammell, W B B (Edinburgh Wands) 1977 I, F, W, 1978 W, E
Geddes, I C (London Scottish) 1906 SA, 1907 W, I, E, 1908 W, E
Geddes, K I (London Scottish) 1947 F, W, I, E
Gedge, H T S (Oxford U, London Scottish, Edinburgh Wands) 1894 W, I, E, 1896 E, 1899 W, E
Gedge, P M S (Edinburgh Wands) 1933 I
Gemmill, R (Glasgow HSFP) 1950 F, W, I, E, 1951 F, W, I
Gibson, W R (Royal HSFP) 1891 I, E, 1892 W, I, E, 1893 W, I, E, 1894 W, I, E, 1895 W, I, E
Gilbert-Smith, D S (London Scottish) 1952 E
Gilchrist, J (Glasgow Acads) 1925 F
Gill, A D (Gala) 1973 P, 1974 W, E, I, F
Gillespie, J I (Edinburgh Acads) 1899 E, 1900 W, E, 1901 W, I, E, 1902 W, I, 1904 I, E
Gillies, A C (Watsonians) 1924 W, I, E, 1925 F, W, E, 1926 F, W, 1927 F, W, I, E
Gilmour, H R (Heriot's FP) 1998 Fj
Gilray, C M (Oxford U, London Scottish) 1908 E, 1909 W, E, 1912 I
Glasgow, I C (Heriot's FP) 1997 F (R)
Glasgow, R J C (Dunfermline) 1962 F, W, I, E, 1963 I, E, 1964 I, E, 1965 W, I

Glen, W S (Edinburgh Wands) 1955 W
Gloag, L G (Cambridge U) 1949 F, W, I, E
Godman, P J (Edinburgh) 2005 R(R), Sm(R), NZ(R), 2006 R, PI(R), A(t&R), 2007 W, It, 2008 Arg 2, NZ, SA, C, 2009 W, F, It, I, E
Goodfellow, J (Langholm) 1928 W, I, E
Goodhue, F W J (London Scottish) 1890 W, I, E, 1891 W, I, E, 1892 W, I, E
Gordon, R (Edinburgh Wands) 1951 W, 1952 F, W, I, E, 1953 W
Gordon, R E (Royal Artillery) 1913 F, W, I
Gordon, R J (London Scottish) 1982 A 1, 2
Gore, A C (London Scottish) 1882 I
Gossman, B M (W of Scotland) 1980 W, 1983 F, W
Gossman, J S (W of Scotland) 1980 E (R)
Gowans, J J (Cambridge U, London Scottish) 1893 W, 1894 W, E, 1895 W, I, E, 1896 I, E
Gowland, G C (London Scottish) 1908 W, 1909 W, E, 1910 F, W, I, E
Gracie, A L (Harlequins) 1921 F, W, I, E, 1922 F, W, I, E, 1923 F, W, I, E, 1924 F
Graham, G (Newcastle) 1997 A (R), SA (R), 1998 I, F (R), W (R), 1999 F (R), Arg (R), R, [SA, U, Sm, NZ (R)], 2000 I (R), US, A, Sm, 2001 I (R), Tg (R), Arg (R), NZ (R), 2002 E (R), It (R), I (R), F (R), W (R)
Graham, I N (Edinburgh Acads) 1939 I, E
Graham, J (Kelso) 1926 I, E, 1927 F, W, I, E, A, 1928 F, W, I, E, 1930 I, E, 1932 SA, W
Graham, J H S (Edinburgh Acads) 1876 E, 1877 I, E, 1878 E, 1879 I, E, 1880 I, E, 1881 I, E
Grant, D (Hawick) 1965 F, E, SA, 1966 F, W, I, E, A, 1967 F, W, I, E, NZ, 1968 F
Grant, D M (East Midlands) 1911 W, I
Grant, M L (Harlequins) 1955 F, 1956 F, W, 1957 F
Grant, T O (Hawick) 1960 I, E, SA, 1964 F, NZ, W
Grant, W St C (Craigmount) 1873 E, 1874 E
Gray, C A (Nottingham) 1989 W, E, I, F, Fj, R, 1990 I, F, W, E, NZ 1, 2, Arg, 1991 F, W, E, I, [J, I, WS, E, NZ]
Gray, D (W of Scotland) 1978 E, 1979 I, F, NZ, 1980 I, F, W, E, 1981 F
Gray, G L (Gala) 1935 NZ, 1937 W, I, E
Gray, S D (Borders, Northampton) 2004 A3, 2008 NZ(R), SA(R), C(R), 2009 W(R), It(R), I(R), E
Gray, T (Northampton, Heriot's FP) 1950 E, 1951 F, E
Greenlees, H D (Leicester) 1927 A, 1928 F, W, 1929 I, E, 1930 E
Greenlees, J R C (Cambridge U, Kelvinside Acads) 1900 I, 1902 W, I, E, 1903 W, I, E
Greenwood, J T (Dunfermline and Perthshire Acads) 1952 F, 1955 F, W, I, E, 1956 F, W, I, E, 1957 F, W, E, 1958 F, W, A, I, E, 1959 F, W, I
Greig, A (Glasgow HSFP) 1911 I
Greig, L L (Glasgow Acads, United Services) 1905 NZ, 1906 SA, 1907 W, 1908 W, I
Greig, R C (Glasgow Acads) 1893 W, 1897 I
Grieve, C F (Oxford U) 1935 W, 1936 E
Grieve, R M (Kelso) 1935 W, I, E, NZ, 1936 W, I, E
Grimes, S B (Watsonians, Newcastle) 1997 A (t+R), 1998 I (R), F (R), W (R), E (R), Fj, A 1, 2, 1999 W (R), E, It, I, F, Arg, R, [SA, U, Sm, NZ (R)], 2000 It, I, F (R), W, US, A, Sm (R), 2001 F (R), W (R), E, It, I (R), Tg, Arg, NZ, 2002 E, It, I, F (R), W (R), C, US, R, SA, Fj, 2003 I 1, F, W 1, E(R), It 1(R), W 2, I 2, [J, US, F, Fj, A], 2004 W, E, It, F, I, Sm, A1, J, A4, SA, 2005 F, I, It, W, E(R)
Gunn, A W (Royal HSFP) 1912 F, W, I, SA, 1913 F
Hall, A J A (Glasgow) 2002 US (R)
Hall, D W H (Edinburgh, Glasgow Warriors) 2003 W 2(R), 2005 R(R), Arg, Sm(R), NZ(R), 2006 F, E, I, It(R), SA 1(R), 2, R, PI, A, 2007 E, W, It, I1, F(R), 2008 Arg 2(R), NZ(R), SA(R), C(R), 2009 W(R), F(R), It(R), I(R), E(R)
Hamilton, A S (Headingley) 1914 W, 1920 F
Hamilton, C P (Newcastle) 2004 A2(R), 2005 R, Arg, Sm, NZ
Hamilton, H M (W of Scotland) 1874 E, 1875 E
Hamilton, J L (Leicester, Edinburgh) 2006 R(R), A(R), 2007 E, W, It(R), I1(R), F(R), I2, SA, [R, NZ(R), It, Arg], 2008 F, W, I(R), NZ, SA, C, 2009 W, F, I2, SA, E
Hannah, R S M (W of Scotland) 1971 I
Harrower, P R (London Scottish) 1885 W
Hart, J G M (London Scottish) 1951 SA
Hart, T M (Glasgow U) 1930 W, I
Hart, W (Melrose) 1960 SA
Harvey, L (Greenock Wands) 1899 I

McHarg, A F (W of Scotland, London Scottish) 1968 I, E, A, 1969 F, W, I, E, 1971 F, W, I, E (2[1C]), 1972 F, E, NZ, 1973 F, W, I, E, P, 1974 W, E, I, F, 1975 I, F, W, E, NZ, A, 1976 F, W, E, I, 1977 E, I, F, W, 1978 I, F, W, NZ, 1979 W, E

McIlwham, G R (Glasgow Hawks, Glasgow, Bordeaux-Bègles) 1998 Fj, A 2(R), 2000 E (R), NZ 2(R), US (R), A (R), Sm (R), 2001 F (R), W (R), E (R), It (R), 2003 SA 2(R), It 2(R), W 2(R), I 2, [A(R)]

McIndoe, F (Glasgow Acads) 1886 W, I

MacIntyre, I (Edinburgh Wands) 1890 W, I, E, 1891 W, I, E

McIvor, D J (Edinburgh Acads) 1992 E, I, F, W, 1993 NZ, 1994 SA

Mackay, E B (Glasgow Acads) 1920 W, 1922 E

McKeating, E (Heriot's FP) 1957 F, W, 1961 SA, W, I, E

McKelvey, G (Watsonians) 1997 A

McKendrick, J G (W of Scotland) 1889 I

Mackenzie, A D G (Selkirk) 1984 A

Mackenzie, C J G (United Services) 1921 E

Mackenzie, D D (Edinburgh U) 1947 W, I, E, 1948 F, W, I

Mackenzie, D K A (Edinburgh Wands) 1939 I, E

Mackenzie, J M (Edinburgh U) 1905 NZ, 1909 W, I, E, 1910 W, I, E, 1911 W, I

McKenzie, K D (Stirling County) 1994 Arg 1, 2, 1995 R, [Iv], 1996 I, F, W, E, NZ 1, 2, A, It, 1998 A 1(R), 2

Mackenzie, R C (Glasgow Acads) 1877 I, E, 1881 I, E

Mackie, G Y (Highland) 1975 A, 1976 F, W, 1978 F

MacKinnon, A (London Scottish) 1898 I, E, 1899 I, W, E, 1900 E

Mackintosh, C E W C (London Scottish) 1924 F

Mackintosh, H S (Glasgow U, W of Scotland) 1929 F, W, I, E, 1930 F, W, I, E, 1931 F, W, I, E, 1932 SA, W, I, E

MacLachlan, L P (Oxford U, London Scottish) 1954 NZ, I, E, W

Maclagan, W E (Edinburgh Acads) 1878 E, 1879 I, E, 1880 I, E, 1881 I, E, 1882 I, E, 1883 W, I, E, 1884 W, I, E, 1885 W, I 1, 2, 1887 I, W, E, 1888 W, I, 1890 W, I, E

McLaren, A (Durham County) 1931 F

McLaren, E (London Scottish, Royal HSFP) 1923 F, W, I, E, 1924 F

McLaren, J G (Bourgoin, Glasgow, Bordeaux-Bègles, Castres) 1999 Arg, R, [Sp, Sm], 2000 It (R), F, E, NZ 1, 2001 F, W, E (R), I, Tg, Arg, NZ, 2002 E, It, I, F, W, 2003 W 1, E, It 1, SA 1(R), It 2, I 2(R), [J, F(R), Fj(t&R), A(R)]

McLauchlan, J (Jordanhill) 1969 E, SA, 1970 F, W, 1971 F, W, I, E (2[1C]), 1972 F, W, E, NZ, 1973 F, W, I, E, P, 1974 W, E, I, F, 1975 I, F, W, E, NZ, A, 1976 F, W, E, I, 1977 W, 1978 I, F, W, E, NZ, 1979 W, E, I, F, NZ

McLean, D I (Royal HSFP) 1947 I, E

Maclennan, W D (Watsonians) 1947 F, I

MacLeod, D A (Glasgow U) 1886 I, E

MacLeod, G (Edinburgh Acads) 1878 E, 1882 I

McLeod, H F (Hawick) 1954 F, NZ, I, E, W, 1955 F, W, I, E, 1956 F, W, I, E, 1957 F, W, I, E, 1958 F, W, A, I, E, 1959 F, W, I, E, 1960 F, W, I, E, SA, 1961 F, SA, W, I, E, 1962 F, W, I, E

MacLeod, K G (Cambridge U) 1905 NZ, 1906 W, I, E, SA, 1907 W, I, E, 1908 I, E

MacLeod, L M (Cambridge U) 1904 W, I, E, 1905 W, I, NZ

MacLeod, S J (Borders, Llanelli Scarlets) 2004 A3, J(t&R), A4(R), SA(R), 2006 F(R), W(R), E, SA2(R), 2007 I2(R), [Pt(R), R(R), NZ, It(R), Arg(R)], 2008 F(R), W(R), I, E, It, Arg 1, 2

Macleod, W M (Fettesian-Lorettonians, Edinburgh Wands) 1886 W, I

McMillan, K H D (Sale) 1953 F, W, I, E

MacMillan, R G (London Scottish) 1887 W, I, E, 1890 W, I, E, 1891 W, I, E, 1892 W, I, E, 1893 W, E, 1894 W, I, E, 1895 W, I, E, 1897 I, E

MacMyn, D J (Cambridge U, London Scottish) 1925 F, W, I, E, 1926 F, W, I, E, 1927 E, A, 1928 F

McNeil, A S B (Watsonians) 1935 I

McPartlin, J J (Harlequins, Oxford U) 1960 F, W, 1962 F, W, I, E

Macphail, J A R (Edinburgh Acads) 1949 E, 1951 SA

Macpherson, D G (London Hospital) 1910 I, E

Macpherson, G P S (Oxford U, Edinburgh Acads) 1922 F, W, I, E, 1924 W, E, 1925 F, W, E, 1927 F, W, I, E, 1928 F, W, E, 1929 I, E, 1930 F, W, I, E, 1931 W, E, 1932 SA, E

Macpherson, N C (Newport) 1920 W, I, E, 1921 F, E, 1923 I, E

McQueen, S B (Waterloo) 1923 F, W, I, E

Macrae, D J (St Andrew's U) 1937 W, I, E, 1938 W, I, E, 1939 W, I, E

Madsen, D F (Gosforth) 1974 W, E, I, F, 1975 I, F, W, E, 1976 F, 1977 E, I, F, W, 1978 I

Mair, N G R (Edinburgh U) 1951 F, W, I, E

Maitland, G (Edinburgh Inst FP) 1885 W, I 2

Maitland, R (Edinburgh Inst FP) 1881 E, 1882 I, E, 1884 W, 1885 W

Maitland, R P (Royal Artillery) 1872 E

Malcolm, A G (Glasgow U) 1888 I

Manson, J J (Dundee HSFP) 1995 E (R)

Marsh, J (Edinburgh Inst FP) 1889 W, I

Marshall, A (Edinburgh Acads) 1875 E

Marshall, G R (Selkirk) 1988 A (R), 1989 Fj, 1990 Arg, 1991 [Z]

Marshall, J C (London Scottish) 1954 F, NZ, I, E, W

Marshall, K W (Edinburgh Acads) 1934 W, I, E, 1935 W, I, E, 1936 W, 1937 E

Marshall, T R (Edinburgh Acads) 1871 E, 1872 E, 1873 E, 1874 E

Marshall, W (Edinburgh Acads) 1872 E

Martin, H (Edinburgh Acads, Oxford U) 1908 W, I, E, 1909 W, E

Masters, W H (Edinburgh Inst FP) 1879 I, 1880 I, E

Mather, C G (Edinburgh, Glasgow) 1999 R (R), [Sp, Sm (R)], 2000 F (t), 2003 [F, Fj, A], 2004 W, E, F

Maxwell, F T (Royal Engineers) 1872 E

Maxwell, G H H P (Edinburgh Acads, RAF, London Scottish) 1913 I, E, 1914 W, I, E, 1920 W, E, 1921 F, W, I, E, 1922 F, E

Maxwell, J M (Langholm) 1957 I

Mayer, M J M (Watsonians, Edinburgh) 1998 SA, 1999 [SA (R), U, Sp, Sm, NZ], 2000 It, I

Mein, J (Edinburgh Acads) 1871 E, 1872 E, 1873 E, 1874 E, 1875 E

Melville, C L (Army) 1937 W, I, E

Menzies, H F (W of Scotland) 1893 W, I, 1894 W, E

Metcalfe, G H (Glasgow Hawks, Glasgow) 1998 A 1, 2, 1999 W, E, It, I, F, Arg, R, [SA, U, Sm, NZ], 2000 It, I, F, W, E, 2001 I, Tg, 2002 E, It, I, F, W (R), C, US, 2003 I 1, F, W 1, E, It 1, SA 1, 2, W 2, I 2, [US, F, Fj, A]

Metcalfe, R (Northampton, Edinburgh) 2000 E, NZ 1, 2, US (R), A (R), Sm, 2001 F, W, E

Methuen, A (London Scottish) 1889 W, I

Michie, E J S (Aberdeen U, Aberdeen GSFP) 1954 F, NZ, I, E, 1955 W, I, E, 1956 F, W, I, E, 1957 F, W, I, E

Millar, J N (W of Scotland) 1892 W, I, E, 1893 W, 1895 I, E

Millar, R K (London Scottish) 1924 I

Millican, J G (Edinburgh U) 1973 W, I, E

Milne, C J B (Fettesian-Lorettonians, W of Scotland) 1886 W, I, E

Milne, D F (Heriot's FP) 1991 [J(R)]

Milne, I G (Heriot's FP, Harlequins) 1979 I, F, NZ, 1980 I, F, 1981 NZ 1, 2, R, A, 1982 E, I, F, W, A 1, 2, 1983 I, F, W, E, NZ, 1984 W, I, E, F, A, 1985 F, W, E, 1986 F, W, E, I, R, 1987 I, F, W, E, [F, Z, NZ], 1988 A, 1989 W, 1990 NZ 1, 2

Milne, K S (Heriot's FP) 1989 W, E, I, F, Fj, R, 1990 I, F, W, E, NZ 2, Arg, 1991 F, W (R), E, [Z], 1992 E, I, F, W, A 1, 1993 I, F, W, E, NZ, 1994 W, E, I, F, SA, 1995 C, I, F, W, E, [Tg, F, NZ]

Milne, W M (Glasgow Acads) 1904 I, E, 1905 W, I

Milroy, E (Watsonians) 1910 W, 1911 E, 1912 W, I, E, SA, 1913 F, W, I, E, 1914 I, E

Mitchell, G W E (Edinburgh Wands) 1967 NZ, 1968 F, W

Mitchell, J G (W of Scotland) 1885 W, I 1, 2

Moffat, J S D (Edinburgh, Borders) 2002 R, SA, Fj(R), 2004 A3

Moir, C C (Northampton) 2000 W, E, NZ 1

Moncreiff, F J (Edinburgh Acads) 1871 E, 1872 E, 1873 E

Monteith, H G (Cambridge U, London Scottish) 1905 E, 1906 W, I, E, SA, 1907 W, I, 1908 E

Monypenny, D B (London Scottish) 1899 I, W, E

Moodie, A R (St Andrew's U) 1909 E, 1910 F, 1911 F

Moore, A (Edinburgh Acads) 1990 NZ 2, Arg, 1991 F, W, E

Morgan, D W (Stewart's-Melville FP) 1973 W, I, E, P, 1974 I, F, 1975 I, F, W, E, NZ, A, 1976 F, W, 1977 I, F, W, 1978 I, F, W, E

Morrison, G A (Glasgow Warriors) 2004 A1(R), 2(R), 3, J(R), A4(R), SA(R), 2008 W(R), E, It, Arg 1, 2, 2009 W, F, It, I, E

Morrison, I R (London Scottish) 1993 I, F, W, E, 1994 W, SA, 1995 C, I, F, W, E, R, [Tg, F, NZ]

Morrison, M C (Royal HSFP) 1896 W, I, E, 1897 I, E, 1898 I, E, 1899 I, W, E, 1900 W, E, 1901 W, I, E, 1902 W, I, E, 1903 W, I, 1904 W, I, E

Morrison, R H (Edinburgh U) 1886 W, I, E

Morrison, W H (Edinburgh Acads) 1900 W

Morton, D S (W of Scotland) 1887 I, W, E, 1888 W, I, 1889 W, I, 1890 I, E

Mowat, J G (Glasgow Acads) 1883 W, E

Mower, A L (Newcastle) 2001 Tg, Arg, NZ, 2002 It, 2003 I 1, F, W 1, E, It 1, SA 1, 2, W 2, I 2

Muir, D E (Heriot's FP) 1950 F, W, I, E, 1952 W, I, E

Munnoch, N M (Watsonians) 1952 F, W, I

Munro, D S (Glasgow High Kelvinside) 1994 W, E, I, F, Arg 1, 2, 1997 W (R)

Munro, P (Oxford U, London Scottish) 1905 W, I, E, NZ, 1906 W, I, E, SA, 1907 I, E, 1911 F, W, I

Munro, R (St Andrew's U) 1871 E

Munro, S (Ayr, W of Scotland) 1980 I, F, 1981 F, W, E, I, NZ 1, 2, R, 1984 W

Munro, W H (Glasgow HSFP) 1947 I, E

Murdoch, W C W (Hillhead HSFP) 1935 E, NZ, 1936 W, I, 1939 E, 1948 F, W, I, E

Murray, C A (Hawick, Edinburgh) 1998 E (R), Fj, A 1, 2, SA, 1999 W, E, It, I, F, Arg, [SA, U, Sp, Sm, NZ], 2000 NZ 2, US, A, Sm, 2001 F, W, E, It (R), Tg, Arg

Murray, E A (Glasgow, Northampton) 2005 R(R), 2006 R, PI, A, 2007 E, W, It, I1, F, I2, SA, [Pt, R, It, Arg], 2008 F, W, I, E, It, Arg 1, 2, NZ, SA, C, 2009 It, I, E

Murray, G M (Glasgow Acads) 1921 I, 1926 W

Murray, H M (Glasgow U) 1936 W, I

Murray, K T (Hawick) 1985 I, F, W

Murray, R O (Cambridge U) 1935 W, E

Murray, S (Bedford, Saracens, Edinburgh) 1997 A, SA, 1998 It, Fj, A 1, 2, SA, 1999 W, E, It, I, F, Arg, R, [SA, U, Sm, NZ], 2000 It, I, F, W, E, NZ 1, US, A, Sm, 2001 F, W, E, It, I, Tg, Arg, NZ, 2002 E, It, I, F, W, R, SA, 2003 I 1, F, W 1, E, It 1, SA 1, 2, It 2, W 2, [J, F, A(R)], 2004 W, E, It, F, I, Sm, A1, 2, 2005 F, I, It, W, E, R, Arg, Sm, NZ, 2006 F, W, I, It, SA1, R, PI, A, 2007 E(t&R), W, It, I1, F, SA(R), [Pt, NZ]

Murray, W A K (London Scottish) 1920 F, I, 1921 F

Mustchin, M L (Edinburgh) 2008 Arg 1, 2, NZ(R), SA(R), C(R)

Napier, H M (W of Scotland) 1877 I, E, 1878 E, 1879 I, E

Neill, J B (Edinburgh Acads) 1963 E, 1964 F, NZ, W, I, E, 1965 F

Neill, R M (Edinburgh Acads) 1901 E, 1902 I

Neilson, G T (W of Scotland) 1891 W, I, E, 1892 W, E, 1893 W, 1894 W, I, 1895 W, I, E, 1896 W, I, E

Neilson, J A (Glasgow Acads) 1878 E, 1879 E

Neilson, R T (W of Scotland) 1898 I, E, 1899 I, W, 1900 I, E

Neilson, T (W of Scotland) 1874 E

Neilson, W (Merchiston Castle School, Cambridge U, London Scottish) 1891 W, E, 1892 W, I, E, 1893 I, E, 1894 E, 1895 W, I, E, 1896 I, 1897 I, E

Neilson, W G (Merchistonians) 1894 E

Nelson, J B (Glasgow Acads) 1925 F, W, I, E, 1926 F, W, I, E, 1927 F, W, I, E, 1928 I, E, 1929 F, W, I, E, 1930 F, W, I, E, 1931 F, W, I

Nelson, T A (Oxford U) 1898 E

Nichol, J A (Royal HSFP) 1955 W, I, E

Nichol, S A (Selkirk) 1994 Arg 2(R)

Nicol, A D (Dundee HSFP, Bath, Glasgow) 1992 E, I, F, W, A 1, 2, 1993 NZ, 1994 W, 1997 A, SA, 2000 I (R), F, W, E, NZ 1, 2, 2001 F, W, E, I (R), Tg, Arg, NZ

Nimmo, C S (Watsonians) 1920 E

Ogilvy, C (Hawick) 1911 I, E, 1912 I

Oliver, G H (Hawick) 1987 [Z], 1990 NZ 2(R), 1991 [Z]

Oliver, G K (Gala) 1970 A

Orr, C E (W of Scotland) 1887 I, E, W, 1888 W, I, 1889 W, I, 1890 W, I, E, 1891 W, I, E, 1892 W, I, E, 1893 I, E

Orr, H J (London Scottish) 1903 W, I, E, 1904 W, I

Orr, J E (W of Scotland) 1889 I, 1890 W, I, E, 1891 W, I, E, 1892 W, I, E, 1893 I, E

Orr, J H (Edinburgh City Police) 1947 F, W

Osler, F L (Edinburgh U) 1911 F, W

Park, J (Royal HSFP) 1934 W

Parks, D A (Glasgow Warriors) 2004 W(R), E(R), F(R), I, Sm (t&R), A1, 2, 3, J, A4, SA, 2005 F, I, It, W, R, Arg, Sm, NZ, 2006 F, W, E, I, It(R), SA1, PI, A, 2007 I1, F, I2(R), SA(R), [Pt, R, NZ(R), It, Arg], 2008 F, W, I(R), E(R), It, Arg 1, 2(R), NZ(R), SA(t), C(R)

Paterson, C D (Edinburgh, Gloucester) 1999 [Sp], 2000 F, W, E, NZ 1, 2, US, A, Sm, 2001 F, W, E, It, I, NZ, 2002 E, It, I, F, W, C, US, R, SA, Fj, 2003 I 1, F, W 1, E, It 1, SA 1, 2, It 2(R), W 2(R), I 2, [J, US, F, Fj, A], 2004 W, E, It, F, I, Sm, A3, J, A4, SA, 2005 F, I, It, W, E, R, Arg, Sm, NZ, 2006 F, W, E, I, It, SA

1, 2, R(R), PI, A, 2007 E, W, It, I1, F, I2, SA, [Pt(R), R, NZ, It, Arg], 2008 F(R), W, I, E, It, Arg 1, 2, NZ, SA, 2009 W(R), F(R), It(t&R), I, E

Paterson, D S (Gala) 1969 SA, 1970 I, E, A, 1971 F, W, I, E (2[1C]), 1972 W

Paterson, G Q (Edinburgh Acads) 1876 E

Paterson, J R (Birkenhead Park) 1925 F, W, I, E, 1926 F, W, I, E, 1927 F, W, I, E, A, 1928 F, W, I, E, 1929 F, W, I, E

Patterson, D (Hawick) 1896 W

Patterson, D W (West Hartlepool) 1994 SA, 1995 [Tg]

Pattullo, G L (Panmure) 1920 F, W, I, E

Paxton, I A M (Selkirk) 1981 NZ 1, 2, R, A, 1982 E, I, F, W, A 1, 2, 1983 I, E, NZ, 1984 W, E, I, F, 1985 I (R), F, W, E, 1986 W, E, I, F, 1987 I, F, W, E, [F, Z, R, NZ], 1988 I, E, A

Paxton, R E (Kelso) 1982 I, A 2(R)

Pearson, J (Watsonians) 1909 I, E, 1910 F, W, I, E, 1911 F, 1912 F, W, SA, 1913 I, E

Pender, I M (London Scottish) 1914 E

Pender, N E K (Hawick) 1977 I, 1978 F, W, E

Penman, W M (RAF) 1939 I

Peterkin, W A (Edinburgh U) 1881 E, 1883 I, 1884 W, I, E, 1885 W, I 1, 2

Peters, E W (Bath) 1995 C, I, F, W, E, R, [Tg, F, NZ], 1996 I, F, W, E, NZ 1, 2, A, It, 1997 A, SA, 1998 W, E, Fj, A 1, 2, SA, 1999 W, E, It, I

Petrie, A G (Royal HSFP) 1873 E, 1874 E, 1875 E, 1876 E, 1877 I, E, 1878 E, 1879 I, E, 1880 I, E

Petrie, J M (Glasgow) 2000 NZ 2, US, A, Sm, 2001 F, W, It (R), I (R), Tg, Arg, 2002 F (t), W (R), C, R(R), Fj, 2003 F(t+R), W 1(R), SA 1(R), 2 (R), It 2, W 2, I 2(R), [J, US, F(t&R), A(R)], 2004 It(R), I(R), Sm(R), A1(R), 2(t&R), 3(R), J, A4, SA(R), 2005 F, I, It, W, E(R), R, 2006 F(R), W(R), I(R), SA 2

Philip, T K (Edinburgh) 2004 W, E, It, F, I

Philp, A (Edinburgh Inst FP) 1882 E

Pinder, S J (Glasgow) 2006 SA 1(R), 2(R)

Pocock, E I (Edinburgh Wands) 1877 I, E

Pollock, J A (Gosforth) 1982 W, 1983 E, NZ, 1984 E (R), I, F, R, 1985 F

Polson, A H (Gala) 1930 E

Pountney, A C (Northhampton) 1998 SA, 1999 W (t+R), E (R), It (t+R), I (R), F, Arg, [SA, U, Sm, NZ], 2000 It, I, F, W, E, US, A, Sm, 2001 F, W, E, It, I, 2002 E, I, F, W, R, SA, Fj

Proudfoot, M C (Melrose, Glasgow) 1998 Fj, A 1, 2, 2003 I 2(R)

Purdie, W (Jedforest) 1939 W, I, E

Purves, A B H L (London Scottish) 1906 W, I, E, SA, 1907 W, I, E, 1908 W, I, E

Purves, W D C L (London Scottish) 1912 F, W, I, SA, 1913 I, E

Rea, C W W (W of Scotland, Headingley) 1968 A, 1969 F, W, I, SA, 1970 F, W, I, A, 1971 F, W, E (2[1C])

Redpath, B W (Melrose, Narbonne, Sale) 1993 NZ (t), 1994 E (t), F, Arg 1, 2, 1995 C, I, F, W, E, R, [Iv, F, NZ], WS, 1996 I, F, W, E, A (R), It, 1997 E, I, F, 1998 Fj, I, A 1, 2, SA, 1999 R (R), [U (R), Sp], 2000 It, I, US, A, Sm, 2001 F (R), E (R), It, I, 2002 E, It, I, F, W, R, SA, Fj, 2003 I 1, F, W 1, E, It 1, SA 1, 2, [J, US(R), F, Fj, A]

Reed, A I (Bath, Wasps) 1993 I, F, W, E, 1994 E, I, F, Arg 1, 2, SA, 1996 It, 1997 W, E, I, F, 1999 It (R), F (R), [Sp]

Reid, C (Edinburgh Acads) 1881 I, E, 1882 I, E, 1883 W, I, E, 1884 W, I, E, 1885 W, I 1, 2, 1886 W, I, E, 1887 I, W, E, 1888 W, I

Reid, J (Edinburgh Wands) 1874 E, 1875 E, 1876 E, 1877 I, E

Reid, J M (Edinburgh Acads) 1898 I, E, 1899 I

Reid, M F (Loretto) 1883 I, E

Reid, R E (Glasgow) 2001 Tg (R), Arg

Reid, S J (Boroughmuir, Leeds, Narbonne) 1995 WS, 1999 F, Arg, [Sp], 2000 It (t), F, W, E (t)

Reid-Kerr, J (Greenock Wand) 1909 E

Relph, W K L (Stewart's Coll FP) 1955 F, W, I, E

Rennie, R M (Edinburgh) 2008 I(R)

Renny-Tailyour, H W (Royal Engineers) 1872 E

Renwick, J M (Hawick) 1972 F, W, E, NZ, 1973 F, 1974 W, E, I, F, 1975 I, F, W, E, NZ, A, 1976 F, W, E (R), 1977 I, F, W, 1978 I, F, W, E, NZ, 1979 W, E, I, F, NZ, 1980 I, F, W, E, 1981 F, W, E, I, NZ 1, 2, R, A, 1982 E, I, F, W, 1983 I, F, W, E, 1984 R

Renwick, W L (London Scottish) 1989 R

Renwick, W N (London Scottish, Edinburgh Wands) 1938 E, 1939 W

Richardson, J F (Edinburgh Acads) 1994 SA

Ritchie, G (Merchistonians) 1871 E

Ritchie, G F (Dundee HSFP) 1932 E
Ritchie, J M (Watsonians) 1933 W, E, I, 1934 W, I, E
Ritchie, W T (Cambridge U) 1905 I, E
Robb, G H (Glasgow U) 1881 I, 1885 W
Roberts, G (Watsonians) 1938 W, I, E, 1939 W, E
Robertson, A H (W of Scotland) 1871 E
Robertson, A W (Edinburgh Acads) 1897 E
Robertson, D (Edinburgh Acads) 1875 E
Robertson, D D (Cambridge U) 1893 W
Robertson, I (London Scottish, Watsonians) 1968 E, 1969 E, SA, 1970 F, W, I, E, A
Robertson, I P M (Watsonians) 1910 F
Robertson, J (Clydesdale) 1908 E
Robertson, K W (Melrose) 1978 NZ, 1979 W, E, I, F, NZ, 1980 W, E, 1981 F, W, E, I, R, A, 1982 E, I, F, A 1, 2, 1983 I, F, W, E, 1984 E, I, F, R, A, 1985 I, F, W, E, 1986 I, 1987 F (R), W, E, [F, Z, NZ], 1988 E, A, 1989 E, I, F
Robertson, L (London Scottish United Services) 1908 E, 1911 W, 1912 W, I, E, SA, 1913 W, I, E
Robertson, M A (Gala) 1958 F
Robertson, R D (London Scottish) 1912 F
Robson, A (Hawick) 1954 F, 1955 F, W, I, E, 1956 F, W, I, E, 1957 F, W, I, E, 1958 W, A, I, E, 1959 F, W, I, E, 1960 F
Rodd, J A T (United Services, RN, London Scottish) 1958 F, W, A, I, E, 1960 F, W, 1962 F, 1964 F, NZ, W, 1965 F, W, I
Rogerson, J (Kelvinside Acads) 1894 W
Roland, E T (Edinburgh Acads) 1884 I, E
Rollo, D M D (Howe of Fife) 1959 E, 1960 F, W, I, E, SA, 1961 F, SA, W, I, E, 1962 F, W, E, 1963 F, W, I, E, 1964 F, NZ, W, I, E, 1965 F, W, I, E, SA, 1966 F, W, I, E, A, 1967 F, W, E, NZ, 1968 F, W, I
Rose, D M (Jedforest) 1951 F, W, I, E, SA, 1953 F, W
Ross, A (Kilmarnock) 1924 F, W
Ross, A (Royal HSFP) 1905 W, I, E, 1909 W, I
Ross, A R (Edinburgh U) 1911 W, 1914 W, I, E
Ross, E J (London Scottish) 1904 W
Ross, G (Edinburgh, Leeds) 2001 Tg, 2002 R, SA, Fj(R), 2003 I 1, W 1(R), SA 2(R), It 2, I 2, [J], 2004 Sm, A1(R), 2(R), J(R), SA(R), 2005 It(R), W(R), E, 2006 F(R), W(R), E(R), I(R), It, SA 1(R), 2
Ross, G T (Watsonians) 1954 NZ, I, E, W
Ross, I A (Hillhead HSFP) 1951 F, W, I, E
Ross, J (London Scottish) 1901 W, I, E, 1902 W, 1903 E
Ross, K I (Boroughmuir FP) 1961 SA, W, I, E, 1962 F, W, I, E, 1963 F, W, E
Ross, W A (Hillhead HSFP) 1937 W, E
Rottenburg, H (Cambridge U, London Scottish) 1899 W, E, 1900 W, I, E
Roughead, W N (Edinburgh Acads, London Scottish) 1927 A, 1928 F, W, I, E, 1930 I, E, 1931 F, W, I, E, 1932 W
Rowan, N A (Boroughmuir) 1980 W, E, 1981 F, W, E, I, 1984 R, 1985 I, 1987 [R], 1988 I, F, W, E
Rowand, R (Glasgow HSFP) 1930 F, W, 1932 E, 1933 W, E, I, 1934 W
Roxburgh, A J (Kelso) 1997 A, 1998 It, F (R), W, E, Fj, A 1(R), 2(R)
Roy, A (Waterloo) 1938 W, I, E, 1939 W, I, E
Russell, R R (Saracens, London Irish) 1999 R, [U (R), Sp, Sm (R), NZ (R)], 2000 I (R), 2001 F (R), 2002 F (R), W (R), 2003 W 1(R), It 1(R), SA 1 (R), 2 (R), It 2, I 2(R), [J, F(R), Fj(t), A(R)], 2004 W(R), E(R), F(R), I(R), J(R), A4(R), SA(R), 2005 It(R)
Russell, W L (Glasgow Acads) 1905 NZ, 1906 W, I, E
Rutherford, J Y (Selkirk) 1979 W, E, I, F, NZ, 1980 I, F, E, 1981 F, W, E, I, NZ 1, 2, A, 1982 E, I, F, W, A 1, 2, 1983 E, NZ, 1984 W, E, I, F, R, 1985 I, F, W, E, 1986 F, W, E, I, R, 1987 I, F, W, E, [F]
Sampson, R W F (London Scottish) 1939 W, 1947 W
Sanderson, G A (Royal HSFP) 1907 W, I, E, 1908 I
Sanderson, J L P (Edinburgh Acads) 1873 E
Schulze, D G (London Scottish) 1905 E, 1907 I, E, 1908 W, I, E, 1909 W, I, E, 1910 W, I, E, 1911 W
Scobie, R M (Royal Military Coll) 1914 W, I, E
Scotland, K J F (Heriot's FP, Cambridge U, Leicester) 1957 F, W, I, E, 1958 E, 1959 F, W, I, E, 1960 F, W, I, E, 1961 F, SA, W, I, E, 1962 F, W, I, E, 1963 F, W, I, E, 1965 F
Scott, D M (Langholm, Watsonians) 1950 I, E, 1951 W, I, E, SA, 1952 F, W, I, 1953 F
Scott, J M B (Edinburgh Acads) 1907 E, 1908 W, I, E, 1909 W, I, E, 1910 F, W, I, E, 1911 F, W, I, 1912 W, I, E, SA, 1913 W, I, E

Scott, J S (St Andrew's U) 1950 E
Scott, J W (Stewart's Coll FP) 1925 F, W, I, E, 1926 F, W, I, E, 1927 F, W, I, E, A, 1928 F, W, E, 1929 E, 1930 F
Scott, M (Dunfermline) 1992 A 2
Scott, R (Hawick) 1898 I, 1900 I, E
Scott, S (Edinburgh, Borders) 2000 NZ 2 (R), US (t+R), 2001 It (R), I (R), Tg (R), NZ (R), 2002 US (R), R(R), Fj(R), 2004 Sm(R), A1(R)
Scott, T (Langholm, Hawick) 1896 W, 1897 I, E, 1898 I, E, 1899 I, W, E, 1900 W, I, E
Scott, T M (Hawick) 1893 E, 1895 W, I, E, 1896 W, E, 1897 I, E, 1898 I, E, 1900 W, I
Scott, W P (W of Scotland) 1900 I, E, 1902 I, E, 1903 W, I, E, 1904 W, I, E, 1905 W, I, E, NZ, 1906 W, I, E, SA, 1907 W, I, E
Scoular, J G (Cambridge U) 1905 NZ, 1906 W, I, E, SA
Selby, J A R (Watsonians) 1920 W, I
Shackleton, J A P (London Scottish) 1959 E, 1963 F, W, 1964 NZ, W, 1965 I, SA
Sharp, A V (Bristol) 1994 E, I, F, Arg 1, 2 SA
Sharp, G (Stewart's FP, Army) 1960 F, 1964 F, NZ, W
Shaw, G D (Sale) 1935 NZ, 1936 W, 1937 W, I, E, 1939 I
Shaw, I (Glasgow HSFP) 1937 I
Shaw, J N (Edinburgh Acads) 1921 W, I
Shaw, R W (Glasgow HSFP) 1934 W, I, E, 1935 W, I, E, NZ, 1936 W, I, E, 1937 W, I, E, 1938 W, I, E, 1939 W, I, E
Shedden, D (W of Scotland) 1972 NZ, 1973 F, W, I, E, P, 1976 W, E, I, 1977 I, F, W, 1978 I, F, W
Shepherd, R J S (Melrose) 1995 WS, 1996 I, F, W, E, NZ 1, 2, A, It, 1997 W, E, I, F, SA, 1998 It, I, W (R), Fj (t), A 1, 2
Shiel, A G (Melrose, Edinburgh) 1991 [I (R), WS], 1993 I, F, W, E, NZ, 1994 Arg 1, 2, SA, 1995 R, [Iv, F, NZ], WS, 2000 I, NZ 1(R), 2
Shillinglaw, R B (Gala, Army) 1960 I, E, SA, 1961 F, SA
Simmers, B M (Glasgow Acads) 1965 F, W, 1966 A, 1967 F, W, I, 1971 F (R)
Simmers, W M (Glasgow Acads) 1926 W, I, E, 1927 F, W, I, E, A, 1928 F, W, I, E, 1929 F, W, I, E, 1930 F, W, I, E, 1931 F, W, I, E, 1932 SA, W, I, E
Simpson, G L (Kirkcaldy, Glasgow) 1998 A 1, 2, 1999 Arg (R), R, [SA, U, Sm, NZ], 2000 It, I, NZ 1(R), 2001 I, Tg (R), Arg (R), NZ
Simpson, J W (Royal HSFP) 1893 I, 1894 W, I, E, 1895 W, I, E, 1896 W, I, 1897 E, 1899 W, E
Simpson, R S (Glasgow Acads) 1923 I
Simson, E D (Edinburgh U, London Scottish) 1902 E, 1903 W, I, E, 1904 W, I, E, 1905 W, I, E, NZ, 1906 W, I, E, 1907 W, I, E
Simson, J T (Watsonians) 1905 NZ, 1909 W, I, E, 1910 F, W, 1911 I
Simson, R F (London Scottish) 1911 E
Sloan, A T (Edinburgh Acads) 1914 W, 1920 F, W, I, E, 1921 F, W, I, E
Sloan, D A (Edinburgh Acads, London Scottish) 1950 F, W, E, 1951 W, I, E, 1953 F
Sloan, T (Glasgow Acads, Oxford U) 1905 NZ, 1906 W, SA, 1907 W, E, 1908 W, 1909 I
Smeaton, P W (Edinburgh Acads) 1881 I, 1883 I, E
Smith, A R (Oxford U) 1895 W, I, E, 1896 W, I, 1897 I, E, 1898 I, E, 1900 I, E
Smith, A R (Cambridge U, Gosforth, Ebbw Vale, Edinburgh Wands) 1955 W, I, E, 1956 F, W, I, E, 1957 F, W, I, E, 1958 F, W, A, I, 1959 F, W, I, E, 1960 F, W, I, E, SA, 1961 F, SA, W, I, E, 1962 F, W, I, E)
Smith, C J (Edinburgh) 2002 C, US (R), 2004 Sm(t&R), A1(R), 2(R), 3(R), J(R), 2005 Arg(R), Sm, NZ(R), 2006 F(R), W(R), E(R), I(R), It(R), SA 1(R), 2, R(R), 2007 I2(R), [R(R), NZ, It(R), Arg(R)], 2008 E(R), It(R)
Smith, D W C (London Scottish) 1949 F, W, I, E, 1950 F, W, I, 1953 I
Smith, E R (Edinburgh Acads) 1879 I
Smith, G K (Kelso) 1957 I, E, 1958 F, W, A, 1959 F, W, I, E, 1960 F, W, I, E, 1961 F, SA, W, I, E
Smith, H O (Watsonians) 1895 W, 1896 W, I, E, 1898 I, E, 1899 W, I, E, 1900 E, 1902 E
Smith, I R (Gloucester, Moseley) 1992 E, I, W, A 1, 2, 1994 E (R), I, F, Arg 1, 2, 1995 [Iv], WS, 1996 I, F, W, E, NZ 1, 2, A, It, 1997 E, I, F, A, SA
Smith, I S (Oxford U, Edinburgh U) 1924 W, I, E, 1925 F, W, I,

Veitch, J P (Royal HSFP) 1882 E, 1883 I, 1884 W, I, E, 1885 I 1, 2, 1886 E
Villar, C (Edinburgh Wands) 1876 E, 1877 I, E
Waddell, G H (London Scottish, Cambridge U) 1957 E, 1958 F, W, A, I, E, 1959 F, W, I, E, 1960 I, E, SA, 1961 F, 1962 F, W, I, E
Waddell, H (Glasgow Acads) 1924 F, W, I, E, 1925 I, E, 1926 F, W, I, E, 1927 F, W, I, E, 1930 W
Wade, A L (London Scottish) 1908 E
Wainwright, R I (Edinburgh Acads, West Hartlepool, Watsonians, Army, Dundee HSFP) 1992 I (R), F, A 1, 2, 1993 NZ, 1994 W, E, 1995 C, I, F, W, E, R, [Iv, Tg, F, NZ], WS, 1996 I, F, W, E, NZ 1, 2, 1997 W, E, I, F, SA, 1998 It, I, F, W, E, Fj, A 1, 2
Walker, A (W of Scotland) 1881 I, 1882 E, 1883 W, I, E
Walker, A W (Cambridge U, Birkenhead Park) 1931 F, W, I, E, 1932 I
Walker, J G (W of Scotland) 1882 E, 1883 W
Walker, M (Oxford U) 1952 F
Walker, N (Borders, Ospreys) 2002 R, SA, Fj, 2007 W(R), It(R), F, I2(R), SA, [R(R), NZ], 2008 F, W, I, E, C
Wallace, A C (Oxford U) 1923 F, 1924 F, W, E, 1925 F, W, I, E, 1926 F
Wallace, W M (Cambridge U) 1913 E, 1914 W, I, E
Wallace, M I (Glasgow High Kelvinside) 1996 A, It, 1997 W
Walls, W A (Glasgow Acads) 1882 E, 1883 W, I, E, 1884 W, I, E, 1886 W, I, E
Walter, M W (London Scottish) 1906 I, E, SA, 1907 W, I, 1908 W, I, 1910 I
Walton, P (Northampton, Newcastle) 1994 E, I, F, Arg 1, 2, 1995 [Iv], 1997 W, E, I, F, SA (R), 1998 I, F, SA, 1999 W, E, It, I, F (R), Arg, R, [SA (R), U (R), Sp]
Warren, J R (Glasgow Acads) 1914 I
Warren, R C (Glasgow Acads) 1922 W, I, 1930 W, I, E
Waters, F H (Cambridge U, London Scottish) 1930 F, W, I, E, 1932 SA, W, I
Waters, J A (Selkirk) 1933 W, E, I, 1934 W, I, E, 1935 W, I, E, NZ, 1936 W, I, E, 1937 W, I, E
Waters, J B (Cambridge U) 1904 I, E
Watherston, J G (Edinburgh Wands) 1934 I, E
Watherston, W R A (London Scottish) 1963 F, W, I
Watson, D H (Glasgow Acads) 1876 E, 1877 I, E
Watson, W S (Boroughmuir) 1974 W, E, I, F, 1975 NZ, 1977 I, F, W, 1979 I, F
Watt, A G J (Glasgow High Kelvinside) 1991 [Z], 1993 I, NZ, 1994 Arg 2(t & R)
Watt, A G M (Edinburgh Acads) 1947 F, W, I, A, 1948 F, W
Weatherstone, T G (Stewart's Coll FP) 1952 E, 1953 I, E, 1954 F, NZ, I, E, W, 1955 F, 1958 W, A, I, E, 1959 W, I, E
Webster, S L (Edinburgh) 2003 I 2(R), 2004 W(R), E, It, F, I, Sm, A1, 2, 2005 It, NZ(R), 2006 F(R), W(R), E(R), I(R), It(R), SA 1(R), 2, R, PI, A, 2007 W(R), I2, SA, [Pt, R, NZ, It, Arg], 2008 F, I, E, It, Arg 1(R), 2, C, 2009 W
Weir, G W (Melrose, Newcastle) 1990 Arg, 1991 R, [J, Z, I, WS, E, NZ], 1992 E, I, F, W, A 1, 2, 1993 I, F, W, E, NZ, 1994 W (R), E, I, F, SA, 1995 F (R), W, E, R, [Iv, Tg, F, NZ], WS, 1996 I, F, W, E, NZ 1, 2, A, It (R), 1997 W, E, I, F, 1998 It, I, F, W, E, SA, 1999 W, Arg (R), R (R), [SA (R), Sp, Sm, NZ], 2000 It (R), I (R), F
Welsh, R (Watsonians) 1895 W, I, E, 1896 W
Welsh, R B (Hawick) 1967 I, E
Welsh, W B (Hawick) 1927 A, 1928 F, W, I, 1929 I, E, 1930 F, W, I, E, 1931 F, W, I, E, 1932 SA, W, I, E, 1933 W, E, I

Welsh, W H (Edinburgh U) 1900 I, E, 1901 W, I, E, 1902 W, I, E
Wemyss, A (Gala, Edinburgh Wands) 1914 W, I, 1920 F, E, 1922 F, W, I
West, L (Edinburgh U, West Hartlepool) 1903 W, I, E, 1905 I, E, NZ, 1906 W, I, E
Weston, V G (Kelvinside Acads) 1936 I, E
White, D B (Gala, London Scottish) 1982 F, W, A 1, 2, 1987 W, E, [F, R, NZ], 1988 I, F, W, E, A, 1989 W, E, I, F, Fj, R, 1990 I, F, W, E, NZ 1, 2, 1991 F, W, E, I, R, [J, Z, I, WS, E, NZ], 1992 E, I, F, W
White, D M (Kelvinside Acads) 1963 F, W, I, E
White, J P R (Glasgow, Sale) 2000 E, NZ 1, 2, US (R), A (R), Sm, 2001 F (R), I, Tg, Arg, NZ, 2002 E, It, I, F, W, C, US, SA(R), Fj, 2003 F(R) W 1, E, It 1, SA 1, 2, It 2, [J, US(R), F, Fj(R), A], 2004 W(R), E, It, F, I, Sm, A1, 2, J(R), A4(R), SA, 2005 F, I, E, Arg, Sm, NZ, 2006 F, W, E, I, It, SA 1, 2, R, 2007 I2, SA, [Pt, R, It, Arg], 2008 F, W, F(R), It(R), NZ, SA, 2009 W, F, It, I, E
White, T B (Edinburgh Acads) 1888 W, I, 1889 W
Whittington, T P (Merchistonians) 1873 E
Whitworth, R J E (London Scottish) 1936 I
Whyte, D J (Edinburgh Wands) 1965 W, I, E, SA, 1966 F, W, I, E, A, 1967 F, W, I, E
Will, J G (Cambridge U) 1912 F, W, I, E, 1914 W, I, E
Wilson, A W (Dunfermline) 1931 F, I, E
Wilson, A W (Glasgow) 2005 R(R)
Wilson, G A (Oxford U) 1949 F, W, E
Wilson, G R (Royal HSFP) 1886 E, 1890 W, I, E, 1891 I
Wilson, J H (Watsonians) 1953 I
Wilson, J S (St Andrew's U) 1931 F, W, I, E, 1932 E
Wilson, J S (United Services, London Scottish) 1908 I, 1909 W
Wilson, R (London Scottish) 1976 E, I, 1977 E, I, F, 1978 I, F, 1981 R, 1983 I
Wilson, R L (Gala) 1951 F, W, I, E, SA, 1953 F, W, E
Wilson, R W (W of Scotland) 1873 E, 1874 E
Wilson, S (Oxford U, London Scottish) 1964 F, NZ, W, I, E, 1965 W, I, E, SA, 1966 F, W, I, A, 1967 F, W, I, E, NZ, 1968 F, W, I, E
Wood, A (Royal HSFP) 1873 E, 1874 E, 1875 E
Wood, G (Gala) 1931 W, I, 1932 W, I, E
Woodburn, J C (Kelvinside Acads) 1892 I
Woodrow, A N (Glasgow Acads) 1887 I, W, E
Wotherspoon, W (W of Scotland) 1891 I, 1892 I, 1893 W, E, 1894 W, I, E
Wright, F A (Edinburgh Acads) 1932 E
Wright, H B (Watsonians) 1894 W
Wright, K M (London Scottish) 1929 F, W, I, E
Wright, P H (Boroughmuir) 1992 A 1, 2, 1993 F, W, E, 1994 W, 1995 C, I, F, W, E, R, [Iv, Tg, F, NZ], 1996 W, E, NZ 1
Wright, R W J (Edinburgh Wands) 1973 F
Wright, S T H (Stewart's Coll FP) 1949 E
Wright, T (Hawick) 1947 A
Wyllie, D S (Stewart's-Melville FP) 1984 A, 1985 W (R), E, 1987 I, F, [F, Z, R, NZ], 1989 R, 1991 R, [J (R), Z], 1993 NZ (R), 1994 W (R), E, I, F
Young, A H (Edinburgh Acads) 1874 E
Young, E T (Glasgow Acads) 1914 E
Young, R G (Watsonians) 1970 W
Young, T E B (Durham) 1911 F
Young, W B (Cambridge U, London Scottish) 1937 W, I, E, 1938 W, I, E, 1939 W, I, E, 1948 E

Scottish Hydro

AYR FINALLY GET THEIR HANDS ON SILVERWARE

It had been a long, long time coming but Ayr finally ended their 112-year wait for major honours when they dethroned Boroughmuir as the Scottish Hydro Electric Premiership champions, recording a convincing 18-point winning margin over second placed Heriots.

Founded back in 1897, the Alloway-based club had finished a distant fifth in the table in 2008 and although they were outscored by both Heriots and third place Boroughmuir, their miserly defence proved the bedrock of their success as they wrapped up the title in early March with three games still to play.

On average, Ayr conceded less than 11 points per game throughout their 22-match campaign and the club's coronation as champions was confirmed with their 20–8 victory over Academicals at Millbrae, breaking Edinburgh and the Borders' traditional dominance of domestic honours.

"We've never won anything in over 100 years, so this is fantastic," said Ayr coach Kenny Murray, who marked his first season in charge at Millbrae in spectacular style. "We put a lot of hard work in this season, from June onwards and right through the pre-season. They've worked hard for seven or eight months, but it's worth it when you get to this stage.

"I think we have added another dimension to our play. We took our foot off the gas in the second half, but I think we did enough to merit the win early on. I don't think anyone can argue that the right team has won. We have been consistent throughout the season. It is fantastic for everyone involved."

The 2008–09 season began in late August and Ayr were out of the blocks quickly with three successive wins before an eagerly-anticipated clash with Heriots at Goldenacre and the first real test of their title credentials.

It was to prove a pulsating clash which Ayr could have settled inside the first 40 minutes and then looked to have lost early in the second half, but they rallied and sealed a 29–25 win in the 77th minute courtesy of flanker Jeff Wilson's pivotal try.

Two more victories followed for Murray's team, but in October they suffered their first major setback at newly-promoted Selkirk. The home side boasted an impressive unbeaten record at Philiphaugh that stretched back to September 2007 but despite their own commanding start to the campaign, Ayr were unable to bring the sequence to an end.

Selkirk scored the only try of the match when Fraser Harkness chipped and chased to set up Lee Jones in the corner and although Ayr's New Zealand fly-half Frazier Climo landed five penalties, the home side held on for a surprise 16–15 triumph for the Premiership new boys.

"We play with confidence, a belief and passion," said Selkirk coach Kevin Barrie. "It was a great for me to see the boys perform. We knew Ayr were a big physical team but we just concentrated on ourselves and played our normal game, putting the ball through our hands."

The reverse, however, failed to derail Ayr's challenge. Seven days later they bounced back with a convincing and morale-boosting 34–10 demolition of defending champions Boroughmuir at Millbrae and three more league wins followed to banish any doubts whether the club were capable of taking the title.

Melrose halted their run in late November with their 26–21 win at the Greenyards, but it was a temporary blip to what was turning out to be a procession for Ayr and with both Heriots and Boroughmuir failing to exert any significant pressure, the question became when and not if they would be crowned champions.

Their first opportunity came at the end of January and a trip to face Boroughmuir. Victory would have given Ayr the title but they were uncharacteristically nervous at Meggetland and were held to a 13–13 draw that meant the champagne stayed on ice.

The visitors got off to a flyer when Climo charged down a clearance to run in under the posts. The Kiwi number 10 converted but the seven points failed to ease Ayr's obvious anxieties and 'Muir hit back with tries from wing Tom Bury and centre Malcolm Clapperton to ensure the points were shared.

The weather wiped out the fixture list in February which meant Ayr had to wait more than a month for another chance to lift the trophy but it finally came in early March with the arrival of Edinburgh Academicals at Millbrae.

A crowd of more than 1,500 came to watch what they hoped would be the victory their side needed and this time they were not disappointed, despite the Millbrae pitch doing a passable impression of a mud bath.

The first score came on 10 minutes and crucially it went to Ayr. Climo's cross-field kick was neatly collected by Florian Marin, who offloaded to full back Andy Wilson for a try. The sin-binning of centre Julian Montoro after a skirmish that involved all 30 players did little to disrupt the home side's rhythm and moments before half-time, they scored again through Wilson to establish a vital 20–0 advantage.

Accies refused to play the role of sacrificial lambs to the champions elect and haunted by their own relegation fears, they mounted a sustained second half fightback that culminated in lock Ed Stuart crashing over to reduce the arrears.

Ayr, however, did not panic and although they were unable to add to their first half points tally, they kept their visitors at arms' length and when the final whistle sounded, the score was 20–8 and the Millbrae side were champions.

"It means everything to us," said Ayr captain Damien Kelly. "A lot of people have worked hard for this, including the fellows behind the scenes. I'm lost for words. I've been here eight years and it's been eight long years winning nothing, so it means everything to win this.

"We usually get better in the second half but the weather was against us and there was a bit of niggle in the game. It was disappointing to lose a try right at the end but that's what happened and we still won the title."

In the Scottish Hydro Electric Cup, however, Ayr came up short and were eliminated at the quarter-final stage by Melrose, who battled past second division Haddington in the last four to set up a showdown with old rivals Heriots at Murrayfield in May and a repeat of the 2008 final.

Twelve months earlier it had been Melrose who emerged victorious but a year on it was Heriots' turn to lift the trophy after the Edinburgh-based club won a thrilling contest in the most dramatic of circumstances.

Melrose drew first blood with an early Scott Wight penalty but the local boys hit back with a converted Struan Dewar try and a deftly-taken Johnny Alston drop goal and Heriots were 10–3 to the good at half-time.

Dave McCall ensured Heriots got the second half off to the perfect start with his side's second try and a further penalty seemed to have settled the issue. But Melrose were far from finished and a 77th-minute try from James Lew made it 19–18 in their favour. The next three minutes, however, were to be even more dramatic.

Heriots scrum half Graham Wilson stepped up for a testing late penalty chance near the touchline and held his nerve to make it 21–19 to the Edinburgh team, but they failed to keep their discipline and conceded a penalty shortly afterwards. Wight stepped up for Melrose but his superb effort from near the halfway line hit the upright and Heriots were Scottish cup kings courtesy of an obdurate piece of woodwork.

"That was just incredible," said Heriots coach Bob McKillop as he caught his breath after the final whistle. "It was tense most of the way through but very tense in that last minute and a half.

"Graham Wilson did something similar as a schoolboy here when winning the Scottish Schools Cup with Dollar Academy and we thought this one was a bit too far for him, so we're delighted with him."

Melrose were understandably distraught at the manner of their defeat but coach Craig Chalmers refused to lay any of the blame on Wight after his kick came up agonisingly short.

"Scott has been magnificent for us and it should never have come to a kick at the end like that," Chalmers said. "Fair play to Heriots, they stuck in well, but I thought we played most of the rugby and that hurts more. We created chances last year and took them and we created a lot more chances this year but didn't take them and that was the difference.

"We've had disappointing segments of the league, but had good moments and to get to the cup final and finish fourth isn't bad. But this was a cup final we should have won really and that's what hurts most I think. But we'll get the heads up and come back."

SCOTLAND

SCOTTISH HYDRO ELECTRIC PREMIERSHIP 2008–09 RESULTS

30 August: Ayr 23 Melrose 0, Boroughmuir 34 Edinburgh Academicals 14, Heriots 22 Hawick 18, Selkirk 28 Currie 24, Stirling County 28 Watsonians 42, West of Scotland 29 Glasgow Hawks 13. **6 September:** Currie 37 Boroughmuir 17, Glasgow Hawks 24 Selkirk 25, Watsonians 35 Heriots 28, Edinburgh Academicals 29 Stirling County 25, Hawick 11 Ayr 17, Melrose 19 West of Scotland 11. **13 September:** Selkirk 28 Melrose 6, Ayr 47 Watsonians 14, West of Scotland 22 Hawick 12, Edinburgh Academicals 17 Currie 10, Stirling County 3 Heriots 23, Boroughmuir 66 Glasgow Hawks 10. **20 September:** Melrose 20 Boroughmuir 27, Hawick 42 Selkirk 15, Glasgow Hawks 17 Edinburgh Academicals 32, Currie 13 Stirling County 13, Heriots 25 Ayr 29, Watsonians 38 West of Scotland 12. **27 September:** Edinburgh Academicals 13 Melrose 20, Stirling County 16 Ayr 22, Boroughmuir 21 Hawick 17, Selkirk 32 Watsonians 28, Currie 25 Glasgow Hawks 26, West of Scotland 13 Heriots 7. **4 October:** Heriots 31 Selkirk 21, Glasgow Hawks 42 Stirling County 8, Watsonians 9 Boroughmuir 35, Hawick 11 Edinburgh Academicals 16, Ayr 27 West of Scotland 0, Melrose 12 Currie 20. **11 October:** Boroughmuir 23 Heriots 33, Glasgow Hawks 21 Melrose 25, Selkirk 16 Ayr 15, Currie 41 Hawick 24, Stirling County 3 West of Scotland 53, Edinburgh Academicals 20 Watsonians 38. **18 October:** Heriots 49 Edinburgh Academicals 15, Melrose 44 Stirling County 23, Watsonians 32 Currie 8, Ayr 34 Boroughmuir 10, West of Scotland 29 Selkirk 17, Hawick 23 Glasgow Hawks 16. **25 October:** Edinburgh Academicals 0 Ayr 28, Melrose 21 Hawick 3, Boroughmuir 22 West of Scotland 6, Glasgow Hawks 16 Watsonians 16. **1 November:** Watsonians 17 Melrose 24, Heriots 27 Glasgow Hawks 12, Selkirk 6 Boroughmuir 0, Stirling County 34 Hawick 22, West of Scotland 22 Edinburgh Academicals 19, Ayr 41 Currie 5. **8 November:** Glasgow Hawks 0 Ayr 14, Currie 34 West of Scotland 8, Hawick 13 Watsonians 13, Edinburgh Academicals 16 Selkirk 24, Melrose 28 Heriots 22. **9 November:** Boroughmuir 54 Stirling County 13. **16 November:** Stirling County 29 Selkirk 30, Currie 12 Heriots 20. **21 November:** Glasgow Hawks 20 West of Scotland 15. **22 November:** Melrose 26 Ayr 21, Edinburgh Academicals 30 Boroughmuir 19, Hawick 7 Heriots 43, Currie 62 Selkirk 20. **23 November:** Watsonians 16 Stirling County 24. **29 November:** Boroughmuir 11 Currie 35, Selkirk 22 Glasgow Hawks 15, Heriots 20 Watsonians 18, Stirling County 31 Edinburgh Academicals 13, Ayr 29 Hawick 0, West of Scotland 15 Melrose 20. **6 December:** Heriots 26 Stirling County 32, Melrose 20 Selkirk 23. **13 December:** West of Scotland 20 Watsonians 10, Selkirk 28 Hawick 3, Edinburgh Academicals 25 Glasgow Hawks 18, Stirling County 16 Currie 38, Ayr 24 Heriots 8. **14 December:** Boroughmuir 26 Melrose 11. **20 December:** Heriots 52 West of Scotland 26, Melrose 26 Edinburgh Academicals 27, Ayr 63 Stirling County 7, Hawick 20 Boroughmuir 15. **21 December:** Glasgow Hawks 33 Currie 20. **10 January:** Glasgow Hawks 29 Boroughmuir 10. **17 January:** Edinburgh Academicals 21 Hawick 25, West of Scotland 3 Ayr 15, Stirling County 12 Glasgow Hawks 10, Currie 17 Melrose 30, Boroughmuir 13 Watsonians 10, Selkirk 29 Heriots 11. **24 January:** Heriots 20 Boroughmuir 43, Melrose 22 Glasgow Hawks 18, West of Scotland 23 Stirling County 16, Watsonians 14 Edinburgh Academicals 16, Ayr 18 Selkirk 5, Hawick 30 Currie 10. **31 January:** Boroughmuir 13 Ayr 13, Selkirk 14 West of Scotland 14, Stirling County 11 Melrose 17, Currie 24 Watsonians 12, Glasgow Hawks 30 Hawick 5. **21 February:** Currie 34 Edinburgh Academicals 14. **7 March:** Watsonians 21 Glasgow Hawks 22, Selkirk 20 Stirling County 17, Heriots 32 Currie 20, Ayr 20 Edinburgh Academicals 8, Hawick 9 Melrose 13, West of Scotland 15 Boroughmuir 20. **21 March:** Watsonians 35 Selkirk 14, Edinburgh Academicals 13 West of Scotland 6, Glasgow Hawks 35 Heriots 30, Currie 19 Ayr 22, Hawick 18 Stirling County 29. **28 March:** West of Scotland 46 Currie 15, Watsonians 42 Hawick 22, Selkirk 20 Edinburgh Academicals 19, Heriots 49 Melrose 41, Stirling County 15 Boroughmuir 64, Ayr 21 Glasgow Hawks 19. **7 April:** Boroughmuir 58 Selkirk 0. **8 April:** Watsonians 24 Ayr 22. **25 April:** Hawick 3 West of Scotland 36. **30 April:** Melrose 48 Watsonians 19. **12 May:** Edinburgh Academicals 33 Heriots 27.

FINAL TABLE

	P	W	D	L	F	A	BP	PTS
Ayr	22	18	1	3	565	231	10	84
Heriots	22	12	0	10	600	518	18	66
Boroughmuir	22	13	1	8	609	397	10	64
Melrose	22	14	0	8	493	443	7	63
Selkirk	22	14	1	7	437	516	5	63
West	22	10	1	11	424	409	10	52
Currie	22	9	1	12	523	504	13	51
Watsonians	22	8	2	12	503	508	15	51
Edinburgh	22	10	0	12	412	513	7	47
Glasgow	22	8	1	13	446	500	12	46
Stirling	22	6	1	15	405	684	9	35
Hawick	22	5	1	16	340	534	9	31

SCOTTISH HYDRO ELECTRIC PREMIERSHIP TWO: Winners: Dundee HSFP
SCOTTISH HYDRO ELECTRIC PREMIERSHIP THREE: Winners: Kirkcaldy
SCOTTISH HYDRO ELECTRIC NATIONAL ONE: Winners: Howe of Fife
SCOTTISH HYDRO ELECTRIC NATIONAL TWO: Winners: Whitecraigs
SCOTTISH HYDRO ELECTRIC NATIONAL THREE: Winners: Lasswade

SCOTLAND

SCOTTISH HYDRO ELECTRIC NATIONAL CUP
2008–09 RESULTS

QUARTER-FINALS

16 April, 2009
Selkirk 21 **Edinburgh Academicals** 28

18 April, 2009	
Haddington 39 **Dundee HSFP** 16	**Melrose** 26 **Ayr** 20
Boroughmuir 14 **Heriots** 18	

SEMI-FINALS

25 April, 2009	
Heriots 50 **Edinburgh Academicals** 8	**Melrose** 27 **Haddington** 20

FINAL

10 May, 2009, Murrayfield, Edinburgh

HERIOTS 21 (1G, 2PG, 1T, 1DG)
MELROSE 19 (1G, 4PG)

HERIOTS: J Alston; G Thomson, D McCall, R Mill, C Goudie; O Brown, G Wilson; A Dymock, F Gillies, W Blacklock, T McVie, M Reid, S Dewar, J Syme, C Fusaro.

SUBSTITUTIONS: J Parker for Fusaro (33 mins); G Rutherford for Brown (temp 49–56 mins, 61–70 mins); Fusaro for McVie (70 mins); A Douglas for Alston (73 mins).

SCORERS *Tries:* Dewar, McCall *Conversion:* Wilson *Penalty Goals:* Wilson (2) *Drop Goal:* Wilson.

YELLOW CARDS: Mill (58 mins), Syme (70 mins)

MELROSE: J Macey; C Anderson, J Lew, J King, C Hardie; W Wight, S McCormick; W Williams, W Mitchell, R Higgins, G Dodds, S Johnson, B Wallace, J Dalziel, R Miller.

SUBSTITUTIONS: N Beavon for Higgins (26 mins); J Murray for Hardie (57 mins); A Gillie for Williams (73 mins); L Gibson for Mitchell (77 mins).

SCORERS *Try:* Lew *Conversion:* Wight *Penalty Goals:* Wight (4)

YELLOW CARD: Dodds (53 mins),

REFEREE: A Ireland (Grangemouth)

SOUTH AFRICA

SOUTH AFRICA'S 2008–09 TEST RECORD

OPPONENTS	DATE	VENUE	RESULT
Wales	8 November	A	**Won** 20–15
Scotland	15 November	A	**Won** 14–10
England	22 November	A	**Won** 42–6
Lions	20 June	H	**Won** 26–21
Lions	27 June	H	**Won** 28–25
Lions	4 July	H	**Lost** 9–28
New Zealand	25 July	H	**Won** 28–19
New Zealand	1 August	H	**Won** 31–19
Australia	8 August	H	**Won** 29–17
Australia	29 August	A	**Won** 32–25
Australia	5 September	A	**Lost** 6–21
New Zealand	12 September	A	**Won** 32–29

MIGHTY SPRINGBOKS DOMINATE

By Iain Spragg

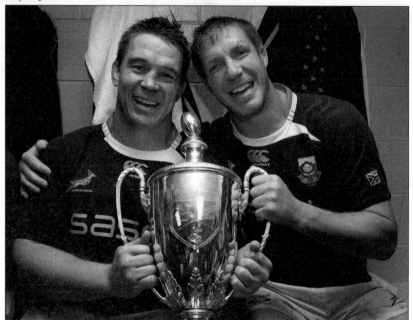

Captain John Smit (left) and lock Bakkies Botha get their hands on the coveted Tri–Nations trophy.

When South Africa captain John Smit held aloft the Tri–Nations trophy in Hamilton in September it represented the culmination of one of the greatest years in the history of Springbok rugby.

Kicking off an incredible nine months for the team with slim victories over Wales and Scotland, who would have thought they would leave Europe last November unbeaten, triumph over the British & Irish Lions and then win their first Tri–Nations crown in five years, beating New Zealand three times in the process. Is this the best Springboks side in their long and illustrious history?

"I've waited a long time for a win here in New Zealand," said Smit as he reflected on his first taste of Test victory on New Zealand soil and a perfect end to a dominant season. "This is the first one that I've ever got. It's very satisfying for me as a person and this team has worked really hard. They've come from a World Cup win and kept that intensity up.

"It was epic. We said at half-time that the All Blacks are always an 00 minute team and they didn't let us down. They came back at us and they showed the character that they've got. I'm happy my boys stuck it out and put on enough pressure to see it through at the end."

At the head of affairs is coach Peter de Villiers, unveiled as the new Springboks coach in January 2008 in succession to Jake White, the man who had famously masterminded South Africa's World Cup triumph. The critics were already sharpening their knives for the new man before a ball had even been kicked or a lineout contested and when South Africa limped home in last place after a disappointing 2008 Tri–Nations campaign, the pressure on De Villiers reached fever pitch.

A year later, however, and the sceptics were glaringly conspicuous by their absence. The much-maligned De Villiers had not only led his side to a 2–1 victory against the Lions, avenging the nation's painful series defeat of 1997, but he had also claimed the Tri–Nations title for his country and in the process ended the All Blacks' four-year triumphant sequence.

The defeat of the Lions was particularly satisfying for South Africa. Forced to wait 12 years for the opportunity to expunge the bitter memories of defeat to the famous tourists, they claimed the series after a dramatic 28–25 win in the second Test at Loftus Versfeld in Pretoria courtesy of Morné Steyn's injury-time penalty.

"The country can now rejoice and be positive. We have beaten a brilliant Lions side. They and their supporters should take it on the chin and say well done for what we have achieved, just as we did in 1997," said De Villiers.

The second season of the De Villiers reign began in November in Cardiff. South Africa had beaten Wales twice on home soil in the summer and they recorded a tenth consecutive triumph over the Welsh with a 20–15 win in the Millennium Stadium. Their victory, however, did not come without a certain amount of second half anxiety as Wales almost overhauled a 17-point deficit on the hour mark and the Springboks were heavily indebted to Jean de Villiers' interception try for their success.

They headed north to Murrayfield to face Scotland a week later and if the performance in Cardiff had been far from convincing, they were hugely fortunate to leave Edinburgh with a victory under their belts.

The Scots led 10–0 at half-time and a shock result looked on the cards, but South Africa regrouped in the dressing room and a try for replacement Jaque Fourie and nine points from the boot of Ruan Pienaar were just enough to earn De Villiers' troops a narrow 14–10 win.

The final leg of their European tour took them to London to tackle England at Twickenham, an unhappy hunting ground for the Springboks.

They had won just once on their last seven visits to the home of English rugby, but after two stuttering performances South Africa suddenly exploded into life with tries from flanker Danie Rossouw, Pienaar, centre Adi Jacobs, Fourie and the irrepressible Bryan Habana as they stormed to a record-breaking 42–6 triumph.

"Coming out of the changing room I had the feeling that something big was about to happen," admitted Smit after the final whistle. "We had a bad start but I deliberately didn't say anything to re-motivate the team and I was delighted with the way the guys came back.

"The character was amazing. To come here and do something like that is pretty special. Guys like Bakkies [Botha] and Victor [Matfield] did not have a Twickenham victory on their CVs and that was what we talked about before the game. It made them even hungrier."

Thoughts now turned to the eagerly-anticipated first Test against the Lions at King's Park in Durban in June. Flanker Heinrich Brussow was named in place of the injured Schalk Burger after impressing for the Lions against the tourists, but otherwise De Villiers was able to select a full-strength line-up.

South Africa exploded out of the blocks, doubtless motivated by 12 years of unhappy reflection on the events of the previous series, and after just four minutes Smit bundled his way over and the home support was delirious.

Pienaar's boot kept the scoreboard ticking over and when Brussow powered his way over for the second try five minutes after the restart, the writing was on the wall for the beleaguered Lions.

To their credit, the tourists rallied with two late tries of their own as South Africa made a raft of changes, but although the final 26–21 scoreline to the Springboks suggested a dramatically tight encounter, the home side and their superior pack had been in complete ascendency for the majority of the match.

A series victory was now within touching distance and De Villiers recalled Burger for the second Test in Pretoria at the expense of Brussow. With the match less than a minute old, Burger gouged the eye of Lions wing Luke Fitzgerald and was sent to the sin-bin, sparing South Africa from having to play the remainder of the match with 14 men.

The Lions led for the first 74 minutes of the match as they rectified their problems in the scrum from the first Test and a converted try from Rob Kearney and five penalties and a drop goal from Stephen Jones saw the visitors amass 25 points.

The Springboks were firmly under the cosh but unbowed and a first half try from JP Pietersen, followed by scores after the break from Habana and Fourie kept De Villiers' side in contention and the stage was set for the most dramatic of denouements in the final five minutes.

With South Africa now leading 25–22, Jones stepped up to land a testing 77th-minute penalty to level the scores only for South Africa to reply through Steyn from more than 50 metres. The ball sailed through the posts and the Springboks took an unassailable 2–0 series lead.

Unsurprisingly, De Villiers made wholesale changes for the third Test at Ellis Park with 10 new faces in his side and it arguably cost South Africa the chance of a series whitewash as the Lions restored a degree of pride with a free-flowing 28–9 victory. It was, however, only a minor blemish on what had been an epic and ultimately victorious series for the coach.

South Africa now prepared for the Tri–Nations bristling with confidence. They began with back-to-back home fixtures with New Zealand and their bruising 28–19 win in Bloemfontein in the first game, followed by a 31–19 victory in Durban – courtesy of a converted try and eight penalties from Morné Steyn, proved the team were determined to add the title to their growing collection of silverware.

The Wallabies were the next visitors and fared little better than the All Blacks had, losing 29–17 at Newlands. The return match in Perth three weeks later was a similar story as two Habana tries secured a 32–25 success at the Subiaco Oval and with four wins from four, the Springboks were desperately close to what would be only their third Tri–Nations triumph.

The champagne, however, had to be put on ice as the two teams decamped to Brisbane and the Suncorp Stadium for the next match. The ground was the scene of South Africa's 49–0 humbling by Australia in 2006 and once again it proved something of a jinxed stadium as Adam Ashley-Cooper and James O'Connor scored the only tries of the game as the Wallabies ran out 21–6 winners.

South Africa now knew they had to beat New Zealand in Wellington in their final fixture to win the tournament. It was to be a fittingly titantic clash between the two old rivals but after 80 minutes of bone-crunching action, the Springboks clung on for an all-important 32–29 win.

The visitors were the first to cross the whitewash when Fourie du Preez scampered over and although the All Blacks remained in the hunt thanks to the boot of Dan Carter, South Africa stretched their lead with a De Villiers intercept score. The home side rallied in the second half with tries from wing Sitiveni Sivivatu and captain Richie McCaw but it was too little too late and the Springboks were the champions.

SOUTH AFRICA INTERNATIONAL STATISTICS

MATCH RECORDS UP TO 30TH SEPTEMBER 2009

MOST CONSECUTIVE TEST WINS

17 1997 A2,It, F 1,2, E,S, 1998 I 1,2,W 1,E 1, A 1,NZ 1,2, A 2, W 2, S, I 3

15 1994 Arg 1,2, S, W 1995 WS, A, R, C, WS, F, NZ, W, It, E, 1996 Fj

MOST CONSECUTIVE TESTS WITHOUT DEFEAT

Matches	Wins	Draws	Period
17	17	0	1997 to 1998
16	15	1	1994 to 1996
15	12	3	1960 to 1963

MOST POINTS IN A MATCH
BY THE TEAM

Pts.	Opponent	Venue	Year
134	Uruguay	E London	2005
105	Namibia	Cape Town	2007
101	Italy	Durban	1999
96	Wales	Pretoria	1998
74	Tonga	Cape Town	1997
74	Italy	Port Elizabeth	1999
72	Uruguay	Perth	2003
68	Scotland	Murrayfield	1997
64	USA	Montpellier	2007
63	Argentina	Johannesburg	2008
62	Italy	Bologna	1997
61	Australia	Pretoria	1997

BY A PLAYER

Pts.	Player	Opponent	Venue	Year
35	P C Montgomery	Namibia	Cape Town	2007
34	J H de Beer	England	Paris	1999
31	P C Montgomery	Wales	Pretoria	1998
31	M Steyn	N Zealand	Durban	2009
30	T Chavhanga	Uruguay	E London	2005
29	G S du Toit	Italy	Port Elizabeth	1999
29	P C Montgomery	Samoa	Paris	2007
28	G K Johnson	W Samoa	Johannesburg	1995
26	J H de Beer	Australia	Pretoria	1997
26	P C Montgomery	Scotland	Murrayfield	1997
25	J T Stransky	Australia	Bloemfontein	1996
25	C S Terblanche	Italy	Durban	1999

MOST TRIES IN A MATCH
BY THE TEAM

Tries	Opponent	Venue	Year
21	Uruguay	E London	2005
15	Wales	Pretoria	1998
15	Italy	Durban	1999
15	Namibia	Cape Town	2007
12	Tonga	Cape Town	1997
12	Uruguay	Perth	2003
11	Italy	Port Elizabeth	1999
10	Ireland	Dublin	1912
10	Scotland	Murrayfield	1997

BY A PLAYER

Tries	Player	Opponent	Venue	Year
6	T Chavhanga	Uruguay	E London	2005
5	C S Terblanche	Italy	Durban	1999
4	C M Williams	W Samoa	Johannesburg	1995
4	P W G Rossouw	France	Parc des Princes	1997
4	C S Terblanche	Ireland	Bloemfontein	1998
4	B G Habana	Samoa	Paris	2007
4	J L Nokwe	Australia	Johannesburg	2008

MOST CONVERSIONS IN A MATCH
BY THE TEAM

Cons	Opponent	Venue	Year
13	Italy	Durban	1999
13	Uruguay	E London	2005
12	Namibia	Cape Town	2007
9	Scotland	Murrayfield	1997
9	Wales	Pretoria	1998
9	Argentina	Johannesburg	2008
8	Italy	Port Elizabeth	1999
8	USA	Montpellier	2007
7	Scotland	Murrayfield	1951
7	Tonga	Cape Town	1997
7	Italy	Bologna	1997
7	France	Parc des Princes	1997
7	Italy	Genoa	2001
7	Samoa	Pretoria	2002
7	Samoa	Brisbane	2003
7	England	Bloemfontein	2007

BY A PLAYER

Cons	Player	Opponent	Venue	Year
12	P C Montgomery	Namibia	Cape Town	2007
9	P C Montgomery	Wales	Pretoria	1998
9	A D James	Argentina	Johannesburg	2008
8	P C Montgomery	Scotland	Murrayfield	1997
8	G S du Toit	Italy	Port Elizabeth	1999
8	G S du Toit	Italy	Durban	1999
7	A O Geffin	Scotland	Murrayfield	1951
7	J M F Lubbe	Tonga	Cape Town	1997
7	H W Honiball	Italy	Bologna	1997
7	H W Honiball	France	Parc des Princes	1997
7	A S Pretorius	Samoa	Pretoria	2002
7	J N B van der Westhuyzen	Uruguay	E London	2005
7	P C Montgomery	England	Bloemfontein	2007

MOST PENALTIES IN A MATCH
BY THE TEAM

Pens	Opponent	Venue	Year
8	Scotland	Port Elizabeth	2006
8	N Zealand	Durban	2009
7	France	Pretoria	1975
7	France	Cape Town	2006
7	Australia	Cape Town	2009
6	Australia	Bloemfontein	1996
6	Australia	Twickenham	1999
6	England	Pretoria	2000
6	Australia	Durban	2000
6	France	Johannesburg	2001
6	Scotland	Johannesburg	2003
6	N Zealand	Bloemfontein	2009

BY A PLAYER

Pens	Player	Opponent	Venue	Year
8	M Steyn	N Zealand	Durban	2009
7	P C Montgomery	Scotland	Port Elizabeth	2006
7	P C Montgomery	France	Cape Town	2006
7	M Steyn	Australia	Cape Town	2009
6	G R Bosch	France	Pretoria	1975
6	J T Stransky	Australia	Bloemfontein	1996
6	J H de Beer	Australia	Twickenham	1999
6	A J J van Straaten	England	Pretoria	2000
6	A J J van Straaten	Australia	Durban	2000
6	P C Montgomery	France	Johannesburg	2001
6	L J Koen	Scotland	Johannesburg	2003

MOST DROPPED GOALS IN A MATCH
BY THE TEAM

Drops	Opponent	Venue	Year
5	England	Paris	1999
4	England	Twickenham	2006
3	S America	Durban	1980
3	Ireland	Durban	1981
3	Scotland	Murrayfield	2004

BY A PLAYER

Drops	Player	Opponent	Venue	Year
5	J H de Beer	England	Paris	1999
4	A S Pretorius	England	Twickenham	2006
3	H E Botha	S America	Durban	1980
3	H E Botha	Ireland	Durban	1981
3	J N B van der Westhuyzen	Scotland	Murrayfield	2004
2	B L Osler	N Zealand	Durban	1928
2	H E Botha	NZ Cavaliers	Cape Town	1986
2	J T Stransky	N Zealand	Johannesburg	1995
2	J H de Beer	N Zealand	Johannesburg	1997
2	P C Montgomory	N Zealand	Cardiff	1999
2	F P L Steyn	Australia	Cape Town	2007

SOUTH AFRICA

CAREER RECORDS

MOST CAPPED PLAYERS

Caps	Player	Career Span
102	P C Montgomery	1997 to 2008
90	J W Smit	2000 to 2009
89	J H van der Westhuizen	1993 to 2003
89	V Matfield	2001 to 2009
80	J P du Randt	1994 to 2007
77	M G Andrews	1994 to 2001
66	A G Venter	1996 to 2001
64	B J Paulse	1999 to 2007
63	J P Botha	2002 to 2009
62	J H Smith	2003 to 2009
56	C J van der Linde	2002 to 2008
54	A-H le Roux	1994 to 2002
54	J de Villiers	2002 to 2009
54	B G Habana	2004 to 2009
53	S W P Burger	2003 to 2009
52	P F du Preez	2004 to 2009
51	P A van den Berg	1999 to 2007
51	J C van Niekerk	2001 to 2008
51	J Fourie	2003 to 2009
47	J T Small	1992 to 1997
43	J Dalton	1994 to 2002
43	P W G Rossouw	1997 to 2003
43	D J Rossouw	2003 to 2009
42	G H Teichmann	1995 to 1999
42	R B Skinstad	1997 to 2007
40	E R Januarie	2005 to 2009

MOST CONSECUTIVE TESTS

Tests	Player	Span
46	J W Smit	2003 to 2007
39	G H Teichmann	1996 to 1999
26	A H Snyman	1996 to 1998
26	A N Vos	1999 to 2001
25	S H Nomis	1967 to 1972
25	A G Venter	1997 to 1999
25	A-H le Roux	1998 to 1999

MOST TESTS AS CAPTAIN

Tests	Captain	Span
64	J W Smit	2003 to 2009
36	G H Teichmann	1996 to 1999
29	J F Pienaar	1993 to 1996
22	D J de Villiers	1965 to 1970
18	C P J Krigé	1999 to 2003
16	A N Vos	1999 to 2001
15	M du Plessis	1975 to 1980
12	R B Skinstad	2001 to 2007
11	J F K Marais	1971 to 1974

MOST POINTS IN TESTS

Pts	Player	Tests	Career
893	P C Montgomery	102	1997 to 2008
312	H E Botha	28	1980 to 1992
240	J T Stransky	22	1993 to 1996
221	A J J van Straaten	21	1999 to 2001
190	J H van der Westhuizen	89	1993 to 2003
181	J H de Beer	13	1997 to 1999
175	B G Habana	54	2004 to 2009
171	A S Pretorius	31	2002 to 2007
156	H W Honiball	35	1993 to 1999
146	A D James	35	2001 to 2008
145	L J Koen	15	2000 to 2003
135*	B J Paulse	64	1999 to 2007
135	J Fourie	51	2003 to 2009
130	P J Visagie	25	1967 to 1971

* includes a penalty try

MOST TRIES IN TESTS

Tries	Player	Tests	Career
38	J H van der Westhuizen	89	1993 to 2003
35	B G Habana	54	2004 to 2009
27*	B J Paulse	64	1999 to 2007
27	J Fourie	51	2003 to 2009
25	P C Montgomery	94	1997 to 2008
21	P W G Rossouw	43	1997 to 2003
20	J T Small	47	1992 to 1997
19	D M Gerber	24	1980 to 1992
19	C S Terblanche	37	1998 to 2003
18	J de Villiers	54	2002 to 2009
14	C M Williams	27	1993 to 2000

* includes a penalty try

MOST CONVERSIONS IN TESTS

Cons	Player	Tests	Career
153	P C Montgomery	102	1997 to 2008
50	H E Botha	28	1980 to 1992
38	H W Honiball	35	1993 to 1999
33	J H de Beer	13	1997 to 1999
31	A S Pretorius	31	2002 to 2007
30	J T Stransky	22	1993 to 1996
25	G S du Toit	14	1998 to 2006
25	A D James	35	2001 to 2008
23	A J J van Straaten	21	1999 to 2001
23	L J Koen	15	2000 to 2003
20	P J Visagie	25	1967 to 1971

MOST PENALTY GOALS IN TESTS

Pens	Player	Tests	Career
148	P C Montgomery	102	1997 to 2008
55	A J J van Straaten	21	1999 to 2001
50	H E Botha	28	1980 to 1992
47	J T Stransky	22	1993 to 1996
31	L J Koen	15	2000 to 2003
28	M Steyn	9	2009
27	J H de Beer	13	1997 to 1999
26	A D James	35	2001 to 2008
25	H W Honiball	35	1993 to 1999
25	A S Pretorius	31	2002 to 2007
23	G R Bosch	9	1974 to 1976
19	P J Visagie	25	1967 to 1971

MOST DROPPED GOALS IN TESTS

Drops	Player	Tests	Career
18	H E Botha	28	1980 to 1992
8	J H de Beer	13	1997 to 1999
8	A S Pretorius	31	2002 to 2007
6	P C Montgomery	102	1997 to 2008
5	J D Brewis	10	1949 to 1953
5	P J Visagie	25	1967 to 1971
4	B L Osler	17	1924 to 1933

TRI-NATIONS RECORDS

RECORD	DETAIL		SET
Most points in season	158	in six matches	2009
Most tries in season	18	in four matches	1997
Highest Score	61	61–22 v Australia (h)	1997
Biggest win	45	53–8 v Australia (h)	2008
Highest score conceded	55	35–55 v N Zealand (a)	1997
Biggest defeat	49	0–49 v Australia (a)	2006
Most appearances	36	V Matfield	2001 to 2009
Most points in matches	210	P C Montgomery	1997 to 2008
Most points in season	95	M Steyn	2009
Most points in match	31	M Steyn	v N Zealand (h),2009
Most tries in matches	7	B J Paulse	1999 to 2007
	7	B G Habana	2005 to 2009
	7	J Fourie	2005 to 2009
Most tries in season	4	J L Nokwe	2008
Most tries in match	4	J L Nokwe	v Australia (h) 2008
Most cons in matches	26	P C Montgomery	1997 to 2008
Most cons in season	12	J H de Beer	1997
Most cons in match	6	J H de Beer	v Australia (h),1997
Most pens in matches	43	P C Montgomery	1997 to 2008
Most pens in season	23	M Steyn	2009
Most pens in match	8	M Steyn	v N Zealand (h),2009

MISCELLANEOUS RECORDS

RECORD	HOLDER	DETAIL
Longest Test Career	J P du Randt	1994–2007
Youngest Test Cap	A J Hartley	18 yrs 18 days in 1891
Oldest Test Cap	J N Ackermann	37 yrs 34 days in 2007

CAREER RECORDS OF SOUTH AFRICA INTERNATIONAL PLAYERS
(UP TO 30TH SEPTEMBER 2009)

PLAYER	DEBUT	CAPS	T	C	P	D	PTS
BACKS							
J de Villiers	2002 v F	54	18	0	0	0	90
P F du Preez	2004 v I	52	12	0	0	0	60
J Fourie	2003 v U	51	27	0	0	0	135
B G Habana	2004 v E	54	35	0	0	0	175
A A Jacobs	2001 v It	28	7	0	0	0	35
C A Jantjes	2001 v It	24	4	1	0	0	22
E R Januarie	2005 v U	40	5	0	0	0	25
Z Kirchner	2009 v Bl	1	0	0	0	0	0
W M Murray	2007 v Sm	3	0	0	0	0	0
A Z Ndungane	2006 v A	11	1	0	0	0	5
O M Ndungane	2008 v It	6	1	0	0	0	5
J L Nokwe	2008 v Arg	4	5	0	0	0	25
W Olivier	2006 v S	24	0	0	0	0	0
R Pienaar	2006 v NZ	34	6	7	13	0	83
J-P R Pietersen	2006 v A	30	11	0	0	0	55
F P L Steyn	2006 v I	36	5	5	14	3	86
M Steyn	2009 v Bl	9	1	8	28	3	114
FORWARDS							
A Bekker	2008 v W	18	1	0	0	0	5
J P Botha	2002 v F	63	7	0	0	0	35
S B Brits	2008 v It	3	0	0	0	0	0
H W Brüssow	2008 v E	10	1	0	0	0	5
S W P Burger	2003 v Gg	53	10	0	0	0	50
P D Carstens	2002 v S	9	0	0	0	0	0
B W du Plessis	2007 v A	30	5	0	0	0	25
J N du Plessis	2007 v A	12	0	0	0	0	0
R Kankowski	2007 v W	9	1	0	0	0	5
V Matfield	2001 v It	89	6	0	0	0	30
T Mtawarira	2008 v W	19	1	0	0	0	5
B V Mujati	2008 v W	12	0	0	0	0	0
G J Muller	2006 v S	23	0	0	0	0	0

M C Ralepelle	2006 v NZ	8	0	0	0	0	0
D J Rossouw	2003 v U	43	7	0	0	0	35
J W Smit	2000 v C	90	5	0	0	0	25
J H Smith	2003 v S	62	10	0	0	0	50
P J Spies	2006 v A	28	4	0	0	0	20
G G Steenkamp	2004 v S	22	1	0	0	0	5
H S van der Merwe	2007 v W	1	0	0	0	0	0
L A Watson	2007 v Sm	10	0	0	0	0	0

SOUTH AFRICA
INTERNATIONAL PLAYERS
UP TO 30TH SEPTEMBER 2009

Note: Years given for International Championship matches are for second half of season; eg 1972 means season 1971–72. Years for all other matches refer to the actual year of the match. Entries in square brackets denote matches played in RWC Finals.

Ackermann, D S P (WP) 1955 BI 2, 3, 4, 1956 A 1, 2, NZ 1, 3, 1958 F 2
Ackermann, J N (NT, BB, N) 1996 Fj, A 1, NZ 1, A 2, 2001 F 2(R), It 1, NZ 1(R), A 1, 2006 I, E1, 2, 2007 Sm, A2
Aitken, A D (WP) 1997 F 2(R), E, 1998 I 2(R), W 1(R), NZ 1, 2(R), A 2(R)
Albertyn, P K (SWD) 1924 BI 1, 2, 3, 4
Alexander, F A (GW) 1891 BI 1, 2
Allan, J (N) 1993 A 1(R), Arg 1, 2(R), 1994 E 1, 2, NZ 1, 2, 3, 1996 Fj, A 1, NZ 1, A 2, NZ 2
Allen, P B (EP) 1960 S
Allport, P H (WP) 1910 BI 2, 3
Anderson, J W (WP) 1903 BI 3
Anderson, J H (WP) 1896 BI 1, 3, 4
Andrew, J B (Tvl) 1896 BI 2
Andrews, E P (WP) 2004 I1, 2, W1(t&R), PI, NZ1, A1, NZ2, A2, W2, I3, E, 2005 F1, A2, NZ2(t), Arg(R), F3(R), 2006 S1, 2, F, A1(R), NZ1(t), 2007 A2(R), NZ2(R)
Andrews, K S (WP) 1992 E, 1993 F 1, 2, A 1(R), 2, 3, Arg 1(R), 2, 1994 NZ 3
Andrews, M G (N) 1994 E 2, NZ 1, 2, 3, Arg 1, 2, S, W, 1995 WS, [A, WS, F, NZ], W, It, E, 1996 Fj, A 1, NZ 1, A 2, NZ 2, 3, 4, 5, Arg 1, 2, F 1, 2, W, 1997 Tg (R), BI 1, 2, NZ 1, A 1, NZ 2, A 2, It, F 1, 2, E, S, 1998 I 1, 2, W 1, E 1, A 1, NZ 1, 2, A 2, W 2, S, I 3, E 2, 1999 NZ 1, 2(R), A 2(R), [S, U, E, A, NZ 3], 2000 A 2, NZ 2, A 3, Arg, I, W, E 3, 2001 F 1, 2, It 1, NZ 1, A 1, 2, NZ 2, F 3, E
Antelme, J G M (Tvl) 1960 NZ 1, 2, 3, 4, 1961 F
Apsey, J T (WP) 1933 A 4, 5, 1938 BI 2
Ashley, S (WP) 1903 BI 2
Aston, F T D (Tvl) 1896 BI 1, 2, 3, 4
Atherton, S (N) 1993 Arg 1, 2, 1994 E 1, 2, NZ 1, 2, 3, 1996 NZ 2
Aucamp, J (WT) 1924 BI 1, 2
Baard, A P (WP) 1960 I
Babrow, L (WP) 1937 A 1, 2, NZ 1, 2, 3
Badenhorst, C (OFS) 1994 Arg 2, 1995 WS (R)
Bands, R E (BB) 2003 S 1, 2, Arg (R), A 1, NZ 1, A 2, NZ 2, [U, E, Sm(R), NZ(R)]
Barnard, A S (EP) 1984 S Am 1, 2, 1986 Cv 1, 2
Barnard, J H (Tvl) 1965 S, A 1, 2, NZ 3, 4
Barnard, R W (Tvl) 1970 NZ 2(R)
Barnard, W H M (NT) 1949 NZ 4, 1951 W
Barry, D W (WP) 2000 C, E 1, 2, A 1(R), NZ 1, A 2, 2001 F 1, 2, US (R), 2002 W 2, Arg, Sm, NZ 1, A 1, NZ 2, A 2, 2003 A 1, NZ 1, A 2, [U, E, Sm, NZ], 2004 PI, NZ1, A1, NZ2, A2, W2, I3, E, Arg(t), 2005 F1, 2, A1, NZ2, W(R), F3(R), 2006 F
Barry, J (WP) 1903 BI 1, 2, 3
Bartmann, W J (Tvl, N) 1986 Cv 1, 2, 3, 4, 1992 NZ, A, F, 1, 2
Bastard, W E (N) 1937 A 1, NZ 1, 2, 3, 1938 BI 1, 3
Bates, A J (WT) 1969 E, 1970 NZ 1, 2, 1972 E
Bayvel, P C R (Tvl) 1974 BI 2, 4, F 1, 2, 1975 F 1, 2, 1976 NZ 1, 2, 3, 4
Beck, J J (WP) 1981 NZ 2(R), 3(R), US

Bedford, T P (N) 1963 A 1, 2, 3, 4, 1964 W, F, 1965 I, A 1, 2, 1968 BI 1, 2, 3, 4, F 1, 2, 1969 A 1, 2, 3, 4, S, E, 1970 I, W, 1971 F 1, 2
Bekker, A (WP) 2008 W1, 2(R), It(R), NZ1(R), 2(t&R), A1(t&R), Arg(R), NZ3, A2, 3, W3(R), S(R), E(R), 2009 BI 1(R), 2(R), NZ2(R), A1(R), 2(R)
Bekker, H J (WP) 1981 NZ 1, 3
Bekker, H P J (NT) 1952 E, F, 1953 A 1, 2, 3, 4, 1955 BI 2, 3, 4, 1956 A 1, 2, NZ 1, 2, 3, 4
Bekker, M J (NT) 1960 S
Bekker, R P (NT) 1953 A 3, 4
Bekker, S (NT) 1997 A 2(t)
Bennett, R G (Border) 1997 Tg (R), BI 1(R), 3, NZ 1, A 1, NZ 2
Bergh, W F (SWD) 1931 W, I, 1932 E, S, 1933 A 1, 2, 3, 4, 5, 1937 A 1, 2, NZ 1, 2, 3, 1938 BI 1, 2, 3
Bestbier, A (OFS) 1974 F 2(R)
Bester, J J N (WP) 1924 BI 2, 4
Bester, J L A (WP) 1938 BI 2, 3
Beswick, A M (Bor) 1896 BI 2, 3, 4
Bezuidenhout, C E (NT) 1962 BI 2, 3, 4
Bezuidenhout, C J (MP) 2003 NZ 2(R), [E, Sm, NZ]
Bezuidenhout, N S E (NT) 1972 E, 1974 BI 2, 3, 4, F 1, 2, 1975 F 1, 2, 1977 Wld
Bierman, J (Tvl) 1931 I
Bisset, W M (WP) 1891 BI 1, 3
Blair, R (WP) 1977 Wld
Bobo, G (GL, WP) 2003 S 2(R), Arg, A 1(R), NZ 2, 2004 S(R), 2008 It
Boome, C S (WP) 1999 It 1, 2, W, NZ 1(R), A 1, NZ 2, A 2, 2000 C, E 1, 2, 2003 S 1(R), 2, Arg (R), A 1(R), NZ 1(R), A 2, NZ 2(R), [U(R), Gg, NZ(R)]
Bosch, G R (Tvl) 1974 BI 2, F 1, 2, 1975 F 1, 2, 1976 NZ 1, 2, 3, 4
Bosman, H M (FS) 2005 W, F3, 2006 A1(R)
Bosman, N J S (Tvl) 1924 BI 2, 3, 4
Botha, B J (N) 2006 NZ2(R), 3, A3, I(R), E1, 2, 2007 E1, Sm, A1, NZ1, Nm(R), S(t&R), [Sm(R), E1, Tg(R), US], 2008 W2
Botha, D S (NT) 1981 NZ 1
Botha, G van G (BB) 2005 A3(R), F3(R), 2007 E1(R), 2(R), Sm(R), A1(R), NZ1, A2, NZ2(R), Nm, S, [Tg]
Botha, H E (NT) 1980 S Am 1, 2, BI 1, 2, 3, 4, S Am 3, 4, F, 1981 I 1, 2, NZ 1, 2, 3, US, 1982 S Am 1, 2, 1986 Cv 1, 2, 3, 4, 1989 Wld 1, 2, 1992 NZ, A, F, 1, 2, E
Botha, J A (Tvl) 1903 BI 3
Botha, J P (BB) 2002 F, 2003 S 1, 2, A 1, NZ 1, A 2(R), [U, E, Gg, Sm, NZ], 2004 I1, PI, NZ1, A1, NZ2, A2, W2, I3, E, S, Arg, 2005 A1, 2, 3, NZ1, A4, NZ2, Arg, W, F3, 2007 E1, 2, A1, NZ1, Nm, S, [Sm, E1, Tg, US(R), Fj, Arg, E2], W, 2008 W1, 2, It, NZ1, 2, A1, Arg, W3, S, E, 2009 BI 1, 2, NZ1, 2, A1, 2, 3, NZ3
Botha, J P F (NT) 1962 BI 2, 3, 4
Botha, P H (Tvl) 1965 A 1, 2
Boyes, H C (GW) 1891 BI 1, 2
Brand, G H (WP) 1928 NZ 2, 3, 1931 W, I, 1932 E, S, 1933 A 1, 2, 3, 4, 5, 1937 A 1, 2, NZ 2, 3, 1938 BI 1
Bredenkamp, M J (GW) 1896 BI 1, 3

SOUTH AFRICA

Breedt, J C (Tvl) 1986 Cv 1, 2, 3, 4, 1989 Wld 1, 2, 1992 NZ, A
Brewis, J D (NT) 1949 NZ 1, 2, 3, 4, 1951 S, I, W, 1952 E, F, 1953 A 1
Briers, T P D (WP) 1955 BI 1, 2, 3, 4, 1956 NZ 2, 3, 4
Brink D J (WP) 1906 S, W, E
Brink, R (WP) 1995 [R, C]
Brits, S B (WP) 2008 It(R), NZ2(R), A1
Britz, G J J (FS, WP) 2004 I1(R), 2(R), W1(R), PI, A1, NZ2, A2(R), I3(t), S(t&R), Arg(R), 2005 U, 2006 E2(R), 2007 NZ2(R)
Britz, W K (N) 2002 W 1
Brooks, D (Bor) 1906 S
Brosnihan, W (GL, N) 1997 A 2, 2000 NZ 1(t+R), A 2(t+R), NZ 2(R), A 3(R), E 3(R)
Brown, C B (WP) 1903 BI 1, 2, 3
Brüssow, H (FS) 2008 E(R), 2009 BI 1, 2(R), 3, NZ1, 2, A1, 2, 3, NZ3
Brynard, G S (WP) 1965 A 1, NZ 1, 2, 3, 4, 1968 BI 3, 4
Buchler, J U (Tvl) 1951 S, I, W, 1952 E, F, 1953 A 1, 2, 3, 4, 1956 A 2
Burdett, A F (WP) 1906 S, I
Burger, J M (WP) 1989 Wld 1, 2
Burger, M B (NT) 1980 BI 2(R), S Am 3, 1981 US (R)
Burger, S W P (WP) 1984 E 1, 2, 1986 Cv 1, 2, 3, 4
Burger, S W P (WP) 2003 [Gg(R), Sm(R), NZ(R)], 2004 I1, 2, W1, PI, NZ1, A1, NZ2, A2, W2, I3, E, 2005 F1, 2, A1, 2(R), 3(R), NZ1, A4, NZ2, Arg(R), W, F3, 2006 S1, 2, 2007 E1, 2, A1, NZ1, Nm, [Sm, US, Fj, Arg, E2], W, 2008 It(R), NZ1, 2, A1, NZ3, A2, 3, W3, S, E, 2009 BI 2, A2(R), 3(R), NZ3
Burger, W A G (Bor) 1906 S, I, W, 1910 BI 2
Carelse, G (EP) 1964 W, F, 1965 I, S, 1967 F 1, 2, 3, 1968 F 1, 2, 1969 A 1, 2, 3, 4, S
Carlson, R A (WP) 1972 E
Carolin, H W (WP) 1903 BI 3, 1906 S, I
Carstens, P D (NS) 2002 S, E, 2006 E1(t&R), 2(R), 2007 E1, 2(t&R), Sm(R), 2009 BI 1(R), 3(t)
Castens, H H (WP) 1891 BI 1
Chavhanga, T (WP) 2005 U, 2007 NZ2(R), 2008 W1, 2
Chignell, T W (WP) 1891 BI 3
Cilliers, G D (OFS) 1963 A 1, 3, 4
Cilliers, N V (WP) 1996 NZ 3(t)
Claassen, J T (WT) 1955 BI 1, 2, 3, 4, 1956 A 1, 2, NZ 1, 2, 3, 4, 1958 F 1, 2, 1960 S, NZ 1, 2, 3, W, I, 1961 E, S, F, I, A 1, 2, 1962 BI 1, 2, 3, 4
Claassen, W (N) 1981 I 1, 2, NZ 2, 3, US, 1982 S Am 1, 2
Claassens, M (FS) 2004 W2(R), S(R), Arg(R), 2005 Arg(R), W, F3, 2007 A2(R), NZ2(R)
Clark, W H G (Tvl) 1933 A 3
Clarkson, W A (N) 1921 NZ 1, 2, 1924 BI 1
Cloete, H A (WP) 1896 BI 4
Cockrell, C H (WP) 1969 S, 1970 I, W
Cockrell, R J (WP) 1974 F 1, 2, 1975 F 1, 2, 1976 NZ 1, 2, 1977 Wld, 1981 NZ 1, 2(R), 3, US
Coetzee, D (BB) 2002 Sm, 2003 S 1, 2, Arg, A 1, NZ 1, A 2, NZ 2, [U, E, Sm(R), NZ(R)], 2004 S(R), Arg(R), 2006 A1(R)
Coetzee, J H H (WP) 1974 BI 1, 1975 F 2(R), 1976 NZ 1, 2, 3, 4
Conradie, J H (WP) 2002 W 1, 2, Arg (R), Sm, NZ 1, A 1, NZ 2(R), A 2(R), S, E, 2004 W1(R), PI, NZ2, A2, 2005 Arg, 2008 W1, 2(R), NZ1(R)
Cope, D K (Tvl) 1896 BI 2
Cotty, W (GW) 1896 BI 3
Crampton, G (GW) 1903 BI 2
Craven, D H (WP) 1931 W, I, 1932 S, 1933 A 1, 2, 3, 4, 5, 1937 A 1, 2, NZ 1, 2, 3, 1938 BI 1, 2, 3
Cronjé, G (BB) 2003 NZ 2, 2004 I2(R), W1(R)
Cronjé, J (BB, GL) 2004 I1, 2, W1, PI, NZ1, A1, NZ2(R), A2(t&R), S(t&R), Arg, 2005 U, F1, 2, A1, 3, NZ1(R), 2(t), Arg, W, F3, 2006 S2(R), F(R), A1(t&R), NZ1, A2, NZ2, A3(R), I(R), E1, 2007 A2(R), NZ2, Nm

Cronje, P A (Tvl) 1971 F 1, 2, A 1, 2, 3, 1974 BI 3, 4
Crosby, J H (Tvl) 1896 BI 2
Crosby, N J (Tvl) 1910 BI 1, 3
Currie, C (GW) 1903 BI 2
D'Alton, G (WP) 1933 A 1
Dalton, J (Tvl, GL, Falcons) 1994 Arg 1(R), 1995 [A, C], W, It, E, 1996 NZ 4(R), 5, Arg 1, 2, F 1, 2, W, 1997 Tg (R), BI 3, NZ 2, A 2, It, F 1, 2, E, S, 1998 I 1, 2, W 1, E 1, A 1, NZ 1, 2, A 2, W 2, S, I 3, E 2, 2002 W 1, 2, Arg, NZ 1, A 1, NZ 2, A 2, F, E
Daneel, G M (WP) 1928 NZ 1, 2, 3, 4, 1931 W, I, 1932 E, S
Daneel, H J (WP) 1906 S, I, W, E
Davidson, C D (N) 2002 W 2(R), Arg, 2003 Arg, NZ 1(R), A 2
Davids, Q (WP) 2002 W 2, Arg (R), Sm (R), 2003 Arg, 2004 I1(R), 2, W1, PI(t&R), NZ1(R)
Davison, P M (EP) 1910 BI 1
De Beer, J H (OFS) 1997 BI 3, NZ 1, A 1, NZ 2, A 2, F 2(R), S, 1999 A 2, [S, Sp, U, E, A 3]
De Bruyn, J (OFS) 1974 BI 3
De Jongh, H P K (WP) 1928 NZ 3
De Klerk, I J (Tvl) 1969 E, 1970 I, W
De Klerk, K B H (Tvl) 1974 BI 1, 2, 3(R), 1975 F 1, 2, 1976 NZ 2(R), 3, 4, 1980 S Am 1, 2, BI 2, 1981 I 1, 2
De Kock, A N (GW) 1891 BI 2
De Kock, D (Falcons) 2001 It 2(R), US
De Kock, J S (WP) 1921 NZ 3, 1924 BI 3
De Kock, N A (WP) 2001 It 1, 2002 Sm (R), NZ 1(R), 2, A 2, F, 2003 [U(R), Gg, Sm(R), NZ(R)]
Delport, G M (GL, Worcester) 2000 C (R), E 1(t+R), A 1, NZ 1, 2, A2, NZ 2, A 3, Arg, I, W, 2001 F 2, It 1, 2003 A 1, NZ 2, [U, E, Sm, NZ]
Delport, W H (EP) 1951 S, I, W, 1952 E, F, 1953 A 1, 2, 3, 4
De Melker, S C (GW) 1903 BI 2, 1906 E
Devenish, C E (GW) 1896 BI 2
Devenish, G St L (Tvl) 1896 BI 2
Devenish, G E (Tvl) 1891 BI 1
De Villiers, D I (Tvl) 1910 BI 1, 2, 3
De Villiers, D J (WP, Bol) 1962 BI 2, 3, 1965 I, NZ 1, 3, 4, 1967 F 1, 2, 3, 4, 1968 BI 1, 2, 3, 4, F 1, 2, 1969 A 1, 4, E, 1970 I, W, NZ 1, 2, 3, 4
De Villiers, H A (WP) 1906 S, W, E
De Villiers, H O (WP) 1967 F 1, 2, 3, 4, 1968 F 1, 2, 1969 A 1, 2, 3, 4, S, E, 1970 I, W
De Villiers, J (WP) 2002 F, 2004 PI, NZ1, A1, NZ2, A2, W2(R), E, 2005 U, F1, 2, A1, 2, 3, NZ1, A4, NZ2, Arg, W, F3, 2006 S1, NZ2, 3, A3, I, E1, 2, 2007 E1, 2, A1, NZ1, Nm, [Sm], 2008 W1, 2, It, NZ1, 2, A1, Arg, NZ3, A2, 3, W3, S, E, 2009 BI 1, 2, NZ1, 2, A1, 2, 3, NZ3
De Villiers, P du P (WP) 1928 NZ 1, 3, 4, 1932 E, 1933 A 4, 1937 A 1, 2, NZ 1
Devine, D (Tvl) 1924 BI 3, 1928 NZ 2
De Vos, D J J (WP) 1965 S, 1969 A 3, S
De Waal, A N (WP) 1967 F 1, 2, 3, 4
De Waal, P J (WP) 1896 BI 4
De Wet, A E (WP) 1969 A 3, 4, E
De Wet, P J (WP) 1938 BI 1, 2, 3
Dinkelmann, E E (NT) 1951 S, I, 1952 E, F, 1953 A 1, 2
Dirksen, C W (NT) 1963 A 4, 1964 W, 1965 I, S, 1967 F 1, 2, 3, 4, 1968 BI 1, 2
Dlulane, V T (MP) 2004 W2(R)
Dobbin, F J (GW) 1903 BI 1, 2, 1906 S, W, E, 1910 BI 1, 1912 S, I, W
Dobie, J A R (Tvl) 1928 NZ 2
Dormehl, P J (WP) 1896 BI 3, 4
Douglass, F W (EP) 1896 BI 1
Drotské, A E (OFS) 1993 Arg 2, 1995 [WS (R)], 1996 A 1(R), 1997 Tg, BI 1, 2, 3(R), NZ 1, A 1, NZ 2(R), 1998 I 2(R), W 1(R), I 3(R), 1999 It 1, 2, W, NZ 1, A 1, NZ 2, A 2, [S, Sp, U, E, A 3, NZ 3]

Le Roux, A H (OFS, N) 1994 E 1, 1998 I 1, 2, W 1(R), E 1(R), A 1(R), NZ 1(R), 2(R), A 2(R), W 2(R), S (R), I 3(R), E 2(t+R), 1999 It 1(R), 2(R), W (R), NZ 1(R), A 1(R), NZ 2(R), A 2(R), [S(R), Sp, U (R), E (R), A 3(R), NZ 3(R)], 2000 E 1(t+R), 2(R), A 1(R), 2(R), NZ 2, A 3(R), Arg (R), I (t), W (R), E 3(R), 2001 F 1(R), 2, It 1, NZ 1(R), A 1(R), 2(R), NZ 2(R), F 3, It 2, E, US (R), 2002 W 1(R), 2(R), Arg, NZ 1(R), A 1(R), NZ 2(R), A 2(R)
Le Roux, H P (Tvl) 1993 F 1, 2, 1994 E 1, 2, NZ 1, 2, 3, Arg 2, S, W, 1995 WS [A, R, C (R), WS, F, NZ], W, It, E, 1996 Fj, NZ 2, Arg 1, 2, F 1, 2, W
Le Roux, J H S (Tvl) 1994 E 2, NZ 1, 2
Le Roux, M (OFS) 1980 BI 1, 2, 3, 4, S Am 3, 4, F, 1981 I 1
Le Roux, P A (WP) 1906 I, W, E
Little, E M (GW) 1891 BI 1, 3
Lobberts, H (BB) 2006 E1(R), 2007 NZ2(R)
Lochner, G P (WP) 1955 BI 3, 1956 A 1, 2, NZ 1, 2, 3, 4, 1958 F 1, 2
Lochner, G P (EP) 1937 NZ 3, 1938 BI 1, 2
Lockyear, R J (GW) 1960 NZ 1, 2, 3, 4, 1960 I, 1961 F 1
Lombard, A C (EP) 1910 BI 2
Lombard, F (FS) 2002 S, E
Lötter, D (Tvl) 1993 F 2, A 1, 2
Lotz, J W (Tvl) 1937 A 1, 2, NZ 1, 2, 3, 1938 BI 1, 2, 3
Loubscher, R I P (EP, N) 2002 W 1, 2003 S 1, [U(R), Gg]
Loubser, J A (WP) 1903 BI 3, 1906 S, I, W, E, 1910 BI 1, 3
Lourens, M J (NT) 1968 BI 2, 3, 4
Louw, F H (WP) 2002 W 2(R), Arg, Sm
Louw, J S (Tvl) 1891 BI 1, 2, 3
Louw, M J (Tvl) 1971 A 2, 3
Louw, M M (WP) 1928 NZ 3, 4, 1931 W, I, 1932 E, S, 1933 A 1, 2, 3, 4, 5, 1937 A 1, 2, NZ 2, 3, 1938 BI 1, 2, 3
Louw, R J (WP) 1980 S Am 1, 2, BI 1, 2, 3, 4 S Am 3, 4, F, 1981 I 1, 2, NZ 1, 3, 1982 S Am 1, 2, 1984 E 1, 2, S Am 1, 2
Louw, S C (WP) 1933 A 1, 2, 3, 4, 5, 1937 A 1, NZ 1, 2, 3, 1938 BI 1, 2, 3
Lubbe, E (GW) 1997 Tg, BI 1
Luyt, F P (WP) 1910 BI 1, 2, 3, 1912 S, I, W, 1913 E
Luyt, J D (EP) 1912 S, W, 1913 E, F
Luyt, R R (W P) 1910 BI 2, 3, 1912 S, I, W, 1913 E, F
Lyons, D J (EP) 1896 BI 1
Lyster, P J (N) 1933 A 2, 5, 1937 NZ 1
McCallum, I D (WP) 1970 NZ 1, 2, 3, 4, 1971 F 1, 2, A 1, 2, 3, 1974 BI 1, 2
McCallum, R J (WP) 1974 BI 1
McCulloch, J D (GW) 1913 E, F
MacDonald, A W (R) 1965 A 1, NZ 1, 2, 3, 4
Macdonald, D A (WP) 1974 BI 2
Macdonald, I (Tvl) 1992 NZ, A, 1993 F 1, A 3, 1994 E 2, 1995 WS (R)
McDonald, J A J (WP) 1931 W, I, 1932 E, S
McEwan, W M C (Tvl) 1903 BI 1, 3
McHardy, E E (OFS) 1912 S, I, W, 1913 E, F
McKendrick, J A (WP) 1891 BI 3
Malan, A S (Tvl) 1960 NZ 1, 2, 3, 4, W, I, 1961 E, S, F, 1962 BI 1, 1963 A 1, 2, 3, 1964 W, 1965 I, S
Malan, A W (NT) 1989 Wld 1, 2, 1992 NZ, A, F 1, 2, E
Malan, E (NT) 1980 BI 3(R), 4
Malan, G F (WP) 1958 F 2, 1960 NZ 1, 3, 4, 1961 E, S, F, 1962 BI 1, 2, 3, 1963 A 1, 2, 4, 1964 W, 1965 A 1, 2, NZ 1, 2
Malan, P (Tvl) 1949 NZ 4
Mallett, N V H (WP) 1984 S Am 1, 2
Malotana, K (Bor) 1999 [Sp]
Mans, W J (WP) 1965 I, S
Marais, C F (WP) 1999 It 1(R), 2(R), 2000 C, E 1, 2, A 1, NZ 1, A 2, NZ 2, A 3, Arg (R), W (R)
Marais, F P (Bol) 1949 NZ 1, 2, 1951 S, 1953 A 1, 2
Marais, J F K (WP) 1963 A 3, 1964 W, F, 1965 I, S, A 2, 1968 BI, 1, 2, 3, 4, F 1, 2, 1969 A 1, 2, 3, 4, S,

E, 1970 I, W, NZ 1, 2, 3, 4, 1971 F 1, 2, A 1, 2, 3, 1974 BI 1, 2, 3, 4, F 1, 2
Maré, D S (Tvl) 1906 S
Marsberg, A F W (GW) 1906 S, W, E
Marsberg, P A (GW) 1910 BI 1
Martheze, W C (GW) 1903 BI 2, 1906 I, W
Martin, H J (Tvl) 1937 A 2
Matfield, V (BB) 2001 It 1(R), NZ 1, A 2, NZ 2, F 3, It 2, E, US, 2002 W 1, Sm, NZ 1, A 1, NZ 2(R), 2003 S 1, 2, Arg, A 1, NZ 1, A 2, NZ 2, [U, E, Sm, NZ], 2004 I1, 2, W1, NZ2, A2, W2, I3, E, S, Arg, 2005 F1, 2, A1, 2, 3, NZ1, A4, NZ2, Arg, W, F3, 2006 S1, 2, F, A1, NZ1, A2, NZ2, 3, A3, 2007 E1, 2, A1, NZ1, Nm, S, [Sm, E1, Tg(R), US, Fj, Arg, E2], 2008 W1(R), 2, It, NZ1, 2, A1, Arg, NZ3, A2, 3, W3, S, E, 2009 BI 1, 2, 3, NZ1, 2, A1, 2, 3, NZ3
Mellet, T B (GW) 1896 BI 2
Mellish, F W (WP) 1921 NZ 1, 3, 1924 BI 1, 2, 3, 4
Mentz, H (N) 2004 I1, W1(R)
Merry, J (EP) 1891 BI 1
Metcalf, H D (Bor) 1903 BI 2
Meyer, C du P (WP) 1921 NZ 1, 2, 3
Meyer, P J (GW) 1896 BI 1
Meyer, W (OFS, GL) 1997 S (R), 1999 It 2, NZ 1(R), A 1(R), 2000 C (R), E 1, NZ 1(R), 2(R), Arg, I, W, E 3, 2001 F 1(R), 2, It 1, F 3(R), It 2, E, US (t+R), 2002 W 1, 2, Arg, NZ 1, 2, A 2, F
Michau, J M (Tvl) 1921 NZ 1
Michau, J P (WP) 1921 NZ 1, 2, 3
Millar, W A (WP) 1906 E, 1910 BI 2, 3, 1912 I, W, 1913 F
Mills, W J (WP) 1910 BI 2
Moll, T (Tvl) 1910 BI 2
Montini, P E (WP) 1956 A 1, 2
Montgomery, P C (WP, Newport, N, Perpignan) 1997 BI 2, 3, NZ 1, A 1, NZ 2, A 2, F 1, 2, E, S, 1998 I 1, 2, W 1, E 1, A 1, NZ 1, 2, A 2, W 2, S, I 3, E 2, 1999 It 1, 2, W, NZ 1, A 1, NZ 2, A 2, [S, U, E, A 3, NZ 3], 2000 C, E 1, 2, A 1, NZ 1, A 2(R), Arg, I, W, E 3, 2001 F 1, 2(t), It 1, F 3(R), It 2(R), 2004 I2, W1, PI, A1, NZ2, A2, W2, I3, E, S, 2005 U, F1, 2, A1, 2, 3, NZ1, A4, NZ2, Arg, W, F3, 2006 S1, 2, F, A1, NZ1, A2, NZ2, 2007 E1, 2, Sm(R), A1, NZ1, Nm, S, [Sm, E1, Tg(R), US, Fj, Arg, E2], 2008 W1(R), 2(R), NZ1(R), 2, Arg(R), NZ3, A2(R), 3(R)
Moolman, L C (NT) 1977 Wld, 1980 S Am 1, 2, BI 1, 2, 3, 4, S Am 3, 4, F, 1981 I 1, 2, NZ 1, 2, 3, US, 1982 S Am 1, 2, 1984 S Am 1, 2, 1986 Cv 1, 2, 3, 4
Mordt, R H (Z-R, NT) 1980 S Am 1, 2, BI 1, 2, 3, 4, S Am 3, 4, F, 1981 I 2, NZ 1, 2, 3, US, 1982 S Am 1, 2, 1984 S Am 1, 2
Morkel, D A (Tvl) 1903 BI 1
Morkel, D F T (Tvl) 1906 I, E, 1910 BI 1, 3, 1912 S, I, W, 1913 E, F
Morkel, H J (WP) 1921 NZ 1
Morkel, H W (WP) 1921 NZ 1, 2
Morkel, J A (WP) 1921 NZ 2, 3
Morkel, J W H (WP) 1912 S, I, W, 1913 E, F
Morkel, P G (WP) 1912 S, I, W, 1913 E, F, 1921 NZ 1, 2, 3
Morkel, P K (WP) 1928 NZ 4
Morkel, W H (WP) 1910 BI 3, 1912 S, I, W, 1913 E, F, 1921 NZ 1, 2, 3
Morkel, W S (Tvl) 1906 S, I, W, E
Moss, C (N) 1949 NZ 1, 2, 3, 4
Mostert, P J (WP) 1921 NZ 1, 2, 3, 1924 BI 1, 2, 4, 1928 NZ 1, 2, 3, 4, 1931 W, I, 1932 E, S
Mtawarira, T (NS) 2008 W2, It, A1(R), Arg, NZ3, A2, 3, W3, S, E, 2009 BI 1, 2, 3, NZ1, 2, A1, 2, 3, NZ3
Muir, D J (WP) 1997 It, F 1, 2, E, S
Mujati, B V (WP) 2008 W1, It(R), NZ1(R), 2(t), A1(R), Arg(R), NZ3(R), A2(R), 3, W3(t), S(R), E(R)
Mulder, J C (Tvl, GL) 1994 NZ 2, 3, S, W, 1995 WS,

[A, WS, F, NZ], W, It, E, 1996 Fj, A 1, NZ 1, A 2, NZ 2, 5, Arg 1, 2, F 1, 2, W, 1997 Tg, BI 1, 1999 It 1(R), 2, W, NZ 1, 2000 C(R), A 1, E 3, 2001 F 1, It 1

Muller, G H (WP) 1969 A 3, 4, S, 1970 W, NZ 1, 2, 3, 4, 1971 F 1, 2, 1972 E, 1974 BI 1, 3, 4

Muller, G J (NS) 2006 S1(R), NZ1(R), A2, NZ2, 3, A3, I(R), E1, 2, 2007 E1(R), 2(R), Sm(R), A1(R), NZ1(R), A2, NZ2, Nm(R), [Sm(R), E1(R), Fj(t&R)], Arg(t&R)], W, 2009 BI 3

Muller, G P (GL) 2003 A 2, NZ 2, [E, Gg(R), Sm, NZ]

Muller, H L (OFS) 1986 Cv 4(R), 1989 Wld 1(R)

Muller, H S V (Tvl) 1949 NZ 1, 2, 3, 4, 1951 S, I, W, 1952 E, F, 1953 A 1, 2, 3, 4

Muller, L J J (N) 1992 NZ, A

Muller, P G (N) 1992 NZ, A, F 1, 2, E, 1993 F 1, 2, A 1, 2, 3, Arg 1, 2, 1994 E 1, 2, NZ 1, S, W, 1998 I 1, 2, W 1, E 1, A 1, NZ 1, 2, A 2, 1999 It 1, W, NZ 1, A 1, [Sp, E, A 3, NZ 3]

Murray, W M (N) 2007 Sm, A2, NZ2

Myburgh, F R (EP) 1896 BI 1

Myburgh, J L (NT) 1962 BI 1, 1963 A 4, 1964 W, F, 1968 BI 1, 2, 3, F 1, 2, 1969 A 1, 2, 3, 4, E, 1970 I, W, NZ 3, 4

Myburgh, W H (WT) 1924 BI 1

Naude, J P (WP) 1963 A 4, 1965 A 1, 2, NZ 1, 3, 4, 1967 F 1, 2, 3, 4, 1968 BI 1, 2, 3, 4

Ndungane, A Z (BB) 2006 A1, 2, NZ2, 3, A3, E1, 2, 2007 E2, Nm(R), [US], W(R)

Ndungane, O M (NS) 2008 It, NZ1, A3, 2009 BI 3, A3, NZ3

Neethling, J B (WP) 1967 F 1, 2, 3, 4, 1968 BI 4, 1969 S, 1970 NZ 1, 2

Nel, J A (Tvl) 1960 NZ 1, 2, 1963 A 1, 2, 1965 A 2, NZ 1, 2, 3, 4, 1970 NZ 3, 4

Nel, J J (WP) 1956 A 1, 2, NZ 1, 2, 3, 4, 1958 F 1, 2

Nel, P A R O (Tvl) 1903 BI 1, 2, 3

Nel, P J (N) 1928 NZ 1, 2, 3, 4, 1931 W, I, 1932 E, S, 1933 A 1, 3, 4, 5, 1937 A 1, 2, NZ 2, 3

Nimb, C F (WP) 1961 I

Nokwe, J L (FS) 2008 Arg, A2, 3, 2009 BI 3

Nomis, S H (Tvl) 1967 F 4, 1968 BI 1, 2, 3, 4, F 1, 2, 1969 A 1, 2, 3, 4, S, E, 1970 I, W, NZ 1, 2, 3, 4, 1971 F 1, 2, A 1, 2, 3, 1972 E

Nykamp, J L (Tvl) 1933 A 2

Ochse, J K (WP) 1951 I, W, 1952 E, F, 1953 A 1, 2, 4

Oelofse, J S A (Tvl) 1953 A 1, 2, 3, 4

Oliver, F (Tvl) 1928 NZ 3, 4

Olivier, E (WP) 1967 F 1, 2, 3, 4, 1968 BI 1, 2, 3, 4, F 1, 2, 1969 A 1, 2, 3, 4, S, E

Olivier, J (NT) 1992 F 1, 2, E, 1993 F 1, 2 A 1, 2, 3, Arg 1, 1995 W, It (R), E, 1996 Arg 1, 2, F 1, 2, W

Olivier, W (BB) 2006 S1(R), 2, F, A1, NZ1, A2, NZ2(R), 3, A3, I(R), E1, 2, 2007 E1, 2, NZ1(R), A2, NZ2, [E1(R), Tg, Arg(R)], W(R), 2009 BI 3, NZ1(R), 2(R)

Olver, E (EP) 1896 BI 1

Oosthuizen, J J (WP) 1974 BI 1, F 1, 2, 1975 F 1, 2, 1976 NZ 1, 2, 3, 4

Oosthuizen, O W (NT, Tvl) 1981 I 1(R), 2, NZ 2, 3, US, 1982 S Am 1, 2, 1984 E 1, 2

Osler, B L (WP) 1924 BI 1, 2, 3, 4, 1928 NZ 1, 2, 3, 4, 1931 W, I, 1932 E, S, 1933 A 1, 2, 3, 4, 5

Osler, S G (WP) 1928 NZ 1

Otto, K (NT, BB) 1995 [R, C (R), WS (R)], 1997 BI 3, NZ 1, A 1, NZ 2, It, F 1, 2, E, S, 1998 I 1, 2, W 1, E 1, A 1, NZ 1, 2, A 2, W 2, S I 3, E 2, 1999 It 1, W, NZ 1, A 1, [S (R), Sp, U, E, A 3, NZ 3], 2000 C, E 1, 2, A 1

Oxlee, K (N) 1960 NZ 1, 2, 3, 4, W, I, 1961 S, A 1, 2, 1962 BI 1, 2, 3, 4, 1963 A 1, 2, 4, 1964 W, 1965 NZ 1, 2

Pagel, G L (WP) 1995 [A (R), R, C, NZ (R)], 1996 NZ 5(R)

Parker, W H (EP) 1965 A 1, 2

Partridge, J E C (Tvl) 1903 BI 1

Paulse, B J (WP) 1999 It 1, 2, NZ 1, A 1, 2(R), [S (R),

Sp, NZ 3], 2000 C, E 1, 2, A 1, NZ 1, A 2, NZ 2, A 3, Arg, W, E 3, 2001 F 1, 2, It 1, NZ 1, A 1, 2, NZ 2, F 3, It 2, E, 2002 W 1, 2, Arg, Sm (R), A 1, NZ 2, A 2, F, S, E, 2003 [Gg], 2004 I1, 2, W1, PI, NZ1, A1, NZ2, A2, W2, I3, E, 2005 A2, 3, NZ1, A4, F3, 2006 S1, 2, A1(R), NZ1, 3(R), A3(R), 2007 A2, NZ2

Payn, C (N) 1924 BI 1, 2

Pelser, H J M (Tvl) 1958 F 1, 1960 NZ 1, 2, 3, 4, W, I, 1961 F, I, A 1, 2

Pfaff, B D (WP) 1956 A 1

Pickard, J A J (WP) 1953 A 3, 4, 1956 NZ 2, 1958 F 2

Pienaar, J F (Tvl) 1993 F 1, 2, A 1, 2, 3, Arg 1, 2, 1994 E 1, 2, NZ 2, 3, Arg 1, 2, S, W, 1995 WS, [A, C, WS, F, NZ], W, It, E, 1996 Fj, A 1, NZ 1, A 2, NZ 2

Pienaar, R (NS) 2006 NZ2(R), 3(R), A3(R), I(t), E1(R), 2007 E1(R), 2(R), Sm(R), A1, NZ1, A2, NZ2, Nm(R), S(R), [E1(t&R), Tg, US(R), Arg(R)], W, 2008 W1(R), It(R), NZ2(R), A1(R), 3(R), W3, S, E, 2009 BI 1, 2, 3(R), NZ1, A1(R), 2, 3

Pienaar, Z M J (OFS) 1980 S Am 2(R), BI 1, 2, 3, 4, S Am 3, 4, F, 1981 I 1, 2, NZ 1, 2, 3

Pietersen, J-P R (NS) 2006 A3, 2007 Sm, A1, NZ1, A2, NZ2, Nm, S, [Sm, E1, Tg, US(R), Fj, Arg, E2], W, 2008 NZ2, A1, Arg, NZ3, A2, W3, S, E, 2009 BI 1, 2, NZ1, 2, A1, 2

Pitzer, G (NT) 1967 F 1, 2, 3, 4, 1968 BI 1, 2, 3, 4, F 1, 2, 1969 A 3, 4

Pope, C F (WP) 1974 BI 1, 2, 3, 4, 1975 F 1, 2, 1976 NZ 2, 3, 4

Potgieter, H J (OFS) 1928 NZ 1, 2

Potgieter, H L (OFS) 1977 Wld

Powell, A W (GW) 1896 BI 3

Powell, J M (GW) 1891 BI 2, 1896 BI 3, 1903 BI 1, 2

Prentis, R B (Tvl) 1980 S Am 1, 2, BI 1, 2, 3, 4, S Am 3, 4, F, 1981 I 1, 2

Pretorius, A S (GL) 2002 W 1, 2, Arg, Sm, NZ 1, A 1, NZ 2, F, S (R), E, 2003 NZ 1(R), A 1, 2005 A2, 3, NZ1, A4, NZ2, Arg, 2006 NZ2(R), 3, A3, I, E1(t&R), 2, 2007 S(R), [Sm(R), E1(R), Tg, US(R), Arg(R)], W

Pretorius, J C (GL) 2006 I, 2007 NZ2

Pretorius, N F (Tvl) 1928 NZ 1, 2, 3, 4

Prinsloo, J (Tvl) 1958 F 1, 2

Prinsloo, J (NT) 1963 A 3

Prinsloo, J P (Tvl) 1928 NZ 1

Putter, D J (WT) 1963 A 1, 2, 4

Raaff, J W E (GW) 1903 BI 1, 2, 1906 S, W, E, 1910 BI 1

Ralepelle, M C (BB) 2006 NZ2(R), E2(R), 2008 E(t&R), 2009 BI 3, NZ1(R), 2(R), A2(R), NZ3(R)

Ras, W J de Wet (OFS) 1976 NZ 1(R), 1980 S Am 2(R)

Rautenbach, S J (WP) 2002 W 1(R), 2(t+R), Arg (R), Sm, NZ 1(R), A 1, NZ 2(R), A 2(R), 2003 [U(R), Gg, Sm, NZ], 2004 W1, NZ1(R)

Reece-Edwards, H (N) 1992 F 1, 2, 1993 A 2

Reid, A (WP) 1903 BI 3

Reid, B C (Bor) 1933 A 4

Reinach, J (OFS) 1986 Cv 1, 2, 3, 4

Rens, I J (Tvl) 1953 A 3, 4

Retief, D F (NT) 1955 BI 1, 2, 4, 1956 A 1, 2, NZ 1, 2, 3, 4

Reyneke, H J (WP) 1910 BI 3

Richards, A R (WP) 1891 BI 1, 2, 3

Richter, A (NT) 1992 F 1, 2, E, 1994 E 2, NZ 1, 2, 3, 1995 [R, C, WS (R)]

Riley, N M (ET) 1963 A 3

Riordan, C A (Tvl) 1910 BI 1, 2

Robertson, I W (R) 1974 F 1, 2, 1976 NZ 1, 2, 4

Rodgers, P H (NT, Tvl) 1989 Wld 1, 2, 1992 NZ, F 1, 2

Rogers, C D (Tvl) 1984 E 1, 2, S Am 1, 2

Roos, G D (WP) 1910 BI 2, 3

Roos, P J (WP) 1903 BI 3, 1906 I, W, E

Rosenberg, W (Tvl) 1955 BI 2, 3, 4, 1956 NZ 3, 1958 F 1

Rossouw, C L C (Tvl, N) 1995 WS, [R, WS, F, NZ], 1999 NZ 2(R), A 2(t), [Sp, NZ 3(R)]
Rossouw, D H (WP) 1953 A 3, 4
Rossouw, D J (BB) 2003 [U, Gg, Sm(R), NZ], 2004 E(R), S, Arg, 2005 U, F1, 2, A1, W(R), F3(R), 2006 S1, 2, F, A1, I, E1, 2, 2007 E1, Sm, A1(R), NZ1, S, [Sm, Tg, Fj, Arg, E2], 2008 W1(t&R), NZ3(R), A3(R), S(R), E, 2009 BI 1(R), 2(R), NZ1(R), 2(R), A1(R), 3(R), NZ3(R)
Rossouw, P W G (WP) 1997 BI 2, 3, NZ 1, A 1, NZ 2(R), A 2(R), It, F 1, 2, E, S, 1998 I 1, 2, W 1, E 1, A 1, NZ 1, 2, A 2, W 2, S, I 3, E 2, 1999 It 1, W, NZ 1, A 1(R), NZ 2, A 2, [S, U, E, A 3], 2000 C, E 1, 2, A 2, Arg (R), I, W, 2001 F 3, US, 2003 Arg
Rousseau, W P (WP) 1928 NZ 3, 4
Roux, F du T (WP) 1960 W, 1961 A 1, 2, 1962 BI 1, 2, 3, 4, 1963 A 2, 1965 A 1, 2, NZ 1, 2, 3, 4, 1968 BI 3, 4, F 1, 2 1969 A 1, 2, 3, 4, 1970 I, NZ 1, 2, 3, 4
Roux, J P (Tvl) 1994 E 2, NZ 1, 2, 3, Arg 1, 1995 [R, C, F (R)], 1996 A 1(R), NZ 1, A 2, NZ 3
Roux, O A (NT) 1969 S, E, 1970 I, W, 1972 E, 1974 BI 3, 4
Roux, W G (BB) 2002 F (R), S, E
Russell, R B (MP, N) 2002 W 1(R), 2, Arg, A 1(R), NZ 2(R), A 2, F, E (R), 2003 Arg (R), A 1(R), NZ 1, A 2(R), 2004 I2(t&R), W1, NZ1(R), W2(R), Arg(R), 2005 U(R), F2(R), A1(t), Arg(R), W(R), 2006 F
Samuels, T A (GW) 1896 BI 2, 3, 4
Santon, D (Bol) 2003 A 1(R), NZ 1(R), A 2(t), [Gg(R)]
Sauermann, J T (Tvl) 1971 F 1, 2, A 1, 1972 E, 1974 BI 1
Schlebusch, J J J (OFS) 1974 BI 3, 4, 1975 F 2
Schmidt, L U (NT) 1958 F 2, 1962 BI 2
Schmidt, U L (NT, Tvl) 1986 Cv 1, 2, 3, 4, 1989 Wld 1, 2, 1992 NZ, A, 1993 F 1, 2, A 1, 2, 3, 1994 Arg 1, 2, S, W
Schoeman, J (WP) 1963 A 3, 4, 1965 I, S, A 1, NZ 1, 2
Scholtz, C P (WP, Tvl) 1994 Arg 1, 1995 [R, C, WS]
Scholtz, H (FS) 2002 A 1(R), NZ 2(R), A 2(R), 2003 [U(R), Gg]
Scholtz, H H (WP) 1921 NZ 1, 2
Schutte, P J W (Tvl) 1994 S, W
Scott, P A (Tvl) 1896 BI 1, 2, 3, 4
Sendin, W D (GW) 1921 NZ 2
Sephaka, L D (GL) 2001 US, 2002 Sm, NZ 1, A 1, NZ 2, A 2, F, 2003 S 1, 2, A 1, NZ 1, A 2(t+R), NZ 2, [U, E(t&R), Gg], 2005 F2, A1, 2(R), W, 2006 S1(R), NZ3(t&R), A3(R), I
Serfontein, D J (WP) 1980 BI 1, 2, 3, 4, S Am 3, 4, F, 1981 I 1, 2, NZ 1, 2, 3, US, 1982 S Am 1, 2, 1984 E 1, 2, S Am 1, 2
Shand, R (GW) 1891 BI 2, 3
Sheriff, A R (Tvl) 1938 BI 1, 2, 3
Shimange, M H (FS, WP) 2004 W1(R), NZ2(R), A2(R), W2(R), 2005 U(R), A1(R), 2(R), Arg(R), 2006 S1(R)
Shum, E H (Tvl) 1913 E
Sinclair, D J (Tvl) 1955 BI 1, 2, 3, 4
Sinclair, J H (Tvl) 1903 BI 1
Skene, A L (WP) 1958 F 2
Skinstad, R B (WP, GL, N) 1997 E (t), 1998 W 1(R), E 1(t), NZ 1(R), 2(R), A 2(R), W 2(R), S, I 3, E 2, 1999 [S, Sp (R), U, E, A 3], 2001 F 1(R), 2(R), It 1, NZ 1, A 1, 2, NZ 2, F 3, It 2, E, 2002 W 1, 2, Arg, Sm, NZ 1, A 1, NZ 2, A 2, 2003 Arg (R), 2007 E2(t&R), Sm, NZ1, A2, [E1(R), Tg, US(R), Arg(R)]
Slater, J T (EP) 1924 BI 3, 4, 1928 NZ 1
Smal, G P (WP) 1986 Cv 1, 2, 3, 4, 1989 Wld 1, 2
Small, J T (Tvl, N, WP) 1992 NZ, A, F 1, 2, E, 1993 F 1, 2, A 1, 2, 3, Arg 1, 2, 1994 E 1, 2, NZ 1, 2, 3(t), Arg 1, 1995 WS, [A, R, F, NZ], W, It, E (R), 1996 Fj, A 1, NZ 1, A 2, NZ 2, Arg 1, 2, F 1, 2, W, 1997 Tg, BI 1, NZ 1(R), A 1(R), NZ 2, A 2, It, F 1, 2, E, S
Smit, F C (WP) 1992 E
Smit, J W (NS, Clermont-Auvergne) 2000 C (t), A 1(R), NZ 1(t+R), A 2(R), NZ 2(R), A 3(R), Arg, I, W, E 3, 2001 F 1, 2, It 1, NZ 1(R), A 1(R), 2(R), NZ 2(R), F 3(R), It 2, E, US (R), [U(R), E(t&R), Gg, Sm, NZ], 2004 I1, 2, W1, PI, NZ1, A1, NZ2, A2, W2, I3, E, S, Arg, 2005 U, F1, 2, A1, 2, 3, NZ1, A4, NZ2, Arg, W, F3, 2006 S1, 2, F, A1, NZ1, A2, NZ2, 3, A3, I, E1, 2, 2007 E1, 2, Sm, A1, [Sm, E1, Tg(R), US, Fj, Arg, E2], W, 2008 W1, 2, NZ1, W3, S, E, 2009 BI 1, 2, 3, NZ1, 2, A1, 2, 3, NZ3
Smith, C M (OFS) 1963 A 3, 4, 1964 W, F, 1965 A 1, 2, NZ 2
Smith, C W (GW) 1891 BI 2, 1896 BI 2, 3
Smith, D (GW) 1891 BI 2
Smith D J (Z-R) 1980 BI 1, 2, 3, 4
Smith, G A C (EP) 1938 BI 3
Smith, J H (FS) 2003 S 1(R), 2(R), A 1, NZ 1, A 2, NZ 2, [U, E, Sm, NZ], 2004 W2, 2005 U(R), F2(R), A2, 3, NZ1, A4, NZ2, Arg, W, F3, 2006 S1, 2, F, A1, NZ1, A2, I, E2, 2007 E1, 2, A1, Nm, S, [Sm, E1, Tg(t&R), US, Fj, Arg, E2], W, 2008 W1, 2, It, NZ1, 2, A1, Arg, NZ3, A2, 3, W3, S, 2009 BI 1, 2, 3, NZ1, 2, A1, 2, 3
Smith, P F (GW) 1997 S (R), 1998 I 1(t), 2, W 1, NZ 1(R), 2(R), A 2(R), W 2, 1999 NZ 2
Smollan, F C (Tvl) 1933 A 3, 4, 5
Snedden, R C D (GW) 1891 BI 2
Snyman, A H (NT, BB, N) 1996 NZ 3, 4, Arg 2(R), W (R), 1997 Tg, BI 1, 2, 3, NZ 1, A 1, NZ 2, A 2, It, F 1, 2, E, S, 1998 I 1, 2, W 1, E 1, A 1, NZ 1, 2, A 2, W 2, S, I 3, E 2, 1999 NZ 2, 2001 NZ 2, F 3, US, 2002 W 1, 2003 S 1, NZ 1, 2006 S1, 2
Snyman, D S L (WP) 1972 E, 1974 BI 1, 2(R), F 1, 2, 1975 F 1, 2, 1976 NZ 2, 3, 1977 Wld
Snyman, J C P (OFS) 1974 BI 2, 3, 4
Sonnekus, G H H (OFS) 1974 BI 3, 1984 E 1, 2
Sowerby, R S (N) 2002 Sm (R)
Spies, J J (NT) 1970 NZ 1, 2, 3, 4
Spies, P J (BB) 2006 A1, NZ2, 3, A3, I, E1, 2007 E1(R), 2, A1, 2008 W1, 2, A1, Arg, NZ3, A2, 3, W3, S, E, 2009 BI 1, 2, 3(R), NZ1, 2, A1, 2, 3, NZ3
Stander, J C J (OFS) 1974 BI 4(R), 1976 NZ 1, 2, 3, 4
Stapelberg, W P (NT) 1974 F 1, 2
Starke, J J (WP) 1956 NZ 4
Starke, K T (WP) 1924 BI 1, 2, 3, 4
Steenekamp, J G A (Tvl) 1958 F 1
Steenkamp, G G (FS, BB) 2004 S, Arg, 2005 U, F2(R), A2, 3, NZ1(R), A4(R), 2007 E1(R), 2, A1, [Tg, Fj(R)], 2008 W1, 2(R), NZ1, 2, A1, W3(R), S(R), 2009 BI 1(R), 3(R)
Stegmann, A C (WP) 1906 S, I
Stegmann, J A (Tvl) 1912 S, I, W, 1913 E, F
Stewart, C (WP) 1998 S, I 3, E 2
Stewart, D A (WP) 1960 S, 1961 E, S, F, I, 1963 A 1, 3, 4, 1964 W, F, 1965 I
Steyn, F P L (NS) 2006 I, E1, 2, 2007 E1(R), 2(R), Sm, A1(R), NZ1(R), S, [Sm(R), E1, Tg(R), US, Fj, Arg, E2], W, 2008 W2(R), It, NZ1(R), 2(R), A1, NZ3(R), A2(R), W3(R), S(R), E(R), 2009 BI 1, 2, 3(t&R), NZ1, 2, A1, 2(R), 3(R), NZ3
Steyn, M (BB) 2009 BI 1(t&R), 2(R), 3, NZ1(R), 2, A1, 2, 3, NZ3
Stofberg, M T S (OFS, NT, WP) 1976 NZ 2, 3, 1977 Wld, 1980 S Am 1, 2, BI 1, 2, 3, 4, S Am 3, 4, F, 1981 I 1, 2, NZ 1, 2, US, 1982 S Am 1, 2, 1984 E 1, 2
Strachan, L C (Tvl) 1932 E, S, 1937 A 1, 2, NZ 1, 2, 3, 1938 BI 1, 2, 3
Stransky, J T (N, WP) 1993 A 1, 2, 3, Arg 1, 1994 Arg 1, 2, 1995 WS, [A, R (t), C, F, NZ], W, It, E, 1996 Fj (R), NZ 1, A 2, NZ 2, 3, 4, 5(R)
Straeuli, R A W (Tvl) 1994 NZ 1, Arg 1, 2, S, W, 1995 WS, [A, WS, NZ (R)], E (R)
Strauss, C P (WP) 1992 F 1, 2, E, 1993 F 1, 2, A 1, 2, 3, Arg 1, 2, 1994 E 1, NZ 1, 2, Arg 1, 2
Strauss, J A (WP) 1984 S Am 1, 2
Strauss, J A (FS) 2008 A1(R), Arg(R), NZ3(R), A2(R), 3(R)
Strauss, J H P (Tvl) 1976 NZ 3, 4, 1980 S Am 1
Strauss, S S F (GW) 1921 NZ 3

Strydom, C F (OFS) 1955 BI 3, 1956 A 1, 2, NZ 1, 4, 1958 F 1,
Strydom, J J (Tvl, GL) 1993 F 2, A 1, 2, 3, Arg 1, 2, 1994 E 1, 1995 [A, C, F, NZ], 1996 A 2(R), NZ 2(R), 3, 4, W (R), 1997 Tg, BI 1, 2, 3, A 2
Strydom, L J (NT) 1949 NZ 1, 2
Styger, J J (OFS) 1992 NZ (R), A, F 1, 2, E, 1993 F 2(R), A 3(R)
Suter, M R (N) 1965 I, S
Swanepoel, W (OFS, GL) 1997 BI 3(R), A 2(R), F 1(R), 2, E, S, 1998 I 2(R), W 1(R), E 2(R), 1999 It 1, 2(R), W, A 1, [Sp, NZ 3(t)], 2000 A 1, NZ 1, A 2, NZ 2, A 3
Swart, J (WP) 1996 Fj, NZ 1(R), A 2, NZ 2, 3, 4, 5, 1997 BI 3(R), It, S (R)
Swart, J J N (SWA) 1955 BI 1
Swart, I S (Tvl) 1993 A 1, 2, 3, Arg 1, 1994 E 1, 2, NZ 1, 3, Arg 2(R), 1995 WS, [A, WS, F, NZ], W, 1996 A 2
Taberer, W S (GW) 1896 BI 2
Taylor, O B (N) 1962 BI 1
Terblanche, C S (Bol, N) 1998 I 1, 2, W 1, E 1, A 1, NZ 1, 2, A 2, W 2, S, I 3, E 2, 1999 It 1(R), 2, W, A 1, NZ 2(R), [Sp, E (R), A 3(R), NZ 3], 2000 E 3, 2002 W 1, 2, Arg, Sm, NZ 1, A 1, 2(R), 2003 S 1, 2, Arg, A 1, NZ 1, A 2, NZ 2, [Gg]
Teichmann, G H (N) 1995 W, 1996 Fj, A 1, NZ 1, A 2, NZ 2, 3, 4, 5, Arg 1, 2, F 1, 2, W, 1997 Tg, BI 1, 2, 3, NZ 1, A 1, NZ 2, A 2, It, F 1, 2, E, S, 1998 I 1, 2, W 1, E 1, A 1, NZ 1, 2, A 2, W 2, S, I 3, E 2, 1999 It 1, W, NZ 1
Theron, D F (GW) 1996 A 2(R), NZ 2(R), 5, Arg 1, 2, F 1, 2, W, 1997 BI 2(R), 3, NZ 1(R), A 1, NZ 2(R)
Theunissen, D J (GW) 1896 BI 3
Thompson, G (WP) 1912 S, I, W
Tindall, J C (WP) 1924 BI 1, 1928 NZ 1, 2, 3, 4
Tobias, E G (SARF, Bol) 1981 I 1, 2, 1984 E 1, 2, S Am 1, 2
Tod, N S (N) 1928 NZ 2
Townsend, W H (N) 1921 NZ 1
Trenery, W E (GW) 1891 BI 2
Tromp, H (NT) 1996 NZ3, 4, Arg 2(R), F 1(R)
Truter, D R (WP) 1924 BI 2, 4
Truter, J T (N) 1963 A 1, 1964 F, 1965 A 2
Turner, F G (EP) 1933 A 1, 2, 3, 1937 A 1, 2, NZ 1, 2, 3, 1938 BI 1, 2, 3
Twigge, R J (NT) 1960 S
Tyibilika, S (N) 2004 S, Arg, 2005 U, A2, Arg, 2006 NZ1, A2, NZ2
Ulyate, C A (Tvl) 1955 BI 1, 2, 3, 4, 1956 NZ 1, 2, 3
Uys, P de W (NT) 1960 W, 1961 E, S, I, A 1, 2, 1962 BI 1, 4, 1963 A 1, 2, 1969 A 1(R), 2
Uys, P J (Pumas) 2002 S
Van Aswegen, H J (WP) 1981 NZ 1, 1982 S Am 2(R)
Van Biljon, L (N) 2001 It 1(R), NZ 1, A 1, 2, NZ 2, F 3, It 2(R), E (R), US, 2002 F (R), S, E (R), 2003 NZ 2(R)
Van Broekhuizen, H D (WP) 1896 BI 4
Van Buuren, M C (Tvl) 1891 BI 1
Van de Vyver, D F (WP) 1937 A 2
Van den Berg, D S (N) 1975 F 1, 2, 1976 NZ 1, 2
Van den Berg, M A (WP) 1937 A 1, NZ 1, 2, 3
Van den Berg, P A (WP, GW, N) 1999 It 1(R), 2, NZ 2, A 2, [S, U (t+R), E (R), A 3(R), NZ 2(R), A 1, NZ 2, A 2, NZ 2(R), A 3(t+R), Arg, I, W, E 3, 2001 F 1(R), 2, A 2(R), NZ 2(R), US, 2004 NZ1, 2005 U, F1, 2, A1(R), 2(R), 3(R), 4(R), F3(R), 2006 S2(R), A1(R), NZ1, A2(R), NZ2(R), A3(R), I, E1(R), 2(R), 2007 Sm, A2(R), NZ2, Nm(t&R), S(R), [Tg, US], W(R)
Van den Bergh, E (EP) 1994 Arg 2(t & R)
Van der Linde, A (WP) 1995 It, E, 1996 Arg 1(R), 2(R), F 1(R), W (R), 2001 F 3(R)
Van der Linde, C J (FS) 2002 S (R), E(R), 2004 I1(R), 2(R), PI(R), A1(R), NZ2(t&R), A2(R), W2(R), I3(R), E(t&R), S, Arg, 2005 U, F1(R), 2, A1(R), 2(R), NZ1, A4, NZ2, I, E1, 2, 2007 E1(R), 2, A1(R), NZ1(R), A2, NZ2, Nm, S, [Sm, E1(R), Tg, US(R), Arg, E2], W, 2008 W1(t&R), It, NZ1, 2, A1, Arg, NZ3, A2

Van der Merwe, A J (Bol) 1955 BI 2, 3, 4, 1956 A 1, 2, NZ 1, 2, 3, 4, 1958 F 1, 1960 S, NZ 2
Van der Merwe, A V (WP) 1931 W
Van der Merwe, B S (NT) 1949 NZ 1
Van der Merwe, H S (NT) 1960 NZ 4, 1963 A 2, 3, 4, 1964 F
Van der Merwe, H S (GL) 2007 W(t+R)
Van der Merwe, J P (WP) 1970 W
Van der Merwe, P R (SWD, WT, GW) 1981 NZ 2, 3, US, 1986 Cv 1, 2, 1989 Wld 1
Vanderplank, B E (N) 1924 BI 3, 4
Van der Schyff, J H (GW) 1949 NZ 1, 2, 3, 4, 1955 BI 1
Van der Watt, A E (WP) 1969 S (R), E, 1970 I
Van der Westhuizen, J C (WP) 1928 NZ 2, 3, 4, 1931 I
Van der Westhuizen, J H (WP) 1931 I, 1932 E, S
Van der Westhuizen, J H (NT, BB) 1993 Arg 1, 2, 1994 E 1, 2(R), Arg 2, S, W, 1995 WS, [A, C (R), WS, F, NZ], W, It, E, 1996 Fj, A 1, 2(R), NZ 2, 3(R), 4, 5, Arg 1, 2, F 1, 2, W, 1997 Tg, BI 1, 2, 3, NZ 1, A 1, NZ 2, A 2, It, F 1, 1998 I 1, 2, W 1, E 1, A 1, NZ 1, 2, A 2, W 2, S, I 3, E 2, 1999 NZ 2, A 2, [S, Sp (R), U, E, A 3, NZ 3], 2000 C, E 1, 2, A 1(R), NZ 1(R), A 2(R), Arg, I, W, E 3, 2001 F 1, 2, It 1(R), NZ 1, A 1, 2, NZ 2, F 3, It 2, E, US (R), 2003 S 1, 2, A 1, NZ 1, A 2(R), NZ 2, [U, E, Sm, NZ]
Van der Westhuyzen, J N B (MP, BB) 2000 NZ 2(R), 2001 It 1(R), 2003 S 1(R), 2, Arg, A 1, 2003 [E, Sm, NZ], 2004 I1, 2, W1, PI, NZ1, A1, NZ2, A2, W2, I3, E, S, Arg, 2005 U, F1, 2, A1, 4(R), NZ2(R), 2006 S1, 2, F, A1
Van Druten, N J V (Tvl) 1924 BI 1, 2, 3, 4, 1928 NZ 1, 2, 3, 4
Van Heerden, A J (Tvl) 1921 NZ 1, 3
Van Heerden, F J (WP) 1994 E 1, 2(R), NZ 3, 1995 It, E, 1996 NZ 5(R), Arg 1(R), 2(R), 1997 Tg, BI 2(t+R), 3(R), NZ 1(R), 2(R), 1999 [Sp]
Van Heerden, J L (NT, Tvl) 1974 BI 3, 4, F 1, 2, 1975 F 1, 2, 1976 NZ 1, 2, 3, 4, 1977 Wld, 1980 BI 1, 3, 4, S Am 3, 4, F
Van Heerden, J L (BB) 2003 S 1, 2, A 1, NZ 1, A 2(t), 2007 A2, NZ2, S(R), [Sm(R), E1, Tg, US, Fj(R), E2(R)]
Van Jaarsveld, C J (Tvl) 1949 NZ 1
Van Jaarsveldt, D C (R) 1960 S
Van Niekerk, J A (WP) 1928 NZ 4
Van Niekerk, J C (GL, WP) 2001 NZ 1(R), A 1(R), NZ 2(t+R), F 3(R), It2, US, 2002 W 1(R), 2(R), Arg (R), Sm, NZ 1, A 1, NZ 2, A 2, F, S, E, 2003 A 2, NZ 2, [U, E, Gg, Sm], 2004 NZ1(R), A1(t), NZ2, A2, W2, I3, E, S, Arg(R), 2005 U(R), F2(R), A1(R), 2, 3, NZ1, A4, NZ2, 2006 S1, 2, F, A1, NZ1(R), A2(R), 2008 It(R), NZ1, 2, Arg(R), A2(R)
Van Reenen, G L (WP) 1937 A 2, NZ 1
Van Renen, C G (WP) 1891 BI 3, 1896 BI 1, 4
Van Renen, W (WP) 1903 BI 1, 3
Van Rensburg, J T J (Tvl) 1992 NZ, A, E, 1993 F 1, 2, A 1, 1994 NZ 2
Van Rooyen, G W (Tvl) 1921 NZ 2, 3
Van Ryneveld, R C B (WP) 1910 BI 2, 3
Van Schalkwyk, D (NT) 1996 Fj (R), NZ 3, 4, 5, 1997 BI 2, 3, NZ 1, 2, 3, 4
Van Schoor, R A M (R) 1949 NZ 2, 3, 4, 1951 S, I, W, 1952 E, F, 1953 A 1, 2, 3, 4
Van Straaten, A J J (WP) 1999 It 2(R), W, NZ 1(R), A 1, 2000 C, E 1, 2, NZ 1, A 2, NZ 2, A 3, Arg (R), I (R), W, E 3, 2001 A 1, 2, NZ 2, F 3, It 2, E
Van Vollenhoven, K T (NT) 1955 BI 1, 2, 3, 4, 1956 A 1, 2, NZ 3
Van Vuuren, T F (EP) 1912 S, I, W, 1913 E, F
Van Wyk, C J (Tvl) 1951 S, I, W, 1952 E, F, 1953 A 1, 2, 3, 4, 1955 BI 1
Van Wyk, J F B (NT) 1970 NZ 1, 2, 3, 4, 1971 F 1, 2, A 1, 2, 3, 1972 E, 1974 BI 1, 3, 4, 1976 NZ 3, 4
Van Wyk, S P (WP) 1928 NZ 1, 2
Van Zyl, B P (WP) 1961 I
Van Zyl, C G P (OFS) 1965 NZ 1, 2, 3, 4

Van Zyl, D J (WP) 2000 E 3(R)
Van Zyl, G H (WP) 1958 F 1, 1960 S, NZ 1, 2, 3, 4, W, I, 1961 E, S, F, I, A 1, 2, 1962 BI 1, 3, 4
Van Zyl, H J (Tvl) 1960 NZ 1, 2, 3, 4, I, 1961 E, S, I, A 1, 2
Van Zyl, P J (Bol) 1961 I
Veldsman, P E (WP) 1977 Wld
Venter, A G (OFS) 1996 NZ 3, 4, 5, Arg 1, 2, F 1, 2, W, 1997 Tg, BI 1, 2, 3, NZ 1, A 1, NZ 2, It, F 1, 2, E, S, 1998 I 1, 2, W 1, E 1, A 1, NZ 1, 2, A 2, W 2, S (R), I 3(R), E 2(R), 1999 It 1, 2(R), W (R), NZ 1, A 1, NZ 2, A 2, [S, U, E, A 3, NZ 3], 2000 C, E 1, 2, A 1, NZ 1, A 2, NZ 2, A 3, Arg, I, W, E 3, 2001 F 1, It 1, NZ 1, A 1, 2, NZ 2, F 3(R), It 2(R), E (t+R), US (R)
Venter, A J (N) 2000 W (R), E 3(R), 2001 F 3, It 2, E, US, 2002 W 1, 2, Arg, NZ 1(R), 2, A 2, F, S (R), E, 2003 Arg, 2004 PI, NZ1, A1, NZ2(R), A2, I3, E, 2006 NZ3, A3
Venter, B (OFS) 1994 E 1, 2, NZ 1, 2, 3, Arg 1, 2, 1995 [R, C, WS (R), NZ (R)], 1996 A 1, NZ 1, A 2, 1999 A 2, [S, U]
Venter, F D (Tvl) 1931 W, 1932 S, 1933 A 3
Versfeld, C (WP) 1891 BI 3
Versfeld, M (WP) 1891 BI 1, 2, 3
Vigne, J T (Tvl) 1891 BI 1, 2, 3
Viljoen, J F (GW) 1971 F 1, 2, A 1, 2, 3, 1972 E
Viljoen, J T (N) 1971 A 1, 2, 3
Villet, J V (WP) 1984 E 1, 2
Visagie, I J (WP) 1999 It 1, W, NZ 1, A 1, NZ 2, A 2, [S, U, E, A 3, NZ 3], 2000 C, E 2, A 1, NZ 1, 2, A 2, NZ 2, A 3, 2001 NZ 1, A 1, 2, NZ 2, F 3, It 2(R), E (t+R), US, 2003 S 1(R), 2(R), Arg
Visagie, P J (GW) 1967 F 1, 2, 3, 4, 1968 BI 1, 2, 3, 4, F 1, 2, 1969 A 1, 2, 3, 4, S, E, 1970 NZ 1, 2, 3, 4, 1971 F 1, 2, A 1, 2, 3
Visagie, R G (OFS, N) 1984 E 1, 2, S Am 1, 2, 1993 F 1
Visser, J de V (WP) 1981 NZ 2, US
Visser, M (WP) 1995 WS (R)
Visser, P J (Tvl) 1933 A 2
Viviers, S S (OFS) 1956 A 1, 2, NZ 2, 3, 4
Vogel, M L (OFS) 1974 BI 2(R)
Von Hoesslin, D J B (GW) 1999 It 1(R), 2, W (R), NZ 1, A 1(R)
Vos, A N (GL) 1999 It 1(t+R), 2, NZ 1(R), 2(R), A 2, [S (R), Sp, E (R), A 3(R), NZ 3], 2000 C, E 1, 2, A 1, NZ 1, A 2, NZ 2, A 3, Arg, I, W, E 3, 2001 F 1, 2, It 1, NZ 1, A 1, 2, NZ 2, F 3, It 2, E, US

Wagenaar, C (NT) 1977 Wld
Wahl, J J (WP) 1949 NZ 1
Walker, A P (N) 1921 NZ 1, 3, 1924 BI 1, 2, 3, 4
Walker, H N (OFS) 1953 A 3, 1956 A 2, NZ 1, 4
Walker, H W (Tvl) 1910 BI 1, 2, 3
Walton, D C (N) 1964 F, 1965 I, S, NZ 3, 4, 1969 A 1, 2, E
Wannenburg, P J (BB) 2002 F (R), E, 2003 S 1, 2, Arg, A 1(t+R), NZ 1(R), 2004 I1, 2, W1, PI(R), 2006 S1(R), F, NZ2(R), 3, A3, 2007 Sm(R), NZ1(R), A2, NZ2
Waring, F W (WP) 1931 I, 1932 E, 1933 A 1, 2, 3, 4, 5
Watson, L A (WP) 2007 Sm, 2008 W1, 2, It, NZ1(R), 2(R), Arg, NZ3(R), A2(R), 3(t&R)
Wegner, N (WP) 1993 F 2, A 1, 2, 3
Wentzel, M van Z (Pumas) 2002 F (R), S
Wessels, J J (WP) 1896 BI 1, 2, 3
Whipp, P J M (WP) 1974 BI 1, 2, 1975 F 1, 1976 NZ 1, 3, 4, 1980 S Am 1, 2
White, J (Bor) 1931 W, 1933 A 1, 2, 3, 4, 5, 1937 A 1, 2, NZ 1, 2
Wiese, J J (Tvl) 1993 F 1, 1995 WS, [R, C, WS, F, NZ], W, It, E, 1996 NZ 3(R), 4(R), 5, Arg 1, 2, F 1, 2, W
Willemse, A K (GL) 2003 S 1, 2, NZ 1, A 2, NZ 2, [U, E, Sm, NZ], 2004 W2, I3, 2007 E1, 2(R), Sm, A1, NZ1, Nm, S(R), [Tg]
Williams, A E (GW) 1910 BI 1
Williams, A P (WP) 1984 E 1, 2
Williams, C M (WP, GL) 1993 Arg 2, 1994 E 1, 2, NZ 1, 2, 3, Arg 1, 2, S, W, 1995 WS, [WS, F, NZ], It, E, 1998 A 1(t), NZ 1(t), 2000 C (R), E 1(t), 2(R), A 1(R), NZ 2, A 3, Arg, I, W (R)
Williams, D O (WP) 1937 A 1, 2, NZ 1, 2, 3, 1938 BI 1, 2, 3
Williams, J G (NT) 1971 F 1, 2, A 1, 2, 3, 1972 E, 1974 BI 1, 2, 4, F 1, 2, 1976 NZ 1, 2
Wilson, L G (WP) 1960 NZ 3, 4, W, I, 1961 E, F, I, A 1, 2, 1962 BI 1, 2, 3, 4, 1963 A 1, 2, 3, 4, 1964 W, F, 1965 I, S, A 1, 2, NZ 1, 2, 3, 4
Wolmarans, B J (OFS) 1977 Wld
Wright, G D (EP, Tvl) 1986 Cv 3, 4, 1989 Wld 1, 2, 1992 F 1, 2, E
Wyness, M R K (WP) 1962 BI 1, 2, 3, 4, 1963 A 2
Zeller, W C (N) 1921 NZ 2, 3
Zimerman, M (WP) 1931 W, I, 1932 E, S

TONGA

TONGA'S 2008–09 TEST RECORD

OPPONENTS	DATE	VENUE	RESULT
Fiji	13 June	H	**Lost** 22–36
Samoa	23 June	N	**Lost** 13–27
Japan	27 June	N	**Lost** 19–21
Junior All Blacks	2 July	N	**Lost** 25–47

PROMISING NEW GENERATION

By Karen Bond

The smallest of the three leading rugby nations in the Pacific Islands, Tonga undoubtedly has raw rugby talent in abundance. The question is how best to harness this talent to ensure the Ikale Tahi's impressive performances at Rugby World Cup 2007 are replicated on the global stage on a consistent basis?

A lack of Test matches in 2008-09 did not help Tonga's attempts to answer this perennial question, the fact that the Pacific Islanders alliance toured Europe in November meaning they had to wait until the ANZ Pacific Nations Cup in June to play once more on the international stage.

The Tongan national side played only four matches – three of them Tests – in the season and failed to win any of them, losing to the Junior All Blacks, Fiji, Samoa and Japan in the Pacific Nations Cup. However, despite this poor return, there were positive signs along the way, most notably in their encounter with the Junior All Blacks in Suva.

Few would have given Tonga much chance against a side who had overcome an opening scare against Samoa to beat Fiji and Japan to secure the title with a round to spare, but the Ikale Tahi had other ideas as tries from lock 'Emosi Kauhenga and flanker Muli Kaufusi gave the underdogs a 20–12 advantage at half-time.

Tries from Rene Ranger and Tonga-born No.8 Sione Lauaki eased the Junior All Blacks into the lead, only for a wonderful team effort to result in a try in the corner for wing Mateo Malupo to cut the deficit to one point, 26–25 with 20 minutes to play.

There was, though, to be no dramatic upset as the Junior All Blacks raised their game to the next level, the arrival of Victor Vito proving the catalyst as the champions added to their tally with tries from Alby Mathewson and Robert Fruean at a time when Tonga had either one or two players in the sin-bin.

Hosea Gear put the gloss on the victory by completing his hat-trick to seal a 47–25 win. Tonga had redeemed themselves after what had been a disappointing tournament, but they still finished bottom of the standings for the second year in succession.

Tonga had begun their Pacific Nations Cup campaign with the visit of Fiji to the Teufaiva Stadium, but despite scoring early tries in both halves there was to be no victory to celebrate in their capital Nuku'alofa with the Fijians running out 36–22 winners.

Ten days later, in a typically physical encounter, Tonga came face to face with Samoa and once again came away with a defeat, this time 27–13 after being outscored by their rivals by four tries to one. The margin of defeat could have been significantly bigger had Samoa capitalised on the numerous try-scoring opportunities that came their way.

Quddus Fielea's side then faced Japan, a side that had beaten them the last two years. Tonga trailed for much of the match at Churchill Park in Lautoka, western Fiji, but hooker Ilaisa Ma'asi touched down and then wing Tevita Halaifonua dotted down at the death, only to then slice his conversion wide to give Japan a 21–19 victory.

There had also been little to smile about for the two Tongan representative sides in the IRB Pacific Rugby Cup a couple of months earlier with Tautahi Gold losing their grip on the silverware after finishing fourth in the round robin, one place above the Tau'uta Reds.

Tautahi Gold had actually gone into the last round with a chance of reaching the final, but with Fiji Warriors and Savai'i Samoa also winning they ultimately came up three points short. Tau'uta Reds managed only one victory from five games, a slender 15–14 defeat of Savai'i in round one, although two of their four defeats did come by a margin of less than seven points.

There was better news for Tonga with the performance of their Under 20s at the IRB TOSHIBA Junior World Championship in Japan. Tonga had finished 13th in 2008, but guaranteed themselves a better finish by beating Canada in their pool after losing to Australia and Wales. This victory was even more important given that the Junior World Championship will be reduced from 16 to 12 participating teams in 2010, ensuring that Tonga remained among the elite nations along with Samoa and Fiji.

There was better to come with Tonga crossing for four tries to beat Argentina 26–17 to ensure a top ten finish. They would ultimately finish tenth, albeit only after a tight battle with Scotland in Osaka when there was barely anything to choose between the teams, the Scots running out 28–25 winners.

Tonga Sevens did manage to beat their Scotland counterparts at the NZI Sevens in Wellington, but failed to replicate their Cup semi-final achievement of 2008 and instead were beaten by the Cook Islands in the Bowl final.

At Rugby World Cup Sevens 2009 in Dubai, Tonga made it through to the Plate semi-finals before narrowly losing 22–19 to Australia. Tonga did though collect some IRB Sevens World Series silverware by winning the Plate in Hong Kong before beating world champions Wales in the Adelaide pool stages.

Tonga also picked up the bronze medal at the Pacific Mini Games in Raratonga at the beginning of October, coming from behind to see off the valiant Niue 38–12 in the third place play-off and join champions Samoa and runners-up Fiji on the medal rostrum.

TONGA

TONGA INTERNATIONAL STATISTICS

MATCH RECORDS UP TO 30TH SEPTEMBER 2009

WINNING MARGIN

Date	Opponent	Result	Winning Margin
21/03/2003	Korea	119–0	119
08/07/2006	Cook Islands	90–0	90
01/01/1979	Solomon Islands	92–3	89
10/02/2007	Korea	83–3	80
15/03/2003	Korea	75–0	75

MOST POINTS IN A MATCH
BY THE TEAM

Date	Opponent	Result	Pts.
21/03/2003	Korea	119–0	119
01/01/1979	Solomon Islands	92–3	92
08/07/2006	Cook Islands	90–0	90
06/12/2002	Papua New Guinea	84–12	84
10/02/2007	Korea	83–3	83

MOST TRIES IN A MATCH
BY THE TEAM

Date	Opponent	Result	Tries
21/03/2003	Korea	119–0	17
08/07/2006	Cook Islands	90–0	14
10/02/2007	Korea	83–3	13
24/06/2006	Cook Islands	77–10	13

MOST CONVERSIONS IN A MATCH
BY THE TEAM

Date	Opponent	Result	Cons
21/03/2003	Korea	119–0	17
08/07/2006	Cook Islands	90–0	10

MOST PENALTIES IN A MATCH
BY THE TEAM

Date	Opponent	Result	Pens
10/11/2001	Scotland	20–43	5
28/06/2008	Samoa	15–20	5

MOST POINTS IN A MATCH
BY A PLAYER

Date	Player	Opponent	Pts.
21/03/2003	Pierre Hola	Korea	39
10/02/2007	Fangatapu Apikotoa	Korea	28
04/05/1999	Sateki Tu'ipulotu	Korea	27
21/03/2003	Benhur Kivalu	Korea	25
06/12/2002	Pierre Hola	Papua New Guinea	24

MOST TRIES IN A MATCH
BY A PLAYER

Date	Player	Opponent	Tries
21/03/2003	Benhur Kivalu	Korea	5
24/06/2006	Viliami Hakalo	Cook Islands	3
08/07/2006	Tevita Vaikona	Cook Islands	3
05/07/1997	Siua Taumalolo	Cook Islands	3
28/03/1999	Siua Taumalolo	Georgia	3
04/05/1999	Jonny Koloi	Korea	3

MOST DROP GOALS IN A MATCH
BY THE TEAM

Date	Opponent	Result	DGS
8 Matches			1

THE COUNTRIES

MOST CONVERSIONS IN A MATCH
BY A PLAYER

Date	Player	Opponent	Cons
21/03/2003	Pierre Hola	Korea	17
08/07/2006	Fangatapu Apikotoa	Cook Islands	9
10/02/2007	Fangatapu Apikotoa	Korea	9
06/12/2002	Pierre Hola	Papua New Guinea	9
05/07/1997	Kusitafu Tonga	Cook Islands	9

MOST PENALTIES IN A MATCH
BY A PLAYER

Date	Player	Opponent	Pens
25/05/2001	Kusitafu Tonga	Fiji	4
10/11/2001	Sateki Tu'ipulotu	Scotland	4
19/02/1995	Sateki Tu'ipulotu	Japan	4
23/07/2005	Fangatapu Apikotoa	Samoa	4
16/09/2007	Pierre Hola	Samoa	4

MOST DROP GOALS IN A MATCH
BY A PLAYER

Date	Player	Opponent	DGS
	8 Matches		1

MOST CAPPED PLAYERS

Name	Caps
'Elisi Vunipola	41
Benhur Kivalu	38
Pierre Hola	34
Manu Vunipola	36
Fe'ao Vunipola	32

LEADING TRY SCORERS

Name	Tries
Siua Taumalolo	12
Fepikou Tatafu	11
Benhur Kivalu	10

LEADING CONVERSIONS SCORERS

Name	Cons
Pierre Hola	65
Sateki Tu'ipulotu	33
Fangatapu 'Apikotoa	30
Kusitafu Tonga	25

LEADING PENALTY SCORERS

Name	Pens
Pierre Hola	34
Sateki Tu'ipulotu	32
Siua Taumalolo	12
Tomasi Lovo	12

LEADING DROP GOAL SCORERS

Name	DGs
Pierre Hola	3

LEADING POINTS SCORERS

Name	Pts.
Pierre Hola	286
Sateki Tu'ipulotu	190
Siua Taumalolo	108
Fangatapu 'Apikotoa	99

TONGA

TONGA INTERNATIONAL PLAYERS
UP TO 30TH SEPTEMBER 2009

Note: Years given for International Championship matches are for second half of season; eg 1972 means season 1971–72. Years for all other matches refer to the actual year of the match.

I Afeaki 1995 F, S, Iv, 1997 Fj, 2001 S, W, 2002 J, Fj, Sa, Fj, 2003 Kor, Kor, I, Fj, Fj, It, C, 2004 Sa, Fj, 2005 It, 2007 Sa, SA, E
P Afeaki 1983 Fj, Sa
S Afeaki 2002 Fj, Fj, PNG, PNG, 2003 Kor, Kor, I, Fj, It, W, NZ
V Afeaki 1997 Sa, 2002 Sa, Fj
J Afu 2008 M, J, AuA, Sa, Fj, 2009 Fj, Sa, J
A Afu Fungavaka 1982 Sa, 1984 Fj, Fj, 1985 Fj, 1986 W, Fj, Fj, 1987 C, W, I, Sa, Fj
M Ahekeheke 1986 Fj
S 'Aho 1974 S, W
T Ahoafi 2007 AuA, Sa
P Ahofono 1990 Sa
K Ahota'e'iloa 1999 Sa, F, Fj, 2000 C, Fj, J
P 'Ake 1926 Fj
A Alatini 2001 S, 2002 J, Fj, 2003 I, Fj
M Alatini 1969 M, 1972 Fj, 1973 M, A, A, Fj, 1974 S, W, C, 1975 M, 1977 Fj
PF Alatini 1995 Sa
S Alatini 1994 Sa, Fj, 1998 Sa, Fj, 2000 NZ, US
S Alatini 1977 Fj, 1979 NC, M, E
T Alatini 1932 Fj
V 'Alipate 1967 Fj, 1968 Fj, Fj, Fj, 1969 M
A Amone 1987 W, I, Sa, Fj
T Anitoni 1995 J, Sa, Fj, 1996 Sa, Fj
V Anitoni 1990 Sa
F Apikotoa 2004 Sa, Fj, 2005 Fj, Sa, Fj, Sa, It, F, 2006 Coo, Coo, 2007 Kor, AuA, J, JAB, 2008 M, J, AuA, Sa, Fj, 2009 Fj, J, JAB
T Apitani 1947 Fj, Fj
S Asi 1987 C
T Asi 1996 Sa
H 'Asi 2000 C
S Ata 1928 Fj
S Atiola 1987 Sa, Fj, 1988 Fj, 1989 Fj, Fj, 1990 Fj, J
K Bakewa 2002 PNG, PNG, 2003 Fj
O Beba 1932 Fj, Fj, Fj
O Blake 1983 M, M, 1987 Sa, Fj, 1988 Sa, Fj, Fj
T Bloomfield 1973 M, A, A, Fj, 1986 W
D Briggs 1997 W
J Buloka 1932 Fj, Fj
D Edwards 1998 A, 1999 Geo, Geo, Kor, US, Sa, F, Fj, C, NZ, It, E
T Ete'aki 1984 Fj, 1986 W, Fj, Fj, 1987 C, W, I, 1990 Fj, J, Sa, Kor, Sa, 1991 Sa
U Fa'a 1994 Sa, W, 1995 J, 1998 Sa, A, Fj
L Fa'aoso 2004 Sa, Fj, 2005 Fj, Sa, Fj, Sa, 2007 US, E
P Fa'apoi 1963 Fj
V Fa'aumu 1986 Fj, Fj
T Fainga'anuku 1999 NZ, It, E, 2000 C, Fj, J, NZ, 2001 Fj, Sa, Fj, Sa
S Faka 'osi'folau 1997 Z, Nm, SA, Fj, Sa, Coo, W, 1998 A, Fj, 1999 Geo, Kor, Fj, 2001 Sa
P Fakalelu 2005 It, 2006 Coo, Coo, 2009 Sa, J, JAB
J Fakalolo 1926 Fj
P Fakana 1963 Fj, Fj
F Fakaongo 1993 S, Fj, 1995 Iv, Sa, Fj, 2000 Fj, J, NZ, Sa, 2001 S, W, 2002 J, Fj, Sa
V Fakatou 1998 Sa, A, Fj, 1999 Kor, NZ

V Fakatulolo 1975 M
P Fakaua 1988 Sa
S Fakaua 2005 Sa
P Faka'ua 1967 Fj, Fj, Fj, 1968 Fj, Fj, Fj, 1969 M, M, 1972 Fj
N Fakauho 1977 Fj, Fj
FP Faletau 1999 Geo, Kor, Kor, J, US, Sa, F, Fj, C
K Faletau 1988 Sa, Fj, 1989 Fj, Fj, 1990 Sa, 1991 Fj, 1992 Fj, 1997 Nm, SA, Fj, Sa, Coo, W, 1999 Sa, F, Fj, C
M Fanga'uta 1982 Fj
MU Fangupo 2009 Sa, J, JAB
F Faotusa 1990 Sa
A Fatafehi 2009 Fj, Sa, JAB
IT Fatani 1992 Fj, 1993 Sa, S, Fj, A, Fj, 1997 Fj, Coo, 1999 Geo, Kor, Kor, J, US, Sa, F, Fj, C, NZ, It, E, 2000 C, Fj, J, NZ, Sa, US
S Fe'ao 1995 F, S
SL Fekau 1983 M, M
K Feke 1988 Fj, Fj, 1989 Fj, 1990 Fj, Sa
M Felise 1987 W, I
I Fenukitau 1993 Sa, S, Fj, A, Fj, 1994 Sa, Fj, 1995 J, J, F, S, 2002 J, Fj, Sa, 2003 It, W, NZ, C
Fetu'ulele 1967 Fj
K Fielea 1987 C, W, I, Sa, Fj, 1990 J, Sa, Kor, Sa, 1991 Sa
P Fifita 1983 Fj
P Fifita 2003 C
S Fifita 1974 S, W, C, 1975 M
T Fifita 1984 Fj, Fj, 1986 W, Fj, Fj, 1987 C, W, I, 1991 Sa, Fj, Fj
T Fifita 2001 Fj, 2003 Fj, 2006 J, 2008 M, J, AuA
V Fifita 1982 Fj
V Fifita 2005 F
F Filikitonga 1990 Fj, Sa
L Fililava 1960 M
M Filimoehala 1968 Fj, 1974 W, C, 1975 M, M
OAML Filipine 2000 C, 2006 J, Fj, Coo, Sa, 2007 US, SA, 2008 M, J, AuA
M Filise 1986 Fj, Fj
T Filise 2001 Fj, Fj, S, W, 2002 Sa, Fj, 2004 Sa, Fj, 2005 Fj, Sa, Fj, Sa, 2007 Fj, Sa, E
S Filo 2004 Sa, Fj
I Finau 1987 Sa, Fj, 1990 Fj, J, Sa
M Finau 1979 NC, M, E, Sa, 1980 Sa, 1984 Fj
M Finau 2007 AuA, 2008 J, 2009 Fj, J, JAB
S Finau 1998 Sa, 1999 Geo, Sa, F, Fj, C, E, 2001 Fj, Fj, S, 2005 It, F
S Finau 1989 Fj, Fj, 1990 Fj, J, Sa, Kor, Sa
S Finau 1926 Fj
T Finau 1967 Fj
V Finau 1987 Sa, Fj
I Fine 2007 Kor, AuA, JAB, Sa
K Fine 1987 C, W, I, 1988 Fj
J Finisi 1932 Fj, Fj, Fj
S Finisi 1928 Fj
P Fisi'iahi 1992 Sa
K Fisilau 1999 J, US, 2000 C, 2005 Fj, Sa, It
K Fokofuka 1995 Sa
K Folea 1991 Fj
S Foliaki 1973 A, A, 1977 Fj
Fololisi 1991 Fj

TONGA

H **Paea** 2007 *Kor*
L **Pahulu** 1973 *A, Fj*, 1974 *S*
V **Pahulu** 1967 *Fj, Fj, Fj*, 1968 *Fj, Fj, Fj*, 1969 *M, M*, 1973 *M*
U **Palavi** 1960 *M*, 1963 *Fj, Fj*
J **Pale** 2001 *S, W*, 2002 *J, Fj, Sa, Sa, Fj*, 2003 *Fj*
M **Pale** 1998 *A*, 1999 *Geo*, 2002 *J, Fj*, 2006 *J, Coo, Sa*
SW **Palei** 2009 *J, JAB*
S **Palenapa** 1990 *Fj, J, Sa, Kor, Sa*, 1996 *Sa, Fj*
D **Palu** 2002 *PNG, PNG*, 2003 *Kor, Kor, I, Fj, C*, 2006 *J, JAB, Coo*, 2007 *AuA, J, JAB*
P **Palu** 1979 *NC*, 1981 *Fj*
T **Palu** 2008 *M, J, AuA*
H **Pau'u** 1983 *Fj, Sa*
T **Pau'u** 1992 *Fj*
J **Payne** 2002 *PNG, PNG*, 2003 *Kor, Kor, I, Fj, It, W, NZ, C*
D **Penisini** 1997 *Nm, Coo*, 1999 *Geo, Kor, C*
'O **Pepa** 1928 *Fj*
H **Petelo** 1982 *Fj*
H **Pierra** 2005 *Sa*
O **Pifeleti** 1983 *Fj, Sa, M, M*, 1984 *Fj, Fj*, 1985 *Fj*, 1989 *Fj, Fj*, 1990 *Sa*, 1991 *Sa, Fj, Fj*
S **Piukala** 2008 *AuA*
H **Pohiva** 1997 *W*, 1998 *Sa, Fj*
THN **Pole** 2007 *Kor, AuA, J, JAB, Fj, Sa, US, Sa, E*, 2008 *M, Sa, Fj*, 2009 *Fj, Sa, J*
S **Pone** 2008 *M, AuA, Sa, Fj*
S **Pongi** 1990 *Sa*
SE **Poteki** 2007 *Kor*
VT **Poteki** 2007 *Kor*, 2008 *M*
S **Pouanga** 1947 *Fj, Fj*
E **Pou'uhila** 1988 *Fj*
K **Pulu** 2002 *Fj, PNG, PNG*, 2003 *Kor, Kor, I, Fj, It, W, NZ*, 2005 *Fj, Sa, Fj, Sa*, 2006 *J*, 2007 *US, Sa, SA, E*, 2008 *Fj*, 2009 *Sa, J*
M **Pulumu** 1979 *NC, Sa, Fj*, 1980 *Sa*, 1981 *Fj, Fj*
T **Pulumufila** 1974 *S, W, C*
H **Saafi** 2000 *NZ*
T **Samiu** 1947 *Fj*
Sanilaita 1981 *Fj*
A **Saulala** 1991 *Fj*
C **Schaumkel** 1992 *Sa, Fj*, 1997 *SA, Fj*
S **Selupe** 1963 *Fj, Fj*, 1967 *Fj, Fj*, 1969 *M, M*, 1972 *Fj*, 1973 *M, A, Fj*
S **Selupe** 1967 *Fj*, 1969 *M*, 1972 *Fj*
S **Selupe** 1928 *Fj*
T **Siale** 1997 *Nm, Sa*
M **Sifa** 1947 *Fj*
S **Sika** 1968 *Fj, Fj, Fj*, 1969 *M, M*
A **Sikalu** 2007 *AuA, J*
T **Sime** 1963 *Fj*
T **Sitanilei** 1932 *Fj*
J **Sitoa** 1998 *A*
T **Soaiti** 1932 *Fj, Fj, Fj*
T **Soane** 1982 *Sa, Fj*, 1983 *Fj, Sa*, 1984 *Fj, Fj*, 1985 *Fj*
L **Stanley** 1985 *Fj*
L **Susimalofi** 1989 *Fj*
L **Tafa** 2007 *J*
S **Tahaafe** 1987 *C*
P **Taholo** 1983 *M*
S **Tai** 1997 *W*, 1998 *A*
U **Tai** 1969 *M*, 1972 *Fj*
E **Taione** 1999 *It, E*, 2000 *Fj, J*, 2001 *S, W*, 2005 *F*, 2006 *JAB, Sa*, 2007 *Fj, Sa, US, Sa, SA, E*, 2008 *M, Sa, Fj*, 2009 *Fj*
K **Take** 1989 *Fj*
E **Talakai** 1993 *Sa, S, Fj, Fj*, 1995 *S, Iv, Sa, Fj*
P **Tanginoa** 1995 *Fj*, 1997 *W*, 1998 *Sa, A*, 1999 *Geo*
T **Tanginoa** 2007 *AuA, J*
F **Taniela** 1982 *Fj*
I **Tapueluelu** 1990 *Fj, J, Sa, Sa*, 1993 *Sa, S*, 1999 *Kor, Kor, J, US, NZ, It, E*
F **Tatafu** 1996 *Fj*, 1997 *Z, Nm, Fj, Sa, Coo, W*, 1999 *Geo, Kor, Kor, J, Sa, Fj, C, NZ, E*, 2002 *J, Fj, Sa, PNG, PNG*
S **Tatafu** 1967 *Fj*
T **Tatafu** 1963 *Fj*
V **Tau** 1999 *US*
A **Taufa** 1993 *A*, 1995 *J, J, F, S*
E **Taufa** 2007 *Sa*, 2008 *M, J, AuA, Sa, Fj*

I **Taufa** 1972 *Fj*
S **Taufa** 1984 *Fj*
S **Taufa** 2005 *Fj, Sa, Fj, Sa*
T **Taufa** 1990 *Fj*
T **Taufahema** 1998 *Sa, A, Fj*, 1999 *Sa, F, NZ, It*, 2000 *C, Fj, J, NZ, Sa*, 2001 *Fj, Sa, Fj, S, W*
M **Taufateau** 1983 *M, M*, 1984 *Fj*, 1987 *Fj*
V **Taufatofua** 1926 *Fj*
A **Ta'ufo'ou** 1997 *Nm, SA, Fj, Sa, Coo*
E **Ta'ufo'ou** 2000 *C, Fj, J, NZ, Sa, US*
N **Taufo'ou** 1996 *Sa, Fj*, 1997 *Nm, SA, Fj, Sa, Coo, W*, 1998 *Sa, A, Fj*, 1999 *Geo, Kor, F, Fj, NZ, It, E*, 2000 *NZ, Sa, US*
E **Taukafa** 2002 *PNG, PNG*, 2003 *Kor, Kor, Fj, Fj, It, W, NZ, C*, 2005 *Fj, Sa, It, F*, 2006 *J, Coo, Sa, Coo*, 2007 *US, Sa, SA, E*, 2008 *Sa, Fj*
S **Taukapo** 2005 *Sa*
P **Taukolo** 1982 *Sa, Fj*
P **Taula** 2009 *Fj, JAB*
S **Taumalolo** 1996 *Sa, Fj*, 1997 *Z, Nm, SA, Coo, W*, 1999 *Geo, Geo, Sa, F, Fj, C, NZ*, 2000 *NZ, Sa, US*, 2001 *Fj, Sa, S, W*, 2006 *J*, 2007 *JAB, Fj, Sa*
P **Taumiuvao** 1986 *Fj*
N **Taumoefolau** 1979 *NC, E, Sa, Fj*
P **Taumoepeau** 1928 *Fj*
T **Taumoepeau** 1999 *Geo, Kor, Kor, J, US, NZ, E*, 2000 *Fj, J, NZ, Sa, US*, 2001 *Fj, Sa, Sa, S, W*, 2002 *J, Fj, Sa*, 2006 *J, Fj, JAB, Coo, Sa, Coo*, 2007 *AuA, J, Fj, Sa*
T **Taumoepeau** 1988 *Fj*
V **Taumoepeau** 1994 *Sa, W*, 1995 *Sa, Fj*
P **Taumoua** 2007 *J*
S **Taupeaafe** 1994 *W, Fj*, 1998 *Sa, A, Fj*, 1999 *Kor, J, NZ, It, E*, 2000 *NZ, US*, 2001 *Fj, Sa*
F **Tautau'a** 2007 *Kor*
S **Tavo** 1959 *Fj*, 1960 *M*, 1963 *Fj, Fj*, 1967 *Fj, Fj, Fj*, 1968 *Fj, Fj, Fj*, 1969 *M, M*
M **Te Pou** 1998 *A, Fj*, 1999 *Geo, Geo, Kor, Kor, J, US, F, NZ, It*, 2001 *S, W*
Telanisi 1967 *Fj*
S **Telefoni** 2008 *M, J, AuA, Sa, Fj*
Teri 1991 *Fj*
Teutau 1991 *Fj*
SLN **Timani** 2008 *J, AuA*, 2009 *Fj, JAB*
D **Tiueti** 1997 *Fj, Sa, W*, 1999 *Geo, Geo, Kor, Sa, F, Fj, C, NZ, It, E*, 2000 *C, Fj, J, NZ, Sa, US*, 2001 *S, W*
T **Tofua** 1926 *W*
T **Toga** 1968 *Fj*
T **Tohi** 1997 *Nm, SA*
T **Toke** 2007 *Kor, J, JAB, Fj, Sa, US, Sa*, 2008 *M, AuA*, 2009 *Fj, JAB*
V **Toloke** 1995 *J, Sa, Fj*, 1996 *Sa, Fj*, 1999 *Geo, Geo, Kor, Kor, US, NZ, E*, 2000 *NZ, Sa, US*, 2002 *J, Sa*
M **Toma** 1988 *Sa, Fj*, 1991 *Sa, Fj, Fj*
G **Tonga** 1997 *Z, W*
K **Tonga** 1996 *Fj*, 1997 *Nm, SA, Fj, Sa, Coo*, 1999 *Geo, Geo, Kor*, 2001 *Fj, Sa*
K **Tonga** 2003 *Fj, C*, 2004 *Sa, Fj*, 2005 *Fj, Fj*
K **Tonga** 1947 *Fj, Fj*
M **Tonga** 2001 *Fj, Sa, Fj, Sa*, 2003 *Kor, Kor*
M **Tonga** 1947 *Fj, Fj*
P **Tonga** 1973 *A*
S **Tonga** 2005 *Sa, Fj, Sa ,*
T **Tonga** 1990 *Sa*
S **Tonga Simiki** 1926 *Fj*
H **Tonga'uiha** 2005 *Fj, Sa, Sa*, 2006 *J, Fj, JAB, Coo, Sa, Coo*, 2007 *Kor, AuA, J, JAB, Fj, Sa, E*, 2008 *M, J, Sa, Fj*, 2009 *Fj, Sa, J*
SL **Tonga'uiha** 2005 *It, F*, 2007 *JAB, US, Sa, SA, E*
'O **Topeni** 2000 *J*
J **Tuamoheloa** 2003 *Fj*
S **Tuamoheloa** 2003 *Fj, C*, 2005 *Fj*
T **Tuavao** 1986 *Fj*
N **Tufui** 1990 *Fj, J, Sa, Sa*, 1992 *Fj*, 1994 *Fj*, 1995 *S, Iv*
S **Tufui** 1926 *Fj*, 1928 *Fj*, 1932 *Fj*
TH **Tu'ifua** 2003 *Fj, It, W, NZ*, 2006 *J, Fj, JAB, Coo, Sa*, 2007 *Fj, Sa, US, Sa, SA, E*
S **Tu'ihalamaka** 1999 *Kor, Kor, J, US*, 2001 *Sa, Fj*

USA

USA'S 2008–09 TEST RECORD

OPPONENTS	DATE	VENUE	RESULT
Uruguay	8 November	H	**Won** 43–9
Japan	16 November	A	**Lost** 19–29
Japan	22 November	A	**Lost** 17–32
Ireland	31 May	H	**Lost** 10–27
Wales	6 June	H	**Lost** 15–48
Argentina Jaguars	10 June	H	**Lost** 14–35
England Saxons	14 June	H	**Lost** 17–56
Georgia	21 June	H	**Won** 31–13
Canada	4 July	H	**Won** 12–6
Canada	11 July	A	**Lost** 18–41

FRESH HOPE FOR EAGLES

By Alex Goff

Limping out of a disappointing two-loss tour of Japan in November, the latest incarnations of the USA's grand new plan had some work to do.

Long dogged by talks of how the Americans could dominate if they lured crossover athletes and got the right coaching in place, the Eagles were instead happy just to tread water as they worked with their third coach in four seasons. This coach, Australian Scott Johnson, had called for a youth movement in the national team, saying he could mould 20-year-olds to be internationals and rejuvenate the programme.

But that all changed as Johnson left to become Director of Rugby at the Ospreys, and in stepped Eddie O'Sullivan, the former Ireland coach who had been an assistant with the USA in 1999 and regularly visited the States to give presentations and coaching clinics.

"I'm not from this country but I understand what the players face," O'Sullivan insisted. "These players are enormously dedicated, but most of them are still amateur. They get up early to do their workouts, go to their jobs, train after that. It's admirable."

O'Sullivan was faced with a daunting schedule and less than three months to create a team to face it – the visits of Ireland on 31 May and Wales a week later, then the Churchill Cup on home soil and finally Rugby World Cup 2011 qualifiers against Canada in July.

Seven internationals in seven weeks for a team of players who have to beg for time off work to play and a group of professionals that desperately needed an off-season.

Against such odds it started well. The Eagles hung on against O'Sullivan's former team and before a sell-out crowd in Santa Clara, California, gave the sort of blue-collar performance fans wanted. It did not yield a victory – Ireland winning 27–10 – but some hard-nosed play for 80 minutes was a good starting point. A week later they faced Wales in Chicago and the Eagles came back down to earth with a 48–15 defeat.

Next stop was the Churchill Cup in Colorado. A young USA squad held the Argentina Jaguars 12–11 at half-time before ultimately losing 35–14. Four days later the Eagles faced the England Saxons, opening the game with a brilliant Mike Petri try and then watching the Saxons run in many, many more to win 56–17.

O'Sullivan insisted his team was putting together some good passages, but correctable penalties and turnovers had scuppered them. A chance for a trophy nonetheless emerged as the Eagles faced Georgia in the Bowl Final. They were a little more daring and emerged 31–13 winners.

With confidence growing the Eagles faced a strong Canada team in the first of two Rugby World Cup 2011 qualifiers in Charleston, North Carolina. In a physical game that threatened to boil over on occasion, the Eagles dominated up front and with Mike Hercus kicking four penalties won 12–6 to claim their first victory over their neighbours since 2005.

Dreams of qualifying ahead of Canada for the first time ever were dashed, though, in a horrendous first half in the return leg in Edmonton a week later. Penalties, poor tackling and a Paul Emerick red card left the Eagles trailing 24–0 at half-time. While the USA scored more points than the Canadians in the second half, the dream of early qualification for New Zealand 2011 was gone and they must now overcome Uruguay in a home and away play-off to qualify as Americas 2.

So no grand milestone for the Eagles. Instead there's just some hope – hope that this coach will stick around long enough to build something.

The hope too is that new plans to develop elite players will pay off. The North America 4 has been discontinued in favour of a new Americas Rugby Championship – involving four Canadian provinces, the Argentina Jaguars and a USA Select side. USA Rugby have also made changes in its Age Grade national team structure, while University teams – Cal-Berkeley, Brigham Young and others – are beginning to develop a network of high performance programmes that produce talented national team players.

But playing overseas remains a big part of making Americans better players, and in that area they took a giant leap forward when, in January, USA captain and flanker Todd Clever signed with South Africa's Xerox Lions to become the first American to play in the Super 14. The Californian became an instant star – his long curly hair putting many in mind of a lion's mane – and whatever he did, whether it be a thundering tackle or a mistake, he did it at 100 miles an hour.

Playing Super 14 meant that Clever could not devote time to the form of rugby that helped make him a star – Sevens. And yet even though Clever played only a small role with the USA Sevens team, it was a big year for the programme.

Under coach Al Caravelli two straight Cup quarter-final appearances in George and Wellington were followed by the team's greatest performance on home soil when they made the Cup semi-finals at the USA Sevens in San Diego, losing to eventual champions Argentina 19–14.

Meanwhile the women's Sevens team had formulated their own plan.

USA

They wanted to claim the first ever Women's Rugby World Cup Sevens title and head coach Julie McCoy worked out a deal to have her players in residency in Little Rock, Arkansas, to train and play for three weeks.

Led by Christy Ringgenberg and the indefatigable neurosurgeon McCoy, the Eagles made the Cup semi-finals only to narrowly lose to New Zealand 14–12, twice being inches away from scoring the try that would have taken them to the inaugural final.

Third in the world would be wonderful for the women's 15-a-side team, which has struggled to find a regular schedule and formulate a domestic competition that challenges the best players.

With a long lay-off between Test matches, head coach Kathy Flores was hard at work trying to find young athletes who can carry the team forward, but who also had the toughness and grit she knew they'd need to beat Canada, England and the rest of the world.

The road to Women's Rugby World Cup 2010 began in Colorado in June with an A-side fixture with Canada that they lost 10–7, followed by a Test which Canada again took 25–17. There was much work to be done, although a second place finish in the Women's Nations Cup in August showed they are moving in the right direction.

On the domestic front, the Super League kicked off in March having discovered less than two weeks before that the St. Louis Bombers would be dropping out. Desperate to make up the numbers, the league asked 2008 Division I champions Life University to join the league and take over the St. Louis schedule.

The Georgia-based chiropractic college promptly won the Eastern Conference with a 7–0 record and met San Francisco Golden Gate in the final. SFFG had always boasted great talent, but never the ability to close out the big play-off games.

But there's also something to be said for a team on a mission, and San Francisco Golden Gate was that team. With Mose Timoteo putting in an man of the match performance and Volney Rouse kicking the points, SFGG beat Life 21–13 in the championship game, made more important because it was televised on ESPN live.

TV coverage improved dramatically for rugby in the USA. ESPN showed live Tests and ABC featured a highlight show of the USA Sevens. More is expected in the coming years, bolstering hopes that the fan base will grow.

As for the Eagles, they must find their way under yet another new coach and new system, while all can point to what the Sevens team has done to improve: nurture crossover athletes, provide a stable and intelligent coaching system, and get your players to believe in themselves.

USA INTERNATIONAL STATISTICS

MATCH RECORDS UP TO 30TH SEPTEMBER 2009

WINNING MARGIN

Date	Opponent	Result	Winning Margin
01/07/2006	Barbados	91–0	91
06/07/1996	Japan	74–5	69
07/11/1989	Uruguay	60–3	57
12/03/1994	Bermuda	60–3	57

MOST POINTS IN A MATCH
BY THE TEAM

Date	Opponent	Result	Pts.
01/07/2006	Barbados	91–0	91
06/07/1996	Japan	74–5	74
17/05/2003	Japan	69–27	69
12/04/2003	Spain	62–13	62
08/04/1998	Portugal	61–5	61

MOST TRIES IN A MATCH
BY THE TEAM

Date	Opponent	Result	Tries
01/07/2006	Barbados	91–0	13
17/05/2003	Japan	69 27	11
07/11/1989	Uruguay	60–3	11
06/07/1996	Japan	74–5	11

MOST CONVERSIONS IN A MATCH
BY THE TEAM

Date	Opponent	Result	Cons
01/07/2006	Barbados	91–0	13
07/11/1989	Uruguay	60–3	8
06/07/1996	Japan	74–5	8

MOST PENALTIES IN A MATCH
BY THE TEAM

Date	Opponent	Result	Pens
18/09/1996	Canada	18–23	6

MOST DROP GOALS IN A MATCH
BY THE TEAM

Date	Player	Opponent	DGS
	16 Matches		1

MOST POINTS IN A MATCH
BY A PLAYER

Date	Player	Opponent	Pts.
07/11/1989	Chris O'Brien	Uruguay	26
31/05/2004	Mike Hercus	Russia	26
01/07/2006	Mike Hercus	Barbados	26
12/03/1994	Chris O'Brien	Bermuda	25
06/07/1996	Matt Alexander	Japan	24

MOST TRIES IN A MATCH
BY A PLAYER

Date	Player	Opponent	Tries
06/07/1996	Vaea Anitoni	Japan	4
07/06/1997	Brian Hightower	Japan	4
08/04/1998	Vaea Anitoni	Portugal	4

MOST CONVERSIONS IN A MATCH
BY A PLAYER

Date	Player	Opponent	Cons
01/07/2006	Mike Hercus	Barbados	13
06/07/1996	Matt Alexander	Japan	8
07/11/1989	Chris O'Brien	Uruguay	7
17/05/2003	Mike Hercus	Japan	7

MOST PENALTIES IN A MATCH
BY A PLAYER

Date	Player	Opponent	Pens
18/09/1996	Matt Alexander	Canada	6
21/09/1996	Matt Alexander	Uruguay	5
02/10/1993	Chris O'Brien	Australia	5
20/10/2003	Mike Hercus	Scotland	5
22/05/1999	Kevin Dalzell	Fiji	5
09/06/1984	Ray Nelson	Canada	5

MOST DROP GOALS IN A MATCH
BY THE TEAM

Date	Player	Opponent	DGS
	16 Players		1

MOST CAPPED PLAYERS

Name	Caps
Luke Gross	62
Mike MacDonald	56
Alec Parker	55
Dave Hodges	53

LEADING TRY SCORERS

Name	Tries
Vaea Anitoni	26
Philip Eloff	10
Riaan van Zyl	10
Paul Emerick	10

LEADING CONVERSIONS SCORERS

Name	Cons
Mike Hercus	86
Matt Alexander	45
Chris O'Brien	24
Grant Wells	14

LEADING PENALTY SCORERS

Name	Pens
Mike Hercus	70
Matt Alexander	55
Mark Williams	35

LEADING DROP GOAL SCORERS

Name	DGs
Mike Hercus	4

LEADING POINTS SCORERS

Name	Pts.
Mike Hercus	439
Matt Alexander	286
Chris O'Brien	144
Mark Williams	143
Vaea Anitoni	130

USA INTERNATIONAL PLAYERS
UP TO 30TH SEPTEMBER 2009

Note: Years given for International Championship matches are for second half of season; eg. 1972 means season 1971–72. Years for all other matches refer to the actual year of the match.

M Alexander 1995 *C*, 1996 *I, C, HK, J, HK, J, Ar, C, Ur*, 1997 *W, C, HK, J, J, HK, C, W, W*, 1998 *Pt, Sp, J, HK, C*
AE Allen 1912 *A*
S Allen 1996 *J*, 1997 *HK, J, J, C, W, W*
T Altemeier 1978 *C*
D Anderson 2002 *S*
B Andrews 1978 *C*, 1979 *C*
VN Anitoni 1992 *C*, 1994 *C, Ar, Ar, I*, 1995 *C*, 1996 *I, C, C, HK, J, HK, J, Ar, C, Ur*, 1997 *W, C, HK, C, W, W*, 1998 *Pt, Sp, J, HK, C, C, J, HK, Fj, Ar, C, Ur*, 1999 *Tg, Fj, J, C, Sa, E, I, R, A*, 2000 *Fj, Sa*
J Arrell 1912 *A*
S Auerbach 1976 *A*, 1913 *NZ*
CA Austin 1912 *A*, 1913 *NZ*
M Aylor 2006 *IrA, M, C, Bar, Ur*, 2007 *S, C, Sa, SA*
A Bachelet 1993 *C, A*, 1994 *Ber, C, Ar, Ar, I*, 1995 *C*, 1996 *I, C, C, HK, J, HK, J, Ar, C*, 1997 *W, C, HK, J, J, HK, C, W, W*, 1998 *Pt, Sp, J, HK, C, C, J*
R Bailey 1979 *C*, 1980 *NZ*, 1981 *C, SA*, 1982 *C*, 1983 *C, A*, 1987 *Tun, C, J, E*
B Barnard 2006 *IrA, M, Bar, C*
I Basauri 2007 *S, E, Tg*, 2008 *Ur, J, J*
D Bateman 1982 *C, E*, 1983 *A*, 1985 *J, C*
P Bell 2006 *IrA, M, C, Bar, C, Ur, Ur*
W Bernhard 1987 *Tun*
C Biller 2009 *I, W, ArJ, E, Geo, C, C*
TW Billups 1993 *C, A*, 1994 *Ber, C, Ar, Ar, I*, 1995 *C*, 1996 *I, C, C, HK, HK, J, Ar, C, Ur*, 1997 *W, C, HK, HK, W, W*, 1998 *Pt, Sp, J, HK, C, C, J, HK, Fj, Ar, C, Ur*, 1999 *Tg, Fj, J, C, Sa, E, I, R, A*
RR Blasé 1913 *NZ*
A Blom 1998 *Sp, J, HK, C, C, HK, Fj, Ar, Ur*, 1999 *Sa*, 2000 *J, C, I*
H Bloomfield 2007 *E, Tg, SA*, 2008 *C*
R Bordley 1976 *A, F*, 1977 *C, E*, 1978 *C*
J Boyd 2009 *I, ArJ*
S Bracken 1994 *Ar*, 1995 *C*
G Brackett 1976 *A, F*, 1977 *E*
N Brendel 1983 *A*, 1984 *C*, 1985 *J, C*, 1987 *Tun, E*
D Briley 1979 *C*, 1980 *W, C, NZ*
J Buchholz 2001 *C*, 2002 *S*, 2003 *Sp, E, Ar, Fj, J, F*, 2004 *C*
B Burdette 2006 *Ur, Ur*, 2007 *E, S, C, E, Tg, Sa, SA*
J Burke 2000 *C, I*
JR Burke 1990 *C, J*, 1991 *J, J, S, C, F, NZ*, 1992 *C*
J Burkhardt 1983 *C*, 1985 *C*
E Burlingham 1980 *NZ*, 1981 *C, SA*, 1982 *C, E*, 1983 *C, A*, 1984 *C*, 1985 *C*, 1986 *J*, 1987 *Tun, C, J, E*
Cabrol 1920 *F*
C Campbell 1993 *C, A*, 1994 *Ber, C, Ar*
D Care 1998 *Pt, J, C*
M Carlson 1987 *W, C*
DB Carroll 1913 *NZ*
L Cass 1913 *NZ*
M Caulder 1984 *C*, 1985 *C*, 1989 *C*
R Causey 1977 *C*, 1981 *C, SA*, 1982 *C, E*, 1984 *C*, 1986 *J*, 1987 *E*
W Chai 1993 *C*
D Chipman 1976 *A*, 1978 *C*
JE Clark 1979 *C*, 1980 *C*
J Clarkson 1986 *J*, 1987 *Tun, C, J, E*

J Clayton 1999 *C, R, A*, 2000 *J, C, I, Fj, Tg, Sa, S, W*
N Cleaveland 1924 *F*
T Clever 2003 *Ar*, 2005 *C, R, W, ArA, C*, 2006 *IrA, M, C, Bar, C, Ur, Ur*, 2007 *E, S, C, E, Tg, Sa, SA*, 2008 *C, Ur, J, J*, 2009 *ArJ, E, Geo, C, C*
R Cooke 1979 *C*, 1980 *W, C, NZ*, 1981 *C, SA*
B Corcoran 1989 *Ur, Ar*, 1990 *Ar*
J Coulson 1999 *A*
M Crick 2007 *E, S, C*, 2008 *C, Ur, J, J*
R Crivellone 1983 *C*, 1986 *C*, 1987 *C*
K Cross 2003 *Sp, Sp, J, C, E, E, Ar, C, Fj, S*, 2004 *C, Rus*
C Culpepper 1977 *E*, 1978 *C*
C Curtis 1997 *C, HK, J*, 1999 *Sa*, 2001 *Ar*
P Dahl 2009 *I, W, E*
B Daily 1989 *Ur, Ar*, 1990 *Ar, C, A, J*, 1991 *J, J, S, F, F, It*
K Dalzell 1996 *Ur*, 1998 *Sp, C, HK, C, Ur*, 1999 *Tg, Fj, J, C, Sa, E, I, R, A*, 2000 *J, C, I, Fj, Tg, Sa, S, W*, 2001 *C, E, SA*, 2002 *S, C, C, Ch, Ur*, 2003 *Sp, Sp, J, C, E, C, Ur, Fj, S, J, F*
P Danahy 2009 *ArJ*
WP Darsie 1913 *NZ*
Davies 1920 *F*
G De Bartolo 2008 *C, Ur, J, J*, 2009 *W, ArJ*
D de Groot 1924 *F*
MG de Jong 1990 *C*, 1991 *J, J, S, C, F, F, It, E*
M Deaton 1983 *A*, 1984 *C*, 1985 *J*
M Delai 1996 *I, HK, J*, 1997 *HK*, 1998 *HK*, 2000 *J, C, I, Fj, Tg, Sa, S, W*, 2001 *C, Ar, Ur*
RH Devereux 1924 *F*
D Dickson 1986 *J*, 1987 *A*
G Dixon 1924 *F*
Doe 1924 *F*
C Doherty 1987 *W*
Doi 1920 *F*
D Dorsey 2001 *SA*, 2002 *S, C, C, Ch, Ur, Ch, Ur*, 2003 *Sp, Sp, J, C, E, Ar, C, Ur, Fj, S, J, F*, 2004 *C, Rus, M, C, F*
G Downes 1992 *HK*
B Doyle 2008 *C*
R Duncanson 1977 *E*
P Eloff 2000 *J, C, I, Fj, Tg, Sa, S, W*, 2001 *C, Ar, Ur, E, SA*, 2002 *S, C, Ch, Ur*, 2003 *Sp, Sp, J, C, E, C, Ur, Fj, S, J, F*, 2006 *Bar, C, Ur, Ur*, 2007 *Tg, Sa, SA*
P Emerick 2003 *Sp, E, Ar, C, Ur, Fj, S, J*, 2004 *M, C, F, I, It*, 2005 *C, R, W, ArA, C*, 2006 *C, Bar, C, Ur, Ur*, 2007 *S, C, E*, 2008 *C, Ur, J, J*, 2009 *E, Geo, C, C*
TV Enosa 2009 *ArJ, E*
BE Erb 1912 *A*
C Erskine 2006 *C, Ur, Ur*, 2007 *E, Tg, Sa, SA*, 2008 *Ur, J, J*
V Esikia 2006 *IrA, M, Bar, C, Ur, Ur*, 2007 *E, E, Tg, Sa, SA*
J Everett 1984 *C*, 1985 *J*, 1986 *J, C*, 1987 *Tun, J, E*
W Everett 1985 *J*, 1986 *J, C*
M Fabling 1995 *C*
M Fanucchi 1979 *C*, 1980 *W*
R Farley 1989 *I, Ur, Ar*, 1990 *Ar, C, A, J*, 1991 *J, J, S, C, F, F, It, E*, 1992 *C*
P Farner 1999 *Tg, Fj, J, C*, 2000 *J, C, I, Fj, Tg, Sa, S, W*, 2002 *C, C, Ch, Ur, Ch, Ur*
L Farrish 1924 *F*
D Fee 2002 *C, C, Ch, Ur, Ch, Ur*, 2003 *Sp, Sp, J, C, E, C,*

468

M **Siano** 1989 *I, C, Ur, Ar*
J **Sifa** 2008 *Ur, J*, 2009 *I, W, ArJ, E*
MK **Sika** 1993 *C, A*, 1994 *Ber, C, Ar, Ar, I*, 1996 *C, C, J, HK, J, Ar, C, Ur*, 1997 *J, W*
S **Sika** 2003 *Fj, J, F*, 2004 *M, C, F, I, It*, 2005 *W, C*, 2006 *IrA, M*, 2007 *S, C, E, Tg, Sa, SA*, 2008 *C, Ur*, 2009 *Geo, C*
C **Slaby** 2008 *C*
C **Slater** 1920 *F*, 1924 *F*
H **Smith** 2008 *Ur, J, J*, 2009 *I, W, E, Geo, C, C*
M **Smith** 1988 *C*
T **Smith** 1980 *C*, 1981 *C, SA*, 1982 *E*
WL **Smith** 1912 *A*
B **Smoot** 1992 *C*
M **Stanaway** 1997 *C, HK, J, C*, 1998 *HK*
L **Stanfill** 2005 *C*, 2006 *C*, 2007 *E, S, C, E, Tg, Sa, SA*, 2009 *I, W, ArJ, E, Geo, C, C*
D **Steinbauer** 1992 *C*, 1993 *C*
J **Stencel** 2006 *C*
D **Stephenson** 1976 *A, F*, 1977 *C*
I **Stevens** 1998 *C*
P **Still** 2000 *S, W*, 2001 *C, Ar, Ur, E, SA*
HR **Stolz** 1913 *NZ*
W **Stone** 1976 *F*
D **Straehley** 1983 *C*, 1984 *C*
G **Sucher** 1998 *C, J, HK, Fj, C, Ur*, 1999 *Tg, Fj, J, C, Sa, E, I, R, A*
R **Suniula** 2009 *I, W, E, C, C*
A **Suniura** 2008 *J*
B **Surgener** 2001 *SA*, 2002 *C, Ur*, 2003 *Sp, E, E*, 2004 *C, F, I, It*, 2005 *W*
E **Swanson** 1976 *A*
C **Sweeney** 1976 *A, F*, 1977 *C, E*
M **Swiderski** 1976 *A*
K **Swiryn** 2009 *I, W, C, C*
B **Swords** 1980 *W, C, NZ*
KR **Swords** 1985 *J, C*, 1986 *C*, 1987 *Tun, C, J, A, W, C*, 1988 *C, R, USS*, 1989 *I, C, Ur, Ar*, 1990 *Ar, C, A, J*, 1991 *J, J, S, C, F, F, It, NZ, E*, 1992 *C*, 1993 *C, A*, 1994 *Ber, C, Ar, Ar*
TK **Takau** 1994 *Ar, Ar, I*, 1996 *C, C, HK, J, HK*, 1997 *C, HK, J, HK, W, W*, 1998 *Sp, HK, C, C, J, HK, Ur*, 1999 *E, I, R, A*
R **Tardits** 1993 *A*, 1994 *Ber, C, Ar, Ar, I*, 1995 *C*, 1996 *I, C, C, J, Ar*, 1997 *W, C*, 1998 *Sp, HK, Fj*, 1999 *Tg, Fj, J, C, Sa, I, R*
J **Tarpoff** 2002 *S, C, C, Ch*, 2003 *Sp, Sp, C, E, E*, 2006 *IrA, M, C, Bar*
Tilden 1920 *F*
M **Timoteo** 2000 *Tg*, 2001 *C, Ar, Ur, SA*, 2002 *S, C, C, Ch, Ur, Ch*, 2003 *Sp, Sp, J, E, Ar, C, F*, 2004 *C, Rus, M, C, F, I, It*, 2005 *C, R*, 2006 *IrA, M, C, Bar*
A **Tuilevuka** 2006 *IrA, M, C*, 2009 *I, W, ArJ, E, Geo, C*
A **Tuipulotu** 2004 *C, Rus, M, C, I, It*, 2005 *C, R, W*, 2006 *C, Bar, C, Ur, Ur*, 2007 *E, S, C, Tg, Sa*
CE **Tunnacliffe** 1991 *F, NZ, E*, 1992 *HK*
JC **Urban** 1913 *NZ*

T **Usasz** 2009 *I, W, ArJ, E, Geo, C, C*
Vaka 1987 *C*
AC **Valentine** 1924 *F*
M **van der Molen** 1992 *C*
R **van Zyl** 2003 *Sp, Sp, J, C, E, C, Ur, Fj, S, J, F*, 2004 *C, F*
J **Vandergeissen** 2008 *C, Ur, J, J*, 2009 *I, W, E, Geo, C, C*
Vidal 1920 *F*
F **Viljoen** 2004 *Rus, M, C, F, I, It*, 2005 *C, R, W, ArA, C*, 2006 *IrA, M, C, Ur, Ur*, 2007 *E, S, C*
T **Vinick** 1986 *C*, 1987 *A, E*
J **Vitale** 2006 *C, Ur*, 2007 *E*
BG **Vizard** 1986 *J, C*, 1987 *Tun, C, J, A, E, W, C*, 1988 *C, R, USS*, 1989 *I, C*, 1990 *C, A*, 1991 *J, J, S, C, F, It*
C **Vogl** 1996 *C, C*, 1997 *W, C, HK, J, J, HK, C*, 1998 *HK, Fj, Ar*
G **Voight** 1913 *NZ*
J **Waasdorp** 2003 *J, E, Ar, Ur, J, F*, 2004 *C, Rus, M, C, F, I, It*, 2005 *C, ArA, C*
D **Wack** 1976 *F*, 1977 *C*, 1978 *C*, 1980 *C*
B **Waite** 1976 *F*
J **Walker** 1996 *I, C, HK, J, Ar, C, Ur*, 1997 *W, J, HK, C, W, W*, 1998 *Sp, J, HK, C, C, J, HK, Ar, C, Ur*, 1999 *Tg, J*
Wallace 1920 *F*
L **Walton** 1980 *C, NZ*, 1981 *C, SA*
A **Ward** 1980 *NZ*, 1983 *C*
B **Warhurst** 1983 *C, A*, 1984 *C*, 1985 *J, C*, 1986 *J*, 1987 *Tun, C, J*
M **Waterman** 1992 *C*
J **Welch** 2008 *J, J*, 2009 *I, Geo, C*
G **Wells** 2000 *J, C, I, Fj, Tg, Sa, S, W*, 2001 *C, Ar, Ur, E*
T **Whelan** 1982 *E*, 1987 *C*, 1988 *C, R, USS*
EA **Whitaker** 1990 *J*, 1991 *F, F, It, NZ*
B **Wiedemer** 2007 *E*, 2008 *C*
L **Wilfley** 2000 *I, Tg, W*, 2001 *Ar, Ur, SA*, 2002 *S, C, C, Ch, Ur, Ch, Ur*, 2003 *Sp, Sp, J, C, E, E, S*
JP **Wilkerson** 1991 *E*, 1993 *A*, 1994 *C*, 1996 *C, Ur*, 1997 *W, C, HK, J, J, C, W, W*, 1998 *Pt, Sp, J, HK*
B **Williams** 1988 *C, R, USS*, 1989 *C*, 1992 *C*
C **Williams** 1990 *C, A, J*, 1991 *J, S, C*
D **Williams** 2004 *C, Rus, M, C, F, I, It*, 2005 *ArA*, 2006 *Ur, Ur*, 2007 *E, C*
MA **Williams** 1987 *W, C*, 1988 *C, R, USS*, 1989 *I, Ur, Ar*, 1990 *Ar, C, A*, 1991 *J, J, F, F, It, NZ, E*, 1992 *HK*, 1994 *C, Ar, Ar, I*, 1996 *I, C, C, HK*, 1997 *W*, 1998 *Fj, Ar, Ur*, 1999 *Tg, J, C, Sa, E, I*
G **Wilson** 1978 *C*, 1980 *W, C*, 1981 *C, SA*
Winston 1920 *F*
Wrenn 1920 *F*
M **Wyatt** 2003 *Ar, C, Ur, J, F*, 2004 *C, Rus, M, C, F, I, It*, 2005 *W, ArA, C*, 2006 *C*
C **Wyles** 2007 *E, S, C, E, Tg, Sa, SA*, 2008 *C, Ur, J, J*, 2009 *I, W, Geo, C, C*
D **Younger** 2000 *J, C, I, Fj*
S **Yungling** 1997 *HK, W*
R **Zenker** 1987 *W, C*

WALES

WALES' 2008–09 TEST RECORD

OPPONENTS	DATE	VENUE	RESULT
South Africa	8 November	H	**Lost** 15–20
Canada	14 November	H	**Won** 34–13
New Zealand	22 November	H	**Lost** 9–29
Australia	29 November	H	**Won** 21–18
Scotland	8 February	A	**Won** 26–13
England	14 February	H	**Won** 23–15
France	27 February	A	**Lost** 16–21
Italy	14 March	A	**Won** 20–15
Ireland	21 March	H	**Lost** 15–17
Canada	30 May	A	**Won** 32–23
USA	6 June	A	**Won** 48–15

GATLAND'S TROOPS DETHRONED AS KINGS OF EUROPE

By Iain Spragg

Wales' best win of the season came over Australia in November.

For most players and coaches, winning a Grand Slam is a career-defining achievement. To record the Championship clean sweep in successive seasons is a feat that has been completed just five times in the 126-year history of the tournament and Wales were unable to emulate the double success in 2009 as they surrendered their Six Nations crown to Ireland.

The euphoria of 2008 and a second Grand Slam in three years was replaced by a new reality as Warren Gatland's side consistently found opposition defences more resolute against their free-flowing style. It was not a season in which the defending champions imploded but the sense they had not kicked on from the previous campaign prevailed.

Wales were denied the possibility of another Grand Slam after their defeat in Paris against France in the third game of the year and were beaten again in their final fixture in Cardiff by Ireland, although their

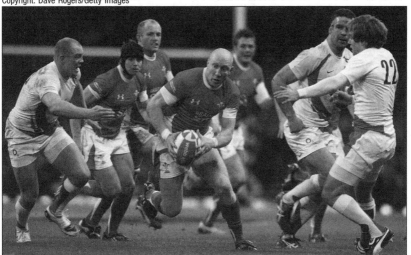

The highlight of the Six Nations was a win over England.

WALES

fourth place finish was deceptive as they were level on points with both England and Les Bleus but recorded an inferior points difference.

There were, however, significant positives for Gatland to reflect on after his second season at the helm. His team's 21–18 triumph over Australia in Cardiff in the autumn was Europe's only success against any of the big three southern hemisphere giants and shorn of the Principality's British & Irish Lions contingent, the unbeaten Wales squad that toured Canada and America in the summer revealed a promising crop of talent coming through the ranks.

"I'm delighted for Declan Kidney," Gatland conceded graciously after Ireland had won in Cardiff. "It was a great game and you've got to give Ireland credit. They've won all the matches and well done to them. It's been a long time coming for Ireland and at the end of it they've deserved their Grand Slam.

"We haven't always played to our potential. Last year we came into the Six Nations completely under the radar and there was no expectation from anybody. And we've had to deal with a lot of different expectations this year, coming in as favourites, every team targeting Wales in terms of seeing us as a big scalp.

"We've had to deal with teams being quite negative in the way they've played against us, not playing a lot of rugby, a lot of pick-and-go, being really competitive at the breakdown, trying to slow the ball down.

"Everyone talks about different plans and that, but it's not about

THE COUNTRIES

Wales struggled to hold France, in Paris, as their Grand Slam dream died.

that. It's about just making sure you're accurate and you learn from things that can hopefully make you a better team."

The season in Wales began acrimoniously with a bitter row between the WRU and the four regions over the old chestnut of player release and was only resolved at the end of October by a High Court decision in favour of the governing body. Gatland had got his wish and his full squad promptly assembled at the start of November to prepare for a four-match series against the Springboks, Canada, New Zealand and the Wallabies.

The coach handed debuts to wing Leigh Halfpenny and No.8 Andy Powell for the South Africa match and the clash between the reigning world and Six Nations champions was as fierce and close as many of the pre-match predictions.

The visitors took the lead through an Adrian Jacobs try in the first half and a second from Jean de Villiers after the break, but Wales rallied and four penalties from James Hook brought them to within five points only for the Springboks to cling on for a 20–15 win.

Six days later Canada provided distinctly more generous opposition in Cardiff as the promising Halfpenny crossed twice in a routine 34–13 victory, but all eyes were on the All Blacks clash the following week and Wales' bid to end a 55-year losing streak against New Zealand.

That Gatland's side went down 29–9 to New Zealand did not tell the full story of the match. Wales led 9–6 at half-time courtesy of three

Stephen Jones penalties and the visitors needed a Ma'a Nonu try after the break to take the lead for the first time in the game. Jerome Kaino added some gloss to the final score with a try in the dying seconds but Wales' impassioned performance deserved better.

The autumn concluded with the match against the Australians and it was to be a genuine thriller in which the home side proudly flew the flag for the northern hemisphere.

Wales drew first blood as early as the third minute when Shane Williams, the IRB Player of the Year, provided the finish to a sweeping move but the Wallabies hit back with a Mark Chisholm try that gave the visitors the lead. The home side rallied with a fine Lee Byrne score and opened up a 21–13 advantage which they desperately clung on to despite a fierce Australian fightback which culminated in a nerve-inducing Digby Ioane try.

"We played some fantastic rugby and I think we proved we are capable of doing it against the top sides," said captain Ryan Jones after leading Wales to a first win over the Wallabies since 2005. "With the work ethic in this team and the coaches we have got, I think the sky is the limit."

The only surprise in Gatland's Six Nations squad was the omission of scrum-half Dwayne Peel and the team to face Scotland in their Murrayfield opener showed just two changes from the XV that started against the Wallabies.

The game in Edinburgh was effectively settled midway through the first half when the Scots were reduced to 14 men and Wales scored twice through Tom Shanklin and Alun Wyn Jones. They added further scores from Halfpenny and Shane Williams and at the final whistle, the visitors were 26–13 winners.

England at the Millennium Stadium were next and although the old enemy pushed Wales all the way, a second half Halfpenny try and five penalties from Stephen Jones were enough to secure a 23–15 victory.

A second successive Grand Slam was still a possibility but Wales' dream was shattered by the French in Paris a week later. An early Byrne try helped establish a 13–3 lead for the visitors after just 24 minutes in the Stade de France, but Les Bleus came storming back with scores from Thierry Dusautoir and Cedric Heymans and 11 points from the boot of scrum-half Morgan Parra sealed a 21–16 victory.

"We have to get over this quickly," said Ryan Jones. "It's not going to be pretty viewing and it will be tough for some individuals, me included. But that's Test match rugby, there's no hiding place. But we've still got a Triple Crown and a Championship to play for. We were beaten by the better team but we will come back stronger from this."

WALES

Redemption was at hand in Rome against Italy a fortnight later, although it did not come in the manner many Wales fans anticipated. Gatland decided to make 10 changes to his starting line-up to face the Azzurri, effectively fielding a shadow XV, and his new-look team struggled and it needed a 72nd-minute score from replacement Shanklin to secure a scrappy 20–15 win.

The result meant Wales needed to beat Ireland by 13 clear points in Cardiff to retain the title. The game was tense throughout but until the dying minutes, it seemed the home side would indeed spoil the Irish party.

Two Stephen Jones penalties gave Gatland's side a 6–0 half-time lead, only for Ireland to reply with tries from Brian O'Driscoll and Tommy Bowe. Two further Jones penalties and a drop goal five minutes from time appeared to have sealed it only for the visitors to hit back with a Ronan O'Gara drop. There was time for one last moment of drama with a long-range penalty attempt from Jones in the final minute but it dropped agonisingly short and Ireland had their Grand Slam.

Gatland spent the summer in South Africa on Lions coaching duty, so it was left to Robin McBryde to lead an inexperienced Wales squad on their two-Test tour of North America.

The first game against Canada in Toronto at the end of May was a disjointed, fractious affair and the tourists were indebted to 22 points from the boot of fly half Dan Biggar in an unconvincing 32–23 victory.

"The feeling is frustration on the whole," conceded McBryde after his first game in charge. "Fair play to Canada, they made it difficult for us, especially at the breakdown. We were unable to build up a head of steam or get any quick ball."

A week later, Wales crossed swords with the USA Eagles in Chicago and the men in red were far more fluent this time around, running in six tries in a 48–15 triumph. Centre Jonathan Davies helped himself to two tries while Mark Jones, Tom James and Gareth Cooper also crossed the whitewash to add to an earlier penalty try.

Wales had at least ended a testing season with victory but after setting themselves such high standards in 2008, it was difficult for the Principality to get unduly carried away with what was an ultimately unspectacular campaign.

WALES INTERNATIONAL STATISTICS

MATCH RECORDS UP TO 30TH SEPTEMBER 2009

MOST CONSECUTIVE TEST WINS

11	1907 I, 1908 E,S,F,I,A, 1909 E,S,F,I, 1910 F
10	1999 F1,It,E,Arg 1,2,SA,C,F2,Arg 3,J
8	1970 F, 1971 E,S,I,F, 1972 E,S,F
8	2004 J, 2005 E,It,F,S,I,US,C

MOST CONSECUTIVE TESTS WITHOUT DEFEAT

Matches	Wins	Draws	Periods
11	11	0	1907 to 1910
10	10	0	1999 to 1999
8	8	0	1970 to 1972
8	8	0	2004 to 2005

MOST POINTS IN A MATCH

BY THE TEAM

Pts.	Opponents	Venue	Year
102	Portugal	Lisbon	1994
98	Japan	Cardiff	2004
81	Romania	Cardiff	2001
77	U S A	Hartford	2005
72	Japan	Cardiff	2007
70	Romania	Wrexham	1997
66	Romania	Cardiff	2004
64	Japan	Cardiff	1999
64	Japan	Osaka	2001
61	Canada	Cardiff	2006
60	Italy	Treviso	1999
60	Canada	Toronto	2005
58	Fiji	Cardiff	2002
57	Japan	Bloemfontein	1995
55	Japan	Cardiff	1993

BY A PLAYER

Pts.	Player	Opponents	Venue	Year
30	N R Jenkins	Italy	Treviso	1999
29	N R Jenkins	France	Cardiff	1999
28	N R Jenkins	Canada	Cardiff	1999
28	N R Jenkins	France	Paris	2001
28	G L Henson	Japan	Cardiff	2004
27	N R Jenkins	Italy	Cardiff	2000
27	C Sweeney	U S A	Hartford	2005
26	S M Jones	Romania	Cardiff	2001
24	N R Jenkins	Canada	Cardiff	1993
24	N R Jenkins	Italy	Cardiff	1994
24	G L Henson	Romania	Wrexham	2003
23	A C Thomas	Romania	Wrexham	1997
23	N R Jenkins	Argentina	Llanelli	1998
23	N R Jenkins	Scotland	Murrayfield	2001
22	N R Jenkins	Portugal	Lisbon	1994
22	N R Jenkins	Japan	Bloemfontein	1995
22	N R Jenkins	England	Wembley	1999
22	S M Jones	Canada	Cardiff	2002
22	J W Hook	England	Cardiff	2007
22	D R Biggar	Canada	Toronto	2009

WALES

THE COUNTRIES

MOST TRIES IN A MATCH
BY THE TEAM

Tries	Opponents	Venue	Year
16	Portugal	Lisbon	1994
14	Japan	Cardiff	2004
11	France	Paris	1909
11	Romania	Wrexham	1997
11	Romania	Cardiff	2001
11	U S A	Hartford	2005
11	Japan	Cardiff	2007
10	France	Swansea	1910
10	Japan	Osaka	2001
10	Romania	Cardiff	2004
9	France	Cardiff	1908
9	Japan	Cardiff	1993
9	Japan	Cardiff	1999
9	Japan	Tokyo	2001
9	Canada	Toronto	2005
9	Canada	Cardiff	2006

BY A PLAYER

Tries	Player	Opponents	Venue	Year
4	W Llewellyn	England	Swansea	1899
4	R A Gibbs	France	Cardiff	1908
4	M C R Richards	England	Cardiff	1969
4	I C Evans	Canada	Invercargill	1987
4	N Walker	Portugal	Lisbon	1994
4	G Thomas	Italy	Treviso	1999
4	S M Williams	Japan	Osaka	2001
4	T G L Shanklin	Romania	Cardiff	2004
4	C L Charvis	Japan	Cardiff	2004

MOST CONVERSIONS IN A MATCH
BY THE TEAM

Cons	Opponents	Venue	Year
14	Japan	Cardiff	2004
11	Portugal	Lisbon	1994
11	U S A	Hartford	2005
10	Romania	Cardiff	2001
8	France	Swansea	1910
8	Japan	Cardiff	1999
8	Romania	Cardiff	2004
8	Canada	Cardiff	2006
7	France	Paris	1909
7	Japan	Osaka	2001
7	Japan	Cardiff	2007

BY A PLAYER

Cons	Player	Opponents	Venue	Year
14	G L Henson	Japan	Cardiff	2004
11	N R Jenkins	Portugal	Lisbon	1994
11	C Sweeney	U S A	Hartford	2005
10	S M Jones	Romania	Cardiff	2001
8	J Bancroft	France	Swansea	1910
8	N R Jenkins	Japan	Cardiff	1999
8	J Hook	Canada	Cardiff	2006
7	S M Jones	Japan	Osaka	2001
7	S M Jones	Romania	Cardiff	2004
6	J Bancroft	France	Paris	1909
6	G L Henson	Romania	Wrexham	2003
6	C Sweeney	Canada	Toronto	2005

MOST PENALTIES IN A MATCH
BY THE TEAM

Pens	Opponents	Venue	Year
9	France	Cardiff	1999
8	Canada	Cardiff	1993
7	Italy	Cardiff	1994
7	Canada	Cardiff	1999
7	Italy	Cardiff	2000
6	France	Cardiff	1982
6	Tonga	Nuku'alofa	1994
6	England	Wembley	1999
6	Canada	Cardiff	2002
6	England	Cardiff	2009
6	Canada	Toronto	2009

BY A PLAYER

Pens	Player	Opponents	Venue	Year
9	N R Jenkins	France	Cardiff	1999
8	N R Jenkins	Canada	Cardiff	1993
7	N R Jenkins	Italy	Cardiff	1994
7	N R Jenkins	Canada	Cardiff	1999
7	N R Jenkins	Italy	Cardiff	2000
6	G Evans	France	Cardiff	1982
6	N R Jenkins	Tonga	Nuku'alofa	1994
6	N R Jenkins	England	Wembley	1999
6	S M Jones	Canada	Cardiff	2002
6	D R Biggar	Canada	Toronto	2009

MOST DROP GOALS IN A MATCH
BY THE TEAM

Drops	Opponents	Venue	Year
3	Scotland	Murrayfield	2001
2	Scotland	Swansea	1912
2	Scotland	Cardiff	1914
2	England	Swansea	1920
2	Scotland	Swansea	1921
2	France	Paris	1930
2	England	Cardiff	1971
2	France	Cardiff	1978
2	England	Twickenham	1984
2	Ireland	Wellington	1987
2	Scotland	Cardiff	1988
2	France	Paris	2001

BY A PLAYER

Drops	Player	Opponents	Venue	Year
3	N R Jenkins	Scotland	Murrayfield	2001
2	J Shea	England	Swansea	1920
2	A Jenkins	Scotland	Swansea	1921
2	B John	England	Cardiff	1971
2	M Dacey	England	Twickenham	1984
2	J Davies	Ireland	Wellington	1987
2	J Davies	Scotland	Cardiff	1988
2	N R Jenkins	France	Paris	2001

MOST CAPPED PLAYERS

Caps	Player	Career Span
100	Gareth Thomas	1995 to 2007
94	C L Charvis	1996 to 2007
92	G O Llewellyn	1989 to 2004
88	M E Williams	1996 to 2009
87	N R Jenkins	1991 to 2002
80	S M Jones	1998 to 2009
72	I C Evans	1987 to 1998
69	D J Peel	2001 to 2009
68	G D Jenkins	2002 to 2009
65	S M Williams	2000 to 2009
63	T G L Shanklin	2001 to 2009
61	I M Gough	1998 to 2009
59	R Howley	1996 to 2002
58	G R Jenkins	1991 to 2000
56	A R Jones	2003 to 2009
55	J P R Williams	1969 to 1981
54	R N Jones	1986 to 1995
54	D J Jones	2001 to 2009
53	G O Edwards	1967 to 1978
53	I S Gibbs	1991 to 2001
52	L S Quinnell	1993 to 2002
52	M Taylor	1994 to 2005
51	D Young	1987 to 2001

MOST CONSECUTIVE TESTS

Tests	Player	Span
53	G O Edwards	1967 to 1978
43	K J Jones	1947 to 1956
39	G Price	1975 to 1983
38	T M Davies	1969 to 1976
33	W J Bancroft	1890 to 1901

MOST TESTS AS CAPTAIN

Tests	Player	Span
28	I C Evans	1991 to 1995
22	R Howley	1998 to 1999
22	C L Charvis	2002 to 2004
21	Gareth Thomas	2003 to 2007
19	J M Humphreys	1995 to 2003
18	A J Gould	1889 to 1897
16	R P Jones	2008 to 2009
14	D C T Rowlands	1963 to 1965
14	W J Trew	1907 to 1913

MOST POINTS IN TESTS

Points	Player	Tests	Career
1049	N R Jenkins	87	1991 to 2002
693	S M Jones	80	1998 to 2009
304	P H Thorburn	37	1985 to 1991
230	S M Williams	65	2000 to 2009
211	A C Thomas	23	1996 to 2000
209	J W Hook	33	2006 to 2009
200	Gareth Thomas	100	1995 to 2007
166	P Bennett	29	1969 to 1978
157	I C Evans	72	1987 to 1998

MOST TRIES IN TESTS

Tries	Player	Tests	Career
46	S M Williams	65	2000 to 2009
40	Gareth Thomas	100	1995 to 2007
33	I C Evans	72	1987 to 1998
22	C L Charvis	94	1996 to 2007
20	G O Edwards	53	1967 to 1978
20	T G R Davies	46	1966 to 1978
20	T G L Shanklin	63	2001 to 2009
18	G R Williams	44	2000 to 2005
17	R A Gibbs	16	1906 to 1911
17	J L Williams	17	1906 to 1911
17	K J Jones	44	1947 to 1957

MOST CONVERSIONS IN TESTS

Cons	Player	Tests	Career
130	N R Jenkins	87	1991 to 2002
117	S M Jones	80	1998 to 2009
43	P H Thorburn	37	1985 to 1991
38	J Bancroft	18	1909 to 1914
34	J W Hook	33	2006 to 2009
30	A C Thomas	23	1996 to 2000
29	G L Henson	31	2001 to 2009
25	C Sweeney	35	2003 to 2007
20	W J Bancroft	33	1890 to 1901
20	I R Harris	25	2001 to 2004

MOST PENALTY GOALS IN TESTS

Penalties	Player	Tests	Career
235	N R Jenkins	87	1991 to 2002
138	S M Jones	80	1998 to 2009
70	P H Thorburn	37	1985 to 1991
36	P Bennett	29	1969 to 1978
35	S P Fenwick	30	1975 to 1981
35	J W Hook	33	2006 to 2009
32	A C Thomas	23	1996 to 2000
22	G Evans	10	1981 to 1983

MOST DROP GOALS IN TESTS

Drops	Player	Tests	Career
13	J Davies	32	1985 to 1997
10	N R Jenkins	87	1991 to 2002
8	B John	25	1966 to 1972
7	W G Davies	21	1978 to 1985

WALES

INTERNATIONAL CHAMPIONSHIP RECORDS

RECORD	DETAIL		SET
Most points in season	151	in five matches	2005
Most tries in season	21	in four matches	1910
Highest Score	49	49–14 v France	1910
Biggest win	39	47–8 v Italy	2008
Highest score conceded	60	26–60 v England	1998
Biggest defeat	51	0–51 v France	1998
Most appearances	47	M E Williams	1998–2009
Most points in matches	406	N R Jenkins	1991–2001
Most points in season	74	N R Jenkins	2001
Most points in match	28	N R Jenkins	v France, 2001
Most tries in matches	18	G O Edwards	1967–1978
Most tries in season	6	M C R Richards	1969
	6	S M Williams	2008
Most tries in match	4	W Llewellyn	v England, 1899
	4	M C R Richards	v England, 1969
Most cons in matches	58	S M Jones	2000–2009
Most cons in season	12	S M Jones	2005
Most cons in match	8	J Bancroft	v France, 1910
Most pens in matches	93	N R Jenkins	1991–2001
Most pens in season	16	P H Thorburn	1986
	16	N R Jenkins	1999
Most pens in match	7	N R Jenkins	v Italy, 2000
Most drops in matches	8	J Davies	1985–1997
Most drops in season	5	N R Jenkins	2001
Most drops in match	3	N R Jenkins	v Scotland, 2001

MISCELLANEOUS RECORDS

RECORD	HOLDER	DETAIL
Longest Test Career	G O Llewellyn	1989 to 2004
Youngest Test Cap	N Biggs	18 yrs 49 days in 1888
Oldest Test Cap	T H Vile	38 yrs 152 days in 1921

CAREER RECORDS OF WALES INTERNATIONAL PLAYERS
(UP TO 30 SEPTEMBER 2008)

PLAYER BACKS	DEBUT	CAPS	T	C	P	D	PTS
D R Biggar	2008 v C	3	0	7	7	0	35
A M Bishop	2008 v SA	6	0	0	0	0	0
L M Byrne	2005 v NZ	27	7	0	0	0	35
G J Cooper	2001 v F	42	9	0	0	0	45
C D Czekaj	2005 v C	7	2	0	0	0	10
J Davies	2009 v C	2	2	0	0	0	10
D J Evans	2009 v C	2	0	0	0	0	0
S L Halfpenny	2008 v SA	6	4	0	2	0	26
G L Henson	2001 v J	31	3	29	18	1	130
J W Hook	2006 v Arg	33	6	34	35	2	209
T James	2007 v E	5	2	0	0	0	10
M A Jones	2001 v E	47	13	0	0	0	65
S M Jones	1998 v SA	80	6	117	138	5	693
D J Peel	2001 v J	69	5	0	0	0	25
W M Phillips	2003 v R	38	4	0	0	0	20
J H Roberts	2008 v S	12	1	0	0	0	5
M Roberts	2008 v C	1	0	0	0	0	0
N J Robinson	2003 v I	13	2	7	5	1	42
T G L Shanklin	2001 v J	63	20	0	0	0	100
J P Spratt	2009 v C	2	0	0	0	0	0
M L Stoddart	2007 v SA	3	2	0	0	0	10
S M Williams	2000 v F	65	46	0	0	0	230
FORWARDS							
H Bennett	2003 v I	23	0	0	0	0	0
L C Charteris	2004 v SA	14	0	0	0	0	0
B S Davies	2009 v S	3	0	0	0	0	0
G L Delve	2006 v S	9	1	0	0	0	5
Ian Evans	2006 v Arg	16	1	0	0	0	5
I M Gough	1998 v SA	61	1	0	0	0	5
R Hibbard	2006 v Arg	9	0	0	0	0	0
G D Jenkins	2002 v R	68	3	0	0	0	15
A R Jones	2003 v E	56	1	0	0	0	5
A-W Jones	2006 v Arg	31	4	0	0	0	20
D A R Jones	2002 v Fj	41	2	0	0	0	10
D J Jones	2001 v A	54	0	0	0	0	0

WALES

D L Jones	2000 v Sm	7	0	0	0	0	0
R P Jones	2004 v SA	33	2*	0	0	0	10
E T Lewis-Roberts	2008 v C	1	0	0	0	0	0
C Mitchell	2009 v C	2	0	0	0	0	0
A Powell	2008 v SA	8	0	0	0	0	0
M Rees	2005 v US	30	2	0	0	0	10
R Sowden-Taylor	2005 v It	8	0	0	0	0	0
J Thomas	2003 v A	47	7	0	0	0	35
R M Thomas	2006 v Arg	7	0	0	0	0	0
T R Thomas	2005 v US	27	1	0	0	0	5
S Warburton	2009 v US	1	0	0	0	0	0
G J Williams	2003 v It	7	0	0	0	0	0
M E Williams	1996 v Bb	88	14	0	0	1	73
J V Yapp	2005 v E	14	0	0	0	0	0

* Ryan Jones's figures include a penalty try awarded against Canada in 2006

WALES INTERNATIONAL PLAYERS
UP TO 30TH SEPTEMBER 2009

Note: Years given for International Championship matches are for second half of season; eg 1972 means season 1971–72. Years for all other matches refer to the actual year of the match. Entries in square brackets denote matches played in RWC Finals.

Ackerman, R A (Newport, London Welsh) 1980 NZ, 1981 E, S, A, 1982 I, F, E, S, 1983 S, I, F, R, 1984 S, I, F, E, A, 1985 S, I, F, E, Fj
Alexander, E P (Llandovery Coll, Cambridge U) 1885 S, 1886 E, S, 1887 E, I
Alexander, W H (Llwynypia) 1898 I, E, 1899 E, S, I, 1901 S, I
Allen, A G (Newbridge) 1990 F, E, I
Allen, C P (Oxford U, Beaumaris) 1884 E, S
Andrews, F (Pontypool) 1912 SA, 1913 E, S, I
Andrews, F G (Swansea) 1884 E, S
Andrews, G E (Newport) 1926 E, S, 1927 E, F, I
Anthony, C T (Swansea, Newport, Gwent Dragons) 1997 US 1(R),2(R), C (R), Tg (R), 1998 SA 2, Arg, 1999 S, I (R), 2001 J 1,2, I (R), 2002 I, F, It, E, S, 2003 R (R)
Anthony, L (Neath) 1948 E, S, F
Appleyard, R C (Swansea) 1997 C, R, Tg, NZ, 1998 It, E (R), S, I, F
Arnold, P (Swansea) 1990 Nm 1, 2, Bb, 1991 E, S, I, F 1, A, [Arg, A], 1993 F (R), Z 2, 1994 Sp, Fj, 1995 SA, 1996 Bb (R)
Arnold, W R (Swansea) 1903 S
Arthur, C S (Cardiff) 1888 I, M, 1891 E
Arthur, T (Neath) 1927 S, F, I, 1929 E, S, F, I, 1930 E, S, I, F, 1931 E, S, F, I, SA, 1933 E, S
Ashton, C (Aberavon) 1959 E, S, I, 1960 E, S, I, 1962 I
Attewell, S L (Newport) 1921 E, S, F
Back, M J (Bridgend) 1995 F (R), E (R), S, I
Badger, O (Llanelli) 1895 E, S, I, 1896 E
Baker, A (Neath) 1921 I, 1923 E, S, F, I
Baker, A M (Newport) 1909 S, F, 1910 S
Bancroft, J (Swansea) 1909 E, S, F, I, 1910 F, E, S, I, 1911 E, F, I, 1912 E, S, I, 1913 I, 1914 E, S, F
Bancroft, W J (Swansea) 1890 S, E, I, 1891 E, S, I, 1892 E, S, I, 1893 E, S, I, 1894 E, S, I, 1895 E, S, I, 1896 E, S, I, 1897 E, 1898 I, E, 1899 E, S, I, 1900 E, S, I, 1901 E, S, I
Barlow, T M (Cardiff) 1884 I
Barrell, R J (Cardiff) 1929 S, F, I, 1933 I
Bartlett, J D (Llanelli) 1927 S, 1928 E, S
Bassett, A (Cardiff) 1934 I, 1935 E, S, I, 1938 E, S
Bassett, J A (Penarth) 1929 E, S, F, I, 1930 E, S, I, 1931 E, S, F, I, SA, 1932 E, S, I
Bateman, A G (Neath, Richmond, Northampton) 1990 S, I, Nm 1,2, 1996 SA, 1997 US, S, F, E, R, NZ, 1998 It, E, S, I, 1999 S, Arg 1,2, SA, C, [J, A (R)], 2000 It, Sm, US, SA, 2001 E (R), It (R), R, I, Art (R), Tg
Bater, J (Ospreys) 2003 R (R)
Bayliss, G (Pontypool) 1933 S
Bebb, D I E (Carmarthen TC, Swansea) 1959 E, S, I, F, 1960 E, S, I, F, SA, 1961 E, S, I, F, 1962 E, S, F, I, 1963 E, F, NZ, 1964 E, S, F, SA, 1965 E, S, I, F, 1966 F, A, 1967 S, I, F, E
Beckingham, G (Cardiff) 1953 E, S, 1958 F
Bennett, A M (Cardiff) 1995 [NZ] SA, Fj
Bennett, H (Ospreys) 2003 I 2(R), S 2(R), [C(R),Tg(R)], 2004 S(R),F(R),Arg 1(R),2, SA1(R), 2006 Arg 2,PI(R), 2007 E2, [J(R)],SA, 2008 E,S,It(R),F, 2009 S(R),E(R),F(R),It,I(R)
Bennett, I (Aberavon) 1937 I
Bennett, P (Cardiff Harlequins) 1891 E, S, 1892 S, I
Bennett, P (Llanelli) 1969 F (R), 1970 SA, S, F, 1972 S (R), NZ, 1973 E, S, I, F, A, 1974 S, I, F, E, 1975 S (R), 1976 E, S, I, F, 1977 I, F, E, S, 1978 E, S, I, F

Bergiers, R T E (Cardiff Coll of Ed, Llanelli) 1972 E, S, F, NZ, 1973 E, S, I, F, A, 1974 E, 1975 I
Bevan, G W (Llanelli) 1947 E
Bevan, J A (Cambridge U) 1881 E
Bevan, J C (Cardiff, Cardiff Coll of Ed) 1971 E, S, I, F, 1972 E, S, F, NZ, 1973 E, S
Bevan, J D (Aberavon) 1975 F, E, S, A
Bevan, S (Swansea) 1904 I
Beynon, B (Swansea) 1920 E, S
Beynon, G E (Swansea) 1925 F, I
Bidgood, R A (Newport) 1992 S, 1993 Z 1,2, Nm, J (R)
Biggar, D R (Ospreys) 2008 C(R), 2009 C,US(R)
Biggs, N W (Cardiff) 1888 M, 1889 I, 1892 I, 1893 E, S, I, 1894 E, I
Biggs, S H (Cardiff) 1895 E, S, 1896 S, 1897 E, 1898 I, E, 1899 S, I, 1900 I
Birch, J (Neath) 1911 S, F
Birt, F W (Newport) 1911 E, S, 1912 E, S, I, SA, 1913 E
Bishop, A M (Ospreys) 2008 SA2(R),C,A(R), 2009 S(R),C,US
Bishop, D J (Pontypool) 1984 A
Bishop, E H (Swansea) 1889 S
Blackmore, J H (Abertillery) 1909 E
Blackmore, S W (Cardiff) 1987 I, [Tg (R), C, A]
Blake, J (Cardiff) 1899 E, S, I, 1900 S, I, 1901 E, S, I
Blakemore, R E (Newport) 1947 E
Bland, A F (Cardiff) 1887 E, S, I, 1888 S, I, M, 1890 S, E, I
Blyth, L (Swansea) 1951 SA, 1952 E, S
Blyth, W R (Swansea) 1974 E, 1975 S (R), 1980 F, E, S, I
Boobyer, N (Llanelli) 1993 Z 1(R),2, Nm, 1994 Fj, Tg, 1998 F, 1999 It (R)
Boon, R W (Cardiff) 1930 S, F, 1931 E, S, F, I, SA, 1932 E, S, I, 1933 E, I
Booth, J (Pontymister) 1898 I
Boots, J G (Newport) 1898 I, E, 1899 I, 1900 E, S, I, 1901 E, S, I, 1902 E, S, I, 1903 E, S, I, 1904 E
Boucher, A W (Newport) 1892 E, S, I, 1893 E, S, I, 1894 E, 1895 E, S, I, 1896 E, I, 1897 E
Bowcott, H M (Cardiff, Cambridge U) 1929 S, F, I, 1930 E, 1931 E, S, 1933 E, I
Bowdler, F A (Cross Keys) 1927 A, 1928 E, S, I, F, 1929 E, S, F, I, 1930 E, 1931 SA, 1932 E, S, I, 1933 I
Bowen, B (S Wales Police, Swansea) 1983 R, 1984 S, I, F, E, 1985 Fj, 1986 E, S, I, F, Fj, Tg, WS, 1987 [C, E, NZ], US, 1988 E, S, I, F, WS, 1989 S, I
Bowen, C A (Llanelli) 1896 S, I, 1897 E
Bowen, D H (Llanelli) 1883 E, 1886 E, S, 1887 E
Bowen, G E (Swansea) 1887 S, I, 1888 S, I
Bowen, W (Swansea) 1921 S, F, 1922 E, S, I, F
Bowen, Wm A (Swansea) 1886 E, S, 1887 E, S, I, 1888 M, 1889 S, I, 1890 S, E, I, 1891 E, S
Brace, D O (Llanelli, Oxford U) 1956 E, S, I, F, 1957 E, 1960 S, I, F, 1961 I
Braddock, K J (Newbridge) 1966 A, 1967 S, I
Bradshaw, K (Bridgend) 1964 E, S, I, F, SA, 1966 E, S, I, F
Brew, A (Newport Gwent Dragons, Ospreys) 2007 I(R),A2,E2
Brew, N R (Gwent Dragons) 2003 R
Brewer, T J (Newport) 1950 E, 1955 E, S
Brice, A B (Aberavon) 1899 E, S, I, 1900 E, S, I, 1901 E, S, I, 1902 E, S, I, 1903 E, S, I, 1904 E, S, I
Bridges, C J (Neath) 1990 Nm 1,2, Bb, 1991 E (R), I, F 1, A
Bridie, R H (Newport) 1882 I

Finlayson, A A J (Cardiff) 1974 I, F, E
Fitzgerald, D (Cardiff) 1894 S, I
Ford, F J V (Welch Regt, Newport) 1939 E
Ford, I R (Newport) 1959 E, S
Ford, S P (Cardiff) 1990 I, Nm 1,2, Bb, 1991 E, S, I, A
Forster, J A (Newport Gwent Dragons) 2004 Arg 1
Forward, A (Pontypool, Mon Police) 1951 S, SA, 1952 E, S, I, F
Fowler, I J (Llanelli) 1919 NZA
Francis, D G (Llanelli) 1919 NZA, 1924 S
Francis, P W (Maesteg) 1987 S
Funnell, J S (Ebbw Vale) 1998 Z (R), SA 1
Fury, W L (London Irish) 2008 SA1(R),2(R)
Gabe, R T (Cardiff, Llanelli) 1901 I, 1902 E, S, I, 1903 E, S, I, 1904 E, S, I, 1905 E, S, I, NZ, 1906 E, I, SA, 1907 E, S, I, 1908 E, S, F, I
Gale, N R (Swansea, Llanelli) 1960 I, 1963 E, S, I, NZ, 1964 E, S, I, F, SA, 1965 E, S, I, F, 1966 E, S, I, F, A, 1967 E, NZ, 1968 E, 1969 NZ 1(R),2, A
Gallacher, I S (Llanelli) 1970 F
Garrett, R M (Penarth) 1888 M, 1889 S, 1890 S, E, I, 1891 S, I, 1892 E
Geen, W P (Oxford U, Newport) 1912 SA, 1913 E, I
George, E E (Pontypridd, Cardiff) 1895 S, I, 1896 S
George, G M (Newport) 1991 E, S
Gething, G I (Neath) 1913 F
Gibbs, A (Newbridge) 1995 I, SA, 1996 A 2, 1997 US 1,2, C
Gibbs, I S (Neath, Swansea) 1991 E, S, I, F 1, A, F 2, [WS, Arg, A], 1992 I, F, E, S, A, 1993 E, S, I, F, J, C, 1996 It, A 3, SA, 1997 US, S, I, F, Tg, NZ, 1998 It, E, S, SA 2, Arg, 1999 S, I, F 1, It, E, C, F 2, [Arg 3, J, Sm, A], 2000 I, Sm, US, SA, 2001 E, S, F, It
Gibbs, R A (Cardiff) 1906 S, I, 1907 E, S, 1908 E, S, F, I, 1910 F, E, S, I, 1911 E, S, F, I
Giles, R (Aberavon) 1983 R, 1985 Fj (R), 1987 [C]
Girling, B E (Cardiff) 1881 E
Goldsworthy, S J (Swansea) 1884 I, 1885 E, S
Gore, J H (Blaina) 1924 I, F, NZ, 1925 E
Gore, W (Newbridge) 1947 S, F, I
Gough, I M (Newport, Pontypridd, Newport Gwent Dragons, Ospreys) 1998 SA 1, 1999 S, 2000 F, It (R), E (R), S, I, Sm, US, SA, 2001 E, S, F, It, Tg, A, 2002 I (R), F, R(R), It, S, 2003 R, 2005 It(R),US(R),SA,A, 2006 E,S,I,It,F,Arg 1,2,A,C,NZ, 2007 I,S(R),F1,It,E1, Arg,F2, [C,A,Fj(R)], 2008 E,S,It,F,SA1,2,3(R),C,A, 2009 S,E,F,I,C(R),US
Gould, A J (Newport) 1885 E, S, 1886 E, S, 1887 E, S, I, 1888 S, 1889 I, 1890 S, E, I, 1892 E, S, I, 1893 E, S, I, 1894 E, S, 1895 E, S, I, 1896 E, S, I, 1897 E
Gould, G H (Newport) 1892 I, 1893 S, I
Gould, R (Newport) 1882 I, 1883 E, S, 1884 E, S, I, 1885 E, S, 1886 E, 1887 E, S
Graham, T C (Newport) 1890 I, 1891 S, I, 1892 E, S, 1893 E, S, I, 1894 E, S, 1895 E, S
Gravell, R W R (Llanelli) 1975 F, E, S, I, A, 1976 E, S, I, F, 1978 E, S, I, F, A 1,2, NZ, 1979 S, I, 1981 I, F, 1982 F, E, S
Gray, A J (London Welsh) 1968 E, S
Greenslade, D (Newport) 1962 S
Greville, H G (Llanelli) 1947 A
Griffin, Dr J (Edinburgh U) 1883 S
Griffiths, C R (Llanelli) 1979 E (R)
Griffiths, D (Llanelli) 1888 M, 1889 I
Griffiths, G (Llanelli) 1889 I
Griffiths, G M (Cardiff) 1953 E, S, I, F, NZ, 1954 I, F, S, 1955 I, F, 1957 E, S
Griffiths, J (Swansea) 2000 Sm (R)
Griffiths, J L (Llanelli) 1988 NZ 2, 1989 S
Griffiths, M (Bridgend, Cardiff, Pontypridd) 1988 WS, R, 1989 S, I, F, E, NZ, 1990 F, E, Nm 1,2, Bb, 1991 I, F 1,2, [WS, Arg, A], 1992 I, F, E, S, A, 1993 Z 1,2, Nm, J, C, 1995 F (R), E, S, I, [J, I], 1998 SA 1
Griffiths, V M (Newport) 1924 S, I, F
Gronow, B (Bridgend) 1910 F, E, S, I
Gwilliam, J A (Cambridge U, Newport) 1947 A, 1948 I, 1949 E, S, I, F, 1950 E, S, I, F, 1951 E, S, I, SA, 1952 E, S, I, F, 1953 E, I, F, NZ, 1954 E
Gwynn, D (Swansea) 1883 E, 1887 S, 1890 E, I, 1891 E, S
Gwynn, W H (Swansea) 1884 E, S, I, 1885 E, S
Hadley, A M (Cardiff) 1983 R, 1984 S, I, F, E, 1985 F, E, Fj, 1986 E, S, I, F, Fj, Tg, 1987 S (R), I, [I, Tg, C, E, NZ, A], US, 1988 E, S, I, F

Halfpenny, S L (Blues) 2008 SA3,C,NZ, 2009 S,E,F
Hall, I (Aberavon) 1967 NZ, 1970 SA, S, E, 1971 S, 1974 S, I, F
Hall, M R (Cambridge U, Bridgend, Cardiff) 1988 NZ 1(R),2, WS, R, 1989 S, I, F, E, NZ, 1990 F, E, S, 1991 A, F 2, [WS, Arg, A], 1992 I, F, E, S, A, 1993 E, S, I, 1994 S, I, F, E, Pt, Sp, C, Tg, R, It, SA, 1995 F, S, I, [J, NZ, I]
Hall, W H (Bridgend) 1988 WS
Hancock, F E (Cardiff) 1884 I, 1885 E, S, 1886 S
Hannan, J (Newport) 1888 M, 1889 S, I, 1890 S, E, I, 1891 E, 1892 E, S, I, 1893 E, S, I, 1894 E, S, I, 1895 E, S, I
Harding, A F (London Welsh) 1902 E, S, I, 1903 E, S, I, 1904 E, S, I, 1905 E, S, I, NZ, 1906 E, S, I, SA, 1907 I, 1908 E, S
Harding, C T (Newport) 1888 M, 1889 S, I
Harding, G F (Newport) 1881 E, 1882 I, 1883 E, S
Harding, R (Swansea, Cambridge U) 1923 E, S, F, I, 1924 I, F, NZ, 1925 F, I, 1926 E, I, F, 1927 E, S, F, I, 1928 E
Harris, C A (Aberavon) 1927 A
Harris, D J E (Pontypridd, Cardiff) 1959 I, F, 1960 S, I, F, SA, 1961 E, S
Harris, I R (Cardiff) 2001 Arg, Tg, A, 2002 I, It (R), E, S (R), Fj(R), C(R), NZ(R), 2003 It, E 1(R), S 1(R), I 1(R), F, I 2, S 2, [C,Tg,It,E], 2004 S,I,F,It
Hathway, G F (Newport) 1924 I, F
Havard, Rev W T (Llanelli) 1919 NZA
Hawkins, F J (Pontypridd) 1912 I, F
Hayward, B I (Ebbw Vale) 1998 Z (R), SA 1
Hayward, D J (Newbridge) 1949 E, F, 1950 E, S, I, F, 1951 E, S, I, F, SA, 1952 E, S, I, F
Hayward, D J (Cardiff) 1963 E, NZ, 1964 S, I, F, SA
Hayward, G (Swansea) 1908 S, F, I, A, 1909 E
Hellings, D (Llwynypia) 1897 E, 1898 I, E, 1899 S, I, 1900 E, I, 1901 E, S
Henson, G L (Swansea, Ospreys) 2001 J 1(R), R, 2003 NZ(R), R, 2004 Arg 1,2,SA1,2,R,NZ,J, 2005 E,It,F,S,I, 2006 I(R),F(R),A,NZ(R), 2007 A1(t&R),2(R), 2008 E,S,It,I,F, 2009 F(R),It,I
Herrerá, R C (Cross Keys) 1925 S, F, I, 1926 E, S, I, F, 1927 E
Hiams, H (Swansea) 1912 I, F
Hibbard, R (Ospreys) 2006 Arg 1(R),2(R), 2007 A1(R),2(R), 2008 SA1(R),2,C, 2009 C,US(R)
Hickman, A (Neath) 1930 E, 1933 S
Hiddlestone, D D (Neath) 1922 E, S, I, F, 1924 NZ
Hill, A F (Cardiff) 1885 S, 1886 E, S, 1888 S, I, M, 1889 S, 1890 S, I, 1893 E, S, I, 1894 E, S, I
Hill, S D (Cardiff) 1993 Z 1,2, Nm, 1994 I (R), F, SA, 1995 F, SA, 1996 A 2, F 2(R), It, 1997 E
Hinam, S (Cardiff) 1925 I, 1926 E, S, I, F
Hinton, J T (Cardiff) 1884 I
Hirst, G L (Newport) 1912 S, 1913 S, 1914 E, S, F, I
Hodder, W (Pontypool) 1921 E, S, F
Hodges, J J (Newport) 1899 E, S, I, 1900 E, S, I, 1901 E, S, 1902 E, S, I, 1903 E, S, I, 1904 E, S, 1905 E, S, I, NZ, 1906 E, S, I
Hodgson, G T R (Neath) 1962 I, 1963 E, S, I, F, NZ, 1964 E, S, I, F, SA, 1966 S, I, F, 1967 I
Hollingdale, B G (Swansea) 1912 SA, 1913 E
Hollingdale, T H (Neath) 1927 A, 1928 E, S, I, F, 1930 E
Holmes, T D (Cardiff) 1978 A 2, NZ, 1979 I, F, E, 1980 F, E, S, I, NZ, 1981 A, 1982 I, F, E, 1983 E, S, I, F, 1984 E, 1985 S, I, F, E, Fj
Hook, J W (Ospreys) 2006 Arg 1(R),2,A(R),PI, C,NZ(R), 2007 I,S,F1,It,E1,A1,2,Arg, F2,[C,A(R),J,Fj],SA, 2008 E,S,It(R), I(R),F,SA1(R),2,3(R),C,NZ(R) , 2009 S(R),F(R),It
Hopkin, W H (Newport) 1937 S
Hopkins, K (Cardiff, Swansea) 1985 E, 1987 F, E, S, [Tg, C (R)], US
Hopkins, P L (Swansea) 1908 A, 1909 E, I, 1910 E
Hopkins, R (Maesteg) 1970 E (R)
Hopkins, T (Swansea) 1926 E, S, I, F
Hopkins, W J (Aberavon) 1925 E, S
Horsman, C L (Worcester) 2005 NZ(R),Fj,SA,A, 2006 PI, 2007 I,F1,It,E1,A2(R),E2, F2, [J,Fj]
Howarth, S P (Sale, Newport) 1998 SA 2, Arg, 1999 S, I, F 1, It, E, Arg 1,2, SA, C, F 2, [Arg 3, J, Sm, A], 2000 F, It, E
Howells, B (Llanelli) 1934 E
Howells, W G (Llanelli) 1957 E, S, I, F
Howells, W H (Swansea) 1888 S, I
Howley, R (Bridgend, Cardiff) 1996 E, S, I, F 1, A 1,2, Bb, F 2, It, A 3, SA, 1997 US, S, I, F, E, Tg (R), NZ, 1998 It, E, S, I, F, Z, SA 2, Arg, 1999 S, I, F 1, It, E, Arg 1,2, SA, C, F 2,

Manfield, L (Mountain Ash, Cardiff) 1939 S, I, 1947 A, 1948 E, S, F, I
Mann, B B (Cardiff) 1881 E
Mantle, J T (Loughborough Colls, Newport) 1964 E, SA
Margrave, F L (Llanelli) 1884 E, S
Marinos, A W N (Newport, Gwent Dragons)) 2002 I (R), F, It, E, S, SA 1,2, 2003 R
Marsden-Jones, D (Cardiff) 1921 E, 1924 NZ
Martin, A J (Aberavon) 1973 A, 1974 S, I, 1975 F, E, S, I, A, 1976 E, S, I, F, 1977 I, F, E, S, 1978 E, S, I, F, A 1,2, NZ, 1979 S, I, F, E, 1980 F, E, S, I, NZ, 1981 I, F
Martin, W J (Newport) 1912 I, F, 1919 NZA
Mason, J E (Pontypridd) 1988 NZ 2(R)
Mathews, Rev A A (Lampeter) 1886 S
Mathias, R (Llanelli) 1970 F
Matthews, C M (Bridgend) 1939 I
Matthews, J (Cardiff), 1947 E, A, 1948 E, S, F, 1949 E, S, I, F, 1950 E, S, I, F, 1951 E, S, I, F
May, P S (Llanelli) 1988 E, S, I, F, NZ 1,2, 1991 [WS]
Meek, N N (Pontypool) 1993 E, S, I
Meredith, A (Devonport Services) 1949 E, S, I
Meredith, B V (St Luke's Coll, London Welsh, Newport) 1954 I, F, S, 1955 E, S, I, F, 1956 E, S, I, F, 1957 E, S, I, F, 1958 A, E, S, I, 1959 E, S, I, F, 1960 E, S, I, F, SA, 1961 E, S, I, 1962 E, S, F, I
Meredith, C C (Neath) 1953 S, NZ, 1954 E, I, F, S, 1955 E, S, I, F, 1956 E, I, 1957 E, S
Meredith, J (Swansea) 1888 S, I, 1890 S, E
Merry, J A (Pill Harriers) 1912 I, F
Michael, G M (Swansea) 1923 E, S, F
Michaelson, R C B (Aberavon, Cambridge U) 1963 E
Millar, W H (Mountain Ash) 1896 I, 1900 E, S, I, 1901 E, S, I
Mills, F M (Swansea, Cardiff) 1892 E, S, I, 1893 E, S, I, 1894 E, S, I, 1895 E, S, I, 1896 E
Mitchell, C (Ospreys) 2009 C(R),US(R)
Moon, R H StJ B (Llanelli) 1993 F, Z 1,2, Nm, J, C, 1994 S, I, F, E, Sp, C, Fj, WS, R, It, SA, 1995 E (R), 2000 S, I, Sm (R), US (R), 2001 E (R), S (R)
Moore, A P (Cardiff) 1995 [J], SA, Fj, 1996 It
Moore, A P (Swansea) 1995 SA (R), Fj, 1998 S, I, F, Z, SA 1, 1999 C, 2000 S, I, US (R), 2001 E (R), S, F, It, J 1,2, R, I, Arg, Tg, A, 2002 F, It, E, S
Moore, S J (Swansea, Moseley) 1997 C, R, Tg
Moore, W J (Bridgend) 1933 I
Morgan, C H (Llanelli) 1957 I, F
Morgan, C I (Cardiff) 1951 I, F, SA, 1952 E, S, I, 1953 S, I, F, NZ, 1954 I, S, 1955 E, S, I, F, 1956 E, S, I, F, 1957 E, S, I, F, 1958 E, S, I, F
Morgan, C S (Cardiff Blues) 2002 I, F, It, E, S, SA 1,2, R(R), 2003 F, 2005 US
Morgan, D (Swansea) 1885 S, 1886 E, S, 1887 E, S, I, 1889 I
Morgan, D (Llanelli) 1895 I, 1896 E
Morgan, D E (Llanelli) 1920 I, 1921 E, S, F
Morgan, D R R (Llanelli) 1962 E, S, F, I, 1963 E, S, I, F, NZ
Morgan, E (Swansea) 1914 E, S, F, I
Morgan, E (London Welsh) 1902 E, S, I, 1903 I, 1904 E, S, I, 1905 E, S, I, NZ, 1906 E, S, I, SA, 1908 F
Morgan, F L (Llanelli) 1938 E, S, I, 1939 E
Morgan, G R (Newport) 1984 S
Morgan, H J (Abertillery) 1958 E, S, I, 1959 I, F, 1960 E, 1961 E, S, I, F, 1962 E, S, F, I, 1963 S, I, F, 1965 E, S, I, F, 1966 E, S, I, F, A
Morgan, H P (Newport) 1956 E, S, I, F
Morgan, J L (Llanelli) 1912 SA, 1913 E
Morgan, K A (Pontypridd, Swansea, Newport Gwent Dragons) 1997 US 1,2, C, R, NZ, 1998 S, I, F, 2001 J 1,2, R, I, Arg, Tg, A, 2002 F, It, E, S, SA 1,2, 2003 E 1, S 1, [C,It], 2004 J(R), 2005 E(R),It(R),F,S,I,US,C,NZ,Fj, 2006 A,PI, NZ, 2007 I,S,It,E1,Arg,F2, [C,A(R),J]
Morgan, M E (Swansea) 1938 E, S, I, 1939 E
Morgan, N H (Newport) 1960 S, I, F
Morgan, P E J (Aberavon) 1961 E, S, F
Morgan, P J (Llanelli) 1980 S (R), I, NZ (R), 1981 I
Morgan, S (Cardiff Blues) 2007 A2(R)
Morgan, T (Llanelli) 1889 I
Morgan, W G (Cambridge U) 1927 F, I, 1929 E, S, F, I, 1930 I, F
Morgan, W I (Swansea) 1908 A, 1909 E, S, F, I, 1910 F, E, S, I, 1911 E, F, I, 1912 S
Morgan, W L (Cardiff) 1910 S
Moriarty, R D (Swansea) 1981 A, 1982 I, F, E, S, 1983 E, 1984

S, I, F, E, 1985 S, I, F, 1986 Fj, Tg, WS, 1987 [I, Tg, C (R), E, NZ, A]
Moriarty, W P (Swansea) 1986 I, F, Fj, Tg, WS, 1987 F, E, S, I, [I, Tg, C, E, NZ, A], US, 1988 E, S, I, F, NZ 1
Morley, J C (Newport) 1929 E, S, F, I, 1930 E, I, 1931 E, S, F, I, SA, 1932 E, S, I
Morris, D R (Neath, Swansea, Leicester) 1998 Z, SA 1(R),2(R), 1999 S, I, It (R), 2000 US, SA, 2001 E, S, F, It, Arg, Tg, A, 2004 Arg 1(R),2(R),SA1(R)
Morris, G L (Swansea) 1882 I, 1883 E, S, 1884 E, S
Morris, H T (Cardiff) 1951 F, 1955 I, F
Morris, J I T (Swansea) 1924 E, S
Morris, M S (S Wales Police, Neath) 1985 S, I, F, 1990 I, Nm 1,2, Bb, 1991 I, F 1, [WS (R)], 1992 E
Morris, R R (Swansea, Bristol) 1933 S, 1937 S
Morris, S (Cross Keys) 1920 E, S, F, I, 1922 E, S, I, F, 1923 E, S, F, I, 1924 E, S, F, NZ, 1925 E, S, F
Morris, W (Llanelli) 1896 S, I, 1897 E
Morris, W D (Neath) 1967 F, E, 1968 E, S, I, F, 1969 S, I, F, E, NZ 1,2, A, 1970 SA, S, E, I, F, 1971 E, S, I, F, 1972 E, S, F, NZ, 1973 E, S, I, A, 1974 S, I, F, E
Morris, W G H (Abertillery) 1919 NZA, 1920 F, 1921 I
Morris, W J (Newport) 1965 S, 1966 F
Morris, W J B (Pontypool) 1963 S, I
Moseley, K (Pontypool, Newport) 1988 NZ 2, 1989 S, I, 1990 F, 1991 F 2, [WS, Arg, A]
Murphy, C D (Cross Keys) 1935 E, S, I
Mustoe, L (Cardiff) 1995 Fj, 1996 A 1(R),2, 1997 US 1,2, C, R (R), 1998 E (R), I (R), F (R)
Nash, D (Ebbw Vale) 1960 SA, 1961 E, S, I, F, 1962 F
Newman, C H (Newport) 1881 E, 1882 I, 1883 E, S, 1884 E, S, 1885 E, S, 1886 E, 1887 E
Nicholas, D L (Llanelli) 1981 E, S, I, F
Nicholas, T J (Cardiff) 1919 NZA
Nicholl, C B (Cambridge U, Llanelli) 1891 I, 1892 E, S, I, 1893 E, S, I, 1894 E, S, 1895 E, S, I, 1896 E, S, I
Nicholl, D W (Llanelli) 1894 I
Nicholls, E G (Cardiff) 1896 S, I, 1897 E, 1898 I, E, 1899 E, S, I, 1900 S, I, 1901 E, S, I, 1902 E, S, I, 1903 I, 1904 E, 1905 I, NZ, 1906 E, S, I, SA
Nicholls, F E (Cardiff Harlequins) 1892 I
Nicholls, H C W (Cardiff) 1958 I
Nicholls, S H (Cardiff) 1888 M, 1889 S, I, 1891 S
Norris, C H (Cardiff) 1963 F, 1966 F
Norster, R L (Cardiff) 1982 S, 1983 E, S, I, F, 1984 S, I, F, E, A, 1985 S, I, F, E, Fj, 1986 Fj, Tg, WS, 1987 F, E, S, I, [I, C, E], US, 1988 E, S, I, F, NZ 1, WS, 1989 F, E
Norton, W B (Cardiff) 1882 I, 1883 E, S, 1884 E, S, I
Oakley, R L (Gwent Dragons) 2003 I 2, S 2(R)
O'Connor, A (Aberavon) 1960 SA, 1961 E, S, 1962 F, I
O'Connor, R (Aberavon) 1957 E
O'Neil, W (Cardiff) 1904 S, I, 1905 E, S, I, 1907 E, I, 1908 E, S, F, I
O'Shea, J P (Cardiff) 1967 S, I, 1968 S, I, F
Oliver, G (Pontypool) 1920 E, S, F, I
Osborne, W T (Mountain Ash) 1902 E, S, I, 1903 E, S, I
Ould, W J (Cardiff) 1924 E, S
Owen, A D (Swansea) 1924 E
Owen, G D (Newport) 1955 I, F, 1956 E, S, I, F
Owen, M J (Pontypridd, Newport Gwent Dragons) 2002 SA 1,2, R, C(R), NZ(R), 2003 It, I 2, S 2, 2004 S(R),I(R),F,E,It,Arg 1,2,SA2,R,NZ,J, 2005 E,It,F,S,I,NZ,Fj,SA,A, 2006 E,S,I,It,F,PI, 2007 A1(R),2,E2, [C(R),A(R),J(R),Fj(R)]
Owen, R M (Swansea) 1901 I, 1902 E, S, I, 1903 E, S, I, 1904 E, S, I, 1905 E, S, I, NZ, 1906 E, S, I, SA, 1907 E, S, 1908 F, I, A, 1909 E, S, F, I, 1910 F, E, 1911 E, S, F, I, 1912 E, S
Packer, H (Newport) 1891 E, 1895 S, I, 1896 E, S, I, 1897 E
Palmer, F C (Swansea) 1922 E, S, I
Parfitt, F C (Newport) 1893 E, S, I, 1894 E, S, I, 1895 S, 1896 S, I
Parfitt, S A (Swansea) 1990 Nm 1(R), Bb
Parker, D S (Swansea) 1924 I, F, NZ, 1925 E, S, F, I, 1929 F, I, 1930 E
Parker, E T (Swansea) 1919 NZA, 1920 E, S, I, 1921 E, S, F, I, 1922 E, S, I, F, 1923 E, S, F
Parker, S T (Pontypridd, Celtic Warriors, Newport Gwent Dragons, Ospreys) 2002 R, Fj, C, NZ, 2003 E 2, [C,It,NZ], 2004 S,I,Arg 1,2,SA1,2,NZ, 2005 Fj,SA,A, 2006 PI,C,NZ, 2007 A1,2,F2(t&R), [C,A],SA, 2008 E,S(R),It(R),SA1
Parker, W J (Swansea) 1899 E, S

Parks, R D (Pontypridd, Celtic Warriors) 2002 SA 1(R), Fj(R), 2003 I 2, S 2
Parsons, G (Newport) 1947 E
Pascoe, D (Bridgend) 1923 F, I
Pask, A E I (Abertillery) 1961 F, 1962 E, S, F, I, 1963 E, S, I, F, NZ, 1964 E, S, I, F, SA, 1965 E, S, I, F, 1966 E, S, I, F, A, 1967 S, I
Payne, G W (Army, Pontypool) 1960 E, S, I
Payne, H (Swansea) 1935 NZ
Peacock, H (Newport) 1929 S, F, I, 1930 S, I, F
Peake, E (Chepstow) 1881 E
Pearce, P G (Bridgend) 1981 I, F, 1982 I (R)
Pearson, T W (Cardiff, Newport) 1891 E, I, 1892 E, S, 1894 S, I, 1895 E, S, I, 1897 E, 1898 I, E, 1903 E
Peel, D J (Llanelli Scarlets, Sale) 2001 J 2(R), R (R), Tg (R), 2002 I (R), It (R), E (R), S (R), SA 1,2, I (R), Arg (R), S 1(R), I 1(R), F, NZ(R), I 2, S 2, [C(R),Tg(R),It,NZ(R),E(R)], 2004 S(R),I(R),F(R),E(R),It(R),Arg 1,2,SA1,2,R,NZ, 2005 E,It,F,S,I, 2006 E,S,I,It,A,C,NZ, 2007 I,S,F1,It,E1,Arg,F2, [C,A,Fj],SA, 2008 S(R),It, SA3(R),C(R),NZ(R), 2009 S(R),E(R),F(R),C(R),US
Pegge, E V (Neath) 1891 E
Perego, M A (Llanelli) 1990 S, 1993 F, Z 1, Nm (R), 1994 S, I, F, E, Sp
Perkins, S J (Pontypool) 1983 S, I, F, R, 1984 S, I, F, E, A, 1985 S, I, F, E, Fj, 1986 E, S, I, F
Perrett, F L (Neath) 1912 SA, 1913 E, S, F, I
Perrins, V C (Newport) 1970 SA, S
Perry, W J (Neath) 1911 E
Phillips, A J (Cardiff) 1979 E, 1980 F, E, S, I, NZ, 1981 E, S, I, F, A, 1982 I, F, E, S, 1987 [C, E, A]
Phillips, B (Aberavon) 1925 E, S, I, F, 1926 E
Phillips, D H (Swansea) 1952 F
Phillips, H P (Newport) 1892 E, 1893 E, S, I, 1894 E, S
Phillips, H T (Newport) 1927 E, S, F, I, A, 1928 E, S, I, F
Phillips, K H (Neath) 1987 F, [I, Tg, NZ], US, 1988 E, NZ 1, 1989 NZ, 1990 F, S, I, Nm 1,2, Bb, 1991 E, S, I, F 1, A
Phillips, L A (Newport) 1900 E, S, I, 1901 S
Phillips, R D (Neath) 1987 US, 1988 E, S, I, F, NZ 1,2, WS, 1989 S, I
Phillips, W D (Cardiff) 1881 E, 1882 I, 1884 E, S, I
Phillips, W M (Llanelli Scarlets, Cardiff Blues, Ospreys) 2003 R, 2004 Arg 1(R),2(R), J(R), 2005 US,C,NZ,Fj(R),SA(R), 2006 S(R),It(R),F,Arg 1,2,PI,C(R),NZ(R), 2007 I(R), F1(R),E1(R), A1,2,F2(R), [C(R),A(R),J,Fj(R)],SA(R), 2008 E,S,It(R),I,F, 2009 S,E,F,It,I
Pickering, D F (Llanelli) 1983 E, S, I, F, R, 1984 S, I, F, E, A, 1985 S, I, F, E, Fj, 1986 E, S, I, F, Fj, 1987 F, E, S
Plummer, R C S (Newport) 1912 S, I, F, SA, 1913 E
Pook, T R (Newport) 1895 S
Popham, A J (Leeds, Llanelli Scarlets) 2003 A (R), I 2, R, S 2, [Tg,NZ], 2004 I(R),It(R),SA1,J(R), 2005 C,Fj(R), 2006 E(R),It(R),F,Arg 1,2,PI,NZ(R), 2007 I S,F1,It,E1,2(R),Arg,F2, [C,A(t),J,Fj],SA(R), 2008 E(R)
Powell, A (Blues) 2008 SA3,C(R),NZ,A, 2009 S,E,F,It
Powell, G (Ebbw Vale) 1957 I, F
Powell, J (Cardiff) 1923 I
Powell, J A (Cardiff) 1906 I
Powell, R D (Cardiff) 2002 SA 1(R),2(R), C(R)
Powell, R W (Newport) 1888 S, I
Powell, W C (London Welsh) 1926 S, I, F, 1927 E, F, I, 1928 S, I, F, 1929 E, S, I, F, 1930 S, I, F, 1931 E, S, F, I, SA, 1932 E, S, I, 1935 E, S, I
Powell, W J (Cardiff) 1920 E, S, F, I
Price, B (Newport) 1961 I, F, 1962 E, S, 1963 E, S, F, NZ, 1964 E, S, I, F, SA, 1965 E, S, I, F, 1966 E, S, I, F, A, 1967 S, I, F, E, 1969 S, I, F, NZ 1,2, A
Price, G (Pontypool) 1975 F, E, S, I, A, 1976 E, S, I, F, 1977 I, F, E, S, 1978 E, S, I, F, A, 1979 S, I, F, 1980 F, E, S, I, NZ, 1981 E, S, I, F, A, 1982 I, F, E, S, 1983 E, I, F
Price, M J (Pontypool, RAF) 1959 E, S, I, F, 1960 E, S, I, F, 1962 E
Price, R E (Weston-s-Mare) 1939 S, I
Price, T G (Llanelli) 1965 E, S, I, F, 1966 E, A, 1967 S, F
Priday, A J (Cardiff) 1958 I, 1961 I
Pritchard, C C (Newport, Pontypool) 1904 S, I, 1905 NZ, 1906 E, S
Pritchard, C C (Pontypool) 1928 E, S, I, F, 1929 E, S, F, I
Pritchard, C M (Newport) 1904 I, 1905 E, S, NZ, 1906 E, S, I, SA, 1907 E, S, I, 1908 E, 1910 F, E

Proctor, W T (Llanelli) 1992 A, 1993 E, S, Z 1,2, Nm, C, 1994 I, C, Fj, WS, R, It, SA, 1995 S, I, [NZ], Fj, 1996 It, E, S, I, A 1,2, Bb, F 2, It, A 3, 1997 E(R), US 1,2, C, R, 1998 E (R), S, I, F, Z, 2001 A
Prosser, D R (Neath) 1934 S, I
Prosser, F J (Cardiff) 1921 I
Prosser, G (Pontypridd) 1995 [NZ]
Prosser, I G (Neath) 1934 E, S, I, 1935 NZ
Prosser, T R (Pontypool) 1956 S, F, 1957 E, S, I, F, 1958 A, E, S, I, F, 1959 E, S, I, F, 1960 E, S, I, F, SA, 1961 I, F
Prothero, G J (Bridgend) 1964 S, I, F, 1965 E, S, I, F, 1966 E, S, I, F
Pryce-Jenkins, T J (London Welsh) 1888 S, I
Pugh, C H (Maesteg) 1924 E, S, I, F, NZ, 1925 E, S
Pugh, J D (Neath) 1987 US, 1988 S (R), 1990 S
Pugh, P (Neath) 1989 NZ
Pugh, R (Ospreys) 2005 US(R)
Pugsley, J (Cardiff) 1910 E, S, I, 1911 E, S, F, I
Pullman, J (Neath) 1910 F
Purdon, F T (Newport) 1881 E, 1882 I, 1883 E, S
Quinnell, D L (Llanelli) 1972 F (R), NZ, 1973 E, S, A, 1974 S, F, 1975 E (R), 1977 I (R), F, E, S, 1978 E, S, I, F, A 1, NZ, 1979 S, I, F, E, 1980 NZ
Quinnell, J C (Llanelli, Richmond, Cardiff) 1995 Fj, 1996 A 3(R), 1997 US (R), S (R), I (R), E (R), 1998 SA 2, Arg, 1999 I F 1, It, E, Arg 1,2, SA, C, F 2, [Arg 3, J, A], 2000 It, E, 2001 S (R), F (R), It (R), J 1,2, R (R), I (R), Arg, 2002 I, F
Quinnell, L S (Llanelli, Richmond) 1993 C, 1994 S, I, F, E, Pt, Sp, C, WS, 1997 US, S, I, F, E, 1998 It, E, S (R), Z, SA 2, Arg, 1999 S, I F 1, It, E, Arg 1,2, SA, C, F 2, [Arg 3, Sm, A], 2000 F, It, E, Sm, US, SA, 2001 E, S, F, It, Arg, Tg, A, 2002 I, F, It, E, R, C(R)
Radford, W J (Newport) 1923 I
Ralph, A R (Newport) 1931 F, I, SA, 1932 E, S, I
Ramsay, S (Treorchy) 1896 I, 1904 E
Randall, R J (Aberavon) 1924 I, F
Raybould, W H (London Welsh, Cambridge U, Newport) 1967 S, I, F, E, NZ, 1968 I, F, 1970 SA, E, I, F (R)
Rayer, M A (Cardiff) 1991 [WS (R), Arg, A (R)], 1992 E (R), A, 1993 E, S, I, Z 1, Nm, J (R), 1994 S (R), I (R), F, E, Pt, C, Fj, WS, R, It
Rees, A (Maesteg) 1919 NZA
Rees, A (Maesteg) 1962 E, S, F
Rees, A M (London Welsh) 1934 E, 1935 E, S, I, NZ, 1936 E, S, I, 1937 E, S, I, 1938 E, S
Rees, B I (London Welsh) 1967 S, I, F
Rees, C F W (London Welsh) 1974 I, 1975 A, 1978 NZ, 1981 F, A, 1982 I, F, E, S, 1983 E, S, I, F
Rees, D (Swansea) 1900 E, 1903 E, S, 1905 E, S
Rees, D (Swansea) 1968 S, I, F
Rees, E B (Swansea) 1919 NZA
Rees, H E (Neath) 1979 S, I, F, E, 1980 F, E, S, I, NZ, 1983 E, S, I, F
Rees, H T (Cardiff) 1937 S, I, 1938 E, S, I
Rees, J (Swansea) 1920 E, S, F, I, 1921 E, S, I, 1922 E, 1923 E, F, I, 1924 E
Rees, J I (Swansea) 1934 E, S, I, 1935 S, NZ, 1936 E, S, I, 1937 E, S, I, 1938 E, S, I
Rees, L M (Cardiff) 1933 I
Rees, M (Llanelli Scarlets) 2005 US, 2006 Arg 1,A,C,NZ(R), 2007 I(R),S(t&R),F1,It, E1,A1,Arg,F2, [C,A,Fj], 2008 E(R),S(R), It,I,F(R),SA1,3,NZ,A, 2009 S,E,F,It(R),I
Rees, P (Llanelli) 1947 F, I
Rees, P M (Newport) 1961 E, S, I, 1964 I
Rees, R (Swansea) 1998 Z
Rees, T A (Llandovery) 1881 E
Rees, T E (London Welsh) 1926 I, F, 1927 A, 1928 E
Rees, T J (Newport) 1935 S, I, NZ, 1936 E, S, I, 1937 E, S
Rees-Jones, G R (Oxford U, London Welsh) 1934 E, S, 1935 I, NZ, 1936 E
Reeves, F C (Cross Keys) 1920 F, I, 1921 E
Reynolds, A D (Swansea) 1990 Nm 1,2(R), 1992 A (R)
Rhapps, J (Penygraig) 1897 E
Rice-Evans, W (Swansea) 1890 S, 1891 E, S
Richards, D S (Swansea) 1979 F, E, 1980 F, E, S, I, NZ, 1981 E, S, I, F, 1982 I, F, 1983 E, S, I, R (R)
Richards, E G (Cardiff) 1927 S
Richards, E I (Cardiff) 1925 E, S, F
Richards, E S (Swansea) 1885 E, 1887 S
Richards, H D (Neath) 1986 Tg (R), 1987 [Tg, E (R), NZ]

Thomas, D J (Swansea) 1904 E, 1908 A, 1910 E, S, I, 1911 E, S, F, I, 1912 E

Thomas, D J (Swansea) 1930 S, I, 1932 E, S, I, 1933 E, S, 1934 E, 1935 E, S, I

Thomas, D L (Neath) 1937 E

Thomas, D L (Aberavon) 1961 I

Thomas, E (Newport) 1904 S, I, 1909 S, F, I, 1910 F

Thomas, E J R (Mountain Ash) 1906 SA, 1908 F, I, 1909 S

Thomas, G (Newport) 1888 M, 1890 I, 1891 S

Thomas, G (Bridgend, Cardiff, Celtic Warriors, Toulouse, Cardiff Blues) 1995 [J, NZ, I], SA, Fj, 1996 F 1, A 1,2, Bb, F 2, It, A 3, 1997 US, S, I, F, E, US 1,2, C, R, Tg, NZ, 1998 It, E, S, I, F, SA 2, Arg, 1999 F 1(R), It, E, Arg 2, SA, F 2, [Arg 3, J (R), Sm, A], 2000 F It, E, S, I, US (R), SA, 2001 E, F, It, J 1,2, R, Arg, Tg, A, 2002 E, R, Fj, C, NZ, 2003 It, E 1, S 1, I 1, F, I 2, E 2, [C,It,NZ(R),E], 2004 S,I,F,E,It,SA2,R,NZ, 2005 E,It,F,NZ,SA,A, 2006 E,S,A,C, 2007 It(t&R),E1,A1,2,E2,Arg,F2, [C(R),A,Fj]

Thomas, G V (Bath, Ospreys, Llanelli Scarlets) 2001 J 1,2, R, I (R), Arg, Tg (R), A (R), 2002 S (R), SA 2(R),R(R), 2003 It(R), E 1, S 1, F, E 2(R), R, 2006 Arg 1,2,PI, 2007 I(t&R),A1,2

Thomas, H M (Llanelli) 1912 F

Thomas, H W (Swansea) 1912 SA, 1913 E

Thomas, H W (Neath) 1936 E, S, I, 1937 E, S, I

Thomas, I (Bryncethin) 1924 E

Thomas, I D (Ebbw Vale, Llanelli Scarlets) 2000 Sm, US (R), SA (R), 2001 J 1,2, R, I, Arg (R), Tg, 2002 It, E, S, SA 1,2, Fj, C, NZ, 2003 It, E 1, S 1, I 1, F, A, NZ, E 2, [Tg, NZ,E], 2004 I,F, 2007 A1,2,E2

Thomas, J (Swansea, Ospreys) 2003 A, NZ(R), E 2(R), R, [It(R),NZ,E], 2004 S(t&R),I, F,E,Arg 2(R),SA1(R),R(t&R),J, 2005 E(R),It,F(R),S(R),US,C,NZ, 2006 It(R),F(R),A, PI(R),C,NZ, 2007 S(R),F1(R),It(R),E1(R),A1,2,Arg,F2, [C,A],SA, 2008 E,S,It,I,F,SA1, 2, 2009 It

Thomas, J D (Llanelli) 1954 I

Thomas, L C (Cardiff) 1885 E, S

Thomas, M C (Newport, Devonport Services) 1949 F, 1950 E, S, I, F, 1951 E, S, I, F, SA, 1952 E, S, I, F, 1953 E, 1956 E, S, I, F, 1957 E, S, 1958 E, S, I, F, 1959 I, F

Thomas, N (Bath) 1996 SA (R), 1997 US 1(R),2, C (R), R, Tg, NZ, 1998 Z, SA 1

Thomas, R (Swansea) 1900 E, S, I, 1901 E

Thomas, R (Pontypool) 1909 F, I, 1911 S, F, 1912 E, S, SA, 1913 E

Thomas, R C C (Swansea) 1949 F, 1952 I, F, 1953 S, I, F, NZ, 1954 E, I, F, S, 1955 S, I, 1956 E, S, I, 1957 E, 1958 A, E, S, I, F, 1959 E, S, I, F

Thomas, R L (London Welsh) 1889 S, I, 1890 I, 1891 E, S, I, 1892 F

Thomas, R M (Newport Gwent Dragons) 2006 Arg 2(R), 2007 E2(R),SA, 2008 It,SA2, C, 2009 It

Thomas, S (Llanelli) 1890 S, E, 1891 I

Thomas, S G (Llanelli) 1923 E, S, F, I

Thomas, T R (Cardiff Blues) 2005 US(R),C,NZ(R),Fj,SA,A, 2006E,S,I,It,F,PI,C(R),NZ, 2007 I,S,F1(R),It(R),E1(R),2(R),F2(R), [C(R),A(R),J,Fj(R)],SA(R), 2008 SA2(R)

Thomas, W D (Llanelli) 1966 A, 1968 S, I, F, 1969 E, NZ 2, A, 1970 SA, S, E, I, F, 1971 E, S, I, F, 1972 E, S, F, NZ, 1973 E, S, I, F, 1974 E

Thomas, W G (Llanelli, Waterloo, Swansea) 1927 E, S, F, I, 1929 E, 1931 E, S, SA, 1932 E, S, I, 1933 E, S, I

Thomas, W H (Llandovery Coll, Cambridge U) 1885 S, 1886 E, S, 1887 E, S, 1888 S, I, 1890 E, I, 1891 S, I

Thomas, W J (Cardiff) 1961 E, 1963 F

Thomas, W J L (Llanelli, Cardiff) 1995 SA, Fj, 1996 It, E, S, F 1, 1996 Bb (R), 1997 US

Thomas, W L (Newport) 1894 S, 1895 E, I

Thomas, W T (Abertillery) 1930 E

Thompson, J F (Cross Keys) 1923 E

Thorburn, P H (Neath) 1985 F, E, Fj, 1986 E, S, I, F, 1987 F, [I, Tg, C, E, NZ, A], US, 1988 S, I, F, WS, R (R), 1989 S, I, F, E, NZ, 1990 F, E, S, I, Nm 1,2, Bb, 1991 E, S, I, F 1, A 1985 S, I, Fj, 1986 F, Fj, Tg, WS, 1987 F, E, Fj

Titley, M H (Bridgend, Swansea) 1983 R, 1984 S, I, F, E, A, 1985 S, I, Fj, 1986 F, Fj, Tg, WS, 1987 F, E

Towers, W H (Swansea) 1887 I, 1888 M

Travers, G (Pill Harriers, Newport) 1903 E, S, I, 1905 E, S, I, NZ, 1906 E, S, I, SA, 1907 E, S, I, 1908 E, S, F, I, A, 1909 E, S, I, 1911 S, F, I

Travers, W H (Newport) 1937 S, I, 1938 E, S, I, 1939 E, S, I, 1949 E, S, I, F

Treharne, E (Pontypridd) 1881 E, 1883 E

Trew, W J (Swansea) 1900 E, S, I, 1901 E, S, 1903 S, 1905 S, 1906 S, 1907 E, S, 1908 E, S, F, I, A, 1909 E, S, F, I, 1910 F, E, S, 1911 E, S, F, I, 1912 S, 1913 S, F

Trott, R F (Cardiff) 1948 E, S, F, I, 1949 E, S, I, F

Truman, W H (Llanelli) 1934 E, 1935 E

Trump, L C (Newport) 1912 E, S, I, F

Turnbull, B R (Cardiff) 1925 I, 1927 E, S, 1928 E, F, 1930 S

Turnbull, M J L (Cardiff) 1933 E, I

Turner, P (Newbridge) 1989 I (R), F, E

Uzzell, H (Newport) 1912 E, S, I, F, 1913 S, F, I, 1914 E, S, F, I, 1920 E, S, F, I

Uzzell, J R (Newport) 1963 NZ, 1965 E, S, I, F

Vickery, W E (Aberavon) 1938 E, S, I, 1939 E

Vile, T H (Newport) 1908 E, S, 1910 I, 1912 I, F, SA, 1913 E, 1921 S

Vincent, H C (Bangor) 1882 I

Voyle, M J (Newport, Llanelli, Cardiff) 1996 A 1(t), F 2, 1997 E, US 1,2, C, Tg, NZ, 1998 It, E, S, I, F, Arg (R), 1999 S (R), I (t), It (R), SA (R), F 2(R), [J, A (R)], 2000 F (R)

Wakeford, J D M (S Wales Police) 1988 WS, R

Waldron, R G (Neath) 1965 E, S, I, F

Walker, N (Cardiff) 1993 I, F, J, 1994 S, F, E, Pt, Sp, 1995 F, E, 1997 US 1,2, C, R (R), Tg, NZ, 1998 E

Waller, P D (Newport) 1908 A, 1909 E, S, F, I, 1910 F

Walne, N J (Richmond, Cardiff) 1999 It (R), E (R), C

Walters, N (Llanelli) 1902 E

Wanbon, R (Aberavon) 1968 E

Warburton, S (Blues) 2009 US(R)

Ward, W S (Cross Keys) 1934 S, I

Warlow, D J (Llanelli) 1962 I

Waters, D R (Newport) 1986 E, S, I, F

Waters, K (Newbridge) 1991 [WS]

Watkins, D (Newport) 1963 E, S, I, F, NZ, 1964 E, S, I, F, SA, 1965 E, S, I, F, 1966 E, S, I, F, 1967 I, F, E

Watkins, E (Neath) 1924 E, S, I, F

Watkins, E (Blaina) 1926 S, I, F

Watkins, E V (Cardiff) 1935 NZ, 1937 S, I, 1938 E, S, I, 1939 E, S

Watkins, H V (Llanelli) 1904 S, I, 1905 E, S, I, 1906 E

Watkins, I J (Ebbw Vale) 1988 E (R), S, I, F, NZ 2, R, 1989 S, I, F, E

Watkins, L (Oxford U, Llandaff) 1881 E

Watkins, M J (Newport) 1984 I, F, E, A

Watkins, M J (Llanelli Scarlets) 2003 It(R), E 1(R), S 1(R), I 1(R), R, S 2, 2005 US(R), C(R),Fj,SA(R),A, 2006 E,S,I,It,F,Arg 1,2(R)

Watkins, S J (Newport, Cardiff) 1964 S, I, F, 1965 E, S, I, F, 1966 E, S, I, F, A, 1967 S, I, F, E, NZ, 1968 E, S, 1969 S, I, F, E, NZ 1, 1970 E, I

Watkins, W R (Newport) 1959 F

Watts, D (Maesteg) 1914 E, S, F, I

Watts, J (Llanelli) 1907 E, S, I, 1908 E, S, F, I, A, 1909 S, F, I

Watts, W H (Newport) 1892 E, S, I, 1893 E, S, I, 1894 E, S, I, 1895 E, I, 1896 E

Watts, W J (Llanelli) 1914 E

Weatherley, D J (Swansea) 1998 Z

Weaver, D S (Swansea) 1964 E

Webb, A (Jim) (Abertillery) 1907 S, 1908 E, S, F, I, A, 1909 E, S, F, I, 1910 F, E, S, I, 1911 E, S, F, I, 1912 E, S

Webb, J (Newport) 1888 M, 1889 S

Webbe, G M C (Bridgend) 1986 Tg (R), WS, 1987 F, E, S, [Tg], US, 1988 F (R), NZ 1, R

Webster, R E (Swansea) 1987 [A], 1990 Bb, 1991 [Arg, A], 1992 I, F, E, S, A, 1993 E, S, I, F

Wells, G T (Cardiff) 1955 E, S, 1957 I, F, 1958 A, E, S

Westacott, D (Cardiff) 1906 I

Wetter, J J (Newport) 1914 S, F, I, 1920 E, S, F, I, 1921 E, 1924 I, NZ

Wetter, W H (Newport) 1912 SA, 1913 E

Wheel, G A D (Swansea) 1974 I, E (R), 1975 F, E, I, A, 1976 E, S, I, F, 1977 I, E, S, 1978 E, S, I, F, A 1,2, 1979 S, I, 1980 F, E, S, I, 1981 E, S, I, F, A, 1982 I

Wheeler, P J (Aberavon) 1967 NZ, 1968 E

Whitefoot, J (Cardiff) 1984 A (R), 1985 S, I, F, E, Fj, 1986 E, S, I, F, Fj, Tg, WS, 1987 F, E, S, I, [I, C]

Whitfield, J J (Newport) 1919 NZA, 1920 E, S, F, I, 1921 F, 1922 E, S, I, F, 1924 S, I

Whitson, G K (Newport) 1956 F, 1960 S, I

Wilkins, G (Bridgend) 1994 Tg

Williams, A (Ospreys, Bath) 2003 R (R), 2005 v US(R),C(R), 2006 Arg 2(R), 2007 A2(R)

Williams, B (Llanelli) 1920 S, F, I

Williams, B H (Neath, Richmond, Bristol) 1996 F 2, 1997 R, Tg, NZ, 1998 It, E, Z (R), SA 1, Arg (R), 1999 S (R), I, It (R), 2000 F (R), It (R), E (t+R), 2001 R (R), I (R), Tg (R), A (R), 2002 I (R), F (R), It (R), E (R), S

Williams, B L (Cardiff) 1947 E, S, F, I, A, 1948 E, S, F, I, 1949 E, S, I, 1951 I, SA, 1952 S, 1953 E, S, I, F, NZ, 1954 S, 1955 E

Williams, B R (Neath) 1990 S, I, Bb, 1991 E, S

Williams, C (Llanelli) 1924 NZ, 1925 E

Williams, C (Aberavon, Swansea) 1977 E, S, 1980 F, E, S, I, NZ, 1983 E

Williams, C D (Cardiff, Neath) 1955 F, 1956 F

Williams, D (Ebbw Vale) 1963 E, S, I, F, 1964 E, S, I, F, SA, 1965 E, S, I, F, 1966 E, S, I, A, 1967 F, E, NZ, 1968 E, 1969 S, I, F, E, NZ 1,2, A, 1970 SA, S, E, I, 1971 E, S, I, F

Williams, D (Llanelli) 1998 SA 1(R)

Williams, D A (Bridgend, Swansea) 1990 Nm 2(R), 1995 Fj (R)

Williams, D B (Newport, Swansea) 1978 A 1, 1981 E, S

Williams, E (Neath) 1924 NZ, 1925 F

Williams, E (Aberavon) 1925 E, S

Williams, F L (Cardiff) 1929 S, F, I, 1930 E, S, I, F, 1931 F, I, SA, 1932 E, S, I, 1933 I

Williams, G (London Welsh) 1950 I, F, 1951 E, S, I, F, SA, 1952 E, S, I, F, 1953 NZ, 1954 E

Williams, G (Bridgend) 1981 I, F, 1982 E (R), S

Williams, G (Bridgend, Cardiff, Blues) 2003 It(R), E 1(R), S 1, F(R), E 2(R), 2009 C(R),US

Williams, G M (Aberavon) 1936 E, S, I

Williams, G P (Bridgend) 1980 NZ, 1981 E, S, A, 1982 I

Williams, G R (Cardiff Blues) 2000 I, Sm, US, SA, 2001 S, F, It, R (R), I (R), Arg, Tg (R), A (R), 2002 F (R), It (R), E (R), S, SA 1,2, R, Fj, C, NZ, 2003 It, E 1, S 1, I 1, F, A, NZ, E 2, [Tg,It(R)], 2004 S,I,F,E,It,Arg1,R,J, 2005 F(R),S,US,C

Williams, H R (Llanelli) 1954 S, 1957 F, 1958 A

Williams, J F (London Welsh) 1905 I, NZ, 1906 S, SA

Williams, J J (Llanelli) 1973 F (R), A, 1974 S, I, F, E, 1975 F, E, S, I, A, 1976 E, S, I, F, 1977 I, F, E, S, 1978 E, S, I, F, A 1,2, NZ, 1979 S, I, F, E

Williams, J L (Cardiff) 1906 SA, 1907 E, S, I, 1908 E, S, I, A, 1909 E, S, F, I, 1910 I, 1911 E, S, F, I

Williams, J L (Blaina) 1920 E, S, F, I, 1921 S, F, I

Williams, J P R (London Welsh, Bridgend) 1969 S, I, F, E, NZ 1,2, A, 1970 SA, S, E, I, F, 1971 E, S, I, F, 1972 E, S, F, NZ, 1973 E, S, I, F, A, 1974 S, I, F, 1975 F, E, S, I, A, 1976 E, S, I, F, 1977 I, F, E, S, 1978 E, S, I, F, A 1,2, NZ, 1979 S, I, F, E, 1980 NZ, 1981 E, S

Williams, L H (Cardiff) 1957 S, I, F, 1958 E, S, I, F, 1959 E, S, I, 1961 F, 1962 E, S

Williams, M E (Pontypridd, Cardiff Blues) 1996 Bb, F 2, It (t), 1998 It, E, Z, SA 2, Arg, 1999 S, I, C, J, [Sm], 2000 E (R), 2001 E, S, F, It, 2002 I, F, It, E, S, SA 1,2, Fj, C, NZ, 2003 It, E 1, S 1, I 1, F, A, NZ, E 2, [C,Tg(R),It,E(R)], 2004 S,I, F(t&R),E(R),It, SA2(t&R),R(R),NZ(R),J(R), 2005 E,It,F,S,I,Fj,SA,A, 2006 E,S,I,It,F,A,C,NZ, 2007 I,S,F1,It,E1,Arg,F2, [C,A,J,Fj], 2008 E,S,It,I,F,SA3,NZ,A, 2009 S,E,F,I

Williams, M T (Newport) 1923 F

Williams, O (Llanelli) 1947 E, S, A, 1948 E, S, F, I

Williams, O L (Bridgend) 1990 Nm 2

Williams, R D G (Newport) 1881 E

Williams, R F (Cardiff) 1912 SA, 1913 E, S, 1914 I

Williams, R H (Llanelli) 1954 I, F, S, 1955 S, I, F, 1956 E, S, I, 1957 E, S, I, F, 1958 A, E, S, I, F, 1959 E, S, I, F, 1960 E

Williams, S (Llanelli) 1947 E, S, F, I, 1948 S, F

Williams, S A (Aberavon) 1939 E, S, I

Williams, S M (Neath, Cardiff, Northampton) 1994 Tg, 1996 E (t), A 1,2, Bb, F 2, It, A 3, SA, 1997 US, S, I, F, E, US 1,2(R), C, R (R), Tg (R), NZ (t+R), 2002 SA 1,2, R, Fj(R), 2003 It, E 1, S 1, F(R)

Williams, S M (Neath, Ospreys) 2000 F (R), It, E, S, I, Sm, SA (R), 2001 J 1,2, I, 2003 R, [NZ,E], 2004 S,I,F,E,It,Arg 1,2,SA1,2,NZ,J, 2005 E,It,F,S,I,NZ,Fj,SA,A, 2006 E,S, It,F,Arg 1,2,A,PI(R),C,NZ, 2007 F1,It,E1,F2, [C,A,J,Fj], 2008 E,S,It,I,F,SA1,2,3,NZ,A, 2009 S,F,It,I

Williams, T (Pontypridd) 1882 I

Williams, T (Swansea) 1888 S, I

Williams, T (Swansea) 1912 I, 1913 F, 1914 E, S, F, I

Williams, T (Swansea) 1921 F

Williams, T G (Cross Keys) 1935 S, I, NZ, 1936 E, S, I, 1937 S, I

Williams, W A (Crumlin) 1927 E, S, F, I

Williams, W A (Newport) 1952 I, F, 1953 E

Williams, W E O (Cardiff) 1887 S, I, 1889 S, 1890 S, E

Williams, W H (Pontymister) 1900 E, S, I, 1901 E

Williams, W L T (Llanelli, Cardiff) 1947 E, S, F, I, A, 1948 I, 1949 E

Williams, W O G (Swansea, Devonport Services) 1951 F, SA, 1952 E, S, I, F, 1953 E, S, I, F, NZ, 1954 E, I, F, S, 1955 E, S, I, F, 1956 E, S, I

Williams, W P J (Neath) 1974 I, F

Williams-Jones, H (S Wales Police, Llanelli) 1989 S (R), 1990 F (R), I, 1991 A, 1992 S, A, 1993 E, S, I, F, Z 1, Nm, 1994 Fj, Tg, WS (R), It (t), 1995 E (R)

Willis, W R (Cardiff) 1950 E, S, I, F, 1951 E, S, I, F, SA, 1952 E, S, 1953 S, NZ, 1954 E, I, F, S, 1955 E, S, I, F

Wiltshire, M L (Aberavon) 1967 NZ, 1968 E, S, F

Windsor, R W (Pontypool) 1973 A, 1974 S, I, F, E, 1975 F, E, S, I, A, 1976 E, S, I, F, 1977 I, F, E, S, 1978 E, S, I, F, A 1,2, NZ, 1979 S, I, F

Winfield, H B (Cardiff) 1903 I, 1904 E, S, I, 1905 NZ, 1906 E, S, I, 1907 S, I, 1908 E, S, F, I, A

Winmill, S (Cross Keys) 1921 E, S, F, I

Wintle, M E (Llanelli) 1996 It

Wintle, R V (London Welsh) 1988 WS (R)

Wooller, W (Sale, Cambridge U, Cardiff) 1933 E, S, I, 1935 E, S, I, NZ, 1936 E, S, I, 1937 E, S, I, 1938 S, I, 1939 E, S, I

Wyatt, C P (Llanelli) 1998 Z (R), SA 1(R),2, Arg, 1999 S, I, F 1, It, E, Arg 1,2, SA, C (R), F 2, [Arg 3, J (R), Sm, A], 2000 F, It, E, US, SA, 2001 E, R, I, Arg (R), Tg (R), A (R), 2002 I, It (R), S, F, 2003 A(R), NZ(t+R), E 2, [Tg(R),NZ(R)]

Wyatt, G (Pontypridd, Celtic Warriors) 1997 Tg, 2003 R (R)

Wyatt, M A (Swansea) 1983 E, S, I, F, 1984 A, 1985 S, I, 1987 E, S, I

Yapp, J V (Cardiff Blues) 2005 E(R),It(R),F(R),S(R),I(R),C(R),Fj, 2006 Arg 1(R), 2008 C,NZ(R), 2009 S(R),It,C,US

Young, D (Swansea, Cardiff) 1987 [E, NZ], US, 1988 E, S, I, F, NZ 1,2, WS, R, 1989 S, NZ, 1990 F, 1996 A 3, SA, 1997 US, S, I, F, E, NZ, 1998 It, E, S, I, F, 1999 I, E (R), Arg 1(R),2(R), SA, C (R), F 2, [Arg 3, J, Sm, A], 2000 F, It, E, S, I, 2001 E, S, F, It, R, I, Arg

Young, G A (Cardiff) 1886 E, S

Young, J (Harrogate, RAF, London Welsh) 1968 S, I, F, 1969 S, I, F, E, NZ 1, 1970 E, I, F, 1971 E, S, I, F, 1972 E, S, F, NZ, 1973 E, S, I, F

Young, P (Gwent Dragons) 2003 R (R)

WALES

CAPITAL END TO DROUGHT

Cardiff claimed the Principality Premiership title for the first time in almost a decade and in the process ended Neath's four-year monopoly of league honours in Welsh club rugby. Cardiff had last been crowned champions in 2000 but returned to winning ways nine years later after holding off the determined challenge of second place Newport.

The club has struggled in the semi-professional era in the Principality, but revived memories of their glory days with an ultimately convincing campaign that culminated in a 27–22 victory over Pontypridd at the end of April – their 15th consecutive win in the league – to confirm the side as Premiership top dogs. It was Cardiff's third title since the inception of league rugby in Wales.

The nerves were initially jangling against Pontypridd at the Arms Park as the visitors took a 17–7 half-time lead and with two further league fixtures on the calendar, it seemed the title celebrations would have to be postponed. Cardiff, however, had no intention of delaying the party and late tries from Adam Powell and Chris Czekaj wrapped up an all-important 27–22 triumph and the players were able to celebrate in front of their own fans.

"It was a tremendous advert for the league and naturally, I was pleased with the way we came back from a 17–7 interval deficit," said Phil Davies, Cardiff's coaching consultant, after witnessing the tense denouement to the side's season.

Pontypridd head coach Paul John added: "Obviously we would have liked to have won this match but I agree that it was a wonderful advert for the Premiership."

Cardiff's chief rivals for the title throughout the campaign were Newport and Aberavon and based on the three sides' performances in the early games of the season, few would have bet on Davies' outfit challenging for honours.

In fact, the Blue and Blacks began in September against Newport at

Rodney Parade. It was the 415th meeting between the two clubs and Cardiff were looking for a first-ever Premiership win in Newport but they were completely outplayed by their hosts. Newport wing Mike Poole bagged a brace of tries and further scores from full-back Jason Tovey and replacement hooker Andrew Brown gave the home side a thumping 30–3 victory and a bonus point.

The victory gave Newport vital impetus under their newly-appointed head coach Steve Cronk and in their next six games they recorded five more victories to establish themselves as one of the division's leading contenders.

Aberavon also made a strong start. Four wins from their opening five games were followed by a surprise reverse against Bedwas but they bounced back and strung together a run of five victories from their next six, including a 17–12 triumph over Newport at Rodney Parade.

In contrast, Cardiff went from bad to worse. They did bounce back from the Newport defeat to see off Bridgend 30–23 at the Arms Park seven days later but there was more misery at the end of September when they were beaten 32–28 by Pontypridd at Sardis Road and when they went down 26–25 at home to Ebbw Vale and then 32–3 to Llanelli in mid-November, there was a full-blown crisis developing at the Arms Park.

It was now make-or-break time for the Blue and Blacks but their season was about to take a dramatic turn for the better. Their next fixture was away to Pontypool in early December and although Cardiff scored an early try through full-back Roger Davies, the visitors were far from fluent. But as the match meandered to its conclusion, Cardiff suddenly exploded into life with injury-time scores from Richard Cornock and Czekaj to record a morale-boosting 36–6 victory.

The late flourish was exactly what the side needed and the win was to be the first of 15 on the bounce that ultimately broke Newport and Aberavon's challenge.

The two most significant results in the run came in January and early February. The first was the return match against Newport at the Arms Park and the boot was firmly on the other foot this time as the Blue and Blacks exacted their revenge for that defeat on the opening day of the season, scoring five tries in a 36–26 triumph over the Black and Ambers.

A month later Aberavon came to the Arms Park and once again Cardiff were too strong for one of their main rivals. Tries from Damian Welch, Ryan Howells, Gareth Davies and Roger Davies did the damage and the home side cantered to a comprehensive 29–3 win and a bonus point.

From there Cardiff powered on and seven more victories put them on the verge of the title. At the end of April, Llanelli were beaten 36–9 at the Arms Park and with Pontypridd the next opponents, the capital side were just one win away from being crowned champions.

With the finishing line in sight, the Pontypridd clash was understandably a tense affair as the Arms Park faithful held their collective breath and their nerves were not helped when Ponty wing Chris Clayton crossed for the first try of the game. Cardiff scrum half Andy Williams replied but another Clayton try gave the visitors a 17–7 lead as the two teams headed to the dressing room.

Cardiff emerged for the second half in determined mood and No.8 Adam Powell crashed over in the 47th minute only for flanker Rhys Lloyd to hit back for the Sardis Road club. A Gareth Davies penalty reduced the arrears for the home team but the coup de grace came with a late score from Czekaj and although Ponty applied all the pressure in the dying minutes, Cardiff held their nerve to cling on for a 27–22 victory and the title.

In the SWALEC Cup, Neath put aside their league woes to beat Llanelli 27–21 in the final at the Millennium Stadium and banish the memories of what was a dismal defence of their Premiership title.

The Welsh All Blacks began the game on the front foot and scored the first try of the match through scrum-half Kevin Farrell and he was followed over the white wash by Luke Ford and Gareth King. The Scarlets replied with scores from lock Aaron Shingler and fly half Luke Richards but it was not enough to prevent the All Blacks claiming victory in the final for a second successive year.

"We knew it would be a tough game because Llanelli have been very competitive throughout the season in the league," admitted Neath coach Rowland Phillips. "They have played some good rugby as well. Llanelli have a good cup tradition and they stretched us at times but our boys showed a lot of resolve defensively."

PRINCIPALITY PREMIERSHIP 2008–09 RESULTS

6 September: **Ebbw Vale** 6 **Bedwas** 6, Llandovery 8 **Bridgend** 20, **Llanelli** 24 Wanderers 13, **Neath** 36 Pontypool 31, Swansea 27 **Aberavon** 29. 13 September: **Aberavon** 31 Llandovery 9, **Bedwas** 28 Wanderers 29, **Bridgend** 33 Ebbw Vale 19, Cross Keys 22 Swansea 21, Newport 30 Cardiff 3, Pontypool 26 **Llanelli** 42, Pontypridd 15 Neath 8. 20 September: **Cardiff** 30 Bridgend 23, Ebbw Vale 13 Pontypridd 3, **Llanelli** 27 Aberavon 23,

Neath 62 Cross Keys 20, Newport 67 Llandovery 5, Swansea 23 Bedwas 15, Wanderers 42 Pontypool 31. 27 September: Aberavon 38 Wanderers 17, Bedwas 20 Neath 57, Bridgend 17 Newport 18, Cross Keys 17 Ebbw Vale 19, Llanelli 24 Llandovery 15, Pontypool 20 Swansea 17, Pontypridd 32 Cardiff 28. 4 October: Aberavon 28 Pontypool 0, Ebbw Vale 3 Newport 9, Llandovery 9 Cardiff 15, Llanelli 25 Bedwas 8, Neath 15 Bridgend 16, Swansea 23 Pontypridd 7, Wanderers 27 Cross Keys 8. 11 October: Cardiff 25 Ebbw Vale 26, Bedwas 25 Aberavon 23, Bridgend 24 Swansea 24, Cross Keys 17 Llanelli 21, Neath 29 Newport 19, Pontypool 13 Llandovery 11, Pontypridd 25 Wanderers 5. 18 October: Aberavon 36 Cross Keys 7, Llandovery 9 Ebbw Vale 15, Llanelli 10 Pontypridd 16, Neath 27 Cardiff 29, Newport 65 Swansea 21, Pontypool 18 Bedwas 13, Wanderers 30 Bridgend 12. 25 October: Bedwas 17 Llandovery 22, Bridgend 18 Llanelli 25, Cross Keys 30 Pontypool 16, Ebbw Vale 29 Neath 10, Pontypridd 27 Aberavon 14, Swansea 26 Cardiff 28, Wanderers 16 Newport 28. 1 November: Aberavon 52 Bridgend 15, Bedwas 10 Cross Keys 13, Cardiff 26 Wanderers 21, Llandovery 8 Neath 28, Newport 13 Llanelli 17, Swansea 20 Ebbw Vale 20, Pontypool 12 Pontypridd 30. 7 November: Newport 35 Pontypool 0. 15 November: Bridgend 23 Pontypool 14, Cross Keys 27 Llandovery 25, Ebbw Vale 9 Wanderers 13, Llanelli 32 Cardiff 3, Neath 14 Swansea 9, Newport 12 Aberavon 17, Pontypridd 23 Bedwas 14. 25 November: Bedwas 36 Bridgend 25, Cross Keys 0 Pontypridd 60, Ebbw Vale 17 Llanelli 25, Llandovery 18 Swansea 13, Wanderers 20 Neath 3. 28 November: Newport 19 Pontypool 9. 6 December: Bridgend 29 Cross Keys 36, Ebbw Vale 11 Aberavon 14, Llandovery 23 Pontypridd 7, Neath 15 Llanelli 13, Newport 31 Bedwas 20, Pontypool 6 Cardiff 36, Swansea 23 Wanderers 26. 13 December: Bedwas 8 Ebbw Vale 0, Bridgend 13 Llandovery 9, Cardiff 22 Cross Keys 15, Pontypool 18 Neath 33, Aberavon 29 Swansea 16. 26 December: Llanelli 42 Swansea 23. 27 December: Aberavon 15 Neath 17, Bedwas 0 Cardiff 43, Cross Keys 13 Newport 9, Pontypool 17 Ebbw Vale 23, Wanderers 33 Llandovery 9. 17 January: Cardiff 36 Newport 26, Ebbw Vale 19 Bridgend 19, Llandovery 18 Aberavon 10, Llanelli 46 Pontypool 8, Neath 21 Pontypridd 17, Swansea 39 Cross Keys 3, Wanderers 9 Bedwas 3. 31 January: Bedwas 16 Llanelli 22, Cardiff 22 Llandovery 13, Cross Keys 14 Wanderers 16, Newport 37 Ebbw Vale 7, Pontypool 17 Aberavon 48, Pontypridd 25 Swansea 19, Bridgend 11 Neath 29. 10 February: Bridgend 10 Bedwas 18, Neath 41 Wanderers 0. 13 February: Cardiff 29 Aberavon 3, Swansea 22 Llandovery 21. 28 February: Aberavon 38 Bedwas 10, Ebbw Vale 13 Cardiff 15, Llandovery 6 Pontypool 10, Llanelli 20 Cross Keys 25, Newport 34 Neath 32, Swansea 39 Bridgend 3, Wanderers 13 Pontypridd 13. 7 March: Bedwas 33 Pontypool 14, Cardiff 25 Neath 19, Cross Keys 14 Aberavon 31, Ebbw Vale 3 Llandovery 27, Pontypridd 21 Llanelli 16, Swansea 18 Newport 29. 8 March: Bridgend 11 Wanderers 3. 10 March: Llanelli 35 Ebbw Vale 13. 14 March: Llandovery 20 Llanelli 15. 15 March: Pontypool 16 Wanderers 31. 17 March: Cross Keys 18 Cardiff 27. 19 March: Neath 32 Bedwas 17. 20 March: Newport 39 Bridgend 15, Wanderers 14 Llanelli 20. 28 March: Bridgend 13 Cardiff 20, Pontypridd 51 Ebbw Vale 12. 31 March: Pontypool 12 Newport 9. 4 April: Aberavon 22 Pontypridd 17, Cardiff 33 Swansea 22, Llandovery 11 Bedwas 34, Llanelli 31 Bridgend 27, Neath 15 Ebbw Vale 20, Newport 39, Wanderers 6, Pontypool 47 Cross Keys 26. 7 April: Pontypridd 28 Newport 26. 10 April: Swansea 31 Llanelli 23. 11 April: Bridgend 7 Pontypridd 28, Cardiff 39 Bedwas 18, Ebbw Vale 12 Pontypool 34, Llandovery 22 Wanderers 19, Neath 19 Aberavon 10, Newport 17 Cross Keys 32. 14 April: Ebbw Vale 18 Swansea 5. 17 April: Wanderers 13 Cardiff 29. 18 April: Cross Keys 13 Bedwas 22, Llandovery 16 Newport 32, Pontypridd 23 Pontypool 22. 21 April: Ebbw Vale 17 Cross Keys 33, Pontypridd 42 Bridgend 13. 22 April: Llanelli 10 Newport 36, Wanderers 23 Aberavon 22. 24 April: Swansea 36 Neath 8. 25 April: Aberavon 20 Newport 34, Bedwas 41 Pontypridd 27, Llandovery 16 Cross Keys 15, Pontypool 26 Bridgend 20, Wanderers 31 Ebbw Vale 29, Cardiff 36 Llanelli 9. 28 April: Cardiff 27 Pontypridd 22, Cross Keys 19 Neath 19. 29 April: Aberavon 46 Llanelli 10, Swansea 22 Pontypool 6. 2 May: Aberavon 32 Ebbw Vale 24, Bedwas 22 Newport 33, Cardiff 15 Pontypool 32, Cross Keys 18 Bridgend 21, Llanelli 30 Neath 25, Pontypridd 22 Llandovery 22, Wanderers 26 Swansea 42. 4 May: Neath 20 Llandovery 17, Bridgend 16 Aberavon 19. 8 May: Aberavon 41 Cardiff 40, Pontypridd 30 Cross Keys 21, Bedwas 22 Swansea 36.

FINAL TABLE

	P	W	D	L	F	A	BP	PTS
Cardiff	26	20	0	6	681	509	13	**93**
Newport	26	18	0	8	746	418	18	**90**
Aberavon	26	17	0	9	691	481	16	**84**
Llanelli	26	17	0	9	614	525	10	**78**
Pontypridd	26	16	2	8	611	467	9	**77**
Neath	26	15	1	10	634	498	14	**76**
Wanderers	26	13	1	12	496	565	9	**63**
Swansea	26	10	2	14	617	576	14	**58**
Cross Keys	26	9	1	16	476	679	8	**46**
Ebbw Vale	26	8	3	15	397	543	6	**44**
Bedwas	26	8	1	17	476	622	8	**42**
Llandovery	26	8	1	17	389	547	8	**42**
Pontypool	26	9	0	17	469	674	5	**41**
Bridgend	26	7	2	17	454	647	9	**41**

THE COUNTRIES

LEAGUE ONE EAST
Winners: Blackwood

LEAGUE ONE WEST
Winners: Carmarthen

LEAGUE TWO EAST
Winners: Tredegar

LEAGUE TWO WEST
Winners: Bridgend Athletic

LEAGUE THREE EAST
Winners: Garndiffaith

LEAGUE THREE SOUTH EAST
Winners: Treorchy

LEAGUE THREE SOUTH WEST
Winners: Aberavon Quins

LEAGUE THREE WEST

Winners: Pontyberem

LEAGUE FOUR EAST

Winners: Llandaff

LEAGUE FOUR SOUTH EAST

Winners: Pentyrch

LEAGUE FOUR SOUTH WEST

Winners: Bryncoch

LEAGUE FOUR WEST

Winners: Llandeilo

LEAGUE FOUR NORTH

Winners: Nant Conwy

LEAGUE FIVE EAST

Winners: Abercarn

LEAGUE FIVE SOUTH EAST

Winners: Pontyclun

LEAGUE FIVE SOUTH CENTRAL

Winners: Pyle

LEAGUE FIVE SOUTH WEST

Winners: Abercrave

LEAGUE FIVE WEST

Winners: Cefneithin

LEAGUE FIVE NORTH

Winners: Bro Ffestiniog

LEAGUE SIX EAST

Winners: Hartridge

LEAGUE SIX CENTRAL

Winners: Wattstown

LEAGUE SIX WEST

Winners: Penlan

WALES

SWALEC CUP 2008–09
RESULTS
QUARTER-FINALS

30 March, 2009

Neath 32 **Cross Keys** 31

Llanelli 27 **Wanderers** 20

Aberavon 20 **Newport** 10

Swansea 62 **Caerphilly** 3

SEMI-FINALS

20 April, 2009

Swansea 16 **Neath** 32

Llanelli 26 **Aberavon** 23

FINAL

9 May, Millennium Stadium, Cardiff

NEATH 27 (3G, 2PG) LLANELLI 21 (1G, 3PG, 1T)

NEATH: G King; J Spratt, S Thomas, L Ford, D Evans; A Thomas, K Farrell; N Downs, A James, C Mitchell, N Edwards, E Evans, L Evans, L Beach (captain), G Gravell.

SUBSTITUTIONS: M Jones for Mitchell (31 mins); H Pugh for L Evans (40 mins); K James for Ford (57 mins); M James for Thomas (68 mins); G Price for James (73 mins); T Knoyle for Farrell (79 mins).

SCORERS *Tries*: Farrell, Ford, King *Conversions*: Thomas (3) *Penalty Goals*: Thomas (2)

LLANELLI: D Newton; M Jacob, N Reynolds, M Brayley, N Jones; L Richards, G Davies; I Jones, C Hawkins (captain), S Gardner, A Powell, A Shingler, L Jones, D Godfrey, S Peters.

SUBSTITUTIONS: A Banfield for Brayley (63 mins); J James for G Davies (67 mins); S Hopkins for I Jones (67 mins); A Davies for Powell (73 mins); A Hopkins for Gardner (75 mins).

SCORERS *Tries*: Shingler, Richards *Conversion*: Richards *Penalty Goals*: Richards (3).

REFEREE P Fear (Fleur de Lys)

THE COMBINED TEAMS

A BREATHTAKING SPECTACLE

By Paul Wallace

Although I firmly believe there were many positives both on and off the field to take from the British & Irish Lions tour of South Africa, there is no disguising the fact the Lions were beaten in two of the three Tests and the target was always to beat the Springboks and record a first series victory since 1997.

The Lions ultimately failed to achieve that but there was no disgrace in the way they set about their task and I would have to say that after the first hour of the opening Test in Durban, when the Springboks were the dominant side, Ian McGeechan's side outplayed South Africa in the remainder of the series. It all came down to the finest of margins, particularly in the second Test in Pretoria, and ultimately South Africa were clinical and calm enough to close it out.

Despite Lions' series wins being infrequent events, there were huge expectations of the squad but the Springboks were always going to be a monumental challenge. They are not the reigning world champions for nothing and they have a group of players who have been together for a number of seasons and the team has matured into a tight, combative and experienced unit. I think South Africa will get even better over the next couple of years and at this stage look capable of successfully defending their World Cup crown.

I was lucky enough to spend a lot of time around the Lions squad during the tour covering the series with Sky TV, talking to players and the coaching staff, and although the history books will record a 2–1 loss, I'm convinced the tour was a personal triumph for McGeechan and the way in which he restored many of the traditional values associated with the red jersey.

The 2005 tour to New Zealand, led by Sir Clive Woodward, was an unsuccessful one both on and off the pitch and although the side that went to Australia four years earlier under Graham Henry did win the first Test in Brisbane, there were already signs then that things behind the scenes weren't right.

Both tours were bloated in terms of the size of the squads and the number of backroom staff. The divisions between the Test match players and the midweekers became more and more pronounced and the players became distanced from the supporters.

McGeechan consciously reversed that trend in South Africa. He didn't exactly go back to basics, because I feel his squad was as well prepared as possible, but he deliberately reintroduced a sense of the wider picture and what a Lions tour is all about. It may have been the fourth tour of the professional era but the atmosphere he created harked back to the amateur days and that for me was an important statement.

I know the players enjoyed the tour. They repeatedly told me as much and it was great to see them mixing with the fans and the media in and around the team hotel rather than being cocooned in an artificial bubble, as they had increasingly been on the previous two tours.

The other big difference was the sense that every single player had a fair chance of selection for the Test team. McGeechan repeatedly said before the tour that he would pick on the basis of form rather than reputation and he was true to his word. You can't have harmony within a squad if some players feel they are not getting a fair crack of the whip and McGeechan's Test sides proved that he was selecting purely based on form and that nurtured a sense of camaraderie and unity that had been lacking in both 2001 and 2005.

A good example of this was the relationship between Lee Byrne and Rob Kearney. I was talking to Lee early on the tour and mentioned how well everyone was saying he was playing. His immediate response was to talk up Rob's form. For me, it was reminiscent of the spirit within the squad in 1997 and the mutual support amongst the players, even if they were rivals for the same position.

Looking specifically at the Tests, hindsight reveals that the Lions were to pay a very heavy price for a sluggish start in the opener in Durban. Their backs were firmly against the wall from the moment John Smit crashed over in the fourth minute and it was not until late in the second half that they looked like they had recovered mentally from the Springboks' early onslaught.

The big talking point of the match was Phil Vickery's problems against Tendai Mtawarira up front and the destruction of the Lions scrum. Although the buck often stops with the props, I don't think you can single Vickery out because without the bulk of someone like Simon Shaw behind and a big scrummaging hooker to add some weight, the odds were always stacked against him.

With no real forward platform, the Lions did well to get within five points of South Africa by the final whistle and I thought some of their

BRITISH & IRISH LIONS

back play was very impressive considering the pack were on the back foot. Saying that, I'm convinced the Springboks would have coasted to an altogether more comfortable victory had they not taken off Mtawarira, Bakkies Botha, Fourie du Preez and Jean de Villiers in the second half.

South Africa's scramble defence, which denied Ugo Monye two tries that could have turned the match, impressed me but the Lions backs still showed they were capable of picking holes in the Springboks front-up defence.

The second Test at Loftus Versfeld began and ended in dramatic fashion and if the Lions had been able to cling on to the lead they held for much of the game, they would have gone into the third Test with all the momentum. It ultimately wasn't to be and you have to give South Africa immense credit for reeling the Lions back in and to Morné Steyn for his nerveless penalty to win the match in the final minute.

The game began with Schalk Burger's disgraceful gouge on Luke Fitzgerald in the opening minute. Burger should have been dismissed. I don't however necessarily go along with the theory that the Lions would have definitely won the game if the Springboks had to play for 79 minutes with only 14 men. It's an overly simplistic argument and a bit of wishful thinking.

The disappointing aspect for the Lions was the fact they led the match for 74 minutes but could not close it out. Burger may have got away with it, but the Lions were in the driving seat and didn't finish the job.

Injuries certainly played their part. Losing both Brian O'Driscoll and Jamie Roberts in the second half was a body blow and left the midfield defence exposed, but perhaps even more significant were the departures of props Gethin Jenkins and Adam Jones, which led to uncontested scrums for the majority of the second period.

The Lions scrum had been a disaster in the first Test but the selection of Jones from the start in Pretoria transformed the front row contest and the Lions at last had a platform. The uncontested scrums denied them that and also allowed South Africa to attack from the base of the scrum at speed through Pierre Spies.

There was, of course, criticism of Ronan O'Gara after he conceded the fatal penalty late on by clattering into Du Preez when he was in the air. O'Gara's state of consciousness may have meant he wasn't thinking straight after being run over by Spies and Du Preez earlier but it was still his responsibility not to give away the penalty, whether or not his eyes were on the ball and not the man.

The history books will show it was the wrong thing to do. I don't think he was wrong to go for the Garryowen, to try and keep the ball alive and go for the victory, but conceding the penalty was certainly a huge mistake.

The third Test at Ellis Park in Johannesburg was a cracking game even though the Springboks made 10 changes to their starting XV and McGeechan was also forced to shuffle his deck after all the injuries. It may have been a dead rubber in terms of the outcome of the series but it was still vitally important to the Lions.

It was obviously a huge match for the Lions because they had not been whitewashed by South Africa in over 100 years and the way they came out all guns blazing was an immense achievement that ensured the tour ended on a high and restored a degree of pride. They needed the win badly and the style in which they achieved it was superb.

It would be naive to argue the Springboks were the same force they were in the first two Tests. Of course, they wanted to make it 3–0 but they had one eye on the upcoming Tri Nations and that must have had some impact on their mentality going into the game.

Looking at the individual performances from both camps throughout the series, there were certainly some eye-catching displays with many players standing out.

From a South African perspective, I was hugely impressed in particular with Botha and the hooker Bismarck du Plessis. They say matches are won and lost up front and they both epitomised the Springboks' physicality and power. Neither took a backward step and along with the rest of the Springbok pack, they controlled possession and bullied the Lions, especially in the first Test. Botha was superb in the lineout as well and for me his overall contribution was crucial to South Africa winning the series.

It was a relatively quiet series for Bryan Habana by his own high standards but he did show glimpses of his brilliance when the opportunity came his way, particularly with his try in the second Test in Pretoria.

There were plenty of Lions players who enhanced their reputations despite finishing on the beaten side. I thought Adam Jones was a revelation in the second half of the first Test and the first 45 minutes of the second and Jamie Heaslip really came into his own, showing his dynamism and power, in Johannesburg. He's a relatively young player and I'm sure there's plenty more to come from him.

In the midfield, O'Driscoll and Roberts were superb before both were forced home with injury and I thought Stephen Jones gave the Lions good control and a sense of authority at fly half, as well as kicking well. Kearney was another who did himself proud after missing out on selection for the starting XV for the first Test and his catching under the high balls the Springboks bombarded him with was faultless.

But for me, the Lions player who made the greatest individual contribution had to be Shaw. Winning his first Lions cap at the age of 35 after touring South Africa back in 1997 was a great story and I felt the Lions looked a different side when he came in for the game in Pretoria alongside Paul O'Connell. He certainly made the most of his chance and his impact in the tight and loose was amazing.

He energised the Lions pack and I also think he gave O'Connell a new

BRITISH & IRISH LIONS

lease of life. I was pushing hard for Shaw to be selected ahead of the first Test and I couldn't understand why he didn't get the nod.

The combination of Shaw and O'Connell worked much better than O'Connell and Alun Wyn Jones, which I thought was always going to be lacking in physical presence against the Botha and Victor Matfield combination. Shaw used his bulk, ball carrying ability and good hands to make an impact, which allowed O'Connell to work hard at the breakdown.

I thought O'Connell's captaincy was very positive and he helped set the tone that McGeechan wanted. There was a lot of debate before the tour about the decision to appoint O'Connell ahead of O'Driscoll but the pair are virtually a double act when it comes to leadership in any case and it was business as usual irrespective of who was awarded the captaincy. As expected, O'Connell led by example and particularly in the second and third Tests I thought his form was excellent.

There were heavy sighs of relief after the final whistle in Johannesburg from everyone who loves the Lions. The last Lions Test victory had come back in 2001 in Australia and it was important that however successful the tour was off the pitch that they also made their mark in terms of a tangible result.

There wasn't a huge amount to choose between the two sides overall, which was reflected in the final points tally, but it would be churlish to suggest that South Africa didn't deserve their victory. They are a hugely accomplished side with the most powerful pack in world rugby and they showed with their Tri Nations victories over New Zealand and Australia a few weeks later that they are a force to be reckoned with at home.

When push came to shove, their experience together as a team, their successful World Cup challenge and their determination to avenge the series loss in 1997 just gave them that edge.

McGeechan and the players did a lot to restore the credibility of the Lions as a side and as an entity and the doom merchants who questioned the future of the Lions concept before the tour will have had little to say after what were three thrilling and dramatic Tests.

Ironically, 2009 was the mirror image of the tour 12 years earlier. In 1997, South Africa scored more points and more tries than the Lions but lost the series. The situation was reversed in 2009, which just goes to prove that Lions tours are all about Test match results.

Looking ahead, I genuinely believe the signs are positive for the 2013 tour to Australia. The likes of Roberts, Heaslip, Kearney and Monye, plus Stephen Ferris, Keith Earls, Fitzgerald, James Hook, Leigh Halfpenny and Tom Croft are all young players who will have gained invaluable experience in South Africa and if the next head coach sticks with the McGeechan template, the Lions will have a great chance against the Wallabies.

THE COMBINED TEAMS

BRITISH & IRISH LIONS INTERNATIONAL STATISTICS

UP TO 30TH SEPTEMBER 2009

MATCH RECORDS

MOST CONSECUTIVE TEST WINS

6	1891	SA 1,2,3,	1896 SA 1,2,3
3	1899	A 2,3,4	
3	1904	A 1,2,3	
3	1950	A 1,2,	1955 SA 1
3	1974	SA 1,2,3	

MOST CONSECUTIVE TESTS WITHOUT DEFEAT

Matches	Wins	Draws	Period
6	6	0	1891 to 1896
6	4	2	1971 to 1974

MOST POINTS IN A MATCH
BY THE TEAM

Pts	Opponents	Venue	Year
31	Australia	Brisbane	1966
29	Australia	Brisbane	2001
28	S Africa	Pretoria	1974
28	S Africa	Johannesburg	2009
26	S Africa	Port Elizabeth	1974
25	S Africa	Cape Town	1997
25	Argentina	Cardiff	2005
25	S Africa	Pretoria	2009
24	Australia	Sydney	1950
24	Australia	Sydney	1959

BY A PLAYER

Pts	Player	Opponents	Venue	Year
20	J P Wilkinson	Argentina	Cardiff	2005
20	S M Jones	S Africa	Pretoria	2009
18	A J P Ward	S Africa	Cape Town	1980
18	A G Hastings	N Zealand	Christchurch	1993
18	J P Wilkinson	Australia	Sydney	2001
17	T J Kiernan	S Africa	Pretoria	1968
16	B L Jones	Australia	Brisbane	1950

MOST TRIES IN A MATCH
BY THE TEAM

Tries	Opponents	Venue	Year
5	Australia	Sydney	1950
5	S Africa	Johannesburg	1955
5	Australia	Sydney	1959
5	Australia	Brisbane	1966
5	S Africa	Pretoria	1974

BY A PLAYER

Tries	Player	Opponents	Venue	Year
2	A M Bucher	Australia	Sydney	1899
2	W Llewellyn	Australia	Sydney	1904
2	C D Aarvold	N Zealand	Christchurch	1930
2	J E Nelson	Australia	Sydney	1950
2	M J Price	Australia	Sydney	1959
2	M J Price	N Zealand	Dunedin	1959
2	D K Jones	Australia	Brisbane	1966
2	T G R Davies	N Zealand	Christchurch	1971
2	J J Williams	S Africa	Pretoria	1974
2	J J Williams	S Africa	Port Elizabeth	1974
2	T Croft	S Africa	Durban	2009
2	S M Williams	S Africa	Johannesburg	2009

MOST CONVERSIONS IN A MATCH
BY THE TEAM

Cons	Opponents	Venue	Year
5	Australia	Brisbane	1966
4	S Africa	Johannesburg	1955
3	Australia	Sydney	1950
3	Australia	Sydney	1959
3	Australia	Brisbane	2001
3	S Africa	Durban	2009

BY A PLAYER

Cons	Player	Opponents	Venue	Year
5	S Wilson	Australia	Brisbane	1966
4	A Cameron	S Africa	Johannesburg	1955
3	J P Wilkinson	Australia	Brisbane	2001
3	S M Jones	S Africa	Durban	2009

BRITISH & IRISH LIONS

MOST PENALTIES IN A MATCH
BY THE TEAM

Pens	Opponents	Venue	Year
6	N Zealand	Christchurch	1993
6	Argentina	Cardiff	2005
5	S Africa	Pretoria	1968
5	S Africa	Cape Town	1980
5	Australia	Sydney	1989
5	S Africa	Cape Town	1997
5	S Africa	Durban	1997
5	S Africa	Pretoria	2009

BY A PLAYER

Pens	Player	Opponents	Venue	Year
6	A G Hastings	N Zealand	Christchurch	1993
6	J P Wilkinson	Argentina	Cardiff	2005
5	T J Kiernan	S Africa	Pretoria	1968
5	A J P Ward	S Africa	Cape Town	1980
5	A G Hastings	Australia	Sydney	1989
5	N R Jenkins	S Africa	Cape Town	1997
5	N R Jenkins	S Africa	Durban	1997
5	S M Jones	S Africa	Pretoria	2009

MOST DROPPED GOALS IN A MATCH
BY THE TEAM

Drops	Opponents	Venue	Year
2	S Africa	Port Elizabeth	1974

BY A PLAYER

Drops	Player	Opponents	Venue	Year
2	P Bennett	S Africa	Port Elizabeth	1974

CAREER RECORDS

MOST CAPPED PLAYERS

Caps	Player	Career Span
17	W J McBride	1962 to 1974
13	R E G Jeeps	1955 to 1962
12	C M H Gibson	1966 to 1971
12	G Price	1977 to 1983
10	A J F O'Reilly	1955 to 1959
10	R H Williams	1955 to 1959
10	G O Edwards	1968 to 1974

MOST CONSECUTIVE TESTS

Tests	Player	Span
15	W J McBride	1966 to 1974
12	C M H Gibson	1966 to 1971
12	G Price	1977 to 1983

MOST TESTS AS CAPTAIN

Tests	Captain	Span
6	A R Dawson	1959
6	M O Johnson	1997 to 2001

MOST POINTS IN TESTS

Points	Player	Tests	Career
67	J P Wilkinson	6	2001 to 2005
66	A G Hastings	6	1989 to 1993
53	S M Jones	6	2005 to 2009
44	P Bennett	8	1974 to 1977
41	N R Jenkins	4	1997 to 2001
35	T J Kiernan	5	1962 to 1968
30	S Wilson	5	1966
30	B John	5	1968 to 1971

MOST TRIES IN TESTS

Tries	Player	Tests	Career
6	A J F O'Reilly	10	1955 to 1959
5	J J Williams	7	1974 to 1977
4	W Llewellyn	4	1904
4	M J Price	5	1959

MOST CONVERSIONS IN TESTS

Cons	Player	Tests	Career
7	J P Wilkinson	6	2001 to 2005
7	S M Jones	6	2005 to 2009
6	S Wilson	5	1966
4	J F Byrne	4	1896
4	C Y Adamson	4	1899
4	B L Jones	3	1950
4	A Cameron	2	1955

THE COMBINED TEAMS

MOST PENALTY GOALS IN TESTS			
Penalties	Player	Tests	Career
20	A G Hastings	6	1989 to 1993
16	J P Wilkinson	6	2001 to 2005
13	N R Jenkins	4	1997 to 2001
12	S M Jones	6	2005 to 2009
11	T J Kiernan	5	1962 to 1968
10	P Bennett	8	1974 to 1977
7	S O Campbell	7	1980 to 1983

MOST DROPPED GOALS IN TESTS			
Drops	Player	Tests	Career
2	P F Bush	4	1904
2	D Watkins	6	1966
2	B John	5	1968 to 1971
2	P Bennett	8	1974 to 1977
2	C R Andrew	5	1989 to 1993

SERIES RECORDS

RECORD	HOLDER	DETAIL
Most team points		79 in S Africa 1974
Most team tries		10 in S Africa 1955 & 1974
Most points by player	N R Jenkins	41 in S Africa 1997
Most tries by player	W Llewellyn	4 in Australia 1904
	J J Williams	4 in S Africa 1974

MAJOR TOUR RECORDS

RECORD	DETAIL	YEAR	PLACE
Most team points	842	1959	Australia, NZ & Canada
Most team tries	165	1959	Australia, NZ & Canada
Highest score & biggest win	116-10	2001	v W Australia President's XV
Most individual points	188 by B John	1971	Australia & N Zealand
Most individual tries	22 by A J F O'Reilly	1959	Australia, NZ & Canada
Most points in match	37 by A G B Old	1974 v SW Districts	Mossel Bay, S Africa
Most tries in match	6 by D J Duckham	1971 v W Coast/Buller	Greymouth, N Zealand
	6 by J J Williams	1974 v SW Districts	Mossel Bay, S Africa

MISCELLANEOUS RECORDS

RECORD	HOLDER	DETAIL
Longest Test Career	W J McBride	13 seasons, 1962–1974
Youngest Test Cap	A J F O'Reilly	19 yrs 91 days in 1955
Oldest Test Cap	N A Back	36 yrs 160 days in 2005

BRITISH & IRISH LIONS

BRITISH & IRISH LIONS INTERNATIONAL PLAYERS
UP TO 30TH SEPTEMBER 2009

From 1891 onwards.

* Indicates that the player was uncapped at the time of his first Lions Test but was subsequently capped by his country.

Aarvold, C D (Cambridge U, Blackheath and England) 1930 NZ 1,2,3,4, A
Ackerman, R A (London Welsh and Wales) 1983 NZ 1,4 (R)
Ackford, P J (Harlequins and England) 1989 A 1,2,3
Adamson, C Y (Durham City) 1899 A 1,2,3,4
Alexander, R (NIFC and Ireland) 1938 SA 1,2,3
Andrew, C R (Wasps and England) 1989 A 2,3, 1993 NZ 1,2,3
Arneil, R J (Edinburgh Acads and Scotland) 1968 SA 1,2,3,4
Archer, H A (Guy's H and *England) 1908 NZ 1,2,3
Ashcroft, A (Waterloo and England) 1959 A 1, NZ 2
Aston, R L (Cambridge U and England) 1891 SA 1,2,3
Ayre-Smith, A (Guy's H) 1899 A 1,2,3,4
Back, N A (Leicester and England) 1997 SA 2(R),3, 2001 A 2,3, 2005 NZ 1
Bainbridge, S J (Gosforth and England) 1983 NZ 3,4
Baird, G R T (Kelso and Scotland) 1983 NZ 1,2,3,4
Baker, A M (Newport and Wales) 1910 SA 3
Baker, D G S (Old Merchant Taylors' and England) 1955 SA 3,4
Balshaw, I R (Bath and England) 2001 A 1(R),2(R),3(R)
Bassett, J A (Penarth and Wales) 1930 NZ 1,2,3,4, A
Bateman, A G (Richmond and Wales) 1997 SA 3(R)
Bayfield, M C (Northampton and England) 1993 NZ 1,2,3
Beamish, G R (Leicester, RAF and Ireland) 1930 NZ 1,2,3,4,A
Beattie, J R (Glasgow Acads and Scotland) 1983 NZ 2(R)
Beaumont, W B (Fylde and England) 1977 NZ 2,3,4, 1980 SA 1,2,3,4
Bebb, D I E (Swansea and Wales) 1962 SA 2,3, 1966 A 1,2, NZ 1,2,3,4
Bedell-Sivright, D R (Cambridge U and Scotland) 1904 A 1
Bell, S P (Cambridge U) 1896 SA 2,3,4
Belson, F C (Bath) 1899 A 1
Bennett, P (Llanelli and Wales) 1974 SA 1,2,3,4, 1977 NZ 1,2,3,4
Bentley, J (Newcastle and England) 1997 SA 2,3
Bevan, J C (Cardiff Coll of Ed, Cardiff and Wales) 1971 NZ 1
Bevan, T S (Swansea and Wales) 1904 A 1,2,3, NZ
Black, A W (Edinburgh U and Scotland) 1950 NZ 1,2
Black, B H (Oxford U, Blackheath and England) 1930 NZ 1,2,3,4, A
Blakiston, A F (Northampton and England) 1924 SA 1,2,3,4
Bowcott, H M (Cambridge U, Cardiff and Wales) 1930 NZ 1,2,3,4, A
Bowe, T J (Ospreys and Ireland) 2009 SA 1,2,3
Boyd, C A (Dublin U and *Ireland) 1896 SA 1
Boyle, C V (Dublin U and Ireland) 1938 SA 2,3
Brand, T N (NIFC and *Ireland) 1924 SA 1,2
Bresnihan, F P K (UC Dublin and Ireland) 1968 SA 1,2,4
Bromet, E (Cambridge U) 1891 SA 2,3
Bromet, W E (Oxford U and England) 1891 SA 1,2,3
Brophy, N H (UC Dublin and Ireland) 1962 SA 1,4
Brown, G L (W of Scotland and Scotland) 1971 NZ 3,4, 1974 SA 1,2,3, 1977 NZ 2,3,4
Bucher, A M (Edinburgh Acads and Scotland) 1899 A 1,3,4
Budge, G M (Edinburgh Wands and Scotland) 1950 NZ 4

Bulger, L Q (Lansdowne and Ireland) 1896 SA 1,2,3,4
Bulloch, G C (Glasgow and Scotland) 2001 A I(t), 2005 NZ 3(R)
Burcher, D H (Newport and Wales) 1977 NZ 3
Burnell, A P (London Scottish and Scotland) 1993 NZ 1
Bush, P F (Cardiff and *Wales) 1904 A 1,2,3, NZ
Butterfield, J (Northampton and England) 1955 SA 1,2,3,4
Byrne, J F (Moseley and England) 1896 SA 1,2,3,4
Byrne, J S (Leinster and Ireland) 2005 Arg, NZ 1,2(R),3
Byrne, L M (Ospreys and Wales) 2009 SA 1
Calder, F (Stewart's-Melville FP and Scotland) 1989 A 1,2,3
Calder, J H (Stewart's-Melville FP and Scotland) 1983 NZ 3
Cameron, A (Glasgow HSFP and Scotland) 1955 SA 1,2
Campbell, S O (Old Belvedere and Ireland) 1980 SA 2(R),3,4, 1983 NZ 1,2,3,4
Campbell-Lamerton, M J (Halifax, Army and Scotland) 1962 SA 1,2,3,4, 1966 A 1,2, NZ 1,3
Carey, W J (Oxford U) 1896 SA 1,2,3,4
Carleton, J (Orrell and England) 1980 SA 1,2,4, 1983 NZ 2,3,4
Carling, W D C (Harlequins and England) 1993 NZ 1
Catt, M J (Bath and England) 1997 SA 3
Cave, W T C (Cambridge U and *England) 1903 SA 1,2,3
Chalmers, C M (Melrose and Scotland) 1989 A 1
Chapman, F E (Westoe, W Hartlepool and *England) 1908 NZ 3
Charvis, C L (Swansea and Wales) 2001 A 1(R),3(R)
Clarke, B B (Bath and England) 1993 NZ 1,2,3
Clauss, P R A (Oxford U and Scotland) 1891 SA 1,2,3
Cleaver, W B (Cardiff and Wales) 1950 NZ 1,2,3
Clifford, T (Young Munster and Ireland) 1950 NZ 1,2,3, A 1,2
Clinch, A D (Dublin U and Ireland) 1896 SA 1,2,3,4
Cobner, T J (Pontypool and Wales) 1977 NZ 1,2,3
Colclough, M J (Angoulême and England) 1980 SA 1,2,3,4, 1983 NZ 1,2,3,4
Collett, G F (Cheltenham) 1903 SA 1,2,3
Connell, G C (Trinity Acads and Scotland) 1968 SA 4
Cookson, G (Manchester) 1899 A 1,2,3,4
Cooper, G J (Newport Gwent Dragons and Wales) 2005 Arg
Corry, M E (Leicester and England) 2001 A 1,2(t+R),3, 2005 Arg, NZ 1,2(R),3(R)
Cotton, F E (Loughborough Colls, Coventry and England) 1974 SA 1,2,3,4, 1977 NZ 2,3,4
Coulman, M J (Moseley and England) 1968 SA 3
Cove-Smith, R (Old Merchant Taylors' and England) 1924 SA 1,2,3,4
Cowan, R C (Selkirk and Scotland) 1962 SA 4
Crean, T J (Wanderers and Ireland) 1896 SA 1,2,3,4
Croft, T R (Leicester and England) 2009 SA 1,2,3(t&R)
Cromey, G E (Queen's U, Belfast and Ireland) 1938 SA 3
Crowther, S N (Lennox) 1904 A 1,2,3, NZ
Cueto, M J (Sale and England) 2005 NZ 3
Cunningham, W A (Lansdowne and Ireland) 1924 SA 3
Cusiter, C P (Borders and Scotland) 2005 Arg (R)
Dallaglio, L B N (Wasps and England) 1997 SA 1,2,3
Dancer, G T (Bedford) 1938 SA 1,2,3
D'Arcy, G (Leinster and Ireland) 2005 Arg

Davey, J (Redruth and England) 1908 NZ 1
Davidson, I G (NIFC and Ireland) 1903 SA 1
Davidson, J W (London Irish and Ireland) 1997 SA 1,2,3
Davies, C (Cardiff and Wales) 1950 NZ 4
Davies, D M (Somerset Police and Wales) 1950 NZ 3,4, A 1
Davies, D S (Hawick and Scotland) 1924 SA 1,2,3,4
Davies, H J (Newport and Wales) 1924 SA 2
Davies, T G R (Cardiff, London Welsh and Wales) 1968 SA 3, 1971 NZ 1,2,3,4
Davies, T J (Llanelli and Wales) 1959 NZ 2,4
Davies, T M (London Welsh, Swansea and Wales) 1971 NZ 1,2,3,4, 1974 SA 1,2,3,4
Davies, W G (Cardiff and Wales) 1980 SA 2
Davies, W P C (Harlequins and England) 1955 SA 1,2,3
Dawes, S J (London Welsh and Wales) 1971 NZ 1,2,3,4
Dawson, A R (Wanderers and Ireland) 1959 A 1,2, NZ 1,2,3,4
Dawson, M J S (Northampton, Wasps and England) 1997 SA 1,2,3, 2001 A 2(R),3, 2005 NZ 1(R),3(R)
Dibble, R (Bridgwater Albion and England) 1908 NZ 1,2,3
Dixon, P J (Harlequins and England) 1971 NZ 1,2,4
Dobson, D D (Oxford U and England) 1904 A 1,2,3, NZ
Dodge, P W (Leicester and England) 1980 SA 3,4
Dooley, W A (Preston Grasshoppers and England) 1989 A 2,3
Doran, G P (Lansdowne and Ireland) 1899 A 1,2
Down, P J (Bristol and *England) 1908 NZ 1,2,3
Doyle, M G (Blackrock Coll and Ireland) 1968 SA 1
Drysdale, D (Heriot's FP and Scotland) 1924 SA 1,2,3,4
Duckham, D J (Coventry and England) 1971 NZ 2,3,4
Duggan, W P (Blackrock Coll and Ireland) 1977 NZ 1,2,3,4
Duff, P L (Glasgow Acads and Scotland) 1938 SA 2,3
Easterby, S H (Llanelli Scarlets and Ireland) 2005 NZ 2,3
Edwards, G O (Cardiff and Wales) 1968 SA 1,2, 1971 NZ 1,2,3,4, 1974 SA 1,2,3,4
Edwards, R W (Malone and Ireland) 1904 A 2,3, NZ
Ellis, H A (Leicester and England) 2009 SA 3(R)
Evans, G (Maesteg and Wales) 1983 NZ 3,4
Evans, G L (Newport and Wales) 1977 NZ 2,3,4
Evans, I C (Llanelli and Wales) 1989 A 1,2,3, 1993 NZ 1,2 3, 1997 SA 1
Evans, R T (Newport and Wales) 1950 NZ 1,2,3,4, A 1,2
Evans, T P (Swansea and Wales) 1977 NZ 1
Evans, W R (Cardiff and Wales) 1959 A 2, NZ 1,2,3
Evers, G V (Moseley) 1899 A 2,3,4
Farrell, J L (Bective Rangers and Ireland) 1930 NZ 1,2,3,4,A
Faull, J (Swansea and Wales) 1959 A 1, NZ 1,3,4
Fenwick, S P (Bridgend and Wales) 1977 NZ 1,2,3,4
Fitzgerald, C F (St Mary's Coll and Ireland) 1983 NZ 1,2,3,4
Fitzgerald, L M (Leinster and Ireland) 2009 SA 2
Flutey, R J (Wasps and England) 2009 SA 3
Ford, R W (Edinburgh and Scotland) 2009 SA 3(R)
Foster, A R (Queen's U, Belfast and Ireland) 1910 SA 1,2
Francombe, J S (Manchester) 1899 A 1

Gabe, R T (Cardiff and Wales) 1904 A 1,2,3, NZ
Gibbs, I S (Swansea and Wales) 1993 NZ 2,3, 1997 SA 1,2,3
Gibbs, R A (Cardiff and Wales) 1908 NZ 1,2
Gibson, C M H (Cambridge U, NIFC and Ireland) 1966 NZ 1,2,3,4, 1968 SA 1(R),2,3,4, 1971 NZ 1,2,3,4
Gibson, G R (Northern and England) 1899 A 1,2,3,4
Gibson, T A (Cambridge U and *England) 1903 SA 1,2,3
Giles, J L (Coventry and England) 1938 SA 1,3
Gillespie, J I (Edinburgh Acads and Scotland) 1903 SA 1,2,3
Gould, J H (Old Leysians) 1891 SA 1
Gravell, R W R (Llanelli and Wales) 1980 SA 1(R),2,3,4
Graves, C R A (Wanderers and Ireland) 1938 SA 1,3
Gray, H G S (Scottish Trials) 1899 A 1,2
Greenwood, J T (Dunfermline and Scotland) 1955 SA 1,2,3,4
Greenwood, W J H (Harlequins and England) 2005 NZ 1(R),3

Greig, L L (US and *Scotland) 1903 SA 1,2,3
Grewcock, D J (Bath and England) 2001 A 1,2,3, 2005 Arg, NZ 1(R)
Grieve, C F (Oxford U and Scotland) 1938 SA 2,3
Griffiths, G M (Cardiff and Wales) 1955 SA 2,3,4
Griffiths, V M (Newport and Wales) 1924 SA 3,4
Guscott, J C (Bath and England) 1989 A 2,3, 1993 NZ 1,2,3, 1997 SA 1,2,3
Hall, M R (Bridgend and Wales) 1989 A 1
Hammond, J (Cambridge U, Blackheath) 1891 SA 1,2,3, 1896 SA 2,4
Hancock, P F (Blackheath and England) 1891 SA 1,2,3, 1896 SA 1,2,3,4
Hancock, P S (Richmond and *England) 1903 SA 1,2,3
Handford, F G (Manchester and England) 1910 SA 1,2,3
Harding, A F (London Welsh and Wales) 1904 A 1,2,3, NZ, 1908 NZ 1,2,3,4
Harding, R (Cambridge U, Swansea and Wales) 1924 SA 2,3,4
Harris, S W (Blackheath and England) 1924 SA 3,4
Harrison, E M (Guy's H) 1903 SA 1
Hastings, A G (London Scottish, Watsonians and Scotland) 1989 A 1,2,3, 1993 NZ 1,2,3
Hastings, S (Watsonians and Scotland) 1989 A 2,3
Hay, B H (Boroughmuir and Scotland) 1980 SA 2,3,4
Hayes, J J (Munster and Ireland) 2005 Arg, 2009 SA 3(R)
Hayward, D J (Newbridge and Wales) 1950 NZ 1,2,3
Healey, A S (Leicester and England) 1997 SA 2(R),3(R)
Heaslip, J P R (Leinster and Ireland) 2009 SA 1,2,3
Henderson, N J (Queen's U, Belfast, NIFC and Ireland) 1950 NZ3
Henderson, R A J (Wasps and Ireland) 2001 A 1,2,3
Henderson, R G (Northern and Scotland) 1924 SA 3,4
Hendrie, K G P (Heriot's FP and Scotland) 1924 SA 2
Henson, G L (Neath-Swansea Ospreys and Wales) 2005 NZ 2
Hewitt, D (Queen's U, Belfast, Instonians and Ireland) 1959 A 1,2, NZ 1,3,4, 1962 SA 4
Hickie, D A (Leinster and Ireland) 2005 Arg
Higgins, R (Liverpool and England) 1955 SA 1
Hill, R A (Saracens and England) 1997 SA 1,2, 2001 A 1,2, 2005 NZ 1
Hind, G R (Guy's H and *England) 1908 NZ 2,3
Hinshelwood, A J W (London Scottish and Scotland) 1966 NZ 2,4, 1968 SA 2
Hodgson, J McD (Northern and *England) 1930 NZ 1,3
Holmes, T D (Cardiff and Wales) 1983 NZ 1
Hopkins, R (Maesteg and Wales) 1971 NZ 1(R)
Horgan, S P (Leinster and Ireland) 2005 Arg (R),NZ 1(R),2(R),3(R)
Horrocks-Taylor, J P (Leicester and England) 1959 NZ 3
Horton, A L (Blackheath and England) 1968 SA 2,3,4
Howard, W G (Old Birkonians) 1938 SA 1
Howie, R A (Kirkcaldy and Scotland) 1924 SA 1,2,3,4
Howley, R (Cardiff and Wales) 2001 A 1,2
Hulme, F C (Birkenhead Park and England) 1904 A 1
Irvine, A R (Heriot's FP and Scotland) 1974 SA 3,4, 1977 NZ 1,2,3,4, 1980 SA 2,3,4
Irwin, D G (Instonians and Ireland) 1983 NZ 1,2,4
Isherwood, G A M (Old Alleynians, Sale) 1910 SA 1,2,3
Jackett, E J (Falmouth, Leicester and England) 1908 NZ 1,2,3
Jackson, F S (Leicester) 1908 NZ 1
Jackson, P B (Coventry and England) 1959 A 1,2, NZ 1,3,4
James, D R (Llanelli and Wales) 2001 A 1,2,3
Jarman, H (Newport and Wales) 1910 SA 1,2,3
Jarman, J W (Bristol and *England) 1899 A 1,2,3,4
Jeeps, R E G (Northampton and *England) 1955 SA 1,2,3,4, 1959 A 1,2, NZ 1,2,3,4, 1962 SA 1,2,3,4
Jenkins, G D (Cardiff Blues and Wales) 2005 NZ 1,2,3, 2009 SA 1,2
Jenkins, N R (Pontypridd, Cardiff and Wales) 1997 SA 1,2,3, 2001 A 2(R)
Jenkins, V G J (Oxford U, London Welsh and Wales) 1938 SA 1
John, B (Cardiff and Wales) 1968 SA 1, 1971 NZ 1,2,3,4
John, E R (Neath and Wales) 1950 NZ 1,2,3,4, A 1,2

Johnson, M O (Leicester and England) 1993 NZ 2,3, 1997 SA 1,2,3, 2001 A 1,2,3

Johnston, R (Wanderers and Ireland) 1896 SA 1,2,3

Jones, A R (Ospreys and Wales) 2009 SA 1(R),2

Jones, A-W (Ospreys and Wales) 2009 SA 1,2(R),3(R)

Jones, B L (Devonport Services, Llanelli and Wales) 1950 NZ 4, A 1,2

Jones, D K (Llanelli, Cardiff and Wales) 1962 SA 1,2,3, 1966 A 1,2, NZ 1

Jones, E L (Llanelli and *Wales) 1938 SA 1,3

Jones, I E (Llanelli and Wales) 1930 NZ 1,2,3,4, A

Jones, J P "Jack" (Newport and *Wales) 1908 NZ 1,2,3, 1910 SA 1,2,3

Jones J P "Tuan" (Guy's H and *Wales) 1908 NZ 2,3

Jones K D (Cardiff and Wales) 1962 SA 1,2,3,4

Jones K J (Newport and Wales) 1950 NZ 1,2,4

Jones R N (Swansea and Wales) 1989 A 1,2,3

Jones, R P (Neath-Swansea Ospreys and Wales) 2005 NZ 1(R),2,3

Jones, S M (Clermont Auvergne, Llanelli Scarlets and Wales) 2005 NZ 1,2(R),3, 2009 SA 1,2,3

Jones S T (Pontypool and Wales) 1983 NZ 2,3,4

Judkins, W (Coventry) 1899 A 2,3,4

Kay, B J (Leicester and England) 2005 Arg (R),NZ 1

Keane, M I (Lansdowne and Ireland) 1977 NZ 1

Kearney, R D J (Leinster and Ireland) 2009 SA 1(R),2,3

Kennedy, K W (CIYMS, London Irish and Ireland) 1966 A 1,2, NZ 1,4

Kiernan, M J (Dolphin and Ireland) 1983 NZ 2,3,4

Kiernan, T J (Cork Const and Ireland) 1962 SA 3, 1968 SA 1,2,3,4

Kininmonth, P W (Oxford U, Richmond and Scotland) 1950 NZ 1,2,4

Kinnear, R M (Heriot's FP and *Scotland) 1924 SA1,2,3,4

Kyle, J W (Queen's U, Belfast, NIFC and Ireland) 1950 NZ 1,2,3,4, A 1,2

Kyrke, G V (Marlborough N) 1908 NZ 1

Laidlaw, F A L (Melrose and Scotland) 1966 NZ 2,3

Laidlaw, R J (Jedforest and Scotland) 1983 NZ 1(R),2,3,4

Lamont, R A (Instonians and Ireland) 1966 NZ 1,2,3,4

Lane, M F (UC Cork and Ireland) 1950 NZ 4, A 2

Larter, P J (Northampton, RAF and England) 1968 SA 2

Laxon, H (Cambridge U) 1908 NZ 1

Leonard, J (Harlequins and England) 1993 NZ 2,3, 1997 SA 1(R), 2001 A 1(R),2(R)

Lewis, R A (Abertillery and Wales) 1966 NZ 2,3,4

Lewsey, O J (Wasps and England) 2005 NZ 1,2,3

Llewellyn, W (Llwynypia, Newport and Wales) 1904 A 1,2,3, NZ

Lynch, J F (St Mary's Coll and Ireland) 1971 NZ 1,2,3,4

McBride, W J (Ballymena and Ireland) 1962 SA 3,4, 1966 NZ 2,3,4, 1968 SA 1,2,3,4, 1971 NZ 1,2,3,4, 1974 SA 1,2,3,4

Macdonald, R (Edinburgh U and Scotland) 1950 NZ 1, A 2

McEvedy, P F (Guy's H) 1904 A 2,3, NZ, 1908 NZ 2,3

McFadyean, C W (Moseley and England) 1966 NZ 1,2,3,4

McGeechan, I R (Headingley and Scotland) 1974 SA 1,2,3,4, 1977 NZ 1,2,3(R),4

McGown, T M W (NIFC and Ireland) 1899 A 1,2,3,4

McKay, J W (Queen's U, Belfast and Ireland) 1950 NZ 1,2,3,4, A 1,2

McKibbin, H R (Queen's U, Belfast and Ireland) 1938 SA 1,2,3

Mackie, O G (Wakefield Trinity and *England) 1896 SA 1,2,3,4

Maclagan, W E (London Scottish and Scotland) 1891 SA 1,2,3

McLauchlan, J (Jordanhill and Scotland) 1971 NZ 1,2,3,4, 1974 SA 1,2,3,4

McLeod, H F (Hawick and Scotland) 1959 A 1,2, NZ 1,2,3,4

McLoughlin, R J (Gosforth, Blackrock Coll and Ireland) 1966 A 1,2, NZ,4

Macmillan, R G (London Scottish and Scotland) 1891 SA 1,2,3

MacNeill, H P (Oxford U and Ireland) 1983 NZ 1,2,4 (R)

Macpherson, N C (Newport and Scotland) 1924 SA 1,2,3,4

Macrae, D J (St Andrew's U and Scotland) 1938 SA 1

McVicker, J (Collegians and Ireland) 1924 SA 1,3,4

Magee, A M (Bective R and Ireland) 1896 SA 1,2,3,4

Magee, J M (Bective R) 1896 SA 2,4

Marques, R W D (Harlequins and England) 1959 A 2, NZ 2

Marsden-Jones, D (London Welsh and Wales) 1924 SA 1,2

Marshall, H (Blackheath and *England) 1891 SA 2,3

Martin, A J (Aberavon and Wales) 1977 NZ 1

Martelli, E (Dublin U) 1899 A 1

Martindale, S A (Kendal and England) 1930 A

Massey, B F (Hull and ER) 1904 A 3

Matthews, J (Cardiff and Wales) 1950 NZ 1,2,3,4, A 1,2

Maxwell, R B (Birkenhead Park) 1924 SA 1

Mayfield, W E (Cambridge U) 1891 SA 2,3

Mayne, R B (Queen's U, Belfast and Ireland) 1938 SA 1,2,3

Meares, A W D (Dublin U and *Ireland) 1896 SA 3,4

Mears, L A (Bath and England) 2009 SA 1

Meredith, B V (Newport and Wales) 1955 SA 1,2,3,4, 1962 SA 1,2,3,4

Meredith, C C (Neath and Wales) 1955 SA 1,2,3,4

Millar, S (Ballymena and Ireland) 1959 A 1,2, NZ 2, 1962 SA 1,2,3,4, 1968 SA 1,2

Miller, E R P (Leicester and England) 1997 SA 2(R)

Milliken, R A (Bangor and Ireland) 1974 SA 1,2,3,4

Milne, K S (Heriot's FP and Scotland) 1993 NZ 1

Mitchell, W G (Richmond and England) 1891 SA 1,2,3

Monye, Y C C (Harlequins and England) 2009 SA 1,3

Moody, L W (Leicester and England) 2005 Arg, NZ 2,3

Moore, B C (Nottingham, Harlequins and England) 1989 A 1,2,3, 1993 NZ 2,3

Morgan, C I (Cardiff and Wales) 1955 SA 1,2,3,4

Morgan, D W (Stewart's-Melville FP and Scotland) 1977 NZ 3(R),4

Morgan, E (London Welsh, Guy's H and Wales) 1904 A 1,2,3, NZ

Morgan, E (Swansea and *Wales) 1908 NZ 2,3

Morgan, G J (Clontarf and Ireland) 1938 SA 3

Morgan, H J (Abertillery and Wales) 1959 NZ.3,4, 1962 SA 2,3,4

Morgan, M E (Swansea and Wales) 1938 SA 1,2

Morgan, W (Cardiff and *Wales) 1908 NZ 2,3

Morley, J C (Newport and Wales) 1930 NZ 1,2,3

Morris, C D (Orrell and England) 1993 NZ 1,2,3

Morris, D R (Swansea and Wales) 2001 A 3(R)

Morrison, M C (Royal HSFP and Scotland) 1903 SA 1,2,3

Mortimer, W (Marlborough N and *England) 1896 SA 1,2,3,4

Mulcahy, W A (UC Dublin and Ireland) 1959 A 1, NZ 4, 1962 SA 1,2,3,4

Mullen, K D (Old Belvedere and Ireland) 1950 NZ 1,2, A 2

Mulligan, A A (Wanderers, London Irish and Ireland) 1959 NZ 4

Mullin, B J (London Irish and Ireland) 1989 A 1

Mullineux, M (Blackheath) 1896 SA 1, 1899 A 1

Mullins, R C (Oxford U) 1896 SA 1,3

Murphy, G E A (Leicester and Ireland) 2005 Arg, NZ 3

Murphy, N A A (Cork Const and Ireland) 1959 A 2, NZ 1,2,4, 1966 A 1,2, NZ 2,3

Murray, P F (Wanderers and Ireland) 1930 NZ 1,2,4, A

Neale, M E (Bristol, Blackheath and *England) 1910 SA 1,2,3

Neary, A (Broughton Park and England) 1977 NZ 4

Neill, R M (Edinburgh Acads and Scotland) 1903 SA 2,3

Nelson, J E (Malone and Ireland) 1950 NZ 3,4, A 1,2

Nicholls, E G (Cardiff and Wales) 1899 A 1,2,3,4

Nicholson, B E (Harlequins and England) 1938 SA 2

Nicholson, E T (Birkenhead Park and *England) 1899 A 3,4

Norris, C H (Cardiff and Wales) 1966 NZ 1,2,3

Norster, R L (Cardiff and Wales) 1983 NZ 1,2, 1989 A 1

Novis, A L (Blackheath and England) 1930 NZ 2,4, A

O'Brien, A B (Guy's H) 1904 A 1,2,3, NZ

O'Callaghan, D P (Munster and Ireland) 2005 Arg, NZ 2,3, 2009 SA 1(R)

O'Connell, P J (Munster and Ireland) 2005 NZ 1,2,3, 2009 SA 1,2,3

BAA-BAAS TOPPLE ENGLAND

I**t was a mixed** season in terms of results for the famous Barbarians in 2008–09, winning on four of their seven outings in the 119th year since the invitational side's creation, but the undisputed highlight of their campaign was victory over England at Twickenham at the end of May.

In front of a crowd of over 40,000, the Baa-Baas were in irrepressible form as they emerged 33–26 victors from a hugely entertaining, eight-try thriller to record their first win over the men in white for four years.

The season began in November in Plymouth for the 11th annual Remembrance Match against the Combined Services and the game produced seven tries, five of which went to the Barbarians as they registered a 33–14 win.

The following month brought a high profile encounter with Australia at Wembley in the Olympic Centenary Match to commemorate the London Games of 1908. The Baa-Baas fielded one of their strongest sides in recent history, including All Black captain Richie McCaw and Springbok skipper John Smit, but the star-studded line-up was to prove not quite cohesive enough and it was the Wallabies, ending their six-match European tour, who held out for a narrow 18–11 victory.

In January, the Barbarians were in Wales to face Llanelli for a match to mark the official opening of the club's new stadium, the Parc y Scarlets, and the 14,479 fans who attended were not disappointed as the two sides shared ten tries. Llanelli were the first on the scoreboard after just three minutes with a Matthew Jacobs try and although the Baa-Baas rallied in the second half, the Scarlets christened their new ground with a 40–24 triumph.

Victories over Blackheath (57–45) at the Rectory Field and Bedford (76–45) at Goldington Road in March and April followed before the match with England at Twickenham.

Captained by Martin Corry in his last senior appearance in England, the Baa-Baas drew first blood through Iain Balshaw and added a second try from lock Chris Jack. The home side replied with a Ben Foden try in the first half but the match was effectively settled in a ten-minute salvo after the restart as the Barbarians pulled away with scores from Australia's Rocky Elsom, Balshaw and Ireland's Gordon D'Arcy. England scored three late tries to leave the result in doubt but at the final whistle, the visitors were 33–26 winners.

"This game was about enjoyment and I thought some of the rugby was absolutely mercurial," said Baa-Baas wing Josh Lewsey. "The whole week had been about sharing some of rugby's greatest qualities which are enjoyment and companionship.

"The Corinthian spirit was there. The aim was to have a good time and deliver on the field as well and we did that. A lot of the rugby in the Premiership is quite structured and controlled but the Barbarians is about putting a lot of good players on the field and letting them play."

The euphoria of their Twickenham victory quickly dissipated, however, as the side travelled to Australia a week later and were put to the sword by the Wallabies in Sydney. The game was played for the inaugural Nick Shehadie Cup, in honour of the eponymous former ARU President, but any hopes the Barbarians had of lifting the new trophy were dashed as Australia cut loose in a 55–7 victory, condemning the tourists to their heaviest ever defeat against southern hemisphere opposition.

Elsewhere, the Penguin International Club were as busy as ever as they celebrated their 50th year after Sidcup RFC members Tony Mason and Alan Wright sat down and decided to set up a travelling club with the aim of fostering the sense of fraternity of the game worldwide.

November saw the Penguins head off for the Borneo 10s at the Sandakan Rugby Club in Bandar Utama, one of seven foreign sides in the competition and looking to avenge their defeat in the finals of the two previous years.

"This will be our third visit to the 10s and after twice finishing as runners-up, we'll be aiming to go one better this time," said Penguins team manager Craig Brown before the tournament. "The competition will, as always, be tough but we're looking forward to playing some strong, attacking rugby in the Penguins tradition and hopefully this will be our year."

The Penguins duly battled their way through to the final again where they faced the hosts, Borneo Eagles, who had beaten them 24–0 at the same stage 12 months earlier. This time it was the visitors who got their hands on the silverware after a 19–5 win. "It was not an easy game," said Brown after the final whistle. "It was a close match and difficult at times but I am happy that we won today."

The Penguins, however, did not fare as well in March at the Hong Kong Football Club 10s. Despite being top seeds in the tournament, they were beaten 12–7 by New Zealand side Aliens in the Cup quarter-final and had to content themselves with success in the Plate competition, beating German debutants Wild Titans 33–12 in the final.

CROSS-BORDER TOURNAMENTS

LEINSTER COMPLETE EURO DREAM

By Will Greenwood

Leinster's players finally get their hands on the Heineken Cup.

It may have been a long time coming but Leinster finally got their hands on the Heineken Cup and based on their spectacular destruction of provincial rivals Munster in the semi-final at Croke Park and the way in which they held their nerve in a tense final against Leicester at Murrayfield, I don't think anyone could seriously argue they were not worthy champions.

They had gone close before, losing in the semi-finals in 1996, 2003 and 2006 but Michael Cheika's side had a confident, ruthless edge about them in 2008–09 and under the superb captaincy of Leo Cullen they got better as the tournament progressed. The Tigers pushed them all the way in the final in Edinburgh to set up a dramatic climax but they were not to be denied and their victory capped an incredible season for Irish rugby at both provincial and international level.

Defeat was a bitter pill to swallow for Leicester after losing in the final in 2007 but shouldn't distract from the fantastic job Richard Cockerill did as head coach in the wake of Heyneke Meyer's resignation earlier in the season. Cockerill was only confirmed as the Tigers' permanent coach in April and to take the side through to the final was a great achievement but Leinster ultimately played a bit more rugby, which I thought was the difference between the two sides.

I have to admit I initially felt it was going to be Munster's year again when the group stages kicked off in October. They qualified for the quarter-finals from Pool One with five wins from six but with the benefit of hindsight, their 25–19 loss to Clermont Auvergne in December was the first sign that the defending champions were perhaps not going to be the force they had been the previous season. Despite boasting a squad bursting with talent, Clermont failed to reach the last eight and then went on to lose the Top 14 Championship final against Perpignan which underlined their lack of consistency and Jekyll and Hyde personality.

Pool Two was a scrappy affair which Leinster emerged from ahead of Wasps courtesy of picking up more bonus points. The Irishmen got off to a flying start with an impressive 27–16 win over Edinburgh in Scotland and although they were narrowly beaten by Castres in France in their fourth outing, they did just enough to make it through to the last eight. Wasps for me were disappointing and I think they got their tactics wrong.

Bonus points were also pivotal in Pool Three. Leicester, Ospreys and Perpignan all won four of their six games but it was the Tigers who emerged as group winners with the Ospreys booking themselves one of the best runners-up spots. It was arguably the strongest pool in the competition but Leicester's innate knack of getting the results they need at crucial times saw them through. The Ospreys' star-studded line-up flattered to deceive again and Perpignan, who joined the list of the French sides who didn't make the knockout stages, at least had the consolation of securing their first Top 14 title in over 50 years later in their campaign.

Harlequins topped Pool Four and the undoubted highlight for the Londoners was their superb 15–10 victory over Stade Français in Paris in early December. They also beat the Scarlets away from home, as well as completing the double over Stade, and with Jordan Turner-Hall and

Chris Robshaw both enhancing their reputations, Quins comfortably progressed to the last eight.

Bath made it three Guinness Premiership sides into the quarter-finals as they won Pool Five but they were ultimately to pay a heavy price for failing to close the match out in their opener in Toulouse. Bath got themselves in front in the dying minutes only to gift David Skrela a late penalty opportunity, which he kicked, and Toulouse snatched the victory. It meant Bath were away from home in the last eight and they were to miss out on the semi-finals as a result.

Pool Six was a procession for Cardiff and the Blues were the only side to qualify for the knockout phase with an unblemished record. They were particularly impressive in the wet against Biarritz and at Kingsholm against Gloucester when they were reduced to 14 men after Tom James was sent off in the first half but were still able to close out a 16–12 victory.

The first of the quarter-finals saw Cardiff continue what was increasingly looking like their march to the final, beating Toulouse 9–6 at the Millennium Stadium. The scoreline suggests it was a terrible game but the truth was it was a fierce and at times epic clash which the Blues just shaded courtesy of three penalties from Ben Blair.

I thought Xavier Rush was outstanding for the Blues and it was also the day I felt Leigh Halfpenny, Andy Powell, Tom Shanklin, Jamie Roberts, Gethin Jenkins and Martyn Williams all booked their places on the Lions tour for the summer. Defeat for Toulouse meant there was to be no French side in the semi-finals for only the second time in the competition's history.

The second quarter-final was an all-English affair as Leicester entertained Bath at the Walkers Stadium and as I mentioned earlier, it was a match the West Country side might well have won had they played at the Recreation Ground. As it transpired, the Tigers clinched a 20–15 victory thanks to Julien Dupuy's superb solo score in the last minute of the game and it was a result that embodied Leicester's gritty character.

I felt sorry for Bath fly-half Butch James, who missed the kicks that could have won the match for his side. He had had a brilliant season up until then but against the Tigers it seemed to me his body had all but given out on him and his mind followed.

The following day Munster hosted Ospreys at Thomond Park and once again the Welsh side packed with internationals failed to live up to expectations as they were demolished 43–9. Credit has to go Munster and Man of the Match Paul Warwick but the Ospreys really should have offered a little more resistance.

Harlequins faced Leinster in London in the last quarter-final and a match that has now become infamous for the fake blood incident. I don't think there's much more I can add to what has already been said on that but it is important to pay tribute to Leinster's superb defence at the Stoop in their 6–5 win and in particular the midfield combination of Brian O'Driscoll and Gordon D'Arcy.

The all-Ireland semi-final clash between Leinster and Munster at Croke Park in May produced one of the greatest team efforts I can remember and although few gave Leinster a prayer before kick-off, they were absolutely magnificent on their way to their 25–6 victory and a place in the final.

Cullen and Malcolm O'Kelly were outstanding in the second row for Leinster but the player who really impressed me was Johnny Sexton, who was pressed into action at 10 in the first half after Felipe Contepomi was injured and held his nerve in the cauldron of Croke Park and didn't put a foot wrong.

The second semi between Leicester and the Blues in the Millennium Stadium was the definition of an epic drama and after 80 minutes of cut and thrust in normal time and an additional 20 minutes of extra-time, the two sides were locked at 26–26 and it all came down to a historic penalty shootout.

It was the Tigers who eventually claimed their place in the record books with a 7–6 triumph after Martyn Williams missed for Cardiff and Jordan Crane landed the last kick for Leicester and like many, I felt desperately sorry for Williams, especially because he had had such a fine match.

As the dust settled, there was much debate about the concept of a penalty shootout to decide such an important game. In principle, I don't think it's a terrible idea but I do believe forwards should not be asked to step up and take a kick. They have no business taking penalties. For me, a shootout should be limited to designated backs, with the degree of difficulty of the kick being incrementally increased each time by moving the ball closer and closer to the touchline.

The final took place three weeks later at Murrayfield but for once Leicester's dogged determination was not quite enough to get them over the line, even though Leinster did have to haul themselves back from a 16–9 deficit in the second half to lift the trophy.

It was another huge match from Rocky Elsom in the backrow for the Irishmen and I also thought Chris Whitaker at scrum-half was hugely influential and that inner confidence Leinster's Ireland contingent had after claiming the Grand Slam was very much in evidence as the match reached its climax and it could have gone either way. Sexton was again admirably calm and controlled to land what was the winning penalty and overall Leinster did just enough to take the Heineken Cup to Ireland for a fourth time and the second year in succession.

HEINEKEN CUP 2008–09 RESULTS

ROUND ONE

10 October, 2008	
Munster 19 Montauban 17	Perpignan 27 Treviso 16

11 October, 2008	
Calvisano 20 Cardiff 56	Scarlets 22 Harlequins 29
Clermont Auvergne 15 Sale 32	Ulster 10 Stade Français 26
Edinburgh 16 Leinster 27	Gloucester 22 Biarritz
Dragons 32 Glasgow 22	

12 October, 2008	
Leicester 12 Ospreys 6	Toulouse 18 Bath 16
Wasps 25 Castres 11	

ROUND TWO

17 October, 2008	
Glasgow 16 Toulouse 22	

18 October, 2008	
Treviso 16 Leicester 60	Biarritz 41 Calvisano 10
Stade Français 37 Scarlets 15	Castres 6 Edinburgh 13
Harlequins 42 Ulster 21	Leinster 41 Wasps 11
Ospreys 15 Perpignan 9	

19 October, 2008	
Bath 13 Dragons 9	Cardiff 37 Gloucester 24
Sale 16 Munster 24	Montauban 19 Clermont Auvergne 24

CROSS-BORDER TOURNAMENTS

5 December, 2008	
Edinburgh 16 **Wasps** 25	**Cardiff** 21 Biarritz 17
Sale 36 Montauban 6	**Ulster** 26 Scarlets 16

6 December, 2008	
Calvisano 17 **Gloucester** 40	**Ospreys** 68 Treviso 8
Leinster 33 Castres 3	Stade Français 10 **Harlequins** 15
Toulouse 26 Dragons 7	**Leicester** 38 Perpignan 27

7 December, 2008	
Bath 35 Glasgow 31	**Clermont Auvergne** 25 Munster 19

ROUND FOUR

12 December, 2008	
Castres 18 Leinster 15	Scarlets 16 Ulster 16

13 December, 2008	
Harlequins 19 Stade Français 17	Dragons 13 **Toulouse** 26
Montauban 16 Sale 12	**Gloucester** 48 Calvisano 5
Treviso 16 **Ospreys** 36	**Munster** 23 Clermont Auvergne 13
Biarritz 6 **Cardiff** 10	

14 December, 2008	
Wasps 19 Edinburgh 11	**Perpignan** 26 Leicester 20
Glasgow 19 **Bath** 25	

ROUND FIVE

16 January, 2009	
Edinburgh 32 Castres 14	**Munster** 37 Sale 14
Clermont Auvergne 43 Montauban 10	

17 January, 2009	
Calvisano 15 **Biarritz** 23	**Leicester** 52 Treviso 0
Toulouse 26 **Glasgow** 33	**Perpignan** 17 Ospreys 15
Ulster 21 Harlequins 10	**Wasps** 19 Leinster 12

18 January, 2009	
Dragons 12 **Bath** 15	**Scarlets** 31 Stade Français 17
Gloucester 12 **Cardiff** 16	

ROUND SIX

23 January, 2009	
Biarritz 24 Gloucester 10	Cardiff 62 Calvisano 20

24 January, 2009	
Harlequins 29 Scarlets 24	Treviso 16 Perpignan 48
Stade Français 24 Ulster 19	Ospreys 15 Leicester 9
Sale 26 Clermont Auvergne 17	

25 January, 2009	
Castres 21 Wasps 15	Bath 3 Toulouse 3
Leinster 12 Edinburgh 3	Glasgow 13 Dragons 10
Montauban 13 Munster 39	

GROUP TABLES

POOL ONE

	P	W	D	L	F	A	BP	PTS
Munster	6	5	0	1	161	98	3	23
Sale	6	3	0	3	136	115	3	15
Clermont	6	3	0	3	137	129	1	13
Montauban	6	1	0	5	81	173	2	6

POOL FOUR

	P	W	D	L	F	A	BP	PTS
Harlequins	6	5	0	1	144	115	2	22
Stade Français	6	3	0	3	131	109	3	15
Ulster	6	2	1	3	113	134	1	11
Scarlets	6	1	1	4	124	154	2	8

POOL TWO

	P	W	D	L	F	A	BP	PTS
Leinster	6	4	0	2	140	70	4	20
Wasps	6	4	0	2	114	112	1	17
Edinburgh	6	2	0	4	91	103	1	9
Castres	6	2	0	4	73	133	1	9

POOL FIVE

	P	W	D	L	F	A	BP	PTS
Bath	6	4	1	1	107	92	3	21
Toulouse	6	4	1	1	121	88	2	20
Glasgow	6	2	0	4	134	150	4	12
Dragons	6	1	0	5	83	115	3	7

POOL THREE

	P	W	D	L	F	A	BP	PTS
Leicester	6	4	0	2	191	90	5	21
Ospreys	6	4	0	2	155	71	4	20
Perpignan	6	4	0	2	154	120	2	18
Treviso	6	0	0	6	72	291	0	0

POOL SIX

	P	W	D	L	F	A	BP	PTS
Cardiff	6	6	0	0	202	99	3	27
Biarritz	6	3	0	3	121	88	3	15
Gloucester	6	3	0	3	156	109	3	15
Calvisano	6	0	0	6	87	270	0	0

11 April, 2009	
Leicester 20 Bath 15	Cardiff 9 Toulouse 6
12 April, 2009	
Harlequins 5 Leinster 6	Munster 43 Ospreys 9

SEMI-FINALS

2 May, Croke Park, Dublin

MUNSTER 6 (2PG)
LEINSTER 25 (2G, 1T, 1PG, 1DG)

MUNSTER: P Warwick; D Howlett, K Earls, L Mafi, I Dowling; R O'Gara, P Stringer; M Horan, J Flannery, J Hayes, D O'Callaghan, P O'Connell (captain), A Quinlan, D Leamy, D Wallace Substitutions: B Murphy for Warwick (66 mins), N Ronan for Leamy (66 mins), T Buckley for Hayes (67 mins); D Fogarty for Flannery (72 mins); M Prendergast for Stringer (74 mins); M O'Driscoll for O'Callaghan (74 mins); D Hurley for Earls (78 mins)

SCORERS *Penalty Goals*: O'Gara (2)

LEINSTER: I Nacewa; S Horgan, B O'Driscoll, G D'Arcy, L Fitzgerald; F Contepomi, C Whitaker; C Healy, B Jackman, S Wright, L Cullen (captain), M O'Kelly, R Elsom, J Heaslip, S Jennings Substitutions: R McCormack for Jennings (temp 19–28 mins); J Sexton for Contepomi (26 mins); G Dempsey for O'Driscoll (temp 38–39 mins); Dempsey for Fitzgerald (59 mins); D Toner for Cullen (80 mins)

SCORERS *Tries*: D'Arcy, Fitzgerald, O'Driscoll *Conversions*: Sexton (2) *Penalty Goal*: Sexton *Drop Goal*: Contepomi

YELLOW CARD Healy (17 mins)

REFEREE N Owens (Wales)

HEINEKEN CUP

3 May, Millennium Stadium, Cardiff

CARDIFF 26 (2G, 4PG)
LEICESTER 26 (2G, 4PG) AET

Leicester win 7–6 on penalties

CARDIFF: B Blair; L Halfpenny, T Shanklin, J Roberts, T James; N Robinson, R Rees; G Jenkins, G Williams, F Filise, B Davies, P Tito (captain), M Molitika, M Williams, X Rush Substitutions: D Jones for Tito (9 mins); A Powell for Molitika (60 mins); J Yapp for Filise (81 mins); C Sweeney for Roberts (99 mins)

SCORERS *Tries*: Roberts, James *Conversions*: Blair (2) *Penalty Goals*: Blair (2), Halfpenny (2)

LEICESTER: G Murphy (captain); S Hamilton, D Hipkiss , S Vesty, J Murphy; T Flood, J Dupuy; M Ayerza, G Chuter, M Castrogiovanni, T Croft, B Kay, C Newby, B Woods, J Crane Substitutions: A Mauger for Hipkiss (temp 47 to 49 mins); J White for Castrogiovanni (51 mins); Mauger for Flood (61 mins); M Smith for J Murphy (temp 64 to 75 mins); L Moody for Woods (74 mins); H Ellis for Dupuy (75 mins); Castrogiovanni for Ayerza (90 mins); M Wentzel for Kay (93 mins); Dupuy for Hipkiss (99 mins)

SCORERS *Tries*: Hamilton, G Murphy *Conversions*: Dupuy (2) *Penalty Goals*: Dupuy (4)

YELLOW CARDS Newby (61 mins), G Murphy (67 mins)

REFEREE A Rolland (Ireland)

FINAL

23 May, Murrayfield, Edinburgh

LEICESTER 16 (1G, 3PG)
LEINSTER 19 (1G, 2PG, 2DG)

LEICESTER: G Murphy (captain); S Hamilton, A Erinle, D Hipkiss, A Tuilagi; S Vesty, J Dupuy; M Ayerza, G Chuter, M Castrogiovanni, T Croft, B Kay, C Newby, J Crane, B Woods Substitutions: L Deacon for Crane (30 mins); M Smith for Murphy (47 mins); J White for Castrogiovanni (53 mins); B Kayser for Chuter (55 mins); L Moody for Woods (61 mins); H Ellis for Dupuy (75 mins)

SCORERS *Try*: Woods *Conversion*: Dupuy *Penalty Goals*: Dupuy (3)

LEINSTER: I Nacewa; S Horgan, B O'Driscoll, G D'Arcy, L Fitzgerald; J Sexton, C Whitaker; C Healy, B Jackman, S Wright, L Cullen (captain), M O'Kelly, R Elsom, J Heaslip, S Jennings Substitutions: R McCormack for Jennings (temp 36–42 mins); J Fogarty for Jackman (55 mins); McCormack for Healy (temp 61–64 mins); R Kearney for Fitzgerald (71 mins)

SCORERS *Try*: Heaslip *Conversion*: Sexton *Penalty Goals*: Sexton (2) *Drop Goals*: O'Driscoll, Sexton

YELLOW CARD Wright (33 mins)

REFEREE N Owens (Wales)

SAINTS CLAIM EUROPEAN PRIZE

By Iain Spragg

Northampton celebrate getting their hands on some silverware.

Northampton Saints marked their first season back in the top tier of English club rugby with victory over Bourgoin in the final of the European Challenge Cup and in the process earned themselves a place in the 2009–10 Heineken Cup.

The Saints suffered the anguish of relegation in 2007, but bounced back at the first time of asking after an unbeaten National League One promotion campaign and went further towards erasing the painful memories of their demotion with a 15–3 victory over their French rivals in an ill-tempered clash at The Stoop.

It was the club's first piece of silverware since they claimed the EDF National Trophy in 2008 and their first taste of success in Europe since they famously lifted the Heineken Cup in 2000.

Northampton were grateful for the kicking prowess of young English fly-half Stephen Myler, who landed five penalties, but the match was marred in the latter stages by a number of scuffles and in the dying minutes Bourgoin replacement Thomas Genevois was shown a red card for a punch on Courtney Lawes.

The unsavoury incident, however, could not take the gloss of Northampton's victory and the result meant the Challenge Cup remained in England following Bath's triumph over Worcester Warriors 12 months earlier. It was also the eighth English success in the competition in the previous nine years, a sequence broken only by Clermont Auvergne's win over Bath in 2007.

"To win a trophy in our first season back in the Premiership is a really good achievement," said the Saints' director of rugby Jim Mallinder. "It wasn't pretty, it was a tough cup final. We knew there might be a bit of niggle and I thought we kept our composure well, particularly towards the end.

"It was a real steely performance from Stephen Myler and he's maturing all the time. He was brilliant in the semi-final and today he was great in defence and attack and to have a goal-kicker like him means a lot to the team. There will be some great teams in the Heineken Cup next season but we're a big club with great support and it's where we deserve to be."

Mallinder's team were drawn in Pool Two of the qualifying phase of the Challenge Cup alongside Bristol and two French sides, Montpellier and Toulon, and they were to be the dominant force with six wins from six to leave the rest trailing in their wake.

They opened up with a crushing 56–3 victory over Toulon at the Stade Félix Mayol and the deluge of points continued with comprehensive wins over Montpellier (51–7), Bristol (66–3) and a 52–11 mauling of Toulon again in the return match at Franklin's Gardens.

In Pool One, London Irish were even more prolific and amassed a staggering 300 points in their six matches. The Exiles twice surpassed the 70-point mark in beating Rovigo 78–3 at the Madejski Stadium and then Connacht 75–5 to stroll into the knockout phase. The Irish provincial side also made it through to the quarter-finals as one of the three best runners-up.

In Pool Three, Worcester were the top side but could not record an unblemished record. The Warriors began with back-to-back wins but in round three they were beaten 29–14 by Bourgoin at the Stade Pierre Rajon, only to return the favour with a 27–6 triumph over the French side at the Sixways Stadium in round four. Both sides progressed to the last eight.

In Pool Four, Brive restored a degree of Gallic pride and finished above second place Newcastle, Parma and El Salvador. Brive were surprisingly beaten 34–29 in their opening fixture by Parma but recovered to claim victories in their next five games and were joined by the Falcons in the quarter-finals.

In Pool Five, Saracens were the team to beat but Viadana, Bayonne and Mont-de-Marsan were not up to the challenge and the London side qualified with a 100 per cent record. Saracens were rarely troubled en route to the knockout stages and the closest they came to defeat was in round three against Bayonne in the Stade Jean Dauger, but the English side held their nerve for a 16–6 win.

It was now time for the quarter-finals with five English sides, two French and one Irish province still in the hunt for honours.

The first game was an Anglo-French affair with London Irish entertaining Bourgoin, but the home side's hopes of reaching the last four were dashed when replacement Mathieu Nicolas scored an interception

Mike Hewitt/Getty Images

Bob Casey's London Irish scored 300 points in their six pool matches.

try four minutes from time to record a dramatic 32–30 win for the visitors.

Two days later, Worcester played host to Brive, only this time it was the English side who were celebrating at the final whistle after a brace of tries from Marcel Garvey and further scores from captain Pat Sanderson and Alex Grove secured a 29–18 victory.

On the same day Northampton played Connacht at Franklin's Gardens and the Saints enjoyed a comfortable 80 minutes against the Irish, with fly half Myler slotting six successive penalties before second half tries from Neil Best, Joe Ansbro, Bruce Reihana and Chris Mayor set up a 42–13 triumph.

The last quarter-final 24 hours later at Vicarage Road saw Saracens face Newcastle and it was the home side's number 10 Glen Johnson who stole the show with 22 points from the boot in a 32–13 victory.

Early May saw the semi-finals staged. The first game was at Franklin's Gardens between the Saints and Saracens and was the scene of a dramatic denouement as Northampton clinched a late win. Bruce Reihana crossed for Saints for the game's first try but Saracens hit back with a Rodd Penney score and as full-time approached, the two teams were locked at 13–13. The dreaded extra-time looked a real possibility until Myler's late drop stole it for Saints.

"We were excellent in the first half, played some really good rugby and I thought we deserved our lead at half-time," said Mallinder after his side's last-gasp triumph. "Full credit to Saracens for coming back at us.

"We defended well and even after they got the try, we came back, got the drop goal and then looked after the ball well. That really showed the maturity in the side and that they are improving. But we won't get carried away. We have a three-week break now but we will come back and work very hard for the final."

The second semi-final between Bourgoin and Worcester at the Stade Pierre Rajon saw the Warriors looking for a second successive appearance in the final, but it was the French side who won out on home turf. Kicking dominated the game until the 62nd minute when Bourgoin's Coenie Basson went over for the first try and although Miles Benjamin touched down for the Premiership club in the 79th minute, it was not enough to stop Bourgoin recording a 22–11 win.

"We had opportunities but we didn't take them," admitted Worcester captain Sanderson. "We spoke about it at half-time and said we would create another chance.

"Injuries didn't help us. We had players playing out of position in the front row and that showed in the first half. But credit to them for playing out of position and hanging in there. There's no criticism levelled towards them because Bourgoin were excellent in that area and made their dominance tell."

The build-up to the final itself was marred by a row about the venue, which was eventually switched from Gloucester's Kingsholm to Harlequins' Stoop at Bourgoin's request and as the game unfolded the pre-match friction seemed to boil over onto the pitch.

While Myler was kicking the points for the Saints, with Bourgoin replying with a solitary penalty, some players seem more intent on finding trouble and Northampton scrum half Lee Dickson was involved in a couple of spats with his opposite number Morgan Parra, who typified the French side's feisty spirit.

It was Parra at the centre of things minutes later after a scuffle with Neil Best which saw both players sent to the sin bin. In the final 10 minutes, Parra was carried off after a big tackle from Lawes, which in turn led to Genevois' dismissal for retaliation, but Northampton were already comfortably in front. In fact, there was just enough time to give club stalwart Tom Smith a few minutes of action before his retirement.

After the final whistle, hooker Dylan Hartley was named Man of the Match as the Saints' celebrations began in earnest.

Mike Hewitt/Getty Images

Stephen Myler's kicking was crucial in the final against Bourgoin.

EUROPEAN CHALLENGE CUP

EUROPEAN CHALLENGE CUP 2008–09 RESULTS

ROUND ONE	
9 October, 2008	
Toulon 3 **Northampton** 56	
10 October, 2008	
Dax 12 **Connacht** 30	Bayonne 10 **Viadana** 21
Montpellier 33 Bristol 15	
11 October, 2008	
Padova 6 **Worcester** 55	**Newcastle** 63 El Salvador 0
London Irish 78 Rovigo 3	
12 October, 2008	
Parma 34 Brive 29	**Saracens** 53 Mont-de-Marsan 3
Bucharest 10 **Bourgoin** 21	
ROUND TWO	
16 October, 2008	
Brive 36 Newcastle 22	
17 October, 2008	
Mont-de-Marsan 8 **Bayonne** 26	Bourgoin 28 **Padova** 29
Connacht 10 **London Irish** 27	**Bristol** 39 Toulon 11
18 October, 2008	
Rovigo 24 Dax 11	**Northampton** 51 Montpellier 7
Viadana 12 **Saracens** 35	
19 October, 2008	
El Salvador 21 **Parma** 59	Bucharest 17 **Worcester** 53
ROUND THREE	
4 December, 2008	
Montpellier 14 Toulon 10	
5 December, 2008	
Dax 0 **London Irish** 38	**Bourgoin** 29 Worcester 14
Brive 84 El Salvador 6	
6 December, 2008	
Parma 14 **Newcastle** 20	**Northampton** 66 Bristol 3
Rovigo 20 **Connacht** 35	Bayonne 6 **Saracens** 10
Mont-de-Marsan 15 **Viadana** 21	
7 December, 2008	
Bucharest 14 **Padova** 20	

ROUND FOUR
11 December, 2008

London Irish 59 **Dax** 7

12 December, 2008

Connacht 30 **Rovigo** 3

13 December, 2008

Padova 15 **Bucharest** 17   **Viadana** 25 **Mont-de-Marsan** 6

Worcester 27 **Bourgoin** 6   **Toulon** 30 **Montpellier** 9

14 December, 2008

El Salvador 5 **Brive** 55   **Newcastle** 21 **Parma** 16

Bristol 21 **Northampton** 25   **Saracens** 36 **Bayonne** 0

ROUND FIVE
15 January, 2009

Montpellier 24 **Northampton** 28

16 January, 2009

Toulon 19 **Bristol** 37   **Bayonne** 33 **Mont-de-Marsan** 19

Dax 22 **Rovigo** 20

17 January, 2009

Parma 29 **El Salvador** 0   **Worcester** 38 **Bucharest** 19

Padova 25 **Bourgoin** 24   **Newcastle** 9 **Brive** 10

London Irish 75 **Connacht** 5

18 January, 2009

Saracens 36 **Viadana** 19

ROUND SIX
22 January, 2009

Brive 29 **Parma** 13

23 January, 2009

Mont-de-Marsan 3 **Saracens** 24   **Bourgoin** 50 **Bucharest** 10

Connacht 49 **Dax** 3

24 January, 2009

Rovigo 9 **London Irish** 23   **Worcester** 68 **Padova** 17

Northampton 52 **Toulon** 11   **Viadana** 22 **Bayonne** 24

25 January, 2009

El Salvador 14 **Newcastle** 43   **Bristol** 25 **Montpellier** 14

GROUP TABLES

POOL ONE

	P	W	D	L	F	A	BP	PTS
London Irish	6	6	0	0	300	34	5	29
Connacht	6	4	0	2	159	140	3	19
Rovigo	6	1	0	5	79	199	1	5
Dax	6	1	0	5	55	220	0	4

POOL FOUR

	P	W	D	L	F	A	BP	PTS
Brive	6	5	0	1	243	89	4	24
Newcastle	6	4	0	2	178	90	3	19
Parma	6	3	0	3	165	120	4	16
El Salvador	6	0	0	6	46	333	0	0

POOL TWO

	P	W	D	L	F	A	BP	PTS
Northampton	6	6	0	0	278	69	5	29
Bristol	6	3	0	3	140	168	2	14
Montpellier	6	2	0	4	101	159	1	9
Toulon	6	1	0	5	84	207	1	5

POOL FIVE

	P	W	D	L	F	A	BP	PTS
Saracens	6	6	0	0	200	43	2	26
Viadana	6	3	0	3	120	126	1	13
Bayonne	6	3	0	3	99	122	0	12
Mont-de-Marsan	6	0	0	6	54	182	1	1

POOL THREE

	P	W	D	L	F	A	BP	PTS
Worcester	6	5	0	1	255	94	4	24
Bourgoin	6	3	0	3	158	115	3	15
Padova	6	3	0	3	112	206	1	13
Bucharest	6	1	0	5	87	197	1	5

Getty Images

Saracens topped Pool Five, including this 36–0 win over Bayonne.

CROSS-BORDER TOURNAMENTS

9 April, 2009	
London Irish 30 **Bourgoin 32**	
11 April, 2009	
Worcester 29 Brive 18	**Northampton 42** Connacht 13
12 April, 2009	
Saracens 32 Newcastle 13	

SEMI-FINALS

1 May, Franklin's Gardens, Northampton

NORTHAMPTON 16 (1G, 2PG, 1DG)
SARACENS 13 (1G, 2PG)

NORTHAMPTON: B Foden; P Diggin, J Clark, J Downey, B Reihana (captain); S Myler, L Dickson; S Tonga'uiha, D Hartley, E Murray, I Fernandez Lobbe, J Kruger, N Best, S Gray (B Sharman 21–31), M Easter.

SUBSTITUTIONS: B Sharman for Gray (temp 21–31 mins); C Lawes for Fernandez Lobbe (57 mins); A Dickens for L Dickson (68 mins); T Smih for Tonga'uiha (70 mins); J Ansbro for Clark (75 mins).

SCORERS *Try*: Reihana *Conversion*: Myler *Penalty Goals*: Myler (2) *Drop Goal*: Myler

SARACENS: C Wyles; R Penney, F Leonelli, B Barritt, N Cato; G Jackson, N de Kock; M Aguero , F Ongaro, C Johnston, S Borthwick (captain), T Ryder, C Jack, A Saull, B Skirving.

SUBSTITUTIONS: M Cairns for Ryder (temp 21–31 mins); D Barrell for Saull (36 mins); T Mercey for Aguero (41 mins); A Farrell for Barritt (56 mins); H Vyvyan for Ryder (57 mins); A Powell for Leonelli (69 mins); Cairns for Ongaro (69 mins).

SCORERS *Try*: Penney *Conversion*: Jackson *Penalty Goals*: Jackson (2)

REFEREE: R Poite (France)

EUROPEAN CHALLENGE CUP

2 May, Stade Pierre Rajon, Bourgoin

BOURGOIN 22 (1G, 4PG, 1DG)
WORCESTER 11 (2PG, 1T)

BOURGOIN: F Denos; D Janin, M Viazzo, Y David, R Coetzee; B Boyet, M Parra; A Tchougong, J Genevois, K Wihongi, C Basson, C Levast, J Frier (captain), W Jooste, Y Labrit.

SUBSTITUTIONS: A Forest for Denos (48 mins); P Cardinali for Tchougong (62 mins); S Laloo for Janin (64 mins); R Vigneaux for Genevois (65 mins); T Genevois for Labrit (72 mins); M Forest for Boyet (76 mins); S Nicolas for Jooste (76 mins).

SCORERS *Try*: Basson *Conversion*: Parra *Penalty Goals*: Parra (4) *Drop Goal*: Boyet

WORCESTER: R Gear; C Fellows, A Grove, D Rasmussen, M Benjamin; J Carlisle, R Powell; C Black, A Lutui, D Morris, G Rawlinson, G Kitchener, T Wood, P Sanderson (captain), N Talei.

SUBSTITUTIONS: S Ruwers for Morris (39 mins); W Bowley for Rawlinson (39 mins); C Fortey for Black (62 mins); G King for Rasmussen (65 mins); M Powell for R Powell (65 mins); J Collins for Wood (75 mins); M Penn for Sanderson (80 mins).

SCORERS *Try*: Benjamin *Penalty Goals*: Carlisle (2)

REFEREE: P Fitzgibbon (Ireland)

FINAL

22 May, Twickenham Stoop, London

NORTHAMPTON 15 (5PG) BOURGOIN 3 (1PG)

NORTHAMPTON: B Foden; P Diggin, J Clarke, J Downey, B Reihana; S Myler, L Dickson; S Tongauiha, D Hartley, E Murray, I Fernández Lobbe, J Kruger, N Best, S Gray, M Easter.

SUBSTITUTIONS: C Lawes for Fernández Lobbe (40 mins); A Dickens for Dickson (65 mins); C Day for Kruger (69 mins); J Ansbro for Clarke (69 mins); T Smith for Tongauiha (73 mins); B Sharman for Hartley (77 mins); G Everitt for Myler (79 mins).

SCORERS *Penalty Goals*: Myler (5)

YELLOW CARD: Best (35 mins)

BOURGOIN: A Forest; R Coetzee, M Viazzo, Y David, J-F Coux; B Boyet, M Parra; A Tchougong, J-P Genevois, K Wihongi, C Basson, C Levast, J Frier, W Jooste, Y Labrit.

SUBSTITUTIONS: S Nicholas for Basson (51 mins); F Denos for Coux (55 mins); T Genevois for Labrit (57 mins); P Cardinali for Wihongi (67 mins); M Forest for Parra (73 mins).

SCORERS *Penalty Goal*: Parra

YELLOW CARD: Parra (35 mins)

RED CARD: Genevois (75 mins)

REFEREE: G Clancy (Ireland)

IRELAND END SAXONS DOMINANCE

Doug Pensinger/Getty Images

Ireland A celebrate lifting the Churchill Cup, after the win over England Saxons.

An inspired performance from Ireland's second string in the final of the Churchill Cup in Denver dethroned England Saxons as the reigning champions and in the process provided a fitting climax to a glorious season for sides from the Emerald Isle.

The Saxons had won the tournament in both 2007 and 2008 but were outclassed and outmuscled in the final by Ireland A, who outscored their opponents by six tries to two in a resounding 49–22 triumph to lift the trophy for the first time in the competition's six-year history.

The New Zealand Maori and the Saxons had monopolised the silverware in previous seasons but Declan Kidney's side were simply irresistible in 2009 as they added another trophy to a bulging Irish trophy cabinet following the senior side's Six Nations Grand Slam, Leinster's Heineken Cup success and Munster's Magners League triumph.

First half tries from Devon Toner and Isaac Boss gave the Irish a tentative 20–12 half-time lead but a third score from Sean Cronin just 24 seconds after the restart opened the floodgates. Felix Jones, Johne Murphy and John Muldoon all duly helped themselves to further tries and although Tom Varndell scored late on for the Saxons, it was no more than a hollow consolation.

"We as coaches came over here to see what was coming through," said Kidney after the match. "We are delighted. We told the boys it was their day and to show what they wanted out of it and they showed us that. England are a very good team. I'm not going to say we smashed them in every facet but we had the hunger."

For England Saxons, defeat was a body blow. The Saxons had won four of the previous six tournaments but after cantering through the pool phase with comfortable wins over the Argentina Jaguars and hosts USA, they were dispatched with ruthless efficiency by Ireland A.

"I'm shell shocked," said dejected Saxons captain Phil Dowson. "We took a pasting and there are no excuses."

The tournament began in early June with Infinity Park in Glendale, Colorado, playing host to the pool phase matches.

The Saxons had the honour of playing the first match, tackling the Jaguars on the same day as the two country's senior sides crossed swords in a full Test match at Old Trafford in Manchester. That encounter ended in an English victory and it was a similar story in North America as second half tries from Matt Smith, Varndell and Man of the Match Joe Simpson earned the Saxons a 28–20 victory.

The day's second game at Infinity Park saw Canada take on tournament debutants Georgia and the Canucks proved too strong for the East Europeans as Matt Evans helped himself to a brace of tries and James Pritchard kicked 17 points in a 42–10 win.

Four days later, Ireland A were in action against the buoyant Canadians and for much of the game it seemed as though the Canucks might pull off a major shock. Leading 16–13 for much of the second half, Canada were eventually overhauled by a late penalty try and another score from Dennis Hurley and their chance of reaching the Cup final was gone.

Hours later Argentina Jaguars made amends for their opening defeat to the Saxons with a 35–14 success over USA. They left it late, however, and needed 16 points in the final 20 minutes to book their place in the Plate final against Canada.

The final day in the pool phase saw the Saxons maul the Eagles 56–17 in a seven-try romp while Ireland A were equally emphatic in their 40–5 demolition of Georgia.

Unfortunately, the Lelos were unable to make the necessary improvements during their final game of the Churchill Cup – the Bowl final clash with the USA – and it was the hosts who emerged 31–13 victors at Dick's Sporting Goods Park in Denver, Colorado.

The Eagles were looking to end a six-match losing run and gained the upper hand in the eighth minute when Tim Usasz scored from a lineout and although the Georgians briefly levelled the match in the first half with an Alexander Todua score, tries from Paul Emerick and Colin Hawley after the break wrapped up the victory.

In the Plate final, the Jaguars took on Canada and it was South rather than North American celebrations at the final whistle as the Argentineans survived a spirited second half fightback from the Canadians to record a 44–29 win.

Tries from captain Agustín Creevy and Francisco Jose Merello gave the Jaguars an early 14–3 lead before Canada crossed the whitewash with a superb try from wing Matt Evans. Centre Benjamin Urdapilleta stretched the lead with a third try for his side but Evans hit back with his second of the match and at half-time it was 21–15 to the Argentineans.

They stretched this advantage with tries from Tomás De Vedia and Leonardo Senatore and the boot of Urdapilleta, who finished the game with a personal haul of 24 points, and although the Canucks rallied with a DTH van der Merwe try, they had left themselves too much to do.

The Cup final between Ireland A and the Saxons was equally free-scoring but for the first time in the tournament it was the English side who found themselves on the wrong end of a heavy scoreline.

The men in white drew first blood in the Dick's Sporting Goods Park with two early penalties from Steven Myler, but Ireland A were quickly into their stride when Toner crashed over and once Boss had added the second, the Irish were never behind again.

Both sides were reduced to 14 men in the 33rd minute when Chris Henry and Dan Cole were both yellow carded, but it did little to disrupt the impressive rhythm of Kidney's side and they had their third try just seconds after the restart courtesy of Cronin. There was brief hope for England Saxons when Ben Woods crossed the whitewash for Stuart Lancaster's team but it was to be a temporary respite and when Jones raced over for Ireland A's fourth score, the game was effectively over as a genuine contest.

The best try of the match was scored by the Irish near the hour mark when Murphy and Fergus McFadden combined beautifully to send the former over and Muldoon rubbed salt into the Saxons' gaping wounds with a sixth try with just minutes left on the clock. Varndell's late effort gave the scoreline a modicum of gloss but in truth Ireland A had put the defending champions to the sword.

CHURCHILL CUP

CHURCHILL CUP 2009 RESULTS
POOL PHASE

6 June, Infinity Park, Colorado	
England Saxons 28	**Argentina Jaguars** 20
Georgia 10	**Canada** 42
10 June, Infinity Park, Colorado	
Ireland A 30	**Canada** 19
Argentina Jaguars 35	**USA** 14
14 June, Infinity Park, Colorado	
England Saxons 56	**USA** 17
Georgia 5	**Ireland A** 40

POOL TABLES

POOL A

	P	W	D	L	F	A	BP	Pts
Ireland A	2	2	0	0	70	24	2	**10**
Canada	2	1	0	1	61	40	1	**5**
Georgia	2	0	0	2	15	82	0	**0**

POOL B

	P	W	D	L	F	A	BP	Pts
England Saxons	2	2	0	0	84	37	1	**9**
Jaguars	2	1	0	1	55	42	0	**4**
USA	2	0	0	2	31	91	0	**0**

CROSS-BORDER TOURNAMENTS

CHURCHILL CUP FINAL

21 June, Dick's Sporting Goods Park, Denver

Ireland A 49 (5G 1T 3PG)
England Saxons 22 (2T 4PG)

IRELAND A: F Jones; D Hurley, F McFadden, K Matthews, J Murphy; J Sexton, I Boss; C Healy, S Cronin, T Buckley, D Ryan, D Toner, N Best (captain), N Ronan, C Henry.

SUBSTITUTIONS: N O'Connor for Henry (43 mins); D Fogarty for Cronin (60 mins); B Young for Healy (75 mins); T Hogan for Toner (75 mins); S Geogh for Boss (75 mins); J Downey for Matthews (75 mins).

SCORERS *Tries*: Toner, Boss, Cronin, Jones, J Murphy, Muldoon *Conversions*: Sexton (3), McFadden (2) *Penalty Goals*: Sexton (3)

YELLOW CARDS: Henry (33 mins), Best (40 mins)

ENGLAND SAXONS: N Abendanon; N Cato, D Waldouck, B Barritt, T Varndell; S Myler, M Young; D Flatman, R Webber, D Cole, S Hooper, N Kennedy, P Dowson (captain), B Woods, L Narraway.

SUBSTITUTIONS: D Schofield for Hooper (54 mins); T Mercey for Cole (56 mins); T Guest for Narraway (56 mins); D Cipriani for Myler (60 mins); S Geraghty for Barritt (60 mins); J Simpson for Young (65 mins); J Ward for Webber (70 mins).

SCORERS *Tries*: Woods, Varndell *Penalty Goals*: Myler (4)

YELLOW CARDS: Cole (33 mins), Woods (73 mins)

REFEREE: M Goddard (Australia)

CHURCHILL PLATE FINAL

21 June, Dick's Sporting Goods Park, Denver

Argentina Jaguars 44 (5G 3PG)
Canada 29 (3G 1T 1PG)

ARGENTINA JAGUARS: L Oro; F Merello, M Viazzo, B Urdapilleta, T De Vedia; I Mieres, M Landajo; J Figallo, A Creevy (captain), P Ledesma, M Sambucetti, C Cáceres, A Campos, L Senatore, T Leonardi.

SUBSTITUTIONS: J Gomez for Ledesma (temp 40 to 50 mins); M Guidone for Creevy (59 mins); H San Martin for Mieres (62 mins); B Agulla for Merello (62 mins); A Guzman for Senatore (66 mins); F Cubelli for Landajo (66 mins).

SCORERS *Tries*: Creevy, Merello, Urdapilleta, De Vedia, Senatore, *Conversions*: Urdapilleta (5) *Penalty Goals*: Urdapilleta (3)

YELLOW CARD: Ledesma (40 mins)

CANADA: J Pritchard; S Duke, DTH van der Merwe, B Keys, M Evans; A Monro, E Fairhurst; F Walsh, M Pletch, D Pletch, J Sinclair, T Hotson, S McKeen, N Dala, A Carpenter (captain).

SUBSTITUTIONS: P Riordan for M Pletch (47 mins); A Kleeberger for Dala (47 mins); D Van Camp for Pritchard (56 mins); D Woolbridge for D Pletch (58 mins); P Mack for Fairhurst (59 mins); C O'Toole for McKeen (62 mins).

SCORERS *Tries:* Evans (2), van der Merwe (2) *Conversions:* Pritchard, Monro, van der Merwe *Penalty Goal:* Pritchard

YELLOW CARDS: Sinclair (40 mins), Kleeberger (51 mins)

REFEREE: P Fitzgibbon (Ireland)

CHURCHILL BOWL FINAL

21 June, Dick's Sporting Goods Park, Denver

USA 31 (2G 1T 4PG) Georgia 13 (1G 2PG)

USA: C Wyles; T Ngwenya, P Emerick, S Sika, C Hawley; M Hercus, T Usasz; M Moeakiola, C Biller, S Pittman, L Stanfill, J Van Der Giessen, JJ Gagiano, T Clever (captain), N Johnson.

SUBSTITUTIONS: A Parker for Stanfill (temp 48 to 63 mins); A Tuilevuka (54 mins); M MacDonald for Moeakiola (58 mins); Parker for Gagiano (63 mins); N Malifa for Hercus (72 mins); M Petri for Usasz (75 mins); J Welch for Biller (76 mins).

SCORERS *Tries:* Usasz, Emerick, Hawley *Conversions:* Hercus (2) *Penalty Goals:* Hercus (4)

YELLOW CARD: Emerick (74 mins)

GEORGIA: M Kvirikashvili; A Todua, D Kacharava, R Gigauri, I Machkhaneli; L Malaguradze, G Rokhvadze; D Dadunashvili, I Natriashvili, G Jgenti, R Urushadze, G Nemsadze, G Labadze (captain), S Maisuradze, D Basilaia.

SUBSTITUTIONS: Z Maisuradze for Labadze (40 mins); V Kakovin for Jgenti (57 mins); L Datunashvili for Nemsadze (59 mins); I Gundishvili for Basilaia (59 mins); G Lomgadze for Dadunashvili (74 mins); T Sokhadze for Kvirikashvili (79 mins); L Gugava for Todua (79 mins).

SCORERS *Tries:* Todua *Conversion:* Kvirikashvili *Penalty Goals:* Kvirikashvili (2)

YELLOW CARDS: Maisuradze (7 mins), Kacharava (74 mins)

REFEREE: G Garner (England)

TROPHY TIME FOR THE BLUES

By Iain Spragg

The Cardiff players celebrate on their lap of honour.

Cardiff destroyed Gloucester 50–12 in the final of the EDF Energy Cup at Twickenham to give the Blues their first silverware since the inception of regional rugby in the Principality and maintain Wales's recent dominance of the tournament.

Dai Young's rampant side ran in seven tries against the hapless Cherry and Whites, notching up a half century of points with their final conversion to lift the cup and so succeed the Ospreys, victors over Leicester 12 months earlier, as EDF champions.

The Blues were born when Welsh rugby opted for a regional structure in 2003 but the ensuing six years had been barren for the newly-formed club until their resounding triumph at Twickenham, a result which reflected the growing strength of Magners League sides against English teams in cross-border competition.

Cardiff had already beaten Gloucester home and away in the group stages of the Heineken Cup and they decimated Dean Ryan's side in London to complete the hat-trick.

Two tries apiece from Leigh Halfpenny and Ben Blair did the damage and with British & Irish Lions head coach Ian McGeechan watching from the stands, it was little surprise that when he named his squad to tackle the Springboks three days later there were six Cardiff players – Halfpenny, Jamie Roberts, Martyn Williams, Tom Shanklin, Gethin Jenkins and Andy Powell – in his tour party.

"We didn't think we'd score 50 points against a team like Gloucester," said Young afterwards. "I'm very proud of the effort and the skills. It's been a long journey at the Blues because of the restrictions in place. We had to work with the younger players.

"We had to make sure everything was right with recruitment and today the seasoned internationals really stood up and led us. It's been a lot of hard graft but days like today make it worthwhile. The players were determined to make sure they came here and achieved something because they deserved it."

For Gloucester, defeat was their fourth successive disappointment in a final at Twickenham and as Ryan surveyed the wreckage after the final whistle, the Cherry and Whites' coach made it clear the result would spark major changes at Kingsholm over the summer.

"We've been successful in reaching finals, we just haven't won trophies," he said. "We must start the journey again with another group of players. Today we were significantly second best and we can't hide from that.

"This group isn't good enough to compete at this level. We have to accept that and it will be part of our review over the summer. You have got to recognise when the learning process is over and I think everyone at this club is at that point.

"We will look at taking the club in a different direction with a different group of people in the next year. We must address the problem with recruitment. It's no accident that some of this squad haven't gone on to become internationals and it's no accident we don't have five or six Lions contenders."

The fourth season of the Anglo-Welsh Cup had begun in early October **543** with Cardiff in Pool B alongside Leicester, Bath and Sale. On paper, it looked the hardest of the competition's four qualifying groups but the Blues were undaunted and were quickly into their stride.

Their opening fixture was against Sale at Edgeley Park and although the Sharks pushed the visitors all the way, a late try from Richard Mustoe sealed an 18–17 victory and Young's team were up and running.

The Blues had home advantage for their clashes with Leicester and Bath and made it count with a 23–9 win over the Tigers before confirming their progress through to the semi-finals with a 24–18 triumph over Bath.

In Pool A, Gloucester proved to be the dominant force with three wins from three, seeing off Wasps (24–19), the Dragons (25–20) and Newcastle at Kingston Park in an 11–10 cliffhanger courtesy of Apo Satala's try four minutes from time.

The Ospreys qualified for the last four from Pool C, narrowly edging out London Irish. The Welsh region opened up with a 24–23 win over Harlequins and then beat Worcester 37–22. They were defeated by the Exiles at the Madejski Stadium in the final game but still reached the knockout phase courtesy of an extra bonus point.

In Pool D, Northampton topped the group ahead of the Scarlets and Saracens with Bristol a distant fourth. The Saints were beaten by Saracens at Vicarage Road in their second match but bounced back with victory over the Scarlets and progressed thanks to their two bonus points.

The first of the semi-finals saw Gloucester tackle the Ospreys at the Ricoh Arena in Coventry but there was to be no return to Twickenham for the Welsh holders as the Cherry and Whites produced a gritty performance to reach the final.

Gloucester were heavily indebted to the boot of fly-half Ryan Lamb who landed three penalties and a drop goal to establish a 12–0 lead against the run of play and when Iain Balshaw went over in the 76th minute for the only try of the match, the English side were 17–0 winners.

"It's not often the Ospreys get nilled," said coach Sean Holley after his side relinquished their grip on the cup. "Full credit to Gloucester, they did a job on us at the breakdown and I thought they defended really, really well.

"We came out with a really positive attitude and probably played all the rugby, but couldn't get on the score sheet. We missed a couple of early penalties so I think the boys felt the game was going our way. We had a lot of momentum, a lot of territory and they really wanted to get a score on the board and at half-time we still felt the game was in our favour."

The second semi was between Cardiff and Northampton at the same venue, but this time it was the Welsh fans celebrating at the final whistle as the Blues claimed a thrilling 11–5 win.

Young's team dominated the first half but only had a Blair penalty and Jason Spice try to show for their efforts and the Saints came back into it after the break when Joe Ansbro crashed over. Cardiff's nerves were now jangling but a second Blair penalty closed out the match and ensured a fourth successive Anglo-Welsh clash in the final.

"I am disappointed for the team to lose a game like that," said Saints boss Jim Mallinder. "We defended really well because Cardiff have got some big physical threats but it just wasn't our day.

"I am really proud where this team has come from in 18 months. After being relegated and spending a season in the first division, we have come a long way. We have improved this year as well and we are moving forward."

The big day at Twickenham was, of course, to be agony for Gloucester and ecstasy for the Blues and the writing was on the wall for the Englishmen as early as the 11th minute when Nicky Robinson's incisive break set up Halfpenny for the first of his tries. The Welsh youngster went over for his second just nine minutes later, Cardiff were already 17–0 up and the match was effectively over as a contest.

The Cherry and Whites finally troubled the scorers on the half hour mark when Mark Foster stretched out for a try, but it was merely a temporary reprieve and Cardiff helped themselves to a third try two minutes before half time when the video referee adjudged that wing Tom James had managed to get the ball down.

For 27 minutes of the second half Gloucester did at least manage to keep Cardiff at bay but further scores were inevitable and the Welsh side crossed again through Blair to extend their advantage.

The score seemed to break the English side's already fragile confidence and the Blues mercilessly went for the jugular and scored three more tries.

Replacement fly half Ceri Sweeney got his side's fifth of the match, Blair the sixth and the rout was completed by Shanklin in the final minute. Gloucester were awarded a penalty try at the other end but when Blair stroked over the conversion to Shanklin's score, the 50 was up and the Cherry and Whites had to suffer the indignity of looking up at a Twickenham scoreboard registering a half century of points.

"I could not have asked any more of them," said Young as the celebrations began. "The players have put in a lot of work but there has been a lot of work behind the scenes as well. It is great to see a lot of smiling faces."

EDF ENERGY CUP 2008–09 RESULTS
GROUP STANDINGS

POOL A

	P	W	D	L	F	A	BP	Pts
Gloucester	3	3	0	0	60	49	1	13
Wasps	3	2	0	1	66	47	2	10
Dragons	3	1	0	2	55	60	1	5
Newcastle	3	0	0	3	37	62	1	1

POOL C

	P	W	D	L	F	A	BP	Pts
Ospreys	3	2	0	1	80	68	2	10
London Irish	3	2	0	1	60	58	1	9
Harlequins	3	1	0	2	67	70	1	5
Worcester	3	1	0	2	58	69	1	5

POOL B

	P	W	D	L	F	A	BP	Pts
Cardiff	3	3	0	0	65	44	0	12
Leicester	3	2	0	1	58	58	0	8
Bath	3	1	0	2	57	64	2	6
Sale	3	0	0	3	58	72	2	2

POOL D

	P	W	D	L	F	A	BP	Pts
Northampton	3	2	0	1	82	70	2	10
Scarlets	3	2	0	1	73	50	0	8
Saracens	3	2	0	1	74	67	0	8
Bristol	3	0	0	3	39	81	1	1

SEMI-FINALS

28 March, Ricoh Arena, Coventry

GLOUCESTER 17 (3PG, 1T, 1DG) OSPREYS 0

GLOUCESTER: O Morgan; I Balshaw, M Tindall (captain), A Allen, J Simpson-Daniel; R Lamb, R Lawson; A Dickinson, O Azam, G Somerville, W James, A Brown, A Strokosch, A Hazell, G Delve.

SUBSTITUTIONS: M Bortolami for Brown (temp 5–14 mins); M Watkins for Tindall (29 mins); O Barkley for Simpson-Daniel (40 mins); C Nieto for Dickinson (40 mins); A Qera for Hazell (52 mins); Bortolami for James (67 mins).

SCORERS: *Try*: Balshaw, *Penalty Goals*: Lamb (3), *Drop Goal*: Lamb

OSPREYS: G Henson; T Bowe, S Parker, A Bishop, S Williams; J Hook, J Nutbrown; P James, R Hibbard, A Jones, I Gough, A Lloyd, T Smith, M Holah, R Jones (captain).

SUBSTITUTIONS: A-W Jones for Gough (26 mins); J Spratt for Henson (38 mins); M Phillips for Nutbrown (53 mins); H Bennett for Hibbard (58 mins); F Tiatia for Lloyd (62 mins); D Biggar for Bishop (69 mins).

REFEREE: N Owens (Wales)

EDF ENERGY CUP

28 March, Ricoh Arena, Coventry

CARDIFF 11 (2PG, 1T) NORTHAMPTON 5 (1T)

CARDIFF: B Blair; L Halfpenny, T Shanklin, J Roberts, T James; N Robinson, J Spice; G Jenkins, G Williams, T Filise, D Jones, P Tito (captain), M Molitika, R Sowden-Taylor, X Rush.

SUBSTITUTIONS: B Davies for Jones (58 mins); R Thomas for Williams (65 mins); J Yapp for Filise (70 mins); S Morgan for Rush (82 mins)

SCORERS: *Try*: Spice, *Penalty Goals*: Blair (2)

NORTHAMPTON: B Foden; P Diggin, J Ansbro, J Downey, B Reihana (captain); S Myler, L Dickson; T Smith, D Hartley, E Murray, I Fernandez Lobbe, J Kruger, N Best, S Gray, R Wilson.

SUBSTITUTIONS: S Tonga'uiha for Smith (50 mins); B Everitt for Myler (63 mins); C Lawes for Gray (68 mins); A Dickens for Dickson (72 mins); M Easter for Fernandez Lobbe (72 mins).

SCORERS: *Try*: Ansbro

REFEREE: G Clancy (Ireland)

FINAL

18 April, Twickenham, London

CARDIFF 50 (6G, 1PG, 1T) GLOUCESTER 12 (1G, 1T)

CARDIFF: B Blair; L Halfpenny, T Shanklin, J Roberts, T James; N Robinson, J Spice; G Jenkins, G Williams, T Filise, B Davies, P Tito (captain), M Molitika, M Williams, X Rush.

SUBSTITUTIONS: R Rees for Spice (2 mins); A Powell for Molitika (60 mins); R Thomas for G Williams (65 mins); D Jones for Davies (69 mins); G Thomas for Halfpenny (72 mins); C Sweeney for Robinson (72 mins); J Yapp for Filise (72 mins).

SCORERS: *Tries*: Halfpenny (2), Blair (2), James, Sweeney, Shanklin, *Conversions*: Blair (6), *Penalty Goal*: Blair

GLOUCESTER: O Morgan; M Foster, J Simpson-Daniel, A Allen, M Watkins; R Lamb, R Lawson; N Wood, O Azam, G Somerville, W James, A Brown, L Narraway, A Qera, G Delve (captain).

SUBSTITUTIONS: M Bortolami for James (53 mins); G Cooper for Lawson (59 mins); A Hazell for Qera (59 mins); O Barkley for Lamb (63 mins); S Lawson for Hazell (64 mins); C Nieto for Wood (70 mins).

SCORERS: *Tries*: Foster, *Penalty*: Barkley, *Conversion*: Barkley

REFEREE: A Rolland (Ireland)

RAMPANT BULLS VICTORIOUS

By Iain Spragg

Celebrate good times! The Bulls start the party after winning the 2009 Super 14.

The Blue Bulls ran riot against the Waikato Chiefs in the Super 14 final with a scintillating display of attacking rugby at Loftus Versfeld, scoring eight tries to secure the trophy for the second time in three years and underline the pre-eminence of South African sides in the southern hemisphere in 2009.

With the Springboks going on to claim the Tri-Nations title a little more than three months later, the Bulls' triumph in Pretoria was firm

No one scored more points in the Super 14 than Morné Steyn.

CROSS-BORDER TOURNAMENTS

evidence of South African rugby's rise and a fitting end to an impressive campaign that saw them bring the trophy back to the Rainbow Nation for only the second time.

The Bulls had won the Super 14 in 2007 after a dramatic 20–19 victory over the Sharks in Durban courtesy of a late try from Bryan Habana, converted by Derick Hougaard. However, two years on there was no need for a repeat of such last-gasp heroics as they put the Chiefs to the sword in a one-sided rout that set a new record for the margin of victory in the final.

Defeat was a bitter pill to swallow for the hapless New Zealanders appearing in their first final, and although they were the first to draw blood with a try from wing Lelia Masaga in the seventh minute, it was to prove only a brief respite from the Bulls' relentless onslaught.

"The last two weeks have been the best two weeks of my life," Bulls captain Victor Matfield said after lifting the trophy. "We started working for this in November. It showed that if you work hard you'll get the result on the field. We had no injuries in the last few weeks and that helped. We all know how hard it is to travel and come all this way. The Chiefs had an awesome year."

In hindsight, the final was a fitting climax to the 14th year of Super

14 competition. The Bulls and the Chiefs were the two strongest sides during the league phase of the tournament but it was essentially a five-way tussle between the two eventual finalists, the Hurricanes, defending champions the Crusaders and 2008 runners-up NSW Waratahs for a place in the semi-finals.

It was the Bulls and the Waratahs who had made the most convincing starts to their respective campaigns in February. The South Africans kicked off with five successive wins, while the Australians recorded four straight victories to set the early pace.

In stark contrast, both the Chiefs and Crusaders initially struggled. The Chiefs lost their opening three matches and while the defending champions did manage a 19–13 victory over the Chiefs in Christchurch in their first outing courtesy of a brace of tries from centre Casey Laulala, they were brought firmly back down to earth with defeats to the Brumbies (18–16) in Canberra in week two, followed by reverses against the Hurricanes (30–24) in Christchurch and the Highlanders (6–0) in Dunedin.

But just as it looked like the Bulls and the Waratahs were threatening to run away it, they both hit indifferent form which coincided with the Chiefs, Hurricanes and Crusaders all rediscovering their own winning formula.

One of the pivotal clashes came in early April when the Bulls travelled to New Zealand to face the Crusaders in Christchurch. The South Africans outscored the Kiwis two tries to one but a conversion, a drop goal and two penalties from Stephen Brett proved the difference between the two teams as the Crusaders edged the contest 16–13.

The Chiefs also began to enjoy a rich vein of form. They broke their duck in week four with a 31–13 victory over the Western Force in Hamilton thanks to a man of the match performance from captain Liam Messam and the result was the catalyst for a superb run of eight wins in their remaining nine games to ensure their place in the knockout stages.

A late charge also ensured the Hurricanes would be involved beyond the regular season. Two defeats in their first five games suggested a difficult campaign lay ahead for the Wellington-based outfit but the side, coached by Colin Cooper, turned the corner in week six. Facing the Lions in Johannesburg, the Kiwis ran in five tries to four, two from All Black Conrad Smith, for a 38–32 success and a bonus point. Five more victories were just enough to earn them a place in the semi-finals.

The final weekend of action saw all five leading contenders record wins, which meant the Bulls topped the table ahead of the Chiefs. The Hurricanes finished third while the Crusaders secured the final remaining place in the last four. It was agony, however, for the Waratahs, who finished level with the Crusaders on 41 points but were denied a semi-final berth on account of their inferior points difference.

The first of the semi-finals was an all-Kiwi affair as the Chiefs entertained the Hurricanes in Hamilton and the local rivalry, let alone the prize of a place in the final on offer, produced a predictably frenetic, bruising encounter that the home side eventually edged 14–10. The visitors drew first blood with a Ma'a Nonu try but the Chiefs hit back with scores from Sione Lauaki and captain Mils Muliaina and were on their way to a first appearance in the final.

"I thought we did really well but a couple of things let us down," admitted Hurricanes captain Rodney So'oialo after the defeat. "We gave away a bit too many penalties and missed a few tackles. I'm proud of the boys for the way they played tonight and all year. They never really gave it up and took it to the Chiefs tonight."

The second semi-final saw the Crusaders fly to South Africa to face the Bulls in Pretoria. The home side had won nine successive Super 14 fixtures at the Loftus Versfeld but at one stage they trailed the defending champions 20–7 and looked in serious danger of fluffing their lines.

It was the cue for an irrepressible rally. First, Akona Ndungane

Phil Walter/Getty Images

The Chiefs led the New Zealand charge in 2009, making the final.

sprinted over to reduce the arrears and when Crusaders No.8 Thomas Waldrom was yellow carded minutes before the break, the Bulls sensed blood and a third try from Pierre Spies and the third and fourth drop goals of the match from Morné Steyn were enough to wrap up a 36–23 win.

"We felt as if we had momentum when we scored our two tries early on," said Crusaders captain Richie McCaw. "But those 10 minutes before half-time really turned things around for the Bulls, and in the end we were beaten by a team that was hungry enough."

When the Bulls won the title in 2007 they had to do it away from home, but in 2009 they had the benefit of running out in the familiar surroundings of the Loftus Versfeld and they took full, devastating advantage as the Chiefs crumbled under their barrage.

The early score from Masaga did temporarily silence the home crowd but they found their collective and vociferous voice just a minute later when Fourie du Preez burst through for the Bulls' first score. The conversion levelled things up at 7–7 but when Du Preez raced 45 metres for his second try only three minutes later, the writing was on the wall for the beleaguered Kiwis.

The Bulls went on to cross the whitewash six more times. Habana helped himself to a brace and was followed over the line by Matfield, Wynand Olivier, Spies and substitute Danie Rossouw to record an historic 61–17 victory and in the process eclipse both the Brumbies 30-point winning margin in the 2001 final and the total of 47 points the Australians amassed in 2004 in their demolition of the Crusaders. Steyn's drop goal in the final also took him to 11 for the season and another record.

"We weren't allowed to play by the Bulls," admitted Muliaina as he began to come to terms with his side's record loss. "That was a world-class performance and well done to them. They thoroughly deserved their win and the title. They showed us how to play and we just couldn't get going. The Bulls have had a fantastic season and I wish them all the best for Springboks selection."

Victory for the Bulls reaffirmed their status as South Africa's leading Super 14 side. The Sharks' three appearances in the final had been the closest the country had come to claiming the title before the Bulls triumphed in 2007 and their second success merely underlined the team's growing strength.

"We have a very special group of players here," enthused Habana as the celebrations began. "It's amazing to be part of an unbelievable team and we have laid the foundations for future generations of this team. We knew the Chiefs would come at us and they scored that first try but we knew if we could keep our composure things would come good."

SUPER 14

Australia had three sides in the top eight, with the Waratahs leading the way for them in fifth.

13 February, 2009: **Highlanders** 31 **Brumbies** 33, **Force** 19 **Blues** 25, **Lions** 34 **Cheetahs** 28. 14 February, 2009: **Crusaders** 19 **Chiefs** 13, **Hurricanes** 22 **Waratahs** 26, **Stormers** 15 **Sharks** 20, **Bulls** 33 **Reds** 20. 20 February, 2009: **Hurricanes** 22 **Highlanders** 17, **Waratahs** 11 **Chiefs** 7, **Force** 16 **Cheetahs** 10, **Stormers** 27 **Reds** 24. 21 February, 2009: **Brumbies** 18 **Crusaders** 16, **Bulls** 59 **Blues** 26, **Sharks** 25 **Lions** 10. 27 February, 2009: **Crusaders** 24 **Hurricanes** 30, **Waratahs** 34 **Highlanders** 16. 28 February, 2009: **Chiefs** 15 **Sharks** 22, **Brumbies** 16 **Force** 25, **Lions** 9 **Bulls** 16, **Stormers** 8 **Blues** 14. 1 March, 2009: **Reds** 22 **Cheetahs** 3. 6 March, 2009: **Chiefs** 31 **Force** 13, **Waratahs** 15 **Reds** 11. 7 March, 2009: **Hurricanes** 29 **Cheetahs** 12, **Blues** 31 **Sharks** 35, **Highlanders** 6 **Crusaders** 0, **Bulls** 14 **Stormers** 10. 13 March, 2009: **Blues** 46 **Cheetahs** 12, **Brumbies** 21 **Waratahs** 11. 14 March, 2009: **Crusaders** 23 **Force** 23, **Highlanders** 10 **Chiefs** 14, **Reds** 25 **Sharks** 13, **Stormers** 56 **Lions** 18. 20 March, 2009: **Hurricanes** 14 **Bulls** 19. 21 March, 2009: **Highlanders** 32 **Cheetahs** 8, **Chiefs** 63 **Blues** 34, **Waratahs** 13 **Crusaders** 17, **Force** 10 **Sharks** 22, **Lions** 25 **Brumbies** 17. 27 March, 2009: **Blues** 22 **Waratahs** 27. 28 March, 2009: **Highlanders** 36 **Bulls** 12, **Crusaders** 11 **Stormers** 7, **Reds** 26 **Chiefs** 50, **Sharks** 35 **Brumbies** 14, **Lions** 32 **Hurricanes** 38. 3 April, 2009: **Crusaders** 16 **Bulls** 13, **Force** 39 **Reds** 7. 4 April, 2009: **Chiefs** 36 **Lions** 29, **Waratahs** 12 **Stormers** 6, **Cheetahs** 27 **Brumbies** 40, **Sharks** 33 **Hurricanes** 17. 10 April, 2009: **Blues** 36 **Lions** 12, **Force** 27 **Hurricanes** 28. 11 April, 2009: **Highlanders** 24 **Reds** 19, **Brumbies** 17 **Stormers** 10, **Waratahs** 6 **Bulls** 20, **Cheetahs** 31 **Sharks** 6. 17 April, 2009: **Blues** 26 **Highlanders** 6, **Brumbies** 32 **Bulls** 31. 18 April, 2009: **Hurricanes** 34 **Stormers** 11, **Reds** 20 **Lions** 31, **Waratahs** 14 **Force** 15, **Cheetahs** 10 **Chiefs** 28, **Sharks** 10 **Crusaders** 13. 24 April, 2009: **Highlanders** 11 **Stormers** 18, **Force** 55 **Lions** 14. 25 April, 2009: **Blues** 24 **Reds** 31, **Hurricanes** 56 **Brumbies** 7, **Cheetahs** 20 **Crusaders** 13, **Bulls** 33 **Chiefs** 27. 1 May, 2009: **Hurricanes** 45 **Blues** 27, **Lions** 20 **Crusaders** 32, **Cheetahs** 10 **Waratahs** 18. 2 May, 2009: **Reds** 13 **Brumbies** 52, **Sharks** 23 **Highlanders** 15, **Bulls** 32 **Force** 29, **Stormers** 14 **Chiefs** 28. 8 May, 2009: **Crusaders** 32 **Reds** 12, **Lions** 27 **Highlanders** 22. 9 May, 2009: **Chiefs** 16 **Hurricanes** 8, **Brumbies** 37 **Blues** 15, **Sharks** 12 **Waratahs** 16, **Bulls** 29 **Cheetahs** 20, **Stormers** 25 **Force** 24. 15 May, 2009: **Chiefs** 10 **Brumbies** 7, **Lions** 33 **Waratahs** 38. 16 May, 2009: **Blues** 13 **Crusaders** 15, **Reds** 28 **Hurricanes** 37, **Force** 33 **Highlanders** 28, **Cheetahs** 22 **Stormers** 28, **Sharks** 26 **Bulls** 27.

FINAL TABLE

	P	W	D	L	F	A	BP	Pts
Bulls	13	10	0	3	338	271	6	46
Chiefs	13	9	0	4	338	236	9	45
Hurricanes	13	9	0	4	380	279	8	44
Crusaders	13	8	1	4	231	198	7	41
Waratahs	13	9	0	4	241	212	5	41
Sharks	13	8	0	5	282	239	6	38
Brumbies	13	8	0	5	311	305	6	38
Western Force	13	6	1	6	328	275	10	36
Blues	13	5	0	8	339	369	12	32
Stormers	13	5	0	8	235	249	7	27
Highlanders	13	4	0	9	254	269	10	26
Lions	13	4	0	9	294	419	9	25
Reds	13	3	0	10	258	380	7	19
Cheetahs	13	2	0	11	213	341	4	12

SEMI-FINALS

22 May, Waikato Stadium, Hamilton

CHIEFS 14 (2G)
HURRICANES 10 (1G, 1PG)

CHIEFS: M Muliaina (captain); L Masaga, D Sweeney, C Bruce, S Sivivatu; S Donald, T Morland; S Taumalolo, A de Malmanche, J McGougan, C Clarke, K O'Neill, L Messam, T Latimer, S Lauaki.

SUBSTITUTES: H Elliot, J Savage, T Lynn, S Lilo, B Goodin, M Delany, S Anesi

SCORERS *Tries:* Lauaki, Muliaina *Conversions*: Donald (2)

HURRICANES: C Jane; T Ellison, C Smith, M Nonu, D Smith; W Ripia, P Weepu; J Schwalger, A Hore, N Tialata, J Thrush, J Eaton, V Vito, S Waldrom, R So'oialo (captain).

SUBSTITUTES: G Robinson, J Ellison, B Evans, K Lowe, A Mathewson, J Kawau, Z Guildford

SCORERS *Tries:* Nonu *Conversion*: Weepu *Penalty Goal:* Weepu

YELLOW CARD Schwalger (25 mins)

REFEREE S Dickinson (Australia)

BULLS 36 (3G, 1PG, 4DG)
CRUSADERS 23 (2G, 2PG, 1DG)

BULLS: Z Kirchner; A Ndungane, M Delport, J Pretorius, B Habana; M Steyn, F du Preez; G Steenkamp, D Kuün, W Kruger, B Botha, V Matfield (captain), D Stegmann, D Potgieter, P Spies.

SUBSTITUTES: C Ralepelle, R Gerber, D Rossouw, P Wannenburg, H Adams, B Francis, G van den Heever

SCORERS *Tries*: Habana, Ndungane, Spies *Conversions*: Steyn (3) *Penalty Goal*: Steyn *Drop Goals*: Steyn (4)

CRUSADERS: L MacDonald; J Payne, T Bateman, R Crotty, A Whitelock; S Brett, A Ellis; W Crockett, J MacDonald, O Franks, B Thorn, I Ross, K Read, R McCaw (captain), T Waldrom.

SUBSTITUTES: D Perrin, B Franks, M Paterson, G Whitelock, K Fotuali'i, C Slade, H Gard

SCORERS *Tries*: Read, Whitelock *Conversions*: MacDonald (2) *Penalty Goals*: Brett, MacDonald *Drop Goal*: Ellis

YELLOW CARD Waldrom (35 mins)

REFEREE B Lawrence (New Zealand)

FINAL

BULLS 61 (6G, 2T, 2PG, 1DG)
CHIEFS 17 (2G, 1PG)

Bulls: Z Kirchner; A Ndungane, J Pretorius, W Olivier, B Habana; M Steyn, F du Preez; G Steenkamp, D Kuün, W Kruger, B Botha, V Matfield (captain), D Stegmann, D Potgieter, P Spies.

SUBSTITUTES: C Ralepelle, R Gerber, D Rossouw, P Wannenburg, H Adams, B Francis, M Delport

SCORERS *Tries*: Du Preez (2), Habana (2), Matfield, Olivier, Spies, Rossouw *Conversions*: Steyn (5), Francis *Penalty Goals*: Steyn (2)

Chiefs: M Muliaina (captain); L Masaga, R Kahui, C Bruce, D Sweeney; S Donald, T Morland; S Taumalolo, A de Malmanche, J McGougan, C Clarke, K O'Neill, L Messam, T Latimer, S Lauaki.

SUBSTITUTES: H Elliot, J Savage, T Lynn, S Lilo, D Bason, M Delany, S Anesi

SCORERS *Tries*: Masaga, Muliaina *Conversions*: Donald (2) *Penalty Goal*: Donald

REFEREE J I Kaplan (South Africa)

Paul O'Connell tasted Magners League glory with Munster before heading off on the Lions tour.

RED ARMY MARCHES ON

Dave Rogers/Getty Images

Munster's loyal fans had something else to shout about in 2009.

Munster claimed their second Magners League crown to maintain Ireland's recent run of success in the cross-border competition, dethroning their provincial rivals Leinster as champions and handing Tony McGahan a trophy in his first season as the side's new Director of Coaching.

Irish sides had triumphed in two of the previous three tournaments – a sequence broken by the Ospreys in 2007 – and Munster, the defending Heineken Cup champions, maintained the Emerald Isle's impressive recent Magners League record with a robust campaign that saw McGahan's side crowned champions ahead of second place Edinburgh at the end of April.

The coronation came with two games to spare and without the Red Army even having to play. The Ospreys faced the Dragons at the Liberty Stadium and although the home side beat their compatriots 27–18, they failed to secure the bonus point required to keep the title race alive and Munster were Celtic champions for the first time in six years.

For McGahan, his side's success was vindication of the province's decision to hand him the coaching reins in the summer. The Australian certainly had big shoes to fill when Declan Kidney left to take up the Ireland job having led the club to Heineken Cup glory and although the names of Michael Bradley, Niall O'Donovan and Eddie O'Sullivan were all mentioned as possible successors, Munster opted for continuity and promoted McGahan.

"Having been involved with Munster for the past three seasons, I fully realise what the expectations of all the supporters are," he acknowledged after replacing Kidney. "It is a privilege and a great honour to be asked to lead one of the top clubs and biggest brand names in world rugby.

"With a solid group of senior players at my disposal, plus an exciting batch of young players coming through, a talented management group and strong administration, I hope to continue and fulfil those expectations in the short and long term. I am looking forward to the challenges ahead."

It was an ironic twist of fate that Munster were to relinquish their grip on the Heineken Cup just two days after they were confirmed as Magners champions, losing to Leinster in the semi-finals, but the setback should not unduly detract from what was a solid debut season for McGahan.

The season began in September and Munster's first assignment was a trip to Murrayfield to tackle Edinburgh. The Scots were to prove the Red Army's main rivals for the title over the campaign but it was the Irish team that gained the early psychological advantage with a hard-fought 20–15 win courtesy of tries from Keith Earls and David Wallace.

McGahan's side were up and running and four further victories followed, including an 18–0 shutout of provincial rivals Leinster in front of 18,000 fans at the RDS in late September.

Their first defeat of the season came the following month when they travelled to Ravenhill to face Ulster, who were bottom of the table and desperately struggling for form.

The form book, however, was well and truly ripped up as Timoci Nagusa scored twice and replacement scrum half Isaac Boss added a third try for the home side for a well-earned 22–6 win that saw Ulster leapfrog both Connacht and the Dragons in the wrong half of the league table.

"Obviously there were some great players missing from that Munster side but I know to beat Munster any day you have to be playing well," said Ulster coach Matt Williams. "I think we just really needed to win that a lot more. We've played a lot of good rugby without the results. Our biggest plus tonight was our defence which I thought was superb. To keep Munster tryless, not many other teams can do that."

The defeat was the catalyst for Munster's least convincing phase of the season. They recovered in their following fixture to defeat the Scarlets 18–16 in Wales but their next two games against Connacht and the return match with Ulster were to see the Red Army wobble dramatically.

The Connacht game was nothing if not a shock. They had not beaten Munster since 1986 but four penalties from man of the match Ian Keatley at the Sportsground sealed a famous 12–6 win and ended their 22-year long losing sequence.

Worse was to follow early in the New Year when Ulster came calling and made a mockery of Thomond Park's reputation as a fortress. No Irish side had won at Munster's home ground since 1995 and Ulster themselves had not tasted victory at Thomond Park for 19 years but tries from Paddy Wallace, Darren Cave, Mark McCrea, Tom Court and Andrew Trimble rewrote history as the Red Army were beaten 37–11 and in the process surrendered top spot in the table to the Ospreys.

"To come to one of the greatest grounds in the world and to win the way we did with ball in hand and to score so many tries is a real achievement," said Williams. "The players stood up in every aspect of the game and were magnificent. We put out nine players who are 23 or under and most of them only 21 – it's an incredible statistic for the province."

Munster had the chance to atone for their back-to-back defeats six days later in a top of the table clash with the Ospreys at the Liberty Stadium. It was a game the Irishmen desperately needed to win and when the chips were down, McGahan's side showed their mettle.

Ospreys' fly-half James Hook landed an incredible seven penalties to give the Welshman 21 points, but a superb individual performance from scrum-half Tomas O'Leary inspired the visitors. O'Leary scored Munster's second try of the match and then switched to fly-half and landed a penalty and when the final whistle sounded, the Irishmen were 25–21 winners.

It was the Ospreys' first defeat at the Liberty Stadium in eight matches and Munster's first success on the road against the Welsh side for five years. More significantly, the Red Army were back to winning ways.

"It's brilliant to get the result," O'Leary said after the game. "We've

MAGNERS LEAGUE

got a great pack and traditionally we've always been strong. This week we concentrated on keeping it basic and keeping it tight and the forwards delivered. It was an easy ride to be behind them to be honest."

Next up were fifth placed Edinburgh at Musgrave Park and it was obvious Munster had regained some of their old verve when Doug Howlett raced over after just 10 minutes. Tony Buckley added a second try before the break and although Edinburgh replied with scores from Ben Cairns and Chris Paterson, further tries from Earls and Ciaran O'Boyle completed a 28–14 win. The bonus point meant McGahan's team went back to the top of the table with Leinster second and the Ospreys dropping down to third.

Munster would not relinquish top spot for the remainder of the campaign. Four more wins on the bounce against the Dragons at Rodney Parade, Glasgow at Firhill, and then Leinster and Connacht at Thomond Park put the Red Army on the verge of the title and with the Scarlets their next opposition at Musgrave Park, they were almost there.

If the Irishmen were nervous at being so close to the finishing line, they did not show it and after just six minutes a Howlett break led to an Ian Dowling try and Munster were in the driving seat. They crossed three more times through David Wallace, Earls and Denis Leamy to earn a 29–10 win and a bonus point.

The only dark cloud on the horizon was a 10th-minute injury to Ireland scrum half O'Leary, who was stretchered off with a suspected broken ankle after getting caught under a pile of bodies. The 25-year-old had been selected for the British & Irish Lions squad earlier in the month but the injury was to cruelly deprive him of the opportunity to tour South Africa.

But on a collective note at least, it had been a more than satisfactory 80 minutes for Munster and six days later, without having to take to the field again, they were confirmed as champions when Ospreys handed it to them on a plate after their failure to secure a bonus point against the Dragons.

"Winning the Magners League is reward for all the players who have played for Munster this season," said club chief executive Garrett Fitzgerald when the news broke the Red Army were champions.

"It is a significant achievement for a new management team and the leaders within our squad. Our support at Magners League games has steadily increased in a difficult economic climate. We would like to thank our supporters, sponsors and everyone else who has helped throughout the campaign."

MAGNERS LEAGUE 2008–09 RESULTS

5 September: **Connacht** 3 **Ospreys** 16, **Dragons** 6 **Glasgow** 12, **Edinburgh** 15 **Munster** 20, **Ulster** 9 **Scarlets** 16. 6 September: **Cardiff** 16 **Leinster** 16. 9 September: **Ospreys** 32 **Cardiff** 10. 10 September: **Dragons** 25 **Scarlets** 27. 12 September: **Cardiff** 16 **Ulster** 15, **Glasgow** 18 **Ospreys** 21, **Leinster** 52 **Edinburgh** 6. 13 September: **Scarlets** 45 **Connacht** 3. 14 September: **Munster** 50 **Dragons** 6. 19 September: **Connacht** 15 **Glasgow** 8, **Edinburgh** 32 **Scarlets** 12, **Ulster** 14 **Dragons** 16, **Leinster** 19 **Ospreys** 13. 20 September: **Munster** 28 **Cardiff** 20. 26 September: **Cardiff** 58 **Connacht** 0, **Glasgow** 34 **Scarlets** 20, **Dragons** 11 **Edinburgh** 9. 27 September: **Ospreys** 43 **Ulster** 0. 28 September: **Leinster** 0 **Munster** 18. 3 October: **Ulster** 13 **Edinburgh** 9. 4 October: **Munster** 25 **Glasgow** 17. 5 October: **Connacht** 19 **Leinster** 18. 24 October: **Connacht** 14 **Edinburgh** 27, **Glasgow** 15 **Leinster** 12. 25 October: **Ulster** 22 **Munster** 6. 28 November: **Scarlets** 16 **Munster** 18, **Edinburgh** 32 **Ospreys** 16, **Glasgow** 28 **Cardiff** 0, **Ulster** 53 **Connacht** 13. 29 November: **Leinster** 29 **Dragons** 13. 19 December: **Dragons** 30 **Ospreys** 24. 20 December: **Scarlets** 27 **Cardiff** 13. 26 December: **Dragons** 19 **Cardiff** 21, **Edinburgh** 39 **Glasgow** 6. 27 December: **Ospreys** 20 **Scarlets** 6, **Ulster** 13 **Leinster** 21. 28 December: **Connacht** 12 **Munster** 6. 31 December: **Cardiff** 12 **Ospreys** 16. 1 January: **Scarlets** 29 **Dragons** 24. 2 January: **Glasgow** 25 **Edinburgh** 20, **Leinster** 26 **Connacht** 18. 3 January: **Munster** 11 **Ulster** 37. 9 January: **Connacht** 14 **Scarlets** 17, **Ospreys** 21 **Munster** 25, **Glasgow** 20 **Dragons** 25, **Edinburgh** 21 **Ulster** 15. 10 January: **Leinster** 21 **Cardiff** 20. 20 February: **Cardiff** 34 **Glasgow** 30. 21 February: **Scarlets** 17 **Leinster** 31, **Munster** 28 **Edinburgh** 14. 22 February: **Ospreys** 22 **Connacht** 10, **Dragons** 26 **Ulster** 16. 6 March: **Connacht** 14 **Cardiff** 19, **Ospreys** 8 **Leinster** 13. 7 March: **Dragons** 9 **Munster** 20, **Ulster** 12 **Glasgow** 0. 8 March: **Scarlets** 13 **Edinburgh** 6. 27 March: **Edinburgh** 32 **Connacht** 5, **Glasgow** 13 **Munster** 26. 29 March: **Leinster** 32 **Ulster** 6. 3 April: **Connacht** 39 **Dragons** 17, **Edinburgh** 16 **Cardiff** 3, **Ulster** 13 **Ospreys** 16. 4 April: **Scarlets** 21 **Glasgow** 38, **Munster** 22 **Leinster** 5. 17 April: **Glasgow** 19 **Ulster** 20, **Edinburgh** 27 **Leinster** 16. 18 April: **Scarlets** 19 **Ospreys** 28, **Munster** 25 **Connacht** 10. 24 April: **Ulster** 9 **Cardiff** 11, **Munster** 29 **Scarlets** 10. 25 April: **Ospreys** 30 **Edinburgh** 32, **Leinster** 36 **Glasgow** 13. 26 April: **Dragons** 27 **Connacht** 14. 30 April: **Ospreys** 27 **Dragons** 18. 6 May: **Cardiff** 26 **Dragons** 12. 8 May: **Connacht** 12 **Ulster** 14, **Leinster** 45 **Scarlets** 8. 9 May: **Edinburgh** 43 **Dragons** 3. 10 May: **Ospreys** 34 **Glasgow** 23, **Cardiff** 20 **Munster** 12. 13 May: **Cardiff** 9 **Scarlets** 30. 15 May: **Glasgow** 30 **Connacht** 9, **Munster** 36 **Ospreys** 10. 16 May: **Dragons** 18 **Leinster** 9, **Scarlets** 43 **Ulster** 17. 17 May: **Cardiff** 14 **Edinburgh** 36.

FINAL TABLE

	P	W	D	L	F	A	BP	PTS
Munster	18	14	0	4	405	257	7	63
Edinburgh	18	11	0	7	416	296	11	55
Leinster	18	11	1	6	401	270	6	52
Ospreys	18	11	0	7	397	319	8	52
Scarlets	18	9	0	9	376	395	4	40
Cardiff	18	8	1	9	322	361	4	38
Glasgow	18	7	0	11	349	375	9	37
Ulster	18	7	0	11	298	331	8	36
Dragons	18	7	0	11	305	429	5	33
Connacht	18	4	0	14	224	460	4	20

PREVIOUS WINNERS

Celtic League Winners

2001/02: **Leinster**
2002/03: **Munster**
2003/04: **Llanelli Scarlets**

2004/05: **Neath Swansea Ospreys**
2005/06: **Ulster**

Magners League Winners

2006/07: **Ospreys**
2007/08: **Leinster**
2008/09: **Munster**

Warren Little/Getty Images

Ben Cairns' Edinburgh created history with their runners-up spot.

CROSS-BORDER TOURNAMENTS

BACK TO TAKE THE TITLE

By Karen Bond

It's all smiles for the Junior All Blacks.

The silverware may have remained in New Zealand hands once more with the returning Junior All Blacks going through the tournament unbeaten, but the ANZ Pacific Nations Cup broke new ground in 2009 with a condensed format which saw all bar the opening round of matches played in one country – Fiji.

A new title sponsor and tournament format were not the only changes for this year with Australia A having withdrawn and two-time champions the Junior All Blacks replacing 2008 winners New Zealand Maori as their country's representatives to give the Pacific Nations Cup the same line-up as its inaugural year in 2006.

"The hosting of the majority of the ANZ Pacific Nations Cup matches for the first time in a single country is a very exciting development for a tournament which is now a major event in the global rugby calendar," said IRB Chairman Bernard Lapasset.

The three previous editions of the Pacific Nations Cup – a key element of the IRB's Strategic Investment Programme – have gradually seen the divide between the second strings of New Zealand and Australia and the other four nations narrow, and with the new condensed format enabling Fiji, Tonga and Samoa in particular to secure the services of their overseas based players the 2009 competition continued this trend.

The tournament kicked off on 12 June at Apia Park as Samoa took on a Junior All Blacks side captained by centre Tamati Ellison and without the services of Luke McAlister after his elevation to the All Blacks to replace the injured Richard Kahui.

Tries from Hosea Gear and Israel Dagg helped the Junior All Blacks establish a 14–0 half-time lead, but the visitors had not counted on Samoa coming roaring back in an enthralling second half with Gavin Williams kicking two penalties and crossing for a try before Esera Lauina's effort forced the tournament favourites to hang on for 13 minutes for a 17–16 victory.

The next day Tonga welcomed Fiji to the Teufaiva Stadium in Nuku'alofa. However while Tonga started each half with a try, they couldn't maintain that momentum against a Fijian side who crossed for five tries in total to secure a bonus point 36–22 win and the perfect warm up for their meeting with the Junior All Blacks five days later in Lautoka.

Japan had sat out the opening round and so began their campaign against Samoa in the only match of the 17-day festival of rugby on Fijian soil at Lawaqa Park in Sigatoka. The match did not begin well for the Japanese with a penalty try and another from Justin Va'a giving the Samoans a 12–3 half-time advantage.

However within 10 minutes of the restart Japan lead following tries from Jack Tarrant and Hirotoki Onozawa, although this would be their final act on the scoreboard as Samoa took control with Mahroni Schwalger, Lauina and Semo Sititi touching down to seal a 34–15 victory and a second bonus point of the competition.

An expectant 10,000 fans converged on Lautoka hoping to see Fiji upset the Junior All Blacks, but the majority of them left Churchill Park disappointed with Gear scoring the first and last of seven tries as the well-drilled New Zealanders ran out 45–17 winners to leave them sitting atop the standings after two rounds with nine points, three clear of Samoa.

The third round provided the first double header with Samoa taking on Tonga and the Junior All Blacks facing the Japanese. Samoa came out on top in a typically physical encounter with Tonga, recording a 27–13 victory, but while they outscored their rivals by four tries to one, they were also guilty of failing to capitalise on a number of opportunities.

The Junior All Blacks wrapped up the second match with a 40–0 lead at half-time, but the improving Japanese didn't let the floodgates open and actually 'won' the second half with Hitoshi Ono, Tarrant and Koji Taira crossing for tries before the New Zealanders rediscovered their scoring touch with Gear and Sione Lauaki touching down in the 52–21 win.

Undoubtedly the fourth round highlight Fiji versus Samoa, one which had been the talk of the town leading up to the Churchill Park tie. The expectant crowd were treated to a spectacle, Samoa dominating early possession and territory, their centre pairing of Gavin Williams and Seilala Mapusua shutting down the dangerous Fijian backline for much of the first half as their side went in 9–3 ahead.

With Fiji's backline looking more dangerous, Vereniki Goneva was denied a stunning try, but within minutes the Sevens star touched down to move the hosts into a 16–9 lead. It remained that way until 12 minutes from time when Samoa turned down a quick tap and were rewarded when Notise Tauafao pounced on a loose ball in-goal.

The conversion was missed and Seremaia Bai had the raucous crowd on their feet when his penalty extended Fiji's lead to 19–14. Samoa threw everything at their hosts, but the defence held firm to spark celebrations when referee Jonathan Kaplan blew for full-time. The celebrations were not only Fiji's though as their victory meant the Junior All Blacks would keep the silverware in New Zealand hands.

The day also yielded a first win for Japan, who edged a tight battle with Tonga 21–19 to record their third successive PNC victory over the islanders. Only resolute Tonga defence kept Japan at bay, although two tries from Shaun Webb did give Asia's top side a 15–7 half-time lead.

A brilliant solo effort from hooker 'Iliasi Ma'asi cut the deficit, but two Ryan Nicholas penalties edged Japan out to 21–14 as the attack-minded sides kept the crowd enthralled. Tonga hit back with Tevita Halaifonua darting down the right wing to score, but crucially he missed the conversion to level the scores.

The focus moved to the National Stadium in Suva for the final round with the Junior All Blacks defending their unbeaten PNC record against winless Tonga and Fiji needing to beat Japan to overhaul Samoa for second spot. The New Zealanders, though, didn't have it all their own way against Tonga, despite the seemingly convincing 47–25 scoreline, and trailed 18–12 at half-time despite two tries in three minutes by Gear.

The introduction of Victor Vito re-energised the pack and three tries in the last eight minutes put a gloss on the final score. This match, though, was merely an appetiser for a master class of adventurous running rugby between Fiji and Japan the following day, one decided only at the death with Netani Talei's try sealing a 40–39 win for the hosts.

Japan made the early running and led 14–3, but Goneva's try gave the Fijians an unlikely 20–14 half-time advantage. There was no let up when play resumed, Japan scoring three tries – two of them by captain Takashi Kikutani – to move out to 36–26 with 10 minutes remaining. There was to be no first win over Fiji in 15 years for Japan as, roared on by their vociferous fans, first Sireli Ledua and then Talei crossed the try-line.

The ANZ Pacific Nations Cup was as successful off the pitch as it was on it with the teams buying into the whole event – the Junior All Blacks often took 30 minutes to make it to their match day bus to satisfy the amassed autograph hunters – and the Fijian public enjoying top class international matches and extending a warm welcome to all with referee Kaplan enjoying the same celebrity status as the players.

ANZ PACIFIC NATIONS CUP 2009 RESULTS		
12/06/09	Samoa 16–17 **Junior All Blacks**	Apia Park, **Samoa**
13/06/09	Tonga 22–36 **Fiji**	Teufaiva Stadium, **Nuku'alofa**
18/06/09	Japan 15–34 **Samoa**	Lawaqa Park, **Sigatoka**
18/06/09	**Junior All Blacks** 45–17 Fiji	Churchill Park, **Lautoka**
23/06/09	**Samoa** 27–13 Tonga	Churchill Park, **Lautoka**
23/06/09	Japan 21–52 **Junior All Blacks**	Churchill Park, **Lautoka**
27/06/09	Tonga 19–21 **Japan**	Churchill Park, **Lautoka**
27/06/09	Samoa 14–19 **Fiji**	Churchill Park, **Lautoka**
02/07/09	Tonga 25–47 **Junior All Blacks**	National Stadium, **Suva**
03/07/09	**Fiji** 40–39 Japan	National Stadium, **Suva**

FINAL TABLE

Team	P	W	D	L	F	A	BP	PTS
Junior All Blacks	4	4	0	0	161	79	3	**19**
Fiji	4	3	0	1	112	120	2	**14**
Samoa	4	2	0	2	91	64	4	**12**
Japan	4	1	0	3	96	145	2	**6**
Tonga	4	0	0	4	79	131	1	**1**

FIJIANS TASTE FIRST SUCCESS

By Karen Bond

The Fiji Warriors are ecstatic with their victory in the final over Upolu Samoa.

Fiji Warriors had contested the inaugural IRB Pacific Rugby Cup final in 2006, but they had to wait three years before they finally got their hands on the trophy with a hard-fought 19–7 defeat of Upolu Samoa at Apia Park giving them the honour of becoming their country's first champions of the six-team representative tournament.

The victory was extra sweet for the Fijians, not only because they had never beaten Upolu in the competition's history, but that it came against the side that had left them heartbroken in round four after Samoa international Roger Warren kicked a penalty with the last play of the match to snatch a 23–21 away win at Churchill Park in Lautoka.

Fijian sides are known for their flair and speed, but the bedrock of the Warriors' success was their resolute defence as they resisted the relentless onslaught of Upolu attacks, particularly in the last quarter as the Samoan side threw everything they had in an attempt to send the 3,000 strong crowd home happy with a second title in three years.

Upolu had dominated the early exchanges with George Stowers in imperious form, but Warriors' captain Alefoso Yalayalatabua, leading his fellow forwards by example, scored the only try of the half in the 26th minute to ensure the visitors led 7–0 at the break.

Two tries in the opening 10 minutes of the second half proved crucial for the Warriors with first flanker Samu Bola and then hooker Viliame Veikoso touching down. Upolu did finally get on the scoreboard with Anitele'a Tuilagi 69th minute try, but the Fijians were determined their line would not be breached again whatever the Samoan side threw at them.

"The boys played with their heart and our defence won the game. I am very proud of the boys," said Warriors coach Ifereimi Tawake. "This win is important for our RWC 2011 preparations and these players are the future. This is great for Fiji rugby, I told them we were leaving our shores to win the IRB Pacific Rugby Cup and we did."

Upolu, the 2007 champions and runners-up to Tongan side Tautahi Gold in 2008, had contested the final without their influential fly-half Warren, the leading point scorer in this year's competition with 57, who had picked up an injury in the all-Samoan affair with Savai'i Samoa the previous week.

That match had, until the final, been the only blemish on Upolu's record with 2006 champions Savai'i having triumphed 26–6 at Apia Park. The loss of Warren – himself a first minute injury replacement – did not help Upolu's cause, although they were already assured of a place in the final having won their first four matches in the round robin stages.

Savai'i were one of three sides hoping to join Upolu in the title decider going into the final round of pool matches, when the Warriors and Tautahi Gold also tasted victory over Tau'uta Reds and Fiji Barbarians respectively. The trio all finished with a record of won three, lost two but the Warriors had claimed an impressive five bonus points along the way and ended up level on 17 points with Upolu. Savai'i finished third on 15, then Gold with 14, Tau'uta Reds six and Fiji Barbarians five.

The Barbarians may have propped up the standings, but this was perhaps understandable, given that they were also their country's Under 20 side who were using the Pacific Rugby Cup to warm up for the IRB TOSHIBA Junior World Championship in Japan during June.

The tournament didn't get off to the best of starts for the young Fijians with a 47–8 loss to the Warriors in Sigatoka, but despite conceding nearly 50 points in two others matches their development over the five weeks as a result of playing against senior sides was evident and they fully deserved their solitary victory, 26–15 over Tau'uta Reds in the Tongan capital Nuku'alofa in round four.

"The main purpose for us to participate in the tournament was to compete against the big boys," said Fiji Under 20 coach Osea Umuumulovo on the eve of Junior World Championship. "We did great and beat one of the Tongan teams. We learned how to improve all the set pieces and how to play against big boys because South Africa and France are slightly bigger than us."

The participation of Fiji's Under 20 side under the banner of the Barbarians – it will be interesting to see if Samoa and Tonga follow their example next year – was not the only first in 2009 as the Pacific Rugby Cup finally saw the first hat-tricks scored since its introduction as a key element in the player development pathway in the Pacific Islands.

Samoa Sevens captain Ofisa Treviranus claimed that honour during Upolu's 49–13 defeat of the Barbarians in Apia during round three, although Warriors full-back Iliesa Keresoni then repeated the feat the following day in their 39–22 defeat of Savai'i.

"This tournament just continues to grow in stature, in popularity and in standard and not only in the standard of the players, but the standard of coaching and match officiating," Will Glenwright, the IRB's Regional General Manager for Oceania, admitted on the eve of the final in a Samoan capital that was "a buzz" with excitement.

"It has been another successful tournament, what we are starting to see now is the quality of athlete participating in the Pacific Rugby Cup improve significantly. All of these players have now been in a High Performance programme within their respective countries for three years, so the athletes are fitter, bigger and stronger and we are seeing that reflected on the field."

One thing that was also evident was the ultra-competitive nature of the 2009 competition with seven matches decided by less than seven points. Tau'uta Reds were involved in three of these encounters, but unfortunately for the 2007 runners-up they only won one of them, 15–14 against Savai'i on the opening weekend.

IRB PACIFIC RUGBY CUP 2009 RESULTS		
24/04/09	Fiji Barbarians 8–47 Fiji Warriors	Lawaqa Park, Sigatoka
24/04/09	Savai'i Samoa 14–15 Tau'uta Reds	Apia Park, Apia
25/04/09	Tautahi Gold 9–17 Upolu Samoa	Teufaiva Stadium, Nuku'alofa
01/05/09	Fiji Barbarians 17–23 Savai'i Samoa	Churchill Park, Lautoka
01/05/09	Upolu Samoa 19–15 Tau'uta Reds	Apia Park, Apia
02/05/09	Tautahi Gold 26–21 Fiji Warriors	Teufaiva Stadium, Nuku'alofa
08/05/09	Upolu Samoa 49–13 Fiji Barbarians	Apia Park, Apia
09/05/09	Tautahi Gold 14–12 Tau'uta Reds	Teufaiva Stadium, Nuku'alofa
09/05/09	Fiji Warriors 39–22 Savai'i Samoa	Churchill Park, Lautoka
15/05/09	Fiji Warriors 21–23 Upolu Samoa	Churchill Park, Lautoka
16/05/09	Tau'uta Reds 15–26 Fiji Barbarians	Teufaiva Stadium, Nuku'alofa
16/05/09	Savai'i Samoa 18–14 Tautahi Gold	Prince Edward Park, Iva
22/05/09	Fiji Barbarians 10–47 Tautahi Gold	Lawaqa Park, Sigatoka
22/05/09	Savai'i Samoa 26–6 Upolu Samoa	Apia Park, Apia
23/05/09	Tau'uta Reds 15–40 Fiji Warriors	Teufaiva Stadium, Nuku'alofa

FINAL STANDINGS

	P	W	D	L	F	A	BP	PTS
Upolu Samoa	5	4	0	1	114	84	1	**17**
Fiji Warriors	5	3	0	2	168	94	5	**17**
Savai'i Samoa	5	3	0	2	103	91	3	**15**
Tautahi Gold	5	3	0	2	110	78	2	**14**
Tau'uta Reds	5	1	0	4	72	113	2	**6**
Fiji Barbarians	5	1	0	4	74	181	1	**5**

FINAL		
29/05/09	Upolu Samoa 7–19 Fiji Warriors	Apia Park, Apia

NATIONS ARE EMERGING

By Karen Bond

AFP

Kazakhstan claimed second in this year's championship.

Japan may have retained their HSBC Asian Five Nations crown with four emphatic bonus point victories just as they had done in the inaugural competition last year, but behind them the race for second place was hotly contested by Korea, Hong Kong and Kazakhstan.

Korea had claimed that mantle in 2008 and were favourites to be 'best of the rest' once more, particularly with Hong Kong finding their feet under new national coach Dai Rees. However, both nations had to travel to Almaty to face Kazakhstan, one of the most improving nations in Asia, in their own backyard.

The Koreans were the first to discover that playing in Kazakhstan's largest city was no easy task in the second round of the competition spanning five consecutive weekends in April and May – even though their visit to the Central Stadium came on the back of the Kazakhs suffering a heavy 87–10 loss to Japan in Osaka seven days earlier.

Kazakhstan had finished fourth last year – needing a win on the final weekend over Arabian Gulf to avoid relegation – with coach Valeriy Popov admitting at the time that their first taste of the Top 5 had been a learning experience and one to motivate them to make the next step up. The visit of Korea provided them with the perfect opportunity to show to the world of rugby that they were a nation on the rise in Asia.

Inspired by their veteran stars, flanker Anton Rudoy and full-back Maxim Lifontov, Kazakhstan led 13–3 at half-time in an entertaining encounter. Two tries in quick succession after the break not only saw Rudoy complete his hat-trick, but took the hosts out to 27–10 with 30 minutes remaining.

Korea, though, weren't finished and fought back to level the match following tries from Jeong Dae Ik and Han Kun Kyu, full-back Kim Huen Hyun converting both and kicking a penalty. However, there was to be no fairytale comeback with Lifontov – last year's leading point-scorer – slotting the winning penalty to the delight of the 2,600 crowd.

Kazakhstan were nearly brought back down to earth with a bang a week later when they only scraped past Singapore 22–19 in humid conditions, but after sitting out round four they returned home and braved the torrential rain that fell for long periods to beat Hong Kong 25–6 and clinch the runners-up spot.

"Today's win is going to be a great boost for rugby in Kazakhstan," captain and try scorer Timur Mashurov said afterwards. "We are really happy to win in front of our home crowd today, but we know we have to do it all again next year if we want to go to the Rugby World Cup in 2011."

Next year's champions will qualify for Rugby World Cup 2011 with the runners-up entering the cross-continental play-off. One side that will not be part of that process is Singapore, having finished bottom with a solitary bonus point on their debut in the Top 5 as last year's Division One winners.

Singapore, though, like Kazakhstan and Arabian Gulf before them, have learned from their experiences and players now realise the difference between local rugby and representing their country against Asia's elite. Beaten by Korea 65–0 and Hong Kong 64–6, Singapore ended the campaign with a 45–15 defeat by Japan at Yio Chu Kang Stadium.

While they were the only side to keep Japan below 50 points, and scored the most points against them, Singapore did face a starting XV containing only four players from the previous week's 80–9 defeat of Korea. For coach Danny Tauroa, though, the performance was "all about character and restoring the pride in wearing the Singapore jersey".

There were other positives to emerge from the Top 5 with Hong

Kong unearthing a new talent in Adam Raby, the wing helping himself to seven tries in his first two internationals, three as his side fought back from 31–3 down at half-time to narrowly lose 36–34 to Korea in round three and then four against Singapore.

While Rees was taking his first steps as Hong Kong coach, his Japanese counterpart John Kirwan has had one eye on RWC 2011 for a while. The former All Black admitted before the Top 5 kicked off that "last year was a transition for us, where we kept some of the older players to help the younger guys, but this year we've only selected players who will still be playing at the 2011 Rugby World Cup."

This meant only one player in his 30s got the nod – Hirotoki Onozawa, who reached a personal milestone by marking his 50th Test for Japan against Korea with a four-try haul to surpass Kirwan's own tally of 35 Test tries, his coach saying afterwards he would "probably buy him a bottle of champagne and share it with him".

Away from the Top 5, Arabian Gulf ensured their RWC 2011 dream lives on by winning Division I. Led by Taif Al Delamie, the first ever Arabian Gulf national to captain the side, they ran out 44–24 winners over Chinese Taipei in the final played at The Sevens in Dubai, while Sri Lanka beat last year's Division II winners Thailand 51–17 to finish third.

Former England wing Rory Underwood joked he must be Malaysia's "lucky charm" after watching the Division II hosts secure promotion by beating an under strength China 43–15 in Kuala Lumpur in June. China had only brought 19 players and, having led by a point at half-time, inevitably tired to allow Malaysia to run riot.

"It was great to be back in a rugby environment in Asia," admitted Underwood. "I am really delighted to see that the Game continues to grow in Asia, particularly through the influence of the HSBC Asian Five Nations . . . I am excited to see some of the native talent in Asia."

Pakistan will play in Division III in 2010 after losing 44–3 to India in the third place play-off – a big improvement on last year's 92–0 defeat, filling the void left by the Philippines' promotion following a 25–0 win over Guam in Manila in early July. This new tier involved the three Regional tournament winners in 2008 – Philippines, Iran and Indonesia – along with Guam, but while the winner would be promoted, there would be no relegation in the first year.

In the bottom tier of the Asian Five Nations pyramid, the two Regional tournaments brought success for hosts Laos and Uzbekistan. Laos got the 2009 competition underway in March, but needed a late 70-metre breakaway try from Packham Sensourivong to beat Cambodia 8–3 and claim the honours. Uzbekistan proved too strong for Kyrgyzstan – a side they had drawn 15–15 with in 2008 – to run out 31–12 winners in Tashkent.

HSBC ASIAN FIVE NATIONS
2009 RESULTS

TOP FIVE

Korea 65–0 Singapore, Japan 87–10 Kazakhstan, Hong Kong 6–59 Japan, Kazakhstan 30–27 Korea, Korea 36–34 Hong Kong, Singapore 19–22 Kazakhstan, Japan 80–9 Korea, Hong Kong 64–6 Singapore, Singapore 15–45 Japan, Kazakhstan 25–6 Hong Kong.

DIVISION I

Chinese Taipei 36–24 Sri Lanka, Arabian Gulf 36–17 Thailand, Sri Lanka 51–17 Thailand, Arabian Gulf 44–24 Chinese Taipei

DIVISION II

China 25–19 Pakistan, Malaysia 43–29 India, India 44–3 Pakistan, Malaysia 43–15 China

DIVISION III

Guam 23–3 Indonesia, Philippines 15–0 Iran, Iran 48–13 Indonesia, Philippines 25–0 Guam

REGIONAL TOURNAMENTS

LAOS: Laos 28–8 Brunei, Brunei 21–10 Cambodia, Laos 8–3 Cambodia
UZBEKISTAN: Kyrgyzstan 38–21 Mongolia, Uzbekistan 31–12 Kyrgyzstan

FINAL STANDINGS

Team	P	W	D	L	F	A	BP	PTS
Japan	4	4	0	0	271	41	4	**24**
Kazakhstan	4	3	0	1	88	139	0	**15**
Korea	4	2	0	2	218	144	3	**13**
Hong Kong	4	1	0	3	110	126	3	**8**
Singapore	4	0	0	4	40	196	1	**1**

ROBINSON ENJOYS DREAM START

By Iain Spragg

Chris Cusiter (with trophy) leads the celebrations.

Scotland supporters may have had scant opportunity for celebration after the performances of the senior side in 2008–09 but they finally had something to cheer about after their second XV triumphed at the fourth IRB Nations Cup in Romania.

Competing in the tournament for the first time, Scotland A dispatched

Russia and Uruguay in the six-team event staged in Bucharest before beating France A 22–12 in their final match to claim the title and start Andy Robinson's reign as Scotland head coach with a bang.

Robinson was named as Frank Hadden's successor in early June and just 17 days later Scotland had lifted its first piece of international silverware since winning the Five Nations Championship 10 years earlier after what was ultimately a convincing victory over the French in the stadionul National Arcul de Triumf.

Both sides went into the final, winner-takes-all game unbeaten but once Scotland A had drawn first blood with an early penalty from Glasgow Warriors fly half Ruaridh Jackson they never surrendered their lead. Jackson landed four more penalties as well as converting Richie Vernon's pivotal late try and Scotland A were the champions.

"I was very pleased with the attitude of the team," Robinson said after his side's triumph. "If we retain that and produce that kind of work rate, we will continue to win games. We got the lead and sat back on it a bit, but we scored a great try at the end. We have to focus on a winning mentality and take that into our next game against Fiji in the autumn.

"France played some sublime rugby in the second half but credit to our boys, they stuck to their guns and managed to contain the French revival and in the end scored a beautiful try."

The tournament began in mid-June with an opening match between the A teams of Italy and France. The Italians were severely hampered by the early loss of props Alberto de Marchi and Michele Rizo to injury and five minutes into the second half the referee was forced to order uncontested scrums.

However, the French, also making their tournament debut, were already in the ascendency and scored five unanswered tries. Italy A replied with five Riccardo Bocchino penalties but were ultimately outclassed in their 31–15 defeat.

The second match on day one saw Scotland A take on Russia and although the final 49–7 scoreline in their favour suggests the Scots were utterly dominant, the Russians more than played their part in an entertaining encounter but ultimately paid a heavy price for mistakes at crucial times in the match.

Wing Rob Dewey scored the first of Scotland A's nine tries in the opening minute. Full back Jim Thompson helped himself to two tries with Russia replying in the 77th minute with a consolation try from Andrey Lugin.

"It is disappointing to see how much good work goes down the drain due to these unforced errors," said Russia coach Steve Diamond. "You pay for your errors straight away, no matter how much hard work you put into it."

The final match on the opening day in Bucharest was between hosts Romania, captained by Brive No 8 Alexandru Manta, and Uruguay. The Oaks dominated in the opening 40 minutes only for the South Americans to rally after the break.

Romania scored first half tries through Florin Vlaicu and Manta to establish an early lead but Los Teros rallied in the second half with a late score from Juan Campomar and the home side were ultimately relieved to clinch a 17–11 win.

Four days later the six teams were in action again. Scotland and Uruguay were first up and Robinson made 11 changes to his starting line-up for the game, obviously mindful of the third match in the punishing Bucharest heat on the horizon.

Wing Simon Webster was the star turn for Scotland with a brace of tries but Los Teros acquitted themselves well just as it seemed the Scots would cut loose and although they could only muster a solitary penalty from fly half Jeronimo Etcheverry in a 27–3 defeat, they were far from disgraced.

Italy A played Russia next with both sides looking for their first win of the tournament and after 80 minutes, it was the Azzurri who had broken their duck as Bocchino scored 15 points and number 8 Manoa Vosawai scored two second half tries in a comfortable 35–3 victory.

The closing game of the day saw Romania tackle France A and it was certainly a case of saving the best for last as the supporters in the stadionul National Arcul de Triumf were treated to an absorbing clash that ebbed and flowed throughout.

The French dominated the early exchanges and scored the first try on 20 minutes through Romain Martial. Four minutes later they added a second from Yannick Forestier and with the Oaks' only first half score coming from an Iulian Dumitras penalty, it seemed that Les Bleus' second string would emerge comfortable winners.

The Romanians had other ideas, however, and came storming back with a Dumitras try and two Vlaicu penalties to trail just 17–16 as the game went into its final 10 minutes. The result was hanging in the balance but France held their nerve and when captain Julien Audy landed a last-minute penalty, Romania were condemned to a heartbreaking 20–16 defeat.

The final day of the tournament would decide the standings and the battle to avoid last place was between Russia and Uruguay. Both sides were clearly desperate to record their first win but the difference between the two teams proved to be impressive Bears' fly half Alexander

Yanyushkin, who scored 17 points, including two tries either side of the break to see off Los Teros and set up a narrow 29–26 Russian victory.

The second match saw Romania play Italy A and the two teams produced a woeful first half spectacle in which they could only muster a single penalty apiece. The second half, however, was a far more entertaining affair. Romania made the early running with a second penalty and when scrum half Valentin Calafeteanu crashed over for a try, converted by Vlaicu, the hosts suddenly found themselves 13–3 up. Italy A were stung into action and replied with three converted tries from captain Antonio Pavanello, Andrea Pratichetti and Andrea Bacchetti to wrap up a 24–13 triumph.

The stage was now set for the denouement of the competition and the showdown between Scotland A and their French counterparts for the title.

Les Bleus were the greater attacking threat for much of the game but the Scots stood firm and their resolute defence repeatedly repelled the French attacks. At the other end of the pitch, Jackson was in prime form with the boot and three successive penalties gave Robinson's side a 9–0 platform. The French replied with a penalty from centre Fabrice Estebanez but Jackson landed a fourth shot at goal moments before the break and at half-time Scotland were 12–3 up.

A fifth successful Jackson penalty after the restart extended the lead but it was the cue for a concerted French rally and they clawed their way back into the contest with two further Estebanez penalties. The Scottish lead was now down to six points and when Bleus fly half Régis Lespinas landed a 61st-minute drop goal, the score was 15–12 and the result in the balance.

There were no further scores for the next 10 minutes but just as France A seemed poised to deliver a knockout blow as they pressed the Scottish line, Robinson's side produced a dramatic coup de grace, counterattacking from long range to send number 8 Vernon over for the only try of the game. Jackson duly converted and Scotland A were the champions.

"I'm absolutely delighted," admitted Scotland A captain Chris Cusiter. "We prepared for a few days and the win was the only thing that was going to be acceptable. There are a lot of young guys playing for Scotland for the first time and I'm pretty confident that a lot of guys are going to make the step up to the full international squad and we can build on something for the future.

"It's been a good tournament and we have enjoyed working under Andy Robinson. He is a great coach. I am heading for Glasgow next season, but I finished my time with Perpignan by winning the French title and it was good to finish the season with another win."

Scotland A's 22–12 win was also good news for the Italians, who leapfrogged the French into second place in the final table courtesy of a superior points difference. Hosts Romania finished in a creditable fourth place, with Russia in fifth and Uruguay, who ironically earned more bonus points than any of the other five teams, in sixth.

IRB NATIONS CUP 2009 RESULTS

12/06/2009	Italy A	15–31	France A	Bucharest
12/06/2009	Scotland A	49–7	Russia	Bucharest
12/06/2009	Uruguay	11–17	Romania	Bucharest
16/06/2009	Scotland A	27–3	Uruguay	Bucharest
16/06/2009	Italy A	35–3	Russia	Bucharest
16/06/2009	France A	20–16	Romania	Bucharest
21/06/2009	Russia	29–26	Uruguay	Bucharest
21/06/2009	Italy A	24–13	Romania	Bucharest
21/06/2009	France A	12–2	Scotland	Bucharest

FINAL STANDINGS

	P	W	D	L	F	A	BP	PTS
Scotland A	3	3	0	0	98	22	1	13
Italy A	3	2	0	1	74	47	1	9
France A	3	2	0	1	63	53	1	9
Romania	3	1	0	2	46	55	1	5
Russia	3	1	0	2	39	110	1	5
Uruguay	3	0	0	3	40	73	2	2

MAJOR RUGBY TOURS 2008–09

By Chris Rhys

BLEDISLOE CUP

1 November 2008, Hong Kong Stadium, Hong Kong
New Zealand 19 (2T 3PG) Australia 14 (2G)

NEW ZEALAND: I Toeava (Auckland); HE Gear (Wellington), CG Smith (Wellington), DW Carter (Canterbury), SW Sivivatu (Waikato); SR Donald (Waikato), QJ Cowan (Southland); TD Woodcock (North Harbour), AK Hore (Wellington), NS Tialata (Wellington), BC Thorn (Tasman), AJ Williams (Auckland), J Kaino (Auckland), R So'oialo (Wellington), RH McCaw (Canterbury, captain)
SUBSTITUTIONS: KF Mealamu (Auckland) for Hore (4 mins), MA Nonu (Wellington) for Donald (48 mins), PAT Weepu (Wellington) for Cowan (50 mins), AF Boric (North Harbour) & GM Somerville (Canterbury) for Thorn & Tialata (63 mins), AJ Thomson (Otago) for Kaino (71 mins), CS Jane (Auckland) for Toeava (75 mins)
SCORERS: *Tries*: Sivivatu, McCaw *Penalty goals*: Carter (3)
AUSTRALIA: AP Ashley–Cooper (ACT Brumbies); PJ Hynes (Queensland Reds), RP Cross (Western Force), SA Mortlock (ACT Brumbies), DA Mitchell (Western Force); MJ Giteau (Western Force), L Burgess (NSW Waratahs); BA Robinson (NSW Waratahs), ST Moore (Queensland Reds), AKE Baxter (NSW Waratahs), MD Chisholm (ACT Brumbies), NC Sharpe (Western Force), DW Mumm (NSW Waratahs), RN Brown (Western Force), GB Smith (ACT Brumbies)
SUBSTITUTIONS: BS Barnes (Queensland Reds) for Cross (52 mins), PR Waugh (NSW Waratahs) for Sharpe (64 mins), MJ Dunning (NSW Waratahs) for Baxter (71 mins), DW Pocock (Western Force) for Smith (74 mins)
SCORERS: *Tries*: Mitchell (2) *Conversions*: Giteau (2)
REFEREE: DA Lewis (Ireland)

AUSTRALIA TO EUROPE 2008

TOUR PARTY

FULL BACKS: AP Ashley–Cooper (ACT Brumbies), LD Turner (NSW Waratahs)
THREE QUARTERS: PJ Hynes (Queensland Reds), DN Ioane (Queensland Reds), DA Mitchell (Western Force), LD Tuqiri (NSW Waratahs), RP Cross (Western Force), SA Mortlock (ACT Brumbies), PJA Tahu (NSW Waratahs)
HALF BACKS: L Burgess (NSW Waratahs), S Cordingley (Queensland Reds), S Sheehan (NSW Waratahs), MJ Giteau (Western Force), BS Barnes (Queensland Reds), JD O'Connor (Western Force), QS Cooper (Queensland Reds)
FORWARDS: ST Moore (Queensland Reds), AL Freier (NSW Waratahs), T Polota–Nau (NSW Waratahs), BA Robinson (NSW Waratahs), AKE Baxter (NSW Waratahs), MJ Dunning (NSW Waratahs), BE Alexander (ACT Brumbies), SM Kepu (NSW Waratahs), MD Chisholm (ACT Brumbies), NC Sharpe (Western Force), P Kimlin (ACT Brumbies), HJ McMeniman (Queensland Reds), DW Mumm (NSW Waratahs), RN Brown (Western Force), GB Smith (ACT Brumbies), PR Waugh (NSW Waratahs), DW Pocock (Western Force), WL Palu (NSW Waratahs)

MANAGER P Thomson **COACH** RM Deans **ASSISTANT COACHES** MA Foley, J Williams **CAPTAIN** SA Mortlock

Match 1, 8 November, Stadio Euganeo, Padova
Italy 20 (1T 4PG 1DG) Australia 30 (1G 1T 6PG)

ITALY: A Masi (Biarritz Olympique); K Robertson (Viadana), G–J Canale (ASM Clermont–Auvergne), G Garcia (Calvisano) Mi Bergamasco (Stade Français); A Marcato (Treviso), P Canavosio (Viadana); S Perugini (Stade Toulousain), L Ghiraldini (Calvisano), C Nieto (Gloucester), C–A del Fava (Ulster), M Bortolami (Gloucester), J Sole (Viadana), S Parisse (Stade Français, captain), Ma Bergamasco (Stade Français)
SUBSTITUTIONS: L Orquera (CA Brive) for Marcato (46 mins), F Ongaro (Saracens) & M Aguero (Saracens) for Ghiraldini & Perugini (51 mins), G Toniolatti (Capitolina) for Canavosio (62 mins), T Reato (Rovigo) for Bortolami (70 mins), A Zanni (Calvisano) for Sole (75 mins)
SCORERS: *Try*: Mi Bergamasco *Penalty goals*: Marcato (2), Orquera (2) *Drop goal*: Marcato
AUSTRALIA: Ashley–Cooper; Turner, Mortlock (captain), Tahu, Ioane; Barnes, Burgess; Alexander, Moore, Dunning, Chisholm, McMeniman, Mumm, Brown, Waugh
SUBSTITUTIONS: Giteau for Barnes (14 mins), Cooper for Tahu (63 mins), Kepu & Palu for Alexander & McMeniman (67 mins), O'Connor for Ashley–Cooper (74 mins), Polota–Nau & Pocock for Moore & Waugh (76 mins)
SCORERS: *Tries*: Turner, Cooper *Conversion*: Giteau *Penalty goals*: Giteau 5, Mortlock
REFEREE: BJ Lawrence (New Zealand)

Match 2, 15 November, Twickenham, London
England 14 (1T 2PG 1DG) Australia 28 (1G 7PG)

ENGLAND: DA Armitage (London Irish); PH Sackey (London Wasps), JD Noon (Newcastle Falcons), RJ Flutey (London Wasps), UCC Monye (Harlequins); DJ Cipriani (London Wasps), DS Care (Harlequins); AJ Sheridan (Sale Sharks), LA Mears (Bath), PJ Vickery (London Wasps), SW Borthwick (Saracens, captain), TP Palmer (London Wasps), TR Croft (Leicester Tigers), NJ Easter (Harlequins), T Rees (London Wasps)
SUBSTITUTIONS: MJH Stevens (Bath) for Sheridan (temp from 33 to 40 mins) & Vickery (54 mins), JAW Haskell (London Wasps) for Easter (58 mins), SD Shaw (London Wasps) & MR Lipman (Bath) for Palmer & Rees (64 mins), HA Ellis (Leicester Tigers) for Care (66 mins), DM Hartley (Northampton Saints) for Mears (69 mins), TGAL Flood (Leicester Tigers) for Cipriani (71 mins)
SCORERS: *Try*: Easter *Penalty goals*: Cipriani (2) *Drop goal*: D Armitage
AUSTRALIA: Ashley–Cooper; Hynes, Cross, Mortlock (captain), Mitchell; Giteau, Burgess; Robinson, Moore, Baxter, Chisholm, Sharpe, McMeniman, Brown, Smith
SUBSTITUTIONS: Palu for Brown (44 mins), Mumm for Chisholm (64 mins), Polota–Nau for McMeniman (80 mins)
SCORERS: *Try*: Ashley–Cooper *Conversion*: Giteau *Penalty goals*: Giteau (6), Mortlock
REFEREE: M Jonker (South Africa)

Match 3, 22 November, Stade de France, Paris
France 13 (1G 1PG 1DG) Australia 18 (1G 1T 2PG)

FRANCE: M Medard (Stade Toulousain); J Malzieu (ASM Clermont–Auvergne), B Baby (ASM Clermont–Auvergne), Y Jauzion (Stade Toulousain), C Heymans (Stade Toulousain); D Skrela (Stade Toulousain), S Tillous–Borde (Castres Olympique); L Faure (Sale Sharks), D Szarzewski (Stade Français), N Mas (USA Perpignan), S Chabal (Sale Sharks), L Nallet (Castres Olympique, captain), T Dusautoir (Stade Toulousain), I Harinordoquy (Biarritz Olympique), F Ouedraogo (RC Montpellier–Herault)
SUBSTITUTIONS: D Traille (Biarritz Olympique) for Baby (36 mins), R Millo–Chluski (Stade Toulousain) for Nallet (43 mins), B Kayser (Leicester Tigers) for Szarzewski (57 mins), B Lecouls (Stade Toulousain) for Mas (59 mins), L Picamoles (RC Montpellier–Herault) for Dusautoir (70 mins), A Palisson (CA Brive) & J Tomas (CA Bourgoin–Jallieu) for Malzieu & Tillous–Borde (79 mins)
SCORERS: *Try*: Penalty try *Conversion*: Skrela *Penalty goal*: Skrela *Drop goal*: Medard
AUSTRALIA: Mitchell; Hynes, Ashley–Cooper, Mortlock (captain), Ioane; Giteau, Burgess; Alexander, Moore, Baxter, McMeniman, Sharpe, Mumm, Palu, Smith
SUBSTITUTIONS: Chisholm for Palu (59 mins), Cordingley & Kepu for Burgess & Alexander (65 mins), Cooper for Ashley–Cooper (76 mins)
SCORERS: *Tries*: Moore, Hynes *Conversion*: Giteau *Penalty goals*: Giteau (2)
REFEREE: C Joubert (South Africa)

Match 4, 29 November, Millennium Stadium, Cardiff
Wales 21 (1G 1T 2PG 1DG) Australia 18 (1G 1T 1PG 1DG)

WALES: LM Byrne (Ospreys); MA Jones (Scarlets), TGL Shanklin (Blues), JH Roberts (Blues), SM Williams (Ospreys); SM Jones (Scarlets), GJ Cooper (Gloucester); GD Jenkins (Blues), M Rees (Scarlets), AR Jones (Ospreys), IM Gough (Ospreys), A–W Jones (Ospreys), RP Jones (Ospreys, captain), A Powell (Blues), ME Williams (Blues)
SUBSTITUTIONS: A Bishop (Ospreys) for Roberts (17 mins), DAR Jones (Scarlets) for Powell (61 mins)
SCORERS: *Tries*: SM Williams, Byrne *Conversion*: SM Jones *Penalty goals*: SM Jones (2) *Drop goal*: SM Jones
AUSTRALIA: Mitchell; Hynes, Cross, Mortlock (captain), Ioane; Giteau, Burgess; Robinson, Moore, Baxter, Chisholm, Sharpe, McMeniman, Brown, Waugh
SUBSTITUTIONS: Cooper for Mortlock (2 mins), Tuqiri for Hynes (33 mins), Freier for Waugh (temp 34 to 37 mins) & Moore (69 mins), Smith for Waugh (61 mins), Mumm for McMeniman (69 mins)
SCORERS: *Tries*: Chisholm, Ioane *Conversion*: Giteau *Penalty goal*: Giteau *Drop goal*: Giteau
REFEREE: DA Lewis (Ireland)

Match 5, 3 December, Wembley Stadium (non-cap match)
Barbarians 11 (1T 2PG) Australia XV 18 (1G 1T 2PG)

Barbarians scorers: *Try*: J Collins *Penalty goals*: PC Montgomery (2)
Australia XV scorers: *Tries*: Tuqiri, Turner *Conversion*: O'Connor *Penalty goals*: O'Connor (2)
Referee: C White (England)

NEW ZEALAND TO EUROPE 2008

TOUR PARTY

FULL BACKS: I Toeava (Auckland), CS Jane (Wellington), JM Muliaina (Waikato)
THREE QUARTERS: JT Rokocoko (Auckland), HE Gear (Wellington), SW Sivivatu (Waikato), AT Tuitavake (North Harbour), CG Smith (Wellington), RD Kahui (Waikato), MA Nonu (Wellington)
HALF BACKS: PAT Weepu (Wellington), QJ Cowan (Southland), AM Ellis (Canterbury), * A Mathewson (Wellington), DW Carter (Canterbury), SR Donald (Waikato)
FORWARDS: CR Flynn (Canterbury), KF Mealamu (Auckland), * HT Elliot (Wellington), B Franks (Tasman), IF Afoa (Auckland), TD Woodcock (North Harbour), NS Tialata (Wellington), JL Mackintosh (Southland), BC Thorn (Tasman), AJ Williams (Auckland), AF Boric (North Harbour), JJ Eaton (Taranaki), RA Filipo (Wellington), J Kaino (Auckland), R So'oialo (Wellington), KJ Read (Canterbury), RH McCaw (Canterbury), S Waldrom (Taranaki), LJ Messam (Waikato), AJ Thomson (Otago)

* Replacement on tour

MANAGER D Shand **COACH** G Henry **ASSISTANT COACHES** W Smith, S Hansen
CAPTAIN RH McCaw

Match 1, 8 November, Murrayfield, Edinburgh
Scotland 6 (2PG) New Zealand 32 (3G 1T 2PG)

SCOTLAND: CD Paterson (Edinburgh); TH Evans (Glasgow Warriors), BJ Cairns (Edinburgh), NJ de Luca (Edinburgh), SF Lamont (Northampton Saints); PJ Godman (Edinburgh), MRL Blair (Edinburgh, captain); AF Jacobsen (Edinburgh), RW Ford (Edinburgh), EA Murray (Northampton Saints), NJ Hines (USA Perpignan), JL Hamilton (Edinburgh), JPR White (Sale Sharks), A Hogg (Edinburgh), J Barclay (Glasgow Warriors)
SUBSTITUTIONS: HFG Southwell (Edinburgh) for S Lamont (41 mins), AG Dickinson (Gloucester) & ML Mustchin (Edinburgh) for E Murray & Hines (54 mins), SD Gray (Northampton Saints) for White (61 mins), DWH Hall (Glasgow Warriors) for Ford (63 mins), DA Parks (Glasgow Warriors) & RGM Lawson (Gloucester) for Godman & Blair (70 mins)
SCORER: *Penalty goals*: Paterson (2)
NEW ZEALAND: Toeava; Tuitavake, Kahui, Nonu, Rokocoko; Donald, Weepu; Mackintosh, Mealamu (captain), Afoa, Boric, Williams, Read, Messam, Thomson
SUBSTITUTIONS: Jane for Toeava (40 mins), Ellis for Weepu (52 mins), Tialata for Mackintosh (54 mins), McCaw & Flynn for Thomson & Mealamu (59 mins), Filipo for Williams (64 mins), Carter for Ellis (69 mins)
SCORERS: *Tries*: Tuitavake, Weepu, Kahui, Boric *Conversions*: Donald (2), Carter *Penalty goals*: Donald (2)
REFEREE: W Barnes (England)

Match 2, 15 November, Croke Park, Dublin
Ireland 3 (1PG) New Zealand 22 (2G 1PG 1T)

IRELAND: GT Dempsey (Leinster); TJ Bowe (Ospreys), BG O'Driscoll (Leinster, captain), LM Fitzgerald (Leinster), RDJ Kearney (Leinster); RJR O'Gara (Munster), TG O'Leary (Munster); MJ Horan (Munster), RD Best (Ulster), JJ Hayes (Munster), DP O'Callaghan (Munster), PJ O'Connell (Muster), AN Quinlan (Munster), JPR Heaslip (Leinster), DP Wallace (Munster)
SUBSTITUTIONS: JP Flannery (Munster) for R Best (57 mins), SPH Ferris (Ulster) for O'Connell (61 mins), EG Reddan (London Wasps) for O'Leary (67 mins), KG Earls (Munster) for Dempsey (70 mins), PW Wallace (Ulster) for Fitzgerald (74 mins), TD Buckley (Munster) & S Jennings (Leinster) for Hayes and D Wallace (76 mins)
SCORER: *Penalty goal*: O'Gara
NEW ZEALAND: Muliaina; Rokocoko, Smith, Nonu, Sivivatu; Carter, Cowan; Woodcock, Mealamu, Tialata, Thorn, Williams, Kaino, So'oialo, McCaw (captain)
SUBSTITUTIONS: Afoa for Tialata (44 mins), Weepu for Cowan (59 mins), Toeava for Smith (63 mins), Flynn for Mealamu (65 mins), Read for So'oialo (70), Donald for Rokocoko (75 mins)
SCORERS: *Tries*: Penalty try, Nonu, Thorn *Conversions*: Carter 2 *Penalty goal*: Carter
REFEREE: SM Lawrence (South Africa)

Match 3, 22 November, Millennium Stadium, Cardiff
Wales 9 (3PG) New Zealand 29 (2G 5PG)

WALES: LM Byrne (Ospreys); SL Halfpenny (Blues), TGL Shanklin (Blues), JH Roberts (Blues), SM Williams (Ospreys); SM Jones (Scarlets), GJ Cooper (Gloucester); GD Jenkins (Blues), M Rees (Scarlets), AR Jones (Ospreys), AW Jones (Ospreys), I Evans (Ospreys), RP Jones (Ospreys, captain), A Powell (Blues), ME Williams (Blues)
SUBSTITUTIONS: LC Charteris (Dragons) for Evans (59 mins), DJ Peel (Sale Sharks) & JW Hook (Ospreys) for Cooper & SM Jones (58 mins), DAR Jones (Scarlets) for Powell (75 mins), JV Yapp (Blues) for Jenkins (79 mins)
SCORER: *Penalty goals*: SM Jones (3)
NEW ZEALAND: Muliaina; Rokocoko, Kahui, Nonu, Sivivatu; Carter, Cowan; Woodcock, Mealamu, Tialata, Thorn, Williams, Kaino, So'oialo, McCaw (captain)
SUBSTITUTIONS: Afoa for Tialata (48 mins), Weepu for Cowan (56 mins)
SCORERS: *Tries*: Nonu, Kaino *Conversions*: Carter (2) *Penalty goals*: Carter (5)
REFEREE: JI Kaplan (South Africa)

Match 4, 29 November, Twickenham, London
England 6 (2PG) New Zealand 32 (1G 2T 5PG)

ENGLAND: DA Armitage (London Irish); PH Sackey (London Wasps), JD Noon (Newcastle Falcons), RJ Flutey (London Wasps), UCC Monye (Harlequins); TGAL Flood (Leicester Tigers), DS Care (Harlequins); TAN Payne (London Wasps), LA Mears (Bath), PJ Vickery (London Wasps), SW Borthwick (Saracens, captain), NJ Kennedy (London Irish), JAW Haskell (London Wasps), NJ Easter (Harlequins), MR Lipman (Bath)
SUBSTITUTIONS: MJH Stevens (Bath) for Vickery (52 mins), T Rees (London Wasps) for Lipman (57 mins), HA Ellis (Leicester Tigers) for Care (60 mins), DM Hartley (Northampton Saints) & TR Croft (Leicester Tigers) for Care & Easter (66 mins), DJ Hipkiss (Leicester Tigers) for Sackey (72 mins), DJ Cipriani (London Wasps) for Noon (74 mins)
SCORERS: *Penalty goals*: Flood, D Armitage
NEW ZEALAND: Muliaina; Rokocoko, Smith, Nonu, Sivivatu; Carter, Cowan; Woodcock, Mealamu, Tialata, Thorn, Williams, Kaino, So'oialo, McCaw (captain)
SUBSTITUTIONS: Read & Afoa for Kaino & Tialata (54 mins), Toeava & Boric for Smith & Thorn (68 mins), Weepu for Cowan (69 mins)
SCORERS: *Tries*: Muliaina (2), Nonu *Conversion*: Carter *Penalty goals*: Carter (5)
REFEREE: AC Rolland

MAJOR TOURS

TOUR PARTY

FULL BACKS: CA Jantjies (Western Province)
THREE QUARTERS: BG Habana (Blue Bulls), J–PR Pietersen (Sharks), OM Ndungane (Sharks), JL Nokwe (Free State Cheetahs), AA Jacobs (Sharks), J de Villiers (Western Province), J Fourie (Golden Lions), FPL Steyn (Sharks)
HALF BACKS: PF du Preez (Blue Bulls), ER Januarie (Western Province), R Pienaar (Sharks), E Rose (Golden Lions)
FORWARDS: JW Smit (Sharks), BW du Plessis (Sharks), M Ralepelle (Blue Bulls), GG Steenkamp (Blue Bulls), T Mtawarira (Sharks), BV Mujati (Western Province), * JN du Plessis (Sharks), A Bekker (Western Province), JP Botha (Blue Bulls), V Matfield (Blue Bulls), SWP Burger (Stormers), HW Brussow (Free State Cheetahs), R Kankowski (Sharks), DJ Rossouw (Blue Bulls), JH Smith (Free State Cheetahs), PJ Spies (Blue Bulls)

* Replacement on tour

MANAGER A Petersen **COACH** P de Villiers **ASSISTANT COACHES** G Gold, D Muir **CAPTAIN** JW Smit

Match 1, 8 November, Millennium Stadium, Cardiff
Wales 15 (5PG) South Africa 20 (2G 2PG)

WALES: LM Byrne (Ospreys); SL Halfpenny (Blues), TGL Shanklin (Blues), JH Roberts (Blues), SM Williams (Ospreys); SM Jones (Scarlets), GJ Cooper (Gloucester); GD Jenkins (Blues), M Rees (Scarlets), AR Jones (Ospreys), AW Jones (Ospreys), I Evans (Ospreys), RP Jones (Ospreys, captain), A Powell (Blues), ME Williams (Blues)
SUBSTITUTIONS: DJ Peel (Sale Sharks) & JW Hook (Ospreys) for Cooper & SM Jones (51 mins), IM Gough (Ospreys) for Evans (64 mins)
SCORERS: *Penalty goals:* Hook (4), Halfpenny
SOUTH AFRICA: Jantjies; Pietersen, Jacobs, De Villiers, Habana; Pienaar, Du Preez; Mtawarira, BW du Plessis, Smit (captain), Botha, Matfield, Smith, Spies, Burger
SUBSTITUTIONS: Bekker for Botha (40 mins), Kankowski for Spies (50 mins), Steyn for Jacobs (59 mins), Januarie & Fourie for Du Preez & Habana (60 mins), Mujati for Smit (66–74 mins), Steenkamp for Mtawarira (74 mins)
SCORERS: *Tries:* Jacobs, De Villiers *Conversions:* Pienaar (2) *Penalty goals:* Pienaar (2)
REFEREE: AC Rolland (Ireland)

Match 2, 15 November, Murrayfield, Edinburgh
Scotland 10 (1G 1PG) South Africa 14 (1T 3PG)

SCOTLAND: CD Paterson (Edinburgh); TH Evans (Glasgow Warriors), BJ Cairns (Edinburgh), NJ de Luca (Edinburgh), RP Lamont (Sale Sharks); PJ Godman (Edinburgh), MRL Blair (Edinburgh, captain); AF Jacobsen (Edinburgh), RW Ford (Edinburgh), EA Murray (Northampton Saints), NJ Hines (USA Perpignan), JL Hamilton (Edinburgh), JPR White (Sale Sharks), A Hogg (Edinburgh), JA Barclay (Glasgow Warriors)
SUBSTITUTIONS: HGF Southwell (Edinburgh) for Paterson (20 mins), DA Parks (Glasgow Warriors) for Godman (temp 10 to 20, 40 to 42 mins), SD Gray (Northampton Saints) for White (58 mins), AG Dickinson (Gloucester) for Jacobsen (64 mins), RGM Lawson (Gloucester) for TH Evans (73 mins), ML Mustchin (Edinburgh) for Hines (74 mins), DWH Hall (Glasgow Warriors) for Ford (76 mins)
SCORERS: *Try:* Hines *Conversion:* Godman *Penalty goal:* Godman
SOUTH AFRICA: Jantjies; Pietersen, Jacobs, De Villiers, Habana; Pienaar, Januarie; Mtawarira, BW du Plessis, Smit (captain), Botha, Matfield, Smith, Spies, Burger
SUBSTITUTIONS: Mujati for BW du Plessis (4 mins), Fourie for Habana (53 mins), Bekker for Botha (53 mins), Steyn for De Villiers (65 mins), Steenkamp, Kankowski & Rossouw for Mtawarira, Burger & Spies (74 mins)
SCORERS: *Try:* Fourie *Penalty goals:* Pienaar (3)
REFEREE: D Pearson (England)

Match 3, 22 November, Twickenham, London
England 6 (2PG) South Africa 42 (4G 1T 3PG)

ENGLAND: D Armitage (London Irish); PH Sackey (London Wasps), JD Noon (Newcastle Falcons), RJ Flutey (London Wasps), UCC Monye (Harlequins); DJ Cipriani (London Wasps), DS Care (Harlequins); TAN Payne (London Wasps), LA Mears (Bath), PJ Vickery (London Wasps), SW Borthwick (Saracens, captain), TP Palmer (London Wasps), JAW Haskell (London Wasps), NJ Easter (Harlequins), T Rees (London Wasps)

SUBSTITUTIONS: TGAL Flood (Leicester Tigers) for Flutey (29 mins), SD Shaw (London Wasps) for Palmer (31 mins), MJH Stevens (Bath) for Vickery (51 mins), DM Hartley (Northampton Saints) for Mears (57 mins), HA Ellis (Leicester Tigers) for Care (65 mins), J Crane (Leicester Tigers) for Easter (68 mins), TR Croft (Leicester Tigers) for Rees (77 mins)

SCORER: *Penalty goals:* Cipriani (2)

SOUTH AFRICA: Jantjies; Pietersen, Jacobs, De Villiers, Habana; Pienaar, Januarie; Mtawarira, Smit (captain), JN du Plessis, Botha, Matfield, Smith, Spies, Burger

SUBSTITUTIONS: Ralepelle for Rossouw (temp 31 to 40 mins) & Smit (75 mins), Kankowski & Fourie for Rossouw & Jacobs (57 mins), Steyn & Bekker for Pienaar & Botha (63 mins), Mujati for JN du Plessis (67 mins), Brussow for Spies (76 mins)

SCORERS: *Tries:* Rossouw, Pienaar, Jacobs, Fourie, Habana *Conversions:* Pienaar (3), Steyn *Penalty goals:* Pienaar (3)

REFEREE: N Owens (Wales)

PACIFIC ISLANDERS TO EUROPE 2008

TOUR PARTY

FULL BACKS: K Ratuvou (Saracens & Fiji), G Williams (US Dax & Samoa)
THREE QUARTERS: S Tagicakibau (London Irish & Samoa), V Delasau (Montauban & Fiji), S Mapusua (London Irish & Samoa), S Rabeni (Leicester Tigers & Fiji), E Taione (Harlequins & Tonga)
HALF BACKS: M Rauluni (Saracens & Fiji), S Martens (Scarlets & Tonga), S Bai (ASM Clermont Auvergne & Fiji), P Hola (Kobelco & Tonga)
FORWARDS: A Lutui (Worcester Warriors & Tonga), S Koto (London Welsh & Fiji), * T Fuga (Harlequins & Samoa), J Va'a (Glasgow Warriors & Samoa), K Pulu (USA Perpignan & Tonga), K Lealamanua (US Dax & Samoa), C Johnston (Saracens & Samoa), * T Lea'aetoa (London Irish & Tonga), P Hehea (Metro Racing Paris & Tonga), K Leawere (Hino Motors & Fiji), F Levi (Ricoh & Samoa), N Latu (NEC & Tonga), S Naevo (NEC & Fiji), G Stowers (World Kobe & Samoa), H T–Pole (Suntory & Tonga), V Vaki (USA Perpignan & Tonga), F Maka (Stade Toulousain & Tonga), * S Koyamaibole (Padova & Fiji)

* Replacement on tour

MANAGER S Rabuka **COACH** Q Fielea **ASSISTANT COACHES** G Ella, P Fatialofa, J Mckee **CAPTAIN** M Rauluni

Match 1, 8 November, Twickenham, London
England 39 (4G 1T 2PG) Pacific Islanders 13 (1G 2PG)

ENGLAND: DA Armitage (London Irish); PH Sackey (London Wasps), JD Noon (Newcastle Falcons), RJ Flutey (London Wasps), UCC Monye (Harlequins); DJ Cipriani (London Wasps), DS Care (Harlequins); AJ Sheridan (Sale Sharks), LA Mears (Bath), MJH Stevens (Bath), SW Borthwick (Saracens, captain), NJ Kennedy (London Irish), TR Croft (Leicester Tigers), NJ Easter (Harlequins), T Rees (London Wasps)

SUBSTITUTIONS: JAW Haskell (London Wasps) for Croft (40–52 mins) & Easter (68 mins), PJ Vickery (London Wasps) & TP Palmer (London Wasps) for Stevens & Kennedy (58 mins), HA Ellis (Leicester Tigers) & MR Lipman (Bath) for Care & Rees (61 mins), TGAL Flood (Leicester Tigers) & DM Hartley (Northampton Saints) for Cipriani & Mears (75 mins)

SCORERS: *Tries:* Sackey (2), Cipriani, Kennedy, Mears *Conversions:* Cipriani (4) *Penalty goals:* Cipriani (2)

PACIFIC ISLANDERS: Ratuvou; Delasau, Rabeni, Mapusua, Tagicakibau; Hola, Rauluni (captain); Va'a, Lutui, Johnston, Levi, Leawere, Naevo, Maka, Latu

SUBSTITUTIONS: Stowers for Maka (16 mins), Bai for Hola (47 mins), Taione & Pulu for Rabeni & Johnston (58 mins), T–Pole for Levi (61 mins), Koto for Lutui (68 mins), Martens for Rauluni (78 mins)

SCORERS: *Try:* Rabeni *Conversion:* Hola *Penalty goals:* Hola, Bai

REFEREE: G Clancy (Ireland)

Match 2, 15 November, Stade Auguste Bonal, Sochaux
France 42 (4G 1T 3PG) Pacific Islanders 17 (1T 4PG)

FRANCE: M Medard (Stade Toulousain): J Malzieu (ASM Clermont–Auvergne), B Baby (ASM Clermont–Auvergne), Y Jauzion (Stade Toulousain), C Heymans (Stade Toulousain); D Skrela (Stade Toulousain), J–B Elissalde (Stade Toulousain); L Faure (Sale Sharks), D Szarzewski (Stade Français), N Mas (USA Perpignan), R Millo–Chluski (Stade Toulousain), L Nallet (Castres Olympique, captain), T Dusautoir (Stade Toulousain), I Harinordoquy (Biarritz Olympique), F Ouedraogo (RC Montpellier–Herault)
SUBSTITUTIONS: S Tillous–Borde (Castres Olympique) for Elissalde (17 mins), B Kayser (Leicester Tigers) & S Chabal (Sale Sharks) for Szarzewski & Nallet (46 mins), D Traille (Biarritz Olympique) for Jauzion (57 mins), L Picamoles (RC Montpellier–Herault) for Dusautoir (70 mins), B Lecouls (Stade Toulousain) & A Palisson (CA Brive) for Mas & Heymans (72 mins)
SCORERS: *Tries*: Szarzewski, Tillous–Borde, Heymans, Picamoles, Medard *Conversions*: Skrela (4) *Penalty goals*: Skrela (3)
PACIFIC ISLANDERS: Williams; Delasau, Rabeni, Mapusua, Tagicakibau; Hola, Rauluni (captain), Lealamanua, Fuga, Pulu, Hehea, Leawere, T–Pole, Koyamaibole, Vaki
SUBSTITUTIONS: Johnston for Lealamanua (46 mins), Levi for Leawere (48 mins), Latu for T–Pole (51 mins), Ratuvou for Williams (58 mins), Martens for Rauluni (67 mins), Mapusua for Koyamaibole (70 mins), Koto for Fuga (72 mins)
SCORERS: *Try*: Taione *Penalty goals*: Bai (4)
REFEREE: N Owens (Wales)

Match 3, 22 November, Stadio Giglio, Reggio Emilia
Italy 17 (2G 1PG) Pacific Islanders 25 (2G 1T 2PG)

ITALY: A Masi (Biarritz Olympique); K Robertson (Viadana), Mi Bergamasco (Stade Français), G Garcia (Calvisano), M Pratichetti (Calvisano); A Marcato (Treviso), P Travagli (Parma); M Aguero (Saracens), L Ghiraldini (Calvisano), C Nieto (Gloucester), M Bortolami (Gloucester), T Reato (Rovigo), J Sole (Viadana), S Parisse (Stade Français, captain), Ma Bergamasco (Stade Français)
SUBSTITUTIONS: A Zanni (Calvisano) for Sole (6 mins), F Ongaro (Saracens) for Ghiraldini (17–21 mins & 56 mins), L McLean (Calvisano) for Masi (62 mins), A Lo Cicero (Racing Metro Paris) for Aguero (70 mins), S Perugini (Stade Toulousain) for Nieto (72 mins)
SCORERS: *Tries*: Ghiraldini, Ma Bergamasco *Conversions*: Marcato (2) *Penalty goal*: Marcato
PACIFIC ISLANDERS: Ratuvou; Delasau, Mapusua, Taione, Tagicakibau; Bai, Martens; Va'a, Fuga, Pulu, Levi, Hehea, Vaki, Koyamaibole, Latu (captain)
SUBSTITUTIONS: Rabeni for Taione (temp 33 to 35 mins & 62 mins), Lea'aetoa & T–Pole for Pulu & Koyamaibole (56 mins), Naevo & Rauluni for Vaki & Martens (62 mins), Williams for Mapusua (72 mins)
SCORERS: *Tries*: Delasau (2), Ratuvou *Conversions*: Bai (2) *Penalty goals*: Bai (2)
REFEREE: W Barnes (England)

CANADA TO EUROPE 2008

TOUR PARTY

FULL BACKS: J Pritchard (Bedford Blues)
THREE QUARTERS: C Hearn (Baymen), J Mensah–Coker (Plymouth Albion), D van Camp (Velox Valhallians), S Duke (University of Victoria), B Keys (University of Victoria), R Smith (Calgary Irish), P Mackenzie (University of Victoria), S White (James Bay AA)
HALF BACKS: E Fairhurst (Cornish Pirates), M Williams (James Bay AA), A Monro (Colorno) M Evans (Hartpury College, Gloucester), N Hirayama (University of Victoria)
FORWARDS: P Riordan (University of Victoria), K Tkachuk (Glasgow Wanderers), J Thiel (Bayside Sharks), M Pletch (Oakville Crusaders), F Walsh (Vandals), T Robertson (Velox Valhallians), * S Franklin (CA Brive), M Burak (Cornish Pirates), J Jackson (Stade Bordelais), T Hotson (Northern Suburbs), S Ault (Barrhaven Scottish), L Cudmore (Capilano), J Sinclair (Castaway Wanderers), S–M Stephen (Plymouth Albion), A Kleeberger (University of Victoria), A Fagan (Swilers), J Marshall (Capilano), A Carpenter (Brantford Harlequins)

* Replacement on tour

MANAGERS R Swany, D Lynch **COACH** KJ Crowley **ASSISTANT COACHES** J Tait, M Williams, K Wirachowski
CAPTAIN P Riordan

Match 1, 1 November. Estadio Universitario, Lisbon
Portugal 13 (1G 2PG) Canada 21 (1G 1T 3PG)

PORTUGAL: P Silva; A Esteves, Da Mateus, Di Mateus, G Foro; P Cabral, P Leal; J Junior, J Correia (captain), D Fialho, D dos Reis, J Severino Somoza, V Uva, T Girão, S Palha
SUBSTITUTIONS: D Figueiredo for D Fialho (49 mins), D Cardoso Pinto for P Cabral (60 mins), J Bardy for S Palha (65 mins), V Jorge for J Severino Somoza (69 mins), D Gama for G Foro (73 mins), JM Muré for J Junior (75 mins)
SCORERS: *Try*: P Silva *Conversion*: P Leal *Penalty goals*: P Leal (2)
CANADA: J Pritchard; D van Camp, B Keys, R Smith, P MacKenzie; A Monro, M Williams; K Tkachuk, P Riordan (captain), M Pletch, T Hotson, S Ault, A Fagan, A Kleeberger, A Carpenter
SUBSTITUTIONS: N Hirayama for A Monro (20 mins), J Sinclair for A Fagan (temp 35 to 41 mins & 53 mins)
SCORERS: *Tries*: Kleeberger, Pritchard *Conversion*: Pritchard *Penalty goals*: Pritchard (3)
REFEREE: P Allan (Scotland)

Match 2, 8 November, Thomond Park, Limerick
Ireland 55 (6G 2T 1PG) Canada 0

IRELAND: KG Earls (Munster); TJ Bowe (Ospreys), BG O'Driscoll (Leinster, captain), LM Fitzgerald (Leinster), RDJ Kearney (Leinster); RJR O'Gara (Munster), EG Reddan (London Wasps), MJ Horan (Munster), JP Flannery (Munster), TD Buckley (Munster), DP O'Callaghan (Munster), PJ O'Connell (Munster), SPH Ferris (Ulster), JPR Heaslip (Leinster), S Jennings (Leinster)
SUBSTITUTIONS: RD Best (Ulster) & JJ Hayes (Munster) for Flannery & Buckley (40 mins), AN Quinlan (Munster), DP Wallace (Munster), PA Stringer (Munster), PW Wallace (Ulster) & SP Horgan (Leinster) for O'Connell, Heaslip, Reddan, O'Gara & O'Driscoll (55 mins)
SCORERS: *Tries*: Kearney (2), Bowe (2), Earls, Heaslip (2), D Wallace *Conversions*: O'Gara (5), P Wallace *Penalty goal*: O'Gara
CANADA: Pritchard; Hearn, Keys, Smith, Mensah–Coker; Monro, Fairhurst; Tkachuk, Riordan (captain), Thiel, Burak, Jackson, Stephen, Carpenter, Kleeberger
SUBSTITUTIONS: Sinclair for Stephen (45 mins), Mackenzie for Pritchard (60 mins), Hotson & Evans for Burak & Monro (64 mins), Walsh for Tkachuk (70 mins), M Pletch for Riordan (74 mins)
REFEREE: C Berdos (France)

Match 3, 14 November, Millennium Stadium, Cardiff
Wales 34 (3G 2T 1PG) Canada 13 (1G 2PG)

WALES: ML Stoddart (Scarlets); SL Halfpenny (Blues), TGL Shanklin (Blues), A Bishop (Ospreys), MA Jones (Scarlets); JW Hook (Ospreys), M Roberts (Scarlets); JV Yapp (Blues), R Hibbard (Ospreys), Rhys Thomas (Dragons), IM Gough (Ospreys), LC Charteris (Dragons), DAR Jones (Scarlets), RP Jones (Ospreys, captain), R Sowden–Taylor (Blues)
SUBSTITUTIONS: DR Biggar (Ospreys) for Hook (18 mins), JH Roberts (Blues) for Shanklin (45 mins), A Powell (Blues) & DJ Peel (Sale Sharks) for RP Jones & M Roberts (51 mins), ET Lewis–Roberts (Sale Sharks) for Rhys Thomas (64 mins)
SCORERS: *Tries*: Halfpenny (2), Penalty tries (2), Stoddart *Conversions*: Biggar (3) *Penalty goal*: Biggar
CANADA: Pritchard; Hearn, Keys, Smith, Mensah–Coker; Monro, Fairhurst; Tkachuk, Riordan (captain), Thiel, Hotson, Jackson, Sinclair, Carpenter, Kleeberger
SUBSTITUTIONS: Williams for Fairhurst (temp 22 to 32 & 57 mins), M Pletch for Thiel (25 mins), Van Camp for Keys (51 mins), Stephen for Carpenter (53 mins), Burak for Hotson (59 mins), Evans for Hearn (68 mins), Walsh for Tkachuk (71 mins)
SCORERS: *Try*: Smith *Conversion*: Pritchard *Penalty goals*: Pritchard (2)
REFEREE: SJ Dickinson (Australia)

Match 4, 22 November, Pittodrie Stadium, Aberdeen
Scotland 41 (4G 2T 1PG) Canada 0

SCOTLAND: RP Lamont (Sale Sharks); SL Webster (Edinburgh); BJ Cairns (Edinburgh), NJ de Luca (Edinburgh), N Walker (Ospreys); PJ Godman (Edinburgh), MRL Blair (Edinburgh, captain); AF Jacobsen (Edinburgh), RW Ford (Edinburgh), EA Murray (Northampton Saints), NJ Hines (USA Perpignan), JL Hamilton (Edinburgh), AK Strokosch (Gloucester), SM Taylor (Stade Français), JA Barclay (Glasgow Warriors)
SUBSTITUTIONS: AG Dickinson (Gloucester) and SD Gray (Northampton Saints) for Jacobsen & Barclay

MAJOR TOURS

(51 mins), RGM Lawson (Gloucester) & DA Parks (Glasgow Warriors) for Blair & Godman (59 mins), MB Evans (Glasgow Warriors) & DWH Hall (Glasgow Warriors) for Webster & Ford (64 mins), ML Mustchin (Edinburgh) for Hines (72 mins)

SCORERS: *Tries*: Walker (2), Barclay, Cairns, Strokosch, R Lamont *Conversions*: Godman (3), Parks *Penalty goal*: Godman

CANADA: Pritchard; Duke, Hearn, Smith, Mensah–Coker; Evans, Fairhurst; Tkachuk, Riordan (captain), Franklin, Hotson, Jackson, Sinclair, Carpenter, Kleeberger

SUBSTITUTIONS: Hirayama for Evans (48 mins), Burak & Williams for Jackson & Fairhurst (52 mins), Keys for Hearn (61 mins), Walsh for Tkachuk (67 mins), Marshall & Stephen for Kleeberger & Carpenter (72 mins)

REFEREE: G Clancy (Ireland)

ARGENTINA TO EUROPE 2008

TOUR PARTY

FULL BACKS: B Stortoni (Glasgow Warriors), M Comuzzi (Pucara)

THREE QUARTERS: H Agulla (CA Brive), R Carballo (Castres Olympique), F Leonelli (Saracens), M Avramovic (Montauban), FM Aramburu (US Dax), GP Tiesi (Harlequins)

HALF BACKS: N Vergallo (US Dax), A Figuerola (CA San Isidro), N Bruzzone (San Isidro Club), F Contepomi (Leinster), JM Hernandez (Stade Français), S Fernandez (Hindu)

FORWARDS: ME Ledesma (ASM Clermont–Auvergne), A Vernet Basualdo (Stade Toulousain), R Roncero (Stade Français), M Ayerza (Leicester Tigers), J Figallo (Jockey Club, Salta), E Guinazu (SU Agen), JP Orlandi (Rovigo), P Albacete (Stade Toulousain), R Alvarez–Kairelis (USA Perpignan), E Lozadoa (Toulon), M Galarza (Universitario de La Plata), A Campos (Pueyrredon), A Galindo (Racing Metro Paris), MA Durand (RC Montpellier–Herault), JM Leguizamon (Stade Français), JM Fernandez–Lobbe (Sale Sharks)

MANAGER A Cubelli **COACH** F Turnes **ASSISTANT COACHES** M Reggiardo, M Gaitan, M Bandarian, G Fernandez **CAPTAIN** F Contepomi

Match 1, 8 November, Stade Velodrome, Marseille
France 12 (3PG 1DG) Argentina 6 (2PG)

FRANCE: M Medard (Stade Toulousain): J Malzieu (ASM Clermont–Auvergne), B Baby (ASM Clermont–Auvergne), Y Jauzion (Stade Toulousain), C Heymans (Stade Toulousain); D Skrela (Stade Toulousain), J–B Elissalde (Stade Toulousain); F Barcella (Biarritz Olympique), D Szarzewski (Stade Français), B Lecouls (Stade Français), R Millo–Chluski (Stade Toulousain), L Nallet (Castres Olympique, captain), T Dusautoir (Stade Toulousain), L Picamoles (RC Montpellier–Herault), I Harinordoquy (Biarritz Olympique)

SUBSTITUTIONS: N Mas (USA Perpignan) for Lecouls (47 mins), S Chabal (Sale Sharks) for Nallet (57 mins), B Kayser (Leicester Tigers) for Szarzewski (64 mins), F Ouedraogo (RC Montpellier–Herault) for Picamoles (64 mins), M Parra (CS Bourgoin–Jallieu) & A Palisson (CA Brive) for Elissalde & Medard (73 mins)

SCORERS: *Penalty goals*: Skrela (2), Baby *Drop goal*: Skrela

ARGENTINA: Stortoni; Leonelli, Tiesi, F Contepomi (captain), Agulla; Hernandez, Vergallo; Roncero, Ledesma, Orlandi, Alvarez–Kairelis, Albacete, Durand, JM Fernandez–Lobbe, Galindo

SUBSTITUTIONS: Campos for Durand (temp 33 to 37 mins) & Alvarez–Kairelis (temp 67 to 69 mins), Aramburu for Tiesi (40 mins), Lozada for Galindo (51 mins), Ayerza for Orlandi (58 mins)

SCORER: *Penalty goals*: F Contepomi (2)

REFEREE: JI Kaplan (South Africa)

Match 2, 15 November, Stadio Olimpico, Turin
Italy 14 (1T 2PG 1DG) Argentina 22 (1G 5PG)

ITALY: A Masi (Biarritz Olympique); K Robertson (Viadana), Mi Bergamasco (Stade Français), G Garcia (Calvisano), M Pratichetti (Calvisano); A Marcato (Treviso), P Canavosio (Viadana); M Aguero (Saracens), F Ongaro (Saracens), C Nieto (Gloucester), C–A del Fava (Ulster), M Bortolami (Gloucester), J Sole (Viadana), S Parisse (Stade Français, captain), Ma Bergamasco (Stade Français)

SUBSTITUTIONS: A Lo Cicero (Racing Metro Paris) for Aguero (50 mins), P Travagli (Parma) for Canavosio (51 mins), L Ghiraldini (Calvisano) for Ongaro (55 mins), T Reato (Rovigo) for Bortolami (temp 43 to 48 mins) & Del Fava (67 mins), L Orquera (CA Brive) for Marcato (60 mins), S Perugini (Stade Toulousain) for Nieto (69 mins)

SCORERS: *Try*: Masi *Penalty goals*: Marcato (2) *Drop goal*: Marcato

ARGENTINA: Stortoni; Aramburu, Tiesi, F Contepomi (captain), Carballo; Hernandez, Vergallo; Roncero, Ledesma, Orlandi, Lozada, Albacete, Durand, JM Fernandez–Lobbe, Alvarez–Kairelis

SUBSTITUTIONS: Galindo for Lozada (58 mins), Figuerola & Agulla for Vergallo & Tiesi (59 mins), Campos for Durand (65 mins), Ayerza for Orlandi (69 mins), Fernandez for Aramburu (75), Vernet Basualdo for Ledesma (77 mins)

SCORERS: *Try*: Carballo *Conversion*: F Contepomi *Penalty goals*: F Contepomi (5)

REFEREE: C White (England)

Match 3, 22 November, Croke Park, Dublin
Ireland 17 (1T 3PG 1DG) Argentina 3 (1PG)

IRELAND: GEA Murphy (Leicester Tigers); TJ Bowe (Ospreys), BG O'Driscoll (Leinster, captain), LM Fitzgerald (Leinster), RDJ Kearney (Leinster); RJR O'Gara (Munster), TG O'Leary (Munster); MJ Horan (Munster), JP Flannery (Munster), JJ Hayes (Munster), DP O'Callaghan (Munster), PJ O'Connell (Muster), SPH Ferris (Ulster), JPR Heaslip (Leinster), DP Wallace (Munster)

SUBSTITUTIONS: RD Best (Ulster) for Flannery (13 mins), D Ryan (Munster) for D Wallace (75 mins)

SCORERS: *Try*: Bowe *Penalty goals*: O'Gara (3) *Drop goal*: O'Gara

ARGENTINA: Agulla; Leonelli, Aramburu, Avramovic, Carballo; Fernandez, Vergallo; Roncero, Ledesma, Orlandi, Alvarez–Kairelis, Albacete, Durand, Leguizamon, JM Fernandez–Lobbe (captain)

SUBSTITUTIONS: Ayerza for Orlandi (48 mins), Lozada for Alvarez–Kairelis (55 mins), Stortoni & Figuerola for Leonelli & Vergallo (60 mins)

SCORER: *Penalty goal*: Fernandez

REFEREE: BJ Lawrence (New Zealand)

IRELAND TO NORTH AMERICA 2009

FULL BACKS: GW Duffy (Connacht)

THREE QUARTERS: BJ Murphy (Munster), I Dowling (Munster), DM Cave (Ulster), I Whitten (Ulster), D Hurley (Munster), K Matthews (Munster)

HALF BACKS: PA Stringer (Munster), EG Reddan (London Wasps), IJ Keatley (Connacht), N O'Connor (Ulster)

FORWARDS: RD Best (Ulster), S Cronin (Connacht), TD Buckley (Munster), TG Court (Ulster), MR Ross (Harlequins), B Young (Ulster), RE Casey (London Irish), MR O'Driscoll (Munster), RJ Caldwell (Ulster), J Muldoon (Connacht), N Ronan (Munster), D Ryan (Munster), C Henry (Ulster), DP Leamy (Munster)

MANAGER P McNaughton **COACH** D Kidney **ASSISTANT COACHES** A Gaffney, L Kiss, P Pook, M Tainton

CAPTAIN RD Best

Match 1, 23 May, Thunderbird Stadium, Vancouver
Canada 6 (2PG) Ireland 25 (2G 1T 2PG)

CANADA: J Pritchard (Bedford Blues); D van Camp (Velox Valhallians), C Hearn (Castaway Wanderers), RJ Smith (Calgary Irish), DTH van der Merwe (James Bay AA); D Spicer (University of Victoria), E Fairhurst (Cornish Pirates); K Tkachuk (Glasgow Warriors), P Riordan (University of Victoria, captain), S Franklin (Cornish Pirates), T Hotson (UBC Old Boys), M Burak (Cornish Pirates), C O'Toole (Castaway Wanderers), A Carpenter (Brantford Harlequins), AR Kleeberger (University of Victoria)

SUBSTITUTIONS: D Wooldridge (Cowichan) for Franklin (20 mins), J Sinclair (Castaway Wanderers) for Carpenter (40 mins), A Monro (Colorno) for Van Camp (54 mins), L Tait (Stade Montois) & N Dala (Castaway Wanderers) for Hotson & O'Toole (58 mins), P Mack (James Bay AA) for Fairhurst (66 mins), S–M Stephen (Plymouth Albion) for Burak (76 mins)

SCORERS: *Penalty goals*: Pritchard (2)

IRELAND: Duffy; B Murphy, Cave, Whitten, Dowling; Keatley, Stringer; Court, R Best (captain), Buckley, Casey, M O'Driscoll, Muldoon, Leamy, Ronan

SUBSTITUTIONS: Ross & Caldwell for Court & Casey (54 mins), Reddan & Ryan for Stringer & Muldoon (71 mins)

SCORERS: *Tries*: B Murphy, Whitten, Buckley *Conversions*: Keatley (2) *Penalty goals*: Keatley (2)

REFEREE: C White (England)

Match 2, 31 May, Buckshaw Stadium, Santa Clara
USA 10 (1G 1DG) Ireland 27 (2G 2T 1PG)

USA: CT Wyles (Saracens); K Swiryn (Old Pugest Sound Beach), JL Sifa (Midleton), R Suniula (Pearl City Rugby), J Boyd (Dallas Harlequins); M Hercus (Sunshine Coast Stingrays), M Petri (New York AC, captain); MS MacDonald (Leeds Carnegie), C Biller (California), W Johnson (Oxford University), J van der Giessen (Denver Barbarians), H Smith (Saracens), LE Stanfill (New York AC), N Johnson (Denver Barbarians), P Dahl (Belmont Shore)
SUBSTITUTIONS: J Welch (Belmont Shore) for Biller (44 mins), A Malifa (Belmont Shore) & M Moeakiola (Park City Haggis) for Hercus & MacDonald (59 mins), AEJ Tuilevuka (Provo Steelers) for Sifa (61 mins), JJ Gagiano (University of Cape Town) for Stanfill (68 mins), C Mackay (Counties Manakau) & T Usasz (Nottingham) for Van der Giessen & Petri (73 mins)
SCORERS: *Try*: Suniula *Conversion*: Malifa *Drop goal*: Malifa
IRELAND: Duffy; B Murphy, Cave, Whitten, Dowling; Keatley, Stringer, Buckley, R Best (captain), Ross, Casey, M O'Driscoll, Muldoon, Leamy, Ronan
SUBSTITUTIONS: Hurley for Cave (temp 22 to 31 & 68 mins), Court for Ross (50 mins), Ryan & Reddan for Muldoon & Stringer (60 mins), Caldwell for Casey (64 mins),
SCORERS: *Tries*: Casey, Whitten, Penalty try, R Best *Conversions*: Keatley (2) *Penalty goal*: Keatley
REFEREE: C White (England)

ENGLAND V BARBARIANS and ARGENTINA 2009

SQUAD

FULL BACKS: DA Armitage (London Irish), BJ Foden (Northampton Saints), OC Morgan (Gloucester)
THREE QUARTERS: MJ Cueto (Sale Sharks), D Strettle (NEC Harlequins), MA Banahan (Bath), J Turner–Hall (NEC Harlequins), DJ Hipkiss (Leicester Tigers), TA May (Newcastle Falcons), JD Noon (Newcastle Falcons), MJM Tait (Sale Sharks), SB Vesty (Leicester Tigers)
HALF BACKS: DS Care (NEC Harlequins), PK Hodgson (London Irish), REP Wigglesworth (Sale Sharks), AJ Goode (CA Brive)
FORWARDS: GS Chuter (Leicester Tigers), DM Hartley (Northampton Saints), SG Thompson (CA Brive), TAN Payne (London Wasps), JM White (Leicester Tigers), DG Wilson (Newcastle Falcons), N Wood (Gloucester), BJ Kay (Leicester Tigers), NJ Kennedy (London Irish), SW Borthwick (Saracens), LP Deacon (Leicester Tigers), SE Armitage (London Irish), JS Crane (Leicester Tigers), T Rees (London Wasps), CDC Robshaw (Harlequins), JAW Haskell (London Wasps), LS Moody (Leicester Tigers), NJ Easter (Harlequins)

TEAM MANAGER MO Johnson **ASSISTANT COACHES** B Smith, J Wells, M Ford, JEB Callard **CAPTAIN** SW Borthwick

Match 1, 30 May, Twickenham (non-cap match)
England XV 26 (3G 1T) Barbarians 33 (4G 1T)

England XV scorers: *Tries*: Foden, Turner–Hall, May, Banahan *Conversions*: Goode (3)
Barbarians scorers: *Tries*: Balshaw 2, Jack, Elsom, D'Arcy *Conversions*: B Blair (4)

Match 2, 6 June, Old Trafford, Manchester
England 37 (2G 1T 4PG 2DG) Argentina 15 (4PG 1DG)

ENGLAND: D Armitage; Cueto, Hipkiss, May, Banahan; Goode, Care; Payne, Hartley, Wilson, Borthwick (captain), L Deacon, Haskell, Easter, S Armitage
SUBSTITUTIONS: White, Crane & Hodgson for Wilson, Easter & Care (63 mins), Vesty for May (72 mins), Tait for Banahan (75 mins), Kay for L Deacon (76 mins), Thompson for Hartley (78 mins)
SCORERS: *Tries*: D Armitage (2), Banahan *Conversions*: Goode (2) *Penalty goals*: Goode (4) *Drop goals*: Goode (2)
ARGENTINA: H Agulla (CA Brive); F–M Aramburu (US Dax), G–P Tiesi (Harlequins), MB Avramovic (Montauban), GO Camacho (Buenos Aires CRC); J–M Hernandez (Stade Français), N Vergallo (US Dax); R Roncero (Stade Français), A Vernat Basualdo (Stade Toulousain), J–P Orlandi (Rovigo), M Carizza (Biarritz Olympique), PE Albacete (Stade Toulousain), A Galindo (Racing Metro Paris), JM Fernandez–Lobbe (Sale Sharks, captain), JM Leguizamon (Stade Français)

SUBSTITUTIONS: MI Ayerza (Leicester Tigers) for JP Orlandi (56 mins), S Fernandez (Hindu) for Avramovic (67 mins), E Lozada (Toulon) for Carizza (67 mins), E Guinazu (SU Agen) for Vernet Basualdo (70 mins), LG Amorosino (Pucara) for Aramburu (75 mins)
SCORERS: *Penalty goals*: Hernandez (4) *Drop goal*: Hernandez
REFEREE: C Berdos (France)

Match 3, 13 June, Estadio Padre Ernesto Martearena, Salta
Argentina 24 (1G 1T 3PG 1DG) England 22 (1G 5PG)

ARGENTINA: H Agulla (CA Brive); F–J Leonelli (Saracens), G–P Tiesi (Harlequins), S Fernandez (Hindu), GO Camacho (Buenos Aires CRC); J–M Hernandez (Stade Français), A Lalanne (London Irish); R Roncero (Stade Français), ME Ledesma (ASM Clermont–Auvergne), MI Ayerza (Leicester Tigers), RE Alvarez–Kairelis (USA Perpignan), PE Albacete (Stade Toulousain), G Fessia (Cordoba Athletic), JM Fernandez–Lobbe (Sale Sharks, captain), JM Leguizamon (Stade Français)
SUBSTITUTIONS: LPG Amorosino (Pucara) for Leonelli (13 mins), E Lozada (Toulon) for Alvarez–Kairelis (70 mins), A Vernet Basualdo (Stade Toulousain) for M Ledesma (73 mins), JP Orlandi (Rovigo) for Ayerza (74 mins)
SCORERS: *Tries*: Leguizamon, Camacho *Conversion*: Hernandez *Penalty goals*: Hernandez (3) *Drop goal*: Hernandez
ENGLAND: D Armitage; Cueto, Hipkiss, May, Banahan; Goode, Care; Payne, Hartley, White, Borthwick (captain), L Deacon, Robshaw, Easter, S Armitage
SUBSTITUTIONS: Tait for Hipkiss (16 mins), Kay for Borthwick (46 to 60 mins) & L Deacon (70 mins), Haskell for Robshaw (53 mins), Wilson & Vesty for White & May (62 mins), Chuter for Hartley (70 mins), Hodgson for Care (71 mins)
SCORERS: *Try*: Banahan *Conversion*: Goode *Penalty goals*: Goode (5)
REFEREE: DA Lewis (Ireland)

WALES TO NORTH AMERICA 2009

TOUR PARTY

FULL BACKS: J Tovey (Newport Gwent Dragons), DJ Evans (Scarlets)
THREE QUARTERS: MA Jones (Scarlets), R Mustoe (Cardiff Blues), T James (Cardiff Blues), CD Czekaj (Cardiff Blues), A Bishop (Ospreys), JP Spratt (Ospreys), J Davies (Scarlets), S Parker (Ospreys)
HALF BACKS: DJ Peel (Sale Sharks), GJ Cooper (Gloucester), DR Biggar (Ospreys), NJ Robinson (Cardiff Blues)
FORWARDS: R Hibbard (Ospreys), GJ Williams (Cardiff Blues), P James (Ospreys), JV Yapp (Cardiff Blues), DJ Jones (Ospreys), C Mitchell (Ospreys), BS Davies (Cardiff Blues), IM Gough (Ospreys), DL Jones (Cardiff Blues), * LC Charteris (Newport Gwent Dragons), DAR Jones (Scarlets), R Sowden–Taylor (Cardiff Blues), RP Jones (Ospreys), L Evans (Newport Gwent Dragons), R McCusker (Scarlets), J Turnbull (Scarlets), S Warburton (Cardiff Blues), D Lydiate (Newport Gwent Dragons)

* Replacement on tour

MANAGER COACH R McBryde **ASSISTANT COACHES** NR Jenkins, S Holley **CAPTAIN** RP Jones

Match 1, 30 May, York University Stadium, Toronto
Canada 23 (2G 3PG) Wales 32 (2G 6PG)

CANADA: J Pritchard (Bedford Blues); C Hearn (Castaway Wanderers), R Smith (Calgary Irish), DTH van der Merwe (James Bay AA), S Duke (University of Victoria); A Monro (Colomo, E Fairhurst (Cornish Pirates); K Tkachuk (Glasgow Warriors), P Riordan (University of Victoria, captain), A Tiedemann (University of Victoria), M Burak (Cornish Pirates), L Tait (Stade Montois), J Sinclair (Castaway Wanderers), A Carpenter (Brantford Harlequins), A Kleeberger (University of Victoria)
SUBSTITUTIONS: D Spicer (University of Victoria) for Monro (25 mins), M Evans (Hartpury College, Gloucester) for Duke (56 mins), M Pletch (Velox Valhallians) for Tiedemann (57 mins), T Hotson (UBC Old Boys) for Tait (61 mins), S–M Stephen (Plymouth Albion) for Dala (69 mins), P Mack (James Bay AA) for Smith (70 mins)
SCORERS: *Tries*: Duke, Fairhurst *Conversions*: Pritchard (2) *Penalty goals*: Pritchard (3)
WALES: DJ Evans; James, J Davies, Bishop, Czekaj; Biggar, Cooper; DJ Jones, Hibbard, Yapp; B Davies, DL Jones, DAR Jones, RP Jones (captain), Sowden–Taylor

SUBSTITUTIONS: Peel for Cooper (40 mins), Mitchell for Yapp (61 mins), Gough for B Davies (63 mins), Spratt for J Davies (75 mins), G Williams for Hibbard (76 mins)
SCORERS: *Tries*: Czekaj, James *Conversions*: Biggar (2) *Penalty goals*: Biggar (6)
REFEREE: M Goddard (Australia)

> **Match 2, 6 June, Toyota Park, Bridgeview, Chicago**
> **USA 15 (1G 1T 1PG) Wales 48 (6G 2PG)**

USA: CT Wyles (Saracens); GL DeBartolo (Eastern Suburbs), AE Tuilevuka (Provo Steelers), R Suniula (Pearl City Rugby) K Swiryn (Old Pugest Sound Beach); A Malifa (Belmont Shore), M Petri (New York AC, captain); M Moeakiola (Park City Haggis), C Biller (California), W Johnson (Oxford University), J van der Giessen (Denver Barbarians), H Smith (Saracens), LE Stanfill (New York AC), N Johnson (Denver Barbarians), P Dahl (Belmont Shore)
SUBSTITUTIONS: M Hercus (Sunshine Coast Stingrays) for Malifa (40 mins), B McClenahan for Biller (51 mins), MS MacDonald (Leeds Carnegie) for Moeakiola (55 mins), LJ Sifa (Midleton) for Swiryn (59 mins), C Mackay (Counties Manakau) for Smith (66 mins), T Usasz (Nottingham) for Petri (67 mins), JJ Gagiano (University of Cape Town) for W Johnson (72 mins)
SCORERS: *Tries*: Tuilevuka, Gagiano *Conversion*: DeBartolo *Penalty goals*: DeBartolo
WALES: DJ Evans; James, J Davies, Bishop, MA Jones; N Robinson, Peel; DB Jones, G Williams, Yapp; Gough DL Jones, DAR Jones, RP Jones (captain), Sowden–Taylor
SUBSTITUTIONS: Warburton for RP Jones (19 mins), Hibbard for Sowden–Taylor (26 mins), Mitchell & Charteris for Yapp & Gough (48 mins) Spratt for DJ Evans (54 mins), Biggar for N Robinson (64 mins), Cooper for Peel (70 mins)
SCORERS: *Tries*: J Davies (2), MA Jones, Penalty try, James, Cooper *Conversions*: N Robinson (4), Biggar (2) *Penalty goals*: N Robinson (2)
REFEREE: M Goddard (Australia)

FRANCE TO NEW ZEALAND AND AUSTRALIA 2009

> **TOUR PARTY**

FULL BACKS: M Medard (Stade Toulousain)
THREE QUARTERS: V Clerc (Stade Toulousain), C Heymans (Stade Toulousain), D Traille (Biarritz Olympique), A Palisson (CA Brive), M Bastareaud (Stade Français), F Fritz (Stade Toulousain), Y Jauzion (Stade Toulousain), M Mermoz (USA Perpignan), J Arias (Stade Français)
HALF BACKS: D Yachvili (Biarritz Olympique), J Dupuy (Leicester Tigers), L Beauxis (Stade Français), F Trinh–Duc (RC Montpellier–Herault)
FORWARDS: D Szarzewski (Stade Français), G Guirado (USA Perpignan), W Servat (Stade Toulousain), F Barcella (Biarritz Olympique), T Domingo (ASM Clermont–Auvergne), S Marconnet (Stade Français), N Mas (USA Perpignan), *L Ducalcon (Castres Olympique), L Nallet (Castres Olympique), S Chabal (Sale Sharks), R Millo–Chluski (Stade Toulousain), P Pape (Stade Français), D Chouly (USA Perpignan), L Picamoles (RC Montpellier–Herault), F Ouedraogo (RC Montpellier–Herault), T Dusautoir (Stade Toulousain), R Martin (Aviron Bayonnais), J Puricelli (Aviron Bayonnais)

*Replacement on tour

MANAGER J Maso **COACH** M Lièvremont **ASSISTANT COACHES** E Ntamack, D Retiere, D Ellis, G Quesada
CAPTAIN T Dusautoir

> **Match 1, 13 June, Carisbrook, Dunedin**
> **New Zealand 22 (2T 4PG) France 27 (3G 2PG)**

NEW ZEALAND: JM Muliaina (Waikato, captain); JT Rokocoko (Auckland), I Toeava (Auckland), MA Nonu (Wellington), CS Jane (Wellington); SR Donald (Waikato), QJ Cowan (Southland), TD Woodcock (North Harbour), AK Hore (Taranaki), NS Tialata (Wellington), BC Thorn (Canterbury), IB Ross (Canterbury), KJ Read (Canterbury), LJ Messam (Waikato), AJ Thomson (Otago)
SUBSTITUTIONS: KF Mealamu (Auckland) for Hore (20 mins), PAT Weepu (Wellington) for Cowan (51 mins), TD Latimer (Bay of Plenty) & CL McAlister (North Harbour) for Thomson & Toeava (60 mins), IF Afoa (Auckland) for Tialata (63 mins), BR Evans (Hawke's Bay) for Ross (74 mins)
SCORERS: *Tries*: Messam, Nonu *Penalty goals*: Donald (4)

FRANCE: Medard; Clerc, Bastareaud, Traille, Heymans; Trinh–Duc, Dupuy; Barcella, Servat, Marconnet, Pape, Millo–Chluski, Dusautoir (captain), Picamoles, Ouedraogo

593

SUBSTITUTIONS: Szarzewski for Servat (51 mins), Chabal for Pape (53 mins), Mas for Marconnet (59 mins), Puricelli for Picamoles (62 mins), Jauzion for Bastareaud (69 mins) Yachvili for Dupuy (73 mins)
SCORERS: *Tries*: Trinh–Duc, Servat, Medard *Conversions*: Dupuy (3) *Penalty goals*: Dupuy (2)
REFEREE: G Clancy (Ireland)

Match 2, 20 June, Westpac Stadium, Wellington
New Zealand 14 (1T 3PG) France 10 (1G 1PG)

NEW ZEALAND: JM Muliaina (Waikato, captain); CS Jane (Wellington), CG Smith (Wellington), MA Nonu (Wellington), JT Rokocoko (Auckland); SR Donald (Waikato), QJ Cowan (Southland), TD Woodcock (North Harbour), KF Mealamu (Auckland), NS Tialata (Wellington), BC Thorn (Canterbury), IB Ross (Canterbury), J Kaino (Wellington), KJ Read (Canterbury), TD Latimer (Bay of Plenty)
SUBSTITUTIONS: IF Afoa (Auckland) & PAT Weepu (Wellington) for Tialata & Toeava (56 mins), CL McAlister (North Harbour) for Donald (63 mins), I Toeava (Auckland) & BR Evans (Hawke's Bay) for Smith & Ross (67 mins)
SCORERS: *Try*: Nonu *Penalty goals*: Donald (2), McAlister
FRANCE: Medard; Clerc, Mermoz, Traille, Heymans; Trinh–Duc, Dupuy; Barcella, Servat, Mas, Chabal, Millo–Chluski, Dusautoir (captain), Picamoles, Ouedraogo
SUBSTITUTIONS: Szarzewski, Domingo & Chouly for Servat, Barcella & Picamoles (40 mins), Martin for Chabal (56 mins), Yachvili for Dupuy (58 mins), Fritz for Clerc (71 mins)
SCORERS: *Try*: Heymans *Conversion*: Dupuy *Penalty goal*: Yachvili
REFEREE: M Jonker (South Africa)

Match 3, 27 June, ANZ Stadium, Sydney
Australia 22 (1G 5PG) France 6 (2PG)

AUSTRALIA: AP Ashley–Cooper (ACT Brumbies); LD Turner (NSW Waratahs), SA Mortlock (ACT Brumbies, captain), BS Barnes (Queensland Reds), DA Mitchell (Western Force); MJ Giteau, (Western Force) L Burgess (NSW Waratahs); BA Robinson (NSW Waratahs), ST Moore (ACT Brumbies), AKE Baxter (NSW Waratahs), JE Horwill (Queensland Reds), NC Sharpe (Western Force), DW Mumm (NSW Waratahs), RN Brown (Western Force), GB Smith (ACT Brumbies)
SUBSTITUTIONS: BE Alexander (ACT Brumbies) for Baxter (53 mins), T Polota–Nau (NSW Waratahs) for Moore (59 mins), DW Pocock (Western Force) for Mumm (62 mins), JD O'Connor (Western Force) for Barnes (70 mins), PR Waugh (NSW Waratahs) & JJ Valentine (Western Force) for Brown & Burgess (72 mins), RP Cross (Western Force) for Mortlock (76 mins)
SCORER: *Try*: Giteau *Conversion*: Giteau *Penalty goals*: Giteau (5)
FRANCE: Traille; Medard, Fritz, Mermoz, Heymans; Beauxis, Yachvili; Barcella, Szarzewski, Marconnet, Pape, Millo–Chluski, Dusautoir (captain), Puricelli, Ouedraogo
SUBSTITUTIONS: Mas & Clerc for Marconnet & Beauxis (53 mins), Arias for Fritz (56 mins), Guirado & Martin for Szarzewski & Millo–Chluski (61 mins), Chouly for Puricelli (67 mins), Dupuy for Yachvili (76 mins)
SCORERS: *Penalty goals*: Beauxis, Yachvili
REFEREE: D Pearson (England)

ITALY TO AUSTRALIA AND NEW ZEALAND 2009

TOUR PARTY

FULL BACKS: L McLean (Calvisano), G Rubini (Overmach Cariparma)
THREE QUARTERS: M Pratichetti (Calvisano), PK Robertson (Viadana), Mi Bergamasco (Stade Français), G–J Canale (ASM Clermont–Auvergne), G Garcia (Calvisano), A Sgarbi (Treviso), R Quartaroli (Overmach Cariparma)
HALFBACKS: P Canavosio (Viadana), T Tebaldi (Gran Parma), G Toniolatti (Capitolina), C Gower (Aviron Bayonnais), CS Burton (Prato)
FORWARDS: LL Ghiraldini (Calvisano), HF Sbaraglini (Treviso), F Staibano (Castres Olympique), S Perugini (Stade Toulousain), M Aguero (Saracens), IF Rouyet (Viadana), C–A del Fava (Ulster), M Bortolami (Gloucester), Q Geldenhuys (Viadana), T Reato (Rovigo), Ma Bergamasco (Stade Français), S Favaro (Rovigo), J–F Montauriol (Casino di Venezia), SM Parisse (Stade Français), A Zanni (Calvisano), P Derbyshire (Padova)

MANAGER C Checchinato **COACH** NWH Mallett **ASSISTANT COACHES** C Orlandi, J–P Cariat, A Troncon
CAPTAIN SM Parisse

Match 1, 13 June, Canberra Stadium, Canberra
Australia 31 (3G 2T) Italy 8 (1T 1PG)

AUSTRALIA: JD O'Connor (Western Force); LD Turner (NSW Waratahs), SA Mortlock (ACT Brumbies, captain), BS Barnes (Queensland Reds), DA Mitchell (Western Force); MJ Giteau, (Western Force) L Burgess (NSW Waratahs); BA Robinson (NSW Waratahs), ST Moore (ACT Brumbies), AKE Baxter (NSW Waratahs), JE Horwill (Queensland Reds), NC Sharpe (Western Force), DW Mumm (NSW Waratahs), RN Brown (Western Force), GB Smith (ACT Brumbies)
SUBSTITUTIONS: AP Ashley–Cooper (ACT Brumbies) for Turner (40 mins), BE Alexander (ACT Brumbies) for Baxter (58 mins), T Polota–Nau (NSW Waratahs) & PJ Kimlin (ACT Brumbies) for Moore & Horwill (60 mins), DW Pocock (Western Force) & QS Cooper (Queensland Reds) for Brown & Mortlock (66 mins)
SCORERS: *Tries*: O'Connor (3), Giteau, Mortlock *Conversions*: Giteau (3)
ITALY: McLean; Robertson, Mi Bergamasco, Pratichetti, Sgarbi; Gower, Canavosio; Perugini, Ghiraldhini, Staibano, Geldenhuys, Del Fava, Zanni, Parisse (captain), Ma Bergamasco
SUBSTITUTIONS: Tebaldi for Canavosio (40 mins), Rouyet for Staibano (57 mins), Bortolami for Del Fava (59 mins), Derbyshire for Ma Bergamasco (67 mins)
SCORERS: *Try*: Robertson *Penalty goal*: McLean
REFEREE: R Poite (France)

Match 2, 20 June, Etihad Stadium, Melbourne
Australia 34 (3G 2T 1PG) Italy 12 (4PG)

AUSTRALIA: JD O'Connor (Western Force); LD Turner (NSW Waratahs), RP Cross (Western Force), QS Cooper (Queensland Reds), PJ Hynes (Queensland Reds); BS Barnes (Queensland Reds), L Burgess (NSW Waratahs); PJM Cowan (Western Force), T Polota–Nau (NSW Waratahs), BE Alexander (ACT Brumbies), JE Horwill (Queensland Reds), DW Mumm (NSW Waratahs), PJ Kimlin (ACT Brumbies), GB Smith (ACT Brumbies, captain), DW Pocock (Western Force)
SUBSTITUTIONS: AP Ashley–Cooper (ACT Brumbies) for Hynes (temp 3 to 16 & 27 to 32 mins) & O'Connor (70 mins), PR Waugh (NSW Waratahs) for Kimlin (67 mins), JJ Valentine (Western Force) for Burgess (73 mins)
SCORERS: *Tries*: Ashley–Cooper (2), Cross, Polota–Nau, Turner *Conversions*: O'Connor (2), Barnes *Penalty goal*: O'Connor
ITALY: McLean; Rubini, Canale, Garcia, Sgarbi; Gower, Tebaldi; Aguero, Sbaraglini, Staibano, Reato, Bortolami, Montauriol, Parisse (captain), Favaro
SUBSTITUTIONS: Quartaroli for Sgarbi (6 mins), Perugini for Staibano (40 mins), Zanni & Geldenhuys for Montauriol & Reato (52 mins), Toniolatti for Tebaldi (60 mins), Ghiraldini for Sbaraglini (62 mins), Burton for Canale (77 mins)
SCORER: *Penalty goals*: McLean (4)
REFEREE: D Pearson (England)

Match 3, 27 June, AMI Stadium, Christchurch
New Zealand 27 (3G 2PG) Italy 6 (2PG)

NEW ZEALAND: JM Muliaina (Waikato, captain); LTC Masaga (Counties Manakau), I Toeava (Auckland), MA Nonu (Wellington), JT Rokocoko (Auckland); CL McAlister (North Harbour) , BG Leonard (Waikato); WWV Crockett (Canterbury), KF Mealamu (Auckland), IF Afoa (Auckland); BC Thorn (Canterbury), IB Ross (Canterbury), J Kaino (Wellington), KJ Read (Canterbury), TD Latimer (Bay of Plenty)
SUBSTITUTIONS: TD Woodcock (North Harbour), GB Whitelock (Canterbury) & PAT Weepu (Wellington) for Crockett, Latimer & Leonard (50 mins), OT Franks (Canterbury) for Afoa (59 mins), CS Jane (Wellington) for Masaga (68 mins), AP de Malmanche (Waikato) for Mealamu (74 mins)
SCORERS: *Tries*: Rokocoko, Ross, Whitelock *Conversions*: McAlister (3) *Penalty goals*: McAlister (2)
ITALY: McLean; Robertson, Canale, Garcia, Mi Bergamasco; Gower, Tebaldi; Perugini, Ghiraldini, Rouyet, Geldenhuys, Bortolami, Zanni, Parisse (captain), Ma Bergamasco
SUBSTITUTIONS: Staibano for Rouyet (50 mins), Pratichetti for Canale (52 mins), Favaro for Zanni (57 mins), Sbaraglini & Del Fava for Ghiraldini & Bortolami (62 mins), Burton for Garcia (71 mins), Toniolatti for Tebaldi (74 mins)
SCORER: *Penalty goals*: McLean (2)
REFEREE: G Clancy (Ireland)

THE BACK ROW

PENALTY KICK
Shoulders parallel with the touchline.
Arm angled up, pointing towards
non-offending team.

FREE KICK
Shoulders parallel with touchline. Arm bent
square at elbow, upper arm pointing towards
non-offending team.

TRY AND PENALTY TRY
Referee's back to dead ball line.
Arm raised vertically.

ADVANTAGE
Arm outstretched, waist high, towards non-
offending team, for a period of approximately
five seconds.

SCRUM AWARDED
Shoulders parallel with touchline. Arm horizontal, pointing towards team to throw in the ball.

FORMING A SCRUM
Elbows bent, hands above head, fingers touching.

THROW FORWARD/FORWARD PASS
Hands gesture as if passing an imaginary ball forward.

KNOCK ON
Arm out-stretched with open hand above head, and moves backwards and forwards.

REFEREES' SIGNALS

NOT RELEASING BALL IMMEDIATELY IN THE TACKLE

Both hands are close to the chest as if holding an imaginary ball.

TACKLER NOT RELEASING TACKLED PLAYER

Arms brought together as if grasping a player and then opening as if releasing a player.

TACKLER OR TACKLED PLAYER NOT ROLLING AWAY

A circular movement with the finger and arm moving away from the body.

ENTERING TACKLE FROM THE WRONG DIRECTION

Arm held horizontal then sweep of the arm in a semi-circle.

INTENTIONALLY FALLING OVER ON A PLAYER
Curved arm makes gesture to imitate action of falling player. Signal is made in direction in which offending player fell.

DIVING TO GROUND NEAR TACKLE
Straight arm gesture, pointing downwards to imitate diving action.

UNPLAYABLE BALL IN RUCK OR TACKLE
Award of scrum to team moving forward at time of stoppage. Shoulders parallel with the touchline, arm horizontal pointing towards the team to throw in the ball, then pointing the arm and hand towards the other team's goal line whilst moving it backwards and forwards.

UNPLAYABLE BALL IN MAUL
Arm out to award scrummage to side not in possession at maul commencement. Other arm out as if signalling advantage and then swing it across body with hand ending on opposite shoulder..

REFEREES' SIGNALS

THE BACK ROW

JOINING A RUCK OR A MAUL IN FRONT OF THE BACK FOOT AND FROM THE SIDE
The hand and arms are held horizontally. Moving sideways.

INTENTIONALLY COLLAPSING RUCK OR MAUL
Both arms at shoulder height as if bound around opponent. Upper body is lowered and twisted as if pulling down opponent who is on top.

PROP PULLING DOWN OPPONENT
Clenched fist and arm bent. Gesture imitates pulling opponent down.

WHEELING SCRUM MORE THAN 90 DEGREES
Rotating index finger above the head.

THROW IN AT SCRUM NOT STRAIGHT
Hands at knee level imitating throw
not straight.

FAILURE TO BIND FULLY
One arm out-stretched as if binding. Other
hand moves up and down arm to indicate the
extent of a full bind.

HANDLING BALL IN RUCK OR SCRUM
Hand at ground level, making sweeping action,
as if handling the ball.

THROW IN AT LINEOUT NOT STRAIGHT
Shoulders parallel with touchline. Hand above
head indicates the path of the ball, not straight.

REFEREES' SIGNALS

CLOSING GAP IN LINEOUT
Both hands at eye level, pointing up, palms inward. Hands meet in squeezing action.

LEANING ON PLAYER IN LINEOUT
Arm horizontal, bent at elbow, palm down. Downward gesture.

PUSHING OPPONENT IN LINEOUT
Both hands at shoulder level, with palms outward, making pushing gesture.

EARLY LIFTING AND LIFTING IN LINEOUT
Both fists clenched in front, at waist level, making lifting gesture.

OBSTRUCTION IN GENERAL PLAY
Arms crossed in front of chest at right angles to each other, like open scissors.

OFFSIDE AT SCRUM, RUCK OR MAUL
Shoulders parallel with touchline. Arm hanging straight down, swings in arc along offside line.

OFFSIDE CHOICE: PENALTY KICK OR SCRUM
One arm is for penalty kick. Other arm points to place where scrum may be taken instead of a kick.

OFFSIDE UNDER 10-METRE LAW OR NOT 10 METRES AT PENALTY AND FREE KICKS
Both hands held open above head.

REFEREES' SIGNALS

HIGH TACKLE (FOUL PLAY)
Hand moves horizontally in front of neck.

**STAMPING (FOUL PLAY: ILLEGAL
USE OF BOOT)**
Stamping action or similar gesture to
indicate the offence..

PUNCHING (FOUL PLAY)
Clenches fist punches open palm.

**DISSENT (DISPUTING REFEREE'S
DECISION)**
Outstretched arm with hand opening and
closing to imitate talking.

**AWARD OF DROP-OUT ON
22-METRE LINE**
Arm points to centre of 22-metre line.

BALL HELD UP IN IN-GOAL
Space between hands indicates that the ball
was not grounded.

BALL IN TOUCH
Flag raised in one hand, the other used to
indicate the team to throw in the ball.

FOUL PLAY
Flag held horizontally in front indicating the
assistant referee has observed foul play

INTERNATIONAL REFEREES
DISMISSALS IN MAJOR
INTERNATIONAL MATCHES

Up to 30 September 2009 in major international matches. These cover all matches for which the eight senior members of the International Board have awarded caps, and also all matches played in Rugby World Cup final stages.

A E Freethy	sent off	C J Brownlie (NZ)	E v NZ	1925
K D Kelleher	sent off	C E Meads (NZ)	S v NZ	1967
R T Burnett	sent off	M A Burton (E)	A v E	1975
W M Cooney	sent off	J Sovau (Fj)	A v Fj	1976
N R Sanson	sent off	G A D Wheel (W)	W v I	1977
N R Sanson	sent off	W P Duggan (I)	W v I	1977
D I H Burnett	sent off	P Ringer (W)	E v W	1980
C Norling	sent off	J–P Garuet (F)	F v I	1984
K V J Fitzgerald	sent off	H D Richards (W)	NZ v W	*1987
F A Howard	sent off	D Codey (A)	A v W	*1987
K V J Fitzgerald	sent off	M Taga (Fj)	Fj v E	1988
O E Doyle	sent off	A Lorieux (F)	Arg v F	1988
B W Stirling	sent off	T Vonolagi (Fj)	E v Fj	1989
B W Stirling	sent off	N Nadruku (Fj)	E v Fj	1989
F A Howard	sent off	K Moseley (W)	W v F	1990
F A Howard	sent off	A Carminati (F)	S v F	1990
F A Howard	sent off	A Stoop (Nm)	Nm v W	1990
A J Spreadbury	sent off	A Benazzi (F)	A v F	1990
C Norling	sent off	P Gallart (F)	A v F	1990
C J Hawke	sent off	F E Mendez (Arg)	E v Arg	1990
E F Morrison	sent off	C Cojocariu (R)	R v F	1991
J M Fleming	sent off	P L Sporleder (Arg)	WS v Arg	*1991
J M Fleming	sent off	M G Keenan (WS)	WS v Arg	*1991
S R Hilditch	sent off	G Lascubé (F)	F v E	1992
S R Hilditch	sent off	V Moscato (F)	F v E	1992
D J Bishop	sent off	O Roumat (Wld)	NZ v Wld	1992
E F Morrison	sent off	J T Small (SA)	A v SA	1993
I Rogers	sent off	M E Cardinal (C)	C v F	1994
I Rogers	sent off	P Sella (F)	C v F	1994
D Mené	sent off	J D Davies (W)	W v E	1995
S Lander	sent off	F Mahoni (Tg)	F v Tg	*1995
D T M McHugh	sent off	J Dalton (SA)	SA v C	*1995
D T M McHugh	sent off	R G A Snow (C)	SA v C	*1995
D T M McHugh	sent off	G L Rees (C)	SA v C	*1995
J Dumé	sent off	G R Jenkins (W)	SA v W	1995
W J Erickson	sent off	V B Cavubati (Fj)	NZ v Fj	1997
W D Bevan	sent off	A G Venter (SA)	NZ v SA	1997

C Giacomel	sent off	R Travaglini (Arg)	F v Arg	1997
W J Erickson	sent off	D J Grewcock (E)	NZ v E	1998
S R Walsh	sent off	J Sitoa (Tg)	A v Tg	1998
R G Davies	sent off	M Giovanelli (It)	S v It	1999
C Thomas	sent off	T Leota (Sm)	Sm v F	1999
C Thomas	sent off	G Leaupepe (Sm)	Sm v F	1999
S Dickinson	sent off	J–J Crenca (F)	NZ v F	1999
E F Morrison	sent off	M Vunibaka (Fj)	Fj v C	*1999
A Cole	sent off	D R Baugh (C)	C v Nm	*1999
W J Erickson	sent off	N Ta'ufo'ou (Tg)	E v Tg	*1999
P Marshall	sent off	B D Venter (SA)	SA v U	*1999
P C Deluca	sent off	W Cristofoletto (It)	F v It	2000
J I Kaplan	sent off	A Troncon (It)	It v I	2001
R Dickson	sent off	G Leger (Tg)	W v Tg	2001
P C Deluca	sent off	N J Hines (S)	US v S	2002
P D O'Brien	sent off	M C Joubert (SA)	SA v A	2002
P D O'Brien	sent off	J J Labuschagne (SA)	E v SA	2002
S R Walsh	sent off	V Ma'asi (Tg)	Tg v I	2003
N Williams	sent off	S D Shaw (E)	NZ v E	2004
S J Dickinson	sent off	P C Montgomery (SA)	W v SA	2005
S M Lawrence	sent off	L W Moody (E)	E v Sm	2005
S M Lawrence	sent off	A Tuilagi (Sm)	E v Sm	2005
S R Walsh	sent off	S Murray (S)	W v S	2006
J I Kaplan	sent off	H T-Pole (Tg)	Sm v Tg	*2007
A C Rolland	sent off	J Nieuwenhuis (Nm)	F v Nm	*2007
N Owens	sent off	N Nalaga (PI)	F v PI	2008

* Matches in World Cup final stages

REFEREES

OBITUARIES

By Adam Hathaway

JOHN DRAKE, who died suddenly on 13 December 2008 aged 49, was a key member of the New Zealand side that won the first Rugby World Cup in 1987 and rated one of the best tight-head props to play for the All Blacks by John Hart. Drake, a product of Auckland Grammar School, played for Otago Juniors before returning to Auckland and making it into the senior side. Drake spent three off-seasons playing for Bourg-en-Bresse in France and during the last of these was called into the All Blacks tour party of Argentina. He played five games during New Zealand's first World Cup which culminated with the All Blacks beating France in the final. Drake was a respected television commentator, with SKY, and newspaper columnist, with the Herald, when he finished playing. Auckland and Bay of Plenty now contest the 'John Drake Boot' commemorating his playing career and later move to Mount Maunganui.

MIKE JEFFERIES, who died of cancer on 30 August 2009 aged 61, was a leading administrator with the Welsh Rugby Union where he served as Head of Legal Affairs. As a partner with the law firm Hugh James in Cardiff one of his most high profile projects was overseeing the legal detail of the contract to fund and complete the building of the Millennium Stadium. Jefferies was born in Crickhowell and educated at King Henry VIII School in Abergavenny before studying law at University College London, joining Hugh James in 1969 and becoming a partner in 1972 as soon as he qualified as a solicitor. During his career at Hugh James his clients included the University of Aberystwyth, Glamorgan County Cricket Club, The Environment Agency and Cardiff Council.

SHAWN MACKAY, who died in Durban on 6 April 2009 aged 26, was a former Australian Sevens captain who played in the back or second row for the Brumbies and for a period coached the Australian Women's Sevens squad. After five years at the Sydney Roosters playing rugby league Mackay joined the Waratahs, playing six games in 2006 and touring the UK with them that year before being offered a one-year deal with the Brumbies in 2009. Mackay's second Super 14 appearance for the Brumbies – against the Sharks – was his last. That night, following a 34–15 defeat, he was hit by a car while out with team-mates and died in a South African hospital nine days later.

COLIN HILLMAN, who died on 2 July 2009 after a long illness aged 46, was a former Wales Sevens national coach and a hooker for Bridgend, Swansea, South Wales Police and Merthyr. Hillman played for the Wales Youth team that beat their South African counterparts 30–25 in Cape Town in 1980, a match that remains the only Welsh international win over a South African international side in Springbok territory. After his playing days he turned to coaching at Nantymoel rugby club and became Director of Rugby at the Bridgend Ravens while featuring on the international stage as the Wales Sevens coach. He remained Director of Rugby at Bridgend and was still a WRU Technical Advisor to the Wales Sevens team at the time of his death. Away from rugby he worked as a South Wales Police Officer and served for part of his career as a South Wales Police Armed Response Officer.

BLEDDYN WILLIAMS, who died on 6 July 2009 aged 86, was known as the 'Prince of Centres' and had the unique distinction of captaining his club (Cardiff) and country (Wales) to wins over the touring All Blacks in 1953. A fly-half originally he switched to the centre where with Billy Cleaver and Dr Jack Mathews they made up one of Wales' best midfield trios. Williams won 22 Welsh caps between 1947 and 1955 and led the side to five wins out of five. Williams was vice-captain to Karl Mullen on the 1950 British & Irish Lions tour to New Zealand and Australia, playing in 20 matches, scoring 12 tries and captaining the Lions in second and third Tests against the All Blacks and leading them to a 19–6 win over the Wallabies in Brisbane. Born in Taffs Well on 22 February 1923, Williams was one of eight brothers who played for Cardiff and was a glider pilot in the Second World War. On his return, he went on to amass 185 tries for Cardiff RFC before retiring in 1955. He went on to become rugby correspondent of the Sunday People, president of Cardiff and was awarded an MBE in the 2005 New Year's Honours List.

HAYDN TANNER, who died on 5 June 2009 aged 92, was the oldest living Welsh international and British Lion when he passed away. He was never dropped by his country and stands comparison with Gareth Edwards in the annals of Welsh rugby. A scrum-half for Swansea and Cardiff, he won his first Welsh cap as an 18-year-old in the win over New Zealand in 1935, after he and his cousin Willie Davies had inspired Swansea to victory over the tourists, and would play 25 times over 15 years. Picked for the 1938 Lions tour of South Africa, he played in the second Test and the Lions won eight of ten matches with him on the field. Tanner was born in Penclawdd and with Davies, who lived next door, played for the local side in his early teens and then aged 17, while still at Gowerton Grammar School, he joined Swansea. Renowned for his reverse pass, Tanner worked as an industrial chemist in London before going to Harvard Business School and becoming a purchasing director for Reed Paper and Board UK. He was a member of London Welsh and helped to coach Esher.

VAUGHAN WILLIAMS, who died on 21 June 2009 aged 63, was a respected RFU Council member who worked tirelessly on behalf of student rugby. His appointments included acting as team manager of the English Universities from 1985 to 1999, as a Students RFU Committee member and as their Community Rugby representative. He was also on the British Universities Sports Association (BUSA) Rugby Management Group, was Chairman of their Rugby Management Group and Chairman of the English Universities/BUSA Rugby Union Management Group. Williams was also Director of Physical Recreation & Sport for the University of Nottingham, and was their coach from 1976 to 2004. He also served as president of Nottinghamshire and Notts, Lincs & Derbyshire (NLD), was an RFU 'A' List Panel Referee from 1987 to 1994 and coached Nottinghamshire Under 23s and the NLD county XV.

DAVID GRAY, who died while out jogging on 2 April 2009 aged 56, was a Scottish second row forward and a key figure in a strong West of Scotland and Glasgow pack that also included fellow internationals Gordon Brown and Sandy Carmichael. Measuring 6ft 8in and weighing in at 17st 10lbs, Gray won nine Scotland caps from 1978 and was ever-present in the 1980 Five Nations. Educated at Kilmarnock Academy, Gray also played for Kilmarnock and Ayrshire and followed his brother Ian, also a lock, into the Scotland B team. After rugby Gray indulged his love of the wilds of Scotland, walking the 200 miles of the Great Outdoors Challenge from Knoydart to the east coast in May 2008. Gray was preparing to compete in the event again when he collapsed while training at Ayr's Dam Park Stadium.

Dr KARL MULLEN, who died on 27 April 2009 aged 82, was the captain of Ireland's Grand Slam winners in 1948, the last Irish side to complete the clean sweep until Brian O'Driscoll's men 61 years later. Mullen was a fellow of the Royal College of Obstetricians and Gynaecologists and helped found the Irish Hospital Consultants Association. He worked at Mount Carmel Hospital in Dublin for more than 40 years until retiring in 2002. A hooker, Mullen left his bedside manner in the dressing room when playing, describing Ireland's tactics as 'Boot, bollock and bite'. Mullen was made Ireland captain, aged 21, for the second game of the 1948 campaign – following the opening 13–6 win against France – and rounded off the Grand Slam with a win over Wales in Belfast. The term Grand Slam was not used in those days – the Triple Crown was the big one – but as the years passed until Ireland's next Slam the legend of the 1948 side grew and Mullen was regularly sought out by journalists. Mullen's team won another Triple Crown in 1949 and he captained the British & Irish Lions to New Zealand and Australia in 1950, playing 17 games, including three Tests on the trip. On retiring he served as President of the Leinster Branch (1963–64) and also as Chairman of the Irish selectors.

FENWICK ALLISON, who died on 13 April 2009 aged 77, was a member of England's Grand Slam-winning side of 1957 and won seven caps, all under the captaincy of Eric Evans. Allison, a place-kicker who played in cotton mittens, played initially for Northern and Northumberland while studying metallurgy at King's, Newcastle, but it was during his time with Coventry and Warwickshire that he won all of his caps. His first cap came in the 8–3 loss to Wales in 1956 and he was ever-present that season. His only appearance in the Grand Slam campaign was in the opener against Wales. Allison was a stalwart of the outstanding Coventry and Warwickshire sides in the late 1950s, leading Warwickshire to the 1957–58 County Championship with a side that included England internationals Peter Jackson and Phil Judd. Work commitments took Allison to Leeds where he coached the Roundhay club. His son-in-law Ian Metcalfe was a replacement for England against New Zealand in 1979, although he did not win a cap and is an RFU Council member.

RUSSELL BRUCE, who died on 17 April 2009 aged 90, was a centre and fly-half for Scotland, winning eight caps between 1947 and 1949. Educated at Glasgow Academy and a surveyor by profession, Bruce also played in six 'Victory' internationals in 1946 to mark the end of the Second World War. One of these ended in a 27–0 win over England at Murrayfield on the same day that Scotland's football team beat the Auld Enemy at Hampden Park. Scotland won five of these six games with Bruce contributing four tries. Bruce won his first cap against France at Stade Colombes and in the last game of that season captained Scotland from stand-off in their 24–5 defeat by England at Twickenham. He missed the 1948 season but played all four games in 1949 when Scotland beat France and Wales.

AIR COMMODORE PADDY FORSYTHE CBE, who died on 28 August 2009 aged 89, was a former Chairman and President of London Irish as well as chairing the RAF Rugby Union and the Combined Services

Rugby Union. But it was for his exploits in World War Two that Forsythe is best remembered. He was one of the last survivors of Bomber Command and piloted his Lancaster on more than 30 missions over Germany. His last flight was Operation Manna dropping food to the freed Dutch near The Hague. Forsythe remained in the RAF until 1975, serving as director of public relations at Far East Command, Singapore, and finally as RAF director of public relations. On retirement he became Chief Executive of the Look Ahead Housing Association.

WALLY HOLMES, who died on 6 April 2009 aged 83, was a front row stalwart for England in the 1950s, winning 16 caps and was the first senior international to come out of the Nuneaton Club. Holmes made his debut in the 11–5 defeat by Wales in 1950 but England struggled that season and the next before enjoying success with three wins in 1952 and topping the Championship in 1953 when a 9–9 draw with Ireland deprived them of the Grand Slam. A conscripted mineworker – or Bevin Boy after the scheme's architect, the Minister for Labour Aneurin Bevin – in the latter part of the Second World War, Holmes went on to work in factories in Coventry for Morris Engines and Massey Ferguson. He played on into the 1960s for Nuneaton and also appeared for Warwickshire, the Midlands Counties and the Barbarians. He played in all three rows of the scrum: usually in the back row for his club and in the second row for his county. Three brothers – Bill, Harry and Sam – also played for the club and all four took to the field together in the 1949–50 season. His grandson Gary has captained Nuneaton.

MAC HENDERSON, who died on 5 March 2009 aged 101, was the Grand Old Man of Scottish rugby, playing in all three matches of Scotland's 1933 Triple Crown. Henderson was the country's oldest international player and a well-known farmer and champion of the organic food movement. Born in May 1907, Henderson played for Edinburgh Accies, Dunbar and Haddington. He also spent three years in New Zealand in the late 1920s, during which time he worked on sheep stations and played for Waipukurau Rugby Club. A flanker, Henderson won all his caps in 1933 and thus never played in a losing Scotland side but his playing days ended when he suffered a serious knee injury playing for the Barbarians against Cardiff. Henderson's farming interests extended to more than 1,000 acres of prime East Lothian land and he and his wife Janet became the first farmers in Scotland to embrace organic methods of growing vegetables. In 1962, the couple opened a farm shop in Edinburgh and a year later their eponymous restaurant, which has since become an institution in the city.

MEMBER UNIONS OF THE INTERNATIONAL RUGBY BOARD

ANDORRA Federació Andorrana de Rugby
www.far.ad

ARABIAN GULF Arabian Gulf Rugby
Football Union
www.agrfu.com

ARGENTINA Union Argentina de Rugby
www.uar.com.ar

AUSTRALIA Australian Rugby Union
www.rugby.com.au

AUSTRIA Osterreichischer Rugby Verband
www.rugby-austria.at

BAHAMAS Bahamas Rugby Football Union
www.rugbybahamas.com

BARBADOS Barbados Rugby Football Union
www.rugbybarbados.com

BELGIUM Fédération Belge de Rugby
www.rugby.be

BERMUDA Bermuda Rugby Union
www.bermudarfu.com

BOSNIA & HERZEGOVINA Ragbi Savez
Republike Bosne

BOTSWANA Botswana Rugby Union

BRAZIL Associação Brasileira de Rugby
www.brasilrugby.com.br

BULGARIA Bulgarian Rugby Federation
www.bfrbg.org

CAMEROON Fédération Camerounaise de
Rugby

CANADA Rugby Canada
www.rugbycanada.ca

CAYMAN Cayman Rugby Union
www.caymanrugby.com

CHILE Federación de Rugby de Chile
www.feruchi.cl

CHINA Chinese Rugby Football Association
www.rugbychina.com

CHINESE TAIPEI Chinese Taipei Rugby
Football Union

COLOMBIA Union Colombiana de Rugby
www.rugbycolombia.blogspot.com

COOK ISLANDS Cook Islands Rugby Union

CROATIA Hrvatski Ragbijaški Savez
www.rugby.hr

CZECH REPUBLIC Ceska Rugbyova Unie
www.rugbyunion.cz

DENMARK Dansk Rugby Union
www.rugby.dk

ENGLAND Rugby Football Union
www.rfu.com

FIJI Fiji Rugby Union
www.fijirugby.com

FINLAND Suomen Rugbyliitto
www.rugbyliitto.sporttisaitti.com

FRANCE Fédération Française de Rugby
www.ffr.fr

GEORGIA Georgian Rugby Union
www.rugby.ge

GERMANY Deutscher Rugby Verband
www.rugby.de

GUAM Guam Rugby Football Union

GUYANA Guyana Rugby Football Union

HONG KONG Hong Kong Rugby Football
Union
www.hkrugby.com

HUNGARY Magyar Rögbi Szövetség
www.mrgsz.hu

INDIA Indian Rugby Football Union
www.rugbyindia.in

IRELAND Irish Rugby Football Union
www.irishrugby.ie

ISRAEL Israel Rugby Union
www.rugby.org.il

ITALY Federazione Italiana Rugby
www.federugby.it

IVORY COAST Fédération Ivoirienne de Rugby

JAMAICA Jamaica Rugby Football Union

JAPAN Japan Rugby Football Union
www.rugby-japan.jp

KAZAKHSTAN Kazakhstan Rugby Football
Federation

KENYA Kenya Rugby Football Union
www.kenyarfu.com

KOREA Korea Rugby Union
www.rugby.or.kr

LATVIA Latvijas Regbija Federācija
www.rugby.lv

LITHUANIA Lietuvos Regbio Federacija
www.litrugby.lt

LUXEMBOURG Fédération Luxembourgeoise
de Rugby
www.rugby.lu

MADAGASCAR Fédération Malagasy de
Rugby

MALAYSIA Malaysia Rugby Union
www.mru.org.my

MALTA Malta Rugby Football Union
www.maltarugby.com

MAURITIUS Rugby Union Mauritius
www.mauritiusrugby.mu

MEXICO Federación Mexicana de Rugby
www.mexrugby.com

MOLDOVA Federatia de Rugby din Moldovei

MONACO Fédération Monégasque de Rugby
www.monaco-rugby.com

MOROCCO Fédération Royale Marocaine de
Rugby
www.rugbymaroc.com

NAMIBIA Namibia Rugby Union

NETHERLANDS Nederlands Rugby Bond
www.rugby.nl

NEW ZEALAND New Zealand Rugby
Football Union
www.allblacks.com

NIGERIA Nigeria Rugby Football Association

NIUE ISLANDS Niue Rugby Football Union

NORWAY Norges Rugby Forbund
www.rugby.no

PAKISTAN Pakistan Rugby Union
www.pakistanrugby.com

PAPUA NEW GUINEA Papua New Guinea
Rugby Football Union

PARAGUAY Union de Rugby del Paraguay
www.urp.org.py

PERU Federación Peruana de Rugby
www.rugbyperu.org

PHILIPPINES The Philippines Rugby Football Union
www.prfu.com

POLAND Polski Związek Rugby
www.pzrugby.pl

PORTUGAL Federação Portuguesa de Rugby
www.fpr.pt

ROMANIA Federatia Romana de Rugbi
www.rugby.ro

RUSSIA Rugby Union of Russia
www.rugby.ru

SAMOA Samoa Rugby Union
www.samoarugbyunion.ws

SCOTLAND Scottish Rugby Union
www.scottishrugby.org

SENEGAL Fédération Sénégalaise de Rugby
www.senegal-rugby.com

SERBIA Rugby Union of Serbia

SINGAPORE Singapore Rugby Union
www.singaporerugby.com

SLOVENIA Rugby Zveza Slovenije
www.rugby.si

SOLOMON ISLANDS Solomon Islands Rugby Union Federation

SOUTH AFRICA South African Rugby Union
www.sarugby.co.za

SPAIN Federación Española de Rugby
www.ferugby.com

SRI LANKA Sri Lanka Rugby Football Union

ST. VINCENT & THE GRENADINES St. Vincent & The Grenadines Rugby Union Football
www.svgrugby.netfirms.com

SWAZILAND Swaziland Rugby Union
www.swazilandrugby.com

SWEDEN Svenska Rugby Forbundet
www.rugby.se

SWITZERLAND Fédération Suisse de Rugby
www.rugby.ch

TAHITI Fédération Tahitienne de Rugby de Polynésie Française

THAILAND Thai Rugby Union
www.thairugbyunion.com

TONGA Tonga Rugby Football Union

TRINIDAD & TOBAGO Trinidad and Tobago Rugby Football Union
www.ttrfu.com

TUNISIA Fédération Tunisienne de Rugby

UGANDA Uganda Rugby Football Union
www.urfu.org

UKRAINE National Rugby Federation of Ukraine

URUGUAY Union de Rugby del Uruguay
www.uru.org.uy

USA USA Rugby Football Union
www.usarugby.org

VANUATU Vanuatu Rugby Football Union

VENEZUELA Federación Venezolana de Rugby Amateur

WALES Welsh Rugby Union
www.wru.co.uk

ZAMBIA Zambia Rugby Football Union

ZIMBABWE Zimbabwe Rugby Union
www.zimbabwerugby.com

THE DIRECTORY

REGIONAL ASSOCIATIONS

ARFU Asian Rugby Football Union
www.arfu.com

CAR Confédération Africaine de Rugby
www.carugby.com

CONSUR Confederacion Sudamericana de
Rugby
www.consur.org

FIRA-AER FIRA Association Européenne de
Rugby
www.fira-aer-rugby.com

FORU Federation of Oceania Rugby Unions
www.oceaniarugby.com

NACRA North America and Caribbean
Rugby Association
www.nacrugby.com

ASSOCIATE MEMBERS

AMERICAN SAMOA American Samoa Rugby
Football Union

ARMENIA Rugby Federation of Armenia
www.armrugby.am

AZERBAIJAN Azerbaijan Rugby Union
www.rugby.az

BRITISH VIRGIN ISLANDS British Virgin
Islands Rugby Union
www.bvirugby.com

BURUNDI Fédération Burundaise de Rugby

CAMBODIA Cambodia Federation of Rugby
www.cambodiarugby.org

GHANA Ghana Rugby Union

INDONESIA Indonesian Rugby Football Union
www.indonesianrugby.com

KYRGYZSTAN Kyrgyzstan Rugby Union

LAO Lao Rugby Federation
www.laorugby.com

MALI Fédération Malienne de Rugby

MAURITANIA Fédération Mauritanienne de
Rugby

MONGOLIA Mongolia Rugby Union

RWANDA Fédération Rwandaise de Rugby

ST. LUCIA St. Lucia Rugby Football Union

TANZANIA Tanzania Rugby Union

TOGO Fédération Togolaise de Rugby
www.fetogrugby.com

UZBEKISTAN Uzbekistan Rugby Union

THE BACK ROW